Cases in Strategic Management

6th EDITION

Charles W. L. Hill
University of Washington

Gareth R. Jones
Texas A&M University

Houghton Mifflin Company

Boston   New York

To my wife, Alexandra Hill, for her ever increasing support and affection
Charles W. L. Hill

For Nicholas and Julia and Morgan and Nia
Gareth R. Jones

Editor-in-Chief: George T. Hoffman
Associate Sponsoring Editor: Susan M. Kahn
Senior Project Editor: Rachel D'Angelo Wimberly
Editorial Assistant: May Jawdat
Senior Production/Design Coordinator: Jennifer Meyer Dare
Senior Manufacturing Coordinator: Marie Barnes
Marketing Manager: Steven W. Mikels
Marketing Associate: Lisa Boden

Cover image and design: © Ron Chapple/Getty Images

Printed in the U.S.A.

Library of Congress Control Number: 2002109474

ISBN: 0-618-31818-6

1 2 3 4 5 6 7 8 9 — VHP — 07 06 05 04 03

Contents

Introduction: Analyzing a Case Study and Writing a Case Study Analysis   C1

Cases

v

Preface

In its fifth edition, *Strategic Management: An Integrated Approach* became the most widely used strategic management textbook on the market. This overwhelming support and acceptance has led us to build on this foundation for this new edition of *Cases in Strategic Management*. We have continued to strive for currency to ensure that cutting edge issues are addressed, and we believe that we have written and collected a set of strategic management cases that are the best ever.

The 43 cases that we have selected for this edition will appeal, we are certain, to students and professors alike, both because these cases are intrinsically interesting and because of the number of strategic management issues they illuminate. These cases will provide students with a broad overview of the field of strategic management and will give them the opportunity to do some in-depth analysis of strategic issues.

The cases fall into three clearly defined categories: cases dealing with small business, which highlight problems and issues in running entrepreneurially based companies; business-level cases, which focus on the way that companies create value and competitive advantage in different industry conditions; and corporate-level cases, which examine how value is created or lost through such strategies as diversification and merger. The organizations discussed in the cases range from large, well-known ones, for which students can do research in order to update the information, to small, entrepreneurial businesses that illustrate the uncertainty and challenge of the strategic management process. In addition, the selections include many international cases, and most of the other cases contain some element of global strategy. There is enough variety in these cases and depth and breadth of coverage to satisfy the needs of most professors. Refer to the table of contents for a complete listing of cases with brief descriptions. A grid that outlines the topical coverage of each case can be found in the *Instructor's Resource Manual: Cases*.

To help students learn how to effectively analyze and write a case study, we continue to include a special section on this subject. This section includes a checklist and explanation of areas to consider when analyzing, writing, and presenting a case study, suggested research tools, and an explanation of the role and methods of financial analysis.

We feel that our entire selection is unrivaled in breadth and depth. We have been fortunate to have a large number of cases to draw on from case authors, many of whom use our books. We are grateful to the other case authors who have contributed to this edition.

Larry D. Alexander, *Virginia Tech*

Simon Algar, *Thunderbird, The American Graduate School of International Management*

A. J. Almaney, *DePaul University*

Bharat Anand, *Harvard Business School*

Steven Angga-Prana, *New York University*

Frank C. Barnes, *University of North Carolina–Charlotte*

M. Edgar Barrett, *Thunderbird, The American Graduate School of International Management*

Chad Beaupierre, *New York University*

Scott Bevier, *New York University*

Herman L. Boschken, *San Jose State University*

James W. Camerius, *Northern Michigan University*

Jonathan Charlton, *Virginia Tech*

Joyce A. Claterbos, *University of Kansas*

Billy Cockrell, *Adrenaline Air Sports*

Gabriella Del Carro, *St. John's University*

Dorothy G. Dologite, *Baruch College, City University of New York*

John Dunkelberg, *Wake Forest University*

Harold Dyck, *California State University*

Roberto Ekesi, *New York University*

Joseph N. Fry, *Richard Ivey School of Business*

Marc E. Gartenfeld, *St. John's University*

Tim Goho, *Wake Forest University*

Sue Greenfeld, *California State University*

Myra Hart, *Harvard Business School*

Andrew C. Inkpen, *Thunderbird, The American Graduate School of International Management*

Lawrence R. Jauch, *University of Louisiana at Monroe*

Min Yee Ji, *New York University*

Andrew Kimbrough, *Thunderbird, The American Graduate School of International Management*

Suresh Kotha, *University of Washington*

David Lane, *Harvard Business School*

Vipon Kumar, *Thunderbird, The American Graduate School of International Management*

Vicken Librarikian, *New York University*

Meredith Martin, *Thunderbird, The American Graduate School of International Management*

Melissa V. Melancon, *University of Louisiana at Monroe*

Robert J. Mockler, *St. John's University*

Chiaki Moriguchi, *Harvard Business School*

Richard Moxon, *University of Washington*

Vincent Pawlowski, *St. John's University*

Elizabeth Petrovski, *St. John's University*

Sharon I. Peyus, *Harvard Business School*

Taz Pirmohamed, *Harvard Business School*

Steve Preziosi, *St. John's University*

Frank T. Rothaermel, *Michigan State University*

George C. Rubenson, *Salisbury University*

Melissa A. Schilling, *New York University*

Frank M. Shipper, *Salisbury University*

Damon Swaner, *St. John's University*

Norihito Tanaka, *Kanagawa University*

Marilyn L. Taylor, *University of Missouri at Kansas City*

Beverly B. Tyler, *North Carolina State University*

Roderick E. White, *Richard Ivey School of Business*

Teaching and Learning Aids

Taken together, the teaching and learning features of *Cases in Strategic Management* provide a package that is unsurpassed in its coverage.

For the Instructor

■ A comprehensive **Instructor's Resource Manual** created especially to accompany the casebook offers complete teaching notes for each case in this collection. These teaching notes cover all aspects of a company's strategy and structure. We also provide a series of questions that can be given to students to help them focus on the significant issues in each case. We have found these to be useful in leading students to think strategically, especially at the beginning of the strategy course, when they lack the tools to pull out the significant issues.

■ New **Videos** from CNN's award-winning "CEO Exchange" series are available to adopters. This series uses in-depth interviews with internationally recognized and respected CEOs to shed light on those managerial, organizational, and technological issues that are shaping the marketplace of ideas. In addition, this series explores the personal side of commerce, as industry icons discuss the values and experiences that shape and influence their business philosophies, strategies, and decisions. The programs that accompany this book are "Jack Welch: Icon of Leadership," "Creating New Categories, Businesses, and Markets" (featuring Thomas Stemberg, chairman and CEO of Staples, and Carl Yankowski, former CEO of Palm, a market leader in handheld computers), "The Built to Order Revolution" (featuring Michael Dell, chairman and CEO of Dell Computer Corporation, and Frederick Smith, chairman, president, and CEO of FedEx Corporation), and "Innovators of Silicon Valley" (featuring Scott McNealy, chairman and CEO of Sun Microsystems, and Marc Andreessen, chairman of Loudcloud and co-founder of Netscape). Each program includes business students and faculty asking questions of the discussants. We are confident this video series will help highlight many issues of interest and can be used to spark class discussion.

■ A **web site** contains features to aid instructors including downloadable files from the *Instructor's Resource Manual* and the Video Guide. Additional materials on the student web site may also be of use to instructors.

For the Student

■ A student **web site** provides help for students as they make their way through the course. The web site features links to the companies highlighted in the cases and links to other sites of general interest while studying strategic management. It also includes the section on analyzing a case study and writing a case study analysis.

Acknowledgments

This book is the product of far more than two authors. We are grateful to George Hoffman, our editor-in-chief, and Steve Mikels, our marketing manager, for their help in promoting and developing the book and for providing us with timely feedback and information from professors and reviewers that have allowed us to shape the book to meet the needs of its intended market. We are also grateful to Susan Kahn, associate sponsoring editor, for ably coordinating the planning of our book and for managing the creation of the ancillary materials; and grateful to Rachel D'Angelo Wimberly, senior project editor, and May Jawdat, editorial assistant, for their adept handling of production. We are also grateful to the case authors for allowing us to use their materials. We also want to thank the departments of management at the University of Washington and Texas A&M University for providing the setting and atmosphere in which the book could be written, and the students of these universities who reacted to and provided input for many of our ideas. In addition, the following reviewers of this and earlier editions gave us valuable suggestions regarding the case selection.

Ken Armstrong, *Anderson University*

Kunal Banerji, *West Virginia University*

Glenn Bassett, *University of Bridgeport*

Thomas H. Berliner, *The University of Texas at Dallas*

Richard G. Brandenburg, *University of Vermont*

Steven Braund, *University of Hull*

Philip Bromiley, *University of Minnesota*

Geoffrey Brooks, *Western Oregon State College*

Lowell Busenitz, *University of Houston*

Gene R. Conaster, *Golden State University*

Steven W. Congden, *University of Hartford*

Catherine M. Daily, *Ohio State University*

Robert DeFillippi, *Suffolk University Sawyer School of Management*

Helen Deresky, *SUNY–Plattsburgh*

Gerald E. Evans, *The University of Montana*

John Fahy, *Trinity College, Dublin*

Patricia Feltes, *Southwest Missouri State University*

Mark Fiegener, *Oregon State University*

Isaac Fox, *Washington State University*

Craig Galbraith, *University of North Carolina at Wilmington*

Scott R. Gallagher, *Rutgers University*

Eliezer Geisler, *Northeastern Illinois University*

Gretchen Gemeinhardt, *University of Houston*

Lynn Godkin, *Lamar University*

Robert L. Goldberg, *Northeastern University*

Graham L. Hubbard, *University of Minnesota*

Tammy G. Hunt, *University of North Carolina at Wilmington*

James Gaius Ibe, *Morris College*

W. Grahm Irwin, *Miami University*

Jonathan L. Johnson, *University of Arkansas Walton College of Business Administration*

Marios Katsioloudes, *St. Joseph's University*

Robert Keating, *University of North Carolina at Wilmington*

Geoffrey King, *California State University–Fullerton*

Rico Lam, *University of Oregon*

Robert J. Litschert, *Virginia Polytechnic Institute and State University*

Franz T. Lohrke, *Louisiana State University*

Lance A. Masters, *California State University–San Bernardino*

Robert N. McGrath, *Embry-Riddle Aeronautical University*

Charles Mercer, *Drury College*

Van Miller, *University of Dayton*

Joanna Mulholland, *West Chester University of Pennsylvania*

Francine Newth, *Providence College*

Paul R. Reed, *Sam Houston State University*

Rhonda K. Reger, *Arizona State University*

Malika Richards, *Indiana University*

Ronald Sanchez, *University of Illinois*

Joseph A. Schenk, *University of Dayton*

Brian Shaffer, *University of Kentucky*

Pradip K. Shukla, *Chapman University*

Dennis L. Smart, *University of Nebraska at Omaha*

Barbara Spencer, *Clemson University*

Lawrence Steenberg, *University of Evansville*

Kim A. Stewart, *University of Denver*

Ted Takamura, *Warner Pacific College*

Bobby Vaught, *Southwest Missouri State*

Robert P. Vichas, *Florida Atlantic University*

Daniel L. White, *Drexel University*

Edgar L. Williams, Jr., *Norfolk State University*

Charles W. L. Hill
Gareth R. Jones

Cases in
Strategic Management

Introduction:
Analyzing a Case Study and
Writing a Case Study Analysis

What Is Case Study Analysis?

Case study analysis is an integral part of a course in strategic management. The purpose of a case study is to provide students with experience of the strategic management problems that actual organizations face. A case study presents an account of what happened to a business or industry over a number of years. It chronicles the events that managers had to deal with, such as changes in the competitive environment, and charts the managers' response, which usually involved changing the business- or corporate-level strategy. The cases in this book cover a wide range of issues and problems that managers have had to confront. Some cases are about finding the right business-level strategy to compete in changing conditions. Some are about companies that grew by acquisition, with little concern for the rationale behind their growth, and how growth by acquisition affected their future profitability. Each case is different because each organization is different. The underlying thread in all cases, however, is the use of strategic management techniques to solve business problems.

Cases prove valuable in a strategic management course for several reasons. First, cases provide you, the student, with experience of organizational problems that you probably have not had the opportunity to experience firsthand. In a relatively short period of time, you will have the chance to appreciate and analyze the problems faced by many different companies and to understand how managers tried to deal with them.

Second, cases illustrate the theory and content of strategic management. The meaning and implications of this information are made clearer when they are applied to case studies. The theory and concepts help reveal what is going on in the companies studied and allow you to evaluate the solutions that specific companies adopted to deal with their problems. Consequently, when you analyze cases, you will be like a detective who, with a set of conceptual tools, probes what happened and what or who was responsible and then marshals the evidence that provides the solution. Top managers enjoy the thrill of testing their problem-solving abilities in the real world. It is important to re-member that no one knows what the right answer is. All that managers can do is to make the best guess. In fact, managers say repeatedly that they are happy if they are right only half the time in solving strategic problems. Strategic management is an uncertain game, and using cases to see how theory can be put into practice is one way of improving your skills of diagnostic investigation.

C1

Third, case studies provide you with the opportunity to participate in class and to gain experience in presenting your ideas to others. Instructors may sometimes call on students as a group to identify what is going on in a case, and through classroom discussion the issues in and solutions to the case problem will reveal themselves. In such a situation, you will have to organize your views and conclusions so that you can present them to the class. Your classmates may have analyzed the issues differently from you, and they will want you to argue your points before they will accept your conclusions, so be prepared for debate. This mode of discussion is an example of the dialectical approach to decision making. This is how decisions are made in the actual business world.

Instructors also may assign an individual, but more commonly a group, to analyze the case before the whole class. The individual or group probably will be responsible for a thirty- to forty-minute presentation of the case to the class. That presentation must cover the issues posed, the problems facing the company, and a series of recommendations for resolving the problems. The discussion then will be thrown open to the class, and you will have to defend your ideas. Through such discussions and presentations, you will experience how to convey your ideas effectively to others. Remember that a great deal of managers' time is spent in these kinds of situations: presenting their ideas and engaging in discussion with other managers who have their own views about what is going on. Thus, you will experience in the classroom the actual process of strategic management, and this will serve you well in your future career.

If you work in groups to analyze case studies, you also will learn about the group process involved in working as a team. When people work in groups, it is often difficult to schedule time and allocate responsibility for the case analysis. There are always group members who shirk their responsibilities and group members who are so sure of their own ideas that they try to dominate the group's analysis. Most of the strategic management takes place in groups, however, and it is best if you learn about these problems now.

Analyzing a Case Study

The purpose of the case study is to let you apply the concepts of strategic management when you analyze the issues facing a specific company. To analyze a case study, therefore, you must examine closely the issues confronting the company. Most often you will need to read the case several times—once to grasp the overall picture of what is happening to the company and then several times more to discover and grasp the specific problems.

Generally, detailed analysis of a case study should include eight areas:

1. The history, development, and growth of the company over time

2. The identification of the company's internal strengths and weaknesses

3. The nature of the external environment surrounding the company

4. A SWOT analysis

5. The kind of corporate-level strategy that the company is pursuing

6. The nature of the company's business-level strategy

7. The company's structure and control systems and how they match its strategy

8. Recommendations

To analyze a case, you need to apply the concepts taught in this course to each of these areas. To help you further, we next offer a summary of the steps you can take to analyze the case material for each of the eight points we just noted:

1. *Analyze the company's history, development, and growth.* A convenient way to investigate how a company's past strategy and structure affect it in the present is to chart the critical incidents in its history—that is, the events that were the most unusual or the most essential for its development into the company it is today. Some of the events have to do with its founding, its initial products, how it makes new-product market decisions, and how it developed and chose functional competencies to pursue. Its entry into new businesses and shifts in its main lines of business are also important milestones to consider.

2. *Identify the company's internal strengths and weaknesses.* Once the historical profile is completed, you can begin the SWOT analysis. Use all the incidents you have charted to develop an account of the company's strengths and weaknesses as they have emerged historically. Examine each of the value creation functions of the company, and identify the functions in which the company is currently strong and currently weak. Some companies might be weak in marketing; some might be strong in research and development. Make lists of these strengths and weaknesses. The SWOT Checklist (Table 1) gives examples of what might go in these lists.

3. *Analyze the external environment.* To identify environmental opportunities and threats, apply all the concepts on industry and macroenvironments to analyze the environment the company is confronting. Of particular importance at the industry level are Porter's five forces model and the stage of the life cycle model. Which factors in the macroenvironment will appear salient depends on the specific company being analyzed. Use each factor in turn (for instance, demographic factors) to see whether it is relevant for the company in question.

   Having done this analysis, you will have generated both an analysis of the company's environment and a list of opportunities and threats. The SWOT Checklist table also lists some common environmental opportunities and threats that you may look for, but the list you generate will be specific to your company.

4. *Evaluate the SWOT analysis.* Having identified the company's external opportunities and threats as well as its internal strengths and weaknesses, consider what your findings mean. You need to balance strengths and weaknesses against opportunities and threats. Is the company in an overall strong competitive position? Can it continue to pursue its current business- or corporate-level strategy profitably? What can the company do to turn weaknesses into strengths and threats into opportunities? Can it develop new functional, business, or corporate strategies to accomplish this change? *Never merely generate the SWOT analysis and then put it aside.* Because it provides a succinct summary of the company's condition, a good SWOT analysis is the key to all the analyses that follow.

5. *Analyze corporate-level strategy.* To analyze corporate-level strategy, you first need to define the company's mission and goals. Sometimes the mission and goals are stated explicitly in the case; at other times, you will have to infer them from available information. The information you need to collect to find out the company's corporate strategy includes such factors as its lines of business and the nature of

TABLE 1

A SWOT Checklist

Potential internal strengths	Potential internal weaknesses
Many product lines?	Obsolete, narrow product lines?
Broad market coverage?	Rising manufacturing costs?
Manufacturing competence?	Decline in R&D innovations?
Good marketing skills?	Poor marketing plan?
Good materials management systems?	Poor material management systems?
R&D skills and leadership?	Loss of customer good will?
Information system competencies?	Inadequate human resources?
Human resource competencies?	Inadequate information systems?
Brand name reputation?	Loss of brand name capital?
Portfolio management skills?	Growth without direction?
Cost of differentiation advantage?	Bad portfolio management?
New-venture management expertise?	Loss of corporate direction?
Appropriate management style?	Infighting among divisions?
Appropriate organizational structure?	Loss of corporate control?
Appropriate control systems?	Inappropriate organizational
Ability to manage strategic change?	structure and control systems?
Well-developed corporate strategy?	High conflict and politics?
Good financial management?	Poor financial management?
Others?	Others?
Potential environmental opportunities	Potential environmental threats
Expand core business(es)?	Attacks on core business(es)?
Exploit new market segments?	Increases in domestic competition?
Widen product range?	Increase in foreign competition?
Extend cost or differentiation advantage?	Change in consumer tastes?
Diversify into new growth businesses?	Fall in barriers to entry?
Expand into foreign markets?	Rise in new or substitute products?
Apply R&D skills in new areas?	Increase in industry rivalry?
Enter new related businesses?	New forms of industry competition?
Vertically integrate forward?	Potential for takeover?
Vertically integrate backward?	Existence of corporate raiders?
Enlarge corporate portfolio?	Increase in regional competition?
Overcome barriers to entry?	Changes in demographic factors?
Reduce rivalry among competitors?	Changes in economic factors?
Make profitable new acquisitions?	Downturn in economy?
Apply brand name capital in new areas?	Rising labor costs?
Seek fast market growth?	Slower market growth?
Others?	Others?

its subsidiaries and acquisitions. It is important to analyze the relationship among the company's businesses. Do they trade or exchange resources? Are there gains to be achieved from synergy? Alternatively, is the company just running a portfolio of investments? This analysis should enable you to define the corporate strategy that the company is pursuing (for example, related or unrelated diversification, or a combination of both) and to conclude whether the company operates in just one core business. Then, using your SWOT analysis, debate the merits of this strategy. Is it appropriate given the environment the company is in? Could a change in corporate strategy provide the company with new opportunities or transform a weakness into a strength? For example, should the company diversify from its core business into new businesses?

Other issues should be considered as well. How and why has the company's strategy changed over time? What is the claimed rationale for any changes? Often, it is a good idea to analyze the company's businesses or products to assess its situation and identify which divisions contribute the most to or detract from its competitive advantage. It is also useful to explore how the company has built its portfolio over time. Did it acquire new businesses, or did it internally venture its own? All of these factors provide clues about the company and indicate ways of improving its future performance.

6. *Analyze business-level strategy.* Once you know the company's corporate-level strategy and have done the SWOT analysis, the next step is to identify the company's business-level strategy. If the company is a single-business company, its business-level strategy is identical to its corporate-level strategy. If the company is in many businesses, each business will have its own business-level strategy. You will need to identify the company's generic competitive strategy—differentiation, low cost, or focus—and its investment strategy, given its relative competitive position and the stage of the life cycle. The company also may market different products using different business-level strategies. For example, it may offer a low-cost product range and a line of differentiated products. Be sure to give a full account of a company's business-level strategy to show how it competes.

Identifying the functional strategies that a company pursues to build competitive advantage through superior efficiency, quality, innovation, and customer responsiveness and to achieve its business-level strategy is very important. The SWOT analysis will have provided you with information on the company's functional competencies. You should investigate its production, marketing, or research and development strategy further to gain a picture of where the company is going. For example, pursuing a low-cost or a differentiation strategy successfully requires very different sets of competencies. Has the company developed the right ones? If it has, how can it exploit them further? Can it pursue both a low-cost and a differentiation strategy simultaneously?

The SWOT analysis is especially important at this point if the industry analysis, particularly Porter's model, has revealed threats to the company from the environment. Can the company deal with these threats? How should it change its business-level strategy to counter them? To evaluate the potential of a company's business-level strategy, you must first perform a thorough SWOT analysis that captures the essence of its problems.

Once you complete this analysis, you will have a full picture of the way the company is operating and be in a position to evaluate the potential of its strategy. Thus, you will be able to make recommendations concerning the pattern of its future actions. However, first you need to consider strategy implementation, or the way the company tries to achieve its strategy.

7. *Analyze structure and control systems.* The aim of this analysis is to identify what structure and control systems the company is using to implement its strategy and to evaluate whether that structure is the appropriate one for the company. Different corporate and business strategies require different structures. You

need to determine the *degree of fit between the company's strategy and structure.* For example, does the company have the right level of vertical differentiation (e.g., does it have the appropriate number of levels in the hierarchy or decentralized control?) or horizontal differentiation (does it use a functional structure when it should be using a product structure?)? Similarly, is the company using the right integration or control systems to manage its operations? Are managers being appropriately rewarded? Are the right rewards in place for encouraging cooperation among divisions? These are all issues to consider.

In some cases, there will be little information on these issues, whereas in others there will be a lot. In analyzing each case, you should gear the analysis toward its most salient issues. For example, organizational conflict, power, and politics will be important issues for some companies. Try to analyze why problems in these areas are occurring. Do they occur because of bad strategy formulation or because of bad strategy implementation?

Organizational change is an issue in many cases because the companies are attempting to alter their strategies or structures to solve strategic problems. Thus, as part of the analysis, you might suggest an action plan that the company in question could use to achieve its goals. For example, you might list in a logical sequence the steps the company would need to follow to alter its business-level strategy from differentiation to focus.

8. *Make recommendations.* The quality of your recommendations is a direct result of the thoroughness with which you prepared the case analysis. Recommendations are directed at solving whatever strategic problem the company is facing and increasing its future profitability. Your recommendations should be in line with your analysis; that is, they should follow logically from the previous discussion. For example, your recommendation generally will center on the specific ways of changing functional, business, and corporate strategies and organizational structure and control to improve business performance. The set of recommendations will be specific to each case, and so it is difficult to discuss these recommendations here. Such recommendations might include an increase in spending on specific research and development projects, the divesting of certain businesses, a change from a strategy of unrelated to related diversification, an increase in the level of integration among divisions by using task forces and teams, or a move to a different kind of structure to implement a new business-level strategy. Make sure your recommendations are mutually consistent and written in the form of an action plan. The plan might contain a timetable that sequences the actions for changing the company's strategy and a description of how changes at the corporate level will necessitate changes at the business level and subsequently at the functional level.

After following all these stages, you will have performed a thorough analysis of the case and will be in a position to join in class discussion or present your ideas to the class, depending on the format used by your professor. Remember that you must tailor your analysis to suit the specific issue discussed in your case. In some cases, you might completely omit one of the steps in the analysis because it is not relevant to the situation you are considering. You must be sensitive to the needs of the case and not apply the framework we have discussed in this section blindly. The framework is meant only as a guide, not as an outline.

Writing a Case Study Analysis

Often, as part of your course requirements, you will need to present a written case analysis. This may be an individual or a group report. Whatever the situation, there are certain guidelines to follow in writing a case analysis that will improve the evaluation your work will receive from your instructor. Before we discuss these guidelines and before you use them, make sure that they do not conflict with any directions your instructor has given you.

The structure of your written report is critical. Generally, if you follow the steps for analysis discussed in the previous section, *you already will have a good structure for your written discussion.* All reports begin with an *introduction* to the case. In it, outline briefly what the company does, how it developed historically, what problems it is experiencing, and how you are going to approach the issues in the case write-up. Do this sequentially by writing, for example, "First, we discuss the environment of Company X. . . . Third, we discuss Company X's business-level strategy. . . . Last, we provide recommendations for turning around Company X's business."

In the second part of the case write-up, the *strategic analysis* section, do the SWOT analysis, analyze and discuss the nature and problems of the company's business-level and corporate strategies, and then analyze its structure and control systems. Make sure you use plenty of headings and subheadings to structure your analysis. For example, have separate sections on any important conceptual tool you use. Thus, you might have a section on Porter's five forces model as part of your analysis of the environment. You might offer a separate section on portfolio techniques when analyzing a company's corporate strategy. Tailor the sections and subsections to the specific issues of importance in the case.

In the third part of the case write-up, present your *solutions and recommendations.* Be comprehensive, and make sure they are in line with the previous analysis so that the recommendations fit together and move logically from one to the next. The recommendations section is very revealing because your instructor will have a good idea of how much work you put into the case from the quality of your recommendations.

Following this framework will provide a good structure for most written reports, though it must be shaped to fit the individual case being considered. Some cases are about excellent companies experiencing no problems. In such instances, it is hard to write recommendations. Instead, you can focus on analyzing why the company is doing so well, using that analysis to structure the discussion. Following are some minor suggestions that can help make a good analysis even better:

1. Do not repeat in summary form large pieces of factual information from the case. The instructor has read the case and knows what is going on. Rather, use the information in the case to illustrate your statements, defend your arguments, or make salient points. Beyond the brief introduction to the company, you must avoid being *descriptive;* instead, you must be *analytical.*

2. Make sure the sections and subsections of your discussion flow logically and smoothly from one to the next. That is, try to build on what has gone before so that the analysis of the case study moves toward a climax. This is particularly important for group analysis, because there is a tendency for people in a group to split up the work and say, "I'll do the beginning, you take the middle, and I'll do the end." The result is a choppy, stilted analysis; the parts do not flow from one to the next, and it is obvious to the instructor that no real group work has been done.

3. Avoid grammatical and spelling errors. They make your work look sloppy.

4. In some instances, cases dealing with well-known companies end in 1998 or 1999 because no later information was available when the case was written. If possible, do a search for more information on what has happened to the company in subsequent years.

   Many libraries now have comprehensive web-based electronic data search facilities that offer such sources as *ABI/Inform*, *The Wall Street Journal Index*, the *F&S Index*, and the *Nexis-Lexis* databases. These enable you to identify any article that has been written in the business press on the company of your choice within the past few years. A number of nonelectronic data sources are also useful. For example, *F&S Predicasts* publishes an annual list of articles relating to major companies that appeared in the national and international business press. *S&P Industry Surveys* is a great source for basic industry data, and *Value Line Ratings and Reports* can contain good summaries of a firm's financial position and future prospects. You will also want to collect full financial information on the company. Again, this can be accessed from web-based electronic databases such as the Edgar database, which archives all forms that publicly quoted companies have to file with the Securities and Exchange Commission (SEC; e.g., 10-K filings can be accessed from the SEC's Edgar database). Most SEC forms for public companies can now be accessed from Internet-based financial sites, such as Yahoo's finance site (**http://finance.yahoo.com/**).

5. Sometimes instructors hand out questions for each case to help you in your analysis. Use these as a guide for writing the case analysis. They often illuminate the important issues that have to be covered in the discussion.

   If you follow the guidelines in this section, you should be able to write a thorough and effective evaluation.

The Role of Financial Analysis in Case Study Analysis

An important aspect of analyzing a case study and writing a case study analysis is the role and use of financial information. A careful analysis of the company's financial condition immensely improves a case write-up. After all, financial data represent the concrete results of the company's strategy and structure. Although analyzing financial statements can be quite complex, a general idea of a company's financial position can be determined through the use of ratio analysis. Financial performance ratios can be calculated from the balance sheet and income statement. These ratios can be classified into five subgroups: profit ratios, liquidity ratios, activity ratios, leverage ratios, and shareholder-return ratios. These ratios should be compared with the industry average or the company's prior years of performance. It should be noted, however, that deviation from the average is not necessarily bad; it simply warrants further investigation. For example, young companies will have purchased assets at a different price and will likely have a different capital structure than older companies do. In addition to ratio analysis, a company's cash flow position is of critical importance and should be assessed. Cash flow shows how much actual cash a company possesses.

Profit Ratios

Profit ratios measure the efficiency with which the company uses its resources. The more efficient the company, the greater is its profitability. It is useful to compare a company's profitability against that of its major competitors in its industry to determine whether the company is operating more or less efficiently than its rivals. In addition, the change in a company's profit ratios over time tells whether its performance is improving or declining.

A number of different profit ratios can be used, and each of them measures a different aspect of a company's performance. Here, we look at the most commonly used profit ratios.

Return on Invested Capital. This ratio measures the profit earned on the capital invested in the company. It is defined as follows:

$$\text{Return on invested capital (ROIC)} = \frac{\text{Net profit}}{\text{Invested capital}}$$

Net profit is calculated by subtracting the total costs of operating the company away from its total revenues (total revenues − total costs). Total costs are the (1) costs of goods sold, (2) sales, general, and administrative expenses, (3) R&D expenses, and (4) other expenses. Net profit can be calculated before or after taxes, although many financial analysts prefer the before-tax figure. Invested capital is the amount that is invested in the operations of a company, that is, in property, plant, equipment, inventories, and other assets. Invested capital comes from two main sources: interest-bearing debt and shareholders' equity. Interest-bearing debt is money the company borrows from banks and from those who purchase its bonds. Shareholders' equity is the money raised from selling shares to the public, *plus* earnings that have been retained by the company in prior years and are available to fund current investments. ROIC measures the effectiveness with which a company is using the capital funds that it has available for investment. As such, it is recognized to be an excellent measure of the value a company is creating.[1] Remember that a company's ROIC can be decomposed into its constituent parts.

Return on Total Assets (ROA). This ratio measures the profit earned on the employment of assets. It is defined as follows:

$$\text{Return on total assests} = \frac{\text{Net profit}}{\text{Total assets}}$$

Return on Stockholders' Equity (ROE). This ratio measures the percentage of profit earned on common stockholders' investment in the company. It is defined as follows:

$$\text{Return on stockholders' equity} = \frac{\text{Net profit}}{\text{Stockholders' equity}}$$

If a company has no debt, this will be the same as ROIC.

Liquidity Ratios A company's liquidity is a measure of its ability to meet short-term obligations. An asset is deemed liquid if it can be readily converted into cash. Liquid assets are current assets such as cash, marketable securities, accounts receivable, and so on. Two liquidity ratios are commonly used.

---

[1] Tom Copeland, Tim Koller, and Jack Murrin, *Valuation: Measuring and Managing the Value of Companies* (New York: Wiley, 1996).

Current Ratio. The current ratio measures the extent to which the claims of short-term creditors are covered by assets that can be quickly converted into cash. Most companies should have a ratio of at least 1, because failure to meet these commitments can lead to bankruptcy. The ratio is defined as follows:

$$\text{Current ratio} = \frac{\text{Current assets}}{\text{Current liabilities}}$$

Quick Ratio. The quick ratio measures a company's ability to pay off the claims of short-term creditors without relying on selling its inventories. This is a valuable measure since in practice the sale of inventories is often difficult. It is defined as follows:

$$\text{Quick ratio} = \frac{\text{Current assets 2 inventory}}{\text{Current liabilities}}$$

Activity Ratios

Activity ratios indicate how effectively a company is managing its assets. Two ratios are particularly useful.

Inventory Turnover. This measures the number of times inventory is turned over. It is useful in determining whether a firm is carrying excess stock in inventory. It is defined as follows:

$$\text{Inventory turnover} = \frac{\text{Cost of goods sold}}{\text{Inventory}}$$

Cost of goods sold is a better measure of turnover than sales because it is the cost of the inventory items. Inventory is taken at the balance sheet date. Some companies choose to compute an average inventory, beginning inventory, and ending inventory, but for simplicity, use the inventory at the balance sheet date.

Days Sales Outstanding (DSO) or Average Collection Period. This ratio is the average time a company has to wait to receive its cash after making a sale. It measures how effective the company's credit, billing, and collection procedures are. It is defined as follows:

$$\text{DSO} = \frac{\text{Accounts receivable}}{\text{Total sales/360}}$$

Accounts receivable is divided by average daily sales. The use of 360 is the standard number of days for most financial analysis.

Leverage Ratios

A company is said to be highly leveraged if it uses more debt than equity, including stock and retained earnings. The balance between debt and equity is called the *capital structure*. The optimal capital structure is determined by the individual company. Debt has a lower cost because creditors take less risk; they know they will get their interest and principal. However, debt can be risky to the firm because if enough profit is not made to cover the interest and principal payments, bankruptcy can result. Three leverage ratios are commonly used.

Debt-to-Assets Ratio. The debt-to-assets ratio is the most direct measure of the extent to which borrowed funds have been used to finance a company's investments. It is defined as follows:

$$\text{Debt-to-assets ratio} = \frac{\text{Total debt}}{\text{Total assets}}$$

Total debt is the sum of a company's current liabilities and its long-term debt, and total assets are the sum of fixed assets and current assets.

Debt-to-Equity Ratio. The debt-to-equity ratio indicates the balance between debt and equity in a company's capital structure. This is perhaps the most widely used measure of a company's leverage. It is defined as follows:

$$\text{Debt-to-equity ratio} = \frac{\text{Total debt}}{\text{Total equity}}$$

Times-Covered Ratio. The times-covered ratio measures the extent to which a company's gross profit covers its annual interest payments. If this ratio declines to less than 1, the company is unable to meet its interest costs and is technically insolvent. The ratio is defined as follows:

$$\text{Times-covered ratio} = \frac{\text{Profit before interest and tax}}{\text{Total interest charges}}$$

Shareholder-Return Ratios

Shareholder-return ratios measure the return that shareholders earn from holding stock in the company. Given the goal of maximizing stockholders' wealth, providing shareholders with an adequate rate of return is a primary objective of most companies. As with profit ratios, it can be helpful to compare a company's shareholder returns against those of similar companies as a yardstick for determining how well the company is satisfying the demands of this particularly important group of organizational constituents. Four ratios are commonly used.

Total Shareholder Returns. Total shareholder returns measure the returns earned by time $t + 1$ on an investment in a company's stock made at time t. (Time t is the time at which the initial investment is made.) Total shareholder returns include both dividend payments and appreciation in the value of the stock (adjusted for stock splits) and are defined as follows:

$$\text{Total shareholder returns} = \frac{\begin{array}{c}\text{Stock price } (t + 1) - \text{stock price } (t) \\ + \text{ sum of annual dividends per share}\end{array}}{\text{Stock price } (t)}$$

If a shareholder invests \$2 at time t and at time $t + 1$ the share is worth \$3, while the sum of annual dividends for the period t to $t + 1$ has amounted to \$0.20, total shareholder returns are equal to $(3 - 2 + 0.2)/2 = 0.6$, which is a 60 percent return on an initial investment of \$2 made at time t.

Price-Earnings Ratio. The price-earnings ratio measures the amount investors are willing to pay per dollar of profit. It is defined as follows:

$$\text{Price-earnings ratio} = \frac{\text{Market price per share}}{\text{Earnings per share}}$$

Market-to-Book Value. Market-to-book value measures a company's expected future growth prospects. It is defined as follows:

$$\text{Market-to-book value} = \frac{\text{Market price per share}}{\text{Earnings per share}}$$

Dividend Yield. The dividend yield measures the return to shareholders received in the form of dividends. It is defined as follows:

$$\text{Dividend yield} = \frac{\text{Dividend per share}}{\text{Market price per share}}$$

Market price per share can be calculated for the first of the year, in which case the dividend yield refers to the return on an investment made at the beginning of the year. Alternatively, the average share price over the year may be used. A company must decide how much of its profits to pay to stockholders and how much to reinvest in the company. Companies with strong growth prospects should have a lower dividend payout ratio than mature companies. The rationale is that shareholders can invest the money elsewhere if the company is not growing. The optimal ratio depends on the individual firm, but the key decider is whether the company can produce better returns than the investor can earn elsewhere.

Cash Flow

Cash flow position is cash received minus cash distributed. The net cash flow can be taken from a company's statement of cash flows. Cash flow is important for what it reveals about a company's financing needs. A strong positive cash flow enables a company to fund future investments without having to borrow money from bankers or investors. This is desirable because the company avoids paying out interest or dividends. A weak or negative cash flow means that a company has to turn to external sources to fund future investments. Generally, companies in strong-growth industries often find themselves in a poor cash flow position (because their investment needs are substantial), whereas successful companies based in mature industries generally find themselves in a strong cash flow position.

A company's internally generated cash flow is calculated by adding back its depreciation provision to profits after interest, taxes, and dividend payments. If this figure is insufficient to cover proposed new investments, the company has little choice but to borrow funds to make up the shortfall or to curtail investments. If this figure exceeds proposed new investments, the company can use the excess to build up its liquidity (that is, through investments in financial assets) or repay existing loans ahead of schedule.

Conclusion

When evaluating a case, it is important to be *systematic*. Analyze the case in a logical fashion, beginning with the identification of operating and financial strengths and weaknesses and environmental opportunities and threats. Move on to assess the value of a company's current strategies only when you are fully conversant with the SWOT analysis of the company. Ask yourself whether the company's current strategies make sense given its SWOT analysis. If they do not, what changes need to be made? What are your recommendations? Above all, link any strategic recommendations you may make to the SWOT analysis. State explicitly how the strategies you identify take advantage of the company's strengths to exploit environmental opportunities, how they rectify the company's weaknesses, and how they counter environmental threats. Also, do not forget to outline what needs to be done to implement your recommendations.

1

Vail Resorts, Inc.

This case was prepared by Herman L. Boschken, San Jose State University.

In 1962, Pete Seibert and Earl Eaton, along with several associates, opened the Vail Ski Resort, which is located in a long narrow valley known for its remoteness and spectacular alpine splendor. Previously home only to mountain ranchers and sheep herders, this area beckoned the ambitious developers because of its ideal ski terrain and a proposed interstate freeway, which was to traverse the valley floor on its way westward from Denver. The partnership would be called Vail Associates and over the remainder of the twentieth century, it would become a premier developer of world-class ski resorts. By the late 1990s, the firm had changed its name to Vail Resorts (VR) and had built or acquired three more Colorado ski resorts, all located within forty-five minutes of each other. In 2000, it expanded into summer venues with the acquisition of the Grand Teton Lodge Co. near Yellowstone, and in 2002, added Heavenly, its first ski resort outside Colorado, to its holdings.

By its fortieth anniversary season, the firm held the most-esteemed reputation in a mountain resort industry that included other prestigious names such as the Aspen Ski Co., Intrawest, and American Ski Co. But in many ways, VR had reached a crossroads by the turn of the century. The industry had been changing

for several years: an aging population was shrinking demand for skiing; snowboarding had encroached on the traditional alpine downhill skiing; competitors were making vast new investments in on-mountain and village facilities; several well-financed consolidations and mergers had reduced the field of resort providers to "the big four"; and newer resorts, like Whistler-Blackcomb (in Canada), were taking an increasing share of the maturing market.

Several things had happened internally as well. Over the course of thirty years, the firm Seibert and Eaton had founded was sold first to Texas oil entrepreneur Harry Bass in 1976 and then to Denver businessman George Gillett in 1985. Gillett, who had previously owned the Harlem Globetrotters, invested heavily in new ski facilities at Vail. His development plan led the resort to a commanding lead in customer popularity and growing profitability. By the early 1990s, however, bad management at Gillett's other enterprises led to his personal bankruptcy, which stranded Vail in a vicious struggle among his creditors. The spoils went to a New York investment firm led by junk-bond specialist Leon Black, who gained control of Vail in 1992. Black retained Gillett as the resort's chairman until the firm's IPO in 1997 installed a new chair and CEO: Adam Aron.

Aron came from the travel and leisure industry, where he had been president of Norwegian Cruise Lines and vice president of marketing for United Airlines. His reputation included recognition as one of the "100 best marketers in the U.S." Black also retained Andy Daly, Gillett's senior operations man, as the firm's president. Combined, the new leadership provided both "fresh eyes from the outside" and a topnotch seasoned industry professional to lead the firm into the new century. The two men wasted no time in setting an agenda. In the summer of 1996, the firm acquired the ski resort division of Ralcorp, which included Vail's primary competition—Breckenridge and Keystone, both located in adjacent Summit County. With a name change to Vail Resorts, the firm went public in early 1997 (NYSE ticker symbol: MTN) and opened its first corporate web site: www.snow.com.

Even with this rapid-fire agenda, it was clear nevertheless that it was time to ponder VR's strategy for the new century. How should the parts of this much larger firm fit together? How might the firm broaden its offerings to an all-season resort theme without losing the sense of an integrated product family? What alternatives lay ahead to maintain momentum, enhance profitability, and retain its world-class status in providing destination resort facilities?

Vail Resorts's Facilities

By the year 2000, the firm owned and operated four major destination winter resorts in Colorado, all located along the Rocky Mountain I-70 corridor in Eagle and Summit counties, and the Grand Teton summer resort in Jackson Hole, Wyoming. All the ski properties included long-term leases from the U.S. Forest Service for the mountain terrain, centrally located retail and commercial structures in the ski-in/ski-out villages, a few quaint hotels and hotel/convention centers, some golf courses, and other strategic facilities. Each resort is distinctive in theme and atmosphere, but all ascribe to Vail Resorts's reputation for quality service, all-season excellence, and trademark in providing a unique upscale experience to discerning customers.

As the firm's marquis resort, Vail is the largest single-mountain ski resort in North America. Built from the ground up, its village has the appearance and ambience of a traditional European alpine setting. Paralleling the interstate, the resort provides all the conveniences of a large rural town. It has two pedestrian-only village centers, which are connected to each other and the town's outer areas (some of which are four miles up or down the freeway) by a complimentary bus system. Vail has accommodations for over 30,000 people and contains over 100 restaurants and bars, 225 shops and markets, a skating arena, outdoor amphitheater, a PGA golf course, regional hospital, transportation center, schools, and a library. It is the primary or second home to professionals and executives from numerous blue-chip companies, "new economy" firms, and Wall Street investment houses. As a group, this clientele prefers anonymity outside their professional careers, and it has chosen Vail because of the resort's relaxed but discrete atmosphere.

With 12,500 acres under Forest Service permit, the resort has developed over 5,000 acres within its boundary of skiable terrain. Skiing is provided on both sides of a seven-mile ridge paralleling the village and interstate, and in an adjacent back-bowl called Blue Ski Basin. Within its skiable boundary, the mountain sports 174 trails serviced by thirty-two lifts with a capacity to handle 51,781 skiers per hour. Vertical drop (a measure of terrain steepness and ski-run length) is 3,330 feet, and the longest run is 4.5 miles. Snow is generally reliable January through April and averages 335 inches annually. Its vast size and varied terrain offer the most diversity of any resort in North America. In a week's stay, few are able to explore all its possibilities.

Ten miles to the west of Vail and located three miles off the interstate is the firm's smallest but most upscale resort, Beaver Creek. The resort actually contains three separate villages at different locations along the skirts of the mountain. Originally conceived as Colorado's location for the 1976 Olympics (which was aborted by a state referendum), the first of these is the core village of Beaver Creek. Opened in 1980, it was planned and designed by a state-of-the-art CAD system to fit a European elegance and environmental sophistication into the constrained setting of a tiny valley and stream. Emphasizing exclusivity, first-class accommodations, and "family friendliness," the alpine village sports twenty-five restaurants, over seventy shops, an outdoor ice-skating arena, the Hyatt Regency and Conference Center, the Vilar Performing Arts Center, and overnight capacity for 5,000 people. The second oldest village is Arrowhead, which VR purchased in the mid 1990s. Although it contains a couple of restaurants and some shopping, it is primarily residential, with condominiums for an additional 1,000 people. The third and newest village is Bachelor Gulch, located partway up the ski mountain between the other two villages.

It is an enclave of million-dollar homes and condominiums along ski runs and has gated-access to limit the nonskiing public. Like Arrowhead, it has limited public facilities, but the village is anchored with a prestigious Ritz-Carlton Hotel.

With over 1,600 acres of skiable terrain (most of which is under lease from the Forest Service), Beaver Creek Resort offers exceptional variety for families whose members exhibit different levels of skiing ability. Beginners can learn on gently sloping terrain at the very top of the mountain adjacent to intermediate and advanced runs (an unusual opportunity), while experts are challenged by some of the most difficult terrain in the industry. Its Birds of Prey downhill course is recognized by World-Cup skiers as the most challenging in North America. Within its official boundaries, the mountain contains 146 trails fed by thirteen lifts having a combined capacity of 24,739 skiers per hour. Vertical drop is 4,040 feet. Snowfall and winter conditions are similar to those at Vail, but the western part of the mountain (containing the Arrowhead and Bachelor Gulch villages) usually closes a few weeks earlier than the rest of the mountain.

VR's two other Colorado winter facilities are located off I-70 about an hour east of Vail and Beaver Creek along the Continental Divide. Opening as a ski resort in 1961, the largest of these is Breckenridge, which consists of a vast range of treeless peaks and an historical western mining town. Although being somewhat remolded to fit VR's family clientele, this resort community's reputation has emphasized the youthful exuberance of singles and couples seeking an active social life. As a consequence, it has more bars but fewer restaurants (totaling over fifty) than Vail and over 100 shops. In addition, the town has a performing-arts theater, museums, a golf course, and a large convention center. It has overnight accommodations for 25,000 people. The clientele of this historically preserved, year-round resort often cite the unique "sense of place and fabled Main Street experience" as a prime reason for coming.

The resort's linear sequence of mountain peaks contains 2,043 acres of skiable terrain, nearly all of which are leased from the Forest Service. As a craggy high-alpine backdrop to the town, the mountain offers 139 ski trails fed by twenty-five lifts, several of which provide direct access from different points in the town. Free buses also circulate from town to higher points on the mountain at peaks 7 and 8. Catering to all levels of skier proficiency, the moun-

tain has lift capacity for 30,656 skiers per hour, and a vertical drop of 3,398 feet. Being on the Continental Divide (the location of many of Colorado's highest elevations), Breckenridge gets slightly less snowfall (about 300 inches annually) than the Vail Valley resorts, but it comes earlier and is more reliable.

Vail Resort's forth winter resort is Keystone. Like Beaver Creek in origin and family focus, its off-mountain facilities were crafted along meadowland as a freestanding, planned unit development. Opened in 1970, the resort has steadily expanded over the years but has acquired a reputation for putting guests close to nature. Its trademark, "Nature of the Rockies," indicates more rustic facilities and accommodations than VR's other three winter resorts. It contains two main villages—the original Keystone Village and the new River Run (a joint partnership with Intrawest)—surrounded by residential areas containing homes and condominiums. The resort provides accommodations for about 5,000 people and contains about fifty shops and restaurants, a convention center for 1,800 people, and a PGA golf course. Additional housing and amenities are located about two miles away in the town of Dillon, the primary service area for Summit County.

Producing 1,861 acres of skiable terrain, Keystone has developed three successive on-mountain areas along a ridge emanating from the two adjacent village areas. With a focus on beginner and intermediate skiers, over 50 percent of the 116 trails are on more difficult slopes by Colorado standards. The three areas are serviced by twenty-two lifts having a combined capacity of 27,873 skiers per hour. Vertical drop is 2,900 feet. Although it receives less snowfall (about 230 inches) than the other three resorts, Keystone opens among the earliest and is one of the last to close during the season.

The four winter resorts are accessible by air and ground. Vail and Beaver Creek are located at the eastern edge of Eagle County, about 100 miles west of Denver. Breckenridge and Keystone are about sixty miles west of Denver. All are along or very near Interstate 70, which passes through the Denver metropolitan area on its way westward. Air transportation is available year-round through Denver International Airport (DIA) and seasonally through the Vail/Eagle County Airport. Ground transportation from both airports is provided by car-rental agencies, Greyhound Bus, and the Rocky Mountain Express van service. The ride from Denver traverses spectacular scenery but takes about two and one-half hours to Vail and Beaver Creek (the most distant). The ride from Eagle Airport is about forty-five minutes to the Vail Valley, but up to one and a half hours to the Summit County resorts.

The Recreation Resort Industry

With its emphasis on skiing and mountain sports, Vail Resorts operates in the "destination" segment of the recreation resort industry. As part of the sprawling vacation and leisure industry, this subindustry is itself a conglomerate of parts having no exact boundaries. According to the U.S. Department of Commerce, recreation resorts also overlap other related industries composed of segments such as amusement parks (e.g., Disney), gaming (e.g., Harrahs Entertainment), cruises (e.g., Princess Cruise Lines), and sporting events (e.g., the NFL). In this ill-defined industry category, competition therefore includes a vast assemblage of direct offerings and marginally substitutable products and services. With loosely segmented markets, strategic opportunities tend to be more elusive and potentially conflicting because they consist of different but partially overlapping customer profiles and product-market relationships.

Traditionally, customers in the recreation resort industry have been distinguished in the population by income, age, and family status (i.e., married/unmarried, with/without children). These factors often differentiated people inclined toward large-scale or mass recreational services coupled with less expensive accommodations (like the makeup of Disney World) from people seeking a more exclusive and intimate resort setting featuring high-value or high-status vacation venues (like those provided by Vail Resorts).

But in the opening years of the twenty-first century, a greater variety of demographic factors became determinants in customer demand analysis, which included educational level attained, occupational status (i.e., professional/managerial employment versus blue-collar/clerical jobs), lifestyle and other psychographic characteristics (cosmopolitan versus parochial awareness), and family makeup (i.e., singles/couples versus families), in addition to the traditional demographics. Looking forward, as industry producers figure out ways of assembling new customer profiles, novel services are likely to appear to keep this dynamic industry in flux.

Competition in the industry was also changing in dramatic ways. Ski resorts had divided into two types, partly the result of a maturing demand since the late 1980s. For those having limited access to capital, expansion into off-mountain amenities and overnight accommodations was sacrificed for development focused on mountain facilities like high-speed detachable chair lifts and snowmaking equipment. As result, most (the best known of which is Squaw Valley) became known as windshield resorts having principally day-use ski slopes with few accommodations on site, and usually requiring a daily roundtrip drive from home. For those resorts with deep pockets, investments in new "villages" with ski-in/ski-out access transformed the sites to "destination" resorts providing a complete experience, including not only accommodations but also "après-ski" activities for people who typically stay a week or longer. Extending this distinction, most of the better-financed destination resorts had also been shifting in the 1990s from a ski resort image to an integrated all-season setting offering winter recreation as well as golf and tennis, on-mountain summer activities, convention programs, world-class performing arts, and international festivals. A recent entry in this new approach is Squaw Valley, which is attempting a catch-up strategy in the destination market in a partnership with Intrawest and others.

With destination resorts having the most market reach demographically and geographically, Colorado claims several of the best known because of its central location in the scenic Rockies and between population centers on the East and West Coasts. Within the state, Vail Resorts competes with the Aspen Ski Company (which owns the three Aspen mountains and Snowmass, all proximally located in the Roaring Forks Valley), Intrawest (which owns controlling interest in Copper Mountain), American Ski Company (which owns Steamboat Springs), the city of Denver (which owns Winter Park), Telluride Golf and Ski, and several small destination operators (including Crested Butte and Purgatory).

Beyond Colorado, destination resort operators are spread out, with most having facilities in other parts of the Rockies, along the Pacific Crest/Sierras, in the northeastern United States, and southern Canada. In California, the major players until 2002 had been Intrawest (with interests at Squaw and Mammoth) and American Ski Company (which had owned Heavenly Valley until the resort's sale to VR). In Utah, most of the operators are small, privately held firms (which own Park City and Snowbird), with the exception of American Ski, which recently redeveloped a resort now called the Canyons. In Canada, Intrawest is the only major operator and owns Whistler-Blackcomb, Mt. Tremblant, and others.

Much of the current market structure of *destination* ski-resort competitors came about in the 1990s, when a rash of consolidations and mergers reduced the field to the "big four" and a few small specialized firms. Nearly all other firms that remain independent are operators of day-use resorts, which have lower capital costs because they offer few off-mountain activities. Figure 1 lists the principal firms and summarizes the site statistics for a selected list of their North American ski resorts.

During this period of consolidation, a technology-driven "arms race" in new development ensued. The target areas of primary investment included (1) thematic, planned-unit development villages at the ski-mountain base; (2) costly snowmaking equipment to guarantee visitors a quality skiing experience regardless of the vagaries of natural precipitation; (3) luxurious on-mountain restaurants to meet the cosmopolitan tastes of high-end skiers; and (4) state-of-the-art lift designs that provide faster, more comfortable access to the mountain top.

On the demand side of the market, destination-resort visitors were becoming more choosy at the turn of the century about the price-to-value of individual resorts. It had become clear that most destination visitors sought additional "creature comforts" both on and off the mountain, and they were willing to pay for exceptional luxury where quality was assured. VR's industry leadership in moving toward this high end market is reflected in an interfirm comparison of market position. Figure 2 compares market penetration for a selection of destination resorts according to each resort's annual skier days (calculated as one skier purchasing a lift ticket for one day).

For many years, VR's resorts have been ranked at or near the top of annual ski magazine surveys. Indeed, as the firm's flagship resort, Vail Mountain was ranked first for much of the 1990s and maintained that status into the twenty-first century. To a great extent, the firm's persistent market position is attributable to the fact that VR is the only firm in the industry that can achieve a cooperative administrative control over all aspects of the destination environment (i.e., mountain activities, local accommoda-

tions, village concessions, entertainment venues, airline and ground transportation), even though much of it is managed by a host of other firms acting as an integrated network of coproducers. As a result of its management of this multiple-partner strategic alliance, VR stood out among its competition in creating a superbly packaged product for the customer.

Nevertheless, the firm's market growth seemed to be stunted by events in the industry generally. As shown in Figure 3, the industry's long-term trend in skier-day visits had been persistently flat throughout the 1990s. An aging population of postwar baby boomers was thought to be a primary cause of this maturing demand. Skiing is a rigorous and potentially dangerous outdoor recreational activity and requires much physical stamina and a dose of youthful abandon. By contrast, baby boomers were moving into middle age during the 1990s and, as family responsibilities became more important in determining types of vacation venues, skiing's reputation as an expensive, singles-oriented, and physically exhausting sport came up short. Many former skiers and many others who might have tried skiing were moving to other segments of the vacation and leisure industry where less physical activity was required.

Besides aging of the population and intense, development-based competition, doing business in this industry had become more difficult because of a growing environmental ethic emerging among recreation and leisure customers. Over the thirty years since landmark legislation of the early 1970s, environmentalism not only had become institutionalized (by the inception of new laws, organizations, and processes) but also had acquired much broader appeal culturally. The impact of this growing respect for environmental concerns was especially felt by firms dealing with or affecting natural resources, a prime example of which were ski-resort operators.

Much of the public's awareness of a degraded environment came from individual experiences and knowledge of a loss in biodiversity and growing problems of pollution. But some public attention was heightened by protests made directly against target firms, some of it involving ecoterrorism. While most in the industry were subject to environmental litigation, varying degrees of nonviolent demonstrations, and media editorializing, Vail Resorts felt the full brunt of protestor anger. In the early morning hours of Monday, October 19, 1998, an ecoterrorist group firebombed Vail Mountain's premier restaurant

FIGURE 1

Destination Ski Resort Firms and Facilities (2000–2001 Summary of Resort Statistics)

Firm/Resort	Location	Lift Ticket Price	Skiable Acreage	Vertical Drop (Feet)	Number of Lifts	Number of Trails	Lift Capacity (Skiers/Hour)
Vail Resorts							
Vail Mountain	Colorado	$61	5,289	3,450	33	193	51,781
Breckenridge	Colorado	$57	2,043	3,398	25	139	30,656
Keystone	Colorado	$57	1,861	2,900	22	116	27,873
Beaver Creek	Colorado	$61	1,625	4,040	14	146	24,739
Aspen Ski and Golf							
Aspen/Snowmass	Colorado	$62	4,780	4,405	44	270	31,310
Intrawest							
Whistler/Blackcomb	British Columbia	$61CN	7,071	5,280	32	223	45,000
Mt. Tremblant	Quebec	$55CN	502	2,131	10	70	15,000
Mammoth Mountain	California	$54	3,500	3,100	28	150	42,100
Copper Mountain	Colorado	$55	2,433	2,601	23	125	31,000
American Ski Co.							
Steamboat Springs	Colorado	$58	2,500	3,668	20	107	30,000
Heavenly Valley	California	$56	4,800	3,500	27	82	40,000
Others							
Telluride	Colorado	$61	1,050	3,165	12	66	14,946
Winter Park	Colorado	$53	1,373	3,060	20	113	32,450
Park City	Utah	$60	2,200	3,100	14	83	19,700
Taos	New Mexico	$45	1,100	2,612	11	72	15,000

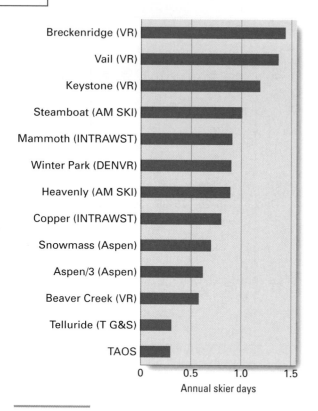

FIGURE 2

Annual Skier Days for Destination Resorts (Selected North American Resorts, 1999–2000 Season)

Sources: Colorado Ski Country; NSAA.

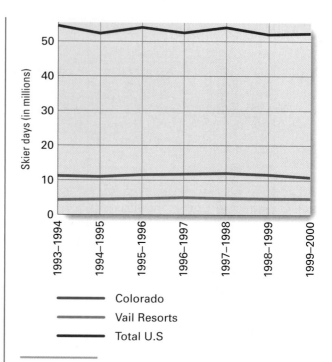

FIGURE 3

Trends in Skier Demand (Annual Skier Days, 1993–2000)

Sources: NSAA, Colorado Ski Country, Vail Resorts.

facility and damaged four ski lifts and the mountain-top headquarters of the Ski Patrol, all of which resulted in $12 million in damage.

Ostensibly done to protest Vail's development of Blue Ski Basin, a 650-acre addition to the mountain's skiable terrain, the act not only galvanized public disdain for the perpetrators, but also awakened a sense of urgency in VR's management. Although Aspen Ski and Golf was the industry's best-known firm for environmental sensitivity, VR had a far more substantial but unorganized environmental management ap-proach. In an effort to improve the firm's systematic handling of environmental issues, it began to give thought in 1999 to integrating the disparate components by drawing them together organizationally. What was taking form was a unifying, policy-driven approach to manage both the daily operations of resource sustainability and recycling and the longer-term planning requirements of the firm's continued development at its individual resorts.

The Vail Resorts Vision

Until its merger with Ralcorp and subsequent IPO in 1997, Vail Resorts had been a privately held firm made up of a closely knit family of managerial employees sharing a common interest in skiing. But under the new controlling ownership of Apollo Investors (Leon Black's holding company), the culture and leadership atmosphere changed dramatically. These corporate transitions raised several new managerial issues, but chief among them was the need for a fresh strategic outlook. During the firm's first year after the merger, the new executive team led by CEO Aron and president Daly articulated a long-term growth strategy to replace what Aron referred to as the "quick hits" of past years.

To launch the new vision, Aron set forth an explicit statement about strategic intent: "At Vail Resorts, we are focused on expanding and enhancing our core ski operations while increasing the scope, diversity and quality of the activities and services we offer our guests—skiers and nonskiers—throughout the year." Along with this declaration, he offered for the first time a set of five policy guidelines to drive the firm's strategic-action agenda: (1) create new attractions to enhance consumer appeal, (2) broaden participation in varied guest experiences (produce services previously provided by coproducers), (3) provide value through the firm's passion for-quality, (4) leverage the firm's strong market position, and (5) capitalize on industry consolidation. All but one of these alluded unambiguously to a need for vertical integration of resort services and a development strategy involving significant on-mountain expansion and new venturing in the villages.

Although bringing greater strategic focus to development, for the most part, the guidelines sought to retain and buttress the firm's historical domain of customers and integrated product lines, which had been at the core of its past success as a destination resort provider. That strategic domain included a product image of world-class destination skiing, which imparted high status and upscale appeal to a youthful but financially well-off clientele. Unlike many other recreational sports, skiing invites the agile risk-taker. As shown in Figure 4, however, it is also associated with household wealth. In VR's case, more than 50 percent of customers have incomes exceeding $100,000, and 31 percent report incomes over $200,000. The firm's domination of the high-end segment of this income-driven market was central to making Vail number 1 in ski-magazine surveys during most of the 1980s and 1990s, as well as cultivating its image as a "playland of the rich."

During the 1990s, however, the Vail Resorts customer began to exhibit a more-accomplished set of demographic and psychological attributes. While income certainly still mattered, the typical VR customer was now also likely to be college educated, have a professional career (i.e., business executive, engineer, doctor, lawyer, academic, government official), and hold significant family responsibilities. As a result, VR's visitor today is more likely to be widely traveled, with global experience and a cosmopolitan outlook. Due in part to their professional responsibilities and institutional work environment, the firm's customer also tends to seek anonymity while on vacation and to prefer a resort environment that encourages others to share this desire. Indeed, this trait in the Vail customer is often mentioned in comparisons with Aspen's customer base, which reputedly is more likely to exhibit a want-to-be-seen Hollywood outlook.

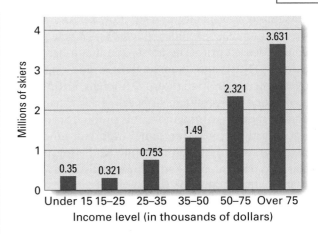

FIGURE 4

The Skiing Population, Distributed by Household Income (United States Population, 1997)

Source: U.S. Bureau of the Census.

In actual application, VR's strategic customer profile is an umbrella for different visitor subtypes. The largest of these are families (about 50 percent of visitations), many of which are multigenerational "boomer" families (i.e., a unit consisting of parents, children, and grandchildren). Although the exact mix varies from resort to resort, the remainder of visitations is about evenly divided among thirty-something couples, corporate and professional conference attendees, and college students. About 10 percent of visitations are made by foreign nationals who fit the demographic profile (especially those from Europe, South America, Japan, and Oceana, where skiing is very popular).

Such variety does not signal incompatible customer segments but rather variance in emphasis within the firm's multiple-attribute strategic profile. For example, although the multigenerational family perhaps represents the best all-round fit with the profile, college students are also a strategic fit. Even though typically lacking high-income professional employment, students often see a college degree as pursuant to the rewards of upper-middle-class status, suggesting even that this customer may become a quintessential replacement for aging boomers.

Until the 1990s, most in the destination ski-resort business saw little basis to differentiate the customer beyond household affluence and a passion for skiing. Providing faster ski lifts, well-manicured ski runs, and high-priced hotels seemed to be what the market recognized as a quality upscale product. As a result, the product most providers offered was *alpine skiing*, which focused primarily on ski-mountain hardware (mostly lifts and snowmaking) and opulent overnight accommodations. Although setting the terms for what president Daly called an "arms race" among industry competitors, this product vision did not directly account for some important emerging psychographic desires for friendly gathering places, spiritual renewal, novel adventure, stylistic flare, and cosmopolitan ambience.

While many in the industry ignored the implications and continued to promote the hardware-driven vision, VR began to cultivate skiing as a product of "luxurious pastoral serenity" and to offer an upscale opportunity to reconnect with the holistic self and valued friends, at least partially within the context of an international village setting. This new product vision was characterized as a *seamless experience*, blending together an uninterrupted progression of ski-resort pleasures while minimizing hassles and tradeoffs. For example, the pedestrian village (invented at Vail in the late 1970s) provides a ski-in/ski-out setting for visitors, placing stylistic ambience and the immediacy of mountain and village activities at the whim of customers without having to drive.

Although originally pioneered by Walt Disney half a century earlier, the emerging concept of seamlessness allowed VR to see opportunity in the threat of an aging population, and it resulted in the firm experiencing industry stability (even growth) in its financials. What many of the firm's competitors had missed in sticking with the old model was the opportunity to derive income from skier visits in ways other than the purchase of a lift ticket or an on-mountain sandwich. By upscaling its on-mountain restaurants, redefining ski school, buying some resort venues previously left to its network of coproducers (particularly classy hotels and resort retail and village commons), and becoming the primary on-line reservations agent for the four-resort packages, VR was able to generate a far greater revenue stream from each visitor than its competition. With the coming of the new millennium, the firm's refocus on an aging boomer as head of a multigenerational family was beginning to pay off. As Figure 5 shows, even though its skier visits followed the industry's flattened trend, the firm was generating revenues from each visitor that were as much as 50 percent greater than its destination-market competition.

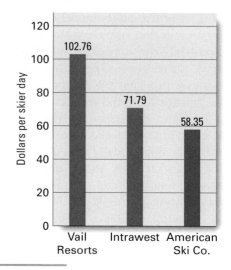

FIGURE 5

Ski Resort Revenue per Skier Day—Industry Comparison (Public Firms, 1999–2000 Ski Season)

During the 1990s, Vail Resorts had been a heavy investor in new facilities. It finished, for example, several eye-catching developments, including the well-known Beaver Creek village and launch of its sister village at Bachelor Gulch; a 650-acre north-face addition at Vail called Blue Sky Basin, along with Vail's redevelopment of the Eagle's Nest gondola and Adventure Ridge recreation area; and construction at Keystone of a new theme village called River Run, along with a golf community called River Ranch (both a joint venture with Intrawest).

Even with this sustained investment level, VR's new-found domain of product-market relationships spurred the firm to escalate substantially its investments into the twenty-first century. Although the firm doubled its size in 1997 with the Ralcorp resorts acquisition, as shown in Figure 6, it increased its capital development expenditures sixfold. Between 1997 and 2000, its capital improvement program for the four ski resorts (excluding acquisitions) averaged over $60 million annually and was allocated among projects such as redevelopment of the Lionshead gondola and pedestrian village at Vail, completion of Blue Sky Basin at Vail, completion of the outdoor ice-skating arena and Vilar performing arts center at Beaver Creek village, and launch of the Bachelor Gulch village and ski area at Beaver Creek.

Even though numerous environmental issues have been and continue to be voiced by local and national organizations concerned about pollution,

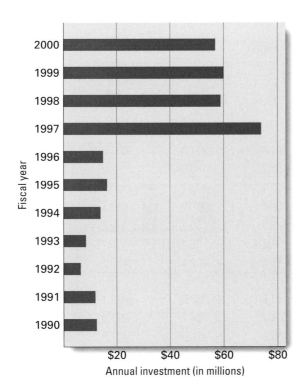

FIGURE 6

Four-Resort Capital Improvements Budget (Vail Resorts, Inc., 1990–2000)

biodiversity, and sustainability, the firm intends to continue its high level of capital investment for the strategic future (perhaps covering the next ten years). Current planning and environmental analysis, for example, is underway on a completely new 264-acre ski-in/ski-out village adjoining the firm's peaks 7 and 8 staging area above the town of Breckenridge. It will contain a mix of 430 "hot-bed" condominiums (individually owned rentals) and 110,000 square feet of retail space, which will be connected to the town center below by a twelve-passenger gondola. At Keystone, another development plan envisions a new base village and ski-mountain addition called Jones Gulch. At Beaver Creek, a new gondola is planned to connect the rapidly developing town of Avon to Bachelor Gulch and continue to the western ridge above Beaver Creek. Significant development is also underway at VR's summer-use Grand Teton resort, including a golf course and residential community. With the 2002 acquisition of Heavenly Resort, early planning is calling for major renewal of on-mountain facilities and new village initiatives.

The Firm's Financial Position

Vail Resorts is a mid-sized firm with assets of slightly over $1 billion and annual revenues of about $500 million (see Figure 7 for selected financial trends). Regarding contributions to revenue by the individual resorts, Vail accounts for about 33 percent of the total, Breckenridge and Keystone each about 25 percent, Beaver Creek 12 percent, and Grand Teton about 5 percent. As a result of varying year-to-year ski conditions (including two of the poorest winters on record), VR's recent financial results have been mixed. Revenues have consistently improved and operating margins are strong but have trended downward since the IPO. Compared with its public competitors, the firm has a far better record than American Ski Company (which merged in 2000 into Doral Corp due in part to its financial stress) but not as robust as that of Intrawest (which focuses more on real estate development than on resort operations). Although not a public firm (requiring SEC reporting), Aspen is rumored to be experiencing substantial financial problems and a declining market share.

To spread financial risk, VR has been diversifying its product line. Historically, more than 95 percent of its revenues came from the five-month ski season. With implementation of its all-season strategy at the ski resorts and its acquisition of summer resorts like the Grand Teton, the winter contribution was reduced in 2001 to about 70 percent. Risk of single-source income was also reduced in part from the firm's vertical integration of activities making up the seamless experience. As shown in Figure 8, nonlift-ticket sources of revenue (e.g., from ski school, on- and off-mountain dining, village retail/rental, hospitality management) represented more than 70 percent of the total in 2001 and have been steadily increasing over recent years. Real estate sales make up only about 10 percent of total revenues on average. They are important to the firm's growth strategy, however, because they feed future resort revenues by expanding the visitor bed base of the area (especially when it involves guest rental units, known as "hot beds").

The firm's 2001 asset base of $1.2 billion consists mainly of resort facilities (58 percent), which include retail/commercial buildings, corporation headquarters, lift and gondola terminals, on-mountain restaurants, land for facilities (such as golf courses, corporation yards, and village commons), and machinery and equipment (ski-lift towers and lines, snowmaking equipment, and snow-grooming

FIGURE 7

Trends in Selected Financial Data (Vail Resorts, Inc., 1997–2001)

Fiscal Year Ended July 31 (In Millions)	2001	2000	1999	1998	1997
Statement of operations					
Revenue					
From resorts	$524.1	$501.4	$431.8	$350.5	$292.1
From real estate	35.2	51.7	43.9	84.2	74.4
Total revenue	559.3	553.1	475.7	434.7	366.5
Operating expenses (excluding D&A)	430.7	430.4	380.0	318.5	269.4
Operating net (EBITDA)	128.6	122.7	95.7	116.2	97.1
Gross operating margin	23.0%	22.2%	20.1%	26.7%	26.5%
Net income	$ 18.7	$ 15.3	$ 12.8	$ 30.1	$ 26.0
Balance sheet data					
Total assets	$1,181.0	$1,127.8	$1,089.2	$912.1	$814.8
Long-term debt	388.4	394.2	398.2	284.0	236.3
Stockholders' equity	519.2	493.8	476.8	462.6	417.2

machines). The second largest asset category is intangibles (17 percent) and includes mostly trademarks and goodwill. The third major component is real estate held for sale (13 percent), which consists mostly of undeveloped or developing land. Nearly all of the on-mountain ski terrain is property leased for forty years from the U.S. Forest Service, which owns this land as part of the White River National Forest. Current assets account for slightly less than 10 percent of the firm's total asset base.

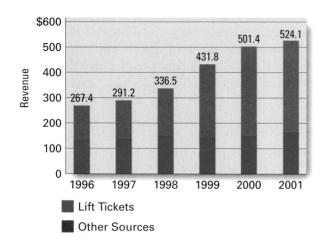

FIGURE 8

Lift Ticket Sales As a Percentage of Resort Revenues (Vail Resorts, Inc., 1997–2001)

Several recent acquisitions are not reflected in the 1997–2001 figures. They include the 2001 end-of-year purchase of Rock Resorts, owner of eleven small high-end resort hotels, and the 2002 purchase of the Heavenly Ski Resort in South Tahoe, California, for $96 million.

The Vail Resorts Organization

With Vail Resorts's new growth strategy, the ensuing changes unleashed a cascade of managerial events and consequences. Indeed, the sheer complexity of the combined resources from the 1997 merger made necessary a massive reorganization of authority. Over the years, the original organization structure provided well for the privately held Vail Valley firm. However, with the acquisition of Ralcorp's two Summit County resorts located an hour away, the purchase of Grand Teton Lodge Company in Wyoming, and the resultant doubling of the firm's asset size and employment base (at seasonal peak, the firm now employs over 12,000, of which half hold permanent year-round status), the existing structure was no longer suitable for the complex integration of diverse new resources, product markets, managerial cultures, personalities, and expertise.

By 2000, the reorganization was almost complete. As shown in Figure 9, the firm's new organization

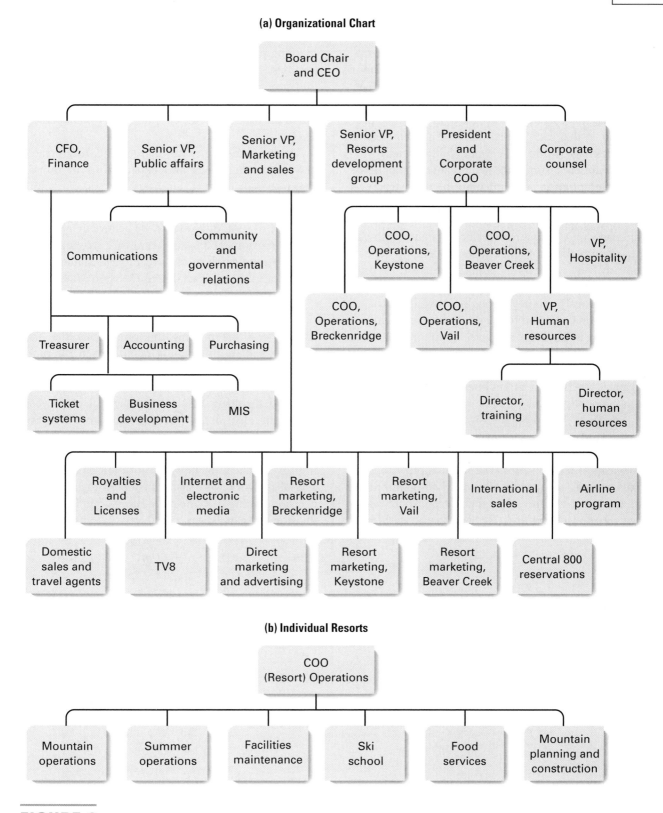

FIGURE 9

Vail Resorts, 2001 (Organization Chart)

chart contained a mix of structural forms, including functional hierarchy, product-line divisions, and a partial matrix. The major accomplishment of the reorganization was to separate management of the four resorts and other product divisions from general management functions. Applying its brand management approach to resort operations, the firm separated production so that each resort would be able to create a distinct image within the VR family of products.

To preserve simultaneous organizational needs for differentiation and integration, two structural components were put in place. First, each resort was given a separate production authority headed by a division COO. To assure overall consistency with Vail Resorts's quality image, each resort division reports to Andy Daly, who acts as "peak coordinator." Second, each resort has a marketing brand manager who simultaneously reports through a partial matrix to the division COO and to the senior vice president for marketing at the corporate level. The reorganization, however, remains incomplete regarding some key integration issues and insufficient in some critical strategic areas, such as environmental management and hospitality management.

At first, the comprehensive reorganization left managerial employees feeling ambiguous about what to expect in the new structure of authority and communication relationships. The months prior to 2000 had created "somewhat of a survival-of-the-fittest environment around here," said Daly. There was a new corporate culture that was being fashioned around the impersonality that comes with the large organizational size of a public company. With the merging of two former competitors, old managerial loyalties, although persistent for a time, were no longer relevant. There were now heightened expectations about what was required in professional behavior in all functional aspects and at all management levels.

At the same time, the merger and IPO created new corporate needs and expectations in human resource management. Driving both was the adoption of a new management credo:

> At Vail Resorts, we believe in
> Customer-Focused Teamwork striving to
> Continuously Improve our Process Management
> Skills through Fact-Based Decision Making to
> Enhance Customer (satisfaction and retention)
> and Shareholder Value (company profits).

As part of implementing this philosophy, the firm was engaged in an ongoing talent search for more and different professional expertise, and this change would require new approaches to motivating, retaining, and directing the best managerial employees. The firm also determined a need for dramatic improvements in employee productivity at both management and nonmanagement levels. Major improvements in the flow of information in the managerial network were also considered to handle the decisionmaking demands of a more complex, multidivisional organization.

Adrenaline Air Sports: Where the Speed Limit Is 120 Miles Per Hour … or More

(condensed version)

2

This case was prepared by Larry D. Alexander (Associate Professor of Business Strategy at Virginia Tech), Billy Cockrell (owner of Adrenaline Air Sports, at Smith Mountain Lake Airport, Smith Mountain Lake, Virginia), and Jonathan Charlton (parachutist and Industrial and Systems Engineering student at Virginia Tech, Blacksburg, Virginia).

Billy Cockrell graduated from Botetourt High School in Roanoke, Virginia, on a Saturday in June 1990. His family had a small party for him later that day at their home to celebrate his graduation. At that gathering, his uncle J. C. Cockrell approached Billy and told him of the unique present he was giving Billy for graduation. He invited Billy to come to his parachute drop zone and take a tandem parachute jump free of charge. Billy's instant response to his uncle was, "No way I'm jumping out of a plane."

After High School

Billy did not feel mature enough to go on to college after high school. Instead, he enlisted for six years in the navy in December 1990, six months after graduating from high school. In the navy, he was trained and worked as a fire-control technician, radar operator, and, occasionally, a search-and-rescue swimmer.

At times in the navy, he would be out to sea on a cruise for three months at a stretch. In

August 1992, he was stationed in Charleston, South Carolina. While many other sailors spent much of their spare time drinking in bars, Billy was looking for something different. One day while visiting on the telephone with his grandmother, Grosejean, she reminded him of the free tandem parachute jump that J. C., his uncle, had offered Billy two years before. This time Billy moved fast on the offer and made the jump the next Saturday at his uncle's drop zone in Greensboro, North Carolina.

Parachute drop-industry statistics show that only a few people who take a first parachute jump ever jump again. This was not the case with Billy Cockrell. He took his second jump the very next day, on Sunday. He became hooked on parachuting and thought he would like to someday work full-time at his own parachute drop zone.

Billy was transferred to various land and sea locations during his six-year navy stint. In 1993, he was sent to San Diego, California, for three months to go through more-advanced naval training. While there, he parachuted at Air Adventures, also located in San Diego, which was a fairly large drop zone operation. Billy was so enthused with his new-found sport that he recruited between forty and fifty people to take their first jump at that drop zone.

According to the United States Parachute Association (Exhibit 1), about 540,000 parachutists worldwide made about 5,563,000 jumps in 1998 alone. In the United States, 317,741 people made 3,500,000 combined jumps in the year 2000 and 34,217 people were members of the United States Parachute Association, headquartered in Alexandria, Virginia, near Washington, D.C. While approximately 300,000 people in the United States took a once-in-a-lifetime jump during 2000, other parachutists made multiple jumps in just one weekend. These veterans of the sport often took up to five or even ten jumps in a single day. At the extreme, Mike Zang made an amazing 500 parachute jumps in a 24-hour period in April of 2001. This amounted to one jump from a Porter type airplane at just 2,100 feet elevation every two minutes and 53 seconds.

A typical parachute jump by experienced jumpers can be described as follows. Four parachuters took off

EXHIBIT 1

U.S. Parachute Association Skydiving Stats

Number of Skydivers worldwide (last reported in 1998 by FAI): 540,000

Number of Skydives worldwide (last reported in 1998 by FAI): 5,563,000

Number of people making a Skydive in the U.S., 2000: 317,741 [1999: 311,511]

Number of Skydives U.S., 2000: 3,500,000

USPA Members, end of 2000: 34,217

Number of Student Jumps:

Student Method	2000	1999
AFF	32,410	31,775
Tandem	185,410	181,775
Static Line	60,338	59,155
Total	278,158	277,366

Number of Members by Total Jump Numbers:

0–25	21.7%
26–250	33.2%
250+	45.1%

Members by Age Group:

0–29	21.0%
30–39	34.4%
40–49	25.7%
50–59	11.2%
60+	3.3%

Gender:

Male	82.0%
Female	14.7%
Unknown	3.3%

with a pilot in a small Cessna-type propeller airplane. It took about twenty to twenty-five minutes to reach 10,000 feet, where the pilot positioned the plane so that the jumpers could parachute and maneuver themselves back to the drop zone. When ready, the parachutists opened the Cessna's passenger door and briefly stood on a step outside the plane or jumped out from inside the plane.

The parachutist initially did a freefall—from 10,000 down to 3,000 feet, usually—with the main chute closed. The jumper's speed quickly accelerated to about 120 miles per hour. On average, a skydiver fell the first thousand feet in about ten seconds and then accelerated, falling each additional thousand feet in about six seconds. Thus, to freefall from 10,000 to 3,000 feet, it took only about forty-six seconds. At 3,000 feet, the jumper pulled a ripcord, which first opened the small pilot chute, then the large main parachute. At that point, the parachutist was "under canopy," slowly descending from the "adrenaline high" of freefall, enjoying the view, and pulling various steering cords to maneuver his parachute back to the drop zone landing area.

All parachute gear was required to have a separate reserve chute in case the main chute did not open or opened incorrectly. Many jumpers paid $500 or more to have an optional automatic activation device attached to their packs so that their second, or reserve, chute opened at a preset altitude. The industry was so safety conscious that all reserve chutes had to be repacked by a rigger, a professional parachute packer, every four months even though it had not been used. This person also checked the two chutes for wear and tear and made any necessary repairs.

During freefall, some parachutists did what was called relative work with other parachutists before opening their parachutes. If four people were jumping together and doing relative work, they might start off in a star formation or point (all holding hands in a square with their feet farthest out), then go to a diamond for a second point, and then to a donut for a third point; if time permitted, they might form an open accordion for a fourth point.

The record number of skydivers to join hands and legs in a free fall pattern was 286 people, accomplished over Ottawa, Illinois in 1998. These very experienced skydivers jumped out of several different planes very quickly and then joined up in just one preplanned pattern. It was planned months in advance and rehearsed to accomplish it and to do it.

Other parachutists did free flying before they opened their parachutes. This was similar to the standard technique of "belly flying" except that the skydiver typically rotated through three positions: head down, feet first, and sitting. These skydivers often did relative work with other free flyers as they moved from one position to another in a choreographed plan. They might come together in a formation or spin and turn relative to each other without touching.

Free flyers going headfirst with their arms at their side could at times exceed 200 miles an hour. These speeds were measured by a Pro-Track helmet computer, which calculates the jumper's statistics, such as his elevation when jumping out of the plane, time in freefall, average speed in freefall, maximum speed in freefall, total elapsed time, and altitude at which the parachute opened.

Another activity performed by parachutists was canopy relative work. In this exercise, the parachutists opened their canopies quickly after exiting the airplane. Then they came together and hooked their feet into the lines of the parachute immediately beneath them. Thus, the parachuters were stacked on top of each other's canopy, the top parachutist controlling the direction of all those below him. This activity was riskier and was done at only a few drop zones throughout the United States, but Adrenaline Air Sports was not included.

Occasionally, some parachutists requested a "hop and pop" jump. This involved a shorter, and therefore, cheaper airplane ride to just 3,000 or 4,000 feet. The parachutists opened their chute a very short time after exiting the plane to test out equipment or to keep the costs down per jump.

The highest parachute jump ever made was by Captain Joseph Kittinger on August 16, 1960. He jumped using bottled oxygen from a balloon at an altitude of 102,800 feet, approximately 20 miles high. As he free fell down past about 80,000 feet in very thin air, he was traveling in excess of 600 miles an hour. Thus, he almost became the first person to break the speed of sound barrier without flying a plane or space vehicle. He also set another record for free falling 84,700 feet, some 16 miles, before opening his chute. As of 2002, Kittinger's records had never been broken, although recently several people were considering trying to break them.

Perhaps more amazing was the highest survived fall without a parachute by Vesna Vulovic on January 26, 1972. She was a stewardess on a DC-9 jet that blew up at 33,330 feet over Czechoslovakia. Everyone on the plane died. She was thrown free of the plane, fell some six miles, hit a snow drift, and amazingly lived.

Adrenaline Air Sports Opens for Business in November 1999

In the fall of 1999, Billy Cockrell signed a five-year lease to open his Adrenaline Air Sports drop zone at Smith Mountain Lake Airport. His rent paid for a hangar, a business office, an adjacent grassy area for parachutists to land on, and rights to take off and land on an unlimited basis from the airport, which was owned and operated by Joe Borgess.

The airport had an elevation of 940 feet and was located about a half mile from the beautiful and large Smith Mountain Lake, which offered boating, sailing, water skiing, swimming, fishing, golf, and parasailing. According to one statistic, up to 10,000 boats could be found on the lake on a busy weekend day. Billy Cockrell had heard from the local realtors that 10,000 new people came to stay at the lake each week during the busy, warm months.

Adrenaline Air Sports's scenic drop zone was located thirty-five miles southeast of Roanoke, Virginia, a city of 94,911 people that was adjacent to Salem to the west. Salem had a population of 24,747 people. Some forty-three miles west of downtown Roanoke (and further west of Salem) was Blacksburg, a college town of 39,573 people. It was the home of Virginia Tech, the largest college in the state, with an enrollment of 25,000 students.

Billy started getting his drop zone underway in fall of 1999. A major goal was to acquire an airplane to take jumpers up. In December 1999, he purchased a 1959 Cessna 182 for $45,000. He arranged to pay for it over a ten-year period with a loan from the Navy Credit Union, which he was eligible to borrow from as a navy veteran.

Billy used eBay and other Internet sources to get most of the equipment he needed to start up his operation. This included helmets and jump suits, which were both fairly expensive. From a Las Vegas supplier on the Internet, he purchased two tandem chutes and two student chutes, larger-sized parachutes used by parachutists starting to jump by themselves. In all, he paid some $15,000 for much of his equipment.

As the year 2000 approached, Billy gradually prepared to open for business and waited for the warm weather in March and April, during which, he hoped, he would attract more customers. As customers increased, Billy realized he needed more equipment.

In May 2000, he bought a third tandem chute, and then in August a fourth one.

In calendar year 2000, Adrenaline Air Sports's total sales amounted to about $90,000—a surprisingly good start for the first year of operations.

Adrenaline Air Sports in Summer 2001

The year 2001 was even better, particularly from April through October. Total sales for the year were $154,000.

Adrenaline Air Sports used part-time employees exclusively. Even Billy worked part-time for Adrenaline even though he might average forty hours a week. And that was on top of his regular full-time job at Luna Innovations in Blacksburg.

In addition, there was his weekend work at the Adrenaline Air Sports' drop zone. During the many bad-weather weekends from late fall to early spring, Billy often went down to his drop zone to get work done, even if no customers were likely to come in. Once the good weather arrived, he would put in a forty-hour weekend, beginning Friday night and ending Sunday night.

After work ended at Luna Innovations at 5 p.m. on Friday, Billy went home for a short time and then drove or flew the seventy miles to his drop zone at Smith Mountain Lake, usually arriving there between 7 and 8 p.m. He usually went first to Adrenaline's office building, which had lights, water, heat, lounge chairs, a bathroom, and some office space. As of March 2002, it also had a shower with hot and cold water, which Billy and some customers helped install. The term "customer" probably sounded strange to him because these people were fellow skydivers who were almost as committed to the sport as Billy.

The manifest on the computer listed all people who had reserved tandem-jump slots for Saturday or Sunday. Tandem jumps were made by first-time parachuters hooked to experienced and certified tandem instructors using one large canopy or parachute.

Most of these people made a reservation with Billy during the week, calling him either at his full-time job or at night at his home. Billy said that he got the most telephone calls on Mondays for parachuting the following weekend. He speculated that first-time jumpers convinced themselves and/or their friends the prior weekend to jump as something of a dare. Then they would call on Monday because if they waited beyond that day, they would often decide not to do it after all.

At Billy's office, he made sure that the various forms jumpers would have to complete were assembled. This included five pages of waivers of liability the jumpers would have to fill out before they were permitted to skydive.

Billy then went to the hangar. There was no heat in the hangar, but it did have lights. He cleaned the hangar and moved items to the wall so that parachuters could repack their chutes on the floor over the weekend or pay a packer to do it. Friday night Billy often repacked any parachutes that his customers would need for Saturday morning.

He owned eight parachutes, which he stored at Adrenaline Air Sports. In addition, some customers stored their own chutes in Billy's hangar when they were not using them. Billy's chutes included four tandem canopies, used for beginners who were attached to their instructor or tandem master, two for accelerated freefall for the next level of skydiving, and two used by just Billy himself. By late Sunday afternoon, nearly everyone was tired, so often nobody would repack these parachutes for the next weekend. Billy would therefore pack them Friday night if necessary. He would then sleep in his office, along with any parachuting customers and/or employees who had arrived early for the weekend. During warm months, they would sleep in the hangar. Everyone slept in sleeping bags, often on air mattresses for some added comfort.

Billy usually started working on Saturday morning by 7 a.m. The manifest was again rechecked and any additional paperwork for that day's jumpers assembled. Training aids were made available. First-time tandem jumpers started arriving by 8 a.m. or soon thereafter for their 8:30 jumps. As first-time jumpers arrived, they filled out forms and paid their $189 fee. They then met their instructor, who gave them ground training, and were asked if they wanted a videotape of their jump, which cost $60. The majority of first-time jumpers purchased the videotape so that they would have a souvenir of their skydiving adventure.

Marketing

Billy used a variety of strategies to get customers to try parachuting at his drop zone. They all helped, though it was hard to pinpoint which marketing approaches were the most effective.

One very helpful advertising technique involved using posters with the headline "Skydive Adrenaline Air Sports." The posters contained such statements as "Skydive at Virginia's Most Scenic Skydiving Center,"

"Specializing in Tandem and Accelerated Freefall," and "Your SAFETY is our FIRST PRIORITY!"

At the bottom of each sheet were tear-off strips of paper that had the name of Adrenaline Air Sports, a telephone number, and a web address. The posters were put up on bulletin boards, walls, and doors at colleges, grocery stores, strip shopping centers, and other places where likely first-time parachuters might see them. Billy also gave them to his loyal customers, asking them to put them up where they worked or near where they lived.

Another marketing strategy was advertising in the Yellow Pages of area telephone directories. Adrenaline Air Sports' ad in Verizon's November 2000 Yellow Pages for Montgomery County of Virginia, whose center was sixty-five miles from Billy's drop zone, read as follows:

> SKYDIVE AT VIRGINIA'S MOST
> SCENIC DROP ZONE
> Located at Smith Mtn Lake Airport
> LEARN TO SKYDIVE
> WITH PROFESSIONALS
> YOUR SAFETY
> IS OUR #1 PRIORITY
> Tandem AFF, Video
> www.air-sports.com
> Smith Mountain Lake . . . 296-1100

The problem with this was that since telephone directories covered such small geographic areas, a business had to spend a lot of money for ads if it was going to cover a large region. Billy paid approximately $18,000 for his numerous Yellow Pages ads per year.

Also appearing in this telephone directory were ads for two of Billy's main competitors, Skydive Orange and Skydive Virginia, both located northeast of Smith Mountain Lake and Charlottesville, 140 miles away from his drop zone.

Billy had tried radio advertising briefly, but never had run a television commercial. Because he had only used radio occasionally, he was not sure of its effectiveness.

Adrenaline Air Sports also placed a small monthly ad in the *Parachutist: Official Publication of the United States Parachute Association*. Adrenaline's three-line monthly ad usually read as follows:

> Adrenaline Air Sports-Skydive Blue Ridge
> Smith Mountain Lake Airport, Moneta
> 30 minutes southeast of Roanoke
> (540) 296-1100
> www.air-sports.com

Like all ads, this appeared along with six others from parachute drop zones in Virginia. Both Skydive Orange and Skydive Virginia were listed. Members of the U.S. Parachute Association automatically got this monthly magazine as part of their yearly membership dues. Over four hundred drop zones were listed in it by state and country.

Adrenaline Air Sports also had eye-catching bumper stickers. They contained one large A for both Adrenaline and Air. The stickers also said "SKYDIVE BLUE RIDGE" and gave a telephone number and web site address. They were given out free of charge to Billy's customers, their friends, and anyone who wanted one.

For first-time parachutists, another form of advertising was the videotape they could purchase as a souvenir of their adventure. Billy was convinced that these jumpers showed their videotapes to many of their friends, helping to stimulate an interest in parachuting. The cost of this advertising was free to Adrenaline Air Sports because beginners paid $60 to get their jumps videotaped.

Tracy Harris did almost all of the skydiving photography at Adrenaline Air Sports. He was about thirty-five years old and ran his own construction business during the week. On the weekends, he worked part-time for Billy with his video camcorder affixed to the top of his helmet. He would go up with every first-time jumper who wanted a videotape, and exited the plane just before the jumper and his tandem instructor. Tracy would record their exit, their freefall, the opening of the parachute (also called canopy), and some of their descent. He then quickly landed so that he could record the pair when they came in for their landing.

So popular were the videotapes that of Tracy Harris's four hundred jumps in 2001, about three hundred were made taking videos. Since Tracy was Adrenaline's sole skydive photographer, he could only handle one videotaping at a time.

Once Tracy finished recording one jumper's landing, he went up almost immediately in another plane with the next jumper. He stored his tapes and worked on them between jumps, on Saturday evenings, and on Sundays. Billy tried to deliver the finished videotapes by the end of Sunday night, if at all possible. Often, Billy or someone else would deliver the videotape to the jumper's home on Sunday night so he or she could have it almost immediately. Billy felt that the videotape was his best marketing tool because the proud first-time parachuter would want to show it to everyone he or she knew.

Flight Operations

Billy purchased his second Cessna 182 in April 2001 to handle the increased number of customers coming to his drop zone. Both planes were being purchased by him with bank loans he obtained from the Navy Credit Union and a local bank in southwest Virginia. With an average purchase price in excess of $40,000, these two small, single-engine propeller planes were a major investment.

Aviation fuel was another significant cost. During 2001, he purchased 11,000 gallons of aviation fuel, which cost almost $26,000, or $2.34 a gallon. On a busy weekend, each plane would consume about $400 in aviation fuel, or one refill every three flights.

Some simple maintenance Billy did on his own. For example, he replaced the oil on each plane frequently every twenty-five hours. Billy felt it was a cheap investment considering the age of the planes.

However, he had a problem getting his planes maintained on a regular basis. No one at his small airport did maintenance, so his planes had to be taken elsewhere to get maintenance. He couldn't ask his three pilots to fly his planes in the middle of the week because they all had regular jobs. One day in February 2001, Billy called the airport in Harrisonburg, Virginia. He said he needed to learn to fly for his business. He got started that day, and just seven days later, he had soloed and received his pilot's license. This changed one aspect of Billy's Adrenaline Air Sports operations.

At the end of a weekend of running his drop zone, Billy often flew one of his planes back to the Virginia Tech airport in Blacksburg, near where he lived and worked during the week. He left the plane there, got into his car, which was parked there for the weekend, and drove a few miles to his home. Then during the week, Billy would fly his plane late in the afternoon a hundred miles to Greensboro, North Carolina. There, his mechanic did routine maintenance on the plane and checked its airworthiness.

That same evening, Billy would fly the plane back to either Blacksburg or his drop zone. If he dropped it off at Adrenaline Air Sports, then someone—often one of his customers—would pick him up and take him back to the Blacksburg area. In this way, Billy's planes received regular maintenance checks in North Carolina during the week. While maintaining the planes took time, Billy was committed to running a very safe skydiving operation, and this started with safe airplanes.

On a busy weekend of good weather, both planes were used all day long. Each plane could take a max-

imum of four skydivers (or parachuters) and the pilot. Seats were removed from the planes, except for the pilot's seat, to accommodate the jumpers and their parachutes.

Billy recently changed the maximum altitude at which his planes would release skydivers. The new policy was that jumpers would be taken to a maximum of 10,000 feet. The Smith Mountain Airport was at an elevation of 1,130 feet, so jumpers could skydive and parachute a total of 8,870 feet. Previously, Billy would take jumpers up to 12,000 feet, charging them more. But he realized that it was not worth it because of the extra ten to fifteen minutes it took to climb to 12,000 feet. The new fee schedule was simple: $6 for a plane ride, plus $1 for each thousand feet. Thus, a ride to 10,000 feet cost $16 and a low-level "hop and pop" (hop out of the plane and pop the parachute) at, say, 4,000 feet would cost $10.

By 8 a.m., the two pilots had arrived to fly the jumpers. The strategy was to keep taking jumpers up as quickly as possible. Adrenaline Air Sports was lucky to have three competent part-time pilots:

J. D. Shumate—A 22-year-old full-time flight instructor at Averett College in Danville, Virginia. He had been a pilot at Adrenaline since it opened in 1999, and had approximately 40 jumps himself.

Jeff "Maverick" Perkins—A 26-year-old UPS (United Parcel Service) truck driver, who previously was a scheduler for U.S. Air Express. He also served as a paramedic in his hometown.

Bobby Bruch—A 42-year-old electrician who worked for Norfolk Southern railroad. He had been a pilot for Billy for one year.

After the first-time tandem jumpers, other parachuters went. This was based on the order in which they had signed up during the preceding week. Experienced jumpers usually had their own parachutes, gear, and clothing, so all they needed was a plane ride, which cost $16 and which took from twenty to twenty-five minutes. Some of these experienced jumpers had been in the sport for ten, twenty, or more years and had several thousand jumps to their credit.

This routine of taking jumpers up, letting them exit the plane, landing the plane, refueling when needed, and taking the next group up continued all morning. At 1 p.m., another set of first-time parachuters arrived.

Billy Cockrell paid approximately $8,000 for insurance each year. This covered his two Cessna planes and provided protection for lawsuits from customers that might get hurt.

Skydiving Instruction

Another key element of Billy's operations was skydiving instruction. Billy had several instructors, Richard Wagner being his lead one. Richard was an interesting person, like most of the people in the sport. He was forty-two years old, first started parachuting at age nineteen, and had over 2,500 jumps. He was vice president of a company in Mount Airy, North Carolina, that made steel reinforcing wire used in building construction.

Richard, who had been a friend of Billy's since 1993, usually came to the drop zone one day of the weekend. He was willing to do whatever Billy asked him to do, such as doing tandem jumps with beginners or coaching others doing accelerated-freefall jumps.

If Richard was not needed as a paid instructor, he would rehearse some four-way skydive patterns called relative work and then jump them. This so-called relative work was done during the fifty seconds or so that four jumpers were in freefall.

Billy had other part-time flight instructors. They included Miles Peters, aged thirty-five, who instructed tandem and accelerated freefall jumpers. Miles had over 1,900 jumps and had been skydiving for ten years. Randy Fields, aged thirty-three, also instructed accelerated freefall jumpers. Randy had over 2,000 jumps and had been with the sport over ten years. Tracy Gasperini, aged thirty-six, instructed tandem jumpers.

Beginning jumpers paid $189 for their tandem jump with an instructor. If they continued, the prices for the next set of jumps were as follows:

2nd jump – $	189	with tandem instructor
Before 3rd jump – $	100	for six-hour ground school
3rd jump – $	189	student with own chute, but two instructors jumping holding on to the student's sides until the student opens chute
4th jump – $	189	same as jumps 1 and 2
5th jump – $	189	jump with own chute with one coach with his own chute nearby
6th jump – $	179	jump with own chute with one coach nearby
7th jump – $	179	jump with own chute with one coach nearby
8th jump – $	179	jump with own chute with one coach nearby
9th jump – $	0	free jump for completing basic set of jumps; own chute and one coach nearby
	$1,582	total price for basic instructional jumps
10th jump – $	41	$16 to be taken to 10,000 feet and $25 to rent one parachute per jump; no charge for instructor or instructor's helper
11th–14th jump – $	41	same as jump 10 each
15th jump – $	41	first solo jump; one-way walkie-talkie provided to communicate with instructor on the ground who helps maneuver and land.

If a beginning jumper who was enthusiastic about the sport wanted to get his own equipment, he would probably purchase used equipment. Prices for good used parachute equipment might fall in the following range:

$	750–$1,000	for main parachute
$	750–$1,000	for reserve second chute
$	750–$1,000	for pack containing both chutes
$	750–$1,000	for automatic-activation device to open second parachute automatically (optional but good to have)
$	3,000–$4,000	total price

If the skydiver wanted all new equipment, then the price range would be $4,000 to $6,000, depending on the quality of the parachute gear. Thus, if a parachuter made a significant investment in used or new equipment and packed his own chutes as well, the price per jump would be just $16.

After taking the twenty basic jumps, a parachuter could look forward to a solo jump and getting an A license. After that, a jumper could work toward getting B, C, and D licenses and then perhaps a coaching rating and an instructor's rating. How long it took to get these various licenses varied widely. Karen Alexander, aged eighteen, got all four licenses plus her coaching certificate in just ten months. Other jumpers might take several years to obtain their A and B licenses.

Another type of very unique parachuting was BASE jumping, which could not be done at Adrenaline Air Sports. BASE jumping involved parachuting off a building for B, off an antenna (radio tower or antenna on top of a building) for A, off a span of a bridge for S, and off the earth for E. A person who parachuted off all four was a true base jumper. Since many of these challenges were from low elevations, the jumper had no time to use a reserve chute if the first one failed. For example, on "Bridge Day" in October on the New River Valley Gorge Bridge, BASE jumpers can jump legally all day from the bridge, which is just 876 feet. On the high side was the Great Trango Tower, in Pakistan, which was BASE jumped by two people, Nicholas Feteris and Glen Singleman, from an elevation of 19,300. This mountain shaped like a pickle on its end required more vertical and difficult climbing than going up Mt. Everest. While BASE jumping could not be practiced at Billy's drop zone, one regular customer, Johnny Woody, was a qualified base jumper and was getting ready to jump into a 1,000 foot vertical cave in Mexico in the next few months.

Repacking Parachutes

Another support operation at Billy's drop zone was the repacking of parachutes so that someone else, or the same person, could make another jump. Experienced parachutists often repacked their own parachute, called the main chute.

For $5, they could have Karen Alexander or someone else at Adrenaline Air Sports pack their chute. Repacking of the larger tandem chute that all beginners used cost $10. Karen had learned to pack chutes from Billy and Billy's rigger, Buzz Conner, so she could earn enough money to take more jumps herself to pay for her new hobby. Other people were available to pack chutes if the demand was high enough.

It must be emphasized that each parachute pack had two chutes: the main chute and the backup chute. Only the main chute was repacked by an experienced parachuter or by a trained person, usually for a fee. The backup or reserve chute was packed only by a "rigger" who was certified by the Federal Aviation Administration to do this important, backup safety procedure. A malfunction with the main chute constituted an emergency situation; the parachutist would then cut away that chute, allowing it to drift down by itself, and open the backup chute. The U.S. Parachute Association standards required that only a rigger pack this life-saving, backup chute.

Finance

Billy Cockrell's sales for 2001 were $154,000. This marked a very good year, and an amazing increase in sales from 2001, which had only $90,000. The 2001 sales were the result of approximate 6,000 total jumps, of which about 500 were tandem jumps with beginners.

Human Resources

As briefly mentioned, all people who worked at Adrenaline Air Sports worked part-time. Furthermore, that work was done primarily on weekends when weather conditions made parachuting possible and enjoyable. Billy, as the owner, was the only one who came close to being a full-time employee.

The pilots and some of the instructors worked regularly for Billy. Most of the other employees came out to Adrenaline Air Sports not knowing if they would pay to jump for fun or if they would be paid to jump with others or if they would pack parachutes. Because they loved skydiving, liked Billy, and enjoyed the people at the drop zone, they would instantly switch from being a customer to an employee if asked to do so.

Competition
Skydive Orange

Located in Orange, Virginia, Skydive Orange was probably the largest parachute operation in the state of Virginia, which had seven major drop zones. Skydive Orange, which was about three hours from Billy's Adrenaline Air Sports, was usually open Friday, Saturday, and Sunday during the season. It also was open on Wednesdays from late April to midfall. During the colder months, it was only open on Saturday and Sunday, weather permitting. Some young, committed skydivers were there seven days a week, however, living in school buses that the drop zone rented out.

This drop zone operated two Cessna 182s and a Twin Otter (a twin-engine propeller plane). The Otter took approximately fourteen skydivers as high as 14,000 feet in just twenty minutes. More jumpers in less time generated much higher revenues per hour of operation. While Skydive Orange had this bigger plane, it also had higher prices for beginners and experienced jumpers. Videotapes also cost more.

Skydive Virginia

Somewhat close to Skydive Orange's operation was Skydive Virginia. It was located between Fredericksburg and Charlottesville, near Lake Anna, and was also about three hours from Adrenaline Air Sports. It was somewhat larger than Billy's operation and smaller than Skydive Orange's. It was usually open four days a week during the season: Friday, Saturday, Sunday, and Monday; during the colder months, it was open just on Saturday and Sunday.

Like Skydive Orange, Skydive Virginia had a couple of Cessnas capable of taking up four parachuters at once. This operation also used a King Air twin-engine plane (similar to Skydive Orange's Twin Otter) that could carry twelve jumpers at a time.

Skydive the Point

Skydive the Point was located in West Point, Virginia, forty miles east of Richmond, the state's capital. It was open Saturday and Sunday twelve months a year. For key weekends like Memorial Day, Skydive the Point would be open Thursday through Monday. It used a Twin Otter plane that fit twenty-two jumpers and flew up to 13,500 or 14,500 feet. The cost per jump for parachutists who owned their own gear was $20, or $19 if they were a member of the club. Since Skydive the Point was between Richmond and the greater Virginia Beach coastal area, and south of the Washington, D.C.–northern Virginia area, it drew upon a huge population base.

Skydive Suffolk

Skydive Suffolk was located at the Suffolk Airport, twenty-five miles west of Norfork and near the Atlantic Ocean. Like Skydive the Point, this drop zone was near a number of populated areas, particularly the Norfork–Virginia Beach area. Open Friday, Saturday, and Sunday year-round, Skydive Suffolk used a King Air, which took fourteen jumpers with their own parachute gear up to 14,000 feet for a price of $19. The company also had a Cessna, which took five jumpers up to 10,500 feet for $13.

Strategic Issues Facing Adrenaline Air Sports

A major issue facing Billy and all parachute drop zones was getting first-time jumpers to come back. According to statistics, only 3 percent of all first-time jumpers ever took a second jump even though most first-time jumpers had a favorable experience. The first jump cost $189 at Adrenaline Air Sports, and somewhat more at other drop zones. Furthermore, the cost for jump 2 was also $189, there was a $100 additional charge for ground school before jump 3 is made. By jump 6, the price reduced a little to $179. The ninth jump was thrown in free by Billy. Thus, the cost for the first nine jumps was about $1,582, or $175 per jump. After that, the price fell to $41 if the jumper was taken to 10,000 feet and rented a parachute.

Jared Campbell's first jump was taken in March 2001 and was somewhat typical of many first-time jumpers' experiences.

Jared had once told his friends that he wanted to take a parachute jump someday. His friend and past roommate Chris Sides therefore picked up one of Adrenaline Air Sports's cards from a poster on a bulletin board at Virginia Tech, where Jared was a student, eighty miles from Billy's drop zone. Chris then privately collected about $200 from Jared's friends to pay for one jump. Then on the Saturday after his twenty-second birthday, Chris and several of these "paying" friends told Jared they were taking him to see an air show that would include a flyby by the B2 Stealth Bomber.

Jared became suspicious after being driven for one and a half hours. Finally, when they turned onto a dirt road miles past Roanoke, he began to doubt that they were going to the air show.

His friend Chris said, "I guess by now you've guessed that there is no air show." Jared, while still puzzled, agreed. Chris then said, "The air show is you, Jared. We came here to see you parachute." So Jared received some training and went on a tandem jump with an instructor attached to him.

Most of the friends who had paid for Jared's jump came along to watch. While this meant a lot to him, little did he know that some of them had made informal bets on whether or not he would follow through. Chris chipped in an extra $60 to have the jump videotaped and then gave Jared the tape of his jump—before, during, and after—set to music.

A year after the jump, Jared was still interested in jumping again. However, he lacked funds to do so.

An unusual example of someone taking a second and third jump is former president George Bush senior. During World War II, he was a fighter pilot whose plane was shot down. Fortunately, he was able to parachute to safety and later get picked up by our troops. Amazingly, after being president from 1989 to 1993, at age 71 he took his second parachute jump in

March 1995 with the Golden Knights, the Army elite parachute team. Several years later, Bush did another jump, in 1999, at age 75. Still older is the record setter for age, Edwin Townsend, who parachuted with his own chute in 1987 at age 89.

Another strategic issue was determining how best to market this sport. What type of customer group should Adrenaline Air Sports target? What form of advertising would best reach these daredevils? Should Billy go after other sports enthusiasts, such as winter and summer skiiers, skateboarders, bicyclists, scuba divers, and cavers? Should he pursue more first-time jumpers, who often were young people in college, even though they almost never jumped again? (People had to be at least eighteen to parachute unless the drop zone allowed them to jump younger with their parents' written permission, in which case they had to be at least sixteen. Adrenaline Air Sports did not allow anyone under eighteen to jump at its drop zone.)

Other possible market segments existed. He could target married, childless men and women who were looking for some new excitement and challenge in their lives. Another possible target was men in their mid thirties to fifties facing midlife crises wanting a challenge to prove themselves. These and other groups continually came to mind when Billy considered which customer segments to focus on. Irrespective of the particular target, which marketing media would best reach them still needed to be determined.

A third issue facing Adrenaline Sports was what could be done, if anything, to make the sport more affordable for new skydivers. Once a person had an A license, after twenty or so jumps, the cost dropped considerably, but it was still an expensive sport. Billy's students paid for the first eight jumps, then received the ninth free. One parachutist at Billy's drop zone commented that people who had already taken eight jumps would undoubtedly pay for the ninth one. Billy considered offering a free jump earlier to encourage a person to continue.

At $189, Adrenaline Air Sports's fee for first-time jumpers was a little cheaper than most other drop zones'. And while the first jumps were expensive, Billy made money from these people, who often never jumped again; he claimed that he didn't make money off the veteran jumpers, who owned their own gear

and paid just $16 a jump. Perhaps there was some way for Billy to lower the price of the instructors' jumps with new parachutists and increase rates for veteran jumpers. However, if rates were raised too much for the experienced jumpers, they might go elsewhere.

Another strategic issue was whether Billy could make Adrenaline Air Sports his job full-time. While Billy clearly was off to a good start with his drop zone, his location was not as suitable to year-round operations as locations in California or Florida, where mild winters made this possible. Still, some of the mid-Atlantic drop zones like Skydive Virginia were full-time businesses for the owners, even if they were open just on weekends during cold months.

What Billy needed to do was get more customers to come to his drop zone, which was beautiful when viewed from the air, during good-weather periods. Unfortunately, Billy had two small planes, Cessna 182s, which could only take up four jumpers at a time. Billy also lacked enough parachutes to rent if he were to get more customers during prime weekends and months. Finally, his location was far away from major metropolitan areas, such as Richmond, northern Virginia, and the Tidewater–Virginia Beach area. And while the Greensboro area of North Carolina was only eighty miles away, larger North Carolina cities like Durham, Raleigh, Winston-Salem, and Charlotte were further.

A final issue was safety. For most people, the thought of "jumping out of a perfectly good airplane," as military pilots like to put it, sends chills down their spine. The sport was, out of necessity, very safety conscious, but with speeds exceeding 120 miles an hour and no safety device resembling a seat belt, accidents were often fatal. Most nonjumpers felt parachuting was extremely dangerous. The type of people who were attracted to the sport were often outdoor types oriented to extreme sports. Jim Crouch, the safety and training coordinator of the U.S. Parachute Association, has noted that jumpers are "lacking in emergency canopy procedures, which causes accidents." He added that parachutists should not "downsize too quickly" to smaller-sized, higher-performance parachutes as this also increases risk.

Overall, expert opinion and industry statistics showed that skydiving was a safe, wholesome sport that had very loyal customers enjoying the sport.

General Aviation: an Industry Note

3

This case was prepared by Harold Dyck and Sue Greenfeld, California State University, San Bernardino.

General aviation is all "civil aviation activity except that of scheduled air carriers. This includes business transportation, air charter, air taxis, personal and recreational flying, emergency medical evacuation, agricultural flying, traffic and aerial observation, and flight training." The Federal Aviation Administration (FAA) counted 192,414 general aviation (GA) aircraft in the United States in 1997 and 612,298 active pilots in 1998. These pilots include student, recreational, private, commercial, airline-transport, helicopter, glider, and lighter-than-air ones. The FAA projects 231,000 active GA aircraft for 2011. Most GA aircraft are for personal use (34.8%); other uses are instructional (17.9%), business (10.8%), and corporate (10.4%) (**http://generalaviation.org/pages/faq.shtml,** January 22, 2001).

General aviation is part of the 1998–2002 National Plan of Integrated Airport Systems (NPIAS), which is "submitted to Congress. . . . The plan identifies 3,344 existing airports that are significant to national air transportation and contains estimates that $35.1 billion in infrastructure development is eligible for Federal aid . . . to meet the needs of all segments of civil avi-

ation" (**www.faa.gov/arp/410home.htm,** January 26, 2001). There are 15,000 non-NPIAS "low activity landing areas," including private airstrips away from populated areas.

While GA pilots are allowed to land at large airports such as LAX or La Guardia, they rarely do. Of the 3,344 airports in the NPIAS, only twenty-nine are identified as "large hubs" that concentrate on airline passengers and freight operations. These hubs accounted for 67.3% of all passenger enplanments in 1998, but only 1.3% of active GA aircraft. Only five of them (Salt Lake City, Las Vegas, Honolulu, Miami, and Phoenix) have a significant number (averaging 343) of GA aircraft. The other twenty-four have fewer than thirty-four based aircraft each (**www.faa.gov/arp/410home.htm,** January 26, 2001).

Therefore, 69% of all active aircraft are based either at the 334 "reliever" airports or the 2,472 GA airports. Reliever airports are located in major metropolitan areas and allow pilots to avoid congested hub airports. They average 181 aircraft each, accounting for 32% of U.S. aircraft. Of the $35.1 billion in NPIAS development monies, reliever airports are allocated 7%, or $7.35 million each. GA airports are located in "communities that do not receive scheduled commercial service" and have "at least 10 locally owned aircraft." These GA airports receive 11% of the NPIAS development monies, or $1.56 million each (**www.faa.gov/arp/410home.htm,** January 26, 2001).

This case is presented as the basis for educational discussion rather than to illustrate either effective or ineffective handling of an administrative situation. Special appreciation is given to Ilia Adami for her research assistance. Reprinted by permission of the authors.

Those Who Fly

To become a pilot in the United States, a person must be at least sixteen years old, be in good health, and read, speak, and understand English. In 1998, there were around 618,000 certified pilots, including almost 98,000 student pilots, 247,000 private pilots, 122,000 commercial pilots, and 134,000 airline transport pilots (**http://www.api.faa.gov/airmen/toc.htm,** March 20, 2001, Table 1). For each type of certificate, a candidate must pass proficiency examinations as well as possess sufficient aeronautical experience.

Student pilots must pass a so-called Class III biannual medical exam given by an FAA-designated physician. This medical clearance lasts for three years for individuals under forty years and two years for those over forty. Students fly with their instructors until their instructors sign them off for their first solo fight usually after about ten to twelve hours of instruction. A student pilot earns his or her private-pilot's certificate with a minimum of thirty-five or forty hours, a written exam, and a check ride with an examiner. To earn a private-pilot's license, a person can expect to spend between $2,500 and $4,000. This includes plane rental at $45 to $60 per hour, an instructor's fee of $15 to $20 per hour, and $150 for ground-school instruction.

Commercial pilots can "fly for hire." They must be at least eighteen years old, should have an instrument rating, must hold a Class II annual medical certificate, must have at least 250 hours of flying time, and must pass a written exam and a check ride with an examiner. Airline-transport pilots can work for the major airlines, must be at least twenty-three years old, are required to log 1,500 hours of flight time, and must hold a Class I semiannual medical certificate, in addition to having to pass more stringent proficiency exams.

Pluses and Minuses of General Aviation Airports

Why would a community want a GA airport? GA airports provide a number of benefits and services to a community. Activities associated with GA airports include agriculture, firefighting, law enforcement, business, cargo, charter, corporate, disaster relief, glider, medical emergency, military, parachute, recreational flying, search and rescue, tourism, training, and ultralights (California Department of Transportation [DOT], 1998). The California DOT differentiates business from corporate activity in this way: business activity involves an individual who flies out of an airport for business without compensation to the pilot, while a corporate activity involves compensating a professional pilot who flies an aircraft owned or leased by the company.

In describing the economic impact of GA on the U.S. economy, Zuelsdorf and McClellan estimated that GA provided 638,000 jobs in 1998. These jobs include those directly related to GA as well as jobs that are indirectly related, such as restaurant workers at airports. They also estimated the total GA economic impact in the United States to be $64.5 billion in 1998, of which $21.8 billion was generated through GA airports (**http://api.hq.faa.gov/conference/procdoc2000/zuelsdor.pdf,** June 20, 2001).

On the other hand, the disadvantages of an airport in a community include noise, safety, air pollution, lower property values, and loss of tax revenue for the next-best use of the land. These affect a community's quality of life and excessive noise can affect children's learning. A study by Gary Evans and Lorraine Maxwell at Cornell University (1997) found that "children whose schools were affected by aircraft noise did not learn to read as well as those who were in quiet schools. The researchers compared children in a noisy school (in the flight path of a major international airport) with similar students in a quiet school and found that children in the noisy school had difficulty acquiring speech recognition skills, impacting on the ability to learn to read" (**http://www. lhh.org/noise/children/learning.htm,** May 7, 2001).

Airports also have certain inherent risks. Many airport neighbors have concerns about aircraft accidents, especially injuries and deaths to individuals on the ground. Table 1 shows data from the National Transportation Safety Board (NTSB) on GA accidents and fatalities from 1982 to 2000. The difference between total and onboard fatalities represents individuals killed on the ground by GA aircraft.

In terms of air pollution, the GA industry has made some movement towards a cleaner environment. For example, small GA aircraft now use low-lead gasoline. Lead has been identified as the second leading hazardous substance emitted into the environment. Lead poisoning can damage the central nervous system, the immune system, and kidneys (**http://www.atsdr.cdc.gov/cxcx3.html,** May 23, 2001). Another example of increased sensitivity to

TABLE 1

U.S. General Aviation Accidents, Fatalities, and Rates, 1982–2000

Year	Accidents		Fatalities		Flight Hours	Accidents Per 100,000 Flight Hours	
	All	**Fatal**	**Total**	**Aboard**		**All**	**Fatal**
1982	3,233	591	1,187	1,170	29,640,000	10.90	1.99
1983	3,077	556	1,069	1,062	28,673,000	10.73	1.94
1984	3,017	545	1,042	1,021	29,099,000	10.36	1.87
1985	2,739	498	956	945	28,322,000	9.66	1.75
1986	2,582	474	967	879	27,073,000	9.54	1.75
1987	2,495	447	838	823	26,972,000	9.25	1.65
1988	2,385	460	800	792	27,446,000	8.69	1.68
1989	2,232	431	768	765	27,920,000	7.98	1.53
1990	2,215	443	767	762	28,510,000	7.77	1.55
1991	2,175	433	786	772	27,678,000	7.85	1.56
1992	2,073	446	857	855	24,780,000	8.36	1.80
1993	2,039	398	736	732	22,796,000	8.94	1.74
1994	1,994	403	725	718	22,235,000	8.96	1.80
1995	2,053	412	734	727	24,906,000	8.23	1.64
1996	1,909	360	632	615	24,881,000	7.67	1.45
1997	1,851	352	641	635	25,464,000	7.27	1.38
1998	1,909	368	631	625	25,349,000	7.53	1.45
1999	1,913	342	630	622	29,496,000	6.49	1.16
2000	1,835	341	592	582	30,800,000	5.96	1.11

Notes: Data are preliminary for 2000. Flight hours are preliminary for 1999. Flight hours are estimated by the Federal Aviation Administration. Since April, 1995, the NTSB has been required by law to investigate all public-use accidents. The effect upon the number of general-aviation accidents has been an increase of about 1.75%.

Source: **http://www.ntsb.gov/aviation/Table10.htm,** May 7, 2001.

pollutants emitted into the air is the preflight safety test. Pilots are expected to inspect their fuel levels on the ground and drain fuel into a small gauge to check for water in the tanks. Water in the tanks could lead to carburetor ice, endangering the pilot and passengers if the engine should fail. A negative consequence of this safety test is the evaporation of discarded fuel, resulting in the pollutants benzene and 1,3-butadiene. However, pilots are now beginning to put this drained fuel back into the tanks.

According to the Aircraft Owners and Pilots Association (AOPA), "oftentimes property values are lower for residential areas surrounding an operating airport" (p. 8). The airport's master plan could affect development in the area. Government agencies may enforce zoning regulations. Building codes may require soundproofing for structures near airports. Real estate disclosures may be required to inform potential buyers of these land-use controls.

Also, a community-owned airport may reduce the tax base. This shows up as "in-lieu" property tax in the airport's accounting records, is an opportunity cost for the next-best use of the land, and can make the GA airport appear as a loss to the city. Other economic users, including developers and cities in search of new park land, have been increasing the pressure to close GA airports. Two recent examples include Meigs Field in Chicago and, in California, Santa

Monica's airport. Both of these GA airports are located in densely populated areas with high property values. Thus, a balanced approach would take into account GA's positive economic effects and the value of the next-best alternative.

Legislation Affecting General Aviation Airports

In the early days, aviation was largely unregulated. The passage of the Air Commerce Act of 1926 created the Department of Commerce Aeronautical Division to enforce Civil Air Regulations, the precursor of the Federal Aviation Regulations (FARs). The federal government became responsible for building airports, creating federal airways to separate aircraft, and testing pilots for aeronautical knowledge and physical capabilities for flying (**http://avstop.com/news/ac.html,** June 20, 2001). In 1938, the federal government created the Civil Aeronautics Authority (CAA), which existed until 1958, when Congress passed the Federal Aviation Act and transferred administration and enforcement to the Federal Aviation Agency, later called the Federal Aviation Administration (FAA).

Today, in the twenty-first century, airways and pilots are highly regulated. For example, in the congested area around Los Angeles International Airport (LAX), there are special flight rules that a pilot must follow regarding the shoreline. The rules say the pilot must be flying at a specific altitude, airspeed, and direction, must be on a special radio frequency and transponder code, and must have a special chart in the aircraft. Special flight rules may also apply above unpopulated areas, such as the Grand Canyon. To help preserve the natural beauty and provide a true wilderness experience, the FAA limits flight over the Grand Canyon to narrow air corridors at precise altitudes. Except in an emergency, no aircraft may fly below the rim of the canyon.

The most recent major federal legislation, passed in 2000, is the Aviation Investment and Reform Act for the 21st Century, known as AIR-21. While this five-year authorization of funds is designed to address the issues of airport capacity, technological updates of air-traffic control, airline competition, and aviation safety, it also affects GA. For small airports, AIR-21 triples the funding from $500,000 to $1.5 million per year, provides them with entitle-ment money based on their needs (up to $200,000 per year), and provides incentives to realize the benefits of air-traffic-control services. Finally, AIR-21 "creates a new funding program to help small under-served airports market and promote their air service" (**http://www.house.gov/transportation/press/air21sum2.html,** July 3, 2001).

The Future of General Aviation

Today, GA pilots have computerized flight-management information systems with satellite-based GPS moving maps, sophisticated flight-planning software linked to real-time weather services through the Internet, and onboard radar storm displays. This is a far cry from 1927, when Charles Lindbergh flew across the Atlantic with "No parachute, no radio, no brakes, not even a forward-facing window (a small periscope would do)" (**http://www.acepilots.com/lindbergh.html,** July 5, 2001). Despite the challenges of regulation, pollution, noise, increasing gas prices and insurance rates, and closing airports, the General Aviation Manufacturers Association forecasts increases through 2010 in the numbers of aircraft, pilots, flight hours, and fuel use, with only the number of hours per pilot decreasing:

	1999	2010	C (%)
Aircraft	219,500	229,100	4.4
Pilots	640,100	810,000	26.5
Flight Hours	31,800,000	38,100,000	19.8
Fuel (mil. gal.)	1,313	2,133	62.5
Hours per Pilot	49.7	47.0	−5.3

Source: General Aviation Manufacturers Association (GAMA), *General Aviation 2000 Statistical Databook* (Washington, D.C.: GAMA, 2000).

In addition, a wealth of information concerning GA and its future is available on the Web at the following addresses:

> **http://www.aopa.org/** AOPA (Airplane Owners and Pilots Association)

http://www.generalaviation.org/ GAMA (General Aviation Manufacturers Association

http://www.faa.gov/ FAA (Federal Aviation Administration)

http://www.nata-online.org/ NATA (National Air Transportation Association)

http://www.nbaa.org/ NBAA (National Business Aircraft Association)

Impact of the 9/11 Tragedy on General Aviation

Airport closures Numerous airports shut down nationwide, including the Redlands Municipal Airport for two weeks.

Airspace changes Both the FAA and the military upgraded their efforts to create and enforce temporary flight restrictions such as those protecting the president and vice president of the United States and nuclear reactors and other facilities of national importance.

Legislation Legislators passed a flurry of new legislation, including:

A massive victim's compensation and airline bailout bill

A major aviation and transportation security act affecting flight schools with increased screening of flight-instruction candidates and enhanced airspace restrictions

A bill making airport-security personnel employees of the federal government

The GA Industry Reparation Act of 2001 (Lobbyists claimed that small GA businesses were as adversely affected by the tragedy as the airlines.)

Industry forecasts The Airplane Owners and Pilots Association predicts a gradual increase in the number of student pilots over the next five years, but the FAA forecasts 15,000 fewer student pilots.

References

Aircraft Owners and Pilots Association (AOPA) (1999). *Airports, A Valuable Community Resource: A Guide to Obtaining Community Support for Your Local Airport.* Frederick, MD: AOPA.

California Department of Transportation (1998). *The California Aviation System: 1998 Inventory Element.*

Eckrose, Roy A., and William H. Green (1988). *How to Assure the Future of Your Airport.* Madison, WI: Ecrose/Green Associates.

Evans, G. W., and L. Maxwell (1997). Environment and Behavior, 29, Fay, T. W., Noise and health. New York, NY: The New York Academy of Medicine, in **http://www.lhh.org/noise/children/learning.htm,** May 7, 2001.

FAR/AIM 2001: Federal Aviation Regulations/Aeronautical Information Manual. Newcastle, WA: Aviation Supplies and Academics, Inc., 2000.

General Aviation Manufacturers Association (GAMA) (2000). *General Aviation 2000 Statistical Databook.* Washington, D.C.: GAMA.

Zuelsdorf, Robert J., and Eric B. McClellan "The Economic Impact of Civil Aviation on the U.S. Economy—2000," **http://api.hq.faa.gov/conference/procdoc2000/zuelsdor.pdf,** Wilbur Smith Associates, June 20, 2001.

http://generalaviation.org/pages/faq.shtml, January 22, 2001.

http://www.acepilots.com/lindbergh.html, July 5, 2001.

http://www.atsdr.cdc.gov/cxcx3.html, May 22, 2001.

http://www.api.faa.gov/airmen/toc.htm, March 20, 2001, Table 1.

http://www.faa.gov/arp/410home.htm, January 26, 2001.

http://www.house.gov/transportation/press/air21sum2.html, July 3, 2001.

http://www.ntsb.gov/aviation/Table10.htm, May 7, 2001.

Nomani, Asra Q., and Nancy Keates (1999), "A Tragedy Puts Small Planes in the Spotlight," *Wall Street Journal,* July 19, B1, B4.

Wells, Alexander T. (1996). *Airport Planning & Management.* 3d ed. New York: McGraw-Hill.

4 Redlands Municipal Airport

This case was prepared by Sue Greenfeld and Harold Dyck, California State University, San Bernardino.

Introduction and Background

Ron Mutter, public works director for the city of Redlands, reflects about broadening public use of the Redlands Municipal Airport. Acquired in 1962, the airport never quite lived up to expectations. While selling fuel and providing flight instruction, the airport did not succeed in establishing air ambulance services or charter flights or in enticing a Cessna pilot center to locate at the airport (Redlands City Council Minutes, 1962). However, the new mayor, Patricia (Pat) Gilbreath, a CPA-firm partner and pilot, sees the potential of the airport to be more economically viable and is working with Ron, the city council, and the city airport advisory board to encourage this to happen. In addition, an entrepreneur has approached the city with a three-phase plan to add new facilities to the airport.

Located in San Bernardino County, California, the 194-acre Redlands Municipal Airport is about sixty miles east of Los Angeles, four miles northeast of charming downtown Redlands, and three miles north of Interstate 10. The airport serves single- and small twin-engine general-aviation aircraft weighing less than 12,500 pounds. A few ultralights—hang gliders with motors—are also based at the airport. The airport has no tower, but is served by an automated twenty-four-hour "unicom" radio frequency for advising pilots of landing conditions and allowing pilots to make position reports. This type of airport usually does not have a precision-instrument approach, but it recently acquired a geographic position system (GPS). The Redlands Municipal Airport bases 9%, or around 204 airplanes, of the county's 2,254 registered aircraft, is one of the county's eighteen paved airports, and is one of California's 257 airports (California Department of Transportation, 1998). In California, there are thirty-three primary and commercial-service airports and 176 reliever and general-aviation airports.

As city officials think about the airport, they wonder the following. Was purchasing the airport beneficial to the city of Redlands? Is the airport capable of generating enough resources to become self-supporting? Should the city be doing more to entice new business and/or pilots to the airport? Whose job is it to promote the airport? Are there important safety issues, such as allowing ultralights to land at the airport? Is the land surrounding the airport used to its potential? Is the airport capable of growing beyond the 204 aircraft now based there? How can the city predict changes in the demand for airport services? To what extent should the city consider the impact of nearby airports? And finally, how should the city balance the competing interests of the various public and private stakeholders?

City of Redlands

Founded in 1888, the city of Redlands sprang up around Assistencia Mission de San Gabriel, an outpost of Los Angeles's San Gabriel mission about fifty-five miles west of Redlands. According to "Redlands History" (**http://www.redlands-aor.com/history.htm,** May 8, 2000), Redlands was named for the color of its adobe soil. Most of the early settlers were from the Chicago area, including a few who were quite wealthy. The San Bernardino Mountains to the north provide a picturesque backdrop to the city, which flourished as a result of a burgeoning citrus industry until World War II—and then everything changed. The creation of a nearby army air corps depot (later Norton U.S. Air Force Base) led to a building boom.

In 1978, county Proposition R was passed to limit growth. Today, Redlands is known for its balanced approach to growth and its preservation of citrus acreage, which local residents refer to as the emerald necklace. This alludes to the dark-green citrus leaves and open-space areas that, when viewed from the air, look like emeralds encircling the city. The population in 1999 was 65,500 and has been fairly stable for the last ten years (**http://www.redlands-aor.com/main .htm,** May 8, 2000).

Exhibit 1 shows the relationships among the airport, the public works department of Redlands, and the city council. The citizens of Redlands elect all five city council members. The mayor is selected from the five by a vote of the city council. The city council appoints seven members to an airport advisory board. These nonpaid members are mostly pilots who meet monthly to discuss issues associated with the airport. According to the Redlands's web site, the

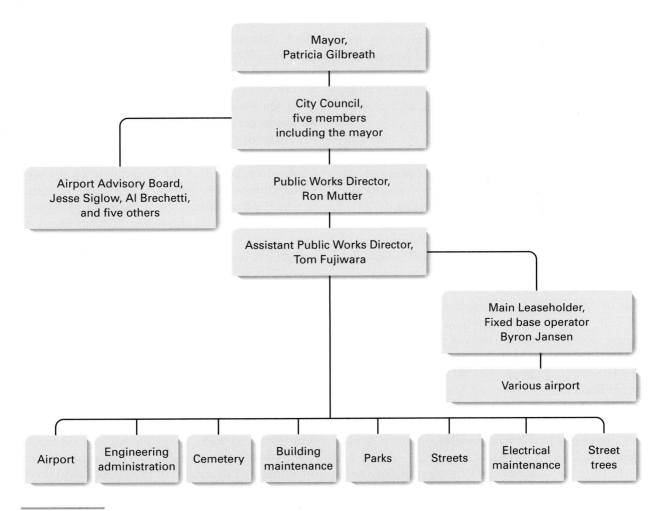

EXHIBIT 1

City Organizational Chart for Redlands Municipal Airport

airport advisory board shall have the power and duty to act in an advisory capacity to the city council in all matters pertaining to the administration, operation, development, improvement, and maintenance of the Redlands Municipal Airport (**http://www.alphais .com/redlands/3006.html#airport,** May 20, 2000). The assistant director and public works director serve as ex-officio members of this board.

History of the Airport

The history of the Redlands Airport can be divided into two periods. From 1945 to 1962 the airport was privately held, and from 1962 to the present it has been owned by the city of Redlands. In 1945, pilot Robert Kanaga, a returning U.S. Army Air Corps veteran of World War II, started laying plans for the Redlands Airport with the financial assistance of a Redlands optometrist, Austin Welch. The bulk of the land was leased from San Bernardino County for ten years at $150 a year. Kanaga was granted permission from the Civil Aeronautics Administration (the forerunner of the FAA) to operate an air agency facility. This business included training pilots, selling new Cessna aircrafts and repair.

When Kanaga was called back to active duty for the Korean War by the U.S. Air Force (formerly the U.S. Army Air Corps) in 1952, the airport was sold to the Southern California Turkey Growers Association, which used the hangar for turkey processing.

In 1955, Roy Haskins and Al Theos bought the airport and asked for help from their family members. . . . Denny Haskins started Red Aero Aviation, an aircraft-maintenance operation.

The Haskins family lengthened the runway twice, once in 1958 and again, in 1959, to the current length of 4,500 feet. Runway lights and fourteen **shade** hangars were also added. The Haskins set up a coffee shop, "but never made money," says Denny Haskins. Roy Haskins made an offer to sell the runway to the city of Redlands in October 1962 to enable the city to apply for federal-aid grants: city ownership of the airport was a prerequisite for obtaining funds for airport development. "It was free federal money," says Denny Haskins.

In 1964, the Redlands City Council authorized an FAA-recommended purchase of about ten acres of property adjoining the runway. A fire truck was added in 1965. Matching funds from the FAA and California State Aeronautics Division helped fund drainage, fencing, underground telephone lines, and other capital improvements in the 1960s. In 1967 and 1968, the city was engaged in promising talks with Golden West Airlines about offering flights, but these did not work out. In 1970, the airport added T-hangars (so-called because of the practice of alternating airplanes backwards and forwards in a long row).

The city continued to get funds from federal and state sources in the decades to follow. These funds were used for flood control, land acquisition, runway improvements, and a runway safety area, among other items. In 1985, a visual approach slope indicator was installed on Runway 8, the runway used for landings to the east. Additional improvements included security fencing and lighting, taxiway reconstruction, and paving an adjacent area for airplane tiedowns.

In order to receive federal and state funding, the city commissioned master plans for the airport in 1962, 1980, and 1991. The last plan, completed in November 1993 and costing $44,000, was financed in part by a grant from the U.S. Department of Transportation (DOT) and the FAA.

When the economic recession of the early 1990s hit California a year after the rest of the nation, the Redlands Airport was affected. Furthermore, nearby Norton U.S. Air Force base was slated for closure in 1994, which added to the uncertainty of the economic climate. Civic leaders did not know the extent to which a base closure would harm the local communities, but 4,250 military and 2,133 civilian jobs were expected to be lost. These figures did not include any indirect losses.

In 1996, the Redlands City Chamber of Commerce helped sponsor the fiftieth anniversary of the establishment of the Redlands Airport. Unfortunately, the June weekend selected for the air show was unseasonably warm; temperatures broke 100 degrees Fahrenheit, and the event lost over $10,000 for the Chamber.

Reflecting on the current situation, Ron Mutter states that in 1991, the Redlands Airport received almost $1,000,000 to create a ramp area to "tie down" airplanes adjacent to the taxiway, but, with the downturn of the economy, many pilots could no longer "afford their expensive toys. . . . Planes were sold, and the number of aircraft based in Redlands went down as much as 10%. . . . Right now we are renting only fifteen to twenty tiedowns out of 100, [but] all our hangars are rented out. We even have a waiting list. All we have available is outside tiedown spaces."

Another concern—mentioned by airport advisory-board members Jesse Siglow and Al Brechetti—revolves around the landing of ultralights at the airport. The Federal Aviation Regulations (FARs) define ultralights as powered or unpowered vehicles that are used in the air for recreational purposes by a single person and that do not need aircraft registration or an airworthiness certificate. The powered ultralights have less than five gallons of fuel and fly at speeds below fifty-five knots. The pilot does not need a license, medical certificate, or biennial flight review as would a general-aviation pilot. Ultralights may only be flown during daylight hours and never over populated areas (U.S. DOT, 1999). Due to the slow speed of ultralights, other pilots perceive them as a hazard. While there is some sentiment against allowing ultralights to be based at the airport, the FAA says they must be allowed to land, and some say that basing more ultralights at Redlands would benefit the airport by increasing the demand for tiedown space and services.

Existing Facilities

As visitors approach the airport, they pass by orange groves and a few scattered houses. They then see the airport's beacon light before parking outside the small terminal building (1,000 sq. ft.). This building has a lounge area with a few vending machines, restrooms, an office, and a counter, where a few pilot supplies are sold. The airport has no cafe or restaurant, but visitors can sit outside in the shade at picnic tables and watch planes take off and land on the east-west runway. Occasionally, a plane or two may taxi up to the fuel island. An "itinerant" or "transient" (i.e., a plane based at another airport) may tie down in the spaces provided for that purpose. The airport has 122 hangars, 349 outdoor tiedown spaces, and 185 additional spaces for transient planes. Hangars rent in the neighborhood of $250 per month.

In terms of future development, the south side of the airport has the most desirable terrain. Gil Brown and his partner, George Saliba, have petitioned the city to allow them to build sixteen new T-hangars. These would be larger than the existing hangars, would run between 1,300 and 1,600 square feet, have electric doors, and rent for around $300 per month. Brown and Saliba call their company Coyote Aviation and have a list of twenty-two people who want to buy or rent these hangars. The north side of the airport

borders the Santa Ana Wash, which is part of a hundred-year floodplain. This is "difficult terrain with numerous slope changes, poor drainage and poor quality soil" (Coffman Associates, Inc., 1993).

Most of the airport's surrounding terrain is owned by the city, so municipal codes regulate or place restrictions on the height of buildings in the vicinity of plane takeoff and landing. New residential developments in the "airport influence area" are required to include an "avigation" easement: the homeowner must disclose to potential buyers the fact that the area has aircraft flights and/or noise.

Airport Businesses

Currently, one major leaseholder and three other fixed-base operators (FBOs) are leasing airport property from the city. The lease allows them to operate a private business at the airport as long it is related to the aviation industry. They can build hangars and rent those hangars out. They can operate offices that handle everything from flight training to selling airplane parts and avionics. They can run maintenance facilities for aircraft, operate emergency medical flight response facilities, and so forth.

The fifty-year leases are now about twenty years old, with three ten-year renewable options. The rates are very favorable to the leaseholders because the city wanted to attract businesses to develop the airport and generate revenue. In hindsight, says Mutter, there should have been other clauses of escalation factors (e.g., cost of living).

Redlands Municipal Airport houses sixteen organizations. Redlands Aviation holds the master lease, currently owned by the Jansen family: Byron and his father, mother, and two brothers. Byron Jansen's job is to open up the public lobby, rent out hangars and tiedown spaces, and sell fuel. With assistance, he staffs the lobby 8 a.m. to 5 p.m., Monday through Friday. Redlands Aviation feels the city is not compensating their company adequately for keeping the public lobby open.

The largest organization at the airport is Mission Aviation Fellowship (MAF), with ninety employees. MAF set up operations in Redlands in 1980 and has a fleet of seventy-five aircraft on forty-one bases flying in remote and isolated regions of twenty countries. Their literature describes their organization this way: "Serving God and responding to human needs since 1945, MAF US spans the globe to serve the needy with aviation and telecommunications service" (**http://www.maf.org/01_who.we.are/1-3who.html,** July 15, 1999). Previously, the technical support (flight and maintenance) was at Ramona, California, while administration was based one hundred miles away, in Fullerton, California.

According to Denny Hoekstra, director of aviation for MAF, the reason MAF selected Redlands as its main base was to merge the technical support with administration. "After doing a study and a matrix . . . , it was felt that Redlands was the best place to come to. Because of the local mountains here, we do a lot of mountain flying and training of our pilots . . . they go into third-world countries, [which] involves mountain flying, landing on unimproved airstrips on the sides of mountains, dirt strips with slope on them (Redlands' runway has a 3% slope). Some of them have peculiar approaches and some of them have illusions. The San Bernardino Mountains around here give us excellent opportunities for training."

Other businesses at the airport include Mercy Medical Airlift, a nonprofit organization whose mission is to "facilitate a charitable means of long distance medical air transport for all medically indigent, low-income and financially vulnerable patients" (**http://www.mercymedical.org,** July 28, 2000). Another business is M.I. Air Corp., run by Masa and Marjo Mitsutomi. This organization specializes in providing flight training for airplane and helicopter pilots, especially students coming from Japan. Many international students train in the United States because it can cost three times or more to fly in their home countries. Exhibit 2 provides a complete list of businesses at the airport. Many of these are sole proprietorships.

Forecasting and Planning Issues Associated with the Airport

To receive federal funds for airport development and improvement, a city must submit a master plan. Redlands commissioned plans in 1962, 1980, and 1991. After commissioning the last plan, the city established the Planning Advisory Committee (PAC), which provided information to the airport consultants, Coffman Associates. The PAC members included "representatives of the City of Redlands, San Bernardino County, the Southern California Association of Government, the State of California, the FAA

EXHIBIT 2

Organizations Operating at Redlands Municipal Airport

Aero Tech Academy
  Flight training & aircraft rental

Aerodynamics, Inc.
  Fuel service & hangar rental

The Book Craftsman
  Custom binding, books/Bible restoration

Inland Aviation
  Aircraft maintenance & inspections

Mercy Medical Airlift
  Air medical transportation

Mission Aviation Fellowship
  Missionary pilot training

Redlands Aviation Corp.
  Aircraft maintenance & repair, annual inspections, flight training, aircraft rental, fuel, hangar & tiedown rentals

Redlands Propeller Service
  Aircraft maintenance & repair

Aerodrome Plane Rental & Flight Training
  Flight training & aircraft rental

Auto Pilot West, Inc.
  Aircraft electronics & avionics

City of Redlands
  Tiedown rental

Instrument Flight Simulation
  Flight training

M.I. Air Corp.
  Aircraft maintenance, repair, flight training & aircraft rental

Red Aero Aviation
  Aircraft maintenance & repair

Redlands Hangar Owners Association
  Hangar rental

Suhay Aircraft Co.
  Aircraft maintenance, repair, & annual inspections

and various aviation personnel, business and community leadership" (Coffman Associates, Inc., 1993). The consultants—located in Kansas City, Missouri, and Phoenix, Arizona—produced the 165-page report in November 1993.

The master plan covers facilities, socioeconomic characteristics (i.e., population, employment, and climate), aviation-demand forecasts, capacity analysis and facility requirements, development alternatives, environmental evaluation, airspace and land-use plans, and a financial program. The forecasts predict activity for the airport up through the year 2015. Among the tables and exhibits in the master plan is one showing the history of aircraft activity (see Exhibit 3).

The purpose of forecasting demand is to assist in planning for facilities, budgeting, and alternative development actions. The master plan provides ten identifying forecasts of the number of aircraft to be based at the Redlands Municipal Airport (see Exhibit 4). The first forecast shown is a trend line, which is a regression on the variable time. The next three forecasts (methods 2–4) are linear regressions, using expected city, county, and state population growth to predict the number of aircraft. The next two forecasts (methods 5–6) use population projections of 2.6% growth for the county and 1.1% for the state and assume a constant number of aircraft per capita and historical population growth. Methods 7 and 8 use a ratio of aircraft based at Redlands Municipal Airport in comparison to other markets, San Bernardino County and California. Methods 9 and 10 are used by two governmental agencies, the California Department of Transportation (CalTrans) and Southern California Association of Governments (SCAG). Using these methods of calculation, aircraft usage at the Redlands Municipal Airport for the year 2000 was

EXHIBIT 3

History of Aircraft Activity

	Based Aircraft				Operations			
Year	Single Engine	Multi-engine	Heli-copters	Total	Local	Itinerant	Air Taxi	Total
1961	44	1	3	48	3,600	3,600	0	7,200
1962	48	0	0	48	3,600	3,600	0	7,200
1963	48	0	0	48	6,000	4,000	0	10,000
1964	46	3	0	49	6,000	7,000	0	13,000
1965	59	3	0	62	6,000	7,000	0	13,000
1966	62	6	0	68	11,000	13,000	0	24,000
1967	60	6	0	66	11,000	12,000	0	23,000
1968	90	6	0	96	11,000	12,000	0	23,000
1970	80	6	0	86	30,000	6,000	0	36,000
1971	82	5	0	87	30,000	6,000	0	36,000
1975	95	5	0	100	24,150	3,000	0	27,150
1977	126	6	0	132	25,200	3,100	0	28,300
1984	N/A	N/A	N/A	320	N/A	N/A	N/A	N/A
1985	192	26	0	218	26,000	26,000	240	52,240
1986	204	26	0	230	26,000	26,000	240	52,240
1987	190	24	0	214	24,000	24,000	240	48,240
1988	190	24	0	214	24,000	24,000	240	48,240
1989	190	24	0	214	24,500	24,000	300	48,800
1990	200	30	0	230	33,600	31,200	300	65,100
1991	200	30	0	230	33,000	32,000	300	65,300

EXHIBIT 4

Ten Forecasts for the Number of Aircraft Based at Redlands Airport

Methods/Year	1995	2000	2005	2010	2015
Trend line	260	293	326	358	391
Pop. Regression, Redlands	294	325	357	388	419
Pop. Regression, San Bernardino County	301	345	388	431	497
Pop. Regression, CA	258	287	313	339	366
Per-capita based Aircraft, San Bernardino	239	267	295	323	366
Per-capita based Aircraft, CA	239	254	267	280	294
Market share, San Bernardino	238	247	256	267	274
Market share, CA	254	259	264	269	274
CalTrans	262	275	285	297	309
SCAG	298	325	352	378	405

Source: Coffman Associates, Inc. (1993).

estimated at between 247 and 345. By 1999, however, only about 230 aircraft were based at the airport.

In reviewing these forecasts, a statistician might ask the following questions: "Why were these ten forecasts so far off the mark? Why did no forecast include income as a variable? Or interest rates? Or some other aspect of the U.S. economy? Why were all the estimates assuming growth? And what about the supply of hangars? Could owners of airplanes prefer hangars that protect the airplane over tiedowns that leave the plane exposed to the elements? What about other competing airports in the vicinity?" Within twenty-five miles of the Redlands Airport, there are seven general-aviation airports: Flabob, Riverside, Rialto, Hesperia, Big Bear, Banning, and San Bernardino International (formerly, Norton U.S. Air Force Base).

The Relationship Between the Airport and the City of Redlands

As owner of the airport, the city is responsible for the runway, taxiway, and electrical beacon. The city grades the shoulders, paints markings on the runway, and keeps the weeds down. In addition, the city police patrol the premises, and city firefighters and paramedics respond to any emergency, such as when a pilot makes a wheel-up landing (when the pilot forgets to put the landing gear down).

Mayor Pat Gilbreath says, "One of the problems we have as a municipality is that Redlands is 'full service . . .' and part of that full service is operating parts of it . . . [without] good business sense. The airport is a classic case of that. . . . We can't let the airport get into terrible shape, and so it becomes an obligation of the General Fund." She notes that dollars spent by businesses at the airport have a multiplier effect on the city and believes that a number of intangibles help the airport be an economic generator. For example, she says, because she is a CPA, some of her clients will fly into Redlands to meet with her and she occasionally will fly out to meet them.

Whose job is it to create businesses at the airport, she wonders, noting that up to this point, the responsibility has been "entrepreneurial." "If somebody has an idea, they can bring it to the city council. . . . We need a restaurant, we need hangars . . . but the city should not really be running the airport, and that is why we are using these lease arrangements. It is like a franchise. We own it, but somebody else runs it."

Leaseholder Byron Jansen of Redlands Aviation remarks, "Our FBO is in sort of a unique position being that we have a public lobby. A lot of times we are thought of as running the Redlands Airport and we have a burden not to be seen that way. This is not our airport. We are not running this airport. We are leasing this building back to the city as a public lobby, but our business is simply to rent hangars and tiedowns and to sell some fuel, to enjoy flying our own airplanes, and we are not really very enthusiastic about politics or that end of things." Redlands Aviation's old lease expired in 1993, putting the arrangement with the city on a month-to-month basis. If a new lease is not negotiated, the lobby will close.

For many years, airport revenues closely matched expenses. The city deliberately kept expenses down so that they would not exceed revenues. In 1978, California passed Proposition 13, which tended to lock in property taxes and force cities to find other sources of revenue. In response to this, in 1989 the city drafted a new financial package, which created an in-lieu $40,000 property tax charged against airport revenues. This accounts for the opportunity cost of lost taxes from the next-best use of the land. Ron Mutter is expected to recover this lost tax revenue for the city. However, the revenues generated by the leases are fixed by their long-term (fifty-year) nature, and the airport now annually shows a loss.

In addition to the in-lieu property tax fee, the city has a general government overhead charge of 13.5%, which includes such items as time put in by the city attorney, finance department, director of public works, and so forth. Ron Mutter says, "Since I can't raise rates [on the long-term leases] or anything else, how do we deal with this? We did develop the west end of the runway some years ago. We built a number of tiedown spaces. We used a federal grant to do it. Our goal was to start renting some spaces and to open up a couple of leases down there. It would be used to start to make up this difference. No sooner did we finish the construction of that ramp than the [California] recession hit."

The Future

Mayor Pat Gilbreath is looking for reasons why both pilots and the general public would want to go to the airport. She wants to shake off the image of the airport as a **place for the rich to play with their toys**—an attitude expressed by a previous mayor, who even suggested the city council look at ways to get rid of the airport.

As the director of public works, Ron Mutter has a vision for the surrounding area. He has architectural plans for a nearby soccer field and restaurant. The emphasis would be on youth-oriented sports so that families could congregate, play sports, and eat at the airport restaurant. He also notes that the city of Redlands has never made a serious marketing effort, unlike the other local airports (such as Rialto, Banning, and Riverside). With all his other major responsibilities, he wonders how much he should get involved in promoting the airport.

Mayor Pat Gilbreath notes that Coyote Aviation originally proposed a three-phase project, only the first of which has been approved. This first phase consists of a fifty-year lease for the sixteen T-hangars being built. The city will break even for the first time, despite the $40,000 in-lieu tax, notes the mayor. Coyote Aviation also has a ten-year option to begin phase 2: constructing a restaurant/sandwich shop that may include a public lobby. Phase 3 would entail the construction of a large maintenance hangar, shade ports, and storage area. Other entrepreneurs are looking at aviation-based housing so that people could park their planes at the airport and live nearby.

Finally, the airport advisory board is proposing a committee to develop the airport. With all this renewed interest, the mayor wants to know how best to enhance the economic viability of the Redlands Airport while balancing the varied interests of her constituency.

REFERENCES

California Department of Transportation (1998). *The California Aviation System: 1998 Inventory Element,* September 7: 222, 268, 257–274.

Coffman Associates, Inc. (1993). *Master Plan for Redlands Municipal Airport, Redlands, California,* November.

http://www.alphais.com/redlands/3006.html#airport, May 20, 2000.

http://www.alphais.com/redlands/40737.html#9, August 10, 2000.

http://www.cedar.ca.gov/military/current_reuse/norton.htm, February 29, 2000.

http://www.faa.gov/arp/arphome.htm, July 19, 1999.

http://www.maf.org/01_who.we.are/1–3who.htm, July 15, 1999.

http://www.mercymedical.org, July 28, 2000.

http://www.redlands-aor.com/history.htm, May 8, 2000.

http://www.redlands-aor.com/main.htm, May 8, 2000.

Redlands City Council Minutes (1962), Book 20, June 6.

U.S. Department of Transportation (1999). *FAR/AIM 2000: Federal Aviation Regulations/Aeronautical Information Manual.* Newcastle, WA: Aviation Supplies & Academics, Inc.

5 Perdue Farms Inc.: Responding to Twenty-First-Century Challenges

This case was prepared by George C. Rubenson and Frank M. Shipper, Salisbury University.

I have a theory that you can tell the difference between those who have inherited a fortune and those who have made a fortune. Those who have made their own fortune forget not where they came from and are less likely to lose touch with the common man.

—Bill Sterling

Background and Company History

The history of Perdue Farms Inc. is dominated by seven themes: quality, growth, geographic expansion, vertical integration, innovation, branding, and service. Arthur W. Perdue, a Railway Express agent and descendant of a French Huguenot family named Perdeaux, founded the company in 1920 when he left his job with Railway Express and entered the egg business full-time near the small town of Salisbury, Maryland. Salisbury is located in a region immortalized in James Michener's *Chesapeake* and alternately known as the Eastern Shore or the DelMarVa peninsula. It includes parts of Delaware, Maryland, and Virginia. Arthur Perdue's only child, Franklin Parsons Perdue, was born in 1920, the year the company was founded.

Perdue Farms's mission statement (Exhibit 1) emphasizes quality. In the 1920s, Mr. Arthur, as he was called, bought leghorn breeding stock from Texas to improve the quality of his flock. He soon expanded his egg market and began shipments to New York. By practicing small economies such as mixing his own chicken feed and using leather from his old shoes to make hinges for his chicken coops, he stayed out of debt and prospered. He tried to add a new chicken coop every year.

By 1940, Perdue Farms was already known for quality products and fair dealing in a tough, highly competitive market. The company began offering chickens for sale when Mr. Arthur

The authors are indebted to Frank Perdue, Jim Perdue, and the numerous associates at Perdue Farms Inc., who generously shared their time and information about the company. In addition, the authors would like to thank the anonymous librarians at Blackwell Library, Salisbury State University, who routinely review area newspapers and file articles about the poultry industry—the most important industry on the DelMarVa peninsula. Without their assistance, this case study would not have been possible. This case is intended to be used as a basis for class discussion rather than as an illustration of either effective or ineffective handling of the situation. Reprinted by permission of George C. Rubenson and Frank M. Shipper.

EXHIBIT 1

Perdue Farms's Mission for the Year 2000

Stand on Tradition

Perdue was built upon a foundation of quality, a tradition described in our Quality Policy . . .

Our Quality Policy

"We shall produce products and provide services
at all times that meet or exceed the expectations of our customers."

"We shall not be content to be of
equal quality to our competitors."

"Our commitment is to be increasingly superior."

"Contribution to quality is a responsibility
shared by everyone in the Perdue organization."

Focus on Today

Our mission reminds us of the purpose we serve . . .

Our Mission

"Enhance the quality of life with great food and agricultural products."

While striving to fulfill our mission, we use our values to guide our decisions . . .

Our Values

- **Quality:** We value the needs of our customers. Our high standards require us to work safely, make safe food, and uphold the Perdue name.
- **Integrity:** We do the right thing and live up to our commitments. We do not cut corners or make false promises.
- **Trust:** We trust each other and treat each other with mutual respect. Each individual's skill and talent are appreciated.
- **Teamwork:** We value a strong work ethic and the ability to make each other successful. We care what others think and encourage their involvement, creating a sense of pride, loyalty, ownership, and family.

Look to the Future

Our vision describes what we will become and the qualities that will enable us to succeed . . .

Our Vision

"To be the leading quality food company with $20 billion in sales in 2020."

Perdue in the Year 2020

- **To our customers:** We will provide food solutions and indispensable services to meet anticipated customer needs.
- **To our consumers:** A portfolio of trusted food and agricultural products will be supported by multiple brands throughout the world.
- **To our associates:** Worldwide, our people and our workplace will reflect our quality reputation, placing Perdue among the best places to work.
- **To our communities:** We will be known in the community as a strong corporate citizen, trusted business partner, and favorite employer.
- **To our shareholders:** Driven by innovation, our market leadership and our creative spirit will yield industry-leading profits.

realized that the future lay in selling chickens, not eggs. In 1944, Mr. Arthur made his son, Frank, a full partner, calling the company A. W. Perdue and Son, Inc.

In 1950, Frank took over leadership of the company, which employed forty people. By 1952, revenues were $6 million from the sale of 2.6 million broilers. During this period, the company began to vertically integrate, operating its own hatchery, starting to create its own feed formulations, and operating its own feed mill. Perdue Farms also began to contract with others to grow chickens for them. By furnishing the growers with peeps (baby chickens) and feed, the company was able to maintain control of quality.

In the 1960s, Perdue Farms continued to vertically integrate by building its first grain-receiving and -storage facilities and Maryland's first soybean-processing plant. By 1967, annual sales had increased to about $35 million. By then, it became clear to Frank that profits lay in processing chickens. In an interview for *Business Week* (September 15, 1972), Frank recalled that "processors were paying us 10 cents a live pound for what cost us 14 cents to produce. Suddenly, processors were making as much as 7 cents a pound."

A cautious, conservative planner, Arthur Perdue had not been eager for expansion, and Frank was reluctant to enter poultry processing. But economics forced his hand, and, in 1968, the company bought its first processing plant, a Swift and Company operation in Salisbury.

From the first batch of chickens that it processed, Perdue's standards were higher than those of the federal government. The state grader on the first batch has often told the story of how he was worried that he had rejected too many chickens as not Grade A. As he finished his inspections for that first day, he saw Frank Perdue headed his way and he could tell that Frank was not happy. Frank started inspecting the birds and never argued over one that was rejected. Next, he saw Frank start to go through the ones that the state grader had passed and began to toss some of them over with the rejected birds. Finally, realizing that few met his standards, Frank put all of the birds in the reject pile. Soon, however, the facility was able to process 14,000 broilers per hour.

From the beginning, Frank Perdue refused to permit his broilers to be frozen for shipping, arguing that it resulted in unappetizing black bones and loss of flavor and moistness when cooked. Instead, Perdue chickens were—and some still are—shipped to the market packed in ice, justifying the company's advertisements at that time that it sold only "fresh, young broilers." However, this policy also limited the company's market to locations that could be serviced overnight from the Eastern Shore of Maryland. Thus, Perdue chose for its primary markets the densely populated towns and cities of the East Coast, particularly New York City, which consumes more Perdue chicken than all other brands combined.

Frank Perdue's drive for quality became legendary both inside and outside the poultry industry. In 1985, Frank and Perdue Farms Inc. were featured in the book *A Passion for Excellence*, written by Tom Peters and Nancy Austin.

In 1970, Perdue established its primary breeding and genetic-research programs. Through selective breeding, Perdue developed a chicken with more white breast meat than the typical chicken. Selective breeding has been so successful that Perdue's chickens are desired by other processors. Rumors have even suggested that Perdue chickens have been stolen on occasion in an attempt to improve competitor flocks.

In 1971, Perdue Farms began an extensive marketing campaign featuring Frank Perdue. In his early advertisements, he became famous for saying things like "If you want to eat as good as my chickens, you'll just have to eat my chickens." He is often credited with being the first to brand what had been a commodity product. During the 1970s, Perdue Farms expanded to areas north of New York City, such as Massachusetts, Rhode Island, and Connecticut.

In 1977, Mr. Arthur died at the age of ninety-one, leaving behind a company with annual sales of nearly $200 million, an average annual growth rate of 17% (compared to an industry average of 1%), the potential for processing 78,000 broilers per hour, and annual production of nearly 350 million pounds of poultry. Frank Perdue has said of his father, "I learned everything from him."

In 1981, Frank Perdue went to Boston for his induction into the Babson College Academy of Distinguished Entrepreneurs, an award established in 1978 to recognize the spirit of free enterprise and business leadership. Babson College president Ralph Z. Sorenson inducted Perdue into the academy, which then numbered eighteen men and women from four continents. Perdue had the following to say to the college students:

There are none, nor will there ever be, easy steps for the entrepreneur. Nothing, absolutely nothing, replaces the willingness to work earnestly, intelligently towards a goal. You have to be willing to pay the price. You have to have an insatiable appetite for detail, have to be willing to accept constructive criticism, to ask questions, to be fiscally responsible, to surround yourself with good people and, most of all, to listen.

The early 1980s saw Perdue Farms expand southward into Virginia, North Carolina, and Georgia. It also began to buy out other producers, such as Carroll's Foods, Purvis Farms, Shenandoah Valley Poultry Company, and Shenandoah Farms. The last two acquisitions diversified the company's markets to include turkey. New products included value-added items, such as "Perdue Done It!" a line of fully cooked chicken products.

James A. (Jim) Perdue, Frank's only son, joined the company as a management trainee in 1983 and became a plant manager. The latter half of the 1980s tested the mettle of the firm. Following a period of considerable expansion and product diversification, Perdue was told by a consulting firm to form several strategic business units that would be responsible for their own operations. In other words, the firm should decentralize. Soon after, the chicken market leveled off and then declined. In 1988, the firm experienced its first year in the red. Unfortunately, the decentralization had created duplication and enormous administrative costs. The firm's rapid plunge into the processing of turkey and other food it had little experience with contributed to the losses. As in the past, the company refocused, concentrating on efficiency of operations, improving communications throughout the company, and paying close attention to detail.

On June 2, 1989, Frank celebrated fifty years with Perdue Farms Inc. At a morning reception in downtown Salisbury, the governor of Maryland proclaimed it "Frank Perdue Day." The governors of Delaware and Virginia did the same. In 1991, Frank was named chairman of the executive committee and Jim Perdue became chairman of the board. Quieter, gentler, and more formally educated than his father, Jim Perdue focused on operations, renewing the company's commitment to quality control and strategic planning. Frank Perdue continued to do advertising and public relations. As Jim Perdue matured as the company leader, he took over the role of company spokesperson and began to appear in advertisements.

Under Jim Perdue's leadership, Perdue Farms expanded into Florida and west to Michigan and Missouri during the 1990s. In 1992, the international business segment was formalized as Perdue Farms and began serving customers in Puerto Rico, South America, Europe, Japan, and China. By 1998, international sales were $180 million per year. International markets are beneficial for the firm because U.S. customers prefer white meat, while customers in most other countries prefer dark meat.

Food-service sales to commercial consumers have also become a major market. New retail-product lines focus on value-added items, individually quick-frozen items, home-meal replacement items, and products for the delicatessen. The Fit 'n Easy label continues as part of a nutrition campaign using skinless, boneless chicken and turkey products.

The 1990s also saw the increased use of technology and the building of distribution centers. For example, all over-the-road trucks were equipped with satellite two-way communications and geographic positioning, allowing for real-time tracking, rerouting if needed, and accurate information for customers as to when products would arrive.

Nearly 20,000 employees have helped Perdue Farms increase revenues to more than $2.5 billion.

Management and Organization

From 1950 until 1991, Frank Perdue was the primary force behind Perdue Farms's growth and success. During Frank's years as the company leader, the poultry industry entered its high-growth period. Industry executives had typically developed professionally during the industry's infancy. Many had little formal education and started their careers in the barnyard, building chicken coops and cleaning them out. They often spent their entire careers with one company, progressing from supervisor of grow-out facilities to manager of processing plants to corporate executive. Perdue Farms was not unusual in that respect. An entrepreneur through and through, Frank lived up to his marketing image: "It takes a tough man to make a tender chicken." He mostly used a centralized management style that kept decision-making authority in his hands and those of a few trusted, senior executives, whom he had known for a lifetime. Workers were expected to do their jobs.

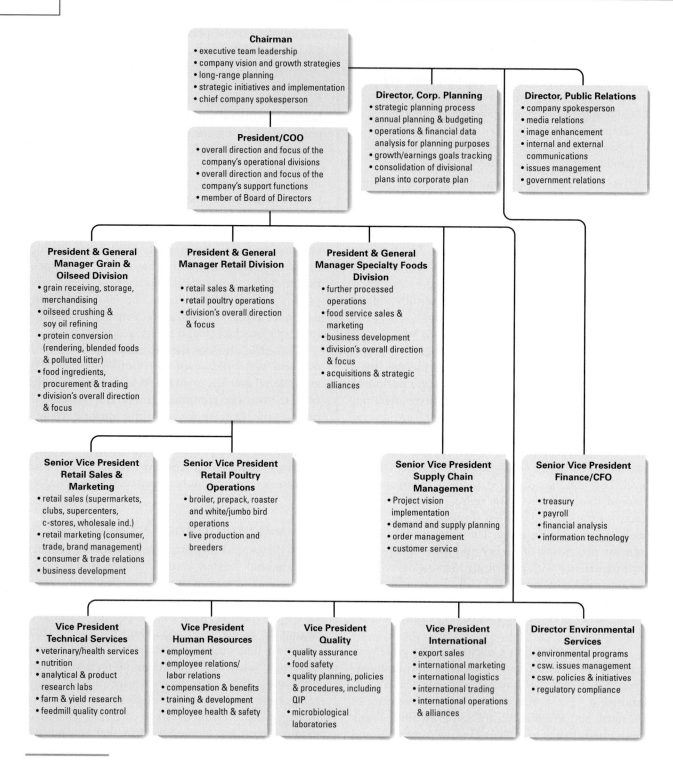

EXHIBIT 2

Perdue Farms Senior-Management Organizational Chart

In later years, Frank increasingly emphasized the involvement of employees—or "associates," as they are referred to—in quality issues and operational decisions. This emphasis on employee participation undoubtedly eased the transfer of power in 1991 from Frank to his son, Jim. Although Jim grew up in the family business, he spent almost fifteen years earning an undergraduate degree in biology from Wake Forest University, a master's degree in marine biology from the University of Massachusetts at Dartmouth, and a doctorate in fisheries from the University of Washington in Seattle. Returning to Perdue Farms in 1983, he earned an MBA from Salisbury State University and was assigned the positions of plant manager, divisional quality-control manager, and vice president of quality improvement process prior to becoming chairman.

Company goals center on the three ps: people, products, and profitability. With a people-first management style, Jim believes that success rests on satisfying customer needs with quality products and putting associates first because "if they come first, they will strive to assure superior product quality—and satisfied customers." This view has had a profound impact on the company culture, which is based on Tom Peters's view that "nobody knows a person's twenty square feet better than the person who works there." In other words, management tries to gather ideas and information from everyone and to maximize productivity by transmitting these ideas throughout the organization.

Key to carrying out this policy is work force stability, a difficult goal in an industry that employs a growing number of associates working in physically demanding and sometimes stressful conditions. A significant number of associates are Hispanic immigrants who may have a poor command of the English language, are sometimes undereducated, and often lack basic health care. In order to increase these associates' opportunities for advancement, Perdue Farms focuses on helping them overcome their disadvantages.

For example, the firm provides English-language classes to help non–English-speaking employees assimilate and earn the equivalent of a high school diploma. To deal with physical stress, the company has an ergonomics committee in each plant that studies job requirements and seeks ways to redesign those jobs that put workers at the greatest risk. The company also has an impressive wellness program, which operates clinics at ten plants. The clinics are staffed by medical professionals working for medical-practice groups under contract to Perdue Farms. Employees can visit a doctor for anything from muscle strain to prenatal care to screening tests for a variety of diseases, and they have access to all Perdue-operated clinics. Care for dependents is also available. Benefits to the employees are obvious; the company also benefits through a reduction in time lost for medical office visits, lower turnover, and a happier, more productive, and more stable work force.

Marketing

In the early days, chicken was sold to butcher shops and neighborhood groceries as a commodity; that is, producers sold it in bulk, and butchers cut and wrapped it. The customer had no idea what firm grew or processed the chicken. Frank Perdue was convinced that higher profits could be made if the firm's products could be sold at a premium price. But the only reason a product can command a premium price is if customers ask for it by name—and that means the product must be differentiated and "branded." Hence, Perdue Farms emphasized superior quality, broader-breasted chickens, and a healthy golden color (the result of adding marigold petals in the feed to enhance the natural color of corn).

In 1968, Frank Perdue spent $50,000 on radio advertising. In 1969, he added $80,000 in TV advertising to his radio budget—against the advice of his advertising agency. Although his early TV ads increased sales, he decided the agency he was dealing with didn't match one of the basic Perdue tenets: "The people you deal with should be as good at what they do as you are at what you do." That decision set off a storm of activity on Frank's part. In order to select an ad agency that met his standards, Frank learned more about advertising than any poultry man before him and, in the process, catapulted Perdue Farms into the ranks of the top poultry producers in the country.

He began a ten-week immersion in the theory and practice of advertising. He read books and papers on advertising. He talked to sales managers of every newspaper, radio, and television station in the New York area, consulted experts, and interviewed forty-eight ad agencies. During April 1971, he selected Scali, McCabe, Sloves as his new advertising agency. As the agency tried to figure out how to successfully "brand" a chicken—something that had never been done—they realized that Frank Perdue was their greatest asset. "He looked a little like a chicken himself, and he sounded a little like one, and he squawked a lot!"

McCabe decided that Perdue should be the firm's spokesman. Frank initially resisted, but in the end, he accepted the role, and the campaign based on the slogan "It takes a tough man to make a tender chicken" was born. The firm's first TV commercial showed Frank on a picnic in the Salisbury City Park saying:

> A chicken is what it eats . . . And my chickens eat better than people do . . . I store my own grain and mix my own feed . . . And give my Perdue chickens nothing but pure well water to drink . . . That's why my chickens always have that healthy golden yellow color . . . If you want to eat as good as my chickens, you'll just have to eat my chickens.

Later ads touted high quality and the broader-breasted chicken:

> Government standards would allow me to call this a grade A chicken . . . but my standards wouldn't. This chicken is skinny . . . It has scrapes and hairs . . . The fact is, my graders reject 30% of the chickens government inspectors accept as grade A . . . That's why it pays to insist on a chicken with my name on it . . . If you're not completely satisfied, write me and I'll give you your money back . . . Who do you write in Washington? . . . What do they know about chickens?

> The Perdue roaster is the master race of chickens.

> Never go into a store and just ask for a pound of chicken breasts . . . Because you could be cheating yourself out of some meat . . . Here's an ordinary one-pound chicken breast, and here's a one-pound breast of mine . . . They weigh the same. But as you can see, mine has more meat, and theirs has more bone. I breed the broadest-breasted, meatiest chicken you can buy . . . So don't buy a chicken breast by the pound . . . Buy them by the name . . . and get an extra bite in every breast.

The ads paid off. In 1968, Perdue had about 3% of the New York market. By 1972, one out of every six chickens eaten in New York was a Perdue chicken, and 51% of New Yorkers recognized the label. Scali, McCabe, Sloves credited Perdue's "believability" for the success of the campaign. "This was advertising in

which Perdue had a personality that lent credibility to the product. If Frank Perdue didn't look and sound like a chicken, he wouldn't be in the commercials."

Frank had his own view. As he told a Rotary audience in Charlotte, North Carolina, in March 1989, "The product met the promise of the advertising and was far superior to the competition. Two great sayings tell it all: 'nothing will destroy a poor product as quickly as good advertising,' and 'a gifted product is mightier than a gifted pen!'"

Today, branded chicken is ubiquitous. The new task for Perdue Farms is to create a single theme for a wide variety of products (e.g., from fresh meat to fully prepared and frozen products) to a wide variety of customers (e.g., retail, food-service, and international markets). Industry experts believe that the market for fresh poultry has peaked and that sales of value-added and frozen products continue to grow at a healthy rate. Although domestic retail sales account for about 60% of Perdue Farms's revenues in 2000, food-service sales now account for 20%, international sales account for 5%, and grain and oilseed contribute the remaining 15%. The company expects food-service, international, and grain-and-oilseed sales to continue to grow as a percentage of total revenues.

Domestic Retail

Today's retail grocery customer is increasingly looking for ease and speed of preparation. To meet this need, Perdue Farms is concentrating on value-added products. The move toward value-added products has significantly changed the meat department in the modern grocery. There are now five distinct meat outlets for poultry:

1. The fresh meat counter—traditional, fresh meat; includes whole chicken and parts.

2. The delicatessen—processed turkey, rotisserie chicken.

3. The frozen counter—individually quick-frozen items such as frozen whole chickens, turkeys, and Cornish hens.

4. Home-meal replacement—fully prepared entrees, such as Perdue's Short Cuts and Deluca brand entrees, which are sold along with salads and desserts so that customers can assemble their own dinners. (The Deluca brand was acquired by Perdue Farms but is sold under its own name.)

5. Shelf stable—canned products.

Because Perdue Farms has always used the phrase "fresh young chicken" as the centerpiece of its marketing, value-added products and the retail frozen counter create a possible conflict for the company. Are these products compatible with the company's marketing image? If so, how does the company present the notion of quality in this broader product environment? To answer that question, Perdue Farms has been studying what "fresh young chicken" means to customers who consistently demand quicker and easier preparation and who admit that they freeze most of their fresh-meat purchases once they get home. One response is that "fresh young chicken" means that "quality" and "freshness" are closely associated. Thus, the real issue may be trust: the customer must believe that the product, whether fresh or frozen, is of the freshest, highest quality possible. Future marketing efforts must develop that concept.

Food Service

The food-service business consists of a wide variety of public and private customers, including restaurant chains, governments, hospitals, schools, prisons, transportation facilities, and the institutional contractors who supply meals to them. Historically, these customers have not been brand conscious, instead requiring the supplier to meet strict specifications at the lowest price, thus making this category a less than ideal fit for Perdue Farms. However, as Americans continue to eat a larger percentage of their meals away from home, traditional grocery sales have flattened and the food-service sector has shown strong growth. Across the domestic poultry industry, food service accounts for about 50% of total poultry sales; for Perdue Farms, about 20% of its revenues come from this category. Clearly, Perdue Farms is playing catch-up in this critical market.

Because Perdue Farms has neither strength nor expertise in the food-service market, management believes that acquiring companies with food-service expertise is the best strategy. One such acquisition is the purchase in September 1998 of Gol-Pak Corporation, based in Monterey, Tennessee. A further processor of products for the food-service industry, Gol-Pak had about 1,600 employees and revenues of about $200 million per year.

International

International markets have generally been a happy surprise. In the early 1990s, Perdue Farms began exporting specialty products such as chicken feet (known as paws) to customers in China. Although not approved for human consumption in the United States, paws are considered a delicacy in China. By 1992, international sales, which consisted principally of paws, had become a small but profitable business of about 30 million pounds per year. Building on this "toehold" over the next six years, Perdue Farms quickly had an international business of more than 500 million pounds per year (see Exhibit 3); annual revenues were more than $140 million from selling a wide variety of products to China, Japan, Russia, and the Ukraine.

In some ways, Japan is an excellent fit for Perdue Farms's products because customers there demand high quality. Furthermore, all Asian markets prefer dark meat, which means that what in America is excess meat can be sold in Asia at a premium price. On the downside, Perdue Farms gains much of its competitive advantage from branding (e.g., trademarks, processes, and technological and biological know-how), but this has little value internationally because most of Asia has not yet embraced the concept of branded chicken.

To better serve export markets, Perdue Farms has developed a portside freezing facility in Newport News, Virginia. This permits poultry to be shipped directly to the port, reducing processing costs and helping to balance ocean shipping costs to Asia, which are in the range of .66 cent per pound (contracting an entire ship is equal to contracting 300 to 500 truckloads).

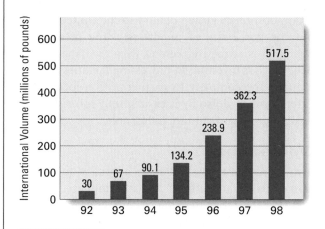

EXHIBIT 3

Perdue Farms's International Sales, 1992–1998

Shipping poultry to Asia is not without problems. For example, in China delivery trucks are seldom refrigerated. Thus, the poultry can begin to thaw as it is being delivered, limiting the distance it can be transported prior to sale. One shipload of Perdue Farms chicken bound for Russia actually vanished and was later discovered to have been impounded using forged documents; eventually, most of its dollar value was recovered.

Initial demand for Perdue Farms's products in Russia, Poland, and eastern Europe was huge. By 1998, a significant portion of the international volume was going to Russia. Unfortunately, the crumbling of Russia's economy has had a devastating effect on imports, and sales have dropped significantly. Such instability of demand, coupled with rampant corruption, makes risking significant capital in Russia unacceptable.

Import duties and taxes for poultry are also a barrier. According to the U.S. Department of Agriculture (USDA), import duty rates in China are a whopping 45% for favored countries and 70% for unfavored countries; in addition, there is a 17% value-added tax for all countries. Import duties and taxes in Russia have been similarly high. Hence, profits can be expected to be slim.

Perdue Farms has created a joint partnership with the Jiang Nan Feng brand in order to develop a small processing plant in Shanghai. Brand recognition is being built with usual marketing tools. The products use the first "tray pack" wrapping available in Shanghai supermarkets. This new business shows promise because the sale in China of homegrown, fresh dark meat is a significant competitive advantage. Furthermore, government regulations do not permit exportation of foreign-grown poultry to the United States, but the possibility of importing white meat from Shanghai is attractive. Perdue Farms's management believes that investing in processing facilities in Asia requires the company to partner with a local firm. Attempting to do so by itself is simply too risky due to the significant cultural differences.

Operations

Two words sum up the Perdue approach to operations: quality and efficiency, with emphasis on the first. Perdue more than most companies embodies the total quality management slogan, "Quality: a journey without end." Some of the key events in this journey are listed in Exhibit 4.

EXHIBIT 4

Milestones in the Quality-Improvement Process at Perdue Farms

1924 –	Arthur Perdue buys leghorn roosters for $25
1950 –	Company adopts logo of a chick under a magnifying glass
1984 –	Frank Perdue attends Philip Crosby's Quality College
1985 –	Perdue recognized for its pursuit of quality in *A Passion for Excellence*
–	Two-hundred Perdue managers attend Quality College
–	Quality Improvement Process adopted
1986 –	Corrective Action Teams established
1987 –	Quality training for all associates established
–	Error Cause Removal Process implemented
1988 –	Steering committee formed
1989 –	First annual quality conference held
–	Team management implemented
1990 –	Second annual quality conference held
–	Values and corporate mission codified
1991 –	Third annual quality conference held
–	Customer satisfaction defined
1992 –	Fourth annual quality conference held
–	How to implement customer satisfaction explained to team leaders and quality improvement teams
–	Quality index created
–	Customer satisfaction index created
–	"Farm to Fork" quality program created
1999 –	Raw material quality index launched
2000 –	High performance team process initiated

Both quality and efficiency are improved through the management of details. Exhibit 5 is a diagram of the structure and product flow of a generic, vertically integrated broiler company. This company can choose which steps in the process it wants to take and which it wants suppliers to take. For example, the company could purchase all grain, oilseed, meal, and other feed; or it could contract with hatcheries to supply primary breeders and hatchery-supply flocks.

Perdue Farms chose maximum vertical integration in order to control every detail. It breeds its own chickens and hatches its own eggs (nineteen hatcheries),

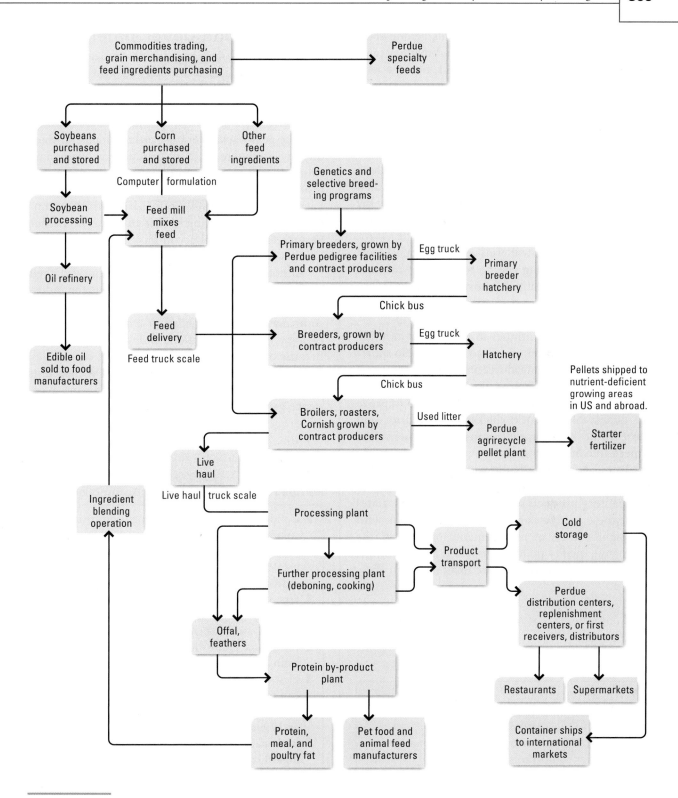

EXHIBIT 5

Perdue Farms's Integrated Operations

selects its own contract growers, builds Perdue-engineered chicken houses, formulates and manufactures its own feed (twelve poultry feedmills, one specialty feedmill, and two ingredient-blending operations), oversees the care and feeding of chicks, operates its own processing plants (twenty-one processing and further-processing plants), distributes with its own trucking fleet, and does its own marketing. Total control of this process formed the basis for Frank Perdue's early claims that his poultry was of higher quality than other poultry: "A chicken is what it eats . . . I store my own grain and mix my own feed . . . and give my Perdue chickens nothing but well water to drink."

Total process control also enables Perdue Farms to ensure that nothing goes to waste. Eight measurable items—hatchability, turnover, feed conversion, livability, yield, birds per man-hour, utilization, and grade—are routinely tracked.

Perdue Farms continues to ensure that nothing artificial is fed to or injected into the birds. No shortcuts are taken. A chemical-free and steroid-free diet is fed to the chickens. Young chickens are vaccinated against disease. Selective breeding is used to improve the quality of the stock: chickens are bred to yield more white breast meat because that is what the American consumer wants.

To ensure that its poultry continues to lead the industry in quality, Perdue Farms buys and analyzes competitors' products regularly. Inspection associates grade these products and share the information with the highest levels of management. In addition, the company's quality policy is displayed at all locations and taught to all associates (see Exhibit 6).

EXHIBIT 6

Quality Policy

- WE SHALL produce products and provide services at all times that meet or exceed the expectations of our customers.
- WE SHALL not be content to be of equal quality to our competitors.
- OUR COMMITMENT is to be increasingly superior.
- CONTRIBUTION TO QUALITY is a responsibility shared by everyone in the Perdue organization.

Research and Development

Perdue is an acknowledged industry leader in the use of research and technology to provide quality products and service to its customers. The company spends more on research (as a percentage of revenues) than any other poultry processor. This practice goes back to Frank Perdue's focus on finding ways to differentiate his products by quality and value. It was research into selective breeding that resulted in the broader breast, an attribute of Perdue Farms chicken that was featured in the company's early advertising. A list of some of Perdue Farms's technological accomplishments is found in Exhibit 7.

Although other processors have improved their stock, Perdue Farms believes that it leads the industry. Attempting to leave nothing to chance, the company employs specialists in avian science, microbiology, genetics, nutrition, and veterinary science. Because of its research and development capabilities, Perdue Farms is often involved in USDA field tests with pharmaceutical suppliers; knowledge and experience gained from these tests sometimes leads to a

EXHIBIT 7

Perdue Farms's Technological Accomplishments

- Conducts more research than all competitors combined
- Breeds chickens that consistently have more breast meat than any other bird produced in the industry
- First to use digital scales to guarantee weights
- First to package fully cooked chicken products in microwaveable trays
- First to have a box lab to define quality of boxes from different suppliers
- First to measure its chickens and competitors' chickens on fifty-two quality factors every week
- Improved 20% on time deliveries between 1987 and 1993
- Built state-of-the-art analytical and microbiological laboratories for feed and end-product analysis
- First to develop food-safety management practices for all areas of the company
- First to develop commercially viable litter pellets for poultry

competitive advantage. For example, Perdue has the most extensive and expensive vaccination program in the industry. The company is also working with, and studying the practices of, several European producers who use completely different methods.

The company has used research to significantly increase productivity. For example, in the 1950s, it took fourteen weeks to grow a 3-pound chicken; today, it takes only seven weeks to grow a 5-pound chicken. This gain in efficiency is due principally to improvements in the feed-to-chicken conversion rate. The current rate of conversion is about 2 pounds of feed to produce 1 pound of chicken, and feed represents about 65% of the cost of growing a chicken. Thus, if additional research can further improve the feed-to-chicken conversion rate by just 1%, the company would see additional income of $2.5 million to $3 million per week, or $130 million to $156 million per year.

Finance

Perdue Farms is privately held and considers financial information to be proprietary. Hence, available financial data are limited. Stock is primarily held by the family; a limited amount is held by management. Numbers commonly used by the media and the poultry industry peg Perdue Farms's revenues for 2000 at about $2.5 billion and the number of associates at nearly 20,000. *Forbes* magazine has estimated 2000 operating profits at about $160 million and net profits at about $22 million.

The firm's compound sales growth rate has been slowly decreasing during the past twenty years, mirroring the industry, which has been experiencing market saturation and overproduction. However, Perdue has compensated by using manpower more efficiently through such improvements as automation. For example, twenty years ago a 1% increase in associates resulted in a 1.6% increase in revenue; currently, a 1% increase in associates results in an 8.5% increase in revenues (see Exhibit 8).

Poultry operations can be divided into four segments: retail chicken (growth rate of 5%), food-service chicken and turkey (growth rate of 12%), international sales (growth rate of 64% over past six years), and grain and oilseed (growth rate of 10%). The bulk of sales continues to come from retail chicken, the sector with the slowest growth rate. The greatest opportunities appear to lie in food-service sales, where the

EXHIBIT 8

Annual Compound Growth Rate for Perdue Farms, 1980–2000

	Revenue	Associates	Sales/ Associate
Past 20 years	10.60%	6.48%	3.87%
Past 15 years	8.45%	4.48%	4.48%
Past 10 years	7.39%	4.75%	2.52%
Past 5 years	8.39%	0.99%	7.33%

company is admittedly behind, and international sales, where political and economic instability in target countries makes the risk to capital significant.

Perdue Farms has been profitable every year since its founding, with the exception of 1988 and 1996. Company officials believe the loss in 1988 was caused by overproduction by the industry and higher administrative costs resulting from a decentralization effort begun during the mid eighties. At that time, there was a concerted effort to push decisions down through the corporate ranks to provide more autonomy. When the new strategy resulted in significantly higher administrative costs due to duplication of effort, the company responded quickly by returning to the basics, reconsolidating, and downsizing. The loss in 1996 was due to the impact of high corn prices. Currently, the goal is to constantly streamline in order to be cost effective.

Perdue Farms approaches financial management conservatively, using retained earnings and cash flow to finance most asset-replacement projects and normal growth. When planning expansion projects or acquisitions, long-term debt is used. The target debt limit is 55% of equity. Such debt is normally provided by domestic and international bank and insurance companies. The debt strategy is to match asset lives with liability maturities and have a mix of fixed-rate and variable-rate debt. Growth plans require about two dollars in projected incremental sales growth for each dollar invested.

Environment

Environmental issues present a constant challenge to all poultry processors. Growing, slaughtering, and processing poultry is a difficult and tedious process that demands absolute efficiency in order to keep operating costs at an acceptable level. Inevitably, detractors argue that the process is dangerous to workers, inhumane to the poultry, and hard on the environment and that it results in food that may not be safe. Thus, media headlines such as "Human Cost of Poultry Business Bared," "Animal Rights Advocates Protest Chicken Coop Conditions," "Processing Plants Leave a Toxic Trail," and "EPA Mandates Poultry Regulations" are routine.

Perdue Farms tries to be pro-active in managing environmental issues. In April 1993, the company created an environmental steering committee. Its mission is "to provide all Perdue Farms work sites with vision, direction, and leadership so that they can be good corporate citizens from an environmental perspective today and in the future." The committee is responsible for overseeing how the company is doing in such environmentally sensitive areas as waste water, storm water, hazardous waste, solid waste, recycling, bio-solids, and employee health and safety.

For example, disposing of dead birds has long been an industry problem. Perdue Farms developed small composters for use on each farm. Using this approach, carcasses resemble soil in a matter of a few days. The disposal of hatchery waste is another environmental challenge. Historically, manure and unhatched eggs were shipped to a landfill. However, Perdue Farms developed a way to reduce the waste by 50% by selling the liquid fraction to a pet-food processor that cooks it for protein. The other 50% is recycled through a rendering process. In 1990, Perdue Farms spent $4.2 million to upgrade its treatment facility with a state-of-the-art system at its Accomac, Virginia, and Showell, Maryland, plants. These facilities use forced air heated to 120 degrees, which causes the microbes to digest all traces of ammonia, even during the winter months.

More than ten years ago, North Carolina's Occupational Safety and Health Administration cited Perdue Farms for an unacceptable level of repetitive stress injuries at its Lewiston and Robersonville, North Carolina, processing plants. This sparked a major research program in which Perdue Farms worked with Health and Hygiene Inc., of Greensboro, North Carolina, to learn more about ergonomics: the repetitive movements required to accomplish specific jobs. Results have been dramatic. Launched in 1991 after two years of development, the program videotapes employees at all of Perdue Farms's plants in order to assign stress values to their tasks. Although

the cost to Perdue Farms has been significant, results have been dramatic: workers' compensation claims went down 44%; lost-time recordables were just 7.7% of the industry average; serious repetitive-stress cases decreased by 80%, and there was a 50% reduction in lost time or surgery due to back injuries (Shelley Reese, "Helping Employees Get a Grip," *Business and Health,* August 1998).

Despite these advances, serious problems continue to develop. In 1997, the organism pfiesteria burst into media headlines when massive numbers of dead fish with lesions turned up along the Chesapeake Bay in Maryland. Initial findings pointed to manure runoff from the poultry industry as the cause. Political constituencies quickly called for increased regulation to insure proper manure storage and fertilizer use. Perdue Farms readily admits that "the poultry process is a closed system. There is lots of nitrogen and phosphorus in the grain, and it passes through the chicken and is returned to the environment as manure. Obviously, if you bring additional grain into a closed area such as the DelMarVa peninsula, you increase the amount of nitrogen and phosphorus in the soil unless you find a way to get rid of it." Nitrogen and phosphorus from manure normally make excellent fertilizer, which moves slowly in the soil. However, scientists speculate that erosion speeds up runoff, threatening the health of nearby streams, rivers, and larger bodies of water, such as the Chesapeake Bay. The problem for the industry is that proposals to control the runoff are sometimes driven more by politics and emotion than research, which is not yet complete.

Although it is not clear what role poultry-related nitrogen and phosphorus runoff played in the pfiesteria outbreak, regulators believe the microorganism feeds on the algae that grows when too much of these nutrients is present in the water. Thus, the EPA and various states are considering new regulations. Currently, contract growers are responsible for either using or disposing of the manure from their chicken houses. But some regulators and environmentalists believe that (1) it is too complicated to police the utilization-and-disposal practices of thousands of individual farmers, and (2) only the big poultry companies have the financial resources to properly dispose of the waste. Thus, they want to make poultry companies responsible for all waste disposal—a move that the industry strongly opposes.

Some experts have called for conservation measures that limit the density of chicken houses in a given area or require a percentage of chicken houses to be taken out of production periodically. Obviously this would be very hard on the farm families who own chicken houses, and the measure could result in fewer acres devoted to agriculture. Working with AgriRecycle Inc. of Springfield, Missouri, Perdue Farms has developed a possible solution: turn excess manure into pellets for use as fertilizer. This would permit sale outside the poultry-growing region, better balancing the input of grain. Spokesmen estimate that as much as 120,000 tons (nearly one-third of the surplus nutrients from manure produced each year on the DelMarVa peninsula) could be sold to corn growers in other parts of the country. Prices would be market driven but could be $25 to $30 per ton, suggesting a potential, small profit. Still, almost any attempt to control the problem potentially raises the cost of growing chickens, forcing poultry processors to look for locations where the chicken population is less dense.

In general, solving environmental problems attributable to the industry presents at least five major challenges to the poultry processor:

- how to maintain the trust of the poultry consumer

- how to ensure that the poultry remain healthy

- how to protect the safety of the employees and the integrity of the process

- how to satisfy legislators, who need to show their constituents that they are taking concrete action when environmental problems occur, and

- how to keep costs at an acceptable level.

Jim Perdue sums up Perdue Farms's position as follows: "We must not only comply with environmental laws as they exist today, but look to the future to make sure we don't have any surprises. We must make sure our environmental policy statement [see Exhibit 9] is real, that there's something behind it, and that we do what we say we're going to do."

Logistics and Information Systems

The recent explosion of poultry products and increase in customers placed a severe strain on Perdue Farms's logistical system, which was developed at a time when there were far fewer products, fewer delivery points, and lower volume. Hence, the company had limited ability to improve service levels, could not support further growth, and could not introduce services that might give it a competitive advantage.

In the poultry industry, companies are faced with two significant problems: time and forecasting. Fresh poultry has a limited shelf life, measured in days. Thus, forecasts must be extremely accurate and deliveries timely. On the one hand, estimating requirements too conservatively results in product shortages. High-volume customers such as Wal-Mart will not tolerate product shortages that lead to empty shelves and lost sales. On the other hand, if estimates are too high, the results are outdated products that cannot be sold and losses for Perdue Farms. A common expression in the poultry industry is "You either sell it or smell it."

Forecasting has always been extremely difficult in the poultry industry because the processor needs to know approximately eighteen months in advance how many broilers will be needed in order to size hatchery-supply flocks and contract with growers to provide live broilers. Most customers (e.g., grocers and food-service buyers) have a much smaller planning window. Additionally, Perdue Farms cannot know when rival poultry processors will discount a particular product reducing Perdue Farms sales, or when bad weather and other factors beyond the company's control may reduce demand.

Historically, poultry companies have based their estimates on past demand and information from industry networks and other contacts. Although product complexity has exacerbated the problem, the steady movement away from fresh product to frozen product (which has a longer shelf life) offers some relief.

Information technology (IT) has helped by shortening the distance between the customer and Perdue Farms. As far back as 1987, PCs were placed on the desks of customer-service associates, allowing each of them to enter customer orders directly. Next, a system was developed to put dispatchers in direct contact with every truck so that the dispatchers would have accurate information about product inventory and delivery at all times. Now, IT is moving to further shorten the distance between the customer and the Perdue Farms service representative by putting a PC on the customer's desk. All of these steps improve communication and shorten the time from order to delivery.

Today, poultry products fall into four channels of distribution:

1. Bulk fresh. **Timeliness and frequency of delivery are critical to ensure freshness.** Distribution requirements are high-volume and low-cost delivery.

EXHIBIT 9

Perdue Farms's Environmental Policy Statement

Perdue Farms is committed to environmental stewardship and shares that commitment with its farm family partners. We're proud of the leadership we're providing our industry in addressing the full range of environmental challenges related to animal agriculture and food processing. We've invested—and continue to invest—millions of dollars in research, new technology, equipment upgrades, and awareness and education as part of our ongoing commitment to protecting the environment.

▍ Perdue Farms was among the first poultry companies with a dedicated Environmental Services department. Our team of environmental managers is responsible for ensuring that every Perdue facility operates with *100 percent compliance of all applicable environmental regulations and permits.*

▍ Through our joint venture, Perdue AgriRecycle, Perdue Farms is investing $12 million to build in Delaware a first-of-its-kind pellet plant that will convert surplus poultry litter into a starter fertilizer that will be marketed internationally to nutrient deficient regions. The facility, which will serve the entire DelMarVa region, is scheduled to begin operation in April 2001.

▍ We continue to explore new technologies that will reduce water usage in our processing plants without compromising food safety or quality.

▍ We invested thousands of man-hours in producer education to assist our family farm partners in managing their independent poultry operations in the most environmentally responsible manner possible. In addition, all our poultry producers are required to have nutrient management plans and dead-bird composters.

▍ Perdue Farms was one of four poultry companies operating in Delaware to sign an agreement with Delaware officials outlining our companies' voluntary commitment to help independent poultry producers dispose of surplus chicken litter.

▍ Our Technical Services department is conducting ongoing research into feed technology as a means of reducing the nutrients in poultry manure. We've already achieved phosphorus reductions that far exceed the industry average.

▍ We recognize that the environmental impact of animal agriculture is more pronounced in areas where development is decreasing the amount of farmland available to produce grain for feed and to accept nutrients. That is why we view independent grain *and* poultry producers as vital business partners and strive to preserve the economic viability of the family farm.

At Perdue Farms, we believe that it is possible to preserve the family farm; provide a safe, abundant, and affordable food supply; and protect the environment. However, we believe that can best happen when there is cooperation and trust between the poultry industry, agriculture, environmental groups, and state officials. We hope Delaware's effort will become a model for other states to follow.

2. Domestic frozen and further-processed products. **Temperature integrity is critical.** Distribution requirements are frequency and timeliness of delivery. This channel lends itself to dual-temperature trailer systems and load consolidation.

3. Export. **Temperature integrity, high volume, and low cost are critical.** This channel lends itself to inventory consolidation and custom loading of vessels.

4. Consumer-packaged goods (packaged-fresh, prepared, and deli products). **Differentiate via inno-** **vative products and services.** Distribution requirements are reduced lead time and low cost.

Thus, forecasting now requires the development of a sophisticated **supply-chain management system** that can efficiently integrate all facets of operations, including grain and oilseed activities, hatcheries and growing facilities, processing plants (which now produce more than four hundred products at more than twenty locations), distribution facilities and the distributors, supermarkets, food-service customers, and export markets (see Exhibit 5). Perdue Farms underlined the importance of the successful implementation of supply-chain management by creating a new executive position, senior vice president for supply-chain management.

A key step in overhauling the distribution infrastructure is building replenishment centers that will, in effect, be intermediaries between the processing plants and the customers. The portside facility in Norfolk, Virginia, which serves the international market, is being expanded and a new domestic freezer facility added.

Products are directed from the processing plants to the replenishment and freezer centers based on customer forecasts, which have been converted to an optimized production schedule. Perdue Farms trucks deliver these bulk products to the centers in finished or partly finished form. At the centers, finishing and packaging are completed. Finally, customer orders are custom-palletized and loaded on trucks (either Perdue owned or contracted) for delivery. All shipments are produced from replenishment-center inventory. Thus, the need for accurate forecasting by the distribution centers is critical.

In order to control the entire supply-chain management process, Perdue Farms purchased a multi-million-dollar IT system that represents the biggest nontangible expense in the company's history. This integrated, state-of-the-art information system required total process reengineering—a project that took eighteen months and required training 1,200 associates. Major goals of the system were to:

1. Make it easier and more desirable for the customer to do business with Perdue Farms.

2. Make it easier for Perdue Farms associates to do their jobs.

3. Reduce costs as much as possible.

Industry Trends

The poultry industry is affected by consumer and regulatory trends. Currently, chicken is the number-one meat consumed in the United States, with a 40% market share (Exhibits 10 and 11). A typical American consumes about 81 pounds of chicken, 69 pounds of beef, and 52 pounds of pork annually (USDA data). Chicken is also becoming the most popular meat in the world; in 1997, poultry set an export record of $2.5 billion. Although exports fell 6% in 1998—a decrease attributed to Russia's and

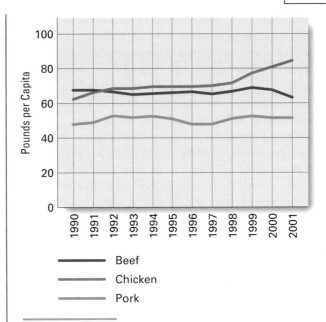

EXHIBIT 10

Consumption per Capita of Chicken, Beef, and Pork in the 1990s and Projected Consumption for 2000 and 2001

Asia's financial crises—food-industry experts expect this to be temporary. Hence, the world market is clearly a growth opportunity.

The popularity and growth of poultry products are attributed to both nutritional and economic issues. Poultry products contain significantly less fat and cholesterol than other meat products. In the United States, the demand for boneless, skinless

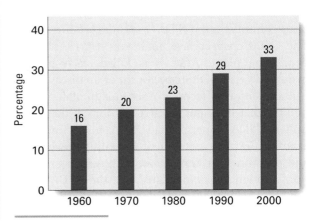

EXHIBIT 11

Chicken as a Percentage of Overall Meat, Poultry, and Fish Consumption, 1960–2000 breast meat, the leanest meat on poultry, is so great that dark meat is often sold at a discount in the United States or shipped overseas, where it is preferred to white meat.

Another trend is a decrease in demand for whole birds as the base dish for home meals and an increase in demand for products that have been further processed for either home or restaurant consumption. For example, turkey or chicken hot dogs, fully cooked sliced chicken or turkey, and turkey pastrami—which neither looks nor tastes like turkey—can be found in most deli cases. Many supermarkets sell either whole rotisserie chicken or parts of it. Almost all fast-food restaurants have at least one sandwich based on poultry products. Many up-scale restaurants feature poultry products that are partially prepared and then shipped to them frozen in order to simplify restaurant preparation. All these products have been further processed, adding value and potentially increasing the profit margin.

The industry is consolidating; that is, the larger companies in the industry are continuing to buy smaller firms. There are about thirty-five major poultry firms in the United States, but this number is expected to drop to twenty to twenty-five within the next ten years. There are several reasons for this. Stagnant U.S. demand and general product oversupply create downward price pressure, which makes it difficult for smaller firms to operate profitably. In addition, efficiency improvements require huge capital outlays. Finally, high-volume retailers such as Sam's Club and Royal Ahold (the Dutch owner of several U.S. supermarket chains) prefer to deal with large suppliers rather than many smaller processors.

The industry is heavily regulated. The Food and Drug Administration (FDA) monitors product safety. The USDA inspects live poultry as it arrives at the processing plant. After it is killed, each bird is inspected by a USDA inspector for avian diseases and contamination of feces or other foreign material. All poultry that does not meet regulations is destroyed under USDA supervision. USDA inspectors also examine the plant, equipment, operating procedures, and personnel for compliance with sanitary regulations. Congress has mandated that the USDA make this information available online. Additional intensive inspections of statistically selected product samples have been recommended by the National Academy of Sciences, so more FDA regulations are anticipated.

Although poultry produces less waste per pound of product than cattle or hogs, all meat industries are being scrutinized more closely by the EPA with regard to waste disposal. In general, waste generated at processing plants is well controlled by regulation, monitoring, and such penalties as fines. When an EPA violation occurs, the company that operates the plant may receive a substantial fine—potentially, millions of dollars.

Still, the most difficult problems to deal with are those that occur as a cumulative result of numerous processors operating in a relatively small area. For example, increasing poultry production in a given area intensifies the problem of disposal of manure. In manmade fertilizer, phosphorus and nitrogen exist in approximately a 1:8 ratio, whereas in poultry manure the ratio can be 1:1. Thus, the production of too much poultry manure can result in excessive phosphorus runoff into streams and rivers, potentially causing aquatic disease and degradation of water quality. This was the case in the 1997 outbreak of pfiesteria, a toxic microbe, in the tributaries of the Chesapeake Bay. Although the poultry industry insisted that there were many possible reasons for the problem, the media and most regulatory spokespersons attributed it primarily to phosphorus runoff from chicken manure. After much negative publicity and extensive investigation by both poultry processors and state regulatory agencies, Maryland passed the Water Quality Act of 1998, which required the industry to formulate nutrient-management plans. However, many environmentalists still believe that the EPA must create stricter regulations. Recent regulatory activity has continued to focus on Eastern Shore agriculture, especially the poultry industry. However, new studies from the U.S. Geological Survey suggest that the vast majority of nutrients affecting the Chesapeake Bay come from rivers that do not flow through the poultry-producing areas of the Eastern Shore. The studies also found that improved agricultural management practices have reduced nutrient runoff from farmlands. Jim Perdue says, "While the poultry industry must accept responsibility for its share of nutrients, public policy should view the watershed as a whole and address all the factors that influence water quality."

Other government agencies whose regulations impact the industry include the Occupational Safety and Health Administration (OSHA) and the Immigration and Naturalization Service (INS). OSHA enforces its employee-safety regulations via periodic inspections and levies fines when noncompliance is discovered. For example, a Hudson Foods poultry plant was fined more than a million dollars for alleged willful violations causing ergonomic injury to workers. The INS also uses periodic inspections to find undocumented workers. It estimates that the percentage of undocumented aliens working in the industry ranges from 3 to 78% of the work force, depending on the plant. Plants found to employ undocumented workers, especially those that are repeat offenders, can be heavily fined.

The Future

The marketplace for poultry in the twenty-first century will be very different from that of the past. Understanding the wants and needs of generation Xers and echo-boomers will be key to responding successfully to these differences.

Quality will continue to be essential. In the 1970s, quality was the cornerstone of Frank Perdue's successful marketing campaign to brand his poultry. However, in the twenty-first century, quality will not be enough. Today's customers expect—even demand—all products to be of high quality. Thus, Perdue Farms plans to use customer service to further differentiate the company from its competitors. The focus will be on learning how to become indispensable to the customer by reducing cost and delivering the product exactly the way the customer wants it, where and when the customer wants it. In short, as Jim Perdue says, "Perdue Farms wants to become so easy to do business with that the customer will have no reason to do business with anyone else."

In the poultry business, customer-purchase decisions, as well as company profitability, hinge on mere pennies. Thus, the location of processing facilities is critical. Historically, Perdue Farms has been an Eastern Shore company and has maintained major processing facilities there. However, it currently costs about 1.5 cents more per pound to grow poultry on the Eastern Shore than in Arkansas. This difference results from the cost of labor, compliance with federal and state environmental laws, resource costs (e.g., feed grain), and other variables. If regulations will permit the importation of foreign-grown poultry in the future, producers could even use inexpensive international labor markets to further reduce costs. The opportunity for large growers to reduce costs in these ways puts increased pressure on small poultry companies, which suggests further consolidation of the industry.

Grocery companies are also consolidating in order to compete with huge food-industry newcomers, such as Wal-Mart and Royal Ahold. These new competitors increase efficiency by minimizing the number of their suppliers and buying huge amounts from each at the lowest possible price. In effect, suppliers and buyers become dependent on each other, and buyers expect their suppliers to do more for them. For example, Perdue Farms considers it possible that, using sophisticated distribution-information programs, they will soon be able to manage the entire meat-department requirements for several supermarket chains. Providing this service would support Perdue Farms's goal of becoming indispensable to its first-line retail customer, the grocer.

The twenty-first-century consumer will demand many options. Clearly, the demand for uncooked, whole chickens purchased at the meat counter has peaked. Demand is moving toward further-processed poultry. To support this trend, Perdue Farms plans to open several cooking plants. In addition, a criterion for future acquisitions will be whether they support value-added processing. Products from these plants will fill food-service requirements and grocery sales of prepared foods, such as delicatessen, frozen, home meal-replacement, and shelf-stable items. Additionally, the twenty-first-century customer will be everywhere. Whether at work, at a sports event, in school, or traveling on the highway, customers will expect to have convenient refreshment options and a wide selection of wholesome, ready-to-eat products.

Designing a distribution system that can handle all of these options is extremely difficult. For example, the system must be able to efficiently organize hundreds of customer orders for more than four hundred different products, which are processed and further prepared at more than twenty facilities throughout the southeast for delivery by one truck—a massive distribution task. As executives note, the company survived until now using distribution techniques created as long ago as the eighties, when there were a handful of products and processing facilities. However, the system approached gridlock during the late 1990s. Thus, Perdue Farms invested in a state-of-the-art information-processing system—a tough decision because "we could build two new processing plants for the price of this technology package."

International markets are a conundrum. On one hand, Perdue Farms's international market has grown from an insignificant side business in 1994 to one generating $140 million in 1999, about 5% of total revenues. Further, its contribution to profits is significant. Poultry is widely accepted around the world, providing opportunities for further growth. However, different places value different parts of the chicken and demand different meat color, preparation, and seasoning. Thus, products must be customized. Parts that are not in demand in one country must be sold at severely reduced prices, used as feed, or shipped frozen to a market where demand exists. While this can be done, it is a distribution problem that significantly complicates an already difficult forecasting model.

International markets can also be very unstable, exposing Perdue Farms to significant demand instability and potential losses. For example, in 1997, about 50% of Perdue Farms's international revenues came from Russia. However, political and economic problems there reduced 1999 revenues significantly. This high level of instability, coupled with the corruption that thrives in a country experiencing severe political and economic turmoil, introduces significant risk to investment.

Clearly, the future holds many opportunities. But none of them comes without risk, and Perdue Farms must carefully choose where it wants to direct its limited resources.

Wizards of the Coast 1990–2001

6

This case was prepared by Charles W. L. Hill, Suresh Kotha, and Richard Moxon, all from the University of Washington, and Frank Rothaermel from Michigan State University.

The excitement was high among the top managers of Wizards of the Coast, the world's leading adventure gaming company, as they sat down to review the company's progress during the first half of 1997. The company had just completed the acquisition of a major competitor, and with the opening of its first gaming entertainment center, it was pioneering a new retail concept. Fueled by one hit product, three years of tremendous growth had been followed by an unexpected downturn in revenues in 1996. Wizards now looked to be on the rebound, but everyone knew that the company still had to prove it had a sustainable-growth strategy for the future.

Creating the Magic

Wizards of the Coast was a privately held company best known for creating the world's leading adventure trading card game, Magic: The Gathering. Since its release in 1993, over five million consumers worldwide had embraced the game, which was available in nine languages and played in over fifty countries. See Exhibit 1 for a brief description of Magic.

This case is based primarily on field research and is intended to be used as a basis for class discussion rather than as an illustration of either effective or ineffective handling of the situation. Reprinted by permission of Frank T. Rothaermel, Suresh Kotha, and Charles W. L. Hill.

The Genesis

Wizards of the Coast was founded by Peter Adkison and a group of other young professionals in 1990 to develop role-playing games. Adkison had been intrigued by strategy and role-playing games ever since he was eleven, and in high school had developed a passion for the Dungeons & Dragons adventure role-playing game. He was working for Boeing as a computer-systems analyst, but was eager to start his own venture. Recalls Adkison, "I was a small cog in a huge machine that itself was a small cog in a huge machine." He and his friends kept their jobs but began developing role-playing games in their spare time.

In 1991, Adkison was introduced to Richard Garfield, a doctoral student in combinational mathematics at the University of Pennsylvania and an avid game player who had been designing his own games since he was a teenager. When the two got together at a game convention, the concept for Magic was born. Adkison had the idea that there was a need for a fantasy role-playing game that was portable and could be played anywhere in no more than an hour. He thought that it could be a card game. Garfield had also been interested in fantasy games since playing a game called Cosmic Encounter in the 1980s. One of the pieces in Cosmic Encounter had special powers. By invoking these powers, a player could change the rules of the game. This intrigued Garfield,

EXHIBIT 1

Magic: The Gathering

The game Magic: The Gathering combines elements of chess, bridge, and the role-playing game of Dungeons & Dragons. Magic is a trading-card game in which two players are rival wizards dueling for control of a magical "multiverse" called Dominia. Each player starts out with twenty life points. The goal is to reduce the opponent's life points to zero before the opponent can do the same—to kill the opponent.

Before starting the game, each player builds a deck of at least forty cards from his or her collection. Each player begins by shuffling the deck and drawing seven cards. Players alternate turns, with each turn a series of actions, such as attacking and defending. There are several types of illustrated cards. Lands are the most basic, providing the magical energy a player needs to play other cards. Others represent creatures, and still others represent spells that a player can cast. The basic strategy lies in choosing when to play what card and when to use what creatures for what purposes. Games usually last fifteen to thirty minutes, but some can last hours.

One of the key features of Magic is that each game played is unique: each player starts out with a deck of forty cards selected from among the more than four thousand sold. It is not uncommon for a player to own several hundred cards. This encourages players to buy or trade cards to enhance their powers and increase their strategic options.

The game is in perpetual evolution because new cards are released periodically and older ones retired by Wizards of the Coast. Retired cards gained instant status as collectibles and can be bought, sold, and traded between individuals, in hobby stores, and on the Internet. New cards are issued in different sets and limited editions. These expansions have kept the game novel and contributed to its phenomenal growth. Since the basic strategy in Magic is assembling the unassailable deck, serious players invest heavily in their collections.

In addition, with each edition of new cards the fantasy multiverse expands. Magic has undergone many extensions, and further expansion is limited only by the players' willingness to remain bewitched.

and he wondered what would happen if all the pieces were magic, each one altering the game in some unique way. He believed that this idea could lead to a fantasy board game, but Adkison persuaded him to focus on cards instead and to think about a format in which players could trade cards, buying and selling collectible cards similar to those of their sports heroes.

Garfield came back a few weeks later with a prototype of Magic: The Gathering. The idea was to combine trading cards and a fantasy game in which players controlled the acts of mystical characters. Recalls Garfield, "The concept of a trading-card game was one of the only 'Eureka!' experiences I've had."

Operating out of the basement of Adkison's home, Wizards of the Coast released Magic: The Gathering in August 1993. The game became an overnight success. The first printing of ten million cards, which was expected to last a year, sold out in six weeks. According to one game-store owner, "My initial was for 24 units, my second was for 572, and my third was, 'Send everything you've got in the warehouse.'" With sales success also came critical acclaim, Magic's winning several game and toy industry awards. Soon,

Adkison left Boeing, and Garfield a new teaching job, to work full-time on Wizards of the Coast.

Products and Customers

Magic cards were sold in starter decks of sixty randomly selected cards for about $8.95 and booster packs of eight or fifteen cards for about $2.95. Even though these were the recommended retail prices, it was not uncommon for retailers to unbundle decks and mark up the prices of cards in great demand. Because the cards also had original artwork that appealed to fantasy-game players and collectors, they were both collected and traded, their price determined by their strategic role and collector value. Each deck was unique, so no two players had identical sets of cards. Players traded cards in order to create a deck with desired characteristics.

According to the chief game developer for Wizards of the Coast, the typical Magic player was a person with a good education, a high household income, and an interest in computers. While the game was most popular with males in their teens or twenties, it had also caught on with younger teens and older men and women. College dormitories had been a breeding ground for new "gamers." Compared to the typical players of a board game such as Monopoly, the players of Magic saw the game more as a hobby—something on which they spent a significant amount of time and money.

Manufacturing and Distribution

Wizards contracted out the design, manufacturing, and packaging of its cards and other products. Most of its cards were designed by independent artists, who earned royalties from their Wizards' sales. In the beginning, the company relied on one supplier, Carta Mundi in Belgium, because no other firm could deliver the quality needed and do the sophisticated card sorting required. During the first two years of booming popularity, manufacturing capacity was the single biggest constraint on the growth of Wizards. Carta Mundi remained the largest supplier, but other suppliers were contracted as the game grew and they were able to meet Wizards' standards.

Wizards had built a widespread retail network to market its cards. Most adventure games were sold through small game, comic, or hobby shops, often mom-and-pop stores supplied by relatively small distributors. These shops were critical to reaching the serious gamers and accounted for about 75% of the company's sales. Wizards allocated new card series to these stores, and there was often a feeding frenzy as consumers rushed to get an advantage by buying the cards. With the popularity of Magic, Wizards was able to enter such national chains as Toys "R" Us, Barnes & Noble, and Target. These stores did not have the special atmosphere of the small retailers, but were more effective for reaching the mass market.

Growth Problems

The success of Magic put Wizards on an explosive growth trajectory. Sales of about $200,000 in 1993 rocketed to $57 million in 1994 and $127 million in 1995. Wizards and Adkison became entrepreneurial superstars. The company grew to about five hundred employees, moved in 1994 to new corporate offices, and opened several international sales offices.

Growth also brought problems. Many of the gamers who started with the company were not ready to move into managerial roles, and some managers who had been brought in could not work well with the gamers. In one case, Adkison found that someone who had been on the payroll for several months had never been hired by or reported to anybody. As Adki-

son said, "I've made so many mistakes, it's not even funny."

But growth came to a sudden halt in 1996, when sales fell off to $117 million. Moving quickly to control costs, Wizards had its first layoffs. According to Adkison, part of the cause was the inevitable leveling off of Magic's customer base and another was the fragmentation of the retail game stores. The success of Magic had drawn too many entrepreneurs into the game-store business, and the resulting shakeout caused some distributors to go under, affecting Wizards too.

While sales in 1997 were expected to be about at the 1996 level, Adkison was aiming at future growth. "We certainly can operate in a slow-growth mode and make nice profits," he said. "But we are focused on growing the company more rapidly in the future." Part of the pressure for growth was coming from its original investors. Many of them were friends of the original entrepreneurs, came from modest backgrounds, and had become rich from their investment in Wizards; but this wealth was all on paper, and many wanted to cash out part of their investments. To take the company public at an attractive price, Wizards would need to have a good growth plan. Coming up with a sustainable-growth strategy was therefore critical.

The Wizards Culture

While developing the systems needed to manage a much larger enterprise, Adkison tried to preserve the creative culture in which the company had been formed. For many years, he refused to have his own office or even a cubicle. On his business cards and memos, his position and title were given as "CEO and janitor." He saw the company as a kind of small software firm with a casual, creative atmosphere that tolerated individualism and creativity—expressed, for example, in eccentric clothing, body piercing, and frequent nerf wars among the employees. Over the years, however, the atmosphere became more reserved and Peter even acquired a corner office.

Wizards executives and employees tended to be very committed to the gaming concept. Richard Garfield, the inventor of Magic, saw adventure games as the "intellectual counterpart of sports: they keep you mentally fit." He believed that with playing Magic came "a lot of stealth education," whether it was art appreciation because of the beautiful cards or enhanced literacy because of the occasional quote from Shakespeare. Garfield also believed that Magic was a strategic game that could be played successfully only when the player had a good understanding of strategy, probability, and chance.

However, Adkison recognized that devoted gamers did not always make good executives. "There's nobody in the company who's ever managed a company this size, including me," he said. "We're trying to balance the desire for top-notch people to take us to the next level with the desire to stay true to people who founded the company." The firm had hired experienced managers from established toy companies, used consultants on strategic and operational issues, and brought outsiders onto its board of directors. Adkison himself obtained a master's degree from the University of Washington Business School, knowing that he would need to continue strengthening the organization and help it develop a strategy for sustainable growth.

The Adventure Gaming Industry

Wizards executives defined the company as part of the adventure gaming industry, which was itself part of the much larger toy industry. They followed publications of the Toy Manufacturers of America, as well as the more specialized *Comics Retailer,* a monthly publication with in-depth reports on gaming developments. Total U.S. toy-industry sales in 1996 were estimated at over $17 billion, of which the biggest single category was video games. The games and puzzles category accounted for approximately $1.4 billion in sales. Role-playing, trading-card, and war games—the segments in which Wizards competed most directly—accounted for about $350 million to $500 million in 1996 sales, according to *Comics Retailer.* The Game Manufacturers Association estimated gaming sales at $750 million.

The adventure gaming industry began in the 1960s with the development of a number of war games. The industry was revolutionized in the early 1970s with the introduction of Dungeons & Dragons, the first popular role-playing game. The game attracted players by being complex and by giving players the opportunity to exercise their creativity. The industry was revolutionized once again in the early 1990s with the introduction of Magic. By 1997, Dungeons & Dragons and Magic were still the top-selling role-playing and trading-card games. Wizards' acquisition in 1977 of TSR, the developer of Dun-

geons & Dragons, brought the two largest game manufacturers under one roof. The rest of the industry consisted of companies that were much smaller. Industry observers predicted that the most serious competition would come from companies in other industries invading adventure games.

Although there was no clear distinction between adventure and family games, people pursued adventure games as a serious hobby, sometimes dedicating many hours a week to playing a certain game. This led some critics to characterize players of Dungeons & Dragons and Magic as members of a "cult." Industry executives felt that this was an unfair image and saw most "gamers" as devoted to the games' intellectual and creative challenges. According to a survey by the Game Manufacturers Association, adventure-game enthusiasts were young and literate and did well in school.

One issue facing the gaming industry was the rise of the Internet and computer-based games. While most people in the industry considered typical video games to represent either lonely quests through fantasy worlds or "shoot-'em-up" arcade-like games, the Internet offered the possibility of role-playing and trading cards in a virtual world. Whether or not games would prefer this to the face-to-face experiences of Dungeons and Magic was of concern to Wizards executives.

Growing the Magic

As the dominant adventure trading-card game, Magic did not have much potential for increasing its share of this market. Wizards focused instead on extending the Magic brand name into other products and targeting the mass market to increase the size of the adventure trading-card industry. At the same time, the company had begun promoting Magic tournaments in an effort to increase the game's legitimacy and defend it from its competition.

Extending the Brand

Adkison was now attempting through licensing, to leverage the Magic brand name into books, computer games, and other products. With the popularity of Magic, Wizards was able to pick and choose its opportunities.

Magic also appeared as a book series by Harper-Collins, selling over half a million copies, and came out as part of two CD-ROM computer games. Wizards executives felt that bookstores were a logical market for its products because Magic players tended to be heavy readers and the game was often played in bookstores.

Also through licensing agreements, Magic merchandise had been extended into prepaid phone cards, clothing, card albums and protectors, a Magic strategy guide and encyclopedia, and calendars. Wizards had also reached an agreement with an Internet development and design company to produce interactive CD-ROM products that would serve as guides to the fantasy worlds created by Wizards. The company also received movie and television offers, but no agreements were reached. Licensing revenues were estimated to be about $1 million annually.

Going for the Mass Market

The dream of Wizards and other adventure-game developers was the mass-market role-playing game. Selling a typical board game brought in revenue of less than $10 a game to a company, but customers could spend up to $500 per year on a role-playing game. A mass-market hit could easily generate a billion dollars.

Wizards introduced a more mainstream version of Magic named Portal, which was targeted at a broader audience (younger teens and families) and was launched with a media campaign costing nearly $5 million. This new game used card decks based on a variety of popular TV characters—such as Xena the Warrior Princess—and allowed these decks to be intermingled. The aim was to interest a consumer other than the gamer who had made Magic a success. Portal was to be distributed through mass-market retailers such as Toys "R" Us and Target.

But Wizards saw risks with the mass market also. Magic gamers were attracted to the atmosphere of game stores and to the experience of the game, not just the game itself. Mass-market retailers, on the other hand, saw games as "boxes." And with retailers' tremendous buying power, Wizards would not enjoy the same margins that it did on its Magic sales.

Developing Tournaments

To increase Magic sales, Wizards attempted to professionalize the activity of playing Magic, transforming it into a legitimate sport. Noted Adkison, "It's been proven that sports are very sustainable. They hold people's attention for a long time." One part of the strategy was to create players who had celebrity

standing and who could popularize the game in the mass market.

Tournaments had been organized informally in the first years of Magic, many held in and sponsored by stores selling the game. Hundreds of these were held each year. In 1996, the company organized a six-city professional tournament series that offered $1 million in prizes and scholarships. Wizards also created a global-ranking system for all professional players that was accessible at its home page (**www.wizards.com**). In the United States, over fifty thousand tournament players competed in thirty leagues.

The Magic world-championship series generated such interest that in 1997 it was carried on television by ESPN. Players from over forty countries competed for individual and team titles and for $250,000 in prize money. Wizards was able to attract a corporate partner, MCI Telecommunications, to sponsor the series. According to one news analysis, the partnership gave legitimacy to Wizards and provided the game with a mass audience, while MCI was able to tap an attractive audience by associating itself with a "cool" event. According to the company that brokered the deal, Magic players were considered a good market due to their passion for the game and their desire to collect everything associated with it. "You've never seen loyalty like this. It's unrivaled across any other product or service category." MCI agreed to sponsor Wizards' Magic tournaments in exchange for exclusive worldwide rights to produce and distribute Magic prepaid telephone cards featuring the artwork of Magic cards.

Wizards also published a variety of magazines connected with its games. *The Duelist* contain articles, tips from celebrity players, and information on upcoming Magic tournaments. *Dragon* magazine, which came to Wizards with the acquisition of the Dungeons & Dragons game, had been published since the 1970s.

Defending the Brand

In addition to aggressively promoting Magic, Wizards of the Coast had applied for a patent covering not the design of the cards but the method of play. Entry barriers to the game industry were relatively low, and Wizards estimated that there were over one hundred games trying to compete with Magic. The company was set on collecting royalty payments from imitators.

Beyond Magic

The success of Magic had not blinded the Wizards executives to the need to seek new sources of revenue. As the leading trading-card game company, it was the target of game developers constantly looking for the next hit. Wizards's response was to develop new games and to acquire other game companies.

Product Development

Wizards developed and marketed what were considered to be great games, but none was able to replicate Magic. Adkison remained optimistic, but realized that repeating that success would be difficult. "We have several things we're working on in R&D that could turn out to be like Magic," he said. "But in the gaming business, you can't bank on past success. We have to learn to make money with smaller releases."

The adventure-game industry had developed largely as a result of two runaway hits: Dungeons & Dragons, then Magic. Adkison expected that another hit would again revolutionize the industry one day. But it seemed unlikely that the same company would be responsible. Wizards needed to position itself to succeed even if it was not the one to develop the next hit.

Acquisitions

After completing two major acquisitions, Wizards was considering others. One acquisition was Five Rings Publishing, developer of the Legends of the Five Rings trading-card game; the other was TSR Inc., creator of Dungeons & Dragons. Integrating these acquisitions had been a major challenge for Wizards. TSR had serious financial difficulties that Wizards had to sort out, and the company was in the process of moving TSR operations and many of TSR's staff from Wisconsin to its Seattle headquarters.

Wizards confirmed reports that it had held discussions with Westend Games, which had the licenses to a Star Wars role-playing game and a DC Comics role-playing game. Other small game companies also looked like attractive acquisition candidates.

Global Magic

Wizards estimated that Magic was played in over fifty countries by more than five million players. Successful, the company had international offices in Antwerp, London, Milan, and Paris and planned to open offices in Asia. Adkison noted that international sales had been very important to sustaining the company during the downturn in U.S. sales in 1996 and there was still a lot of expansion potential in the international market.

Game Centers

In May 1997, Wizards of the Coast opened its first retail and gaming store, a 34,000-square-foot Wizards of the Coast Game Center, located in Seattle close to the campus of the University of Washington. Designed as the first entertainment center for adventure gamers, it offered an extensive array of arcade video games, sold games and associated merchandise, offered food and beverages, and provided a place for trading-card gamers to meet and compete with others. It was also intended to be a site for tournaments.

According to Adkison, the game center was "sort of like Niketown or Planet Hollywood. We have the opportunity to create the ultimate gaming atmosphere. This is a club, a hangout, a place for the devoted game players to go and play anytime." Wizards hoped that game centers would create an even stronger game-playing community by encouraging people to consider games an entertainment choice, like going to the movies or dining out. Just as the cineplex concept broadened the movie-going public, Wizards hoped that "gameplexes" would encourage the growth of the game-playing community. The Seattle Game Center carried many competitive games, but Wizards games were featured most prominently.

Another function of the game centers was to improve the retail distribution of the Wizards' product line. The company was disappointed with the support given by traditional retailers to the games and felt that it knew better than retailers how to sell and support its games.

Wizards also knew that the success of game centers was not a sure thing. Companies like Gameworks had introduced family-entertainment centers with very limited success. Wizards was encouraged, however, by the success of Games Workshop—the developer of the popular Warhammer game—with a similar concept.

Lightning Strikes Twice: Pokemon

In 1998, Adkison recognized that Wizards of the Coast was still a one-product company whose future was tightly linked to the success of Magic. He said, "Magic provides over 90% of our cash flow. It is obviously our primary focus. The big strategic issue with Magic is to develop its potential to become a 'classic game' that yields steady profits year after year. I wouldn't mind being a $500 million to $1 billion company. We want to make games as big as the movies." As he thought about the company's future strategy, the possibility that Wizards would have another hit like Magic seemed highly unlikely.[1] How wrong he was, for within a year Wizards would be riding a wave much bigger than that generated by Magic.

Named after the endearing set of characters invented by Nintendo, Pokemon had begun life in Japan as a game for Nintendo's N64 and Game Boy video-game platforms. In 1997, one of Nintendo's employees developed the Pokemon trading-card game. The Nintendo employee was an avid player of Magic, and he had simply taken the underlying structure of the game—referred to in the industry as the "game mechanic"—and inserted a new set of characters: those of the Pokemon world. The resulting trading-card game was a sensation in Japan.

Seeing the potential, Nintendo decided to sell the trading-card game in the rest of the world. However, it faced two problems in selling Pokemon outside of Japan. First, it lacked the distribution required to sell the game; and second, Wizards of the Coast had applied for and received a patent on the game mechanic underlying Magic. Since the Pokemon trading-card game used the same game mechanic, Nintendo might be in violation of this patent. The obvious solution to this dilemma was for Nintendo to license the ex-Japanese rights to the Pokemon game to the company with the patent on the underlying game mechanic and with an established distribution system, brand name, and industry expertise: Wizards of the Coast.

The results of the deal soon exceeded the expectations of both companies. Pokemon quickly became a global phenomenon among the six- to twelve-year-old set. Sales of the trading cards rocketed, along with sales of the video games, and the growing popularity of an associated TV series. For Wizards, the result was an unexpected bonanza. The company's sales surged from $150 million in 1998 to an estimated $400 million in 1999. The popularity of Pokemon trading cards accounted for some $225 million of this increase.[2] As with Magic, Wizards quickly issued expansion sets that emphasized new themes and generated incremental sales revenues. The collectible aspect of Pokemon trading cards was, if anything, greater than that of Magic. Kids competed with each other to collect a full set of trading cards, including highly valued rare cards.

Another appealing aspect of the Pokemon phenomenon was that it broadened Wizards' appeal to a demographic that it had not been able to reach with Magic: six- to twelve-year-old kids. The "dark themes" of Magic had put off many parents, but appealed to fourteen- to twenty-five-year-olds with a passion for strategy games. At Wizards, the hope emerged that kids would cut their teeth on Pokemon and, when they grew older, move on to Magic. Moreover, Pokemon allowed Wizards to widen its distribution system, selling in mainstream locations that had not sold Magic.

The Hasbro Acquisition

With Pokemon emerging as *the* theme of the 1999/2000 Christmas season, the success of Wizards attracted the attention of major players in the toy industry, including, most notably, Hasbro. In September 1999, Hasbro made a $325 million bid to acquire Wizards, which the company quickly accepted.[3] Under the terms of the deal, Peter Adkison would continue as CEO of Wizards for at least four years, the company would remain at its current location, and it would be granted a high degree of operating autonomy. Hasbro was looking to Wizards to broaden its offering of Pokemon toys and games in advance of the holiday season. In addition, the growing presence of Wizards in the hobby niche of the gaming industry, along with its growing retail presence, appealed to Hasbro, which was suffering from stagnating sales of many of its traditional toy offerings.

From Wizards' perspective, the bid from Hasbro had a number of attractive features. Wizards had long planned to take the company public, but recognized that executing an Initial Public Offering (IPO) might be very difficult given the skeptical view of the hobby gaming industry held on Wall Street. Many of Wizards' key employees hold significant stock holdings in the company, but in the absence of an IPO, this stock was not very liquid. The market was very thin because there were only about three hundred stockholders. The Hasbro bid allowed these employees to turn their illiquid Wizards' stock into cash—a very appealing option to many. Moreover, an acquisition by Hasbro gave Wizards the opportunity to use

Hasbro's brand name to open certain doors, such as those of mass-market retailers who had traditionally been reluctant to stock the products of the hobby gaming industry. Hasbro's financial muscle could also help Wizards' to accelerate its retail-store strategy, to make further acquisitions in the industry, and to fund the advertising required to strengthen its brand.

Strategy Going Forward

The acquisition by Hasbro did not signal any big change in strategy at Wizards. The company continued to take steps to build its Magic and Pokemon trading-card games, hoping that like Monopoly and Risk, these games would become "classics." These steps included an extension of the organized-play concept to the Pokemon game, issuing of more expansion packs and new editions for Magic and Pokemon, television advertising campaigns, and broadening the distribution for Magic. In addition, the company continued to look for other opportunities to add to its franchise in the trading-card arena. In February 2000, Wizards announced that it had reached an agreement with Warner publishing to create a Harry Potter trading-card game that would employ a game mechanic similar to that of Magic and Pokemon and be marketed to ten- to fourteen-year-olds, the prime demographic for the best-selling Harry Potter books.[4] The game was scheduled to be released in late 2000. In February 2000, the company also announced that it had reached an agreement with the Major League Baseball Association and the Major League Baseball Players Association to create a trading-card game with a baseball theme, using league players as its central characters.

Wizards also continued to aggressively pursue its retail strategy, making a major strategic move prior to the Hasbro acquisition. In May 1999, Wizards acquired The Game Keeper Inc., which owned a chain of fifty-three retail stores that sold chess, puzzles, backgammon, dominoes, and family board games. Most of the stores were located in malls on the West Coast. The plan was to sell the full range of Wizards games in these stores and gradually convert them over to the Wizards brand name.[5] The company also continued to steadily expand the bigger game centers. In mid-1999, it had six game centers. By April 2000, the number had risen to eighteen and the company announced plans to open another thirty-four that year. Of these thirty-four, six would be converted from Game Keeper stores; the remaining game centers would be net additions. Not all of the game centers would be as large as the one in Seattle, but the average size would remain around 2,700 square feet, encompassing a retail store, an area for game play, and an area dedicated to coin-operated video games. The combination seemed to be a winning formula; the video-game and game-play areas drew in customers (and money, in the case of the video games), who would make purchases from the retail store.[6]

ENDNOTES

1. Charles Hill assisted in the facilitation of strategic planning sessions at Wizards that helped produce this strategy.
2. J. Milliot. Hasbro to acquire Wizards of the Coast. *Publishers Weekly,* September 20, 1999, p. 12.
3. J. Pereira and D. Golden. Games: With Wizards and Dragons, Hasbro expands its reach. *Wall Street Journal,* September 10, 1999, p. B1.
4. S. P. Chan. Wizards to make Harry Potter cards. *Seattle Times,* February 12, 2000, p. B1.
5. B. Ramsey. Wizard buys chain of stores. *Seattle Post Intelligencer,* May 6, 1999, p. D2.
6. D. Scheraga. Would you like to play a game? *Chain Store Age,* April 2000, pp. 50–51.

Napster 7

This case was prepared by Charles W. L. Hill, the University of Washington.

Lou Reed (artist): *"Artists, like anyone else, should be paid for their work."* [1]

Alanis Morissette (artist): *"Napster presents huge problems for the artists. It raises the question—which is positive—of where and how artists are compensated. But I don't agree with the model they have set up. The artist should be the person who's ultimately in a position to decide when and how something should be shared with whomever they choose to share it."* [2]

Eminem (artist): *"Whoever put my s**t on the Internet, I want to meet that mother****** and beat the s**t out of him."* [3]

Ted Cohen (record industry executive): *"I think it (Napster) is one of the coolest things to come around. I also thought the moment I saw it, 'My God! This could destroy the whole business.'"* [4]

Shawn Fanning (Napster founder) on hearing that the rock group Metallica had filed suit against Napster: *"Napster respects the role of artists and is very interested in working with Metallica and the music industry to develop a workable model that is fair to everyone while unleashing the power of the Internet to build enthusiasm for music."* [5]

Steven Wendell Isaacs (independent artist): *"I believe that Napster is a powerful promotional tool for the many artists and bands that want to reach large numbers of listeners but have not been able to get, or are disappointed by, the support provided by large recording labels."* [6]

James Breyer (venture capitalist): *"Napster is truly revolutionary—and it will be a precursor of some of the most important web applications over the next several years."* [7]

Introduction

Sometime in fall 1998, an indifferent eighteen-year-old student at Northeastern University in Boston had an epiphany. Wouldn't it be great, he thought, if people could share their music with each other over the Internet.[8] The student's name was Shawn Fanning, and the service that grew out of his epiphany, Napster, would shake the very foundations of the music recording industry. By 2000, Napster had taken

This case is intended to be used as a basis for class discussion rather than as an illustration of either effective or ineffective handling of the situation. Reprinted by permission of Charles W. L. Hill.

center stage in a pivotal struggle for the future of the industry. On one side was the Recording Industry Association of America (RIAA), the big five music recording labels, and several high profile recording artists, including Lars Ulrich of Metallica. On the other was a small company with less than fifty employees and limited funds, over thirty million users of Napster's service, and several artists who believed that supporting Napster was in their best interests, including Pearl Jam. In the middle was the U.S. judicial system.

The Music Industry

The music industry grew at a robust rate throughout the 1990s, registering global sales of $38.5 billion in 1999. The largest markets were the United States (37%), Japan (16.7%), the United Kingdom (7.6%), Germany (7.4%), France (5.2%), and Canada (2.3%). This growth came to an end in 2000, when global sales fell 5%, and again in 2001, when global sales slumped to $33.7 billion.

Despite the fall in sales, the International Federation of the Phonographic Industry (IFPI) claimed that demand for music was higher than ever, but that the decline in sales reflected the fact that "the commercial value of music is being widely devalued by mass copying and piracy."[9] According to the IFPA, one-third of all CDs and cassettes around the globe in 2000 were illegally produced and sold, suggesting that piracy cost the industry over $10 billion per annum.[10] Although illegal plants in Asia have long been the source of many pirated CDs and tapes, by 2001 the IFPI was getting increasingly concerned about consumers "burning" songs downloaded over the Internet onto CDs. In Germany, 18% of 10,000 consumers surveyed said burning CDs resulted in their buying less music. In the United States, nearly 70% of people who downloaded music burned the songs onto a CD-R disc, while 35% of people downloading more than twenty songs per month said they now buy less music as a result.[11]

As a result of consolidation, by 2001 the industry was dominated by five large recording companies that collectively accounted for over 90% of global recorded music sales. The five were Sony Music, Universal Music Group (which was owned by Vivendi, a French media conglomerate), EMI, Warner Music Group (owned by AOL Time Warner), and Bertelsmann Music Group or BMG (owned by Bertels-

mann, a large German media conglomerate). In 2000, Warner Music Group and EMI had attempted to merge their activities, but were prohibited from doing so by antitrust authorities in Europe, who believed that the merger would put too much market power in the hands of a small number of recording labels.

Music companies sign artists in return for royalties on units sold, which generally run between 12% and 16% of net revenues. The typical contract specifies that in return for royalties on future sales, the copyright of the artists' creations becomes the property of the music companies. The music companies then bear the costs of recording and producing the music, pressing the CDs, marketing, and distribution. It can cost around $1 million to produce and launch a new act, not counting the costs of manufacturing and distributing the CDs. These upfront costs are normally deducted from the artists' royalties. Although there are rare cases of instant hits, with an album selling over a million copies, the vast majority of new CDs are never profitable. Each year the major labels issue about 7,000 new CDs (and minor labels issue another 20,000). Most never recover the upfront recording and marketing costs. In the end, some 10% are profitable.[12] The low success rate implies that many artists never make a dime from their work. Moreover, under an industry practice known as cross-collateralization, the deficit from an artist's first album is added to the deficit from the second album, making it very difficult for some artists to ever make a profit on their work.

Since CDs were first introduced in 1983, their average price in real terms has fallen significantly. Between 1983 and 1996, the average price of a CD fell by more than 40%, while the consumer price index rose by nearly 60%. Despite the price fall, antitrust authorities on both sides of the Atlantic have investigated the music recording industry for alleged price fixing. In May 2000, the big five companies settled a suit with the United States Federal Trade Commission, agreeing to end a requirement that retail stores adhere to minimum prices in advertisements.[13] The agreement was expected to open the way for more price discounting of CDs in retail stores.[14] In August 2001, the European Union ended a similar investigation after three major recording companies agreed to end minimum price requirements.

Historically, the other big players in the music industry have been retailers. In 2000, 95% of CD sales in the United States were still made through music stores. However, the nature of distribution was changing, with discount stores such as Wal-Mart beginning to account for a larger proportion of total CD sales. **Amazon.com** was also emerging as an important distributor of CDs. In addition, experiments by the big five music companies in the online distribution of music were causing tensions with retailers, who started to fear that store sales might suffer.

Intellectual Property Rights and Technology

In the United States, the rights given to copyright holders are based on the Copyright Protection Act of 1976. (Similar legislation exists in other nations, and intellectual property is protected under World Trade Organization agreements, which over 120 countries have signed on to.) Under the 1976 act, copyright holders have the exclusive right to control the reproduction, modification, distribution, public performance, and public displays of their copyrighted material. This set of rights can be violated in three ways:[15]

1. **Direct copyright infringement:** The direct infringer violates any of the copyright holder's exclusive rights, for example, producing and selling a CD without obtaining permission from the copyright holder.

2. **Vicarious copyright infringement:** The vicarious infringer has the right and ability to control the direct infringer's actions and reap financial benefits from those actions. For example, the courts have held that swap meet organizers vicariously infringed if they knowingly created and administered a market in which bootleg music is bought and sold, and were paid a fee for admission.

3. **Contributory copyright infringement:** The infringer knowingly induced or caused the directly infringing conduct. For example, an electronic bulletin-board service was found liable when it encouraged subscribers to upload *Playboy* pictures so that other subscribers could download them.

Historically, the music industry has always been concerned about the potential for piracy of copyrighted material. New technology has often facilitated the low-cost copying and distribution of music. In the 1960s and 1970s, the advent of the audio cassette tape led to widespread illegal copying and distribution of music. In the early 1990s, the industry was deeply concerned about attempts by Sony to commercialize its Digital Audio Tape (DAT) technology, which they felt would facilitate high fidelity copying of recorded music and thus lead to greater piracy. Although the RIAA initially opposed Sony, they switched to supporting the technology once Sony agreed to incorporate software that would make it difficult to use DAT technology to make multiple copies of a music recording. In addition, in 1992 the Audio Home Recording Act required DAT manufacturers to pay a royalty on each blank tape they sold to compensate music companies for the piracy that would take place through DAT. DAT technology was not accepted by consumers, but it was clear the underlying copyright issues would not go away.

Another technology that raised the specter of copyright infringement was MP3. Originally developed in the 1980s, MP3 is a software technology for creating compressed digital music files which could be downloaded for free from the Internet. MP3 music files were created through a process known as "ripping," in which computer owners copy a CD into MP3's digital format, which is about one-twelfth the size of the original file. This compression was achieved by eliminating overlapping sound waves and digital audio signals that fell outside of human hearing range. The great virtue of compressed MP3 files is that they take up less space on a hard drive and can be transferred more easily over the Internet. Until the late 1990s, however, the speed of most Internet connections was so slow that there was little online demand for MP3 music files. Three things changed: the emergence of high-speed Internet connections, especially on college campuses; the growth of web sites such as **MP3.com,** which archived MP3 files; and the introduction of portable MP3 players.

In November 1997 **MP3.com** launched its site. **MP3.com** had purchased thousands of CDs and converted their contents into MP3 files which were stored on its web servers, where subscribers to **MP3.com**'s service could access and download them. In an attempt to protect itself from legal problems, **MP3.com** required a user to demonstrate that he owned the CD for which he was downloading MP3 files by inserting a copy of the CD into his computer

CD-Rom drive, where it could be detected by software **MP3.com** used. In the same year, Diamond Multimedia introduced the Rio, a small portable device that could play up to two hours of MP3s.

The music industry immediately saw the threat: consumers could use high-speed Internet connections to download MP3 files over the Internet and store them on their Rios, circumventing copyright in the process. The RIAA filed a temporary restraining order against Diamond in October 1998, but the U.S. Court of Appeals ruled that converting the digital content of a CD to other formats for personal use was protected by the so-called fair-use doctrine contained in the 1976 Copyright Act. (The fair-use doctrine basically allows individuals to make copies from copyright material they have purchased for their personal use—i.e. not for resale or distribution.)

Having failed to halt the sale of the Rio, Universal Music Group (UMG) immediately went after web sites from which MP3 files could be downloaded. **MP3.com** was the obvious first target. In May 2000, the U.S. District Court ruled that **MP3.com** had directly infringed on music companies' copyright, noting that in actuality, **MP3.com** was "replaying for the subscribers converted versions of the recordings it copied, without authorization, from plaintiffs' copyrighted CDs."[16] On September 6, Judge Jed Rakoff delivered his ruling that **MP3.com** would have to pay the music companies $25,000 for each of the CDs it had copied to stream to consumers who also owned those discs. It looked as if **MP3.com** would have to pay UMG between $118 million and $250 million. In making his judgment, Rakoff stated that "some companies operating in the area of the Internet seemed to believe that because their technology is somewhat novel, they are somehow immune from the ordinary application of the law."[17] Around the same time, the RIAA was also trying to shut down another Internet music service: Napster.

In addition to seeking legal recourse against copyright violators, the music industry tried to develop technology that would protect digital audio recordings from piracy and counterfeiting. The RIAA recruited Leonard Chiariglione, inventor of the MP3 format, to head up the effort. Chiariglione pulled together a consortium of 180 firms, including record companies and consumer electronics and software firms, in an attempt to create the Security Digital Music Initiative (SDMI), a set of technological guidelines that were intended to reduce the risk of copyright infringements of digital audio media. The SDMI tried to develop guidelines for two types of security measures:

1. Digital watermarks would be embedded in digital music, which then could only be played on SDMI compliant music players.

2. Digital rights management technology would embed digital music with an encrypted digital package that would limit the number of times a CD could be copied.

Unfortunately, the SDMI made little progress, reportedly because there were too many competing voices, all with veto power. Apparently, different sides in the industry kept vetoing each other's schemes for copyright protection.[18]

The Birth of Napster

While the music industry was struggling with the SDMI, Shawn Fanning was giving birth to its biggest challenge yet: Napster. There was nothing remarkable about Fanning that would lead one to believe that he would spawn a potentially world shattering idea.[19] One of five children, he grew up in Brockton, Massachusetts, a small town some twenty miles south of Boston. His family was solidly working class with one exception: his uncle, John Fanning, was a computer industry entrepreneur who ran a company called NetGames. During summers at high school, Shawn worked at John's company, where he picked up programming skills from other interns who were studying computer science at Carnegie Mellon. It was at this time that he also became a regular visitor to Internet chat rooms, and particularly Internet Rely Chat, or IRC, which had become a de facto meeting place in cyberspace for hackers, traders of copied software and music, and so on. To enter IRC rooms, Fanning had to give a user name, so he chose his nickname from high school, Napster.

Although Fanning tried to get into Carnegie Mellon, he had to settle for Northeastern. As luck would have it, one of Fanning's roommates was obsessed with MP3 technology, which he used to download music from Internet sites and play on his computer. What caught Fanning's interest was not so much the ability to trade music files over the Internet using MP3 technology, but his roommate's frequent complaints about the process. Internet music sites were not always easy to find, they were unreliable, the links were often broken, and the indices listing music on a site were out of date more often than not. At the time, Fanning was disenchanted with his courses at Northeastern, which he found to be pretty basic, and was looking around for something to do. Solving his roommate's problems seemed to fit the bill.

As it developed, Fanning's approach to fixing this problem was relatively straightforward. He envisioned an index managed by a central server that would list all of the MP3 music files that people had on their hard drives and were willing to share, along with the embedded web addresses of their location. The list could be created if people downloaded a piece of "client" software onto their PCs. This software would update the central list every time someone logged onto or off of the Internet. The MP3 files themselves would continue to reside on the hard drives of individual PCs. To download a file, a user simply had to click on the title of the song, and if the PC with that title was logged on, the file would be transferred from one PC to the other over the Internet.

In essence, Fanning was proposing to create a peer-to-peer network of personal computers, coordinated by a central server which managed the index of MP3 files. The idea itself was not that new, although Fanning's application was. The entire Internet is basically nothing more than a huge peer-to-peer network. In 1998, another attempt to utilize peer-to-peer technology, **SETI@home,** had caused a stir in the high-tech community. **SETI@home** was a program that harnessed the unused computing power of thousands of personal computers to analyze data from radio telescopes for evidence of signals from potential alien civilizations. The program that did this was embedded in a screensaver that could be downloaded from the **SETI@home** site. The basic idea was that when the computers were unused (and the screensaver was on), the SETI program would communicate with a central server, which would download data to the PC, where it would be analyzed and then uploaded back to the central server. After fifteen months, some two million volunteers had downloaded the screen saver; **SETI@home** had received the equivalent of 345,000 years' worth of computing time from its volunteers; and it was estimated that the distributed network of PCs allowed **SETI@home** to tap into computing power about ten times faster than that of a conventional supercomputer.[20]

It is not clear whether Fanning was aware of the parallel development of **SETI@home,** which demonstrated the remarkable potential of peer-to-peer computing. Fanning would provide an even more compelling demonstration. First of all, however, he had to get the program written, and he needed some help. Fanning roped in two friends, Jordan Ritter and Sean Parker, whom he had met through an online hacker group called w00w00. Together they would develop the core of Napster. As Ritter later commented, "At that stage, Napster was really just Shawn and a bunch of friends trying to help out. There were no venture capitalists, no uncles on the scene, and no shady hangers-on."[21] What drove Fanning on, according to another friend, was that people kept telling him it wouldn't work. They said that people would not be willing to share their music files. According to this friend, Fanning was "driven more by the desire to prove everyone that he was right than he was by any realization or recognition of a potential revolution."[22]

By early 1999, Shawn Fanning had dropped out of Northeastern and was working around the clock writing code for the server and client. To prove his doubters wrong, he decided to try out an early version of his software, which he had christened Napster, giving out the client software to around thirty friends. He asked them not to pass it on, an instruction that several ignored, and within a few days the software had been downloaded by some 3,000 to 4,000 people. Many of these early adopters proved to be an invaluable resource, providing feedback that helped Fanning to improve the software.

It was around this time that Shawn Fanning told his uncle, thirty-six-year-old John Fanning, what he was up to. John quickly saw the commercial potential of Napster. In May 1999 he incorporated Napster as a company and went looking for investors. According to *Business Week*, when the company was incorporated, John took 70% of the equity and Shawn 30%.[23] One insider reportedly commented, "I am told that this was done without Shawn Fanning's immediate knowledge or involvement. Newspapers have accurately reported the morally deplorable distribution of equity."[24]

Napster's Takeoff

The embryonic company clearly had a number of problems to solve. First, it needed capital; second, it had to develop a business model that would enable it to profit from the service it provided; and third, it needed to prepare itself for the inevitable challenge from the RIAA. Very early on, John Fanning began to explore the legal ramifications of Napster's business. Among others, he consulted with the law firm of Wilson, Sonsini, Goodrich & Rosati, which had successfully defended Diamond Multimedia against the RIAA. The conversations reportedly gave John the confidence to push the business forward, and the belief that if Napster were sued, the company would have a good shot at winning in court.[25] John seemed to think that because Napster did not actually copy and distribute MP3 files, but simply put people who wanted to swap files in touch with each other, it was not breaking the law.

In summer 1999, John Fanning started to get initial funding for Napster. His first calls were to high-net-worth individuals he knew personally. A friend, Yosi Amram, kicked in $250,000, and another added $100,000. By the end of the summer John had raised enough capital to keep Napster going through to the year's end. Napster moved to Silicon Valley in fall 1999, primarily on John's suggestion that being in the Valley would help in the quest to raise more capital. Shawn and his friends (now all Napster employees) were working sixteen- to twenty-hour days writing code while John was out looking for more venture capital.

In September, realizing that the company needed a CEO who could develop a business model, Eileen Richardson, who had ten years' experience in the venture capital world—but had never run a company—was hired. Richardson's main claim to fame was that she had led an investment in Firefly, an Internet service that recommends music, which was subsequently purchased by Microsoft. Her task was to help secure additional funding, develop a business model, and then hand off the job to her replacement. In October 1999, Napster had raised $2 million in series B venture capital funding from a number of wealthy Silicon Valley executives, including Angel Investors' founding partner, Ron Conway, and Joe Kraus, founder of **Excite@Home.** What helped to secure the funds for the fledgling company was the extraordinary growth of Napster over the previous few months.

Formally launched in June 1999, the program spread with unprecedented speed. There was no marketing or advertising to sell the service, which was given away for free. The service spread through word of mouth. The early adopters were students on university campuses with access to personal computers and high-bandwidth Internet connections. In the fall of 1999 Napster was featured on the web site **download.com,** helping to raise the service to new heights. In July 1999, the Napster community was estimated at 4.9 million. By October 2000, it was thirty-two million and the site was growing by a million users a week, with some 800,000 logged on at any one time.

Among the first to take notice were the administrators of university computing and communications resources. The utilization of their networks was skyrocketing as students used them to transfer MP3 files. By October 1999, Napster was already occupying 10% of the Internet bandwidth capacity at Oregon State University, which became the first to ban the service. At Florida State University, Napster was taking up 20% to 30% of the bandwidth, and at the University of Illinois, the figure at times soared to 75%–80%. Soon, university after university banned Napster. In almost all cases, the primary motive was not the protection of copyright, but a desire to protect scarce computing resources from being soaked up by Napster. By February 2000, for example, the popularity of Napster had pushed network utilization at New York University to 98%, slowing down access and impeding its value as an academic tool. Once Napster was banned, network utilization dropped immediately to 60% of capacity.[26] Not all universities banned Napster, however. Several Ivy League universities, including MIT and Harvard, continued to allow students to use the service, citing their commitment to providing Internet access for all of their community and noting that they did not regulate or monitor a user's choice of sites to visit. Moreover, in many universities that did ban Napster, students fought back, using 1960s-style rhetoric to claim that a ban on Napster amounted to censorship and a violation of free speech.

Why was Napster so attractive? The obvious appeal was that users could download music for free. Why pay $17.95 for a CD that contained ten tracks, only three of which you wanted, when you could download the best three from the Internet for free and leave out the rest? Others cite the convenience of the technology. To get new music, you didn't have to go down to a music store. You just booted up your computer, logged on to the service, and quickly downloaded what you wanted. Many also found it interesting to browse through the playlists of other users, finding music that they would not otherwise listen to. And you could find music on Napster that you could not find in a retail store: old music recordings, esoteric music, unpopular noncommercial music, and so on. Napster also seemed to go hand in hand with two other developments: the spread of portable MP3 players, and new technology that allowed PC users to burn or create customized CDs. In both cases, users could create personal collections or playlists of music tracks from Napster downloads.

According to an RIAA survey of 1,015 music consumers on the attractions of peer-to-peer file-sharing services, having access to a large selection and variety of artists ranked highest (87%), followed by the capability to download files quickly (84%), the ability to download individual songs (83%), a convenient search feature (81%), and the ability to get music for free (79%). Ability to access songs not commercially available ranked lowest (64%).[27]

Collision Course

It was soon apparent that Napster was on a collision course with the music industry. The core of the problem, according to the RIAA, was that Napster's service was violating copyright, facilitating massive piracy of intellectual property, and, consequently, stealing. The RIAA, along with executives from several music companies, started informal discussions with Napster during the late summer of 1999. Record-industry executives insisted that the talks were a sincere attempt to find some common ground. One idea being explored at the time was for Napster to sell a minority stake to the record companies, which in turn would allow Napster to license a host of content. However, many Napster insiders believed that the record-industry executives were never serious about negotiating a deal, and they were just biding time. Whatever the truth, many observers do agree that Napster's new CEO, Eileen Richardson, did nothing to help matters. By all reports, Richardson had an abrasive and combative manner in her dealings with the record companies and RIAA, which only served to distance the two sides.[28] The following exchange apparently occurred in a CNN online chat room:

> *RIAA:* While there are many legitimate uses of MP3s, don't you feel that your service will be primarily used by music pirates?

> *Eileen Richardson:* We are about enabling amateur and unknown artists to share their music on this new medium. Our job is not to stop pirating; that is your job.[29]

According to other sources, Richardson was once heard yelling on the phone to Frank Creighton, head of the RIAA's anti-piracy group. Richardson also had face-to-face meetings with Hilary Rosen, RIAA's president, that apparently did not go too well. One observer noted that "Eileen got into fights with Hilary. . . . Eileen was fairly arrogant and thought what they were doing was right."[30]

Whatever the truth of the situation, on December 7, 1999, with talks between Napster and the RIAA at an impasse, the RIAA filed suit against Napster on behalf of eighteen record companies, citing copyright infringement. Several songwriters filed suit a few days later, and others were to follow. The RIAA alleged that Napster was vicariously infringing copyright, and that it contributed to the direct infringement of copyright held by members of the music industry. The RIAA claimed damages of $100,000 for each copyrighted musical work that was copied with Napster's software. For its part, Napster contended that its users did not infringe copyright because they only made personal copies and used the service in a way that amounted to sampling. The fair-use section of the 1976 Copyright Protection Act stated: "The fair use of a copyrighted work, including such use by reproduction in copies or phonorecords or by any other means specified by that section, for purposes such as criticism, comment, news reporting, teaching (including multiple copies for class room use), scholarship, or research, is not an infringement of copyright."[31]

One of the most high profile suits filed by songwriters was that of the music group Metallica. Metallica had protested that Napster's users were engaged in the unauthorized copying and distribution of copyrighted material. Napster responded that if Metallica could identify users that were violating copyright law, it would remove them from the service. In April 2000, the band's attorney, Howard King, filed suit against Napster and several of the universities that allowed the service to continue, alleging that Napster and the universities were violating the Racketeering Influenced and Corrupt Organizations Act, legislation that was originally aimed at organized crime. King and the band's drummer, Lars Ulrich, also turned up at Napster's headquarters with thirteen boxes of computer print-outs that contained the names of 335,435 Napster users who had swapped Metallica MP3 files and asked Napster to take them off the service. According to Ulrich, their complaint was that "Napster hijacked our music without asking . . . my band authored the music which is Napster's lifeblood. We should decide what happens to it, not Napster—a company with no rights in our recordings which has never invested a penny in Metallica's music or had anything to do with its creation."[32] Shawn Fanning, a Metallica fan himself, was somewhat disturbed by the criticism made by one of his heroes. Thereafter, he would frequently appear in public wearing a Metallica T-shirt, most notably at the MTV Music Awards, where Ulrich sat in the audience.

One of the defenses often voiced by Napster at this time was that far from hurting CD, Napster actually encouraged them. The basic argument was that Napster was dispensing free samples. When something was appealing enough as a sound file on a home computer, people would go out to a record store and buy the entire CD, just as they would if they had heard the song on the radio.[33] In early 2000, 'N Sync, Britney Spears, and Eminem each had huge hits. In the weeks before their records came out, these were the three most heavily trafficked artists on Napster's services, causing some to wonder if marketing departments at their respective labels had seeded Napster with prerelease copies of their music as a promotional tool.[34] In contrast to Metallica, some musicians openly supported Napster. Smashing Pumpkins broke with its label, Virgin, and gave away the group's final album for free via Napster, a move that met with a massive response. Even some senior record-industry executives seemed to exhibit a degree of schizophrenia. Thomas Middlehoff, the CEO of Bertelsmann, owner of BMG, admitted, "Let's be honest; despite all the dangers, Napster is pretty cool." He thought that file sharing as a system was a great idea, but that Fanning's mistake was "not having developed a complementary system for the protection of intellectual property rights and combining the two."[35]

Roadblock

By late spring Napster had its back against the wall. Not only was the company the object of several law-suits, but it was also fast running out of cash. Into the breach stepped Hummer Winblad, a high-profile Silicon Valley venture-capital firm. On May 21, Hummer Winblad announced that it would invest $15 million in Napster. A Hummer Winblad partner, Hank Barry, was brought in as CEO, replacing Richardson, while Hummer co-founder John Hummer joined Napster's board. Hank Barry was an interesting choice for CEO. A former lawyer with a strong background in intellectual property law, he promised to build a working business model for the company and to solve its legal problems. One of Barry's first actions was to bring in David Boies, who had led the Justice Department to victory in the Microsoft anti-trust case, to defend Napster against the RIAA. He also hired two seasoned record-industry executives to round out the senior-management team.

However, Barry had little breathing room. The pace of the legal assault against Napster was quickening. On June 12, 2000, the RIAA filed for a preliminary injunction that would shut down Napster pending trial, citing ongoing and widespread copyright infringement that was causing the industry great harm. On July 26, 2000, Napster had its day in court. Inside Napster, there seemed to be a strong belief that the company would triumph. John Fanning sent around an internal e-mail stating that "if the motion is granted, the order will be stayed pending appeal to the Ninth Circuit, where the motion will be decided . . . and if they rule against us, which I view as a 10% chance, we would be appealing to the Supreme Court, where the future of the world will be hanging in the balance."[36] It was not to be. After a two-hour hearing and a brief fifteen-minute recess, the presiding judge dismissed virtually every argument that Boies could muster for Napster and granted the injunction. In making her ruling Judge Marilyn Patel noted that there was a big difference between making copies for friends, which might be protected by the fair-use section of the 1976 Act, and making copies available via Napster, where a music file could be downloaded by millions of anonymous users.[37]

With the injunction granted and the service shut down, Barry scrambled to develop a business model that would both make sense and facilitate an alliance with Napster's opponents: the music labels. With the cash burn rate running in excess of $500,000 a month, Barry realized that he needed to move as expeditiously as possible. Again, Napster considered selling a minority stake in the company to the music labels, and then splitting subscription, sponsorship, and advertising revenues. The economics seemed compelling; if 20 million users (half of Napster's total in mid 2000) paid $100 a year for subscriptions that would allow for unlimited downloads, that would be $2 billion a year for Napster and the record labels. One survey found that 68% of Napster users would be prepared to pay a $15 monthly subscription for the service. Barry himself was reportedly contemplating a subscription of $4.95 a month.[38]

In the interim, Napster continued to hope that it would ultimately win in court. That hope was dashed when on February 12, 2001, a three judge panel from the Ninth Circuit Court of Appeals issued its ruling. The appeals court upheld Patel's injunction and determined that Napster should be held liable for copyright infringement. The judges stated that using Napster to "get something for free they would ordinarily have to buy" was a commercial use, and thus copyright infringement. Although the appeals court did send the injunction back to Patel for clarification, it was clear that Napster would get little relief from the courts.

BMG to the Rescue?

While the court drama was still unfolding, on October 31, 2000, Bertelsmann (owner of BMG, the fifth biggest record label in the world) broke ranks with the other major labels and announced that it was forming an alliance with Napster to develop a subscription-based music-distribution service based on Napster's peer-to-peer technology. As part of the alliance, Bertelsmann provided Napster with a $60 million loan, buying the service much-needed time. In explaining the decision, Bertelsmann's CEO Thomas Middlehoff indicated that the genie was already out of the bottle with respect to file-swapping technology. Indeed, with two other Napster alternatives, Gnutella and FreeNet, already making an appearance, Middlehoff suggested that the industry needed to embrace the technology, not rail against it in the courts.

Middlehoff's goal was that BMG and Napster would introduce a paid-subscription service by mid 2001. However, progress was slow. In November 2001, with no subscription service in sight, Bertelsmann kicked in an additional $25 million loan to help Napster. By early 2002, Bertelsmann was reportedly contemplating a bid to buy out Napster for $15 million.[39] However, the bid was in risk of being derailed by internal strife at Napster. On March 25, board member John Fanning filed a lawsuit against two fellow directors, John Hummer and Hank Barry, claiming that the two venture capitalists were no longer directors because they were voted out on March 24, 2002. Napster's new CEO (the third), Konrad Hilbers, issued a statement calling the lawsuit "legally groundless." Observers speculated that the reason for the lawsuit was that Napster was running out of cash and might have to file for bankruptcy, leaving John Fanning (and very possibly Shawn Fanning) with no return from Napster. On April 12, Napster announced that it would lay off 30% of its work force, and this followed a 10% reduction in the previous month.[40]

In the interim, the major record labels continued to push ahead with plans to introduce their own online music service. In early 2002, the big five companies launched two services. Both services sell monthly subscriptions that allow users to listen to songs without downloading using streaming audio technology. Alternatively, subscribers can download versions of songs that in most cases cannot be burned onto a CD or transferred to a portable device. Each service only has songs from certain labels.

MusicNet, which offers songs from Warner Music, BMG, and EMI, has one subscription plan: $9.85 a month for 100 streams and 100 downloads. Downloads expire after thirty days and can't be played. Pressplay, which offers music from Sony, Universal, and EMI, offers four subscription plans, ranging in price from $9.95 to $24.95 a month, for up to 1,000 streams and 100 downloads. The higher subscription fee service from Pressplay will let users burn up to twenty songs a month onto CDs that will not expire, but no more than two songs from any one artist can be burned.[41]

ENDNOTES

1. Trevor Merriden. *Irresistible Forces.* Capstone Books, Oxford, U.K., 2001, p. 45.
2. Trevor Merriden. *Irresistible Forces.* Capstone Books, Oxford, U.K., 2001, p. 45.
3. John Alderman. *Sonic Boom.* Perseus Publishing, Cambridge Mass, 2001, p. 114.
4. John Alderman. *Sonic Boom.* Perseus Publishing, Cambridge Mass, 2001, p. 116.
5. John Alderman. *Sonic Boom.* Perseus Publishing, Cambridge Mass, 2001, p. 10.
6. Trevor Merriden. *Irresistible Forces.* Capstone Books, Oxford, U.K., 2001, p. 26.

7. S. P. Ante, S. V. Brull, D. K. Berman, and M. France. "How the music sharing phenomenon began, where it went wrong, and what happens next." *Business Week,* August 14, 2000, p. 114.

8. Trevor Merriden. *Irresistible Forces.* Capstone Books, Oxford, U.K., 2001.

9. IFPI News release. Global music sales down 5% in 2001. **www.ifpi.org.**

10. International Federation of the Phonographic Industry, Fighting Piracy, 2001. **www.ifpi.org.**

11. IFPI News release. Global music sales down 5% in 2001. **www.ifpi.org.**

12. RIAA. How much does it cost to make a CD? **www.riaa.org.**

13. J. R. Wilke. Music firms, U.S. hold settlement talks. *Wall Street Journal,* December 16, 1999, p. A3.

14. J. R. Wilke. FTC move expected to bring lower CD prices, *Wall Street Journal,* May 10, 2000, p. A3.

15. D. Kiron, C. E. Bagley, and M. J. Roberts. Napster. *Harvard Business School Case # 801–219,* March 29, 2001.

16. UMG Recordings v MP3.com Inc., 92 F. Supp 2d 349 (S.D.N.Y. 2000).

17. John Alderman. *Sonic Boom.* Perseus Publishing, Cambridge Mass, 2001, p. 143.

18. John Alderman. *Sonic Boom.* Perseus Publishing, Cambridge Mass, 2001, p. 91.

19. John Alderman. *Sonic Boom.* Perseus Publishing, Cambridge Mass, 2001.

20. Anonymous. Divide and Conquer. *The Economist,* July 29, 2002.

21. Trevor Merriden. *Irresistible Forces.* Capstone Books, Oxford, U.K., 2001, p. 6.

22. Trevor Merriden. *Irresistible Forces.* Capstone Books, Oxford, U.K., 2001, p. 7.

23. S. P. Ante, S. V. Brull, D. K. Berman, and M. France. "How the music sharing phenomenon began, where it went wrong, and what happens next." *Business Week,* August 14, 2000, pp. 112–120.

24. Trevor Merriden. *Irresistible Forces.* Capstone Books, Oxford, U.K., 2001, p. 9.

25. S. P. Ante, S. V. Brull, D. K. Berman, and M. France. "How the music sharing phenomenon began, where it went wrong, and

what happens next." *Business Week,* August 14, 2000, pp. 112–120.

26. S. P. Ante, S. V. Brull, D. K. Berman, and M. France. "How the music sharing phenomenon began, where it went wrong, and what happens next." *Business Week,* August 14, 2000, p. 112–120.

27. RIAA. Market Data, **www.riaa.org.**

28. S. P. Ante, S. V. Brull, D. K. Berman, and M. France. "How the music sharing phenomenon began, where it went wrong, and what happens next." *Business Week,* August 14, 2000, p. 112–120.

29. Cited in D. Kiron, C. E. Bagley, and M. J. Roberts. Napster. *Harvard Business School Case # 801–219,* March 29, 2001.

30. S. P. Ante, S. V. Brull, D. K. Berman, and M. France. "How the music sharing phenomenon began, where it went wrong, and what happens next." *Business Week,* August 14, 2000, pp. 112–120.

31. Section 107 of the Copyright Act of 1976.

32. **Salon.com** magazine, May 1, 2000.

33. J. Selvin. Did Napster help boost record sales? *San Francisco Chronicle,* August 5, 2001.

34. John Alderman. *Sonic Boom.* Perseus Publishing, Cambridge Mass, 2001, p. 1117.

35. John Alderman. *Sonic Boom.* Perseus Publishing, Cambridge Mass, 2001, p. 116.

36. Quoted in S. P. Ante, S. V. Brull, D. K. Berman, and M. France. "How the music sharing phenomenon began, where it went wrong, and what happens next." *Business Week,* August 14, 2000, pp. 112–120.

37. Anonymous. Rewired for sound. *The Economist,* August 5, 2000, pp. 59–60.

38. S. Ante. Napster: Tune in, turn on, pay up. *Business Week,* November 13, 2000, p. 52.

39. L. Himelstein and T. Lowry. The sound at Napster: tick, tick, tick. *Business Week,* April 8, 2002, p. 73.

40. N. Wingfield. Napster lays off 30% of workers. *Wall Street Journal,* April 12, 2002, p. A16.

41. W. S. Mossberg. Record labels launch two feeble services to replace Napster. *Wall Street Journal,* February 7, 2002, p. B1.

AtomFilms

8

This case was prepared by Taz Pirmohamed (MBA '01) under the supervision of Professor Bharat Anand, Harvard Business School.

We are building an entertainment platform so that we can take advantage of any and all opportunities to lead the next-generation entertainment market. That is why I named the company Atom Corporation instead of AtomFilms or Atom Games—like an atom we are a building block in the entertainment space.

Mika Salmi, CEO, Atom Corporation—
December, 2000

Mika Salmi rushed into the "Holiday Romance" conference room carrying the term sheets from several different deals. In the past month, potential partners, including Hollywood studios, online entertainment start-ups, telecom companies, and peer-to-peer applications providers, had approached him. Now, he needed to determine which deals were critical to the long-term sustainability of the company.

In the past two years, Salmi had grown AtomFilms from an idea to a successful short-film distribution company. By December 2000, AtomFilms licensed and syndicated films to hundreds of companies, including major airlines and cable television stations. In addition, AtomFilms had built a strong presence on the web with its award-winning consumer website. The business-to-business (B2B) film distribution business was growing quickly, and the business-to-consumer (B2C) website was one of the only remaining online entertainment sites on the web. Since 1997, almost all of the traditional Hollywood studios had either built or acquired an online entertainment property. But, many of their original business models had failed. Similarly, numerous online entertainment start-ups, without the backing of a Hollywood name, had either filed for bankruptcy or had initiated layoffs. By all accounts, "digital Hollywood"—the name given to the online entertainment industry—was a huge disappointment. With this in mind, Salmi wanted to ensure that both the B2C and B2B divisions of the business were profitable and sustainable in the long-term. Thus far, the B2C side of the business had been lagging.

In January 2001, after considering many alternative options to finance and grow the company, AtomFilms merged with Shockwave, a private company that supplied consumers with media players and entertainment content through its website. Shockwave's online advertising revenue model complemented AtomFilms' offline distribution revenue model. The combined entity would have several million users visiting its website, and Salmi wanted to employ a revenue model that could monetize site traffic without compromising growth. The options to do this included charging subscription fees to access site content, focusing solely on site advertising revenues, or selling the best short-film submissions to TV networks and movie studios so that they could be developed into a TV series or a feature film. Salmi was intent on selecting a revenue model that would best position the company in the rapidly evolving entertainment industry.

At the same time, AtomFilms viewed itself as uniquely positioned to take advantage of emerging content distribution channels, including mobile phones and personal digital assistants (PDAs). Short films were ideal for consumers seeking entertainment "on the go" since they could be compressed into files small enough to be downloaded and viewed in a few minutes. A few weeks earlier, a major European telecommunications company seeking to license AtomFilms content had approached Salmi. By enabling cellular subscribers to download short films onto their phones, the company would be able to increase airtime usage. Salmi had to decide whether or not this was the right deal to launch AtomFilms into the wireless space in Europe.

Finally, Salmi pondered the importance of emerging peer-to-peer (P2P) applications. P2P applications created by companies such as Napster and Scour had facilitated content distribution amongst users logged onto their networks. However, the increased popularity of P2P distribution networks might cause content sites such as AtomFilms to become redundant. Flycode—a new P2P start-up that specialized in both audio and visual (A-V) content transfer—wanted to license AtomFilms' content. In exchange, AtomFilms would be provided with a permanent space on Flycode's website. Even though Flycode lacked a working prototype or a clearly defined revenue model, the reputation of the founders was impressive. Salmi wondered whether the P2P space was an opportunity or threat to the B2C side of AtomFilms' business.

Salmi again examined the term sheets in his hands again. As he glanced at his watch, he realized how little time he had to act on each deal.

Landscape

Offline Entertainment Space

Movies   Theatrical movies were a cornerstone of domestic entertainment spending. In 2000, U.S. consumers purchased 1.5 billion movie tickets worth approximately $7.8 billion at the box office. Although box office sales had been growing only at a moderate pace over the past decade, exhibition on the big screen was considered to be a key driver of film viewing in other channels—for example, television and home video.

Movie releases from six film distribution companies (see Exhibit 1a)—the Walt Disney Co., Viacom Inc., Sony Corp., Fox Entertainment Group (majority owned by News Corp. Ltd.), Time Warner Inc., and Universal Studios Group (majority owned by Seagram Co.)—typically accounted for at least 80% of box office revenues. These distributors provided some or all of the financing required to produce a film. In addition, the distribution company that handled the theatrical release often owned the rights to distribute the film through other channels such as pay-per-view television, cable television, and home video (Exhibit 1b). Disney's Buena Vista film business had consistently captured the highest theatrical market share (17% in 1999), followed by Warner Bros. (14%), Universal (13%), Paramount (11%), and Fox Entertainment (11%).[1] In addition, in 1999, U.S. films generated almost $7 billion in international box office sales—matching the size of domestic box office sales. The globalization of the film market, in turn, had helped bolster the independent film movement—since independent films often performed better in foreign markets.

Prior to 1989, the market for independent films was relatively small and fragmented. Independent films had trouble finding distribution outside the small circuit of "art-house" theatres across the country. Rarely would a major studio acquire and then distribute an independent film. However, in 1989 Miramax Films purchased the rights to Steven Soderbergh's *Sex, Lies and Videotape*. The film cost only $1.2 million to produce and grossed over $20 million at the box office, making it the first bona fide inde-

EXHIBIT 1A

Ownership of Properties by Media Conglomerates

Media Conglomerate	Film	TV	Music	Publishing	E-Commerce
Disney	Buena Vista Caravan Pictures Miramax Touchstone	ABC A&E ESPN Disney Channel		Hyperion Press	Go Network
Viacom	Paramount Pictures Blockbuster Ent.	MTV Nickelodeon VH1 TV Land Paramount TV Showtime Spelling Ent.		MacMillan Publishing	CBS Sportsline
Sony	Columbia/Tri-star Sony Pictures Studios	Columbia/Tri-star TV	Columbia Epic Relativity Red Inc.		
AOL/Time Warner	Castle Rock New Line Cinema Warner Brothers	HBO CNN TBS TNT Cartoon Network Comedy Central Cinemax	Atlantic Elektra Sire Records WB Records	Little, Brown Warner Books Time Magazine Fortune Sports Illustrated	AOL Hoover's
Bertelsmann		Largest radio/TV owner in Europe	BMG Arista	Random House Bantam	Barnes & Noble
Seagram	Universal Studios		Universal/ Polygram		

pendent blockbuster. The success of the film marked the beginning of a mergers and acquisition frenzy as major studios either bought or merged with smaller production houses specializing in independent films. Independent films enabled studios to identify fresh talent for their studio divisions and create a more diverse portfolio of films. In 1994, Turner Entertainment acquired an independent film house called New Line Cinema. That same year, Twentieth Century Fox and Sony each created independent film divisions.

Television   Based on ratings data from Nielsen Media Research, Inc., the four major broadcast networks—ABC (owned by Walt Disney), CBS, FOX (majority owned by News Corp Ltd.) and NBC (owned by General Electric Co.) attracted close to 55% of U.S. primetime viewers in 2000. Increasingly, major broadcast networks were taking an ownership interest in the shows they aired. By doing so, they could share the syndication revenues generated from reruns if a show turned out to be a hit.

Over-the-air broadcast stations not affiliated with any major network achieved roughly 10% market share. The remainder of the primetime audience was split between dozens of cable and satellite channels, none of which averaged more than 5% market share. Roughly 75% of all U.S. households subscribed to cable networks delivered through wired cable or satellite services. Cable networks fell into one of two categories. Most advertiser-supported networks, such as ESPN and CNN, were advertiser-supported and were delivered to the consumer via a cable system

EXHIBIT 1B

Typical Life Cycle of a
Motion Picture

Box Office Release (34%)
- Theatre sources of revenue
  - admissions
  - screen advertising
  - concessions
- Foreign release

Pay-per-view/Cable (8–10%)
- Seek continued growth in asset
  base (with return above COC)
  - expand product line
  - enter new geographies
  - increase penetration
- Invest to protect position

Television (6–8%)
- Improve returns through pricing,
  cost reductions and/or asset
  productivity enhancements
- Sell or exit if returns cannot be
  improved
- Television

Home Video (48%)
- Primary strategies
  - severe limits to growth in
    assets (investments)
  - improve returns through pricing
    and/or cost reductions, e.g.,
    reduce complexity
- Secondary strategies
  - maintain growth if returns can
    be quickly raised above COC
  - sell or exit if returns cannot be
    improved

operator as part of a "basic" cable subscription package. Other networks, such as HBO, were pay-TV channels—to receive them, subscribers paid a fee in addition to the basic rates for cable or satellite service. ESPN and CNN had carved out a profitable niche with a relatively narrow range of programming, whereas USA Network and TBS SuperStation featured a broad sampling of broadcast network reruns, movies, and sports. Recently, many cable networks had invested more heavily in original program content. For example, Comedy Central won a sizeable audience when it aired the first-run series of *South Park* and HBO had garnered huge audience shares with *The Sopranos* and *Sex in the City*.

Video The home video market was a major revenue source for movie distributors. Consumers were now spending nearly three times as much per year to watch films on videocassette or DVD as in the theatre. In 1999, the market for video rentals was $10 billion. Videotape and DVD purchases accounted for an additional $10 billion. Movie distributors often sold videos to video retailers. The two largest video retailers were Blockbuster Inc. (4,795 stores) and Hollywood Entertainment Corp. (1,615 stores). The rest of the video rental market was extremely fragmented and mainly comprised smaller, specialty video retailers with fewer than five locations.

Recently, movie distributors and video retailers were making greater use of revenue sharing agreements. Under this arrangement, distributors sold videos to a retailer for a lower price in exchange for sharing a portion of the future rental revenues. This practice had encouraged video retailers to carry more copies of popular titles in their stores to satisfy consumer demand, without the risk of inflating their inventory.

Online Entertainment

The world wide web In 1991, Tim Berners-Lee, a researcher at the European Laboratory for Particle Physics, wrote the basic parameters of a new language for describing computer documents. The language, known as hypertext mark-up language or HTML, could describe text, data, graphics, video, and audio. As individual computer users wrote documents in HTML, and placed them on host computers that constituted the Internet, the World Wide Web emerged. In January 1999, more than 100 million individuals used the World Wide Web.

As World Wide Web usage increased, the variety of web sites appearing on the Internet also exploded. Early entertainment sites were furnished with only simple text-based content. By 2000, some websites featured live webcasts and interactive programming. However, in 1998, many major film studios were still

Digital Content

	Set-top Boxes/TV	PC
Type of Content	• Sit-up (active) and sit-back (passive) content • Original and existing • TV, film and interactive	• Sit-up (active) content • Original content • Existing content not well-suited to PC viewing • Interactive
Length	• Any	• <30 mins
Revenue Sources	• Contextual and traditional advertising • Subscription/PPV • E-commerce	• Advertising • E-commerce • Offline mass advertising if content adapted for TV/cable broadcast
Audience	• Broad	• Niche audiences • Primarily teen/college segments
Growth Levers	• Penetration of set-top boxes	• Broadband access • Production of content suitable for PC viewing

EXHIBIT 1C

Broadband and Convergence

wary of making a major web site investment, hoping that the Internet would not have a significant impact on their revenue streams for many years. Jake Winebaum, chairman of Disney's Buena Vista Internet Group, noted that "it took decades for a medium like cable television to economically sustain original programming. But after years of thriving on material repackaged from broadcast TV and movies, cable networks are increasingly producing original (con-

tent). You'll see the same thing on the Net that happened with cable TV—Disney wants to be there when it happens."

Moves by Hollywood

By 1999, despite the lack of compelling business models, the major film studios were financing online ventures. At the outset, studios simply transferred existing content and programming information to the Internet.

EXHIBIT 1D

Broadband Penetration

Projected Broadband Penetration	2000	2001	2002	2003	2004	2005
Number of PCs connected to BB	6.2	15.2	25.2	38.2	53.5	69.2
Satellite, web-enabled box	0.5	1.8	3.0	4.1	6.4	7.7
Satellite, advanced box	3.8	1.8	9.8	10.3	10.6	11.0
Cable, advanced digital box	0.1	1.8	4.0	10.6	23.8	36.4
Cable, basic digital box	4.1	1.8	7.4	7.1	2.6	1.9
Total BB consoles	—	1.8	7.4	16.2	30.9	43.5
	14.6	24.2	56.8	86.5	127.9	169.7

Source: Bruce Kasrel, "Broadband Content Splits," Forrester Research, Inc., October 2000.

DreamWorks SKG In late 1999, Ron Howard of Imagine Entertainment and Steven Spielberg of DreamWorks SKG announced the creation of a new Internet-only entertainment company, POP.com. Funded by Paul Allen's Vulcan Ventures and launched in spring 2000, POP.com offered aspiring artists the opportunity to submit films that might be produced by POP.com, community-oriented features aimed at filmmakers, and short form content. Despite the fanfare that accompanied the site launch, POP.com announced major layoffs in September 2000 and a change in focus—from producing mass-market Internet content to running a movie news portal. POP.com was viewed as one of the several major start-up failures in the online entertainment space.

Sony Mirroring its broad, offline entertainment-based revenue stream, Sony developed several online entertainment properties ranging from interactive gaming to multi-media content creation. The most profitable of Sony's online ventures was aimed at the 280,000 subscribers to the role-playing game *Everquest*. Subscribers would pay approximately $50 to buy the game on a CD-ROM and would then pay approximately $10 a month to play. In 2000, the *Everquest* site generated approximately $100 million in revenues.[2] Sony also planned to rollout an experimental online movie service in 2001, with a broader rollout once consumer broadband became more pervasive. The multi-media platform would enable users to download movies onto PCs, digital video recorders (for example, TiVo and Replay), cable set- top boxes, TV sets with built-in hard drives, and video game consoles like the Sony PlayStation. Meanwhile, a Sony unit called Sony Pictures Digital Entertainment had begun developing original, interactive content for the Internet. One example of Sony's content offering was an online show called Dawson's Desktop, an Internet brand extension of the popular teen drama *Dawson's Creek*. Fans could go deeper into the story by reading the lead character's e-mail or diary and by watching his home videos.

Disney After launching its first major online property in 1995, Disney's Blast website quickly became the leading kids and family entertainment site, according to Media Metrix.[3] The site offered subscribers' access to games, stories, arts-and-crafts activities, message boards, and live events for $5.95 a month or $39.95 a year. Ken Goldstein, general manager of Disney Online, said that "Disney plans to revamp the site to add more sophisticated content, with a particular eye for collaborative activities aimed at children, such as a group treasure hunt." Disney also planned to add features to enable up to 24 players to collaborate in the same game and to allow them to type their comments into a chat layer of the game. The site also offered more free content in order to attract a larger base of users. Underlying all content on Disney's online property was the company's corporate philosophy—to develop the most innovative and parent-trusted content for both kids and families.

Warner Brothers Warner Brothers created Warner Online in 1999 to develop a hallmark entertainment property called Entertaindom.com. The site was divided into four areas: Playdom, for online games; Toondom, for children's programming; Screendom, for television and movies; and Rhythmdom, for music. The site featured original programming produced by Warner Brothers and others. Warner Brothers planned to offer free content and to generate revenues from selling advertising, capturing a percentage of gross merchandise sales, and from pay-per-view events. It was also examining the feasibility of a subscription-based revenue model. Following the merger announcement of Time Warner with AOL in January 2000, the site was shut down.

Digital Entertainment Network (DEN) In 1999, Marc Collins-Rector created DEN to develop and broadcast brief, episodic online shows aimed at 14- to 24-year-olds with a particular emphasis on gay, Christian, Hispanic, and Asian young adults. The online entertainment start-up attracted a blue-chip group of investors and partners before the site launch. By June 1999, over $33 million had been invested by Chase Capital Partners, Microsoft, and Dell Computer, and DEN was in production to create 13 online shows. At its peak, DEN employed more than 300 technical and creative staffers led by executives from Disney, Channel One, and other top-notch entertainment companies. However, after launching its website in late 1999, DEN ran into a series of financial difficulties and unfavorable press coverage regarding the conduct of its management team. In addition, DEN was criticized for freely using its venture capital dollars to pay huge management salaries and exorbitant program development costs. In early 2000, DEN failed to raise a new round of financing, withdrew its planned IPO, and ran out of cash. By May 2000, DEN had laid off its remaining 150 employees and announced it would file for bankruptcy reorganization or liquidation by the end of 2000.[4]

The Founding of AtomFilms

The European Market for Short Films

Short films or "shorts" were loosely defined as films that were shorter than a feature-length film. In general, shorts ranged from one to twenty minutes in length. Short films could be shown before feature films in theatres, as stand-alone films, or as a bundle of several shorts broadcast in one-half or one-hour time-slots. Short films were pervasive in Europe, because European television schedules offered more pockets of programming time that were ideal for broadcasting short content. By contrast, short films occupied a different niche in the U.S. entertainment market. There, short films were often used to showcase the talent of an actor, director, or producer in order to gain access to the financing or support required to produce a feature film. As a consequence of these differences, the commercial U.S. short-film industry was much smaller than its European counterpart.[5]

Discovery of Market Need

Mika Salmi, CEO and founder of AtomFilms, was the son of a professional hockey player from the National Hockey League in Finland. Growing up in Europe, Salmi acquired a passion for the entertainment industry while viewing innovative short-form content on Finnish television networks. From a very young age, Salmi demonstrated a keen interest in the entertainment industry. As a teen, he was a deejay, a rave promoter, and manager of a rock band. He recalled his instinct for identifying trends in popular culture: "I could always see where trends were moving, since I personally was always searching for the next new, new thing."

In 1992, Salmi was completing an MBA degree at INSEAD in Fontainebleau, France, when he discovered the French television station M6. M6 broadcast short-form entertainment of all kinds, including short films, music videos, and animation. Salmi, immediately struck by the innovative content that aired on the station, later recalled:

> My reasons for loving the content on M6 in the early 90s are the same reasons why I love MTV today. I can tune in anytime and be entertained. I don't have to commit myself to watching for half an hour, and I don't have to plan in advance when to tune in.

Although Salmi was convinced of the potential of providing short-form content to consumers, he was not sure how to leverage this idea into an entrepreneurial opportunity. In late 1994, Salmi moved to New York to work for Sony International Music and immediately noticed the lack of short-form content in the U.S. entertainment industry. He recounted:

> After I moved to New York, I felt deprived of the short-form content I was viewing in theatres and TV stations in Europe. There was a huge entertainment industry America, and yet short-form content was nowhere to be found in the mainstream U.S. market.

Salmi had dreamed of creating a cable channel similar to M6. Despite this, his first business plan was on a short-film distribution company that modeled itself on an independent label in the music industry. While writing the business plan, Salmi began to research the short film-industry by purchasing compilation videotapes of short films that had been published by local film festivals and distribution companies. He was amazed at what he found: "There were hundreds of distribution companies ranging in size from one-person shops to 100-person shops. I had no idea this was such a huge business and still invisible to the consumer."

The dearth of venture capital funding in the mid-nineties for film distribution companies led Salmi to realize that in order to build a sustainable revenue stream, any business model that focused on short-form content would need to encompass multiple distribution channels (e.g., theatre, TV, CD-ROM). But, still unsure about how to make the business plan a reality, Salmi moved to Seattle to join Real Networks as Director of Business Development for their entertainment division. After successfully launching *Real Audio*—a software "player" that enabled consumers to listen to digital music files on a PC—the company began to develop an audio-visual player. Salmi recalled:

> Our (market research) studies showed that people had very short attention spans while watching their PC, but they were actively engaged in the content. We also learned that the content

had to be unique, because consumers believed that if you could find it anywhere on the web, it couldn't be very good.

The dearth of web-friendly entertainment content led Real Networks to commission Spike Lee to create four short films specifically for the launch. Meanwhile, Salmi noticed that his clients also shared his frustration with the lack of unique content:

> Companies were trying to take movie trailers or live broadcasts and shoehorn them into the category of Internet entertainment. Neither the big studios nor the networks were set up to license, borrow, or lend content to web companies. There was no central clearinghouse for Internet-friendly entertainment content.

At this point, Salmi realized that his original business plan could deliver short-form entertainment using another channel—the Internet. So the AtomFilms business model was finally complete. His plan was further bolstered by the fact that "the U.S. market for short films was under-developed relative to Europe. Therefore, high-quality content would be more readily available in the United States and at a lower price." Salmi was finally ready to launch the company.

Visions of a B2B Company

Early on, Salmi recognized that AtomFilms could generate the most stable revenue stream from offline—not online—channels. Although consumer demand for online entertainment was growing, few entertainment companies had figured out how to build a viable entertainment business on the Internet. Salmi determined that the company needed to balance two critical issues—content acquisition and content distribution—to quickly reach profitability. With this in mind, Salmi hired Jannat Gargi and Brian Burke to build the content acquisition and content distribution departments.

The content acquisition side of the business was fueled by a grassroots public relations strategy that encompassed all the major film festivals:

> We tried to make a splash at every single film festival by giving away free stuff and by hosting big parties for our artists. One of our best publicity stunts was at the 1998 Sundance Film Festival when we rented a bus and showed short films inside. We built our brand, product recognition, and respect from industry professionals inside a bus! Everybody—including the press—loved it.

Soon, the AtomFilms brand became synonymous with short, independent filmmaking. The first film acquired by AtomFilms—entitled *Holiday Romance*—was nominated for an Academy Award for best short film in 1999. Recognition for AtomFilms products helped gain the trust and support of filmmakers across the globe. Salmi recalled that "pretty soon, our office was flooded with thousands of short-film reels from amateur and professional filmmakers."

The content distribution side of the business was also built using grassroots tactics. As Salmi described: "Brian was calling every single airline and TV station in the United States. He was attached to the telephone from morning until night calling every possible distribution channel to figure out who might buy our content."

In December 1998, Air Canada became the first paying customer of AtomFilms by purchasing five films for broadcast during their short-haul flights. Shortly afterward, several other airlines and cable television stations, such as the Sundance channel, also began to purchase content. Salmi noted: "All we needed was one customer in each channel to prove that the model worked. After that point, we were confident that we could raise enough money to build a larger sales force and really grow our business."

By mid 1999, AtomFilms' initial efforts had paid off. The company appeared to have created a cycle of growth: for every successful film it licensed, the company attracted more film submissions, more customers seeking to license its content, and more press detailing its success.

Incorporation of B2C

Although AtomFilms was a business-to-business (B2B) company, it built its first web site in November 1998 as a "live brochure" for its clients. Salmi recalled that: "the site was very functional—it simply detailed our company history and product line." However, in early 1999, Salmi spoke to several of his Internet clients, including @Home and the Go Network, to better understand how industry leaders were using A/V content over the web. He recalled: "I always thought we had the vision to use our content in much more innovative ways than our clients did. I was right. The web was full of lackluster entertainment sites that were *not* entertaining."

Armed with the belief that AtomFilms could create a superior web entertainment experience, Salmi prepared to launch a consumer web site. The site would showcase the company's best short films, create a community for short-film makers, and generate more public interest in short films. Salmi recalled that "on the day we launched the consumer web site, *USA Today* published an article about our innovative content, and we were instantly a huge hit . . . site traffic has been sky-rocketing ever since."

The traffic and registered users on the AtomFilms site experienced exponential growth. (See Exhibits 1–3.) However, the advertising and merchandise revenue stream from the website was still overshadowed by the licensing and syndication revenues generated from offline distribution channels. In addition, whereas the B2C revenue stream was small, the people and technology required to support site maintenance and development was substantial. Still, Salmi viewed the AtomFilms site as an important component of the company's brand identity, marketing strategy, and consumer outreach. With many people visiting the site and sharing AtomFilms content with their friends, the intangible impact of the site was significant.

Growth of AtomFilms

As the confidence of Salmi and his new management team began to grow, so did the revenues and client base of AtomFilms. By year-end 2000, AtomFilms had generated almost $5.8 million in revenues, including approximately $3 million in licensing and syndication revenue, $1.7M in advertising and sponsorship revenue and an additional $.1 million in revenue from merchandise sold through the company's web site. (Company financials for 1999, and projected figures for 2000–2001 are in Exhibit 2). The website was experiencing a similar level of success: by Q4 2000, AtomFilms had accumulated a total of 15.2M unique visitors and 1.8 million registered users or Atom "insiders." Users, who were spending an average of 15 minutes per session on the site, had viewed over 31 million films (see Exhibits 3a–d, 4, and 5 for additional information). Website visitors were mostly young, middle-income, males; about 21% of site visitors were females. Along the way, several major deals contributed to the rapid growth of AtomFilms.

Content Acquisition

By year-end 2000, AtomFilms had amassed more than 1,500 short-films sourced from 350 filmmakers worldwide. The acquisition cost per film had stabilized at approximately $2,400 per film, despite increased competition for short-form content in the marketplace. A series of partnership deals enabled AtomFilms to acquire a bundle of short films at a low cost. One such agreement was signed in February 2000 with the University of Southern California's (USC) film school. AtomFilms bought the online distribution rights for 100 films from USC's School Cinema and Television—including shorts made by George Lucas and Robert Zemeckis when they were film students.[6]

Another major deal involved the first Internet-only animated characters for exclusive viewing on the AtomFilms site. Aardman Animations—the production company that had created the film *Chicken Run* in early 2000—produced the *Angry Kid* series for AtomFilms. Within seven weeks, *Angry Kid*, watched by over one million people, set an Internet record as one of the most popular characters in the history of the Internet.

Syndication and Licensing

Creating a large client base of syndication clients in a nascent market for short films was one of the greatest challenges facing AtomFilms. Several unique syndication deals helped the company convince clients of the value of syndicating a short film. In November 1999, Intel had created the WebOutfitter site for exclusive use by purchasers of the Pentium III processor. The site demonstrated the potential of rich broadband content when coupled with broadband access and a high-speed microprocessor. Since high bandwidth was required to enjoy audio-visual content over the web, AtomFilms' shorts helped to demonstrate the power of Intel's microprocessors to its customers.

By late 2000, AtomFilms had tapped almost every entertainment distribution channel except movie theatres. In November 2000, Century Theatres—which owned and operated over 700 screens in 11 Western states—agreed to feature short films for the launch of their CineArts 6 multiplex in Evanston, Illinois. Since short films had not preceded a feature length film in a theatre for over 25 years, the deal represented an important victory for AtomFilms.

Advertising and Sponsorship

In 2000, AtomFilms' innovative deal with Volkswagen presented a unique model for advertising and sponsorship. Volkswagen (VW) developed a new site—vw.com—to expose young people to the carefree and fun lifestyle the company promoted. VW agreed to

EXHIBIT 2

AtomFilms Income Statement

	1999	2000E	2001E
Revenue			
Ads	136	1,488	1,081
Sponsorships	—	2,682	2,322
Total Ads and Sponsorships	—	4,170	3,404
Syndication—Business	187	3,954	5,681
Subscription—Consumer	—	71	225
Total Syndication and Subscription	—	4,025	5,906
Merchandise	67	354	—
Service	—	71	—
Total Merchandise and Service	—	424	—
Total Revenue	390	8,619	9,310
COGS—Royalties and Investments	88	2,396	630
COGS—Other Costs	87	2,239	2,105
Gross Margin	215	3,984	6,575
Operating Expenses			
Sales and Marketing			
Labor	670	3,002	3,031
Advertising	—	10,031	2,000
Other Costs	1,412	1,864	1,421
Total Sales and Marketing	2,082	14,897	6,453
Content Acquisition and Display	—	—	—
Labor	590	4,155	3,724
Content Acquisition Costs	—	1,021	600
Other Costs	693	1,937	1,858
Total Content Acquisition and Display	1,283	7,113	6,182
General, Administrative and IT	—	—	—
Labor	560	2,947	3,276
Other Costs	236	1,987	1,947
Total General, Administrative and IT	796	4,934	5,223
Facilities	520	1,776	2,550
Research and Development	—	445	—
Depreciation and Amortization	180	1,917	2,200
Total Operating Expenses	4,161	31,081	22,608
Income From Operations	(3,946)	(27,096)	(16,033)
Metrics			
Page Views		549,730	404,472
Total Content under Syndication		1,576	4,139

Source: AtomFilms. All numbers (except page views and total content under syndication) are in thousands of U.S. dollars.

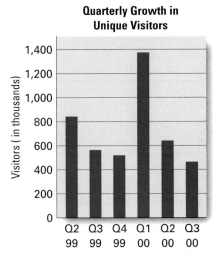

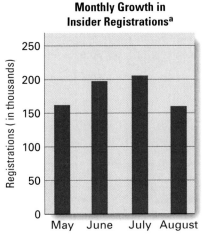

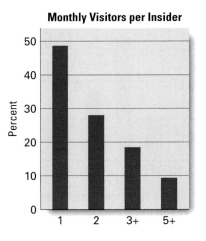

EXHIBIT 3A

Site Traffic at AtomFilms

Source: AtomFilms 1999/2000.

ªRegistration wall on site removed in August 2000; data collected between May–August 2000.

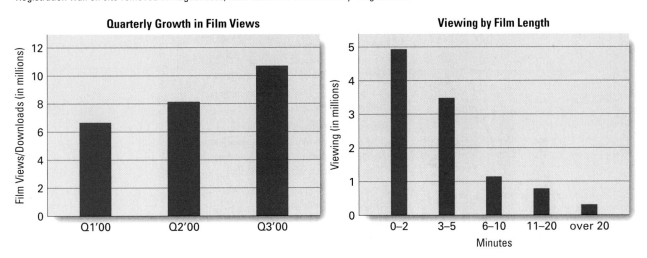

EXHIBIT 3B

Film Downloads on AtomFilms Website

Source: AtomFilms 1999/2000.

sponsor the "Journey Tour"—a cross-country tour in a VW van while showing Eric Saperston's short film entitled *The Journey*—at major college campuses in the United States. VW paid for a portion of the tour expenses, advertised on the AtomFilms site, and showed live webcasts of the trip on vw.com. In addition, VW mentioned the AtomFilms partnership in a series of national print and radio advertisements aimed at drawing traffic to the vw.com website.

Competition

IFILM   Created by Kevin Wendle, the founder of CNet and E Online, iFILM raised $37.5 million to host original short films by amateur filmmakers on its website. In 2000, however, iFILM changed its business model to become an online film directory while continuing to host original short films. The site also launched the iFILM Screening Network—a 14-day advance showcase where agencies could evaluate a

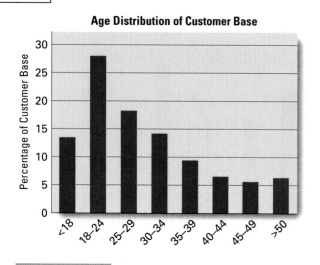

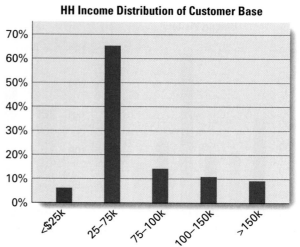

EXHIBIT 3C

User Demographics on AtomFilms Website

Source: AtomFilms 1999/2000.

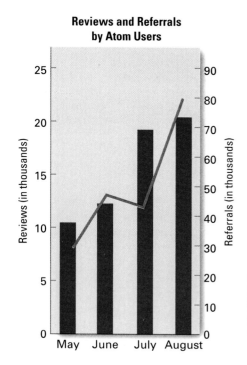

**Marketing/Promotions Reinforce
Current Segment of Users**

Film Festival Promotions
- Sponsorship of events, parties at film festivals
- Coverage in industry and popular press

Strong appeal to film-maker and indie film enthusiast communities

Journey Promotion
- Tour of Journey film to all college campuses
- Supporting sponsors are VW and Swatch, who wish to reach young, college kids

Strong appeal to indie film enthusiast and college student communities

Maverick Program
- Aimed at creating offline brand awareness
- Heavy users selected as 'Mavericks' to throw local Atom Film parties

Strong appeal to indie film enthusiast and college student communities

EXHIBIT 3D

Reviews and Referrals by AtomFilms Users

Source: AtomFilms 1999/2000.

filmmaker's work prior to the piece being viewed by a broader web audience. This portion of the site was created when the Creative Artists Agency (CAA) signed filmmakers Jeremy Hunt and Bruce Branit after their short film *405* appeared on iFILM. iFILM's revenue model involved securing 1% of the revenue from a successful filmmaker and agency relationship, instead of paying filmmakers directly for distribution rights. In December 2000, iFILM announced layoffs of 10% of total payroll for undisclosed reasons.[7]

Reelshort In partnership with Universal Pictures, Jeremy Bernard founded Reelshort in order to use short-film submissions to connect up-and-coming talent with big-name directors and actors. Reelshort paid filmmakers for the rights to a film and then

EXHIBIT 4

Management and Board Bios

Mika Salmi, CEO

Mika Salmi is CEO of AtomShockwave. In 1998, Salmi founded AtomFilms with the vision to discover and create new entertainment formats, marketed towards a wide array of distribution channels. Prior to AtomShockwave, Salmi was in charge of business development for media and entertainment at RealNetworks. He also spent seven years in the music industry for both Sony and EMI discovering bands such as Nine Inch Nails and Presidents of the United States of America. Salmi graduated Phi Beta Kappa with honors from the University of Wisconsin and earned his MBA from INSEAD in Fountainebleau, France.

Matt Hulett, President

Matt Hulett is President of AtomShockwave, responsible for operating and leading the business. Previously, as Chief Marketing and Online Officer for AtomFilms, Hulett led worldwide marketing, business, and online strategy. Prior to joining Atom, he was influential in the rise of RealNetworks. As group product manager, Hulett helped to make the RealPlayer streaming-media software the most popular non-browser product on the Web. Hulett was also responsible for founding the e-commerce and retail software distribution channels as well as popular consumer products, including RealPlayer Plus's and RealNetworks's subscription software services. Prior to RealNetworks, he spent five years as the worldwide marketing manager for WRQ's industry-leading Reflection PC-UNIX connectivity software. Hulett is a graduate of the University of Washington with a bachelor's degree in marketing and information systems.

Michael Comish, President, International

Based in London, Michael Comish manages AtomShockwave's international operations in Europe and Asia. Prior to joining AtomShockwave, Comish spent eight years in consulting, most recently as a partner in London with Mercer Management Consulting, one of the world's premier corporate strategy firms. At Mercer, he developed strategies for a number of leading technology and media companies such as Deutsche Telekom, Phillips, and Sprint, as well as branded-good companies such as Campbell's soups. Comish graduated with an honors degree in Business Administration from the University of Western Ontario, Canada, and earned his MBA from INSEAD in Fountainebleau, France.

Heather Redman, Executive Vice President, Corporate Strategy

Heather Redman leads corporate strategy and development at AtomShockwave. Prior to joining AtomShockwave, Redman was Senior Vice President, General Counsel and Secretary of Getty Images, Inc. Prior to its merger with Getty, she served as Vice President and General Counsel of digital photography pioneer PhotoDisc, Inc. Redman brings legal experience from the law firm Heller Ehrman White & McAuliffe. Redman graduated Phi Beta Kappa from Reed College and holds a law degree from Stanford Law School.

Eric Cansler, Senior Vice President, Finance and Operations

Eric Cansler is in charge of all financial operations at AtomShockwave. Cansler joins AtomShockwave from Headbone Interactive, where he was Vice President of Finance and Operations. At Headbone, Cansler worked to secure financing and led the company's transition from a CD-Rom to an Internet-focused content and entertainment company. Before Headbone, he was with Pantheon, Inc., a provider of software tools for Internet applications. Cansler spent six years with Arthur Andersen, LLP, as a consultant to high-tech clients. He graduated from the University of North Carolina and holds a Master degree in Accounting from the University of Colorado.

(continued)

EXHIBIT 4

Management and Board Bios *(continued)*

Michael Yanover, Senior Vice President, Entertainment

Michael Yanover heads the entertainment group at AtomShockwave. Since joining AtomShockwave, Yanover has initiated and is overseeing its key entertainment content, including some of its high profile Hollywood deals, such as that with acclaimed film director Tim Burton. Prior to joining AtomShockwave, Yanover started and ran independent TV, video game, and publishing companies, with some notable accomplishments being the creation of the "Men in Black" franchise and first prize at the 1999 Annecy International Animation Festival. Before that, he practiced as a transactional entertainment attorney in Los Angeles, representing clients such as Mel Gibson and Ridley Scott, and as a corporate and venture capital attorney in New York at Stroock, Stroock & Lavan, representing clients such as Warburg Pincus. Yanover holds an MBA in Finance from the University of Chicago and a J.D. from the University of Toronto.

Mike Edmunds, Senior Vice President, Interactive Products

Mike Edmunds leads AtomShockwave's Interactive Products Group, overseeing the acquisition and production of interactive entertainment content ranging from casual Web games to personal media creativity applications. Edmund has over eleven years experience in product development and technical management. As Vice President of Engineering at Macromedia, he was responsible for the Shockwave Player technology and Director multimedia authoring software. He also designed user interfaces and developed search engines at Verity, Inc. Edmunds holds a degree in computer science from the Massachusetts Institute of Technology.

Toni Marinovich, Chief Marketing Officer

Toni Marinovich leads the marketing and brand strategy for AtomShockwave. Marinovich joins AtomShockwave from Getty Images, where she held the position of Vice President of Global Marketing. While at Getty, she was responsible for the strategic direction and marketing of eight brands. She successfully developed marketing and creative services teams throughout Europe, resulting in several prestigious design awards. Marinovich has over twelve years of marketing experience working with Corbis Corporation, Apple Computer & Global Village Communications, among others. Marinovich holds a degree in Political Science from California State University in San Jose.

Seth Levenson, Vice President, Advertising Sales

Seth Levenson is responsible for driving AtomShockwave's advertising, sponsorship, and partnership revenue. Levenson joins AtomShockwave from Go.com, where he was Director of Advertising for the ESPN Internet Group. Having joined the Seattle-based Starwave Corporation in 1996, Levenson was the top revenue producer for the company's sites, such as ESPN.com, ABCNews.com, and Mr. Showbiz. Levenson has created and sold innovative cross-media advertising programs for major national advertisers, such as the Ford Motor Company, General Motors, MBNA, Intel, McDonald's and Universal Pictures. Levenson brings 14 years of media marketing and sales experience to AtomShockwave, including 5 years at Condé Nast Publications as Advertising Manager with Gourmet magazine and CondeNet. He earned his BA degree from Oberlin College and completed graduate programs at Harvard-Radcliffe College.

Lee Crawford, Vice President, Engineering

Lee Crawford leads Engineering and Operations teams at AtomShockwave and has over ten years experience directing the development of complex software systems. Prior to joining AtomShockwave, Crawford was Director of Engineering at Segasoft Networks, Inc., where he lead the Dreamcast Network project. Prior to Segasoft, he co-ran Twofish Technology, a consulting company guiding large, traditional corporations in shifting their applications to the web. Before that, he was a Senior Software Engineer at Thinking Machines Corporation. Crawford graduated from Florida State University with a degree in Computer Science.

EXHIBIT 5

AtomFilms Venture Financing

COMPANY OVERVIEW:

Business Brief:	Acquirer of exclusive licenses to films, animations, and digital content for distribution to a broad range of traditional and new media channels
Founded:	03/99
Status:	Private & Independent
Employees:	140
Stage:	Shipping Product
Industries:	Consumer & Business Services: Other

INVESTORS

Investment Firm	Participating Round
Warner Bros. Online	1
WaterView Advisors	1
Arts Alliance (London)	1, 2
Individual Investors	1, 2
Allen & Company Incorporated	1
Chase Capital Partners	2*
Intel Corporation	2
Trans Cosmos	2

* = Lead Investor

FINANCINGS TO DATE:

Round #	Round Type	Date	Amount Raised	Post $ Valuation (SMM)	Company Stage
1	Corp	5/99	5.0	NA	Product Development
2	First	12/99	20.0	NA	Shipping Product

EXECUTIVES AND BOARD MEMBERS:

Name	Title	Background/Former Employer
Heather Redman	SVP, Business Affair	SVP, General Counsel & Secretary, Getty Images; VP & General Counsel, PhotoDisc;
Eric Cansler	VP, Finance and Operations	CFO, Headbone Interactive; VP Finance, Pantheon
Irl Nathan	VP, Entertainment Technology	President & Cofounder, Pixel/Wave Entertainment
Frank Biondi	Board Member, Venture Investor	Senior Managing Director, Waterview Advisors
Robert Egan	Board Member, Venture Investor	Executive, Chase Capital Partners
Thomas Hoegh	Board Member, Venture Investor	Partner, Arts Alliance
Richard Barton	Board Member, Outsider	CEO, Expedia
Bill Heston	Board Member, Outsider	VP, Business Development, Getty Images
Mark Torrance	Board Member, Outsider	Chairman & Founder, Getty Images

Source: Compiled from VentureOne.

resold it through multiple distribution channels. Universal Pictures was one of the major investors in Reelshort. In return, Universal's development and production executives were given two weeks to view films on a private site prior to the work "going live" to the public. In addition, Reelshort could draw on the resources of Universal and its production partners to help nurture new talent.

Icebox   Icebox was launched in early 1999 by Steve Stanford, from Citysearch.com; Rob LaZebnik, a writer of *The Simpsons;* and Howard Gordon, a writer and producer of *The X-Files.* Icebox featured animated shorts that were both created in-house and submitted by amateur filmmakers. The site had signed over 100 established writers and producers hailing from *South Park, The Simpsons,* and *King of the Hill* to develop web-friendly animated content. Revenue was generated from three sources: advertising, merchandise sales, and licensing content to production studios and TV networks. In August 1999, Icebox announced a partnership with the Showtime cable network to produce a live action series based on the Icebox original animated series *Starship Regulars.*[8] In November 2000, Icebox laid off 50% of its staff for undisclosed reasons.[9] Then, in early 2001, Icebox officially closed down its site.

Pseudo programs   Created by Josh Harris, founder of the Internet market research firm Jupiter Communications, Pseudo produced and aired more than 40 non-mainstream, youth-oriented, interactive shows every week from its studio. Programming, which included games, music, fashion, and performing arts, featured interactive tools to facilitate communication between show hosts and web users. Pseudo generated revenues from advertising contracts with leading consumer brands, such as Arizona Jeans, Sprite, and Levi Strauss.[10] Pseudo.com closed its doors in December 2000. (See Exhibit 6).

Z.com   Z.com was a privately held company backed by the prolific Internet incubator Idealab! Z.com launched its site with original programming that included animation, short films, live events, and interactive games. Z.com was backed by several big-name Hollywood artists, including Brad Grey, the television producer of *The Sopranos* and Jerry Bruckheimer, one of Hollywood's top film producers whose credits included *Flashdance, Beverly Hills Cop,*

Top Gun, The Rock, and *Armageddon.* In late 2000, the company announced it had purchased the website Comedy.com and planned to integrate its programs with the Z.com offering.[11]

Emerging Technologies and Devices

Broadband

The term "broadband" was used to refer to a two-way, digital service that transmitted a minimum of 1.5 megabits per second (mbps) in at least one direction.[12] Narrowband devices, on the other hand, included an ordinary dial-up modem, which handled 28.8 or 56 kilobits per second (kbps). Still images and text could be adequately downloaded using narrowband devices. However, data-intensive applications like video-on-demand (VOD) required broadband connections. Broadband networks promised to unleash the Internet's full potential by providing high-speed data access to consumers' homes. In the United States, Internet access was expected to be a $13 billion business by 2002, and even larger if a portion of the $44 billion pay TV industry and the $110 billion local telephone market was included. The total addressable market was this large because broadband access could take place over one of three pipelines: high-speed telephone lines or DSL (Digital Subscriber Line), cable lines, or satellite connections.

DSL   By 1999, all the major local carriers were beginning to offer some form of DSL, since almost every household in the country had a phone line and roughly 60–70% could support DSL. The relatively slow rate at which consumers subscribed to DSL services, however, was attributed to three factors: limited geographic availability, difficulties in arranging installation, and high prices. In early 1999, the number of subscribers was roughly 75,000—a figure much lower than the local carriers had anticipated.

Cable   By 1999, 68% of U.S. households subscribed to cable television. Since the growth of cable subscribers had leveled out at 1% to 2% per year, the cable industry embraced high-speed Internet access as an opportunity to defend and grow its revenue base. All major cable operators were investors in one of two leading cable modem Internet service providers

(ISPs): @Home and Road Runner. @Home's service was available to 5.7 million of the 60 million homes reached by its cable partners' networks, whereas Road Runner was available to 3.6 million of the 27 million homes in its network. By 2000, fewer than 1.5 million homes subscribed to broadband services through either service. Despite the low adoption rates, cable companies also explored the possibility of offering telephone service over cable lines.

Satellite   Satellites provided a third alternative to new terrestrial fiber networks. However, whereas satellites were extremely efficient at broadcasting, they could transmit signals in one direction only. Although the technology for two-way communication was being developed, it was not ready for commercial introduction by early 2001. Hughes Network Systems used geo-stationary satellites to offer Internet access but required subscribers to use a dial-up modem and telephone line for upstream access. The difficulties in convincing consumers to purchase this complicated system had slowed the growth of satel-lite Internet access. By 2000, only 500,000 homes in the United States subscribed to this service.

Convergence

Nicholas Negroponte, a technology futurist and co-founder of the MIT Media Laboratory, had, in his description of convergence in 1995, declared that there would be no distinction between the TV and the PC in the future.[13] Nearly six years later, most U.S. households still did not use a "convergence" device in their homes. Although computers had persisted as a tool primarily associated with work, television was a tool used primarily for relaxation. Still, several companies and technologies had developed new devices that might help convergence take root in all households.[14]

Interactive television   The device created to facilitate convergence became more prolific once Microsoft bought Web TV—a Silicon Valley start-up—in 1997. Microsoft believed that Web TV devices could reach every American without a PC. But by 2000, Web TV

Technology Enablers	Pre-production	Online Film Distribution	Online Entertainment Content Distribution
Sightsound	ScriptShark	Atomfilms	Den
Shockwave	Medialive	Lemontv	Wirebreak
Real Networks	Idealive	Icebox	Pseudo
Windows Media Player	Patronet	Thebitscreen	Sputnik7
Apple Quick-time Player	Creativeplanet	Joecartoon	Movietv
		eveo	Metv
		Mediatrip	Regenerationtv
		iFILM	Broadcast
		Filmunderground	zchannel.net
		Raindance	Escreeningroom
		Shootingpeople	footage.net
		Alwaysindependentfilms	Internetv
		Movieflix	kkrs.net
		Thesync	
		Undergroundfilm	
		Zeroonefilms	
		Cinemanow	
		Bijoucafe	
		Pop	
		Scour	

EXHIBIT 6

Players in Online Entertainment

Source: Press clippings, web search; all underlined companies have filed for bankruptcy protection or closed site.

had sold only 1 million subscriptions and reached only 1% of U.S. households. In addition, many consumers seeking Internet access had purchased PCs—a trend aided by rapidly decreasing prices of personal computer hardware and software.

A recent example of a device the increased "interactivity" with the television was the Personal Video Recorder (PVR). PVRs performed the same functions as a videocassette recorder but used digital technology and a memory. PVRs allowed consumers to skip ads, pause live programming and then watch it later, and record programs on a particular topic so that consumers were able to program their own "channel." However, by year-end 2000, TiVo and Replay, two San Francisco-based start-ups that created PVR systems, had sold only 100,000 boxes between them. Microsoft had recently developed UltimateTV, an enhanced version of the PVR that was bundled with set-top boxes installed as part of a cable or satellite package. To date, several cable operators, including DirecTV and British satellite operator BskyB, had begun inserting PVRs into their boxes.

Game consoles   Using the PC as the primary game platform was expected to diminish because several game console manufacturers created convergence-oriented consoles with features such as Internet access, DVD, and CD players. These features were expected to transform gaming from a solitary to a group event, thus generating potential network effects in the retail gaming markets. These network effects, and the increased production of interactive game content, were expected to be the key drivers behind the projected 16.2 million U.S. households that would purchase Internet-connected consoles by 2003.[15] As delivery platforms evolved, revenue streams were expected to shift to advertising, pay-per-use, and product placement fees linked to Internet-based gaming.

The Sony Playstation2 (PS2)—released in the fall of 2000 was expected to capture nearly 90% of total new console sales. Sony, in a joint venture with Toshiba Corp., had spent more than $2 billion developing the PS2. The machine included a built-in video game console, DVD player, and CD-ROM drive. Even with all the accruements, it still had reserve space for a high-speed Internet connection and a hard drive for storing and playing music, movies and games. Sony Corporation envisioned the

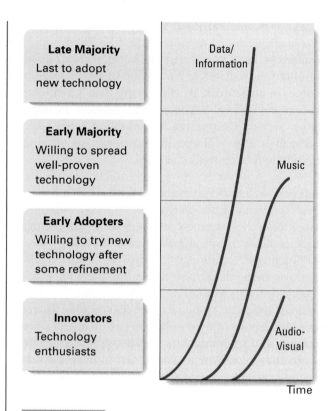

EXHIBIT 7

Adoption Curves for Data, Music, and Audio-Visual

PS2 emerging as the new "home-theatre-in-a-box" solution for families.[16]

Other game console makers had followed suit. The latest version of Sega's Dreamcast offered comparable graphics to the PS2 and a link to the Internet, but lacked a hard drive for storing media content. In 2001, Microsoft launched a new gaming console called X-Box that included an Internet connection and storage capacity similar to the PS2. However, without Sony or Sega's library of established games and characters, the X-Box was not expected to rival the sales of Sony's console for many years.[17]

Wireless   By 2000, total penetration of wireless devices was large enough that mobile phones were designed to function as convergence devices. Industry insiders envisioned mobile phones as devices for sending and receiving email messages, surfing the Internet, sending files from person-to-person, and storing digital music or audio-visual files. In several international markets that lacked the broadband infrastructure for cable or DSL connections, mobile

| How? | "A distributed computing architecture that allows client systems to communicate directly with other clients, with or without a single administrative server to coordinate and manage interactions between peers"[a] |

| What? | • Documents sent via email
• MP3 files with digital music
• Budweiser "Wassup" video clip |

| Who? | • Napster (music)
• Scour (A/V)
• Gnutella/Freenet (all) |

| Why? | • Efficient sharing and distribution of content
• Free, open to any user
• Lack of external control/monitoring |

| Why not? | • Intellectual property rights
• Security of data files on individual PCs |

EXHIBIT 8A

Overview of Peer-to-Peer Networks

[a] "P2P: Publishing Computing Power to the Edge," Forrester Research, October 26, 2000.

phones were viewed as the ideal convergence device.[18]

By early 2000, Japan boasted mobile phone penetration rates of 46% in urban areas. NTT, Japan's largest local carrier, responded to this trend by developing a new wireless entertainment product. The i-Mode—an application developed in partnership with Sanyo and Liquid Audio Japan—sent top 10 music lists to i-Mode subscribers' cell phones. Subscribers could then purchase and burn an album onto a minidisk at the nearest music kiosk.

Emerging Applications: Peer-to-Peer Networks

A peer-to-peer (P2P) network was defined as a distributed computing architecture that allowed client systems to communicate directly with other clients, with or without a single administrative server to coordinate and manage interactions between peers.[19] (See Exhibits 8a–b.) In essence, P2P networking allowed peers to freely share files over an unregulated network. Following the rise of Napster, a communal music file-sharing application that became one of the most popular destinations on the web, P2P networks were being hailed as the next killer application for the web. By year-end 2000, Napster had attracted over 38 million users and had become the quintessential archetype for a successful P2P application.

Some observers argued that widespread usage of P2P technologies would be hampered by concerns regarding security and piracy. Although P2P networking enabled two disparate computers to communicate without a central server, it lacked the protection inherent in the traditional client/server model. Even with newly developed security measures, many individuals and companies distrusted applications that might make their PC vulnerable to outsiders.

B2C Applications of P2P Networking

The most profound P2P networking applications applied to sharing digital entertainment. In particular, many within the music industry felt the industry was undergoing a dramatic transformation as a result of an effective compression technology combined

EXHIBIT 8B

Applications of P2P Networks

Source: "P2P: Publishing Computing Power to the Edge," Forrester Research, October 26, 2000.

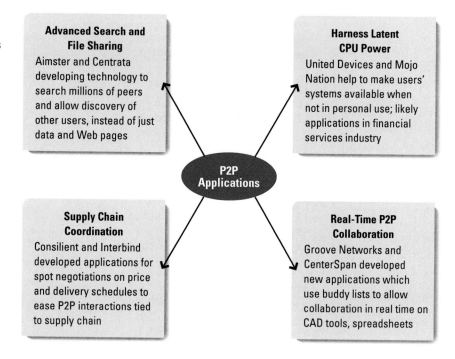

Advanced Search and File Sharing
Aimster and Centrata developing technology to search millions of peers and allow discovery of other users, instead of just data and Web pages

Harness Latent CPU Power
United Devices and Mojo Nation help to make users' systems available when not in personal use; likely applications in financial services industry

P2P Applications

Supply Chain Coordination
Consilient and Interbind developed applications for spot negotiations on price and delivery schedules to ease P2P interactions tied to supply chain

Real-Time P2P Collaboration
Groove Networks and CenterSpan developed new applications which use buddy lists to allow collaboration in real time on CAD tools, spreadsheets

with a file-sharing application. Although several different compression technologies had emerged via the Internet, MP3's technology enabled users to compress digital music files to an easily downloadable size while preserving the quality of the music file. Two companies, MP3 and Napster, had developed the most popular file sharing applications for Internet users. Their service was, in effect, a computer-based jukebox that allowed music fans to access songs, via the Internet, that they already possessed in physical compact disk form. Once the user logged in with a password, he or she could access the service from computers around the world.

P2P file-sharing applications posed several threats to the music industry. These included the prospects that music fans would access the Internet service with CDs borrowed from friends (i.e., for which they did not pay), that groups of fans would share passwords and be able to access one another's recordings via the Internet, and that copies of copyrighted music would be downloaded and stored from the Internet site and then passed along to others. The Recording Industry Association of America (RIAA), a trade group, had identified more than 4,500 music websites in the United States that illegally carried copyrighted recordings. Moreover, they predicted that by 2005 more than $3 billion of annual revenue would be lost as a result of illegal file sharing.[20] To

stem the tide, the RIAA filed copyright infringement litigation against MP3.com, calling for a halt to that firm's My.MPe.com service.[21]

Napster, the most successful file-sharing application with a community of 38 million users, had succeeded in creating so much consumer and media interest that the major music labels took notice. On October 31, 2000, Bertelsmann—the world's largest publishing and music company—announced a deal to offer a subscription service on Napster's site. Consumers would pay $4.95 per month to download music from Bertelsmann's BMG label alongside Napster's free download service. No other major music labels had signed up for a paid subscription service on Napster, although most offered secure paid downloads on their own sites (Exhibit 8c).

Recently, new companies had been created to replicate the Napster application for sharing audiovisual content rather than digital music. Scour, created in early 2000 and backed by Hollywood power broker Michael Ovitz, was the first of these companies. Despite strong consumer usage of the Scour application, the company filed for bankruptcy in November 2000 after being sued for copyright infringement by the film and music industries.[22]

Next, Bill Bales—a Napster co-founder and investor—created Flycode, a company whose seed money was obtained from senior managers at large

EXHIBIT 8C

Online Strategies of Major Music Companies

Distributor	Key Labels	Online Initiatives
BMG Entertainment	Arista RCA Zomba	▪ Offers secure downloads of 50+ albums and singles ▪ Retails CDs via GetMusic.com; a joint venture with UMG ▪ Acquired CDNow, July 2000 ▪ Partnership with Napster
EMI Recorded Music	Capitol Priority Virgin	▪ Offers secure downloads of 100 albums and 40 singles
Sony Music Entertainment	Columbia Epic	▪ Partnered with UMG to develop subscription services
Universal Music Group	Interscope MCA Mercury	▪ Partnered with UMG to develop subscription services ▪ Retails CDs via GetMusic.com; a joint venture with BMG ▪ Testing Bluematter multimedia format for downloads
Warner Music Group[a]	Atlantic Elektra Reprise Warner Bros	▪ Launching secure singles downloads in November 2000 ▪ Investments in ArtistDirect, Launch.com, and DiscoverMusic.com

[a] "Online Music: Napster and After," The Yankee Group, September 2000.

technology companies in Silicon Valley. Flycode aimed to develop a file-sharing application to enable distribution of video content and photographs with a more intelligent software interface. Having experienced the difficulty associated with controlling illegal content transfer while at Napster, Bales aimed to solve many of Napster's problems by using newly created technologies. Flycode intended to develop a new form of digital rights management software to protect copyrighted materials from piracy.

The Flycode business model differed from Napster. It planned to secure content from both amateur and professional artists and to provide artists with the option to give away ad-supported content, sell files individually, or sell subscriptions to Flycode's site. In addition, Flycode intended to collect ancillary revenue streams from site advertising, sponsorships, and by selling demographic user data to content providers. Flycode's target content partners included movie studios, television networks, and other content providers.

Recent Developments at AtomFilms

Deals

Wireless   As new wireless platforms emerged, Salmi realized that feature films and television shows required too much bandwidth to view on a wireless device. By contrast, AtomFilms content was small enough to be transmitted at lower speeds. In April 2000, Microsoft and ActiveSky launched the new Windows-powered PocketPC devices. The ActiveSky Media Player was specifically developed to bring media streaming technology to small devices. AtomFilms entered into a partnership with Microsoft and ActiveSky that would enable short films to be pre-loaded into the new PDAs, to promote the viewing of short-form entertainment on large-screen mobile devices.

A second deal involved a telecommunications company. In November 2000, AtomFilms signed a syndication deal with Schibsted Telecom, the largest media company in Scandinavia. Schibsted, which attracted an estimated 50% of Scandinavian online traffic to its online properties, was seeking content for its new media portal. Schibsted syndicated 100 short films from AtomFilms for Internet distribution to its customers for their mobile and handheld devices.

Flycode   Flycode approached AtomFilms in the summer of 2000 with a content partnership opportunity. AtomFilms would supply content to the Flycode network for a small fee per file. AtomFilms' content would be wrapped in Flycode's proprietary technology to enable real-time tracking of content viewing. The data generated from the Flycode technology "wrapper" could be used to garner higher advertising dollars from companies that posted ads in Atom-Films content. Although a letter of intent had been signed, the final terms of the deal were undecided.

Financing

After witnessing a rather chilly climate for Internet start-ups following the precipitous drop in the NASDAQ in early 2000, Salmi was concerned about raising an additional $30M in a series D round of financing. Existing investors in AtomFilms contributed $5M in a bridge loan while Salmi sought other financing options. By Q4 2000, AtomFilms had attracted the attention of an Asian investor seeking to acquire the company to help develop its broadband and wireless platform in Asia; and interest in a merger with a leading online entertainment destination—Shockwave. After carefully considering both options, Salmi agreed to a merger between Atom-Films and Shockwave on December 15, 2000.

Shockwave was a private company with 57% of pre-merger ownership belonging to the online powerhouse Macromedia. The Shockwave site featured cutting-edge games, shows, music, and creativity applications, along with the Flash player—software required for viewing most animated works on the web. The revenue model of Shockwave stemmed from site advertising and totaled roughly three times AtomFilms' revenues in 2000. Monthly site traffic comparisons from Q4 2000 pegged Shockwave's traffic at approximately 12 million visits and AtomFilms' traffic at approximately 1.2 million visits.

Shockwave had accumulated a large roster of blue-chip advertisers and millions of site visitors seeking to download its free media player. However, the company was seeking to build both a global and offline channel presence. AtomFilms, on the other hand, had acquired the licensing rights to a massive content library, had developed many lucrative syndication relationships in offline channels, and had built offices and partnerships in the United States, Europe, and Asia. A merger with Shockwave would enable AtomFilms to reduce consumer marketing expenditures, to increase the breadth of content available on its site to include games and music, and to reach a much larger audience (See Exhibit 9). Although the cost-savings from the merger had not been fully explored, Salmi believed that the new entity could cut payroll from 300 to 200 persons, reduce lease costs by moving AtomFilms' staff to San Francisco, and decrease overall marketing costs by at least one-third.

Major Issues

Internal Resource Allocation

One of the key issues Salmi confronted, as he tried to steer the company to profitability, was financial and human resource allocation between the B2C and B2B sides of the business. The B2B licensing and syndication business generated sizeable revenues and profits for the company. Yet, Salmi believed that the size of the overall B2B film distribution market was relatively small. On the other hand, the B2C side of the business generated significant traffic and public relations for the company, but web surfers were notoriously difficult to monetize. This raised the question about which side of the AtomFilms business model was most sustainable in the long term. As the company expanded in size and scope, Salmi needed to decide where to focus precious time and resources.

Branding

The company also grappled with issues about its brand. So far, AtomFilms had built a strong brand connoting images such as "independent," "hip," and "short-form entertainment." It had also built a strong following among young, college-age males and the independent filmmaking community. However, the company now sought to broaden its viewer base in order to increase overall market demand for short-film entertainment. Salmi was uncertain about several issues regarding the company's brand. First, how could AtomFilms reposition its brand to appeal to a broad range of consumers? Second, which channels were most appropriate to reach out to new consumer segments? Third, should the online and offline channels deliver distinct messages to consumers? And, finally, what types of consumer marketing campaigns were appropriate for a company of this size and scope for each channel?

Wireless

Salmi was convinced that emerging wireless platforms were the ideal conduit for AtomFilms content. The company's vast library of short-form content was perfect for the new digital consumer. Consumers in Japan had already embraced technologies such as the I-Mode. However, the delivery of audio-visual content via wireless devices was largely untapped, and Salmi was not sure about how aggressively to tap this market.

EXHIBIT 9

AtomShockwave Fact Sheet

The Mission

To be the world's leading entertainment provider for businesses and consumers in emerging media formats.

The Company

AtomShockwave offers world-class entertainment, spanning games, films, and animations, driving distribution across the Internet, mobile devices, television, airlines and more. AtomShockwave is a pioneer and innovator in technology and content. The company is headquartered in San Francisco with regional offices in Los Angeles, New York, London and Tokyo. For more information, please visit **www.atomfilms.com** and **www.shockwave.com.**

The Catalog

The AtomShockwave catalog is as diverse as it is distinguished, offering groundbreaking games and interactive entertainment as well as an award-winning library of quality short films and animations from around the world, in every genre and style. With these original games, films, and animations, ranging from 30 seconds to 30 minutes in length, AtomShockwave is capable of offering entertainment anytime, everywhere.

Partnerships

AtomShockwave's breadth of advertising and sponsorship partners and syndication customers includes major television networks, theaters, Web sites broadband services, airlines, handheld and wireless devices and film institutes:

Acura	The Ford Motor Company	Palm IIIc
Adobe	F/X Networks	Real Networks
Altoids	HBO/Cinemax	Sci-Fi Channel
AMC Theaters	Hewlett-Packard	Sharper Image
Apple QuickTime	IBM	Showtime Networks
Blockbuster	Intel	Skyy Vodka
British Airways	Eastman Kodak	Sony
Camera World	Levi Strauss & Co.	Sony Playstation 2
Cartoon Network	Lexus	Swatch
Cathay Pacific	LucasFilm	Symantec
Century Theaters	Lugz	TiVo
Columbia Pictures	Maxim Online	United Airlines
Continental Airlines	Microsoft Pocket PC	Universal Pictures
Compaq	Microsoft Windows Media	20th Century Fox
Dell	New Line Cinema	Volkswagen
Delta Airlines	Nintendo	Warner Brothers
Finlandia Vodka	Nike	

Doing so might expose the AtomFilms brand to potential consumer dissatisfaction, owing to the slow speed or inefficiency of wireless content transfer. In addition, the telecom partners that had approached AtomFilms wanted to license its content but would not allow Salmi to decide how to market or deliver the content to consumers. How could he mitigate the risks of a poorly executed deal that exposed AtomFilms content to millions of European consumers?

Peer-to-Peer Networks

Despite the recently signed letter of intent to partner with Flycode on its audio-visual peer-to-peer net-work, Salmi wondered whether the evolution of new peer-to-peer models might make AtomFilms redundant in the consumer content distribution space. A successful P2P site could become the leading distribution platform for entertainment content—particularly if more intelligent applications could be developed that enabled consumers to navigate the vast array of content more efficiently. In addition, if filmmakers chose to distribute content via P2P networks, AtomFilms would find it increasingly difficult to search and secure high-quality content. The deal with Flycode had not yet been signed, and Salmi needed to determine the costs and benefits associated with joining forces with an unproven P2P networking company.

Future of the Company

Salmi also faced important strategic choices regarding the AtomFilms business model. During a recent senior management meetings, three models had been put on the table. First, AtomFilms could forge ahead with its current business model but place more emphasis on seeking several core corporate sponsors for its website. So far, several consumer products companies, including Ford and Volkswagen, had expressed interest in paying to maintain a constant presence on the AtomFilms site.

The second option was to introduce a subscription or pay-per-use fee on the AtomFilms website, in order to monetize consumer traffic on the site. However, fears of both radically diminished traffic and high consumer dissatisfaction upon the introduction of such a subscription fee had prevented the company from implementing this model in the past.

Finally, AtomFilms might leverage its relationships with filmmakers, talent agencies, production houses, and movie studios to gain a stronger foothold in the offline entertainment market. Under this scenario, AtomFilms would scan its thousands of film submissions to identify talent or scripts that might be useful to a talent agency or production house. In exchange, AtomFilms might participate in future revenue streams if the talent or scripts were used to produce a major feature film.

Ultimately, AtomFilms could not pursue all three strategies simultaneously. With a post-merger integration underway and with more announcements regarding failed online entertainment start-ups,

Salmi wanted to stay focused on his original mission—to create an entertainment company that delivered content to consumers anytime, anyplace, and through every channel imaginable.

ENDNOTES

1. "S&P Movies and Home Entertainment Industry Survey," May 2000.
2. Article in the October 9, 2000 issue of *Fortune* Magazine.
3. "Organization Profile: Disney Online," *PR Newswire*, December 27, 2000.
4. *Los Angeles Times*, May 18, 2000.
5. *The Wall Street Journal Europe*, August 14, 2000.
6. Bill Richards, Entertainment & Technology—Short and Sweet: "The Internet isn't quite ready for movies yet; But AtomFilms wants to be ready when it is," *The Wall Street Journal*, March 20, 2000.
7. Michelle Botwin, "Cybertainment 2000 Shakeout Hook Up Online Entertainment," *Los Angeles Times*, December 29, 2000.
8. Red Herring Company Profile Icebox.com, October 2000.
9. Michelle Botwin, "Cybertainment 2000 Shakeout Hook Up Online Entertainment," *Los Angeles Times*, December 29, 2000.
10. Red Herring Company Profile: Pseudo Programs, August, 2000.
11. Article in the June 1, 2000 edition of the *Associated Press Newswires*.
12. Some of the information in this section is drawn from Mark Kwak and David Yoffie, "The Broadband Race: Industry Note," Harvard Business School note No. 799-106, May 3, 1999.
13. "A Survey of E-Entertainment," *The Economist*, October 7, 2000.
14. Ibid.
15. Ibid.
16. Christopher Stern, "Sony's Serious About PlayStation 2; Company Sees Console As the Centerpiece of Home Entertainment," *Washington Post*, October 28, 2000.
17. Ibid.
18. Japanese Market Primed for Subscriptions: Jupiter Concept Report, October 4, 2000.
19. "1 P2P: Pushing Computing Power to the Edge," Forrester Research, October 26, 2000.
20. Lee Bruno, "Peer Review," Red Herring, December 4, 2000.
21. "S&P Movies and Home Entertainment Industry Survey," May 2000.
22. *Los Angeles Times*, May 18, 2000.

ZOOTS—The Cleaner Cleaner

9

This case was prepared by Myra Hart and Research Associate Sharon I. Peyus, Harvard Business School.

When we did the research, we found that dry cleaning does not scream, "Opportunity!" All our interviews and our industry analysis indicated that people were willing to accept the mediocrity they were getting. They weren't particularly price sensitive; they weren't worried about the environment; all they wanted was to get their clothes back—clean, on time, and with all the buttons on.

Todd Krasnow, CEO, ZOOTS

On October 29, 1998, Todd Krasnow, CEO and co-founder of ZOOTS, welcomed the entire "clean team" staff, investors and friends to the company's grand opening. The "invitation only" party began in the late afternoon at ZOOTS' first retail dry cleaning establishment (Store #001) in Danvers, MA. It then moved on to ZOOTS' state-of-the-art central cleaning facility in Wilmington, MA. For the team, the party was an opportunity to share with family and friends the results of nine months of work that included securing funding, finding the right retail locations, staffing and training, and

designing the firm's Internet site. For Krasnow, it was the first time he was willing to provide anyone outside ZOOTS' immediate family a look at what they were doing.

Still, he was extremely cautious about calling attention to the new enterprise. Because of his high profile in the retail community, members of the press were very interested in learning what his new venture was all about. Krasnow, however, was not interested in the notoriety. He was determined to launch ZOOTS quietly so that he and his team could work out any operational issues in relative obscurity. His plans called for running in "stealth mode" until he had at least three ZOOTS stores open, so even as he acted the genial host of the party, he kept an eye out for uninvited guests. When he discovered some gatecrashers, he quietly escorted them out. It was clear they had not crashed for the "party experience."

Though the mood was festive, the celebration was deliberately kept simple. No champagne or chocolate truffles were served in the new 10,000-sq. ft. cleaning lab—only white wine, finger sandwiches, and packaged cookies. Nonetheless, the opening was a momentous event. On the one hand, it represented the culmination of extraordinary efforts. On the other hand, it marked the beginning of ZOOTS' "real work." Shortly after the party trimmings came down the next morning, the lab would be filled with thousands of pounds of dirty clothes that would have to be sorted, repaired, cleaned, packaged, and delivered back to their rightful owners within days.

Krasnow moved among the guests, chatting with employees and investors, laughing easily and congratulating each individual on his or her accomplishments. As he walked to the front of the room to offer the evening's few formal remarks, he chuckled to himself. He wondered what his Harvard Business School (HBS) classmates would think of his career in dry cleaning. Certainly, neither he nor they could have foreseen his choice when they graduated from HBS 15 years earlier.

Origins

Todd Krasnow

Todd Krasnow grew up in Westchester County, New York. He graduated from Cornell University in 1979 with a BS in Chemistry and, for the next 2 years, he applied his knowledge of chemistry as a food technologist at General Foods. His product line, Crispy Cookin', was intended to bring the taste of fast food into the home. His group patented a process that made it possible to retain the crispness of frozen fried food when heated in the oven. Krasnow himself received a patent for a quick frying process he developed that sealed a batter dipped piece of fish without cooking the fish itself. The finished frozen product bore a strong resemblance in taste, texture, and appearance to the fish served at the Arthur Treacher's restaurants.

Krasnow enjoyed the challenges of his work, but he was well aware that the technologists were not the key decision-makers in the company. After 2 years at General Foods, Krasnow left for Harvard Business School where he received his MBA in 1983. During his 2nd year at HBS, Krasnow took time out from his studies to co-author the school's annual musical. The 1983 spoof, *Soul Proprietors*, was a take off on *Damn Yankees*, in which two prospective HBS students sold their souls to the devil to get into HBS. "It had a happy ending however," Krasnow recalled.

Krasnow worked at Star Market, a division of the Chicago-based Jewel Companies in the summer between his first and second years (1982). He joined the food and drug retailer after graduation, becoming one of the company's select group for fast track management trainees, informally (and somewhat irreverently) referred to as the "Jewel Jets." Krasnow's first 18 months on the job included a rotation through store operations areas including grocery, produce, deli, service, and store management.

He became Marketing and Media Coordinator in 1985. He worked closely with marketing director Myra Hart (HBS MBA '81) and took responsibility for preparing the weekly sales forecasts for the chain. After Hart told her marketing group that she would be leaving to join Tom Stemberg in the Staples start-up as vice president of operations, Krasnow approached her privately and indicated that he would be interested in joining the team. A few months later, in March 1986, he became Staples' Director of Marketing, charged with responsibility for selling the public on the office superstore's value proposition. His success with both traditional and direct marketing campaigns later earned him the title of Executive Vice President of Marketing. Krasnow maintained a strong role in setting the chain's marketing direction throughout his years at Staples, though his career path included several years in California helping to launch the west coast operations, an assignment running the company's international joint ventures, and the launch of the company's catalog operation. Along the way, Krasnow introduced many innovations, among them free *next day* delivery of office supplies.

For 10 years, Krasnow never considered looking outside the company for new opportunities. In 1996, the Executive Vice President of Sales and Marketing was completely committed to the company and to his longtime friend and mentor, Tom Stemberg who was the President and CEO of Staples. He was continually challenged by the work and, even more important, he was still having fun. However, when a group of investors approached him in late 1996 and asked him to consider joining their new venture as CEO, he found that he was tempted—not so much by the specific opportunity as by the idea of taking such a step. Stemberg was still young and deeply engaged in the leadership of Staples. It was unlikely that Krasnow would have the opportunity to lead Staples for many years to come, yet he was ready for such a challenge. He decided to discuss the offer with Stemberg.

Tom Stemberg

Tom Stemberg was a retailer through and through. After completing his education at Harvard (AB, 1971; MBA, 1973), he joined the Jewel Companies as a "mentored" management trainee. During his first months on the job, he spent his days bagging groceries, stocking shelves, and cleaning fish, but he also had regular meetings with a senior officer who had agreed to be his mentor during the training period. Assigned to Jewel's Star Market division in Boston, Stemberg quickly moved up the ladder. When he was named Vice President of Sales and Marketing just before his twenty-eighth birthday, he was the youngest senior officer in Jewel's history. His innovative marketing programs bolstered the supermarket's business and his aggressive leadership in marketing caught the attention of other major supermarket chains.

In late 1982, Stemberg joined Ohio-based First National Supermarkets (FNS) as Senior Vice President of Sales and Merchandising of its eastern division. In 1983, he was named president of the Connecticut-headquartered Edwards-Finast division. While at FNS, Stemberg concentrated his efforts on building a network of Edwards Food Warehouse stores, a high-volume, no-frills operation that offered low-priced merchandise, much of it under the Edwards-Finast label. In spite of his division's success, Stemberg decided to leave First National when, in January 1985, he realized that his differences with board chairman, Bob Samuels, were irreconcilable.

Stemberg conferred with his old friend and supermarketing colleague, Leo Kahn, as he sought the right opportunity. The two agreed to join forces and, with Kahn's encouragement, Stemberg wrote the business plan for Staples, the Office Superstore. Over the next 12 months, Stemberg recruited a senior management team, raised more than $4 million in initial funding, and opened the first of over 1000 retail stores in the US. His Staples concept and the team's execution of the concept changed the way small businesses and consumers bought office products. Initially, Stemberg was President and CEO and Kahn was Chairman of the Board. When Krasnow

approached him in 1996 to discuss the possibility of leaving Staples to become the chief executive of another business, Stemberg was Chairman and Chief Executive Officer of Staples. He was also a director of both PETsMart and Cornerstone Brands. He served on the executive committees of the City of Hope, the National Office Products Council and was co-chair of the Friends of Harvard Basketball.

Searching for Opportunity

When Krasnow told him about the offer, Stemberg agreed that the time was right to consider such a move—Krasnow should either start his own venture or take over the helm of a substantial existing enterprise. Stemberg cautioned him, however, to think carefully about which opportunity to pursue, reminding him that there would be many good ones out there. Stemberg then went a step further, offering to help Krasnow develop a viable business concept, work with him to test the idea, write the plan, and secure funding.

Stemberg recalled the process he had used in 1985. When he decided to launch his own venture, he had started by taking a personal inventory of his skills and knowledge (which were in high-volume, low-margin retailing and distribution), then looked for market needs that could be served by these skills. After determining which areas of specialty retailing were growing the fastest, he conducted an industry analysis to determine what the size of the opportunity might be and what competitive action he could anticipate. Stemberg and Krasnow agreed to undertake a similar quest in February 1997, with Stemberg playing much the same role for Krasnow that Leo Kahn had done for him in 1985.

As a starting point, they determined that the new business venture should be in retail, should serve very basic needs, and should provide goods or services that required frequent "repeat" purchases. Krasnow was also committed to building a business that was based on strong customer relationships. As the two thought about the business models they might choose, they agreed that large-footprint category-killer stores (e.g., Staples, Home Depot, and Toys 'R Us) no longer represented the unique opportunity they had 10–15 years earlier. This decision freed them to explore business opportunities that would be profitable with much smaller scale operating units. One idea on which Stemberg had been keeping a file for several years was "dry cleaning."

They met frequently and compared notes on the retail experiences that they had personally found were less than satisfactory. They considered what it would take to change the way the products or services were delivered, then reviewed the industry structure and the likelihood of competitive or imitative responses. As Krasnow and Stemberg sifted through the many ideas they generated, they found that dry cleaning continued to intrigue them. Both had more than their share of frustrating dry cleaning experiences, with complaints ranging from missing shirt buttons to inconvenient hours, poor customer service, and cash only operations.

Each put up $250,000 to underwrite the research process and organized the new venture as a limited liability corporation that they called C.C., LLc (Limited Liability company). The "C.C." represented their commitment to building a Cleaner Cleaner, but their use of initials only was one of many steps they took to keep the focus of their new venture under wraps for as long as possible. A dozen years earlier, they had learned how quickly "me too" operations would spring up in the wake of a new concept introduction. Staples saw 22 office superstore operators open within 2 years of its launch. With both men even more visible in the retailing industry in 1997, they chose to delay the inevitable imitative flurry for as long as possible.

Defining the Territory

Krasnow began to research the dry cleaning universe, using both "bottom up" and "top down" approaches. He interviewed family and friends to get more information about their customer experiences. He was particularly interested in identifying individual hot buttons. He used the data he collected to build a profile of customer expectations about quality convenience service, and turnaround time. He also began to get a sense of the product mix his acquaintances had cleaned or laundered and what their heavy usage times were.

At the same time, Krasnow wanted to learn more about the business from the supplier's point of view. He convinced a local dry cleaner to help him understand all aspects of the business, particularly the marketing and operating issues. Using a year's worth of the cleaner's point-of-sale data provided, Krasnow

built a more robust model of usage, product mix, and general cleaning requirements. He also gained new insights about the demographics of heavy cleaning users. Though the research was conducted in Boston, he felt confident that he could extrapolate from these findings and make projections for other East Coast markets.

Krasnow also hired a consulting firm to survey 13 local area dry cleaners. In return for their cooperation, he agreed to share the survey results with all of them. He began to build a database of dry cleaning transactions in the greater Boston area with the expectation that he could use the information to develop more detailed demand and demographic information. He charted seasonality, consumer cycle times (time between drop-off and pick-up), and geographic concentration of customers. The survey corroborated his earlier findings and provided additional demographic data, product mix details, and even some information about individual business operating characteristics. He was pleased with the information he was able to amass through his own research and that of his consultants. He recalled:

I'd never been a dry cleaner, but we were able to gather all kinds of knowledge—of how many shirts a dry cleaner does; how many and how often people come back (the next day, a week later, or more than six months later). We learned how often people come in only once and you never see them again. We determined how often high income people use dry cleaners versus low-income people, whether they were homeowners or renters, single or married, male or female. All of it was information that we could get our hands around. One thing that the research made clear was that customers were generally accepting of the status quo in the industry.

The Dry Cleaning Industry

For the most part, the business units in the highly fragmented industry were family owned. The low capital required for start-up and the relatively low level of skill needed made the industry particularly attractive to immigrants who often employed their entire families in the business. The International Fabricare Institute (IFI), a non-profit founded in 1883, was the industry association of dry cleaners, wet cleaners, launderers, apparel and textile manufacturers, suppliers, and other practitioners in the fabricare industry that kept track of business growth and development. IFI estimated that in 1999 there were approximately 45,000 dry-cleaning stores generating approximately $8 billion in revenues. Projected sales for 2000 were $9 billion industry-wide (IFI). The 50 largest operators in the industry captured approximately 5% of total market share; 97% of all companies in the industry operated five stores or fewer.

One of the largest companies in the industry, Johnson Service Group PLC, operated dry cleaning companies in the UK and posted annual sales in 1999 close to $327 million.[1] The group also operated franchise dry cleaning outlets in the United States under the name Dryclean USA.

There were some newer venture capital backed companies that had national aspirations. For example, *Hangers of New England,* a retail franchise of professional garment care stores, operated one store in Wilmington, North Carolina and had announced plans to open up to 100 retail stores in 7 states (including Massachusetts) by the end of 2000. *Hangers* was unique because it used the patented and environmentally friendly Micare system developed by Micell Technologies. The cleaning process used no heat and relied on liquid carbon dioxide (CO_2)—a natural substance found in carbonated soft drinks—to remove spots and dirt rather than on traditional dry cleaning solvents.

Anton's Cleaners, a Tewksbury, MA–based chain of 40 stores was another potentially formidable competitor. Anton's was one of the largest dry cleaners operating stores and plants in Krasnow's target area of eastern Massachusetts and southern New Hampshire. Because Anton's provided on-site cleaning, it was able to offer same-day service to customers.

In spite of the fact that there were a few larger players, competition was generally assessed on a very local basis. Every dry cleaner within a three-minute radius of a retail outlet was considered a potential competitor. Because of this, each of the retail cleaning stores in a chain—even those within the radius of a single central cleaning plant—would operate in its own distinct competitive market. The fact that an individual dry cleaning establishment might be a part of a larger chain did not necessarily

make it any more formidable than a well-run "mom and pop" operation.

Building the Business
Defining the Business Concept

In spite of the fact that customers seemed to be willing to put up with inadequate dry cleaning service and that the dry cleaning industry appeared to defy rationalization, Krasnow was determined to go ahead. He planned to build a nationwide dry cleaning chain that focused on the customer experience. Though his new venture would use the web to attract customers and to track orders, the concept was, at its core a "brick and mortar" business. Stemberg and Krasnow believed that the hundreds of branded stores they envisioned would do for dry cleaning what Staples had done for office products—provide better service at reasonable prices.

The value proposition was simple. Their new venture would get the customers' cleaning done right, reliably, and conveniently. "We know that it's a winning formula and the customer is telling us that it's a winning formula," Krasnow emphasized. His cleaning team would not only meet, but also would surpass the expectations of the new economy's time-challenged consumers. It would offer customers a variety of convenient ways in which to take care of their dry cleaning needs.

Financing the Start-Up

Krasnow used the data he collected from customers, cleaners, consultants and industry information to build his financial assumptions. The revenues (pricing, average order size, customer counts, individual store volume) and operating costs (rents, store staffing, central facility operations) were estimates well documented by research. Krasnow relied on his own marketing experience and industry data to estimate other costs. He went so far as to have his team conduct time and motion studies of employee activities (shirt pressing, clothes sorting, as well as counter service at the retail stores) to provide the detail necessary for staffing and payroll models. He developed multiple scenarios that allowed comparison of revenues and profits for alternative operating models (e.g. on-site cleaning vs. centralized plant).

Though he did careful planning, Krasnow did not create a formal business plan. Since the first round of financing was provided by Stemberg, Krasnow, and a

1. Source: One Source

few selected associates, such a document was not required. "We had every important data point we needed in the plan that we circulated. We didn't include the market potential—but we thought we knew the answer based on our preliminary research."

In May 1998, Krasnow closed a $3.5 million series A round of financing. He and Stemberg contributed $1 million each and they raised an additional $1.5 million from a small group of family and friends. Krasnow also put in place a $5 million line of credit with a major Boston bank that was to be used to fund equipment purchases and working capital needs.

More Research

Krasnow hired independent marketing consultant, Phyllis Wasserman (HBS 1977), to conduct additional customer research. Wasserman, who had worked with Krasnow at Staples for seven years, had recently retired from her position as Sr. Vice President of Advertising and Communications. Krasnow had been deeply involved in creating and executing Staples' marketing strategy, but in his new venture, he found that his responsibilities as CEO consumed most of his time. His experience in working with Wasserman and his trust in her abilities led him to call her in on a consulting basis to take charge of several important marketing projects.

As Wasserman dug into the research, she found that dry cleaning was "a low-interest" category. Customers apparently gave little thought to choosing a dry cleaner, even though most expressed some dissatisfaction with the dry cleaning service they currently used. Wasserman noted that quality was a major weakness in the existing dry cleaning environment. "I pushed very hard on that score, and we wasted about a month trying to articulate our brand positioning statement—trying to define what we meant by quality and how we would communicate that to our potential customers," she recalled.

Krasnow recalled, "We started out thinking that we should emphasize environmental friendliness, convenience, and price, but the environmental piece didn't resonate with potential customers." The message that he believed would be most powerful was one of unequalled convenience and uncompromising quality. The C.C., Llc customer should be able to drop off or pick up clothes at any hour of the day or night and do so with the assurance that a favorite shirt or skirt wouldn't be missing any buttons when it was returned. If an item of clothing were missing a button,

it should be replaced automatically. The company's quality pledge would be, "Cleaning Done Right Or It's Free." In spite of his insistence on getting things done right, Krasnow believed it was most important to emphasize the convenience message, rather than quality. Wasserman agreed that convenience was a clearer and more concrete message around which she could build the brand. She elaborated:

> Building a brand name that would convey that message was critical. It was to be our unique selling proposition. Furthermore, convenience would be as our customers defined it—not as we defined it. We wanted to give our customers as many different ways to do business with us as they wanted, and we asked them to choose. Our message was, "We're not asking you to do business in our way, rather tell us how you want to do business with us."

Some of the conveniences the company would offer were extended hours, drive through drop off and pick up, and secure lockers that would provide the same kind of round-the-clock access that ATM's had introduced to banking customers. Computer systems would be built to provide customers order-tracking capabilities. Though there were still many logistical issues to work through, total customer convenience would be the company's defining difference.

Real Estate and Store Planning

Krasnow determined that centralized cleaning was the most efficient way to run the business. He planned to create regional "hub and spoke" networks of 7–10 retail stores serviced by a central cleaning plant. He anticipated that one of his prototype stores could produce three times the industry's average revenue, but he planned to use the Boston market to test his hypotheses and refine the operating model.

The store design would be kept clean and simple. Though not all locations would be built to exactly the same specifications, the prototype would include a 2400-sq. ft. facility with dedicated parking and space to accommodate a drive-through lane. In addition, each store would have a secure lobby area stocked with individual clothes lockers that would be accessible 24 hours a day. A proprietary system would enable customers to pick up and drop off clothes at any hour of the day or night using a key coded locker system and personalized garment bags. (See Exhibit 1.)

STORE CONFIGURATION

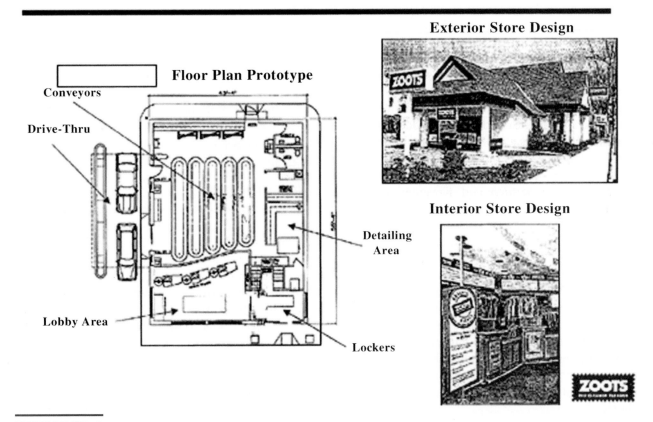

Floor Plan Prototype

Conveyors

Drive-Thru

Lobby Area

Detailing Area

Lockers

Exterior Store Design

Interior Store Design

EXHIBIT 1

Store Prototype

Densely populated, affluent areas, which had been identified as pockets of "heavy users" were targeted first. In early 1998, Krasnow signed leases for a retail store in Danvers and a site in Wilmington, MA, to be the "cleaning lab." He began looking for additional locations in metro Boston Nashua, NH, and Worcester and Springfield, MA. All of these stores were to be serviced by the Wilmington plant. The initial stores leased were in suburban locations. Once the Boston hub was functioning well, Krasnow planned to replicate it in other high volume markets.

Building the Brand

Krasnow and Stemberg had already selected a company name and logo, but they wanted Wasserman to take the next steps in developing the company's iden-

tity. She was delighted with the name, which she described as, "*in your face,* bold, different, yet likable." She believed that people not only noticed, but also remembered **ZOOTS** because the name was short, playful, and easy to remember. It conjured up images of slightly zany "Zoot suits" and its individual components worked well. The letter "Z" was unusual both usually and audibly and the double "O's" lent themselves to bold graphics. Wasserman was confident that the ZOOTS name would translate well to electronic as well as print media.

She focused her energies on the challenge of store design. The operations group determined the physical layout of the facility, but she was responsible for creating ZOOTS' visual identity. She hired an experienced retail design firm and set out on her own to visit the best of branded retailers to see how they conveyed their messages through physical space. She and Krasnow spent hours discussing the image that they wanted ZOOTS to convey and ways in which they could express that image through the store design and décor. A dark wood interior would create a relaxed and comfortable store environment, but a minimalist approach with stark white surfaces would convey the "clean" image. Bold colors and powerful graphics would be more memorable. Wasserman argued for a clean and modern look—one that signaled fast and efficient service. "Everything we do needs to communicate *bold, different, revolutionary, modern,* and *fast,*" she told Krasnow.

Together, Wasserman and Krasnow reviewed design proposals, selecting elements they liked from each. Light colored woods, bold graphics, and crisp, bright colored signage were combined to create the ZOOTS image. Blue was the background color of choice because of its association with water and cleanliness. Once they agreed on the key elements, Wasserman and her design team completed a set of drawings for Krasnow. She dropped them off early on a Friday, then left for a long weekend on Nantucket with her family. When Stemberg looked over the package later that afternoon, he was disappointed because he thought the overall effect was "boring."

Wasserman had been at her "getaway retreat" only moments when the phone rang. When she picked up the receiver, she heard Krasnow's voice, in which she detected a note of barely controlled panic. He quickly brought her up to date on Stemberg's reaction and asked, "What can we do about it now?" Because the Danvers project was set to break ground on the following Monday, there was little time for making substantive changes. Wasserman looked down at the purple jacket that she had tossed on the bed when she came in. She told Krasnow to relax. She would have the problem solved by Monday. She called the design firm, described the color of her jacket, and asked them to change all the blue surfaces to purple in the drawings.

When she handed the revised drawings to Krasnow on Monday morning, his first response was, "Oh my God, they are really *purple.*" She tacked the drawings to his walls and suggested he live with them for a few hours. Twenty four hours later, he concurred, "We're going to be purple." "The color shouts,"

Wasserman declared. "The first thing that you see is a building that is different and announces, 'I'm here.'"

Wasserman selected an ad agency and began hiring staff. In the summer of 1999, Krasnow asked her to come on board as the full-time senior marketing person or to find her own replacement. She agreed to join the ZOOTS team because, as she recalled, "It was a marketer's dream opportunity to develop a brand that hasn't existed before as opposed to trying to communicate and enhance or change a brand that already has an image in customers' minds."

Operational Plans

Store Operations

Krasnow's decision to focus on convenience defined the kind of services that would be available. ZOOTS customers could expect courtesy and efficiency at the counter, as well as reliability and quality in cleaning services. However, the real ZOOTS' difference lay in extended store hours (7:00 am–8:00 pm daily, 8:00 am–6:00 pm Saturday, and 11:00 am–6:00 pm Sunday), drive-through drop off and pick up facilities, and 24 hour access through a secure personal locker system. ZOOTS planned to offer Internet access to track order information, web-based coupons and promotions, and automated credit card billing. ZOOTS also provided Goodwill Industries drop boxes in every store. Customers could bring in their discarded clothing and get a receipt for the donations. ZOOTS then cleaned and delivered the donated clothing free of charge.

Though some of these services were available at competing dry cleaning establishments, others were completely novel—for example, the 24-hour pick up service. Customers interested in the service pre-registered, then received a personalized, bar coded ZOOTS garment bag and a personal pin number. Clothes could be packed in the garment bag and deposited in store drop boxes at any hour. When customers wanted to pick up their orders, they could call the store (or enter the request through the web site) to request that their clothes be put in a locker. An electronic bulletin board inside the store vestibule/locker area would display the customer's name and locker number that could be accessed by keying in the pin number.

Drive-through accommodations provided a more conventional convenience alternative for customers who wanted to avoid the hassle of parking. A ZOOTS customer service representative came out to greet the customer and pick up any dirty clothing, then returned with finished cleaning orders and hung them up in the back seat. Consumers who rated this service particularly convenient were likely to have children or dogs in the car. In spite of the many alternatives available, the vast majority of customers preferred the more conventional way of doing business, taking the time to come inside so that they could point out spots and discuss special handling with the counter person.

Inside each ZOOTS store, large menu boards displayed available services and their costs. (ZOOTS services included laundering, clothing repair and alteration, professional wet cleaning, shoe polishing and repair, garment storage, wedding gown cleaning and boxing, drapery and curtain cleaning, and leather cleaning and restoration in addition to dry cleaning.) These menu board also informed customers what was included in normal processing and what was not. For example, repairing hems and cuffs was complimentary, but ironing a garment that had eight or more narrow pleats would cost an additional $4.

Home delivery service was one convenience that was *not* part of the business model that Krasnow crafted in 1998. Although he knew that some dry cleaners offered that amenity, he decided that he would not include that service, at least initially, choosing to focus all attention on opening retail stores.

Each store had a full time manager and several regular part time counter people who worked at least 20 hours per week. All went through a training program and were actively encouraged to make suggestions for operational improvements.

Store personnel greeted customers, cataloged and "detailed" the garments (entered a description of the garment and how each was to be cleaned or handled into the computer). They asked questions about any unusual fabrics, noticeable stains or damage, specific customer requests and preferences, and the date the items were required. While creating the customer invoice, the counter person also generated a "quick slip" with the detailed instructions that was inserted into an individual cleaning bag with the customer's order. The store clerks then sorted the individual orders according to the specific services required

(cleaning, laundering, rush, repair) and bundled them in large transport bags marked with its own store number.

Plant Operations

ZOOTS' trucks picked up dirty laundry and returned finished orders to the retail stores twice daily, dropping dozens of clearly marked bags of dirty clothes at the central cleaning facility as it made its circuit. At the plant handlers opened the transport bags and removed the smaller detail bags, each of which included a copy of the "quick slip" with cleaning instructions, total number of pieces, and expected return date.

Approximately 20 people were stationed in booths tagging the garments individually. They used the quick slips inside each bag to determine what tags to affix. The tags denoted the originating store, special handling or repair instructions, and rush status. Because one garment could have multiple instructions, it was possible to have as many as 4 or 5 tags attached by staple, plastic tag, or safety pin through the manufacturer's label. Once the items were tagged, they were put into lots of approximately 100 garments, sorted by date needed and type of handling required.

After this initial tagging and sorting, the bins were moved to the cleaning area where there were five large (80 lb.) and three small hydrocarbon processing machines. Though the machines did a good job, many items had to pre-washed or pre-spotted before going into the machines. The plant team put pressure on the stores to tag spots more carefully so that they wouldn't be missed the first time around.

The cleaning process took approximately one hour. When it was completed, the clothes were again sorted. Shirts were batched for pressing while sweaters were sent through a steam tunnel on hangers. Approximately 40% of the items placed on hangers did not have to be pressed, including such items as silk blouses and dresses. These garments were placed on a conveyor rack that took them directly to the assembly area.

Suits, shirts, and pants generally required pressing. Once a garment had been pressed, it too was placed on the conveyor and sent to the assembly area where the garment was inspected for missing buttons, stains, or incorrect pressing. Experienced tailors were on hand to make repairs or mend any items that were discovered during the cleaning process whether or not the customer had pointed the problem out at the store. When process was completed, garments were sorted and hung on racks that corresponded to the tag color and delivery date.

An inspector then verified that the tags matched the garments and that the overall quality of the cleaned garments was acceptable. A "completion inspector" put a hole punch through the invoice and then a "bagger" bagged the garments using twist ties to secure all the items listed on the invoice. Depending on the number of steps required in the processing of a garment, as many as 10 or more people might handle a particular garment between drop off and pick up by the customer.

Running the Business
Off to a Rocky Start

When the last remains of the opening night party were swept away on the morning of October 30, 1998, the cleaning lab was ready "to let the games begin." The Danvers store was open and ready for business. All the systems were in place, the staff had been hired and trained, and the plant had already completed several test runs. However, all the best-laid plans quickly began to unravel. The office manager of ZOOTS headquarters failed to show up for work that morning. Not only had she decided to quit without giving notice, but she also drove off with all the cash register forms, garment tags, store coupons, and bank deposit slips in the trunk of her car. The Danvers store team had to scramble with manual back up systems while the plant had to make the best of a jerry-rigged tracking system.

Fortunately the business started slowly. Just as Krasnow had deliberately kept a low profile on the business start up, he also planned a very soft opening for the first store. No major fanfare, no radio or TV ads, only some local mailings with coupons. He wanted to start on a small scale so that he and the team could work through all the details. In the face of this minor opening disaster, he was relieved that they could make the necessary adjustments in relative obscurity. After a quick recovery from the opening fiasco, the ZOOTS team settled down to work on perfecting its systems for handling high volume and delivering on its promise of high quality service.

Quality and Efficiency Challenges

Soon after the cleaning lab opened, one of the cleaning lab employees stood at the entrance to the manager's door lamenting, "This shirt used to have sequins." The denuded shirt was one of many problems that surfaced as the crew learned the dry cleaning process—certain clothes just shouldn't be cleaned. What were occasional problems in "mom and pop" operations could easily become an almost daily occurrence at ZOOTS because of its anticipated high volume. "Rejects" or problem garments provided learning opportunities that enabled improvement, not only at the lab, but also at the retail store where garments were first received and inspected. The plant manager saw the sequined shirt as a call to action to develop a handbook for store personnel that would provide detailed instructions on what items should and should not be accepted for cleaning. Her goal was to eliminate unnecessary disappointment for the customers, but at the same time to control damage claims.

Claims were made because of damage to delicate fabrics or unusual materials, shrinkage, mysterious holes, fading, or missing buttons, but the most significant losses were those created by lost or missing items. If a tag fell off a garment or if the wrong tag was attached at the outset, it was extremely difficult for that garment to find its way back to its rightful owner. Because of the high volume at the ZOOTS plant, several new "orphaned" articles of clothing were created daily.

One member of the lab's management team took the initiative to create a spreadsheet of "orphan garments." He sent the sheet, which included detailed descriptions of the garments and their manufacturers, to the stores daily. Store personnel would then try to match up the items against specific customer complaints. Once the formal "orphan garment" program was organized, the average number of garments needing to be matched to their rightful owners was reduced from several full racks to approximately 15-20 at any given time. (Orphaned garments were donated to Goodwill Industries if they were unclaimed after 90 days.) Krasnow commented on how and why garments got lost in the first place:

> One problem we had initially was losing garments. The computer system we had was a store-based system and it didn't allow us to split an order in the production facility. If a garment/order had 5

pieces and one piece got pulled out for a stain or extra treatment or something, we didn't have a good system for matching it back up with the original order. It would get into a different queue that might take a couple of days. By the time it got back to the re-assembly point, the lot number sequences were cycling through again. This "old" piece would come up and somebody assembling the order at 2:00 am in the morning would just look at a number and stick it on in with the next round of lot numbers. Then, off went the shirt to another customer who was expecting to get a dress back. We have fixed that, but it's the kind of problem you don't anticipate until it happens.

The operating part of the business is proving to be absolutely mind-boggling in terms of the challenge to have good service recovery and not make the mistakes in the first place. That's really where the opportunity . . . it's not like other dry cleaners have solved the problem—they just have it on a much smaller scale. We need to do it at scale.

A five-person team was established to identify critical problem areas and to develop solutions. Krasnow reviewed the store and plant problems daily and made frequent site visits as he and the team struggled to get the operations running smoothly. The items that topped their list included: accurate order assembly, increased efficiency and streamlined handling, improved handling of special care garments. The ZOOTS team regarded the customer complaints as a report card. Though they might be specific, they almost always raised issues that could be addressed and corrected across the board with all accounts, stores, and customers.

When there were damages, as in the case of the once-sequined shirt, ZOOTS used the Fabricare Institute's guide for determining claims or appropriate reimbursement to the customer. In some instances, a claim could be made against the manufacturer for faulty merchandise. As far as meeting efficiency goals, the cleaning lab still had a long way to go. Seasoned pressers could handle up to 50 shirts an hour, but the new pressers in the ZOOTS' lab averaged far less than that.

Cranking Up the Volume

The second and third ZOOTS stores opened in West Roxbury and South Attleboro, MA, in early 1999. When it had operated only one store, the ZOOTS team could overwhelm operating challenges with personal attention from the store manager, the plant supervisor, or headquarters staff. However, with multiple stores up and running, the systems had to take over.

ZOOTS ran its first major promotion, an insert ad in the Boston Globe with a $5 coupon, in late March 1999. At the same time, Krasnow granted his first newspaper interview to an old friend at the Boston Globe. At long last, he was willing to disclose the basic business concept and outline his plans for ZOOTS' growth (Exhibit 2).

The article was very positive and the $5 coupon that ran with the ad brought people into the stores in droves. However, the incredible spike in demand resulted in a ZOOTS systems meltdown. The Wilmington facility knew it was coming, but was simply not ready to handle the volume. Krasnow was the first to admit that, in spite of his retailing experience, the operations in this service-intensive business were quite different than they were in office supplies and food retailing. He recalled:

> Many people in dry cleaning have run
> $1 million dry cleaners. The issues that we have
> with dry cleaning are not the actual dry cleaning or the pressing. It's the process management of thousands and thousands of garments a day that are all different, that have to go through the factory and come out on time—all while dealing with exceptions or premium service for special treatments—it adds to the complexity.

The marketing group immediately cut back on advertising and promotions. The challenge the ZOOTS team faced going forward was not in getting customers to try the service, but in figuring out how to get the dry cleaning done to their satisfaction. Krasnow admitted that the team underestimated the "manufacturing" process. He elaborated,

> If I've made a mistake it's been in not being
> quick enough to bring in a full partner who was
> an operator, because we underestimated just how difficult the executional side of the cleaning production is. It is outside of my range of previous experience. We went in thinking that it was not that hard, but what has been hard is the execution.

Business

THE BOSTON GLOBE • WEDNESDAY, MARCH 31, 1999

Looking to clean up

With Zoots, duo that helped create Staples aim to be national players in dry-cleaning business

By Chris Reidy
GLOBE STAFF

PAULA NEWTON, WHO commutes nearly 100 miles a day, is delighted with Zoots, the new dry-cleaning chain started by some of the same folks who made Staples Inc. a retail phenomenon.

Unlike the dry cleaners near her home in the Magnolia section of Gloucester, she can drop off or pick up her laundry 24 hours a day. And thanks to the drive-through window at the Zoots in Danvers, "I don't even have to get out of my car," she says.

Zoots is the brainchild of Staples co-founder Thomas G. Stemberg and Todd Krasnow, one of Staples's first employees.

For Stemberg, Zoots may represent a retail hat trick of sorts, certifying his status as a serial entrepreneur.

In 1986, he helped launch Staples, going from zero to $7.12 billion in sales in 12 years. He's a key investor in KaBloom, a new, local chain of flower stores.

And now he and partner Krasnow look to be national players in dry cleaning, with Krasnow running the day-to-day operations of Zoots while Stemberg remains as chief executive of Staples.

Will the Staples golden touch rub off on the mundane world of pressed pants and starched shirts?

Some in the dry-cleaning industry don't think so. They note that many

ZOOTS, Page D4

Zoots CEO Todd Krasnow showed off some dry cleaning outside the West Roxbury store.

Retail hat trick

A cofounder of Staples Inc., Thomas G. Stemberg is a major force, and investor, in two new retail chains with ideas of going national. Staples, KaBloom, and Zoots each entered a fragmented mom-and-pop industry. All three chains seem to share the same belief: that size and efficiency will allow a big chain to better serve customers and underprice smaller rivals.

STAPLES

Established in 1986, Westborough-based Staples has gone from zero to $7.12 billion in annual sales in a mere 12 years. It operates 913 stores worldwide that sell a wide variety of office supplies at lower prices than many competitors. Stemberg is chief executive.

KaBloom

Wowed by a flower shop he saw in Germany, Stemberg helped launch a US knockoff called KaBloom last year that is trying to make Americans think about low-price flowers as an everyday purchase. Plans calls for KaBloom to grow from three stores into a national chain. Stemberg plays no role in day-to-day operations.

ZOOTS

Zoots, a dry-cleaning venture Stemberg cofounded with Todd Krasnow, opened its first store last year. The three-store chain looks to go national with Krasnow in charge of day-to-day operations, offering low prices and conveniences such as drive-through service and 24-hour access.

EXHIBIT 2

Boston Globe Article

Source: Copyright © 1999 by Globe Newspaper Co (MA). Reproduced with permission of Globe Newspaper Co (MA) via Copyright Clearance Center.

Another Option

The ZOOTS news item piqued the interest of Cliff Sirlin, a co-founder and owner of Cleaner Options. Sirlin's partner, Andy Applebaum, was on his honeymoon in Hawaii, but Sirlin was so intrigued by the article, which a Boston friend had faxed to him, that he picked up the phone and called Krasnow immediately. He explained that he and Applebaum owned a home delivery dry cleaning business that operated in joint ventures and franchising agreements with local dry cleaners. He wanted to know how the two companies could work together. Within 2 months, Krasnow had completed his due diligence, had acquired the business, and had introduced ZOOTS first home delivery route in the Boston market.

Growth Plans

ZOOTS raised a $9 million second round of angel funding in January 1999. Individual investors included Stemberg, Krasnow, and friends and family. By April 1999, Krasnow and Stemberg began to discuss raising a large round of venture capital to fund more aggressive growth. The first 3 stores were performing well against the targets that Krasnow had established, based on the performance data he had gleaned from the 13 dry cleaners included in his original research. The board urged him to accelerate the rollout of the business. Though Boston was a promising market and its expansion was a priority, finding good real estate was extremely difficult, so growth there would be slower than anticipated.

EXHIBIT 2 (*continued*)

THE BOSTON GLOBE • WEDNESDAY, MARCH 31, 1999

Emerging **Business**

A REPORT ON NEW ENGLAND'S GROWING COMPANIES

Duo look to clean up with Zoots

■ ZOOTS
Continued from Page D1

Americans have gone casual, and khakis in the office often translate into flat sales at the dry cleaners.

What's more, people are emotionally attached to their clothes and don't like entrusting them to strangers; instead, folks tend to patronize family-owned dry cleaners that have been in business for two or three generations. Get too big and risk losing that all-important personal touch. That's why no dry-cleaning chain has yet managed to expand nationwide.

"This is one business you can't McDonald's-ize," says Charles Anton, vice president of Anton's Cleaners, a 40-store, Tewksbury-based chain that's one of the largest in Massachusetts.

As a customer, Newton seems less concerned with a dry-cleaner's pedigree than with price and convenience.

"By the time I get home from work, the dry cleaners near my home are closed," she says.

According to Newton, Zoots provides her with lower prices and added conveniences: She can check in advance whether her husband's shirts are ready by visiting the company's Web site at Zootscleaner.com.

Krasnow and Stemberg are betting that there are a lot of busy people like Newton from two-worker households.

"We're trying to make [dry cleaning] less of a hassle for customers," Krasnow says.

In Zoots, the pair envision a national chain with hundreds of stores that does for dry cleaning what Staples has done for office products – offering better service at a lower price.

Last week, Zoots opened a store in West Roxbury, the third in the chain. By year's end, plans call for 20 stores. Most will have drive-through windows and special lockers where customers can drop off or pick up their clothing 24 hours a day.

According to Krasnow and Stemberg, there are similarities between the highly fragmented dry-cleaning industry of mom-and-pop stores today and the office-supply market of the late 1980s.

With so many mom-and-pop stores, there's an opportunity for Krasnow and Stemberg to apply their Harvard Business School training to devise a more efficient dry-cleaning operation.

One way to achieve efficiencies is to have most of the cleaning done at a central location that serves a network of stores. Mom-and-pop dry cleaners, in contrast, tend to do most of their cleaning in the back of their stores.

Centralizing operations may offer another bonus. Many mom-and-pops use harsh cleaning solvents that can hurt the environment.

By using one cleaning facility to serve a number of stores, Zoots claims it can use "greener" high-tech cleaning techniques, something many customers seem to be interested in.

Sometime later this year, plans call for Zoots to test its business model in another, as-yet-undisclosed market.

On paper, the strategy makes sense, but there are skeptics.

"You have all these guys in the ivory tower making assumptions, but most of them have never pressed a pair of pants," says Anton of Anton's Cleaners.

These aren't the best of times for the industry. Not only is there a trend toward casual clothing, but there's always the possibility that some new miracle fabric will come along that doesn't require as much dry-cleaning as worsteds and wools.

When "polyester was a tacky fad" in the 1970s, a lot of dry cleaners went under, notes David Uchic, a vice president of the International Fabricare Institute, an industry trade group.

Today Uchic estimates there are about 34,000 dry-cleaning stores in a nearly $7 billion industry. While some stores are doing quite well, generally business is "soft," he says.

Soft sales haven't deterred others from exploring the possibility of building a large dry-cleaning chain with stores in many different states.

Outside of New England, a company called DryClean Depot seeks to slash prices by operating giant stores with on-site facilities designed to clean large volumes of clothing.

Meanwhile, another company is pushing a technology that cleans without harsh solvents; using this technique, dry-cleaning franchises called Hangers will market themselves as an environmentally friendly alternative to old-fashioned methods.

Sam Brickle, the Rhode Island investor who holds the New England franchise, predicts 20 Hangers could be up and running in the region by the end of the year.

Zoots also has big plans with an initial investment of $20 million. Of that amount, Stemberg contributed $5 million, Krasnow $2 million.

What inspired two men who had devoted more than a decade of their lives to paper clips and legal pads to try dry cleaning?

Stemberg, it seems, keeps files on ideas for new retail chains, and his file on dry cleaning had achieved critical mass.

"I experienced a lot of problems as a customer," Stemberg says, adding: "You'd get your shirts back with two buttons missing, and the stores were never open when you wanted."

From such discontent, the idea for Zoots was born.

Anton's Cleaners once had visions of being a big chain, operating more than 100 stores in the early 1990s.

In those days, it, too, used centralized cleaning facilities. But ultimately, it decided to retrench and went back to having its stores do most of their cleaning on the premises.

The cost of shipping clothes back and forth from stores to a central facility erased any savings, Anton says, and cleaning on-site makes it easier to offer same-day service.

"This is a business about personal relationships," he says. Dry cleaning is "not a commodity. . . . The minute you have to get on a plane, you know your [dry-cleaning] chain is too big."

Krasnow and Stemberg have heard nay-saying before.

In its early days, no one gave Staples much of a chance either; the computer was to make office supplies obsolete.

"Society was going to go paperless," Stemberg recalls.

It's the same thing with dry cleaning and casual days, he thinks. Jeans may be showing up more at the office, but many people have less time than ever to wash and press them.

"Staples was a revolutionary idea, and this could be as revolutionary as Staples," Stemberg says of Zoots.

It won't be industry experts who will determine whether Zoots succeeds, adds Krasnow. "It will be the customers."

Chely La Pointe, manager of the West Roxbury Zoots, checked finished laundry.

Thomas G. Stemberg

Furthermore, once news of the ZOOTS concept was public knowledge, the board felt it was important to claim as many geographic markets as possible before competitors blossomed in every city. The Connecticut market was the most obvious next step. It would be a new hub with its own cleaning facility and a separate marketing umbrella, but it was proximate enough to headquarters for frequent site visits and close management supervision. Several sites were leased in the Hartford, CT, market and a central facility was underway in Wallingford, CT. The ZOOTS management team expected that the new stores would produce revenues and, eventually, profits at the same rate as the three stores already operating in Massachusetts.

Krasnow and his board began to push beyond the Connecticut borders to consider markets that were not so real estate-constrained. The goal was to locate profitable markets where more stores could be opened quickly. Krasnow, Stemberg, and other Staples board members pointed out that Staples had initially concentrated its growth in major metropolitan areas thinking that secondary markets would be more difficult to run efficiently and that they would be less profitable. When they opened those markets in later years, they discovered that, in fact, these investments were very profitable. That experience suggested that if ZOOTS ran into difficulties finding locations in the major metropolitan areas, it could move directly into secondary markets and build a profitable enterprise much more quickly.

When Boston Markets (formerly Boston Chicken) declared bankruptcy, it closed a number of stores and put the real estate on the block. Krasnow's team reviewed the list and found that there were sites available in the Virginia Beach, VA area that might provide ZOOTS a strong entry opportunity. Several members of the senior management team flew to Virginia Beach to investigate the potential of the Boston Market sites. Though the team rejected all of the Boston Market sites, they did find several other potential stores available that met their expansion criteria. They also found satisfactory space for the central plant. The operating economics looked good, and a large labor force was nearby.

In July 1999, Krasnow signed a lease for a new cleaning lab in Portsmouth, Virginia. The team spent the next few months working on getting permits, building the central facility, and securing store sites. Krasnow was closing in on his goal of creating a profitable business model that could be replicated in multiple geographic locations.

Krasnow was also making plans for entering the Philadelphia market. His real estate team located a site for the central cleaning facility and was scouting the neighborhoods for appropriate store locations.

Another major consideration was the purchase of a chain of dry cleaning stores in Ohio. Widmer's had both brick and mortar retail stores and a successful home delivery service. The Cleaner Options acquisition and integration had gone smoothly and Kras-

October 12, 1999

Dear valued shareholders,

The third quarter has been an active one for Zoots. We have seen our business develop in a number of important ways, but we have also missed several targets.

1   Acquisitions: On September 15th, we acquired Widmer's, the leading dry cleaning chain in Cincinnati. Widmer's operates 8 stores and 15 home delivery routes. In addition, they use a 30,000 square foot production facility for their cleaning, which is consistent with Zoots' centralized production philosophy. Given the excess capacity of this plant, we believe we can more than double the volume processed there, by opening Zoots stores and routes in areas not currently served by Widmer's.

2. Real Estate: We finished the quarter with 8 Zoots stores in operation, 2 fewer than our target. We believe that we will miss our year end target (20 stores) as 4 stores slide into early 2000. The delays have been caused by challenges in financing development sites and permitting. More importantly, the missed targets tell us we need a far more robust real estate pipeline to meet our 2000 objectives. In part, the pipeline is behind because of difficulty in staffing the real estate department. We anticipate resolving our staffing issues in the 4th quarter.

    During the quarter, we began construction on two 30,000 square foot cleaning laboratories: one in Portsmouth, Virginia and the other in Wallingford, Connecticut, just outside of Hartford. Both are scheduled to open late this year or early next year.

3. Operations: Store revenue has continued to exceed our expectations for the stores that are open, although, in total, store revenue is behind our budget due to the delayed openings. Home pick-up and delivery revenue is also exceeding our plans. At the end of the quarter nine routes were in operation in the Boston market. Store, cleaning lab and delivery expenses were in line with expectations.

    On October 4th, we began providing dry cleaning service for Streamline.com, a Boston based home delivery grocery service. Streamline.com is a publicly traded company that has offered dry cleaning as part of its service mix since its inception. We are providing the dry cleaning under the Clean'r Cleaner name (a trademark owned by Zoots).

4. Human resources: Bob Anarumo joined us in August as Chief Operating Officer. A copy of our internal announcement about Bob is attached.

EXHIBIT 3

October 1999 Letter to Shareholders

now saw acquisition of well-operated chains as another way to speed ZOOTS growth.

In June 1999, ZOOTS completed a confidential offering memorandum for 14,000,000 Class G shares at $2.50. Krasnow arranged his schedule to meet with venture capitalists around the country. In September 1999, ZOOTS closed a $38 million round of financing with Charlesbank Capital Partners, Chase Venture Capital, Weston Presidio Partners, and Dorset Capital as well as Krasnow, Stemberg and many of the individual investors who participated in the earlier rounds.

Getting Results

In August 1999, ZOOTS had broken ground for the Porstmouth/Virginia Beach cleaning facility and it was building out several retail store sites. The grand opening was planned for December 1999, but Krasnow was very uneasy about the decision long before the first store opened. He commented:

> The plan going into Portsmouth—it's almost laughable now—if it weren't so painful. We were going to open up 8 stores in the Virginia Beach/Portsmouth market by the end of 1999. That's how easy we thought the real estate was going to be. It turned out that getting the right real estate was every bit as hard as it was in New England. Our initial assessment of easy real estate was incorrect.
>
> Besides the real estate challenge, another important obstacle surfaced in mid-to-late August. We began to develop a new sales

Phyllis Wasserman joined us as Vice President, Marketing. Phyllis had been Senior Vice President, Advertising at Staples, where she successfully built a strong brand image through print, catalog and broadcast advertising. After leaving Staples, Phyllis consulted to a number of companies, including Zoots.

Paul Tritman joined us on October 11th, as Vice President, Production. Paul fills a critical position in which he will lead our efforts to improve cleaning quality and reliability while increasing efficiency. He was Director of Manufacturing and Controls Engineering for Kidde-Fenwal, Inc.

5. Financial: We recently closed a $38,000,000 equity financing, our first financing involving institutional investors. Our lead investor was Charlesbank Capital Partners. Other institutional investors include Chase Venture Capital Associates, Weston Presidio, and Dorset Capital. Mike Eisenson of Charlesbank and Steve Murray of Chase have joined our Board.

We expect to extend our bank credit facility from $5 million to $12 million in the coming month.

Finally, it is worth noting that our Danvers store celebrated its first anniversary last week. It has certainly been an exciting year since that first store opening day in October, 1998. On behalf of everyone at Zoots, thank you for giving us the support which has allowed us to build our business quickly.

Sincerely,

Todd Krasnow
C.E.O.

EXHIBIT 3 *(continued)*

EXHIBIT 3 (continued)

August, 1999

To the Zoots Family:

I am delighted to announce that Bob Anarumo will be joining Zoots on August 30th as Chief Operating Officer.

For the past six years, Bob has been President and CEO of the largest franchise group in Boston Market, with a territory spanning from Canada to Virginia and revenue of over $400 million. Bob opened or acquired 360 restaurants, and ran the most (and often only) profitable franchise group within the Boston Market network. Prior to Boston Market, Bob ran a 300 restaurant division of Pizza Hut. He also led the development of Pizza Hut delivery, which required the creation of locations and processes completely outside of the existing restaurant business. His drive to create well-run, customer focused operations are clearly demonstrated and fit our own culture exceptionally well.

As soon as Bob learns the Zoots business and gets to know our people, he will assume responsibility for all day-to-day operations. This includes store, home delivery and cleaning lab operations, as well as our distribution, logistics and human resource functions. This will allow me to spend more time with our marketing team to drive sales and our real estate team to explore significant real estate opportunities. Marketing and real estate will report to me. In addition, I shall focus on Zoots' long range development, including acquisition opportunities, financing, and other projects. Tom Sager and his team, along with JJ Pellegrino will report to me in these efforts. Larry Kennedy and the systems team will work closely with Bob, Tom and me to insure the continued development of systems that support our operation and enable rapid growth.

Bob and his family will be relocating from New Jersey. Please join me in welcoming him to Zoots.

Sincerely,

Todd Krasnow

19 Needham Street, Suite #2, Newton, MA 02461-1622
Tel: 617-558-9666 Fax: 617-558-9667

---

projection model based on the data we were getting from our own stores and it really gave me cause to worry. Our initial real estate model was based on the 13 dry cleaners that we had gotten data from before we started ZOOTS. When we began to get reliable data from our own stores—which, by mid summer, included good and bad stores—we tightened up the criteria. The new model we built indicated that there was far less potential for building strong new stores in the Portsmouth market than we had anticipated. We ran the new model for the first time in mid-summer. We realized, 'Oops, because of the tight real estate market, we aren't going to have the number of stores we anticipated and the stores we do have aren't going to produce the sales we projected. How are we going to achieve the economies of scale we need in the plant?'

Based on our new info, it was clear that the Portsmouth and Virginia Beach sites didn't have as much potential as we had first thought. We did the math and discovered that we would not be able to fill the Portsmouth facility with the eight stores we had planned in the Virginia Beach and Norfolk markets.

We were under construction and couldn't turn the process around. We had just started the delivery business (the acquisition of Cleaner Options in NY), and had to ask the question of 'how are we ever going to get ourselves working properly in Virginia Beach?'

The original model had indicated that ZOOTS could open eight stores in the Portsmouth/Virginia Beach area, each of which would do "x" amount of business. By late August, Krasnow concluded that,

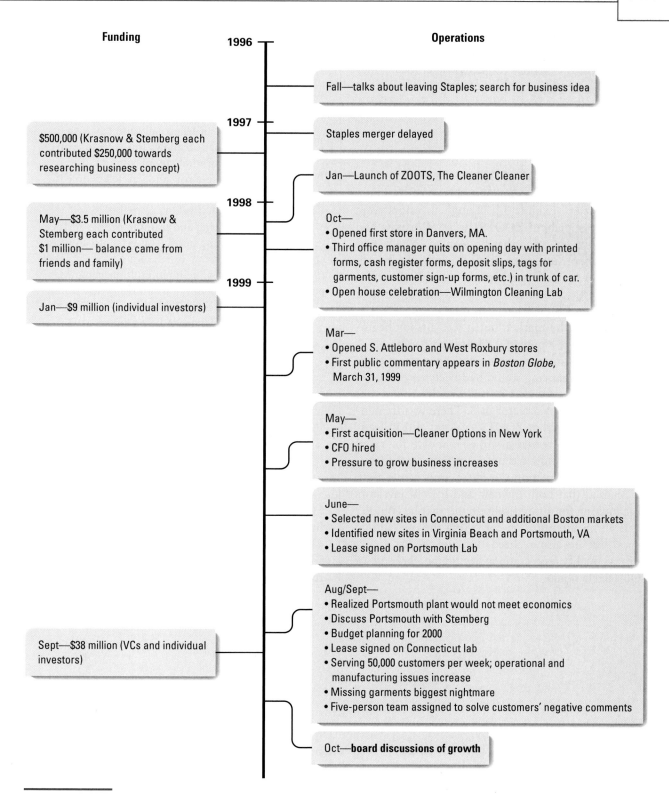

Funding

1996

Operations

Fall—talks about leaving Staples; search for business idea

1997

Staples merger delayed

$500,000 (Krasnow & Stemberg each contributed $250,000 towards researching business concept)

Jan—Launch of ZOOTS, The Cleaner Cleaner

1998

May—$3.5 million (Krasnow & Stemberg each contributed $1 million— balance came from friends and family)

Oct—
• Opened first store in Danvers, MA.
• Third office manager quits on opening day with printed forms, cash register forms, deposit slips, tags for garments, customer sign-up forms, etc.) in trunk of car.
• Open house celebration—Wilmington Cleaning Lab

1999

Jan—$9 million (individual investors)

Mar—
• Opened S. Attleboro and West Roxbury stores
• First public commentary appears in *Boston Globe*, March 31, 1999

May—
• First acquisition—Cleaner Options in New York
• CFO hired
• Pressure to grow business increases

June—
• Selected new sites in Connecticut and additional Boston markets
• Identified new sites in Virginia Beach and Portsmouth, VA
• Lease signed on Portsmouth Lab

Aug/Sept—
• Realized Portsmouth plant would not meet economics
• Discuss Portsmouth with Stemberg
• Budget planning for 2000
• Lease signed on Connecticut lab
• Serving 50,000 customers per week; operational and manufacturing issues increase
• Missing garments biggest nightmare
• Five-person team assigned to solve customers' negative comments

Sept—$38 million (VCs and individual investors)

Oct—**board discussions of growth**

EXHIBIT 4
ZOOTS Timeline

"we could only open four stores, not the eight as planned, and that each of the stores would only do two thirds of the business expected. That means that we would have only one third of the volume that we used to justify this move. More sales were needed—the question was 'from where?'"

October 1999

The shareholders letter of October 12, 1999 chronicled both the successes and the misses of the most recent quarter (Exhibit 3). Though investors were very optimistic about ZOOTS' future, Krasnow had some serious concerns that he wanted to talk over with Stemberg first, then bring them to the board. The first of his concerns was the quality of service and efficient operations. The second had to do with the specifics of the Portsmouth market. ZOOTS was committed to the market, but it was already beginning to look like a potential disaster on paper.

An overarching concern was how to manage growth. The financing round had been very successful. Though they took $38 million, the round was over-subscribed by a factor of 3. There was tremendous optimism about ZOOTS' concept and its leadership team. There was a strong mandate for rapid growth, but Krasnow did not want to grow the business without correcting the operational issues first. He realized that both his new and his old investors were looking for a rapid rollout and that he couldn't focus all his attention on correcting the operational issues, but he also realized that not meeting customers' quality expectations would be the end of ZOOTS. He noted:

That's the balancing act. We've been all over this issue and have gone from 'let's open in 20 markets in two years' to 'let's shut down the growth and focus on getting the operational stuff perfect.'

There is a very big difference between understanding this stuff intellectually and having a little spreadsheet that calculates this stuff for you and actually doing what you need to do. If it snows for 3 days in a row and you tell people to go home, they quit because they think, 'What kind of job is that, if I don't get paid?' Now you're back to hiring and training people and they are performing poorly—it gets into all those human dynamics.

The challenge of being in multiple geographies while still identifying and really fine tuning the business model, while also trying to grow, those are the challenges of being a start-up. I actually don't think there's anything particularly unique about these challenges. Individual elements are specific to my business, but this is what it means to be a start-up. I think that every business that has a lot of growth potential goes through this. My belief is even companies that are incredibly sexy from the outside, like e-Bay, etc. totally different type of business and workforce—everything is different—but they have the same issues.

Krasnow considered all the many challenges he had already overcome in launching ZOOTS (Exhibit 4) and knew that he would have to come up with some good answers about how to balance the operating challenges with the imperative for growth.

Nike: Sweatshops and Business Ethics

10

This case was prepared by Charles W. L. Hill, the University of Washington.

Introduction

Nike is in many ways the quintessential global corporation. Established in 1972 by former University of Oregon track star Phil Knight, Nike is now one of the leading marketers of athletic shoes and apparel on the planet. The company has $10 billion in annual revenues and sells its products in some 140 countries. Nike does not do any manufacturing. Rather, it designs and markets its products, while contracting for their manufacture from a global network of 600 factories scattered around the globe that employ some 550,000 people.[1] This huge corporation has made founder Phil Knight into one of the richest people in America. Nike's marketing phrase "Just do it!" and "swoosh" logo have become as recognizable in popular culture as the faces of its celebrity sponsors, such as Michael Jordan and Tiger Woods.

For all of its successes, the company has been dogged for more than a decade by repeated and persistent accusations that its products are made in "sweatshops" where workers, many of them children, slave away in hazardous conditions for below-subsistence wages. Nike's wealth, its detractors claim, has been built upon the backs of the world's poor. To many, Nike has become a symbol of the evils of globalization: a rich Western corporation exploiting the world's poor to provide expensive shoes and apparel to the pampered con-

sumers of the developed world. Nike's Niketown stores have become standard targets for anti-globalization protestors. Nike has been the target of repeated criticism and protests from several nongovernmental organizations, such as San Fransisco–based Global Exchange, a human-rights organization dedicated to promoting environmental, political, and social justice around the world.[2] News media have run exposés on working conditions in foreign factories that supply Nike. Students on the campuses of several major U.S. universities with which Nike has lucrative sponsorship deals have protested against the ties, citing Nike's use of sweatshop labor.

For its part, Nike has taken many steps to counter the protests. Yes, it admits, there have been problems in some overseas factories. But the company has signaled a commitment to improving working conditions. It requires that foreign subcontractors meet minimum thresholds for working conditions and pay. It has arranged for factories to be examined by independent auditors and terminated contracts with factories that do not comply with its standards. But for all this effort, the company continues to be a target of protests.

The Case Against Nike

Typical of the exposés against Nike was a *CBS 48 Hours* news report that aired on October 17, 1996.[3] Reporter Roberta Basin visited a Nike factory in Vietnam. With a shot of the factory, her commentary began:

This case is intended to be used as a basis for class discussion rather than as an illustration of either effective or ineffective handling of the situation. Reprinted by permission of Charles W. L. Hill.

C129

The signs are everywhere of an American invasion in search of cheap labor. Millions of people who are literate, disciplined, and desperate for jobs. This is Niketown near what used to be called Saigon, one of four factories Nike doesn't own but subcontracts to make a million shoes a month. It takes 25,000 workers, mostly young women, to "Just Do It."

But the workers here don't share in Nike's huge profits. They work six days a week for only $40 a month, just 20 cents an hour.

Baskin interviews one of the workers in the factory, a young woman named Lap. Baskin tells the listener:

Her basic wage, even as a sewing team leader, still doesn't amount to the minimum wage. . . . She's down to 85 pounds. Like most of the young women who make shoes, she has little choice but to accept the low wages and long hours. Nike says that it requires all subcontractors to obey local laws; but Lap has already put in much more overtime than the annual legal limit: 200 hours.

Baskin then asks Lap what would happen if she wanted to leave, if she was sick or had to take care of a sick relative: could she leave the factory? Through a translator, Lap replies:

It is not possible if you haven't made enough shoes. You have to meet the quota before you can go home.

The clear implication of the story was that Nike was at fault for allowing such working conditions to persist in the Vietnamese factory (which, incidentally, was owned by a Korean company).

Another example of an attack on Nike's subcontracting practices occurred in June 1996. It was launched by USA, a foundation largely financed by labor unions and domestic-apparel manufacturers that oppose free trade with low-wage countries. According to Joel Joseph, chairman of the foundation, a popular line of high-priced Nike sneakers, the "Air Jordans," were put together by eleven-year-olds in Indonesia making 14 cents per hour. A Nike spokeswoman, Donna Gibbs, countered that this was false. According to Gibbs, the average worker made 240,000 *rupiah* ($103) a month working a maximum fifty-four-hour week, or about 45 cents per hour. Moreover, Gibbs noted, Nike had staff members in each factory monitoring conditions to make sure that they obeyed local minimum-wage and child-labor laws.[4]

Another example of the criticism against Nike is the following extracts from a newsletter published by Global Exchange:[5]

During the 1970s, most Nike shoes were made in South Korea and Taiwan. When workers there gained new freedom to organize and wages began to rise, Nike looked for "greener pastures." It found them in Indonesia and China, where Nike started producing in the 1980s, and most recently in Vietnam.

The majority of Nike shoes are made in Indonesia and China, countries with governments that prohibit independent unions and set the minimum wage at rock bottom. The Indonesian government admits that the minimum wage there does not provide enough to supply the basic needs of one person, let alone a family. In early 1997 the entry-level wage was a miserable $2.46 a day. Labor groups estimate that a livable wage in Indonesia is about $4.00 a day.

In Vietnam the pay is even less—20 cents an hour, or a mere $1.60 a day. But in urban Vietnam, three simple meals cost about $2.10 a day, and then of course there is rent, transportation, clothing, health care, and much more. According to Thuyen Nguyen of Vietnam Labor Watch, a living wage in Vietnam is at least $3 a day.

In another attack on Nike's practices, Global Exchange published a report in September 1997 on working conditions in four Nike and Reebok subcontractor's factories in southern China.[6] Global Exchange, in conjunction with two Hong Kong human-rights groups, had interviewed workers at the factories in 1995 and again in 1997. According to Global Exchange, in one factory, a Korean-owned subcontractor for Nike, workers as young as thirteen earned as little as 10 cents an hour and toiled up to seventeen hours daily in enforced silence. Talking during work was not allowed, and violators were fined $1.20 to $3.60, according to the report. The practices were in violation of Chinese labor law, which states that no child under sixteen may work in a factory, and the Chinese minimum-wage requirement of $1.90 for an eight-hour day. Nike condemned the study as "erroneous," charging that it incorrectly stated the wages of workers and made irresponsible accusations.

Global Exchange, however, continued to be a major thorn in Nike's side. In November 1997, the organization obtained and then leaked a confidential report by Ernst & Young of an audit that Nike had commissioned of a factory in Vietnam owned by a Nike subcontractor.[7] The factory had 9,200 workers and made 400,000 pairs of shoes a month. The Ernst & Young report painted a dismal picture of thousands of young women, most under age twenty-five, laboring ten and a half hours a day, six days a week, in excessive heat, noise, and foul air, for slightly more than $10 a week. The report also found that workers with skin or breathing problems had not been transferred to departments free of chemicals, and that more than half the workers who dealt with dangerous chemicals did not wear protective masks or gloves. It claimed workers were exposed to carcinogens that exceeded local legal standards by 177 times in parts of the plant and that 77% of the employees suffered from respiratory problems.

Put on the defensive yet again, Nike called a news conference and pointed out that it had commissioned the report, and had acted on it.[8] The company stated that it had formulated an action plan to deal with the problems cited in the report, and had slashed overtime, improved safety and ventilation, and reduced the use of toxic chemicals. The company also asserted that the report showed that Nike's internal monitoring system had performed exactly as it should have. According to one spokesman:

> This shows our system of monitoring works. . . . We have uncovered these issues clearly before anyone else, and we have moved fairly expeditiously to correct them.

Nike's Responses

Unaccustomed to playing defense, Nike formulated a number of strategies and tactics over the years to deal with the problems of working conditions and pay in subcontractor facilities. In 1996, Nike hired one-time U.S. ambassador to the United Nations, representative, and former Atlanta mayor Andrew Young to assess working conditions in subcontractors' plants around the world. The following year, after a two-week tour of three countries that included inspections of fifteen factories, Young released a mildly critical report. He informed Nike it was doing a good job in its treatment of workers, though it should do better. According to Young, he did not see:

> sweatshops, or hostile conditions. . . . I saw crowded dorms . . . but the workers were eating at least two meals a day on the job and making

what I was told were subsistence wages in those cultures.[9]

Young was widely criticized by human-rights and labor groups for not taking his own translators and for doing slipshod inspections, an assertion he repeatedly denied.

In 1996, Nike joined a presidential task force designed to find a way of banishing sweatshops in the shoe and clothing industries. The task force included industry leaders, representatives from human-rights groups, and labor leaders. In April 1997, they announced an agreement for workers' rights that U.S. companies could agree to when manufacturing abroad. The accord limited the work week to sixty hours, and called for paying at least the local minimum wage in foreign factories. The task force also agreed to establish an independent monitoring association—later named the Fair Labor Association (FLA)—to assess whether companies are abiding by the code.[10]

The FLA now includes among its members the Lawyers Committee for Human Rights, the National Council of Churches, the International Labor Rights Fund, 135 universities (universities have extensive licensing agreements with sports-apparel companies), and companies such as Nike, Reebok, and Levi Strauss.

In early 1997, Nike also began to commission independent organizations such as Ernst & Young to audit the factories of its subcontractors. In September 1997, Nike tried to show its critics that it was involved in more than just a public-relations exercise when it terminated its relationship with four Indonesian subcontractors, stating that they had refused to comply with the company's standards for wage levels and working conditions. Nike identified one of the subcontractors, Seyon, which manufactured specialty sports gloves for Nike, saying that Seyon refused to meet a 10.7% increase in the monthly wage, to $70.30, required by the Indonesian government in April 1997.[11]

On May 12, 1998, in a speech given at the National Press Club, Phil Knight spelled out in detail a series of initiatives designed to improve working conditions for the 500,000 people that make products for Nike at subcontractor facilities.[12] Among the initiatives Knight highlighted were the following:

> We have effectively changed our minimum age limits from the ILO (International Labor

Organization) standards of 15 in most countries and 14 in developing countries to 18 in all footwear manufacturing and 16 in all other types of manufacturing (apparel, accessories and equipment). Existing workers legally employed under the former limits were grandfathered into the new requirements.

During the past 13 months we have moved to a 100 percent factory audit scheme, where every Nike contract factory will receive an annual check by PricewaterhouseCoopers teams who are specially trained on our Code of Conduct Owner's Manual and audit/monitoring procedures. To date they have performed about 300 such monitoring visits. In a few instances in apparel factories they have found workers under our age standards. Those factories have been required to raise their standards to 17 years of age, to require three documents certifying age, and to redouble their efforts to ensure workers meet those standards through interviews and records checks.

Our goal was to ensure workers around the globe are protected by requiring factories to have no workers exposed to levels above those mandated by the permissible exposure limits (PELs) for chemicals prescribed in the OSHA indoor air quality standards.[13]

These moves were applauded in the business press, but they were greeted with a skeptical response from Nike's long-term adversaries in the debate over the use of foreign labor. While conceding that Nike's policies were an improvement, one critic writing in the *New York Times* noted that:

> Mr. Knight's child labor initiative is . . . a smokescreen. Child labor has not been a big problem with Nike, and Philip Knight knows that better than anyone. But public relations is public relations. So he announces that he's not going to let the factories hire kids, and suddenly that's the headline.
>
> Mr. Knight is like a three-card monte player. You have to keep a close eye on him at all times.
>
> The biggest problem with Nike is that its overseas workers make wretched, below-subsistence wages. It's not the minimum age that needs raising, it's the minimum wage. Most of the workers in Nike factories in China and Vietnam make less than $2 a day, well below the subsistence levels in those countries. In Indonesia the pay is less than $1 a day.

The company's current strategy is to reshape its public image while doing as little as possible for the workers. Does anyone think it was an accident that Nike set up shop in human rights sinkholes, where labor organizing was viewed as a criminal activity and deeply impoverished workers were willing, even eager, to take their places on assembly lines and work for next to nothing?[14]

Other critics question the quality of Nike's auditors, PricewaterhouseCoopers (PwC). Dara O'Rourke, an assistant professor at MIT, followed the PwC auditors around several factories in China, Korea, and Vietnam. He concluded that although the auditors found minor violations of labor laws and codes of conduct, they missed major labor-practice issues, including hazardous working conditions, violations of overtime laws, and violation of wage laws. The problem, according to O'Rourke, was that the auditors had limited training and relied on factory managers for data and for setting up interviews with workers, all of which were performed in the factories. The auditors, in other words, were getting an incomplete and somewhat sanitized view of conditions in the factory.[15]

The Controversy Continues

Fueled perhaps by the unforgiving criticisms of Nike that continued after Phil Knight's May 1998 speech, a wave of protests against Nike occurred on many university campuses from 1998 to 2001. The moving force behind the protests was the United Students Against Sweatshops (USAS). The USAS argued that the Fair Labor Association (FLA), which grew out of the presidential task force on sweatshops, was an industry tool, and not a truly independent auditor of foreign factories. The USAS set up an alternative independent auditing organization, the Workers Rights Consortium (WRC), which they charged with auditing factories that produce products under collegiate licensing programs (under which Nike is a high-profile supplier of products). The WRC is backed, and partly funded, by labor unions and refuses to cooperate with companies, arguing that doing so would jeopardize its independence.

By mid 2000, the WRC had persuaded some forty-eight universities to join, including all nine campuses of the University of California systems, the University of Michigan, and the University of

Oregon, Phil Knight's alma mater. When Knight heard that the University of Oregon would join the WRC, as opposed to the FLA, he withdrew a planned $30 million donation to the university.[16] Despite this, in November 2000 another major northwest university, the University of Washington, announced that it too would join the WRC, although it would also retain its membership in the FLA.[17]

Nike continued to push forward with its own initiatives, updating progress on its web site. In April 2000, in response to accusations that it was still hiding conditions, it announced that it would release the complete reports of all independent audits of its subcontractors' plants. Global Exchange continued to criticize the company, arguing in mid 2001 that the company was not living up to Phil Knight's 1998 promises and that it was intimidating workers from speaking out about abuses.[18]

ENDNOTES

1. From Nike's corporate web site at **www.nikebiz.com.**
2. **www.globalexchange.org.**
3. "Boycott Nike," *CBS News 48 Hours*, October 17, 1996.
4. D. Jones. "Critics tie sweatshop sneakers to 'Air Jordan,'" *USA Today*, June 6, 1996, p. 1B.
5. Global Exchange Special Report: Nike Just Don't Do It. **http://www.globalexchange.org/education/publications/ newsltr6.97p2.html#nike.**
6. V. Dobnik. "Chinese workers abused making Nikes, Reeboks," *Seattle Times*, September 21, 1997, p. A4.
7. S. Greenhouse. "Nike shoeplant in Vietnam is called unsafe for workers," *New York Times*, November 8, 1997.
8. S. Greenhouse. "Nike shoeplant in Vietnam is called unsafe for workers," *New York Times*, November 8, 1997.
9. Quoted in: V. Dobnik. "Chinese workers abused making Nikes, Reeboks," *Seattle Times*, September 21, 1997, p. A4.
10. W. Bounds and H. Stout. "Sweatshop pact: Good fit or threadbare?" *Wall Street Journal*, April 10, 1997, p. A2.
11. Associated Press Reporter. "Nike gives four factories the boot," *Los Angeles Times*, September 23, 1997, p. 20.
12. Archived at **http://www.nikebiz.com/labor/speech_trans.shtml.**
13. OSHA is the United States Occupational Safety and Health Agency.
14. B. Herbert. "Nike Blinks," *New York Times*, May 21, 1998.
15. Dara O'Rourke. Monitoring the monitors: A critique of the PricewaterhouseCoopers (PwC) labor monitoring. Department of Urban Studies and Planning, MIT.
16. L. Lee and A. Bernstein. Who says student protests don't matter? *Business Week*, June 12, 2000, pp. 94–96.
17. R. Deen. UW to join anti-sweatshop group. *Seattle Post Intelligencer*, November 20, 2000, p. B2.
18. Anonymous. Rights group says Nike isn't fulfilling promises. *Wall Street Journal*, May 16, 2001.

11

WestJet Looks East[1]

Professors Joseph N. Fry and Roderick E. White prepared this case solely to provide material for class discussion. The authors do not intend to illustrate either effective or ineffective handling of a managerial situation. The authors may have disguised certain names and other identifying information to protect confidentiality.

In August 1999, the Canadian airline industry was taken by surprise when the Onex Corporation proposed to acquire and merge Canada's two large system carriers, Canadian Airlines and Air Canada. A long and debilitating rivalry between the two airlines was being pushed to a conclusion. Air Canada countered with a merger proposal of its own and ultimately prevailed in a high-profile takeover battle. With Onex out of the picture, the way was clear for Air Canada to achieve a near monopoly of domestic, regularly scheduled air travel. Meanwhile, the federal government, which had helped to begin the merger initiatives, insisted that it would sustain competition in the industry.

In light of these developments, the management of WestJet Airlines of Calgary were reviewing their growth plans and wondering, in particular, if they should shift from their focus on building and reinforcing their Western Canadian markets to expanding in the East. WestJet was a young, successful, low-fare airline patterned after Southwest Airlines, the most successful U.S. air carrier. WestJet had been profitable from its start-up in early 1996, and by 1999 was flying 13 Boeing 737s approximately 517 flights per week between 11 destinations in Western Canada. WestJet had just recently completed a $25 million initial public offering and planned to purchase three additional aircraft with the proceeds. At the time of the offering, WestJet's plan was to use the increased flight capacity for further penetration of the western market. A summary of WestJet's financial performance is given in Exhibit 1.

Industry Background: Domestic Warfare

The epic battle between Air Canada and Canadian had started with the deregulation of Canada's domestic airline industry in the mid-

One-time permission to produce Ivey cases granted by Ivey Management Services, 2002.

1. This case has been written on the basis of public sources only. Consequently, the interpretation and perspectives presented in this case are not necessarily those of WestJet or any of its employees.

EXHIBIT 1

Selected Financial Information for WestJet,
1998 and Projected 1999 ($000)

	12/31/1999	12/31/1998
Operating Revenues	$204,000	$125,000
Operating expenses	173,000	112,000
Operating income	30,000	13,000
Income before taxes	29,000	12,000
Net Income	16,000	7,000
Current assets	61,000	23,000
Capital and other assets	126,000	85,000
Total Assets	187,000	108,000
Current liabilities	50,000	29,000
Long-term debt	30,000	22,000
Deferred income tax	13,000	8,000
Shareholders equity	94,000	49,000
Total Liabilities and Shareholder Equity	187,000	108,000

Source: Company Financial Reports.

1980s.[2] At that time, Pacific Western Airlines, a successful regional carrier, spurned a potential marriage with Air Canada and set out to become a full-fledged national and international carrier. To achieve this, the company, renamed Canadian Airlines, acquired Canadian Pacific Airlines (which itself had just swallowed Eastern Provincial Airways, Nordair, and Quebecair) and a few years later, Wardair. As it emerged from this process, Canadian Airlines had assembled the essentials of an international air carrier; in particular, it held a strong position in Western Canada and important flag carrier routes across the Pacific and to Mexico and South America. On the other hand, Canadian was working from a relatively weak position in Eastern Canada and across the Atlantic. It was experiencing integration difficulties with the acquisitions, and it was saddled with significant debt. Canadian chose, nevertheless, to persist and to engage Air Canada in a winner-takes-all contest to

2. After deregulation, the government would license airlines to fly any domestic route, any time, at any price, subject only to safety requirements. The government also retained provisions requiring that at least 75 per cent of the voting interests of air carrier license holders be owned and controlled by Canadians and that control of the airline be held in fact by Canadians.

become Canada's dominant, regularly scheduled domestic and international carrier.

In the meantime, Air Canada was in transition from government ownership to publicly traded company. When full privatization was achieved in 1989, Air Canada was seen on the one hand as a carrier that was quite well-off in routes, equipment and finance, but, on the other hand, limited in its potential by overstaffing, low productivity and a pervasive attitude of entitlement.

A 10 Year Dog Fight

While cumbersome, Air Canada was the stronger airline. In a continuing war of attrition—marked by over-capacity in overlapping routes and frequencies, and corresponding price pressures—Canadian, with its burdensome debt, was soon in financial trouble. In 1992, with the economy in recession, Canadian posted a loss of over $500 million, reducing its accumulated equity to zero. Air Canada took note and pursued the possibility of a merger. The reaction from Canadian and its employees ranged from uncooperative to hostile, and Air Canada withdrew, reportedly to wait and pick up the pieces when Canadian fell into bankruptcy. Canadian soon got back into the thick of it, however, largely by way of a strategic alliance with AMR Corp., parent of American Airlines. The alliance provided for a critical $246 million equity investment in return for a service agreement that secured Canadian as a customer for AMR's Sabre information systems business and significant concessions by Canadian's employees, shareholders and creditors.

But, by 1995, Canadian was in serious trouble again. For that matter, Air Canada was suffering too—but it was somewhat better-off in scale, market position and financing. (Collectively, in their six fiscal years from 1990 through 1995, the two airlines posted cumulative losses of $2.15 billion, of which Canadian accounted for $1.26 billion.) Given the circumstances, Canadian management took a serious look at downsizing its domestic operations and retrenching to its more profitable international routes. As attractive as this idea looked in concept, there were serious obstacles to successful implementation, ranging from the maintenance of effective domestic feed and distribution for the international routes to absorbing the tangible and intangible costs of major layoffs and facility closings. Management chose instead to seek further payroll concessions and productivity improvements to sustain their now-quixotic all-fronts contest with Air Canada.

Air Canada was not prepared to disengage, of course, and pressed on with the battle. The inevitable outcome was painfully slow to emerge. But over the next three years, Canadian lost a cumulative $3.19 million, and by late 1998, the airline was clearly having trouble assembling the cash needed to stay in the air. In March 1999, Canadian approached Federal Transport Department officials to explain its situation and to request that the government use Section 47 of the Transport Act to allow Canada's main airlines to enter into discussions that would normally be forbidden under competition regulations. Meanwhile, with the encouragement of Canadian, Onex Corporation and American Airlines executives were engaged in on and off talks about a venture to merge Canadian and Air Canada. When Section 47 was formally invoked in August, Air Canada was the first mover, with an offer to buy Canadian's international routes. Canadian rejected this out of hand. Then, in short order, Onex announced a plan to buy and merge both airlines in a deal that was heavily backed by American Airlines. Air Canada management was dismayed, to say the least, at the prospect of falling short so close to victory and outraged at the seeming complicity of the government in the process.

The Last Weeks of Canadian Airlines

A fierce takeover battle was joined, full of rancor, legal maneuvering, bids and counter-bids. The stakes were unprecedented. The competing proposals put forward by Onex and Air Canada were both structured such that the winner would emerge with control of a single airline serving over 80 per cent of Canada's regularly scheduled domestic air travel. Public relations programs were cranked up to a fever pitch. Both sides claimed that they would generate the greatest shareholder benefits, without, of course, abusing their monopoly position. One of Air Canada's promises—which seemed aimed at the not necessarily consistent goals of tying up yet another domestic market segment, while reassuring the public that price competition would continue—was that it would set up a separate low-fare carrier at Hamilton airport.[3] Just to make sure of its position, Air

---

3. Hamilton airport was located 60 kilometres south-west of Toronto's international airport. It was used by airfreight carriers, local air traffic and the occasional charter flight, but had no regularly scheduled passenger traffic.

Canada took a pre-emptive step in locking up all of Hamilton's available gates.

After 10 weeks of a very public contest, both sides were claiming that they would emerge the winner. Then, in early November, one of Air Canada's legal defenses came through: a judge in the Quebec Superior Court ruled that Onex's bid contravened the terms of the legislation under which Air Canada was privatized. Under the Air Canada Public Participation Act, no single party could control more than 10 per cent of Air Canada. Onex decided to withdraw, leaving Canadian hanging by a thread and looking for further backing from American Airlines and its Oneworld alliance partners. These last-ditch efforts were unsuccessful, and in early December, the Canadian board announced its approval of a $98 million takeover offer from Air Canada.

All that remained for the acquisition to proceed was approval from the federal government. This was expected, although some conditions would be imposed. The government was concerned about domestic competition, and as a condition for approving the merger, Air Canada would be required to hand over some gates at major airports.

Industry Background: Concurrent Developments

Passenger Traffic

From a historic high point reached in 1990, the number of passengers carried by Canada's domestic airlines dipped about 15 per cent in the recession of the early 1990s and did not recover to prerecession levels until 1995. Thereafter, growth was strong; overall, from 1990 through 1998, passenger counts grew 23 per cent, from 36.8 million to 45.4 million and the number of revenue passenger kilometres flown increased 41.5 per cent, from 66.8 billion to 94.5 billion. The distribution of demand by major airline and service is given in Table 1.

By Sector The components of passenger traffic growth over the 1990 to 1998 period reflected the increasing importance of transborder (United States) and other international traffic. Passenger traffic carried by domestic airlines grew 14 per cent over the period, transborder traffic grew 39 per cent and other international traffic grew 53 per cent. A particularly important event during the period was the signing of an "Open Skies" agreement with the United States in

TABLE 1

Passenger Kilometres Flown by Canadian Carriers—1990 and 1998 (millions)

	Air Canada	%	Canadian	%	Other Sch.*	%	Charter	%	Total	%
1990	25,504	37.6	21,624	31.9	3,975	5.9	16,675	24.6	67,778	100
1998	37,296	39.5	26,544	28.1	10,784	11.4	19,843	21.0	94,467	100

*The growth in "other scheduled" reflected the practice of most charter carriers in the 1990s to add some form of seasonal or peak-time scheduled carriage.

Source: Drawn from Transport Canada, Air Information in Canada, T-Facts. Includes domestic and international carriage.

1995. This treaty essentially removed pre-existing restrictions on air traffic between the two countries over a three-year period. It sustained the competitive status quo within each country, however, by not providing for cabotage—the right of an airline to carry local traffic within a foreign country. The revenue mix of the two major airlines in 1998, as shown in Table 2, reflected the results of these trends.

By Region   The distribution of passenger traffic carried by domestic carriers by region was six per cent for Atlantic Canada, 13 per cent for Quebec, 37 per cent for Ontario, 21 per cent for the Prairies and North, and 23 per cent for the Pacific.

By Airport   Passenger traffic in Canada was concentrated in relatively few airports. Toronto alone accounted for 31 per cent of the passenger traffic flown by Canadian carriers in 1998. Put together, the country's seven largest airports—Toronto, Vancouver, Montreal-Dorval, Calgary, Edmonton, Ottawa, Halifax, and Winnipeg—accounted for 83 per cent of all traffic flown by Canadian carriers. By sector, these same airports accounted for 75 per cent of the domestic, 97 per cent of the transborder and 90 per cent of the international passenger traffic flown by Canadian carriers.

By City Pair   Passenger traffic data for origin/destination traffic, or point-to-point traffic, further emphasizes the importance of the Toronto market in domestic air travel. The 10 highest-traffic domestic city pairs is presented in Table 3. Toronto anchored one end for seven of the top 10 city pairs.

Competition

The competitive context of the air travel market in Canada in the 1990s was a reflection of the seemingly irrational duel between Air Canada and Canadian. It was a hostile environment, marked by over-capacity, price-cutting and heavy losses for the two big airlines. It was remarkable that, under these circumstances, a number of relatively small carriers—namely, Royal Airlines, Canada 3000, AirTransat, Skyservice and WestJet—found viable market niches and were able to stay aloft and to grow. There were also notable failures—Greyhound, Vistajet and Astoria.

In the spring of 1996, Greyhound attempted to set up a low-fare, transcontinental service with its hubs in Winnipeg. Greyhound's low fares generated reasonable load factors and, interestingly, passenger profiles that were much further upscale than expected by industry observers. However, Greyhound was also saddled by costly delays in securing regulatory approvals, by inefficient secondhand 727 aircraft, by

TABLE 2

Passenger Revenue Mix for Major Airlines—1998 ($ millions)

	Domestic	Transborder	International	Total
Air Canada	2,294	1,426	1,257	4,977
Canadian	1,403	355	993	2,751

Source: Company Annual Reports.

TABLE 3

Point-to-Point Traffic for Selected City Pairs—1997 (thousands)*

Carriers	Scheduled	Charter	Total
Toronto to Montreal	1,182	NA	1,182
Toronto to Vancouver	830	233	1,063
Toronto to Ottawa	684	NA	684
Toronto to Calgary	495	95	590
Calgary to Vancouver	520	50	570
Toronto to Winnipeg	347	56	403
Toronto to Halifax	289	77	366
Edmonton to Vancouver	312	48	360
Calgary to Edmonton	308	NA	308
Toronto to Edmonton	282	44	326

*Excludes passengers flying the city pair as part of a connecting flight itinerary.

Source: Drawn from Transport Canada, Air Information in Canada, T-Facts Air Folder.

expensive aircraft lease arrangements, and by some questionable operating decisions, such as selling airline tickets in bus stations to avoid travel agent commissions. When the parent bus company was sold to Laidlaw Inc. in the summer of 1997, the airline was cut loose and quickly shut down.

Vistajet hardly got off the ground. It was to be a London, Ontario-based discount airline, but after four months of operation with one 30-year-old 737 and a bird strike that disabled the plane at a critical juncture, the new venture called it quits. Astoria, a two aircraft airline offering business class-only service between Toronto and Montreal, also folded after only four months of operation.

Competition and Government Policy

The federal government may have hoped that deregulation and the privatization of Air Canada would free it from some messy obligations. How wrong. By the early 1990s, Canadian's financial problems had become high-profile political issues. And, for the government, there were no easy solutions. Any significant effort to help Canadian—by, for example, providing financial assistance, moderating competition through reregulation, or dropping domestic ownership provisions—would fly in the face of the government's political and economic objectives to be and to be seen to be even-handed, to avoid interference with market mechanisms and to maintain a domestically controlled industry. Not helping Cana-

dian could result in an Air Canada monopoly, jeopardizing the government's goal of maintaining a healthy and competitive market, and, in the process, generating no small amount of criticism. Caught on the horns of a dilemma, the government tried to provide some aid to Canadian,[4] but it only bought some time for Canadian to pursue its own fate.

Faced with Canadian's failure, the government suspended competition rules, leading to the Air Canada—Onex takeover battle. In the furore that ensued, which included heated attacks on the government's actions and on the motives and intelligence of the transport minister, critics were nevertheless short on constructive alternatives. What the government did do was advise both Air Canada and Onex that it would be taking steps to protect the public interest, including provisions to:

▌ Prevent price gouging by any emerging monopoly carrier;

▌ Enhance competition in the domestic market, particularly by ensuring ease of entry and policing predatory practices;

▌ Maintain Canadian ownership and control of the industry;

▌ Maintain service to small communities;

▌ Ensure fair treatment of employees.

4. For example, the government purchased some of Canadian's aircraft in what some thought was a sweetheart deal.

The precise legislation to accomplish these aims was yet to be tabled, and some critics questioned whether these objectives could ever be achieved. In response, the government promised that if a competitive industry did not evolve in a reasonable time, it would have no hesitation about initiating further steps, such as the discussion of cabotage with the United States.

The Competitive Situation in Late 1999

As the new Air Canada took shape, the industry was rife with speculation about its strategic intentions and the consequences for travelers and industry players alike. Given the government's position on sustaining competition, it looked as if there would be opportunities for Canada's existing airlines and possibly for new entrants; the issues for the airlines were how and when to take advantage of these possibilities. Following is a brief review of the positions and apparent intentions of the incumbent and announced players.

The New Air Canada   Despite the turmoil of the moment, complete with pending but uncertain government approvals and conditions, union clashes, and unresolved financial and operating issues at Canadian, there were some broad, if not settled, themes in Air Canada's positions. It was expected that as the air cleared the company would: Rationalize Air Canada's and Canadian's regional feeder carriers to eliminate gross duplication of capacity; Rationalize the domestic trunk routes of the two airlines to cut capacity by 15 per cent or more; Rationalize and expand its transborder operations (where it already held over 50 per cent of the market) and its other international operations, and use these dominant positions as forcefully as possible to influence domestic patronage and pricing; Increase prices and cut promotional spending as much as legally, politically and commercially feasible; Air Canada had already announced plans to create a stand-alone low fare airline based in Hamilton, and perhaps parallel stand-alone businesses for the leisure (charter) market and for cargo. This theme was a sore point with Air Canada's union since the company had made no secret of its desire for concessions in wages and work rules for the new entities. The initiatives for a separate low-fare airline within the Air Canada family remained unclear. Was it a public relations ploy to help gain approval for the acquisition of Canadian; or was it a strategic move to pre-empt other low-fare players, like WestJet?

Most observers doubted that Air Canada would be able, or would be allowed, to sustain all of the market share accrued through the merger. Air Canada clearly thought otherwise and appeared to be developing all segments of the industry.

Royal Airlines   Royal was founded in 1979, and for many years operated as a Quebec-based charter carrier with additional cargo, water bombing and aircraft maintenance services. In the early 1990s, the company went public and expanded into charter operations in Canada and abroad. By 1999, Royal's fleet encompassed 11 large passenger aircraft. In anticipation of the opportunities that might be created by an Air Canada–Canadian merger, Royal added domestic scheduled services in October, 1999, with flights at peak times from Toronto, Montreal, Ottawa, Winnipeg, Halifax and Vancouver.

Canada 3000   Canada 3000 was a privately owned carrier that started business in 1988 as a dedicated charter carrier for international pleasure travel, and gradually added scheduled carrier operations in Canada and abroad. By 1999, the company's fleet of 15 large aircraft were focused on long-haul domestic and international routes that varied with seasonal traffic patterns. It was anticipated that Canada 3000 would expand its operations in response to industry restructuring, possibly with an IPO to finance fleet additions.

AirTransAt   The parent of AirTransat, Transat A.T. Inc., operated an integrated vacation travel business encompassing every aspect of holiday travel organization and distribution. The airline's fleet of 20 large charter aircraft was dedicated to the vacation travel market in Canada and Europe. There were no indications that Transat intended to change its focus in response to the domestic market turmoil.

Skyservice   Skyservice Airlines flew a charter fleet of four large aircraft mainly for two big tour operators, but also for incidental hire. The airline was a division of privately owned Skyservice Investments. This was an aggressive company and it was expected that it would attempt to expand its operations, possibly by way of long-haul scheduled domestic service.

CanJet   The CanJet Corp. of Toronto had been working since the summer of 1999 on plans for a low-fare airline that would fly out of Hamilton to Montreal, Ottawa, Halifax and Winnipeg. Although the prospective venture was backed by a well-known industry figure, Kenneth Rowe, chairman of the IMP Group Ltd. of Halifax, as of early December it was still regarded as very much a paper airline.

Canadian Regional Airlines There was an expectation the government would insist that Air Canada try to sell Canadian's regional feeder subsidiary as a condition of the acquisition. The airline consisted of 54 aircraft, most notably a fleet of 30 20-to-30-year-old, 60-to-85 passenger Fokker F 28 jets. These aircraft had been described uncharitably, but with some accuracy, by Robert Milton, Air Canada's CEO, as planes that "are rarely flown in the Third World anymore."

Although the strategic role of the regional airlines in Canada was to feed the hub-based trunk flights of their parents, up to 80 per cent of the passengers on regional airlines flew between cities without ongoing connections on the larger jet aircraft.[5] It was not clear in December 1999 whether or not there would be a buyer at an acceptable price, although one industry entrepreneur, Jim Deluce of Regional Airlines Holdings, had proposed purchasing both the Canadian and Air Canada regional subsidiaries.

WestJet and the 'Southwest' Business Model

WestJet commenced operations out of Calgary in 1996. The airline was the brainchild of several local businessmen unhappy with the price and service being provided in the West by the major carriers (and this at the height of a price and frequency battle!). The founders went into business with a strategy that copied the Southwest model, "rivet-for-rivet, stitch-for-stitch."

Other airlines had adopted this formula with varying degrees of success, including Morris Air (now part of Southwest) and Spirit Airlines in the United States, and easyJet, Ryanair and Virgin Express[6] in Europe. Interestingly, major system carriers on both continents had, by and large, experienced serious difficulties in their attempts to establish similar low-fare operating units.

5. Joe Randall, president of Air Canada's regional airline business, in The Globe and Mail, January 21, 2000.
6. Created when Virgin acquired EuroBelgian Express.

The Southwest Low-Fare Airline Model

In the United States, Southwest Airlines had pioneered, developed, and exploited a low-fare airline model to the point of becoming the most consistently profitable airline in the world. Founded in 1971, with three planes serving three Texas cities, Southwest had overcome early problems and had steadily grown its fleet, route structure and financial record. Over the years, Southwest had become well known for its employee-oriented, irreverent, work-hard-play-hard culture which was epitomized in the iconoclastic management style of Herb Kelleher, chairman and CEO.

The Southwest business model departed from the conventional system-airline, hub-and-spoke model in three principal ways, by: (1) focusing on price-sensitive passengers; (2) employing a short-haul, point-to-point route system, and; (3) running a low-cost, no-frills operation. An outline of further differences in the conventional hub-and-spoke and Southwest models is presented in Table 4. There were, of course, other business models being pursued in the industry such as charter, scheduled charter, and full- or luxury-service medium- to long-haul point-to-point carriage, but these were less central to the WestJet situation.

The Competitive Features of the Southwest Model

The Southwest-style airlines took some pains to emphasize that their low-fare/short-haul operations were a complement to the traditional airlines in that they aimed primarily at budget-conscious travellers who might otherwise drive, use a bus or train, or not travel at all. While this was undoubtedly accurate as a point of focus, it was also true that as their systems expanded, low-fare airline routes overlapped city pairs served by the large system carriers, or by their subsidiary regional feeder operations. Indeed, the average length of a Southwest flight had been steadily increasing over the years and it was estimated that currently 40 per cent of passengers were either through or connecting.[7] As a result, the two airline system types invariably ended up in competition for at least part of the potential market. This was not a happy circumstance for the major carriers

7. Connecting passengers landed at an intermediate airport and changed planes to complete their flight; through passengers landed at one or more intermediate airports but did not change planes to complete their flight.

TABLE 4

Comparison of the Hub-and-Spoke and Southwest Models

	Hub-and-Spoke	Southwest
Market Focus	Business travel	Personal travel
Value Proposition	Frequency, system, amenities	Low fare
Route System	Integrated hub-and-spoke	Point-to-point
Stage Length	Medium- and long-haul	Short-haul
Seating	Reserved	Open
Baggage	Transfer and interline	Check in/pick up only
Airport Requirements	Major metropolitan hubs	Secondary airports
Aircraft Turn Time (at gate)	30 to 60 minutes	15 to 20 minutes
Fleet	Multi-role/type	Single role/type 1 aircraft type
Ticketing	Travel Agents	Direct
Product	Multi-class, frills	Single class, no-frills
Promotional Focus	Service, loyalty programs, restricted price deals	Low price, few restrictions
Culture	Formal	Casual
Structure	Hierarchical, defined roles and relationships	Flat, multi-task
Personnel Systems	Union work rule driven	Task, enterprise success driven

who were already locked in a tough competitive battle with each other.

The response of the major carriers to the advent of low-fare competitors followed two avenues. First, they counter-attacked through their regular operations—by measures that included selective fare cuts, enhanced promotional incentives, and shifts in frequencies and equipment. Second, if low fare operators continued to grow, some of the majors tried the more direct counter of creating captive low-fare subsidiary operations. All these responses, however, were ultimately limited by the higher cost structures of the conventional airlines and by the difficulty of disentangling a subsidiary from the route structure and traditional practices, of the parent, including most notably union restrictions and cultural habits.

The Southwest formula was designed to achieve low cost. The key elements highlighted in Table 1 and other operational practices were designed to contribute to this end. The focus on one aircraft type, for example, contributed to lower employee-to-aircraft ratios, greater flexibility in crew assignments, and simplified maintenance, training programs and administrative procedures relative to the multi-aircraft system carriers. The result of this dedication to low cost meant the low-fare carriers had substantially lower operating costs per unit of capacity than those of the conventional airlines. WestJet estimated, for example, that its operating costs, after equalization for stage length, were 40 per cent to 50 per cent lower than those of Canadian and Air Canada. This difference put conventional carriers at a terrific disadvantage if they chose to compete on price on any given city pair. Some comparative financial and operating statistics for selected airlines are presented in Exhibit 2.

Setting up a competitive, profitable, low-fare subsidiary had also proven to be a problematic endeavor for the traditional airlines. In the early 1990s, Continental Airlines launched Continental Life and closed it after a few years of substantial losses. Other entrants included, in the United States. United Airlines' United Shuttle, Delta Airlines' Delta Express and U.S. Airways' MetroJet, and in Europe, British Airways' GO. Although specific financial results were not available for these ventures, industry observers were generally skeptical about their profitability on any kind of fully allocated cost basis. United, for

EXHIBIT 2

Comparative Financial and Operating Performance for Selected Airlines*

	Southwest	WestJet	easyJet	Air Canada	Canadian	United
Financial Results						
Operating Revenues	6,226	126	184	5,932	3,171	26,257
Operating Expenses	5,203	112	181	5,788	3,173	24,016
Operating Income	1,022	14	3	144	(22)	2,209
Net Income	647	7	6	(16)	(138)	1,227
Operating Statistics**						
Average Stage Length (miles)***	450	378	NA	955	1,325	NA
Rev. Pass. Miles (RPM, millions)	31,419	639	1,302	23,212	16,695	124,609
Avail. Seat Miles (ASM, millions)	47,544	893	1,737	32,719	23,217	174,008
Load Factor (%)	66	72	75	71	72	72
Pass. Revenue/RPM (cents)****	19	19	NA	19	14	19
Pass. Revenue/ASM (cents)	13	13	NA	13	10	13
Oper. Revenue/ASM (cents)	13	14	11	16	11	15
Oper. Cost/ASM (cents)	11	13	10	16	11	14
Employees	25,844	629	394	23,000	14,123	91,000
ASM/Employee (millions)	1,840	1,420	4,410	1,430	1,640	1,910
Aircraft	280	11	8	157	81	577

* For fiscal year end, 1998.
** Air Canada, Canadian statistics exclude regional subsidiaries.
*** Typically, airline operating costs per mile decrease with longer flights. WestJet estimated, for example, that its operating costs per available seat mile if it operated with an average stage length of 1,113 miles (Calgary-Thunder Bay) would be about 8.2 cents per mile.
**** Simple passenger revenue comparisons are also confounded by stage length. As costs per mile fall with longer stage lengths, the tendency, under competition, is for prices per mile to fall as well.

Source: Company financial reports. All currencies converted to Canadian dollars.

example, had started United Shuttle to compete with Southwest in the Western United States, but had backed off from direct competition after reported losses of $200 million and repositioned the Shuttle as a feeder to its West Coast hubs. British Airways, which had launched GO in 1998 to compete with the challenge of Ryanair and easyJet, had reported operating losses of $32 million in GO's first year of operation—much to the delight of easyJet, which sponsored a contest offering prizes for the most accurate forecast of the losses.

Whatever their willingness to subsidize losses, whether it be on particular routes or with new entries, the conventional airlines faced the limitations of their own fiscal abilities and beyond this, the prospect of legal challenge for engaging in

predatory competition. In the United Kingdom, for example, easyJet made a big thing of their underdog status by suing British Airways under Article 26 of the Treaty of Rome, which says that dominant players in a market should not operate below the cost of production.

WestJet's Progress

By late 1999, WestJet was on a roll. The company had overcome some early problems with safety regulations; acquired a fleet; established a route structure; built a reputation as an efficient and reliable, if unconventional operator; grown passenger volumes; fought off competitive challenges; completed a successful IPO; and was increasingly profitable.

TABLE 5

WestJet Service Coverage and Weekly Departures, Summer 1999

Airport Departures	Service Commenced	Aircraft in Service	Weekly Departures
Calgary	February, 1996	3	156
Vancouver	February, 1996		94
Kelowna	February, 1996		61
Edmonton	February, 1996		88
Victoria	March, 1996		27
Regina	June, 1996	4	21
Saskatoon	August, 1996		28
Abbotsford, B.C.	June, 1997	6	20
Winnipeg	March, 1998	8	27
Prince George	March, 1999		26
Thunder Bay	March, 1999	12	7

Source: WestJet Prospectus, April 1999.

Route Network

WestJet's route network focused on short-haul point-to-point service in Western Canada. This structure allowed WestJet to provide frequent service and dispense with many of the amenities usually provided on longer flights. The company's service coverage and departure frequencies as of late 1999 are summarized in Table 5. Whenever possible, WestJet picked niche routes where it could compete with non-stop jet service against the turbo-prop service of the majors' regional subsidiaries. On all its routes, WestJet sought to offer low everyday fares while maintaining a friendly service environment. Consistent with the Southwest model, WestJet offered a single class of service, did not interline baggage with other airlines, nor offer meal service, city ticket offices, frequent-flier programs, airport lounges or business class amenities.

Passenger Traffic

The impact of WestJet's entry, coupled with the competitive response of the majors, contributed to large increases in traffic on the targeted city pairs, as illustrated in Table 6. It appeared, indeed, that WestJet was correct in claiming that it was opening new demand segments for the industry.

Competitive Reaction

Air Canada and Canadian counter-attacked in predictable ways. They sought to match WestJet's everyday low prices—which were up to 60 per cent less than the nominal economy prices of the majors—but in doing so they raised "fences" to limit their overall revenue erosion—such as by limiting the number of seats available in varying discount ranges, by restricting the times when the low fares were available and by requiring minimum stay-overs. On the promotional

TABLE 6

Growth in Passenger Traffic for Largest City Pairs* (000 passengers)

	Cal-Van	Edm-Van	Cal-Edm	Kel-Van	Cal-Vic	Edm-Vic
1995	422	243	271	87	63	43
1997	674	438	375	192	162	123
% Inc.	60	80	38	119	155	186

Source: WestJet Prospectus, April 1999.

* For cities served by WestJet; all domestic carriers; traffic does not include domestic portion of international flights.

front, both airlines used occasional bonus point offers in their frequent-flyer programs to help stem the loss of high yield customers. Similarly, on occasion, the majors would price under on selected routes. Finally, the majors shuffled equipment and frequencies to try to improve their offering. At one point, for example, Air Canada attempted to compete in some city pairs by introducing its new 50-seat CRJ 700 regional jet, but had backed off after 10 months and little progress. Throughout these various forays, WestJet claimed that it made money on all routes.

In WestJet's assessment, Air Canada and Canadian were engaging in harassment and containment, rather than in trying to "blow 'em out of the sky"—although the two majors would no doubt have been happy to see this happen. The company was confident that, under these circumstances, it had room for continuing profitable growth.

WestJet's Options

In early September 1999, WestJet's CEO, Stephen Smith, reiterated the company's original plan: "We have a business plan we've been following and that plan contemplates the addition of three or four aircraft per year focused primarily on Western Canada . . . the company doesn't plan to fly further east than Thunder Bay for the foreseeable future . . . at least three to five years."[8] WestJet was, quite logically, concerned about not overextending itself. The airline had prospered in a tough market by following conservative policies with respect to growth and financing. It took pride, for example, in the fact that it had minimized the use of debt and owned 11 of its 13 aircraft.

As the events of the fall of 1999 unfolded, however, WestJet management was more or less compelled to take the possibility of eastern expansion into consideration. First, there was a matter of growth potential. If the company remained in Western Canada there was growth potential to perhaps 30 to 40 aircraft. A successful move to the East would more than double the potential. Second, there was a matter of timing, and particularly concerns about first-mover advantages. It was quite apparent that it would be just a matter of time before someone entered the East with a low-fare strategy—be it Air Canada or CanJet, or another start-up. As a condition of its merger with Canadian, Air Canada undertook not to start up a low-fare airline in eastern Canada until September 2001, provided there was a low-fare entrant within the next year.[9] If no other low-fare entrant stepped forward Air Canada could enter the eastern market as soon as September 2000. Air Canada also promised to facilitate gate access for newcomers at Hamilton airport. Finally, there was a chance that by remaining solely in the West, WestJet might become vulnerable to competition reaching out from their Eastern bases.

There was a strong temptation to push east, probably with an operation based at Hamilton airport. Beyond this, WestJet's management had to consider immediate and fundamental questions of pace—how fast and how significant an entry was necessary from a competitive standpoint, how fast and how significant an entry could the company digest, and how it would connect (if at all) to the company's routes in the West? And, finally, in the longer haul, what were WestJet's prospects against Air Canada and others?

---

8. The Globe and Mail, September 7, 1999.

9. There was no restriction of Air Canada launching a low-fare operation in Western Canada.

Avon Products, Inc.: The Personal-Care Industry

12

This case was prepared by Gabriela Del Carro and Marc E. Gartenfeld under the direction of Dr. Robert J. Mockler, St. John's University.

In spring 2000, Andrea Jung, president and CEO since November 1999 at Avon Products, Inc., faced the strategic decision of developing a growth strategy for the 115-year-old company. Avon Products, Inc., the world's largest direct seller of beauty and related personal-care products, sold to women in 137 countries via three million independent sales representatives who generated approximately $5.1 billion in annual revenues. Upon reviewing the financial statistics of Avon, Jung discovered that not only had earnings risen in the low-single digits in the past few years, but—also more disturbing—the growth rate had shrunk during the same time. In light of this problem, Jung faced significant strategic decisions in growing the company in lieu of its stagnant sales, limited distribution capabilities, and shifts in personal-care preferences and spending habits in this rapidly changing industry.

For 115 years, Avon had enjoyed worldwide success mainly due to its unique direct-selling distribution channel and worldwide brand-name recognition. However, recent single-digit growth indicated that the company needed to

This case is intended to be used as a basis for class discussion rather than as an illustration of either effective or ineffective handling of the situation. This case was prepared by Gabriella Del Carro, Marc E. Gartenfeld, and Robert J. Mockler, under whose supervision the case was written. Reprinted by permission of the authors.

make significant improvements in its overall operations. In 1999, sales increased approximately 1% as gains in fashion, jewelry and accessories, and noncore categories offset declines in cosmetics, fragrances, toiletries, and apparel. The single-digit growth rate had declined each year. Avon's direct-selling model generated 95% of the company's revenues. In 2000, Jung was deciding whether or not to enter Avon into a nonexclusive partnership with J C Penney and Sears to supplement its sales representatives, expand its distribution capabilities, and attract new customers in order to increase sales and earnings.

Under careful consideration was the type of products to be sold in these stores. The company was leaning towards higher-priced cosmetics, which would be sold exclusively in these department stores. By partnering with J C Penney and Sears, considered to be the weakest portion of the brand-name retail market, the company ran the risk of a possible further weakening of its brand image. Also, in marketing a higher-priced Avon line in those department stores, the company might be sending an unintentional message to consumers that the current Avon line was not of high enough quality to be sold in J C Penney and Sears. Avon had faced significant hard times in the past, and past efforts in diversifying products and distribution had put them at risk of debt and takeover.

Avon was also spending $30 million to re-launch **Avon.com,** in order to enable consumers to buy products from sales representatives online or directly through the company. The company was intending to allow each sales representative to customize his or her own web site, which would be linked to the company's home page. However, personalized inconsistent web sites could further erode Avon's already weakened image.

The global personal-care market was valued at $171.39 billion in 1999, with overall growth of 2.8% from 1995 through 1999 (Agos, 2000). The industry had had to deal with significant changes: shifting distribution channels and market demands as well as new consumer groups. Due to the ease of entry and aggressive competition in the industry, personal-care-product companies began to utilize the Internet as a distribution channel for their products. However, many of the well-established retail and direct-selling companies had been overly cautious in developing extensive web sites due to the fear of possible cannibalization. Younger companies, less-established retailers, and niche operators, however, recognized the opportunities of the Internet and were increasingly eroding the market share of major players. Expanding target markets had also restructured personal-care marketing and product plans. As a result of sustained marketing campaigns and greater product knowledge, consumers began to display more-sophisticated buying behavior. This trend was attributed to the rising spending power of the younger generations and their corresponding demand for high-quality beauty products. However, the young and affluent customer rarely shopped for personal-care products via the direct-selling channel. Other attractive customer segments in the industry included the Generation Y market, the ethnic market, and, increasingly, the men's personal-care market.

In light of Avon's disappointing financial situation and new retail initiatives, as well as changing market demands, Jung was considering the following strategic decisions. What type of product-line extensions or divestitures should Avon undertake? How should the company establish a successful Internet presence? If the company ventured into retail outlets, which would best suit the company's current structure and future goals? How could the company create a consistent and strong image? These and other decisions would have to be made if Avon was to grow, prosper, and triumph against competitors in the near, intermediate, and longer-term future.

The Personal-Care Industry and Competitive Market

Overall View of the Industry

The personal-care industry, as shown in Figure 1, was defined by the Food and Drug Administration (FDA) as all products intended to be applied to the body for cleansing, beautifying, promoting attractiveness, or altering the body's appearance (U.S. FDA, 2000A). The products in the personal-care industry were divided into skin care, makeup/color cosmetics, hair care, personal hygiene products, perfumes/fragrances, spa services, and other related items. The customers in the industry could be segmented according to their age (mature market, baby boomers, Generation X, Generation Y), by gender (male, female), and by ethnic origin (African American, Asian American, Latin American). Products in the industry were distributed and sold via three methods: direct selling, retail selling, and online selling. The personal-care industry was prominent in both the domestic and international markets and was regulated by the FDA, Federal Trade Commission, and Department of Transportation. Competition mainly came from Mary Kay Inc. and L'Oreal.

In 1999, the global market for personal-care products was valued at $171.39 billion, with overall growth of 2.8% from 1995 through 1999 (Agos, 2000). Overall, the market for personal-care products was expected to increase steadily in the future, reaching $197.97 billion in 2003, as seen in Figure 2.

Products/Services

Skin Care   Skin-care products, valued at $29.44 billion in 1999, were comprised of facial products, hand and body products, and cosmeceuticals (Agos, 2000). Approximately 39% of households purchased facial cleansers and lotions at least once a year with expenditures averaging $14.41; 22% of the purchases were attributed to perceived price savings (Grossman, 1999). Consumers tended to buy larger sizes and use larger quantities of hand and body lotion than the facial segment: approximately 73.7% of households bought skin and hand lotions, with yearly expenditures averaging $21.33 (Cooney-Curran, 2000). Consumers bought the products about four times a year, with 21.3% purchasing the products due to perceived price savings or deals (Cooney-Curran, 2000). Consumers were becoming increasingly price sensitive to hand and body lotion products, and at the same time,

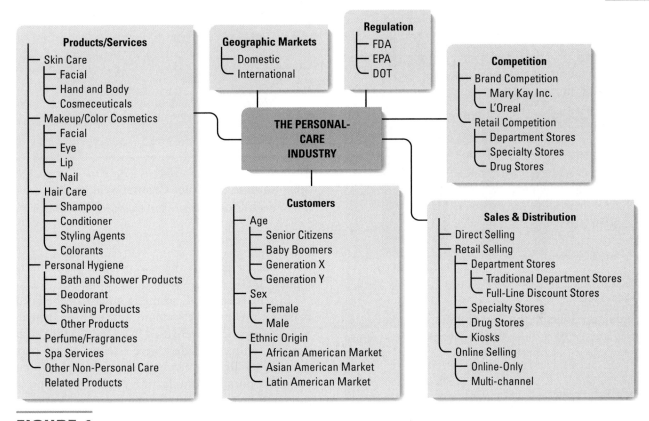

FIGURE 1

The Personal-Care Industry

they demanded quality and effectiveness in the products they purchased.

Personal-care products considered to be drugs or "cosmeceuticals" were articles intended to cleanse, beautify, or promote attractiveness as well as treat or prevent disease or otherwise affect the structure or any function of the human body (U.S. FDA, 2000A). Skin cosmeceuticals comprised 25% of the total skin-care market in 1999 with sales of $1.5 billion (Bittar, 2000). The growth was driven by the introduction of cosmeceutical ingredients in mass products—once the exclusive domain of high-quality product manufacturers. It was projected that in the following years, the skin-care market would be dominated by cosmeceuticals, especially in the more-advanced economies. The entry of many mass companies into the market was likely to drive average prices up, which in turn would increase revenue growth (Bittar, 2000).

The most common skin cosmeceuticals were anti-wrinkle cosmeceuticals and sun cosmeceuticals.

Anti-wrinkle cosmeceuticals contained ingredients such as Retinal (a vitamin A derivative), which served to maintain the skin's youthful appearance. Product claims of "anti-aging," "wrinkle reduction," and "improves fine lines" dominated the skin-care segment, as consumers were eager to purchase products that delivered a glimmer of hope for healthier-looking skin and body. Sun cosmeceuticals came in two types: sunscreens and sun blocks. Sunscreens were creams, lotions, or oils that were SPF-rated and that reacted with chemicals in the skin to offer protection from the sun for a predetermined period without risking sunburn. Sun blocks were opaque creams or pastes containing zinc oxide or titanium dioxide, which prevented all ultraviolet radiation from reaching the skin, and, therefore, did not carry an SPF rating. Sunscreens with an SPF above 15 were sometimes referred to as sun blocks even though they still allowed some UV-light to pass through. Sun cosmeceuticals mainly protected individuals from

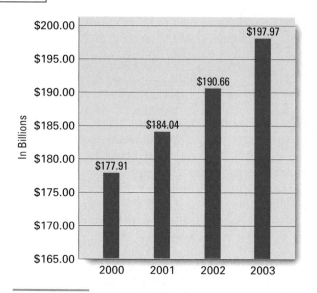

FIGURE 2

Expected Sales in the Personal-Care Market

Source: F. Agos (2000). "State of the Industry: 2000," *Global Cosmetic Industry,* June 1, vol. 166, no. 6, p. 22.

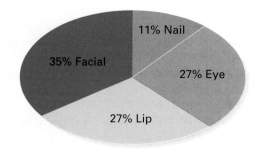

FIGURE 3

1998 Sales in the Color Cosmetic Segment

Source: Market Share Reporter (2000). Detroit, MI: Gale Research.

sunlight-induced skin aging and melanoma, a form of skin cancer responsible for a 191% increase in mortality rates for men and 84% in women between 1950 and the mid 1990s (Altruis Biomedical Network, 2000C).

Keys to success with skin-care products were tailoring the products to specific needs and frequently introducing new products. Successful introduction of new skin-care products required strong company research and development. Other keys to success were strong brand loyalty and strong brand image, which made product claims viable.

Makeup/Color Cosmetics The makeup/color cosmetic segment, valued at $19.1 billion in 1999, was the highest revenue-generating one in the personal-care industry. Figure 3 illustrates the components of the makeup/color cosmetic segment in order of sales volume.

Facial makeup/color cosmetic products included foundation, face powder, concealer, and rouge. Facial cosmetics were the highest revenue-generating segment in the makeup/color cosmetic market. Sales for foundation (a vanishing cream) were $602.7 million in 1999, a 19.1% gain over 1998. Foundation experienced the most growth of any color cosmetic cate-

gory, due in part to the use of sheer-skin effects (Sauer, 2000).

Eye makeup/color cosmetic products included mascara, eyeliner, eye shadow, and eyebrow pencil. Since eye cosmetics were used in a very sensitive area, product testing and safety were essential. Customers were increasingly demanding new products with an emphasis on all-in-one features, such as new brow products that emphasized definition and contour, mascara products with gel-based consistency to promote thickness and shine, and monochromatic and metallic colors for eye shadows.

Lip makeup/color cosmetic products were comprised of lipstick, lip gloss, and lip pencil. The trend in lip products was towards all-in-one products that provided color and moisturizing capabilities while also protecting the lips from harmful UV-rays and that contained SPF, vitamins, botanicals, antioxidants, and exfoliators.

Nail makeup/color cosmetic products consisted of nail varnish or enamel, nail varnish remover, and nail-treatment products. Nail cosmetics experienced the lowest growth in the personal-care industry due to fashion-related cycles and lack of new shades, colors, and product launches.

Growth in the overall makeup/color cosmetic segment was expected to remain strong in the future, especially as new products were expected to hit the market. Cosmetics were considered basic necessities and were purchased regardless of the health of the economy. Sales of cosmetics relied on disposable personal income, which was expected to increase 2.4% through 2003 (Sanabria, 2000A). However, the segment was heavily influenced by prevalent fashion trends, as shown at beauty web sites, in magazines, or at runway shows. Cosmetics were becoming more innovative and sophisticated; the popularity of multi-functional, all-in-one products was evidence of this trend. Consumers of makeup/color cosmetics were also seeking products tailored to their specific needs, and their increased product knowledge led to the demand for selection. Female consumers began to purchase cosmetics by the age of twelve. By the age of thirteen, 90% of them regularly used cosmetic products (Sanabria, 2000A).

Keys to success in the makeup/color cosmetics industry were developing products according to fashion trends, having a wide range of selection in each subcategory, and creating products according to needs. An additional key to success was developing product awareness and recognition among young consumers. Also, since makeup/color cosmetics were at times used on very sensitive areas of the body, strong quality control was required.

Hair Care   The hair-care segment was comprised of shampoo, conditioner, styling agents, and colorants. Shampoo was the most popular hair-care product. Due to consumer demand, special formulation shampoos were developed for particular hair types or for hair that had been subjected to a treatment such as coloring. Similarly, many new conditioning products offered a combination of benefits, such as protecting and strengthening the hair. Hair colorants were leading the hair-care segment, being driven by increased purchases by women, men, baby boomers, and Generation Y. It was reported that 50% of women colored their hair and 35% of them did it at home with a consistent growth rate projected for upcoming years (In Cosmetics99, 1999). Those who began to color their hair in their midthirties were likely to color it for life.

Additionally, there was social pressure for baby boomers to maintain a young-looking image, particularly for women of this age group who were pursuing careers. Hair colorants led to the introduction of styling products formulated for colored or UV-damaged hair that could intensify color and longevity. The hair-color category had grown 12% over the past year (Sanabria, 2000A). All hair types experienced problems to some degree. Thus, hair structure and physical properties of hair care were important factors to consider in developing new hair-care products, as were the specific needs for the hair types of different ethnic groups. Use of natural ingredients in

hair products was expected to drive growth in the hair-care segment for the next ten years, due to consumers' recognition that herbs had fewer side effects, promoted health, and were perceived to be cleaner and simpler (Altruis Biomedical Network, 2000A). In 1999, there were two to three times more brands than in 1990, causing market saturation in the hair-care segment (Sanabria, 2000B).

In order to succeed in this market, value-added products needed to be introduced in order to distinguish between the numerous products, and then a complete line of hair-care products would need to be developed in order to increase profits. Keys to success in marketing hair-care products were tailoring them to special needs, using natural ingredients, developing value-added products, and offering a complete line of products. Keys to success also included brand loyalty with existing consumers and awareness and recognition for younger consumers by offering trendy coloring products.

Personal Hygiene   The personal-hygiene segment included bath and shower products, deodorants, shaving products, and related items. Bath and shower products included bubble bath and cleansing products such as bar soap and body wash. Approximately 93% of the population used personal wash products, with above-average growth in shower gels and antibacterial products. However, bar soaps constituted two-thirds of bath product sales. Shaving products included razors, both electric and manual, and shaving creams. Competition among electric razors was expected to increase due to technological innovations. Manual razors were considered commodities that were easily interchangeable. As a result, many companies reduced prices and sustained smaller profit margins with this product in order to gain customer loyalty (Altruis Biomedical Network, 2000B). Other products in the personal-hygiene segment included oral-hygiene products and feminine-hygiene products.

In 1999, the total global market value of personal hygiene was $22.4 billion (Agos, 2000). Personal-hygiene products did not always follow the same trends as other personal-care items, since many personal-hygiene products were considered staples, as opposed to luxuries. Sales of personal-hygiene products designed exclusively for men were estimated at $1.7 billion in 1999 (NPD Group, 2000A). Manufacturers were increasingly targeting the "wellness" market, attempting to derive value from aromatherapeutic products advertised as relieving the stresses of modern life. These included essential oils like eucalyptus and menthol in bath additives, shower gels, and soaps. Many companies not primarily involved in personal-care products diversified their product line with personal-hygiene products, due to the non-cyclical market. Due to increased competition and number of products offered, a key to success was developing all-in-one products and utilizing aromatherapeutic ingredients. Most personal-hygiene products were distributed via retail outlets, and often the companies with the strongest brand names and largest profit margins would get premium shelf space. Many generic brands were available for price-conscious consumers.

Therefore, keys to success in this market were developing good relations with storeowners in order to obtain premium shelf space and increase sales and building strong brand loyalty.

Perfumes/Fragrances   The global fragrance market was valued at $22.2 billion in 1999 (NPD Group, 2000A). Sales of men's prestige fragrances rose to $960 million in 1999, a 6% increase from the previous year. Women's fragrances decreased by 1% in the same year (NPD Group, 2000A). Unisex fragrances were driving the market globally, growing from 6% of overall sales in 1995 to 8% in 1999 (NPD Group, 2000A). The fragrance market was highly sensitive to the marketing strategies of major fragrance houses.

The association with clothing and sports was expected to drive the market in the future. During the 1990s, a thousand new perfumes were launched (NPD Group, 2000A). Future trends included invisible scents which only reached the brain; microencapsulation, which would allow scents to remain on the skin for days; and natural aromatherapeutic scents, which stimulated mood, enhanced the senses, and reduced stress. Many companies offered single-use sprays in order to increase brand awareness. Also, companies were offering refillable perfumes, which were 20% to 40% cheaper than nonrefillables, in order to ensure repeat sales. Overall, companies participating in the fragrance industry were subjected to rising price competition, price transparency, and limited future-growth prospects. The fragrance market was heavily influenced by prevailing trends and further characterized by low-level brand loyalty. Consumers were becoming increasingly fashion and value conscious. Recent product launches indicated that mental well-being was having an impact on innovation, encouraging consumers to purchase value-added products (Anonymous, 2000).

Keys to success in the fragrance industry were new product introductions with an emphasis on mental well-being, increased brand awareness through the increased distribution of samples, and strong brand loyalty.

Figure 4 indicates the expected future sales growth of personal-care products from 1998 to 2005 segmented by type of product.

FIGURE 4

Expected Future Sales Growth of Personal-Care Products, 1998–2005

Low Growth ($<$ 12%)	Premium women's fragrances, hand care, baby hair care, face masks, bath additives, styling agents, home perms, conditioners
Medium Growth (12–18%)	Facial makeup, baby toiletries, mass women's fragrances, baby skin care, premium's men's fragrances, 2-in-1 hair-care products, mass unisex fragrances, suntan products, after-sun products, bar soaps, toners, mass men's fragrances
High Growth (18–25%)	Shower products, eye makeup, post-shave products, salon hair care, body care, solid deodorants, talcum powder, premium unisex fragrances, cleansers, shampoo, spray deodorants
Exceptionally High Growth ($>$ 25%)	Baby sun care, hair colorants, lip products, self-tanning products, cream deodorants, facial moisturizers

Source: F. Agos (2000). "State of the Industry: 2000," *Global Cosmetic Industry,* June 1, vol. 166, no. 6, p. 22.

Spa Services   Spas, also known as wellness centers, were places where individuals received therapeautic and beautifying services such as massages, body wraps, manicures, pedicures, and haircuts, hair colorants, and hair styling. Many spas sold a variety of prestigious, premium-priced personal-care products. Spas were becoming more commonplace for both men and women. Most consumers received samples of the products that were used in the services they received. As a result, many developed brand loyalty to products they perceived to be superior and specific to their needs.

Keys to success with spa services were offering samples of products used during the services, developing a strong brand image by developing and selling prestigious, high-priced products, and creating products tailored to needs.

Other Nonpersonal-Care Products   A few personal-care companies went beyond normal personal-care product line extensions and offered nonpersonal-care products such as jewelry, apparel, gift and decorative products, and home-entertainment items. The key to success with such products was to analyze each segment to see if it was profitable and fit the company's brand image.

Customers

Customers in the personal-care industry could be categorized according to age, gender, and ethnic origin.

Age   Customers could be segmented by age in four distinct markets: the mature market, baby boomers, Generation X, and Generation Y. Figure 5 illustrates the age ranges and size of each age segment.

Senior Citizens. The senior citizen segment was comprised of individuals aged fifty-four and over. The number of individuals in the United States aged sixty-five and older increased by over 3.7 million since 1990, reaching approximately 35 million people (Francese, 2000). The average household of senior citizens aged 65 to 74 spent nearly $30,000 a year on goods and services (Francese, 2000). However, as senior citizens aged, they tended to reduce their purchases of personal-care products. In recent years, department stores, malls, and specialty stores showed the greatest net declines in senior citizens' personal-care purchases. The preferred channels of distribution were drugstores, mass merchandisers, and, most

FIGURE 5

Customers in the Personal-Care Industry Segmented by Age

Senior Citizens 54 and above years old	34.8 million people (over age 65)
Baby Boomers 35–53 years old	81 million people 30% of the population
Generation X 23–34 years old	46 million people 17% of the population
Generation Y 5–22 years old	73 million people 28% of the population

Source: Global Cosmetic Industry (2000). "GENERATION GAPS: Global Cosmetic Industry Takes a Look at the Personal-Care Preferences, Spending Habits, and Power of Generation Y and X and Baby Boomers," [Online]. http://www.findarticles.com/cf_0/ m0HLW/6_166/63411614/p1/ article.jhtml. Accessed November 1.

important, direct selling due to its convenience (Francese, 2000).

Baby Boomers. The baby-boomer segment, estimated at 81 million people or 30% of the population, was comprised of individuals aged 35 to 53 years old and the largest demographic segment (Global Cosmetic Industry, 2000). Within this segment, households headed by 45- to 53-year-olds had the highest median income and a median net worth of $57,755, higher than any other personal-care product customer age group, with increases expected (Global Cosmetic Industry, 2000). Their disposable income was valued at $930 billion in 1998, an increase of 7% in 1996. The boomers' spending power was expected to grow 16% over the next five years, reaching $1,080 billion by 2003 (Global Cosmetic Industry, 2000). This segment outspent all age groups in virtually every category, including categories not targeted to them (Brookman, 1999). Due to the age of this large demographic segment, they sought products that could reverse or halt the aging process, protect the skin from environmental stresses, and color gray hair.

Figure 6 portrays the personal-care items purchased regularly by baby boomers. The top five purchases in this segment were shampoo, deodorant, bath soap, hand and body lotion, and hair conditioner. Figure 7 illustrates the products that baby boomers were most likely to buy in the future. As

FIGURE 6

Personal-Care Items Purchased Regularly by Baby Boomers

Product	% Who Purchase Item Regularly
Shampoo	84
Deodorant	83
Bath soap	78
Hand and body lotion	53
Conditioner	46
Hair styling products	36
Men cologne	33
Lipstick	32
Facial moisturizer	32
Mascara	32
Facial cleanser	31
Eye makeup	28
Perfume—women's	25
Foundation	24
Nail polish	23
Hair colorant	22
Sunscreens	21
Blush	20
Face powder	17
OVERALL	98%

Source: Global Cosmetic Industry (2000). "GENERATION GAPS: Global Cosmetic Industry Takes a Look at the Personal-Care Preferences, Spending Habits, and Power of Generation Y and X and Baby Boomers," [Online]. **http://www.findarticles.com/cf_0/ m0HLW/6-166/63411614/p1/ article.jhtml**. Accessed November 1.

FIGURE 7

Personal-Care Products That Baby Boomers Were Most Likely to Buy

Category	Volume Index*
Feminine hygiene products	230
Pain remedies for back and leg	164
Hair colorants—women's	158
Ethnic hair products	155
Eyebrow and eyeliner cosmetics	155
Cream foundations	152
Dieting aids—appetite suppressants	150
Bath oil	147
Hand cream	146
Mascara	145
Perfume—women's	143
Skin cream—all purpose	141

*Volume indices above 120 indicate that dollar sales among households headed by women ages 45–54 were notably above expected levels.

Source: Global Cosmetic Industry (2000). "GENERATION GAPS: Global Cosmetic Industry Takes a Look at the Personal-Care Preferences, Spending Habits, and Power of Generation Y and X and Baby Boomers," [Online]. **http://www.findarticles.com/cf_0/m0HLW/ 6_166/63411614/p1/article.jhtml**. Accessed November 1.

indicated, personal-care-product purchases that were above expected levels and expected to increase in popularity were hair colorants, feminine-hygiene products, ethnic hair products, and various eye-makeup products.

Both men and women baby boomers were value- and quality-conscious, but not necessarily price-sensitive. Baby boomers were recreational shoppers and status-brand purchasers. Baby boomers shopped via numerous channels of distribution (including high-end specialty stores, department stores, full-line discount stores, and direct selling). Due to their hectic lifestyles and time constraints, keys to success were providing product information and education, creat-ing products according to needs, and cultivating strong brand loyalty.

Generation X. The Generation X segment, averaging 46 million people, or 17% of the population, spent approximately $125 billion yearly (Global Cosmetic Industry, 2000). Figure 8 illustrates the most regularly purchased items by Generation X. The five most regular purchases by Generation X were shampoo, deodorant, bath soap, hair conditioner, and hand and body lotion. This age segment tended to purchase personal-care products they perceived to be unique and was expected to have increasing disposable income to spend in the coming years on luxury goods. In the future, they were expected to be loyal to the companies/brands from which they made purchases in the past (typically, well-known brand names). They also tended to be loyal to companies that demonstrated support of women's issues. Therefore, keys to success were a strong brand image, strong brand loyalty, offering of unique products, and sponsorship of women's issues.

FIGURE 8

Personal-Care Items Purchased Regularly by Generation X

Product	% Who Purchase Item Regularly
Shampoo	83
Deodorant	79
Bath soap	77
Hair conditioner	52
Hand and body lotion	51
Hair styling products	40
Men's cologne	35
Deodorant soap	34
Lipstick	32
Facial cleanser	31
Mascara	29
Facial moisturizer	26
Women's Perfume	26
Eye makeup	25
Foundation	22
Nail polish	21
Face powder	19
Blush	17
Sunscreens	16
Hair colorant	14
OVERALL	97%

Source: Global Cosmetic Industry (2000). "GENERATION GAPS: Global Cosmetic Industry Takes a Look at the Personal-Care Preferences, Spending Habits, and Power of Generation Y and X and Baby Boomers," [Online]. **http://www.findarticles.com/cf_0/m0HLW/ 6_166/63411614/p1/article.jhtml.** Accessed November 1.

Generation Y. Generation Y was the 73 million 5- to 22-year-old people who comprised 28% of the population. According to U.S. census projections, Generation Y, nearly three times the size of Generation X, was expected to reach 33.6 million by 2005, making for the largest teen population in U.S. history (Anonymous, 1999). According to Teen Research Unlimited, Generation Y spent $150 billion in 1999 and influenced $450 billion in purchases. Spending in this segment centered mainly on food, clothing, entertainment, and personal-care items (Anonymous, 1999). Generation Y purchased what they perceived to be quality yet affordable personal-care products. They tended to prefer products created for them and that addressed their needs. Most informed of all the populations, they used the Internet for all of their needs, including product information and purchasing, chatting with friends, and education. Generation Y was heavily influenced by the fashion and music industries and was responsive to advertisements in these channels. However, they also developed brand loyalty to companies that subtly marketed to them. Since they tended to value self-expression and individualism, many experimented with hair coloring and were inclined to purchase nonpermanent hair colorants. Also, Generation Y was expected to increase sales in the skin-care market. As their bodies began changing and developing, skin-care issues, especially blemish concerns, were expected to proliferate.

Keys to success with Generation Y were quality products at affordable prices, products tailored to their specific needs, and trendy, fashionable, youth-oriented products. Keys to success were brand awareness and recognition, subtle marketing techniques, and promotions targeted specifically to Generation Y. The ability to distribute products through various distribution channels was an additional key to success.

Gender   Females influenced an average of 90% of all household purchase decisions and were the main personal-care-product consumers (Mallory, 1995). Approximately 72% of American women worked full-time. The number of working wives with children under the age of six had risen by more than 400% since 1948, earning more than $1 trillion in 1994, a fivefold increase over 1975 (Mallory, 1995). Working women spent less time shopping and were more brand- and store-loyal than nonworking women. Working women were less likely to shop during evening hours and on the weekend, as well as less likely to buy through direct-mail catalogs. The key to success in targeting to women in general was utilizing various distribution channels.

The male consumer was increasingly purchasing personal-care products, especially hair colorants and fragrances. Although hair colorants for men grew at a very slow pace from the 1950s to the 1990s, the last five years presented a 13.1% increase in this sector (Sanabria, 2000B). The reason for this growth was twofold: first, the stereotype that once discouraged men from using products to enhance their appearance was virtually nonexistent by 1999; second, the baby-boomer males, who were still in the work force, were striving to maintain a youthful appearance in their work environment. The growth in the male fragrance market had been attributed in part to aggressive advertising in magazines targeted at males, which were increasing in number. Male consumers were increasingly shopping for personal-care products in convenient retail locations. The most powerful driver for men was a brand name; while very loyal, they were also open to trying new products (NPD Group, 2000A). Nine out of ten men who wore a fragrance chose it and purchased it by themselves, which was a significant change from a decade earlier, when men were influenced by and reliant on women to make this decision. Men were increasingly purchasing hair-styling aids in hair-dressing salons. They were less price-sensitive than women and also more service-dependent. However, they demanded products created for them since they did not have an interest in purchasing personal-care products made for women.

Keys to success with males were promotions specifically targeting them, brand awareness through trials, masculine packaging, retail presence, and providing services to influence decisions. Additional keys to success were a strong brand name and brand loyalty.

Ethnic Origin By the year 2050, nearly half of all Americans will be non-Caucasian (Herman, 2000). The three main segments in the personal-care ethnic market were African Americans, Asian Americans, and Latin Americans. African American growth figures had been fairly constant, while tremendous growth occurred in the Asian and Latin American segments. Consumers of non-Caucasian ethnicity spent more on personal-care products than any other consumer group, and subsequently demanded products tailored to their unique needs (Herman, 2000). Figure 9 illustrates personal-care products in greatest demand in this market: hair-care products dominated all other product segments in the personal-care industry. Figure 10 shows the top selling items in the ethnic hair-care market. Again, chemical hair products and hair stylants were the preferred items.

The second largest segment in the ethnic market was color cosmetics, though most ethnic users were limited to using products tailored for Caucasian skin and needed specialized skin-care products.

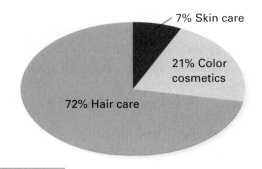

FIGURE 9

1999 Ethnic Market Expenditures in the Personal-Care Industry

Source: Market Share Reporter 2000. Detroit, MI: Gale Research.

African American Segment. The African American consumers, comprising approximately 34 million people, constituted the largest ethnic group in the United States and represented 12% of the population. With a growth rate of 11% annually, the African American segment was expected to grow to 45 million by 2020 (Kyriakos, 1999). Annual expenditures were expected to rise from $308 billion in 1990 to $532 billion in 1999, up 72.9% in nine years for a compound annual growth of 6.3%. About 50% of African Americans were considered middle class, up from only 16% in 1990 (Kyriakos, 1999). Unlike other ethnic groups that were clustered in a few geographic or metropolitan areas, African Americans drove the market in many U.S. cities (Herman, 2000).

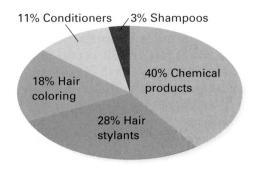

FIGURE 10

1999 Ethnic Market Expenditures in the Hair-Care Segment

Source: Market Share Reporter 2000. Detroit, MI: Gale Research.

African American consumers tended to prefer popular or leading brands, were brand loyal, and were unlikely to purchase private-label and generic products. To satisfy the need in the marketplace, many personal-care companies developed products targeted to African American women, with an emphasis on hair care. It was noted that 64% of African Americans (compared to 51% of Caucasians) were willing to spend more for what they considered to be superior quality, which in turn led them to be 25% more likely to buy premium or brand names (Kyriakos, 1999). African American women spent three times more on hair-care products than the rest of the population. African American women were influenced by their individual lifestyles and required hair designs that were versatile. Because their hair was naturally fragile, to successfully target this market the industry needed to create products that were gentle and rich in moisturizing and conditioning agents. The biggest need in this industry was for a relaxer that did not damage hair, since 80% of African American women used chemicals on their hair, relaxers being most popular. Nearly 75% of African American women had six perfumes on average. African Americans demanded specialized skin products suited for their needs since dry skin was a common skin problem in this segment (Rocafort, 2000). In selling personal-care products, it was determined that mass media did not communicate well in the African American market. Many marketers supplemented their advertisements in magazines, newspapers, and media directed specifically to African Americans. African Americans were also more brand loyal to companies who sought to build relationships.

Keys to success with the African American segment were a premium brand name, products targeted to needs—specifically hair-care and skin-care products—specialized promotions, building relationships, and developing brand loyalty.

Asian American Segment. The Asian American population, at approximately 7 million and encompassing 3% of the population, was the fastest-growing minority in the United States (Shiffman, 1997). Asian Americans were considered to be better educated and more computer literate than the rest of the population. They spent more than $38 billion on consumer goods and services annually, and they valued quality and were willing to pay for it. This ethnic segment tended to be very loyal consumers, especially to retailers who made it known that they valued

Asian American patronage. They were more responsive to advertisements featuring models of their ethnicity (Shiffman, 1997). Asian Americans sought products tailored specifically to their unique sensitive-skin needs, the reason many Asian immigrants continued to use products from Asia. Keys to success with Asian Americans were products targeted to needs, high-quality products, promotions targeted specifically to them, and developing brand awareness.

Latin American Segment. Latin Americans represented about 9% of the United States population, with a combined buying power of $205 billion. With a 53% population increase during the decade from 1980 to 1990 (and a 27% growth rate expected for the decade 2000 to 2010), Latin Americans were projected to surpass African Americans within twenty years as the largest American ethnic group (Shiffman, 1997). Latin Americans preferred well-known or familiar brands and purchased those they perceived to be more prestigious. They generally enjoyed shopping more than other ethnic groups did, but tended not to be impulse buyers and were increasingly utilizing promotions and price reductions offered by companies. They also appeared to be engaged in the process of acculturation, adopting the consumption patterns of the majority of U.S. consumers. Latin Americans also spent more time with mass media in their first language. Latin Americans were beginning to be targeted by some larger cosmetic companies.

Keys to success with Latin Americans were brand recognition, price reductions/discounts, and foreign-language advertisements.

Sales and Distribution

Personal-care products were sold and distributed via three main channels: direct, retail, and Internet.

Direct Selling   Direct selling, which comprised face-to-face selling and remote selling, included both personal contact with consumers in their homes (and other non–store locations, such as offices) and telephone solicitations initiated by the retailer, emphasizing convenience and personalization. Consumers were often more relaxed in their homes than in retail stores, and were more likely to be attentive in the absence of competing brands. Senior citizens and those with children benefited from direct selling due to their limited mobility. For the company, direct selling presented lower overhead costs since store locations and fixtures were not necessary (Berman,

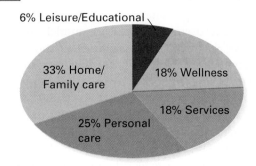

FIGURE 11

1999 Direct Selling—Percentage of
Sales by Major Product Group

Source: The Direct Selling Industry (2000). "2000 Direct Selling
Growth & Outlook Survey," [Online]. **http://www.dsa.org/
factsht00.stm.** November 7.

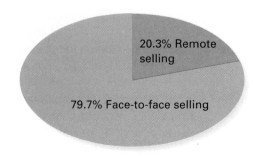

FIGURE 12

Percentage of Sales by Type of
Direct-Selling Medium

Source: The Direct Selling Industry (2000). "2000 Direct Selling
Growth & Outlook Survey," [Online]. **http://www.dsa.org/
factsht00.stm.** November 7.

1997). Figure 11 illustrates the major product groups involved in direct selling, with personal-care items the second most popular products sold via this channel. Figure 12 illustrates the popularity of face-to-face and remote selling.

Figures 13 and 14 indicate the percentage of sales attributed to the subsegments of face-to-face selling and remote selling.

However, in recent times, sales from direct selling—especially in the personal-care industry—were rising at a slow pace, for several reasons. More women were working and were not interested or available to purchase items at home. Improved job

opportunities in other fields and the interest in full-time, career-oriented positions reduced the number of people interested in direct-selling jobs. Sales productivity was low because the average transaction was small and consumers were increasingly unreceptive to this type of selling; many would not open their doors to salespeople or talk to telephone sales representatives (The Direct Selling Industry, 2000). Keys to success with direct selling were recruiting and maintaining quality and enthusiastic sales representatives. A key to success with current sales representatives was to offer incentives. Also, having strong internal relations was another important key to success.

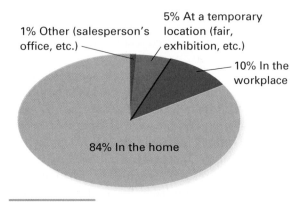

FIGURE 13

Percentage of Sales by Face-to-Face Selling

Source: The Direct Selling Industry (2000). "2000 Direct Selling
Growth & Outlook Survey," [Online]. **http://www.dsa.org/
factsht00.stm.** November 7.

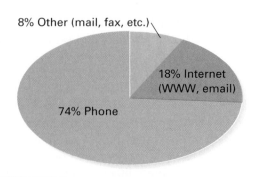

FIGURE 14

Percentage of Sales by Remote Selling

Source: The Direct Selling Industry (2000). "2000 Direct Selling
Growth & Outlook Survey," [Online]. **http://www.dsa.org/
factsht00.stm.** November 7.

Retail Selling   Personal-care products were sold mainly through four retail outlets: department stores, specialty stores, drugstores, and kiosks. Department stores had the greatest selection of any general-merchandise retailers, and often served as the anchor store in a shopping center or district, had strong credit-card penetration, and were usually part of a chain. Traditional department stores, such as Macy's and Bloomingdale's, merchandised average- to high-quality products with moderate to above-average pricing. Customer services ranged from medium to high levels of sales assistance, credit, and delivery. Macy's strategy was aimed at middle-class shoppers interested in a wide assortment and moderate prices, while Bloomingdale's aimed at upscale consumers through more trendy merchandise and higher prices.

During the past decade, sales growth in traditional department stores was behind that of the full-line discount stores. There were several reasons for this decline. Traditional department stores no longer had brand exclusivity for the items they sold because manufacturers' brands were also available at specialty and discount outlets. Many stores were too large and had too much unproductive selling space and low-turnover personal-care merchandise. Also, price-conscious consumers were increasingly attracted to discount retailers. Department stores, which represented approximately $80 billion in annual sales, cited a 1% decline in same-store sales from January 2000 to August 2000, despite a 7% increase in the overall retail industry (Berman, 1997). This was partly due to their high reliance on apparel, which comprised 75% of department stores' inventory, and their vulnerability to changes in consumer buying habits. In the past, consumers shopped at department stores for their merchandise selection and service; however, they now purchased at mass merchants for the same reasons—as well as for convenience and price. Traditional department stores were trying to target Generation Y by offering more fashion-conscious products combined with a more exciting decor. Keys to success with traditional department stores were offering medium- to high-priced quality products, having a wide assortment in the product mix, maintaining relationships with store managers for optimal displays and space, and hiring and maintaining qualified sales representatives for point-of-purchase assistance.

A full-line discount store was a high-volume, low-cost, fast-turnover outlet selling a broad range of merchandise for less than conventional prices. Its products were normally sold with minimal assistance in any single department, and catalogs were normally not available. Durable goods accounted for approximately 60% of all sales (Berman, 1997). In 1993, Wal-Mart, Kmart, and Target expanded operations to include almost 5,000 full-line discount stores that accounted for nearly $70 billion in sales that year. The average outlet tended to be smaller than the traditional department store, which improved productivity. The growth in most of the personal-care categories was stronger in full-line discount stores, since they were able to attract some of the drugstore customers. These locations were able to fuel growth by feeding off the heavy volume of customer traffic in their stores. Sales for facial cosmetics increased 15.7% in this outlet for 1999. Men's fragrances rose 12.5%, and women's fragrances rose 6.7%. Full-line discount stores catered to the middle- to lower-class consumer seeking average- to good-quality merchandise at competitive prices (Berman, 1997). Keys to success with full-line discount stores were products that required minimal assistance and stressed convenience and variety; average- to good-quality products that attracted more price-sensitive middle-class consumers; and creating strong relationships with store managers for optimal displays and space.

Specialty stores carried a narrow product line with a wide assortment of products within that category, and tailored their strategy to selected market segments. This method allowed the specialty store to maintain better selections, flexibility, and sales expertise than department stores. Specialty stores increased in popularity in the 1990s due to their image and their strong consumer focus. For the first half of 2000, specialty stores experienced a 4% increase in sales (D'Innocenzio, 2000). Specialty stores tended to target medium- to high-income baby-boomer and Generation X consumers. An example of a personal-care specialty store was Sephora, a company offering a hands-on shopping environment. Customers had the ability to browse through the various international, unique, and prestigious cosmetic selections that were organized alphabetically and by specific categories, and had the choice of shopping with no sales assistance or with detailed expert advice. The company was formed in 1993, and with 143 international stores, was the leading chain of perfume and cosmetic stores in France and the second in Europe. Keys to success in selling to specialty stores were unique and prestigious cosmetics and qualified sales representatives for point-of-purchase assistance.

Drugstores mainly sold mass-market personal-care products, with sales that increased steadily in 2000 and strong growth expected in the near future. New brands, such as Olay and Neutrogena, as well as advanced product formulations from established mass-market brands, helped drugstore chains gain loyalty from department-store shoppers. Although space remained tight in chain drugstore cosmetics departments, there was a growing trend to balance out the department with a product mix that was geared to a greater variety of consumers.

In addition to carrying traditional mainstream mass-market brands, drugstore chains were adding a broader assortment of products targeted toward professional, middle- to high-income women. In addition, chains were looking at brands targeting less affluent women or women looking for a broad selection of fashion shades in their cosmetics. Drugstores attributed their growth to strong marketing and merchandising initiatives, a marketing emphasis on cosmetics as a core department, and partnerships with manufacturers resulting in customized promotions (Parks, 1999B). Although full-line discount stores generated more customer traffic, drugstores were able to drive growth through prominent window displays, aggressive and consistent advertising, competitive prices, in-store service, and new products. Manufacturers were able to capitalize on these opportunities by maintaining good relations with storeowners. As a result, drugstores managed their marketing mix effectively while providing high levels of consumer satisfaction (Parks, 1999B). In 1999, chain drugstores experienced 9.6% gains in facial cosmetics. However, sales of nail cosmetics decreased 10.7% in the same year. Sales of men's and women's fragrances rose 5% and 2.2%, respectively. Other personal-care sales rose 3.9% to $1.42 billion, while unit volume fell 3.9% (Parks, 1999B).

Keys to success with drugstores were maintaining good relations with storeowners through a wide assortment of products in each category; gearing products towards both affluent and nonaffluent customers; introducing new products; advertising aggressively and consistently; and offering competitive prices.

A kiosk was an attractive freestanding structure located in malls, airports, and other high-traffic areas. A kiosk showcased a company's products and services and provided product information and, in some cases, purchasing opportunities. Mall owners had increasingly utilized kiosks as a strategic tool to raise sales-per-square-foot. Kiosks ranged in price from $4,000–$20,000, depending on the level of complexity and technology utilized in the design. The kiosk needed to be secure, well ventilated, and accessible to people of different sizes, physical abilities, and language skills. Currently, kiosks were becoming more computerized and offered video, audio, and interactivity, making the experience of using a kiosk more friendly and accessible. Although many personal-care companies did not utilize kiosks in malls, those that did stressed the need for exciting new products, enthusiastic and knowledgeable sales representatives, and samples and trials to distribute in order to increase brand awareness and product trial. These, along with strong brand image and prime location, were keys to success with kiosks.

Online Selling   With the emergence of the Internet as a shopping channel, many new personal-care companies developed web sites. This allowed them to utilize the Internet as a marketing tool by providing extensive company and product information on the site, as well as presenting brand images and advertising. However, many older companies had been cautious in using the Internet as a shopping channel since they considered it beyond their core competencies and were concerned that Internet sales might undermine their retail position and cannibalize product sales. Less-established companies were quicker in developing e-commerce sites, and as a result enjoyed increasing market share and international sales (Croft, 1997). Retail sales on the Internet were growing rapidly. In 1998, online retailers in the United States generated $14.9 billion in revenues, with a 140% increase expected for 1999 (NPD Group, 2000B). This trend was expected to continue as more consumers experimented with online access and e-commerce shopping. Unlike some other industries, the personal-care market was not yet saturated online. Therefore, personal-care companies could still develop loyal customer bases that could allow for stronger market dominance (Davis, 2000).

In 1998, there were two types of personal-care retailers online. Online-only retailers existed solely on the Internet and did not have physical locations.

Their advertising and marketing budget was directed towards customer acquisition and retention and brand awareness. Multi-channel retailers had established brands and a physical presence, and therefore did not need to spend as much as the online-only companies to build their brand online. Multi-channel retailers were able to leverage existing marketing efforts by adding their web address to promotions and encouraging customers to go online, an effort to capture an even larger share of their spending. Supplemental revenue accounted for less than half of 1% of their revenues, as opposed to 12% for online-only retailers (D'Innocenzio, 2000).

Online selling posed a major problem for direct-selling companies in general. Direct sellers' sales forces were usually partially or fully compensated based on a percentage of sales. With the introduction of online selling, sales representatives feared cannibalization of sales and loss of customers. As a result, many direct sellers were faced with strategic decisions on how to include the Internet as a channel of distribution while placating their sales representatives. At the end of 1999, more than 17 million households were shopping online, purchasing $20.2 billion over the Internet during the year. The number of online shoppers was expected to level off at about 50 million, but that trend was expected to be offset by a surge in average online spending per household, increasing from $1,167 in 1999 to $3,738 in 2004. At that point, online spending in the United States was expected to total $184 billion (NPD Group, 2000B).

Figure 15 illustrates the behavior of consumers when purchasing personal-care products via the Internet. In 1999, online personal-care sales accounted for 1% of the personal-care industry. Fragrance, makeup, and skin care accounted for 2% of all products sold online. A recent NPD report stated that 62% of polled consumers would consider purchasing personal-care products online and cited convenience as the most influential factor, as seen in Figure 16.

Only 31% of those polled considered price to influence shopping online versus in a retail store. In response to this, many online companies did not offer discounted prices, but rather coupons and other incentives to shop online. Another important factor influencing online purchasing decisions was brand names. Of those polled, 64% stated that they would buy products they had tried before. However, the type of products purchased influenced online pur-

FIGURE 15

Types of Online Personal-Care Purchases

Source: NPD Group (2000C). "Media Metric Beauty Visory," [Online]. **http://www.npd.com/corp/content/special/ evisory.htm.** Accessed November 1.

chasing behavior. For example, those purchasing fragrance, makeup, and skin products were brand loyal when purchasing online. However, consumers seeking bath and body products tended to try to find the lowest price for their preferred brand. Another trend in online beauty retailing was the diminishing distinction between brands: prestige beauty products traditionally sold only in department stores were featured next to mass beauty products at some sites (NPD Group, 2000C).

FIGURE 16

Reasons for Purchasing Beauty Products Online Instead of in Traditional Stores

Shop any time	75%
Delivery of purchases	54%
Ease of comparison shopping	46%
Faster	42%
Avoid sales tax	38%
Find hard-to-find/exclusive brands	37%
Better prices	31%
Avoid interacting with salespeople	19%
Stores too far away	13%

Source: NPD Group (2000B). "NPD and Media Metrix e-Visory Report Anticipates Dramatic Growth of Online Beauty Sales," [Online]. **http://www.npd.com/corp/content/news/releases/press_000321.htm.** Accessed October 9.

The most successful and popular personal-care web sites were those that had existed for some time and had a high level of advertising. Web sites that featured health and beauty products were more visited than cosmetics-only web sites. Health-related sites typically carried mass-merchandise beauty brands. Cosmetics-only sites tended to carry only prestige or exclusive brands. Personal-care web sites offered value-added incentives to enhance their positions. All of the companies provided quick, easy returns; many offered free shipping, and some sent free samples with orders. Increasingly, most sites were also providing a wealth of consumer information in the form of magazine-type articles, reviews, directories for purchasing and service, and makeup tips (NPD Group, 2000C). However, almost two-thirds of consumers said they were unlikely or certain not to buy personal-care products or services from the Internet since it was stated to be difficult to purchase cosmetics without a trial or sample. This was most true with new product offerings.

In the future, the Internet is expected to become more popular and more acceptable among consumers as a shopping method. It was expected that conventional direct-selling personal-care companies would face exceptional competition in countries where computer use and penetration was high, such as in North America, Western Europe, and parts of the Asia-Pacific region. By the year 2003, the Internet is expected to account for 8.2% of overall home-shopping sales (NPD Group, 2000C).

Keys to success with the Internet were offering a convenient and easy-to-navigate site, having online selling capabilities, providing coupons and price incentives to shop online, providing enhanced features at the web site—such as product information and articles—offering samples and trials, and advertising to get the consumer to the web site. Additional keys to success were a strong brand name to generate traffic and encourage customer loyalty at an early stage.

Geographic Markets

Personal-care products were sold in both the domestic and international markets. The information provided in the following sections pertains to the domestic personal-care market. Overall, the largest continental market in the personal-care industry was North and South America in 1999, with total sales of $43 billion (Dutton, 1999). The increasing globalization of the world's economy presented significant opportunities for consumer-goods manufacturers. Barriers to investment in emerging markets were dropping, and disposable income in these regions was gradually increasing, bringing with it demand for staple consumer products (Dutton, 1999).

The global personal-care industry was expected to experience continued growth in the future, as levels of consumption in undeveloped markets were significantly lower than those in Western Europe and North America. However, personal-care companies in Western Europe were under increasing pressure to come up with new products to meet consumer demands for both wider choice and higher quality. In 1998, personal-care and cosmetics companies experienced the impact of the economic downturn in Asia in both regional and global sales. To help minimize declining profits, firms restructured, focused on their core businesses, and, in some cases, expanded to gain a foothold in Asian countries in preparation for their economic recovery. Asia and Latin America were considered to have huge growth potential even though they were subject to economic downturns. The products with the greatest global growth potential were basic items such as deodorant, shampoo, and soap, especially in developing regions. For example, since 1994, deodorant experienced an 18.2% sales growth globally, compared to only 11.6% growth for the personal-care and cosmetics market overall. New or improved formulas emphasizing health and well-being and cosmeceuticals were common among products launched in 1999 (Dutton, 1999). European consumers wanted more variety now that they had more outlets from which to buy personal-care products. Supermarket chains, which in some European countries had pharmacies inside their stores, had been anxious to establish themselves as providers of quality cosmetics and toiletries. In the global market, market share of the top twenty players grew from 68% in 1996 to 72% in 1998, with the top ten companies holding 54%. These top ten companies were L'Oreal, Unilever, Procter & Gamble, Johnson & Johnson, Avon, Shiseido, Colgate-Palmolive, Revlon, Amway, and Bristol-Myers Squibb (Dutton, 1999).

Keys to success in the international market were tailoring products to needs, utilizing various distribution outlets, and creating a presence in emerging countries.

Regulation

Cosmetics marketed in the United States need to comply with the provisions of the 1938 Federal Food, Drug, and Cosmetic Act (FD&C) and the Fair Packaging and Labeling Act (FPLA). The FD&C Act was passed by Congress to protect consumers from unsafe or deceptively labeled or packaged products by prohibiting the movement in interstate commerce of adulterated or misbranded food, drug devices, and cosmetics. The FPLA was passed by Congress to ensure that packages and their labels provided consumers with accurate information about the quantity of contents in order to facilitate value comparisons (U.S. FDA, 2000A). The FD&C Act prohibited the distribution of cosmetics that were adulterated or misbranded. A cosmetic was considered adulterated if it met one of the following conditions:

▪ Contained a substance that might have made the product harmful to consumers under typical conditions of use

▪ Contained a filthy, putrid, or decomposed substance

▪ Was manufactured or held under unsanitary conditions in which it might have become contaminated or harmful to consumers

▪ Was not a hair dye and contained an unpermitted color additive

A cosmetic was considered misbranded if it met one of the following conditions:

▪ Its labeling was false or misleading

▪ It did not bear the required labeling information

▪ Its container was made or filled in a deceptive manner (U.S. FDA, 2000B)

For enforcement of the law, the FDA conducted examinations and investigations of products, inspected establishments in which products were manufactured or held, and seized adulterated and misbranded products.

Another regulating agency was the Environmental Protection Agency (EPA), which regulated products so that they complied with the limitations on using and storing volatile organic compounds. The EPA also regulated the manufacturing process, including wastewater and toxic emissions. At the manufacturing level, the Department of Transportation controlled how raw materials were labeled and shipped.

Keys to success in regards to federal regulation were adherence to good manufacturing practices, effective self-inspections, and maintaining good relations with regulation authorities.

Competition

Mary Kay Inc.   Mary Kay Inc. was the number two direct seller of beauty products in the United States. It sold more than two hundred products in eight product categories—facial skin care, cosmetics, fragrances, wellness products, sun protection, nail care, body care, and men's skin care—with a fairly good brand name and loyalty. It sold quality products at affordable prices. In regards to its skin-care line, the company tended to have weak research and development capabilities and therefore had limited new product introductions and a weak brand image. Its skin-care and color-cosmetic product lines included all-in-one features and products tailored to meet needs. However, the company had a limited selection within each product category (Hoovers Online Network, 2000B).

The company's color-cosmetic line had products tailored to needs and developed according to fashion trends, but the selection of color cosmetics was limited. The company had a relatively weak personal-hygiene segment and did not have either a spa line or a hair-care line. Mary Kay had good brand awareness and loyalty with its fragrance line but was weak in the areas of new product introductions—particularly those promoting mental well-being—and distributing samples and trials.

Mary Kay had a limited customer base of women. Its most loyal customers were senior citizens due to the convenience of the company's direct-selling channel. Baby-boomer customers were attracted to the company's high-quality products, which were tailored to their needs, resulting in sufficient brand loyalty. However, boomers were not completely satisfied with shopping at Mary Kay since they desired product information and education and a variety of channels of distribution.

The company did not target Generation X or Generation Y. Although ethnic models were used in advertising and promotions, the company did not have products tailored to any ethnic segment. African Americans valued a premium brand name, products targeted to needs, specialized promotions, and strong internal relations—areas in which Mary Kay was weak. Its quality products appealed to Asian Americans, but the company was weak in targeting products to their needs, targeting them in its promotions, and developing brand awareness. Mary Kay did not have success with Latin Americans since the company was weak in brand recognition, price reductions and discounts, and foreign-language advertisements. It was attempting to reach the male market by selling fragrances, personal-hygiene, and skin products in masculine packaging, but it targeted women in its promotions and advertising for these products, resulting in a generally weak male customer base (Mary Kay Inc. Company Website, 2000).

Mary Kay's products were distributed via 600,000 direct-sales consultants in approximately thirty-six countries. Sales for the company reached $1 billion in 1999, and the company posted a one-year sales growth of 0.0% and a one-year employee growth of 7.1% (Hoovers Online Network, 2000B). Although Mary Kay was experiencing virtually no growth with its direct-selling model, the company decided not to expand into retail distribution in the near, intermediate, or long-term future in order to maintain strong internal relations. The company felt that expansion would affect their core sales representatives. The company successfully recruited and motivated their enthusiastic sales force through bonuses ranging from jewelry to the company's trademark pink Cadillac. The company did have a convenient and easy-to-navigate web site, but it did not offer a community site linking consumers to articles and advice on subjects related to personal-care products (Hoovers Online Network, 2000B).

The company did not advertise its web site because it was not being used for online selling. Consumers who reached the web site were directed to a page that allowed them to locate a consultant in their area. Consumers had the ability to order from the consultant's web site, allowing the company to develop a loyal customer base and a good brand name. Samples, trials, coupons, and price incentives were not readily available to customers either through the web site or direct selling (Mary Kay Inc. Company Website, 2000).

L'Oreal   L'Oreal was the world's largest beauty company, with products ranging from makeup and perfume to apparel leading to a very strong brand image in the personal-care market. L'Oreal was comprised of numerous brands, including L'Oreal and May-belline, which were quality, unique, and affordable product lines; Lancôme, featuring more upscale, premium-priced products for more affluent customers; and Redken and Soft Sheen, which included hair products (L'Oreal Company Website, 2000).

L'Oreal's diverse product lines were sold in a variety of outlets, including department stores, full-line discount stores, drugstores, specialty stores, and the Internet. The company did not use kiosks or direct selling. L'Oreal sold its average- to good-quality products to attract more price-sensitive, middle-class consumers in full-line discount stores. These products required minimal assistance from sales people and stressed convenience and variety. The company was successful via this channel due to its strong relations with store managers, obtaining optimal displays and space. L'Oreal also distributed this type of product line via drugstores. The company enjoyed success due to its wide assortment of competitively priced products in each category, products geared to both affluent and non-affluent consumers, frequent new product introductions, and aggressive and frequent advertising.

L'Oreal conducted cosmetology and dermatology research and had a 19.5% stake in a pharmaceutical company. Its diverse product mix enabled the company to enjoy worldwide success and create strong customer bases in every category. The company's research department employed approximately 2,100 scientists and filed for about 400 patents a year—77 of them in 1999—with numerous product introductions each year. It devoted 3% of sales to cosmeceutical research (anti-aging products and sunscreen products). It sold its products in 150 countries, with products tailored according to regional needs and demands via various distribution channels. The company sold 56% of its products in Western Europe, 27% in North America, and 17% in the rest of the world (Hoovers Online Network, 2000C).

Almost 90% of the company's sales were generated from ten brands: Biotherm, Laboratoires GARNIER, Lancôme, L'Oreal, Maybelline, Redken, Helena Rubinstein, Vichy, and perfumes Giorgio Armani and Ralph Lauren. The Helena Rubinstein line consisted of products emphasizing natural ingredients and wellness targeted to the baby-boomer segment of the market. Lanvin, a subsidiary of the Group L'Oreal, developed a wide range of ready-to-wear fashion for men and women, made-to-measure fashion for men, and accessories and perfumes (Hoovers Online Network, 2000C).

Maybelline was a leader in quality, affordable, innovative, and trendy color cosmetics sold both in the United States and internationally. Maybelline products are distributed in 40,000 retail outlets, including drugstores, discount stores, supermarkets, and personal-care specialty stores, and are also carried in more than seventy countries worldwide. Due to its well-known brand name and good relations with store employees, the company was able to obtain optimal shelf space. Maybelline products were available on the Internet and featured trendy fashionable products in order to develop product awareness and recognition with Generation Y customers. The Maybelline web site offered content, community, price incentives, and purchasing options (Hoovers Online Network, 2000C).

In July 1998, L'Oreal acquired Soft Sheen Products, a large manufacturer of ethnic hair-care products. Soft Sheen, a major marketer in the United States, also had distribution in Africa. As a result, the company was considering distributing its numerous other brands in Africa. L'Oreal also owned Carson Inc., supposedly the largest marketer of ethnic hair- and skin-care products with global sales of $176 million. As a result, African Americans perceived the L'Oreal brands as having a premium brand name. They responded to the company's specialized promotions and efforts to build relationships. Asian Americans responded to the company's quality products. Latin Americans were also purchasers of L'Oreal products due to brand recognition, price reductions/discounts, and foreign-language advertisements.

L'Oreal also successfully launched a complete hair-care line both domestically and internationally. Its hair colorants, available in a variety of shades and including value-added features, targeted senior citizens, baby boomers, and Generation Y and men (L'Oreal Company Website, 2000). The company also had strong relations with male customers due to targeted promotions, creating brand awareness through trials, masculine packaging, having a retail presence, providing services to influence decisions, and having a strong brand name.

L'Oreal's convenient and easy-to-navigate main web site gives customers extensive product and company information. Not all its brands are available for online purchasing. It currently was expanding its L'Oreal web site internationally, which in turn developed customized web sites for each region, offering editorial content in the local language. At the time,

only L'Oreal and Maybelline products could be purchased online. Through the samples and trials offered online as well as through advertisements to get customers to the site, L'Oreal was able to build a strong brand name and loyal customer base.

The Lancôme line was mainly distributed in traditional department stores due to its superior quality, premium pricing, wide assortment of product mix, relationships with store managers for optimal displays and space, and qualified sales representatives for point-of-purchase assistance. However, the product was available online and was highly successful. Approximately 52% of the visitors made a purchase and spent more than 30% more than consumers who bought via the traditional retail outlet (L'Oreal Company Website, 2000). This line was popular with affluent senior citizens, baby boomers, and Generation X customers. Its Lancôme line, which was a unique and prestigious cosmetic collection, was also sold via specialty stores since they provided qualified sales representatives for point-of-purchase assistance.

The company utilized a quality control department to ensure that all products were developed, designed, and delivered according to the highest standards. It conducted its own self-examinations to see if the company was growing and continuing according to specifications. The company advertised its numerous brands in various magazines and television spots according to its target market. For example, the company often sponsored events in order to develop brand awareness in its younger customers. Also, the company often issued samples and rebate coupons to develop brand awareness and recognition (L'Oreal Company Website, 2000).

Retail Competition Traditional department stores offered a wide range of personal-care products with an emphasis on skin care, color cosmetics, personal hygiene, and perfumes/fragrances. The brands sold via this channel were usually prestigious, high-priced products geared toward medium- to highly affluent consumers: Christian Dior, Elizabeth Arden, Hard Candy, Lorac, and L'Ancome. They also appealed to affluent, young senior citizens. Department stores were strong in the baby-boomer market by offering high-quality and high-value products. Traditional department stores within themselves also sold via the Internet and were therefore strong in providing boomers with numerous channels of distribution. The department stores generally featured personal-care counters where consumers obtained personal assistance and product information via employees. Due to the higher price range of department stores' personal-care products, they were highly tailored to baby-boomer needs, thereby strengthening consumer loyalty. Traditional department store brands were also becoming increasingly popular with Generation X. Traditional department stores brands such as Polo Sport, Biotherm, Calvin Klein, and Nautica appealed to male customers since they contained masculine packaging, targeted promotions at the male sector, provided services to influence decisions, and created brand awareness through trials.

Full-line discount stores sold personal-care products in the skin-care, color-cosmetics, hair-care, personal-hygiene, and perfumes/fragrances categories. The brands sold via this channel included many private-label product lines such as My Generation and Sonia Kashuk, and affordable product lines including Vidal Sassoon, Pantene, Maybelline, Cover Girl, L'Oreal, and Revlon. The product lines were geared towards Generation X and Generation Y. The reason that full-line discount stores were so successful with Generation Y was due to its quality products at affordable prices, its trendy, fashionable, youth-oriented products tailored to needs, and strong brand awareness and recognition.

Specialty stores seemed to be in competition with traditional department stores since both channels carried high-quality, high-priced personal-care products. However, specialty stores such as Sephora tended to carry more obscure international brands such as Anna Sui, Benetton, Bvlgari, Nino Cerutti, and Poppy. As a result, specialty stores had high loyalty and recognition with both affluent baby boomers and Generation X. At a store like Sephora, customers had the ability to browse through the various unique and prestigious cosmetic selections that were organized alphabetically and by specific categories and had the choice to shop with no sales assistance or detailed expert advice.

Drugstores such as Genovese, CVS, and Rite Aid carried affordable mass-merchandise personal-care brands such as Oil of Olay, Neutrogena, Jane Cosmetics, Maybelline, and Revlon. Drugstores tended to compete with full-line discount stores in attracting Generation Y consumers, with quality products tailored to needs at affordable prices. However, drugstores also carried personal-care product lines geared

towards both non-affluent and affluent male customers. Certain personal hygiene items, such as razors, toothpaste, and shampoo and conditioner, were nonelastic generic products purchased by both affluent or non-affluent men and women customers.

The Company
Overview of the Company

Avon Products, Inc. (Avon) was a manufacturer and marketer of personal-care products, including skin-care, hair-care, color cosmetics, fragrances, personal hygiene, and a limited line of nonpersonal-care products such as jewelry, apparel, decorative and home entertainment products and a provider of spa services. Avon commenced operations in 1886 and was incorporated on January 27, 1916. It provided one of the first opportunities for American women to be financially independent at a time when their place was traditionally at home. Avon distributed its products primarily through the direct-selling channel. It was considered the world's largest direct-seller of affordable, quality beauty products. However, the company also utilized kiosks and the Internet to increase its consumer base. The company marketed its products through its sales campaign brochures, sponsorship of women-related issues, and print and television advertisements.

Avon's main customers were women of all ethnic races with a concentration of those aged thirty-five and over. Avon had a prominent presence in the United States and 137 countries. The company had revenues of $5.3 billion in 1999 compared to $5.2 billion in 1998 (Avon, 2000). In 1999, through their three million representatives, Avon handled over one billion customer transactions and sold over two billion units, making it the sixth largest global beauty company (Avon, 2000). Figure 17 gives a detailed overview of Avon Products, Inc.

Products/Services

In the past, Avon carried various product lines targeted to specific regional needs. However, in doing so, the company obtained a fragmented brand image. To rectify this problem, Avon developed universal global brands. Avon had distinguished itself as the supplier of high-quality beauty products at affordable prices. More beauty products carried the Avon brand name than any other in the world (Avon,

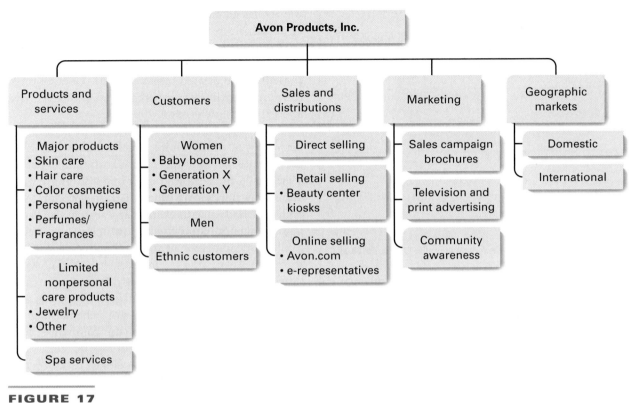

FIGURE 17

Avon Products, Inc.

1999). Figure 18 illustrates Avon's product lines as a percentage of sales. It can be noted that skin care, hair care, color cosmetics, and fragrances were the largest grossing product lines. Figure 19 indicates the actual sales dollars generated by Avon's diverse product lines.

Major Product Lines   Avon was the creator of the first alpha-hydroxy skin-care products developed by a strong research and development department that was concurrently devising alternative skin-care regimes and anticipating frequent new product introductions (Parks, 2000). Its skin-care products were tailored to needs being demanded by the market, specifically those of aging consumers and female consumers by offering high-quality and high-value products at affordable prices. By developing its ANEW product line, Avon was able to tap into the growing cosmeceutical market. It also fulfilled skin-care market opportunities by offering products that

included anti-aging features, natural ingredients, environmental protection lotions for the face, and complete skin-care regimes (Bittar, 2000). Due to this, Avon had a strong brand loyalty and brand image in the skin-care market.

Avon's line of value-added shampoos, conditioners, treatments, and styling products were somewhat tailored to consumer needs. The company developed many types of shampoos and conditioners to treat the major types of hair problems and colored or graying hair. It also had a line of hair-stylant products, although they were designed for normal (not ethnic-specific) hair types. Avon also sold an Herbal Care line that utilized natural ingredients to achieve healthier-looking hair (Hoovers Online Network, 2000A). The company did not have a hair-coloring product line and therefore did not successfully build brand recognition and awareness among younger consumers; nor did it capitalize on the need for this product by aging consumers. The company therefore

FIGURE 18

Avon Product Lines as a Percentage of
1999 Sales

Source: Hoovers Online Network (2000). "Avon Products, Inc.,"
[Online]. **http://www.hoovers.com/premium/profile/2/0,2147,10152,00**
.htm. Accessed October 11.

was weak in developing a complete hair-care line.
Since Avon's customers needed to shop elsewhere for
these products, the company had a weak brand image
and loyalty in the hair-care segment.

With the largest color palette in the world, Avon
had superior quality and quantity of makeup products. Its main cosmetic line, Avon Color, included a
wide range of face, eye, lip, and nail cosmetics, which
were customized according to various skin tones and
prevailing fashion trends. The line was the company's
largest global brand and the leading cosmetics brand
in the world (Avon, 1999). Beyond Color was Avon's
innovative anti-aging line, which combined anti-
aging treatments with color cosmetics. Color Trend

FIGURE 19

Avon Product Lines: Actual Sales in 1999

Product	$ Millions
Skin-care, hair-care, color cosmetics & fragrances	3,226
Gift & decorative	1,052
Apparel	556
Jewelry & accessories	455
Total	5,289

Source: Hoovers Online Network (2000A). "Avon Products, Inc.,"
[Online]. **http://www.hoovers.com/premium/profile/2/0,2147,10152,00**
.htm. Accessed October 11.

was Avon's global brand embracing trendy cosmetics
at affordable prices. Color Trend's full- and mini-
sized products were gradually becoming known.
However, they were not yet being aggressively purchased by the desired target market—Generation Y.
Currently, the line was offered only in Europe, Asia,
and Latin America (Avon, 1999).

Avon sold a number of personal-hygiene products, most of which fell into the bath-and-body category. It sold these products individually and as part of
a gift set, which allowed consumers to enjoy price
savings by purchasing more than one product. The
bath-and-body products included aromatherapeutic
ingredients and comprised all-in-one features. As a
result, the company had strong brand loyalty in this
segment (Avon, 2000). However, it was not established in the retail industry, so it did not yet have
strong relations with store managers, which was necessary for the long-term success of personal-hygiene
products. Skin-So-Soft, one of the company's best-
known brands, was first introduced in 1961. Currently, the Skin-So-Soft brand included products that
ranged from the original bath oil to Bug Guard Plus
with IR3535, a breakthrough technology that combined DEET-free bug repellent and PABA-free sunscreen. Naturals was a line of gentle and moisturizing
cleansers and bubble-bath products. The Aromatherapy line included candles, creams, lotions, bath products, and sprays that helped create a sense of mental
well-being and revitalization (Avon, 2000).

Avon was the world's leader in perfume sales, selling more units of fragrance than any other company
in the world. It released one global fragrance brand
per year, launched at the end of the year to coincide
with the holiday season. Avon's first new fragrance of
the millennium would be Incandessence, to be
launched worldwide in October. Incandessence also
would incorporate a unique perfume design. The
company developed a special time-released construction that changed the scent as the day progressed.
Each phase was composed of flowers, which reached
their peak of fragrance release in the given time
frame. The result was a prolonged experience and
enjoyment of the fragrance (Avon, 1999). The company's global fragrances, Women of Earth and Perceive, were the best-selling fragrance launches in the
world. Its Perceive fragrance included mood-enhanc-
ing pheromone technology, which was intended to
enhance feelings of confidence and well-being. The
company had a number of fragrances for both male

and female customers. However, Avon did not its issuing of samples throughout the years, which was imperative in the fragrance market. Despite this, it had good brand awareness and brand loyalty with its fragrance customers (Avon, 1999).

Limited Nonpersonal-Care Products   Avon's limited nonpersonal-care products were considered to be part of the "Beyond Beauty" or "Beauty Plus" category. Avon specialized in exclusively designed fashion jewelry, including pierced and clip earrings, necklaces, bracelets, rings, and watches. Avon developed gold- and silver-tone costume jewelry, and genuine 925 sterling silver, featuring genuine and simulated stones and pearls. Jewelry designs were developed in small local markets before they were distributed globally, allowing the company to have the leading market share of costume jewelry worldwide (Avon, 2000). While jewelry represented approximately 13% of Avon's domestic business, it accounted for a much smaller percentage of the company's international sales. Sales of fashion jewelry and accessories rose significantly in 1999, reflecting the success of sterling silver and bolder jewelry designs, the introduction of licensed luggage, and a strong performance in watches and handbags (Avon, 2000).

Home entertainment and gift and decorative items also posted strong growth, which was due to the increased sales of inspirational and religious products. Avon's apparel line noted decreases in sales due to the underperformance of new product introductions (Avon, 1999). Not all the segments were profitable, and some contributed to Avon's fragmented brand image. Therefore, Avon was weak in analyzing each business segment in order to gauge profitability and brand-image development.

Spa Services   Avon's spa services include hair care (cuts, style, and color), nail care (manicures and pedicures), personal hygiene (nutrition and lifestyle counseling, waxing), skin care (facials and body treatments), and cosmetics (makeup applications). New services include the opening of Eliza's Eyes at the Avon Centre, which was a boutique exclusively dedicated to the eyebrow. Also, in April 2000, the Avon Centre introduced Endermologie, a proven technique to reduce the appearance of cellulite, and Dermabrasion, a technique known to treat hyperpigmentation, acne scars, and fine lines and wrinkles (Byrnes, 2000). Avon developed a complete line of spa products, which complemented the services at the centre. These products were priced higher and were more value-driven than those featured in the brochure, resulting in an increase in more affluent consumers and brand image. These products, which were tailored to various customer needs, could be purchased either at the spa itself or on the company's web site. The company did not offer samples of the products it used in the services, which was a common practice in the industry.

Customers

Avon's customers included women—senior citizens, baby boomers, Generation X, and Generation Y—men, and consumers of ethnic origin.

Women   Nearly half the women in the United States (48 million) relied on Avon and its personal-care products. Approximately 50% of American women had purchased from Avon in 1999 and 90% had purchased from Avon in their lifetime. The company was hoping to tap into the 59% of women who said they would purchase Avon products if they were more accessible (Nelson, 2000). Although some 70% of adult women in the United States said they would consider buying Avon through its direct-selling channel, nearly half of them were not served by a representative, while one million more would buy Avon's products but preferred not to shop through a representative. With women in general, Avon was weak in providing various distribution channels.

Avon had a strong senior-citizen customer base for two reasons. First, senior citizens had begun purchasing Avon products decades earlier and had developed strong loyalty to both the company and its product lines. Second, Avon's unique direct-selling channel was convenient for senior citizens due to their possible limited mobility.

Avon's customers included those of various ages and ethnic origins. Avon had fairly strong brand loyalty with older women consumers, since they had grown accustomed to purchasing Avon's products through a sales representative who visited them at home. Women in the baby-boomer segment were partial to Avon's high-quality, high-value products, wellness products, and products tailored specifically to their needs, and as a result had strong brand loyalty to the company. However, due to Avon's limited distribution channel and lack of extensive product information and education, the company did not provide an extremely satisfactory shopping experience to these customers.

Avon had good brand image and brand loyalty to Generation X due in part to its charitable sponsorship of women's issues and its unique products. With Generation Y, Avon had yet to establish brand recognition and awareness, since the company had not targeted this demographic segment with specific products tailored to their needs or with trendy, fashionable youth-oriented products. Those in this segment who did shop with Avon did so due to its quality products at affordable prices. Also, Avon was weak in advertising to this segment and in providing various distribution outlets in which to purchase products.

Men Avon had extremely few male customers, since the company built its brand image as being a women's beauty and personal-care company. For male consumers, Avon was weak in targeting promotions specifically to them as well as generating brand awareness with trials and samples and creating a strong brand name and brand loyalty. The company did offer masculine packaging. Despite the fact that Avon was strong in providing services to influence decisions, it did not utilize the preferred male distribution outlet—retail stores.

Ethnic Customers Avon was increasingly gaining foothold in the African American market. The company had just begun to develop color-cosmetic products targeted towards darker skin tones. As a result, the company had good brand loyalty with this customer segment. The company featured African American models in their sales brochures and found this to be an influencing factor in gaining brand recognition. It was building good relationships with those of this ethnic origin through its direct-selling model and sponsorships. Since it was one of the few personal-care companies to begin to develop products geared specifically towards African Americans, Avon was considered a premium brand name. Avon was not very focused on creating products specifically geared towards Latin Americans and Asian Americans, despite the fact that the company had developed some regional product modifications in Latin America and Asia in order to satisfy needs. The company did feature some Latin Americans in their promotions with copy written in Spanish at times. However, they were just beginning to include Asian models in their advertisements. Although the company offered quality products, which Asians considered pertinent, and price discounts, which were of value to Latin Americans, the company had not developed sufficient brand recognition and awareness with either of these consumer segments.

Sales and Distribution

Avon's products were distributed via three methods: direct selling, limited retail selling (kiosks), and online selling. To accelerate growth in the United States, Avon was seeking new channels to reach more customers and improve access to its products.

Direct Selling Three million representatives, approximately 500,000 of whom worked in the United States, sold Avon's products worldwide (Byrnes, 2000). Almost all the representatives were women who sold on a part-time basis. Representatives were independent contractors or independent dealers, and were not agents or employees of Avon. Representatives purchased products directly from Avon and sold them to their customers, both in the home and in the workplace. In the United States, the representative contacted customers, selling primarily through the use of brochures, which highlighted new products and specially priced items, while also utilizing product samples, demonstration products, and selling aids such as makeup color charts. Through phone calls and personal visits Avon representatives built personal relationships with customers, issuing samples and brochures and making recommendations. Purchasing through Avon representatives allowed consumers the convenience of purchasing items beyond normal business hours and avoiding the lineups associated with retail shopping. Avon had strong monetary and flexibility incentives for its sales representatives, who generated 98% of the company's revenues. For independent Avon sales representatives, earnings were based on total sales, with total dollar amount increasing as the percentage increased. However, to encourage and motivate new representatives, Avon automatically guaranteed personal earnings of 40% on their first order, regardless of the dollar amount. Avon again guaranteed 40% personal earnings on the second, third, and fourth orders if the order was $50 or more. After the fifth order, earnings were based upon actual total dollar sales (Avon, 2000).

The company also built strong internal relations. In 1998, Avon launched its Leadership Representatives Program. Sales representatives were offered the opportunity to become leadership representatives, allowing them to receive significant cash bonuses for recruiting, training, and developing others in the field. Leadership representatives were able to earn from 2% to 14% of the sales of the representatives they successfully recruited and motivated. The United States had more than 12,000 leadership representatives, an increase of 6,000 in 1998. Sales districts with the highest level of leadership participation grew their sales in 1999 at more than double the rate of districts with the lowest participation (Byrnes, 2000). Also, since the representatives dedicated extensive time and energy into building their businesses, the company recognized individual achievements on all levels through its President's Recognition Program, which allowed representatives to set their own sales goals and rewarded them based on these achievements.

However, the company was weakening in its ability to recruit and retain quality employees since rumors of retail expansion proliferated throughout the company and the media.

Retail Selling—Beauty Centre Kiosks   Avon Beauty Centre kiosks, freestanding mini display stores measuring approximately 10 feet by 14 feet and located in select urban malls across the United States, were designed to display an upscale beauty image, showcase the company's beauty brands, and encourage customer trial of product. The kiosks, first developed in 1998, were mainly created to attract the approximately twenty to thirty million women who currently did not purchase Avon products (Parks, 1999). Each kiosk carried more than 350 Avon personal-care products and offered makeovers and beauty product advice from beauty consultants as well as samples and trials to increase brand awareness, thereby improving Avon's brand image. Avon was currently evaluating the performance of its approximate thirty-nine kiosk locations. Due to the infancy of the Beauty Centre kiosks, Avon did not have accurate sales figures and projections to utilize in measuring their performance (Parks, 1999). At this point, the kiosks only sold Avon color cosmetics, fragrances, and skin-care products. On average, each carried only 400 products out of more than 5,000 that constituted Avon's full line (Parks, 1999). By focusing on these three categories, Avon elevated its image as a beauty-care brand. The Beauty Centre personnel, who were enthusiastic and knowledgeable, were trained not to place too much pressure on consumers to make a purchase after a makeover or manicure. And, unlike department-store brands, the Avon makeovers emphasized not only a trial of the product but a learning experience on applying cosmetics, thereby successfully increasing product knowledge and education (Parks, 1999). Thus far, Avon had done an average of 230 manicures and 250 makeovers per location. About 95% of kiosk consumers were new to Avon, and approximately 70% made a purchase, requested a brochure, and/or asked to be directed to a local Avon representative. The company planned to utilize the kiosks for new product launches in the future (Parks, 1999).

In 2000, Jung was deciding whether or not to enter Avon into a nonexclusive partnership with J C Penney and Sears to supplement its sales representatives, expand its distribution capabilities, and attract new customers in order to incite sales and earnings. Under careful consideration was the type of products to be sold in these stores. The company was leaning towards higher-priced cosmetics, which would be sold exclusively in the department stores. By partnering with J C Penney and Sears, considered to be the weakest portion of the brand retail market, the company ran the risk of the possible further reduction of its brand name. Also, in marketing a higher-priced Avon line in the department stores, the company might be sending an unintentional message to consumers that the current Avon line was not of high enough quality to be sold in J C Penney and Sears. Avon had faced significant hard times in the past. Past efforts at diversification in products and distribution had put them at risk of debt and takeovers (Nelson, 2000).

Online Selling   Avon's products were distributed online via the company's own web site, **Avon.com,** and with the emerging e-representatives. In 1997, the company attempted to create a basic web site and did so by offering only a small fraction of its products for sale. Management consciously downplayed the web site's role to avoid problems with its representatives. However, as the importance of the Internet in the industry became evident, the company struggled with a strategy that would capitalize on the advantages of online selling while placating their core sales representatives. Sales representatives even protested when the company attempted to print its web address on brochures; then covered up the address with stickers, thereby forcing the company to quickly remove it. They also voiced strong opinions regarding the fairness of Avon selling online while prohibiting its representatives to create their own sites (Hoovers Online Network, 2000A). The internal struggle with an Internet strategy spanned three years and, as a result, Avon lost its opportunity to be a market leader. Less-established companies immediately took advantage of the explosive growth of the Internet and secured approximately $1 billion online (Hoovers Online Network, 2000A).

Currently, the company offers online shopping in the United States, Brazil, Germany, Italy, and Japan. Domestically, since the company did not advertise the web site to a great extent, it was weak in driving consumers to the site. The company was slowly building a loyal customer base since its global brand name attracted consumers to the site. The company was strong in offering a simple and easy to navigate web site, but weak in offering samples or trials online. Also weak was its lack of community and content, which were further drivers to a web site. The company did not offer price incentives or coupons to shopping online. Prices for items online were relatively comparable to those offered in the bimonthly sales brochure.

In order to increase the company's Internet presence and appease its sales representatives, Avon planned to invest $60 million in the next three years to develop customized Internet sites for its sales representatives, thereby creating "e-representatives." The e-representatives would extend to consumers the opportunity to order Avon products twenty-four hours a day, seven days a week, while still offering free delivery and personal service. Visitors would connect to **Avon.com** and locate e-representatives within their zip code.

The cost to become an e-representative was $15, with commissions raging from 20% to 25% for orders shipped direct or 30% to 50% for ones the e-representative delivered. The program would significantly reduce organizational costs. Prior to the development of **Avon.com,** representatives completed a forty-page paper order form, which they submitted to the company via mail or fax. With the ability to complete online forms, the cost of processing the order would decrease from 90¢ per order to 30¢ per order (Avon, 2000). In total, e-representatives were expected to save the company $10 million by 2002 and were expected to add 1% to Avon's U.S.

sales growth annually. The e-representative initiative program seemed to be successful in placating the sales representatives and integrating Avon's channels of distribution. However, top managers at Avon struggled with the possibility that this chosen Internet strategy may not have been the best solution for the company. If every sales representative participated in the program, then Avon would have approximately 500,000 web sites. It was impossible to control the quality and content of each site, thereby leaving the possibility of an inconsistent and misrepresentative Avon brand image. As a result, the company was pondering alternative Internet strategies.

Marketing

Avon's products were marketed through sales campaign brochures during twelve to twenty-six individual sales campaigns each year. Each campaign was conducted using a brochure offering a wide assortment of products, many of which changed from campaign to campaign based on changing fashion trends and consumer tastes. Each year, Avon printed over 600 million sales brochures in more than twelve languages. In the United States alone, the brochure was distributed to fourteen million women every two weeks. Avon planned to allocate $20 million to upgrade the campaign sales brochure in order to project Avon's high-quality image to its varied customers (Avon, 1999), and $40 million to create a more successful television- and print-marketing plan for Avon in its domestic market. One idea was to target women over the age of 20 with an emphasis on cosmeceutical products. The company was also developing a global brand campaign featuring a new theme, "Let's Talk." Most of its advertising dollars were being planned for print ads in women's magazines such as *Ladies Home Journal, Glamour, O,* and *Cosmopolitan* and television advertising on networks (except ABC), syndicated programming, and cable. The idea of devoting about 15% of its budget to Hispanic advertisement efforts was under debate (Bittar, 2000).

Avon had sought to develop brand awareness through various charitable sponsorships devoted to women issues. Some activities included the Breast Cancer Awareness Crusade, the Avon Running—Global Women's Circuit (which promoted the importance of fitness in women's lives), Women of Enterprise Program (which recognized five women entrepreneurs who had overcome incredible obstacles to achieve business success), and the Avon

Worldwide Fund for Women's Health. These programs raised millions of dollars for health-related problems of concern to women (Hoovers Online Network, 2000A). Each of these initiatives had also been a lucrative incentive for the company to expand its product line by correlating the event with a profitable item. For example, Avon created an attractive **Avon Breast Cancer Crusade** from which part of the proceeds went to research. Avon was the official cosmetics, fragrance, and skin-care sponsor for the 1996 Summer Olympics Game and was the first major U.S. cosmetics company to announce a permanent end to animal testing (Hoovers Online Network, 2000A).

Geographic Markets

Avon was present in both the domestic and international personal-care markets. Avon's sales per geographic region are shown in Figure 20.

The company currently had operations in 51 markets and sold its products in 137 countries. Latin America posted strong results in 2000 with revenues from Brazil, Venezuela, and Central America offsetting declines in Argentina that were caused by economic conditions there. The Asia/Pacific regions had strong growths in China, which helped compensate for the weakening Philippine *peso*. Sales in Europe were not as strong as in other markets, due mainly to currency weaknesses (Company Sleuth, 2000). The company was aggressively pursuing new customers in emerging economies such as Taiwan, Malaysia, and Russia (Hoovers Online Network, 2000). Avon has a small retail presence in Asia and Latin America,

FIGURE 20

Avon's Sales by Geographic Region

Geographic Area	$ Millions	% of Total
North America		
United States	1,809	34
Other countries	274	5
Latin America	1,608	30
Europe	878	17
Asia/Pacific	720	14
Total	**5,289**	**100**

Source: Hoovers Online Network (2000A). "Avon Products, Inc.," [Online]. **http://www.hoovers.com/premium/profile/2/0,2147,10152,00.htm.** Accessed October 11.

mainly in small boutiques sometimes run by its sales representatives. The success in the international sector could be partly attributed to Avon's ability to culturally adapt products according to regional needs. For example, Avon's Color Trend product line is featured mainly in Europe, Asia, and Latin America. The line features trendy and fashionable color cosmetics at affordable prices targeted specifically to younger personal-care customers. Several of its global brands were not available in the United States since they were created exclusively with a particular international market in mind.

Management

When Andrea Jung was promoted from Chief Operating Officer to Chief Executive Officer in November 1999, she became the first female CEO in the company's 115-year history. Jung emphasized open communication with all levels and sought to create a CEO advisory council of the ten top performers from every level of the company and from all around the world (Byrnes, 2000). Sixteen senior operating and other key executives comprised Avon Operating Council (AOC). With Andrea Jung as its leader, the AOC met bimonthly to review global operations and strategic initiatives in order to maximize shareholder wealth. The AOC's members represented an average of more than twenty years' experience with the company (Avon, 1999). Avon had more women in management positions (89%) than any other Fortune 500 company. Of Avon's officers, 47% were women, and five women sat on Avon's board of directors. The management of Avon was attempting to instill a sense of urgency around the need for decisive action and calculated risk taking. As one manager stated, "Pride, speed, and performance have become the watchwords for all of our associates as we strive to foster a high-performance culture around the Avon world" (Avon, 1999).

Avon's top managers were currently disputing strategic alternatives for growing the company. The most significant issues among management were Avon's slow earning growth, stagnant sales, limited distribution capabilities, and shifts in personal-care preferences and spending habits. The AOC members' views on how to expand the company differed: some favored Avon's gradual involvement in retail with a focus on current customers, while others preferred an aggressive retail growth strategy in order to obtain new and emerging personal-care customers. The company would remain in a stagnant position until a consensus could be reached.

Regulatory

Avon maintained strong relations with government officials through its strong adequate manufacturing practices and internal quality controls and self-inspections.

Financial

Figure 21 illustrates Avon's stock performance over the past five years.

The volatility evident in Figure 21 was due in part to earnings growth falling short of targets, unprecedented stock market volatility, and negative investor sentiment toward consumer-products companies in general. In 1999, the stock price dropped sharply in the second half and finished the year down 25% (Avon, 1999).

Avon's five-year net sales comparison is shown in Figure 22.

Although the company had positive net sales and earnings growth for the past five years, the increases were in the single digits and were declining each year. In fact, 1999's one-year revenue growth was a minute 1.5%. Most of Avon's product lines had single- to double-digit growth except apparel, which fell in the single digits. As Allan Mottus, a consultant to beauty

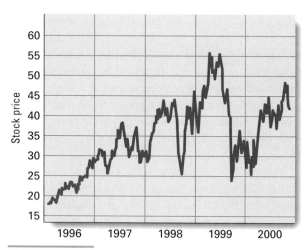

FIGURE 21

Avon's Stock Chart 1995–2000

Source: Bloomberg. "Avon Products Chart Center," [Online].
**http://quote.bloomberg.com/gcenter/gcenter.cgi?iquote
=AVP&PERIOD=5Y&equote1=&equote2=&equote3=&EXCH=
US&T=markets_gcenter99.ht&x=36&y=6**. Accessed November 30.

FIGURE 22

Avon's Five-Year Net Sales Comparison
(in millions)

	1995	1996	1997	1998	1999
Net sales	$4,492	$4,814	$5,079	$5,213	$5,289

Source: Avon (1999). *Annual Report.*

and retail companies, stated in *Business Week,* "We're in one of the greatest economies of all times, and Avon's still finding it hard to increase sales" (Byrnes, 2000).

Towards the Future

At the bimonthly meeting of the Avon Operating Council, Andrea Jung decided to present her retail objectives to the other sixteen members of the board. She felt this was imperative since, although earnings were expected to remain positive for the future, the company's single-digit growth, volatile stock, and seemingly archaic and limited distribution channel did not bode well for the company's intermediate and long-term future. Avon needed a new strategic plan, emphasizing where to sell its products, who would be its target market, and which product lines best fit its brand image.

As she stood in front of the members, Andrea Jung articulated her retail idea to broaden Avon's reach in the United States. Jung stated her main objectives, which were to partner with Sears and J C Penney department stores and create a store-within-a-store, where it could introduce a new and more upscale exclusive product line. This retail initiative would be done in conjunction with direct selling. In implementing both strategies, Avon would benefit from increased profits, sales, and nationwide exposure, allowing the company to continue attracting the baby-boomer segment. The plan was financially appropriate, since the company would only invest $15 to $20 million to launch the products in these locations and a bulk of the expenses (such as advertising, overhead, and employee salary) would be carried by the department stores.

Jung argued that such a strategy was feasible since retail selling was on the rise, with an increase in customer traffic in virtually all traditional department stores. Baby boomers, whose spending power was

Byrnes, N. (2000). "Avon: The New Calling," *Business Week*, September 18, iss. 3699, pp. 136–148.

Company Sleuth (2000). "Avon Reports Record Third Quarter Results." [Online]. **http://www.companysleuth.com.** Accessed October 22.

Cooney-Curran, J. (2000). "Deliveries of Hope," *Global Cosmetic Industry*, September, vol.167, iss.3, p. 6.

Croft, M. (1999). "Changing Face of Cosmetics; Consumers' Growing Ease with Internet Shopping Is Forcing Store-Based Cosmetic Companies to Tread the Home-Shopping Pathway," *Marketing Week*, May 27, pp. 40–41.

D'Innocenzio, A. (2000). "Specialty Retailers Gain More Customers Who Want Fresh Fashions and Good Service." *Associated Press.* [Online]. **http://www.mcall.com/html/business/news/d_g001_ fistores.htm.** Accessed September 24.

Davis, D. (2000). "Cyberphobia! E-Commerce Poses a Serious Threat to Brick and Morter Retailers," *Global Cosmetics Industry*, March.

Dutton, G. (1999). "A Changing Landscape for Cosmetics and Personal Care," *Chemical Market Reporter*, April 5.

Francese, P. (2000). "With Senior Citizens, Population Growth Has Been a Gray Area," *Wall Street Journal*, NW3, May 24.

Global Cosmetic Industry (2000). "GENERATION GAPS: Global Cosmetic Industry takes a Look at the Personal-Care Preferences, Spending Habits, and Power of Generation Y and X and Baby Boomers." [Online]. **http://www.findarticles.com/cf_0/m0HLW/ 6_166/63411614/p1/article.jhtml.** Accessed November 1.

Grossman, A. (1999). "Facial Cleansers Trend Toward Ease, Quick Results," *Drug Store News*, February 1.

Herman, S. (2000). "Skin Deep," *Global Cosmetic Industry*. September 1, vol. 167, no.3, p. 50.

Hoovers Online Network (2000A). "Avon Products, Inc." [Online]. **http:// www.hoovers.com/premium/profile/2/0,2147,10152,00.htm.** Accessed October 11.

Hoovers Online Network (2000B). "Mary Kay Inc." [Online]. **http:// www.hoovers.com/co/capsul/8/0,2163,40298,00.html.** Accessed October 19.

Hoovers Online Network (2000C). "L'Oreal SA." [Online]. **http:// www.hoovers.com/co/capsul/2/0,2163,41772,00.html.** Accessed October 19.

In Cosmetics99 (1999). "Shampoo and Styling Lead in the Hair Sector." [Online]. **http://www.dotfinechem.com/incos/s. . .atures/ nov_dec99/sh ampoo/index.htm.** Accessed November 1.

Kyriakos, T. (1999). "Growing Wealth Creates Increased Spending," *Drug Store News*, June 7.

L'Oreal Company Website (2000). **http://www.loreal.com.** Accessed November 5.

Mallory, M. (1995). "Women on a Fast Track," *U.S. News and World Report*, November 6, vol. 119, no.18, p. 60.

Market Share Reporter (2000). Detroit, MI: Gale Research.

Mary Kay Inc. Company Website (2000). **http://www.marykay.com.** Accessed November 5.

Nelson, E. (2000). "Avon Expects Boutiques in Sears, Penneys to Break Even by 2002," *Wall Street Journal*, September 28, Eastern Edition, p. B14.

NPD Group (2000A). "NPD Fragrancetrack Reports Men Who Wear Fragrance Are Wearing It More Often." [Online]. **http://www.npd .com/corp/content/news/releases/press_000926.htm.** Accessed October 30.

NPD Group (2000B). "NPD and Media Metrix e-Visory Report Anticipates Dramatic Growth of Online Beauty Sales." [Online]. **http:// www.npd.com/corp/content/news/releases/press_000321.htm;** Accessed October 9.

NPD Group (2000C). "Media Metrix NPD Beauty Visory, Summer 2000." [Online]. **http://www.npd.com/corp/content/special/ evisory.htm.** Accessed November 1.

Parks, L. (1999A). "Avon Reaching Out to New Customers with Upscale Beauty Center Kiosks," *Drug Store News*, April 26.

Parks, L. (1999B). "Drug buyers optimistic about cosmetics sales.(New lines from Olay and Neutrogena helping)," *Drug Store Newsletter*, June 7.

Parks, L. (2000). "Beauty Makers Respond to Myriad of Needs, Creating Products Perfect for Everyone," *Drug Store Newsletter*, September 25, p. 37.

Rocafort, C. (2000). "Formulating for the Ethnic Hair Care Marketplace," *Soaps & Cosmetics*. [Online]. **http://www.wysiwyg://102/ http://206.0.199.8/sc/mag/sc1.html.** Accessed November 9.

Sanabria, V. (2000A). "The Inner Hue: Self-Expression Dominates the Color Cosmetic Category," *Global Cosmetic Industry*, April.

Sanabria, V. (2000B). "Hair-Care Update: Innovative, Multifunctional Products and Emerging Market Segments Drive the Hair-Care Industry," *Global Cosmetic Industry*, May 1, vol.166, no. 5, p.18.

Sauer, P. (2000). "Varying Shades of Profitability Uncovered in Cosmetics and Personal Care," *Chemical Market Reporter*, May 8.

Schiffman, L. (1997). *Consumer Behavior*. Upper Saddle River, N.J. Prentice-Hall.

The Direct Selling Industry (2000). "2000 Direct Selling Growth & Outlook Survey." [Online]. **http://www.dsa.org/factsht00.stm.** November 7.

U.S. Food and Drug Administration (2000A). "Cosmetic Handbook." [Online]. **http://www.fda.org.** Accessed October 11.

U.S. Food and Drug Administration (2000B). "Cosmetic Labeling Manual." [Online]. **http://www.fda.org.** Accessed October 11.

13

The Body Shop International: U.S. Operations

This case was prepared by A. J. Almaney, Professor of Management at DePaul University.

Anita Roddick was instantly recognizable behind the wheel of a green Volkswagen Golf as she roared up to her Littlehampton headquarters in Sussex, England. With her hair flying and the sleeves of her shirt rolled like an army sergeant major's, the founder of the Body Shop International (BST), Britain's most successful global retailer, paused just long enough to admire her latest pet project: an enormous electronic sign that blared "STEER CLEAR OF SHELL—BOYCOTT NOW" at a Shell service station sitting across the road.

The question of the oil giant's responsibility for human-rights abuse in Nigeria was a current preoccupation of the perpetually crusading Roddick. But on this morning, she was scowling at some equally disquieting news from her board of directors: the profit figures from the United States were dismal. The company's U.S. division lost 3 million pounds in 1997, compared with a loss of 1.3 million pounds in 1996 and a profit of 4.9 million pounds in 1995. In addition, the company's share price, which was 365 pence in 1993, dropped to 121 pence in 1997.

This case is intended to be used as a basis for class discussion rather than as an illustration of either effective or ineffective handling of the situation. Reprinted by permission.

Weak U.S. sales and a slumping share price were just two of the problems that threw the cosmetics concern into a midlife crisis. Competition was also increasing. A host of imitators, notably the Bath and Body Works, began to invade the company's market niche. On top of that, the company that boasted of putting principles before profits was accused of engaging in unethical practices. Its critics alleged that the company had misled the public about everything from its stand against animal testing to the ingredients in its products. Even though the company strenuously denied the allegation, the bad publicity had tarnished its image as one of the most glamorous growth stocks.[1]

The challenge facing the company was this: Did the entrepreneurial Roddick have what it would take to run a large company, and could it compete effectively against such aggressive and nimble competitors as the Bath and Body Works?

History

On a fact-finding trip Anita Roddick had made for the United Nations to study women in the Third World, she learned that for centuries women in underdeveloped countries had used organic potions to care for their skin, so she decided to open a cosmetics shop that would sell natural products in cheap containers. The shop, which later was named The BST, was started in 1976 in Brighton, England. The thirty-three-year-old housewife with two young daughters started the business to earn enough money to care for her family while her husband, Gordon Roddick, pursued a dream of horseback riding from Buenos Aires to New York.

With a bank loan of about 10 million British pounds, Roddick opened the first store carrying only twenty-five naturally based skin-care and hair-care products which were sold in clear urine sample bottles purchased from a local hospital. When supply of the bottles ran out, she began a refill policy. Handwritten labels with product information were pasted on the bottles. Before her husband had left for Buenos Aires, he told her she had to make 300 pounds a week in order to stay in business. "What happens, Gordon, if I don't?" she asked. He said, "Give it six months and then pack it up and meet me with the kids in Peru."[2]

The store proved to be so successful that another was opened within a year. When Gordon Roddick returned home in 1977, he joined his wife in the business. At first, he took over the tasks of filling bottles and handling the finances, teaching himself what he needed to learn as he went along. Although he later became the company's chairman, he continued to handle the financial side of the business while keeping a low profile. Gordon attributed the company's success to his wife. "Creatively, this is Anita's company entirely. She says what she wants, and we make all her dreams come true," he said.[3] A year later, they began to franchise the business.

The 1980s witnessed the company's explosive growth. Sales and profits grew on average 50% a year. In 1984, the company went public with the Roddicks' retaining 27.6% of the company's stock. Gordon continued to be the chairman while Anita served as managing director. In the same year, the company had 138 stores, 87 of which were located outside the United Kingdom. By the end of the decade, pretax profits climbed to an estimated 35 million pounds on sales of 212 million pounds despite the onset of a withering recession in British retailing.[4]

In 1988, the first Body Shop opened in the United States. All stores were owned by the company as franchising was not permitted until 1990. In 1992, a new U.S. headquarters opened in Raleigh, North Carolina, to make and distribute products to U.S. stores. In 1997, the number of stores reached 287; 138 of these were company owned. The Roddicks set as an objective increasing the number of stores in the United States to 500 by the year 2000.

Corporate Governance

The board of directors of the BST consisted of eleven members. As shown in Exhibit 1, all but three of them were company officers. While Anita held the chief executive officer's position, her husband was the chairman of the board.

The board met regularly throughout the year. Its functions included overall company strategy and future development, allocation of financial resources, acquisitions and divestitures, approval of major investments, annual budgets, senior executive appointments, budget policy, and risk management.

In 1997, the company came under criticism for not complying with The Code of Best Practices as defined in the United Kingdom by the Cadbury Committee. One of the recommendations of the Cadbury Committee was that an audit committee should consist of at least three non-executive directors. At the Body Shop, the committee consisted of only two such directors. A year later, however, the company complied with the committee's recommendation.

Profile of the CEO

Anita Roddick, the daughter of Italian immigrants, was born on October 23, 1942. She was educated at an all-girls high school in Littlehampton, Sussex, and graduated from Newton Park College of Education in Bath, England. When she was eighteen, Roddick learned from her mother that her much-loved stepfather was in fact her real father—a product of a love affair her mother had while she was still married to her first husband, whom she divorced when Roddick was eight.

As a young adult, Roddick traveled the world over. In a visit to Johannesburg, South Africa, she was arrested by the police for attending a jazz club on "black night." Upon her return home, she was introduced by her mother to her future husband, Gordon. The couple had two daughters.

For several years, she ran a cafe but became tired of the "crazy" hours. She began to look for a job with "sensible hours." That led her to open her own shop.

EXHIBIT 1

Board of Governance

Director	Age	Title
Anita L. Roddick	54	Chief executive officer
T. Gordon Roddick	55	Chairman
Stuart A. Rose	47	Managing director
Eric G. Helyer	61	Executive director
Jane Reid	44	Strategic development director and company secretary
Jeremy A. Kett	49	Finance director
Terry G. Hartin	51	Executive director
Ivan C. Levy	40	Executive director
Penny L. Houghes	37	Non-executive director
Aldo Papone	64	Non-executive director
Adrian D. Bellamy	55	Non-executive director

Source: The Body Shop International, *1998 Annual Report,* p. 40.

Anita Roddick was funny, provocative, and a great talker whose language was peppered with four-letter words. She attributed her bawdy language and feisty nature to her Italian heritage. When she was growing up, she felt different from her neighbors in Littlehampton. "We were noisy, always screaming and shouting. We played music loudly, ate pasta, and smelled of garlic," she said. She attributed her rebellious personality to her mother, who was not afraid to challenge the status quo.[5] She acquired a strong work ethic as a child, waiting tables in her parent's cafe. Highly emotional, she would jump up and down at board meetings and scream and clap her hands if she liked something. If she did not, she would dismiss it with a four-letter word.

Throughout her career, Roddick received many accolades. In 1985, for example, she was named Britain's Business Woman of the Year, and three years later she was awarded an Order of the British Empire by the royal family. In 1992, she won the Business Leader of the Year Award from the National Association of Women Business Owners in the United States.

Anita's Management Style

For many years, the BST was not managed professionally. It had no business plan and no job descriptions. In Roddick's own words, "You'd bury your head with laughter if you saw how unprofessional we were."[6] Working for Roddick, according to a former employee, was "like being in a circus parade. Your job is to follow behind the elephants and scoop up the dung."[7]

As a result, when the company expanded, it became difficult to retain managers who sought to run the organization more professionally. One such manager was Robert Cluckman, a retailing expert who had been recruited as the company's international general manager. He left in 1992, complaining about the BST's unstructured environment and lack of a strategic plan. Another manager, Janet Swaysland, lasted less than a year as vice president for communications and later said, "They were clueless about what they wanted."

Anita on Company Bigness

Roddick did not reconcile herself to the idea of having to run a big business. She thought that one could lose the sense of being remarkable by just being big. To her, wanting to be big was very much a male pathological trait. Roddick did not want the BST to be a McDonald's, where customer relationships would be lost. But she could not escape the fact that she was an entrepreneur who had created a big, bureaucratic organization. She was annoyed by the language being used: her staff talked about three-year plans, net income, and average sales, all of which she did not like. She was also annoyed with what she called the "obsession with meetings." "We are getting to a point where we can't fart without calling a meeting,"[8] she said.

She expressed concern over the fat-cat mentality that was creeping into her company. People would carelessly spill coffee on a new carpet, did not recycle newspapers, and left lights on after a meeting, all of which went against her philosophy of running a lean and green company.[9]

Anita on Profit

Ever since the company went public in 1984, Roddick struggled against what she described as "pressure from money men" who told her how to run the company and what she should be doing with her money. The sense of conflict kept growing, leading her to think seriously about taking the company private again. She thought financial figures were not unimportant, but to concentrate only on the figures was, in her view, "dumb." She also disputed the notion that shareholders should have more rights and influence on the company than employees, the community, and the environment.

Roddick had several reasons for taking the company public in the first place. For one thing, she felt that her business needed credibility to get good retail sites, and she was not being taken seriously by property owners who controlled retailing. For another, it was the "sexy" thing to do at the time. "When you have a crazy idea that should never have existed, all you want to do is push it to see how far it would go. It was a huge barometer of reassurance and a way of getting more money. It was like growing up."[10] She also admitted that vanity played a role in her decision.

Company Mission

In 1995, the BST retained a management consulting firm to undertake an appraisal of its structure, objectives, and methods of decision making and problem solving. One outcome of this process was the formulation of a mission statement (see Exhibit 2).

Company Vision

Roddick articulated the BST's vision in the following way:

> I believe quite passionately that there is a better way. I think you can rewrite the book on business. I think you can trade ethically; be committed to social responsibility, global

EXHIBIT 2

BST Mission Statement

To dedicate our business to the pursuit of social and environmental change.

To creatively balance the financial and human needs of our stakeholders: employees, customers, franchisees, suppliers, and shareholders.

To courageously ensure that our business is ecologically sustainable: meeting the needs of the present without compromising the future.

To meaningfully contribute to local, national and international communities in which we trade, by adopting a code of conduct which ensures care, honesty, fairness, and respect.

To passionately campaign for the protection of the environment, human and civil rights, and against animal testing within the cosmetics and toiletries industry.

To tirelessly work to narrow the gap between principle and practice, whilst making fun, passion, and care part of our daily lives.

Source: The Body Shop International, *1998 Annual Report,* p. 1.

responsibility; empower your employees without being afraid of them. I think you can really rewrite the book. That is the vision, and the vision is absolutely clear.[11]

Values

In addition to the mission and vision statements, the company also adopted a statement of values articulating its philosophy toward its stakeholders (see Exhibit 3).

1. To develop and build relationships with our shareholders and prospective shareholders, with the aim of creating a base of well-informed investors who fully understand the company's aims and objectives.

2. To operate a progressive dividend policy.[12]

Objectives

The BST set the following objectives, all of which pertained to the company's relations with its stakeholders:

1. To manage the business with the aim of maximizing shareholder interests, while also balancing the needs of other stakeholder groups.

EXHIBIT 3

Statement of Values

> We aim to ensure that human and civil rights, as set out in the Universal Declaration of Human Rights, are respected throughout our business activities. We will establish a framework based on this declaration to include criteria for workers' rights embracing a safe, healthy working environment, fair wages, no discrimination on the basis of race, creed, gender or sexual orientation, or physical coercion of any kind.
>
> We will support long-term, sustainable relationships with communities in need. We will pay special attention to those minority groups, women and disadvantaged peoples who are socially and economically marginalized.
>
> We will use environmentally sustainable resources wherever technically and economically viable. Our purchasing will be based on a system of screening and investigation of the ecological credentials of our finished products, ingredients, packaging, and suppliers.
>
> We will promote animal protection throughout our business activities. We are against animal testing in the cosmetics and toiletries industry. We will not test ingredients or products on animals, nor will we commission others to do so on our behalf. We will use our purchasing power to stop suppliers' animal testing.
>
> We will institute appropriate monitoring, auditing, and disclosure mechanisms to ensure our accountability and demonstrate our compliance with these principles.

Source: The Body Shop International, *The Body Shop Approach to Ethical Auditing.* Undated company document.

2. To develop and build relationships with our shareholders and prospective shareholders, with the aim of creating a base of well-informed investors who fully understand the company's aims and objectives.

3. To operate a progressive dividend policy.[13]

Strategy

In the mid 1980s, the company followed a strategy of growth through geographic expansion. With the UK market nearly saturated, Anita hoped that, in a decade, a map of the world would be dotted with the Body Shops.

Franchising served as a strategic tool for the company's growth. The first franchise shop opened in 1977 in Bognor Regis, West Sussex, in the United Kingdom. When Roddick entered the U.S. market in 1988, she opted to open her own stores instead of immediately franchise. She thought this would give the company time to adjust to the new market. When Roddick decided to franchise in the United States in 1990, she had more than 2,000 applicants. The BST's U.S. subsidiary acted as head franchisee in the United States. The head office, filling facilities, and main distribution center were based in Wake Forest, North Carolina. The subsidiary granted sub-franchise rights to individuals and organizations. In 1997, the company had 278 stores in the United States, 128 of which were company-owned.

Franchisees paid a flat fee of 60,000 pounds to buy into the business and then invested a minimum of 375,000 pounds to get the store built, stocked, and running. To determine whether the potential franchisees shared her passion for global issues, Roddick required them to take a comprehensive test that included questions about their taste in music, books, and film as well as their thoughts on how they would like to die. Because most of the franchisees had no formal business experience, Roddick had them work in a store where the existing staff could evaluate how they would fit in. Then the candidates went through extensive interviews at headquarters with Roddick and other top executives. Because of time constraints, Roddick had to develop ways to implement the same rigorous procedures in the United States without having to conduct the interviews personally. Once selected, the franchisees had to undergo extensive training in London or at one of the area development offices in the United States, where they learned the details of each product and the rules of merchandising and running the stores.

Organizational Structure

The BST was segmented into four divisions: the Body Shop UK, the Body Shop USA, the Singapore Operation, and Independent Overseas Franchisees. The Body Shop USA was broken down into Mail Order, Company Shops, Franchise Shops, and Area Distributors. Each of the Area Distributors was segmented into smaller units.

Strategy-Implementation Problems

Before long, the company's rapid expansion began to create difficulties. Instead of patiently learning the unique characteristics of the U.S. market and perfecting sales in its existing shops, the company charged into the top malls, to which it was not accustomed, in hopes of beating its competitors.[14]

Furthermore, Roddick's relationship with franchisees began to deteriorate. Some of them did not share her enthusiasm about certain causes. Although the typical franchisee—young, well educated, female—generally shared Anita's ideas and wanted to be part of the "family" structure, others were fearful that her radical ideas drove some customers away. They were also concerned that the company's rapid expansion had a cannibalizing effect, taking 4% away from their sales[15] and damaging the company's image by turning it into another McDonald's.[16] Some franchisees were unhappy about having to pay the 60,000 pounds purchase fee—something that their counterparts in the United Kingdom were exempted from.

Also, as the company expanded, its communication with its franchisees worsened. In a survey of the franchisees conducted by the company itself, it was found that 48% of them did not think the company's long-term strategy was clearly communicated to them.

Products

The company marketed over six hundred different products, which could be classified in seven broad groups:

1. Skin products: lotions and gels

2. Body products: bars and deodorants

3. Makeup products: lipstick, mascara, eye definer, and eye shadow

4. Fragrance products: body spray, perfume oil, and eau de toilettes

5. Hair products: shampoo, conditioners, and scalp treatment

6. Aromatherapy products: bath oil, massage oil, and relaxing body lotion

7. Hands and feet products: foot scrub, cooling leg gel, foot spray, hand cream, footsie roller, and file-a-foot

The BST's approach to packaging was to make it simple yet attractive.[17] All shampoos and lotions were sold in identical plastic bottles with black caps and green labels. The packing material was a vegetable-based starch, puffed into shape with no chemical binders. This material was biodegradable, dissolving in water in five minutes. The products were placed in clear containers with factual information of what was inside and what the product was good for.

Suppliers

In 1987, Roddick began the BST's Trade-Not-Aid program which involved purchasing natural ingredients from Third World countries, thus benefiting both the company and native communities. To find such ingredients, Anita traveled several times a year to remote areas of the Third World where she observed local customs and talked with native people about their methods of skin and hair care. Several indigenous groups signed agreements with BST to supply it with natural ingredients.

Industry

The personal-care products industry in the United States was about 39 billion pounds, which accounted for more than one-third of the total world market. In 1995, the industry grew by 11% to 3.3 billion pounds. The surge capped four years of strong industry growth that spawned scores of bath boutiques. Even retailers, such as the Gap, began to enter the market or expand their product line. By 1996, the number of soap and scent boutiques, which came to be known as The Body Shop Crowd reached 1,400, not counting such scent-purveying stores as Victoria's Secret, Fredrick's of Hollywood, and Banana Republic.[18]

Entry and exit barriers were relatively low because retail space was widely available and there were many suppliers of products for the industry. It was estimated that the average cost per store for leasehold improvement and furniture and fixtures was about 338,000 pounds, average pre-opening costs were about 7,500 pounds, and working capital requirements (mainly inventory purchases) were about 60,000 pounds.[19]

Being cyclical, with future growth expected to be 1% to 2% annually, and glutted with so many stores, the industry was ripe for a shakeout. Some stores were already beginning to slip, among them Nature's Elements, which filed for bankruptcy reorganization.

The one bright spot in this picture was the ethnic health and beauty aids market, which by 2001 was expected to grow by 6% to almost 3 billion pounds.

Competitors

The personal-care products market in the United States was highly segmented and included specialty stores, chains, and department stores. Packaging, price, selection, service, and quality were the principal attributes on which companies competed. Most competitors relied heavily on advertising that created unrealistic ideas of what people should look like and how their skin should feel and smell to others.

BST's major competitors included Bath and Body Works, Crabtree and Evelyn, Aveda, H2O plus, and Garden Botanika.

Bath and Body Works

The most successful of the competitors was Bath and Body Works, part of Intimate Brands, Inc., which itself was 83% owned by the Limited. Bath and Body Works benefited from the strength and experience of its parent company, the Limited.

The chief executive of Bath and Body Works (BBW) was Beth Pritchard, a hands-on executive who each month spent two days in one of her boutiques, wearing reindeer antlers and serving as a salesperson. To get a feel for her products, she tested them on herself, her daughter, and her friends. Pritchard's personal touch and her drive catapulted the company from being a blip in the personal-care product industry to being an industry leader. When she took over in 1991, the company had 95 stores and 30 million pounds in sales. By 1997, she expanded the chain to 750 stores with sales of 11 million pounds, leaving the BST a distant second (it had 287 U.S. stores). Like the BST, BBW did not advertise. Its success was attributed to word-of-mouth recommendations and in-store promotions, such as special offers.

The promotional theme BBW focused on was not natural products or animal protection but Americana. The shops were colorful places that evoked rural America and were designed to have a welcome, down-home feel. Checkered cloths covered the tables, and the merchandise sat in old barrels while the scents of fresh-baked pies emanated from the perfumes. Pritchard made innovation a priority. Roughly 30% of the company's products were new each season, far more than rivals'.[20]

In commenting on the ability of BBW to compete with BST in the United States, Leslie H. Wexner, the Limited's chairman, said his rival's background as a manufacturer and foreigner worked against her in the United States "They were not retailers," he said. "We have an advantage—we know the territory."[21]

Aveda

Aveda was founded by Horst Rechellbacher, an Austrian hairdresser, in 1977. Headquartered in Minneapolis, Minnesota, the company had 140 stores worldwide, 60 of them freestanding stores in the United States. Of its 80 international outlets, 50 were stores-within-stores in department stores and the rest were freestanding. Its sales in 1996 were estimated at 263 million pounds, an 80% increase over 1995.[22]

Aveda developed and marketed scent, hair, skin, makeup, and other lifestyle products created from flower and plant essences. Rechellbacher staked his company's existence on plants, believing that plants, if properly harvested and utilized, could offer powerful and complex ingredients for use in an unlimited range of products. Also, unlike petrochemically derived ingredients, plants were a renewable resource. The company established state-of-the-art research and manufacturing facilities in Minneapolis to develop technologies by which pure plant and flower essences could be extracted, and it was successful in targeting black consumers with such products as the Self Control Hair Styling Stick. These and other products were sold at thousands of beauty salons across the country.[23]

H2O Plus

A privately held company, H2O Plus opened its first store in Chicago in 1989, and within a year had 27 stores in mall locations stretching from San Francisco to Palm Beach, Florida. The company was created by Cindy Melk, a twenty-eight-year-old entrepreneur who said she wanted to offer a no-nonsense, affordable alternative to overpriced and overpackaged products sold in department stores.[24] The company distributed its products through fifty-eight company-owned stores, nine franchises, and four hundred department stores, including Marshall Field's, Dillard Department Stores, Macy's, and Federated Department Stores. Its target market consisted of women between the ages of 18 and 39, and its prices were about 15% to 20% lower than department-store designer lines of similar quality. Despite that, the company's sales volume dropped to 45 million pounds from 50 million. The decline was attributed to growing competition and lack of differentiation among the company's own products.[25]

Garden Botanika

Garden Botanika was established in 1990 in Redmond, Washington. The company sold high-quality, reasonably priced, botanically based personal-care products and cosmetics. The company began with three stores but grew to 196 stores by 1996. In 1997, it had 259 stores and planned to open 30 more that year. It introduced new products on a continuous basis, thus offering the customer an extensive product assortment. Its products, which targeted women between 30 and 49, ranged from makeup to perfume and bath gel. In 1997, the company mailed a thirty-six-page holiday catalog to nearly 3 million mail-order and retail customers. The catalog contained fragrance samples of some of the company's products. Although the company's sales increased from 9.6 million pounds in 1993 to over 138.6 million in 1997, its net losses rose from 2.1 million in 1993 to 7.4 million in 1997.

Crabtree and Evelyn

A private company, Crabtree and Evelyn had 115 stores. It tried to create the feel of an English sitting room in its stores. It sold British baked goods and china along with floral soaps. The company was acquired by Kepon Berhad (KLK), based in Kuala Lumpur, Malaysia. KLK had businesses in Malaysia, the United Kingdom, and Australia involving the production and processing of palm products, natural rubber, and cocoa. The acquisition was viewed as a means of expanding the company's retail outlets worldwide.[26]

Drugstores

Drugstore chains were initially slow to react to specialty stores such as the BST and BBW. As a result, they began to lose sales. To prevent further losses, the drugstore chains began to copy the specialty stores' concept. Their market research showed that consumers who shopped at drugstores cited familiarity with the store, its proximity to their home or workplace, and one-stop shopping as the main reasons for preferring their drugstore. Those who shopped at specialty stores did so when choosing gifts or when in a self-indulgent mood.[27]

Stores

Most of the BST's stores in the United States were small and had shelves too cluttered to appeal to American consumers. On the shelves were note cards with stories about the products or their ingredients. But there were also stacks of pamphlets with titles such as "Animal Testing and Cosmetics" and "What is natural?" The stores appeared dull and outdated and had shoddy-looking products such as spangly purses made out of bubble wrap, Day-Glo plastic hair clips, velvet alice bands, multicolored mascara, and pencil-case goodies. The stores were designed to be self-service: though the sales people were pleasant and knowledgeable about the products, they were trained not to be forceful with customers and to offer advice only when asked.[28]

Customers

The BST's target market consisted primarily of females over twenty-five years old. In 1997, females twenty-five to seventy-four years old numbered about 68 million and were expected to number 90 million by the year 2005.[29]

When the BST opened its stores in the United States, its counterculture approach to cosmetics appealed to many women. It aroused in them the feelings of enthusiasm, commitment, and loyalty more appropriate to a political movement than a store. Like missionaries selling Bibles, they even pitched its products to their friends.[30]

However, American consumers gradually grew lukewarm to the company's political messages, which continued to be popular in Europe. They were also not as loyal as the Europeans. More than European customers, Americans were influenced by price. Furthermore, Americans were used to shopping in malls, where storefronts tended, to blur together and shopkeepers were not connected to the community, as was the case in Europe. Reflecting on the company's failure to relate to American consumers, Roddick said, "It was a different culture which we did not understand."[31]

Employees

The total number of employees at the Wake Forest, North Carolina, site was 240 including office, warehouse, and production personnel. In addition, the company employed 2,500 sales people in its stores.

Generally, the employees were very motivated and loyal to the company, often talking about the difficulty they would have working for an "ordinary company." Anita believed that employees of other companies were cynical about their employers and did not buy the argument that the companies cared about them. According to Anita, profits were "boring" to most employees even if they got a piece of the action.

The BST attacked employee cynicism in the same manner it attacked customers' cynicism about corporate advertising—with information. All employees could attend the company's training school where the emphasis was placed not on making profit but on the nature and uses of the products. They were encouraged to spend half a day each month volunteering in a community project—time for which they were paid. And after five years, they were also allowed a six-month sabbatical. Many of them used the time to travel or volunteer at the company-sponsored orphanages in Romania and Albania.

To find out employees' feelings about the company, the BST conducted surveys and focus groups. The results showed that 92% lauded the company's efforts on human rights, environmental protection, and animal welfare, and 75% were proud to tell others they were part of the BST family.

Communication

Anita attached a great deal of importance to communication as a means of getting the company's values across to its employees. She did that through face-to-face communication as well as through the company's newsletter. The newsletter, resembling an underground newspaper, devoted more space to the company's campaigns to save the rain forest and ban the ozone-depleting chemicals than to the opening of a new branch or the dropping of an old product. Anita was personally involved in determining the newsletter's content. She would suggest articles, check copy, choose illustrations, and change design. She viewed the newsletter as a direct line of communication from the leader to the rest of the organization.[32]

Advertising and Promotion

Anita Roddick learned how to use free publicity early on when her first store was threatened with a lawsuit by two neighboring funeral parlors which objected to having a store named The BST so near their corpses. She contacted the local paper with the sad story of a struggling mother about to lose her small shop and received generous press coverage. This resulted in a large number of sympathetic readers filing through her doors. Ever since, Anita chose not to market or advertise, believing it to be a waste of time and money that the consumer would end up paying for. This strategy also reflected her belief that customers were so overmarketed that they became increasingly cynical about advertising which told them half truths or untruths. That is why she was heavily criticized when she appeared in an American Express commercial to promote her Trade-Not-Aid program.[33]

Thus, instead of traditional advertising she relied on the generosity of the press which courted her company as it became the darling of the City (London's Wall Street). The BST actually racked up about 5.25 million pounds worth of free publicity a year from various articles about the entrepreneurial Anita. "I am always available to the press," Anita said. "I fervently believe that passion persuades, and I emit a lot of enthusiasm."[34] The only promotion the company used was limited to window displays, catalogs, and point-of-purchase displays. In such promotions, the marketing theme stressed the customer's "well-being" rather than glamor and instant rejuvenation as is the norm in this industry.[35] To strengthen its credibility with the customers, the company sought to educate them by telling them where the product came from, how it was made, what was in it, how it was tested, and what it could be used for."[36]

To generate more publicity for her company, Anita hired two public-relations firms, one in New York and one in London. Their job was to make sure Anita would keep a high profile in both the general and beauty press. In the United States she was written about in several publications, including *Time, Newsweek,* and *Inc.* She was also profiled on CBS television.

Research and Development

In the early 1990s, the company did not introduce any significant new products. It was too busy opening new stores in the United States. Instead of revamping the company's aging product line, top management devoted an increasing amount of time launching environmental projects. This provided its competitors with an opening to steal market share by offering new products.

In the mid 1990s, the company sought to introduce several new products and enhance existing products. The revamped product line, however, had mixed results. While a nonaerosol hair mousse flopped, a new line of cosmetics called "Colorings" did well.[37] In 1998, new products comprised 15% of the product mix. But that still fell below the industry average of 25%.

In developing new products, top management required that they should meet demanding safety and environmental standards, adopting a policy that opposed the use of animals in testing raw materials. The company used human volunteers to evaluate product safety prior to launch. The company also required suppliers of raw materials to provide written confirmation every six months that no raw materials were tested on animals.

Social Responsibility

Anita believed that business should do more than make money, create decent jobs, or sell good products. Rather, business should help solve major social problems by using its resources to come up with answers to such questions as: "How do we bring human fulfillment?" "How do we address mass unemployment?" "How do we prevent social alienation?"[38] In line with this philosophy, the company encouraged and contributed to social and environmental programs by helping such groups as Greenpeace, Amnesty International, and Friends of the Earth. All franchisees were asked to participate in the campaigns.

Anita also launched the Trade-Not-Aid program which included buying blue corn from the Pueblo Indians in New Mexico and Brazil's nut oil from the Kayapo Indians of the Amazon River Basis. The company also donated seed money to launch the *Big Issue*—a London weekly newspaper sold by the homeless.[39]

The company pursued a policy against animal testing. However, a 1992 British television documentary charged that the BST did use ingredients that had been tested on animals. In a public statement, the company asserted that its policy was never to use ingredients until five years after they had been tested on animals. A company spokesman said, "We are trying to give [suppliers] an incentive to stop testing on animals by telling them that if you stop testing and find other ways, we will buy your stuff."[40] The Roddicks sued for libel and won more than 800,000

pounds in damages. In 1994 an American journalist, writing in the magazine *Business Ethics,* broadened the charge of hypocrisy to include the BST's environmental standards, charitable contributions, and efforts to buy materials from the Third World. Anita dismissed the allegations as "recycled rubbish," and an independent research group later concluded that the charges were "broadly unfair."[41]

In response to these charges and to make sure that its values were adhered to, the company created a self-scrutinizing mechanism called the "Social Audit" to examine every aspect of the company such as corporate giving, community projects, animal testing, and trade-and-not aid programs. It also looked at human-resources issues such as staff conditions and family leave. The audit was verified by an outside auditor and released each year along with the company's financial results.

Finance

In 1997, the BST's share price dropped to 121 pence from its peak of 365 pence in 1993. This was due primarily to the poor performance of the company's U.S. division which lost 3 million pounds in 1997, compared with a loss of 1.3 million pounds in 1996 and a profit of 4.9 million pounds in 1995. Even though the total retail sales were 1% higher in 1997 than in 1996, comparable store sales showed a 4% decline.[42] (For the company's sales and profit by region, see Exhibit 4.)

EXHIBIT 4

BST Sales and Operating Profit for 1997

Region	Sales (in millions of British pounds)	Operating Profit (in millions of British pounds)
UK	106.1	13.6
USA	73.1	(3.0)
Europe	39.3	8.1
Asia	35.7	14.7
Americas (excluding USA)	9.9	3.1
Australia and New Zealand	6.7	2.0

Source: The Body Shop International, *1998 Annual Report,* p. 34.

The pressure on the company to place the bottom line ahead of its environmental concerns began to mount. It came not only from shareholders and franchisees who wanted to maximize their earnings but also from some employees and managers who were willing to sacrifice some of the company's ideals for the job security that profitability would allow.

The decline in profit was caused by higher overheads and an increase in the cost of promotion. Also contributing to the company's financial woes was the emergence of copycat retailers who stole some of the company's market share with aggressive discounting. Additionally, many customers were turned off by the company's politically correct message. "You can't be a flower child your whole life," said Allan Mottus, publisher of a cosmetics-

trade publication. "They have been relying on that friendly green message that worked well in Europe, but that wasn't enough in the States,"[43] he added. Reflecting on the company's poor performance in the United States, Gordon Roddick, the company's chairman, said, "The USA continues to pose our greatest challenge. The USA is one of the toughest marketplaces in the world."[44] (For the balance sheet and cash-flow statements, see appendixes A and B.)

The company's troubles in the U.S. market highlighted top management's lack of retail and marketing know-how. Although the company essentially pioneered the specialty bath-products concept, it faced agile competitors and high real-estate costs, something it was not accustomed to in the United Kingdom. In one Pennsylvania mall alone, the BST had eight direct competitors.[45]

APPENDIX A

BST Balance Sheet
(for the 52 weeks ended February 28, 1998)

	1998 (in millions of British pounds)	1997 (in millions of British pounds)
Fixed assets		
Tangible assets	50.7	52.7
Investments	50.5	15.8
	101.2	68.5
Current assets		
Stocks	28.5	21.2
Debtors	59.5	65.6
Cash at bank and in hand	21.3	39.0
	109.3	125.8
Creditors: amounts falling due within one year	59.3	44.9
Net current assets	50.0	80.9
Total assets less current liabilities	151.2	149.4
Creditors: amounts falling due after more than one year	—	0.1
Deferred tax	1.9	0.6
	149.3	148.7
Capital and reserves		
Called up share capital	9.7	9.7
Share premium account	42.8	42.1
Profit and loss account	96.8	96.9
Shareholders funds	149.3	148.7

Source: The Body Shop International, *1998 Annual Report,* p. 39.

APPENDIX B

BST Consolidated Cash Flow Statements
(for the 52 weeks ended February 28, 1998)

	1998 (in millions of British pounds)		1997 (in millions of British pounds)	
Net cash inflow from operating activities		41.5		51.7
Returns on investments and servicing of finance				
Interest received	1.5		1.7	
Interest paid	(1.6)	(0.1)	(1.7)	—
Taxation				
UK corporate tax	(16.3)		(14.7)	
Overseas corporate tax	(0.3)	(16.6)	(0.5)	(15.2)
Capital expenditure and financial investment				
Purchase of tangible fixed assets	(11.6)		(8.8)	
Purchase of EST shares	(1.5)		—	
Sale of tangible fixed assets	0.1	(13.0)	0.2	(8.6)
Acquisitions and disposals				
Cash consideration	(18.3)		(1.9)	
Cash and cash equivalents acquired	(0.7)		0.3	
Cash received on disposal	0.3	(18.7)	—	(1.6)
Equity dividends paid		(9.7)		(7.3)
Cash flow (outflow) before use of liquid resources and financing		(16.6)		19.0
Management of liquid resources				
Short-term deposits		5.3		(15.0)
Financing				
Issue of ordinary share capital	0.7		5.1	
Syndicated loan	18.3			
Loan repayments	(20.3)	(1.3)	(6.8)	(1.7)
Increase (decrease) in cash		(12.6)		2.3

Source: The Body Shop International, *1998 Annual Report,* p. 41

Economy

In 1997, the U.S. economy entered its seventh year of solid expansion, and the outlook remained optimistic. From 1997 through 2002, the economy would continue to grow, although at a more modest pace than in the past years.[46] Job growth would continue to be strong; and unemployment, inflation, and interest rates would continue to be relatively low. Until the year 2006, personal consumption expenditures were projected to increase by 2.1%, compared with 2.3% for 1986 to 1997. Personal income would increase by 4.8% and disposable income by 4.9%, compared with 5.9% and 5.8% for the previous ten years.[47]

Demographics

The growth rate of the total population was expected to slow down during 1997–2006 to an average annual rate of 0.8%, from 0.1% for the previous ten years.

The U.S. female population was projected to increase from about 137 million in 1997 to about 146 million in 2005 and to about 158 million in 2015.[48]

Ethnic diversity in the United States would become more pronounced. By the year 2001, nearly 30% of the population would be non–Anglo-Saxon. The number of Hispanic Americans was expected to double by 2010 to surpass African Americans as the largest ethnic group.[49] The Pacific Islander and Asian populations would quadruple by then. As a result, sales of ethnic hair-care products were expected to rise about 6% by 1999.

Culture

As baby boomers aged, the market for anti-aging products grew. This group numbered 43.2 million and accounted for the largest share of skin-care sales: almost 23%.

Widespread work stress contributed to the popularity of bath products. Customers, eager to soothe frazzled nerves and pamper themselves, began snapping up bath accessories ranging from shower puffs and bath salts to body scrubs and rubber duckies. The desire by baby boomers to spend more time at home and find more ways to relax would help feed the body-and-bath-products market. At the same time, new home designs that transformed bathrooms from closets into lounges promoted more leisure time in the bath. The bathing-as-leisure trend was expected to help the industry generate more sales in the foreseeable future.

Technology

Online sales of products of all types hit 1 billion in 1994 and 2.3 billion in 1995. Retail sales of products purchased on the Internet was expected to surpass 92 billion as the number of subscribers to the World Wide Web would reach 300 million by 2000. Beauty products accounted for an estimated 2% of all online sales but were predicted to reach 8% in five years.[50]

Conclusion

In the past, the BST stood alone in the U.S. natural-care-products market. However, as savvy competitors began to invade its turf and steal its market, key questions were raised about the company. For example, was the management style of the visionary and entrepreneurial Anita Roddick unsuitable for a large, publicly owned company? Why did the company stumble in the U.S. market? Should Anita be removed from her position and replaced with a professional manager? And how can the company regain its former competitive position?

ENDNOTES

1. Charles P. Wallace, "Can the Body Shop Shape Up?" *Fortune,* April 15, 1996, pp. 119–120.
2. Bo Burlingham, "This Woman Has Changed Business Forever," *Inc.,* June 1990, p. 46.
3. *Ibid.*
4. *Ibid.,* p. 34.
5. Adrienne Sanders, "Success Secrets of the Successful," *Forbes,* vol. 62, no. 10, November 2, 1998, pp. 22–24.
6. Tara Parket-Pope, "Body Shop Prepares U.S. Image Makeover," *Wall Street Journal,* November 12, 1996, p. B5.
7. "Anita Roddick," *Management Today,* March 1996, p. 45.
8. Burlingham, *op. cit.,* p. 34.
9. *Ibid.*
10. *Management Today, op. cit.*
11. Burlingham, *op. cit.,* p. 46.
12. The Body Shop International, *Our Agenda.* Undated company document.
13. *Ibid.*
14. Wallace, *op. cit.*
15. Jennifer Conlin, "Survival of the Fittest: Anita Roddick, Founder of the Body Shop," *Working Women,* vol. 19, no. 2, p. 28.
16. Wallace, *op. cit.*
17. Carolyn J. Poppe, "The New Look of Cosmetics Packaging," *Soap Cosmetics and Cosmetics Specialties,* vol. 72, no. 6, June 1996, p. 26.
18. Donald A. Davis, "Glut Indeed," *Drug and Cosmetic Industry,* vol. 159, no. 5, November 1996, p. 22. Also, see "Shoppers Just Want to Be Entertained," *Household and Personal Products Industry,* vol. 34, no. 11, November 1997, p. 12.
19. Intibrands, Inc., *1995 Annual Report,* p. 10.
20. Lori Bengiorno, "The McDonald's of the Toiletries," *Business Week,* August 4, 1997, pp. 79–80.
21. Wallace, *op. cit.,* p. 119.
22. "A Who's Who of Cosmetics—1997 . . . ," *Women's Wear Daily: Holiday Supplement,* vol. 34, September 1997.
23. "Aveda: Creating a Healthy Business," *Drug and Cosmetic Industry,* vol. 161, no. 2, August 1997, pp. 16–20.
24. Lauri Freeman, "Personal Care Products Fill Specialty Niche," *Stores,* vol. 73, no. 5, May 1991.
25. Cara Kagan, "H2O Dives into Relaunch Plans," *Women's Wear Daily,* vol. 171, no. 33, February 16, 1996, p. 6.
26. "Crabtree and Evelyn Sold," *European and Cosmetic Markets,* vol. 13, no. 8, August 1996, p. 277.
27. "Drugstores Turn Tide in Battle of the Bath," *Women's Wear Daily,* June 1997, p. 4.
28. Parker-Pope, *op. cit.*
29. U.S. Bureau of the Census, *Current Population Reports,* 1996, p. 17.
30. Burlingham, *op. cit.,* p. 36.
31. Earnest Beck, "Body Shop Founder Roddick Steps Aside As CEO," *Wall Street Journal,* May 13, 1998, p. B8.
32. Burlingham, *op. cit.,* pp. 40–41.

33. Connie Wallace, "Lessons in Marketing—from a Maverick, Anita Roddick," *Working Woman*, vol. 15, no. 10, October 1990, p. 81.

34. *Ibid.*

35. Burlingham, *op. cit.*, p. 37.

36. Conlin, *op. cit.*

37. Wallace, *op. cit.*

38. Eric Hollreiser, "The Body Shop Founder Seeks Site for Her Biz School with Heart," *Philadelphia Business Journal,* September 29, 1995, vol. 14, no. 31, p. 7.

39. Jennifer Conlin, *op. cit.*

40. *Ibid.*

41. Charles P. Wallace, *op. cit.*

42. The Body Shop International, *1997 Annual Report,* p. 33.

43. Parket-Pope, *op. cit.*

44. The Body Shop International, *1996 Annual Report,* p. 1.

45. Parke-Pope, *op. cit.*

46. Ray M. Perryman, "The Short-Term U.S. Outlook," *Journal of Business Forecasting and Methods,* vol. 6, no. 4, winter 1997, pp. 38–40.

47. Thomas Boustead, "The U.S. Economy to 2006," *Monthly Labor Review,* November 1997, pp. 6–22.

48. U.S. Bureau of the Census, *op. cit.*

49. "Demographic changes alter equation for chains," *Chain Drug Review,* vol. 18, no. 8, April 8, 1996, p. 35.

50. "Beware of the Web," *Non-Foods Merchandising,* vol. 38, no. 2, February 1996, p. 33.

14

J. P. Morgan Chase & Co.: The Credit Card Segment of the Financial Services Industry

This case was prepared by Steven Preziosi, Damon Swaner, and Marc E. Gartenfeld, all of St. John's University, and Dorothy G. Dologite, Baruch College, under the direction of Dr. Robert J. Mockler, St. John's University.

In January 2001, Chase Cardmember Services (CCS) executive Richard Srednicki was faced with the task of turning around the industry's fifth-largest credit card issuer. CCS's success over the next two years would determine its fate. While the U.S. credit card market had been saturated for several years, other firms had still managed to grow by introducing new products or finding profitable niches. CCS had done neither. Because the recent J. P. Morgan–Chase Manhattan merger involved pooling of interests, the newly created financial services giant was unable to sell off its credit card business for two years. This gave CCS twenty-four months to develop, implement, and begin to reap the benefits of a new long-term, enterprisewide, winning strategy.

All of the players in this industry faced the same problem: how to acquire and retain profitable customers. This made for a competitive, mostly zero-sum game. As a result, there had been rapid consolidation in the industry, with the largest firms controlling an increasing percentage of the total market.

This case is intended to be used as a basis for class discussion rather than as an illustration of either effective or ineffective handling of the situation. This case was prepared by Steven Preziosi, Damon Swaner, and Robert J. Mockler, under whose supervision the case was written. Reprinted by permission of the authors.

CCS was in a unique position in the market. It had grown into a large player primarily as the result of combining other portfolios in several large bank mergers during the 1990s. Now it needed to find a way to grow internally. A new management team installed in early 2000 had reenergized the business and had worked diligently to build momentum and focus the employees on growth and profitability. However, the desired result of changing CCS into a long-term winner in the market was still far off.

In order to determine how it would position itself in the industry and convince customers that CCS could service them better than the other card issuers in the market, CCS management had to resolve a number of strategic questions. A strong customer service focus was an absolute necessity to retain customer loyalty. A focus on new products, underserved segments, new technologies, and value-added services was also required. Finally, a strong financial discipline and high return on investment were needed to continue to secure capital from its parent company. These and other strategic questions needed to be answered if CCS was to differentiate itself and so win against the competition in the near, intermediate, and long-term time frames.

Industry and Competitive Market

The Financial Services Industry

The financial services industry consists of investment banks, insurance companies, broker/dealers, asset managers, venture capital firms, and commercial banks, as shown in Figure 1. Investment banks provide services that include underwriting of public and private offerings, research, trading of advisory services for mergers and acquisitions, and financial engineering. Insurance companies provide a means of decreasing one's exposure to risk through policies that pay on the occurrence of some event. Broker/dealers perform two different functions: acting as agents bringing buyers and sellers of securities together and also acting as market makers standing ready to buy and sell securities by presenting a bid-ask spread at all times. Asset managers provide pension and mutual fund management services. Venture capital firms provide funding to start-up companies and firms looking to expand. Commercial banks include the traditional branch banking functions of deposit taking and lending. This sector also includes mortgage banking, small business and middle market banking activities, and credit card issuance.

Investment Banks   One of the many important roles of the investment bank is to assist companies in raising capital through its function as underwriter. Investment banks buy securities from a company and then sell them in secondary markets. Types of underwriting activities include initial public offerings; sale of bonds, commercial paper, and private debt; and equity offerings. Investment banks also play an important role in the creation of value for companies through mergers and acquisitions. In this capacity investment banks bring companies together with the end result of either combining the firms or facilitating the exchange of assets. Finally, one of the most important functions of the investment bank is to provide research and assessments of individual companies and sectors as a basis for its own investment or for sale to other investors.

Insurance Companies   Insurance companies provide a means of dealing with risk. They will pay out an agreed-upon sum contingent upon the occurrence of some event. Typical insurance policies include life insurance, auto insurance, medical insurance, and various types of disaster insurance. The insurance company is compensated for absorbing this risk by a premium that is paid periodically, usually monthly, by the insured.

Broker/Dealers   The broker/dealers, although usually the same firm, provide two different types of services. As a broker, the firm acts as an agent bringing buyers and sellers of securities together and executing transactions on their behalf in the over-the-counter markets and at the exchanges. Brokers are not participants in the transaction and do not take on any risk but rather are compensated exclusively

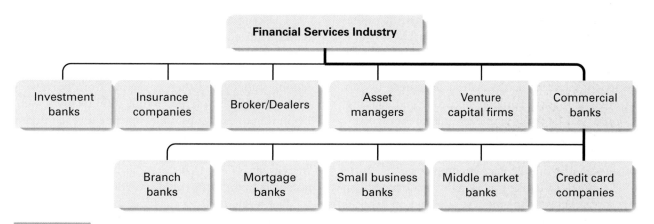

FIGURE 1

Structure of the Financial Services Industry

through commissions. As a dealer, the firm is party to the transactions in which it participates. Dealers must stand ready to buy and sell at any time and must provide a bid price, which is what the dealer is willing to pay for a certain security, and an ask price, which is the price at which the dealer is willing to sell. Dealers are compensated by the spread between the price paid for the security and the price at which it is sold.

Asset Managers   Asset managers include various large investors like pension funds, mutual funds, hedge funds, and 401(k)'s. All of these types of funds fall under the rubric of institutional investors. Institutional investors increasingly play a larger role in the secondary market by allowing small investors to diversify their portfolios into investments that they would not normally be able to afford. By pooling the assets of many investors, large funds are able to participate in IPOs, commercial paper markets, and bond markets, all of which are normally beyond the reach of the smaller investor.

Venture Capital Firms   Venture capital firms provide funding to start-up companies, expanding companies, and companies that are restructuring. Generally venture capitalists take on great risk in their investments. However, the venture capitalists ask much in return for their investment. They may take a large share in ownership of the company along with a seat on the board of directors. Investments are made by venture capital firms with one of three types of exit strategies in mind: taking the company public, selling to a larger company, or filing for bankruptcy. Although a large number of all investments fail, the remaining investments generally yield venture capital firms a very high return on their money.

Commercial Banks   Commercial banks perform a variety of services, such as cash management, usually through a branch banking network, and lending. Commercial bank lending encompasses several different types of credit, including mortgages and credit cards, and also provides banking services to small businesses and middle market companies.

Commercial banks traditionally made money on the spread between the interest rate paid on deposits and the rate at which they lent. However, because of the competitive pressures brought on by globalization and the Financial Services Modernization Act of 1999, the face of banking in the United States has dramatically changed. Under the old law (Glass-Steagall) the businesses of investment banking, commercial banking, and insurance were either not allowed to mix with each other or only allowed to mix in a very limited way. The passage of the Financial Services Modernization Act allowed these three businesses to operate under a new type of holding company and paved the way for much of the consolidation that was occurring in the financial services industry. In addition, the financial services industry, especially commercial banking, had been forced to change because of the arrival of the Internet. Every aspect of commercial banking operations had been modified in some way in order to accommodate Internet use.

This study focuses on the credit card segment of the commercial banking sector of the financial services industry.

The Credit Card Segment

History and Trends   The credit card industry in the United States can trace its roots to just prior World War I. In 1914, Western Union began to provide a deferred-payment service to its most credit-worthy customers. Over the next several decades, department stores and other retailers began to provide revolving credit accounts to many of their customers as well. In the 1950s, the popularity of revolving credit accounts grew and the retailers began using imprinted cards to help streamline the transaction process and identify customers. As customers made purchases using their cards, the charges were posted directly to the cardholders' accounts at the store, with bills being sent out monthly.

The biggest advances began to occur when the banks realized the potential of this new payment method. The large U.S. banks discovered that credit cards fit nicely into their current business, which was lending money and then collecting from borrowers over time with interest. While the retailers were beginning to earn substantial revenue on the interest from their credit accounts, the firms also recognized the potential for even larger profits from the increased sales that standardized, universally accepted credit cards could provide.

By the late 1960s, many banks began issuing cards to their customers and merchants began accepting them as payment. These early cards required payment in full within a short period of time, usually less than ninety days. However, banks quickly recognized the revenue potential of simply extending the repayment time while continuing to charge interest. Soon thereafter, banks, led by Bank of America, created associations to act as clearinghouses for credit card transactions. Some of these associations included BankAmericard, BankMark, and MasterCharge and were the forerunners of the current two associations, Visa and MasterCard.

Also in the late 1960s, another use for credit cards began to develop, the Travel and Entertainment (T&E) market. Cards issued by American Express, Diner's Club, and Carte Blanche, called charge cards as opposed to credit cards, became popular with traveling businesspeople. The difference between charge cards and the bank-issued credit cards was that charge cards did not involve the charging of interest, which was the banks' primary motivation for entering the industry. They were paid in full by the cardholder at the end of each billing cycle, which was usually one month. These firms derived revenue from charging the customers higher annual fees and the merchants higher transaction fees for accepting the cards.

By the late 1970s, card usage was commonplace. The bank-issued cards, T&E cards, and the original retailer-issued cards were all flourishing. Technological advances had helped ensure accuracy in the process, and most large merchants were accepting the cards.

In the 1980s Sears, the largest retailer issuer of cards, introduced its DiscoverCard, which included a unique value proposition, an annual rebate on the cardholder's total card purchases. Competition among credit card issuers began to accelerate rapidly. Citibank led the way with the development of the AAdvantage card, which offered American Airlines frequent flyer miles with each purchase. The use of direct mail campaigns increased dramatically as banks searched to expand their customer base beyond the reach of their traditional branch-banking network. During the 1980s the volume of outstanding credit card debt grew from $71 billion in 1980 to $242 billion by 1990 (Nilson Report, 2000).

The increase in credit card usage was even more dramatic in the 1990s, driven by a strong economy, aggressive marketing by credit card issuers, and changes in consumer spending preferences. Outstanding credit card debt grew to $675 billion by the end of the decade (Nilson Report, 2000).

By 2000, the industry had begun to consolidate. The smaller banks did not have the scale to compete with the few remaining large issuers. Competition in the market for credit-worthy customers had grown fierce, forcing banks to look for new niches. MBNA established a niche in an area ignored by large banks, affinity marketing. It focused on partnering with as many local partners as possible, including universities, organizations, and athletic teams. This allowed it to capitalize on the brand loyalty that customers had, not to MBNA, but to its affinity partners. Cap One found a niche with the lower-credit-quality customers offering higher-priced, or secured, lines of credit. Competition also began to come with substitute products, most notably debit cards, which provided the same payment features as credit cards but drew funds from the cardholder's deposit or checking account, as opposed to drawing upon a line of credit (History of the Credit Card, 2001; Credit Card History, 2001).

The growth in credit card usage was expected to continue. Established as the dominant payment method for Internet commerce, credit card usage would grow as web purchasing grew (Lowe, 2001). Also, as consumers' reliance on using cash for purchases continued to decrease, credit cards had additional opportunity for growth. The trend toward consolidation in the industry was likely to continue, as was the impact of technological advancement on credit cards. The credit card segment of the financial services industry is broken down further in Figure 2.

Functions of the Credit Card Segment   The credit card segment served two major functions for its customers (called cardholders). First, it was a payment mechanism that provided a means for cardholders to complete transactions for goods and services. Second, it was a debt access mechanism, allowing cardholders to borrow the funds used in competing transactions.

Payment Mechanism.   The credit card issuers provided cardholders with a means of paying for goods and services. The advantage over other forms of payments (cash, personal checks) was that customers could make purchases without having to physically interact with a merchant (i.e., telephone, Internet). Credit cards also allowed cardholders to keep track of all of their purchases with one monthly statement. In this arena, credit cards faced major competition from debit cards, which allowed cardholders the purchasing

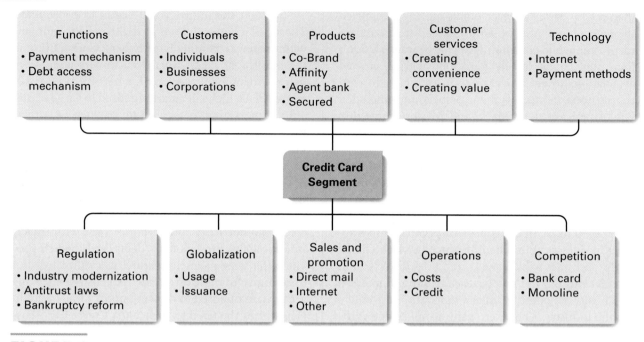

FIGURE 2

Structure of the Credit Card Segment of the Commercial Banking Sector

advantages provided by credit cards but linked the payments to the cardholders' deposit accounts.

Trends in the technology area, such as greater Internet use and the change in lifestyle and buying habits that it had created, increased the average American's credit card use during the 1990s (Lowe, 2001). This created a great opportunity for payment method providers to increase market share. One major key to success in the payment mechanism role was to become the customer's first choice of payment mechanism by maintaining universal acceptance of cards and by using aggressive sales and advertising. Other keys to success were increasing card usage with value-added services like purchase protection or rebates, developing cardholder loyalty by deepening relationships through affinity or cross-selling other products, and developing aggressive advertising campaigns to attract new customers. Also important was leveraging the issuer's other business lines, particularly commercial bank segments, as a means of acquiring new customers.

Debt Access Mechanism. In this role, cards allowed customers to pay for items with borrowed funds. This allowed cardholders to detach their purchasing from their income. With over $600 billion in credit card debt outstanding, credit card purchasing helped drive the U.S. economy. This volume of debt outstanding tripled during the 1990s and was eleven times the 1980 level by the end of the decade (Carney, 2000). The unique advantage of credit cards was the combination of these two functions: allowing cardholders to make all of their purchases when needed and to make payments when available (provided they make their nominal monthly minimum payments).

Credit card issuers earned revenue primarily from interest charged on debt outstanding. Customers that maintain outstanding debt on their credit card are called "revolvers," short for revolving credit users. Customers that use their credit cards primarily for transactions and do not maintain a debt balance are called "transactors." Transactors were much less profitable and were becoming a larger percentage of cardholders. In 1992, 29 percent of all cardholders were transactors; by 1998 the share was 42 percent (Mannix, 1998). This trend was forcing issuers to look for ways to increase customer profitability. One way to increase revenue from transactors was to charge an annual fee. However, given the multitude of choices available, annual fees were unattractive to customers unless they were associated with a value-added service for which customers were willing to pay (such as Citibank's AAdvantage card).

Opportunities had been created for making credits cards a debt access mechanism by increasing credit card usage as a payment mechanism. For example, in 1990 credit cards accounted for only 10.3 percent of total consumer payments, a number that is expected to increase to 23 percent by 2003. Credit card dollar volume is also expected to exceed $2.0 trillion by 2003 (Anonymous, 1998). The keys to success in this area were to attract and maintain debt by offering competitive rates to develop cardholder loyalty through affinity or depth of relationship and to limit loan losses through strong credit and collections policies.

Customers   The credit card industry can be broken down into the three main types of customers served: individuals, businesses, and corporations.

Individuals.   In the individual consumer market, the largest of the three, credit cards allowed cardholders to manage their finances. This market was fiercely competitive, with constant advertising and direct mail campaigns needed to sustain market share. Cardholders with outstanding debt could transfer balances to lower-interest-rate cards with increasing ease. Value-added services, including loyalty programs, rebates, and rewards, were required for customer retention because they increased cardholder attachment to the card and lessened the likelihood that they would switch to a competing card.

Customers were segmented by credit-worthiness. Customers that were considered credit-worthy were called the "prime" market. Issuers usually determined a customer's credit-worthiness by reviewing their credit bureau report, which contained a credit bureau score (FICO score). The higher the score, the more credit-worthy the customer. Customers that had derogatory credit bureau marks, usually caused by missed payments or loan defaults, were considered the "low prime" market. Customers that were the worst credit quality, including customers that had previously filed bankruptcy, were considered "subprime." The low and subprime markets had historically been underserved compared to the prime market in the United States.

The prime customer market had been the most competitive: the average U.S. household already had 2.4 credit cards by the end of 2000 (Coleman, 2001). All issuers were competing to be the card of choice for these customers since they were the most likely to have the means to pay back the borrowed funds. Loan losses were a concern in the credit card industry, and failure to control their level would have a large impact on an issuer's profitability. Opportunities in this area stemmed from trends in increased usage of credit cards (Anonymous, 1998). Additionally, opportunities had been created by the increase in the number of people shopping on the Internet. It was estimated that 17 million U.S. households would be shopping online by the end of 2001 and that 49 million households would be spending as much as $184 billion online by 2004 (Forrester Research, 2001). The keys to success in the prime market were increasing customer card usage by offering value-added services like purchase protection or frequent flyer programs, and attracting new customers through aggressive advertising. Also important was developing cardholder loyalty through affinity or depth of relationship, which made it less likely that cardholders would switch to a new card.

The low and subprime markets had been less saturated than the prime markets, but by 2001 they were becoming increasingly more competitive as issuers sought out new customers (Coleman, 2001). The trends that affected the prime market, including increased card usage and Internet purchasing, also affected this market. However, previously issuers were hesitant to enter this market for fear of high loan loss rates. Opportunities in this area, however, did exist because issuers like Cap One and Providian proved that credit cards to this segment could be issued profitably. Despite higher loan losses, these customers were more likely to revolve than prime customers and were thus incurring higher finance charges. The keys to success in this market were limiting loan losses by maintaining strong credit policies, attracting new customers through aggressive advertising, limiting losses by maintaining a strong collections department, and increasing profitability by selling charged-off accounts.

The loan loss rate, also called the charge-off rate, is shown for various credit card issuers in Table 1. Issuers charge off accounts after they reach 180 days past due. The charge-off rate is calculated by dividing total charge-offs by total average receivables. Companies

TABLE 1

Loan Loss Rates, 1999

Cap One	3.85%
MBNA	4.33
Citigroup	4.56
Amex	5.00
Bank One	5.23
Discover	5.42
Bank of America	5.57
J. P. Morgan Chase	5.66
Household	6.65
Fleet	6.78

Source: CardFlash Company Website (2001) [Online]. **http://www .cardflash.com.** Accessed April 24.

that continually add new accounts, like Cap One and MBNA, tend to have lower charge-off rates. Firms with more mature portfolios and fewer new accounts have higher loss rates. Acquiring new accounts especially in the prime market was the focus for most issuers.

Businesses. Credit cards served both functions, payments and debt access, for small businesses or merchants and organizations. This market was less competitive and smaller than the individual consumer market. Account acquisitions in this market were more heavily dependent upon the businesses' banking relationship with the parent company. Thus firms with a strong commercial bank presence had an advantage. Opportunities in this area stemmed from trends in the Internet's growth as a purchasing tool for consumers and a marketing tool for businesses. For example, 44 percent of U.S. companies were selling online in 2000 and 36 percent more said they would do so by the end of 2001 (Nua Internet Surveys, 2001). Additionally, small businesses that used the Internet had grown 46 percent faster than those that did not (Nua Internet Surveys, 2001). In terms of dollars and cents, Internet advertising generated $1.92 billion in 1998, which was double the 1997 figure, and small and home offices spent over $51 billion on high-tech goods in 1998 (Nua Internet Surveys, 2001).

The keys to success in the business market were maintaining customer loyalty by offering programs and promotions that rewarded businesses for using the card, such as rebates on purchases, and leveraging banking relationships that businesses had with the issuer's parent company to attract new business cardholders. Also important were attracting and maintaining debt by offering competitive rates and creating convenience for businesses through flexible payment arrangements.

Corporations. In the corporate card market, the focus was solely on the payment function of credit cards. Employees of major corporations carried credit cards for travel and entertainment purchases. At the end of each month, the employee submitted the expenses and the corporation paid the credit card bill. American Express had historically been the dominant player in this market. This market was less reliant on direct mail, the traditional form of account acquisition in the credit card segment, and instead relied on a sales force that sought out new corporate clients.

Opportunities in this market stemmed from the development of Internet technologies that allowed networking. One key to success was creating convenience for corporate cardholders through the creation of Intranet-type platforms that allowed online billing, reconciliation, and approval of charges within the corporate structure. Other keys to success were to leverage the parent company's investment bank by using relationships other firms had with the parent as a basis for winning these companies' corporate card business, and to maintain an aggressive sales force that would also seek out new corporate customers.

Products The major products of the credit card segment were Visa- and MasterCard-associated credit cards. However, these cards could also be cobranded cards, affinity cards, agent bank cards, or secured cards, among other types.

Visa and MasterCard controlled over 77 percent of the credit card market (*Star Ledger*, 2000). Most bank card issuers and monolines issued both Visa- and MasterCard-associated cards. Visa and MasterCard were associations on whose networks most credit card transactions were cleared. American Express and Discover each had their own networks and did not issue Visa- or MasterCard-associated cards. Members of the Visa and MasterCard associations were prohibited from issuing American Express or Discover cards but were allowed to issue both MasterCard and Visa cards.

A recent trend in the industry had been issuers choosing either Visa or MasterCard as a primary partner. Citibank and Chase had both chosen MasterCard, while NationsBank and Providian had chosen Visa. In doing so, the issuers were working out more favorable fee arrangements with their primary association. Issuers associated with either Visa or MasterCard in order to geographically extend the areas of acceptance of the issuing bank's cards. The key to success in this area was to create convenience for the cardholder by using the association with Visa or MasterCard to create wider acceptance of the issuing bank's card.

Cobranded Cards.   Cards partnered with large corporations also became an important part of the credit card industry. Partners included airlines, hotel chains, long-distance telephone companies, retailers, and gasoline companies. These cards generally offered cardholders some type of rebate or reward each time the card was used. For example, the Shell Oil card from J. P. Morgan Chase offered cardholders a 1 percent rebate for every dollar charged to the card, plus a 5 percent rebate on any Shell gasoline charged to the card. These rebates could then be used to offset future Shell gasoline purchases. However, the rewards paid to customers reduced the profitability of the relationship for card issuers. As a result, cobranded cards needed to strike a balance between offering attractive rewards to entice customers and remaining profitable. Cards with particularly rich rewards or with high levels of transactors, such as airline cobranded cards, generally charged annual fees.

Opportunities in this area stemmed from the issuers' ability to leverage cardholders' brand loyalty to the co-brand partner and to provide customers with value while remaining profitable. The keys to success were creating brand loyalty by offering discounts and promotions on products and services, increasing card usage by sending cardholders targeted offers or coupons for use with the co-brand partner, and creating value for co-brand partners by giving cardholders rebates when purchasing from the partner, thus increasing the likelihood that these customers would choose to purchase from the partner rather than the partner's competitors. Also important were partnering with large well-known national brands to gain market share and attract new customers, and attracting profitable customers through lucrative rewards programs that added significant value to such a degree that customers would pay an annual fee for the card.

Affinity Cards.   These were also cards that were partnered with a company or organization, but the nature of the relationship was different than with cobranded cards. Affinity cards did not offer cardholders rewards. Instead, they were marketed to potential customers that were or wanted to be identified as being affiliated with the card's partner. Most universities, athletic teams, and professional organizations were currently in affinity partner relationships with card issuers. Since the target market for any affinity card was generally smaller than with cobranded cards, issuers needed to have numerous affinity partners to be successful in this market. Lasting brand loyalty could be created in this market by partnering with various organizations that cardholders were closely associated with.

One of the leading affinity card marketers was MBNA. MBNA had created affinity cards with various causes, such as the United Negro College Fund, developed affinity cards for over five hundred colleges and universities, and developed affinity cards with military and law enforcement agencies such as the U.S. Marine Corps and the National Association of Chiefs of Police. These kinds of affinity partnerships created greater loyalty among cardholders. MBNA lost only 2 percent of its profitable customers annually as compared to the industry average of 15 percent (Wherry, 2000).

A major key to success in this arena was having flexible systems and processes that allowed the issuer to manage thousands of affinity partners. Also important were maintaining an effective sales force that actively sought out new partners and a strong marketing team that was able to identify new segments.

Agent Bank Cards.   The trend in the financial services industry toward consolidation also affected the credit card segment. Many smaller credit card issuers were finding that they did not have the scale to manage a credit card portfolio profitably and were exiting the business. However, the small and mid-sized banks still wanted to be able to issue credit cards to their customers. In an agent banking relationship, a bank was able to provide its customers with a credit card without having to manage a credit card portfolio. An example of an agent banking transaction would be

MBNA's purchase of the credit card portfolio of First Tennessee Bank (Overdorf, 2000).

In an agent bank relationship, the smaller bank's customers were issued a card in the name of their bank, but the cards were owned and serviced by a larger card issuer. The advantage for the smaller company was that it could continue to meet the needs of its clientele. The advantage for the issuing company was the additional loans. The relationship was similar to that of a cobranded or affinity card, but in this case the partner was another financial institution. Since customers tended to be loyal to the bank where they had their accounts, the issuing firm was able to obtain loans from a population to which it would otherwise not have had access. Also, customers were less likely to default on loans to banks in which they had their other accounts. Thus agent banking cards generally had lower loan loss rates.

As the segment continued to consolidate, more portfolios were likely to come up for sale. For the issuers that had the capital to compete for these acquisitions and the ability to integrate new portfolios into their current business, this trend provided a substantial opportunity. Another key to success was to develop effective partnerships with the agent bank partners to ensure that the banks continued to solicit new customers for the agent bank card. Also, it was important to maintain an experienced agent bank team to service the portfolio and manage the relationship with the agent bank.

Since 78 percent of the $675 billion in outstanding credit card debt was controlled by the top ten issuers, the remaining 22 percent represented a lucrative cache of potential loyal customers (Nilson Report, 2000). This 22 percent, or approximately $150 billion, was more than double the portfolio of any one issuer other than Citibank at the end of 2000 (Cardflash, 2001).

Secured Cards. Secured cards were offered to customers with poor credit quality. They required customers to keep cash on deposit with the card issuer. In return customers were given a card with a credit limit equal to the amount of their deposit. This allowed customers to whom issuers were not willing to grant credit to take advantage of the payment function of credit cards. Cap One successfully entered this market. As cardholders demonstrated their ability to use credit, Cap One would then convert them to a regular credit card. The key to success

with secured cards was to aggressively advertise to targeted customers or regions with lower credit quality in order to attract new cardholders.

Customer Services Important to success in the credit card segment was maintaining customer loyalty. With all the brands of credit cards as well as other payment methods available, the one thing that a credit card issuer could do to distinguish itself from the competition was to provide greater convenience and value for its customers. The opportunities to create convenience and value stemmed from several different factors. Innovations in payment methods and the demand for a greater variety of payment methods had forced many payment method providers to create new ways to pay for goods and services. Additionally, technological advances, such as the Internet, had created new methods of buying goods and services and created demand for new and more secure ways to pay for those goods and services.

Creating Convenience. Letting customers choose the way they wished to pay was an important part of creating convenience for customers and ultimately led to the kind of brand loyalty that was desired. One way to provide convenience and choice was to make a number of different payment systems available to the customer. Examples included credit cards; debit cards, which allowed customers to make payments that were directly withdrawn from the checking account; and stored value cards, which allowed customers to place a fixed amount of money on the card to make purchases. The stored value cards protected the customer in case the card was lost or stolen, since only the amount of money that had been placed electronically on the card would be lost. Another payment method, which was a product of the Internet age, was the smart card. The smart card contained an electronic chip that held a great deal of customer information and allowed for greater protection for purchases made over the Internet. Creating cards that combined the functionality of any or all of these types of cards presented a potential opportunity for issuers.

Creating Value. Value for customers came in many forms: services or reward programs such as frequent flyer programs for individual customers, or ease of settlement and usage for business and corporate customers. For all customers a key to success was the development and creation of value-intensifying services in conjunction with payment methods. Examples were adding services to each type of card like extending warranties for goods bought with the card, offering cash back or insurance for goods bought with the card, and cobranding cards with retailers, restaurants, or airlines so that cardholders could get discounts or rebates from those partners.

Offering electronic bill payments created value to both corporate and individual customers. The bills were sent to individuals online and paid for online. This reduced the time and cost of bill collecting for many corporate customers while providing a convenient way to pay bills for individual customers. Additionally, electronic bill payments increased traffic on the payment method provider's web site, and from there a whole array of value-creating services could be provided. For example, purchasing platforms, which are electronic exchanges that connect buyers and sellers, could be linked to the payment provider's web site. These purchasing platforms would be commercial hubs for both business-to-business (B2B) and business-to-consumer (B2C) types of business. These platforms created value for businesses and convenience for their customers while extending the market share of the payment method.

Technology   Technological advances dramatically affected the credit card segment. The Internet and new payment methods like smart cards provided new opportunities for growth for card issuers.

Internet.   The growth of purchasing on the Internet was exponential, as shown in Figure 3. Credit cards were involved in 90 to 95 percent of Internet sales transactions (Lowe, 2001). Because of the Internet's increasing popularity, businesses of all kinds grew and gained access to new customer bases.

Although there had been tremendous growth in e-commerce and the Internet industry, many people who browsed online were still hesitant to shop online for fear of a security breach when placing personal information over the Internet. New security systems were in development but had not yet reached the majority of online consumers. The credit card had a substantial opportunity in this area.

The keys to success were to partner with highly trafficked web sites to attract potential customers, to create value-added services like online purchase protection or rebates for online purchases, and to main-

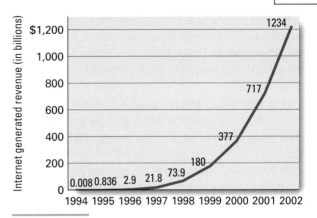

FIGURE 3

Growth of Internet Purchasing

Source: Nua Internet Surveys (2001). "The Internet and Businesses," [Online]. **http://www.nua.net/surveys/index.** Accessed March 1.

tain aggressive customer advertising targeted to online shoppers. It was also important to create a secure Internet environment by developing high-security systems for credit card use over the Internet and to create value and convenience for cardholders and merchants through the development of B2C web sites featuring merchants that accepted an issuer's cards and offered discounts to cardholders.

Payment Methods.   The technological advances that had changed banking and the credit card industry had affected payment methods. The creation and increasing popularity of various payment systems had created greater value and convenience for consumers. One innovation in electronic payments was the smart card, which contained a computer chip that activated a digital wallet when one was making purchases online. The chip contained a digital ID number that authenticated the cardholder and then launched the digital form-filling wallet when one was required to fill out forms to make purchases online.

The smart card gained rapid adoption in Europe and Asia, but growth in the United States was slow. In 2000, the total world market for smart cards was approximately $2.6 billion, but only $100 million was in the United States (Robinson, 2001). The U.S. had a well-developed infrastructure to accept magnetic-strip (traditional) credit cards and had been slow to make the investment to convert to smart cards. However, the potential increases in online purchasing suggested that an opportunity for issuers was to develop cards that contained both a magnetic strip and a smart chip like Amex's Blue card. These cards could still be used within the current infrastructure but also offered the Internet purchasing benefits of a smart card.

The keys to success for issuers in this area were to continuously develop technology, maintain strong advertising to make consumers aware of the technology, and maintain an aggressive sales force that would bring new payment systems to consumers and merchants. Also critical was to make the transition from regular credit cards to new payment methods as cost efficient as possible for merchants and to create convenience and choice for cardholders by offering various products, including dual cards.

Regulation New laws and stricter application of regulations had an effect on the financial services industry, and on commercial banking in particular. In 1999, the Financial Services Modernization Act was passed, ushering in sweeping changes in the banking industry. This legislation, along with the application of antitrust laws and the bankruptcy reform act, had potential effects on the credit card segment.

Industry Modernization. The Financial Services Modernization Act of 1999 repealed the Glass-Steagall Act, which prohibited cross-sector affiliation between the banking and securities industries. It also repealed the 1956 Bank Holding Company Act, which prohibited unions between the banking and insurance industries. The legislation established a new entity called a financial holding company. For a bank holding company to qualify as a financial holding company, all of its depository institution subsidiaries must be well managed and well capitalized and must have a satisfactory Community Reinvestment Act (CRA) rating. A financial institution seeking to become a multipurpose financial institution could structure itself in two ways. It could become a financial holding company and set up affiliates. This provided the most flexibility and greatest possibility for one-stop shopping. Alternatively, it could create subsidiaries. Although the federal government had issued an interim rule stating that those banks and their subsidiaries were allowed to operate many financial services, insurance underwriting, merchant banking, and real estate development were not allowed.

This legislation spurred a flood of mergers and acquisitions among financial institutions. One of the largest mergers in U.S. history resulted, the Travelers–Citigroup merger. This created a financial powerhouse that had operations in investment banking through its Solomon Smith Barney arm, insurance through Travelers, and commercial banking through Citibank.

Antitrust Laws. The antitrust laws have also affected the credit card industry. In October of 1998 the Department of Justice (DOJ) brought an antitrust suit against Visa and MasterCard. The allegations were that Visa and MasterCard were not really competitors. The DOJ claimed that the two associations operated under a "duality" whereby member banks were allowed to issue both Visa- and MasterCard-branded plastic. According to the DOJ, this duality meant that these brands were in effect one business and that this one business held a dominant market position. This enabled them to stifle competition from rivals by forbidding banks from issuing rival cards like American Express or Discover.

The DOJ recommended that major card-issuing banks commit their credit and debit cards exclusively to either Visa or MasterCard. The implications of antitrust charges and subsequent recommendations by the DOJ caused a shift in the allegiance of many major banks. Since the lawsuit was initiated, many banks have chosen to focus their business with one brand or the other. For example, Citigroup and Chase chose to predominately use MasterCard, and Bank One and Bank of America chose to predominately use Visa. The result of this shift to either Visa or MasterCard meant another layer of competition between card issuers.

Bankruptcy Reform. The Bankruptcy Reform Act could also have an impact on the industry. The new law would require all cardholders to meet certain income guidelines and seek out credit counseling before being allowed to file for bankruptcy. This could have long-term positive results for issuers, but it may also result in a short-term dramatic increase in loan losses as cardholders attempt to file before the new law takes effect (Cardflash, 2001). Issuers benefited in 1999 and 2000 from a declining bankruptcy trend, as shown in Table 2, but a dramatic increase, even short-term, would negatively affect issuers' profitability.

TABLE 2

U.S. Bankruptcy Filings

Year	Totals Filings	Business Filings	Consumer Filings
1991	943,987	71,549	872,438
1992	971,517	70,643	900,874
1993	875,202	62,304	812,898
1994	832,829	52,374	780,455
1995	926,601	51,959	874,642
1996	1,178,555	53,549	1,125,006
1997	1,404,145	54,027	1,350,118
1998	1,442,549	44,367	1,398,182
1999	1,319,465	44,367	1,281,581
2000	1,253,444	35,472	1,217,972

Source: ABI World (2001). "Filing Statistics," [Online]. **http://www.abiworld.org/stats/newstatsfront.html**. Accessed April 23.

Globalization   Globalization of the financial services industry has also an impact on the credit card sector. Globalization led to increased worldwide acceptance of credit cards and also led U.S. issuers to begin issuing cards to customers outside the United States.

Usage.   Visa and MasterCard expanded their networks globally, allowing U.S. customers to use their cards around the world. American Express and Discover built proprietary networks to also allow cardholders worldwide usage. Issuers without a proprietary network could take advantage of the Visa and MasterCard networks. This allowed credit cards to act as a universal payment mechanism, with the issuer handling the foreign exchange portion of the transactions. As a result, credit cards brought added convenience for customers traveling abroad.

Issuance.   Some U.S. issuers also built international credit card portfolios. Citibank and American Express were two of the largest U.S. issuers in the global market. American Express operated in the major markets in Europe and Japan, where it had over 1 million cards issued (Harner, 2000). Citibank was able to expand on the basis of its international consumer banking operations and looked to continue to grow in this business. Since international name recognition was required to be a successful international issuer, firms with a worldwide commercial banking presence had the advantage. Also

required was an international operational and legal infrastructure that enabled issuers to lend to customers in other countries. U.S. firms without an international consumer banking presence found it difficult to issue cards in foreign markets partly because of the lack of name recognition but also because of cultural differences (Levinshone, 2000).

Sales and Promotion   The primary account acquisition method used during the 1990s was direct mail. However, a new acquisition channel developed in the Internet, and issuers continued to look for other ways to attract customers.

Direct Mail.   Direct mail acquisitions helped fuel the growth in credit card issuance during the 1990s. By 2001 mailboxes were being stuffed with more credit card solicitations than ever, with the typical U.S. household receiving more than three card offers a month. In 2000, card issuers mailed a record 3.54 billion solicitations, up from 2.87 billion in 1999 (Coleman, 2001).

With this increase in solicitations also came a record-low response rate of 0.6 percent in 2000, compared with 1.0 percent in 1999 (Coleman, 2001). To be successful, issuers needed to develop creative campaigns to attract customers and to use technology to segment and target the base of potential customers. Also, issuers needed to seek out other means of acquiring customers.

Internet. The use of the Internet as an acquisition channel increased dramatically, with many issuers offering online applications and instant approval decisions. Partnering with or advertising on highly trafficked web sites was important to success. Also important was instant decision making, which allowed new cardholders to immediately begin using their new credit card number to make purchases on the Web. However, as this grew, the potential for fraudulent applications also grew.

Other. Other methods of account and customer acquisition included in-branch invitations and cross-selling customers from other businesses within the bank. In-branch invitation acquisitions stemmed from customers applying for credit through a firm's commercial banking branch network. Bank card issuers had an advantage over monolines in this area. Cross-selling also provided an acquisition channel. For firms that operated in other segments besides credit cards, customers of these other products provided acquisition targets. For example, banks that issued mortgages or auto loans could also issue credit cards to these customers.

Operations Credit card issuers needed to manage their operations effectively to remain profitable. One important area was the cost of doing business, including personnel cost. Another important operation was credit, which determined the firms' lending criteria.

Costs. Beyond the costs of acquiring customers, credit card issuers had other costs that needed to be managed effectively. The personnel cost of customer service and collections comprised a considerable portion of the issuer's expenses. The cost of printing and delivering monthly statements to customers was also substantial. The Internet provided an opportunity to reduce this particular cost. As issuers migrated customers to electronic statements, there could be reductions in paper, printing, and postage costs.

Credit. Another important operational area was credit underwriting. This involved determining who should be offered credit and how much they should be offered. Issuers usually developed risk criteria using an individual's credit bureau scores (otherwise called FICO scores). These scores took into account the individual's past credit and payment history.

Cardholders with missed payments or loan defaults would have lower FICO scores. Issuers offering credit to these low or subprime customers usually charged higher rates or fees to compensate for the increased risk of nonpayment.

Competition As a result of credit card industry consolidation, the largest issuers controlled an increasing percentage of the market. At the end of 2000, the top ten issuers controlled 78 percent of the total market (CardFlash, 2001). Competition among the leaders was fierce, and most of the country was saturated with cards and offers from all of the large firms on a regular basis. The growth of the top ten issuers is shown in Table 3.

Low introductory interest rates were common, with issuers content to issue loans for a time below their own cost of funds in hopes that the cardholders would stay long enough to become profitable customers. Value propositions also became increasingly important as issuers vied to become the card of choice, and retaining current cardholders became as important as acquiring new customers.

Bank Card Issuers. Banks historically made up the largest segment of the credit card industry. However, throughout the 1990s, companies whose sole business was credit cards began to take in increased share of the market. These firms, called monolines, used creative advertising and searched out new niches to win customers from the bank card issuers.

Citibank had historically been the largest player in the credit card market. Much of the innovation in the industry (cobranded cards, aggressive direct mail campaigns) began with Citibank. Many of the executives across the credit card industry began their careers with Citibank, including the CCS executive Richard Srednicki. In 1998, Citibank purchased the AT&T Universal Card portfolio, which allowed it to regain the leadership position that was briefly lost to Bank One after the latter's purchase of First USA. In 2000, Citibank purchased the Associates portfolio, signaling to the industry that it would continue to be an aggressive acquirer and would continue to use acquisitions to fuel its growth (McCafferty, 2001).

Citibank's greatest advantages were that it had the worldwide presence that made it attractive to business travelers and vacationers and that it had the scale to operate efficiently. It had credit card operations in forty-eight countries worldwide.

TABLE 3

Top Ten Credit Card Issuers (as of 12/31/00)

Rank/Issuer	4Q/00	4Q/99	Change
1. Citigroup	$87.7b	$72.4b	+21%
2. MBNA America	$70.4b	$58.8b	+20%
3. Bank One/FUSA	$67.0b	$69.4b	−18%
4. Discover	$47.1b	$38.0b	+24%
5. Chase Manhattan	$36.2b	$33.6b	+ 8%
6. American Express	$28.7b	$23.4b	+23%
7. Providian	$26.7b	$18.7b	+43%
8. Bank of America	$24.3b	$20.9b	+16%
9. Capital One	$22.7b	$15.7b	+45%
10. Household	$15.2b	$13.3b	+14%

Source: CardFlash (2001). "U.S. Payment Card Daily—Friday March 16, 2001," [Online]. **http://www.cardweb.com**. Accessed March 16.

Citibank had the top airline co-brand credit card with its partnership with American Airlines. It also had the top telecommunications co-brand from acquisition of the AT&T portfolio. Also, its over 100 million cardholders provided a substantial base from which to cross-sell other products in an attempt to deepen cardholders' relationships with the company and so make it less likely they would switch to another issuer's card (McCafferty, 2001).

Citibank attempted to limit its loan losses by maintaining strong collection departments and policies. It could also effectively integrate acquired portfolios, including agent banking portfolios. However, in 2001 it focused more on acquiring international credit card portfolios, which may have signaled a strategic decision to focus less on domestic portfolio acquisitions. Finally, Citibank had not made an effort to compete in the corporate card business and as a result had not developed the technological platform that would allow it to enter this market in the near term.

Other bank card issuers included most of the U.S. large and mid-sized banks. However, many of these banks did not have the scale to operate a credit card business efficiently, and as a result the trend had been toward exiting this business. Even large banks, like the Bank of New York and First Union, sold off their credit card portfolios.

Bank One became a large credit card issuer with its acquisition of the monoline First USA, which grew dramatically during the 1990s with aggressive direct mail campaigns and very low introductory rates. It had an extensive co-brand network and an affinity relationship network of over 2,000 partners.

However, despite its size, Bank One ran into considerable financial trouble. In 2000, it was forced to take large write-offs associated with the credit quality of its credit card portfolio and then continued to struggle to remain profitable, with large numbers of customers accruing interest rates below the bank's cost of funds. Bank One had the scale to compete effectively but needed to work on strengthening its profitability, as well as its credit and collections policies.

Other bank card issuers faced similar problems. Because of size limitations, most did not have the international name recognition to compete in the international card issuance market, the capital to compete for portfolio acquisitions, or the technology to compete in the corporate card market.

Monoline Issuers.   These firms had unique advantages and disadvantages over the bank card issuers. One disadvantage was that monolines did not have the same access to capital that the larger banks had. However, the credit card segments within the large banks had to compete for that capital with other, possibly more profitable, businesses within the bank. Monolines do not have this dilemma and as a result may be more flexible in their choices of investment projects.

MBNA had one of the most unique situations in the industry. In slightly over a decade, it built its company from a small Maryland bank into one of the largest credit card issuers in the United States. It held a competitive advantage in the sector of affinity marketing, an offshoot of cobranding, with over 4,000 affinity relationship partners.

MBNA built partnerships with thousands of small groups across the United States, from athletic teams to universities to professional groups. It also used its affinity relationship strategy to become a successful issuer in the United Kingdom, Ireland, and Canada.

MBNA's advantage was that it was able to use the affinity that individuals had for any one of its partners as a method for issuing them a credit card. Also, since people were less likely to default on a card that was associated with an organization that they were a part of or had affinity toward, the loan loss rates on MBNA's portfolio continued to be lower than the industry averages. Another advantage was its relentless focus on effective credit underwriting and customer service. Customer service was part of the MBNA culture and was imbued in each function, from account acquisitions through collections. MBNA had not opted to compete in the corporate card market and did not have the investment banking presence to leverage and win corporate card business.

American Express (Amex) was the leader in the corporate card market as well as in the charge card (nonrevolving credit) market. However, it also became an aggressive marketer of revolving credit cards, first with its Optima card and most recently with Blue. It had worldwide name recognition, partially because of the historical popularity of its traveler's check product. However, its worldwide card position is skewed more toward the charge card business than the credit card business.

Amex had several advantages over its competitors. First, it owned a global processing platform and thus did not use the MasterCard or Visa networks. This allowed it to build its brand name while other issuers' names often got lost behind the MasterCard or Visa brands. Amex also had a loyal customer base that paid their bills. As a result, Amex had a lower percentage of delinquent accounts (measured as accounts ninety or more days past due) than any of its competitors (McCafferty, 2001). Amex had also focused on customer service and had maintained a strong collections group that also helped to limit its loan losses. This base of loyal customers also provided a receptive audience for Amex to cross-sell

other products. For example, in 1999 Amex cardholders accounted for 30 percent of all new customers with American Express Financial Advisors (McCafferty, 2001). This helped build the depth of relationship needed to retain customers. Amex's strong brand name also provided a base from which to launch new products, like the Blue card.

The Blue card was unique in that it contained a "smart" chip as well as a magnetic strip as the means of identification. Amex had marketed it as the card for the new economy and had seen rapid growth in this portfolio. The Blue card was able to be marketed as the card for the new economy since the smart chip would allow for secure Internet transactions using a reader hooked up to the user's computer. However, as of early 2001, fewer than 1 percent of Blue cardholders were using the smart chip capability to make Internet purchases. This suggested that the success of the Blue launch was related more to a creative marketing campaign than to a fundamental change in the industry (Fargo, 2001).

In the corporate card market, Amex was the recognized leader. However, smaller competitors had built more flexible technology platforms for servicing corporate clients and had begun winning business away from Amex. In 2000, CCS purchased Paymentech, the largest of these competitors.

Historically, Amex had been an occasional acquirer of portfolios. However, by 2001 it had become a potential target for acquisition by larger financial services organizations like Citigroup and Morgan Stanley Dean Witter. It had run into some financial difficulty and so was less likely to be competing for agent bank acquisitions in the near term.

Other monoline issuers will have an impact on the future of the credit card industry. Discover rebounded after years of stagnation with a strong marketing campaign and its cash-back approach, which allowed cardholders to obtain a rebate in cash each year on a percentage of their purchases. Several other companies, including CCS, attempted a similar card without Discover's success.

Cap One became an aggressive marketer of credit cards during the latter part of the 1990s. It focused on lending to all levels across the credit spectrum, from "superprime," the most credit-worthy customers within the prime market, to subprime, the least credit-worthy customers. It had a very profitable secured card with which it served the subprime market. For a fee and a required up-front cash deposit, a high-credit-risk customer could obtain a low-credit-limit card with which he or she could build or rebuild credit. Once he or she had done so, Cap One would then offer a more flexible credit arrangement.

Cap One continued to grow rapidly using technology to segment the market of potential customers and to target offers specifically to their needs and preferences. During the fourth quarter of 2000, Cap One added three times as many new customers as any other issuer (Condon, 2001).

Providian Financial also grew through marketing to the subprime segment. It was also a buyer of distressed credit card assets, which were loans that other banks had charged off. However, Providian's loan loss rates were double those of Cap One (Condon, 2001).

Besides Amex, and to a lesser degree MBNA, the monolines did not have the international name recognition required to issue internationally. Nor did these firms have the commercial or investment banking presence to leverage for individual and corporate customer businesses. Also, although many of these companies were growing rapidly, they did not have the access to capital needed to be strong competitors for portfolio acquisitions.

The Company

Overview

Chase Cardmember Services (CCS) made up 29 percent of the cash operating earnings of J. P. Morgan Chase's commercial banking sector, as shown in Figure 4, but just over 7 percent of the earnings of the entire J. P. Morgan Chase company (J. P. Morgan Chase, 2000). CCS had benefited from the trend toward consolidation in the financial services industry during the 1990s. It had become one of the few remaining large issuers in the credit card segment as a result of two large bank mergers: Chemical Bank with Manufacturer's Hanover and this combined Chemical Bank with Chase Manhattan. The combination of these companies and the resultant combinations of the credit card portfolios helped CCS grow more than any of the individual firms had been able to do through internal growth or customer acquisitions.

CCS also benefited from the consolidation trend, specifically in the credit card segment, with numerous commercial banks exiting this segment. This was evidenced by its purchase of the entire credit card portfolio of the Bank of New York. While opportunity for CCS abounded as the number of

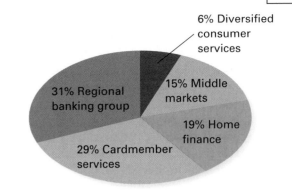

FIGURE 4

J. P. Morgan Chase Commercial Bank

Source: J. P. Morgan Chase (2000). *Annual Report.*

portfolios up for sale, including mid-sized and large portfolios, increased, CCS had still not proven it could expand its business via means other than portfolio acquisitions.

Products

CCS offered Visa and MasterCard products, including cobranded cards, agent bank cards, and a very minor secured card product, but it did not offer affinity cards. CCS also had a small but growing business and corporate card presence.

Cobranded Cards   Cobranded credit cards were one area in which CCS competed strongly, with offerings in various industries, including gasoline, airlines, and retailing.

Shell.   The Shell Oil card was the largest cobranded card that was part of the CCS portfolio. The CCS partnership with Shell began with Chemical Bank and had been maintained through several mergers. This was the one CCS credit card that advertised regularly on television. Advertisements could also be found at Shell gas stations around the United States. The card offered a 5 percent rebate on gas purchases made at Shell gas stations and a 1 percent rebate on all other purchases. These rebates could only be used at Shell gas stations to offset the cost of future gas purchases. The card was similar to cards offered by other oil companies.

The Shell card was the leading gasoline cobranded card. Gasoline cobranded cards developed as an offshoot to the gasoline cards that most oil companies had issued. The advantages for customers were that the cobranded card carried either a Master-Card or Visa logo, could be used for purchases other than gas, and allowed customers to earn rebates on their purchases. The advantage for Shell was the additional business from customers that would only want to buy gas from Shell so they could earn the rebates offered by the card. The advantages for CCS bank were the additional loans and becoming the card of choice for customers loyal to Shell.

The Shell card, like other cobranded cards offering rewards or rebates, tended to attract customers that charged frequently but also paid off their balance each month (called "transactors"). In general, CCS made most of its profits from customers that did not pay their balance each month, thus accruing finance charges (called "revolving"). Many cards that attracted "transactors" attached an annual fee to the card, but the Shell card remained attractive to customers since it did not have an annual fee.

Wal-Mart. The Wal-Mart card was CCS's second largest cobranded card. This card was launched with the nation's largest retailer in 1996. The card did not offer any value enhancement but carried a low fixed interest rate. This strategy was consistent with Wal-Mart's philosophy of everyday low prices. No value enhancement was added to the card because Wal-Mart did not want any customer to receive benefits not available to all of its customers.

This approach worked successfully for several years, and the portfolio grew steadily. However, competition in the industry had reduced interest rates across the board. In order to acquire new customers, most card issuers were offering very low introductory interest rates. Because of the nature of the relationship with Wal-Mart, CCS was prohibited from making similar offers. Thus the portfolio growth slowed considerably as customers became used to receiving low introductory offers.

Continental Airlines. The Continental Airlines card was CCS's airline cobranded card. Prior to 1997, CCS had been the issuer of the British Airways cobranded credit card. This card had a limited appeal outside of East Coast business travelers and wealthy individuals. At the same time, Marine Midland was struggling to maintain its credit card business and was looking for a buyer for the Continental Airlines portfolio. CCS decided to sell the British Airways portfolio and pur-

chase the Continental Airlines portfolio from Marine Midland. This card had a much broader appeal nationwide as a result of Continental's large U.S. presence.

The Continental Airlines card allowed cardholders to earn Continental frequent flyer miles for each dollar charged to the card. The card had a high annual fee compared with other CCS offerings, but it also offered bonus miles for opening the account, helping to overcome cardholders' aversion to annual fees.

The card was primarily marketed through direct mail, but it was also advertised on Continental Airlines flights and in airports at Continental terminals. The appeal was to business travelers, families looking to earn miles toward vacations, and anyone who flew often on Continental. The card was similar to offers by other airlines, particularly the Citibank AAdvantage card, which was partnered with American Airlines.

Toys "R" Us. The Toys "R" Us card was a small portfolio that was obtained when CCS purchased the credit card business of the Bank of New York in 1998. The card appealed primarily to parents with young children.

The card was relaunched in 1999 and allowed cardholders to earn rebate points that could be redeemed at Toys "R" Us and Toys "R" Us.com. The portfolio remained small and was marketed primarily at Toys "R" Us locations and on the Toys "R" Us.com web site.

Verizon. The Verizon card was the descendant of the Bell Atlantic cobranded card prior to the phone company's merger with GTE and its subsequent name change to Verizon. In 2001, CCS chose to terminate its relationship with the telecommunications company.

Like the Shell card and cobranded cards from other issuers, the Verizon card tended to appeal to "transactors," or customers who charged frequently, thus earning significant rebates, but who did not carry a balance monthly and did not accrue interest charges. CCS ending this relationship was possibly a signal that the industry was moving away from "transactor" cards that were unprofitable.

Agent Bank Cards CCS had agent banking relationships with two banks. The first was the Bank of New

York. This was a small portfolio of individuals and businesses that had Bank of New York credit cards that were issued and serviced by CCS. The other, larger relationship was with Huntington Bank. CCS purchased this portfolio in 1999, and it was the first all-agent bank portfolio that CCS purchased.

CCS continued to look to be a portfolio acquirer and recognized that many of the portfolio sales in the future would involve agent banking relationships. It had experience in integrating and managing two agent banking relationships and was looking to build on this experience. Other large firms, like Citibank and MBNA, had also been acquiring agent banking relationships, as evidenced by MBNA's purchase of the First Tennessee Bank portfolio. Agent banking relationships could also be sought out and developed without having to purchase portfolios, but this was less common.

This area represented an opportunity for growth for CCS since it gained experience from its two agent bank relationships, it had the capital to fund agent bank portfolio acquisitions, and portfolios continued to come up for sale.

Business and Corporate Cards   A growing and profitable segment of the CCS portfolio was the business and corporate card sector. The business card market involved cards issued to small businesses, many of them already having a banking relationship with Chase (or the Bank of New York and Huntington Bank, in the case of agent bank business cards).

However, a larger area for growth appeared to be the corporate card market. This involved issuing and servicing the credit cards issued to employees within large corporations. This sector was dominated by American Express. However, CCS had recently acquired the corporate card business of Paymentech. As part of this purchase, CCS acquired Paymentech's industry leading platform for acquiring and servicing corporate cards, and CCS president Richard Srednicki stated that this was a strategic growth area for the business (Dow Jones, 2000).

The corporate card business was less dependent on interest charges, since most corporations paid incurred expenses on a monthly basis. Also, since the corporation guaranteed payment on charges made by its employees, loan losses were not a concern. The revenue was derived mainly from fee income. This reduced CCS's reliance on interest rate–sensitive revenue. Also, J. P. Morgan Chase had a strong invest-

ment bank that CCS could leverage to acquire additional corporate clients.

Technology

CCS made several attempts to incorporate new technology into its business. It worked to incorporate the Internet and was also working to begin incorporating smart card technology.

The Internet   In 1999, CCS launched a cobranded card with the Internet retailer Shopnow.com. The card offered reward points for merchandise purchased at the site. However, in 2000 Shopnow.com realized that the value proposition for general purpose online retailers was limited and decided to change its name to Network Commerce and its business focus to B-to-B commerce (Boone, 2000). As a result, the Shopnow.com card never became the CCS entry into the new economy that it had hoped.

However, the Shopnow.com card was a good example of how CCS might fit into the core business of J. P. Morgan Chase going forward. It was developed after the Chase venture capital business funded Shopnow.com. This card was designed to help not only CCS but also Shopnow.com, which would in turn increase the value of Chase's investment in the company. Although it was unsuccessful, it set a precedent for potential future synergies within J. P. Morgan Chase.

CCS also developed an Internet presence as part of the www.chase.com site. The site allowed cardholders to check their current and previous statements online and, if they had a Chase checking account, pay their bill online.

Payment Methods   By the start of 2001, CCS had not issued a card that incorporated smart card technology. However, it was developing a smart card and was also looking into the possibility of combining smart card technology with its cobranded cards. The Continental Airlines card, which had a more affluent customer base than its other cobranded cards, was one possible alternative.

Regulation

The regulatory environment provided several opportunities and threats for CCS.

Financial Services Modernization   This legislation spurred a flood of mergers and acquisitions among financial institutions; among them was the merger of J. P. Morgan and Chase Manhattan. The resulting company, J. P. Morgan Chase, was a large multifaceted financial services company or one-stop shopping facility for financial services.

The creation of this large financial services conglomerate presented a challenge for CCS. CCS had now become a much smaller part of a larger company, and there was the possibility that it would not be deemed part of the core business of the new firm. The situation also presented an opportunity for CCS. CCS could present itself as an integral part of a financial services team that could provide a true one-stop-shopping financial services experience for customers. For example, for any business that did its investment banking, middle market banking, or branch network banking with J. P. Morgan Chase, CCS could add value by providing various payment methods for these customers. The key to success was to demonstrate to J. P. Morgan Chase that CCS could provide valuable services to existing clients by helping to create a true one-stop-shopping financial services experience for clients.

Antitrust Legislation The pending antitrust suit involving MasterCard and Visa was not likely to have a dramatic impact on CCS. Even if the government forced the Associations to drop the prohibition on member banks issuing American Express or other non-Visa or non-MasterCard cards, CCS would likely opt not to issue American Express cards because it was seen as an independent competitor. By 2000, CCS had already agreed to become primarily a MasterCard issuer.

Globalization

Since CCS cards were affiliated with Visa or MasterCard, its cardholders could use their cards worldwide. However, CCS opted to exit the international card issuance business.

Until mid 2000, CCS had a profitable and growing credit card business in Hong Kong, where it was the third largest credit card issuer. The Manhattan Card, as it was called, was considered the premier elite credit card in Hong Kong. This card portfolio was the largest part of J. P. Morgan Chase's international consumer banking operations, which also included branch banking networks in Hong Kong, Panama, and the Virgin Islands.

However, in 2000 the corporation made the strategic decision to exit the international commercial banking business. As a result, the Hong Kong credit card business was sold to Standard Chartered Bank for $1.32 billion and CCS became a domestic-only card issuer (ChinaOnline, 2000). After the merger with J. P. Morgan, CCS did have an internationally recognized brand name that it could leverage if it decided to reenter the international card issuance business. It also had the capital needed if it wanted to expand internationally via acquisition of foreign credit card businesses.

Finance

CCS had been a profitable and important segment of Chase Manhattan prior to the J. P. Morgan merger. However, as a result of the J. P. Morgan–Chase Manhattan merger, CCS's parent became primarily an investment bank. This could make it difficult for CCS to obtain capital from the corporation to fund portfolio acquisitions and other growth-oriented activities. CCS needed to focus on maintaining a high return on investment, since it has to compete for capital with profitable investment banking and venture capital projects in other parts of the corporation.

CCS made money primarily on interest charged to customers who borrowed money (revolved). It also made money on late fees charged to customers not making timely payments and overlimit fees charged to customers exceeding their credit limit. Another source of profit was insurance premiums

TABLE 4

CCS Charge-Off Rates (losses as % of total loans)

3Q00	4.97%
2Q00	5.09
1Q00	5.39
4Q99	5.25
3Q99	5.57
2Q99	5.85
1Q99	6.18
1999 (full year)	5.66
1998 (full year)	6.02
1997 (full year)	5.58

Source: Chase Manhattan (2000). *Third Quarter Earnings Release.*

charged to customers enrolling in payment insurance, which helped customers maintain their credit rating in the event they became unemployed.

Other CCS revenues included interchange income, which was a transaction-processing fee charged to merchants accepting credit cards as payment, cash advance fees, and annual fees. However, as more customers became transactors, CCS profitability was likely to become challenged as interest income decreased.

Another threat to CCS was the economy, since loan losses also affected its profitability. Bankruptcies had been on the decline during 1999 and 2000 because the economy had been strong. This had helped CCS reduce its overall loan losses. However, if this trend turned around, the credit card industry as a whole would be significantly affected (Lee, 2001). The Bankruptcy Reform Act currently before Congress could help offset some of this risk by making it difficult for some individuals to file bankruptcy. However, if the economy worsened, the volume of bankruptcies was still likely to increase dramatically.

Periodically, Chase securitized a portion of its credit card portfolio by selling a pool of credit card receivables to a trust, which issued securities to investors. The receivables underlying the securities that were sold to investors were not included in Chase's consolidated results. Securitization changed CCS's status from that of a lender to that of a servicer. When credit card receivables were securitized, CCS ceased to derive interest income on those receivables and instead received fees for continuing to service them. As a result, securitization did not significantly affect Chase's reported and operating net income. Table 5 shows CCS revenue for 1998–1999. Operating revenue is the revenue CCS derives from its business activities. Reported revenue includes the additional income CCS derives from its securitization activities.

Management

Richard Srednicki began his career at Citibank and contributed to its growth into the leading U.S. credit card issuer during the 1980s. One of his more recent assignments was as an executive at AT&T in charge of the AT&T Universal Card. During his tenure, the AT&T card business was sold to Citibank as AT&T decided to exit the credit card business. CCS faced a similar situation: it was possible that its parent could possibly someday also want to exit the business.

David Coulter, the former CEO of Bank of America, was now running the J. P. Morgan Chase commercial bank, of which CCS was a major part. The success of CCS would likely be critical to Mr. Coulter's success as head of the commercial bank, and he had said that CCS was not for sale and would continue to look to be a portfolio acquirer (Moyer, 2001).

However, the decision about whether J. P. Morgan Chase would remain in the credit card segment probably rested with the CEO William Harrison and the board of directors. Mr. Harrison's experience had been more on the investment side of the banking industry, and the J. P. Morgan merger solidified that portion of the business without having a dramatic impact on the commercial banking operations. Analysts suggested that the slower-growing commercial banking business might not be a good fit with the expanding investment banking business.

Looking Toward the Future

Given the trends of consolidation and technological advance in the credit card segment, CCS management was exploring a number of strategic alternatives. The pressure was on to begin clarifying its strategic direction to both the investment community and the J. P. Morgan Chase board of directors. One decision that had to be made was the geographic scope CCS would take in expanding its business. Mr. Srednicki was considering two alternatives.

The first alternative for CCS was one centered on growth, both domestically and internationally. In this alternative, CCS would build a global credit card franchise and diversify its current business by expanding into other countries, particularly those

TABLE 5

CCS Revenue, Year Ended December 31, (in millions)

	1999	1998
Reported credit card revenue	$1,698	$1,474
Less impact of credit card securitizations	(318)	(299)
Operating credit card revenue	$1,380	$1,175

Source: Chase Manhattan (1999). *Annual Report.*

countries where the J. P. Morgan and Chase names had substantial name recognition.

This alternative was feasible, since although J. P. Morgan Chase no longer had an international commercial banking presence, it did have a strong international presence in the investment banking sector. CCS could leverage this brand name recognition in countries like Canada, the United Kingdom, and Japan to expand to international consumers. CCS had the capital required to purchase portfolios anywhere in the world, which also made international expansion feasible. Finally, CCS could compete for international corporations' business for its corporate card business as well.

This alternative could win against the competition, because among its competitors, only Citibank and Amex had greater name recognition worldwide, and Amex was more focused on the charge card market. With the trend toward consolidation affecting the international financial services industry along with the domestic industry, the credit card segment worldwide was likely to consolidate faster than one firm alone could absorb. CCS had the capital required to acquire international portfolios as they came up for sale, and as a result, CCS was in a position to win against all of the other competitors except Citibank. If it participated during this consolidation, along with Citibank, it would build an international presence that could be leveraged in the future. If it did not participate in this consolidation in the near term, it would limit its ability to ever compete in this market. It could also win against all competition in the international corporate card business. It had the industry leading technology platform that could be applied to corporate card portfolios domestically and internationally and the worldwide investment banking presence to leverage for acquiring new business.

The main drawbacks to this strategy were CCS's lack of an international commercial banking presence to leverage for acquiring new customers, lack of an international infrastructure for servicing these customers, and Citibank's more dominant position in this area.

However, CCS could find ways around these problems. While Citibank did have a dominate position in this area, the industry was consolidating faster that Citibank alone could absorb. If CCS were to begin competing for and winning portfolios, it could participate with Citibank in absorbing this consolidation. Also, it could develop the required international infrastructure through acquisition. Where Citibank might be more inclined just to purchase the portfolio of an international card issuer, CCS could look to also purchase the issuer's infrastructure.

A second alternative was one centered solely on domestic expansion. Mr. Srednicki had inherited a business that had already determined it would exit the international card business. In doing so it recognized that there was more opportunity domestically that it wished to focus on. This alternative would keep CCS on that path and allow it to focus its resources entirely on opportunities in the domestic market like corporate cards and agent banking cards.

This alternative was feasible, since CCS had the access to capital required to be an acquirer of domestic portfolios and could do so more frequently without having to also acquire the infrastructure that international expansion would require. Also, domestically CCS had a strong commercial banking presence, which was very helpful in acquiring loyal customers.

This alternative would allow CCS to win against the competition, since many competitors did not have the capital needed to be an aggressive acquirer. With this access to capital, and with Citibank focused on building its international business, CCS had a competitive advantage for domestic portfolio acquisitions. Also, most large U.S. corporations already had some relationship with J. P. Morgan Chase. As a result, CCS was in position to leverage these relationships, along with its industry leading technology platform for servicing corporate clients to win against the competition in the corporate card business. Internationally, CCS would have to compete for business with foreign banks whose relationship with foreign corporations might limit CCS's success in the corporate card market.

The major drawback to this alternative was the possibility that Citibank would change its focus from international expansion back to domestic expansion. Citibank's scale made it a difficult head-on competitor that could limit CCS's success in the domestic market.

However, CCS could find ways around this problem. As in the international market, the domestic credit card market was consolidating faster than one company could absorb. As a result, CCS could still succeed by participating along with Citibank in the segment's consolidation. It does have the advantage over Citibank in the corporate card segment, and could use this advantage to become the dominant acquirer of corporate card portfolios.

Mr. Srednicki needed to decide which strategic decision to implement. While CCS had a strong domestic presence and no international presence, the trend toward consolidation internationally made this a good time to build an international business. If he chose not to take advantage of this opportunity now, it was likely that CCS would not be able to enter this market successfully in the future. However, in both domestic and international markets, Citibank had advantages over CCS. With Citibank focusing internationally, this was a good time for CCS to focus on domestic opportunity. Mr. Srednicki's decision would determine what direction CCS would take to win against increasing competition in the near, intermediate, and long term.

REFERENCES

Anonymous (1998). "Expanding Economy Propels Credit Cards," *Industries in Transition*, vol. 25, p. 10.

Boone, R. (2000). "Shopnow.com Changes Name, Set Profit Goal," LocalBusiness.com. [Online]. **http://www.localbusiness.com/Story/0,1118,SEA_134552,00.html.** Accessed April 1, 2001.

CardFlash (2001). "U.S. Payment Card Daily—Friday March 16, 2001." [Online]. **http://www.cardweb.com.** Accessed March 16.

Carney, D. (2000). "Breaking Up the Old Card Game?" *Business Week*, June 12, vol. 3685, p. 98.

ChinaOnline (2001). "Hong Kong's Standard Chartered Bank Buys Chase Manhattan's Retail Credit Card Business." [Online]. **http://www.chinaonline.com/industry/financial/NewsArchive/Secure/2000/november/C00110101.asp.** Accessed March 30.

Coleman, C. (2001). "Credit Card Solicitations Get Record Low in Response Rate," *Wall Street Journal*, March 19.

Condon, B. (2001). "House of Cards," *Forbes*. [Online]. **http://www.forbes.com/forbes/2001/0402/077.html?_requestid=70916.** Accessed April 9.

Credit Card History (2001). "Credit Card History." [Online]. **http://www.worldwidebankcard.net/hist.htm.** Accessed March 1.

Dow Jones Newswire (2000). "Chase to Acquire Paymentech Unit," *Dallas Morning News*, November 21, p. 7D.

Fargo, J. (2001). "Bank Cards Heed the Smart Card Call," *Credit Card Management*, January 2, vol. 13, no. 10, p. 25.

Forrester Research (2001). [Online]. **http://www.forrester.com/ER/Press/Release/0,1769,164, FF.html.** Accessed March 1.

Harner, S. (2000). *Japan's Financial Revolution*. Armonk, N.Y.: M.E. Sharpe, Inc.

History of the Credit Card (2001). [Online]. **http://www.triumphant.com/history.htm.** Accessed March 1.

J. P. Morgan Chase (2000). *Annual Report.*

Lee, W. (2001). "Consumer Pinch Showing Up in Late Payments," *American Banker*, March 16.

Levinshone, A. (2000). "The Coming of a Financial Services Bazaar," *Strategic Finance*, April. [Online]. **http://www.mamag.com/strategicfinance/2000/04g.htm.** Accessed April 8, 2001.

Lowe, F. (2001). "Why Credit Will Still Rule the Web," *Credit Card Management*, February 2. [Online]. **http://www.cardforum.com/html/ccmissue/toc.htm.** Accessed April 8.

Mannix, M. (1998). "Goodbye to Debt," *U.S. News & World Report*, April 23, p. 63.

McCafferty, R. (2001). "Citigroup vs. American Express," *The Motley Fool*. [Online]. **http://www.fool.com/portfolios/rulemaker/2001/rulemaker010 319.htm?source=eheyhopop001101&ref=yhoolnk.** Accessed March 20.

Moyer, L. (2001). "JPM-Chase Retail Plan Goes Heavy on e-Tail," *American Banker*, February 21.

Nilson Report (2000). "The Future of Credit Cards in the United States," December, no. 730, pp. 6–7.

Nua Internet Surveys (2001). "The Internet and Businesses." [Online]. **http://www.nua.net/surveys/index.** Accessed March 1.

Overdorf, J. (2000). "First Tennessee Bank Sells Affinity/Co-Branded Programs." *Dow Jones Newswires*, November 30.

Robinson, Brian (2001). "Is It Too Late for Smart Cards?" Informationweek.com, March 19, pp. 61–64.

"U.S. Takes Visa, MasterCard to Court over Antitrust Concerns." *Star Ledger*, (2000) June 18.

Wherry, R. (2000). "Credit Check," *Forbes*. [Online]. **http://www.forbes.com/forbes/2000/1113/6613148a.html.** Accessed April 8, 2001.

15 Toyota: The Evolution of the Toyota Production System

This case was prepared by Charles W. L. Hill, the University of Washington.

Introduction

The growth of Toyota has been one of the great success stories of Japanese industry during the last half century. In 1947, the company was a little-known domestic manufacturer producing around 100,000 vehicles a year. Today it is the world's third largest automobile company with global production of 5.8 million vehicles and revenues of $108 billion. Toyota operates fifty-six plants in twenty-five countries and has a work force of more than 210,000. It is the market leader in Japan and is threatening to overtake Daimler Chrysler for the number three spot in the United States. In 2000, the Toyota Camry, with sales of 420,000, was the best-selling car in North America for the fourth consecutive year, while the Lexus, at 200,000 units sold, was the best-selling luxury brand in the United States.[1] Toyota's U.S. market share stood at 11 percent in 2000, up from 7.7 percent in 1996. In contrast, Daimler Chrysler's share was 14.7 percent in 2000, down from 16.2 percent in 1996.[2]

This case is intended to be used as a basis for class discussion rather than as an illustration of either effective or ineffective handling of the situation. Reprinted by permission of Charles W. L. Hill.

Toyota's vehicles consistently rank near the top in surveys of customer satisfaction and quality. As stated in the 2001 J. D. Power report on vehicle quality, "Toyota builds vehicles with more consistent quality levels across a platform than any other manufacturer."[3] Of sixteen vehicle segments looked at by J. D. Power, Toyota held the top spot for quality in seven J. D. Power gave the company's Kyushu plant in Japan the highest quality score of any car plant in the world. Moreover, Toyota's plant in Cambridge, Ontario, had the highest quality score of any plant in North America.

Not only does Toyota score well on quality metrics, but its plants also score well on productivity metrics. According to the 2001 Harbour Report, an annual survey of productivity in North American car plants, in 2000 it took Toyota 31.06 hours of employee time to build a car at its average North American plant. Although this is longer than the industry leading performance of Nissan, which can build a car in 27.63 hours, it is considerably less than the 39.94 hours it takes Ford to build a car, or the 40.52 hours at General Motors, or the more than 34 hours it takes Daimler Chrysler to build a car.[4]

This case describes the rise of Toyota from an obscure Japanese automobile company into the giant of today. It explains how the revolutionary production system developed at Toyota during the quarter of a century after 1950 paved the way for the company's current success.

The Origins of Toyota

The original idea behind the founding of the Toyota Motor Company came from the fertile mind of Toyoda Sakichi.[5] The son of a carpenter, Sakichi was an entrepreneur and inventor whose primary interest lay in the textile industry, but he had been intrigued by automobiles since a visit to the United States in 1910. Sakichi's principal achievement was the invention of an automatic loom that held out the promise of being able to lower the costs of weaving high-quality cloth. In 1926 Sakichi set up Toyoda Automatic Loom to manufacture this product. In 1930 Sakichi sold the patent rights to a British textile concern, Platt Brothers, for about 1 million yen, a considerable sum in those days. Sakichi urged his son, Toyoda Kiichiro, to use this money to study the possibility of manufacturing automobiles in Japan. A mechanical engineer with a degree from the University of Tokyo, in 1930 Kiichiro became managing director of loom production at Toyoda Automatic Loom.

Kiichiro was at first reluctant to invest in automobile production. The Japanese market was at that time dominated by Ford and General Motors, both of which imported knock-down car kits from the United States and assembled them in Japan. Given this, the board of Toyoda Automatic Loom, including Kiichiro's brother-in-law and the company's president, Kodama Risaburo, opposed the investment on the grounds that it was too risky. Kiichiro probably would not have pursued the issue further had not his father made a deathbed request in 1930 that Kiichiro explore the possibilities of automobile production. Kiichiro had to push, but in 1933 he was able to get permission to set up an automobile department within Toyoda Automatic Loom.

Kiichiro's belief was that he would be able to figure out how to manufacture automobiles by taking apart U.S.-made vehicles and examining them piece by piece. He also felt that it should be possible to adapt U.S. mass-production technology to manufacture cost efficiently at lower volumes. His confidence was based in large part upon the already considerable engineering skills and capabilities at his disposal through Toyoda Automatic Loom. Many of the precision engineering and manufacturing skills needed in automobile production were similar to the skills required to manufacture looms.

Kiichiro produced his first 20 vehicles in 1935, and in 1936 the automobile department produced 1,142 vehicles—910 trucks, 100 cars, and 132 buses. At this time, however, the production system was essentially craft-based rather than a modern assembly line. Despite some progress, the struggle might still have been uphill had not fate intervened in the form of the Japanese military. Japan had invaded Manchuria in 1931 and quickly found American-made trucks useful for moving men and equipment. As a result, the military felt that it was strategically important for Japan to have its own automobile industry. The result was the passage of an automobile manufacturing law in 1936 which required companies producing more than 3,000 vehicles per year in Japan to get a license from the government. Moreover, to get a license over 50 percent of the stock had to be owned by Japanese investors. The law also placed a duty on imported cars, including the knock-down kits that Ford and GM brought into Japan. As a direct result of this legislation, both GM and Ford exited from the Japanese market in 1939.

Once the Japanese government passed this law, Kodama Risaburo decided that the automobile venture could be profitable and switched from opposing to proactively supporting Kiichiro (in fact, Risaburo's wife, who was Kiichiro's elder sister, had been urging him to take this step for some time). The first priority was to attract the funds necessary to build a mass-production facility. In 1937 Risaburo and Kiichiro decided to incorporate the automobile department as a separate company in order to attract outside investors—which they were successful in doing. Kiichiro Toyoda was appointed president of the new company. The company was named the Toyota Motor Company. (The founding family's name, "Toyoda," means "abundant rice field" in Japanese. The new name had no meaning in Japanese.)

Upon incorporation, Risaburo and Kiichiro's vision was that Toyota should expand its passenger car production as quickly as possible. However, once again fate intervened in the form of the Japanese military. Toyota had barely begun passenger car production when war broke out; in 1939 the Japanese government, on advice from the military, prohibited passenger car production and demanded that the company specialize in the production of military trucks.

The Evolution of the Toyota Production System

After the end of World War II, Kiichiro was determined that Toyota should reestablish itself as a manufacturer of automobiles.[6] Toyota, however, faced a number of problems in doing this:

1. The Japanese domestic market was too small to support efficient-scale mass-production facilities such as those common in America by that time.

2. The Japanese economy was starved of capital, which made it difficult to raise funds to finance new investments.

3. New labor laws introduced by the American occupiers increased the bargaining power of labor and made it difficult for companies to lay off workers.

4. North America and Western Europe were full of large auto manufacturers eager to establish operations in Japan.

In response to the last point, in 1950 the new Japanese government prohibited direct foreign investment in the automobile industry and imposed high tariffs on the importation of foreign cars. This protection, however, did little to solve the other problems facing the company at this time.

From Mass Production to Flexible Production   At this juncture a remarkable mechanical engineer entered the scene: Ohno Taiichi. More than anyone else, it was Ohno who was to work out a response to the above problems. Ohno had joined Toyoda Spinning and Weaving in 1932 as a production engineer in cotton thread manufacture and entered Toyota when the former company was absorbed into the latter in 1943. Ohno worked in auto production for two years, was promoted and managed auto assembly and machine shops between 1945 and 1953, and in 1954 was appointed a company director.

When Ohno Taiichi joined Toyota the mass-production methods pioneered by Ford had become the accepted method of manufacturing automobiles. The basic philosophy behind mass production was to produce a limited product line in massive quantities to gain maximum economies of scale. The economies came from spreading the fixed costs involved in setting up the specialized equipment required to stamp body parts and manufacture components over as large a production run as possible. Since setting up much of the equipment could take a full day or more, the economies involved in long production runs were reckoned to be considerable. Thus, for example, Ford would stamp 500,000 right-hand door panels in a single production run and then store the parts in warehouses until they were needed in the assembly plant, rather than stamp just those door panels that were needed immediately and then change the settings and stamp out left-hand door panels, or other body parts.

A second feature of mass production was that each assembly worker should perform only a single task, rather than a variety of tasks. The idea here was that as the worker became completely familiar with a single task, he could perform it much faster, thereby increasing labor productivity. Assembly line workers were overseen by a foreman who did not perform any assembly tasks himself, but instead ensured that the workers followed orders. In addition, a number of specialists were employed to perform nonassembly operations such as tool repair, die changes, quality inspection, and general "housecleaning."

After working in Toyota for five years and visiting Ford's U.S. plants, Ohno became convinced that the basic mass-production philosophy was flawed. He saw five problems with the mass-production system:

1. Long production runs created massive inventories that had to be stored in large warehouses. This was expensive both because of the cost of warehousing and because inventories tied up capital in unproductive uses.

2. If the initial machine settings were wrong, long production runs resulted in the production of a large number of defects.

3. The sheer monotony of assigning assembly line workers to a single task generated defects, since workers became lax about quality control. In addition, since assembly line workers were not responsible for quality control, they had little incentive to minimize defects.

4. The extreme division of labor resulted in the employment of specialists such as foremen, quality inspectors, and tooling specialists, whose jobs logically could be performed by assembly line workers.

5. The mass-production system was unable to accommodate consumer preferences for product diversity.

In addition to these flaws, Ohno knew that the small domestic market in Japan and the lack of capital for investing in mass-production facilities made the American model unsuitable for Toyota.

Reducing Setup Times.   Given these flaws and the constraints that Toyota faced, Ohno decided to take a fresh look at the techniques used for automobile production. His first goal was to try to make it economical to manufacture autobody parts in small batches. To do this, he needed to reduce the time it took to set up the machines for stamping out body parts. Ohno and his engineers began to experiment with a number of techniques to speed up the time it took to change the dies in stamping equipment. This included using rollers to move dies in and out of position along with a number of simple mechanized adjustment mechanisms to fine-tune the settings. These techniques were relatively simple to master, so Ohno directed production workers to perform the die changes themselves. This in itself reduced the need for specialists and eliminated the idle time that workers previously had enjoyed while waiting for the dies to be changed.

Through a process of trial and error, Ohno succeeded in reducing the time required to change dies on stamping equipment from a full day to fifteen minutes by 1962, and to as little as three minutes by 1971. By comparison, even in the early 1980s many American and European plants required anywhere between two and six hours to change dies on stamping equipment. As a consequence, American and European plants found it economical to manufacture in lots equivalent to ten to thirty days' supply and to reset equipment only every other day. In contrast, since Toyota could change the dies on stamping equipment in a matter of minutes, it manufactured in lots equivalent to just one day's supply, while resetting equipment three times per day.

Not only did these innovations make small production runs economical, but they also had the added benefit of reducing inventories and improving product quality. Making small batches eliminated the need to hold large inventories, thereby reducing warehousing costs and freeing up scarce capital for investment elsewhere. Small production runs and the lack of inventory also meant that defective parts were produced only in small numbers and entered the assembly process almost immediately. This had the added effect of making those in the stamping shops far more concerned about quality. In addition, once it became economical to manufacture small batches of components, much greater variety could be included into the final product at little or no cost penalty.

Organization of the Workplace.   One of Ohno's first innovations was to group the work force into teams. Each team was given a set of assembly tasks to perform, and team members were trained to perform each task that the team was responsible for. Each team had a leader who was himself an assembly line worker. In addition to coordinating the team, the team leader was expected to perform basic assembly line tasks and to fill in for any absent worker. The teams were given the job of housecleaning, minor tool repair, and quality inspection (along with the training required to perform these tasks). Time was also set aside for team members to discuss ways to improve the production process (the practice now referred to as "quality circles"). The immediate effect of this approach was to reduce the need for specialists in the workplace and to create a more flexible work force in which individual assembly line workers were not treated simply as human machines. All of this resulted in increased worker productivity.

None of this would have been possible, however, had it not been for an agreement reached between management and labor after a 1950 strike. The strike was brought on by management's attempt to cut the work force by 25 percent (in response to a recession in Japan). After lengthy negotiations, Toyota and the union worked out a compromise. The work force was cut by 25 percent as originally proposed, but the remaining employees were given two guarantees, one for lifetime employment and the other for pay graded by seniority and tied to company profitability through bonus payments. In exchange for these guarantees, the employees agreed to be flexible in work assignments. In turn, this allowed for the introduction of the team concept.

Improving Quality.   One of the standard practices in the mass-production automobile assembly plants was to fix any errors that occurred during assembly in a rework area at the end of the assembly line. Errors routinely occurred in most assembly plants either because bad parts were installed or because good parts were installed incorrectly. The belief was that stopping an assembly line to fix such errors would cause enormous bottlenecks in the production system. Thus it was thought to be more efficient to correct errors at the end of the line.

Ohno viewed this system as wasteful for three reasons: (1) since workers understood that any errors would be fixed at the end of the line, they had little incentive to correct errors themselves; (2) once a defective part had been embedded in a complex vehicle, an enormous amount of rework might be required to fix it; and (3) since defective parts were often not discovered until the end of the line when the finished cars were tested, a large number of cars containing the same defect may have been built before the problem was found.

In an attempt to get away from this practice, Ohno decided to look for ways to reduce the amount of rework at the end of the line. His approach involved two elements. First, he placed a cord above every workstation and instructed workers to stop the assembly line if a problem emerged that could not be fixed. It then became the responsibility of the whole team to come over and work on the problem. Second, team members were taught to trace every defect back to its ultimate cause and then to ensure that the problem was fixed so that it would not reoccur.

Initially, this system produced enormous disruption. The production line was stopping all the time and workers became discouraged. However, as team members began to gain experience in identifying problems and tracing them back to their root cause, the number of errors began to drop dramatically and stops in the line became much rarer, so that today in most Toyota plants the line virtually never stops.

Developing the *Kanban* System   Once reduced setup times had made small production runs economical, Ohno began to look for ways to coordinate the flow of production within the Toyota manufacturing system so that the amount of inventory in the system could be reduced to a minimum. Toyota produced about 25 percent of its major components in-house (the rest were contracted out to independent suppliers). Ohno's initial goal was to arrange for components and/or subassemblies manufactured in-house to be delivered to the assembly floor only when they were needed, and not before (this goal was later extended to include independent suppliers).

To achieve this, in 1953 Ohno began experimenting with what came to be known as the *kanban* system. Under the *kanban* system, component parts are delivered to the assembly line in containers. As each

container is emptied, it is sent back to the previous step in the manufacturing process. This then becomes the signal to make more parts. The system minimizes work in progress by increasing inventory turnover. The elimination of buffer inventories also means that defective components show up immediately in the next process. This speeds up the processes of tracing defects back to their source and facilitates correction of the problem before too many defects are made. Moreover, the elimination of buffer stocks, by removing all safety nets, makes it imperative that problems be solved before they become serious enough to jam up the production process, thereby creating a strong incentive for workers to ensure that errors are corrected as quickly as possible. In addition, by decentralizing responsibility for coordinating the manufacturing process to lower-level employees, the *kanban* system does away with the need for extensive centralized management to coordinate the flow of parts between the various stages of production.

After perfecting the *kanban* system in one of Toyota's machine shops, Ohno had a chance to apply the system broadly in 1960 when he was made general manager of the Motomachi assembly plant. Ohno already had converted the machining, body stamping, and body shops to the *kanban* system, but since many parts came from shops that had yet to adopt the system, or from outside suppliers, the impact on inventories was initially minimal. However, by 1962 he had extended the *kanban* to forging and casting, and between 1962 and 1965 he began to bring independent suppliers into the system.

Organizing Suppliers   Assembly of components into a final vehicle accounts for only about 15 percent of the total manufacturing process in automobile manufacture. The remaining 85 percent of the process involves manufacturing more than ten thousand individual parts and assembling them into about one hundred major components, such as engines, suspension systems, transaxles, and so on. Coordinating this process so that everything comes together at the right time has always been a problem for auto manufacturers. The response at Ford and GM to this problem was massive vertical integration. The belief was that control over the supply chain would allow management to coordinate the flow of component parts into the final assembly plant. In addition, American firms held the view that vertical integration made them more efficient by reducing their dependence on other firms for materials and components and by limiting their vulnerability to opportunistic overcharging.

As a consequence of this philosophy, even as late as the mid 1990s General Motors makes 68 percent of its own components in-house, while Ford makes 50 percent. When they haven't vertically integrated, U.S. auto companies historically have tried to reduce the procurement costs that remain through competitive bidding—asking a number of companies to submit contracts and giving orders to suppliers offering the lowest price.

Under the leadership of Kiichiro Toyoda during the 1930s and 1940s, Toyota essentially followed the American model and pursued extensive vertical integration into the manufacture of component parts. In fact, Toyota had little choice in this matter, since only a handful of Japanese companies were able to make the necessary components. However, the low volume of production during this period meant that the scale of integration was relatively small. In the 1950s, however, the volume of auto production began to increase dramatically. This presented Toyota with a dilemma: should the company increase its capacity to manufacture components in-house in line with the growth in production of autos, or should the company contract out?

In contrast to American practice, the company decided that while it should increase in-house capacity for essential subassemblies and bodies, it would do better to contract out for most components. Four reasons seem to bolster this decision:

1. Toyota wanted to avoid the capital expenditures required to expand capacity to manufacture a wide variety of components.

2. Toyota wanted to reduce risk by maintaining a low factory capacity in case factory sales slumped.

3. Toyota wanted to take advantage of the lower wage scales in smaller firms.

4. Toyota managers realized that in-house manufacturing offered few benefits if it was possible to find stable, high-quality, and low-cost external sources of component supply.

At the same time, Toyota managers felt that the American practice of inviting competitive bids from suppliers was self-defeating. While competitive bidding might achieve the lowest short-run costs, the practice of playing suppliers off against each other did not guarantee stable supplies, high quality, or cooperation beyond existing contracts to solve design or engineering problems. Ohno and other Toyota managers believed that real efficiencies could be achieved if the company entered into long-term relationships with major suppliers. This would allow them to introduce the *kanban* system, thereby further reducing inventory holding costs and realizing the same kind of quality benefits that Toyota was already beginning to encounter with its in-house supply operations. In addition, Ohno wanted to bring suppliers into the design process since he believed that suppliers might be able to suggest ways of improving the design of component parts based upon their own manufacturing experience.

As it evolved during the 1950s and 1960s, Toyota's strategy toward its suppliers had several elements. First, the company spun off some of its own in-house supply operations into quasi-independent entities in which it took a minority stake, typically holding between 20 percent and 40 percent of the stock. It then recruited a number of independent companies with a view to establishing a long-term relationship with them for the supply of critical components. Sometimes, but not always, Toyota took a minority stake in these companies as well. All of these companies were designated as "first-tier suppliers." First-tier suppliers were responsible for working with Toyota as an integral part of the new product development team. Each first tier was responsible for the formation of a "second tier" of suppliers under its direction. Companies in the second tier were given the job of fabricating individual parts.

Both first- and second-tier suppliers were formed into supplier associations. Thus by 1986 Toyota had three regional supply organizations in Japan with 62, 135, and 25 first-tier suppliers. A major function of the supplier associations was to share information regarding new manufacturing, design, or materials management techniques among themselves. Concepts such as statistical process control, total quality control, and computer-aided design were rapidly diffused among suppliers by this means.

Toyota also worked closely with its suppliers, providing them with management expertise, engineering expertise, and sometimes capital to finance new investments. A critical feature of this relationship was the incentives that Toyota established to encourage its suppliers to focus on realizing continuous process improvements. The basic contract for a component would be for four to five years, with the price being agreed in advance. If by joint efforts the supplier and Toyota succeeded in reducing the costs of manufacturing the components, then the additional profit would be shared between the two. If the supplier by its own efforts came up with an innovation that reduced costs, the supplier would keep the additional profit that the innovation generated for the lifetime of the contract.

As a consequence of this strategy, today Toyota outsources more than almost any other major auto manufacturer. By the late 1980s Toyota was responsible for only about 27 percent of the value going into a finished automobile, with the remainder coming from outside suppliers. In contrast, General Motors was responsible for about 70 percent of the value going into a finished automobile. Other consequences included long-term improvements in productivity and quality among Toyota's suppliers that were comparable to the improvements achieved by Toyota itself. In particular, the extension of the *kanban* system to include suppliers, by eliminating buffer inventory stocks, in essence forced suppliers to focus more explicitly on the quality of their product.

Consequences   The consequences of Toyota's production system included a surge in labor productivity and a decline in the number of defects per car. Table 1 compares the number of vehicles produced per worker at General Motors, Ford, Nissan, and Toyota between 1965 and 1983.

These figures are adjusted for the degree of vertical integration pursued by each company. As can be seen, in 1960 productivity at Toyota already outstripped that of Ford, General Motors, and its main Japanese competitor, Nissan. As Toyota refined its production system over the next eighteen years, productivity doubled. In comparison, productivity essentially stood still at General Motors and Ford during the same period.

Table 2 provides another way to assess the superiority of Toyota's production system. Here the performance of Toyota's Takaoka plant is compared with that of General Motors's Framingham plant in 1987. As can be seen, the Toyota plant was more productive, produced far fewer defects per one hundred cars, and kept far less inventory on hand.

A further aspect of Toyota's production system is that the short setup times made it economical to manufacture a much wider range of models than is feasible at a traditional mass-production assembly plant. In essence, Toyota soon found that it could supply much greater product variety than its competitors with little in the way of a cost penalty. In 1990 Toyota was offering consumers around the world roughly as many products as General Motors (about 150), even though Toyota was still only half GM's size. Moreover, it could do this at a lower cost than GM.

Distribution and Customer Relations

Toyota's approach to its distributors and customers as it evolved during the 1950s and 1960s was in many ways just as radical as its approach toward suppliers. In 1950 Toyota formed a subsidiary, Toyota Motor Sales, to handle distribution and sales. The new subsidiary was headed by Kaymiya Shotaro from its inception until 1975. Kaymiya's philosophy was that dealers should be treated as "equal partners" in the Toyota family. To back this up, he had Toyota Motor Sales provide a wide range of sales training and service training for dealership personnel.

TABLE 1

Vehicles Produced per Worker (adjusted for vertical integration), 1965–1983

Year	General Motors	Ford	Nissan	Toyota
1965	5.0	4.4	4.3	8.0
1970	3.7	4.3	8.8	13.4
1975	4.4	4.0	9.0	15.1
1979	4.5	4.2	11.1	18.4
1980	4.1	3.7	12.2	17.8
1983	4.8	4.7	11.0	15.0

Source: M. A. Cusumano, *The Japanese Automotive Industry* (Cambridge, Mass.: Harvard University Press, 1989), Table 48, p. 197.

TABLE 2

General Motors's Framingham Plant Versus
Toyota's Takaoka Plant, 1987

	GM Framingham	Toyota Takaoka
Assembly hours per car	31	16
Assembly defects per 100 cars	135	45
Inventories of parts (average)	2 weeks	2 hours

Source: J. P. Womack, D. T. Jones, and D. Roos, *The Machines That Changed the World* (New York: Macmillan, 1990), Figure 4.2, p. 83.

Kaymiya then used the dealers to build long-term ties with Toyota's customers. The ultimate aim was to bring customers into the Toyota design and production process. To this end, through its dealers, Toyota Motor Sales assembled a huge database on customer preferences. Much of these data came from monthly or semiannual surveys conducted by dealers. These asked Toyota customers their preferences for styling, model types, colors, prices, and other features. Toyota also used these surveys to estimate the potential demand for new models. This information was then fed directly into the design process.

Kaymiya began this process in 1952 when the company was redesigning its Toyopet model. The Toyopet was primarily used by urban taxi drivers. Toyota Motor Sales surveyed taxi drivers to try to find out what type of vehicle they preferred. They wanted something reliable, inexpensive, and with good city fuel mileage—which Toyota engineers then set about designing. In 1956 Kaymiya formalized this process when he created a unified department for planning and market research whose function was to coordinate the marketing strategies developed by researchers at Toyota Motor Sales with product planning by Toyota's design engineers. From this time on marketing information played a critical role in the design of Toyota's cars and, indeed, in the company's strategy. In particular, it was the research department at Toyota Motor Sales that provided the initial stimulus for Toyota to start exporting during the late 1960s after predicting, correctly, that growth in domestic sales would slow down considerably during the 1970s.

Overseas Expansion

Large-scale overseas expansion did not become feasible at Toyota until the late 1960s for one principal reason: despite the rapid improvement in productivity, Japanese cars were still not competitive.[7] In 1957, for example, the Toyota Corona sold in Japan for the equivalent of $1,694. At the same time the Volkswagen Beetle sold for $1,111 in West Germany, while Britain's Austin company was selling its basic model for the equivalent of $1,389 in Britain. Foreign companies were effectively kept out of the Japanese market, however, by a 40 percent value-added tax and shipping costs.

Despite these disadvantages, Toyota tried to enter the United States market in the late 1950s. The company set up a U.S. subsidiary in California in October 1957 and began to sell cars in early 1958, hoping to capture the American small car market (which at that time was poorly served by the U.S. automobile companies). The result was a disaster. Toyota's cars performed poorly in road tests on U.S. highways. The basic problem was that the engines of Toyota's cars were too small for prolonged high-speed driving and tended to overheat and burn oil, while poorly designed chassis resulted in excessive vibration. As a result, sales were slow and in 1964 Toyota closed down its U.S. subsidiary and withdrew from the market.

The company was determined to learn from its U.S. experience and quickly redesigned several of its models based on feedback from American consumer surveys and U.S. road tests. As a result, by 1967 the picture had changed considerably. The quality of Toyota's cars was now sufficient to make an impact in the U.S. market, while production costs and retail prices had continued to fall and were now comparable with international competitors in the small car market.

In the late 1960s Toyota reentered the U.S. market. Although sales were initially slow, they increased steadily. Then the OPEC-engineered fourfold increase in oil prices that followed the 1973 Israeli/Arab conflict gave Toyota an unexpected boost. U.S. consumers began to turn to small fuel-efficient cars in droves, and Toyota was one of the main beneficiaries. Driven primarily by a surge in U.S. demand, worldwide exports of Toyota cars increased from 157,882 units in 1967 to 856,352 units by 1974 and 1,800,923 units by 1984. Put another way, in 1967 exports accounted for 19 percent of Toyota's total output. By 1984 they accounted for 52.5 percent.

Success brought its own problems. By the early 1980s political pressures and talk of local content regulations in the United States and Europe were forcing an initially reluctant Toyota to rethink its exporting strategy. Toyota already had agreed to "voluntary" import quotas with the United States in 1981. The consequence for Toyota was stagnant export growth between 1981 and 1984. Against this background, in the early 1980s Toyota began to think seriously about setting up manufacturing operations overseas.

Transplant Operations

Toyota's first overseas operation was a 50/50 joint venture with General Motors established in February 1983 under the name New United Motor Manufacturing, Inc. (NUMMI). NUMMI, which is based in Fremont, California, began producing Chevrolet Nova cars for GM in December 1984.[8] The maximum capacity of the Fremont plant is about 250,000 cars per year.

For Toyota, the joint venture provided a chance to find out whether it could build quality cars in the United States using American workers and American suppliers. It also provided Toyota with experience dealing with an American union (the United Auto Workers Union) and with a means of circumventing "voluntary" import restrictions. For General Motors, the venture provided an opportunity to observe in full detail the Japanese approach to manufacturing. While General Motors's role was marketing and distributing the plant's output, Toyota designed the product and designed, equipped, and operated the plant. At the venture's start, thirty-four executives were loaned to NUMMI by Toyota and sixteen by General Motors. The chief executive and chief operating officer were both Toyota personnel.

By the fall of 1986 the NUMMI plant was running at full capacity and the early indications were that the NUMMI plant was achieving productivity and quality levels close to those achieved at Toyota's major Takaoka plant in Japan. For example, in 1987 it took the NUMMI plant nineteen assembly hours to build a car, compared to sixteen hours at Takaoka, while the number of defects per one hundred cars was the same at NUMMI as at Takaoka—forty-five.[9]

Encouraged by its success at NUMMI, in December 1985 Toyota announced that it would build an automobile manufacturing plant in Georgetown, Kentucky. The plant, which came on stream in May 1988, officially had the capacity to produce 200,000 Toyota Camrys a year. Such was the success of this plant, however, that by early 1990 it was producing the equivalent of 220,000 cars per year. This success was followed by an announcement in December 1990 that Toyota would build a second plant in Georgetown with a capacity to produce a further 200,000 vehicles per year.[10]

In 2001, Toyota had four vehicle assembly plants in North America with a total capacity to produce over 1 million vehicles per year. In addition, the company had two engine plants, an aluminum wheel plant, an aluminum casting plant, special parts and body parts plants, and an automatic transmission plant. In totally, these factories employed more than 123,000 Americans, more than Coca-Cola, Microsoft, and Oracle combined. Some 60 percent of all Toyota vehicles sold in the United States are now locally produced, and the company is aiming to add another U.S. plant capable of turning out an additional 250,000 vehicles a year by 2005.[11]

Although many of the senior managers at Toyota's U.S. plants were initially Japanese, increasingly they are American. The Americans are also starting to drive product development decisions. A pivotal event in the changing relationship occurred in the late 1990s, when Japanese managers resisted their U.S. colleagues' idea that the company should produce a V8 pickup truck for the American market. To change their minds, the U.S. executives took their Japanese counterparts to a Dallas Cowboys football game—with a pit stop in the Texas Stadium parking lot. There the Japanese saw row upon row of full-size pickups. Finally, it dawned on them that Americans see the pickup as more than a commercial vehicle, considering it primary transportation. The result of this was Toyota's best-selling V8 pickup truck, the Toyota Tundra.[12]

In addition to its North American transplant operations, Toyota moved to set up production in Europe in anticipation of the 1992 lowering of trade barriers among the twelve members of the European Economic Community. In 1989 the company announced that it would build a plant in England with the capacity to manufacture 200,000 cars per year by 1997.

In 2001, Toyota opened a second European plant in France, raising its total production capacity within the European Union to 370,000. Toyota's goal is to sell 800,000 cars a year in the EU by 2005, which would give the company a 5 percent share of the EU market.[13]

Despite Toyota's apparent commitment to expand U.S.- and European-based assembly operations, it has not all been smooth sailing. A major problem has been building an overseas supplier network that is comparable to Toyota's Japanese network. For example, in a 1990 meeting of Toyota's North American supplier's association, Toyota executives informed their North American suppliers that the defect ratio for parts produced by 75 North American and European suppliers was 100 times greater than the defect ratio for parts supplied by 147 Japanese suppliers—1,000 defects per million parts versus 10 defects per million among Toyota's Japanese suppliers. Moreover, Toyota executives pointed out that parts manufactured by North American and European suppliers tend to be significantly more expensive than comparable parts manufactured in Japan.

Because of these problems, Toyota had to import many parts from Japan for its U.S. assembly operations. However, for political reasons Toyota was being pushed to increase the local content of cars assembled in North America. The company's plan was for 50 percent of the value of Toyota cars assembled in the United States to be locally produced by January 1991. Today the local content of cars produced in North America is over 70 percent. To improve the efficiency of its U.S.-based suppliers, Toyota embarked upon an aggressive supplier education process. In 1992, it established the Toyota Supplier Support Center to teach its suppliers the basics of the Toyota production system. By 2001, eighty-nine supplier companies had been through the center. Many have reportedly seen double- and triple-digit productivity growth as a result, as well as dramatic reductions in inventory levels.[14]

Product Strategy

Toyota's initial production was aimed at the small car/basic transportation end of the automobile market. This was true both in Japan and of its export sales to North America and Europe. During the 1980s, however, Toyota progressively moved up market and abandoned much of the lower end of the market to new entrants such as the South Koreans. Thus, the company's Camry and Corolla models, which initially were positioned toward the bottom of the mar-

ket, have been constantly upgraded and now are aimed at the middle-income segments of the market. This upgrading reflects two factors: (1) the rising level of incomes in Japan and the commensurate increase in the ability of Japanese consumers to purchase mid-range and luxury cars and (2) a desire to hold onto its U.S. consumers, many of whom initially purchased inexpensive Toyotas in their early twenties and who have since traded up to more expensive models.

The constant upgrading of Toyota's models reached its logical conclusion in September 1989 when the company's Lexus division began marketing luxury cars to compete with Jaguars, BMWs, and the like. The Lexus range of cars includes the ES 250, which was initially priced at $22,000, and the LS 400, which comes fully loaded with a $43,000 price tag (for comparison, a Jaguar XJ6 costs $40,000). The initial purpose of Lexus was to go after America's luxury car market, which amounted to about 850,000 unit sales in 1989. The car is also being sold in Japan and Europe.

Encouraged by car testers who rated the Lexus LS 400 the best in its class, Toyota initially projected worldwide sales around 75,000 units for the Lexus models in 1990. The early results for Lexus fell short of expectations. Although the fully loaded LS 400 model appeared to be selling well, the ES 250 model was not, primarily because it was not enough of a luxury car to appeal to luxury buyers. Moreover, a slowdown in the U.S. auto market and the increasing specter of recession during 1990s cut into Lexus's potential sales. As a result, Toyota scaled back its projections for first-year sales from 75,000 to 60,000.[15] Toyota sold 57,162 Lexus models in North America during the 1990 model year.[16] By 2001, Toyota was selling over 200,000 Lexus models a year in the United States, making it the best-selling luxury brand in the country.

Another addition to Toyota's product range in recent years has been a minivan. As with the Lexus range, this vehicle was aimed at the North American market, where the minivan segment has grown most rapidly. Toyota first introduced a minivan in 1986, but it flopped. In typical Toyota fashion, the company dispatched product planners and design engineers to showrooms to find out why. Among the problems they identified were that the minivans lacked an aisle down the center, the short wheelbase gave them a pitchy ride, and the engine was not easy to service. Based on this feedback, Toyota designers completely redesigned the vehicle and reintroduced it in April 1990 as the Previa minivan. The early result exceeded expectations. Toyota sold 50,000 Previas in the first year and projected that it could easily sell 100,000 per year in the future.[17]

Toyota in 2001

As Toyota entered the new millennium, the company's managers could look back upon half a century of remarkable growth. The production system that it had pioneered was recognized as the standard to beat in the industry. From small beginnings in the mid 1980s, it had rapidly established a global production system. Toyota had become the third largest automobile company in the world, and it was still gaining market share in the United States and Europe.

Despite its successes, Toyota is not without problems. Most notably, while its business has blossomed in the United States, things have been tough in Japan for most of the last decade. Although Toyota has held onto its leadership position in Japan, sales have fallen as Japan has struggled with three recessions in ten years. For the first time ever, in 2001 Toyota sold more cars in the United States (1.74 million) than in Japan (1.71 million). More telling still, operating margins on U.S.-produced cars are estimated to run at around 13 percent, compared to 5 percent in Japan. The essence of the problem is that in Japan's shrinking market Toyota faces stiff competition from Nissan and Honda, while in the U.S. market, which is growing faster, Toyota is up against less efficient producers.

ENDNOTES

1. P. Strozniak, "Toyota Alters the Face of Production," *Industry Week*, August 13, 2001, pp. 46–48.
2. Standard & Poors, *Autos and Auto Parts*, December 27, 2001.
3. J. D. Power and Associates, "Toyota Motor Corporation Dominates Vehicle Quality," May 17, 2001, press release.
4. A. Priddle, "Efficiency by the Numbers," *Ward's AutoWorld*, July 2001, pp. 57–59.
5. This section is based primarily on the account given in M. A. Cusumano, *The Japanese Automobile Industry*.
6. The material in this section is drawn from three main sources: M. A. Cusumano, *The Japanese Automobile Industry*; Ohno Taiichi, *Toyota Production System* (Cambridge, Mass.: Productivity Press, 1990; Japanese Edition, 1978); J. P. Womack, D. T. Jones, and D. Roos, *The Machine That Changed the World* (New York: Macmillan, 1990).
7. The material in this section is based on M. A. Cusumano, *The Japanese Automobile Industry*.
8. Niland Powell, "U.S.-Japanese Joint Venture: New United Motor Manufacturing, Inc.," *Planning Review*, January–February 1989, pp. 40–45.
9. From J. P. Womack, D. T. Jones, and D. Roos, *The Machine That Changed the World*.
10. J. B. Treece, "Just What Detroit Needs: 200,000 More Toyotas a Year," *Business Week*, December 10, 1990, p. 29.
11. C. Dawson and L. Armstrong, "The Americanization of Toyota," *Business Week*, April 15, 2002, pp. 52–54.
12. Ibid., pp.
13. W. Kimberley, "Toyota Is Building in France," *Automotive Manufacturing and Production*, December 1999, p. 38.
14. P. Strozniak, "Toyota Alters the Face of Production," *Industry Week*, August 13, 2001, pp. 46–48.
15. "The Next Samurai," *The Economist*, December 23, 1989, pp. 69–72; M. Landler and W. Zellner, "No Joyride for Japan," *Business Week*, January 15, 1990, pp. 20–21.
16. "Elegant Nippon," *The Economist*, December 8, 1990, p. 73.
17. J. Flint, "The New Number Three?" *Forbes*, June 11, 1990, pp. 136–140.

Nucor in 2001

This case was prepared by Frank C. Barnes, University of North Carolina–Charlotte, and Beverly B. Tyler, North Carolina State University.

Nucor grew quickly in size, market share, and profits from 1975 to 1990. In spite of the economic recession in 1991, it appeared that the fastest-growing steel company in America was unstoppable. Customers liked Nucor's innovations and lower costs, investors were pleased with the high P/E ratio, and Nucor, with Ken Iverson as the model company president, was a media darling. But by the fall of 2001, just ten years later, much had changed. The steel industry worldwide was mired in one of its most unprofitable periods ever. The economic recession that hit Asia and Europe in the late 1990s reached the United States, speeded by the September 11 terrorist attack. The slowing economy affected major steel-consuming industries such as construction, automobiles, and farm equipment. Hamstrung by overcapacity, foreign companies with few markets abroad were dumping their steel in the United States. Although many competitors had copied Nucor's mini-mill production processes and reduced costs, over twenty U.S. steel companies had filed for bankruptcy protection since late 1997. As the company faced a new century, strategic thinking was never more important, expansion was not as simple, and opportunities in steel would be harder to come by. Nucor expected to become the largest steel maker in the United States, but the challenges ahead were as great as at any period in the company's history.

Background

Nucor could be traced back to the company that manufactured the first Oldsmobile in 1897 and became the Reo Truck Company. As the company declined into bankruptcy in the postwar years, a 1955 merger created Nuclear Corp. of America. Following the "conglomerate" trend of the period, Nuclear acquired various "high-tech" businesses, such as radiation sensors, semiconductors, rare earths, and air conditioning equipment. However, the company lost money continually, and a fourth reorganization in 1965 put forty-year-old Ken Iverson in charge. The building of Nucor had begun.

Ken Iverson had joined the navy after high school in 1943 and had been transferred from officer training school to Cornell's Aeronautical Engineering Program. On graduation he selected mechanical engineering/metallurgy for a master's degree to avoid the long drafting apprenticeship in aeronautical engineering. His college work with an electron microscope earned him a job with International Harvester. After five years in their lab, his boss and mentor prodded him to expand his vision by going with a smaller company.

Over the next ten years, Iverson worked for four small metals companies, gaining technical knowledge and increasing his exposure to other

This case is intended to be used as a basis for class discussion rather than as an illustration of either effective and ineffective handling of the situation. Reprinted by permission of the authors.

business functions. He enjoyed working with the presidents of these small companies and admired their ability to achieve outstanding results. Nuclear Corp., after failing to buy the company Iverson worked for, hired him as a consultant to find them another metals business to buy. In 1962, the firm bought a small joist plant in South Carolina that Iverson found, on the condition that he would run it.

Over the next four years Iverson built up the Vulcraft division as Nuclear Corp. struggled. The president, David Thomas, was described as a great promoter and salesman but a weak manager. A partner with Bear Stearns actually made a personal loan to the company to keep it going. In 1966, when the company was on the edge of bankruptcy, Iverson, who headed the only successful division, was named president and moved the headquarters to Charlotte, North Carolina, where he focused the company business first on the joist industry and soon moved into steel production.

He immediately began getting rid of the esoteric, but unprofitable, high-tech divisions and concentrated on the steel joist business he found successful. They built more joist plants and in 1968 built their first steel mill in South Carolina to "make steel cheaper than they were buying from importers." By 1984 Nucor had six joist plants and four steel mills, using the new "mini-mill" technology.

From the beginning, Iverson had the people running the various plants, called divisions, make all the major decisions about how to build and run Nucor. The original board was composed of Iverson; Sam Siegel, his financial chief; and Dave Aycock, who had been with the South Carolina joist company before Nuclear acquired it. Siegel had joined Nuclear as an accountant in 1961. He quit Nuclear but in their crisis agreed to return as treasurer if Iverson were named president. Aycock and Siegel were named vice presidents at the time Iverson was named president.

Dave Aycock was the last of eight children raised on a small farm in the poor Wadesboro, North Carolina, community. He attended the University of North Carolina at Chapel Hill for one month, before financial considerations convinced him to join the navy as an enlisted man. For the next three years and eight months his specialty was as a metalsmith. On leaving the service in 1954, he got a job at Vulcraft as a welder. Over the next six years he worked his way up to production supervisor and assistant plant manager, and then to sales manager.

Aycock had been very impressed with the owner of Vulcraft, Sanborn Chase. He described him as "the best person I've ever known" and as "a scientific genius." He said he was a man of great compassion who understood the atmosphere necessary to enable people to self-motivate. Chase, an engineer by training, invented a number of things in diverse fields. He also established the incentive programs for which Nucor later became known. With only one plant, he was still able to operate with a "decentralized" manner. Before his death in 1960, while still in his forties, the company was studying the building of a steel mill using newly developed mini-mill technology. His widow ran the company until it was sold to Nucor in 1962.

Aycock met Ken Iverson when Nuclear purchased Vulcraft, and they worked together closely for the next year and a half. Located in Phoenix at the corporate headquarters, he was responsible to Iverson for all the joist operations and was given the task of planning and building a new joist plant in Texas. In late 1963 he was transferred to Norfolk, where he lived for the next thirteen years and managed a number of Nucor's joist plants. Then in 1977 he was named the manager of the Darlington, South Carolina, steel plant.

Aycock had this to say about Iverson: "Ken was a very good leader, with an entrepreneurial spirit. He is easy to work with and has the courage to do things, to take lots of risks. Many things didn't work, but some worked very well." There is the old saying "failure to take risk is failure." This saying epitomizes a cultural value personified by the company's founder and reinforced by Iverson during his time at the helm. Nucor was very innovative in steel and joists. Their plant was years ahead in wire rod welding at Norfolk. In the late 1960s they had one of the first computer inventory management systems and design/engineering programs. They were very sophisticated in purchasing, sales, and managing, and they often beat their competition by the speed of their design efforts.

In 1984, Aycock became Nucor's president and chief operating officer, while Iverson became chairman and chief executive officer. Whereas Iverson was an enthusiastic spokesman for Nucor's story, Aycock took a more low keyed position. On one occasion he commented, "I was never as consumed by the excitement of making hot metal. To me Nucor is a company with lots of employees and investors." For him

Nucor's purpose was to create value for stockholders and employees. The fact that it did so by making steel was secondary.

By 1984, in just twenty years, a bankrupt conglomerate had become a leading steel company in America. It was a fairytale story. Tom Peters used Nucor's management style as an example of "excellence," while the barons of old steel ruled over creeping ghettos. NBC featured Nucor on television and *New Yorker* magazine serialized a book about how a relatively small American steel company built a team that led the whole world into a new era of steel making. As the NBC program asked: "If Japan Can, Why Can't We?" Nucor had! Iverson was rich, owning $10 million in stock, but with a salary which rarely reached $1 million, compared with some U.S. executives' $50 or $100 million. The forty-year-old manager of the South Carolina Vulcraft plant had become a millionaire. Stockholders chuckled, and nonunionized hourly workers, who had never seen a layoff in twenty years, earned more than the unionized workers of old steel and more than 85 percent of the people in the states where they worked. Many employees were financially quite secure.

Nucor owed much of its success to its benchmark organizational style and the empowered division managers. There were two basic lines of business. The first was the six steel joist plants that made the steel frames seen in many buildings. The second included four steel mills that utilized the innovative mini-mill technology to supply first the joist plants and later the outside customers. Nucor was still only the seventh largest steel company in America. Over its second twenty years, Nucor was to rise to become the second largest U.S. steel company. A number of significant challenges were to be met and overcome to get there, and once that horizon was reached even greater challenges would arise. The following describes the systems Nucor built and its organization, divisions, management, and incentive system.

Nucor's Organization

In the early 1990s, each of Nucor's twenty-two divisions, one for every plant, had a general manager who was also a vice president of the corporation. The divisions were of three basic types: joist plants, steel mills, and miscellaneous plants. The corporate staff consisted of less than twenty-five people. In the beginning Iverson had chosen Charlotte "as the new home base for what he had envisioned as a small cadre of executives who would guide a decentralized operation with liberal authority delegated to managers in the field," according to *South Magazine*. Iverson gave his views on keeping a lean organization:

> Each division is a profit center and the division manager has control over the day-to-day decisions that make that particular division profitable or not profitable. We expect the division to provide contribution, which is earnings before corporate expenses. We do not allocate our corporate expenses, because we do not think there is any way to do this reasonably and fairly. We do focus on earnings. And we expect a division to earn 25 percent return on total assets employed, before corporate expenses, taxes, interest or profit sharing. And we have a saying in the company—if a manager doesn't provide that for a number of years, we are either going to get rid of the division or get rid of the general manager, and it's generally the division manager.

A joist division manager commented on being in an organization with only four levels:

> I've been a division manager four years now and at times I'm still awed by it: the opportunity I was given to be a Fortune 500 vice president. . . . I think we are successful because it is our style to pay more attention to our business than our competitors. . . . We are kind of a "no nonsense" company.

The divisions did their own manufacturing, selling, accounting, engineering, and personnel management. A steel division manager, when questioned about Florida Steel, which had a large plant 90 miles away, commented, "I expect they do have more of the hierarchy. I think they have central purchasing, centralized sales, centralized credit collections, centralized engineering, and most of the major functions."

Nucor strengthened its position by developing strong alliances with outside parties. It did no internal research and development. Instead, it monitored others' work worldwide and attracted investors who brought it new technical applications at the earliest possible dates. Though Nucor was known for constructing new facilities at the lowest possible costs, its engineering and construction team consisted of only three individuals. They did not attempt to specify exact equipment parameters, but instead asked the equipment supplier to provide this information and then held the manufacturer accountable. They had alliances with selected construction companies around the country who knew the kind of work Nucor wanted. Nucor bought 95 percent of its scrap steel from an independent broker who followed the market and made recommendations regarding scrap purchases. It did not have a corporate advertising department, corporate public relations department, or corporate legal or environmental department. It had long-term relationships with outsiders to provide these services.

Because the steel industry had established a pattern of absorbing the cost of shipment, all users paid the same delivered price, regardless of the distance from the mill. Nucor broke with this tradition and stopped equalizing freight. It offered all customers the same sales terms. Nucor also gave no volume discounts, feeling that with modern computer systems there was no justification. Customers located next to the plant guaranteed themselves the lowest possible costs for steel purchases. Two tube manufacturers, two steel service centers, and a cold rolling facility had located adjacent to the Arkansas plant. These facilities accounted for 60 percent of the shipments from the mill. The plants were linked electronically to each other's production schedules and thus could function in a just-in-time inventory mode. All new mills were built on large enough tracks of land to accommodate collaborating businesses.

Iverson didn't feel greater centralization would be good for Nucor. Hamilton Lott, a Vulcraft plant manager, commented in 1997, "We're truly autonomous; we can duplicate efforts made in other parts of Nucor. We might develop the same computer program six times. But the advantages of local autonomy make it worth it." Joe Rutkowski, manager at Darlington steel, agreed, "We're not constrained; headquarters doesn't restrict what I spend. I just have to make my profit contribution at the end of year."

South Magazine observed that Iverson had established a characteristic organizational style described as "stripped down" and "no nonsense." "Jack Benny would like this company," observed Roland Underhill, an analyst with Crowell, Weedon and Co. of Los Angeles, and "so would Peter Drucker." Underhill pointed out that Nucor's thriftiness doesn't end with its "spartan" office staff or modest offices. "There are no corporate perquisites," he recited. "No company planes, no country club memberships, no company

cars." *Fortune* noted, "Iverson takes the subway when he is in New York, a Wall Street analyst reports in a voice that suggests both admiration and amazement." The general managers reflected this style in the operation of their individual divisions. Their offices were more like plant offices or the offices of private companies, built around manufacturing rather than for public appeal. They were simple, routine, and businesslike.

Division Managers

The corporate personnel manager described management relations as informal, trusting, and not "bureaucratic." He felt there was a minimum of paperwork, that a phone call was more common than memos, and that no confirming memo was thought to be necessary.

A Vulcraft manager commented: "We have what I would call a very friendly spirit of competition from one plant to the next. And of course all of the vice presidents and general managers share the same bonus systems so we are in this together as a team even though we operate our divisions individually." He added: "When I came to this plant four years ago, I saw we had too many people, too much overhead. We had 410 people at the plant and I could see, from my experience at the Nebraska plant, we had many more than we needed. Now with 55 fewer men, we are still capable of producing the same number of tons as four years ago."

The divisions managed their activities with a minimum of contact with the corporate staff. Each day disbursements were reported to corporate office. Payments flowed into regional lockboxes. On a weekly basis, joist divisions reported total quotes, sales cancellations, backlog, and production. Steel mills reported tons rolled, outside shipments, orders, cancellations, and backlog.

Each month the divisions completed a two-page (11″ × 17″) "Operations Analysis" which was sent to all the managers. Its three main purposes were (1) financial consolidation, (2) sharing information among the divisions, and (3) corporate management examination. The summarized information and the performance statistics for all the divisions were then returned to the managers.

The general managers met three times a year. In late October they presented preliminary budgets and capital requests. In late February they met to finalize budgets and treat miscellaneous matters. Then, at a meeting in May, they handled personnel matters, such as wage increases and changes of policies or benefits. The general managers as a group considered the raises for the department heads, the next lower level of management for all the plants.

Vulcraft—Joist Divisions

One of Nucor's major businesses was the manufacture and sale of open web steel joists and joist girders at six Vulcraft divisions located in Florence, South Carolina; Norfolk, Nebraska; Ft. Payne, Alabama; Grapeland, Texas; St. Joe, Indiana; and Brigham City, Utah. Open web joists, in contrast to solid joists, were made of steel angle iron separated by round bars or smaller angle iron (Figure 1). These joists cost less, were stronger for many applications, and were used primarily as the roof support systems in larger buildings, such as warehouses and shopping malls.

The joist industry was characterized by high competition among many manufacturers for many small customers. With an estimated 40 percent of the market, Nucor was the largest supplier in the United States. It utilized national advertising campaigns and prepared competitive bids on 80 to 90 percent of the buildings using joists. Competition was based on price and delivery performance. Nucor had developed computer programs to prepare designs for customers and to compute bids based on current prices and labor standards. In addition, each Vulcraft plant maintained its own engineering department to help customers with design problems or specifications. The Florence manager commented, "Here on the East Coast we have six or seven major competitors; of course none of them are as large as we are. The competition for any order will be heavy, and we will see six or seven different prices." He added, "I think we have a strong selling force in the marketplace. It has been said to us by some of our competitors that in this particular industry we have the finest selling organization in the country."

Nucor aggressively sought to be the lowest-cost producer in the industry. Materials and freight were two important elements of cost. Nucor maintained its own fleet of almost 150 trucks to ensure on-time delivery to all of the states, although most business was regional because of transportation costs. Plants were located in rural areas near the markets they served. Nucor's move into steel production was a move to lower the cost of steel used by the joist business.

Joist Production   On the basic assembly line used at the joist divisions, three or four of which might make up any one plant, about six tons of joists per hour would be assembled. In the first stage eight people cut the angles to the right lengths or bent the round bars to the desired form. These were moved on a roller conveyer to six-man assembly stations, where the component parts would be tacked together for the next stage, welding. Drilling and miscellaneous work were done by three people between the lines. The nine-man welding station completed the welds before passing the joists on roller conveyers to two-man inspection teams. The last step before shipment was the painting.

The workers had control over and responsibility for quality. There was an independent quality control inspector who had the authority to reject the run of

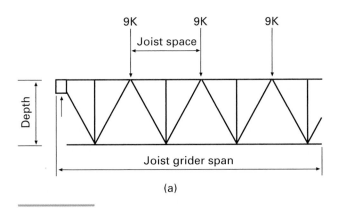

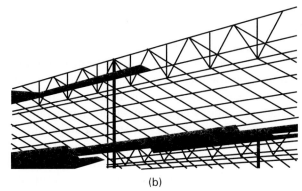

(a)   (b)

FIGURE 1

Illustration of Joists

joists and cause them to be reworked. The quality control people were not under the incentive system and reported to the engineering department.

Daily production might vary widely, since each joist was made for a specific job. The wide range of joists made control of the workload at each station difficult; bottlenecks might arise anywhere along the line. Each workstation was responsible for identifying such bottlenecks so that the foreman could reassign people promptly to maintain productivity. Since workers knew most of the jobs on the line, including the more-skilled welding job, they could be shifted as needed. Work on the line was described by one general manager as "not machine type but mostly physical labor." He said the important thing was to avoid bottlenecks.

There were four lines of about twenty-eight people each on two shifts at the Florence division. The jobs on the line were rated on responsibility and assigned a base wage, from $11 to $13 per hour. In addition, a weekly bonus was paid on the total output of each line. Each worker received the same percent bonus on his base wage. The Texas plant was typical, with the bonus running at 225 percent, giving a wage of $27 an hour in 1999.

The amount of time required to make a joist had been established as a result of experience; the general manager had seen no time studies in his fifteen years with the company. As a job was bid, the cost of each joist was determined through the computer program. The time required depended on the number of panels and the length and depth of the joist. At the time of production, the labor value of production, the standard, was determined in a similar manner. The South Carolina general manager stated, "In the last nine or ten years we have not changed a standard."

The Grapeland plant maintained a time chart, which was used to estimate the labor required on a job. The plant teams were measured against this time for bonus. The chart was based on the historical time required on the jobs. Every few years the time chart was updated. Because some of the changes in performance were due to equipment changes, generally the chart would be increased by half the change and the employee would benefit in pay from the other half. The last change, two years ago, saw some departments' pay increased by as much as 10 percent. The production manager at Grapeland considered himself an example for the Nucor policy—"the sky is the limit." He had started in an entry position and risen to the head of this plant of two hundred people.

Table 1 shows the productivity of the South Carolina plant in tons per man-hour for a number of years. The year 1999 set a record for overall tonnage. The manager explained that the small drop in 2000 was due to managerial changes; he was new to the division and had brought two new managers with him.

Steel Divisions

Nucor moved into the steel business in 1969 to provide raw material for the Vulcraft plants. Iverson said, "We got into the steel business because we wanted to build a mill that could make steel as cheaply as we were buying it from foreign importers or from offshore mills." Thus they entered the industry using the new mini-mill technology after they took a task force of four people around the world to investigate new technological advancements. A case writer from Harvard recounted the development of the steel divisions:

> By 1967 about 60% of each Vulcraft sales dollar was spent on materials, primarily steel. Thus, the goal of keeping costs low made it imperative to obtain steel economically. In addition, in 1967 Vulcraft bought about 60% of its steel from foreign sources. As the Vulcraft Division grew, Nucor became concerned about its ability to obtain an adequate economical supply of steel and in 1968 began construction of its first steel mill in Darlington, South Carolina. By 1972 the Florence, South Carolina, joist plant was purchasing over 90% of its steel from this mill. The Fort Payne, Alabama plant bought about 50% of its steel from Florence. The other joist plants in Nebraska, Indiana and Texas found transportation costs prohibitive and continued to buy their steel from other

---

TABLE 1

Tons per Man-hour

1977—0.163	1982—0.208	1987—0.218
1978—0.179	1983—0.215	1988—0.249
1979—0.192	1984—0.214	1999—0.251
1980—0.195	1985—0.228	2000—0.241
1981—0.194	1986—0.225	

steel companies, both foreign and domestic. Since the mill had excess capacity, Nucor began to market its steel products to outside customers. In 1972, 75% of the shipments of Nucor steel was to Vulcraft and 25% was to other customers.

Between 1973 and 1981 they constructed three more bar mills and their accompanying rolling mills to convert the billits into bars, flats, rounds, channels, and other products. Iverson explained in 1984:

> In constructing these mills we have experimented with new processes and new manufacturing techniques. We serve as our own general contractor and design and build much of our own equipment. In one or more of our mills we have built our own continuous casting unit, reheat furnaces, cooling beds and in Utah even our own mill stands. All of these to date have cost under $125 per ton of annual capacity—compared with projected costs for large integrated mills of $1,200–1,500 per ton of annual capacity, ten times our cost. Our mills have high productivity. We currently use less than four man hours to produce a ton of steel. This includes everyone in the operation: maintenance, clerical, accounting, and sales and management. On the basis of our production workers alone, it is less than three man hours per ton. Our total employment costs are less than $60 per ton compared with the average employment costs of the seven largest U.S. steel companies of close to $130 per ton. Our total labor costs are less than 20% of our sales price.

In 1987 Nucor was the first steel company in the world to begin to build a mini-mill to manufacture steel sheet, the raw material for the auto industry and other major manufacturers. This project opened up another 50 percent of the total steel market. The first plant in Crawfordsville, Indiana, was successful, and three additional sheet mills were constructed between 1989 and 1990. Through the years these steel plants were significantly modernized and expanded until the total capacity was 3 million tons per year at a capital cost of less than $170 dollars per ton by 1999. Nucor's total steel production capacity was 5.9 million tons per year at a cost of $300 per ton of annual capacity. The eight mills sold 80 percent of their output to outside customers and the balance to other Nucor divisions. A new million-ton steel plate mill was under construction in Hartford County, North Carolina.

All four of the bar mills were actually two mills operating side by side. One mill concentrated on the larger bar products, which had separate production and customer demands, while the other mill concentrated on smaller-diameter bar stock. Throughout Nucor each operation was housed in its own separate building with its own staff. Nucor designed its processes to limit work-in-process inventory, to limit space, to utilize a pull approach to material usage, and to increase flexibility.

The Steel-Making Process   A steel mill's work is divided into two phases: preparation of steel of the proper "chemistry" and the forming of the steel into the desired products. The typical mini-mill utilized scrap steel, such as junk auto parts, instead of the iron ore, which would be used in larger, integrated steel mills. The typical bar mini-mill had an annual capacity of 200,000 to 600,000 tons, compared with the 7 million tons of Bethlehem Steel's Sparrow's Point, Maryland, integrated plant.

In the bar mills a charging bucket fed loads of scrap steel into electric arc furnaces. The melted load, called a heat, was poured into a ladle to be carried by overhead crane to the casting machine. In the casting machine the liquid steel was extruded as a continuous red-hot solid bar of steel and cut into lengths weighing some 900 pounds called "billets." In the typical plant the billet, about 4 inches in cross section and about 20 feet long, was held temporarily in a pit where it cooled to normal temperatures. Periodically billets were carried to the rolling mill and placed in a reheat oven to bring them up to 2,000 degrees Fahrenheit, at which temperance they would be malleable. In the rolling mill, presses and dies progressively converted the billet into the desired round bars, angles, channels, flats, and other products. After cutting to standard lengths, they were moved to the warehouse.

Nucor's first steel mill, which employed more than five hundred people, was located in Darlington, South Carolina. The mill, with its three electric arc furnaces, operated twenty-four hours per day, five and a half days per week. Nucor had made a number of improvements in the melting and casting operations. The general manager of the Darlington plant developed a system that involved preheating the ladles, which allowed for the faster flow of steel into the caster and resulted in better control of the steel characteristics. Thus less time and lower capital investment were required at Darlington than at other mini-mills at the time of its construction. The casting machines were "continuous casters," as opposed to the old batch method. The objective in the "front" of the mill was to keep the casters working. At the time the Darlington plant was also perhaps the only mill in the country that regularly avoided the reheating of billets. This saved $10 to $12 per ton in fuel usage and losses due to oxidation of the steel. The cost of developing this process had been $12 million. All research projects had not been successful. The company spent approximately $2 million in an unsuccessful effort to utilize resistance heating. It lost even more on an effort at induction melting. As Iverson told *Metal Producing,* "That costs us a lot of money. Timewise it was very expensive. But you have got to make mistakes and we've had lots of failures."

The Darlington design became the basis for plants in Nebraska, Texas, and Utah. The Texas plant had cost under $80 per ton of annual capacity. Whereas the typical mini-mill at the time cost approximately $250 per ton, the average cost of Nucor's four mills was under $135. An integrated mill was expected to cost between $1,200 and $1,500 per ton.

The Darlington plant was organized into twelve natural groups for the purpose of incentive pay. Two mills each had two shifts with three groups—melting and casting, rolling mill, and finishing. In melting and casting there were three or four different standards, depending on the material, that were established by the department manager years ago based on historical performance. The general manager stated, "We don't change the standards." The caster, key to the operation, was used at a 92 percent level—one percentage point greater than the claims of the manufacturer. For every good ton of billet above the standard hourly rate for the week, workers in the group received a 4 percent bonus. For example, with a common standard of 10 tons per run hour and an actual rate for the week of 28 tons per hour, the workers would receive a bonus of 72 percent of their base rate in the week's paycheck. In the rolling mill there were more than one hundred products, each with a different historical standard. Workers received a 4 to 6 percent bonus over the computed standard for every good ton sheared per hour for the week. A manager stated: "Meltshop employees don't ask me how much it costs Chaparral or LTV to make a billet. They want

to know what it costs Darlington, Norfolk, Jewitt to put a billet on the ground—scrap costs, alloy costs, electrical costs, refractory, gas, etc. Everybody from Charlotte to Plymouth watches the nickels and dimes."

Management Philosophy

Aycock, while still the Darlington manager, stated:

> The key to making a profit when selling a product with no aesthetic value, or a product that you really can't differentiate from your competitors, is cost. I don't look at us as a fantastic marketing organization, even though I think we are pretty good; but we don't try to overcome unreasonable costs by mass marketing. We maintain low costs by keeping the employee force at the level it should be, not doing things that aren't necessary to achieve our goals, and allowing people to function on their own and judging them on their results.
>
> To keep a cooperative and productive work force you need, number one, to be completely honest about everything; number two, to allow each employee as much as possible to make decisions about that employee's work, to find easier and more productive ways to perform duties; and number three, to be as fair as possible to all employees. Most of the changes we make in work procedures and in equipment come from the employees. They really know the problems of their jobs better than anyone else. We don't have any industrial engineers, nor do we ever intend to, because that's a type of specialist who tends to take responsibility off the top division management and give them a crutch.
>
> To communicate with my employees, I try to spend time in the plant and at intervals have meetings with the employees. Usually if they have a question they just visit me. Recently a small group visited me in my office to discuss our vacation policy. They had some suggestions and, after listening to them, I had to agree that the ideas were good.

In discussing his philosophy for dealing with the work force, the Florence manager stated:

> I believe very strongly in the incentive system we have. We are a nonunion shop and we all feel that the way to stay so is to take care of our people and show them we care. I think that's easily done because of our fewer layers of manage-

ment. . . . I spend a good part of my time in the plant, maybe an hour or so a day. If a man wants to know anything, for example an insurance question, I'm there and they walk right up to me and ask me questions, which I'll answer the best I know how.

We don't lay our people off and we make a point of telling our people this. In the slowdown of 1994, we scheduled our line for four days, but the men were allowed to come in the fifth day for maintenance work at base pay. The men in the plant on an average running bonus might make $17 to $19 an hour. If their base pay is half that, on Friday they would only get $8 to $9 an hour. Surprisingly, many of the men did not want to come in on Friday. They felt comfortable with just working four days a week. They are happy to have that extra day off.

About 20 percent of the people took the fifth day at base rate, but still no one had been laid off, in an industry with a strong business cycle.

In an earlier business cycle the executive committee decided in view of economic conditions that a pay freeze was necessary. The employees normally received an increase in their base pay the first of June. The decision was made at that time to freeze wages. The officers of the company, as a show of good faith, accepted a 5 percent pay cut. In addition to announcing this to the workers with a stuffer in their pay envelopes, the executives held meetings. Each production line, or incentive group of workers, met in the plant conference room with all supervisory personnel—foreman, plant production manager, and division manager. The production manager explained the economic crisis the company was facing to the employees, and all of their questions were answered.

Personnel and Incentive Systems

The foremost characteristic of Nucor's personnel system was its incentive plan. Another major personnel policy was providing job security. Also, all employees at Nucor received the same fringe benefits. There was only one group insurance plan. Holidays and vacations did not differ by job. Every child of every Nucor employee received up to $1,200 a year for four years if he or she chose to go on to higher education, including technical schools. The company had no executive dining rooms or restrooms and no fishing lodges, company cars, or reserved parking places.

Jim Coblin, Nucor's vice president of human resources, described Nucor's systems for *HRMagazine* in a 1994 article: "No-frills HR at Nucor: a lean, bottom-line approach at this steel company empowers employees." Coblin, as benefits administrator, received part-time help from one of the corporate secretaries in the corporate office. The plants typically used someone from their finance department to handle compensation issues, although two plants had personnel generalists. Nucor plants did not have job descriptions; they found they caused more problems than they solved, given the flexible work force and nonunion status of Nucor employees. Surprisingly, Coblin also found performance appraisal a waste of time. If an employee was not performing well, the problem would be dealt with directly. He had observed that when promotional opportunities became available, the performance appraisals were not much help in filling the position. So he saw both of these as just more paperwork. The key, he believed, was not to put a maximum on what employees could earn and to pay them directly for productivity. Iverson firmly believed that the bonus should be direct and involve no discretion on the part of a manager.

Employees were kept informed about the company. Charts showing the division's results in return-on-assets and bonus payoff were posted in prominent places in the plant. The personnel manager commented that as he traveled around to all the plants, he found that everyone in the company could tell him the level of profits in his or her division. The general managers held dinners at least once but usually twice a year with their employees. The dinners were held with fifty or sixty employees at a time, resulting in as many as twenty dinners per year. After introductory remarks the floor was open for discussion of any work-related problems. There was a new employee orientation program and an employee handbook that contained personnel policies and rules. The corporate office sent all news releases to each division, where they were posted on bulletin boards. Each employee in the company also received a copy of the annual report. For the last several years the cover of the annual report had contained the names of all Nucor employees.

Absenteeism and tardiness were not a problem at Nucor. Each employee had four days of absences before pay was reduced. In addition to these, missing work was allowed for jury duty, military leave, or the death of close relatives. After this, a day's absence cost an employee bonus pay for that week, and lateness of more than a half hour meant the loss of bonus for that day.

Safety was a concern of Nucor's critics. With ten fatalities in the 1980s, Nucor was committed to doing better. Safety administrators were appointed in each plant, and safety improved in the 1990s. The company also had a formal grievance procedure, although the Darlington manager couldn't recall the last grievance he had processed.

The company had conducted attitude surveys every three years for over two decades. These provided management insight into employee attitudes on twenty issues and allowed comparisons across plants and divisions. There were some concerns and differences, but most employees appeared very satisfied with Nucor as an employer (see appendices 1 and 2). The surveys suggested that pay was not the only thing the workers liked about Nucor. The personnel manager said that an NBC interviewer, working on the documentary "If Japan Can, Why Can't We?" often heard employees say, "I enjoy working for Nucor because Nucor is the best, the most productive, and the most profitable company that I know of."

The average hourly worker's pay was over twice the average earnings paid by other manufacturing companies in the states where Nucor's plants were located. In many rural communities where Nucor had located, it provided better wages than most other manufacturers. The new plant in Hertford County illustrated this point in a June 21, 1998, article in the *Charlotte Observer,* entitled "Hope on the Horizon: In Hertford County, Poverty Reigns and Jobs are Scarce." Here the author wrote, "In North Carolina's forgotten northeastern corner, where poverty rates run more than twice the state average, Nucor's $300 million steel mill is a dream realized." The plant on the banks of the Chowan River in North Carolina's coastal district had their employees earning a rumored $60,000 a year, three times the local average manufacturing wage. Nucor had recently begun developing its plant sites with the expectation that other companies would colocate to save shipping costs. Four companies have announced plans to locate close to Nucor's property, adding another one to two hundred jobs. People couldn't believe such wages, but calls to the plant's chief financial officer got "We don't like to promise too much, but $60,000

might be a little low." The average wage for these jobs at Darlington was $70,000. The plant's CFO added that Nucor didn't try to set pay "a buck over Wal-Mart" but went for the best workers. The article noted that steel work is hot and often dangerous, and that turnover at the plant may be high as people adjust to this and to Nucor's hard-driving team system. He added, "Slackers don't last." The state of North Carolina had given $155 million in tax credits over twenty-five years. The local preacher said, "In fifteen years, Baron (a local child) will be making $75,000 a year at Nucor, not in jail. I have a place now I can hold in front of him and say 'Look, right here. This is for you.'"

The Incentive System There were four incentive programs at Nucor, one each for (1) production workers, (2) department heads, (3) staff people such as accountants, secretaries, or engineers, and (4) senior management, which included the division managers. All of these programs were based on group performance.

Within the production program, groups ranged in size from twenty-five to thirty people and had definable and measurable operations. The company believed that a program should be simple and that bonuses should be paid promptly. "We don't have any discretionary bonuses—zero. It is all based on performance. Now we don't want anyone to sit in judgment, because it never is fair," said Iverson. The personnel manager stated: "Their bonus is based on roughly 90 percent of the historical time it takes to make a particular joist. If during a week they make joists at 60 percent less than the standard time, they receive a 60 percent bonus." This was paid with the regular pay the following week. The complete paycheck amount, including overtime, was multiplied by the bonus factor. A bonus was not paid when equipment was not operating: "We have the philosophy that when equipment is not operating everybody suffers and the bonus for downtime is zero." The foremen were also part of the group and received the same bonus as the employees they supervised.

The second incentive program was for department heads in the various divisions. The incentive pay here was based on division contribution, defined as the division earnings before corporate expenses and profit sharing are determined. Bonuses were reported to run between 0 and 90 percent (average 35–50 percent) of a person's base salary. The base salaries at this level were set at 75 percent of industry norms.

There was a third plan for people who were not production workers, department managers, or senior managers. Their bonus was based on either the division return-on-assets or the corporate return-on-assets, depending on the unit they were a part of. Bonuses were typically 30 percent or more of a person's base salary for corporate positions.

The fourth program was for the senior officers. The senior officers had no employment contracts, pension or retirement plans, or other perquisites. Their base salaries were set at about 75 percent of what an individual doing similar work in other companies would receive. Once return-on-equity reached 9 percent, slightly below the average for manufacturing firms, 5 percent of net earnings before taxes went into a pool, which was divided among the officers based on their salaries. "Now if return-on-equity for the company reaches, say 20 percent, which it has, then we can wind up with as much as 190 percent of our base salaries and 115 percent on top of that in stock. We get both." Half the bonus was paid in cash and half was deferred. Individual bonuses ranged from zero to several hundred percent, averaging 75 to 150 percent.

However, the opposite was true as well. In 1982 the return was 8 percent and the executives received no bonus. Iverson's pay in 1981 was approximately $300,000 but dropped the next year to $110,000. "I think that ranked by total compensation I was the lowest paid CEO in the Fortune 500. I was kind of proud of that, too." In his 1997 book, *Plain Talk: Lessons from a Business Maverick,* Iverson said, "Can management expect employees to be loyal if we lay them all off at every dip of the economy, while we go on padding our own pockets?" Even so, by 1986 Iverson's stock was worth over $10 million dollars and the once Vulcraft manager was a millionaire.

In lieu of a retirement plan, the company had a profit sharing plan with a deferred trust. Each year 10 percent of pretax earnings was put into profit sharing for all people below officer level. Twenty percent of this was set aside to be paid to employees in the following March as a cash bonus, and the remainder was put into trust for each employee on the basis of the percentage of their earnings as a percentage of total wages paid within the corporation. The employee was vested after the first year. Employees received a quarterly statement of their balance in profit sharing.

The company had an Employer Monthly Stock Investment Plan to which Nucor added 10 percent to the amount the employee contributed on the purchase of any Nucor stock, and paid the commission. After each five years of service with the company, the employee received a service award consisting of five shares of Nucor stock. Moreover, if profits were good, extraordinary bonus payments would be made to the employees. For example, in December 1998 each employee received a $800 payment. Iverson said:

> I think the first obligation of the company is to the stockholder and to its employees. I find in this country too many cases where employees are underpaid and corporate management is making huge social donations for self-fulfillment. We regularly give donations, but we have a very interesting corporate policy. First, we give donations where our employees are. Second, we give donations that will benefit our employees, such as to the YMCA. It is a difficult area and it requires a lot of thought. There is certainly a strong social responsibility for a company, but it cannot be at the expense of the employees or the stockholders.

Having welcomed a parade of visitors over the years, Iverson had become concerned with the pattern apparent at other companies' steel plants: "They only do one or two of the things we do. It's not just incentives or the scholarship program; it's all those things put together that results in a unified philosophy for the company."

Building on Success

Throughout the 1980s and 1990s Nucor continued to take the initiative and to be the prime mover in steel and the industries vertically related to steel. For example, in 1984 Nucor broke with the industry pattern of basing the price of an order of steel on the quantity ordered. Iverson noted, "Some time ago we began to realize that with computer order entry and billing, the extra charge for smaller orders was not cost justified." In a seemingly risky move in 1986, Nucor began construction of a $25 million plant in Indiana to manufacture steel fasteners. Imports had grown to 90 percent of this market as U.S. companies failed to compete. Iverson said, "We're going to bring that business back; we can make bolts as cheaply as foreign producers." A second plant, in 1995, gave Nucor 20 percent of the U.S. market for steel fasteners. Nucor also acquired a steel bearings manufacturer in 1986, which Iverson called "a good fit with our business, our policies and our people."

In early 1986 Iverson announced plans for a revolutionary plant at Crawfordsville, Indiana, which would be the first mini-mill in the world to manufacture flat-rolled or sheet steel, the last bastion of the integrated manufacturers. This market alone was twice the size of the existing market for mini-mill products. It would be a quarter of a billion dollar gamble on a new technology. The plant was expected to halve the integrated manufacturer's $3 of labor per ton and save $50 to $75 on a $400-a-ton selling price. If it worked, the profit from this plant alone would come close to the profit of the whole corporation. *Forbes* commented, "If any mini-mill can meet the challenge, it's Nucor. But expect the going to be tougher this time around." If successful, Nucor had the licensing rights to the next two plants built in the world with this technology.

Nucor had spent millions trying to develop the process when it heard of some promising developments at a German company. In the spring of 1986, Aycock flew to Germany to see the pilot machine at SMS Schloemann-Siemag AG. In December the Germans came to Charlotte for the first of what they thought would be many meetings to hammer out a deal with Nucor. Iverson shocked them when he announced Nucor was ready to build the first plant of its kind.

Kieth Busse was given the job of building the Crawfordsville, Indiana, sheet steel plant. Though an accountant by training, Busse had designed and built Nucor's state-of-the-art bolt factory. A midwesterner of German extraction, as a sideline he ran a gun supermarket in Fort Wayne and was the biggest machine gun dealer in northern Indiana. The process of bringing this plant online was so exciting that it became the basis for a best-selling book by Robert Preston, which was serialized in *New Yorker* magazine.

Preston reported on a conversation at dinner during construction between Iverson and Busse. Thinking about the future, Busse was worried that Nucor might someday become like Big Steel. He asked, "How do we allow Nucor to grow without expanding the bureaucracy?" He commented on the vice presidents stacked on vice presidents, research departments, assistants to assistants, and so on. Iverson agreed. Busse seriously suggested, "Maybe we're going to need group vice presidents." Iverson's heated response was "Do you want to ruin the company? That's the old Harvard Business School thinking. They would only get in the way, slow us down." He said the company could at least double, to $2 billion, before it added a new level of management. "I hope that by the time we have group vice presidents I'll be collecting Social Security."

The gamble on the new plant paid off and Busse, the general manager of the plant, became a key man within Nucor. The new mill began operations in August of 1989 and reached 15 percent of capacity by the end of the year. In June of 1990 it had its first profitable month, and Nucor announced the construction of a second plant in Arkansas.

In December 1992, Nucor signed a letter of intent with Oregon Steel Mills to build a sheet mill on the West Coast to begin in 1994. This project was later canceled. The supply and cost of scrap steel to feed the mini-mills was an important future concern to Iverson. So at the beginning of 1993 Nucor announced the construction of a plant in Trinidad to supply its mills with iron carbide pellets. The innovative plant would cost $60 million and take a year and a half to complete. In 1994 the two existing sheet mills were expanded and a new $500 million, 1.8-million-ton sheet mill in South Carolina was announced, to begin operation in early 1997.

In what the *New York Times* called their "most ambitious project yet," in 1987 Nucor had begun a joint venture with Yamato Kogyo, Ltd., to make structural steel products in a mill on the Mississippi River in a direct challenge to the Big Three integrated steel companies. He put John Correnti in charge of the operation.

John Correnti, born in the Finger Lakes region of western New York, received a degree in civil engineering from Clarkson University in 1969. He commented: "I was a C/F student my first two years and an A/B student my last two years." After seventeen offers, he accepted a job with U.S. Steel in their construction department. He was energetic and ambitious and became one of the youngest people to ever become a construction superintendent there. The construction group members were considered mavericks at U.S. Steel and specialized in overcoming the bureaucracy and paperwork. While employed by U.S. Steel, Correnti conducted projects in a wide range of steel operations across the country.

While working on a project in Texas in 1980, Correnti married a Texan and decided to leave U.S. Steel rather than move his wife out of Texas. A headhunter showed him a construction manager job with Nucor, a company he had never heard of. And Ken Iverson convinced him to join the company and move to Salt Lake City to build a bar plant at Plymoth, Utah. Correnti was used to being independent: "I just started doing things, and I figured that when they didn't want me to do something, I'd hear from somebody. I never heard from anybody."

In 1984 he moved to a more-challenging job of vice president and general manager of the Utah bar mill, which was not performing well. He wasted no time getting everyone focused on cost cutting, pointing out examples of wasted pens in one man's desk and the possibility of washing and reusing gloves. The plant office, dubbed the Taj Mahal by people in the plant, was too far from the main operations, so Correnti had it torn down and moved the staff into a nearby engineering building. He wouldn't let the salespeople have carpet until their sales reached the desired level. By the time he left in 1986 to build the Nucor-Yamato plant, the division was turning profitable.

Correnti built and then became the general manager of Nucor-Yamato when it started up in 1988. In 1991 he surprised many people by deciding to double Nucor-Yamato's capacity by 1994. It became Nucor's largest division and the largest wide flange producer in the United States. By 1995, Bethlehem Steel was the only other wide flange producer of structural steel products left and had plans to leave the business.

Nucor started up its first facility to produce metal buildings in 1987. A second metal buildings facility began operations in late 1996 in South Carolina, and a new steel deck facility, in Alabama, was announced for 1997. At the end of 1997 the Arkansas sheet mill was undergoing a $120 million expansion to include a galvanizing facility.

In 1995 Nucor became involved in its first international venture, an ambitious project with Brazil's Companhia Siderurgica National to build a $700 million steel mill in the state of Ceara. While other mini-mills were cutting deals to buy and sell abroad, Nucor was planning to ship iron from Brazil and process it in Trinidad.

Nucor set records for sales and net earnings in 1997 (see appendix 3 for financial reports and appendix 4 for financial ratios). In the spring of 1998, as Iverson approached his seventy-third birthday, he was commenting, "People ask me when I'm going to retire. I tell them our mandatory retirement age is ninety-five, but I may change that when I get there." It surprised the world when, in October 1998, Ken Iverson left the board. He retired as chairman at the end of the year. Although sales for 1998 decreased 1 percent and net earnings were down 10 percent, the management made a number of long-term investments and closed draining investments. Start-up began at the new South Carolina steam mill and at the Arkansas sheet mill expansion. The plans for a North Carolina steel plate mill in Hertford were announced. This would bring Nucor's total steel production capacity to 12 million tons per year. The plant in Trinidad, which had proven much more expensive than was originally expected, was deemed unsuccessful and closed. Finally, directors approved the repurchase of up to 5 million shares of Nucor stock.

Still, the downward trends at Nucor continued. Sales and earnings were down 3 percent and 7 percent, respectively, for 1999. However, these trends did not seem to affect the company's investments. Expansions were under way in the steel mills, and a third building systems facility was under construction in Texas. Nucor was actively searching for a site for a joist plant in the Northeast. A letter of intent was signed with Australian and Japanese companies to form a joint venture to commercialize the strip casting technology. To understand the challenges facing Nucor, industry, technology, and environmental trends in the 1980s and 1990s must be considered.

The U.S. Steel Industry in the 1980s

The early 1980s had been the worst years in decades for the steel industry. Data from the American Iron and Steel Institute showed shipments falling from 100 million tons in 1979 to the mid-80 levels in 1980 and 1981. Slackening in the economy, particularly in auto sales, led the decline. In 1986, when industry capacity was at 130 million tons, the outlook was for a continued decline in per capita consumption and movement toward capacity in the 90- to 100-million-ton range. The chairman of Armco saw "millions of tons chasing a market that's not there: excess capacity that must be eliminated."

The large, integrated steel firms, such as U.S. Steel and Armco, that made up the major part of the industry, were the hardest hit. The *Wall Street Journal* stated, "The decline has resulted from such problems as high labor and energy costs in mining and processing iron ore, a lack of profits and capital to modernize plants, and conservative management that has hesitated to take risks."

These companies produced a wide range of steels, primarily from ore processed in blast furnaces. They had found it difficult to compete with imports, usually from Japan, and had given market share to imports. They sought the protection of import quotas. Imported steel accounted for 20 percent of the U.S. steel consumption, up from 12 percent in the early 1970s. The U.S. share of world production of raw steel declined from 19 to 14 percent over the period. Imports of light bar products accounted for less that 9 percent of the U.S. consumption of those products in 1981, according to the U.S. Commerce Department, while imports of wire rod totaled 23 percent of U.S. consumption.

Iron Age stated that exports, as a percentage of shipments in 1985, were 34 percent for Nippon, 26 percent for British Steel, 30 percent for Krupp, 49 percent for USINOR of France, and less than 1 percent for every American producer on the list. The consensus of steel experts was that imports would average 23 percent of the market in the last half of the 1980s.

Iverson was one of the very few in the steel industry to oppose import restrictions. He saw an outdated U.S. steel industry that had to change.

We Americans have been conditioned to believe in our technical superiority. For many generations a continuing stream of new inventions and manufacturing techniques allowed us to far outpace the rest of the world in both volume and efficiency of production. In many areas this is no longer true and particularly in the steel industry. In the last three decades, almost all the major developments in steel making were made outside the U.S. There were eighteen continuous casting units in the world before there was one in this country. I would be negligent if I did not recognize the significant contribution that the government has made toward the technological deterioration of the steel industry. Unrealistic depreciation schedules, high corporate taxes, excessive regulation and jaw-boning for lower steel prices have make it difficult for the U.S. steel industry to borrow or generate the huge quantities of capital required for modernization.

By the mid 1980s the integrated mills were moving fast to get back into the game: they were restructuring, cutting capacity, dropping unprofitable lines, focusing products, and trying to become responsive to the market. The industry made a pronounced move toward segmentation. Integrated producers focused on mostly flat-rolled and structural grades, reorganized steel companies focused on a limited range of products, mini-mills dominated the bar and light structural product areas, and specialty steel firms sought niches. There was an accelerated shutdown of older plants, elimination of products by some firms, and the installation of new product lines with new technologies by others. High-tonnage mills restructured to handle sheets, plates, structural beams, high-quality bars, and large pipe and tubular products, which allowed a resurgence of specialized mills: cold-finished bar manufacturers, independent strip mills, and mini-mills.

The road for the integrated mills was not easy. As *Purchasing* pointed out, tax laws and accounting rules slowed the closing of inefficient plants. Shutting down a ten-thousand-person plant could require a firm to hold a cash reserve of $100 million to fund health, pension, and insurance liabilities. The chairman of Armco commented: "Liabilities associated with a planned shutdown are so large that they can quickly devastate a company's balance sheet."

Joint ventures had arisen to produce steel for a specific market or region. The chairman of USX called them "an important new wrinkle in steel's fight for survival" and stated, "If there had been more joint ventures like these two decades ago, the U.S. steel industry might have built only half of the dozen or so hot-strip mills it put up in that time and avoided today's over capacity." *Purchasing* observed, "The fact is that these combined operations are the result of a laissez faire attitude within the Justice Department under the Reagan administration following the furor when government restrictions killed the planned USS takeover of National Steel."

The American Iron and Steel Institute reported steel production in 1988 of 99.3 million tons, up from 89.2 million in 1987, and the highest in seven years. As a result of modernization programs, 60.9 percent of production was from continuous casters. Exports for steel increased and imports fell. Some steel experts believed the United States was now cost-competitive with Japan. However, 1989 proved to be a year of "waiting for the other shoe to drop," according to *Metal Center News*. U.S. steel production was hampered by a new recession, the expiration of the voluntary import restraints, and labor negotiations in several companies. Declines in car production and consumer goods hit flat-rolled steel hard. AUJ Consultants told MCN, "The U.S. steel market has peaked. Steel consumption is tending down. By 1990, we expect total domestic demand to dip under 90 million tons."

The U.S. Steel Industry in the 1990s

The economic slowdown of the early 1990s did lead to a decline in the demand for steel through early 1993, but by 1995 America was in its best steel market in twenty years and many companies were building new flat-roll mini-mills. A *Business Week* article at the time described it as "the race of the Nucor look-alikes." Six years after Nucor pioneered the low-cost German technology in Crawfordsville, Indiana, the competition was finally gearing up to compete. Ten new projects were expected to add 20 million tons per year of the flat-rolled steel, raising U.S. capacity by as much as 40 percent by 1998. These mills opened in 1997, just as the industry was expected to move into a cyclical slump. It was no surprise that worldwide competition increased and companies that had previously focused on their home markets began a race to become global powerhouses. The foreign push was new for U.S. firms, which had focused on defending their home markets. U.S. mini-mills focused their international expansion primarily in Asia and South America.

Meanwhile, in 1994 U.S. Steel, North America's largest integrated steel producer, began a major business process reengineering project to improve order fulfillment performance and customer satisfaction on the heels of a decade of restructuring. According to *Steel Times International*, "U.S. Steel had to completely change the way it did business. Cutting labor costs, and increasing reliability and productivity took the company a long way towards improving profitability and competitiveness. However, it became clear that this leaner organization still had to implement new technologies and business processes if it was to maintain a competitive advantage." The goals of the business process reengineering project included a sharp reduction in cycle time, greatly decreased levels of inventory, shorter order lead times, and the ability to offer real-time promise dates to customers. In 1995, the company successfully installed integrated planning/production/order fulfillment software, and the results were very positive. U.S. Steel believed that the reengineering project had positioned it for a future of increased competition, tighter markets, and raised customer expectations.

In late 1997 and again in 1998 the decline in demand prompted Nucor and other U.S. companies to slash prices to compete with the unprecedented surge of imports. By the last quarter of 1998 these imports had led to the filing of unfair trade complaints with U.S. trade regulators, causing steel prices in the spot market to drop sharply in August and September before they stabilized. A press release by the U.S. secretary of commerce, William Daley, stated, "I will not stand by and allow U.S. workers, communities and companies to bear the brunt of other nations' problematic policies and practices. We are the most open economy of the world. But we are not the world's dumpster." In early 1999 American Iron and Steel Institute reported in its Opinion section of its web page the following quotes by Andy Sharkey and Hank Barnette. Sharkey said, "With many of the world's economies in recession, and no signs of recovery on the horizon, it should come as no surprise that the United States is now seen as the only reliable market for manufactured goods. This can be seen in the dramatic surge of imports." Barnette noted, "While there are different ways to gauge the impact of the Asian crisis, believe me, it has already hit. Just ask the 163,000 employees of the U.S. steel industry."

The Commerce Department concluded in March 1999 that six countries had illegally dumped stainless steel in the United States at prices below production costs or home market prices. The Commerce Department found that Canada, South Korea, and Taiwan were guilty only of dumping, while Belgium, Italy, and South Africa also gave producers unfair subsidies that effectively lowered prices. However, on June 23, 1999, The *Wall Street Journal* reported that the Senate decisively shut off an attempt to restrict U.S. imports of steel, despite industry complaints that a flood of cheap imports was driving them out of business. Advisors of President Clinton were reported to have said that the president would likely veto the bill if it passed. Administrative officials opposed the bill because it would violate international trade law and leave the United States open to retaliation.

The American Iron and Steel Institute (AISI) reported that in May 1999 U.S. steel mills shipped 8,330,000 net tons, a decrease of 6.7 percent from the 8,927,000 net tons shipped in May 1998. They also stated that for the first five months of 1999 shipments were 41,205,000 net tons, down 10 percent from the same period in 1998. AISI president and CEO Andrew Sharkey III said, "Once again, the May data show clearly that America's steel trade crisis continues. U.S. steel companies and employees continue to be injured by high levels of dumping and subsidized imports. . . . In addition, steel inventory levels remain excessive, and steel operating rates continue to be very low." Table 2A compares the average import customs value per net ton of steel for May 1999 to the first quarter of 1998, and Table 2B compares U.S. imports of steel mill products by country of origin for the first five months in 1999 to those of 1998 and 1997.

As the 1990s ended, Nucor was the second largest steel producer in the United States, behind USX. The company's market capitalization was about two times that of the next smaller competitor. Even in a tight industry, someone can win. Nucor was in the best position because the industry was very fragmented and there are many marginal competitors.

Steel Technology and the Mini-Mill

A new type of mill, the "mini-mill," had emerged in the United States during the 1970s to compete with the integrated mill. The mini-mill used electric arc furnaces initially to manufacture a narrow product line from scrap steel. The leading U.S. mini-mills in the 1980s were Nucor, Florida Steel, Georgetown Steel, North Star Steel, and Chaparral. Between the late 1970s and 1980s, the integrated mills' market share fell from about 90 percent to about 60 percent, with the integrated steel companies averaging a 7 percent return on equity, the mini-mills averaging 14 percent, and some, such as Nucor, achieving about 25 percent. In the 1990s mini-mills tripled their output to capture 17 percent of domestic shipments. Moreover, integrated mills' market share fell to around 40 percent, while mini-mills' share rose to 23 percent, reconstructed mills' increased their share from 11 to 28 percent, and specialized mills increased their share from 1 to 6 percent.

Some experts believed that a relatively new technology, the twin shell electric arc furnace, would help mini-mills increase production, lower costs, and take market share. According to the *Pittsburgh Business Times*, "With a twin shell furnace, one shell—the chamber holding the scrap to be melted—is filled and heated. During the heating of the first shell, the

TABLE 2A

Average Import Customs Value per Net Ton (selected products)

Product	May 1999	1st Quarter 1998	% Change
Wire rods	$275	$350	−21.50%
Structural shapes	267	379	−29.60
Plates cut lengths	456	490	−6.90
Plates in coils	257	377	−31.70
Reinforcing bars	198	300	−33.90
Line pipe	429	524	−18.20
Black plate	551	627	−12.20
Sheets, hot rolled	242	304	−20.40
Sheets, cold rolled	400	549	−27.10
Sheet & strip galvanized electrolytic	483	609	−20.70
Total, all steel mill products	332	455	−27.00

Source: American Iron and Steel Press Release, June 24, 1999.

TABLE 2B

U.S. Imports of Steel Mill Products by Country of Origin (thousands of net tons)

Country	5 Mos 99 Prelim	5 Mos 98	5 Mos 97	5 Mos 99 vs. 5 Mos 98 % Change	5 Mos 99 vs. 5 Mos 97 % Change
European Union	2,569	2,634	3,048	−2.5%	−15.7%
Canada	2,157	2,146	2,035	0.5	6.0
Japan	1,452	2,099	1,015	−30.8	43.1
Mexico	1,444	1,263	1,432	14.3	0.8
Brazil	1,428	987	1,565	44.7	−8.8
Korea	1,330	1,064	643	25.0	106.8
Russia	343	1,583	1,680	−78.3	−79.6
Australia	316	366	121	−13.7	161.2
South Africa	252	214	120	17.8	110.0
China	243	177	274	37.3	−11.3
India	170	118	90	70.3	123.3
Indonesia	187	116	33	61.2	466.7
Turkey	148	232	209	−36.2	−29.2
Ukraine	105	392	290	−73.2	−63.8
Others	1,546	1,188	1,038	27.5	46.0
Total	**13,690**	**14,578**	**13,593**	**−6.1**	**0.7**

Source: American Iron and Steel Press Release, June 24, 1999.

second shell is filled. When the heating is finished on the first shell, the electrodes move to the second. The first shell is emptied and refilled before the second gets hot." This increased production by 60 percent. Twin shell production had been widely adopted in the last few years. For example, Nucor Steel began running a twin shell furnace in November 1996 in Berkeley, South Carolina, and installed another in Norfolk, Nebraska, which began operations in 1997. "Everyone accepts twin shells as a good concept because there's a lot of flexibility of operation," said Rodney Mott, vice president and general manager of Nucor-Berkeley. However, this move toward twin shell furnaces could mean trouble with scrap availability. According to an October 1997 quote in the *Pittsburgh Business Times* by Ralph Smaller, vice president of process technology at Kvaerner, "Innovations that feed the electric furnaces' production of flat-rolled [steel] will increase the demand on high quality scrap and alternatives. The technological changes

are just beginning and will accelerate over the next few years."

According to a September 1997 *Industry Week* article, steel makers around the world are now closely monitoring the development of continuous "strip casting" technology, which may prove to be the next leap forward for the industry. "The objective of strip casting is to produce thin strips of steel (in the 1-mm to 4-mm range) as liquid steel flows from a tundish— the stationary vessel which receives molten steel from the ladle. It would eliminate the slab-casting stage and all of the rolling that now takes place in a hot mill." Strip casting was reported to have some difficult technological challenges, but companies in Germany, France, Japan, Australia, Italy, and Canada had strip-casting projects under way. In fact, all of the significant development work in strip casting was taking place outside the United States.

Larry Kavanaph, American Iron and Steel Institute vice president for manufacturing and technology, said, "Steel is a very high-tech industry, but nobody knows it." Today's most productive steel-making facilities incorporate advanced metallurgical practices, sophisticated process-control sensors, state-of-the-art computer controls, and the latest refinements in continuous casting and rolling mill technology. Michael Shot, vice president for manufacturing at Carpenter Technology Corp., Reading, Pennsylvania, a specialty steels and premium-grade alloys producer, said, "You don't survive in this industry unless you have the technology to make the best products in the world in the most efficient manner."

Environmental and Political Issues

Not all stakeholders have been happy with the way Nucor does business. In June 1998, *Waste News* reported that Nucor's mill in Crawfordsville, Indiana, was cited by the United States Environmental Protection Agency for alleged violations of federal and state clean air rules. The Pamlico–Tar River Foundation, the NC Coastal Federation, and the Environmental Defense Fund had concerns about the state's decision to allow the company to start building the plant before the environmental review was completed. According to the *News & Observer* web site, "The environmental groups charge that the mill will discharge 6,720 tons of pollutants into the air each year."

There were also concerns about the fast-track approval of the facility being built in Hertford County. First, this plant was located on the banks of one of the most important and sensitive stretches of the Chowan, a principal tributary to the national treasure Albemarle Sound and the last bastion of the state's once vibrant river-herring fishery. North Carolina passed a law in 1997 that required the restoration of this fishery through a combination of measures designed to prevent overfishing, restore spawning and nursery habitats, and improve water quality in the Chowan. "New federal law requires extra care in protecting essential habitat for the herring, which spawn upstream," stated an article in the *Business Journal*. Second, there were concerns regarding the excessive incentives the state gave to convince Nucor to build a $300 million steel mill in the state. Some questioned whether the promise of three hundred well-paying jobs in Hertford County was worth the $155 million in tax breaks the state was giving Nucor to locate there.

Management Evolution

As Nucor opened new plants, each was made a division and given a general manager who had complete responsibility for all aspects of the business. The corporate office did not involve itself in the routine functioning of the divisions. There was no centralized purchasing, hiring and firing, or division accounting. The total corporate staff was still less than twenty-five people, including clerical staff, when 1999 began.

In 1984, Dave Aycock moved into the corporate office as president. Ken Iverson was chief executive officer and chairman. Iverson, Aycock, and Sam Siegel operated as an executive board, providing overall direction to the corporation. By 1990 Aycock, who had invested his money wisely, owned over 600,000 shares of Nucor stock, five hotels and farms in three states, and was ready to retire. He was sixty, five years younger than Iverson, and was concerned that if he waited, he and Iverson might be leaving the company at the same time. Two people stood out as candidates for the presidency, Keith Busse and John Correnti. In November, Iverson called Correnti to the Charlotte airport and offered him the job. Aycock commented, "Keith Busse was my choice, but I got outvoted." In June 1991 Aycock retired and Keith Busse left Nucor to build an independent sheet mill in Indiana for a group of investors.

Thus Iverson, Correnti, and Siegel led the company. In 1993, Iverson had heart problems and major surgery. Correnti was given the CEO role in 1996. The Board of Directors had always been small, consisting of the executive team and one or two past Nucor vice presidents. Several organizations with large blocks of Nucor stock had been pressing Nucor to diversify its board membership and add outside directors. In 1996 Jim Hlavacek, head of a small consulting firm and friend of Iverson, was added to the board.

Only five, not six, members of the board were in attendance during the Board of Directors meeting in the fall of 1998, because of the death of Jim Cunningham. Near its end, Aycock read a motion, drafted by Siegel, that Ken Iverson be removed as chairman. It was seconded by Hlavacek and passed. It was announced in October that Iverson would be a chairman emeritus and a director, but after disagreements Iverson left the company completely. It was agreed that Iverson would receive $500,000 a year for five years. Aycock left retirement to become chairman.

The details of Iverson's leaving did not become known until June of 1999, when John Correnti resigned after disagreements with the board and Aycock took his place. All of this was a complete surprise to investors and brought the stock price down 10 percent. Siegel commented, "The board felt Correnti was not the right person to lead Nucor into the twenty-first century." Aycock assured everyone that he would be happy to move back into retirement as soon as replacements could be found.

In December 1999 Correnti became chairman of rival Birmingham Steel, with an astounding corporate staff of 156 people. With Nucor's organizational changes, he questioned their ability to move as fast in the future. "Nucor's trying to centralize and do more mentoring. That's not what grew the company to what it is today."

Aycock moved ahead with adding outside directors to the board. He appointed Harvey Gantt, principal in his own architectural firm and former mayor of Charlotte; Victoria Haynes, formally B. F. Goodrich's chief technology officer; and Peter Browning, chief executive of Sonoco (biographical sketches of board members and executive management are provided in appendices 5 and 6). Then he moved to increase the corporate office staff by adding a level of executive vice presidents over four areas of business and adding two specialist jobs in strategic planning and steel technology. When Siegel retired, Aycock promoted Terry Lisenby to CFO and treasurer, and hired a director of information technology to report to Lisenby (Figure 2 provides the organization chart).

Jim Coblin, vice president of human resources, believed the additions to management were necessary, saying, "It's not bad to get a little more like other companies." He noted that the various divisions did their business cards and plant signs differently; some did not even want a Nucor sign. Sometimes six different Nucor salesmen would call on the same customer.

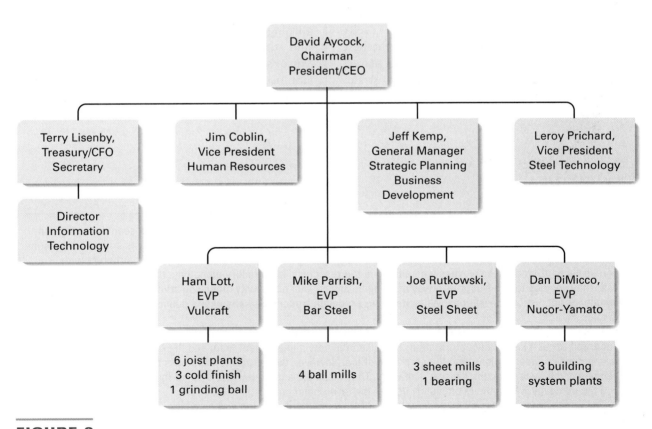

FIGURE 2

Nucor Organization Chart

"There is no manager of human resources in the plants, so at least we needed to give additional training to the person who does most of that work at the plant," he stated. With these new additions there would be a director of information technology and two important committees, one for environmental issues and the second for audit.

Coblin believed that the old span of control of twenty people might have worked well when there was less competition. Aycock considered it "ridiculous," saying, "It was not possible to properly manage, to know what was going own. The top managers have totally lost contact with the company." Coblin was optimistic that the use of executive vice presidents (EVPs) would improve management. The three meetings of the general managers had slowly increased from about one and a half days to about two and a half days and had become more focused. The new EVP positions would add a perspective above the level of the individual plants. Instead of fifteen individual detailed presentations, each general manager would give a five-minute briefing and then there would be an in-depth presentation on the group, with team participation. After some training by Lisenby, the divisions had recently done a pretty good job with a SWOT analysis. Coblin thought these changes would make Nucor a stronger global player.

To **Jeff Kemp,** the new general manager of strategic planning and business development, the big issue was how to sustain earnings growth. In the U.S. steel industry there were too many marginal competitors. The U.S. government had recently added to the problem by giving almost a billion dollars to nine mills, which simply allowed them to limp along and weaken the industry. Kemp was looking for Nucor's opportunities within the steel industry. He asked why Nucor had bought a bearing company. His experience in the chemical industry suggested a need for Nucor to establish a position of superiority and grow globally, driving industry competition rather than reacting. He argued that a company should protect its overall market position, which could mean sacrifices for individual plants. Aycock liked Kemp's background in law and accounting and had specifically sought someone from outside the steel industry to head up Nucor's strategic planning. By June 2000 Kemp had conducted studies of other industries in the U.S. market and had developed a working document that identified opportunities worthy of further analysis.

"Every company hits a plateau," Aycock observed. "You can't just go out and build plants to grow. How do you step up to the next level? I wouldn't say it's a turning point but we have to get our strategic vision and strategic plans." He stated, "We are beginning Nucor's first ever strategic planning sessions; it was not necessary before." They had just received an image survey from a consulting firm (Exhibit 1).

EXHIBIT 1

Nucor's Image Survey

In early 2000, Nucor had an outside consulting firm conduct a survey of the company's image as seen by the top ten to fifteen managers, including the corporate office. They also gathered the views of a few analysts and media personnel. The managers still agreed that Nucor valued risk taking, innovation, and a lean management structure with aggressive, hard-working employees who accepted the responsibility of failure along with the opportunity for success. They seemed to see Nucor as a way of doing business—not just a way of making steel—in terms of values and personality, not just business terms. When asked to associate Nucor's persona with a public figure, John Wayne was the clear choice.

The managers in the field seemed to believe that the new layer of management was needed, and they were not concerned about a loss of decentralization. They liked the new management team and the changes so far, particularly the improved communications with the corporate office. However, the corporate managers thought the company was changing much faster than the division managers. They also held a more positive view of the company regarding how good the company was in their community or with the environment.

The people from the media had positive views of Nucor as hard-working and committed to its employees, and as an innovative risk-taking economic powerhouse. Some who were most familiar with the company believed that it needed to do a better job of communicating its vision during a period of transition.

Aycock believed Nucor needed to be quick to recognize developing technology in all production areas. He noted the joint venture to develop a new "strip caster" that would cast the current flat-rolled material in a more-finished form. The impact could be "explosive," allowing Nucor to build smaller plants closer to markets. This would be particularly helpful on the West Coast. Nucor would own the U.S. and Brazilian rights, and its partners would own the rest. Aycock was also looking forward to the next generation of steel mills and this time wanted to own the rights. He praised Iverson's skill at seeing new technology and committing the company to it.

Aycock was very interested in acquisitions, but he believed "they must fit strategically." A bar mill in the upper central Midwest and a flat-rolled plant in the Northeast would be good. A significant opportunity existed in preengineered buildings. Aycock intended to concentrate on steel for the next five to six years, achieving an average growth rate of 15 percent per year. In about seven years he would like to see Nucor ready to move into other areas. He said Nucor had already "picked the low-hanging grapes" and must be careful in its next moves.

Steel and Nucor in the Twenty-first Century

In September 2000, David Aycock stepped aside as he had planned, and Dan DiMicco was elected president and chief executive officer of Nucor. Peter Browning was elected chairman of the Board of Directors. Aycock retired from the board a year later.

Sales for 2000 increased 14 percent over 1999 to reach a record level. Earnings were also at record levels, 27 percent over 1999. The year had begun on a strong footing, but business had turned weak by the year's end. While Nucor remained profitable, other steel companies faced bankruptcy. A Vulcraft plant was under construction in New York. It was Vulcraft's first northeastern operation and expanded its geographical coverage into a new region. It was also attempting a breakthrough technological step in strip casting at Crawfordsville—the Castrip process. It sold its grinding ball process and the bearing products operation because they were not a part of Vulcraft's core business.

In the company's annual report DiMicco laid out its plans for 2000 and beyond: "Our targets are to deliver an average annual earnings growth of 10 to 15 percent over the next ten years, to deliver a return well in excess of our cost of capital, to maintain a minimum average return on equity of 14 percent, and to deliver a return on sales of 8 to 10 percent. Our strategy will focus on Nucor becoming a "market leader" in every product group and business in which we compete. This calls for significant increases in market share for many of our core products and the maintenance of market share where we currently enjoyed a leadership position." While pointing out that it would be impossible to obtain this success through the previous strategy of greenfield construction, he added, "There will now be a heavy focus on growth through acquisitions. We will also continue growing through the commercialization of new disruptive and leapfrog technologies."

In early 2001 the *Wall Street Journal* predicted that all but two of the United States's biggest steel makers would post fourth-quarter losses. AK Steel Holding Corp. and Nucor Corp. were expected to have profits for the quarter of 2000, while U.S. Steel Group, a unit of USX Corp., was expected to post a profit for the year but not for the fourth quarter. By October 1, more than twenty steel companies in the United States, including Bethlehem Steel Corp. and LTV Corp., the nation's third and fourth largest U.S. steel producers, respectively, had filed for bankruptcy protection. Over a dozen producers were operating under Chapter 11 bankruptcy-law protection, which allows them to maintain market share by selling steel cheaper than non–Chapter 11 steel makers. On October 20, *The Economist* noted that of the fourteen steel companies followed by Standard & Poor, only Nucor was indisputably healthy. In the fall of 2001, 25 percent of domestic steel companies were in bankruptcy proceedings, and the United States was the largest importer of steel in the world. Experts believed that close to half of the U.S. steel industry might be forced to close before conditions improved.

The world steel industry found itself in the middle of one of its most unprofitable and volatile periods, in part because of a glut of steel that has sent prices to twenty-year lows. While domestic steel producers found themselves mired in red ink, many foreign steel makers desperately needed to continue to sell in the relatively open U.S. market to stay profitable. The industry was hovering around 75 percent capacity, a level too low to be profitable for many companies. Three European companies—France's USINOR SA, Luxembourg's Arbed SA, and Spain's

Aceralia Corp.—were in the process of merging to form the world's largest steel company. Two Japanese companies—NKK Corp. and Kawasaki Steel Corp.—were in talks of a merger that would make them the world's second biggest steel maker. These new large steel makers could outmuscle U.S. competitors, which were less efficient, smaller, and financially weaker than their competitors in Asia and Europe. The largest U.S. steel maker, USX-U.S. Steel Group, was currently only the eleventh largest producer in the world, and consolidation in the industry could push it further down the list. In spite of these worsening conditions, global steel production increased 7 percent last year to a record 747 million tons, and efforts were under way to negotiate a worldwide reduction in steel production.

In addition to cheap imports, U.S. steel producers were facing higher energy prices, weakening demand by customer industries, increasingly tough environmental rules, and a changing cost structure among producers. With the declining economy, energy prices could begin to drop. However, so would the demand for construction, automobiles, and farm equipment. Environmental rules could lead to costly modifications and closings of old plants that produced coke along with vast clouds of ash and acrid green smoke. In 1990 mini-mills accounted for 36 percent of the domestic steel market, but by 2000 the more efficient mini-mills had seized 50 percent of the market and the resulting competition had driven prices lower.

In March 2001, Nucor made its first acquisition in ten years, purchasing a mini-mill in New York from Sumitomo Corp. Nucor had hired about five people to help plan for future acquisitions. DiMicco commented, "It's taken us three years before our team has felt this is the right thing to do." In the challenged industry, it would be cheaper to buy than to build plants. During this downturn Nucor was taking advantage of competitors' weaknesses to take market share and invest in new facilities.

In the first quarter, sales decreased 14 percent and earnings were cut in half, despite steel shipments' being at record levels. By the third quarter, sales were down 12 percent, profit was down 70 percent, and earnings per share were down 60 percent from the previous year. In the third quarter Nucor had $20.5 million in net income, compared to $67.8 million from the year before. The company shipped 3.04 million tons of steel, a 10.4 percent increase over the year before, setting a new tonnage record. DiMicco stated, "All the U.S. mills could close and there would still be excess capacity." The year 2001 would indeed be a year to test the metal of the new Nucor!

Appendix 1: Nucor Employee Survey

Question Description	Year*	Almost Never	Seldom	Sometimes	Often	Very Often
1. Meet schedule	5	1	4	22	47	26
	4	1	4	25	48	21
	3	4	10	39	37	9
	2	11	16	40	26	7
	1	10	15	0	0	75
2. Have tools	5	1	4	19	44	32
	4	1	3	21	47	28
	3	2	5	32	46	15
	2	6	10	36	37	10
	1	6	11	0	0	83
3. Open communication	5	7	14	34	29	16
	4	11	19	35	25	11
	3	11	19	37	26	7
	2	24	23	32	16	5
	1	24	25	0	0	51

(continued)

Appendix 1: Nucor Employee Survey *(continued)*

Question Description	Year*	Almost Never	Seldom	Sometimes	Often	Very Often
4. Maintenance	5	5	11	28	37	19
	4	6	11	31	36	16
	3	5	14	32	37	13
	2	13	16	34	28	10
	1	13	16	0	0	71
5. Drug test	5	2	3	9	34	53
	4	4	4	12	35	45
	3	5	4	13	33	44
	2					
	1					
6. Rules fair	5	8	13	24	30	25
	4	9	13	25	31	22
	3	10	11	23	31	25
	2					
	1					
7. Computer systems	5	8	14	32	29	16
	4	10	17	33	27	13
	3	13	18	32	27	10
	2	21	20	34	19	7
	1	23	21	0	0	57
8. Informed	5	5	9	21	34	31
	4	6	9	24	34	26
	3	9	14	27	33	17
	2	15	15	30	28	12
	1	16	16	0	0	69
9. Supervisor fair	5	4	7	20	36	34
	4	6	7	20	35	32
	3	6	9	26	38	21
	2	10	11	32	35	13
	1	13	12	0	0	74
10. Supervisor ideas	5	7	11	24	30	29
	4	8	12	29	30	21
	3	11	15	28	30	16
	2	17	18	31	24	10
	1	18	17	0	0	65
11. Division managers' actions	5	8	12	39	31	19
	4	7	14	33	33	13
	3	9	17	35	30	9
	2	20	21	34	20	6
	1	18	22	0	0	60
12. Division managers informed	5	7	12	27	34	20
	4	6	12	28	35	19
	3	8	15	31	32	14
	2	17	18	33	23	9
	1	15	20	0	0	65

(continued)

Appendix 1: Nucor Employee Survey *(continued)*

Question Description	Year*	Almost Never	Seldom	Sometimes	Often	Very Often
13. General managers' actions	5	6	9	27	35	23
	4	7	14	33	33	13
	3	9	17	35	30	9
	2	20	21	34	20	6
	1	18	22	0	0	60
14. General managers' response	5	8	13	31	30	18
	4	7	14	32	33	14
	3	12	19	34	28	8
	2	19	20	35	21	6
	1	20	22	0	0	58
15. General managers' information	5	4	8	25	38	25
	4	6	12	28	35	19
	3	8	15	31	32	14
	2	17	18	33	23	9
	1	15	20	0	0	65
16. Oa tm gd	5	2	5	19	42	32
	4	6	9	27	35	22
	3	8	11	29	35	17
	2	17	14	32	26	11
	1	13	12	0	0	74
17. Headquarter directions	5	2	3	18	44	33
	4	1	2	17	45	36
	3	1	3	19	47	29
	2					
	1					
18. Paid fr-out	5	6	9	21	31	32
	4	6	9	20	34	30
	3	10	13	24	33	20
	2	14	13	28	31	14
	1	11	13	0	0	75
19. Paid fr-in	5	10	13	24	29	24
	4	10	14	22	31	23
	3	16	16	25	29	14
	2	21	15	26	27	11
	1	19	15	0	0	66
20. Heal care	5	10	14	30	32	14
	4	8	12	31	35	14
	3	19	18	31	24	7
	2	11	13	33	31	12
	1	8	11	0	0	80

* The most recent survey was 5.

Appendix 2: Nucor Survey Plant Comparisons

Question*	Descrpt.	Total Company	V1	V2	V3	V4	V5	V6	S1	S2	S3	S4	S5	01	02	03	04	05	06
			Vulcraft Plants						**Steel Plants**					**Other Plants**					
1	Meet sche	5	4	6	5	6	5	5	5	6	5	4	1	5	11	2	18	6	3
2	Have tools	5	2	4	3	7	3	4	2	8	6	3	2	6	11	3	17	5	6
3	Open com	21	17	23	16	15	18	26	21	26	23	19	15	24	31	23	35	21	30
4	Maint	16	12	13	12	9	22	13	13	26	25	19	9	13	29	11	33	15	29
5	Drug test	5	5	6	5	3	3	5	8	7	4	5	2	4	9	3	4	5	11
6	Rules fair	21	15	24	19	13	12	20	21	31	16	26	15	22	26	32	36	19	37
7	Cmplt sys	22	16	22	18	20	19	31	20	27	28	24	15	28	26	18	55	24	40
8	Informed	14	8	22	12	15	18	17	12	18	19	10	8	22	16	15	23	17	11
9	Supv fair	11	9	21	13	11	12	15	10	13	10	10	4	15	14	13	9	11	10
10	Supv idea	18	14	32	19	20	18	24	15	18	18	13	9	26	25	18	25	20	13
11	Dmgr act	20	13	23	17	14	15	28	23	26	32	16	11	18	18	14	48	24	41
12	Dmgr infm	19	17	16	15	14	14	23	19	27	31	19	13	15	24	9	44	21	36
13	Gmgr act	15	9	17	8	15	9	25	16	17	15	19	5	29	20	4	43	10	43
14	Gmgr gets	21	15	22	12	18	14	24	22	25	24	28	12	30	25	9	45	25	43
15	Gmgr infm	12	11	8	7	14	7	17	15	13	15	18	4	11	15	2	35	13	34
16	Oa tm gd	7	3	7	3	4	7	8	7	9	13	6	1	8	5	2	22	15	13
17	Hq direct	5	3	7	3	2	2	10	6	11	16	4	3	3	4	1	11	4	2
18	Paid fr-out	15	16	26	19	20	19	20	16	15	14	10	6	42	25	8	11	11	19
19	Paid fr-in	23	18	33	21	28	23	26	24	22	25	23	12	45	29	20	28	20	33
20	Heal care	24	14	19	16	34	16	27	22	42	31	12	25	18	8	27	7	29	23

* For text of questions, see appendix 1.

Appendix 3: Financial Report

Annual Report: Consol. Inc Acct., Yrs End. Dec.31 (thousand $)

	12/31/2001	12/31/2000	12/31/1999	12/31/1998	12/31/1997
Net sales	$4,139,248	$4,586,146	$4,009,346	$4,151,232	$4,184,498
Costs and expenses					
Cost of products sold	$3,820,303	$3,925,478	$3,480,479	$3,591,783	$3,578,941
Marketing, administrative and other expenses	$138,559	$183,175	$154,774	$147,972	$145,410
Interest expense (income)	($6,525)	($816)	($5,095)	($3,832)	($35)
	$3,965,387	$4,107,838	$3,630,157	$3,735,924	$3,724,315
Earnings before federal income taxes	$173,861	$487,308	$379,189	$415,309	$460,182
Federal income taxes	$60,900	$167,400	$134,600	$151,309	$165,700
Net earnings	**$112,961**	**$310,908**	**$244,589**	**$263,709**	**$294,482**
Com. divds	—	—	45,354	42,129	35,154
Capital expenditures	$261,145	$415,405	$374,718	$502,910	$306,749
Average number of shares (thousands)	77,814	77,582	87,247	87,862	87,872
Operating income as calculated	—	—	$630,730	$664,595	$677,911
Depreciation	$289,063	$259,365	$256,637	$253,118	$217,764

Consolidated Balance Sheet (thousand $)

	12/31/2001	12/31/2000	12/3 1/1999	12/31/1998	12/31/1997
Assets					
Current assets	$1,373,666	$1,379,539	$1,538,509	$1,129,467	$1,125,508
Property, plant, and equipment	$2,365,655	$2,329,421	$2,191,339	$2,097,079	$1,858,875
Total assets	**$3,759,348**	**$3,710,867**	**$3,729,848**	**$3,226,546**	**$2,984,383**
Liabilities and Stockholders' Equity					
Total current liabilities	$484,159	$558,068	$531,031	$486,897	$524,454
Long-term debt after one year	$460,450	$460,450	$390,450	$215,450	$167,950
Total stockholders' equity	$2,201,460	$2,130,951	$2,262,248	$2,072,552	$1,876,426
Total liabilities	**$3,759,348**	**$3,710,867**	**$3,729,848**	**$3,226,546**	**$2,984,383**
Net working capital	$889,507	$821,460	$1,007,478	$642,570	$601,055
Equity per share	$28.29	$27.47	$25.96	$23.73	$21.32
Capital expenditures	$261,145	$415,405	$374,718	$502,910	$306,749
Number of common shares (thousands)			90,103	90,052	
Number of treasury shares (thousands)			2,969	2,699	

Source: Standard & Poor's Corporate Records.

Appendix 4: Financial Ratios

	1990	1991	1992	1993	1994	1995	1996	1997	1998	1999	2000
Net sales	1,481	1,465	1,619	2,253	2,975	3,462	3,647	4,184	4,151	4,009	4,586
Net earnings	75	65	79	123	227	275	248	294	264	245	311
Current assets	313	334	382	468	639	831	828	1,126	1,129	1,539	1,381
Current liabilities	203	229	272	350	382	447	466	524	487	531	558
Long-term debt > 1 year	29	73	247	352	173	107	153	168	215	390	460
Stockholders' equity	653	712	784	902	1,123	1,382	1,609	1,876	2,973	2, 262	2,131
Total assets	1,036	1,182	1,507	1,829	2,002	2,296	2,620	2,984	3,227	3,730	3,722
COGS	1,293	1,303	1,417	1,966	2,492	2,900	3,139	3,579	3,591	3,480	3,925
Shares out, year end	86	86	87	87	87	88	88	88	88	87	78
Current ratio	1.54	1.46	1.40	1.34	1.67	1.86	1.78	2.15	2.32	2.90	2.47
Long-term debt : equity ratio	0.04	0.10	0.32	0.39	0.15	0.08	0.10	0.09	0.07	0.17	0.22
Profit margin	5.1%	4.4%	4.9%	5.5%	7.6%	7.9%	6.8%	7.0 %	6.4%	6.1%	6.8%
Return on equity	11.5%	9.1%	10.1%	13.6%	20.2%	19.9%	15.4%	15.7%	8.9%	10.8%	14.6%
Return on total assets	7.2%	5.5%	5.2%	6.7%	11.3%	12.0%	9.5%	9.9%	8.2%	6.6%	8.4%
Total asset turnover	143.0%	124.0%	107.0%	123.0%	149.0%	151.0%	139.0%	140.0%	129.0%	107.0%	123.0%
Gross profit margin	12.7%	11.1%	12.5%	12.7%	16.2%	16.2%	13.9%	14.5%	13.5%	13.2%	14.4%
Earning per share	$0.87	$0.76	$0.91	$1.41	$2.61	$3.13	$2.82	$3.34	$3. 00	$2.82	$3.99

Appendix 5: Board of Directors and Executive Management

To 1990

Board: Iverson, Aycock, Siegel, Vandekieft
Executive Office: Iverson, Aycock, Siegel

1990

Board: Iverson, Aycock, Cunningham, Siegel, Vandekieft
Executive Office: Iverson, Aycock, Siegel

1991 to 1994

Board: Iverson, Aycock, Siegel, Cunningham, Correnti
Executive Office: Iverson, Siegel, Correnti, Lisenby, Prichard

1995 to 1996

Board: Iverson, Aycock, Siegel, Cunningham, Correnti, Hlavacek

Executive Office: Iverson, Siegel, Correnti, Doherty, Prichard

1997

Board: Iverson, Aycock, Siegel, Cunningham, Correnti, Hlavacek
Executive Office: Iverson, Siegel, Correnti, Lisenby, Prichard

1998

Board: Aycock, Siegel, Correnti, Hlavacek, Browning, Gantt, Haynes
Executive Office: Aycock, Siegel, Correnti, Parrish, Rutkowski, Lisenby, Prichard

1999 to 2000

Board: Aycock, Siegel, Hlavacek, Browning, Gantt, Haynes
Executive Office: Aycock, Lisenby, DiMicco, Lott, Parrish, Rutkowski, Coblin, Prichard

Appendix 6: Biographies of Board Members and Executive Managers

H. David Aycock joined the predecessor to Nucor in 1962 when it bought the Vulcraft plant in Florence, South Carolina, where he was sales manager. He became the general manager at the Vulcraft plant in Nebraska in 1963. He was instrumental in building and operating the plant, and he also managed the Texas plant. In 1981 he became general manager of the Nucor steel plant in South Carolina. In 1985 he became president and chief operating officer. He retired in June 1991 but remained on the board. In October 1998, Mr. Aycock became chairman and, in June 1999, chief executive officer. In September 2000 he stepped down as Nucor's CEO and chairman of the Board of Directors. He retired from the board in 2001.

Peter C. Browning has been the president and chief executive officer of Sonoco Products Company and was senior officer in 1993. He was previously the president, chairman, and chief executive officer of National Gypsum Company. He was elected chairman of Nucor's Board of Directors in September 2000.

James W. Cunningham was a vice president of Nucor and general manager of the research chemicals division in Phoenix from 1966 until the division was sold in 1998. He died on September 15, 1998, at seventy-seven years of age.

Daniel R. DiMicco was executive vice president of Nucor-Yamato, Nucor Steel Hertford (plate division), and Nucor Building Systems before becoming president. He graduated from Brown University in 1972 with a bachelor of science in engineering, metallurgy, and materials science. He received a master's in metallurgy from the University of Pennsylvania in 1975. He was with Republic Steel in Cleveland as a research metallurgy and project leader until he joined Nucor in 1982 as plant metallurgist and manager of quality control for Nucor Steel in Utah. In 1988 he became melting and castings manager. In 1991 he became general manager of Nucor-Yamato and a vice president in 1992. In September 2000 he was elected president and chief executive officer of Nucor.

John A. Doherty served as vice president and engineering consultant at Nucor.

Harvey B. Gantt was a partner in Gantt Huberman Architects for more than twenty-five years. He also served as mayor of the city of Charlotte, North

Carolina, and was active in civic affairs. He was the first African American graduate of Clemson University. He joined Nucor's Board of Directors in 1998.

Victoria F. Haynes is the president of Research Triangle Institute in Chapel Hill, North Carolina. Until 2000, she was the chief technical officer of the B. F. Goodrich Co. and vice president of its advanced technology group. She started with Goodrich in 1992 as vice president of research and development. She joined Nucor's Board of Directors in 1998.

James D. Hlavacek is the managing director of Market Driven Management. Mr. Hlavacek was a neighbor and long-term friend of Mr. Iverson. He joined Nucor's Board of Directors in 1995.

Terry S. Lisenby is chief financial officer and an executive vice president of Nucor. He graduated from the University of North Carolina at Charlotte in 1976 with a bachelor of science in accounting. Mr. Lisenby held accounting and management positions with Seidman and Seidman, Harper Corporation of America, and Concept Development, Inc. He joined Nucor in September 1985 as manager of financial accounting. He became vice president and corporate controller in 1991 and assumed the role of chief financial officer on January 1, 2000.

Hamilton Lott, Jr., is executive vice president of the Vulcraft operations, cold-finished operations in Nebraska, and the Utah grinding ball plant. He graduated from the University of South Carolina in 1972 with a bachelor of science in engineering and then served in the United States Navy. He joined Nucor in 1975 as a design engineer at Florence. He later served as engineering manager and as sales manager of Nucor's Vulcraft division in Indiana. He was general manager of the Vulcraft division in Texas from 1987 to 1993 and general manager in Florence from 1993 to 1999. He became a vice president in 1988 and joined the Executive Office in 1999.

D. Michael Parrish is executive vice president for the four steel plants and Nucor Fastener. He graduated from the University of Toledo in 1975 with a bachelor of science in civil engineering. He joined Nucor in September 1975 as a design engineer for Vulcraft and became engineering manager at Vulcraft in 1981. In 1986 he moved to Alabama as manufacturing manager and in 1989 returned to Utah as vice president and general manager. In 1991 he took the top job with Nucor Steel Texas and in 1995 with Nucor Steel Arkansas. In January 1999 he moved into the corporate office as executive vice president.

Leroy C. Prichard is vice president, Steel Technologies, at Nucor.

Joseph A. Rutkowski is executive vice president of Nucor Steel in Indiana, Arkansas, Berkeley, and South Carolina and of Nucor Bearing Products. He graduated from Johns Hopkins University in 1976 with a bachelor of science in materials science engineering. He held metallurgical and management positions with Korf Lurgi Steeltec, North American Refractories, Georgetown Steel, and Bethlehem Steel. He joined Nucor in 1989 as manager of cold finish in Nebraska and became melting and casting manager in Utah before becoming vice president and general manager of Nucor Steel in Darlington in 1992. In 1998 he moved to Hertford as vice president and general manager to oversee the building of the new plate mill.

Richard N. Vandekieft is a former vice president of Nucor.

17 Digital Devices: Current and Future Market Opportunities

This case was prepared by Charles W. L. Hill, the University of Washington.

Introduction

The computer industry is now entering its third era.[1] The first era was characterized by the mainframe computer and was dominated by IBM with its proprietary hardware and software standards. The second era was characterized by the personal computer and was dominated by Microsoft with its proprietary software standards, MS-DOS and then Windows. The World Wide Web will characterize the third era of computing. The center of gravity in the vast computing and communications complex is now moving rapidly off the desktop and onto the Web. This shift is being driven by the emergence of web-based "killer applications" that deliver compelling value to users, including email, information retrieval and manipulation, and e-commerce and ebusiness applications. Many of these applications are still in their infancy, and there is the promise of continued rapid growth. For example, online sales in the United States, which reached $9 billion in 1998, are projected to reach anywhere from $75 billion to $147 billion by 2003, according to forecasts from a number of different firms.[2]

Unlike prior eras, it is unclear whether any one company will dominate this new era. Nor is it clear whether proprietary standards will play the central role in this era that they have in prior eras. After all, the key to the rapid growth of the Net has been the development of protocols that are in the public domain, such as TCP/IP, HTML, and XML, not proprietary standards. What does seem increasingly clear, however, is that in this new era users will be able to access and manipulate a vast amount of information and computing power that reside "out there" on the Web using a number of different digital devices in addition to the personal computer. These devices (often called information appliances) are characterized by specialized functionality, technological elegance, ergonomic simplicity, and low device costs (under $500). They include hand-held personal assistants; wireless phones with Internet functionality, including smart phones; web-enabled televisions; Internet-ready video game terminals; and web tablets. As with paradigm shifts in prior eras and other industries, the dominant enterprise in the personal computer era faces special challenges born of its prior dominance as it tries to overcome inertia forces and reposition itself to succeed in a world where the ground is shifting from under its feet and the rules are changing rapidly in ways that are only clear ex post facto. That enterprise, of course, is

This case is intended to be used as a basis for class discussion rather than as an illustration of either effective or ineffective handling of the situation. Reprinted by permission of Charles W. L. Hill.

Microsoft. The emergence of digital devices represents an important competitive arena in which many believe Microsoft must not only participate, but also win, if the company is to be successful going forward.

Technological Trends

The shift to the third era of computing is being facilitated by a number of technological trends that continue to increase the power of computing and drive down its cost, increase the supply and drive down the cost of communications bandwidth, and promise to provide persistent ubiquitous connectivity to the Web through wired and wireless conduits. These trends should ultimately allow individuals to access personal and business information anywhere anytime through any digital device and to draw upon the vast supply of computing power that resides remotely on the Web to manipulate that information and execute economic transactions.

Trends in computing power continue to be driven by the exponential logic of Moore's law. According to computer scientist, entrepreneur, author, and cyber poet Ray Kurzweil, if Moore's law persists for another ten years, a $1,000 personal computer will be able to perform about a trillion calculations a second, up from a "mere billion" today.[3] For sure, Moore's law will probably grind to a halt fifteen to twenty years from now because of the limitations placed on photolithographic technology by quantum physics and the physics of light. But by then, a $4,000 computing device in (1999) dollars will have approximately the same computational capability as the human brain (20 million billion calculations per second). Nor will progress in computing power stop when it becomes impossible to further shrink the geometry of features on a silicon chip. Before then, a new wave of computing devices based on molecular switches, photonic connections, DNA-based computing, and/or quantum computing principles will probably have replaced today's computing paradigm.[4]

But that's all in the future. For now, the point is that exponential progress will enable computer manufacturers to put significant computing power into very small devices within a few very years. When coupled with Internet connectivity, the exponential growth in computing power should be able to support business and consumer software applications that currently are beyond the reach not only of the desktop computer, but also of today's supercomputers, and that stretches our imagination. One example would be autonomous software agents or digital assistants that have the ability to recognize and communicate in natural language, learn from experience, and perform a variety of complex tasks for their owners. Another would be video conferencing using holographic three-dimensional (3D) technology, although for this to become a reality, massive increases in communications bandwidth would also be required; but then again, the supply of bandwidth is also increasing exponentially.

Advances in optical communications technology are driving forward the rapid increase in the supply of bandwidth, while simultaneously driving down the costs of that bandwidth. The speed of this advance is currently most evident in the fiber-optic core or backbone of telecommunications networks, where advances in laser technology coupled with the introduction of dense wave division multiplexing (DWDM) are generating rapid advances in the speed of data transmission. In 1999, the most powerful backbone system transmitted data at a rate of 10 gigabytes per second (a giga is a billion). In early 2000, Nortel Networks was marketing a 40-gigabyte-per-second system, capable of transmitting 90,000 volumes of an encyclopedia every second. By early 2002, Nortel plans to deploy a 6.4-terabit (trillion bit) system. If the current trajectory holds, bandwidth capacity will increase 200 times by 2004—and that may be just the beginning.[5]

Although this surge in bandwidth has yet to dramatically impact the experience of the average computer user, that too may change. Two impediments have limited the supply of bandwidth to end users— the last mile problem and the slow rate of wireless data transmission. The *last mile problem* refers to the inability of business and computer users to access high-bandwidth conduits (fiber-optic cables) at their offices and homes because of the high cost of building out such a network from its core to its periphery. While there is no immediate solution, the rollout of cable modems, DSL lines, and Internet links via satellite television receivers is now proceeding and will bring much faster access and download speeds to many small businesses and residences. More generally, fiber-optic connections are now included as a matter of course in new business construction, and developers are experimenting with the installation of fiber-optic outlets in new residential construction. As demand for bandwidth increases, over time we may see the emergence of all optical networks in which optical switching technology replaces today's electronic routers and most businesses and residences are linked by fiber or fiberless optical networks that rely upon shooting lasers through the air.[6] Such developments will make virtually limitless bandwidth available to the average user—even the residential user.

As for the slow rate of wireless data transmission, here too constraints are being pushed back. As that happens, the wireless Internet will become a technological and commercial reality. One key is the adoption of third-generation (or 3G) digital wireless networks that aim to increase data transmission rates from a paltry 9.5 K per second to a more respectable 2.5 M per second. DoCoMo is now rolling out the world's first 3G network in Japan. Europe should follow in 2002, and the United States, ever the laggard in wireless, sometime between 2003 and 2005.[7]

Although it is already possible to access information stored on the Internet through a wireless phone, the use of wireless phones as Internet terminals will be enhanced by the widespread adoption of another standard that is in the public domain, the emerging Wireless Application Protocol (WAP). Already endorsed by over eight hundred companies worldwide, WAP provides a common standard for developing web content for access by wireless-enabled digital devices with small screens, lower connection speeds, and less memory than a personal computer (PC). WAP is based on a programming language called Wireless Markup Language (WML) that is related to XML. Once companies produce versions of their web sites in WML, they can be accessed by anyone with a wireless-enabled digital device that uses WAP and a microbrowser. This is now beginning to untether much of the Internet, opening it up to the mobile user.

Another technology that feeds into the wireless Internet equation is Bluetooth. Named after a ninth-century Viking chief who united warring tribes, Bluetooth is a public communications protocol that seeks to enable a wide variety of digital devices to communicate with each other and exchange signals via radio waves. Although Bluetooth only works over short distances (no more than 100 feet), it will allow for seamless synchronization between an individual's personal digital devices—such as a smart phone, hand-held PC, and desktop PC—without the need for proprietary data synchronization software. Bluetooth is designed to be compatible with the WAP and

is currently supported by around one thousand companies, including all the major players in the computing and communications space.

Bluetooth may also help make the vision of ubiquitous computing proposed by the late Mark Weiser a reality. Before his untimely death in 1999, Weiser was the chief technologist at Xerox's Palo Alto Research Center. According to Weiser, the coming era of computing will be characterized by a profusion of inexpensive computers with which we will interact on an almost constant basis. Computers, in the form of special-purpose embedded processors, can already be found in watches, ovens, cars, wallets, and cell phones. Inevitably, these computers will become more pervasive, will talk to one another (via Bluetooth), and will form the invisible computational infrastructure of our lives. Ultimately, argued Weiser, "If your refrigerator watches you take the milk carton in and out every day, and if your refrigerator could talk to your wallet, then when you went to the store the wallet could tell the milk cartons that you need milk. And the milk cartons could then say to you, 'Hey buy me, you're out of milk.'"[8]

Some argue that another technological development needed if Weiser's vision is to become a reality is an overarching universal platform or distributed operating system that will allow the devices in a network to locate and work seamlessly with each other. Both Sun Microsystems and Microsoft are attempting to create such a system. Sun's prototype system is Jini, and Microsoft's is known as Universal Plug and Play (Upnp). Jini is the latest addition to Sun's Java vision. What Java aims to do for software Jini hopes to do for the machines that run it: provide a distributed operating system in which devices of every description can meet. Jini is about trying to create an architecture, a universal language, a set of super protocols—to knit together the emerging global computer and communications network and make everything work with, and be accessible by, everything else.[9]

The basic point of Jini is to simplify user interaction with the network. The key to Jini is Java's platform independence and its own innate ability to work over existing network software and protocols. As an extension of the Java code, along with the federation of Java Virtual Machines (JVMs), Jini becomes the universal language for disparate devices. The core of Jini's architecture lies in a "lookup service" knows as JavaSpace. The lookup service acts as an electronic bulletin board that monitors the devices attached to a network. So Java's ability to run on different computers, combined with the ability of Jini-enabled devices to send their own software code to the lookup service and receive instructions from other devices, is what gives a Jini network its potential magic.[10]

To consumers this means the ability to connect, power, and control through the network any appliance with an embedded processor, including hand-held devices, smart phones, set top boxes, and home thermostats. Once connected, the device announces itself to the network, indicates what it is there to do, and then carries out its task. On a corporate scale, Jini has potential for altering the way networks operate, without changing the underlying structure. Computing power would be distributed among devices connected to the computer, letting them share each other's resources. If Jini works, you will be able to sit with your laptop, and it will be able to reach out across the network; for the moments that you need the power, it will become the largest supercomputer in the world.[11] Instead of a platform designed to provide all capabilities in all cases, Jini provides only what is needed. And by using Java as the standard platform, you achieve interoperability. Basically, any device with a link to the network and a programmable ROM can be a network device with Jini.[12]

Microsoft's competing Universal Plug and Play platform was announced in June 1999. Upnp is based on the same open standards that underlie the Internet. To send commands among Upnp appliances, the software would use an in-house wired or wireless (e.g., Bluetooth) network. But like Jini, the software would tap into the Internet to perform more complex tasks. By mid June 2000, Sun reportedly had some 35 partners signed up to develop devices that are Jini-enabled, while Microsoft had about 125 partners working on products and technologies related to Upnp. However, neither company expects products to be commercially available for another twelve to eighteen months.[13]

So where is all this technology leading us? We cannot know for sure, but as science fiction writer William Gibson has pointed out, there is a sense in which the future is already with us; it's just unevenly distributed. Looking at current technological trends can help us discern the shape of things to come through the fog of our ignorance. Gazing dimly through the mist, what we think we see is a world where computing power and communications bandwidth are both abundant and inexpensive, where computational devices surround us, and where these devices talk effortlessly to each other through wired and wireless connections using protocols that are in the public domain, and perhaps a distributed software in a platform such as Jini or Upnp. This does not look like the proprietary segmented world of the mainframe and personal computer eras, but it is a world of infinite profit opportunities waiting to be discovered.

Digital Devices

The term *digital devices* (or *information appliances*) covers a wide range of different devices including hand-held personal digital assistants (PDAs), PC companions, wireless phones with Internet functionality, set top boxes, video game terminals, and web tablets. What these devices have in common right now is that they are all computers, they are not PCs, they are inexpensive (most are priced under $500), and they have mass market potential. Unlike the PC, which is a general-purpose machine, these various devices are specialized appliances designed specifically to perform certain tasks. Their specialized functionality is both their strength and their limitation. While they lack the flexibility of the PC, they are better suited to performing specific tasks, from playing videogames to managing personal information for people not tied permanently to a desk (which means just about everyone). If current trends are any guide, within a very short time most if not all of these devices will be able to access the Internet. Moreover, they should be able to communicate directly with each other using technologies such as Bluetooth. At that point they will become specialized appliances with general-purpose web-browsing capabilities.

Since the early 1980s, the personal computer has been the growth engine of the computer industry. Although some have predicted the demise of the PC, this seems highly unlikely. However, it is true that the growth rate is slowing down in more-developed markets such as the United States, where sales in the first half of 2000 increased at single-digit rates, compared to a 15 percent growth outside the United States. One of the reasons for this is that home penetration now exceeds 50 percent in the United States and business penetration is much higher (International Data Corporation pegged home penetration in the United States at 52 percent in mid 2000 and predicted that it would surpass 60 percent in 2001).[14] Although replacement demand for PCs is likely to remain robust, and although many homes may ultimately have several PCs, the high growth rates of the past seem less likely to continue.

Hand-Held Personal Digital Assistants

While the PC market is maturing, the growth rate of digital devices is accelerating rapidly. Take the hand-held personal digital assistants (PDAs), such as those produced by Palm, Handspring, and Microsoft. These devices are designed to perform basic information management functions associated with scheduling, address books, note taking, email, word processing, and expense tracking. Although there have been experiments with several different form factors—some with miniature keyboards (so-called PC companions) and some without—the form factor that seems to be dominating is the one pioneered by Palm with its original Palm Pilot, which is the essence of simplicity. The Palm Pilot was the brain child of Jeff Hawkins and Donna Dubinsky (who subsequently left Palm to found Handspring). Their vision was to produce a simple electronic device that would function as a calendar, an address book, a to-do list, and a memo writer. They believed that the main competitor for the Pilot would be paper, not computers. Accordingly, they tried hard to make the Pilot a model of simplicity. For example, looking up the day schedule is no more difficult than opening a date book: one push of a button and there it is. They succeeded beyond their expectations.

First introduced in 1996, within eighteen months over 1 million Palm Pilots were shipped. By 1999, some 2.3 million PDAs had been shipped in the United States. IDC projected U.S. sales of 3.6 million PDAs in 2000 and 9.7 million in 2004. The worldwide figure is expected to grow from 4 million PDAs in 2000 to over 17 million devices in 2004, while average selling prices will decline somewhat to $320 a unit. If this comes to pass, worldwide sales will rise from $1.6 billion in 1999 to $5.5 billion in 2004, representing an annual compound growth rate of over 24 percent (see Table 1 for sales forecasts).[15] Following the lead set by the introduction of the Palm VII in mid 1999, an increasing proportion of these PDAs will have wireless functionality and an ability to access the Web through microbrowser technology.

TABLE 1A

Worldwide Unit Sales Forecasts for Digital Devices, 1999–2004 (000)

	1999	2000	2001	2002	2003	2004
Internet-enabled game consoles	1,933	8,400	16,005	25,410	25,603	22,638
Internet-enabled TVs	6,117	13,992	18,334	19,336	18,736	17,808
Smart hand-held devices*	1,723	3,348	6,619	12,592	21,599	33,176

* Includes PDAs, PC companions, and smart wireless phones.

Source: IDC, Review and Forecast of Worldwide Information Appliance Market, 2000.

TABLE 1B

Worldwide Unit Sales Installed Base for Digital Devices, 1999–2004 (000)

	1999	2000	2001	2002	2003	2004
Internet-enabled game consoles	2,841	11,241	27,246	51,809	75,418	85,731
Internet-enabled TVs	10,131	23,564	40,208	56,901	70,888	81,291
Smart hand-held devices*	3,414	6,150	11,691	22,560	40,811	67,367

* Includes PDAs, PC companions, and smart wireless phones.

Source: IDC, Review and Forecast of Worldwide Information Appliance Market, 2000.

Wireless Phones

Projected growth rates for wireless phones that can access the Internet using WAP protocols are similarly dramatic and, significantly, involve much larger unit volumes. Right now there are some 550 million wireless subscribers in the world. Penetration is over 30 percent in the United States and between 30 and 50 percent across much of Europe and Japan. In Finland, close to 70 percent of the population now have cell phones. According to estimates from Nokia, by 2004 the number of wireless subscribers will approach 1.4 billion worldwide. Moreover, an increasing proportion of these wireless subscribers will be using phones that are Internet-enabled and that incorporate larger display screens and microbrowsers that can read WML-formatted web pages. Nokia forecasts that by 2004 some 600 million web-enabled wireless phones will have been sold, surpassing by 50 to 100 million the number of PCs connected to the Internet.[16] The leading edge of this movement can be seen in Japan, where NTT's DoCoMo started a persistent (always-on) wireless Internet phone service in February 1999. By mid 2000, DoCoMo had signed 10 million subscribers and competitors offering similar services had signed another 5 million, so that 12 percent of the Japanese population now has access to persistent wireless data connections. At this rate, soon more Japanese will have Internet connections through wireless phones than via PCs.

IDC forecasts a much smaller number of "smart phone" sales than Nokia, but it defined *smart phones* narrowly to include just those phones that not only have Internet microbrowser functionality but also include personal information management functions in the device (as in a PDA) that work when the phone is not connected to the network. Clearly, such devices will be very close substitutes for the wireless-enabled PDA like the Palm VII. According to IDC, worldwide shipments of the "smart phones" segment will grow from around 1 million units in 2000 to 21.6 million units in 2004 and will generate sales of $7.5 billion at an average selling price of $350.[17]

Videogame Consoles

Videogame consoles represent yet another specialized digital device that is rapidly becoming Internet-enabled. Some 40 percent of United States households already own a videogame console. Videogame players have shown a tendency to upgrade to more powerful machines every time a new generation of hardware comes along. The next generation of videogame consoles now arriving are designed for 128-bit games and include Sega's Dreamcast, Sony's Playstation II, Microsoft's X-Box, and Nintendo's Dolphin. All of these consoles will probably have web-browsing capabilities, since they were initially included to facilitate multiplayer gaming over the Internet. Users will also be able to download games, movies, and music onto their consoles, as well as use their consoles to browse the Web, send email, execute e-commerce transactions, and so on. These capabilities have led some to speculate that videogame terminals are a Trojan horse in the living room that might ultimately hit PC sales.[18]

Sony is the current market leader in the videogame space. The total videogame market is huge, generating $20 billion in worldwide sales annually and $7.1 billion in the United States. U.S. videogame sales are closing in on Hollywood film revenues, and the industry is growing faster than either the music or film business. Sony has sold some 77 million units of its PlayStation console worldwide. It introduced the PlayStation 2 console in Japan in March 2000 and shipped 1.41 million units in just two months.[19] According to IDC, 1.9 million Internet-enabled videogame consoles were shipped in 1999 (primarily the Sega Dreamcast), 8.4 million would be shipped in 2000 (the Dreamcast and PlayStation 2), and 22.6 million would be shipped by 2004 (see Table 1).[20] If the videogame manufacturers are successful in their attempt to broaden the market appeal of their equipment to include a larger proportion of adults, these figures could prove quite conservative.

Set Top Boxes

Another category of digital devices that has garnered significant attention is the web-enabled television category. In the short to medium term, most of the growth here will involve the purchase of set top boxes. Set top boxes can be used to decode and encode digital signals, thereby transforming a standard TV into a more powerful and interactive Internet-enabled device. Set top boxes are needed because the average TV lasts twelve to fifteen years. Such legacy equipment lacks digital capabilities necessary to access Internet media. In the long run, fully integrated digital TVs are expected to reduce the need for set top boxes.

Although the concept of interactive TV has been around for decades and companies have been talking about set top boxes and associated services for some years now, sales have been slow to pick up. In part, this is because the reality of interactive TV has often lagged behind the hype. Microsoft's Web TV, launched in 1996, is one of the more successful attempts to introduce interactive TV services and has more than 1 million subscribers, but by mid 2000 the venture still had not offered users full integration with Microsoft services such as email and instant chat. However, an improved version was scheduled to roll out in fall 2000 with the introduction of Web TV's Ultimate TV platform. More generally, several industry analysts believe that the set top box market is now ready for prime time. For example, Jupiter Communications forecasted that by 2004, 29 percent of U.S. households should have access to some form of interactive television and interactive TV services could generate some $10 billion in revenues.[21] Forrester saw an even quicker ramp up, with 25 percent of U.S. homes having an interactive TV service by 2002.[22] IDC forecasted that between 2000 and 2004 some 45 million set top boxes would be sold in the United States and 90 million would be sold worldwide (see Table 1).[23]

The catalysts for projected growth in the set top box arena include several new service offerings announced in 2000. For example, in mid 2000, AOL announced plans to launch an interactive TV service, AOLTV. Around the same time, Blockbuster Entertainment announced that it had teamed up with Enron to provide video-on-demand service to U.S. households using set top box technology. Under this agreement, Enron would encode and stream movies over its nationwide fiber-optic network and store them on servers at Blockbuster locations as well as near customers' houses. To provide the "last mile" of transport to customers, Enron and Blockbuster signed on as affiliates several providers of high-speed access, including SBC Communications, Qwest, and Covad.[24]

Other Categories

Although PDAs, web-enabled wireless phones and TVs, and videogame consoles are at the leading edge of the digital device revolution, they by no means constitute the full range of actual or potential devices. Other consumer devices include hand-held PC companions, auto PCs, and stand-alone web tablets or screen phones that offer Internet connectivity. So far, the most successful of these formats have been the hand-held PC companions. These compact clam shell devices come equipped with miniature keypads, versions of popular PC applications, and an ability to synchronize information with desktop PCs. However, sales of this category seem to have stalled, particularly in the United States, where shipments fell from 421,000 units in 1998 to a projected 235,000 units in 2000. Nor are things projected to get much better in the United States, where the category seems to be in danger of extinction. However, growth elsewhere, particularly in Europe, where Psion's PC companion offerings have a strong following, could lift worldwide unit sales from around 1 million in 2000 to 1.8 million by 2004.[25]

A number of vertical application devices used in business settings are also often included in the digital device category. Even though they are not mass market consumer devices, they share some features with consumer devices, including the utilization of similar operating systems, such as Windows CE, web functionality, and wireless capabilities. Such VADs include devices used to gather data from the field or in a mobile situation and transmit it to a central point. Familiar examples include the keypad-based handsets used by FedEx delivery and pickup drivers to collect tracking data for packages. Key- or pen-based vertical application devices are also used to collect inventory information from a warehouse, by physicians accessing patient records in a hospital, and so on. These specialized devices cost more than other digital devices—typically between $1,000 and $2,000 each. Worldwide unit sales are projected to grow from 2.25 million in 2000 to 4.66 million in 2004, representing $6.2 billion worth of potential revenues.[26]

Summary

Three points are worth emphasizing at this juncture. First, digital devices seem poised to emerge as a key *complement* to the personal computer. The PC is likely to retain its important role in the home and office, but increasingly consumers and businesses will also use other devises to manage their personal information and access the Web to gather and manipulate information, communicate, and perform economic transactions.

Second, in the consumer space at least, sales of digital devices will probably accelerate more rapidly than sales of PCs, with total shipments of such devices surpassing those of the PC by 2003. IDC projects shipments of PCs to consumers in the United States to grow from 16 million units in 1999 to 25 million units in 2003. Over the same time period, the combined U.S. unit sales to consumers of PDAs, set top boxes, Internet-ready videogame consoles, and smart phones (narrowly defined) are projected to rise from 3 million units in 1999 to around 30 million units in 2003 (see Figure 1).[27] If wireless phones with web-browsing capability are included in these figures, the gap becomes much greater, since many of the 130 million wireless service subscribers expected by then will own wireless phones with microbrowsers that can interpret WML-formatted web data.[28]

Third, in the digital device arena, no single form factor will dominate. If IDC's projections are anywhere close to the mark, there will be a worldwide installed base of some 270 million digital devices by the end of 2004, with Internet-ready game consoles, set top boxes, and a combined PDA/smart phone category, each accounting for roughly 30 percent of the total devices.[29] Again, it is important to emphasize that IDC does not include in its data web-enabled wireless phones that lack the personal information management functionality of smart phones. It is worth emphasizing yet again that Nokia forecasts that by 2004 some 600 million wireless phones will have been sold that contain some form of web functionality.

The Players

There are a large number of companies that play either directly or indirectly in the digital device space. The space itself can be broken down into several categories (see Figure 2), including hardware providers, operating system providers, application software providers, Internet service providers, and providers of Internet servers' software. The categories are broad and can be subdivided still further. For example, PDAs, wireless phones, set top boxes, videogame consoles, and vertical application devices are all subdivisions of the hardware category; operating system providers include providers of device operating systems, such as Palm with its Palm operating system (OS) and Microsoft with Windows CE, and providers of real-time operating systems for embedded microprocessors such as Wind River Systems; application providers include those producing applications aimed at the consumer space (such as Electronic Arts, which produces games that have online multiplayer functionality) and providers of business applications that can be accessed through Internet-enabled digital devices, be they wireless or wired (such as Microsoft, Oracle, SAP); and so on. Some companies play in just one segment. For example, Handspring is currently focused exclusively on the PDA space, while other companies play in multiple segments (such as Microsoft and Sony). Microsoft in particular is now participating in one form or another in all five major categories in the arena, making it the only company with such a broad spread of assets.

The remainder of this case focuses on just one segment of the device space illustrated in Figure 2: the operating system space. Moreover, it focuses on the providers of operating systems for relatively large consumer devices such as PDAs and smart phones (Palm, Microsoft, and Psion/Symbian), rather than providers of embedded real-time operating systems (Wind River Systems). It is important to keep the wider playing field in mind, however, when evaluating the strategy of companies competing in this space. Ultimately, an analysis of the wider arena should inform strategic decisions at the level of device operating systems.

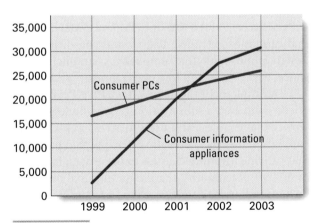

FIGURE 1

United States Sales of Consumer Personal Computers and Digital Devices, 1999–2003

Source: IDC Review and Forecast of Worldwide Information Appliance Market, 2000.

Note: Consumer information appliances include PDAs, PC companions, Internet-enabled TVs, Internet-enabled game consoles, and smart wireless phones.

FIGURE 2

Categories in the Digital Device Space

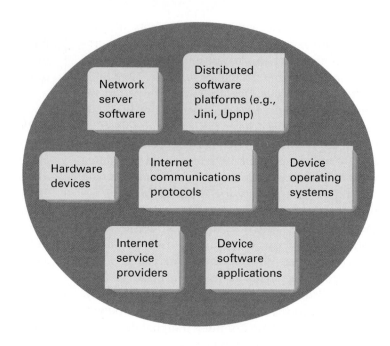

Palm

Palm began selling its pioneering Palm Pilot in 1996 when it was part of U.S. Robotics, which was acquired by 3Com in 1997.[30] Palm was subsequently spun out of 3Com in mid 2000 and now operates as an independent entity. Since the introduction of the Palm Pilot, Palm has emerged as the leader in the hand-held space. In 1999, Palm had a 66 percent share of the worldwide PDA market, and some 75 percent of the PDA's shipped worldwide used the Palm OS (Palm licenses its operating system to other vendors, which now include Handspring and Sony).[31] In the all-important United States market, Palm's lead was stronger still. Palm held 83.5 percent of the hand-held market in the United States in 1999, versus 9.8 percent for PDAs that utilized Microsoft's Windows CE operating system.[32] As of June 2000, Palm had sold over 7 million Palm devices worldwide and revenues had grown from around $1 million in 1995 to over $1 billion in 2000.

The appeal of the original Palm Pilot was based on a combination of functionality, simplicity, mobility, and an ability to synchronize data with a PC. Palm has tried to stay true to its original vision with its current PDA product line, which includes the Palm III, V, VII, and m100 product. The Palm VII comes with wireless capabilities, and the m100 is positioned as an entry-level device and is designed to appeal to a wide range of consumers. Prices range from $450 for the Palm VIIx to $150 for the entry-level m100. Most Palm models utilize monochrome screens—primarily to keep down power consumption—although the Palm IIIc comes with a color screen. Palm's PDAs run on low-speed (16–20 MHz) Motorola Dragon Ball microprocessors, again to keep power consumption down. The systems are shipped with between 2 and 8 MB of RAM and 2 MB of ROM that cannot be extended. Palm seems committed to a design philosophy that emphasizes simplicity, elegance, ease of use, and low power consumption.

To complement the Palm VII, in 1999 Palm introduced Palm.Net, a subscription-based wireless access service that enables Palm users to access web-clipping content on the Internet. Palm offers prepaid packages that provide for limited access to these data, for $9.99 or $24.99 per month (charging additional amounts for network usage in excess of the prepaid package). Unlimited access costs $44.99 a month. Using the Palm VII as a wireless-enabled Internet access device, Palm.Net subscribers can get stock quotes, read news clippings, check airline times, access online shops, and, increasingly, access enterprise data and applications. Palm.Net optimizes web data for display on Palm screens. Palm is also a supporter of the WAP.

Palm's stated strategy is to establish the Palm platform as the industry standard for hand-held devices.

The Palm platform consists of several key components. These include (1) the 16-bit operating system itself, (2) the user interface, (3) application programming interfaces that allow third-party developers to write applications that run on the Palm platform, (4) development tools, (5) HotSync data synchronization technology that allows the Palm to synchronize information with PCs or enterprise databases, (6) Graffiti script recognition technology that enables users to input data through a pen-based interface, and (7) web-clipping software that allows content providers to present, and users to receive, Internet and enterprise data in a format optimized for hand-held devices.

The Palm platform software code is designed to allow applications to run quickly and reliably and to minimize power, processing, and memory requirements without sacrificing performance. Palm designs separations between software layers, the underlying basic code or kernel, and the hardware reference design specific to the Palm devices. This means that the Palm platform can be broken into easily configurable components, allowing the Palm OS to run on a variety of different digital devices. Thus, in addition to the PDA form factor, elements of the Palm platform have been licensed to run on wireless phones, set top boxes, and vertical application devices.

In general, Palm seems committed to licensing its platform on a selective basis to other companies that make a wide range of digital devices. Symbol Technologies has licensed the Palm OS and has used it in a number of vertical application devices. Qualcomm has licensed the Palm OS and has used it in its pdQ digital smart phone. In late 1999, Palm announced a nonexclusive agreement with Nokia (the world's largest producer of wireless handsets) to work jointly on the development of wireless phones that use the Palm platform. Handspring licensed the Palm OS to run its own PDA offering, the Visor, a striking product developed by the inventors of the original Palm Pilot, Jeff Hawkins and Donna Dubinsky. In June 2000, Sony announced that it too would license the Palm OS to run its own line of hand-held PDAs, which were slated for market introduction in late 2000. Palm's decision to license its OS to competing manufacturers of PDAs is an interesting one and reflects the company's belief that it is more important to increase the total market for PDAs using the Palm OS than to monopolize the supply of those PDAs. It is worth noting that, after a slow start, Handspring's Visor seemed in 2000 to be gaining significant share from Palm in retail sales.[33]

Palm's early market lead and broad market adoption has helped to attract a large community of third-party developers who develop software applications that run on the Palm platform. Palm provides tools to this community to help them develop applications. As of June 2000, some 77,000 developers had registered to use Palm developer tools to create applications for the Palm platform, up from 5,000 in only eighteen months. Although Palm extracts no license revenue from these applications, the company believes that the spread of applications will further adoption of its platform and accordingly devotes considerable attention to nurturing third-party developers. Palm has also established a $150 million venture capital fund to invest in promising developers.

Palm sees the enterprise market as a significant opportunity. Most of Palm's devices have been used in professional settings, but historically they have been purchased by individual users rather than by corporations. The introduction of the Palm VII, with its ability to access enterprise data from remote locations, has considerably increased the value of the Palm platform from an enterprise perspective. Palm devices are now on the approved standards list of over three hundred companies, including eighty-nine *Fortune* 500 companies. To further the adoption of the Palm platform in corporate settings, Palm has established relationships with companies like Oracle, People Soft, Sap, Siebel, and Sybase to develop applications that provide access to enterprises databases using the Palm platform. For example, SAP's mobile R/3, introduced in mid 1998, runs on the Palm platform.[34] Similarly, in mid 1998, Oracle announced a partnership with Palm to integrate a 150-kbyte version of the Oracle Lite client database into Palm OS units. Oracle states that this integration will let Palm OS applications and data be replicated, synchronized, and shared with Oracle8 databases. However, most software companies are hedging their bets by developing applications for *both* the Palm OS and Windows CE platforms.

Microsoft

Microsoft competes in this space with its Windows CE operating system. Unlike Palm, Microsoft does not manufacture PDAs itself, but instead works with various computer companies who do, including

Hewlett Packard and Compaq. In April 2000, Microsoft introduced the third version of its operating system for digital devices, Windows CE 3.0. The prior versions had failed to garner significant sales. For example, in the PDA market, devices using the Windows CE OS slipped from 14.5 percent of the worldwide market in 1998 to 12.6 percent in 1999.[35]

Windows CE 3.0 is just part of Microsoft's offering in the device space. Windows NT Embedded, a derivative of Windows NT 4.0, is targeted at devices in the mid to high range of the spectrum that need a more powerful embedded operating system than Windows CE. These devices include office automation systems such as Xerox's Document Center Systems. In addition, the Microsoft Server Appliance Kit, an add-on to Windows 2000, enables development of server appliances based on Windows 2000 technology.[36]

Windows CE is a modular OS that can be configured for different devices. Version 3.0 includes an update of Microsoft's Platform Builder tool, which is used to configure the OS for each specific deployment environment. Using the Platform Builder technology, Microsoft contends that a build of the OS can range from as little as 300 KB to as much as 4 MB. The goal here is to enable an original equipment manufacturer to customized Windows CE to their particular device and application. For applications that can leverage it, Internet Explorer 4.0 is integrated with Windows CE 3.0 along with the Windows Media Player.

Compared to prior versions, Windows CE 3.0 also has improved real-time operating system (RTOS) capabilities. Potentially this extends the reach of Windows CE into a wide range of digital devices that need RTOS capabilities. These include manufacturing process controls, high-speed data acquisition devices, telecommunications switching equipment, medical monitoring equipment, aircraft "fly-by-wire" controls, and weapons delivery, space navigation and guidance, laboratory experiment control, automobile engine control, and robotics systems. While Microsoft's internal tests show that Windows CE 3.0 does now meet the minimum requirements for an RTOS, independent reviewers still believe that the response time of the OS is too slow for it to qualify as a true RTOS.[37]

Windows CE has been ported to twelve different processor architectures and 180 different CPUs. Unlike Palm's 16-bit OS, Windows CE is a 32-bit

operating system. Microsoft contends that without a 32-bit processor, the complex graphical interfaces for Internet-connected devices that it expects developers to create using Windows CE would not be possible. A definite attraction of CE is that developers can use Microsoft Windows development tools and Win 32 APIs to write applications. This leverages the skill base of the large Windows development community. It is estimated that some 5 million developers around the world are currently writing software for Windows. Thus, in theory there is a huge reservoir of talent out there ready to write software for Windows CE while programs for other Windows systems can be quickly modified for CE.[38] To further help a developer, included with Platform Builder is Embedded Visual Tools, a development environment analogous to the Visual Studio product in the general-purpose product line that can be used to build applications on top of Windows CE 3.0.

One of the first Windows CE 3.0 products to hit the market is the Pocket PC, a line of PDAs produced by Hewlett Packard and Compaq, among others. HP's Jornada 548 is at the top end of the range. Priced at $550, it comes with a color screen, a 133-MHz, 32-bit Hitatchi processor, 32 MB of RAM, and 16 MB of ROM. Storage space can be increased using flash memory cards. The battery life is estimated at eight hours. For comparison, the battery life of the Palm VII is several weeks. The Jornada is longer, thicker, and heavier than Palm models (9.1 ounces versus 6.7 ounces for the Palm VIIx).

Most reviews suggest that the Pocket PC is strong in areas where Palm machines are weak and vice versa. The Pocket PCs contain all of the basic PIM (Personal Information Management) functions that come with Palm's devices. In addition, they also let users play games and MP3 digital music files, record voice notes, and read electronic books using Microsoft's Reader that includes Microsoft's Clear Type font display. The Pocket PC will also display Microsoft Word and Excel files, and thus enable the user to open many email attachments. The handwriting recognition software is less demanding than Palm's Graffiti. The Pocket PC offers a fast USB connection to a desktop machine, and, with a modem attached, the Pocket PC can access an Internet standard or AOL email account and surf the Web using pocket Internet Explorer. The device is suited for applications that need SQL, SSL (Secure Sockets Layer) with 128-bit encryption, Windows network authentication and access, guaranteed asynchronous message delivery, or remote procedure calls.

Clearly, Microsoft and its partners are targeting users that need more from a PDA than a basic organizer and are prepared to pay a premium price for that additional functionality. On the downside, the Pocket PC is a bulkier machine with much shorter battery life and less elegance than the minimalist Palm and Handspring devices. For those who want just the basic PIM functions of the Palm, the Pocket PC may prove to be a hard sell. Despite this, most observers now believe that the Pocket PC offers the Palm OS its first credible challenge. IDC, for example, forecasts that with the arrival of Windows CE 3.0, Microsoft's share of the world PDA operating system market will grow from an estimated 18 percent in 2000 to 39 percent in 2004, while Palm's share will slip from 75 percent to 50 percent.[39] Like Palm, Microsoft is committed to licensing Windows CE 3.0 widely. Microsoft has been quietly working with a number of equipment manufacturers and service providers in an attempt to get its technology incorporated into smart phones. In June 2000, the company announced that it would join forces with Samsung to provide a version of Windows CE 3.0 as the OS for Samsung smart phones, along with Microsoft Mobile Explorer, a microbrowser for Internet and email access.[40] Ericsson has also agreed to adopt Mobile Explorer for use in some of its smart phones.[41] Microsoft has also entered into a joint venture with Qualcomm to develop wireless devices and services based on CE and Qualcomm's CDMA digital cellular technology.[42]

Microsoft is pushing Windows CE in the set top box arena. As part of a broad agreement that included a $5 billion investment by Microsoft, AT&T agreed to use Microsoft's Windows CE software in at least 2.5 million set top boxes. This is in addition to a 1998 deal with TCI (now owned by AT&T) to put Windows CE in 5 million set top boxes. However, both deals were nonexclusive, and AT&T has been at pains to indicate that it will also use competing software, such as the Java OS promoted by Sun Microsystems.[43] These nonexclusive agreements reflect one of the biggest fears of device manufacturers and suppliers of complement services, such as cable—namely, that Microsoft will dominate the digital device world in much the same way as it has dominated the PC world. If this were to occur, Microsoft could conceivably capture much of the economic value in the marketplace, leaving device manufacturers and service providers to compete with each other in a commodity world. In the words of TCI president Leo Hinderly, many device manufacturers and complement suppliers "don't want to be a Bill Gates download."[44] This fear adds momentum behind any offering that is perceived as helping to keep Microsoft's ambitions in check. In other words, there is something of a presumption in favor of non-Microsoft solutions on the part of many other participants in the digital device value chain.

More generally, some critics of Microsoft's strategy argue that the company's attempt to modularize Windows CE so that it can be used across a very wide range of devices will not work. A frequently heard argument is that the digital device arena lacks the same compelling need for standardization that Microsoft exploited in the PC arena.[45] The world of digital devices is far more fragmented than that of the PC, so the argument goes; hence standards are naturally less important. This view is reflected in the following quote from Jerry Fidler, CEO of Wind River Systems, whose VxWorks operating system kernel for embedded processors competes in some of the same space as Windows CE. Fidler noted, "It's going to be tough for Microsoft. This isn't a one-size-fits-all market. Applications are specific, not standard like they are in the PC world. This world is chaos."[46]

Psion/Symbian/EPOC

Psion is a British company that was an early leader in the market for hand-held PC companions (which, unlike PDAs, combine a small form factor and screen with a keyboard for data input). Its Series 5 machine was introduced in mid 1997, a full six months before similar devices utilizing Windows CE. The Series 5 was greeted with critical and popular acclaim, especially in Europe. The Series 5, which is a derivative of Psion's popular Series 3 machine, uses Psion's EPOC operating system and a novel and highly usable keyboard that offers far more than the tiny-buttoned keyboards usually associated with hand-held computers. The Psion Series 5 comes with a set of built-in applications that share data formats with popular Microsoft desktop applications. These include a Word-compatible word processor. Psion provides excellent desktop connectivity with Windows through its PsiWin product.[47]

Psion has followed up its successful Series 5 machine with a more powerful Series 7 machine that comes equipped with a modem and has web-browsing functionality. Although the PC companion category is declining in the United States, Psion's strong following in Europe has led to predictions that the category will continue to grow in Western Europe. Moreover, Psion is preparing to introduce a Palm-type PDA in 2001. Because of these factors, IDC believes that Psion's EPOC operating system will continue to be a player in the hand-held computer space (PDAs plus PC companions), accounting for 13.2 percent of worldwide operating system sales for the category in 2004, up from 7.5 percent in 2000 (see Table 2).[48]

It is in the smart phone category, however, that Psion's EPOC is poised for the greatest potential gain. In 1998, Psion pulled an ace out of the hole in the form of Symbian: a joint venture with cellular telephone giants Ericsson, Nokia, and Motorola. The objective of the venture was to adapt Psion's EPOC operating system as the OS for the next generation of smart wireless phones. Subsequently, Matsushita also joined the venture, and Sony has licensed EPOC technology from Symbian for its future smart phone ventures. Collectively, Psion's partners in Symbian and licensees account for more than 80 percent of the global sales of mobile phones. If their share holds and smart phone sales grow as predicted, Psion's EPOC could emerge not only as a significant competitor to Windows CE and the Palm OS, but also as the market leader in the smart phone category.[49] In 2000, IDC predicted that some 60 percent of all smart phones sold in 2004 would utilize an EPOC operating system (see Table 3).[50]

Symbian will license EPOC to all comers for a fee of around $5 to $10 per phone, which compares favorably to the $25 per unit that Microsoft reportedly charges to license CE.[51] Psion claims that EPOC is better suited than CE to cell phones, where long battery life and efficient use of memory are more important than links to a PC desktop. Be this as it may, there is no doubt that EPOC has another attraction to Psion's partners and any potential licensees— it is not a Microsoft product. This point has been underlined by Psion's founder, David Potter, who in outlining the thinking behind Symbian explained that "we looked at the cellular industry, an industry selling 100 million units a year, and asked: 'Are these guys really going to allow the mighty Bill to come in and take their businesses?' It's absolutely obvious that there is no way they are going to do that. We looked at their needs and said, 'Let's make these guys secure.'"[52] Building on this success, Potter has announced his intentions to license EPOC to other electronic hardware manufacturers, such as set top box manufacturers.

However, for all of its promise, Symbian has its detractors and problems. Not least of these is that its EPOC-based Quartz operating system for smart phones is not yet ready for market introduction. More seriously perhaps, Psion's partners in the Symbian venture seem to be hedging their bets. Nokia has also signed a deal with Palm to license the Palm platform, and Ericsson is licensing OS technology from Microsoft. Wireless phone vendors also seem to be developing some of their own software technology, albeit around the Quartz platform, in an attempt to create some unique value. These fractures in the Symbian alliance have prompted some high-level defections from the venture, including that of former Psion and Symbian executive Juha Christensen, who

---

TABLE 2

Worldwide Market Share Forecasts for Hand-Held Computers (PDAs and PC Companions) by Operating System, 1999–2004 (% share)

	1999	2000	2001	2002	2003	2004
Win CE (PC companions)	9.3	7.1	5.6	4.5	3.8	3.1
Win CE (PDAs)	10.0	15.1	20.9	26.5	31.0	34.8
EPOC	8.5	7.5	10.4	11.2	12.3	13.2
Palm OS	60.6	62.3	56.9	52.8	48.9	45.7
Other	11.7	7.9	6.1	5.0	4.0	3.2

Source: IDC Review and Forecast of Worldwide Information Appliance Market, 2000.

TABLE 3

Worldwide Smart Phone Market Share Forecasts by Operating System, 1999–2004 (% share)

	1999	2000	2001	2002	2003	2004
EPOC	0	11.5	50.5	55.7	57.1	59.4
Win CE	0	0	9.8	13.4	16.1	20.0
GEOS	94.8	50	0	0	0	0
Palm OS	2.3	35.6	37.1	28.7	25.0	19.1
Other	3.1	2.9	2.6	2.2	1.8	1.5

Source: IDC Review and Forecast of Worldwide Information Appliance Market, 2000.

left Symbian in March to join rival Microsoft.[53] As a consequence, the most that can be said at this juncture is that Symbian is still in the game with a shot at getting an EPOC-based operating system established as the dominant format in the smart phone arena, but that the probability of this occurring is lower than it was when the venture was established.

Key Strategic Issues

The competitive situation in the digital device arena is still unfolding daily. Huge uncertainties abound as to the future direction of the market. How will the technology evolve? What are the attributes of the technology required to facilitate this development? Will standards be important in the digital device arena, or in segments of that arena? What kind of products will be demanded by mass-market consumers, as opposed to technophiles? Where will the growth be? What product attributes in terms of form factors and functions will be required to drive forward expansions of demand? What is the correct technological, product development and competitive strategy for Microsoft to pursue in order for the company to help the market grow and to position itself to profit from that growth, irrespective of how critical uncertainties resolve themselves? How can Microsoft gain a major share in a market where not only competitors, but also suppliers of important complements, have a vested interest in seeing the company's market share bounded?

ENDNOTES

1. Perhaps the most compelling statement of this was made by the late Mark Weiser, chief technologist at Xerox PARC. See Elizabeth Wasserman, "Electronics Guru Predicts Ubiquitous Computing," *Arizona Republic*, January 19, 1998, p. E1; and Mark Weiser, "The Future of Ubiquitous Computing on Campus," *Communications of the ACM* 41(1), January 1998, p. 41.
2. Kevin Werbach, "Analysts Only Guessing at E-commerce Sales Figures," *Seattle Post Intelligencer*, December 9, 1999, p. C2.
3. Ray Kurzweil, *The Age of Spiritual Machines* (New York: Penguin, 1999).
4. Stan Williams, "The Computer of the Future," *Technology Review*, September–October 1999, pp. 92–96.
5. Stephen Pizzo, "The Race for Fiberspace," *Forbes ASAP*, August 21, 2000, p. 73.
6. See Peter Fairley, "The Microphotonics Revolution," *Technology Review*, July–August 2000, pp. 38–44; and Jeff Hecht, "Light Signals Direct," *Technology Review*, July–August 2000, p. 27. George Gilder sees the emergence of all optical networks, complete with optical switches, fiber in the home, and laser-based local networks, as an inevitable development: Eric Pfeiffer, "Gilder on Optics," *Forbes ASAP*, August 21, 2000, p. 97.
7. M. Hamblem, "3G Wireless," *Computerworld*, p. 63.
8. Wasserman, "Eletronics Guru," p. E1.
9. Kevin Kelly and Spencer Reiss, "One Huge Computer," *Wired*, August 1998.
10. Izarek Shopper, Net Watch: Sun Microsystems and Jini Architecture, October 1998.
11. Ibid.
12. Aaron Goldberg, "I Dream of Jini, and So Should You," *PC Week*, August 3, 1998.
13. Peter Loftus, "Apples and Oranges," *Wall Street Journal*, June 26, 2000, p. R28.
14. David Hamilton, "U.S. PC Sales Slowed During the Second Quarter," *Wall Street Journal*, July 24, 2000, p. A4.
15. Jill House, *Market Mayhem: The Smart Handheld Devices Market Forecast and Analysis* (IDC, 2000). Rex Crum, "Palm and Handspring: The Whole World in Their Hands?" *Upside Today*, August 18, 2000.
16. Jay Palmer, "Palmed Off," *Barron's*, February 28, 2000, pp. 31–34.
17. House, *Market Mayhem*.
18. Dean Takahashi, "Buying Decision, the Big Game: It's Sony Versus Sega Versus Nintendo Versus Microsoft," *Wall Street Journal*, June 26, 2000, p. R16.
19. Alex Pham, "Global Wars," *Boston Globe*, May 29, 2000, p. C1.
20. K. Hause, B. Ma, D. Hwang, and J. House, *Review and Forecast of the World Wide Information Appliance Market, 1999–2004* (IDC 2000).
21. A. E. Cha, "AOL to Meld TV and Internet Services," *Washington Post*, July 27, 2000, p. E1.
22. Mike Snider, "Your TV's Little Black Box Is Growing Up," *USA Today*, July 17, 2000, p. D3.

23. Hause et al., *Review and Forecast.*

24. Sallie Hofmeister, "Blockbuster in Pact with Enron to Offer Demanded Video," *Los Angeles Times,* July 20, 2000, p. C1.

25. House, *Market Mayhem.*

26. Ibid.

27. Hause et al., *Review and Forecast.*

28. C. Pottorf and C. Vyas, *U.S. Wireless Services and Devices Market Assessment, 1999–2004* (IDC, 2000).

29. Hause et al., *Review and Forecast.*

30. Much of the information in this section is derived from the June 2000 Palm 10K.

31. House, *Market Mayhem.*

32. Matt Hamblen, "Pocket PC May Help Microsoft Gain Handheld Market Share," *Computer World,* February 28, 2000.

33. Crum, "Palm and Handspring."

34. Richard Levin and Tom Davey, "Handhelds—Mobile Evolution," *Information Week,* June 15, 1998, p. 20.

35. House, *Market Mayhem.*

36. Al Gillen, *Windows as An Embedded OS: Where Does It Fit In?* (IDC, August 2000).

37. Ibid.

38. Jeff Jurvis, "Business Support Grows for Windows CE," *Information Week,* March 2, 1998.

39. House, *Market Mayhem.*

40. Pui-Wing Tam, "Microsoft, Samsung to Join on 'Smart Phones,'" *Wall Street Journal,* June 14, 2000, p. B6.

41. Matt Hamblen, "Microsoft, Ericsson Partner on Wireless," *Computerworld,* December 13, 1999, p. 30.

42. J. G. Spooner, "Alliance to Bolster CE," *PC Week,* November 9, 1998, p. 16.

43. Dave Bank and Din Clark, "Microsoft Windows Heads for TV Sets," *Wall Street Journal,* May 7, 1999, p. A3.

44. S. Hamm, "Microsoft's Future: A Band of Powerful Foes is Determined to Slow the Gates Juggernaut," *Business Week,* January 19, 1998, p. 58.

45. "Windows CE Falls Short," *Forrester Report* 5(1) May 1998.

46. E. W. Desmond, "Microsoft's Big Bet on Small Machines," *Fortune,* July 20, 1998, p. 86.

47. N. Clayton and S. Vogel, "Palmistry," *The Scotsman,* September 9, 1998, p. 8.

48. House, *Market Mayhem.*

49. C. P. Wallace, "The Man Bill Gates Fears Most," *Fortune,* November 23, 1998, p. 257.

50. House, *Market Mayhem.*

51. Dan Gillmor, "Formidable Force Aims at Microsoft," *San Jose Mercury News,* July 7, 1998, p. E1.

52. Wallace, "The Man Bill Gates Fears Most."

53. S. Baker and K. Capell, "So Much for This Microsoft Rival," *Business Week,* May 1, 2000, p. 66.

Treo: Handspring's Last Stand? 18

This case was prepared by Melissa A. Schilling, Chad Beaupierre, Scott Bevier, Roberto Ekesi, and Vicken Librarikian, New York University.

It was December 2001 and the cofounders of Handspring, Donna Dubinsky and Jeff Hawkins, were sitting on a plane on the way to the CTIA Wireless IT and Internet convention in Las Vegas. Dubinsky and Hawkins were about to unveil their latest product, the Treo Communicator, at the most-recognized trade show for wireless technologies. Unlike Handspring's previous personal digital assistant (PDA) offerings, this product was an integrated "smart phone" and represented Handspring's first attempt to enter the wireless communications market and a fundamental shift in corporate strategy.

Though Handspring was second only to Palm in the worldwide hand-held computer market share, it had yet to turn a profit. PDA price wars and slumping sales had decimated margins in the PDA industry and left producers with large quantities of rapidly obsolescing inventory. Economic conditions had forced Handspring to mark down even its more-advanced models. Facing increased economic pressures, a battered stock price, and increasing competition in the PDA market, Dubinsky and Hawkins were attempting to reinvent Hand-

spring as a leader in the smart phone market (see appendix 1 for an excerpt of a Handspring management discussion on repositioning the company). Smart phone shipments were expected to grow to almost 5 million units in 2002, amounting to $2.3 billion in sales.[1] Smart phones also had higher margins. However, entering the smart phone market also meant pitting the company against very large and established rivals such as Nokia, Samsung, and Ericsson. Could Handspring convince enterprises and individual consumers that it was the right company to deliver a competitive product in the wireless communications market? Would it be able to compete with competitors that had more experience and scale in the telecommunications market? If Handspring was able to successfully penetrate the smart phone market, would that be enough to turn the company's financial situation around?

Background

Handspring was cofounded in July 1998 by Jeff Hawkins and Donna Dubinsky. Hawkins was the original founder of Palm Computing, a company that made handwriting recognition software for PDAs. US Robotics acquired Palm in 1995, bringing badly needed capital to fund development costs, and in 1996 the company introduced the first generation of Palm Pilot PDAs. However, after 3Com acquired US Robotics in 1997, Hawkins and Dubinsky decided to leave the company and start a new venture that would produce PDAs based on the Palm operating system: Handspring.[2] They completed their core management team with Ed Colligan, another former 3Com employee who had been responsible for marketing the Palm PDA devices (see appendix 2 for a full management team description). They positioned Handspring to the public and investors as the same people doing the same thing, this time just better. The executive team's mantra was "Innovate, innovate, and innovate. Yet keep it small, simple, affordable, and connected."

Handspring entered the PDA market in mid 1999 with its Visor device. The Visor was priced lower than Palm's PDAs, and with its Springboard module contained more functions than Palm's devices. The module allowed the PDA to be expanded by inserting a range of components, such as mobile phones, digital cameras, pagers, modems, MP3 players, and additional software applications.[3] Handspring launched a global marketing program for its Visor and Springboard modules, selling through a variety of distribution channels that included the World Wide Web, value-added resellers, international distribution agencies, and retailers. Handspring's largest retailers were Best Buy, Staples, and CompUSA, which accounted for 14, 13, and 10 percent of sales, respectively. Competing primarily on design and price, the consumer segment was Handspring's primary target, while the business segment received only a secondary focus.

Before long it became apparent that the Springboard modules, initially praised by consumers and feared by competitors, were not going to revolutionize the PDA market. The Springboard modules never achieved strong market acceptance because they were expensive and could only make the Visor devices imitate, and not replace, other devices. This lack of a compelling differentiating factor, combined with an increasingly competitive PDA market, had moved Handspring into a very vulnerable competitive position. Since the fall of 2000, investors had seen Handspring's stock price drop from a high of $95 to as low as $1.20. By December 2001, Handspring's stock was trading at just over $6 a share. Facing increasingly difficult economic conditions and a third straight year of increasing operating losses (see Figures 1, 2, and 3 for Handspring's financials), Handspring had

to do something drastic. Though it had already made one foray into merging cell phone and PDA capabilities with the VisorPhone (a Springboard module that acted as a cell phone), that product had received a lukewarm welcome. The module was expensive, and the combination of the module and the PC was bulky and awkward. This time around the company decided to commit fully to the smart phone concept by introducing a product that would put phone capability and styling first, with PDA functionality second: the Treo.

The Treo is a single device that integrates the functionality of a cell phone, PDA, and pager with "always on" capability.[4] Unlike regular cell phones that have some organizer capabilities, smart phones such as the Treo had larger, sharper screens that could display regular web pages rather than the small subset of web pages designed to be readable on cell phone displays.[5] At its launch, it was heralded as the smart phone with the tightest integration of these functions and capabilities. Handspring was betting that it could establish the Treo as the future in handheld communications.

Treo Communicator

The Treo was designed to fit in the palm of one's hand and combined three existing products (cell phone, PDA, and pager) into one small package without compromising functionality or ease of use. It was the first product to come close to realizing the product concept inspired by Gene Roddenberry's *Star Trek*. The Treo was equipped with a dual-band Global System for Mobile Communications (GSM) world phone that would be upgradeable to GPRS (General Packet Radio Service) networks when they became more widely available. Handspring was also developing a version that would run on Sprint's third-generation Code Division Multiple Access (CDMA) networks.

The Treo did not have the Springboard module, but it did feature a display (available in monochrome sixteen-shade gray scale or color) that was only slightly smaller than the standard Handspring Visor display and that acted as a touch screen. Like the Motorola StarTac or Ericsson World Phone (or *Star Trek*'s tricorders, for that matter), the Treo had a flip cover protecting the display and keyboard area. It also came with either a keyboard or writing area (both models were offered to suit different customer prefer-

FIGURE 1

Balance Sheet

Handspring, Inc. Consolidated Balance Sheets (in thousands, except share and per share amounts)

	June 30, 2001	July 1, 2000
Assets		
Current assets		
Cash and cash equivalents	$ 87,580	$196,548
Short-term investments	33,943	—
Accounts receivable, net of allowance for doubtful accounts of $2,239 and $50 as of June 30, 2001, and July 1, 2000, respectively	12,850	20,484
Prepaid expenses and other current assets	19,473	1,776
Inventories	2,857	40
Total current assets	156,703	218,848
Long-term investments	80,237	2,664
Property and equipment, net	15,041	8,280
Intangibles and other assets	1,254	680
Total assets	**$253,235**	**$230,472**
Liabilities and Stockholders' Equity		
Current liabilities		
Accounts payable	$ 37,881	$ 20,152
Accrued liabilities	70,152	16,034
Total current liabilities	108,033	36,186
Long-term liabilities	—	57
Commitments and contingencies		
Stockholders' equity		
Preferred stock, $0.001 par value per share, 10,000,000 shares authorized; nil shares issued and outstanding at June 30, 2001, and July 1, 2000	—	—
Common stock, $0.001 par value per share, 1,000,000,000 shares authorized; 129,949,768 and 125,436,978 shares issued and outstanding at June 30, 2001, and July 1, 2000, respectively	130	125
Additional paid-in capital	368,166	321,116
Deferred stock compensation	(29,445)	(58,268)
Accumulated other comprehensive income (loss)	994	(64)
Accumulated deficit	(194,643)	(68,680)
Total stockholders' equity	145,202	194,229
Total liabilities and stockholders' equity	**$253,235**	**$230,472**

Source: Handspring 10K, June 30, 2001.

ences), a built-in microphone, and an infrared port. It measured 4.3 inches by 2.7 inches by 0.7 inches and weighed only 5.2 ounces. Like other Handspring products, the backbone of the Treo was the Palm operating system. The Treo featured a 33-MHz Motorola Dragonball processor, 16 megabytes of memory, and a rechargeable Lithium Ion battery.

When the Treo model with the monochrome display was purchased with a one-year wireless service contract, the device sold for $399, but as a stand-alone product it was priced at $599 (prices were higher for color displays). To encourage existing Visor users to upgrade to the Treo, Handspring offered a $100 rebate to Treo customers who sent in the serial numbers from their Visors. Existing Visor users were a primary target for the Treo, since one of its key points of differentiation from other smart phones was the option to use the Graffiti handwriting recognition software used on Visor PDAs.

The communicator was fully integrated with the built-in Phone Book, allowing one to dial directly from the contact list. Moreover, the Treo had a

FIGURE 2

Statement of Operations

Handspring, Inc. Consolidated Statements of Operations (in thousands, except per share amounts)

	Year Ended June 30, 2001	Year Ended July 1, 2000	Period from July 29, 1998 (date of inception) to June 30, 1999
Revenue	$ 370,943	$101,937	$ —
Costs and operating expenses			
Cost of revenue	292,311	69,921	—
Research and development	23,603	10,281	2,738
Selling, general and administrative	145,132	42,424	2,451
In-process research and development	12,225	—	—
Amortization of deferred stock compensation and intangibles(*)	32,830	40,077	3,646
Total costs and operating expenses	506,101	162,703	8,835
Loss from operations	(135,158)	(60,766)	(8,835)
Interest and other income, net	12,195	675	446
Loss before taxes	(122,963)	(60,091)	(8,389)
Income tax provision	3,000	200	—
Net loss	**$ (125,963)**	**$ (60,291)**	**$ (8,389)**
Basic and diluted net loss per share	**$ (1.21)**	**$ (1.77)**	**$ (0.71)**
Shares used in calculating basic and diluted net loss per share	**103,896**	**34,015**	**11.772**
(*) Amortization of deferred stock compensation and intangibles			
Cost of revenue	$ 4,521	$ 5,904	$ 526
Research and development	6,926	8,059	1,217
Selling, general and administrative	21,383	26,114	1,903
	$ 32,830	$ 40,077	$ 3,646

Source: Handspring 10K, June 30, 2001.

speaker phone and was compatible with several external headset options. The Treo also possessed common PDA features such as Date Book Plus, Phone Book, To Do List, and Memo Pad, and it allowed its user to organize short-term and long-term schedules. The Treo's paging capabilities enabled users to send and receive email and short SMS text messages from virtually any location. Importantly, the Treo provided web access to its users using Handspring's "Blazer" wireless web browser. To go online, a user had only to push a button and the Treo would connect automatically. It could bookmark up to one hundred web sites and run a wide range of applications, such as one that provided maps of the New York City subway system or a program that translated between English, French, Spanish, German, and Italian. It could transfer data from various other Palm OS devices, and it could even run

applications that were not developed to run on the Palm OS.

Some analysts observed that Handspring's advantage might be that adding voice capabilities to a PDA would be simpler and more effective than adding PDA capabilities to a phone. John Troyer, chief strategy officer at Neomar, remarked, "I think it's a lot easier to put voice into a PDA than it is to jam a PDA into a phone. I think we're seeing the result of that." Critics were quick to point out, however, that the Treo's battery life was subpar, with only 2.5 hours of talk time. Additionally, though the Blazer browser had earned accolades, surfing the Web using GSM was "agonizingly slow," and thus web-surfing functionality was unlikely to become a particularly valuable feature until GPRS network upgrades became available.[6] Furthermore, though the email system shipped with the Treo at its launch was adequate for

FIGURE 3

Statement of Cash Flows

Handspring, Inc. Consolidated Statements of Cash Flows (in thousands)

	Year Ended June 30, 2001	Year Ended July 1, 2000	Period from July 29, 1998 (date of inception) to June 30, 1999
Cash flows from operating activities			
Net loss	$(125,963)	$ (60,291)	$ (8,389)
Adjustments to reconcile net loss to net cash used in operating activities			
Depreciation and amortization	7,104	2,668	70
Amortization of deferred stock compensation and intangibles	32,830	40,077	3,646
In-process research and development	12,225	—	—
Write-off of excess and obsolete inventories	26,811	—	—
Charitable contribution of common stock	—	900	—
Amortization of costs associated with financing agreement	—	568	31
Amortization of premium or discount on available-for-sale securities, net	(1,313)	(118)	(108)
Gain on sale of available-for-sale securities	(277)	—	—
Stock compensation to non-employees	—	815	15
Changes in assets and liabilities			
Accounts receivable	6,625	(20,484)	—
Prepaid expenses and other current assets	(18,219)	(1,751)	(48)
Inventories	(10,011)	(40)	—
Intangibles and other assets	(40)	(616)	(64)
Accounts payable	18,701	18,944	884
Accrued liabilities	34,584	15,941	67
Net cash used in operating activities	**(16,943)**	**(3,387)**	**(3,896)**
Cash flows from investing activities			
Purchases of available-for-sale securities	(244,972)	(4,474)	(10,965)
Sales and maturities of available-for-sale securities	186,866	10,424	4,833
Purchases of investments for collateral on operating leases	(51,287)	(2,106)	(150)
Purchases of property and equipment	(14,283)	(9,818)	(780)
Cash acquired from acquisition	29	—	—
Net cash used in investing activities	**(123,647)**	**(5,974)**	**(7,062)**
Cash flows from financing activities			
Proceeds from borrowings	—	6,000	—
Principal payments on borrowings	(83)	(6,000)	—
Issuance of redeemable convertible preferred stock, net	—	11,490	17,972
Net proceeds from initial public offering and exercise of underwriters' overallotment	27,969	184,928	—
Proceeds from issuance of common stock	3,109	2,012	519
Repurchase of common stock	(41)	—	—
Net cash provided by financing activities	**30,954**	**198,430**	**18,491**
Effect of exchange rate changes on cash	668	(54)	—
Net increase (decrease) in cash and cash equivalents	(108,968)	189,015	7,533
Cash and cash equivalents			
Beginning of period	196,548	7,533	—
End of period	**$ 87,580**	**$196,548**	**$ 7,533**
Supplemental disclosure of cash flow information			
Cash paid for interest	$ 6	$ 37	$ 1
Cash paid for taxes	$ 236	$ 1	$ 1

Source: Handspring 10K, June 30, 2001.

individual consumers, it lacked the security required by corporate users; thus third-party software was initially required for corporate customers. However, Handspring later joined forces with Visto, a leading provider of web-based email and synchronization services, to develop a software program ("Treo Mail") that would bring wireless email from any Microsoft Exchange or standard Internet account, thus meeting the needs of most mobile executives.[7]

Repositioning Handspring

"The theme for the company is Treo."

—*Ed Colligan, Chief Operating Officer, Handspring*

Treo represented more than just an additional product in Handspring's portfolio—Handspring was "betting the farm" on the success of the new device. As stated by CEO Donna Dubinsky, Handspring would be "transitioning out of the organizer business and into the communicator business."[8] Handspring would continue to support the Visor so long as there was demand, but it would direct all of its development and promotion effort toward the communicator. Some analysts wondered why Handspring would abandon the Visor platform, risking alienating third-party developers for the platform and rendering all Springboard development and inventory obsolete.[9]

Treo also represented a shift in market focus for Handspring. Though individual consumers would still be targeted, the Treo would be targeted primarily at the enterprise market. Management believed the integration of phone, PDA, and pager made the Treo an appealing corporate productivity tool and that the growth potential in the business-to-business (B2B) market was greater than that in the business-to-consumer (B2C) market. At a major corporate software convention in Las Vegas, Ed Colligan stated, "We believe that this is a really compelling enterprise device for wireless voice and data. I think as we build critical mass in the enterprise with the Treo, you'll see more applications. It takes a breakthrough device to get developers going."

To attract share in the enterprise market, the product would require great breadth in available software applications and supporting tools. To ensure that a wide range of applications for the device would be available, Handspring formed several comarketing agreements with software companies that had already

developed widely used applications for Visor and Palm PDAs and cell phones, to produce applications for a myriad of purposes like personal use (email, maps, browsers), business use (groupware, sales force automation, CRM, spreadsheets), and entertainment (games, pictures, personal rings).

Handspring marketed and distributed the Treo to both consumers and businesses through various channels, including retail and online stores as well as B2B agreements. For example, Handspring formed sales and marketing relationships with Neomar and Infowave whereby the companies would jointly promote Handspring's Treo and their wireless data access platforms. In addition to its own direct sales, Handspring appointed the major wholesaler Ingram Micro to focus on the enterprise market, and D&H Distributing to promote its products on college campuses.

Because the Treo was the company's first cell phone–based product offering, GSM wireless service providers had become a new and significant retail channel. The company formed partnerships with Cingular Wireless and Voicestream to sell the Treo with wireless service plans. To unlock global markets, Handspring also established similar deals with foreign wireless networks in Europe and Asia. For example, Handspring formed a strategic distribution agreement with APE Telecom, one of Sweden's leading producers of mobile communication products, to cover the marketing and distribution of the Handspring Treo to the Swedish market.

Internal Development

Handspring's products were designed by its internal engineering, marketing, and manufacturing organizations. Technologies required to support product development were either created internally or licensed from external providers. Its internal staff included engineers from many disciplines—software architects, electrical engineers, mechanical engineers, radio specialists, user interface design specialists, and others. Once a project was approved, a cross-functional team was assembled to design the product and transition it into manufacturing. To develop innovative products while minimizing time to market, the company used parallel development teams working on multiple projects. Before products were released into production, they had to pass a series of quality benchmarks and manufacturing guidelines.

Handspring's research and development expenditures in 2001 totaled $23.6 million, up from

$10.3 million in 2000 and $2.7 million in 1999. As of August 31, 2001, it had ninety-three people engaged in research and development activities, and it planned to focus its development efforts on wireless communicators.[10]

Supply-Chain Management

Though design, marketing and sales were conducted primarily in-house, Handspring was the quintessential outsourcer when it came to manufacturing and service. External parties handled manufacturing and assembly, customer and technical support, and repair services. All production of the Visor hand-held computers had been outsourced to Flextronics and Solectron. Visor phones had been built in partnership with Option International of Leuven, Belgium. Motorola provided microprocessors, Wavecom supplied the Treo with its integrated dual-band GSM radio module for wireless voice and data communications, and Acura Tech Ltd. supplied connector systems. Several components (such as the microprocessors) were available only from a single source.

Outsourcing components and manufacturing enabled Handspring to focus on its core competencies and helped to minimize inventory levels. Handspring's supply-chain management techniques backfired, however, when component shortages delayed the Treo's introduction in the United States and prompted the company to lower its production targets.[11] Handspring consequently decided to route most of its early production to Europe, where the GSM standard is more widespread and customers are considered to be more ready for smart phones.[12]

Choosing Sides in Standards Battles

The developers of the Treo had to place bets on who would win in two separate standards battles: operating systems for hand-held computers, and wireless telecommunication standards for mobile phones. The Palm operating system (OS) was an obvious choice given Handspring's history. It also held a commanding 77 percent worldwide market share at the end of 1999, and though estimates indicated that the share declined to 66 percent by the end of 2001, that still represented a significant lead over the next leading contender, Microsoft's Windows CE. However, forecasts for future trends in hand-held operating systems were troubling. Microsoft's share was predicted to gain significantly, mostly at the expense of the Palm OS share (see Figure 4 for worldwide hand-held operating system shares).

In the wireless telecommunications standards battles, Treo had put its money on the Global System for Mobile Communications (GSM). The Treo utilized GSM technology on two bands—900/1,900 MHz in North America, and 900/1,800 MHz in Asia

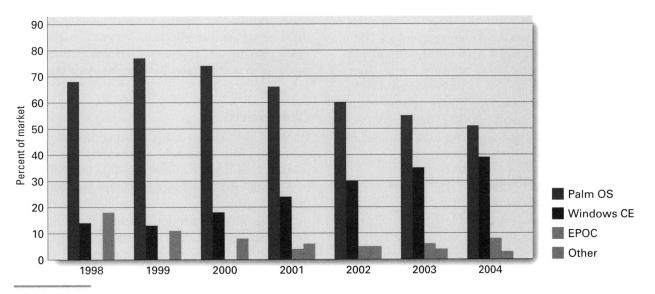

FIGURE 4

Worldwide Hand-Held Operating System Shares for 1998 and 1999, and Forecasts for 2000 to 2004

Source: Salomon Smith Barney, October 18, 2000.

and Europe.[13] Though GSM was the dominant standard globally, in the United States a wireless telecom standards battle was still unfolding. Following deregulation of the telecommunications industry in 1996, several national wireless networks had emerged (such as Cingular, Verizon, VoiceStream, Sprint PCS, and AT&T wireless), and industry players supported different digital voice wireless platforms. Of these platforms, the GSM served as the leading format for second-generation wireless communications with the largest worldwide installed base by 2000 (for an explanation of the various generations of wireless telecommunications service, see Exhibit 1).

GSM was developed in the 1980s to set a common standard for digital wireless voice communication in Europe as European markets began to unify.[14] However, by March 1999 all three of the largest wireless handset makers—Ericsson, Motorola, and Nokia—were also manufacturing wireless phones based on Qualcomm's Code Division Multiple Access (CDMA) second-generation (2G) wireless format.[15] Twenty-five percent of worldwide wireless subscribers were forecasted to have adopted CDMA technology by the end of 2002, making it the second most widely used 2G format.[16] The third most prevalent wireless platform technology, TDMA, was developed by AT&T. It was used primarily in North America and accounted for 9 percent of worldwide cellular subscribers in 2000. Most network system providers, like Ericsson, produced networks for all types of leading network technologies.

Globally, GSM was the dominant standard, and it was also better positioned for the transition to 2.5G and 3G GPRS service. However, in the United States in 2001, GSM only had an 11 percent market share; most U.S. wireless service providers adhered to the CDMA or TDMA standards. The Treo would thus function seamlessly in Europe and Asia, but coverage in the United States would be spotty.

Building a Web of Alliances

To ensure that the Treo would have a wide range of high-quality applications available for it, Handspring built a web of alliances with third-party software developers. In addition to the relationship with Visto described previously, Handspring also teamed with several leading wireless solution providers (including Aether Systems, Infowave, Neomar, Synchrologic, Wireless Knowledge, and others) to ensure that

email delivery would be secure. Handspring forged a relationship with Avantgo for its Internet ability, and with Pumatech for desktop synchronization.

Handspring also established marketing agreements with several other key software developers. It teamed with Extended Systems Inc. to comarket the Treo and other Handspring products with the latter's Xtnd Connect Server, which enabled wireless synchronization between corporate servers and hand-held devices. Handspring partnered with Synchrologic Inc. to market the Treo and other devices with Synchrologic's iMobile Suite software, which allowed wireless access to groupware, sales force automation, and customer relationship management data.

Handspring and Handango combined forces to build two online software stores. One store would be dedicated to individual consumers, while the other store would be dedicated to businesses. The stores would sell products ranging from productivity-enhancing software to games. In addition, each company would actively market the other's products via its company web sites, newsletters, and other media. Handspring also allied with Brightpoint, a large distributor of mobile phones, to distribute the Treo and provide integrated logistics services for the device.[17]

One of Handspring's most important alliance relationships was with Palm. Handspring had entered into a nonexclusive licensing agreement with Palm to use the Palm operating system. This agreement did not expire until the end of 2009, but because of its nonexclusive clause, Handspring would be able to migrate the Treo to another operating system if market demand warranted this. Given the dynamic nature of the marketplace, keeping the Treo flexible was a priority.

Competition

Handspring would be facing an expanded set of competitors in the hand-held communication devices market. It would be competing in a head-to-head battle with established mobile phone manufacturers to obtain market share. In spring of 2002, the global market share leaders in hand-held communications devices were Nokia, Motorola, Ericsson, and Samsung (see Figure 5 for comparative market shares). Whereas the market for mobile phones was mature, the smart phone market was relatively new and growing, and it was expected to attract the attention of most of the major mobile phone manufacturers. In

EXHIBIT 1

Three Generations of Wireless Telecommunications

Original cellular networks (now referred to as first generation) supported only analog voice communication. However, in the 1990s, the second generation (2G) of wireless communication emerged that supported voice and text transmission over digital networks.

2G Wireless. In 2G wireless communications, calls were established using an exclusive circuit so that the connection was lost as soon as such a call was ended. Networks were capable of handling only a certain number of such "circuit-switched" calls.

The 2G wireless industry underwent rapid change in the 1990s. The 1996 Telecommunications Act unleashed rapid increases in competition in the wireless industry, and several national wireless service providers emerged in the United States, including AT&T Wireless, Sprint PCS, Nextel Communications, Verizon Wireless, Cingular Wireless, and VoiceStream Wireless. On a global scale NTT DoCoMo, Vodafone, Telecom Italia, and France Telecom all emerged as leading wireless service providers. Additionally, many smaller carriers emerged in the industry to gain over 17 percent of the wireless market. With the increase in competition, pricing for voice wireless service fell to its most "attractive" prices ever, drawing more users to wireless phones. At the same time, revenue per subscriber had been declining in many countries, like the United States, due to the lingering effects of deregulation as the price of wireless services continued to fall. This shift toward marginal pricing as the wireless voice market matured drove wireless companies to continue differentiating their products through development of new technology. One of the primary areas targeted was the development of networks that would enable broadband Internet access. In the late 1990s, wireless service providers began planning to upgrade their existing networks and to build new wireless transmission systems to incorporate these new wireless technologies. To support the data needs of broadband wireless, networks needed to be updated to "packet-switching networks" that would allow a continuous connection for wireless users to send and receive data at any time.[18]

2.5G Wireless: The Bridge to the Future. Before entirely new 3G wireless systems were installed worldwide to support the needs of emerging wireless technology, many network providers planned to update existing networks to support packet-switching technology that would provide an "always-on" continuous connection, but at slower speeds than would be possible with 3G networks. These "bridging technologies" were known as 2.5G systems because they relied upon equipment from existing 2G networks. CDMA technology proved to be an initial leader in the move to 2.5G systems because the core CDMA technology was already based on an underlying packet-switching technology, requiring only a system upgrade. To upgrade GSM networks, General Packet Radio Service (GPRS) technology was planned to allow handsets an always-on connection by upgrading existing signals.

Most wireless companies saw 2.5G technologies only as a stepping stone to 3G, since 3G systems would ultimately be cheaper to operate and would offer data connection speeds up to ten times faster than 2.5G networks. However, as some industry researchers pointed out, 2.5G phones could "steal 3G's thunder" if users resisted 3G technology in favor of lower usage costs of 2.5G systems, thereby forestalling 3G indefinitely.[19] One of the first operational 2.5G wireless packet transmission networks was NTT DoCoMo's i-mode network that became operational in February 1999. By March 2000, the network, which ran on TDMA technology, had already achieved close to 21 million subscribers.[20]

Planning for 3G Wireless. By 2001 all major wireless manufacturers were active in the development of 3G wireless technologies, and planning had begun for installation of 3G wireless networks across the globe. These new networks would be able to fully support the broadband data needs of emerging wireless technologies, while providing a continuous connection to the wireless Internet.

As 3G wireless systems, based on new frequencies from their 2G predecessors, became closer to a reality, multinational wireless companies worked to band together to ensure compatibility among different 3G systems. By 2001, twenty-seven wireless service providers and vendors, including handset manufacturers Ericsson, Motorola, and Nokia, had joined together to form the 3G.IP group, focused on promoting a common IP-based wireless system for 3G mobile communications technology while ensuring rapid standards development. 3G.IP focused on 3G development using wireless CDMA technology that has CDMA technology at its core, but that could easily be added to the existing global GSM core network.[21] Wireless CDMA appeared to be a leading platform among competing 3G wireless technologies, although no clear standard had yet emerged by early 2001.

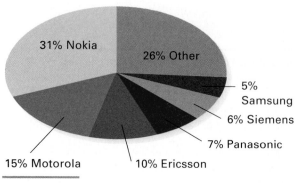

FIGURE 5

Worldwide Wireless Telecommunications
Market Share in 2001

Source: **www.cellular.co.za.**

fact, Nokia, Samsung, and Kyocera already had smart phones available on the market.

The three smart phones that offered the most direct competition for the Treo were the Kyocera QCP 6035, the Samsung SPH-1300, and the Nokia 9290. The functionality provided by each of these phones was nearly identical, offering few opportunities for differentiating the products to consumers. The major differences between the models were in size and weight, with the Treo being the smallest and lightest. It was 11 percent smaller and lighter than Samsung's SPH-I300, 35 percent lighter and 60 percent smaller than the Kyocera QCP 6035, and 20 percent lighter and 35 percent smaller than the Nokia 9290. Handspring hoped that the compact design would prove to be a critical factor in mobile phone purchases. The various models also differed in the included accessories, protective covers, and input methods, where a clear winning approach was not yet evident.

Because it was being heavily marketed as an employee productivity tool for the enterprise, the Treo would also be in competition with PDAs. It would be in most direct competition with products such as the Palm Pilot i705 and the RIM Blackberry 5810, which provided wireless connectivity. Though not nearly as large as the mobile phone competitors, Palm and RIM were both well-recognized and established competitors in the PDA market.

Both of these PDAs offered "always-on" connectivity, though the Palm i705 did not offer voice capability and thus was not truly a mobile phone. RIM's Blackberry 5810's phone capability was available only through an integrated headset jack. The device was priced at $499 and was lighter (but larger) than the Treo, and like the Treo it used the GSM network but did not operate in Europe (a different model, the 5820, was required for use in Europe).[22]

The Future

Handspring shipped 47,000 units of the Treo in the first quarter of 2002, and Wall Street responded warmly, pushing Handspring's stock price up to 34 percent. But both Dubinsky and Hawkins knew that the Treo would be a key inflection point in Handspring's history. Like many young start-ups, Handspring still had not achieved profitability, and the patience of the investing public was wearing thin. The company desperately wanted to avoid the recent fate of many other bankrupt technology companies. Would Handspring have the resources necessary to battle giants like Nokia and Samsung? Would Handspring be able to effectively penetrate the enterprise market, and would this market shift pay off? Would the higher margins of smart phones rescue the company from its financial woes, or were smart phones destined for the same heavy price cutting that had afflicted PDAs? The company had made a serious gamble, and now all eyes were watching to see how the relatively new company would fare in the high-stakes battle to secure the next dominant design in personal computing and communicating technology.

Appendix 1: Excerpt from Management Discussion in Handspring 2001 10K

If we are unable to compete effectively with existing or new competitors, our resulting loss of competitive position could result in price reductions, fewer customer orders, reduced margins, and loss of market share.

The market for hand-held computing and wireless communication products is highly competitive, and we expect competition to increase in the future. Some of our competitors or potential competitors have significantly greater financial, technical, amd marketing resources than we do. These competitors may be able to respond more rapidly than we can to new or emerging technologies or changes in customer requirements. They may also devote greater resources to the development, promotion, and sale of the products than we do.

Our products compete with a variety of hand-held devices, including keyboard-based devices, sub-notebook computers, smart phones, and two-way pagers. Our principal competitors, and possible new competitors, include:

- Palm, from whom we license our operating system;

- licensees of the Microsoft's PocketPC operating system for hand-held devices such as Casio, Compaq, and Hewlett-Packard;

- licensees of Symbian EPOCH operating systems for wireless communication devices such as Panasonic and Siemens;

- other Palm OS operating system licensees, including Acer, Handera, Sony, and Symbol;

- smart phone manufacturers such as Ericsson, Kyocera, Motorola, Nokia, and Samsung;

- Research In Motion Limited, a leading provider of wireless E-mail, instant messaging, and Internet connectivity; and

- a variety of start-up companies looking to compete in our current and future markets.

We expect our competitors to continue to improve the performance of their current products and to introduce new products, services, and technologies. Successful new product introductions or enhancements by our competitors could reduce the sales and market acceptance of our products, cause intense price competition, and result in reduced gross margins and loss of market share.

Our failure to compete successfully against current or future competitors could seriously harm our business. To be competitive, we must continue to invest significant resources in research and development, sales, and marketing. We cannot be sure that we will have sufficient resources to make these investments or that we will be able to make the technological advances necessary to be competitive.

Appendix 2: Handspring Management Team

Jeff Hawkins

Currently chairman and chief product officer of the company, Jeff Hawkins cofounded Handspring with Donna Dubinsky in July 1998 after their incredibly successful run together at Palm Computing. In 1994, Hawkins invented the original PalmPilot products and founded Palm Computing, now a 3Com company. He is often credited as the designer who reinvented the hand-held market.

An industry veteran with nearly twenty years of technical expertise, Hawkins currently holds nine patents for various hand-held devices and features. His vision for hand-held computing dates back to the 1980s, when as vice president of research at GRiD Systems Corporation he served as principal architect and designer for the GRiDPad and GRiD Convertible. Prior to that, he held key technical positions with Intel Corporation. Hawkins earned his B.S. in electrical engineering from Cornell University.

Donna Dubinsky

Currently president and CEO, Donna Dubinsky cofounded Handspring with Jeff Hawkins in July 1998 to create a new breed of hand-held computers for consumers. As president and CEO of Palm Computing, Dubinsky helped make the PalmPilot the best-selling hand-held computer and the most rapidly adopted new computing product ever produced. When Dubinsky first joined Hawkins at Palm Computing in 1992, shortly after the company was founded, she brought with her more than ten years of marketing and logistics experience from Apple and Claris. Dubinsky and Hawkins introduced the original PalmPilot in February 1996, a move that revitalized the hand-held computing industry.

In addition to her position as CEO of Handspring, Dubinsky currently serves as a director of Intuit Corporation and is a trustee of the Computer Museum History Center. She earned her B.A. from Yale University and her M.B.A. from the Harvard Graduate School of Business Administration.

Ed Colligan

Currently chief operating officer, Ed Colligan joined Handspring to lead the development and marketing efforts for a new generation of hand-held computers. As the vice president of marketing for Palm Computing, Ed Colligan worked with Jeff Hawkins and Donna Dubinsky to lead the product marketing and marketing communications efforts for Palm, including the successful positioning, launch, and marketing of the popular Palm product family.

Prior to Palm, Colligan was vice president of strategic and product marketing at Radius Corporation. During his eight years there, Colligan helped make Radius the brand leader in Macintosh graphics, graphic imaging, and hardware development.

Colligan's multiple successes have earned him several marketing industry accolades. *Marketing Computers Magazine* named him the 1997 Marketer of the Year, and *Advertising Age* named him one of the Top 100 Marketers of 1997, an award that spanned all product categories. He holds a B.A. from the University of Oregon.

Bernard Whitney

Bernard Whitney joined Handspring as chief financial officer in June 1999. He comes to Handspring from Sanmina, Inc., an electronics manufacturing company, where he served as executive vice president and chief financial officer. A primary focus at Sanmina was leading the systems technology and strategic development effort that included eight successful acquisitions.

Prior to Sanmina, Whitney served as vice president of finance for Network General Corporation, a network fault tolerance and performance management solutions company.

From 1987 to 1995, Whitney held a variety of positions in corporate finance for mass storage manufacturer Conner Peripherals. He has an M.B.A from San Jose State University and a B.S. in business administration from the California State University at Chico.

ENDNOTES

1. Salomon Smith Barney, "Smart Handheld Device Market Segments, Worldwide, 1998–2004E," October 18, 2000.
2. P. Tjahyadikarta and M. A. Schilling, "Palm Economy," Boston University Teaching Case # 2001-01, and forthcoming in M. Hitt, D. Ireland, and B. Hoskisson, *Strategic Management: Competitiveness and Globalization*, 5th ed. (St. Paul, MN: West Publishing, 2001).
3. Stephanie Miles, "Is Palm Ready for the Handheld Challenge?" CNET News.com, September 13, 1999.
4. "Always on" refers to devices that are capable of remaining continuously connected to the Internet.
5. R. Pegoraro, "Even the Best of the Phone-PDA Combos Aren't Good Enough," *Washington Post,* January 27, 2002, p. H.07.
6. K. Shaw, "Handspring Treo: An End User Review," *Network World,* February 4, 2002: **www.nwfusion.com.**
7. S. Wildstrom, "An E-mailer Out to Squash Blackberry," *Business Week,* April 29, 2002, pp. 24ff.
8. M. Moore, "Treo Melds Phone, Wireless Net, PDA in 'Star Trek' Style," *Houston Chronicle,* January 24, 2002.
9. J. Sullivan, "Handspring Bets the Farm on Treo—Then Postpones It," *Wireless Data News,* January 30, 2002, pp. 1ff.
10. Handspring 10K, 2001.
11. Pegoraro, "Even the Best."
12. Sullivan, "Handspring Bets the Farm."
13. Moore, "Treo Melds Phone."
14. **www.nokia.com.**
15. P. Henning, "Qualcomm, Ericsson Unite over New Wireless Standard," *Red Herring,* 2000: **www.redherring.com.**
16. Anonymous, *S&P Telecommunications Wireless Industry Survey* (New York: McGraw-Hill, December 28, 2000), p. 5.
17. Matthew M. Nordan of Forrester Research, quoted in A. Reinhardt, S. Baker, W. Echikson, K. Carlisle, and P. Schmidt, "Who Needs 3G Anyway?" *Business Week: European Business,* March 26, 2001, p. 18.
18. **www.nttdocomo.com.**
19. **www.ericsson.com.**
20. "Brightpoint Signs Distribution Agreement with Handspring," *Wall Street Research Net,* February 27, 2002.
21. Anonymous, "Two Stumbling Steps Toward 3G," *Economist Technology Quarterly.* December 9, 2000: **www.economist.com.**
22. W. S. Mossberg, "Gadgets—The Mossberg Solution: Which Smart Phone Is the Smartest?" *Wall Street Journal,* April 10, p. D3.

The Home Video Game Industry: From Pong to X-Box

This case was prepared by Charles W. L. Hill, the University of Washington.

An Industry Is Born

In 1968, Nolan Bushell, the twenty-four-year-old son of a Utah cement contractor graduated from the University of Utah with a degree in engineering.[1] Bushnell then moved to California, where he worked briefly in the computer graphics division of Ampex. At home, Bushnell turned his daughter's bedroom into a laboratory. There, he created a simpler version of Space War, a computer game that had been invented in 1962 by an MIT graduate student, Steve Russell. Bushnell's version of Russell's game, which he called Computer Space, was made of integrated circuits connected to a 19-inch black-and-white television screen. Unlike a computer, Bushnell's invention could do nothing but play the game, which meant that, unlike a computer, it could be produced cheaply.

Bushnell envisioned video games like his standing next to pinball machines in arcades. With hopes of having his invention put into production, Bushnell left Ampex to work for a small pinball company that manufactured 1,500 copies of his video game. The game never sold, primarily because the player had to read a full page of directions before he or she could play the game—way too complex for an arcade game. Bushnell left the pinball company and with a friend, Ted Dabney, put up $500 to start a company that would develop a simpler video game. They wanted to call the company Syzygy, but the name was already taken, so they settled on Atari, a Japanese word that was the equivalent of "*check* in the *go.*"

In his home laboratory, Bushnell built the simplest game he could think of. People knew the rules immediately, and it could be played with one hand. The game was modeled on table tennis, and players batted a ball back and forth with paddles that could be moved up and down sides of a court by twisting knobs. He named the game "Pong" after the sonarlike sound that was emitted every time the ball connected with a paddle.

In the fall of 1972, Bushnell installed his prototype for Pong in Andy Capp's tavern in Sunnyvale, California. The only instructions were "avoid missing the ball for a high score." In the first week, 1,200 quarters were deposited in the casserole dish that served for a coin box in Bushnell's prototype. Bushnell was ecstatic; his simple game had brought in $300 in a week. The pinball machine that stood next to it averaged $35 a week.

Lacking the capital to mass-produce the game, Bushnell approached established

This case is intended to be used as a basis for class discussion rather than as an illustration of either effective or ineffective handling of the situation. Reprinted by permission of Charles W. L. Hill.

amusement game companies, only to be repeatedly shown the door. Down but hardly out, Bushnell cut his hair, put on a suit, and talked his way into a $50,000 line of credit from a local bank. He set up a production line in an abandoned roller skating rink and he hired people to assemble machines while Led Zeppelin and the Rolling Stones were played at full volume over the speaker system of the rink. Among his first batch of employees was a skinny seventeen-year-old named Steve Jobs, who would latter found a few companies of his own, including Apple Computer, NeXT, and Pixar. Like others, Jobs had been attracted by a classified ad that read "Have Fun and Make Money."

In no time at all, Bushnell was selling all the machines that his small staff could make—about ten per day—but to grow, he needed additional capital. While the ambience at the rink, with its mix of rock music and marijuana fumes, put off most potential investors, Don Valentine, one of the country's most astute and credible venture capitalists, was impressed with the growth story. Armed with Valentine's money, Atari began to increase production and expand their range of games. New games included Tank and Breakout; the latter was designed by Jobs and a friend of his, Steve Wozniak, who had left Hewlett-Packard to work at Atari.

By 1974, 100,000 Ponglike games were sold worldwide. Although Atari manufactured only 10 percent of the games, the company still made $3.2 million that year. With the Pong clones coming on strong, Bushnell decided to make a Pong system for the home. In fact, Magnavox had been marketing a similar game for the home since 1972, although sales had been modest.[2] Bushnell's team managed to compress Atari's coin-operated Pong game down to a few inexpensive circuits that were contained in the game console. Atari's Pong had a sharper picture and more sensitive controllers than Magnavox's machine. It also cost less. Bushnell then went on a road show, demonstrating Pong to toy buyers, but he received an indifferent response and no sales. A dejected Bushnell returned to Atari with no idea of what to do next. Then the buyer for the sporting goods department at Sears came to see Bushnell, reviewed the machine, and offered to buy every home Pong game Atari could make. With Sears's backing, Bushnell boosted production. Sears ran a major television ad campaign to sell home Pong, and Atari's sales soared, hitting

$450 million in 1975. The home video game had arrived.

Boom and Bust

Nothing attracts competitors like success, and by 1976 about twenty different companies were crowding into the home video game market, including National Semiconductor, RCA, Coleco, and Fairchild. Recognizing the limitations of existing home video game designs, Fairchild came out in 1976 with a home video game system capable of playing multiple games. The Fairchild system consisted of three components—a console, controllers, and cartridges. The console was a small computer optimized for graphics processing capabilities. It was designed to receive information from the controllers, process it, and send signals to a television monitor. The controllers were hand-held devices used to direct on-screen action. The cartridges contained chips encoding the instructions for a game. The cartridges were designed to be inserted into the console.

In 1976, Bushnell sold Atari to Warner Communications for $28 million. Bushnell stayed on to run Atari. Backed by Warner's capital, in 1977 Atari developed and bought out its own cartridge-based system, the Atari 2600. The 2600 system was sold for $200, and associated cartridges retailed for $25–$30. Sales surged during the 1977 Christmas season. However, a lack of manufacturing capacity on the part of market leader Atari and a very cautious approach to inventory by Fairchild led to shortages and kept sales significantly below what they could have been. Fairchild's cautious approach was the result of prior experience in consumer electronics. A year earlier it had increased demand for its digital watches, only to accumulate a buildup of excess inventory that had caused the company to take a $24.5 million write-off.[3]

After the 1977 Christmas season, Atari claimed to have sold about 400,000 units of the 2600 VCA, about 50 percent of all cartridge-based systems in American homes. Atari had also earned more than $100 million in sales of game cartridges. By this point, second-place Fairchild sold around 250,00 units of its system. Cartridge sales for the year totaled about 1.2 million units, with an average selling price of around $20. Fresh from this success and fortified by market forecasts predicting sales of 33 million cartridges and an installed base of 16 million machines by 1980, Bushnell committed Atari to manufacturing 1 million units of the 2600 for the 1978 Christmas season. Atari estimated that total demand would reach 2 million units. Bushnell was also encouraged by signals from Fairchild that it would again be limiting production to around 200,000 units. At this point, Atari had a library of nine games. Fairchild had seventeen.[4]

Atari was not the only company to be excited by the growth forecasts. In 1978, a host of other companies, including Coleco, National Semiconductor, Magnavox, General Instrument, and a dozen other companies, entered the market with incompatible cartridge-based home systems. The multitude of choices did not seem to entice consumers, however, and the 1978 Christmas season brought unexpectedly low sales. Only Atari and Coleco survived an industry shakeout. Atari lost Bushnell, who was ousted by Warner executives. (Bushnell went on to start Chuck E. Cheese Pizza Time Theater, a restaurant chain that had 278 outlets by 1981.) Bushnell later stated that part of the problem was a disagreement over strategy. Bushnell wanted Atari to price the 2600 at cost and make money on sales of software; Warner wanted to continue making profits on hardware sales.[5]

Several important developments occurred in 1979. First, several game producers and programmers defected from Atari to set up their own firm, Activision, and to make games compatible with the Atari 2600. Their success encouraged others to follow suit. Second, Coleco developed an expansion module that allowed its machine to play Atari games. Atari and Mattel (which entered the market in 1979) did likewise. Third, the year 1979 saw the introduction of three new games to the home market—Space Invaders, Asteroids, and Pac Man. All three were adapted from popular arcade games and all three helped drive demand for players.

Demand recovered strongly in late 1979 and kept growing for the next three years. In 1981, U.S. sales of home video games and cartridges hit $1 billion. In 1982, they surged to $3 billion, with Atari accounting for half of this amount. It seemed as if Atari could do no wrong; the 2600 was everywhere. About 20 million units were sold, and by late 1982, a large number of independent companies, including Activision, Imagic, and Epyx, were now producing hundreds of games for the 2600. Second-place Coleco was also doing well, partly because of a popular arcade game,

Donkey Kong, which it had licensed from a Japanese company called Nintendo.

Atari was also in contact with Nintendo. In 1982, the company very nearly licensed the rights to Nintendo's Famicom, a cartridge-based video game system machine that was a big hit in Japan. Atari's successor to the 2600, the 5200, was not selling well and the Famicom seemed like a good substitute. The negotiations broke down, however, when Atari discovered that Nintendo had extended its Donkey Kong license to Coleco. This allowed Coleco to port a version of the game to its home computer, which was a direct competitor to Atari's 800 home computer.[6]

After a strong 1982 season, the industry hoped for continued growth in 1983. Then the bottom dropped out of the market. Sales of home video games plunged to $100 million. Atari lost $500 million in the first nine months of the year, causing the stock of parent company Warner Communications to drop by half. Part of the blame for the collapse was laid at the feet of an enormous inventory overhang of unsold games. About 15 to 20 million surplus game cartridges were left over from the 1982 Christmas season (in 1981, there were none). On top of this, around 500 new games hit the market in 1993. The average price of a cartridge plunged from $30 in 1979 to $16 in 1982, and then to $4 in 1983. As sales slowed, retailers cut back on the shelf space allocated to video games. It proved difficult for new games to make a splash in a crowded market. Atari had to dispose of 6 million ET: The Extraterrestrial games. Meanwhile, big hits from previous years, such as Pac Man, were bundled with game players and given away free to try to encourage system sales.[7]

Surveying the rubble, commentators claimed that the video game industry was dead. The era of dedicated game machines was over, they claimed. Personal computers were taking their place.[8] It seemed to be true. Mattel sold off its game business, Fairchild moved on to other things, Coleco folded, and Warner decided to break up Atari and sell its constituent pieces—at least, those pieces for which it could find a buyer. No one in America seemed to want to have anything to do with the home video game business; no one, that is, except for Minoru Arakawa, the head of Nintendo's U.S. subsidiary, Nintendo of America (NOA). Picking through the rubble of the industry, Arakawa noticed that there were people who still packed video arcades, bringing in $7 billion a year, more money than the entire movie industry. Perhaps it was not a lack of interest in home video games that had killed the industry. Perhaps it was bad business practice.

The Nintendo Monopoly

Nintendo was a century-old Japanese company that had built up a profitable business making playing cards before diversifying into the video game business. Based in Kyoto and still run by the founding Yamauchi family, the company started to diversify into the video game business in the late 1970s. The first step was to license video game technology from Magnavox. In 1977, Nintendo introduced a home video game system in Japan based on this technology that played a variation of Pong. In 1978, the company began to sell coin-operated video games. It had its first hit with Donkey Kong, designed by Sigeru Miyamoto.

The Famicom

In the early 1980s, the company's boss, Hiroshi Yamauchi, decided that Nintendo had to develop its own video game machine. He pushed the company's engineers to develop a machine that combined superior graphics-processing capabilities and low cost. Yamauchi wanted a machine that could sell for $75, less than half the price of competing machines at the time. He dubbed the machine the Family Computer, or Famicom. The machine that his engineers designed was based on the controller, console, and plug in the cartridge format pioneered by Fairchild. It contained two custom chips—an 8-bit central processing unit and a graphics-processing unit. Both chips had been scaled down to perform only essential functions. A 16-bit processor was available at the time, but to keep costs down, Yamauchi refused to use it.

Nintendo approached Ricoh, the electronics giant, which had spare semiconductor capacity. Employees at Ricoh said that the chips had to cost no more that 2,000 yen. Ricoh thought that the 2,000-yen price point was absurd. Yamauchi's response was to guarantee Ricoh a 3-million-chip order within two years. Since the leading companies in Japan were selling, at most, 30,000 video games per year at the time, many within the company viewed this as an outrageous commitment, but Ricoh went for it.[9]

Another feature of the machine was its memory—2,000 bytes of random access memory (RAM), compared to the 256 bytes of RAM in the Atari machine. The result was a machine with superior graphics-processing capabilities and faster action that could handle far more complex games than Atari games. Nintendo's engineers also built a new set of chips into the game cartridges. In addition to chips that held the game program, Nintendo developed memory map controller (MMC) chips that took over some of the graphics-processing work from the chips in the console and enabled the system to handle more complex games. With the addition of the MMC chips, the potential for more-sophisticated and more complex games had arrived. Over time, Nintendo's engineers developed more powerful MMC chips, enabling the basic 8-bit system to do things that originally seemed out of reach. The engineers also figured out a way to include a battery backup system in cartridges that allowed some games to store information independently—to keep track of where a player had left off or to track high scores.

The Games

Yamauchi recognized that great hardware that would not sell itself. The key to the market, he reasoned, was great games. Yamauchi had instructed the engineers, when they were developing the hardware, to make sure that "it was appreciated by software engineers." Nintendo decided that it would become a haven for game designers. "An ordinary man," Yamauchi said, "cannot develop good games no matter how hard he tries. A handful of people in this world can develop games that everyone wants. Those are the people we want at Nintendo."[10]

Yamauchi had an advantage in the person of Sigeru Miyamoto. Miyamoto had joined Nintendo at the age of twenty-four. Yamauchi had hired Miyamoto, a graduate of Kanazawa Munici College of Industrial Arts, as a favor to his father and an old friend, although he had little idea what he would do with an artist. For three years, Miyamoto worked as Nintendo's staff artist. Then in 1980, Yamauchi called Miyamoto into his office. Nintendo had started selling coin-operated video games, but one of the new games, Radarscope, was a disaster. Could Miyamoto come up with a new game? Miyamoto was delighted. He had always spent a lot of time drawing cartoons, and as a student, he had played video games constantly. Miyamoto believed that video games could be used to bring cartoons to life.[11]

The game Miyamoto developed was nothing short of a revelation. At a time when most coin-operated video games lacked characters or depth, Miyamoto created a game around a story that had both. Most games involved battles with space invaders or heroes shooting lasers at aliens; Miyamoto's game did neither. Based loosely on *Beauty and the Beast* and *King Kong,* Miyamoto's game involved a pet ape who runs off with his master's beautiful girlfriend. His master is an ordinary carpenter called Mario, who has a bulbous nose, a bushy mustache, a pair of large pathetic eyes, and a red cap (which Miyamoto added because he was not good at hairstyles). He does not carry a laser gun. The ape runs off with the girlfriend to get back at his master, who was not especially nice to the beast. The man, of course, has to get his girlfriend back by running up ramps, climbing ladders, jumping off elevators, and the like, while the ape throws objects at the hapless carpenter. Since the main character is an ape, Miyamoto called him Kong; because the main character is as stubborn as a donkey, he called the game Donkey Kong.

Released in 1981, Donkey Kong was a sensation in the world of coin-operated video arcades and a smash hit for Nintendo. In 1984, Yamauchi again summoned Miyamoto to his office. He needed more games, this time for Famicom. Miyamoto was made the head of a new research and development (R&D) group and told to come up with the most imaginative video games ever.

Miyamoto began with Mario from Donkey Kong. A colleague had told him that Mario looked more like a plumber than a carpenter, so a plumber he became. Miyamoto gave Mario a brother, Luigi, who was as tall and thin as Mario was short and fat. They became the Super Mario Brothers. Since plumbers spend their time working on pipes, large green sewer pipes became obstacles and doorways into secret worlds. Mario and Luigi's task was to search for the captive Princess Toadstool. Mario and Luigi are endearing bumblers, unequal to their tasks yet surviving. They shoot, squash, or evade their enemies—a potpourri of inventions that include flying turtles and stinging fish, man-eating flowers and fire-breathing dragons—while they collect gold coins, blow air bubbles, and climb vines into smiling clouds.[12]

Super Mario Brothers was introduced in 1985. For Miyamoto, this was just the beginning. Between 1985 and 1991, Miyamoto produced eight Mario games. About 60 to 70 million were sold worldwide, making Miyamoto the most successful game designer in the world. After adapting Donkey Kong for Famicom, he also went on to create other top-selling games, including another classic, The Legend of Zelda. While Miyamoto drew freely from folklore, literature, and pop culture, the main source for his ideas was his own experience. The memory of being lost among a maze of sliding doors in his family's home was re-created in the labyrinths of the Zelda games. The dog that attacked him when he was a child attacks Mario in Super Mario. As a child, Miyamoto had once climbed a tree to catch a view of far-off mountains and had become stuck. Mario gets himself in a similar fix. Once Miyamoto went hiking without a map and was surprised to stumble across a lake. In the Legend of Zelda, part of the adventure is in walking into new places without a map and being confronted by surprises.

Nintendo in Japan

Nintendo introduced Famicom into the Japanese market in May 1983. Famicom was priced at $100, more than Yamauchi wanted, but significantly less than the products of competitors. When he introduced the machine, Yamauchi urged retailers to forgo profits on the hardware because it was just a tool to sell software, and that is where they would make their money. Backed by an extensive advertising campaign, 500,000 units of Famicom were sold in the first two months. Within a year, the figure stood at 1 million, and sales were still expanding rapidly. With the hardware quickly finding its way into Japanese homes, Nintendo was besieged with calls from desperate retailers frantically demanding more games.

At this point Yamauchi told Miyamoto to come up with the most imaginative games ever. However, Yamauchi also realized that Nintendo alone could not satisfy the growing thirst for new games, so he initiated a licensing program. To become a Nintendo licensee, companies had to agree to an unprecedented series of restrictions. Licensees could issue only five Nintendo games per year, and they could not write those titles for other platforms. The licensing fee was set at 20 percent of the wholesale price of each cartridge sold (game cartridges wholesaled for around

$30). It typically cost $500,000 to develop a game and took around six months. Nintendo insisted that games not contain any excessively violent or sexually suggestive material and that they review every game before allowing it to be produced.[13]

Despite these restrictions, six companies (Bandai, Capcom, Konami, Namco, Taito, and Hudson) agreed to become Nintendo licensees, not least because millions of customers were now clamoring for games. Bandai was Japan's largest toy company. The others already made either coin-operated video games or computer software games. Because of these licensing agreements, they saw their sales and earnings surge. For example, Konami's earnings went from $10 million in 1987 to $300 million in 1991.

After the six licensees began selling games, reports of defective games began to reach Yamauchi. The original six licensees were allowed to manufacture their own game cartridges. Realizing that he had given away the ability to control the quality of the cartridges, Yamauchi decided to change the contract for future licensees. Future licensees were required to submit all manufacturing orders for cartridges to Nintendo. Nintendo charged licensees $14 per cartridge, required that they place a minimum order for 10,000 units, (later the minimum order was raised to 30,000), and insisted on cash payment in full when the order was placed. Nintendo outsourced all manufacturing to other companies, using the volume of its orders to get rock bottom prices. The cartridges were estimated to cost Nintendo between $6 and $8 each. The licensees then picked up the cartridges from Nintendo's loading dock and were responsible for distribution. In 1985, there were seventeen licensees. By 1987, there were fifty. By this point, 90 percent of the home video game systems sold in Japan were Nintendo systems.

Nintendo in America

In 1980, Nintendo established a subsidiary in America to sell its coin-operated video games. Yamauchi's American-educated son-in-law, Minoru Arakawa, headed the subsidiary. All of the other essential employees were Americans, including Ron Judy and Al Stone. For its first two years, Nintendo of America (NOA), based originally in Seattle, struggled to sell second-rate games such as Radarscope. The subsidiary seemed on the brink of closing. NOA could not even make the rent payment on the warehouse. Then they received a large shipment from Japan:

2,000 units of a new coin-operated video game. Opening the box, they discovered Donkey Kong. After playing the game briefly, Judy proclaimed it a disaster. Stone walked out of the building, declaring that "it's over."[14] The managers were appalled. They could not imagine a game less likely to sell in video arcades. The only promising sign was that a twenty-year employee, Howard Philips, rapidly became enthralled with the machine.

Arakawa, however, knew he had little choice but to try to sell the machine. Judy persuaded the owner of the Spot Tavern near Nintendo's office to take one of the machines on a trial basis. After one night, Judy discovered $30 in the coin box, a phenomenal amount. The next night there was $35, and $36 the night after that. NOA had a hit on its hands.

By the end of 1982, NOA had sold over 60,000 copies of Donkey Kong and had booked sales in excess of $100 million. The subsidiary had outgrown its Seattle location. They moved to a new site in Redmond, a Seattle suburb, where they located next to a small but fast-growing software company run by an old school acquaintance of Howard Philips, Bill Gates.

By 1984, NOA was riding a wave of success in the coin-operated video game market. Arakawa, however, was interested in the possibilities of selling Nintendo's new Famicom system in the United States. Throughout 1984, Arakawa, Judy, and Stone met with numerous toy and department store representatives to discuss the possibilities, only to be repeatedly rebuffed. Still smarting from the 1983 debacle, the representatives wanted nothing to do with the home video game business. They also met with former managers from Atari and Caloco to gain their insights. The most common response they received was that the market collapsed because the last generation of games were awful.

Arakawa and his team decided that if they were going to sell Famicom in the United States, they would have to find a new distribution channel. The obvious choice was consumer electronics stores. Thus, Arakawa asked the R&D team in Kyoto to redesign Famicom for the U.S. market so that it looked less like a toy (Famicom was encased in red and white plastic), and more like a consumer electronics device. The redesigned machine was renamed the Nintendo Entertainment System (NES).

Arakawa's big fear was that illegal, low-quality Taiwanese games would flood the U.S. market if NES was successful. To stop counterfeit games being played on NES, Arakawa asked Nintendo's Japanese engineers to design a security system into the U.S. version of Famicom so that only Nintendo-approved games could be played on NES. The Japanese engineers responded by designing a security chip to be embedded in the game cartridges. NES would not work unless the security chips in the cartridges unlocked, or shook hands with, a chip in NES. Since the code embedded in the security chip was proprietary, the implication of this system was that no one could manufacture games for NES without Nintendo's specific approval.

To overcome the skepticism and reluctance of retailers to stock a home video game system, Arakawa decided in late 1985 to make an extraordinary commitment. Nintendo would stock stores and set up displays and windows. Retailers would not have to pay for anything they stocked for ninety days. After that, retailers could pay Nintendo for what they sold and return the rest. NES was bundled with Nintendo's best-selling game in Japan, Super Mario Brothers. It was essentially a risk-free proposition for retailers, but even with this, most were skeptical. Ultimately, thirty Nintendo personnel descended on the New York area. Referred to as the Nintendo SWAT team, they persuaded some stores to stock NES after an extraordinary blitz that involved eighteen-hour days. To support the New York product launch, Nintendo also committed itself to a $5 million advertising campaign aimed at the seven- to fourteen-year-old boys who seemed to be Nintendo's likely core audience.

By December 1985, between 500 and 600 stores in the New York area were stocking Nintendo systems. Sales were moderate, about half of the 100,000 NES machines shipped from Japan were sold, but it was enough to justify going forward. The SWAT team then moved first to Los Angeles, then to Chicago, then to Dallas. As in New York, sales started at a moderate pace, but by late 1986 they started to accelerate rapidly, and Nintendo went national with NES.

In 1986, around 1 million NES units were sold in the United States. In 1987, the figure increased to 3 million. In 1988, it jumped to over 7 million. In the same year, 33 million game cartridges were sold. Nintendo mania had arrived in the United States. To expand the supply of games, Nintendo licensed the rights to produce up to five games per year to thirty-one American software companies. Nintendo contin-

ued to use a restrictive licensing agreement that gave it exclusive rights to any games, required licensees to place their orders through Nintendo, and insisted on a 30,000-unit minimum order.[15]

By 1990, the home video game market was worth $5 billion worldwide. Nintendo dominated the industry, with a 90 percent share of the market for game equipment. The parent company was, by some measures, now the most profitable company in Japan. By 1992, it was netting over $1 billion in gross profit annually, or more than $1.5 million for each employee in Japan. The company's stock market value exceeded that of Sony, Japan's premier consumer electronics firm. Indeed, the company's net profit exceeded that of all the American movie studios combined. Nintendo games, it seemed, were bigger than the movies.

As of 1991, there were over 100 licensees for Nintendo, and over 450 titles were available for NES. In the United States, Nintendo products were distributed through toy stores (30 percent of volume), mass merchandisers (40 percent of volume), and department stores (10 percent of volume). Nintendo tightly controlled the number of game titles and games that could be sold, quickly withdrawing titles as soon as interest appeared to decline. In 1988, retailers requested 110 million cartridges from Nintendo. Market surveys suggested that perhaps 45 million could have been sold, but Nintendo allowed only 33 million to be shipped.[16] Nintendo claimed that the shortage of games was in part due to a worldwide shortage of semiconductor chips.

Several companies had tried to reverse-engineer the code embedded in Nintendo's security chip, which competitors characterized as a lockout chip. Nintendo successfully sued them. The most notable was Atari Games, one of the successors of the original Atari, which in 1987 sued Nintendo of America for anticompetitive behavior. Atari claimed that the purpose of the security chip was to monopolize the market. At the same time, Atari announced that it had found a way around Nintendo's security chip and would begin to sell unlicensed games.[17] NOA responded with a countersuit. In a March 1991 ruling, Atari was found to have obtained Nintendo's security code illegally and was ordered to stop selling NES-compatible games. However, Nintendo did not always have it all its own way. In 1990, under pressure from Congress, the Department of Justice, and several lawsuits, Nintendo rescinded its exclusivity requirements, freeing up developers to write games for other platforms. However, developers faced a real problem: what platform could they write for?

Sega's Sonic Boom

Back in 1954, David Rosen, a twenty-year-old American, left the U.S. Air Force after a tour of duty in Tokyo.[18] Rosen had noticed that Japanese people needed lots of photographs for ID cards, but that local photo studios were slow and expensive. He formed a company, Rosen Enterprises, and went into the photo-booth business, which was a big success. By 1957, Rosen had established a successful nationwide chain. At this point, the Japanese economy was booming, so Rosen decided it was time to get into another business—entertainment. As his vehicle, he chose arcade games, which were unknown in Japan at the time. He picked up used games on the cheap from America and set up arcades in the same Japanese department stores and theaters that typically housed his photo booths. Within a few years, Rosen had 200 arcades nationwide. His only competition came from another American-owned firm, Service Games (SeGa), whose original business was jukeboxes and fruit machines.

By the early 1960s, the Japanese arcade market had caught up with the U.S. market. The problem was that game makers had run out of exciting new games to offer. Rosen decided that he would have to get into the business of designing and manufacturing games, but to do that he needed manufacturing facilities. SeGa manufactured its own games, so in 1965 Rosen approached the company and suggested a merger. The result was Sega Enterprise, a Japanese company with Rosen as its CEO.

Rosen himself designed Sega's first game, Periscope, in which the objective was to sink chain-mounted cardboard ships by firing torpedoes, represented by lines of colored lights. Periscope was a big success not only in Japan, but also in the United States and Europe, and it allowed Sega to build up a respectable export business. Over the years, the company continued to invest heavily in game development, always using the latest electronic technology.

Gulf and Western, a U.S. conglomerate, acquired Sega in 1969, with Rosen running the subsidiary. In 1975, Gulf and Western (G&W) took Sega public in the United States, but left Sega Japan as a G&W subsidiary. Hayao Nakayama, a former Sega distributor,

was drafted as president. In the early 1980s, Nakayama pushed G&W to invest more in Sega Japan so that the company could enter the then-booming home video game market. When G&W refused, Nakayama suggested a management buyout. G&W agreed, and in 1984, for the price of just $38 million, Sega became a Japanese company once more. (Sega's Japanese revenues were around $700 million, but by now the company was barely profitable.)

Sega was caught off guard by the huge success of Nintendo's Famicom. Although it released its own 8-bit system in 1986, the machine never commanded more than 5 percent of the Japanese market. Nakayama, however, was not about to give up. From years in the arcade business, he understood that great games drove sales. Nevertheless, he also understood that more powerful technology gave game developers the tools to develop more appealing games. This philosophy underlay Nakayama's decision to develop a 16-bit game system, Genesis.

Sega took the design of its 16-bit arcade machine and adapted it for Genesis. Compared to Nintendo's 8-bit machine, the 16-bit machine featured an array of superior technological features, including high-definition graphics and animation, a full spectrum of colors, two independent scrolling backgrounds that created an impressive depth of field, and near CD quality sound. The design strategy also made it easy to port Sega's catalog of arcade hits to Genesis.

Genesis was launched in Japan in 1989 and in the United States in 1990. In the United States, the machine was priced at $199. The company hoped that sales would be boosted by the popularity of its arcade games, such as the graphically violent Altered Beast. Sega also licensed other companies to develop games for the Genesis platform. In an effort to recruit licensees, Sega asked for lower royalty rates than Nintendo, and it gave licensees the right to manufacture their own cartridges. Independent game developers were slow to climb on board, however, and the $200 price tag for the player held back sales.

One of the first independent game developers to sign up with Sega was Electronic Arts. Established by Trip Hawkins, Electronic Arts had focused on designing games for personal computers and consequently had missed the Nintendo 8-bit era. Now Hawkins was determined to get a presence in the home video game market, and aligning his company's wagon with Sega seemed to be the best option. The Nintendo playing field was already crowded, and Sega offered a far less restrictive licensing deal than Nintendo. Electronic Arts subsequently wrote several popular games for Genesis, including John Madden football and several gory combat games.[19]

Nintendo had not been ignoring the potential of the 16-bit system. Nintendo's own 16-bit system, Super NES, was ready for market introduction in 1989—at the same time as Sega's Genesis. Nintendo introduced Super NES in Japan in 1990, where it quickly established a strong market presence and beat Sega's Genesis. In the United States, however, the company decided to hold back longer to reap the full benefits of the dominance it enjoyed with the 8-bit NES system. Yamauchi was also worried about the lack of backward compatibility between Nintendo's 8-bit and 16-bit systems. (The company had tried to make the 16-bit system so that it could play 8-bit games but concluded that the cost of doing so was prohibitive.) These concerns may have led the company to delay market introduction until the 8-bit market was saturated.

Meanwhile, in the United States, the Sega bandwagon was beginning to gain momentum. One development that gave Genesis a push was the introduction of a new Sega game, Sonic the Hedgehog. Developed by an independent team that was contracted to Sega, the game featured a cute hedgehog that impatiently tapped his paw when the player took too long to act. Impatience was Sonic's central feature—he had places to go, and quickly. He zipped along, collecting brass rings when he could find them, before rolling into a ball and flying down slides with loops and underground tunnels. Sonic was Sega's Mario.

In mid 1991, in an attempt to jump-start slow sales, Tom Kalinske, head of Sega's American subsidiary, decided to bundle Sonic the Hedgehog with the game player. He also reduced the price for the bundled unit to $150, and he relaunched the system with an aggressive advertising campaign aimed at teenagers. The campaign was built around the slogan "Genesis does what Nintendon't." The shift in strategy worked, and sales accelerated sharply.

Sega's success prompted Nintendo to launch its own 16-bit system. Nintendo's Super NES was introduced at $200. However, Sega now had a two-year head start in games. By the end of 1991, about 125 game titles were available for Genesis, compared to twenty-five for Super NES. In May 1992, Nintendo reduced the price of Super NES to $150. At this time

Sega was claiming a 63 percent share of the 16-bit market in the United States, and Nintendo claimed a 60 percent share. By now, Sega was cool. It began to take more chances with mass media–defined morality. When Acclaim Entertainment released its bloody *Mortal Kombat* game in September 1992, the Sega version let players rip off heads and tear out hearts. Reflecting Nintendo's image of their core market, its version was sanitized. The Sega version outsold Nintendo's two to one.[20] Therefore, the momentum continued to run in Sega's favor. By January 1993, there were 320 titles available for Sega Genesis, and 130 for Super NES. In early 1994, independent estimates suggested that Sega had 60 percent of the U.S. market and Nintendo had 40 percent, figures Nintendo disputed.

3DO

Trip Hawkins, whose first big success was Electronic Arts, founded 3DO in 1991.[21] Hawkins's vision for 3DO was to shift the home video game business away from the existing cartridge-based format and toward a CD-ROM-based platform. The original partners in 3DO were Electronic Arts, Matsushita, Time Warner, AT&T, and the venture capital firm Kleiner Perkins. Collectively they invested over $17 million in 3DO, making it the richest start-up in the history of the home video game industry. 3DO went public in May 1993 at $15 per share. By October of that year, the stock had risen to $48 per share, making 3DO worth $1 billion—not bad for a company that had yet to generate a single dollar in revenues.

The basis for 3DO's $1 billion market cap was patented computer system architecture and a copyrighted operating system that allowed for much richer graphics and audio capabilities. The system was built around a 32-bit RISC microprocessor and proprietary graphics processor chips. Instead of a cartridge, the 3DO system stored games on a CD-ROM that was capable of holding up to 600 megabytes of content, sharply up from the 10 megabytes of content found in the typical game cartridge of the time. The slower access time of a CD-ROM compared to a cartridge was alleviated somewhat by the use of a double-speed CD-ROM drive.[22]

The belief at 3DO—a belief apparently shared by many investors—was that the superior storage and graphics-processing capabilities of the 3DO system would prove very attractive to game developers, allowing them to be far more creative. In turn, better games would attract customers away from Nintendo and Sega. Developing games that used the capabilities of a CD-ROM system altered the economics of game development. Estimates suggested that it would cost approximately $2 million to produce a game for the 3DO system and could take as long as twenty-four months to develop. However, at $2 per disc, a CD-ROM cost substantially less to produce than a cartridge.

The centerpiece of 3DO's strategy was to license its hardware technology for free. Game developers paid a royalty of $3 per disc for access to the 3DO operating code. Discs typically retailed for $40 each.

Matsushita introduced the first 3DO machine into the U.S. market in October 1993. Priced at $700, the machine was sold through electronic retailers that carried Panasonic high-end electronics products. Sega's Tom Kalinsky noted, "It's a noble effort. Some people will buy 3DO, and they'll have a wonderful experience. It's impressive, but it's a niche. We've done the research. It does not become a large market until you go below $500. At $300, it starts to get interesting. We make no money on hardware. It's a cutthroat business. I hope Matsushita understands that."[23] CD-ROM discs for the 3DO machine retailed for around $75. The machine came bundled with Crash n Burn, a high-speed combat racing game. However, only eighteen 3DO titles were available by the crucial Christmas period, although reports suggested that 150 titles were under development.[24]

Sales of the hardware were slow, reaching only 30,000 by January 1994.[25] In the same month, AT&T and Sanyo both announced that they would begin to manufacture the 3DO machine. In March, faced with continuing sluggish sales, 3DO announced that it would give hardware manufacturers two shares of 3DO stock for every unit sold at or below a certain retail price. Matsushita dropped the price of its machine to $500. About the same time, Toshiba, LG, and Samsung all announced that they would start to produce 3DO machines.

By June 1994, cumulative sales of 3DO machines in the United States stood at 40,000 units. Matsushita announced plans to expand distribution beyond the current 3,500 outlets to include the toy and mass merchandise channels. Hawkins and his partners announced that they would invest another $37 million in 3DO. By July, there were 750 3DO software

licensees, but only forty titles were available for the format. Despite these moves, sales continued at a very sluggish pace and the supply of new software titles started to dry up.[26]

In September 1996, 3DO announced that it would either sell its hardware system business or move it into a joint venture.[27] The company announced that about 150 people, one-third of the work force, would probably lose their jobs in the restructuring. According to Trip Hawkins, 3DO would now focus on developing software for online gaming. Hawkins stated that the Internet and Internet entertainment constituted a huge opportunity for 3DO. The stock dropped $1.375 to $6.75.

Sega's Saturn

3DO was not alone in moving to a CD-ROM-based format. Both Sega and Sony also introduced CD-ROM-based systems in the mid 1990s. Sega had in fact beaten 3DO to the market with its November 1992 introduction of the Sega CD, a $300 CD-ROM add-on for the 16-bit Genesis. Sega sold 100,000 units in its first month alone. Sales then slowed down, however, and by December 1993 were standing at just 250,000 units. One reason for the slowdown, according to critics, was a lack of strong games. Sega was also working on a 32-bit CD-ROM system, Saturn, which was targeted for a mid-1995 introduction in the United States. In January 1994, Sega announced that Microsoft would supply the operating system for Saturn.[28]

In March 1994, Sega announced the Genesis Super 32X, a $150 add-on cartridge designed to increase the performance of Genesis cartridge and CD-ROM games. The 32X contained the 32-bit Hitachi microprocessor that was to be used in Saturn. Sega called the 32X "the poor man's 32-bit machine" because it sold for a mere $149. Introduced in the fall of 1994, the 32X never lived up to its expectations. Most users appeared willing to wait for the real thing, Sega Saturn, promised for release the following year.

In early 1995, Sega informed the press and retailers that it would release Saturn on "Sega Saturn Saturday, Sept 2nd," but Sega released the 32-bit Saturn in May 1995. It was priced at $400 per unit and accompanied by the introduction of just ten games. Sega apparently believed that the world would be delighted by the May release of the Saturn. However, Saturn was released without the industry fanfare that normally greets a new game machine. Only four retail chains received the Saturn in May, while the rest were told they would have to wait until September. This move alienated retailers, who responded by dropping Sega products from their stores.[29] Sega appeared to have made a marketing blunder.[30]

Sony's PlayStation

In the fall of 1995, Sony entered the fray with the introduction of the Sony PlayStation.[31] PlayStation used a 32-bit RISC microprocessor running at 33 MHz and using a double-speed CD-ROM drive. PlayStation cost an estimated $500 million to develop. The machine had actually been under development since 1991, when Sony decided that the home video game industry was getting too big to ignore. Initially, Sony was in an alliance with Nintendo to develop the machine. Nintendo walked away from the alliance in 1992, however, after a disagreement over who owned the rights to any future CD-ROM games. Sony went alone.[32]

From the start, Sony felt that it could leverage its presence in the film and music business to build a strong position in the home video game industry. A consumer electronics giant with a position in the Hollywood movie business and the music industry (Sony owned Columbia Pictures and the Columbia record label), Sony believed that it had access to significant intellectual property that could form the basis of many popular games.

In 1991, Sony established a division in New York: Sony Electronic Publishing. The division was to serve as an umbrella organization for Sony's multimedia offerings. Headed by Iceland native Olaf Olafsson, then just twenty-eight years old, this organization ultimately took the lead role in both the market launch of PlayStation and in developing game titles.[33] In 1993, as part of this effort, Sony purchased a well-respected British game developer, Psygnosis. By the fall of 1995, this unit had twenty games ready to complement PlayStation: The Haldeman Diaries, Mickey Mania (developed in collaboration with Disney), and Johnny Mnemonic, based on the William Gibson short story. To entice independent game developers such as Electronic Arts, Namco, and Acclaim Entertainment, Olafsson used the promise of low royalty rates. The standard royalty rate was set at $9 per disc, although developers that signed on early enough were given a lower royalty rate. Sony also provided approximately 4,000 game development tools to licensees in an effort to help them speed games to market.[34]

To distribute PlayStation, Sony set up a retail channel separate from Sony's consumer electronics sales force. It marketed the PlayStation as a hip and powerful alternative to the outdated Nintendo and Sega cartridge-based systems. Sony worked closely with retailers before the launch to find out how it could help them sell the PlayStation. To jump-start demand, Sony set up in-store displays to allow potential consumers to try the equipment. Just before the launch, Sony had lined up an impressive 12,000 retail outlets in the United States.[35]

Sony targeted its advertising for PlayStation at males in the eighteen- to thirty-five-year age range. The targeting was evident in the content of many of the games. One of the big hits for PlayStation was Tomb Raider, whose central character, Lara Croft, combined sex appeal with savviness and helped to recruit an older generation to PlayStation.[36] PlayStation was initially priced at $299, and games retailed for as much as $60. Sony's Tokyo-based executives had reportedly been insisting on a $350–$400 price for PlayStation, but Olafsson pushed hard for the lower price. Because of the fallout from this internal battle, in January 1996, Olafsson resigned from Sony. By then, however, Sony was following Olafsson's script.[37]

Sony's prelaunch work was rewarded with strong early sales. By January 1996, more than 800,000 PlayStations had been sold in the United States, plus another 4 million games. In May 1996, with 1.2 million PlayStations shipped, Sony reduced the price of PlayStation to $199. Sega responded with a similar price cut for its Saturn. The prices on some of Sony's initial games were also reduced to $29.99. The weekend after the price cuts, retailers reported that PlayStation sales were up by between 350 percent and 1,000 percent over the prior week.[38] The sales surge continued through 1996. By the end of the year, sales of PlayStation and associated software amounted to $1.3 billion, out of a total for U.S. sales at $2.2 billion for all video game hardware and software. In March 1997, Sony cut the price of PlayStation again, this time to $149. It also reduced its suggested retail price for games by $10 to $49.99. By this point, Sony had sold 3.4 million units of PlayStation in the United States, compared to Saturn's 1.6 million units.[39] Worldwide, PlayStation had outsold Saturn by

13 million to 7.8 million units, and Saturn sales were slowing.[40] The momentum was clearly running in Sony's favor, but the company now had a new challenge to deal with: Nintendo's latest generation game machine, the N64.

Nintendo Strikes Back

In July 1996, Nintendo launched Nintendo 64 (N64) in the Japanese market. This release was followed by a late fall introduction in the United States. N64 is a 64-bit machine developed in conjunction with Silicon Graphics. Originally targeted for introduction a year earlier, N64 had been under development since 1993. The machine used a plug-in cartridge format rather than a CD-ROM drive. According to Nintendo, cartridges allow for faster access time and are far more durable than CD-ROMs (an important consideration with children).[41]

The most-striking feature of the N64 machine, however, was its 3D graphics capability. N64 provides fully rounded figures that can turn on their heels and rotate through 180 degrees. Advanced ray tracing techniques borrowed from military simulators and engineering workstations added to the sense of realism by providing proper highlighting, reflections, and shadows.

N64 was targeted at children and young teenagers. It was priced at $200 and launched with just four games. Despite the lack of games, initial sales were very strong. Indeed, 1997 turned out to be a banner year for both Sony and Nintendo. The overall U.S. market was strong, with sales of hardware and software combined reaching a record $5.5 billion. Estimates suggest that PlayStation accounted for 49 percent of machines and games by value. N64 captured a 41 percent share, leaving Sega trailing badly with less than 10 percent of the market. During the year, the average price for game machines had fallen to $150. By year-end there were 300 titles available for PlayStation, compared to forty for N64. Games for PlayStation retailed for $40, on average, compared to over $60 for N64.[42]

By late 1998, PlayStation was widening its lead over N64. In the crucial North American market, PlayStation was reported to be outselling N64 by a two-to-one margin, although Nintendo retained a lead in the under-twelve category. At this point, there were 115 games available for N64 versus 431 for PlayStation.[43] Worldwide, Sony had now sold close to 55 million PlayStations. The success of PlayStation had a major impact on Sony's bottom line. In fiscal 1998, PlayStation business generated revenues of $5.5 billion for Sony, 10 percent of its worldwide revenues, but accounted for $886 million, or 22.5 percent, of the company's operating income.[44]

The Next Generation

After almost vanishing from the marketplace in 1998, Sega made a bold attempt to retake a leadership position with the late 1998 introduction in Japan of its Dreamcast home video game machine. The Dreamcast is the most powerful home video game machine yet, with the capability to display advanced 3D graphics. The Dreamcast runs on a 128-bit microprocessor at 200 MHz and uses a Microsoft Windows CE operating system. The games are stored on a CD-ROM, and the machine comes equipped with a 56K modem to facilitate multiplayer online game playing. Priced at $240 and launched with only a handful of games, the Dreamcast still sold over 1 million units in its first few months on the Japanese market.

Sega has scheduled a September 1999 date for the U.S. launch of the Dreamcast. The machine is priced at $199. Up to twelve games will be available at launch, including a new version of Sonic the Hedgehog that cost an estimated $30 million to produce. By Christmas 1999, there should be thirty games, and 100 by mid 2000. Sega has licensed approximately 100 independent developers to work on Dreamcast games. The company has plans to spend some $100 million on advertising to launch the system in the United States. Sega has already struck distribution agreements with some of the largest chains in the United States, including Toys "R" Us, Wal-Mart, and Sears. About 20,000 stores should be carrying the Dreamcast. As of spring 1999, advanced orders for the Dreamcast stood at 300,000.[45]

Sony also has plans to launch a 128-bit machine, dubbed PlayStation 2, in 2000. Sony is reportedly investing $1 billion in development of PlayStation 2. The machine is expected to have graphics capabilities 200 times faster than the original PlayStation and will utilize a DVD disk for storage. In an attempt to leverage its huge global base, Sony plans to make its new machine backward compatible with the original PlayStation.[46] Nintendo is also reportedly working on a 128-bit machine, although details are sketchy.

The great unknown is the threat that the personal computer poses to the video game industry. The threat has been discussed for years, but until recently general-purpose PCs have lacked the capabilities of specialized game machines. This may now be changing. Microsoft has provided a direct interface between Windows applications and three-dimensional graphics technology with a variation on its Active X technology, Direct X. According to game developers, the combination of Direct X, fast Pentium microprocessors, faster CD-ROM drives, and graphics accelerator chips has made the PC a much more appealing platform for which to write games. Another attraction of writing for the PC is that game developers do not have to pay royalties to PC manufacturers for the privilege of supplying compatible games.

Since early 1997, most new PCs have been sold with 3D graphics capability. With prices dropping to under $1,000 for high-powered "entry level" PCs, industry estimates suggest that over 100 million PCs may be sold in 1998, all of them with a high enough specification to run advanced games. Indeed, many believe that game software is the only application that really stretches the modern PC.[47]

The New Millennium

In the history of the video game industry, each new chapter has been associated with a launch of a new generation of more powerful machines that can support faster processing, better graphics, and more compelling game play. In each era, a different company has risen to market dominance. The original video game consoles were produced by Atari and were based on 4-bit technology. Nintendo dominated the 8-bit era; Sega, the 16-bit era; and Sony, the 32-bit era. Nintendo launched a 64-bit machine in 1996, but its competitors didn't follow, preferring instead to focus on the development of 128-bit machines. Sega was the first to market a 128-bit video game console, which it launched in Japan in late 1998 and in the United States in late 1999. Sony launched its own 128-bit machine, Sony PlayStation 2, in 2000. Industry newcomer Microsoft and Nintendo are currently developing their own 128-bit machines.

With the possible exception of Nintendo's offering, all these machines will have web-browsing capabilities to facilitate multiplayer gaming over the Internet. Users will also be able to download games, movies, and music onto their consoles and use their consoles to browse the web, send email, execute ecommerce transactions, and so on. These capabilities have led some to speculate that video game consoles might ultimately hit personal computer sales.[48]

The prize that these competitors are going after is a $20-billion-a-year worldwide market that industry analysts say is growing more rapidly than the film or music industries. United States video game sales now rival Hollywood box-office revenues. More people than ever are playing video games and spending more time doing it. More than 40 percent of U.S. households now have at least one game console, according to estimates from International Data Corp.[49]

Sega Dreamcast

Sega introduced its 128-bit console, Sega Dreamcast, in the United States in September 1999 (the Japanese market launch was late 1998). The Dreamcast came equipped with a 56-kilobit modem to allow for online gaming over the Internet. By late 2000, Sega had sold around 6 million Dreamcasts worldwide, accounting for about 15 percent of console sales since its launch. The company has a goal of shipping 10 million units by March 2001.[50] Sega has nurtured Dreamcast sales by courting outside software developers who help keep the pipeline full of new games, including Crazy Taxi, Resident Evil, and Quake III Arena. Another 170 games are scheduled for the 2002 holiday season.

In April 2000, Sega announced that it would provide its Dreamcast video game console at no charge to customers who subscribe to a new Sega web service for two years at $21.95 a month. Customers who have already bought the Dreamcast console, which lists for $199, will get a free keyboard and a $200 check if they subscribe.[51] This represents something of a gamble by Sega. No one really knows whether there's a critical number of game players who want to hook their machines to their television sets and cruise the Web. The business potential of online games has received a lot of attention, but the usual game medium is still the personal computer. Still, by April 2000 company data showed that about 20 percent of Sega Dreamcast owners were already using the console's built-in modem. They were going online to cruise the Internet or send email. In March 2000, the company launched the first Internet game played from a video game console. In the simple game, Chu Chu Rocket, players help lead mice through mazes and escape from pursuing cats.

To run its online operation, Sega set up Sega.com, an independent company headed by Brad Huang, a thirty-five-year-old former hedge-fund manager who pitched the strategy to Sega chairman Isao Okawa a year ago. Sega's online gaming web site, SegaNet, made its debut in August 2000. The web site is Sega's portal to the Internet, providing a gathering place for Sega fans. During 2000, Sega planned to launch 12 online games, including versions of hits like Quake III Arena and Half-Life. In addition, Sega will offer multiplayer online console games like football and basketball. Gamers could play basketball over the Internet, for example, with as many as eight human players on two teams. Eventually, Sega hopes to provide games for which it will be able to charge a premium monthly fee.

Despite its position as first mover with a 128-bit machine, and despite a bold Internet strategy, as of late 2000 the company appeared to be struggling. Sega was handicapped first by product shortages due to constraints on the supply of component parts and then by a lack of demand as consumers waited to see whether PlayStation 2 would be a more attractive machine. In September 2000, Sega responded to the impending launch of Sony's PlayStation 2 by cutting the price for its console from $199 to $149. Then in late October, Sega announced that, due to this price cut, it would probably lose over $200 million for the fiscal year ending March 2001.[52]

Sony PlayStation 2

Sony's first video game console, the original PlayStation, has been a phenomenal success worldwide. Since its release in 1995, more than 27 million units have been sold in the United States and about 80 million worldwide. In 1999, Sony held a 53 percent share in the market for consoles. PlayStation 2 was launched in Japan in mid 2000, and in the United States at the end of October 2000. Initially priced at $299, PlayStation 2 is undoubtedly a powerful machine. At its core is a 300-megahertz graphics processing chip that was jointly developed with Toshiba and consumed about $1.3 billion in R&D. Referred to as the Emotion Engine processor, the chip allows the machine to display stunning graphic images previously found only on supercomputers. The chip makes the PlayStation 2 the most powerful video game machine yet.

The machine is set up to play different CD and DVD formats, as well as proprietary game titles. As is true with the original PlayStation, PlayStation 2 can play audio CDs. The system is also compatible with the original PlayStation: any PlayStation title can be played on the PlayStation 2. To help justify the price tag, the unit doubles as a DVD player with picture quality as good as current players. The PlayStation 2 does not come equipped with a modem, but it does have networking capabilities and a modem can be attached using one of two USB ports.[53]

Despite the raw power of PlayStation 2, a couple of things have blemished the market launch. First, Sony made far-reaching performance claims for PlayStation 2, but it is receiving some criticism from game experts who have suggested that the first games available for the new system have not matched the talk. Although Sony has sold 3 million PlayStation 2 consoles in Japan since the launch in March 2000, the devices have clearly fallen short of expectations. Programmers grumble that the machine is very hard to write games for. Game players in Japan have complained about blurry and "jagged" images. Designers still don't have a blockbuster PlayStation 2 software title after eighteen months on the job. Sony counters that most game developers have not had sufficient time to write games for the new system, and that the second generation of games written for PlayStation 2 should take better advantage if PlayStation's capabilities. Another problem arose in late October 2000, when Sony announced that it expects to ship just 500,000 machines—half the number previously announced—to the United States for the product's launch. Sony blamed the shortfall on a chip shortage. It plans to ship about 100,000 more PlayStations each week until Christmas. Sony's marketers had long anticipated that demand for the "PS 2," as the company calls PlayStation 2, would outstrip supply at first—but not by this much.[54]

Nintendo GameCube

Nintendo has garnered a solid position in the industry with its N64 machine by focusing on its core demographic, seven- to twelve-year-olds. In 1999, Nintendo took 33 percent of the hardware market and 28 percent of the game market. Nintendo's next generation video game machine, code named Dolphin and named GameCube, packs a modem and a powerful 400-megahertz, 128-bit processor made by IBM into a compact cube. GameCube marks a shift away from Nintendo's traditional approach of using proprietary cartridges to hold game software.

Instead, software for the new player will come on 8-centimeter compact disks, which are smaller than music compact disks. The new disks hold 1.5 gigabytes of data each, far greater storage capacity than the old game cartridges. Players will be able to control GameCube using wireless controllers.[55]

Nintendo has tried to make the GameCube easy for developers to work with rather than focusing on raw peak performance. While developers no doubt appreciate this, by the time GameCube hits store shelves, PlayStation 2 will have been on the market for eighteen months and may have a solid library of games. On the other hand, Nintendo's greatest asset is its intellectual property, which is instantly recognizable by its core demographic and includes Donkey Kong, Super Mario Brothers, and the Pokemon characters. Currently, Nintendo expects to introduce the GameCube in Japan in July 2001, and in the United States in October 2001.

Microsoft X-Box

Microsoft was first rumored to be developing a video game console in late 1999. In March 2000, Bill Gates made it official when he announced that Microsoft would enter the home video game market in fall 2001 with a console code named X-Box. In terms of sheer computing power, the 128-bit X-Box towers above its competitors. X-Box will have a 733-megahertz Pentium III processor, a high-powered graphics chip from Nvidia Corp, a built-in broadband cable modem to allow for online game playing and high-speed Internet browsing, 64 megabytes of memory, CD and DVD drives, and an internal hard disk drive, all features no other console has to date. The operating system will be a stripped-down version of its popular Windows system optimized for graphics-processing capabilities. Microsoft claims that because the X-Box will be based on familiar PC technology, it will be much easier for software developers to write games for. It should be relatively easy to convert games from the PC to run on the X-Box, and vice versa.[56]

Although Microsoft will be a new entrant to the video game industry, it is no stranger to games. Microsoft has long participated in the PC gaming industry and is one of the largest publishers of PC games, with hits such as Microsoft Flight Simulator and Age of Empires I and II to its credit. Sales of Microsoft's PC games have increased 50 percent annually over the past four years, and the company now controls about 10 percent of the PC game mar-

ket. The company has also offered online gaming for some time, including its popular MSN Gaming Zone site. Started in 1996, the web site is the largest online PC gaming hub on the Internet. Nearly 12 million subscribers pay $9.95 a month to play premium games such as Asheron's Call or Fighter Ace. Or they can play traditional card and board games for free. Nor is Microsoft new to hardware; its joysticks and game pads outsell all other brands and it has an important mouse business.

Microsoft's entry into the home video game market was in part a response to the potential threat from companies like Sony and Sega. Microsoft worried that Internet-ready consoles like PlayStation 2 and Dreamcast might take over many web-browsing functions from the personal computer. Some in the company described Internet-enabled video game terminals as Trojan horses in the living room. In Microsoft's calculation, it made sense to get in the market to try and keep Sony and others in check. With annual revenues in excess of $20 billion worldwide, the home video game market is huge and an important source of potential growth for Microsoft. Still, by moving away from its core market, Microsoft is taking a huge risk, particularly given the scale of investments required to develop the X-Box, which could run as high as $1.5 billion.

ENDNOTES

1. A good account of the early history of Bushnell and Atari can be found in S. Cohen, *Zap! The Rise and Fall of Atari*, New York: McGraw-Hill, 1984.
2. Isaacs, R., "Video Games Race to Catch a Changing Market," *Business Week*, December 26, 1977, p. 44B.
3. Pagnano, P., "Atari's Game Plan to Overwhelm Its Competitors," *Business Week*, May 8, 1978, p. 50F.
4. Isaacs, R., "Video Games Race to Catch a Changing Market," *Business Week*, December 26, 1977, p. 44B.
5. Pagnano, P., "Atari's Game Plan to Overwhelm Its Competitors," *Business Week*, May 8, 1978, p. 50F; and Sheff, D., *Game Over*, New York: Random House, 1993.
6. Cohen, S., *Zap! The Rise and Fall of Atari*, New York: McGraw-Hill, 1984.
7. Kehoe, L., "Atari Seeks Way out of Video Game Woes," *Financial Times*, December 14, 1983, p. 23.
8. Schrage, M., "The High Tech Dinosaurs: Video Games, Once Ascendant, Are Making Way," *Washington Post*, July 31, 1983, p. F1.
9. Sheff, D., *Game Over*, New York: Random House, 1993.
10. Quoted in Sheff, D., *Game Over*, New York: Random House, 1993, p. 38.
11. Sheff, D., *Game Over*, New York: Random House, 1993.
12. Golden, D., "In Search of Princess Toadstool," *Boston Globe*, November 20, 1988, p. 18.
13. Gross, N., and Lewis, G., "Here Come the Super Mario Bros.," *Business Week*, November 9, 1987, p. 138.
14. Sheff, D., *Game Over*, New York: Random House, 1993.

15. Golden, D., "In search of Princess Toadstool," *Boston Globe,* November 20, 1988, p. 18.

16. Staff Reporter, "Marketer of the Year," *Adweek,* November 27, 1989, p. 15.

17. Lazzareschi, C., "No Mere Child's Play," *Los Angeles Times,* December 16, 1988, p. 1.

18. For a good summary of the early history of Sega, see Battle, J., and Johnstone, B., "The Next Level: Sega's Plans for World Domination," *Wired,* release 1.06, December 1993.

19. Sheff, D., *Game Over,* New York: Random House, 1993.

20. Battle, J., and Johnstone, B., "The Next Level: Sega's Plans for World Domination," *Wired,* release 1.06, December 1993.

21. For background details, see Flower, J., "3DO: Hip or Hype?" *Wired,* release 1.02, May/June 1993.

22. Brandt, R., "3DO's New Game Player: Awesome or Another Betamax?" *Business Week,* January 11, 1993, p. 38.

23. Flower, J., "3DO: Hip or Hype?" *Wired,* release 1.02, May/June 1993.

24. Jacobs, S., "Third Time's a Charm (They Hope)," *Wired,* release 2.01, January 1994.

25. Dunkin, A., "Video Games: The Next Generation," *Business Week,* January 31, 1994, p. 80.

26. Greenstein, J., "No Clear Winners, Though Some Losers; the Video Game Industry in 1995," *Business Week,* December 22, 1995, p. 42.

27. Staff Reporter, "3DO Says 'I Do' on Major Shift of Its Game Strategy," *Los Angeles Times,* September 17, 1996, p. 2.

28. Battle, J., and Johnstone, B., "The Next Level: Sega's Plans for World Domination," *Wired,* release 1.06, December 1993.

29. Greenstein, J., "No Clear Winners, Though Some Losers: The Video Game Industry in 1995," *Business Week,* December 22, 1995, p. 42.

30. Hamilton, D. P., "Sega Suddenly Finds Itself Embattled," *Wall Street Journal,* March 31, 1997, p. A10.

31. Taves, S., "Meet Your New Playmate," *Wired,* release 3.09, September 1995.

32. Kunni, I., "The Games Sony Plays," *Business Week,* June 15, 1998, p. 128.

33. Platt, C., "WordNerd," *Wired,* release 3.10, October 1995.

34. Kunni, I., "The Games Sony Plays," *Business Week,* June 15, 1998, p. 128.

35. Trachtenberg, J. A., "Race Quits Sony Just Before U.S. Rollout of Its PlayStation Video-Game System," *Wall Street Journal,* August 8, 1995, p. B3.

36. Beenstock, S., "Market Raider: How Sony Won the Console Game," *Marketing,* September 10, 1998, p. 26.

37. Trachtenberg, J. A., "Olafsson Calls It Quits as Chairman of Sony's Technology Strategy Group," *Wall Street Journal,* January 23, 1996, p. B6.

38. Greenstein, J., "Price Cuts Boost Saturn, PlayStation Hardware Sales," *Video Business,* May 31, 1996, p. 1.

39. Greenstein, J., "Sony Cuts Prices of PlayStation Hardware," *Video Business,* March 10, 1997, p. 1.

40. Hamilton, D., "Sega Suddenly Finds Itself Embattled," *Wall Street Journal,* March 31, 1997, p. A10.

41. Staff Reporter, "Nintendo Wakes Up," *The Economist,* August 3, 1996, pp. 55–56.

42. Takahashi, D., "Game Plan: Video Game Makers See Soaring Sales Now—And Lots of Trouble Ahead," *Wall Street Journal,* June 15, 1998, p. R10.

43. Takahashi, D., "Sony and Nintendo Battle for Kids Under 13," *Wall Street Journal,* September 24, 1998, p. B4.

44. Kunni, I., "The Games Sony Plays," *Business Week,* June 15, 1998, p. 128.

45. Takahashi, D., "Sega Is Pricing Game Machine on the Low Side," *Wall Street Journal,* April 16, 1999, p. B6.

46. Paradise, J., "Sony to Launch New PlayStation in Coming Year," *Wall Street Journal,* March 3, 1999, p. B1.

47. Fitzgerald, B., "Pieces of the Puzzle—Closer to Reality," *Wall Street Journal,* November 16, 1998, p. R33.

48. Takahashi, D., "Buying Decision, the Big Game: It's Sony Versus Sega Versus Nintendo Versus Microsoft," *Wall Street Journal,* June 26, 2000, p. R16.

49. Hause, K., Ma, B., Hwang, D., and House, J., *Review and Forecast of the World Wide Information Appliance Market,* 1999–2004, IDC, 2000.

50. Guth, R. A., "Sega Cites Dreamcast Price Cuts for Loss Amid Crucial Time for Survival of Firm," *Wall Street Journal,* October 30, 2000, p. A22.

51. Takahashi, D., "Sega Will Give Away Dreamcast Players to Lure Subscribers to the Web," *Wall Street Journal,* April 4, 2000, p. B1.

52. Guth, R. "Sega Cites Dreamcast Price Cuts for Loss Amid Crucial Time for Survival of Firm," *Wall Street Journal,* October 30, 2000, p. A22.

53. Oxford, T., and Steinberg, S. "Ultimate Game Machine Sony's PlayStation 2 Is Due on Shelves Oct. 26. It Brims with Potential—But at This Point Sega's Dreamcast Appears a Tough Competitor," *Atlanta Journal/Atlanta Constitution,* October 1, 2000, p. P1.

54. Hwang, S. "Sony Rolls Out PlayStation Ads Despite Shortage," *Wall Street Journal,* October 6, 2000, p. B1.

55. Guth, R. A., "New Players from Nintendo Will Link to Web," *Wall Street Journal,* August 25, 2000, p. B1.

56. Takahashi, D., "Microsoft's X-Box Impresses Game Developers," *Wall Street Journal,* March 13, 2000, p. B12.

Microsoft Windows Versus Linux

This case was prepared by Charles W. L. Hill, the University of Washington.

Windows is still a no-brainer for most people.

—*Linus Torvalds, August 2000*

Intellectual property is an artificial legal scheme. Companies that keep users from sharing software are antisocial.

—*Richard Stallman, unpaid head,*
Free Software Foundation, April 1998

Companies who think they can give away their products—or build them on the backs of those that have no intellectual-property value—will be unable to sustain their businesses.

—*Craig Mundie, Senior Vice President, Microsoft, May 2001*

Linux is a toy.
—*Steve Ballmer, Microsoft CEO, March 2001*[1]

Linux is a disruptive technology.

—*Michael Dell, CEO,*
Dell Computer Corporation,
Linux World Key Note Address, August 2000

The Accidental Entrepreneur

Linux is an operating system kernel that can be downloaded for free from the Internet. It is the creation not of a company, but of a self-organizing community of developers working together voluntarily over the Internet to improve the source code of the system. The source code is published on the Internet under a general public license. This specifies that licensees must agree to make any improvements or additions to the operating system freely available in the form of source code.

Linus Torvalds initiated the development of Linux in 1991.[2] At the time, Torvalds was a twenty-one-year old computer science student at the University of Helsinki, Finland. He was taking a class on programming for the UNIX operating system, a powerful commercial operating system originally developed by AT&T. Frustrated by the limited availability of UNIX hardware at the university, Torvalds purchased a PC with the intention of writing some basic UNIX-like code that would run on the low-powered machine. He

This case is intended to be used as a basis for class discussion rather than as an illustration of either effective or ineffective handling of the situation. Reprinted by permission of Charles W. L. Hill.

started by writing a task-switching protocol and then added other features as the need arose.

Within six months Torvalds had put together many of the elements of an operating system—task switching, a file management system, and device drivers. At this point, Torvalds realized that he had developed the basic elements of an operating system kernel. Torvalds christened his embryonic operating system Linux, a play on his first name and UNIX.

Torvalds was aided in the development of Linux by software available from the Free Software Foundation's GNU project. (GNU is a recursive acronym that stands for "Gnu's Not UNIX.") Richard Stallman, then a programmer at MIT's artificial intelligence lab, began the GNU project in 1984. The aim of the GNU project was to write a complete and free version of UNIX. Hardly wishing to reinvent the wheel, Torvalds tweaked Linux so that it fit GNU's preexisting library of programs. In his words, "I never ported programs, I ported the kernel to work with the programs."[3]

Torvalds also adopted another of Stallman's ideas, the general public license scheme (GPL), often referred to as a "copyleft" scheme. A GPL allows users to sell, copy, and change copyleft programs—but specifies that any modifications to the source code must be made freely available.

The Open-Source Software Paradigm

In mid-1991, Torvalds posted the source code of Linux on a University of Helsinki FTP server under a GPL so that others could download and use it. In return, he asked for advice on improving the system. Soon the emails started coming in with comments, suggestions, and software patches to improve Linux. Almost by accident, Torvalds had stumbled on a new paradigm for designing software: the open-source software paradigm. A distributed community of Linux users connected only by the Internet had spontaneously organized itself and was working cooperatively, for no pay, to improve the functionality of the operating system.

Like Torvalds, the development community was composed primarily of computer hobbyists whose main motivation was the ego gratification associated with solving complex technical challenges. Some developers cooperated to solve a problem. Others

competed with each other for bragging rights, with the best codes winning through a process of Darwinian selection. If an author drifted away from the process, no longer improving his or her bit of code, other people would pick it up and work on it. Hovering over this entire process was the omnipresent Torvalds, whose role evolved into orchestrator and arbitrator of the "competition" that was emerging among developers to improve Linux.

Several advantages of the open source software development process soon became apparent. First, developers were free to choose what area they worked on, rather than being assigned to a task they might not want. The matching of programmer to task by self-selection increased the speed of development. Second, Linux reflected the diversity of the user base and was quickly adapted to run on a wide range of processor architectures, including processors from Intel (386 to Pentium), Digital Equipment (Alpha), Sun (SPARC), Silicon Graphics (MIPS), and Motorola (Power PC). Third, the open-source process meant that the code was rapidly tested by end users in a diverse range of environments and was quickly debugged, with patches appearing on a weekly basis.

In parallel to this somewhat anarchic process, there was always a stable release distribution that moved forward when new features had been thoroughly tested. Linux moved through a series of point releases—1.1, 1.2, etc.—and subpoint releases—1.2.12, 1.2.13, and so on. When a big enough jump in software functionality occurred, developers moved on to the next version, a process presided over by Torvalds. The result of this process was an operating system kernel that was efficient in its use of computer resources, could run in a diverse set of computer environments, was very stable, and improved at a rapid rate. And the kernel was free.

By 1994, Linux had matured to the point where Torvalds decided to release Linux 1.0. At this juncture, the grassroots movement was gaining momentum, the user base was already large, and the core Linux development team was substantial. Among the thousands of files in Linux 1.0, there was one simply called Credits. This file listed the names, addresses, and contributions of the main participants in the development of the operating system. The list included more than one hundred names scattered around the world.

Building Momentum

With the release of Linux 1.0, Linux began to gain momentum. As befits a grassroots movement, the early adopters of Linux were technically minded individuals and Linux evangelists who started using Linux in the workplace because it suited their individual needs. The early adopters were concentrated in higher education, government agencies such as NASA, and research institutions. Soon, however, the operating system started to penetrate corporations, typically entering individual departments under the radar screen of corporate information officers.

Two developments occurred together to give Linux adoption a big boost. The first was the formation of several companies designed to exploit the Linux phenomenon.[4] These included Caldera and Red Hat Software, both established in 1994. How do you make money out of an operating system that is free? The idea behind Caldera and Red Hat was to bundle Linux together with associated programs on a CD, such as a graphical user interface for Linux; sell it for a low price; and then build a large enough user base to profit by selling services such as installation, customization, and technical support—services that the distributed developers of Linux had no interest in offering, but which Linux would need if it was ever to be more than a cult phenomenon.

Another central idea behind these companies was to provide legitimacy for Linux, which in turn would overcome resistance from corporate information officers, who seemed unlikely to approve adoption of software that was free, written by "hackers," and not backed by any identifiable vendor who could be held accountable and offer help when things went wrong.

The second development that boosted Linux was the rapid growth of the World Wide Web in the mid 1990s. Designed and distributed through the medium of the Internet, Linux itself was a child of the Web. As early as 1995, research suggested that almost 50 percent of new Internet server implementations were Linux based.[5] Free, stable, and platform independent, and placing low demands on computing resources, Linux turned out to be the ideal operating system for an appliance server. (Appliance servers are network-enabled devices designed explicitly to provide a single dedicated service, such as email, file and print, or Internet access, or a predefined suite of services.)

By 1997, Red Hat claimed that Linux had gained a presence in many large organizations. Included among Red Hat's customers were NASA, Disney, Lockheed Martin, General Electric, UPS, NASDAQ, the IRS, and Boeing, as well as most leading U.S. universities. It must be said, however, that most of these customers were individuals or departments, and not the corporation or agency per se. Since the operating system could be downloaded for free from multiple sites, it was very difficult to determine how many people were actually using Linux. Red Hat estimated the number in 1997 to be between 3 and 5 million.[6] International Data Corporation estimated that about 150,000 servers were shipped with a Linux operating system in 1997.[7]

Equally important as adoptions by large organizations was the ability of Linux to gain a foothold among cost- and performance-conscious small and medium-sized businesses. Typical of these businesses was Mahaffey's Quality Printing, an offset and flexographic printer in Jackson, Mississippi. Mahaffey's got a T1 Internet connection in 1996 and originally used Windows NT to run the company's servers. The company was experiencing rapid growth, however, and its servers suffered frequent crashes and restarts running on NT. The production manager had read about Linux in an article in *Wired* magazine and decided to try it as an FTP server. The experience was so positive that Mahaffey's decided to stay with Linux for the FTP server, and the company also decided to stick with the operating system as its server solution. By 1999, the company had seven Linux servers for print-and-file serving: OPI, FTP, mail, DNS, Web, database, and fax serving. The decision gave Mahaffey's significant savings. They did not have to pay for an operating system license, plus the lower power requirements of Linux meant that they could run the operating system on aging Intel hardware. The company calculated that it saved approximately $60,000 and got a stable operating system too.[8]

Going Mainstream

In 1998, Linux started to penetrate the mainstream, but not through any mass-marketing campaign or direct sales effort. No player had the resources to carry out such a campaign. It had simply proved its value again and again in different computing environments, and thus generated support from a growing community of users, service providers, and application providers. The almost religious fervor of the open source movement aided adoption among those looking for an alternative to Microsoft.

On university campuses, courses on Linux were increasingly popular, thereby increasing the supply of developers eager to improve the operating system or work on Linux applications. The ability to look at the source code of an operating system, and manipulate it, was enormously attractive to students. Demand was given a boost by some high-profile implementations of Linux that began to increase its legitimacy, at least in the eyes of corporate information officers. For example, Digital Domain Inc. used workstations running Linux to render many of the stunning graphical images from the blockbuster movie *Titanic*. NASA's Goddard Space Flight Center built a supercomputer out of off-the-shelf PC components and chose Linux to run the machine. When they were reported in industry news media, such implementations helped to get the Linux bandwagon rolling.

The big driver of demand, however, remained the web or appliance server market. According to IDC data, approximately 500,000 copies of Linux were shipped as server operating systems during 1998, making Linux second to Microsoft's Windows NT, which shipped 1.2 million copies.[9] As the year progressed, a growing number of software companies added legitimacy to Linux by aligning themselves with the operating system. In July 1998, database providers Informix, Oracle, and Sybase all announced that they would offer Linux versions of their database software. In September 1998, Intel and Netscape announced that they would invest in Red Hat Software. In November 1998, at the annual Comdex computer trade show in Las Vegas, there was a sharp increase in the number of Linux-oriented companies showing their wares. In December 1998, media reports suggested that IBM would announce a broad service and support agreement for Red Hat's distribution of Linux. Also in December, Coral announced that it would distribute a limited-feature Linux version of its WordPerfect software for free.

Increasing recognition set up a virtuous circle in which growing demand elicited more recognition from software companies, who pledged to support Linux, which generated more demand for Linux and led to more pledges. The process was spurred on by the fact that Linux was not a Microsoft product, and many in the industry had an interest in seeing Microsoft dethroned from its commanding position.

Ironically, a backhanded complement from Microsoft in the form of a leaked internal confidential memo, dubbed the "Halloween memo" because of its release date, added to the growing hype surrounding Linux. In it, a Microsoft employee described Linux as a "direct short term revenue and platform threat to Microsoft, particularly in the server space." The memo also noted that case studies provided "dramatic" evidence that open-source software can match and exceed the quality of commercial software, and that open-source advocates "are making progressively more credible agreements that their products are at least as robust—if not more—than commercial alternatives."[10]

Linux Gets Hyped

In the supercharged economic environment of the late 1990s, it is perhaps not surprising that Linux too became the object of excessive hype. From being the obscure brainchild of one student in Finland, Linux was suddenly transformed in the eyes of certain media sources into a prime-time contender for Microsoft's operating system hegemony.

Calmer voices pointed out that while Linux might be a strong contender in segments of the server market, its appeal in the desktop arena was marginal. The key consideration was a lack of compelling applications, such as the ubiquitous Microsoft Office, financial management software, and games. Even with all of the strengths of the Linux development community, Microsoft could still count on an army of developers schooled in Win 32 API protocols to keep writing applications to run on Windows. Given a choice between writing applications for a platform that had yet to penetrate the desktop and writing for one that dominated the desktop, developers naturally acted according to their economic interests, even if their noneconomic preferences lay elsewhere. In addition, while graphical user interfaces (GUIs) were now available for Linux, it was still regarded by many as a technical system that was intimidating to the average user.

Immersed in the rhetoric of the new economy, however, many anti-Microsoft opinion leaders brushed aside such concerns in their desire to see Linux succeed. It was certainly true that many cost-conscious dot-com start-ups were adopting Linux as the operating system for their web servers precisely because it was free and stable. Since Linux was not the product of a company—a concept that was difficult for many to grasp—attention shifted to the growing list of Linux distributors and complementors, such as Red Hat, Caldera Systems, and VA Linux, several of which went public in 1999 and 2000, and saw dramatic increases in their share prices.

Red Hat was typical: it went public in August 2000 and closed on the first day of trading at $52.06 a share, a gain of 271.88 percent. The shares peaked a few months later at $150, valuing Red Hat at $25 billion. At the time, Red Hat had revenues of $52.8 million and an operating loss of $46.7 million. By mid 2001 the shares had fallen to $3.75, giving Red Hat a more modest market cap of $637 million. In the interim, the company had annual revenues of $102.65 million, but losses of $107.4 million. The Red Hat story and the similar experience of its Linux peers suggest that a profitable business model based on Linux may be difficult to achieve.

Beyond the Hype

Although the implosion of the dot-com bubble and the associated wreckage took some of the steam out of the Linux bandwagon, the underlying trends remained positive, particularly in the server market. Exhibit 1 summarizes the actual and forecasted worldwide server unit shipments by operating system over the 1997–2005 period, as presented by IDC.[11]

Exhibit 1 clearly shows the rapid rise of Linux between 1998 and 2000, and suggests that this growth will continue unabated through 2005, with a compound annual growth rate of 38.8 percent between 2000 and 2005. Also evident is the penetration of Windows NT and now Windows 2000 into the server space. Windows NT beat NetWare as the market leader in 1998, and Windows 2000 is expected to maintain this position for Microsoft through 2005, with a compound annual growth rate of 14.3 percent. The big loser is NetWare from Novell, which is rapidly losing ground to Windows 2000 and Linux. Unix too, is predicted to lose share.

Linux 2.4

The continual improvement in Linux is helping to drive adoption in the server arena. The current version, Linux 2.4, was released in early 2001. Linux 2.4 has many features designed for corporate enterprise computing. The kernel provides improvements in capacity, storage management, and symmetric multiprocessing. Linux 2.4 offers a logical volume manager subsystem to enhance its storage management capabilities. It allows system administrators to add and remove Linux storage disks, without the need for rebooting. It also produces file system snapshots for backup purposes. Linux can now support files larger than 2 GB and addresses up to 64 GB of physical memory on Intel-based servers.

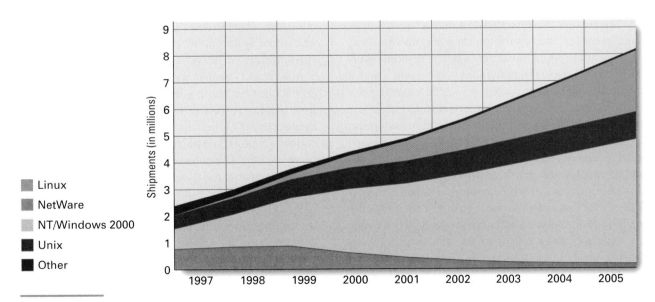

EXHIBIT 1

Worldwide Server Shipments by Operating System, 1997–2005

Linux 2.4 supports three new microprocessor architectures: Intel's Architecture 64 (IA64), which is also known as Itanium; IBM System/390 mainframes; and SuperH, which is the microprocessor used in Windows CE hand-held devices. It also provides support for a wide range of hardware devices, including universal serial bus (UBS) drivers for digital cameras, keyboards, mice, modems, network cards, printers, scanners, and zip drives.

Drivers and Barriers to Linux Adoption

Recent surveys by IDC and Gartner support the perception that the adoption of Linux in the server arena is being driven by a combination of low cost and reliability. In 2001, IDC asked IT managers in approximately 865 organizations to identify the three top reasons why they would consider adopting Linux as a server operating system.[12] Initial price was cited by 41 percent of those surveyed, followed by reliability (27 percent). Availability of specific applications was cited as the third reason for adoption (19 percent). The specific applications include other open source software, such as Apache Web server, Samba for print-and-file serving, and Sendmail for email and messaging solutions, and open-source development tools.

A mid 2000 Gartner survey of 709 decisionmakers for server operating systems yielded similar results.[13] About 54 percent cited the low initial price, 32 percent cited reliability, and 19 percent cited low ongoing operating costs. Interviews of Linux adopters tend to reinforce these results.

The surveys also provided data on barriers to adoption. In the IDC survey, the three top reasons why users decided not to adopt Linux were a lack of in-house skills (39 percent), lack of applications (36 percent), and a desire to limit platform profusion within the enterprise (34 percent). The Gartner survey presented a similar picture, with the three top barriers to Linux adoption identified by respondents being lack of service and support options (22 percent), lack of in-house skills (18 percent), and lack of applications (16 percent).

The low cost of implementing a Linux solution derives not just from the free license, but also from the ability to run Linux on aging hardware, which is a plus for cost-conscious organizations. With the growing interest in Linux on university campuses, it seems unlikely that a lack of in-house skills will remain a long-term barrier to adoption. The lack of a broad portfolio of enterprise applications is currently a problem for Linux both in the server arena and on the desktop.

Commenting on the results of its survey, IDC postulates that Linux is now crossing the chasm from technically minded early adopters to mainstream acceptance. The crossing is essentially summarized by a shift from a belief in the open-source paradigm as an "anything but Microsoft" grassroots movement to a more pragmatic and objective analysis of the economic benefits that Linux offers to adopters.

Linux Use on Servers

The lack of enterprise computing applications explains why most of Linux implementation is currently limited to the application server arena. Linux is still a niche product. Another IDC survey of Linux use reported that respondents overwhelmingly cited Internet/intranet application workloads as the most common use for Linux (78 percent).[14] Strong use was also reported for file and print (58 percent), software development (57 percent), and email messaging (57 percent). Internet service providers (ISPs) in particular are attracted to the low cost of Linux given their own operating environment, which is characterized by extreme pressure on profit margins. Only 7.5 percent of respondents indicated that they used Linux for enterprise applications such as enterprise resource planning, customer relationship management, supply chain management, and human resource functions.

Linux may currently be confined to a niche, but it is worth noting that when Windows NT was launched, it too was supported by very few enterprise grade server applications. As with Linux, the early adoption of Windows NT consisted mostly of a grassroots solution for print-and-file servers and a workgroup mail server for small groups of PCs. As Windows NT gained momentum, enterprise grade application developers began to support NT, which in turn drove forward the adoption of Windows NT in enterprises and elicited more support from application developers. As a result of this virtuous circle, there are very few enterprise server applications that are not available today for Windows 2000.

Could Linux be following a similar development path? It is certainly possible. Like Windows NT, Linux started as a grassroots movement in corporations that entered under the radar screen of corporate information managers. And like Windows NT, as the installed base of Linux servers expands, enterprise application developers are beginning to support the system. Among others, SAP, Oracle, and IBM began announcing applications for Linux in mid to late 2000.

Vendor Support for Linux on the Server

The bullish case for Linux is boosted by the growing list of hardware vendors and software providers that are supporting Linux. Major hardware vendors, including Compaq, Dell, Fujitsu, Hitachi, IBM, and NEC, have embraced Linux and ship the operating system on their servers. As noted earlier, Oracle, Sybase, and Informix have all ported their database management software to Linux. In 2001, Dell and Oracle announced a deal to put Oracle database software on its Linux servers. SAP has ported its enterprise software to Linux. Hewlett Packard offers worldwide support for Linux, and Computer Associates now provides a version of Unicenter TNG for Linux.[15]

IBM's Linux Push

In one of the single biggest commitments to Linux, IBM announced in December 2000 plans to invest nearly $1 billion in Linux software development, hardware, services, the open-source community, and partnerships during 2001.[16] IBM seems to be betting heavily that Linux will become a major operating sys-

tem in the enterprise and will drive IBM's eServer sales growth across all of the company's eServer platforms—from appliances to mainframes. IBM now has more than 1,500 employees focused on Linux hardware and software development. In addition, IBM chairman and CEO Lou Gerstner also announced a deal in which IBM would build what it claims is the world's largest Linux supercomputer. The system, now deployed by Royal Dutch/Shell Group, consists of 1,024 IBM X-series servers packaged in thirty-two racks and all running Linux. The system is designed to analyze seismic data.

IBM apparently sees Linux as a way to compete simultaneously with both Microsoft and Sun. An IBM spokesperson has stated that IBM will discontinue its AIX offerings when Linux contains the enterprise features that customers demand from commercial UNIX products. IBM seems willing to cannibalize its own UNIX business to beat Sun and Microsoft. To support this strategy, IBM has produced the diagram summarized in Exhibit 2, which illustrates how IBM Linux solutions can be used to replace Windows. Some comments from an IBM

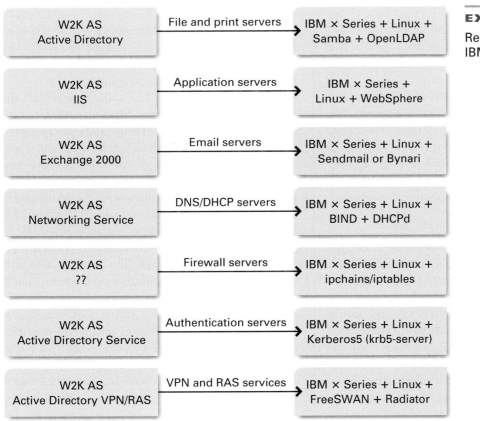

EXHIBIT 2

Replacing Windows with IBM Linux Solutions[17]

EXHIBIT 3

Comments from an IBM Document

The outages in the MSN Messenger emphasize increasing concerns about Microsoft's ability to move from developing software to turning its products into rentable Web services through the .NET and Hailstorm strategies. This . . . is an early example of Microsoft's lack of technical infrastructure and capability to support a large scale, Web-based service and distribution model. This disadvantage for Microsoft is a key advantage for IBM in numerous ways.

Linux is highly stable and reliable—here are the facts: According to a Zona Research report published in October 2000, 80% of respondents replied that stability and reliability were the deciding factors when it came to choosing Linux as their operating system. The Standish group found that Linux servers are more reliable than Microsoft servers when it comes to peak operational downtime. This research shows that Linux servers have about 14 hours of unplanned downtime per year, amounting to 99.6% uptime during average peak operational periods. By comparison, Standish found the average Microsoft Enterprise Cluster to have just over 99% uptime or about 30 hours of downtime during the average peak operational period. Further, according to an article by Alan Radding published in *Information Week* in April 2001, in terms of actual hours, *the Microsoft server cluster will be down more than twice as long as a Linux server.*

Despite Microsoft Corp.'s continued contention that open-source operating systems don't make good business sense, the Transaction Processing Performance Council released new data in mid-May showing that IBM's upcoming DB2 7.2 release running on Linux 2.4.3 outperforms SQL Server 2000 running on Windows 2000 in the 100GB category, by the order of 2,733 queries per hour for DB2 on Linux versus 1,699 per hour on SQL Server 2000. [See complete results on **http://www.tpc.org.**—results are current as of 6/26/01.]

In addition to licensing and auditing costs . . . Microsoft Windows 2000 Advanced Server . . . starts at $4,000 per 25 users. That does not include add-on components and connectors. So, to run a moderately sized eBusiness application, supporting, say, 7,000 possible users, and entry level server costs could start at $1.1 million.

---

document attacking Microsoft and supporting Linux are given in Exhibit 3. The comments give some insights into IBM's likely sales strategy under its Linux initiative.

Despite the rising tide of third-party support from the likes of IBM, there is little sign yet that Linux is moving out of its niche in the server arena. For all of the high-profile announcements of Linux support, Windows 2000 still holds a huge lead in available enterprise applications. For Linux to grow outside its niche, this lead must obviously change.

Linux on the Client

Although Linux is making rapid headway in certain segments of the server market, it is currently a no-show on the desktop. The early hype promoted Linux as an alternative to Windows for the client, but at this point, Linux looks set to join Next OS and IBM's OS/2 as also-rans in a business Microsoft dominates almost completely. Accumulating evidence shows that Linux is making little headway. Eazel, considered by many to be one of the most promising developers of applications for Linux desktops, closed its doors in May 2001. Started by the team that had developed the

interface for the Apple Macintosh, Eazel had been trying to develop a similar interface for Linux. The company failed because it was unable to raise additional funding from venture capitalists.

Eazel's demise followed a similar retreat from the Linux market by Corel, the Canadian software company that owns both WordPerfect Office (a competitor to Microsoft Office) and Corel Draw. Corel had developed Linux versions of WordPerfect Office and Corel Draw and had entered the market as a distributor of the Linux operating system. Corel struggled to become profitable, however, and in October 2000 accepted a $135 million investment by Microsoft in return for a commitment to develop applications for Microsoft's .NET initiative. In January 2001, the company stepped back from its role as a Linux operating system distributor as part of a plan to "return to profitability."[18] In August 2001, Dell Computer announced that it would stop selling desktop and notebook computers pre-installed with the Linux operating system due to a lack of demand.[19]

One does not have to look hard to find reasons for the inability of Linux to establish itself on the desktop. There is no economic reason to switch. In fact, there are economic costs to doing so. The vast bulk of existing applications, including Microsoft Office, are written to run on Windows. Most users have invested in a library of Windows applications, are familiar with the Windows GUI, are content enough with the system they have, and see no compelling reason to bear the costs of switching to another system. Even if the operating system is free, the applications would not be, and there would be a cost involved in learning a new system. The GUIs for Linux, such as KDE and Gnome, are not as user friendly as Windows. Some Linux implementations still use the old command line interface, a format that most desktop users haven't seen since the heyday of MS-DOS in the 1980s.

Some argue that for Linux to start making inroads in mature PC markets such as the United States, new Linux applications would have to offer compelling economic reasons for bearing the costs of switching and installing a Linux operating system. For longtime Windows users, there is no sign of such applications anywhere on the horizon and no indication as to what they might be.

Linux is making some headway, however, in the K–12 educational market.[20] Cash-strapped schools are finding that they can build PC labs for students at a much lower cost by buying old Intel hardware and installing Linux. Applications for Linux, such as StarOffice and Mozilla, meet the bulk of basic educational needs—word processing, spreadsheets, presentation software, Web browsing, and email. Scoffing at the notion that Linux is a more difficult system, a representative of the Open Source Educational Foundation has noted, "We have kindergartners using it [Linux] on a daily basis without any problems."[21]

Linux appears to be gaining traction on the desktop in some foreign markets.[22] To varying degrees, this seems to be the case in Central and Eastern Europe and in China. In general, these markets are price sensitive and the level of PC penetration is currently very low, so widespread attachment to Windows is not a major issue. In these markets, the low cost of Linux is a real benefit to PC vendors and buyers. It is probably no coincidence that the growing popularity of Linux in price-sensitive developing markets is occurring at the same time that Microsoft is stepping up efforts to reduce the level of piracy of its products. Even in these markets though, the lack of Linux applications is hindering adoption. Unless this situation changes, these markets may default toward Windows standardization in the long run.

How Vulnerable Is Microsoft?
The Strengths of Linux

The picture of Linux that is emerging is one of a highly successful niche operating system that is valued in focused segments of the server market for its low cost and stability. ISPs in particular have embraced Linux as a choice for web servers. Outside this niche, however, Linux is currently limited by a lack of enterprise and desktop applications. While Linux supporters, including Linus Torvalds, concede that Linux has a long way to go before it becomes a threat to the hegemony of Windows on the desktop, the situation in the server arena is less clear.

Theoretically at least, the growing installed base of Linux servers, when coupled with the desire of many other enterprises to see a non-Microsoft solution, could trigger an increase in the supply of enterprise applications written to run on Linux. The trick is to get the process going. A larger number of enterprise applications could unleash a bandwagon effect, where the increasing availability of Linux applications drives forward adoption of more Linux servers and induces developers to write more applications based on Linux, which further increases demand for the servers, and so on. If it proceeds far enough, this virtuous circle could result in the market flipping from Microsoft dominated to Linux dominated. Once that happens in the server arena, downward migration of Linux onto the desktop (perhaps using a different computing paradigm where many Office applications reside on servers) could become a possibility.

The commitment of companies such as IBM to promoting Linux should be taken as a signal that this scenario is not entirely remote. Microsoft's history demonstrates that an operating system that enters corporations through a grassroots movement and establishes itself initially in selected niches or beachheads can become an enterprisewide system.

To bolster their case, supporters of Linux point out that in a recent test, Linux outperformed Windows 2000.[23] In May 2001, Transaction Processing Performance Council (TPPC) benchmarks revealed that IBM's DB2 7.2 on Linux 2.4.3 outperformed Microsoft SQL Server and Windows 2000 in a 100 GB database test. In prior TPPC tests, Microsoft has typically won with the SQL Server and Windows 2000 duo across various hardware configurations. Microsoft dismissed the results, arguing that the numbers were more reflective of database performance than of operating system capabilities.

Linux supporters also point to the strong interest in Linux on university campuses. The open-source software model allows students to look at and experiment with the source code of Linux, making it useful for courses on operating systems. In a campus bookstore, one is likely to see rows of books on Linux in the computer section. At the very least, the number of graduates with development talent and training in Linux will alleviate a perceived barrier to Linux adoption cited in corporate surveys—the lack of in-house talent.

Limitations of Linux and the Advantages of Microsoft

Questions about the value and long-term viability of Linux remain. The lack of enterprise and desktop applications remains a vexing problem. Linux may be cheap, and it may be able to take advantage of inexpensive aging hardware, but what about the total cost of ownership? Does the lack of Linux talent strain an organization and give rise to unanticipated costs? The open-source software paradigm may have worked well when the Linux code was relatively compact, but will the paradigm scale to a more complex and bulky code? Between release 1.0 and 2.4, the Linux kernel grew from a few thousand lines of code to over 1 million. At what point does the complexity of the development process overwhelm the open-source model? How practical is it to have a single individual, currently Torvalds, acting as final arbitrator? Can voluntary cooperation and coordination sustain the growth of a system that others are profiting from, including ISPs, Linux distributors, application developers, and service providers? Will developers motivated by ego gratification begin to question why they are working for free on a system so that others can get rich? When does the revolution run out of steam? And if key distributors such as Red Hat begin to take ownership of the system, will Linux splinter into several incompatible versions, as occurred with UNIX?

Then there is the tenacity of Microsoft to consider. Microsoft has also shown a willingness to experiment with licensing its own source code, although not in a manner that is similar to the GNU General Public License under which Linux source code is distributed.[24] During the second half of 2000, Microsoft launched a pilot program that gave a small number of large enterprise customers access to the source code—under strict nondisclosure agreements—for Windows operating environments. The goal was to allow customers to review the code, thereby boosting their confidence in areas such as security and encryption, and helping them to address deployment concerns. In March 2001, the program was expanded to include about 1,000 North American enterprise customers, and in May 2001 the program was expanded internationally. At the same time, Microsoft has licensed the source code for one or more Microsoft products to over 100 universities in the United States and abroad, giving students hands-on experience with Microsoft source code.

Microsoft has many other advantages. While Windows NT was prone to crashing, Windows 2000 has won praise for its stability, thereby reducing one of the factors that induced companies to try Linux in the first place. As noted, Windows has the clear advantage in terms of applications. A large development community is schooled in Win 32 API and ready to write more applications for Windows. Windows 2000 seems to be a secure system, while Microsoft charges that the Linux security model is weak. Microsoft has the advantage of a big support infrastructure, the cost of which can be spread over a vast installed base. Corporate information officers might want to standardize their enterprise software on a single platform for economic reasons. Microsoft is in a unique position to fulfill this need with its offerings from Windows 2000 Datacenter Server: Windows 2000 Server, Windows XP desktop offerings, and Windows CE. All of this suggests that while Linux may continue to make headway in segments of the server market, other market shifts will be required if Linux is to become a viable contender against Windows for enterprise applications and on the desktop.

ENDNOTES

1. Cited in S. Campbell, "Linux Debate," *Crn*, March 26, 2001, p. 3.
2. Background material for this section drawn from the following sources: G. Moody, "The Greatest OS That (N)ever Was," *Wired*, Release 5.08, August 1997; S. Davis, "Linux: Software with a License to Use," *Wall Street Journal*, April 3, 1998, p. B7F; G. Moody, *Rebel Code: Linux and the Open Source Revolution*, 2001.

3. G. Moody, "The Greatest OS That (N)ever Was," *Wired,* Release 5.08, August 1997.

4. J. Burke, "The Finnish Connection," *Red Herring,* August 1, 1996.

5. M. Bolzern, "Public Domain OS Catches On," *Software Magazine,* October 1995, pp. 8–9.

6. G. Moody, "The Greatest OS That (N)ever Was," *Wired,* Release 5.08, August 1997.

7. W. Wilson, "Linux Blazing into Tech Mainstream," *Seattle Post Intelligencer,* December 28, 1998, p. C1.

8. D. Greenlaw, "Linux Illuminations from an Early Adopter," *Printing Impressions,* May 2000, p. 76.

9. W. Wilson, "Linux Blazing into Tech Mainstream," *Seattle Post Intelligencer,* December 28, 1998, p. C1.

10. B. Ploskina, "Halloween Memo: Great Threat or Gobbledygook?" *Ent,* November 18, 1998, pp. 1, 52.

11. International Data Corporation. Worldwide Server Market Forecast and Analysis, 2001–2005, June 2001, IDC Report #25031.

12. International Data Corporation, "Users' Perceptions of Linux: Time to Start Crossing the Chasm," August 2001, IDC Bulletin #25269.

13. "What the Enterprise Thinks of Linux: Service Needs and Adoption Drivers," Garnter Advisory, October 16, 2000.

14. International Data Corporation, "Linux Usage: Enterprise Application Need Not Apply—Yet," IDC Bulletin #23876.

15. C. R. Lubrano, "Linux or Windows: What Should You Do?" *Datapro,* June 14, 2001; M. Hubley, "Major Service Vendors' Commitment to Linux and OSS," Gartner Advisory, June 15, 2001.

16. Anonymous, "IBM Invests Almost $1 Billion in Linux," *InfoWorld,* December 18, 2000.

17. Microsoft Field Bulletin, "Answering the 'Winning with Linux' Letter," August 2001.

18. E. Scannell. "Corel Steps Away from Linux to Focus on Being Profitable," *InfoWorld,* January 29, 2001, p. 24.

19. A. Krauss, "Dell Ends Linux Offering," *New York Times,* August 3, 2001, p. 4.

20. A. Gonzalez, "Penguin Enrolls in U.S. Schools," *Wired News,* August 20, 2001, www.wired.com.

21. A. Gonzalez, "Penguin Enrolls in U.S. Schools," *Wired News,* August 20, 2001, www.wired.com.

22. N. Spit and A. Jump, "Linux in Eastern Europe: More Than Just an Insurance Policy?" Gartner Advisory, September 19, 2000.

23. C. R. Lubrano, "Linux or Windows: What Should You Do?" *Datapro,* June 14, 2001.

24. A. Gillen, "Microsoft Extends Its Source Licensing Efforts," IDC Flash #24643, May 2001.

21

IBM Global Services: The Professional Computer Services Industry

This case was prepared by Vincent Pawlowski and Marc E. Gartenfeld, both of St. John's University, and Dorothy G. Dologite, Baruch College, under the direction of Dr. Robert J. Mockler, St. John's University.

In early 2001, John Joyce, chief financial officer of International Business Machines (IBM), in presenting the company's fourth-quarter and full-year 2000 results to industry securities analysts at the Investors Relations Meeting on January 17, 2001, commented that although IBM Global Services (IGS) had posted growth quarter to quarter and year to year, results for 2000 were not what they wanted (IBM, 2001a). IBM Global Services had not met the company's objectives for the full year or the last quarter in either revenue or pretax income (PTI), and its direct expense grew faster than its revenue. This certainly raised some concerns, considering IGS's position as IBM's growth engine and second largest contributor to the company's bottom line. Joyce was also very careful to remind analysts that a slowing economy and its potential impact on information technology spending were still wild cards for future growth. The main issue to be resolved was to create an enterprisewide strategy that would differentiate IBM Global Services from its competition.

Since December 1996, when IBM established IBM Global Services (IGS), IGS had achieved outstanding business results. IGS had grown faster than the industry, and IBM Global Services was then widely recognized as the largest computer services company in the world, surpassing EDS. Prior to this period, Integrated Systems Solution Corporation (ISSC), an IBM subsidiary and the predecessor of IGS, had similar results. It was accepted that the success of IBM's services business was a major contributor to IBM's overall business recovery and that the future of IBM depended on the future success of IBM Global Services. Figure 1 identifies the segments of IBM (hardware, global services, software, global financing, enterprise investments/other) and the company's percentage of revenue by segment.

The computer services industry includes three broad categories of services: processing services (data entry, credit card authorization, billing payroll processing), network services (electronic data interchange services, electronic mail delivery, file transfer, and electronic funds transfer), and professional computer services (technology consulting, custom programming, systems integration, and outsourcing). The industry had experienced a prolonged period of

FIGURE 1

IBM Company's Percentage of Revenue
by Segment

	2000	1999	1998
Hardware	42.7	43.3	44.2
Global services	37.5	36.7	35.4
Software	14.3	14.5	14.5
Global financing	3.9	3.6	3.5
Enterprise Investments/other	1.6	1.9	2.4
Total	100	100	100

Source: IBM Annual Report (2001).

strong growth, which was expected to continue into 2001 and beyond primarily due to the service demands associated with the use of the Internet in business (Hoovers Online Network, 2001a). This rapid growth was stimulating increased competition as well as high acquisition and alliance activity. However, a major impediment to sustained growth was the shortage of computer professionals, including programmers and system designers. This shortage was also significantly increasing the labor costs within this industry.

Louis V. Gerstner, Jr., chairman and CEO of IBM, had driven IBM to follow an overall strategic focus to maintain a superior standing in the computer industry (hardware, software, services, and financing). However, as IBM entered the twenty-first century a smaller percentage of its customers was expected to buy an item with "IBM" stamped on it. Gerstner made this clear in a statement from late 1999 (IBM, 2001b):

> Sometime within the next five years, more than half of our revenues and workforce will come from services. This will mean that, very soon, revered IBM brand attributes like quality, reliability and innovation will primarily be descriptors of IBM people—their knowledge, ideas and behavior—just as today they describe IBM ThinkPads, servers and software.

The future of IBM was expected to be determined by its effectiveness in competing in the rapidly growing and highly competitive computer services industry, specifically in the professional computer services segment. The overall computer services industry is a segment of the computer industry. The computer industry is comprised primarily of hardware, software, and services.

In light of IGS's declining financials and its overall importance to the future success of the IBM Corporation, Gerstner was asking his IGS executive management team to consider changing the way IGS was doing business. IGS's immediate task was to make several strategic decisions in the areas of target customers, services to be offered, geographic market expansion, and changes to its management system to take advantage of the industry trends, and to attract and retain skilled resources. These and other specific strategic questions needed answering if IBM Global Services was to differentiate itself from its competition and so achieve a winning edge over competitors within intensively competitive, rapidly changing immediate, intermediate, and long-term time frames.

Computer Services Industry

The segment of focus, computer services, can be divided into three main categories: processing services, network services, and professional computer services, as shown in Figure 2.

Computer services firms typically enter long-term relationships with their customers. This is true of all three segments (professional computer, processing, and network services). These firms do so by signing contracts that specify the amount of time the designated services are to be provided and the monetary value of the services. Revenues derived from multiyear contracts can be accurately predicted by the computer services vendor and by financial analysts. Some computer services firms do business through annual or other short-term contracts that are renewed at expiration with great predictability. Computer services vendors undertake efforts to increase their retention rates, or percentage of contract renewals, which usually run well over 90 percent (U.S. Business Reporter, 2001a).

With a solid knowledge of revenues under multiyear contracts and past retention rates for contracts coming up for renewal, computer services firms can predict with a high degree of confidence the amount of revenues that they'll earn in a set time period. Based on these accurate revenue assessments, computer services companies can set and manage their expenses at the levels necessary to earn the required

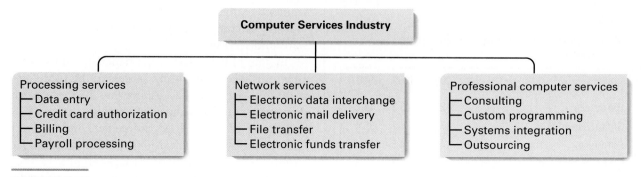

FIGURE 2

The Computer Services Industry

return in each period. Rarely do computer services vendors post results that are materially different from those expected by the company or stock analysts.

According to Standard and Poor's Industry Survey, the computer services industry had experienced a prolonged period of strong growth, which was expected to continue into 2001 and beyond. Spending on computer services was forecasted to rise about 11 percent in 2001, to an estimated $429.9 billion. This figure was in addition to the 11 percent growth in 2000, when sales reached an estimated $387.5 billion (Standard and Poor's Industry Survey, 2001a).

A large percentage of growth in 2000 came in the second half of the year. This concentration reflected the year's having gotten off to a slow start, due to the lack of any year 2000 (Y2K) impact and a corresponding shortfall in spending, as well as a delay in spending by IT managers (Rosen, 2001). In 1999, the sector total of $349 billion represented 13 percent growth over 1998 (Standard & Poor's Industry Survey, 2001b).

According to Standard and Poor's Industry Survey, the global computer services industry would continue growing at a compound annual rate of 11 percent through 2004. The United States accounted for about 46 percent of the worldwide market for computer services in 1999, a percentage that was expected to remain steady over the next several years. The overall computer services business is a broad-based industry and is highly fragmented, with the ten largest firms accounting for about 33 percent of total worldwide services revenues (Standard & Poor's Industry Survey, 2001c).

According to the U.S. Department of Labor, 1.96 million people were employed in the computer and data processing services industry at the end of Octo-

ber 2000, a rise of 6.5 percent from the 1.84 million employed at the end of 1999. The figure in 1999 represented growth of 8.2 percent from the 1.7 million employed at the end of 1998. However, while industry employment has been growing significantly faster than the U.S. economy, a major impediment is a shortage in skilled technology labor (U.S. Business Reporter, 2001b).

The United States is the world's largest producer and consumer of computer products and services. As presented in the U.S. Department of Commerce's Industry Outlook '99, where it referenced a *Datamation* magazine's 1996 survey of computer companies worldwide, this survey indicated that eight of the top ten companies are U.S. companies. The survey results are shown in Figure 3. Within each specific product or service sector, the U.S. portion of leading companies is equally high. Additionally, most of the innovative and fastest growing computer services companies are in the United States. Because of the world dominance of U.S. companies, global trends and issues tend to be the same as those that affect the domestic industry.

One of the most significant trends in the computer services industry was convergence within the overall computer industry. Companies in diverse areas—computer hardware, software, information services, data communications, and telecommunications—were rapidly forming alliances with each other through joint ventures, mergers, and acquisitions. These alliances allowed companies to integrate computer technology products with computer services so that they could offer a greater selection of products and services (services within all three segments). A key objective of these alliances was to remain viable in an increasingly competitive national

FIGURE 3

Top Ten Global Service and Support Suppliers, 1996* (millions of dollars)

Company	Country	Revenues ($)
IBM	United States	22,785
Electronic Data Systems	United States	14,441
Hewlett Packard	United States	9,462
Digital Equipment	United States	5,988
Computer Science	United States	5,400
Accenture (Anderson Consulting)	United States	4,877
Fujitsu	Japan	4,160
Cap Gemini Sogeti	France	4,104
Unisys	United States	3,949
Automatic Data Processing	United States	3,567

*Services and support includes outsourcing, facilities management, systems integration, IT consulting, contract programming, and disaster recovery.

Source: U.S. Department of Commerce's U.S. (2001b), Industry Outlook '99: Information Services, p. 4.

and international marketplace by increasing the company's pool of resources with minimal training expense, increasing revenue growth, and increasing the breadth of service offerings.

In the past, alliances and acquisitions were common among hardware and software companies and hardware and communications equipment companies. In 2001, they were springing up among firms in much more diverse areas: hardware and software, data communications, Internet applications and World Wide Web development, graphics development, networking, and information publishing. Not only were large, well-known companies forming alliances among themselves, they were also forming them with smaller, more obscure companies. Small companies were forming alliances to keep a firm grip on their markets.

These alliances were designed to ensure the participating firm's competitiveness in the marketplace by offering business and residential consumers a broader range of high-quality products and services.

Alliances and acquisitions also gave companies the ability to increase skilled resources without the need for extensive training of existing or newly hired resources. This strategy also offered the opportunity to increase revenues by acquiring the other company's markets and service offerings.

All this was causing a blurring of traditional industry categories in computer information technology and communications. In the past, distinctions among hardware manufacturers, software developers, communication equipment producers, service providers, and telecommunications companies were relatively clear. However, computer companies were diversifying their operations to enter the more lucrative computer services industry. Hewlett-Packard is an example, with its introduction of eservices. Companies were branching out into a wide variety of activities through alliances with or acquisitions of other companies and diversification of their own internally developed services mixes.

Another factor in this increased spending was the trend toward client server architectures and away from traditional mainframe architectures. These factors were providing great opportunities for computer services providers to offer services such as systems integration, consulting, maintenance, outsourcing, and disaster recovery.

As previously stated, the computer services industry can be divided into three main categories: processing services, network services, and professional computer services.

The Processing Services Segment

This segment comprises vendors that process their customers' transactions and data using the vendor-owned computer systems (often with proprietary software). IDC estimates that the sector's revenues were $65.3 billion in 1999, with forecast growth of 6.6 percent in 2000, to $69.6 billion, and 6.5 percent in 2001, to $74.1 billion. IDC expects the sector to grow at about a 6 percent compound annual rate through 2004. The largest independent computer services processing vendor is Automatic Data Processing Inc. (ADP), a major supplier of employer, brokerage, dealer, and claims services, with revenues of $6.3 billion in fiscal 2000 (September) (Standard and Poor's Industry Survey, 2001d).

The outlook was very good for data processing services. Traditional data processing services had strong growth opportunities. These services include data entry, credit card authorization, billing, and payroll processing. They are commonly referred to as back-office functions because they are routine, high-volume, easily automated functions. Many service providers in this area are small companies that target local businesses as their clients. The demand for traditional data processing services is directly related to the strength of the local and national economies.

The Network Services Segment

Network services companies provide a broad range of value-added network services, including electronic interchange services, electronic mail delivery, file transfer, and electronic funds transfer. These firms are increasingly providing more-sophisticated forms of electronic commerce, including services that facilitate sales and customized research over the Internet.

The dominant factor in the growth of network services is the acceptance of the Internet as a business tool. In addition, the growth of the Internet as a means of electronic communications in residential markets will have a positive effect on certain network services companies.

The third segment of the computer services industry is professional computer services, the focus of this case.

The Professional Computer Services Segment

The broad professional services segment, which is the industry's largest, includes services, supported technology platforms, targeted customers, methods of sales and distribution, targeted markets, the competition, and the supportive management system, as shown in Figure 4. The professional computer services segment was expected to experience strong growth, except in certain areas such as custom programming. Growth in this area could level off as a result of the wide selection of sophisticated off-the-shelf hardware and software solutions. Other factors, such as greater hardware compatibility, the efficiencies offered by next-generation languages, and the growing standardization of data types, are contributing trends as well.

Numerous factors were to stimulate growth in this segment overall. Foremost among them are businesses' continued preference for client server architectures, the increased complexity of new information technology products, and the need to integrate them successfully into business operations. Additional factors contributing to the growth of this segment were the many information technology vendors, the convergence of information technology and communications technology products, and the need

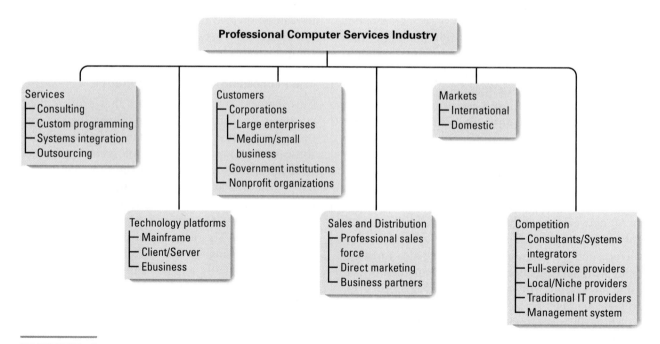

FIGURE 4

The Professional Computer Services Industry

to integrate these products efficiently and effectively into business operations.

An additional trend in global professional computer services was the record levels at which foreign businesses have been purchasing computers, software, and data communication equipment. This buying rush had been stimulated in part by reduced tariffs on information technology products in many countries. This international expansion of the information technology infrastructure benefits the companies offering professional computer services by providing greater opportunities for related services.

Another important trend in this segment industry was the growing proportion of spending on professional services relative to spending in the information technology markets overall, both at the national and international levels. Expenditures on software and computer services have increased continuously compared with those on hardware, particularly in countries whose information technology and telecommunications infrastructure are relatively strong and developed. On average, one-fifth of information technology expenditures go to support services such as outsourcing, systems integration, consulting, customer programming, and disaster recovery. That share of spending was becoming the single largest segment of computer information technology spending (Hoovers Online Network, 2001b).

In a related trend, firms that traditionally specialized in computer products are developing new services and generating a higher proportion of their revenues from them. This has occurred as prices for computer components have fallen in a fiercely competitive environment. According to Standard and Poor's, IBM Corporation earned about $18.4 billion, about 24 percent of its revenues, in the twelve months ending in 1997, from computer-related services. And this figure has been steadily increasing each year since. Digital Equipment Corporation derived about 42 percent of its revenues from computer services, an amount totaling $6.2 billion in that same period ending in 1997. The database market leader Oracle Corporation has expanded its consulting business; in this same period, computer services accounted for $3 billion (51 percent) of the company's revenues. Its closest competitor, Sybase Inc., derived about 46 percent of its revenue from consulting, education, and other computer services associated with sales of its core software products (Standard and Poor's Industry Survey, 2001e).

This increase in spending was due to advances in technology and the growing complexity of computer information technology, communication, and telecommunications systems. In addition, maintaining, supporting, and integrating information technology, computer services, and telecommunications in a multivendor environment generate a greater demand for computer services, such as consulting or outsourcing. This was illustrated by an industry survey performed by Computer Science Corporation in which they surveyed information services executives from several countries. Figure 5 presents the top ten issues, many of which offer opportunities for professional computer services; for example, issues 2 and 3 can be addressed through consulting services; issue 4, through systems integration services; issues 6 and 8, through outsourcing services. Another significant trend was the prevalence of acquisitions as companies scrambled to increase their technical skills, increase their service offerings, enter new markets, or establish themselves in new geographic areas.

Perhaps the most important factor in the growth of professional computer services was the Internet. Businesses were attempting to take advantage of the Internet's potential while maintaining security and control over critical business data and information. This created great demand for systems integration and computer consulting to resolve these sometimes divergent goals.

FIGURE 5

Top Information Technology Issues Worldwide*

1. Organizing and utilizing data.
2. Aligning IS and corporate goals.
3. Connecting electronically to customers, suppliers, and/or partners.
4. Integrating systems.
5. Developing an electronic business strategy.
6. Capitalizing on advances in IT.
7. Instituting cross-functional information systems.
8. Cutting IS costs.
9. Using IT for competitive breakthroughs.
10. Improving IS human resources.

*Based on a November 1999 survey of information services executives.

Source: Standard and Poor's Industry Survey (2001f), Computers: Commercial Services, January 25, p. 9.

A troublesome trend in the industry that could slow future growth was the shortage of skilled professionals. This shortage was affecting the availability of programmers and systems designers. This shortage was also significantly increasing the labor costs within this industry. All service providers faced the challenge of attracting and retaining these highly sought-after skills. However, some studies suggested that this shortage was not as serious as it was being portrayed. These studies suggested that there was no shortage and that the industry created its own problems by using overly specific criteria for employment and by failing to make good use of older workers (Dr. Dobb's Journal, 2000).

Services The services offered in the professional computer services segment are consulting, custom programming, systems integration, and outsourcing. These services are applied across multiple technology platforms, which will be discussed later. The greatest opportunities were available in consulting, systems integration, and outsourcing. These areas had enjoyed the most significant growth and, as previously stated, this trend would continue because of the continued complexity of information technology.

Consulting. Computer consulting firms work with corporations to create and implement strategies to cope with the most complex business problems. Consultants combine their industry specific experience with technology expertise to help clients improve overall performance and competitiveness. These firms address a client's issues by assessing and defining long-term information technology (IT) systems management strategy, designing administrative processes and selecting tools to manage systems, and creating an organizational structure that supports ongoing evaluation of system performance against dynamic business needs.

Many of the same factors driving demand for other technology services are driving demand for consulting services. In the private sector, companies are struggling to deal with continual changes in the regulatory environment, increased global competition, postmerger integration issues, industry consolidation, the new digital economy, and growth strategies. This expected growth is presented in Figure 6.

In the public sector, pressure from taxpayers constantly requires governments to do more with less. The same pressures exist in the private sector as well. To compete more effectively, companies need to look for ways to expand revenues, cut costs, operate more efficiently, manage risk more effectively, and improve their customer service. Consulting organizations help their clients manage these major issues. These services are also crucial for a government agency or company seeking to pursue an Internet strategy.

The keys to success in the area of consulting are offering a wide range of consulting services, including both business and information technology services. Both require business and technical expertise because customers are taking a new look at how business and IT service help them achieve success. These two areas (business and technology) are now tightly integrated. It is equally important to have highly skilled consulting resources. These resources need to have strong consulting skills, technology, and industry knowledge and expertise.

FIGURE 6

Worldwide Consulting Services (millions of dollars)

	1998	1999	2000	2003*	Annual Percentage Growth 1998–2003
Business consulting	6,674	8,118	9,856	17,850	21.7
IT consulting	22,763	26,551	30,887	49,675	16.9
Total	29,437	34,669	40,743	67,525	18.1

*Forecast.

Source: Standard and Poor's Industry Survey (2001g), Computers: Commercial Services, January 25, p. 7.

Custom Programming. Professional services firms involved in custom programming provide clients with programmers on a temporary, per diem basis. Such firms are known as body shops. Fees typically correlate with the technical skill required for the project. Customers of professional services firms include organizations whose current personnel lack the needed expertise, as well as firms undertaking projects that require additional staff but not permanent new employees. Demand for professional computer services, such as custom programming, had been aided by a long-standing shortage of computer professionals, including programmers and systems designers, available to work in business and government.

The general demand for software applications had grown substantially faster than the productivity of computer programmers. Although such an environment should be positive for the computer services industry, revenue growth in the custom programming business was actually slowing. The proliferation of prepackaged software and new software application development tools had decreased the demand for custom programming services. In addition, customer attitudes were changing. Customers were now looking for total, integrated solutions from their service providers. They no longer wanted to purchase the hardware, software, and communications equipment and then have to manage the integration themselves through customer programming.

The keys to success in custom programming are computer programming expertise and a wide range of programming knowledge. Through this expertise, a firm can develop a reputation for quality code. Effective maintenance of the application is another key to success and is related to the overall quality of the code. This will ensure the profitability of the business relationship and continue to enhance the reputation of the custom programming provider.

Systems Integration.   The systems integrator's role is to produce a unique computer system that meets a client's specific needs. The process is generally executed in various phases of a system's life cycle: planning, design, construction, implementation, and operation. A rapidly growing sector, systems integration owes its popularity to quickly advancing technology, a shortage of technical personnel, and the complexity of automating front-office processes. Its two major markets are government and the commercial market.

The outlook for the commercial systems integration market was bright; it was expected to expand significantly faster than the government market. With such attractive prospects, integration firms that traditionally served government agencies have entered the commercial arena. Hardware vendors and the major accounting firms, as well as dedicated systems integrators, all hoped to ride the wave of growth in commercial systems integration. This growth is illustrated in Figure 7.

The key to success in the area of systems integration is the ability to ascertain a client's requirements and to translate them into a total, end-to-end solution. Success requires a thorough knowledge and ability to execute a system's life cycle: planning, design, construction, implementation, and operation. A clear demonstration of these skills leads to another key to success, a reputation as a quality systems integrator.

FIGURE 7

Worldwide Systems Integration Services (millions of dollars)

	1998	1999	2000	2003*	Annual Percentage Growth 1998–2003
Application development	57,028	67,063	78,009	128,595	17.7
Integration	32,815	39,737	48,329	88,863	22.0
Deployment	21,527	25,320	29,718	45,919	16.4
Total	11,370	132,120	156,056	263,377	18.8

* Forecast.

Source: Standard and Poor's Industry Survey (2001h), Computers: Commercial Services, January 25, p. 7.

Outsourcing. In the computer services industry, outsourcing involves a client organization hiring a computer services firm (or outsourcing vendor) to perform a portion of its data processing and data management tasks. As part of the contract (which is often many years in length), the outsourcing vendor typically agrees to purchase the client's computer center facilities to execute the contract. This includes hiring the customer's data processing employees.

Outsourcing helps relieve companies of the task of managing computing resources and thus allows them to focus on their core business. It furnishes the flexibility needed to expand the customer's data processing capabilities on a seasonal or ongoing basis; adopt new technologies; migrate key applications to new platforms; and quickly develop, test, and deploy new applications. It also provides the technical skill and support to supplement the customer's in-house staff as needed. It matches computing resources to changing business requirements and helps minimize the customer's technology investment by leveraging the vendor's expertise. Outsourcing can also provide the flexibility to adopt and deploy new technology.

The outsourcing market is growing as a viable alternative to in-house information systems management. Major players include Andersen Consulting, Computer Sciences, Electronic Data Systems, and IBM. The widespread success of outsourcing is confirmed by the numerous megacontracts that large corporations from various industries have awarded in recent years. Valued at billions of dollars over several years, these megacontracts involve varied types of services. Growth in this segment is presented in Figure 8.

Outsourcing services can include facilities management (in which the outsourcing vendor operates the client's data center on-site); remote computing (in which processing is done off-site); and communications network management, contract software programming, and software maintenance. Because no company can depend on a single customer, vendors generally manage more than one megacontract at a time.

The key to success in this area is to assume quickly the IT support requirements of the client without disrupting its operations. This requires significant investment in data centers strategically placed within the chosen geographic markets and the ability to provide the required resources and/or absorb the resources (both hardware and human resources) transferred from the client to the vendor's operation. The overall key to success in the area of services is to achieve market presence and share by providing a wide range of service offerings and customizing the service to meet the needs of specific industries or businesses. A provider must also have the ability to offer a continuous flow of new services as IT trends evolve. This adaptability is accomplished through strong research and development. Another key to success is to achieve brand identification through

---

FIGURE 8

Worldwide Outsourcing Services (millions of dollars)

	1998	1999	2000	2003*	Annual Percentage Growth 1998–2003
Operational services	44,521	51,532	59,779	92,929	15.9
Application management	7,858	9,412	11,246	18,929	19.2
Help desk	4,178	4,873	5,696	8,926	16.4
Business continuation	6,197	7,264	8,595	14,666	18.8
Asset management	2,637	3,198	3,919	7,144	22.1
Transaction processing	17,874	19,340	21,221	30,544	11.3
Total	83,265	95,619	110,456	173,138	15.8

*Forecast.

Source: Standard and Poor's Industry Survey (2001i), Computers: Commercial Services, January 25, p. 7.

wide advertising. These services must be based on the current technology platforms being utilized by clients.

Supported Technology Platforms   These services cover all technology platforms: mainframe (enterprise systems), client/server, and ebusiness. Each of these platforms presents opportunities to professional computer services providers.

Mainframe.   The mainframe is the largest computer, a powerhouse with extensive memory and extremely rapid processing power. It is used for very large business, scientific, or military applications where a computer must handle massive amounts of data or many complicated processes. The death of the mainframe was prematurely announced in the late 1980s and early 1990s.

This technology made a resurgence due to its relatively cheap support costs compared to client/server technology, its ability to manage huge amounts of data and databases, and its scalability. IBM, the traditional leader in mainframe technology, led this effort by repositioning the mainframe as an enterprise server, which offered continued opportunity for this technology.

Client/Server.   The client/server platform is a model for computing that splits processing between clients and servers on a network and assigns functions to the machine most able to perform the function. The client is the user's point of entry for the required function and is normally a desktop computer, a workstation, or a laptop computer. The server provides the client with services or application access. The server can be a mainframe or a smaller specialized computer. Even though the relative support cost of client/server technology is high, its flexibility and cost of initial hardware investment is an advantage.

The high total cost of ownership, including initial purchase costs, the cost of hardware and software upgrades, maintenance, technical support, and training, is still relatively high for client/server technology. The advent of network computers is helping to address this issue and is a key component of the emerging "network economy."

Network computing utilizes a simplified desktop device that does not store software programs or permanent data. Users download whatever software or data they need from a central computer over the Internet or an organization's own internal network. The high total cost of ownership for client/server technology makes outsourcing of these services very attractive and offers professional computer service providers a clear opportunity. The emergence of network computing, driving the new network economy, offers significant opportunities for the computer industry overall, but especially for the professional computer services segment. Companies will be looking at computer servers as just another utility, with vast networks delivering applications, data, and computing capabilities to an estimated 1 trillion network-connected devices by the year 2005. Companies will be relying on computer services firms to provide all their IT needs. The network economy was expected to bring into question how companies acquire and manage information technology because the IT infrastructure will be moved out of the corporate data center and onto a global network. Companies will be renting it as a service, with the expectation that it will vastly increase a company's access to computing power, expertise, and innovation.

Ebusiness.   This is a suite of products (hardware, software, and services) that enables an organization to use the Internet and other digital mediums for communication and coordination, and the management of the firm. It is an enabler that extends the reach of existing management. It includes, but is not limited to, e-commerce—the process of buying and selling goods and services electronically and involving transactions using the Internet, networks and other digital technologies.

This technology was emerging as the primary technology platform for the new economy. It was revolutionizing the way business operated and was managed, and was providing professional computer service providers significant opportunity in the areas of outsourcing of web content hosting (a company hosting its web site on a vendor's infrastructure and having the vendor provide total management), consulting (providing a client advice and direction as it staked its claim in the ebusiness marketplace safely, quickly, and profitably), and custom programming (providing application development services that understand, use, and expand a client's intranet, extranet, and messaging potential through complex web application development).

This technology offered great opportunity for professional computer service companies because it was estimated that over 50 percent of large companies and 75 percent of small and medium businesses were still in the early stages of web adoption as of 2000. Early adoption is defined as having only a web presence. These companies were still not leveraging the full power of the Internet for transaction processing and delivery services (ebizchronicle.com, 2001). Therefore, these companies would be looking for various services to enable them to conduct business over the Internet.

The key to success in the technology area is to have excessive knowledge across all technology platforms. Although ebusiness was clearly the industry focus at this time, many companies had significant investment in large mainframes, and the client/server was still the predominant architecture used throughout the industry. The ability to build new solutions based on current and future technology was also crucial, and it required a strong research and development capability.

The Growth and Impact of the Internet   Originally, the Internet was an inexpensive and helpful communication device for academics and defense industry engineers. In the mid 1980s, after the invention of the World Wide Web, it began to be used for a broader purpose. The development in the early 1980s of graphic viewers to interface with the Web was the breakthrough that enabled a larger portion of the computer-using population to embrace the Internet. As the Internet grew through the mid 1990s, online transactions remained in its infancy. As the year 2000 approached, however, the ability to buy and sell electronically was refined, and a fundamental transformation occurred in the United States and the global market place.

Internet use became oriented more toward business needs: advertising, marketing, communication, and (to an extent) sales. The corporate world's use of the Internet has outpaced the earlier uses, such as file access and file transfer. Internet technology is having a profound effect on global trade of software products and on technical, financial, professional, and many other services, but especially computer services.

Customers   The customer base for the computer services industry includes a wide range of organizations. It offers services primarily to corporations, including large enterprises and medium and small businesses, as well as government institutions, and private institutions.

Corporations (Large Enterprises).   These companies (with more than 1,000 employees) offered the professional computer services segment an opportunity to provide its broad range of services to a company's management. The large enterprises had several motivations in seeking professional computer services. These companies clearly saw information technology (IT) as critical to their competitive advantage. Its IT executives were involved in business strategy, and the business executives were involved in IT decisions. These companies are typically not IT innovators, but they are fast followers. They are uncomfortable with the Internet but planned significant use of it. They preferred all-in-one solutions, which were often customized solutions, that bundle computer products and professional computer services. They usually preferred long-term relationships with one or two services providers.

The key to success in attracting and retaining large corporations was the ability of the service provider to provide a customized, all-in-one solution. The service provider needed to have a proven track record in providing services to meet the specific needs of the company's industry. Therefore, a broad range of service offerings, skilled resources with the ability to customize these offerings, and the knowledge of the customer's industry were crucial. These ingredients would enable a service provider to attract and retain large corporate customers because it could meet their specific requirements.

Corporations (Medium and Small).   These companies (with less than 1,000 employees) offer the professional computer services segment a significant opportunity because they are one of the untapped growth areas. However, they are very difficult to market to and support. Therefore, a company that can effectively market to and efficiently support medium and small corporations can have a strategic advantage over the competition.

These companies are comfortable with Internet technology and have widely deployed it. They prefer long-term, trusted advisors, and they often purchase services but are highly price sensitive. They typically cannot and do not meet their IT requirements internally (especially small businesses) and they do not want customized solutions. It is estimated that almost half (45 percent) of future opportunities in professional computer services will come from small and medium businesses. This market, for instance, was growing faster than either large enterprise or consumer markets. In the United States alone, there were 22 million small businesses. They typically have simpler business and IT processes. While they are highly diverse and costly to reach, many, but not all, understand that the Web can enable them to compete with much larger firms on an equal footing because everyone is just a click away on the Web.

The keys to success in attracting and retaining medium and small corporations and businesses is the ability to provide standardized solutions at a competitive price. In addition, because of the challenge of effectively marketing to and supporting this type of customer, a strong direct marketing capability is also crucial.

Government Institutions.   These organizations are as large as, if not larger than, large enterprise corporations and require high maintenance. Many government operations, such as NASA and NATO, are technology oriented and therefore present an opportunity for professional computer services providers. For example, the largest user of system integration services is the U.S. government. However, ongoing pressure to reduce government spending in general and to cut defense budgets in particular has produced uncertainties in this segment. This trend is truly global. But it may also have a reverse effect for some government institutions that seek to reduce their cost through efficiencies brought about by computer innovations. This could lead to an increased demand for professional computer services. The keys to success with government institutions is to have knowledge of and the ability to leverage the bureaucracy found in such organizations.

Nonprofit Organizations.   These organizations may be large or small. They include education providers, community organizations, and religious organizations, to name a few. They offer an opportunity because they require computer service solutions just like any other customer; however, they are typically very price sensitive. The key to success for nonprofit organizations is the ability to provide standardized solutions at the lowest cost possible, as it is for medium and small corporations. Overall keys to success in attracting and retaining customers is

knowing how to service customers through knowledge of their specific industry or business, and by targeting the customer segments with the greatest growth potential.

Sales/Distribution   The sales and distribution strategies within the professional computer services industry utilize professional sales forces, direct marketing, and/or working through business partners.

Professional Sales Force.   Typically professional computer service providers employ trained professionals to sell their services. These resources are usually trained to support a specific industry sector (for example, the manufacturing, financial, or entertainment sector). Industry knowledge is crucial in this services segment. Customers want and expect that their providers know their industry-specific requirements and can translate these requirements into meaningful solutions. They may also have skills for a specific technology or offering. These highly skilled and expensive resources are usually applied to the firm's largest customers. These customers require personalized, face-to-face support, and their contract values can support the cost of the sales force. The key to success for a professional sales force is their ability to market the company's services in the context of the client's industry or business. This requires in-depth industry and technology knowledge.

Direct Marketing.   The underlying logic of direct marketing is making direct contact with customers through alternate media (for example, telephone, telemarketing, mail, or the Internet). Many professional computer services companies employ telemarketing and the Internet to sell to customers, especially small to medium-sized customers.

The key to success with direct marketing as a channel is to ensure that customers have ready access to these sales resources. The ability to reach a person, with limited delay, is a must. Many telemarketing functions offer 24/7 coverage, and many firms are incorporating a "call me" facility from their web sites, which allows a customer to receive a call back within a specified period of time.

Business Partners.   Business partners are independent distributors who enter into agreements with professional computer services providers to market and distribute all or part of the provider's solutions. Business partners develop, market, influence, sell, deliver, and/or support solutions with components (hardware, software, and services) from the service company with whom they have partnered. The key to success with business partners is to develop strong relationships with this alternate channel by providing quality services for them to market and offering incentives to ensure your services are reaching the customers. An overall key to success in the area of sales and distribution is to control cost by applying appropriate sales channels to the customer segment.

Domestic and International Markets   Global demand for professional computer services was growing tremendously. The United States accounted for about 46 percent of the worldwide market for professional computer services in 1999. Significant growth was expected for the United States and for Europe and Asia, especially in the areas of system integration and outsourcing. Many leading professional computer services firms generate up to one-third of their revenue abroad, so their performance can be affected by growth trends in the real gross domestic product (GDP) of foreign economies. IT spending as a percentage of GDP was growing in every country, and was led by English-speaking countries. France and Germany were projected to join these leaders as well. Asia, including China, represented another growth area, even though it was behind the worldwide average for IT spending (Standard & Poor's, 2001j).

The size and growth opportunities available in international markets continue to attract professional computer services companies. With a significant percentage of revenues tied to foreign markets, many firms are subject to foreign currency risk. For U.S.-based firms, overseas sales are translated from local currencies into dollars. A strong dollar hurts reported earnings, while a weak dollar helps. The European and Asian markets represented significant opportunity for professional computer services providers. This was especially true for outsourcing opportunities across all technology platforms, but especially true for ebusiness.

The key to success in this area is to maintain and grow market share by servicing a diverse set of markets (geographic and industry specific). This is accomplished from a geographic perspective by having a presence in each of the major markets. A service provider should have data centers strategically located in the geographic areas to provide outsourcing services.

Management System   The sustained growth of computer services, and in particular, professional computer services, triggered a serious shortage of skilled IT professionals, and this has ignited a war for talent among IT service providers. By 2001, an estimated 800,000 IT positions in the United States and Europe were unfilled for lack of qualified candidates, and fewer college graduates were choosing computer sciences. Professional computer service providers faced the challenge of attracting and retaining these required resources. In an industry where skilled resources are the most important, professional computer services providers must have a management system that attracts and retains their employees by enabling them to realize their business and professional growth potential.

Competition   Each of the various computer services market segments is dominated by several large vendors that use their size, reputation, expertise, and marketing prowess to secure the largest contracts awarded by the largest organizations. These companies are likely to bid successfully on the largest contracts in this industry.

Computer services firms are entrusted to install, manage, or otherwise refine an organization's computer networks or perform crucial processing tasks. Therefore, it's rare for a small, unknown computer services firm with limited operating experience to win business with a Fortune 1000 company or other large organization. Opportunities do exist, however, for smaller vendors to service the computing needs of small office, home office, and personal computing markets, where the jobs are less complex.

Customer demand is attracting increasing competition from traditional services competitors and spawning new competition as services providers seek leadership positions across the full spectrum or in elements of the services value chain. The four prevalent types of competitors are:

■ Consultants/systems integrators (like Accenture, formerly Andersen Consulting)

■ Full-service providers (such as EDS and CSC)

■ Local/niche providers (for example, NTT or ADP)

■ Traditional IT providers (like HP or Oracle, Sybase)

In its most recent quarterly report, 4Q 2000, Computer Sciences (CSC) continued showing revenue growth in the 12 percent range. It signed $4.4 billion worth of new contracts in the quarter, with new deals up 45 percent in the first half of its fiscal year. Electronic Data Systems had been harder hit by the Y2K slump, but reported 8 percent growth in its most recent quarter. EDS is starting work on a $6.9 billion deal with the U.S. Navy, signed in the previous quarter. The other services industry news was no news at all: the planned takeover of Pricewaterhouse-Coopers's consulting business by HP was called off, mostly because of HP's inability to pay for the expensive deal with its slumping stock (Hoovers Online Network, 2001).

The following competitive analysis is based on the leader within each of the four types of competitors listed above.

Consultants/Systems Integrators (Accenture).   Accenture (formerly Andersen Consulting, a unit of Andersen Worldwide) is a global management and technology consulting organization generating $8.9 billion in fiscal year 1999, ending December 31, 1999. This represents an 8 percent increase over 1998 results and a 10 percent increase after removing the impact of international exchange rates (Accenture, 2001). The company's mission was to help its clients create the client's future. Accenture was repositioning itself by moving beyond consulting to become a network of businesses that will be a market maker of the new ebusiness economy. To execute this mission, Accenture integrated its various industry specializations with its competencies in strategic services, change management, processes, and technologies to provide a total solution for its customers. To serve its strategic deliverables, the company offers its customers various services addressing supply chain management, electronic commerce, customer relationship management, enterprise business solutions, and knowledge management. The partnership also provides outsourcing of business operations through its business process management operation, along with custom programming and system integration services. Accenture lacked the broad services offerings provided by a full services provider such as IBM Global Services.

After a prolonged two-and-a-half-year struggle, on August 7, 2000, an international arbitrator ruled that the links between accounting firm Arthur Andersen and Andersen Consulting be severed immediately. Under the ruling, the consulting arm lost the right to the Andersen name at the end of the 2000 calendar year, an outcome seen as a victory for the consulting group. Arthur Andersen had claimed that Andersen Consulting should pay a termination fee of $14.5 billion to leave the umbrella organization, a claim that was denied. However, Arthur Andersen retained the right to jointly developed software and gained $1 billion in undistributed funds. The split freed Andersen Consulting from an SEC ruling on conflict of interest between audit and consulting that now limits the kinds of consulting work permitted to Big Five accounting firms. Beginning January 1, 2001, Andersen Consulting operated under its new brand name, Accenture, a combination of "accent" and "future" that means to accelerate, to amplify, and to exceed expectations. This name change triggered a massive advertising campaign to achieve brand identification as a worldwide professional computer services provider.

Accenture announced record global revenue for the fiscal year ending August 31, 2000, a 15.4 percent increase over the previous year. The firm had achieved double-digit growth for the past seven consecutive years and eleven of the past twelve years (Accenture, 2001).

The company was known for the following strengths:

▌ *Global Presence.* Accenture had grown significantly from its formation in 1989, with $1.6 billion in revenue and 21,400 employees, to become a leading management and technology consulting firm, generating $8.9 billion in revenue in 1999, and employing approximately 65,000 people in forty-eight countries. The company claimed 85 percent of the Fortune 100 global companies as customers, which they market to via dedicated sales/consulting resources known for their skills and industry knowledge, and an Internet presence limited to presenting information only (no transactions), and good relationships with business partners. They had effectively marketed and serviced large, small, and medium businesses by providing all-in-one solutions and, to a limited extent, competitively priced standardized solutions. In the e-commerce area, Accenture claimed their clients include more than half of both the Fortune Global 500 and the Industry Standard 100, representing the most important companies of the Internet economy (Accenture, 2001).

■ *Broad Industry Coverage.* Accenture targeted sixteen industry segments, grouped into five global market units: financial services, products, communications and high tech, resources, and government. The firm's government and communications industries led all its industry sectors with 35 percent and 29 percent growth, respectively. The firm estimated its electronic commerce revenue to $1.5 billion in 1999, triple the firm's $500 million e-commerce revenue in 1998. Its consumer and pharmaceutical products, electronics/high-tech, and insurance industries also showed double-digit growth again in 1999. Financial services, which represented the fastest growing global market in 1998 at 33 percent, exhibited 0 percent growth in 1999 resulting from an 18 percent decline in health services that offset an 11 percent gain in insurance. While the communications and high-tech global market also showed significant growth in 1999 at 29 percent, overall it slowed from a 25 percent increase in 1998, reflecting a drop in media and entertainment revenue growth from 31 percent to 4 percent. Professionals in the company's industry form teams with representatives from the firm's competencies in technology, strategy, change management, and process (Accenture, 2001).

■ *Strong Research and Development (R&D) Effort.* Through R&D activities, Accenture assesses the business impact of new technologies and applies emerging technologies to create innovative business solutions. The company operated the Center for Strategic Technology Research (CSTaR) and conducted leading-edge research on technologies. Specifically, CSTaR continually investigates how the convergence of computing, communication, and content technologies changes how we work and live in the next three to five years.

Despite these strengths, Accenture exhibited some weaknesses and faced some risks:

■ *Change in Top Management.* In September 1999, Andersen Consulting managing partner and CEO George Shaheen resigned his position to join an Internet grocer, Webvan Group, with a compensation package estimated at more than $100 million. Shaheen had served as chief executive since the firm's formation in 1989, overseeing the firm's

increase in revenue from $1.3 billion in 1989 to $8.3 billion in 1998. Several industry analysts questioned Accenture's continued success with the departure of Shaheen. In November 1999, the partners appointed a longtime Andersen Consulting partner, Joe W. Forehand, as the new CEO and managing partner. Forehand, who had held leadership positions in eleven of the sixteen industries served by Andersen Consulting, planned to focus on taking Andersen Consulting to its "next level of marketplace leadership." Forehand faced the challenges of the transformation of Accenture into a profitable ebusiness consulting firm, the branding challenge of a name change, and industrywide alteration of the long-standing billing per-hour formula to a fixed-fee market.

■ *Competitive Market.* Accenture faced an increasingly competitive market as management consultants, systems integrators, and systems vendors continued to expand their operations into related technology consulting and outsourcing operations. In addition, the Big Five accounting firms now also relied on the profitable consulting within the professional computer services area. Smaller niche firms had also started to provide more-focused competition in localized markets. The company faced increased competition in the ebusiness area because many consulting firms established ebusiness strategies. In addition, the company competed with smaller firms, which were perceived as providing leading-edge knowledge while being flexible, and were increasingly attracting large corporate clients as well as experienced consultants. However, Accenture had strong market intelligence due to is worldwide network of consultants and the relationships it had developed as part of the Andersen Worldwide team.

■ *Employee Turnover.* Due to industry growth, Accenture faced a tight market for recruiting and retaining employees. While the company had improved its employee turnover rate somewhat, it still saw top employees in the IT field leaving to join Internet start-ups that offered large compensation packages, typically with significant stock options. IPO slowdowns were expected to temper this trend in 2001 but burnout from long hours and travel did remain issues. This was a sign that Accenture did not have an effective management system to attract and retain skilled resources.

■ *Limited Service Offerings.* Accenture had a distinct weakness because it was limited in the services it provided, focusing solely on consulting and systems integration. They did not provide outsourcing services, an area that presented significant opportunity, especially because businesses were implementing ebusiness solutions, and because of the emergence of network computing, both leading to the growth of outsourcing services.

Full Services Providers (EDS). EDS, which takes credit for pioneering the concept of outsourcing nearly four decades ago, was among a handful of large outsourcers offering an end-to-end services portfolio, including management consulting, ebusiness solutions, business process management, and information solutions. Since entering the arena, EDS claimed to have become a global leader in providing ebusiness and information technology services to 9,000 business (large and small, providing all-in-one and standardized solutions) and government clients in approximately fifty-five countries around the world. EDS markets through a worldwide network with a direct sales force with an industry orientation, maintains a limited Internet presence (no transaction capability), and offers good business partner relationships. The company posted revenues of $18.53 billion in 1999 and signed new contracts in 1999 valued at more than $24.9 billion (EDS, 2001).

The company was known for the following strengths:

■ *Global Presence and Broad Industry Coverage.* The company has more than 121,000 employees worldwide and brings deep industry knowledge to solve challenges in a wide variety of industries, including communications, energy, finances, government, health care, manufacturing and retailing, and transportation. Business alliances with industry-leading organizations, including relationships with companies such as WebMethods, SeeBeyond, and SAP America, have been key to EDS's efforts to extend its clients' reach in the marketplace with new services.

■ *Operational Efficiency.* The company has recently set in motion changes designed to streamline its operations, including reducing its work force and rearranging its offerings, to make it a leaner, more efficient competitor and to update its image as a lumbering, stodgy behemoth. EDS increased its investment in research and development to enable a continuous flow of new services supporting current and future technologies.

The company was known for the following weakness:

■ *Aggressive Buying of Market Share.* Several industry analysts were questioning EDS's strategy for competing against outsourcing leader IBM Global Services. EDS was sacrificing profit margin by aggressively buying market share. The concern was that EDS was paying too much to win outsourcing contracts. EDS was paying several times what would have normally been a competitive rate, an example of which was the 2001 contract to assume management of the Sabre's air-travel infrastructure.

Local/Niche Providers (ADP). With nearly 500,000 clients across multiple industries, ADP was one of the largest companies in the world dedicated to providing computerized transaction processing, data communications, and information services for specific niche markets. However, ADP's services were very narrowly focused, allowing them to focus on the customer segments with the greatest growth potential for ADP's service offerings. The company's services included employer services, such as payroll, payroll tax, and human resource management; brokerage services, such as securities transaction processing and investor communication services; industry specific computing and consulting services for auto and truck dealers; and dealer services, such as computerized auto repair estimating and auto parts availability services. All of ADP's computing services enabled clients to process and/or distribute data (their own, ADP's, or that of third parties) and/or to access and utilize ADP and third-party databases and information through the use of ADP's batch, interactive, and client site systems. These services are marketed through a network of highly skilled direct sales force resources. ADP focused on providing custom and standardized solutions at a competitive price. The core services were supported by consulting services, custom programming, and systems integration. ADP's consultancy was very strong due to its narrow focus, which allowed for strong industry and technical expertise in the areas they serviced.

Employer services, brokerage services, dealer services, and claims services were the company's four largest businesses. Together, they represent over 95 percent of ADP's revenue and are the key strategic elements of the company's future growth. The company was very strong financially, with approximately $6.3 billion in annual revenues, over $4.5 billion in shareholders' equity, over 12 percent growth in revenue and earnings, about 20 percent return on equity, 156 consecutive quarters of record revenues and earnings per share, and 39 consecutive years of double-digit increases in EPS (ADP, 2001).

For fiscal 2000, which ended June 30, 2000, revenues grew 13 percent, to about U.S. $6.3 billion. Prior to nonrecurring charges in 1999, pretax earnings increased 21 percent, and diluted earnings per share increased 16 percent, to $1.31. During fiscal year 1999, the company sold several businesses and decided to leave several other businesses and contracts. It also recorded transaction costs and other adjustments related to Employer Services's acquisition of Vincam. The combination of these transactions resulted in nonrecurring charges of $0.03 in fiscal year 1999. Fiscal year 2000 was ADP's thirty-ninth consecutive year of double-digit earnings per share growth since becoming a public company in 1961 (ADP, 2001).

Strengths. ADP continued to operate from a position of solid financial results and liquidity. Standard & Poor's includes ADP among only ten companies to which it gives its highest AAA rating. The company remained very strong financially, with more than $6.3 billion in annual revenues, over $4.5 billion in shareholders' equity, over 12 percent growth in revenue and earnings, about 20 percent return on equity, 156 consecutive quarters of record revenues and earnings per share, and 39 consecutive years of double-digit increases in EPS. The market potential for the company was still excellent. Employer Services (ES) was its oldest business and was the leading provider of outsourced payroll and human resources management services. However, very good potential remained in every ES market segment as the outsourcing trend continued to gain momentum. For instance, ADP's business that provided payroll and other services to small and medium businesses in North America had over 370,000 clients, yet this represented only a fraction of the 11 million companies plus 24 million home-based businesses in the U.S. market that could potentially use the company's services. About 60 percent of middle-market companies

still had not yet chosen to outsource payroll and human resources management. Also, although the company's National Accounts business in North America had grown to over $800 million annually, the market potential among ADP's existing large employer clients was over $11 billion. ADP did not fully leverage these relationships as a distribution channel.

Weaknesses. ADP had grown essentially through an ongoing strategic program of acquisitions rather than through internal growth. Some industry analysts believed that continued growth through acquisition for the company will become increasingly difficult over time and may ultimately lead to the need for costly restructuring. With the continued growth of other competitive organizations, and the advances made in the various technologies required to support customers in the markets in which ADP served, there was an expected increase in competition for the company to deal with in the future. These factors may, at some point, cause the company to be unable to report the same high levels of continuing growth as it had in the past. For example, increased competitive pressures may ultimately prevent ADP from maintaining its string of 156 consecutive quarters of double-digit earnings per share (EPS) growth. In addition, due to its narrow focus and the targeting of local and niche customers, it was weak in addressing the needs of large corporate customers and did not have or need a large Internet presence.

Traditional IT Providers (Hewlett Packard) Much of chairman, president, and CEO Carly Fiorina's tenure at Hewlett Packard (HP) had been focused on the reorganization of a company plagued by high overhead costs and the inability to respond to market conditions. Through a combination of layoffs, product line reorganizations, and a refocusing on the computer services sector, Fiorina transformed HP into a focused competitor. The company's financial results indicated that Hewlett Packard had some success in this area. After posting weak quarter-over-quarter results during much of 1998 and into 1999, results for the quarter ending June 2000 showed a 16 percent revenue increase (HP, 2001a).

However, during the first quarter of fiscal year 2001, revenue grew only 2 percent to $11.9 billion, from $11.6 billion the previous year. Consequently, HP missed the forecast of $12.4 billion on its top line by 4 percent. HP's earnings per share (EPS) for the first quarter of 2001 were $0.16, compared with $0.40 the previous year. HP's officials blamed a slowdown in the U.S. economy, execution issues, pricing pressure on the PC and printing businesses, and adverse currency effects when explaining why the company missed its forecast. The disparity between the contributions of earnings for each business unit was increasingly steady. Its image and printing segment was of increasing importance to HP. The computing system segment's top line increased 2 percent, representing 40 percent of the total revenue. The third major business division, computer services, posted the highest year-over-year growth rate of 13 percent, and represents 15.5 percent of revenue. However, computer services' operational results declined 19 percent, from $125 million to $101 million, when comparing the first quarter of 2000 to the first quarter of 2001 (HP, 2001b). HP should have been concerned with the fact that they were growing faster in this area with diminishing profitability.

HP credited part of its revenue growth to its eservices strategy, designed to highlight the way HP technology supports the growth of electronic services over the Internet. In general, the company's product strategy essentially utilizes all of the company's products, ranging from inkjet printers and consumer appliances to PCs, workstations, and high-end UNIX servers. This strategy had given Hewlett Packard a focused message that appeared to be winning over some customers. Previously, Hewlett Packard seemed to be outmaneuvered by rivals such as Sun Microsystems and IBM. HP had also implemented an industry orientation to its market strategy, but they were still fundamentally a hardware company. As a hardware company, they had a good ability to build new solutions based on current and future technologies due to their research and development capabilities.

As with all of the competitors within the traditional IT provider category, HP was limited in the range of services it provided. Typically these companies focused on their original core product and wrapped services around that competency. In the case of HP, it was equipment; for Oracle and Sybase, it was software, specifically database management software and services. All were seeking to provide ebusiness support and services but did not have the full range of services as did some of the other categories of competitors. They were weak in the areas of consulting, custom programming, systems integration, and outsourcing.

The Company

Since December 1996, when IBM established IBM Global Services (IGS), IGS had achieved outstanding business results. IBM Global Services had grown its business faster than the industry, and IGS was widely recognized as the largest services company in the world, surpassing EDS, as shown in Figure 9. Previously, ISSC, an IBM subsidiary, had similar results. It was accepted that the success of IBM's services business was a major contributor to IBM's overall business recovery.

IBM Global Services's results in 2000 were not what the company's executives wanted. IGS didn't meet its objectives for the full year or last quarter in

FIGURE 9

Top Five Service Providers in 1999

Company	Type of Services	Revenue (U.S.$ in billions)	Market Share (%)
IBM Global Services	Multisegment*	34.6	8.2
EDS	Multisegment	18.6	4.4
Accenture	Consultancy	10.3	2.5
Computer Sciences Corp.	Multisegment	8.9	2.1
Hewlett Packard	Multisegment	7.9	1.9

*Multisegment = full-service provider (consulting, custom programming, system integration, outsourcing).

Source: IBM (2001c), "Services," **http://www.ibm.com/services/fullservice.html#its**. Accessed: February 19, 2001.

either revenue or pretax income (PTI), and its direct expense grew faster than its revenue. IGS's investment in web hosting was showing promise, with revenue growth of more than 200 percent last year. Web hosting, part of ebusiness services, was a new business and had required significant investment, and it has not yet contributed to gross profit.

In the fourth quarter of 2000, IGS grew 5 percent (12 percent at a constant currency rate), to $9.2 billion, reflecting revenue growth across all services categories. Ebusiness services revenues grew more than 70 percent year over year. Revenue comparisons for IBM Global Services were adversely affected by a year-over-year decline in the Y2K services business and the sale of the IBM Global Network to AT&T in 1999, ending IGS's direct involvement in the network services segment. After adjusting for these factors, IBM Global Services revenues (excluding maintenance) increased 10 percent (17 percent at a constant currency rate) (IBM, 2001d).

IGS had been very successful in increasing its revenue, broadening its range of service offerings, and building its pool of resources through acquisitions and alliances. In the first quarter of 2001, they had acquired Mainspring Corporation, an ebusiness consulting firm, for $80 million; and Informix, a database application and consulting company, for $1 billion. They also entered into strategic alliances with Ariba, a provider of business-to-business (B2B) applications and services, and i2, a supply chain management and ebusiness consulting firm.

In light of the significant opportunities presented by the computer services industry and IBM's desire to transform itself into a service company (both IT and business services) through its IGS business unit, IGS will need to consider changing the way they conduct business. This services orientation will require them to answer the following questions: How can they convert the ebusiness mind share that they have developed to true market share? How will IGS expand its outsourcing service to include the other geographic areas, such as Europe and Asia? How can IGS take advantage of the services opportunities in the small and medium business market segment, and be profitable while doing so? And what management systems investments are necessary to support this business transformation? These and other strategic decisions will have to be made if IBM Global Services is to succeed and win against the competition.

Services

IBM Global Services offers consulting services, custom programming, systems integration, and outsourcing services through three lines of businesses (LOBs). Each line of business is segmented along industry lines, so they have an in-depth understanding of the customer's specific challenges and requirements.

Consulting and Custom Programming   Consulting and custom programming services are offered through IGS's Business Innovation Services (BIS) line of business. Business Innovation Services provides business and industry consulting and custom programming. By combining industry expertise with leading-edge technologies, BIS develops innovative solutions to help its customers solve complex challenges associated with business, such as growing revenue and profit, attracting and retaining customers, reducing costs and time to market in inventory, and enabling new business designs and processes.

Business Innovation Services had a network of worldwide consulting practices staffed with highly trained consultants. These practices had an industry orientation and focused on five main industry sectors: communications, distribution, financial services, industrial, and public. The revenue from the consulting practices was steadily increasing, while the revenue from the custom programming services offered by BIS remained flat year to year.

System Integration   This service is provided through IGS's Integrated Technology Services (ITS) LOB. ITS understands that improving the effectiveness and efficiency of computer systems is vital to business growth. It helps companies gain greater productivity and optimizes return on the companies' computer investments. ITS builds the technical infrastructure that enables new business initiatives and helps customers keep pace with rapidly changing technology. ITS can help assure the continued performance and value of a customer's systems and networks. They assess the customer's systems environment, define and prioritize initiatives for improvement, and provide support and training to the customer's IT department and end users.

IBM Global Services's integrated technology services had a proven track record of helping customers pull all their information technology systems together. ITS ensures the reliability of systems and networks, maximizes IT efficiency and flexibility, secures Internet transactions, provides support and training, and maintains server hardware, software, and networks. ITS experts helped companies worldwide to address the total IT picture, from architecture and proof of concept to network consulting and integration. ITS is very strong in providing true end-to-end solutions.

Outsourcing   This service is provided through IGS's Strategic Outsourcing (SO) LOB. SO understands that gaining a competitive advantage through outsourcing involves evaluating the customer's business strategy and differentiating core from noncore operations. SO provided its customers with a flexible management strategy, immediate technological improvements through world-class skills, infrastructure, and management processes, as well as ongoing, reliable, and secure management of business operations. SO takes over all aspects of running a customer's data center or companywide computer infrastructure.

IGS's strategic outsourcing was the world's largest and most-experienced outsourcing provider, with over 73,000 servers and mainframes under its management in 133 global data centers. Fifteen of these centers were focused exclusively on ebusiness (hosting a customer's Internet and/or intranet sites). Although IGS SO has this extensive global reach, they do not have a significant outsourcing market share in Europe and parts of Asia. When putting together an outsourcing deal, IGS believes it is imperative that they protect the interests of both IGS and the customer. They seek to maintain an acceptable level of profitability while guarding the customer's investment by ensuring IGS's ability to deliver a full range of quality services throughout the life of the contract.

Supported Technology Platforms

IGS, as well as IBM overall, offers solutions across all technology platforms: mainframe, client/server, and ebusiness. IGS had been the industry leaders and innovators in all three areas. IBM demonstrated this commitment to technology leadership and the rapid delivery of customer solutions incorporating this technology innovation through its extensive investment in research and development.

IBM had led all companies in the number of patents issued by the U.S. government patent office during the eight years leading up to 2000. IBM led all companies again in 2000 U.S. patents with 2,886 issued patents. As of 2000, IBM held nearly 34,000 patents worldwide, including about 19,000 in the United Sates. In addition, the company is one of the largest non-European patent holders in Europe and one of the largest non-Japanese patent holders in Japan. IBM's expenses in research and development were $5,151 million in 2000, $5,273 million in 1999, and $5,046 million in 1998. Although all of its major competitors had good R&D capabilities, no one matched IBM's investment or success, as illustrated by the number of patents held worldwide.

IBM was the leading manufacturer of mainframes and has successfully repositioned this technology, once thought to be a dinosaur and a dead-end technology, as an enterprise server and a mass-storage access device. Ebusiness spans many of IGS's offerings and contributed significantly to its performance in 2000. The company's total discrete ebusiness revenue grew more than 70 percent, to approximately $5 billion in 2000. This increase was driven by ebusiness consulting, ebusiness systems integration, and ebusiness hosting services (a form of outsourcing).

IBM had been focusing on the Internet, ebusiness, and the network economy enabling technology for several years. The network economy was defined as the expected shift of computing to the network, which represented the next major opportunity for IGS: the emerging model of delivering technology and services on an as-needed, pay-as-you-go basis. This was the basis for what was being called the future "network economy" or "e-utility." It was expected to drive a new emerging world economy, calling attention to the distinct economic behaviors that result from global interconnection of information systems.

IGS had sold IBM Global Network Services to AT&T, but just the network infrastructure, circuits, and switching equipment. That business was very competitive and required constant capital improvements and investment. IGS retained the centralized computing capability that would be the true driver of this next generation of computing.

Customers

IBM Global Services understands that customers are looking to professional computer services providers to guide them in transforming their businesses through the integration of business and information technology strategies. The customers expect to receive value for the dollars spent on information technology. IGS provides that value by helping customers enhance their global reach, strategy execution, competitive advantage, supplier relationship, and customer loyalty. IGS was achieving this once again through its industry orientation, segmenting its customers not only by size but also by the customer's industry (i.e., retail, manufacturing, transportation, and financial).

IGS's broad range of service offerings, industry orientation, extensive research and development capabilities, and strong market intelligence enables them to provide both customizable, all-in-one solutions for large customers and competitively priced standardized solutions for small and medium business customers. IGS services both large companies and small and medium businesses. However, IGS's services, known for their quality and innovation, were more in line with the needs of large companies because of cost and complexity. Therefore, they were not targeting a customer segment with significant revenue potential. However, there was a renewed emphasis on attracting small and medium businesses by including a small and medium sector to IGS's industry alignment.

Sales/Distribution

IBM, including IGS, was world renowned for its superior sales force. For many years, IBM was symbolized by its highly trained and aggressive sales force, known for their skills and trademark blue suits, white shirts, and wingtip shoes. By the mid 1990s, the company's image had softened and there was a more casual approach to sales to match the changing corporate environment, but IBM was still praised for its superior sales force.

IGS had the ability to call upon a wide network of industry specific sales force experts. These resources were also highly trained to market services across industry sectors. This dedicated sales force was skilled and knowledgeable in specific technologies and offerings. IGS ensured the effectiveness of its sales force by requiring them to be certified in specific technology and industry knowledge. The certification was a combination of internal and external education requirements and the successful certification from outside boards (i.e., Microsoft, CISCO, and the Project Management Institute's certifications).

IBM had a worldwide network of telemarketing centers. These centers were established to market specifically to medium-sized customers offering a limited product line (mid-range and personal systems). This strategy had proven successful in North America, so it was being expanded to all the major geographic areas (Latin America, Europe, and Asia).

IBM, including IGS, was also in the process of reinventing itself as an ebusiness. It was using the Internet to market, sell, and deliver certain products. IBM had successfully launched a business-to-consumer site, a business-to-business web site, and an online technical support site. However, these channels were focusing on particular products (mid-range and personal systems, and software that could be delivered electronically). Services were not being aggressively marketed or delivered through the Internet.

IBM had established a strong Business Partner Program. As of 2001, there were approximately 45,000 business partners comprising 90,000 program and contractual relationships across IBM technologies, products, services, and solutions. IGS understood that these relationships were invaluable in the ongoing creation and delivery of solutions that efficiently address customer requirements and market opportunities such as ebusiness. In 2000, revenue growth through business partners was up 11 percent year to year. Business partners generated nearly 35 percent of IBM's revenue in 2000, compared with 20 percent four years previously. A significant portion of this was in the services area. In 1998, business partners were responsible for more than 60 percent of the revenue derived from the medium and small business market, which, many agreed, was a rich services opportunity.

A major strength of IGS was the skills and expertise of its personnel. This is of paramount importance in a services business where a company's skills and expertise are its products. These skills include specific technology knowledge, but even more important, specific industry knowledge.

Markets

IGS's strength was its global reach, providing a customer with services locally and internationally. IGS could provide services consistently across many countries and could be available in multiple locations under a single contract. IGS is the industry's number 1 worldwide provider of professional computer services, with more than 136,000 employees in 160 countries. IGS markets all its services across these global markets. However, it had not fully leveraged its outsourcing capabilities to foreign markets. This was especially true in Europe and Asia.

A major weakness of IGS, which can also be a strength, was its size. It was often slow to bring new services to market due to the size and complexity of the company and its management system. An example of this slow responsiveness was its introduction of ebusiness colocation facilities. Colocation facilities offered Internet start-ups a low-cost hosting facility where they could manage their own application, providing them with the required flexibility, but they did not have to be concerned with the management of the network, infrastructure, and security. IGS introduced this offering at the end of the dot-com boom, thereby losing out on the explosive growth in this area and then being stuck with expensive data-center floor space.

Management System

For many years, perspective employees saw employment at IBM as a great opportunity. Several surveys had identified IBM as one of the best companies in the area of employee benefits. This distinction had eroded since the 1980s, due in part to the company's financial difficulties in the mid 1980s through the early 1990s. Part of the company's recovery plans included mass layoffs and reduction in benefits. Although these were harsh measures, they were effective. By the mid to late 1990s, IBM (in particular, IGS) was once again an industry leader. Other changes in the corporate culture, due to the hard times of the early 1990s, were a flattening of the management structure and the elimination of corporate bureaucracy, which had previously made the company slow to make decisions. The new, more casual management style was more attractive to the personnel the company was then trying to attract.

However, IGS still had not embraced many of the strategies other consulting and services firms were utilizing for some time. These strategies included aggressive stock option programs covering more than just the company's executive ranks, and attractive signing bonuses. A stock option program is an opportunity for employees to share in the company's success over the long term by establishing a financial link to the shareholder value they work to produce. Stock option and signing bonus programs can deliver a competitive edge in employee recruitment, retention, and motivation. In an industry where knowledge represents a key asset, IGS had to continue to recruit and retain top employees. This was a weakness across the industry due to the shortage of IT professionals.

Looking Toward the Future

IBM Global Services is well positioned in the professional computer services industry; however, the company was worried that this position would erode if it did not take advantage of the existing industry trends when making key strategic decisions. The recent financial performance was disappointing, although the company continued to show growth in this important segment for IBM Corporation.

Gerstner, IBM's CEO, stated that the future of IBM would depend on the performance and growth of services, especially in the area of ebusiness, and the emerging "network economy" or "e-utility" model. This would be accomplished by focusing its resources on expanding services across the entire spectrum of ebusiness solutions, and targeting nontraditional customer segments, markets, and geographic locations.

Key IGS executives were proposing one alternative, which was to concentrate solely on ebusiness service offerings. This would limit its expansion in traditional offerings such as client server and enterprise systems (mainframe). IGS's priorities would be to capture a wide set of service opportunities and to secure ebusiness leadership in the marketplace. They would achieve these goals by aggressively increasing ebusiness service offerings, including ebusiness consulting, ebusiness integration services, and ebusiness outsourcing services, while maintaining traditional services.

This strategy was feasible because the Internet and ebusiness services were viewed as the growth engine for this segment, and IBM already had significant brand recognition in this area. They had coined the term *ebusiness*. IGS could turn this ebusiness mind share into true market share by offering all the necessary services a company needs to be successful in the web-based economy. This targeted focus would not dilute IGS resources across multiple service lines, especially custom application development, which this alternative would abandon. This was supported by the fact that ebusiness revenue grew more than 70 percent, to approximately $5 billion in 2000, with expected strong growth in subsequent years.

This alternative could win against the competition because of IGS's existing reputation as a world leader in professional computer services. In addition, the shift of resources to focus on ebusiness service offerings would assist in addressing the shortage of skilled resources and would offer another advantage over its competition (consultants/system integrators, full service providers, local/niche providers, and traditional IT providers). IGS would be positioned as the leader of ebusiness services, the most rapidly growing segment of services. IGS was better than the competition in several areas. Although all the competition had embraced ebusiness (Accenture in the area of consulting services, EDS in the area of outsourcing, and HP in the area of hardware), none had the capability to provide IGS's broad range of ebusiness services. Plus, by focusing its vast resources solely on ebusiness, IGS could bring solutions to market more rapidly. This strategy also has the potential of laying the foundation for exploiting the emerging network economy or e-utility model. This is the reshaping of the IT infrastructure from one that is largely internally built and managed by a company to one that is built and managed by external service providers for on-demand use by a company. This could truly differentiate IGS from its competition. IGS's ability to market using all three challenges of a dedicated professional sales force, direct marketing, and business partners was another advantage.

A major drawback with this shift away from being a full professional services provider to one focusing solely on ebusiness offerings was that IGS would be losing potential future revenue from traditional professional computer services sources. In addition, customers contracted for other services often contract with their existing service provider as they migrate to ebusiness. A way around these drawbacks would be to ensure that IGS is truly positioned as the world leader in ebusiness, which would be accomplished through a worldwide promotion strategy.

Other IGS executives were proposing another alternative, which was to expand the service offerings to provide a full range of professional services, but with an emphasis on ebusiness, network computing, and the future network economy. IGS would offer consulting, systems integration, and outsourcing to accommodate a client's needs and once again abandon a significant focus on custom application development. This strategy was feasible because the Internet and ebusiness services were viewed as the growth engine for this segment, and IBM already had significant brand recognition in these areas. However, this strategy would not limit the targeted services. IGS would provide a full range of services from the traditional client/server and enterprise systems (mainframes) to the emerging ebusiness and the future network computing. This strategy is feasible because it would continue to attract clients with a broad range of requirements, many of whom have not embraced ebusiness or are at various stages of their migration to ebusiness and still require other services. It is also feasible because of IBM's extensive investment in research and development, which ensures a continuous flow of services needed to support this type of strategy.

This alternative could win against the competition because of IGS's existing reputation as a world leader in professional computer services. IGS's brand recognition and global reach provided them advantages in pursuing these opportunities. IGS's competition (consultants/system integrators, full service providers, local/niche providers, and traditional IT providers) did not have the same name recognition with ebusiness as IGS enjoyed. They all faced the increased demands of their large customers to provide all-in-one solutions and at the same time provide standardized solutions at a competitive price, an area in which IGS held an advantage. IGS was better than the competition in several areas, but especially in the ability to provide a continuous flow of new products and services through their extensive investment in research and development (over $5 billion per year) as compared to the research and development of competitors such as EDS and HP.

A drawback to this strategy is the overextension of the company's resources to attempt to be all things to all clients. The size of the company has been a weakness before; offering too broad a range of services can negatively affect IGS's speed in bringing new services to market. Another drawback of offering such a broad range of services is the cost required to build and maintain the required skills, central delivery centers, facilities, and equipment. Ways around these drawbacks are IBM's continued investment in research and development and a continued evolution of the company's management structure, allowing the large company to have the speed of a smaller firm.

Based on these arguments, it was difficult to decide which alternative to choose, or whether to consider a third alternative. In general, Gerstner and the IGS executive team needed to decide which strategic decisions to implement in many different areas. There were many significant decisions to be made relative to which customers, services, and geographic markets to focus on, to name just a few. IBM Global Services can provide a broad range of service choices for companies of all sizes in many different geographic areas. The challenge is to decide which combination of alternatives will take advantage of industry trends, differentiate them from the competition, and secure the continued growth and success of IBM Global Services.

REFERENCES

Accenture (2001), "About Us," http://www.accenture.com/xd/xd.asp?it=enWeb&xd=aboutus\about_home.xml. Accessed February 21, 2001.

ADP (2001), "About the Company," http://www.adp.com/corporate/about.html. Accessed February 21, 2001.

Dr. Dobb's Journal (2001), http://www.ddj.com/articles/2000/0004/0004k/0004k.htm. Accessed April 1, 2001.

ebizchronicle (2001), http://www.ebizchronicle.com/backgrounders/may/summary.htm. Accessed April 3, 2001.

Hoovers Online Network (2001a), "Computer Services Industry," http://www.hoovers.com/industry/snapshot/0,2204,58,00.html. Accessed February 19, 2001.

Hoovers Online Network (2001b), "Computer Services Industry," http://www.hoovers.com/industry/snapshot/0,2204,58,00.html. Accessed February 19, 2001.

HP (2001a), http://www.hp.com/country/us/eng/companyinfo.htm. Accessed February 22, 2001.

HP (2001b), http://www.hp.com/country/us/eng/companyinfo.htm. Accessed February 22, 2001.

IBM (2001a), "Investor Relations," http://www.ibm.com/Investor. Accessed February 19, 2001.

IBM (2001b), "About the Company," http://www.ibm.com/IBM. Accessed February 19, 2001.

IBM (2001c), "Services," http://www.ibm.com/services/fullservice.html#its. Accessed February 19, 2001.

IBM (2001d), "Worldwide Services," http://www.ibm.com/services/worldwide/. Accessed February 19, 2001.

IBM Annual Report (2001).

Rosen, Cheryl (2001), "The Shrinking IT Budget," *Information Week.Com,* March 5, pp. 22–24.

Standard & Poor's Industry Survey (2001a), Computers: Commercial Services, January 25, p. 6.

Standard & Poor's Industry Survey (2001b), Computers: Commercial Services, January 25, p. 7.

Standard & Poor's Industry Survey (2001c), Computers: Commercial Services, January 25, p. 7.

Standard & Poor's Industry Survey (2001d), Computers: Commercial Services, January 25, p. 15.

Standard & Poor's Industry Survey (2001e), Computers: Commercial Services, January 25, p. 9.

Standard & Poor's Industry Survey (2001f), Computers: Commercial Services, January 25, p. 6.

Standard & Poor's Industry Survey (2001g), Computers: Commercial Services, January 25, p. 7.

Standard & Poor's Industry Survey (2001h), Computers: Commercial Services, January 25, p. 7.

Standard & Poor's Industry Survey (2001i), Computers: Commercial Services, January 25, p. 7.

Standard & Poor's Industry Survey (2001j), Computers: Commercial Services, January 25, p. 7.

U.S. Business Reporter, Industry Overview (2001a), "Computer Services Industry," http://www.activemedia-guide.com/computer_services.htm. Accessed February 19, 2001.

U.S. Business Reporter, Industry Overview (2001b), "Computer Services Industry," http://www.activemedia-guide.com/computer_services.htm. Accessed February 19, 2001.

U.S. Department of Commerce's U.S. (2001a), Industry Outlook '99: Information Services, p. 15.

U.S. Department of Commerce's U.S. (2001b), Industry Outlook '99: Information Services, p. 4.

22 SAP and the Evolving Web Software ERP Market

This case was prepared by Gareth R. Jones, Texas A&M University.

In 1972, after the project they were working on for IBM's German subsidiary was abandoned, five German IBM computer analysts left the company and founded Systems Applications and Products in Data Processing, known today as SAP. These analysts had been involved in the provisional design of a software program that would allow information about cross-functional and cross-divisional financial transactions in a company's value chain to be coordinated and processed centrally—resulting in enormous savings in time and expense. They observed that other software companies were also developing software designed to integrate across value chain activities and subunits. Using borrowed money and equipment, the five analysts worked day and night to create an accounting software platform that could integrate across all the parts of an entire corporation. In 1973, SAP unveiled an instantaneous accounting transaction processing program called R/1, one of the earliest examples of what is now called an enterprise resource planning system (ERPS).

Today, ERP is an industry term for the multi-module applications software that allows a company to manage the set of activities and transactions necessary to manage the business processes for moving a product from the input stage, along the value chain, to the final customer. As such, ERPs can recognize, monitor, measure, and evaluate all the transactions involved in business processes such as product planning, the purchasing of inputs from suppliers, the manufacturing process, inventory and order processing, and customer service itself. Essentially, a fully developed ERP provides a company with a standardized Information Technology (IT) platform that gives complete information about all aspects of its business processes and cost structure across functions and divisions so that it can (1) constantly search for ways to perform these processes more efficiently and lower its cost structure, and (2) allow it to improve and service its products and raise their value to customers. For example, ERPs provide information that allows for the design of products that match customer needs and lead to superior responsiveness to customers.

To give one example, Nestlé installed SAP's newest ERP software across its more than 150 U.S. food divisions in 2001. It thus discovered that each division was paying a different price for the same flavoring, vanilla. The same small set of vanilla suppliers was charging each division as much as they could get, so all divisions paid widely different prices depending on their bargaining power with the supplier. Before the

SAP system was installed, managers had no idea this was happening because their IT system could not compare and measure the same transaction (e.g., purchasing vanilla) across divisions. SAP's standardized cross-company software platform revealed this problem, and hundreds of thousands of dollars in cost savings were achieved by solving this one transaction difficulty alone.

SAP focused its R/1 software on the largest multinational companies with revenues of at least $2.5 billion. Although relatively few in number, these companies, most of which were large manufacturers, stood to gain the most benefit from ERP, and they were willing to pay SAP a premium price for its product. Its focus on this influential niche of companies helped SAP develop a global base of leading companies. Its goal, as it had been from the beginning, was to create the global industry standard for ERP by providing the best business applications software infrastructure.

In its first years, SAP not only developed ERP software, it also used its own internal consultants to install it physically on-site at its customers' corporate IT centers, manufacturing operations, and so on. Determined to increase its customer base quickly, however, SAP switched strategies in the 1980s. It decided to focus primarily on the development of its ERP software and to outsource, to external consultants, more and more of the implementation services needed to install and service its software on-site in a particular company. It formed a series of strategic alliances with major global consulting companies such as IBM, Accenture, and Cap Gemini to install its R/1 system in its growing base of global customers.

ERP instillation is a long and complicated process. A company cannot simply adapt its information systems to fit SAP's software; it must use consultants to rework the way it performs its value chain activities so that its business processes, and the information systems that measure these business processes, became compatible with SAP's software. SAP's ERP system provides a company with the information needed to achieve best industry practices across its operations. The more a particular company wishes to customize the SAP platform to its particular business processes, the more difficult and expensive the implementation process and the harder it becomes to realize the potential gains from cost savings and value added to the product.

SAP's outsourcing consulting strategy allowed it to penetrate global markets quickly and eliminated the huge capital investment needed to provide this service on a global basis. For consulting companies, however, the installation of SAP's software became a major money-spinner, and SAP did not enjoy as much of the huge revenue streams associated with providing computer services, such as the design, installation, and maintenance of an ERP platform on an ongoing basis. It did earn some revenue by training consultants in the intricacies of installing and maintaining SAP's ERP system.

By focusing on ERP software development, SAP did not receive any profits from this highly profitable revenue stream, and made itself dependent on consulting companies that now became the experts in the installation/customization arena. This decision had unfortunate long-term consequences because SAP began to lose firsthand knowledge of its customers' problems and an understanding of the changing needs of its customers, especially when the Internet and cross-company integration became a major competitive factor in the ERP industry. For a company whose goal was to provide a standardized platform across functions and divisions, this outsourcing strategy seemed like a strange choice to many analysts. Perhaps SAP should have expanded its own consulting operations to run parallel with those of external consultants, rather than providing a training service to these consultants to keep them informed about its constantly changing ERP software.

To some degree, its decision to focus on software development and outsource at least 80 percent of installation was a consequence of its German founders' "engineering" mindset. Founded by computer program engineers, SAP's culture was built on values and norms that emphasized technical innovation, and the development of leading-edge ERP software was the key success factor in the industry. SAP poured most of its money into research and development (R&D) to fund projects that would add to its platform's capabilities; consequently, it had much less desire and money to spend on consulting. Essentially, SAP was a product-focused company and believed R&D would produce the technical advances that would be the source of its competitive advantage and allow it to charge its customers a premium price for its ERP platform. By 1988, SAP was spending more than 27 percent of gross sales on R&D.

As SAP's top managers focused on developing its technical competency, however, its marketing and sales competency was ignored because managers believed the ERP platform would sell itself. Many of its internal consultants and training experts began to feel they were second-class citizens, despite the fact that they brought in the business and were responsible for the vital role of maintaining good relationships with SAP's growing customer base. It seemed that the classic problem of managing a growing business from the entrepreneurial to the professional management phase was emerging. SAP's top managers were not experienced business managers who understood the problems of implementing a rapidly growing company's strategy on a global basis; the need to develop a sound corporate infrastructure was being shoved aside.

In 1981, SAP introduced its second-generation ERP software, R/2. Not only did it contain many more value-chain/business process software modules, but it also linked its ERP software to the databases and communication systems used on mainframe computers, thus permitting greater connectivity and ease of use of ERP throughout a company. The R/1 platform had been largely a cross-organizational accounting/financial software module; the new software modules could handle procurement, product development, and inventory and order tracking. Of course, these additional components had to be compatible with each other so that they could be seamlessly integrated together on-site, at a customer's operations. SAP did not develop its own database management software package; its system was designed to be compatible with Oracle's database management software, the global leader in this segment of the software industry. Once again, this was to have repercussions later, when Oracle began to develop its own ERP software, essentially moving from database software into ERP development.

As part of its push to make its R/2 software the industry standard, SAP had also been in the process of customizing its basic ERP platform to accommodate the needs of companies in different kinds of industries. The way value chain activities and business processes are performed differs from industry to industry because of differences in the manufacturing processes and other factors. ERP software solutions must be customized by industry to perform most effectively. Its push to become the ERP leader across industries, across all large global companies, and across all value chain business processes required a huge R&D investment. In 1988, the company went public on the Frankfurt stock exchange to raise the necessary cash. By 1990, with its well-received multilingual software, SAP had emerged as one of the leading providers of business applications software, and its market capitalization was soaring. SAP began to dominate ERP software sales in the high-tech and electronics, engineering and construction, consumer products, chemical, and retail industries. Its product was increasingly being recognized as superior to the other ERP software being developed by companies such as PeopleSoft, S. D. Edwards, and Oracle. One reason for SAP's increasing competitive advantage was that it could offer a broad, standardized, state-of-the-art solution to many companies' business process problems, one that spanned a wide variety of value chain activities spread around the globe. By contrast, its competitors, like PeopleSoft, offered more-focused solutions aimed at one business process, such as human resources management.

SAP Introduces the R/3 Solution

SAP's continuing massive investment in developing new ERP software resulted in the introduction of its R/3, or third-generation, ERP solution in 1992. Essentially, the R/3 platform expanded on its previous solutions; it offered seamless, real-time integration for over 80 percent of a company's business processes. It had also embedded in the platform hundreds and then thousands of industry best practice solutions, or templates, that customers could use to improve their operations and processes. The R/3 system was initially composed of seven different modules corresponding to the most common business processes. Those modules are production planning, materials management, financial accounting, asset management, human resources management, project systems, and sales and distribution.

R/3 was designed to meet the diverse demands of its previous global clients. It could operate in multiple languages and convert exchange rates, and so on, on a real-time basis. SAP, recognizing the huge potential revenues to be earned from smaller business customers, ensured that R/3 could now also be configured for smaller customers and be customized to suit the needs of a broader range of industries. Furthermore, SAP designed R/3 to be "open architecturally," meaning that it could operate with whatever kind of computer hardware or software (the legacy system) that a particular company was presently using. Finally, in response to customer concerns that SAP's standardized system meant huge implementation problems in changing their business processes to match SAP's standardized solution, SAP introduced some limited customization opportunity into its software. Using specialized software from other companies, SAP claimed that up to 20 percent of R/3 could now be customized to work with the company's existing operating methods and thus would reduce the problems of learning and implementing the new system. However, the costs of doing this were extremely high and became a huge generator of fees for consulting companies. SAP used a variable-fee licensing system for its R/3 system; the cost to the customer was based on the number of users within a company, on the number of different R/3 modules that were installed, and on the degree to which users utilized these modules in the business planning process.

SAP's R/3 far outperformed its competitors' products in a technical sense and once again allowed it to charge a premium price for its new software. Believing that competitors would take at least two years to catch up, SAP's goal was to get its current customers to switch to its new product and then it could rapidly build its customer base to penetrate the growing ERP market. In doing so, it was also seeking to establish R/3 as the new ERP market standard and lock in customers before competitors could offer a viable alternative. This strategy was vital to its future success because, given the way an ERP system changes the nature of a customer's business processes once it is installed and running, there are high switching costs involved in moving to another ERP product, costs that customers want to avoid.

R/3's growing popularity led SAP to decentralize more and more control of the marketing, sale, and installation of its software on a global basis to its foreign subsidiaries. While its R&D and software development remained centralized in Germany, it began to open wholly owned subsidiaries in most major country markets. By 1995, it had eighteen national subsidiaries; today, it has over fifty. In 1995, SAP established a U.S. subsidiary to drive sales in the huge U.S. market. Its German top managers set the subsidiary a goal of achieving $1 billion in revenues within five years. To implement this aggressive growth strategy, and given that R/3 software needs to

be installed and customized to suit the needs of particular companies and industries, several different regional SAP divisions were created to manage the needs of companies and industries in different U.S. regions. Also, the regional divisions were responsible for training an army of consultants, both internal and external, from companies such as Accenture, on how to install and customize the R/3 software. For every internal lead SAP consultant, there were soon about nine to ten external consultants working with SAP's customers to install and modify the software.

The problems with a policy of decentralization soon caught up with SAP, however. Because SAP was growing so fast and there was so much demand for its product, it was hard to provide the thorough training consultants needed to perform the installation of its software. Once SAP had trained an internal consultant, that consultant would sometimes leave to join the company for which he or she was performing the work or even to start an industry-specific SAP consulting practice, with the result that SAP's customers' needs were being poorly served. Since the large external consulting companies made their money based on the time it took their consultants to install a particular SAP system, some customers were complaining that consultants were deliberately taking too long to implement the new software to maximize their earnings, and were even pushing inappropriate or unnecessary R/3 modules.

The word started to circulate that SAP's software was both difficult and expensive to implement, which hurt its reputation and sales. Some companies had problems implementing the R/3 software; for example, Chevron spent over $100 million and two years installing and getting its R/3 system operating effectively. In one well-publicized case, Foxmeyer Drug blamed SAP software for the supply chain problems that led to its bankruptcy. The firm's major creditors sued SAP in court, alleging that the company had promised R/3 would do more than it could. SAP responded that the problem was not the software but the way the company had tried to implement it, but SAP's reputation was harmed nevertheless.

SAP's policy of decentralization was also somewhat paradoxical because the company's mission was to supply software that linked functions and divisions rather than separated them, and the characteristic problems of too much decentralization of authority soon became evident throughout SAP. In its U.S. subsidiary, each regional SAP division started developing its own procedures for pricing SAP software, offering discounts, dealing with customer complaints, and even rewarding its employees and consultants. There was a total lack of standardization and integration inside SAP America and indeed between SAP's many foreign subsidiaries and their headquarters in Germany. This meant that little learning was taking place between divisions or consultants, there was no monitoring or coordination mechanism in place to share SAP's *own* best practices between its consultants and divisions, and organizing by region in the United States was doing little to build core competences. For example, analysts were asking, If R/3 has to be customized to suit the needs of a particular industry, why didn't SAP use a market structure and divide its activities by the needs of customers based in different industries? These problems slowed down the process of implementing SAP software and prevented quick and effective responses to the needs of potential customers.

SAP's R/3 was also criticized as being too standardized because it forced all companies to adapt to what SAP had decided were best industry practices. When consultants reconfigured the software to suit a particular company's needs, this process often took a long time and sometimes the system did not perform as well as had been expected. Many companies felt that the software should be configured to suit their business processes and not the other way around, but again SAP argued that such a setup would not lead to an optimal outcome. For example, SAP's retail R/3 system could not handle Home Depot's policy of allowing each of its stores to order directly from suppliers, based upon centrally negotiated contracts between Home Depot and those suppliers. SAP's customers also found that supporting their new ERP platform was expensive and that ongoing support cost three to five times as much as the actual purchase of the software, although the benefits they received from its R/3 system usually exceeded these costs substantially.

The Changing Industry Environment

Although the United States had become SAP's biggest market, the explosive growth in demand for SAP's software had begun to slacken by 1995. Competitors such as Oracle, Baan, PeopleSoft, and Marcum were catching up technically, often because they were focusing their resources on the needs of one or a few industries or on a particular kind of ERP module (for example, PeopleSoft's focus on the HRM module). Indeed SAP had to play catch-up in the HRM area and develop its own to offer a full suite of integrated business solutions. Oracle, the second largest software maker after Microsoft, was becoming a particular threat as it expanded its ERP offerings outward from its leading database knowledge systems and began to offer more and more of an Internet-based ERP platform. As new aggressive competitors emerged and changed the environment, SAP found it needed to change as well.

Competitors were increasing their market share by exploiting weaknesses in SAP's software. They began to offer SAP's existing and potential customers ERP systems that could be customized more easily to their situation; systems that were less expensive than SAP's, which still were charged at a premium price; or systems that offered less expensive module options. SAP's managers were forced to reevaluate their business model, and their strategies and the ways in which they implemented them.

New Implementation Problems

To a large degree, SAP's decision to decentralize control of its marketing, sales, and installation to its subsidiaries was due to the way the company had operated from its beginnings. Its German founders had emphasized the importance of excellence in innovation as the root value of its culture, and SAP's culture was often described as "organized chaos." Its top managers had operated from the beginning by creating as flat a hierarchy as possible to create an internal environment where people could take risks and try new ideas of their own choosing. If mistakes occurred or projects didn't work out, employees were given the freedom to try a different approach. Hard work, teamwork, openness, and speed were the norms of their culture. Required meetings were rare and offices were frequently empty because most of the employees were concentrating on research and development. The pressure was on software developers to create superior products. In fact, the company was proud of the fact that it was product driven, not service oriented. It wanted to be the world's leading innovator of software, not a service company that installed it.

Increasing competition led SAP's managers to realize that they were not capitalizing on its main strength—its human resources. In 1997, it established a human resources management (HRM) department and gave it the responsibility to build a more formal organizational structure. Previously it had outsourced its own HRM. HRM managers started to develop job descriptions and job titles, and put in place a career structure that would motivate employees and keep them loyal to the company. They also put in place a reward system, which included stock options, to increase the loyalty of their technicians, who were being attracted away by competitors or were starting their own businesses because SAP did not then offer a future: a career path. For example, SAP sued Siebel Systems, a niche rival in the customer relationship software business, in 2000 for enticing twelve of its senior employees, who it said took trade secrets with them. SAP's top managers realized that they had to plan long term, and that innovation by itself was not enough to make SAP a dominant global company with a sustainable competitive advantage.

At the same time that it started to operate more formally, it also became more centralized to encourage organizational learning and to promote the sharing of its own best implementation practices across divisions and subsidiaries. Its goal was to standardize the way each subsidiary or division operated across the company, thus making it easier to transfer people and knowledge where they were needed most. Not only would this facilitate cooperation, it would also reduce overhead costs, which were spiraling because of the need to recruit trained personnel as the company grew quickly and the need to alter and adapt its software to suit changing industry conditions. For example, increasing customer demands for additional customization of its software made it imperative that different teams of engineers pool their knowledge to reduce development costs, and that consultants should not only share their best practices but also cooperate with engineers so that the latter could understand the problems facing customers in the field.

The need to adopt a more standardized and hierarchical approach was also being driven by SAP's growing recognition that it needed more of the stream of income it could get from both the training and installation sector of the software business. It began to increase the number of its consultants. By having them work with its software developers, they became the acknowledged experts and leaders when

it came to specific software installations and could command a high price. SAP also developed a large global training function to provide the extensive ERP training that consultants needed and charged both individuals and consulting companies high fees for attending these courses so that they would be able to work with the SAP platform. SAP's U.S. subsidiary also moved from a regional to a more market-based focus by re-aligning its divisions, not by geography, but by their focus on a particular sector or industry, for example, chemicals, electronics, pharmaceuticals, consumer products, and engineering.

Once again, however, the lines of authority between the new industry divisions and the software development, sales, installation, and training functions were not worked out well enough and the hoped-for gains from increased coordination and cooperation were slow to be realized. Globally too, SAP was still highly decentralized and remained a product-focused company, thus allowing its subsidiaries to form their own sales, training, and installation policies. Its subsidiaries continued to form strategic alliances with global consulting companies, allowing them to obtain the majority of revenues from servicing SAP's growing base of R/3 installations. SAP's top managers, with their engineering mindset, did not appreciate the difficulties involved in changing a company's structure and culture, either at the subsidiary or the global level. They were disappointed in the slow pace of change because their cost structure remained high, although their revenues were increasing.

New Strategic Problems

By the mid 1990s, despite its problems in implementing its strategy, SAP was the clear market leader in the ERP software industry and the fourth largest global software company because of its recognized competencies in the production of state-of-the-art ERP software. Several emerging problems posed major threats to its business model, however. First, it was becoming increasingly obvious that the development of the Internet and broadband technology would become important forces in shaping a company's business model and processes in the future. SAP's R/3 systems were specifically designed to integrate information about all of a company's value chain activities, across its functions and divisions, and to provide real-time feedback on its ongoing performance.

However, ERP systems focused principally on a company's internal business processes; they were not designed to focus and provide feedback on cross-company and industry-level transactions and processes on a real-time basis. The Internet was changing the way in which companies viewed their boundaries; the emergence of global ecommerce and online cross-company transactions was changing the nature of a company's business processes both at the input and output sides.

At the input side, the Internet was changing the way a company managed its relationships with its parts and raw materials suppliers. Internet-based commerce offered the opportunity of locating new, low-cost suppliers. Developing web software was also making it much easier for a company to cooperate and work with suppliers and manufacturing companies and to outsource activities to specialists who could perform the activities at lower cost. A company that previously made its own inputs or manufactured its own products could now outsource these value chain activities, which changed the nature of the ERP systems it needed to manage such transactions. In general, the changing nature of transactions across the company's boundaries could affect its ERP system in thousands of ways. Companies like Commerce One and Ariba, which offered this supply chain management (SCM) software, were growing rapidly and posing a major threat to SAP's "closed" ERP software.

At the output side, the emergence of the Internet also radically altered the relationship between a company and its customers. Not only did the Internet make possible new ways to sell to wholesalers, its largest customers, or directly to individual customers, it also changed the whole nature of the company–customer interface. For example, using new customer relationship management (CRM) software from software developers like Siebel systems, a company could offer its customers access to much more information about its products so that customers could make more-informed purchase decisions. A company could also understand customers' changing needs so it could develop improved or advanced products to meet those needs; and a company could offer a whole new way to manage after-sales service and help solve customers' problems with learning about, operating, and even repairing their new purchases. The CRM market was starting to boom.

In essence the Internet was changing both industry- and company-level business processes and pro-

viding companies and whole industries with many more avenues for altering their business processes at a company or industry level, so that they could lower their cost structure or increasingly differentiate their products. Clearly, the hundreds of industry best practices that SAP had embedded in its R/3 software would become outdated and redundant as e-commerce increased in scope and depth and offered improved industry solutions. SAP's R/3 system would become a dinosaur within a decade unless it could move quickly to develop or obtain competencies in the software skills needed to develop web-based software.

These developments posed a severe shock to SAP's management, who had been proud of the fact that, until now, SAP had developed all its software internally. They were not alone in their predicament. The largest software companies, Microsoft and Oracle, had been caught unaware by the quickly growing implications of web-based computing. The introduction of Netscape's web browser had led to a collapse in Microsoft's stock price because investors saw web-based computing, not PC-based computing, as the choice of the future. SAP's stock price also began to reflect the beliefs of many people that expensive, rigid, standardized ERP systems would not become the software choice as the Web developed. One source of SAP's competitive advantage was based on the high switching costs of moving from one ERP platform to another. However, if new web-based platforms allowed both internal and external integration of a company's business processes, and new platforms could be customized more easily to answer a particular company's needs, these switching costs might disappear. SAP was at a critical point in its development.

The other side of the equation was that the emergence of new web-based software technology allowed hundreds of new software industry start-ups, founded by technical experts equally as qualified as those at SAP and Microsoft, to enter the industry and compete for the wide-open web computing market. The race was on to determine which standards would apply in the new web computing arena and who would control them. The large software makers like Microsoft, Oracle, IBM, SAP, Netscape, Sun Microsystems, and Computer Associates had to decide how to compete in this totally changed industry environment. Most of their customers, companies large and small, were still watching developments before deciding how and where to commit their IT budgets. Hundreds of billions of dollars in future software sales were at stake, and it was not clear which company had the competitive advantage in this changing environment.

Rivalry among major software makers in the new web-based software market became intense. Rivalry between the major players and new players, like Netscape, Siebel Systems, Marcum, I2 Technology, and SSA, also intensified. The major software makers, each of which was a market leader in one or more segments of the software industry, such as SAP in ERP, Microsoft in PC software, and Oracle in database management software, sought to showcase their strengths to make their software compatible with web-based technology. Thus, Microsoft strove to develop its Windows NT network-based platform and its Internet Explorer web browser to compete with Netscape's Internet browser and Sun Microsystems's open-standard Java web software programming language, which was compatible with any company's proprietary software, unlike Microsoft's NT.

SAP also had to deal with competition from large and small software companies that were breaking into the new web-based ERP environment. In 1995, SAP teamed with Microsoft, Netscape, and Sun Microsystems to make its R/3 software Internet-compatible with any of their competing systems. Within one year, it introduced its R/3 Release 3.1 Internet-compatible system, which was most easily configured, however, when using Sun's Java web-programming language. SAP raised new funds on the stock market to undertake new rounds of the huge investment necessary to keep its web-based R/3 system up to date with the dramatic innovations in web software development and to broaden its product range to offer new, continually emerging web-based applications, for example, applications such as the corporate intranets, business-to-business (B2B) and business-to customer (B2C) networks, web site development and hosting, security and systems management, and streaming audio and video teleconferencing.

Because SAP had no developed competency in web software development, its competitors started to catch up. Oracle emerged as its major competitor; it had taken its core database management software used by thousands of large companies and overlaid it with web-based operating and applications software. Oracle could now offer its huge customer base a growing suite of web software, all seamlessly inte-

grated. The suite of software also allowed them to perform Internet-based ERP value chain business processes. While Oracle's system was nowhere near as comprehensive as SAP's R/3 system, it allowed for cross-industry networking at both the input and output sides, it was cheaper and easier to implement quickly, and it was easier to customize to the needs of a particular customer. Oracle began to take market share away from SAP.

New companies like Siebel Systems, Commerce One, Ariba, and Marcum, which began as niche players in some software applications such as SCM, CRM, intranet, or web site development and hosting, also began to build and expand their product offerings so that they now possessed ERP modules that competed with some of SAP's most lucrative R/3 modules. Commerce One and Ariba, for example, emerged as the main players in the rapidly expanding business-to-business (B2B) industry supply chain management market. B2B is an industry-level ERP solution that creates an organized market and thus brings together industry buyers and suppliers electronically and provides the software to write and enforce contracts for the future development and supply of an industry's inputs. Although these niche players could not provide the full range of services that SAP could provide, they became increasingly able to offer attractive alternatives to customers seeking specific aspects of an ERP system. Also, companies like Siebel, Marcum, and I2 claimed that they had the ability to customize their low-price systems, and prices for ERP systems began to fall.

In the new software environment, SAP's large customers started to purchase software on a "best of breed" basis, meaning that customers purchased the best software applications for their specific needs from different, leading-edge companies rather than purchasing all of their software products from one company as a package—such as SAP offered. Sun began to promote a free Java computer language as the industry "open architecture" standard, which meant that, as long as each company used Java to craft their specific web-based software programs, they would all work seamlessly together and there would no longer be an advantage to using a single dominant platform like Microsoft's Windows or SAP's R/3. Sun was and is trying to break Microsoft's hold over the operating system industry standard, Windows. Sun wanted each company's software to succeed because it was "best of breed," not because it locked customers in and created enormous switching costs for them should they contemplate a move to a competitor's product.

All these different factors caused enormous problems for SAP's top managers. What strategies should they use to protect their competitive position? Should they forge ahead with offering their customers a broad, proprietary, web-based ERP solution and try to lock them in and continue to charge a premium price? Should they move to an open standard and make their R/3 ERP Internet-enabled modules compatible with solutions from other companies, and indeed forge alliances with those companies to ensure that their software operated seamlessly together? Since SAP's managers still believed they had the best ERP software and the capabilities to lead in the web software arena, was this the best long-run competitive solution? Should SAP focus on making its ERP software more customizable to its customers' needs and make it easier for them to buy selected modules to reduce the cost of SAP software? This alternative might also make it easier for them to develop ERP modules that could be scaled back to suit the needs of medium and small firms, which increasingly were becoming the targets of its new software competitors. Once these new firms got a toehold in the market, it would then be a matter of time before they improved their products and began to compete for SAP's installed customer base. SAP realized that it had to refocus its business model, especially because rivals were rapidly buying niche players and, at the same time, filling gaps in their product lines to be able to compete with SAP.

Opportunities and threats were emerging from all sides. The question was how to proceed, especially since the various major software companies were all supporting different industry standards to promote their own competitive advantage in the Internet world. Microsoft was fighting to preserve the dominance of its Windows platform from the encroachments made by Sun's Java platform and the free Linux platform, which was being championed by IBM as the operating platform of the future. Indeed, IBM recognized that lucrative revenues could be earned from computer services and consulting and had changed its strategy in the 1990s. No longer was its major focus the development of proprietary software but the design, installation, and servicing of whatever hardware and software system its customers chose to deploy. For IBM, championing and develop-

ing Linux was a way to increase revenues. By 2001, 7 to 10 percent of companies' operating systems were running on the free Linux system. For IBM, however, promoting Linux, as Sun was promoting Java, was also a way to frustrate Microsoft's aims to control the industry standard for personal computing operating software in a web-based software environment.

The mySAP.com Initiative

In 1997, SAP sought a quick fix to its problems by releasing new R/3 solutions for ERP Internet-enabled supply chain management (SCM) and customer relationship management (CRM) solutions, which converted its internal ERP system into an externally based network platform. SCM, now know as the "back end" of the business, integrates the business processes necessary to manage the flow of goods, from the raw material stage to the finished product. SCM programs forecast future needs, and plan and manage a company's operations, especially its manufacturing operations. CRM, known as the "front-end" of the business, provides companies with solutions and support for business processes directed at improving sales, marketing, customer service, and field service operations. CRM programs are rapidly growing in popularity because they lead to better customer retention and satisfaction and higher revenues. In 1998, SAP followed with industry solution maps, business technology maps, and service maps, all of which were aimed at making its R/3 system dynamic and responsive to changes in industry conditions. In 1998, recognizing that its future rested on its ability to protect its share of the U.S. market, it listed itself on the New York Stock Exchange and began to expand the scope of its U.S. operations.

In 1999, however, the full extent of the change in SAP's business model and strategies became clear when it introduced its mySAP.com (mySAP) initiative to gain control of the web-based ERP, SCM, and CRM markets, and to extend its reach into any e-commerce or Internet-based software applications. The mySAP initiative was a comprehensive ebusiness platform designed to help companies collaborate and succeed, regardless of their industry or network environment. It demonstrated several elements of SAP's changing strategic thinking for how to succeed in the 2000s.

First, to meet its customer's needs in a new electronic environment, SAP used the mySAP platform to change itself from a vendor of ERP components to a provider of ebusiness solutions. The platform was to be the online portal through which customers could view and understand the way its Internet-enabled R/3 modules could match their evolving needs. SAP recognized that its customers were increasingly demanding access to networked environments with global connectivity, where decisions could be executed in real time through the Internet. Customers wanted to be able to leverage new ebusiness technologies to improve basic business goals like increasing profitability, improving customer satisfaction, and lowering overhead costs. In addition, customers wanted total solutions that could help them manage their relationships and supply chains.

MySAP was to offer a total solutions ERP package, including SCM and CRM applications, which would be fundamentally different from the company's traditional business application software. SAP's software would no longer force the customer to adapt to SAP's standardized architecture; mySAP software could be adapted to facilitate a company's transition into an ebusiness. In addition, the solution would create value for a company by building on its already developed core competencies; mySAP would help to leverage those core competencies, thus building a company's competitive advantage from within, rather than by creating it solely through the installation of SAP's industry best practices. SAP created a full range of front- and back-end products such as SCM and CRM software, available through its mySAP.com portal, that are specific to different industries and manufacturing technologies. These changes meant that it could compete in niche markets and make it easier to customize a particular application to an individual company's needs.

Second, mySAP provided the platform that would allow SAP's product offerings to expand and broaden over time, an especially important feature because web-based software was evolving into ever more varied applications. SAP was essentially copying other software makers, who were branching out into more segments of the software industry to capitalize on higher growth software segments and to prevent obsolescence should demand for their core software erode because of technological developments. Henceforth, SAP was not offering product-based solutions but customer-based solutions. Its mySAP ebusiness platform solutions are designed to be a scalable and flexible architecture that supports data-

bases, applications, operating systems, and hardware platforms from almost every major vendor.

Third, SAP realized that cost was becoming a more important issue because competition from low-cost rivals demonstrated that customers could be persuaded to shift vendors if they were offered good deals. Indeed, major companies like Oracle often offered their software at discount prices or even gave it away free to well-known companies to generate interest and demand for their product. SAP focused on making mySAP more affordable by breaking up its modules and business solutions into smaller, separate products. Customers could now choose which particular solutions best met their specific needs; they no longer had to buy the whole package. At the same time, all mySAP offerings were fully compatible with the total R/3 system so that customers could easily expand their use of SAP's products. SAP was working across its whole product range to make its system easier and cheaper to use. SAP realized that repeat business is much more important than a one-time transaction, so they began to focus on seeking out and developing new, related solutions for their customers to keep them coming back and purchasing more products and upgrades.

Fourth, mySAP was aimed at a wider range of potential customers. By providing a simpler and cheaper version of its application software coupled with the introduction of the many mySAP ebusiness solution packages, SAP broadened its offerings targeted not only to large corporations but also small and medium-sized companies. MySAP allowed SAP to provide a low-cost ERP system that could be scaled down for smaller firms. For example, for small to mid-sized companies that lack the internal resources to maintain their own business applications on-site, mySAP offered hosting for data centers, networks, and applications. Small businesses could benefit greatly from the increased speed of installation and reduced cost possible through outsourcing and by paying a fee to use mySAP in lieu of having to purchase SAP's expensive software modules. SAP also focused on making its R/3 mySAP offerings easier to install and use, and reduced implementation times and consulting costs in turn reduced the costs of supporting the SAP platform for both small and large organizations.

To support its mySAP initiative, SAP had continued to build in-house training and consulting capabilities to increase its share of revenues from the services side of its business. SAP's increasing web software services efforts paid off because the company was now better able to recognize the problems experienced by customers. This result led SAP to recognize both the needs for greater responsiveness to customers and customization of its products to make their installation easier. Its growing customer awareness had also led it to redefine its mission as a developer of business solutions, the approach embedded in mySAP, rather than as a provider of software products.

To improve the cost effectiveness of mySAP installations, SAP sought a better way to manage its relationships with consulting companies. It moved to a parallel sourcing policy, in which several consulting firms competed for a customer's business, and it made sure a SAP consultant was always involved in the installation and service effort to monitor external consultants' performance. This helped keep service costs under control for its customers. Because customer needs changed so quickly in this fast-paced market and SAP continually improved its products with incremental innovations and additional capabilities, it also insisted that consultants undertake continual training to update their skills, training for which it charged high fees. In 2000, SAP adopted a stock option program to retain valuable employees after losing many key employees—programmers and consultants—to competitors.

Fifth, SAP increasingly embraced the concept of open architecture, and its mySAP offerings are compatible with the products of most other software makers. It had already ensured that its mySAP platform worked with operating systems such as Microsoft NT, Sun's Java, and UNIX, for example. Now it focused on ensuring that its products were compatible with emerging web applications software from any major software maker—by 2001 SAP claimed to have over 1,000 partners.

Indeed, strategic alliances and acquisitions became increasingly important parts of its strategy to reduce its cost structure, enhance the functionality of its products, and build its customer base. Because of the sheer size and expense of many web-based software endeavors, intense competition, and the fast-paced dynamics of this industry, SAP's top managers began to realize they could not go it alone and produce everything in-house. SAP's overhead costs had rocketed in the 1990s as it pumped money into building its mySAP initiative. Intense competition seemed to indicate that continuing massive expenditures would be necessary. SAP's stock price had decreased because higher overhead costs meant falling profits despite increasing revenues. SAP had never seemed to be able to enjoy sustained high profitability because changing technology and competition had not allowed it to capitalize on its acknowledged position as the ERP industry leader.

Given existing resource constraints and time pressures and the need to create a more profitable business model, in the 2000s SAP's managers realized that they needed to partner with companies that now dominated in various niches of the software market. By utilizing already developed best of breed software, SAP would not have to deploy the capital necessary if it were to go it alone. In addition, synergies across partner companies might allow future development to be accomplished more efficiently and enable it to bring new mySAP products to the market more quickly.

One example of SAP reaping the benefits of such synergies was its alliance with Commerce One, a leading provider of B2B marketplace software and online procurement applications. The alliance created value for SAP, which obtained the skills of Commerce One's engineers and allowed it to share resources and development costs. In 2001, SAP solidified its alliance with Commerce One by making a $250 million investment in the company, and it launched a U.S. subsidiary, SAPMarkets, to compete in the business-to-business e-commerce services market. In another major alliance, it announced in 2002 that it was joining with IBM to speed the delivery of product life-cycle management (PLM) software and services to its growing base of manufacturing customers. PLM offers an integrated environment that ensures that all people involved in product development, manufacturing, and services have quick and secure access to all shared, current information so that they can plan appropriately on a global level. SAP will incorporate IBM's own industry specific solutions into its mySAP PLM software, and IBM will deliver consulting, integration, and implementation services around mySAP PLM solutions. This is a huge potential market; manufacturing companies have always been the main customer base for SAP's ERP systems.

Not only did SAP form alliances with other companies, it also used acquisitions to drive its entry into new segments of the web software market. For example, SAP acquired Top Tier Software Inc. in 2001 to gain access to its iView technology. This technology allows seamless integration between the web software of different companies and is critical for SAP because it lets customers drag-and-drop and mix information and applications from both SAP and non-SAP platform-based systems, and thus enables the open systems architecture SAP has increasingly supported. Top Tier was also an enterprise portal software maker, and in 2001 SAP teamed up with Yahoo to use these competencies to create a new U.S. subsidiary called SAP Portals, which would deliver state-of-the-art enterprise portal products that would enable people and companies to collaborate effectively and at any time. It also opened SAP hosting to provide hosting and web maintenance services.

By 2002, SAP believed that its partnerships and alliances had maneuvered it into a position of continued market dominance for the twenty-first century. Many of the major vendors of the databases, applications, operating systems, and hardware platforms that mySAP supports were once considered the competition, but the companies were now working together to create value by maximizing the range of web-based products that could be offered to customers through a common interface. MySAP adds value to its competitors products by decreasing the exclusivity between the applications of different companies. In essence, SAP was treating these other products as complementary products, which added to the value of its own, promoted mySAP as the industry standard, and increased its dominance of the ERP web software market.

SAP's managers were shocked when it became clear that Microsoft, also recognizing the enormous potential of web software ERP sales, particularly in the small and medium business segment of the market, might be planning to compete in this market segment in 2002. Microsoft had bought two companies that competed in this segment to bolster its own web software offerings. Also, when Microsoft introduced its new XP operating system in 2001, it had not included a Java applications package to allow web software developers to write ebusiness software that would be compatible with XP, undercutting its rival Sun's attempts to bypass the Window's platform using its Java language. However, this also undercut SAP's open architecture initiatives because many of its mySAP installations were based on Java, not Microsoft's NT platform. SAP's managers saw this

move as an attempt by Microsoft to wipe out the competitive advantage SAP had been gaining since the introduction of mySAP in 1999. SAP challenged Microsoft to indicate its support for the Java language. Already under scrutiny and attack by Sun and other software companies for its anticompetitive trade practices, Microsoft seemed to step back when it announced in June 2002 that its next version of XP would contain support for Java-based programming. Clearly, however, an open architecture and industry standard for web-based software are not in Microsoft's interests, especially if word processing and other important office applications become available as part of any e-commerce platform such as mySAP.

Microsoft could well became a formidable potential competitor for SAP because of Microsoft's competencies in a wide area of software products and because it has the resources to develop quickly and easily an ERP system with web-based solutions. In the past, SAP tried to avoid this competition problem by partnering with Microsoft in a wide variety of endeavors and making sure its products were compatible with Microsoft's, thus making their interests mutual rather than divisive. However, if Microsoft sees its Windows platform coming under increasing threat, it could quickly move into SAP's and Oracle's market. The competitive battle over industry standards seems far from over.

The recession that started in 2000 has also increased competition in the ERP industry. SAP and Oracle, in particular, have battled to protect and increase their market share. The huge drop in spending on IT by major companies and the decrease in the number of new customers has hit the industry hard. The stock prices of all these companies have fallen dramatically, with some like I2 Systems, also a provider of SCM solutions, fighting to survive. Competition among software companies has been intense, and customers have taken advantage of this rivalry to demand price discounts from SAP as well as other companies, which hurts revenues and profits. Smaller competitors like I2 and Siebel lowered their prices to the point where they took a loss on a particular sale to gain market share. The weakest companies have been forced to fall back on their main strengths and reduce their range of product offerings. This strategy will help SAP because it has the resources to withstand the current downturn and therefore might emerge stronger as a result.

SAP's number of software installations and customers increased steadily between 1998 and 2002. The number of software installations grew at a faster pace than the number of customers, a characteristic of the lock-in feature of investment in one ERP platform. In 2002, SAP was still the number 1 vendor of standard business applications software, with a worldwide market share of over 30 percent. Oracle was next with a 16 percent share of the market. SAP claimed that it had 10 million users and 50,000 SAP installations in 18,000 companies in 120 countries in 2002, and that half of the world's top 500 companies used its software.

Implementing mySAP

SAP's problems were not just in the strategy area, however. Its mySAP initiative had increased its overhead costs, and it still could not find the appropriate organizational structure to make the best use of its resources and competencies. It continued to search for the right structure for servicing the growing range of its products and the increasing breadth of the companies, in terms of size, industry, and global location, it was now serving.

Recall that in the mid 1990s, SAP had began to centralize authority and control to standardize its own business processes and manage knowledge effectively across organizational subunits. While this reorganization resulted in some benefits, it had the unfortunate result of lengthening the time it took SAP to respond to the fast-changing web software ERP environment. To respond to changing customer needs and the needs for product customization, SAP now moved to decentralize control to programmers and its sales force to manage problems where and when they arose. SAP's managers felt that in an environment where markets are saturated with ERP vendors and where customers want service and systems that are easier to use, it was important to get close to the customer. SAP had now put in place its own applications software for integrating across its operating divisions and subsidiaries, allowing them to share best practices and new developments and thus avoid problems that come with too much decentralization of authority.

To speed the software development process, SAP divided its central German software development group into three teams in 2000. One team works on the development of new products and features, the second refines and updates functions in its existing products, and the third works on making SAP products easier to install. Also, to educate its customers and speed customer acceptance and demand for mySAP, SAP changed its global marketing operations in late 2000. Following its decentralized style, each product group once had its own marketing department that operated separately to market and sell its products. This decentralization had caused major problems because customers didn't understand how the various parts of mySAP fit together. It also wasted resources and slowed the sales effort. Announcing that "SAP had to develop a laserlike focus on marketing," a far cry from its previous focus on its engineering competency, SAP's top managers centralized control of marketing at its U.S. subsidiary and put control of all global marketing into the hands of one executive, who was now responsible for coordinating market efforts across all mySAP product groups and all world regions.

Soon after, in 2001, once again to speed up the implementation of the mySAP initiative, SAP folded the SAPMarkets and SAP Portals subsidiaries into SAP's other operations and split the SAP product line into distinct but related mySAP product groups, each of which was to be treated as an independent profit center, with the head of each product group reporting directly to SAP's chairperson. The type of web software application or ERP industry solution being offered to the customer differentiates each product group (see Exhibit 1).

SAP also changed the way its three German engineering groups worked with the different mySAP products groups. Henceforth, a significant part of the engineering development effort would take place inside each mySAP product group so that program engineers, who write and improve the specific new mySAP software applications, were joined with the sales force for that group. Now they could integrate their activities and provide better customized solutions. The software engineers at its German headquarters, besides conducting basic R&D, would be responsible for coordinating the efforts of the different mySAP engineering groups, sharing new software developments among groups, providing expert solutions, and ensuring all the different mySAP applications worked together seamlessly.

Each mySAP product group is now composed of a collection of cross-functional product development teams focused on their target markets. Teams are

EXHIBIT 1

mySAP.com Product Groups

---

mySAP.com Solutions

▌ Industry solutions

▌ Solutions for small and mid-sized businesses

▌ mySAP enterprise portals

▌ mySAP supply chain management

▌ mySAP customer relationship management

▌ mySAP supplier relationship management

▌ mySAP product life cycle management

▌ mySAP exchanges

▌ mySAP business intelligence

▌ mySAP financials

▌ mySAP human resources

▌ mySAP mobile business

▌ mySAP hosted solutions

▌ mySAP technology

mySAP.com Industry Solutions

▌ mySAP aerospace and defense

▌ mySAP automotive

▌ mySAP banking

▌ mySAP chemicals

▌ mySAP consumer products

▌ mySAP engineering and construction

▌ mySAP financial service provider

▌ mySAP health care

▌ mySAP higher education and research

▌ mySAP high tech

▌ mySAP insurance

▌ mySAP media

▌ mySAP mill products

▌ mySAP mining

▌ mySAP oil and gas

▌ mySAP pharmaceuticals

▌ mySAP public sector

▌ mySAP retail

▌ mySAP service providers

▌ mySAP telecommunications

▌ mySAP utilities

---

given incentives to meet their specific sales growth targets and to increase operating effectiveness, including reducing the length of installation time. The purposes of the new product group/team approach was to decentralize control, make SAP more responsive to the needs of customers and to changing technical developments, and still give SAP centralized control of development efforts. To ensure that its broadening range of software was customizable to the needs of different kinds of companies and industries, SAP enlisted some of its key customers as "development partners" and as members of these teams. Customers from large, mid-sized, and small companies were used to test new concepts and ideas. Within every mySAP product group, cross-functional teams focused on customizing its products for specific customers or industries. SAP opened the development process to its competitors and allowed them to work with SAP teams to make their products compatible with SAP's products and with the computer

platforms or legacy systems already installed in their customers' operations. Through this implementation approach, SAP was striving to pull its actual and potential customers and competitors toward the single, open standard of SAP. The company also instituted stricter training and certification methods for consultants to improve the level of quality control and protect its reputation.

At the global level, SAP grouped is national subsidiaries into three main world regions: Europe, the Americas, and Asia/Pacific. This grouping made it easier to transfer knowledge and information between countries and serve the specific demands of national markets inside each region. Also, this global structure made it easier to manage relationships with consulting companies and to coordinate regional marketing and training efforts, both under the jurisdiction of the centralized marketing and training operations.

Thus, at present SAP operates with a loose form of matrix structure. To increase internal flexibility and responsiveness to customers while at the same time boosting efficiency and market penetration, the world regions, the national subsidiaries, and the sales people and consultants within them constitute one side of the matrix. The centralized engineering, marketing, and training functions and the twenty or so different mySAP product groups compose the other side. The problem facing SAP is to coordinate all these distinct subunits so they will lead to rapid acceptance of SAP's new mySAP platform across all the national markets in which it operates.

In practice, a salesperson in any particular country works directly with a client to determine what type of ERP system he or she needs. Once this system is determined, a project manager from the regional subsidiary or from one of the mySAP groups is appointed to assemble an installation team from members of the different product groups whose expertise is required to implement the new client's system. Given SAP's broad range of evolving products, the matrix structure allows SAP to provide those products that fit the customer's needs in a fast, coordinated way. SAP's policy of decentralizing authority and placing it in the hands of its employees enables the matrix system to work. SAP prides itself on its talented and professional staff who can learn and adapt to many different situations and networks across the globe.

The Future

In April 2002, SAP announced that its revenues had climbed 9.2 percent, but its first-quarter profit fell 40 percent because of a larger-than-expected drop in license revenue from the sale of new software. It seems that many customers have been reluctant to invest in the huge cost of moving to the mySAP system given the recession and continuing market uncertainty. Its rivals have fared worse, however, and SAP announced it had several orders for mySAP in the works, and that the 18,000 companies around the world using its flagship R/3 software would soon move to its new software once their own customers had started to spend more money. In the meantime, SAP announced it would introduce a product called R/3 Enterprise, which would be targeted at customers not yet ready to make the leap to mySAP. R/3 Enterprise is a collection of web software that can be added easily to the R/3 platform to provide a company with the ability to network with other companies and perform many

e-commerce operations. SAP hopes this new software will show its R/3 customers what mySAP can accomplish for them once it is running in their companies. SAP's managers believe the company is poised to jump from being the third largest global software company to being the second, ahead of Oracle, if it can use its mySAP open system architecture to overcome Microsoft's stranglehold on the software market and bypass the powerful Windows standard.

REFERENCES

Boudette, N. E., "E-Business: SAP Boosts Commerce One Stake," *Wall Street Journal,* July 2, 2001, p. B8.

Boudette, N. E., "Germany's SAP Reorganizes Its Marketing, Focuses on Web," *Wall Street Journal,* 2000, August 7, p. A8.

Boudette, N. E., "Results Show SAP Is Waiting to Benefit from Recovery," *Wall Street Journal,* April 19, 2002, p. A16.

"Burger King Corporation Selects SAP to Enable Information Technology Strategy," mySAP.com. Accessed June 25, 2002.

Collett, S., "SAP: Whirlpool's Rush to go Live Led to Shipping Snafus," *www.computerworld,* November 4, 1999.

Conlin, R., "SAP Teams with Yahoo! On Portal Venture," CRMDaily.com, April 4, 2001.

Conlin, R., "SAP Upgrades CRM App, Unveils New Strategy," CRMDaily.com, April 23, 2001.

Edmondson, G., and Baker, S., "Silicon Valley on the Rhine," *Business Week,* November 7, 1997.

Hill, S., "SAP 'Opens Up,'" *Msi,* Oak Brook, August 2001.

Jacobs, F., and Whybark, D. *Why ERP? A Primer on SAP Implementation.* New York: McGraw-Hill, 2000.

Kersteller, J., "Software," *Business Week,* January 8, 2001.

Key, P. "SAP Strategy: Displace All Competing Gateways," *Philadelphia Business Journal,* September 27, 1999.

King, J., "Commerce One Deal Reflects SAP Strategy Shift," Computerworld.com, June 15, 2000.

King, S., and Ohlson, K., "Update: Commerce One Deal Reflects SAP Strategy Shift," Computerworld.com, 2000.

Konicki, S., "Overwhelmed—SAP Regroups Software Business," *Information Week,* June 6, 2000.

Konicki, S., and Maselli, J., "SAP Touts Customers' Experiences," *Informationweek,* June 3, 2002.

Krill, P., "SAP Takes on Its CRM Rivals," *Infoworld,* September 10, 2001.

Maselli, J., "Analysts Steer Customers Away from SAP CRM Upgrade," *Information Week,* September 10, 2001.

Meissner, G. *Inside the Secret Software Power.* New York: McGraw-Hill, 2000.

O'Brien, K., "Many Blows to SAP Strength," http://www.it.mycareer.com.au/software/20000125/A39678-2000Jan21.html. Accessed January 25, 2000.

Pender, L., "SAP CEO: Don't Blame Us for Snafus," www.Zdnet.com, November 10, 1999.

SAP AG, "SAP Transforms E-Business with New mySAP Technology for Open Integration," *Business Wire,* November 6, 2001.

SAP Annual Reports and 10K Reports, 1998–2002.

Scannell, E., "Accenture, SAP Jump into Bed," *Infoworld,* July 9, 2001.

Standard and Poor's Industry Overview—Software, *Industry Survey,* April 26, 2001.

Weston, R., "SAP Strategy Extends Scope," CNETNews.com, September 15, 1998.

www.mySAP.com, 2002.

www.SAP.com, 2002.

Iridium: Communication for the New Millennium

23

This case was prepared by Min Yee Ji and Steven Angga-Prana under the supervision of Melissa A. Schilling, New York University.

The Ice Trek

In November 1998, the Iridium Ice Trek team—Eric Philips, Peter Hillary, and John Muira—set out from the coast of Antarctica to ski to the South Pole and back.[1] The journey was 1,742 miles and was one of the longest unsupported polar treks of any kind. The 100-day trek covered some of the most remote and inhospitable terrain in the world.

The Ice Trek team was the first private expedition to communicate via telephone direct from the Antarctic interior to the outside world. The team used two Kyocera telephones connected to the Iridium satellite system for broadcast of the expedition live to an audience of millions. For the trekkers, Iridium phones offered peace of mind in dangerous times; the ability to keep in touch with family during the Christmas season; and the ability to share the journey's other highs and lows with the outside world through phone calls to print, radio, television, and electronic media. The millions of listeners at home were kept up to date all the way to the end, when the three skiers reached the South Pole on January 26, 1999.

This case is intended to be used as a basis for class discussion rather than as an illustration of either effective or ineffective handling of the situation. The authors would like to acknowledge the help and support of Shawn Kuehn, Ryan Steele, Colin Blaney, Jay Margolis, and Frances Zeon. Reprinted by permission.

Despite the technological benefits of the Iridium system, there was a lack of subscribers using the global telecommunications service in the first year. By April 1999, the company reported 10,230 voice customers and just over 2,000 pager users, out of 200,000 projected for the end of 1998.[2] The future of global communication for trekkers and other adventurers who travel to remote locations was in jeopardy.

Birth of the Satellite Giant

Iridium was the first to market a service that allowed users to communicate anywhere, anytime. It took ten years of hard work and development to make this vision a reality. In 1987, three Motorola engineers—Ray Leopold, Ken Peterson, and Bary Bertiger—proposed a gateway concept costing $5 billion.[3] The gateway allowed the constellation of satellites to communicate with existing terrestrial telephone systems. The idea caught on with executives at Motorola and, in 1990, the Iridium system concept was unveiled at simultaneous press conferences in Beijing, London, Melbourne, and New York City. The press conferences created enough public and institutional confidence that Motorola spun off Iridium as a separate company in 1991. The fledgling company was in charge of deploying and developing the network, and in its first year reserved radio frequencies for the Iridium low earth orbit satellites (LEOs). The following year, the company took the first steps toward creating its constellation of satellites and secured a $3.37 billion contract with Motorola for system development, construction, and delivery.[4] Motorola became the prime contractor supplying satellites, gateways, and communication products for the system. The next four years progressed smoothly; with Motorola's backing, Iridium was able to raise $1.9 billion by 1996.[5] With finances secured, the terrestrial facilities used in operating and monitoring the satellites were completed. By May 1998, Iridium launched sixty-six satellites into orbit with 100 percent launch success, the best launch track record for any developer of low earth orbit satellites for voice communications.

The bad news was the lack of subscribers using the system after its completion. The lack of subscribers resulted in the resignation of Roy Grant, the chief financial officer, in April 1999, and the business was forced to seek an extension from creditors after failing to meet revenue and subscription goals.[6] A few weeks later, vice chairman and chief executive officer Edward Staiano resigned both his positions, as well as his post as chairman of Iridium World Communications Ltd.[7]

Satellite 101

The idea behind satellite communication was the ability to make a call anywhere in the world. While cellular networks covered the densely populated areas, 86 percent of the land remained outside a terrestrial cellular network. A global telecommunication device—one device that could work anywhere, even in the Amazon jungle, Gobi Desert, or Atlantic Ocean—was needed. So the Iridium concept was designed, not to replace or compete with existing cellular networks, but to fill in the holes between them.[8]

Before the Iridium concept was developed, satellite phones were as large and bulky as a briefcase. They had to be aligned with a compass and remain stationary while in use. These phones received transmissions from satellites called geosynchronous earth orbit (GEO). The satellites tracked the Earth at exactly its rotational speed to remain in the same position at 22,300 miles above the Earth.[9] The distance of these satellites from earth required only five GEOs operating in tandem to cover the whole globe. The result, however, was a noticeable delay of at least half a second in the transmitted sound from the GEOs.

The Iridium system, named after the atomic element iridium, used LEO satellites sitting 485 miles above earth. These satellites transmitted service in milliseconds to smaller, compact phones. Since LEOs were closer to earth, each satellite covered a much smaller area compared to GEOs. The Iridium system originally required seventy-seven satellites to cover the whole Earth.[10] The system was later decreased to sixty-six LEO satellites, with eleven spare satellites, to make the system more efficient and cheaper. Iridium's LEO divided the Earth into six orbital planes, eleven operational satellites, and one spare in each orbital plane.[11] Satellite controller stations, called gateways, controlled all of the LEOs, making the Iridium network incompatible with any other system.

Through these LEOs, Iridium provided voice, data, facsimile, and paging services to subscribers with hand-held wireless phones and pagers. The Iridium LEO system worked to provide these services using several frequencies, or bands. A call made from the Iridium handsets was connected directly to the satellites, which then either connected the call to another satellite or a gateway, depending on the receiver's location. This system was capable of handling a maximum of 1,100 simultaneous calls.[12] Calls made to Iridium handsets from landline phones were routed to the public network, the gateway, and then the satellite, which would then connect to the handsets. The system required the use of subscriber identity module (SIM) cards, which identified the caller with information such as phone number and country of origin. Due to the complexities of the Iridium structure, the system was smart enough to reject calls made in areas where no agreements or licensing had been established with the local government.

The Market: Calling Planet Earth!

Iridium was focused toward both the business traveler and workers in highly specialized industries that required connectivity in remote locations, such as mining, maritime, oil and gas exploration, humanitarian organizations, and aeronautics, as well as a list of other potential subscribers. The size of the target market involved in specialized industries was but a handful. In 1999, it was determined that barely 3 percent of America's work force was engaged in farming, mining, or other activities requiring people to live where Mother Nature put the resources.[13] The larger part of the target market was already situated in established centers, where terrestrial cellular networks satisfied their communication needs. Iridium's vice president of marketing and corporate communications, John Windolph, targeted this market as the "affluent business person, the international traveler who spends at least three weeks a year on the road and makes at least $70,000 per annum . . . [and who] use[s] 55 minutes of wireless service a day, and 70 percent of [whose] calling time is spent on international calls."[14] Iridium not only provided continuous satellite coverage but was also seen as a status symbol—an individual could be the first owner of a satellite phone on his or her block. Customers might also adopt satellite services out of fear of losing communication during vacations in areas where telephone service was inconvenient or nonexistent, such as on a sailboat. Iridium saw a market niche that had not been targeted and offered three communication services: world satellite service, world roaming service, and world page service to satisfy the market's needs.[15]

World Satellite Service   World satellite service enabled subscribers to make telephone calls via Iridium's satellite system. This service required the use of a satellite handset or fixed unit on ships, trucks, and airplanes. One satellite handset cost anywhere from $1,000 to $3,500. Unlike cellular, these phones weighed approximately 2 pounds and had nearly 2-foot-long antennas. Even with a huge pipe antenna attached to a brick-sized phone, Iridium's reception quality varied, especially when the phone was used inside a building. However, Iridium officials argued that these phones were not designed for urban use, which is why they teamed with Sprint to offer a world roaming service.[16] Per-minute charges varied depending on where the call was placed. Originally, each call cost anywhere from $2 to $7 per minute, in addition to the $69 monthly fee.[17] Due to the competition, Iridium was forced to reduce these rates by 65 percent. These per-minute charges varied for international satellite service, domestic satellite service, and international water service.[18]

World Roaming Service   World roaming service provided service extension to existing subscribers of cellular for times when they roamed to areas where cellular service was nonexistent or when the local cellular provider technology differed from the subscribers' technology. For example, a code division multiple access (CDMA) phone would not work in a

time division multiple access (TDMA) network. By using a cellular cassette inserted in the Iridium phone's back, Iridium world roam service subscribers could enjoy seamless coverage, even in areas where their cellular provider had no agreement to provide service. In such areas, the handset searched for a wireless network. When one was not available, the handset automatically switched to one of Iridium's satellites. This satellite handset differed, however, from the one required for the world satellite service. Without the rear cellular cassette, the phone acted like a normal cellular phone and, most important, was just as small as any other cellular phone.

Iridium's major partner in the world roaming service, Sprint, made Iridium's service available to all of Sprint's personal communication system (PCS) customers traveling internationally. These customers retained their Sprint PCS phone numbers and were billed to their Sprint PCS statements. Sprint was expected to charge the Iridium-based service at $1.49 a minute for worldwide roaming, $1.99 a minute for domestic satellite calls, and $3.99 a minute for international satellite service.[19]

World Page Service   Iridium's world page service provided global paging services, wireless messaging, and information services. Each pager cost about $500, with a monthly fee of $159. Customers received the benefit of alphanumeric services and could even receive up to 200-word messages emailed from Iridium's web site.[20]

Marketing Campaign

To sell its satellite services, Iridium needed a global advertising campaign appealing to markets worldwide. Iridium looked for an advertising agency that not only exhibited creativity and outstanding service but also achieved positive chemistry throughout the organization. Ammirati Puris Lintus was selected and given a budget of $180 million. In addition to direct mail campaigns in twenty markets and in twenty different languages, Iridium advertised in *Fortune,* the *Wall Street Journal,* the in-flight magazines of thirty-seven airlines, and other publications read by jet-setting business executives. Advertisements were designed to create product awareness and to emphasize that the phones would work anywhere. The marketing campaign's overall objective was to create an aspirational brand that would be associated with exclusive activities. The goal of this advertising was achieved: there were 1.5 million responses to advertisements that ran in the fourth quarter of 1998, which was right on target, according to John Windolph, vice president of marketing and corporate communications.[21] Iridium was creating a brand overnight and educating the market about the use of satellite phones. Iridium also sponsored sporting events in remote locations where the Iridium phones were needed and used as primary communication devices. For example, Iridium sponsored sailing events, road rallies, expeditions, and any activities located outside regular telecommunications services, such as Bitter End Road Rally and Eco Challenge.[22]

Demand

Iridium was a large-scale, technologically advanced system of low-orbit satellites that was conceived many years before cellular phones were used on a widespread basis. The company thus focused on the high end of the market. The consumers in this target market traveled frequently for business or pleasure. Iridium was confident in the growth of this market and forecasted that 240,000 subscribers would use their system in 1999. They also forecasted that this market would roughly double in scope every year thereafter, with 4.5 million subscribers and revenues of $5 billion in 2005 (Exhibit 1).[23] By 1999, however, it was clear that Iridium would not meet forecasted demand, with only 27,000 subscribers.[24]

EXHIBIT 1

Iridium Subscriber Forecasts, 1996–2007
(thousands of satellite voice subscribers)

Year	Old Forecasts	New Forecasts
1998	160	40
1999	796	400
2000	1,259	1,259
2001	1,852	1,852
2002	2,547	2,547
2003	3,226	3,226
2004	3,791	3,791
2005	4,261	4,261
2006	4,652	4,652

Source: Merrill Lynch.

Iridium's Operational Structure

Iridium's system comprised nineteen strategic partners from around the world. Seventeen of these partners participated in the operation and maintenance of twelve ground station gateways.[25] Those twelve gateway operators also served as regional distributors of Iridium services in their commercial territories (Exhibit 2). The gateway operators were segmented according to twelve regions, or territories, which they managed: (1) Iridium Africa Corporation, (2) SudAmerica Corporation, (3) Middle East Corporation, (4) Iridium Canada, (5) Iridium India Telecom Limited, (6) Iridium Italia S.p.A., (7) SK Telecom of Korea, (8) South Pacific Iridium Holding Limited of Indonesia and Thai Satellite Telecom Company, (9) Sprint Iridium of the United States, (10) Nippon Iridium of Bermuda, (11) Verbacom Holdings of Germany, and (12) Pacific Asia Communications Ltd. of Taiwan. Strategic partners not involved in the day-to-day operations of the Iridium system helped to develop the actual constellation. Khrunichev State

EXHIBIT 2

Iridium's Regional Gateways Operating Companies

Regional Gateway	Operating Company
Beijing, China	Iridium China (HK) Ltd.
Seoul, Korea	SK Telecom (Iridium Korea)
Nagano, Japan	Nippon Iridium Telecom Corp.
Taipei, Taiwan	Pacific Iridium Telecom Corp.
Bangkok, Thailand	Thai Satellite Telecom Iridium South Pacific
Tempe, Arizona, United States	Iridium North America Iridium Central America & Mexico
Hawaii, United States	U.S. Government Gateway
Rio de Janeiro, Brazil	Iridium SudAmerica Corp.
Rome, Italy	Iridium Italia Iridium Communications Germany
Moscow, Russia	Iridium Eurasia
Jeddah	Iridium Middle East Corp. Iridium Africa Corp.
Mumbai	Iridium India Telecom Ltd.

Source: C. A. Ingley & Co.

Research and Production Space Center manufactured launch vehicles and orbital stations. As a subcontractor, Khrunichev launched satellites for Iridium. Iridium China, a wholly owned subsidiary of China Aerospace, was responsible for launching satellites over China's air space.

Still other strategic partners developed the hardware and software for the global telecommunications giant. Lockheed Martin Corporation was a major subcontractor to Motorola for the construction of the Iridium satellites. And while Lockheed provided the parts for the satellites, Raytheon was primarily responsible for the design and construction of the main mission antennas of the satellites. Neither partner was involved with the operation of the Iridium gateways, however.

Operating Contracts

Motorola, which owned 19 percent of Iridium, was involved in several contracts amounting to $3.4 billion. Motorola provided overall coordination for several subcontractors for the design, development, production, and delivery in orbit of the space segment. Its terrestrial network development contract required the subcontractors to design the gateway hardware and software. The operations and maintenance contract ensured day-to-day management of the space segment after deployment: the subcontractors were obligated to monitor, upgrade, and replace hardware and software as necessary to maintain performance specifications.[26]

Regional Gateways

Fifteen franchises, which were subsidiaries of Iridium LLC, operated the regional gateways. The business offices of these gateway operators distributed service to end-users directly through cellular operators and regional telecommunications providers.[27] In addition to delivering satellite communication to the appropriate carriers, gateway operators were in charge of identifying and training service providers and their sales staff.[28] Besides marketing and distributing the products and services, each operator franchise was also responsible for negotiating communication rights with eighty nations around the world and developing interfaces with terrestrial phone networks.[29]

Production and Distribution

Production of handsets and pagers were outsourced to a Japanese firm, Kyocera, and to Motorola. Products had to meet stringent quality control standards imposed by Iridium. During the original rollout, Kyocera had difficulties meeting quality control standards and was unable to ship significant quantities of phones until early March 1999. Although Motorola's satellite phones and pagers were available since the commencement of commercial operations, the production of cellular cassettes for its dual-mode satellite/cellular phones and some other accessories were delayed.

Competition for Global Voice

Competition in the global voice market required developing a constellation of satellites that could cover the entire world at once. This setup meant launching enough satellites so that at least one satellite could be seen from every point on the Earth. Iridium faced twelve main contenders, but its closest competitors were Globalstar and ICO (Exhibits 3 and 4).

Globalstar

Globalstar, a global telecommunications service, commenced operations on October 13, 1999. Globalstar was established in 1991 as a consortium of leading international telecommunications companies providing wholesale mobile and fixed satellite-based telephone services. It offered voice calling, short messaging services, roaming, positioning, facsimile, and data transmission on the Globalstar satellite system. It had a constellation of forty-eight LEO satellites and offered services to existing cellular telephone networks in more than 100 countries on six continents.[30]

Products and Services   The competition was fierce for securing the largest market, what Globalstar called the "cellular extension market." This market was an all-encompassing segment that included voice services in vertical and unserved markets, such as industrial and maritime.[31] Globalstar's second largest target market was the market for fixed voice services. This market included rural telephony markets, which slightly overlap the cellular extension market. Globalstar considered the global roamer (Iridium's primary market) to be its smallest market.[32]

Like Iridium, Globalstar offered roaming features that incorporated cellular service. It required dual-mode handsets that were compatible with the

EXHIBIT 3

The Global Mobile Market—Who Owns What?

Iridium	ICO Global	Globalstar	Teledesic (Broadband)
Motorola	Inmarsat	Loral Space Systems	Boeing
Veba	TRW	Qualcomm	AT&T Wireless
RWE	British Telecom	Vodafone Airtouch	Craig McCaw
Bell Canada	Deutsche Telekom	Alcatel	Bill Gates
Telecom Italia	Swisscom	Alenia	Prince Alwaleed
Korea Mobile Telecom	Sonera	Motorola	George Soros
Nippon Iridium	Singapore Telecom	China Telecom	
UCOM	Telefónica de Espana	DACOM	
Lockheed Martin	T_Mobil	France Telecom	
Sprint	Telkom SA	General Electric	
		Daimler Chrysler	
		Aerospace	
		Hyundai	

Source: ArcChart at www.arcchart.com.

cellular network and the satellite network. Similar to Iridium, its services required the use of a cellular cassette, which extended the antennas to receive satellite signals. Globalstar gained a competitive edge through its price points. The Globalstar handsets retailed for $900.[33] The company also offered cheaper domestic pricing plans than did Iridium. Globalstar charged a monthly service charge and fees for satellite connection and use. Its "Beyond Basic" service was priced at $29.99 per month and $1.69 per minute of airtime; the "Beyond 100" plan included 100 minutes for $169.99, with additional minutes at $1.49 each; and the "Beyond 250" plan included 250 minutes for $369.99, with additional minutes at $1.39 each.[34] With its competitive price points and global partners, Globalstar believed it could generate 5,000 subscribers in 1999, 383,000 subscribers in 2000, and an impressive installed base of 850,000 users in 2001.[35]

Partnership Globalstar's competitiveness in the market was enhanced by its reputable founders—Loral Corporation and Qualcomm, Inc.—and its strategic partners representing the world's leading telecommunications service providers and equipment manufacturers. Globalstar's strategic partners included telecommunications service providers AirTouch, Dacom, France Telecom, and Vodafone, who provided on-the-ground marketing and telephony experience, and telecommunications systems manufacturers Alcatel, Alenia, DASA, Hyundai, Loral, Qualcomm, and Space Systems/Loral.[36]

EXHIBIT 4

Cost of Satellite System—Amortized Total by Year, Day, Minute, and Second

System	Total Cost ($ billions)	Lifespan	Yearly Cost ($ millions)	Daily Cost ($)	Per-Minute Cost ($)	Per-Second Cost ($)
Globalstar	2.2	5	440	1,205,479	837	13.95
ICO Global	3.5	12	291.666	799,087	555	9.25
Iridium	5.0	5	1,000	2,739,726	1,903	31.71

Source: L. Swasey, "Sorting Through the Satellite Voice Market," *Advanstar Communications,* July 15, 1999.

ICO Global Communication

ICO Global Communications (ICO) was established in January 1995. It included a holding company and seventeen wholly owned direct and indirect subsidiaries formed to conduct its business worldwide.[37] By August 1999, ICO had filed a voluntary petition for reorganization under Chapter 11 due to insufficient capital before its satellite service started. In March 2000, however, a group of investors led by telecommunications pioneer Craig O. McCaw and his affiliated companies, Teledesic LLC and Eagle River Investments LLC, were talking about leading a group of international investors who would provide up to $1.2 billion to ICO.

Products and Services   ICO's proposed satellite service would commence in the first quarter of 2001 and would deliver digital voice, data, facsimile, and messaging services to users all over the world. In October 1998, ICO established ICO-roam, allowing customers of existing Global System for Mobile Communications (GSM) networks to roam into ANSI-41 cellular networks in North America using their home cellular number. The service was offered through customers' existing cellular network operators or service providers, and all charges were billed on their usual monthly invoices. The phones were similar to any GSM unit but had dual modes: cellular and satellite.

ICO forecasted a demand of 53 million subscribers, which would generate $47.4 billion by the end of 2010.[38] The target markets for ICO were similar to Iridium's and Globalstar's. ICO provided communication for mariners, people in remote areas requiring fixed units, mobile users, land transport operators, and government employees in military and relief agencies.

Unlike Iridium's system, ICO utilized medium Earth orbit (MEO) satellites that circled 6,494 miles above the Earth's surface.[39] This structure gave ICO global coverage with only ten satellites. The total infrastructure cost $3.5 billion, with $292 million in annual operating costs (Exhibit 5).[40] Furthermore, ICO's satellites lasted twelve years—twice the lifespan of Iridium's satellites.

Partnership   A team led by NEC Corporation and including Hughes Network Systems Inc. and Ericsson Limited was responsible for the design, manufacture, construction, installation, and testing of the ICONET ground network. Hughes Space and Communications International Inc. built ICO's satellites and supplied launch services. Mitsubishi, NEC, and Nera developed and manufactured ICO phones. Samsung Electronics supplied ICO with approximately $60 million worth of handsets.[41]

Alternatives for Global Travelers

Another option for international travelers was to use cellular services that operated in multiple countries and regions. In the past, various standards and frequencies, such as TDMA, CDMA, and global system for mobilization (GSM), hindered global roaming into different technological networks. However, cellular phones were becoming more adaptive to such differences through features such as multiple-band operation, which allowed phones to work in two different cellular technology networks.[42] Using their original phone numbers, cellular subscribers could roam into another country at a much lower price. A GSM handset with multiple-band features cost about $300 to $400, while the domestic charges cost $0.35 and roaming charges cost about $2.00 per minute.[43] The GSM network was available in over one hundred countries. Cellular providers had already begun to make mutual agreements to let subscribers roam in their territories.

The Future of Iridium

Although Iridium had a first-mover advantage, its management acknowledged that the transition from a development stage company to an operating stage company was not smooth. A key challenge that confronted Iridium was meeting subscriber forecasts. Iridium needed 27,000 subscribers by March 1999 to fulfill loan agreements with its creditors. In addition to its problems with financing, Iridium had difficulties coordinating its suppliers and service providers. One of its main suppliers, Kyocera, was unable to deliver quality phones on time during the first few months of operation, while its service providers were not trained properly for sales. Another challenge for the company was competing rivals, such as ICO and Globalstar, which were very aggressive in marketing their products through price cuts and services. As revenues began to lag far behind projections, Iridium's managers began to feel increasingly uneasy about Iridium's prospects.

EXHIBIT 5

Financial Statements, Iridium and Competitors, 1996–1998

Iridium—Balance Sheet

Fiscal Year End	12/31/1998	12/31/1997	12/31/1996
Cash	24,756,000	359,260,000	1,889,000
Receivables	93,000	NA	NA
Other current assets	32,052,000	20,216,000	10,630,000
Total current assets	56,901,000	379,476,000	12,519,000
Property/Plant/Equipment	3,584,209,000	3,151,380,000	2,390,385,000
Net property/Equipment	3,584,209,000	3,151,380,000	2,390,385,000
Depreciation and other assets	97,785,000	114,831,000	31,177,000
Total assets	3,738,895,000	3,645,687,000	2,434,081,000
Accounts payable	165,539,000	106,794,000	17,937,000
Other current liabilities	131,532,000	360,601,000	100,563,000
Total current liabilities	297,071,000	467,395,000	118,500,000
Long-term debt	2,530,735,000	1,264,288,000	505,000,000
Other long-term liabilities	433,926,000	279,367,000	238,552,000
Total liabilities	3,261,732,000	2,011,050,000	862,052,000
Retained earnings	−1,680,194,000	−427,393,000	−133,840,000
Other liabilities	2,157,357,000	2,062,030,000	1,705,869,000
Shareholders equity	477,163,000	1,634,637,000	1,572,029,000
Total liability/Net worth	3,738,895,000	3,645,687,000	2,434,081,000

Iridium—Income Statement

Fiscal Year End	12/31/1998	12/31/1997	12/31/1996
Net sales	186,000	NA	NA
Gross profit	186,000	NA	NA
Sell/Gen/Admin	749,162,000	177,474,000	70,730,000
Inc b/Dep & amort	−748,976,000	−177,474,000	−70,730,000
Depreciation and amortization	673,341,000	119,124,000	674,000
Nonoperating income	−249,906,000	3,045,000	2,395,000
Income before taxes	−1,672,223,000	−293,553,000	−69,009,000
Prov for inc tx	7,971,000	NA	4,589,000
N/I b/Ex-item	−1,680,194,000	−293,553,000	−73,598,000
Net income	−1,680,194,000	−293,553,000	−73,598,000

ICO Global—Balance Sheet

Fiscal Year End	12/31/1998	12/31/1997	12/31/1996
Cash	548,692,000	378,780,000	756,385,000
Market securities	228,005,000	NA	NA
Other current assets	11,253,000	59,093,000	8,064,000
Total current assets	787,950,000	437,873,000	764,449,000

(continued)

EXHIBIT 5 *(continued)*

ICO Global—Balance Sheet *(continued)*

Fiscal Year End	12/31/1998	12/31/1997	12/31/1996
Property/Plant/Equipment	1,818,568,000	860,929,000	301,271,000
Accumulated depreciation	NA	NA	NA
Net Property/Equipment	1,818,568,000	860,929,000	01,271,000
Depreciation and other assets	57,466,000	95,138,000	41,000,000
Total assets	2,663,984,000	1,393,940,000	1,106,720,000
Accounts payable	104,851,000	30,313,000	18,929,000
Other current liabilities	57,944,000	27,401,000	1,275,000
Total current liabilities	162,795,000	57,714,000	20,204,000
Long-term debt	533,021,000	4,432,000	NA
Other long-term liabilities	4,409,000	30,348,000	2,608,000
Total liabilities	700,225,000	92,494,000	22,812,000
Comm stock net	2,076,000	1,800,000	1,359,000
Capital surplus	2,305,681,000	1,934,512,000	1,438,848,000
Retained earnings	−342,964,000	−232,288,000	−44,311,000
Other liabilities	−1,034,000	−402,578,000	−311,988,000
Shareholders' equity	1,963,759,000	1,301,446,000	1,083,908,000
Total liability/Net worth	2,663,984,000	1,393,940,000	1,106,720,000

ICO Global—Income Statement

Fiscal Year End	12/31/1998	12/31/1997	12/31/1996
Net sales	142,000	NA	NA
Cost of goods sold	289,000	NA	NA
Gross profit	−147,000	NA	NA
Sell/Gen/Admin	142,189,000	67,569,000	48,913,000
Inc b/Dep & amort	−142,336,000	−67,569,000	−48,913,000
Depreciation and amortization	5,684,000	3,332,000	1,341,000
Nonoperating income	41,127,000	−114,494,000	20,639,000
Income before taxes	−106,893,000	−185,395,000	−29,615,000
Prov for inc tx	3,783,000	2,582,000	1,647,000
N/I b/Ex-item	−110,676,000	−187,977,000	−31,262,000
Net income	−110,676,000	−187,977,000	−31,262,000
Outstanding shares	207,647,618	180,567,513	186,867,513

Globalstar—Balance Sheet

Fiscal Year End	12/31/1998	12/31/1997	12/31/1996
Inv/Adv to subs	612,716,000	482,676,000	173,118,000
Total assets	612,716,000	482,676,000	173,118,000
Accrued expense	1,679,000	1,679,000	NA

(continued)

EXHIBIT 5 *(continued)*

Globalstar—Balance Sheet *(continued)*

Fiscal Year End	12/31/1998	12/31/1997	12/31/1996
Total current liabilities	1,679,000	1,679,000	NA
Total liabilities	1,679,000	1,679,000	NA
Preferred stock	301,410,000	300,358,000	NA
Comm stock net	30,638,000	10,000,000	10,000,000
Capital surplus	318,643,000	175,750,000	175,750,000
Retained earnings	−51,864,000	−27,712,000	−12,632,000
Other liabilities	12,210,000	22,601,000	NA
Shareholders' equity	611,037,000	480,997,000	173,118,000
Total liability/Net worth	612,716,000	482,676,000	173,118,000

Globalstar—Income Statement

Fiscal Year End	12/31/1998	12/31/1997	12/31/1996
Nonoperating income	−2,950,000	2,290,000	−12,632,000
Interest expense	21,202,000	17,370,000	NA
Income before taxes	−24,152,000	−15,080,000	−12,632,000
N/I b/Ex-item	−24,152,000	−15,080,000	−12,632,000
Net income	−24,152,000	−15,080,000	−12,632,000
Outstanding shares	30,638,152	10,000,000	10,000,000

Source: Disclosure Report.

ENDNOTES

1. www.icetrek.org.
2. C. Bulloch, 1999, "Trouble for Big LEOs," *Telecommunications,* Vol 33, Issue 9 (International Edition), pp. S132–S135.
3. www.iridium.com.
4. Ibid.
5. Ibid.
6. Anonymous, 1999, "DOD to Buy Gear for Iridium Use," *Electronic Engineering Times,* April 5, p. 8.
7. Anonymous. 1999, "Iridium's CEO Resigns Due to Dispute with Board of Directors," *Satellite News,* April 26, p. 1.
8. J. Meyers, 1997, "The Final Countdown," *Telephony,* November 17, p. 36.
9. D. Rohde, 1997, "Satellites: Are They for You?" *Network World,* September 8, p. 30.
10. W. Stallings and R. Van Slyke, 1998, *Business Data Communications.*
11. D. Larsen, 1999, "Iridium Takes to the Skies," *Utility Business,* March, pp. 41–45.
12. M. Warwick, 1999, "Up in Smoke," *Communication International,* October, pp. 72–75.
13. P. R. Krugman, 1999, "When Did the Future Get So Boring?" *Fortune,* September 27, pp. 42–44.
14. K. Higgins, 1999, "The Anytime, Anywhere Phone Company," *Marketing Management,* Vol. 8, Issue 1, pp. 4–8.
15. www.iridium.com.
16. J. Sheridan, 1999, "Bullish on Iridium," *Industry Week,* June 21, pp. 46–50.
17. L. Swasey, 1999, "Sorting Through the Satellite Voice Market," *Advanstar Communications,* July 15, pp. 24–26.
18. J. Sheridan, 1999, "Bullish on Iridium," *Industry Week.* June 21, pp. 46–50.
19. Ibid.
20. D. Larsen, 1999, "Iridium Takes to the Skies," *Utility Business,* March, pp. 41–45.
21. K. Higgins, 1999, "The Anytime, Anywhere Phone Company," *Marketing Management,* Vol. 8, Issue 1, pp. 4–8.
22. Ibid.
23. Merrill Lynch, 1999, "Iridium Faces Further Financing Difficulties," *Satellite International.*
24. Ibid.
25. www.iridium.com.
26. Iridium World Communications Ltd., 1998, Annual Report.
27. C. Ingley, 1999, "Global Vision: Making the Right Connections," *Satellite Communications,* February, pp. 38–44.
28. Iridium World Communications Ltd., 1998, Annual Report.
29. K. Higgins, 1999, "The Anytime, Anywhere Phone Company," *Marketing Management,* Vol. 8, Issue 1, pp. 4–8.
30. www.globalstar.com.
31. A. Cosper, 1999, "Globalstar's Grace Under Pressure," *Satellite Communications,* December, p. 26.
32. Ibid.

33. Baskerville Communications Corp., 1998, "Adjusted Capital Expenditures for Major Global MSS Providers," *Satellite International*.

34. K. Carroll, 2000, "Globalstar USA Goes Commercial," *Telephony*, June 19, p. 30.

35. Merrill Lynch, 1999, "Globalstar's Subscriber Forecast," *Satellite International*.

36. www.ee.surrey.ac.uk/Personal/L.Wood/constellations/background .html.

37. www.ico.com.

38. Dresdner Kleinwort Benson, 1998, "ICO Financial and Subscriber Forecasts," *BaskervilleCommunications*.

39. www.Lloyd.com.

40. L. Swasey, 1999, "Sorting Through the Satellite Voice Market," *Advanstar Communications, Inc.,* July 15, pp. 24–26.

41. www.ico.com.

42. C. Mason, 1999, "Does Your Phone Roam in Rome?" *America's Network,* October 1, pp. 51–54.

43. www.omnipoint.com.

24 A Hundred-Year War: Coke vs. Pepsi, 1890s—1990s

This case was prepared by Professor Chiaki Moriguchi and Research Associate David Lane, Harvard Business School. It is a rewrite of cases prepared by Professor Michael E. Porter and Professor David B. Yoffie.

For decades, competition between Coca-Cola and Pepsi-Cola has been labeled "the cola wars." The most intense battles were fought over the $56 billion industry in the United States, where the average American consumed 55 gallons of soft drinks per year. As the U.S. soft drink industry matured, however, the cola wars were moving increasingly to international markets. Coke, the world's largest soft drink company with a 51% share of the worldwide soft drink market, earned 75% of its 1998 profits outside of the United States. Pepsi, with only 15% of its beverage operating profits coming from overseas, continued to challenge Coke in international markets. According to Roger Enrico, CEO of Pepsi-Cola:

> The warfare must be perceived as a continuing battle without blood. Without Coke, Pepsi would have a tough time being an original and lively competitor. The more successful they are, the sharper we have to be. If the Coca-Cola Company

didn't exist, we'd pray for someone to invent them. And on the other side of the fence, I'm sure the folks at Coke would say that nothing contributes as much to the present-day success of the Coca-Cola Company [as] Pepsi.[1]

As the cola wars continued into a second century, Coke and Pepsi faced such perennial questions as: How could they maintain their growth at home? How would the industry's changing landscape affect their profitability? How should they redesign their strategies in response to diverse and constantly evolving market conditions abroad?

Economics of the U.S. Soft Drink Industry

Americans consumed 23 gallons of soft drinks a year in 1970 compared to 55 gallons in 1998 (see Exhibit 1). This growth was fueled by the increasing availability and affordability of soft drinks in the marketplace, and by the introduction and popularity of diet soft drinks. Over the past two decades, the real price of soft drinks fell, and consumer demand appeared responsive

1. Roger Enrico, *The Other Guy Blinked and Other Dispatches From the Cola Wars* (New York: Bantam Books, 1988).

EXHIBIT 1

U.S. Industry Consumption Statistics

	1970	1975	1981	1985	1990	1991	1992	1993	1994	1995	1996	1997	1998
Historical Soft Drink Consumption													
Cases (millions)	3,090	3,780	5,180	6,500	7,914	8,040	8,160	8,395	8,608	8,952	9,489	9,682	9,880
Gallons/capita	22.7	26.6	34.5	40.8	47.7	47.8	48.0	48.4	49.6	51.2	52.6	53.7	54.8
As a % of total beverage consumption	12.4	14.4	18.7	22.4	26.1	26.2	26.3	29.8	27.2	28.1	28.8	29.4	30.0
U.S. Liquid Consumption Trends (gallons/capita)													
Soft drinks	22.7	26.3	34.2	40.8	47.7	47.8	48.0	48.4	49.6	51.2	52.6	53.7	54.8
Coffee	35.7	33.0	27.2	26.8	26.4	26.5	26.1	28.4	29.5	29.9	29.8	29.3	28.9
Milk	18.5	21.6	24.3	23.8	24.1	23.3	23.1	25.1	25.0	24.8	24.5	24.3	24.0
Beer	22.8	21.8	20.6	19.8	19.4	19.4	19.2	22.8	22.7	22.4	22.2	22.1	22.1
Bottled water	—	1.2	2.7	5.2	9.2	9.6	9.9	9.5	10.3	10.9	11.4	11.4	11.3
Tea	5.2	7.3	7.3	7.3	7.0	6.7	6.8	6.9	6.9	6.6	6.6	6.7	6.8
Juices	6.5	6.8	6.9	7.4	6.2	6.4	6.6	6.5	6.5	6.4	6.4	6.4	6.3
Powdered drinks	—	4.8	6.0	6.3	5.7	5.9	5.6	5.2	5.2	5.2	5.1	5.1	5.0
Wine	1.3	1.7	2.1	2.4	2.0	1.9	1.8	1.7	1.8	1.8	1.9	1.9	1.9
Distilled spirits	1.8	2.0	2.0	1.8	1.5	1.4	1.3	1.3	1.3	1.2	1.2	1.2	1.2
Subtotal	114.5	126.5	133.3	141.6	149.2	148.9	148.4	155.8	158.8	160.4	161.7	162.1	162.3
Imputed water consumption	68.0	56.0	49.2	40.9	33.3	33.6	34.1	26.7	23.7	22.1	20.8	20.4	20.2
Total*	182.5	182.5	182.5	182.5	182.5	182.5	182.5	182.5	182.5	182.5	182.5	182.5	182.5

Source: John C. Maxwell, Jr., *Beverage Industry Annual Manual 1992/1993,* and *The Maxwell Consumer Report,* Feb. 3, 1994; *Adams Liquor Handbook,* casewriter estimates.

[a]This analysis assumes that each person consumes on average one-half gallon of liquid per day.

to declining prices.[2] Many alternatives to soft drinks existed, including coffee, beer, milk, tea, bottled water, juices, powdered drinks, wine, distilled spirits, and tap water. Yet Americans drank more soda than any other beverage, with the soft-drink category being the only one with rising consumption every year between 1970 and 1998. The cola segment of the soft drink industry held the dominant share (almost 70%) of the market in the 1990s, followed by lemon/lime, pepper, orange, root beer, and other flavors.

Soft drinks consisted of a flavor base, a sweetener, and carbonated water. Four major participants were involved in the production and distribution of soft drinks: 1) concentrate producers, 2) bottlers, 3) retail channels, and 4) suppliers.

Concentrate Producers

The concentrate producer blended raw material ingredients (excluding sugar or high fructose corn syrup), packaged it in plastic canisters, and shipped the blended ingredients to the bottler. The concentrate producer added artificial sweetener to make diet soda concentrate, while bottlers added sugar or high fructose corn syrup themselves. The process involved little capital investment in machinery, overhead, or labor. A typical concentrate manufacturing plant cost approximately $5–$10 million to build, and one plant could serve the entire United States.

A concentrate producer's most significant costs were for advertising, promotion, market research, and bottler relations. Marketing programs were jointly implemented and financed by concentrate producers and bottlers. Concentrate producers usually took the lead in developing the programs, particularly in product planning, market research, and advertising. They invested heavily in their trademarks over time, with innovative and sophisticated marketing campaigns (see Exhibit 2). Bottlers assumed a larger role in developing trade and consumer promotions, and paid an agreed percentage—typically 50% or more—of promotional and advertising costs. Concentrate producers employed extensive sales and marketing support staff to work with and help improve the performance of their bottlers, setting standards and suggesting operating procedures. Concentrate producers also negotiated directly with the bottlers' major suppliers—particularly sweetener and packaging suppliers—to encourage reliable supply, faster delivery, and lower prices.

Once a fragmented business with hundreds of local manufacturers, the landscape of the U.S. soft drink industry had changed dramatically over time. Among national concentrate producers, Coca-Cola and Pepsi-Cola, the soft drink unit of PepsiCo, claimed a combined 76% of the U.S. soft drink market in sales volume in 1998, followed by Dr Pepper/Seven-Up, Cadbury Schweppes, and Royal Crown (see Exhibit 3).[3] There were also private-label brand manufacturers and several dozen other national and regional producers. Exhibit 4 gives financial data for the leading American soft drink companies.

Bottlers

Bottlers purchased concentrate, added carbonated water and high-fructose corn syrup, bottled or canned the soft drink, and delivered it to customer accounts. Coke and Pepsi bottlers offered "direct store door" delivery (DSD), which involved route delivery sales people physically placing and managing the soft drink brand in the store. Smaller national brands, such as Shasta and Faygo, distributed through food store warehouses. DSD entailed managing the shelf space by stacking the product, positioning the trademarked label, cleaning the packages and shelves, and setting up point-of-purchase displays and end-of-aisle displays. The importance of the bottler's relationship with the retail trade was crucial to continual brand availability and maintenance. Cooperative merchandising agreements (CMAs) between retailers and bottlers were used to promote soft drink sales. Retailers agreed to specified promotional activity and discount levels in the CMA in exchange for a payment from the bottler.

The bottling process was capital-intensive and involved specialized, high-speed lines. Lines were interchangeable only for packages of similar size and construction. Bottling and canning lines cost from $4–$10 million each, depending on volume and package type. The minimum cost to build a small bottling plant, with warehouse and office space, was $20–$30 million. The cost of an efficient large plant, with four lines, automated warehousing, and a capacity of 40 million cases, was $75 million in 1998.[4]

2. Robert Tollison et al., *Competition and Concentration* (Lexington Books, 1991), p. 11.

3. Cadbury Schweppes acquired Dr Pepper and Seven-Up in 1994.

4. "Louisiana Coca-Cola Reveals Crown Jewel," *Beverage Industry*, January 1999.

EXHIBIT 2

Advertising Spending by Brand in the United States ($ millions)

	1975	1980	1985	1990	1995	1996	1997	1998
Coca-Cola Company								
Coca Cola	$25.3	$47.8	$71.6	$90.4	$82.4	$131.6	$112.9	$115.5
Diet Coke			40.6	69.1	72.2	60.4	39.7	39.7
Sprite	2.6	10.7	22.2	23.4	49.6	55.8	58.4	56.5
Diet Sprite			6.7	7.6	2.2	NA	NA	NA
Tab	6.5	12.6	15.6	NA	NA	NA	NA	NA
Pepsi-Cola Company								
Pepsi-Cola	17.9	40.2	56.9	79.4	112.2	90.4	106.0	106.0
Diet Pepsi	3.7	11.6	32.9	76.5	10.8	0.2	19.7	13.9
Mountain Dew	2.8	10.2	9.0	11.7	29.8	29.0	34.0	39.8
Dr Pepper Company								
Dr Pepper	6.2	16.1	9.6	24.1	37.7	40.9	48.5	55.2
Diet Dr Pepper	1.6	2.9	5.7	6.6	24.4	NA	NA	NA
Seven-Up Company								
7-Up	10.2	25.5	22.3	31.4	15.2	33.0	38.5	26.9
Diet 7-Up	3.3	7.9	15.6	8.5	NA	NA	NA	NA
Royal Crown Cola								
Royal Crown	10.9	6.6	5.1	1.4	2.5	NA	NA	NA
Diet Rite Cola	3.5	3.4	3.5	3.2	0.4	NA	NA	NA
Canada Dry	5.2	10.1	12.4	4.5	5.8	NA	NA	NA
All Others	10.5	26.3	30.4	58.3	55.0	112.0	90.1	116.1
Industry Total	**114.0**	**241.0**	**383.0**	**498.0**	**523.3**	**553.3**	**547.8**	**569.6**

Source: Advertising Age, Beverage Industry, company annual reports.

Roughly 80–85 plants were required for full distribution across the United States. Among top bottlers in 1998, packaging accounted for approximately half of bottlers' cost of goods sold, concentrate for one-third, and nutritive sweeteners for one-tenth.[5] Labor accounted for most of the remaining variable costs. Bottlers also invested capital in trucks and distribution networks. Bottlers' gross profits often exceeded 40%, but operating margins were razor thin. See Exhibit 5 for the cost structures of a typical concentrate producer and bottler.

The number of U.S. soft drink bottlers had fallen from over 2,000 in 1970 to less than 500 in 1998.[6] Historically, Coca-Cola was the first concentrate producer to build nation-wide franchised bottling networks, a move that Pepsi and Seven-Up followed. The typical franchised bottler owned a manufacturing and sales operation in an exclusive geographic territory, with rights granted in perpetuity by the franchiser. In the case of Coca-Cola, territorial rights did not extend to fountain accounts—Coke delivered to its fountain accounts directly, not through its bottlers. The rights

5. Calculated from M. Dolan et al., "Coca-Cola Beverages," Merrill Lynch Capital Markets, July 6, 1998.

6. Timothy Muris et al., *Strategy, Structure, and Antitrust in the Carbonated Soft-Drink Industry* (Quorum Books, 1993), p. 63.

EXHIBIT 3

U.S. Soft Drink Market Share by Case Volume (percent)

	1966	1970	1975	1980	1985	1990	1995	1998
Coca-Cola Company								
Classic					5.8	19.4	20.0	20.6
Coca-Cola	27.7	28.4	26.2	25.3	14.4	0.7	0.2	a
Cherry Coke					1.6	0.6	0.9	0.7
diet Coke					6.3	9.1	9.5	8.6
diet Cherry Coke						0.2	0.1	0.1
Tab	1.4	1.3	2.6	3.3	1.1	0.2	0.1	a
Caffeine-Free Coke, diet Coke, and Tab					1.8	3.1	2.5	3.0a
Sprite and diet Sprite	1.5	1.8	2.6	3.0	4.2	4.4	5.6	7.0
Others	2.8	3.2	3.9	4.3	1.9	2.7	4.1	4.3
Total	**33.4**	**34.7**	**35.3**	**35.9**	**37.1**	**40.4**	**42.9**	**44.6**
PepsiCo, Inc.								
Pepsi-Cola	16.1	17.0	17.4	20.4	18.2	17.3	15.4	14.5
Diet Pepsi	1.9	1.1	1.7	3.0	3.7	6.2	5.4	5.0
Caffeine-Free Pepsi, and Diet Pepsi					2.3	2.3	1.9	1.9
Mountain Dew	1.4	0.9	1.3	3.3	2.9	3.8	5.6	6.7
Diet Mountain Dew						0.5	0.7	0.8
Slice					0.7	0.9	0.9	0.6
Diet Slice					0.6	0.4	0.2	0.1
Others	1.0	0.8	0.7	1.1	0.2	0.4	0.5	1.3
Total	**20.4**	**19.8**	**21.1**	**27.8**	**28.6**	**31.8**	**30.6**	**31.0**
Seven-Up	6.9	7.2	7.6	6.3	5.7	4.0	2.7	2.1
Dr Pepper	2.6	3.8	5.5	6.0	4.7	5.8	6.0	6.1
Royal Crown Co.	6.9	6.0	5.4	4.7	2.9	2.6	2.0	1.3
Cadbury Schweppes	NA	NA	NA	NA	4.5	3.2	16.1b	14.4b
Other companies	29.8	28.5	25.1	19.3	16.5	12.2	8.4	8.7
Total (mil. cases)	**2,927**	**3,670**	**4,155**	**5,180**	**6,500**	**7,914**	**8,952**	**9,880**

Source: John C. Maxwell, Jr., *Beverage Industry Annual Manual 1992/1993; The Maxwell Consumer Report,* February 3, 1994; and the Beverage Marketing Corporation, cited in *Beverage World,* March 1996 and March 1999.

aFor 1998, Coca-Cola ("New Coke") and Tab are included, along with Citra, in the caffeine-free category.
bAfter 1995, Cadbury-Schweppes's shares include the shares of Seven-Up and Dr. Pepper.

granted to the bottlers were subject to termination only in the event of default by the bottler. The original Coca-Cola franchise contract, written in 1899, was a fixed-price contract that did not provide for contract renegotiation even if ingredient costs changed. With considerable effort, often involving bitter legal disputes, Coca-Cola amended the contract in 1921 and again in 1978 to adjust concentrate price. In 1986, Coke won a further amendment to the bottling contract that pro-

vided the company with greater pricing flexibility. Pepsi negotiated concentrate prices with its bottler association, and normally based price increases on the Consumer Price Index. According to an industry report, the price of concentrate sold to bottlers had increased at an annual rate of 3%–4% during the 1990s.[7]

7. "Following Coke, Pepsi Will Raise Prices," *New York Times,* November 22, 1999.

Coca-Cola and Pepsi franchise agreements allowed bottlers to handle the non-cola brands of other concentrate producers. Franchise agreements also allowed bottlers to choose whether or not to market new beverages introduced by the concentrate producer. Some restrictions applied, however, as bottlers could not carry directly competitive brands. For example, a Coca-Cola bottler could not sell Royal Crown Cola, but it could distribute Seven-Up, if it decided not to carry Sprite. Franchised bottlers had the freedom to participate in or reject new package introductions, local advertising campaigns and promotions, and test marketing. The bottlers also had the final say in decisions concerning retail pricing, new packaging, selling, advertising, and promotions in its territory, though they could only use packages authorized by the franchiser. Historically, most franchised bottlers in the United States had been small, privately owned, and independent. More recently, the major concentrate producers had initiated consolidation among their bottlers and taken partial equity positions in large franchised bottlers based in urban areas. In addition to franchised bottlers, the major concentrate producers fully owned and operated a number of bottlers on their own.

Retail Channels

In the late 1990s, the distribution of soft drinks in the United States took place through food stores (40%), fountain outlets[8] (17%), convenience stores (14%), vending machines (8%), and other outlets (21%). Mass merchandisers, warehouse clubs, and drug stores made up most of the last category. Bottler's profitability by type of retail outlet is shown in Exhibit 6. Profits were affected by delivery method and frequency, drop size, advertising, and marketing.

The main distribution channel for soft drinks was the supermarket. Soft drinks were among the five largest selling product lines sold by supermarkets, traditionally yielding a 15%–20% gross margin (about average for food products) and accounting for 3%–4% of food store revenues.[9] Soft drinks represented a large percentage of a supermarket's business, and were also a big traffic draw. Bottlers fought for retail shelf space to ensure visibility and accessibility

for their products, and looked for new locations to increase impulse purchases, such as placing coolers at checkout counters. The proliferation of products and packaging types created intense shelf-space pressures. Supermarkets' share of soft drink sales fell in the 1990s due to the rise of new retail formats and widespread price discounting.

Discount retailers, warehouse clubs, and drug stores accounted for about 16% of soft drink sales in 1998.[10] These firms often had their own private label soft drink, or they sold a generic label such as President's Choice. One of the largest private label brand manufacturers was the Cott Corporation. Cott purchased concentrate from Royal Crown, bottled or canned the product, and sold it to more than forty retail chain stores, including Wal-Mart, Sam's Club, and Safeway. Private label soft drinks were usually delivered to a retailer's warehouse, while branded soft drinks were delivered directly to the store. With the warehouse delivery method the retailer was responsible for storage, transportation, merchandising, and stocking the shelves, thus incurring additional costs (see Exhibit 7 for a comparative profit margin analysis). Doug Ivester, Coca-Cola COO in 1993, had this to say, "Coke delivers and stocks its soda, while Cott drops its pop at retailers' warehouses. The trouble is, most retailers have never had a good understanding of what their costs really are."[11]

Historically, Pepsi had focused on sales through retail outlets, while Coke had dominated fountain sales. Coca-Cola had a 65% share of the fountain market in 1998, while Pepsi had 25%.[12] Competition for fountain sales was intense, and was characterized by "significant everyday discounting to national and local customers."[13] National fountain accounts were essentially "paid sampling," with soft drink companies earning pretax operating margins of around 2%. For restaurants, by contrast, fountain was extremely profitable—soft drinks were one of their highest margin products. Coke and Pepsi invested in the development of fountain equipment, such as service dispensers, and provided their fountain customers with cups, point-of-sale material, advertising, and in-store promotions to increase brand presence. After

---

8. The "fountain outlets" traditionally referred to soda fountains, but was later used also for restaurants, cafeterias, and other establishments that served soft drinks by the glass using fountain dispensers.

9. *Progressive Grocer 1998 Sales Manual Databook,* July 1998, p. 68.

10. Greg Johnson, "It's a Take-No-Prisoners Attitude in the Soft Drink Wars," *Los Angeles Times,* May 28, 1998.

11. Patricia Sellers, "Brands—It's Thrive or Die," *Fortune,* August 23, 1993.

12. Sanford C. Bernstein data, in *The Wall Street Journal,* May 8, 1998, p. A3.

13. *Beverage World,* 1989.

EXHIBIT 4

Financial Data for the Leading Soft Drink Companies ($ millions)

	1975	1980	1985	1986	1987	1988
Coca-Cola Company[a]						
Soft drinks, United States						
Sales	NA	1,486	1,865			
Operating profits/sales		11.1%	11.6%			
Soft drinks, International						
Sales	NA	2,349	2,677			
Operating profit/sales		21.0%	22.9%			
Consolidated						
Sales	2,773	5,475	5,879			
Net profit/sales	9.0%	7.7%	12.3%			
Net profit/equity	21.0%	20.0%	24.0%			
Long-term debt/assets	3.0%	10.0%	23.0%			
Coca-Cola Enterprises (CCE)[c]						
Sales						
Operating profit/sales						
Net profit/sales						
Net profit/equity						
Long-term debt/assets						
PepsiCo, Inc.[d]						
Soft drinks, United States						
Sales	1,065	2,368	2,725			
Operating profit/sales	10.4%	10.3%	10.4%			
Soft drinks, International						
Sales	NA	NA	NA			
Operating profit/sales						
Consolidated						
Sales	2,709	5,975	7,585			
Net profit/sales	4.6%	4.4%	5.6%			
Net profit/equity	18.0%	20.0%	30.0%			
Long-term debt/assets	35.0%	31.0%	36.0%			
Dr Pepper Company						
Sales	138	339	174	181	207	244
Net profit/sales	8.6%	7.8%	2.3%	2.5%	−0.1%	−4.5%
Net profit/equity	24.0%	24.0%	30.0%	NA	−1.0%	−30.6%
Long-term debt/assets	NA	38.0%	47.0%	50.0%	38.0%	80.1%
Seven-Up Company[f]						
Sales	214	353	678	271	297	
Net profit/sales	9.5%	NA	NA	−2.4%	2.5%	
Net profit/equity	24.0%	NA	NA	−2.5%	14.8%	
Long-term debt/assets	2.0%	NA	NA	42.0%	66.0%	
Dr Pepper/Seven-Up Companies[g]						
Sales						511
Operating profit/sales						11.7%
Net loss or profit						−79
Long-term debt/assets						140.6
Royal Crown Corporation[h]						
Sales	258	438	986	1,102	1,109	1,122
Net profit/sales	5.2%	2.3%	0.6%	−0.8%	1.6%	3.2%
Net profit/equity	17.0%	10.0%	5.0%	−9.0%	15.0%	23.0%
Long-term debt/assets	NA	38.0%	47.0%	50.0%	38.0%	46.0%

Source: Company annual reports.

[a]Coca-Cola's soft drink sales were comprised primarily of concentrate sales. Coke's 44% stake in CCE was accounted for by the equity method of accounting. Coke's share of CCE's net earnings was included in its consolidated net income figure.

[b]From 1994, Coca-Cola reported U.S. data as part of a North American category that included Canada and Mexico.

[c]CCE's net losses in 1991 and 1992 were due to debt transactions, which increased net income expense.

[d]PepsiCo's soft drink sales included sales by company-owned bottlers.

[e]In 1998, PepsiCo began reporting U.S. data as part of a North American category including Canada.

1989	1990	1991	1992	1993	1994	1995	1996	1997	1998
	2,461	2,646	2,813	2,966	5,327[b]	5,513[b]	6,050[b]	6,443[b]	6,915[b]
	16.5%	17.7%	18.1%	20.8%	17.2%	15.5%	15.7%	20.3%	21.1%
	6,125	7,245	8,551	9,205	10,812	12,559	12,576	12,357	11,898
	29.4%	29.7%	29.5%	29.9%	29.3%	29.1%	28.4%	33.3%	29.5%
	10,236	11,572	13,074	13,957	16,264	18,127	18,673	18,868	18,813
	13.5%	14.0%	12.7%	15.6%	15.7%	16.5%	18.7%	21.9%	18.8%
	36.0%	38.0%	43.0%	51.7%	48.8%	55.4%	56.7%	56.5%	42.0%
	8.0%	10.0%	10.0%	11.9%	10.3%	7.6%	6.9%	4.7%	3.6%
	3,933	3,915	5,127	5,465	6,011	6,773	7,921	11,278	13,414
	8.3%	3.1%	6.0%	7.0%	7.3%	6.9%	6.9%	6.4%	6.5%
	2.4%	−2.1%	3.6%	0.3%	1.1%	1.2%	1.4%	1.5%	1.1%
	6.0%	−5.8%	−14.8%	−1.2%	5.2%	5.7%	7.4%	9.6%	5.8%
	39.0%	51.0%	43.4%	47.0%	47.9%	46.3%	47.2%	50.3%	45.5%
	5,035	5,172	5,485	5,918	7,045	7,427	7,734	7,852	8,266[e]
	13.4%	14.4%	14.6%	15.8%	15.7%	16.7%	18.3%	16.5%	14.7%
	1,489	1,744	2,120	2,720	2,609	3,040	2,853	2,689	2,385
	6.3%	6.7%	6.7%	6.3%	5.6%	3.9%	−29.1%	−5.1%	−9.2%
	17,515	19,292	21,970	25,021	17,984	19,067	20,337	20,917	22,348
	6.2%	5.6%	5.9%	6.4%	7.6%	7.5%	4.6%	7.1%	8.9%
	22.0%	19.5%	23.0%	25.1%	19.9%	19.4%	14.2%	21.5%	31.1%
	33.0%	42.0%	38.0%	31.4%	38.0%	35.9%	36.9%	24.6%	17.8%
267	311	381							
3.0%	5.7%	4.5%							
18.1%	42.5%	−62.2							
78.7%	74.7%	72.3%							
514	540	601	659	707	769				
22.2%	22.8%	23.0%	24.4%	25.9%	26.5%				
−42	−33	−38	−140	78	66				
149.0	152.2	138.5	163.4	116.3	113.9				
1,175	1,231	1,027	1,075	1,058	150.8	214.6	309.1	555.7	736.4
−0.1%	−0.9%	−1.6%	−0.7	−5.7%	2.2%	5.6%	0.3%	9.7%	12.9%
−1.0%	−11.0%	−39.0%	−7.7%	NA					
46.0%	46.0%	34.0%	35.3%	53.7%					

[f]Seven-Up was purchased by Philip Morris in 1978; in 1986, Seven-Up's domestic operation was sold to Hicks and Haas, and its international operation was sold to PepsiCo. Seven-Up had negative shareholders equity in 1988, 1989, and 1990.

[g]Dr Pepper/Seven-Up was formed in 1988. The company experienced net losses due to changes relating to new financial accounting rules and a company recapitalization plan. Cadbury Schweppes acquired the company in 1994, after which figures for Dr Pepper/Seven-Up became unavailable.

[h]Royal Crown was purchased by DWG Corporation in late 1984. Royal Crown Corporation was made up of RC Cola and Arby's, a franchised restaurant system. In 1994, Royal Crown was sold to Triarc Corporation, which acquired Mistic Beverages in 1995, and Snapple and Stewarts in 1997. From 1994, Royal Crown sales were reported jointly with those of Triarc's other beverage brands and net profit/sales is altered to Triarc's beverage operating profit/sales.

EXHIBIT 5

Comparative Cost and Financial Structure of a Typical U.S. Concentrate Producer and Bottler
(per standard case of 24 8-ounce bottles), 1993

	Concentrate Producer		Bottler	
	Dollars per Case	**Percent of Sales**	**Dollars per Case**	**Percent of Sales**
Profit and Loss Data				
Net sales	.66	100%	2.99	100%
Cost of sales	.11	17	1.69	57
Gross profit	.55	83	1.30	43
Selling and delivery	.01	2	.85	28
Advertising and marketing	.26	39	.05	2
General and administration	.05	13	.13	4
Pretax profit	.23	29	.27	9
Balance Sheet Data				
Cash, investments	.12		.16	
Receivables	.32		.30	
Inventories	.02		.16	
Net property, plant & equipment	.07		.82	
Goodwill	.03		1.37	
Total assets	.56		2.81	
Pretax profit/total assets	.41		.10	

Source: Industry analysts and casewriter estimates.

EXHIBIT 6

U.S. Soft Drink Retail Outlets, 1993

	Food Stores	Convenience Stores	Fountain	Vending	Other	Total
Percent of industry volume	40.0%	14.0%	17.0%	8.0%	21.0%	100.0%
Share of channel:						
Coca-Cola (all brands)	32.8	29.6	58.9	48.6	45.4	40.7%
Pepsi-Cola (all brands)	28.5	37.4	27.0	40.6	32.5	31.3%
Other brands	38.7	33.0	14.1	10.8	22.1	28.0%
Bottling Profitability Per Case (192 ounces per case):						
Net Price	$3.14	$3.09	$1.52[b]	$6.05	$1.90	$3.13
NOPBT[a]	$0.25	$0.40	$0.05[b]	$0.69	$0.31	$0.34

Source: Industry analysts and casewriter estimates.

[a]Net Operating Profit Before Tax.
[b]Industry average, excluding Coca-Cola bottlers. The Coca-Cola Company supplies fountain outlets directly.

EXHIBIT 7

Comparative Profit Margin Analysis for Door-Store Delivery, Private Label, and Warehouse Delivered Soft Drinks in the United States, 1993

Category	Retail Price	Cost of Goods	Gross Profit	Handling Costs	Net Profit per Unit	Net Profit per Case	Net Margin
DSD	$1.01	$.86	$.15	$.07	$.08	$.48	7.9%
Private Label	.69	.55	.14	.17	(.03)	(.18)	N/A
Warehouse	.82	.65	.17	.17	.00	.00	.00

Source: *Jesse Meyers' Beverage Digest*, July 1993. Reprinted with permission. Copyright 1993 *Beverage Digest*.

Pepsi entered the first-food restaurant business with the acquisitions of Pizza Hut (1978), Taco Bell (1986), and Kentucky Fried Chicken (1986), Coca-Cola persuaded other chains such as Wendy's and Burger King to switch to Coke. PepsiCo spun its restaurant business off to the public in 1997, while retaining the Frito-Lay snack food business.

Concentrate produces offered bottlers rebates to encourage them to purchase and install vending machines. The owners of the property on which vending equipment was located usually received a sales commission. Coke and Pepsi were the largest suppliers of soft drinks to the vending channel. Juice, tea, and lemonade were also available through vending machines.

Suppliers

Concentrate producers and bottlers purchased two major inputs: packaging, which included $3.4 billion in cans, $1.3 billion in plastic bottles, and $0.6 billion in glass; and sweeteners, which included $1.1 billion in sugar and high fructose corn syrup, and $1.0 billion in artificial sweetener (predominantly aspartame). The majority of U.S. soft drinks were packaged in metal cans (55%), then plastic bottles (40%), and glass bottles (5%). Cans were an attractive packaging material because they were easily handled, stocked, and displayed, weighed little, and were durable and recyclable. Plastic bottles, introduced in 1978, boosted home consumption of soft drinks because of their larger 1-liter, 2-liter, and 3-liter sizes.

The concentrate producers' strategy towards can manufacturers was typical of their supplier relationships. Coke and Pepsi negotiated on behalf of their bottling networks, and were among the metal can industry's largest customers. Since the can constituted

about 40% of the total cost of a packaged beverage, bottlers and concentrate producers often maintained relationships with more than one supplier. In the 1960s and 1970s, Coke and Pepsi backward integrated to make some of their own cans, but largely exited the business by 1990. In 1994, Coke and Pepsi instead sought to establish stable long-term relationships with their suppliers. Major can producers included American National Can, Crown Cork & Seal, and Reynolds Metals. Metal cans were viewed as commodities, and there was chronic excess supply in the industry. Often two or three can manufacturers competed for a single contract, which lowered their margins.

With the advent of diet soft drinks in the 1980s, Coke and Pepsi began purchasing aspartame, most notably from Nutrasweet Company, and selling presweetened diet soda concentrate to bottlers. After the expiration of Nutrasweet's U.S. aspartame patent in 1991, Coke amended its franchise bottler contract to pass along two-thirds of any increase or savings in the cost of artificial sweetener to its bottlers. Though not contractually obligated, Pepsi followed suit.

The Evolution of the U.S. Soft Drink Industry

Early History[14]

Coca-Cola was formulated in 1886 by John Pemberton, a pharmacist in Atlanta, Georgia, who sold it at drug store soda fountains as a "potion for mental and physical disorders." A few years later, Asa Candler acquired

14. See J. C. Louis and Harvey Yazijian, *The Cola Wars* (Everest House, 1980); Mark Pendergrast, *For God, Country, and Coca-Cola* (Charles Scribner's, 1993); David Greising, *I'd Like the World to Buy a Coke* (John Wiley & Sons, 1997).

the formula, established a sales force, and began brand advertising of Coca-Cola. Tightly guarded in an Atlanta bank vault, the formula for Coca-Cola syrup, known as "Merchandise 7X," remained a well-protected secret. Candler granted Coca-Cola's first bottling franchise in 1899 for a nominal one dollar, believing that the future of the drink rested with soda fountains. The company's bottling network grew quickly, however, reaching 370 franchisees by 1910.

In its early years, Coke was constantly plagued by imitations and counterfeits, which the company aggressively fought in court. In 1916 alone, courts barred 153 imitations of Coca-Cola, including the brands Coca-Kola, Koca-Nola, Cold-Cola, and the like. Coke introduced and patented a unique 6.5-ounce "skirt" bottle to be used by its franchisees that subsequently became an American icon.

Robert Woodruff, who became CEO in 1923, began working with franchised bottlers to make Coke available wherever and whenever a consumer might want it. He pushed the bottlers to place the beverage "in arm's reach of desire," and argued that if Coke were not conveniently available when the consumer was thirsty, the sale would be lost forever. During the 1920s and 1930s, Coke pioneered open-top coolers to store-keepers, developed automatic fountain dispensers, and introduced vending machines. Woodruff also initiated "lifestyle" advertising for Coca-Cola, emphasizing the role of Coke in a consumer's life.

Woodruff also developed Coke's international business. In the onset of World War II, at the request of General Eisenhower, he promised that "every man in uniform gets a bottle of Coca-Cola for five cents wherever he is and whatever it costs the company." Beginning in 1942, Coke was exempted from wartime sugar rationing whenever the product was destined for the military or retailers serving soldiers. Coca-Cola bottling plants followed the movements of American troops; sixty-four bottling plants were set up during the war—largely at government expense. This contributed to Coke's dominant market shares in most European and Asian countries, a lead that the company still retained in the 1990s.

Pepsi-Cola was invented in 1893 by a North Carolina pharmacist, Caleb Bradham. Like Coke, Pepsi adopted a franchise bottling system, and by 1910 it had built a network of 270 franchised bottlers. Pepsi struggled, however, declaring bankruptcy in 1923 and again in 1932. Business began to pick up in the midst of the Great Depression, when Pepsi lowered the price for its 12-ounce bottle to a nickel, the same price Coke charged for its 6.5-ounce bottle. When Pepsi tried to expand its bottling network in the late 1930s, its choices were small local bottlers striving to compete with wealthy Coke franchisees.[15] Pepsi nevertheless began to gain the market position.

In 1938, Coke filed suit against Pepsi, claiming that Pepsi-Cola was an infringement on the Coca-Cola trademark. The court ruled in favor of Pepsi in 1941, ending a series of suits and countersuits between the two companies. With its famous radio jingle, "Twice as Much, for Nickel Too," Pepsi's U.S. sales surpassed those of Royal Crown and Dr Pepper in the 1940s, trailing only Coca-Cola. In 1950, Coke's share of the U.S. soft drink market was 47% and Pepsi's was 10%; hundreds of regional soft drink companies continued to produce a wide assortment of flavors.

The Cola Wars Begin

In 1950, Alfred Steele, a former Coca-Cola marketing executive, became Pepsi's CEO. Steele made "Beat Coke" his theme and encouraged bottlers to focus on take-home sales through supermarkets. The company introduced the first 26-ounce bottles to the market, targeting family consumption, while Coke stayed with its 6.5-ounce bottle. Pepsi's growth soon began tracking the growth of supermarkets and convenience stores in the United States: There were about 10,000 supermarkets in 1945, 15,000 in 1955, and 32,000 at the peak in 1962.

In 1963, under the leadership of new CEO Donald Kendall, Pepsi launched its "Pepsi Generation" campaign that targeted the young and "young at heart." Pepsi's ad agency created an intense commercial using sports cars, motorcycles, helicopters, and a catchy slogan. The campaign helped Pepsi narrow Coke's lead to a 2-to-1 margin. At the same time, Pepsi worked with its bottlers to modernize plants and improve store delivery services. By 1970, Pepsi's franchise bottlers were generally larger compared to Coke bottlers. Coke's bottling network remained fragmented, with more than 800 independent franchised bottlers that focused mostly on U.S. cities of 50,000 or less.[16] Throughout this period, Pepsi sold concentrate to its

---

15. Louis and Yazijian, p. 23.
16. Pendergrast, p. 310.

bottlers at a price approximately 20% lower than Coke. In the early 1970s, Pepsi increased the price to equal that of Coca-Cola. To overcome bottlers' opposition, Pepsi promised to use the extra margin to increase advertising and promotion.

Coca-Cola and Pepsi-Cola began to experiment with new cola and noncola flavors and a variety of packaging options in the 1960s. Before then, the two companies had adopted a single product strategy, selling only their flagship brand. Coke introduced Fanta (1960), Sprite (1961), and low-calorie Tab (1963). Pepsi countered with Teem (1960), Mountain Dew (1964), and Diet Pepsi (1964). Each introduced non-returnable glass bottles and 12-ounce metal cans in various packages. Coke and Pepsi also diversified into non-soft drink industries. Coke purchased Minute Maid (fruit juice), Duncan Foods (coffee, tea, hot chocolate), and Belmont Springs Water. Pepsi merged with snack-food giant Frito-Lay in 1965 to become PepsiCo, claiming synergies based on shared customer targets, store-door delivery systems, and marketing orientations.

In the late 1950s, Coca-Cola, still under Robert Woodruff's leadership, began using advertising that finally recognized the existence of competitors, such as "American's Preferred Taste" (1955) and "No Wonder Coke Refreshes Best" (1960). In meetings with Coca-Cola bottlers, however, executives only discussed the growth of their own brand and never referred to its closest competitor by name. During the 1960s, Coke primarily focused on overseas markets, apparently believing that domestic soft drink consumption had neared saturation. Pepsi meanwhile battled aggressively in the United States, doubling its share between 1950 and 1970.

The Pepsi Challenge

In 1974, Pepsi launched the "Pepsi Challenge" in Dallas, Texas. Coke was the dominant brand in the city and Pepsi ran a distant third behind Dr Pepper. In blind taste tests hosted by Pepsi's small local bottler, the company tried to demonstrate that consumers in fact preferred Pepsi to Coke. After its sales shot up in Dallas, Pepsi started to roll out the campaign nationwide, although many of its franchise bottlers were initially reluctant to join.

Coke countered with rebates, rival claims, retail price cuts, and a series of advertisements questioning the tests' validity. In particular, Coke used retail price discounts selectively in markets where the Coke bottler was company owned and the Pepsi bottler was an independent franchisee. Nonetheless, the Pepsi Challenge successfully eroded Coke's market share. In 1979, Pepsi passed Coke in food store sales for the first time with a 1.4 share point lead. Breaking precedent, Brian Dyson, president of Coca-Cola, inadvertently uttered the name "Pepsi" in front of Coke's bottlers at the 1979 bottlers conference.

During the same period, Coke was renegotiating its franchise bottling contract to obtain greater flexibility in pricing concentrate and syrups. Bottlers approved the new contract in 1978 only after Coke conceded to link concentrate price changes to the CPI, adjust the price to reflect any cost savings associated with a modification of ingredients, and supply unsweetened concentrate to bottlers who preferred to purchase their own sweetener on the open market.[17] This brought Coke's policies in line with Pepsi, which traditionally sold its concentrate unsweetened to its bottlers. Immediately after securing bottler approval, Coke announced a significant concentrate price hike. Pepsi followed with a 15% price increase of its own.

Coke's Reawakening

In 1980, Cuban-born Roberto Goizueta was named CEO and Don Keough president of Coca-Cola. In the same year, Coke switched from sugar to the lower-priced high fructose corn syrup, a move Pepsi emulated three years later. Coke also intensified its marketing effort, increasing advertising spending from $74 million to $181 million between 1981 and 1984. Pepsi elevated its advertising expenditure from $66 million to $125 million over the same period. Goizueta sold off most of the non-soft drink businesses he had inherited, including wine, coffee, tea, and industrial water treatment, while keeping Minute Maid.

Diet Coke was introduced in 1982 as the first extension of the "Coke" brand name. Much of Coca-Cola management referred to its brand as "Mother Coke," and considered it too sacred to be extended to other products. Despite internal opposition from company lawyers over copyright issues, Diet Coke was a phenomenal success. Praised as the "most successful consumer product launch of the eighties," it became within a few years not only the nation's most

17. Pendergrast, p. 323.

popular diet soft drink, but also the third-largest selling soft drink in the United States.

In April 1985, Coke announced the change of its 99-year-old Coca-Cola formula. Explaining this radical break with tradition, Goizueta saw a sharp depreciation in the value of the Coca-Cola trademark as "the product had a declining share in a shrinking segment of the market."[18] On the day of Coke's announcement, Pepsi declared a holiday for its employees, claiming that the new Coke tasted more like Pepsi. The reformulation prompted an outcry from Coke's most loyal customers, many of whom consumed large amounts of Coca-Cola daily. Bottlers joined the clamor. Three months later, the company brought back the original formula under the name Coca-Cola Classic, while retaining the new formula as the flagship brand under the name New Coke. Six months later, Coke announced that Coca-Cola Classic (the original formula) would henceforth be considered its flagship brand.

New soft drink brands proliferated in the 1980s. Coke introduced 11 new products, including Cherry Coke, Caffeine-Free Coke, and Minute-Maid Orange. Pepsi introduced 13 products, including Caffeine-Free Pepsi-Cola, Lemon-Lime Slice, and Cherry Pepsi. The number of packaging types and sizes also increased dramatically, and the battle for shelf space in supermarkets and other food stores grew fierce. By the late 1980s, both Coke and Pepsi offered more than ten major brands, using at least seventeen containers and numerous packaging options.[19] The struggle for market share intensified, and the level of retail price discounting increased sharply. Consumers were constantly exposed to cents-off promotions and a host of other supermarket discounts.

Throughout the 1980s, the smaller concentrate producers were shuffled from one owner to another. Over five years, Dr Pepper was sold (all and in part) several times, Canada Dry twice, Sunkist once, Shasta once, and A&W Brands once. Some of the deals were made by food companies, but several were leveraged buyouts by investment firms. Coke and Pepsi did not stand on the sidelines. Each tried to buy the most prominent American niche players. In January 1986,

Pepsi announced its intention to acquire Seven-Up from Philip Morris. One month later, Coca-Cola announced plans to acquire Dr Pepper. In June of that year, the Federal Trade Commission voted to oppose both acquisitions, although Pepsi eventually acquired Seven-Up's international operations. Acquisition effort continued. In June, 1998, Pepsi purchased Tropicana, a premium fruit juice producer, for $3.3 billion. In December 1998, Coca-Cola agreed to pay $1.8 billion for Cadbury Schweppes' soft drink brands for all markets but the U.S., France, and South Africa. Regulatory opposition, however, forced Coke to exclude much of Europe from the deal, and the acquisition remained unapproved by Australia, Canada, and Mexico as of December 1999.

Reorganizing the Bottling System

Relations between Coke and its franchised bottlers had been strained since the contract renegotiation of 1978. Coke struggled to persuade bottlers to cooperate in marketing and promotion programs, upgrade plant and equipment, and support new product launches.[20] The cola wars had particularly weakened small independent franchised bottlers. High advertising spending, product and packaging proliferation, and widespread retail price discounting raised capital requirements for bottlers, while lowering their margins. Many bottlers that had been owned by one family for several generations no longer had the resources or the commitment to be competitive.

At a July 1980 dinner with Coke's fifteen largest domestic bottlers, Goizueta announced a plan to refranchise bottling operations. Coke began buying up poorly managed bottlers, infusing capital, and quickly reselling them to better-performing bottlers. Refranchising allowed Coke's larger bottlers to expand outside their traditionally exclusive geographic territories.

When two of its largest bottling companies came up for sale in 1985, Coke moved swiftly to buy them for $2.4 billion preempting outside financial bidders. Together with other bottlers that Coke had recently bought, these acquisitions placed one-third of Coca-Cola's volume in company-owned bottlers. In 1986, Coke began to replace its 1978 franchise agreement with the Master Bottler Contract that afforded Coke much greater freedom to change concentrate price.

18. *The Wall Street Journal*, April 24, 1986.
19. Timothy Muris, David Scheffman, and Pablo Spiller, *Strategy, Structure, and Antitrust in the Carbonated Soft Drink Industry* (Quorum Books, 1993), p. 73.

20. Greising, p. 88.

Coke reportedly raised its concentrate price significantly under the new contract.[21]

Coke's bottler acquisitions had increased its long-term debt to approximately $1 billion. In 1986, on the initiative of Doug Ivester, who later became CEO, the company created an independent bottling subsidiary, Coca-Cola Enterprises (CCE), and sold 51% of its shares to the public, while retaining the rest. The minority equity position enabled Coke to separate its financial statements from CCE. As Coke's first so-called "anchor bottler," CCE consolidated small territories into larger regions, renegotiated with suppliers and retailers, merged redundant distribution and material purchasing, and cut its work force by 20%. CCE moved towards mega-facilities, investing in 50 million-case production lines with high levels of automation and massive warehouse and delivery capabilities.

Coke continued to acquire independent franchised bottlers and sell them to CCE.[22] "We became an investment-banking firm specializing in bottler deals," reflected Don Keough. In 1997 alone, Coke put together more than $7 billion in deals involving bottlers. By then, CCE was Coke's largest bottler with annual sales of $11 billion, handling over 60% of Coke's North American volume.[23] Some industry observers questioned Coke's accounting practice, as Coke retained substantial managerial influence in its arguably independent anchor bottler.[24]

In the late 1980s, Pepsi also acquired MEI Bottling for $591 million, Grand Metropolitan's bottling operations for $705 million, and General Cinema's bottling operations for $1.8 billion. The number of Pepsi bottlers decreased from more than 400 in the mid-1980s to less than 200 in the mid-1990s. Pepsi owned about half of these bottling operations outright and held equity positions in most of the rest. Experience in the snack food and restaurant businesses boosted Pepsi's confidence in its ability to manage the bottling business.

In 1998, Pepsi separated its bottling operations to form the Pepsi Bottling Group (PBG).[25] By the end of 1998, PBG handled 54% of Pepsi's domestic beverage volume, and 32% of its volume worldwide.[26] In April 1999, PBG went public, with Pepsi retaining a 35% equity stake.

The bottler consolidation of the 1990s made smaller concentrate producers increasingly dependent on the Pepsi and Coke bottling network to distribute their products. In response, Cadbury Schweppes in 1998 bought and merged two large U.S. bottlers to form its own bottler, American Beverage Corporation.

Toward the Total Beverage Company

Although Americans still consumed more soft drinks than any other beverage, the average annual growth of sales volume during the 1990s was 3%, compared to 6% in the previous decade. Some industry analysts argued that U.S. soft drink consumption had approached its limit, while others believed that innovations would continue to fuel consumption. Coke and Pepsi also faced challenges from private label brands and "new age" beverages. Private label brand cola, accounting for 11% of the U.S. soft drink market in 1998, was sold through expanding discount retailers and warehouse chains at up to 35% lower price compared to national brands.[27] New age beverages included naturally flavored soda and tea-based drinks introduced by firms such as Clearly Canadian and Snapple, among others, as well as fruit drinks and sports drinks. In 1998, some 3 billion gallons (11.1 gallons per capita) of new age beverages were consumed in the United States, garnering sales of $7.7 billion, up from $900 million in 1993.[28]

Coke and Pepsi launched new drinks throughout the 1990s, including Power Aide, All Sport, Nordic Mist, and Tropical Chill. Both companies predicted that future increases in market share would come from beverages other than carbonated soft drinks. Pepsi pronounced itself a "total beverage company," and Coca-Cola appeared to be moving in the same direction, recasting its performance metric from share of the soda market to "share of stomach." "If Americans want to drink tap water, we want it to be Pepsi tap water," said Pepsi's vice-president for new

21. Robert McGough, "No More Mr. Nice Guy," *Financial World*, July 25, 1989, pp. 30–34.
22. Greising, p. 292.
23. *Beverage Industry*, January 1999, p. 17.
24. Albert Meyer and Dwight Owsen, "Coca-Cola's Accounting," *Accounting Today*, September 28, 1998.
25. *Beverage World*, October 1998, p. 20.
26. M. Gramig, "Pepsi to Spin Off Bottling Group," *The Atlanta Journal and Constitution*, January 9, 1999, p. D1.
27. *Beverage World*, 1998.
28. *New Age Beverages*, 1998; *Beverage World*, March 1999.

business, describing the philosophy behind the new strategy.[29] Coke's Goizueta echoed that view: "Sometimes I think we even compete with soup."[30]

Internationalizing the Cola Wars

Coke and Pepsi also increasingly looked overseas for new growth. In the 1990s, new access to markets in China, India, and Eastern Europe stimulated some of the most intense battles of the cola wars. In many international markets, per capita consumption levels remained a fraction of those in the United States. For example, while the average American drank 878 eight-ounce cans of soft drinks in 1998, the average Chinese drank 23. In 1998, Coca-Cola held a world market share of 51%, compared to Pepsi's 21% and Cadbury Schweppes' less than 8%. Among major overseas markets, Coke dominated in Western Europe and much of Latin America, while Pepsi had marked presence in the Middle East and Southeast Asia (see Exhibit 8).

By the end of World War II, Coca-Cola was the largest international producer of soft drinks. Coke steadily expanded its overseas operations in the 1950s, and the name Coca-Cola soon became a synonym for American culture. Following Coke, Pepsi entered Europe soon after the war, and—benefiting from Arab and Soviet exclusion of Coke—into the Middle East and Soviet bloc in the early 1970s. However, Pepsi put less emphasis on its international operations during the subsequent decade. In 1980, international sales accounted for 62% of Coke's soft drink volume, in contrast to 20% of Pepsi's. Pepsi rejoined the international battles in the late 1980s, realizing that many of its foreign bottling operations were inefficiently run and "woefully uncompetitive."[31]

Coke and Pepsi approached international markets differently. Coke built brand presence in developing markets where soft drink consumption was low but potential was large, such as Indonesia: With 200 million inhabitants, a median age of 18, and per capita consumption of 9 eight-ounce cans of soda a year, one Coke executive noted that "they sit squarely on the equator and everybody's young. It's soft drink heaven."[32] In order to penetrate Coke strongholds, Pepsi utilized a niche strategy with well-executed blitzes, targeting big cities in Latin America and other countries. At the same time, Pepsi moved broadly into markets where Coke had little or no presence.

Coke and Pepsi also organized their overseas bottlers differently. Coke appointed anchor bottlers—large and experienced bottlers—to swiftly enter new markets and organize local bottling networks. Like its U.S. practice, Coke typically held minority equity in anchor bottlers. By 1998, Coke had 10 anchor bottlers operating in 40 international markets, handling about 47% of its global volume.[33] In contrast, Pepsi formed alliances directly with a large number of local bottlers (through joint ventures, partial ownership, and direct control) and invested heavily with its own money to develop their business skills and infrastructure. Including wholly-owned bottlers, Pepsi maintained equity control in over 20% of its bottling system on a volume basis, or about 50% on a revenue basis. Following Coke's lead, however, Pepsi also began to establish anchor bottlers overseas.

Unlike the U.S. market, the bottling contracts for foreign franchisees were not perpetual but typically ran for 3 to 10 years with no guarantee of renewal. Foreign contracts usually did not contain restrictions on concentrate pricing, providing concentrate producers with more discretion to use the prices for strategic purposes. Coke and Pepsi made pricing decisions on a country-by-country basis, taking local conditions into account. Local bottlers set retail prices on the basis of retail channel development, growth in disposable income, and the availability of alternative beverages. Concentrate producers encountered various obstacles in international operations, including cultural differences, political instability, price controls, advertising restrictions, foreign exchange controls, and lack of infrastructure. Their operating margins, nevertheless, were considerably higher abroad on average than in the United States.[34] The following vignettes illustrate how the cola wars had played out in different foreign markets.

29. Marcy Magiera, "Pepsi Moving Fast To Get Beyond Colas," *Advertising Age,* July 5, 1993.
30. Greising, p. 233.
31. Larry Jabbonsky, "Room to Run," *Beverage World,* August 1993.

32. John Huey, "The World's Best Brand," *Fortune,* May 31, 1993.
33. Pendergrast, p. 280.
34. Greising, p. 180.

EXHIBIT 8

Soft Drink Industry—Selected International Market Shares, 1998

	Population (000)	8-oz Per Capita[a]	Coca-Cola[b]	PepsiCo[b]	Cadbury Schweppes[b]
Asia					
Australia	18,613	449	57.1%	9.8%	16.2%
China	1,236,915	23	33.0	15.5	0.1
India	984,004	6	53.0	41.4	1.4
Indonesia	212,942	9	87.0	5.1	3.2
Japan	125,932	96	55.9	8.2	2.1
Pakistan	135,135	10	27.4	64.7	0.1
Philippines	77,726	208	69.1	18.2	
South Korea	46,417	117	53.3	13.2	0.2
Thailand	60,037	133	50.3	45.7	0.2
Vietnam	76,236	10	61.1	34.0	3.4
Europe					
Czech Republic	10,286	255	34.5	16.5	1.4
France	58,805	161	59.2	7.5	5.1
Germany	82,079	353	55.2	4.9	0.9
Hungary	10,208	303	51.0	44.0	4.7
Italy	56,783	218	45.8	5.9	1.1
Netherlands	15,731	362	45.1	14.5	1.5
Poland	38,607	176	27.9	14.7	0.6
Romania	22,396	109	49.0	8.5	0.3
Russia	146,861	67	33.0	11.7	3.0
Spain	39,134	378	57.8	16.0	4.5
United Kingdom	58,970	360	33.3	11.7	6.3
Latin America					
Argentina	36,265	345	61.0	29.0	2.5
Brazil	169,807	277	48.4	5.8	0.7
Colombia	38,581	181	57.0	8.1	0.2
Mexico	98,553	580	68.4	19.7	4.2
Peru	26,111	115	40.0	15.8	3.5
Venezuela	22,803	321	72.4	22.0	1.5
North America					
Canada	30,675	493	39.4	34.3	9.7
United States	270,312	878	44.5	31.4	14.4
Africa					
Kenya	28,337	30	98.4	1.0	0.6
South Africa	42,835	210	81.7	0.0	16.1
Sudan	33,551	11	4.0	65.8	
Yemen	16,388	40	35.0	15.0	50.0
Zaire (Congo)	49,001	5	75.1	10.5	
Middle East					
Egypt	66,050	49	56.8	38.1	3.1
Israel	5,644	400	67.6	13.6	1.0
Morocco	29,114	78	91.0	4.0	5.0
Saudi Arabia	20,786	237	25.0	74.8	0.2
World Total	**5,927,000**	**125**	**51.0**	**20.8**	**7.4**

Source: Beverage Digest Company, *The Green Sheet,* September 24, 1999. Reprinted with permission. Copyright 1999 *Beverage Digest.*

[a] 128 ounces = 1 gallon.
[b] Corporate share includes local brands, if owned or controlled by Coke, Pepsi, or Cadbury Schweppes.

Japan

Coca-Cola was first introduced to Japan in 1961. By the early 1970s, Japan had become Coke's largest market outside the United States, contributing 18% of Coke's total corporate earnings.[35] Coke took small equity stakes in bottling plants owned by well-connected Japanese business partners, including Mitsubishi, Mitsui, Kirin Brewery, and Kikkoman, a leading soy-source producer. Coca-Cola's direct distribution system, which bypassed the traditional Japanese layers of wholesalers, threw the beverage industry into an uproar. Yet the popularity of the product and Japan's early emulation of all things American promoted acceptance of the new methods.[36] Coke introduced vending machines to Japan, a channel that eventually accounted for more than half of Coke's Japanese sales.[37] Adjusting to local preference, Coke regularly introduced new products—as many as twenty per year—most of which were not carbonated soft drinks but varieties of teas, coffees, juices, and flavored water.

Pepsi had never had a notable presence in Japan until Suntory became its master franchisee in 1997. As Japan's second-largest beverage company, Suntory offered Pepsi access to its broad distribution system and was expected to double Pepsi's market share to about 16%.

Germany and Eastern Europe

Germany, although a profitable market for Coca-Cola, had been for many years a patchwork of 160 small and poorly capitalized bottlers. Under Goizueta's initiative, the bottling network was consolidated to 60 well-capitalized bottlers by the early 1990s. Pepsi went another route, taking control of all its independent German bottler in the mid-1980s. When Coke moved quickly into East Germany and Eastern Europe in 1989, Pepsi remained preoccupied with reorganizing its existing German bottlers.

Pepsi's pre-existing ties to government bureaucrats in Eastern Europe proved insufficient to preserve market dominance in the face of Coke's marketing efforts. By 1992, Coke's market share topped Pepsi's in every country except Poland and Czechoslovakia, and before long, those countries fell as well. Even in Russia, where Pepsi's 60% share led Coca-Cola's 38% as recently as 1994, a strategy focused on ties to the new capitalist elite brought Coca-Cola market supremacy by 1997.[38]

India

Strong nationalist sentiment once forced both Coca-Cola and Pepsi out of India in the 1970s. When the Indian government insisted that Coke disclose its secret formula in exchange for continuing operation, the company closed its business in that hot and thirsty country of 850 million souls.[39] Pepsi was permitted to return in 1988 only upon agreeing to export $5 of Indian-made products for every $1 of materials it imported. Coke returned two years later, agreeing to channel its investment through local joint venture partner Parle Exports. Coke invested $70 million in India's largest bottler, acquiring Parle's own brands as well as immediate access to Parle's 54 bottling plants. Parle, however, continued to bottle and sell its own brands, including local market leader "Thums Up," after having sold the right to do so to Coke. In protest, Coke concentrated marketing support on its own, rather than Parle's former brands. Even so, in 1996, Coca-Cola's own brands held just a 20% share, trailing both Thums Up's 40% share and Pepsi's 30% share of the Indian market.

Mexico

Mexico was the largest soft drink market outside the United States. In the early 1990s, as part of its strategy of attacking "Coke fortresses," Pepsi invested more than $750 million in marketing, bottling, and distribution infrastructure to boost its market share in Monterey.[40] Pepsi moved to refit several of its bottlers with state-of-the-art lines that filled disposable plastic containers, ignoring the fact that for Mexicans—as for most other Latin Americans—a soft drink was to be consumed on the spot in order to return the glass bottle and get a refund.[41] The blitz initially was a success, and Pepsi's local cola share

35. Pendergrast, p. 313.
36. Pendergrast, p. 282.
37. June Preston, "Things May Go Better for Coke amid Asia Crisis, Singapore Bottler Says," *Journal of Commerce*, June 29, 1998, p. A3.

38. Greising, p. 188 and p. 273.
39. Enrico, p. 5.
40. Elisabeth Malkin, Phillip L. Zweig, and Lori Bongiorno, "No Deposit, No Return," *Business Week*, September 23, 1996.
41. David Swafford, "The Fizz that Couldn't Last . . . Pepsi Goes Flat in Latin America," *Latin Finance*, November 1996.

tripled to 24% in four months. Coke, however, hit back with price discounting that reduced Pepsi's margins, and the campaign quickly faltered. Pepsi bottlers were left with expensive and ultramodern production lines running at about 30% capacity. As the peso devaluation hit the economy in 1994, Pepsi's local bottlers with costly dollar-denominated debt began defaulting in 1996.[42] In 1999, Pepsi took over and reorganized the bottlers, merging them into a Mexican anchor bottler, Gemex.

Venezuela

Venezuela was the only South American country in which Pepsi outsold Coke by a margin approaching 4-to-1. That changed overnight in August 1996 when Pepsi's long-time local bottler, Embotelladoros Hit de Venezuela (EHV), switched to Coca-Cola. Pepsi had franchised EHV as its sole Venezuelan bottler in 1940 but had held no equity. EHV had succeeded in selling Pepsi in Venezuela by sweetening the recipe to conform to local taste and by developing its own local advertising. Coke paid $500 million to acquire a 50%

share of the $400 million-per-year bottler. Pepsi filed a complaint with Venezuela's anti-monopoly commission for breach of franchise contract and won a $2 million fine from Coke. Separately, the International Court of Arbitration ordered EHV to pay Pepsi $94 million, the equivalent of a decade of Pepsi's Venezuelan profits. In the meantime, Pepsi found a new joint venture partner and responded to Coke with price discounting and heavy investment in retail distribution. Appealing to loyal customers cultivated over five decades, Pepsi recovered a 29% share of the Venezuelan market by year-end 1998.[43]

As the cola wars continued overseas, the management of Coke and Pepsi faced new and old questions: Could Pepsi catch up with Coke in global market share as it had in the U.S. markets? Would overseas soft drink markets evolve into a duopoly, as in the United States, or might other patterns emerge, with different players, different organizational structures, and different levels of profitability?

---

42. Malkin et al, "No Deposit, No Return."

43. Constance L. Hays, "Coca-Cola Is Battling to Consolidate its Recent Gains over PepsiCo in a Turf War in Venezuela," *New York Times,* December 18, 1998, p. C3.

25 Wal-Mart Stores, Inc.: Strategies for Dominance in the New Millennium

This case was prepared by James W. Camerius, Northern Michigan University.

David Glass had recently announced that he was stepping down from his role as president and chief executive officer (CEO) at Wal-Mart Stores, Inc. He stepped to the podium in early 2000 at a Kansas City convention of the company's store managers to introduce Wal-Mart's new CEO, Lee Scott, fifty-one, to a crowd of cheering executives. "I'm not going anywhere; I'll be around to give everyone more help than they probably would like," Glass suggested. At sixty-four years old, he would remain chairman of the firm's executive committee.

Lee Scott was only the third CEO in the entire history of Wal-Mart. Sam Walton had built the company from the ground up. During the twelve years that David Glass held the position, sales grew from $16 billion to $165 billion. Lee Scott had been personally recruited by David Glass twenty-one years before from a Springdale, Arkansas, trucking company to come to Wal-Mart as manager of the truck fleet. In his years at Wal-Mart he had established himself as a leader, innovator, and team player. Over the last four years he served as chief operating officer (COO) and vice chairman of the company. He was aware that there were

tremendous opportunities to serve new markets with the company's stores. His management mandate was to drive the company to a new level of success in domestic and international markets.

A Maturing Organization

In 2000, Wal-Mart Stores, Inc., Bentonville, Arkansas, operated mass merchandising retail stores under various names and retail formats including Wal-Mart discount department stores; Sam's Wholesale Clubs, wholesale/retail membership warehouses; and Wal-Mart Supercenters, large combination grocery and general merchandise stores in all fifty states. In the international division, it operated stores in Canada, Mexico, Argentina, Brazil, Germany, South Korea, the United Kingdom, and Puerto Rico, and stores through joint ventures in China. It was not only the nation's largest discount department store chain, it had surpassed the retail division of Sears, Roebuck, & Co. in sales volume as the largest retail firm in the United States. It was also considered the largest retailer in the world, with sales of $165 billion in 1999. The McLane Company, Inc., a Wal-Mart subsidiary, sold a wide variety of grocery and nongrocery products to different retailers, including selected Wal-Marts, Sam's Clubs, and

Supercenters. In 1999, *Discount Store News* honored Wal-Mart as "Retailer of the Century" with a commemorative issue of the periodical.

A financial summary of Wal-Mart Stores, Inc., for the fiscal years ended January 31, 1999, and January 31, 2000, is shown in appendixes A and B. An eleven-year financial summary for the fiscal years January 31, 1990, to January 31, 2000, is shown in appendix C. Appendix D lists the Wal-Mart Board of Directors and Executive Officers on January 31, 2000.

The Sam Walton Spirit

Much of the success of Wal-Mart was attributed to the entrepreneurial spirit of its founder and chairman of the board, Samuel Moore Walton (1918–1992). Many considered him one of the most influential retailers of the century. Sam Walton (or "Mr. Sam," as some referred to him) traced his down-to-earth, old-fashioned, homespun, evangelical ways to growing up in rural Oklahoma, Missouri, and Arkansas. Although he was remarkably blasé about his roots, some suggested that it was the simple belief in hard work and ambition that had "unlocked countless doors and showered upon him, his customers, and his employees . . . , the fruits of . . . years of labor in building [this] highly successful company."

"Our goal has always been in our business to be the very best," Sam Walton said in an interview, "and, along with that, we believe that in order to do that, you've got to make a good situation and put the interests of your associates first. If we really do that consistently, they in turn will cause . . . our business to be successful, which is what we've talked about and espoused and practiced. The reason for our success," he said, "is our people and the way that they're treated and the way they feel about their company." Many have suggested it was this people-first philosophy, which guided the company through the challenges and setbacks of its early years, that allowed the company to maintain its consistent record of growth and expansion in later years.

There was little about Sam Walton's background that reflected his amazing success. He was born in Kingfisher, Oklahoma, on March 29, 1918, to Thomas and Nancy Walton. Thomas Walton was a banker at the time and later entered the farm mortgage business and moved to Missouri. Sam Walton, growing up in rural Missouri in the depths of the

Great Depression, discovered early that he "had a fair amount of ambition and enjoyed working," he once noted. He completed high school at Columbia, Missouri, and received a Bachelor of Arts degree in economics from the University of Missouri in 1940. "I really had no idea what I would be," he once said, "At one point in time," adding as an afterthought, "I thought I wanted to become president of the United States."

A unique, enthusiastic, and positive individual, Sam Walton was "just your basic homespun billionaire," a columnist once suggested. "Mr. Sam is a lifelong small-town resident who didn't change much as he got richer than his neighbors," he noted. Walton had tremendous energy, enjoyed bird hunting with his dogs, and flew a corporate plane. When the company was much smaller he could boast that he personally visited every Wal-Mart store at least once a year. A store visit usually included Walton leading Wal-Mart cheers that began, "Give me a W, give me an A . . . ." To many employees he had the air of a fiery Baptist preacher. Paul R. Carter, a Wal-Mart executive vice president, was quoted as saying, "Mr. Walton has a calling." He became the richest man in America, and by 1991 had created a personal fortune for his family in excess of $21 billion. In 1999, despite a division of wealth, five family members were still ranked among the richest individuals in the United States.

Sam Walton's success was widely chronicled. He was selected by the investment publication, *Financial World* in 1989 as the "CEO of the Decade." He had honorary degrees from the University of the Ozarks, the University of Arkansas, and the University of Missouri. He also received many of the most-distinguished professional awards of the industry like "Man of the Year," "Discounter of the Year," and "Chief Executive Officer of the Year," and was the second retailer to be inducted into the Discounting Hall of Fame. He was a recipient of the Horatio Alger Award in 1984 and acknowledged by *Discount Stores News* as "Retailer of the Decade" in December 1989. "Walton does a remarkable job of instilling near-religious fervor in his people," said analyst Robert Buchanan of A. G. Edwards. "I think that speaks to the heart of his success." In late 1989 Sam Walton was diagnosed with multiple myeloma, or cancer of the bone marrow. He planned to remain active in the firm as chairman of the board of directors until his death. He died in 1992.

The Marketing Concept

Genesis of an Idea

Sam Walton started his retail career in 1940 as a management trainee with the JC Penney Co. in Des Moines, Iowa. He was impressed with the Penney method of doing business and later modeled the Wal-Mart chain on "The Penney Idea" (see Exhibit 1). The Penney Company found strength in calling employees associates rather than clerks. Founded in Kemerer, Wyoming, in 1902, Penney's located stores on the main streets of small towns and cities throughout the United States. Early Walton 5 & 10s were on main streets and served rural areas.

Following service in the U.S. Army during World War II, Sam Walton acquired a Ben Franklin variety store franchise in Newport, Arkansas. He operated this store successfully with his brother, James L. "Bud" Walton (1921–1995), until losing the lease in 1950. When Wal-Mart was incorporated in 1962, the firm was operating a chain of fifteen stores. Bud Walton became a senior vice president of the firm and concentrated on finding suitable store locations, acquiring real estate, and directing store construction.

The early retail stores owned by Sam Walton in Newport and Bentonville, Arkansas, and later in other small towns in adjoining southern states, were variety store operations. They were relatively small

EXHIBIT 1

The Penney Idea, 1913

1. To serve the public, as nearly as we can, to its complete satisfaction.
2. To expect for the service we render a fair remuneration and not all the profit the traffic will bear.
3. To do all in our power to pack the customer's dollar full of value, quality, and satisfaction.
4. To continue to train ourselves and our associates so that the service we give will be more and more intelligently performed.
5. To improve constantly the human factor in our business.
6. To reward men and women in our organization through participation in what the business produces.
7. To test our every policy, method, and act in this wise: "Does it square with what is right and just?"

Source: Trimble, Vance H., *Sam Walton: The Inside Story of America's Richest Man,* New York: Dutton, 1990.

operations of 6,000 square feet, were located on main streets, and displayed merchandise on plain wooden tables and counters. Operated under the Ben Franklin name and supplied by Butler Brothers of Chicago and St. Louis, they were characterized by a limited price line, low gross margins, high merchandise turnover, and concentration on return on investment. The firm, operating under the Walton 5 & 10 name, was the largest Ben Franklin franchisee in the country in 1962. The variety stores were phased out by 1976 to allow the company to concentrate on the growth of Wal-Mart discount department stores.

Foundations of Growth

The original Wal-Mart discount concept was not a unique idea. Sam Walton became convinced in the late 1950s that discounting would transform retailing. He traveled extensively in New England, the cradle of off-pricing. After he had visited just about every discounter in the United States, he tried to interest Butler Brothers executives in Chicago in the discount store concept. The first Kmart, as a "conveniently located one-stop shopping unit where customers could buy a wide variety of quality merchandise at discount prices," had just opened in Garden City, Michigan. Walton's theory was to operate a similar discount store in a small community and in that setting, he would offer name brand merchandise at low prices and would add friendly service. Butler Brothers executives rejected the idea. The first "Wal-Mart Discount City" opened in late 1962 in Rogers, Arkansas.

Wal-Mart stores would sell nationally advertised, well-known brand merchandise at low prices in austere surroundings. As corporate policy, they would cheerfully give refunds, credits, and rain checks. Management conceived the firm as a "discount department store chain offering a wide variety of general merchandise to the customer." Early emphasis was placed on opportunistic purchases of merchandise from whatever sources were available. Heavy emphasis was placed upon health and beauty aids (H&BA) in the product line and "stacking it high" in a manner of merchandise presentation. By the end of 1979, there were 276 Wal-Mart stores located in eleven states.

The firm developed an aggressive expansion strategy. New stores were located primarily in communities of 5,000 to 25,000 in population. The stores' sizes ranged from 30,000 to 60,000 square feet, with

45,000 being the average. The firm also expanded by locating stores in contiguous geographic areas. When its discount operations came to dominate a market area, it moved to an adjoining area. While other retailers built warehouses to serve existing outlets, Wal-Mart built the distribution center first and then spotted stores all around it, pooling advertising and distribution overhead. Most stores were less than a six-hour drive from one of the company's warehouses. The first major distribution center, a 390,000-square-foot facility, opened in Searcy, Arkansas, outside Bentonville, in 1978.

National Perspectives

At the beginning of 1991, the firm had 1,573 Wal-Mart stores in thirty-five states, with expansion planned for adjacent states. Wal-Mart became the largest retailer and the largest discount department store in the United States.

As a national discount department store chain, Wal-Mart Stores, Inc., offered a wide variety of general merchandise to the customer. The stores were designed to offer one-stop shopping in thirty-six departments that included family apparel, health and beauty aids, household needs, electronics, toys, fabric and crafts, automotive supplies, lawn and patio, jewelry, and shoes. At certain store locations, a pharmacy, automotive supply and service center, garden center, or snack bar was also operated. The firm operated its stores with "everyday low prices" as opposed to putting heavy emphasis on special promotions, which called for multiple newspaper advertising circulars. Stores were expected to "provide the customer with a clean, pleasant, and friendly shopping experience."

Although Wal-Mart carried much the same merchandise, offered similar prices, and operated stores that looked much like the competition, there were many differences. In the typical Wal-Mart store, employees wore blue vests to identify themselves, aisles were wide, apparel departments were carpeted in warm colors, a store employee followed customers to their cars to pick up their shopping carts, and the customer was welcomed at the door by a "people greeter" who gave directions and struck up conversations. In some cases, merchandise was bagged in brown paper sacks rather plastic bags because customers seemed to prefer them. A simple Wal-Mart logo in white letters on a brown background on the front of the store served to identify the firm. Yellow smiley faces were used on in-store displays. Consumer studies determined that the chain was particularly adept at striking the delicate balance needed to convince customers its prices were low without making people feel that its stores were too cheap. In many ways, competitors like Kmart sought to emulate Wal-Mart by introducing people greeters, upgrading interiors, developing new logos and signage, and introducing new inventory response systems.

A "satisfaction guaranteed" refund and exchange policy was introduced to allow customers to be confident of Wal-Mart's merchandise and quality. Technological advancements like scanner cash registers, hand-held computers for ordering of merchandise, and computer linkages of stores with the general office and distribution centers improved communications and merchandise replenishment. Each store was encouraged to initiate programs that would make it an integral part of the community in which it operated. Associates were encouraged to "maintain the highest standards of honesty, morality, and business ethics in dealing with the public.

The External Environment

Industry analysts labeled the 1980s and early 1990s as eras of economic uncertainty for retailers. Many retailers were negatively affected by increased competitive pressures, sluggish consumer spending, slower-than-anticipated economic growth in North America, and recessions abroad. In 1995, Wal-Mart management felt the high consumer debt level caused many shoppers to reduce or defer spending on anything other than essentials. Management also felt that the lack of exciting new products or apparel trends reduced discretionary spending. Fierce competition resulted in lower margins, and the lack of inflation stalled productivity increases.

By 1998, the country had returned to prosperity. Unemployment was low, total income was relatively high, and interest rates were stable. Combined with a low inflation rate, buying power was perceived to be high and consumers were generally willing to buy. At the beginning of the year 2000, the United States had experienced one of the longest periods of economic expansion in its history.

Many retail enterprises confronted heavy competitive pressure by restructuring. Sears, Roebuck & Company, based in Chicago, became a more-focused retailer by divesting itself of Allstate Insurance

Company and its real estate subsidiaries. In 1993, the company announced it would close 118 unprofitable stores and discontinue the unprofitable Sears general merchandise catalog. It eliminated 50,000 jobs and began a $4 billion, five-year remodeling plan for its remaining multiline department stores. After unsuccessfully experimenting with an everyday low-price strategy, management chose to re-align its merchandise strategy to meet the needs of middle market customers, who were primarily women, by focusing on product lines in apparel, home, and automotive. The new focus on apparel was supported with the advertising campaign, "The Softer Side of Sears." A later companywide campaign broadened the appeal: "The many sides of Sears fit the many sides of your life." Sears completed its return to its retailing roots by selling off its ownership in Dean Witter Financial Services, Discovery Card, Coldwell Banker Real Estate, and Sears mortgage banking operations. In 1999, Sears refocused its marketing strategy with a new program that was designed to communicate a stronger whole-house and event message. A new advertising campaign was introduced with the slogan, "The good life at a great price. Guaranteed." In 2000, a new store format was introduced that concentrated on five focal areas: appliances, home fashions, tools, kids, and electronics. Other departments, including men's and women's apparel, assumed a support role in these stores.

By the early 1990s, the discount department store industry had changed in several ways and was thought to have reached maturity by many analysts. Several formerly successful firms like E. J. Korvette, W. T. Grant, Atlantic Mills, Arlans, Federals, Zayre, Heck's, and Ames had declared bankruptcy and either liquidated or reorganized as a result. Venture announced liquidation in early 1998. Firms like Target Stores and Shopko Stores began carrying more fashionable merchandise in more attractive facilities and shifted their emphasis to more national markets. Specialty retailers such as Toys "R" Us, Pier 1 Imports, and Oshmans had matured and were no longer making big inroads in toys, home furnishings, and sporting goods. The superstores of drug and food chains were rapidly discounting increasing amounts of general merchandise. Some firms, like May Department Stores Company with Caldor and Venture, and Woolworth Corporation with Woolco, had withdrawn from the field by either selling their discount divisions or closing them down entirely. Woolworth's

remaining 122 Woolco stores in Canada were sold to Wal-Mart in 1994. All remaining Woolworth variety stores in the United States were closed in 1997.

Several new retail formats had emerged in the marketplace to challenge the traditional discount department store format. The superstore, a 100,000- to 300,000-square-foot operation, combined a large supermarket with a discount general-merchandise store. Originally a European retailing concept, these outlets where known as "malls without walls." Kmart's Super Kmart, American Fare, and Wal-Mart's Supercenter Store were examples of this trend toward large operations. Warehouse retailing, which involved some combination of warehouse and showroom facilities, used warehouse principles to reduce operating expenses and thereby offer discount prices as a primary customer appeal. Home Depot combined the traditional hardware store and lumberyard with a self-service home improvement center to become the largest home-center operator in the nation.

Some retailers responded to changes in the marketplace by selling goods at price levels (20 to 60 percent) below regular retail prices. These off-price operations appeared as two general types: (1) factory outlet stores like Burlington Coat Factory Warehouse, Bass Shoes, and Manhattan's Brand Name Fashion Outlet, and (2) independents like Loehmann's, T. J. Maxx, Marshall's, and Clothestime, which bought seconds, overages, closeouts, or leftover goods from manufacturers and other retailers. Other retailers chose to dominate a product classification. Some super specialists like Sock Appeal; Little Piggie, Ltd; and Sock Market offered a single, narrowly defined classification of merchandise with an extensive assortment of brands, colors, and sizes. Niche specialists, like Kids Mart, a division of Venator (Woolworth) Corporation, targeted an identified market with carefully selected merchandise and appropriately designed stores. Some retailers like Silk Greenhouse (silk plants and flowers), Office Club (office supplies and equipment), and Toys "R" Us (toys) were called "category killers" because they had achieved merchandise dominance in their respective product categories. Stores like The Limited, Limited Express, Victoria's Secret, and The Banana Republic became minidepartment specialists by showcasing new lines and accessories alongside traditional merchandise lines.

Kmart Corporation, headquartered in Troy, Michigan, became the industry's third largest retailer after Sears, Roebuck & Co. and second largest discount department store chain in the United States in 1990. Kmart had 2,171 stores and $35,925 million in sales at the beginning of 2000. The firm was perceived by many industry analysts and consumers in several independent studies as a laggard. It had been the industry sales leader for several years and had recently announced a turnaround in profitability. In the same studies, Wal-Mart was perceived as the industry leader, even though, according to the *Wall Street Journal*, "they carry much the same merchandise, offer prices that are pennies apart and operate stores that look almost exactly alike." "Even their names are similar," noted the newspaper. The original Kmart concept of a "conveniently located, one-stop shopping unit where customers could buy a wide variety of quality merchandise at discount prices" had lost its competitive edge in a changing market. As one analyst noted in an industry newsletter: "They had done so well for the past 20 years without paying attention to market changes, now they have to." Kmart acquired a new president and chief executive officer in 2000. Wal-Mart and Kmart sales growth over the period 1990–1999 is reviewed in Exhibit 2. A competitive analysis is shown of four major retail firms in Exhibit 3.

Some retailers like Kmart had initially focused on appealing to professional, middle-class consumers who lived in suburban areas and who were likely to be price sensitive. Other firms like Target, which had adopted the discount concept early, attempted to go generally after an upscale consumer. Some firms such as Fleet Farm and Pamida served the rural consumer, while firms like Value City and Ames Discount Department Stores chose to serve the urban consumer.

In rural communities, Wal-Mart's success often came at the expense of established local merchants and units of regional discount store chains. Hardware stores, family department stores, building supply outlets, and stores featuring fabrics, sporting goods, and shoes were among the first either to close or to relocate. Regional discount retailers in the Sunbelt states like Roses, Howard's, T.G.&Y., and Duckwall-ALCO, which once enjoyed solid sales and earnings, were forced to reposition themselves by renovating stores, opening bigger and more modern units, re-merchandising assortments, and offering lower prices. In many cases, stores like Coast-to-Coast and Ben Franklin closed after a Wal-Mart announcement that it was planning to build in a specific community. "Just the word that Wal-Mart was coming made some stores close up," indicated one local newspaper editor.

Domestic Corporate Strategies

The corporate and marketing strategies that emerged at Wal-Mart were based on a set of two main objectives that had guided the firm through its growth years. In the first objective, the customer was featured:

EXHIBIT 2

Competitive Sales and Store Comparison, 1990–1999

Year	Kmart		Wal-Mart	
	Sales (000)	Stores*	Sales (000)	Stores*
1999	$35,925,000	2,171	$165,013,000	3,989
1998	33,674,000	2,161	137,634,000	3,999
1997	32,183,000	2,136	117,958,000	3,406
1996	31,437,000	2,261	104,859,000	3,054
1995	34,389,000	2,161	93,627,000	2,943
1994	34,025,000	2,481	82,494,000	2,684
1993	34,156,000	2,486	67,344,000	2,400
1992	37,724,000	2,435	55,484,000	2,136
1991	34,580,000	2,391	43,886,900	1,928
1990	32,070,000	2,350	32,601,594	1,721

*Number of general merchandise stores.

EXHIBIT 3

An Industry Comparative Analysis, 1999

	Wal-Mart	Sears	Kmart	Target
Sales (millions)	$165,013	$41,071	$35,925	$33,702
Net income (thousands)	$ 5,377	$ 1,453	$ 403	$ 1,144
Net income per share	$ 1.21	$ 3.83	$ 1.29	$ 2.45
Dividends per share	$ .14	$ n/a	$ n/a	$ .40
Percentage sales change	20.0%	2.7%	6.6%	9.9%

Number of stores:
Wal-Mart, United States
    Discount Stores—1,801
    Sam's Clubs—463
    Supercenters—721
Wal-Mart International
    Discount stores—572
    Sam's Clubs—49
    Supercenters—383
Sears Roebuck & Company (all divisions)
    Sears Merchandise Group
        Full-line department stores—858
        Hardware stores—267

    Sears dealer stores—738
    Sears Auto Centers stores—798
    NTB National Tire & Battery stores—310
Kmart Corporation
    Big Kmart—1,860
    Traditional Kmart—206
    Super Kmart—105
Target Corporation
    Target—912
    Mervyn's—267
    Department stores—64

Source: Corporate annual reports.

"customers would be provided what they want, when they want it, all at a value." In the second objective, the team spirit was emphasized: "treating each other as we would hope to be treated, acknowledging our total dependency on our Associate-partners to sustain our success." The approach included aggressive plans for new store openings; expansion to additional states; upgrading, relocating, refurbishing, and remodeling of existing stores; and opening new distribution centers. For Wal-Mart management, the 1990s were considered an era in which the firm grew to become a truly nationwide retailer that operated in all fifty states. At the beginning of 2000, Wal-Mart management predicted that over the next five years, 60 to 70 percent of sales and earnings growth would come from domestic markets with Wal-Mart stores and supercenters, and another 10 to 15 percent from Sam's Club and McLane. The remaining 20 percent of the growth would come from planned growth in international markets. As David Glass once noted, "We'll be fine as long as we never lose our responsiveness to the customer."

In the 1980s, Wal-Mart developed several new retail formats. The first Sam's Club opened in Oklahoma City, Oklahoma, in 1983. The wholesale club was an idea that had been developed earlier by other firms but found its greatest success and growth in acceptability at Wal-Mart. Sam's Clubs featured a vast array of product categories with limited selection of brand and model; cash-and-carry business with limited hours; large (100,000-square-foot), bare-bones facilities; rock-bottom wholesale prices; and minimal promotion. The limited membership plan permitted wholesale members who bought membership and others who usually paid a percentage above the ticket price of the merchandise. A revision in merchandising strategy resulted in fewer items in the inventory mix with more emphasis on lower prices. A later acquisition of 100 Pace warehouse clubs, which were converted into Sam's Clubs, increased that division's units by more than one-third. At the beginning of 2000, there were 463 Sam's Clubs in operation.

Wal-Mart Supercenters were large combination stores. They were first opened in 1988 as Hypermarket*USA, a 222,000-square-foot superstore that combined a discount store with a large grocery store, a food court of restaurants, and other service businesses such as banks or videotape rental stores. A scaled-down version of Hypermarket*USA was called the Wal-Mart Supercenter, and was similar in merchandise offerings, but with about 180,000 to 200,000 square feet of space. These expanded store concepts also included convenience stores and gasoline distribution outlets to "enhance shopping convenience." The company proceeded slowly with these plans and later suspended its plans for building any more hypermarkets in favor of the supercenter concept. At the beginning of 2000, Wal-Mart operated 721 supercenters. The name, Hypermarket*USA, was no longer used to identify these large stores.

Wal-Mart also tested a new concept called the neighborhood market in several locations in Arkansas. Identified by the company as "small-marts," these green-and-white stores were stocked with fresh fruits and vegetables, a drive-up pharmacy, a twenty-four-hour photo shop, and a selection of classic Wal-Mart hard goods. Management elected to move slowly on this concept, planning to open no more than ten a year. The goal was to ring the super-stores with these smaller stores to attract customers who were in a hurry and wanted only a few items.

The McLane Company, Inc., a provider of retail and grocery distribution services for retail stores, was acquired in 1991. It was not considered a major segment of the total Wal-Mart operation.

Several programs were launched in Wal-Mart stores to highlight popular social causes. The "buy American" program was a Wal-Mart retail program initiated in 1985. The theme was "Bring It Home to the USA" and its purpose was to communicate Wal-Mart's support for American manufacturing. In the program, the firm exerted substantial influence to encourage manufacturers to produce goods in the United States rather than import them from other countries. Vendors were encouraged to initiate the process by contacting the company directly with proposals to sell goods that were made in the United States. Buyers also targeted specific import items in their assortments on a state-by-state basis to encourage domestic manufacturing. According to Haim Dabah, president of Gitano Group, Inc., a maker of fashion discount clothing that imported 95 percent of its clothing and now makes about 20 percent of its

products here: "Wal-Mart let it be known loud and clear that if you're going to grow with them, you sure better have some products made in the U.S.A." Farris Fashion, Inc. (flannel shirts); Roadmaster Corporation (exercise bicycles); Flanders Industries, Inc. (lawn chairs); and Magic Chef (microwave ovens) were examples of vendors that chose to participate in the program.

From the Wal-Mart standpoint, the "Buy American" program centered around value—producing and selling quality merchandise at a competitive price. The promotion included television advertisements featuring factory workers, a soaring American eagle, and the slogan: "We buy American whenever we can, so you can too." Prominent in-store signage and store circulars were also included. One store poster read: "Success Stories—These items formerly imported, are now being purchased by Wal-Mart in the U.S.A."

Wal-Mart was one of the first retailers to embrace the concept of "green" marketing. The program offered shoppers the option of purchasing products that were better for the environment in three respects: manufacturing, use, and disposal. The program was introduced through full-page advertisements in the *Wall Street Journal* and *USA Today*. In-store signage identified products that were environmentally safe. As Wal-Mart executives saw it, "Customers are concerned about the quality of land, air, and water, and would like the opportunity to do something positive." To initiate the program, 7,000 vendors were notified that Wal-Mart had a corporate concern for the environment and asked for their support in various ways. Wal-Mart television advertising showed children on swings, fields of grain blowing in the wind, and roses. Green-and-white store signs, printed on recycled paper, marked products or packaging that had been developed or redesigned to be more environmentally sound.

The Wal-Mart private brand program began with the "Ol' Roy" brand, the private-label dog food named for Sam Walton's favorite hunting companion. Introduced to Wal-Mart stores in 1982 as a low-price alterative to national brands, Ol' Roy became the biggest seller of all dog-food brands in the United States. "We are a [national] brand-oriented company first," noted Bob Connolly, executive vice president of merchandising at Wal-Mart. "But we also use private labels to fill value or pricing voids that, for whatever reason, the brands left behind. Wal-Mart's private label program included thousands of products that had brand names such as Sam's Choice, Great Value, Equate, and Spring Valley.

Wal-Mart had become the channel commander in the distribution of many brand-name items. As the nation's largest retailer and in many geographic areas the dominant distributor, it exerted considerable influence in negotiation for the best price, delivery terms, promotion allowances, and continuity of supply. Many of these benefits could be passed on to consumers in the form of quality name-brand items available at lower than competitive prices. As a matter of corporate policy, management often insisted on doing business only with producers' top sales executives rather than going through a manufacturer's representative. Wal-Mart had been accused of threatening to buy from other producers if firms refused to sell directly to it. In the ensuing power struggle, Wal-Mart executives refused to talk about the controversial policy or admit that it existed. As a spokesperson of an industry association of sales agencies' representatives suggested, "In the Southwest, Wal-Mart's the only show in town." An industry analyst added, "They're extremely aggressive. Their approach has always been to give the customer the benefit of a corporate saving. That builds up customer loyalty and market share."

Another key factor in the mix was an inventory control system that was recognized as the most sophisticated in retailing. A high-speed computer system linked almost all the stores to headquarters and the company's distribution centers. It logged electronically every item sold at the checkout counter, automatically kept the warehouses informed of merchandise to be ordered, and directed the flow of goods to the stores and even to the proper shelves. Most important for management, it helped detect sales trends quickly and speeded up market reaction time substantially. According to Bob Connolly, executive vice president of merchandising, "Wal-Mart has used the data gathered by technology to make more inventory available in the key items that customers want most, while reducing inventories overall."

At the beginning of 2000, Wal-Mart set up a separate company for its web site, with plans to go public. Wal-Mart.com Inc., based in Palo Alto, California, was jointly owned by Wal-Mart and Accel Partners, a Silicon Valley venture-capital firm. The site included a wide range of products and services that ranged from shampoo to clothing to lawn mowers, as well as airline, hotel, and rental car bookings. After launching and then closing a Sam's Club web site, Wal-Mart had plans to reopen the site in mid-June 2000 with an emphasis on upscale items such as jewelry, housewares, and electronics and full product lines for small business owners. SamsClub.com would be run by Wal-Mart from the company's Bentonville, Arkansas, headquarters.

International Corporate Strategies

In 1994, Wal-Mart entered the Canadian market with the acquisition of 122 Woolco discount stores from Woolworth Corporation. When acquired, the Woolco stores were losing millions of dollars annually, but operations became profitable within three years. At the end of 1999, the company had 166 Wal-Mart discount stores in Canada and planned to open seventeen new stores in fiscal 2000. The company's operations in Canada were considered a model for Wal-Mart's expansion into other international markets. With 35 percent of the Canadian discount and department store market, Wal-Mart was the largest retailer in that country.

With a tender offer for shares and mergers of joint ventures in Mexico, the company in 1997 acquired a controlling interest in Cifra, Mexico's largest retailer. Cifra, later identified as Wal-Mart de Mexico, operated stores with various concepts in every region of Mexico, ranging from the nation's largest chain of sit-down restaurants to a softline department store. Retail analysts noted that the initial venture involved many costly mistakes. Time after time it sold the wrong products, including tennis balls that wouldn't bounce in high-altitude Mexico City. Large parking lots at some stores made access difficult because many people arrived by bus. In 2000, Wal-Mart operated 397 Cifra outlets in Mexico, in addition to twenty-seven Wal-Mart Supercenters and thirty-four Sam's Club stores.

When Wal-Mart entered Argentina in 1995, it initially faced challenges adapting its United States–based retail mix and store layouts to the local culture. Although globalization and American cultural influences had swept through the country in the early 1990s, the Argentine market did not accept American cuts of meat, bright-colored cosmetics, and jewelry that gave prominent placement to emeralds, sapphires, and diamonds, even though most Argentine women preferred wearing gold and silver. The first stores even had hardware departments full of tools wired for 110-volt electric power; the standard throughout Argentina was 220. Compounding the challenges were store layouts that featured narrow aisles; stores appeared crowded and dirty.

Wal-Mart management concluded that Brazil, with the fifth largest population in the world and people who had a tendency to follow U.S. cultural cues, offered great opportunities for Wal-Mart. Although financial data were not broken out on South American operations, retail analysts cited the accounts of Wal-Mart's Brazilian partner, Lojas Americanas SA, to suggest that Wal-Mart lost $100 million in start-up costs of the initial sixteen stores. Customer acceptance of Wal-Mart stores was mixed. In Canada and Mexico, many customers were familiar with the company from cross-border shopping trips. Many Brazilian customers were not familiar with the Wal-Mart name. In addition, local Brazilian markets were already dominated by savvy local and foreign competitors such as Grupo Pao de Acucar SA of Brazil and Carrefour SA of France. And Wal-Mart's insistence on doing things "the Wal-Mart way" initially alienated many local suppliers and employees. The country's continuing economic problems also presented a challenge. In 2000, Wal-Mart planned to expand its presence by opening three more Sam's Clubs in Brazil.

Because of stubborn local regulations, management felt it would be easier for Wal-Mart to buy existing stores in Europe than to build new ones. The acquisition of twenty-one "hypermarkets" in Germany at the end of 1997 marked the company's first entry into Europe, which management considered "one of the best consumer markets in the world." These large stores offered one-stop shopping facilities similar to Wal-Mart supercenters. In early 1999, the firm also purchased seventy-four Interspar hypermarket stores. All of these German stores were identified with the Wal-Mart name and restocked with a new and revamped selection of merchandise. In response to local laws that forced early store closings and banned Sunday sales, the company simply opened stores earlier to allow shopping to begin at 7 A.M.

Wal-Mart acquired ASDA, Britain's third largest supermarket group, for $10.8 billion in July 1999. With its own price rollbacks, people greeters, "permanently low prices," and even smiley faces, ASDA had emulated Wal-Mart's store culture for many years. Based in Leeds, England, the firm had 232 stores in England, Scotland, and Wales. While the culture and pricing strategies of the two companies were nearly identical, there were differences, primarily in the size and product mix of the stores. The average Wal-Mart Supercenter in 1999 was 180,000 square feet in size and had about 30 percent of its sales in groceries. In contrast, the average ASDA store had only 65,000 square feet and did 60 percent of sales in grocery items.

The response in Europe to Wal-Mart was immediate and dramatic. Competitors scrambled to match Wal-Mart's low prices, long hours, and friendly service. Some firms combined to strengthen their operations. For example, France's Carrefour SA chain of hypermarkets combined forces with competitor, Promodes, in a $16.5 billion deal. In 1999, Carrefour dominated the European market with 9,089 locations. It was also one of the world's largest retailers with market dominance in Europe and in Latin America and Asia.

Wal-Mart's initial effort to enter China fell apart in 1996 when Wal-Mart and Thailand's Charoen Pokphand Group terminated an eighteen-month-old joint venture because of management differences. Wal-Mart decided to consolidate its operations with five stores in the Hong Kong border city of Shenzhen, one in Dalian, and another in Kumming. Although management had plans to open ten additional stores in China by the end of 2000, analysts concluded that the company was taking a low-profile approach because of possible competitive response and government restrictions. Beijing restricted the operations of foreign retailers in China, requiring them, for instance, to have government-backed partners. In Shenzhen, it limited the number of stores Wal-Mart could open. Planned expansion in the China market came as China prepared to enter the World Trade Organization and its economy showed signs of accelerating. At the beginning of 2000, Wal-Mart operated five supercenters in South Korea.

The international expansion accelerated management's plans for the development of Wal-Mart as a global brand along the lines of Coca-Cola, Disney, and McDonald's. "We are a global brand name," said Bobby Martin, an early president of the international division of Wal-Mart. "To customers everywhere it means low cost, best value, greatest selection of quality merchandise and highest standards of customer service," he noted. Some changes were mandated in Wal-Mart's international operations to meet local tastes and intense competitive conditions. "We're building companies out there," said Martin. "That's like starting Wal-Mart all over again in South America or Indonesia or China." Although stores in different international markets would coordinate purchasing to gain leverage with suppliers, developing new technology and planning overall strategy would be done from Wal-Mart headquarters in Bentonville, Arkansas. At the beginning of 2000, the international division of Wal-Mart operated 572 discount stores, 383 supercenters, and forty-nine Sam's Clubs. Wal-Mart's international unit accounted for $22.7 billion in sales in 1999. Exhibit 4 shows the countries in which stores were operated and the number of units in each country.

Decisionmaking in a Market-Oriented Firm

One principle that distinguished Wal-Mart was the unusual depth of employee involvement in company affairs. Corporate strategies put emphasis on human resources management. Wal-Mart employees became associates, a name borrowed from Sam Walton's early association with the JC Penney Co. Input was encouraged at meetings at both the store and corporate level. The firm hired employees locally and provided training programs. Through a "letter to the president" program, management encouraged employees to ask questions, and made words like *we, us,*

EXHIBIT 4

Wal-Mart International Division, 1999

Country	Stores
Mexico	460
United Kingdom	236
Canada	166
Germany	95
Brazil	16
Puerto Rico	15
Argentina	10
China	8
South Korea	5

Source: Wal-Mart, Hoover's Online.

and *our* part of the corporate language. Several special award programs recognized individual, department, and division achievement. Stock ownership and profit-sharing programs were introduced as part of a partnership concept

The corporate culture was complimented by the editors of the trade publication, *Mass Market Retailers,* when they recognized all 275,000 associates collectively as the "Mass Market Retailers of the Year." "The Wal-Mart associate," the editors noted, "in this decade that has come to symbolize all that is right with the American worker, particularly in the retailing environment and most particularly at Wal-Mart." The "store within a store" concept, as a Wal-Mart corporate policy, trained individuals to be merchants by being responsible for the performance of their own departments as if they were running their own businesses. Seminars and training programs afforded them opportunities to grow within the company. "People development, not just a good program for any growing company but a must to secure our future," is how Suzanne Allford, vice president of the Wal-Mart people division, explained the firm's decentralized approach to retail management development.

"The Wal-Mart way" was a phase that was used by management to summarize the firm's unconventional approach to business and the development of the corporate culture. As noted in a report referring to a recent development program: "We stepped outside our retailing world to examine the best managed companies in the United States in an effort to determine the fundamentals of their success and to 'benchmark' our own performances." "The name 'total quality management' (TQM) was used to identify this vehicle for proliferating the very best things we do while incorporating the new ideas our people have that will assure our future." In 1999, *Discount Store News* honored Wal-Mart Stores, Inc., as "Retailer of the Century" with a commemorative 200-page issue of the magazine.

The Growth Challenge

H. Lee Scott, Jr., indicated that he would never forget his first meeting with Sam Walton. "How old are you?" Walton asked the then thirty-year-old Scott, who had just taken a job overseeing the Wal-Mart trucking fleet. "Do you think you can do this job?" asked Walton. When Scott said yes, Walton agreed and said, "I reckon you can." More than twenty years later, as Wal-Mart's new CEO, Scott was facing his toughest challenge yet: keeping the world's biggest retailer on its phenomenal roll and delivering the huge sales and earnings increases that investors had come to expect from Wal-Mart over the years. Analysts had correctly projected that Wal-Mart would surpass General Motors to be ranked number 1 in revenue on the Fortune 500 list in 2000. The combination of growth and acquisition had caused revenue to make huge leaps every year. In 1999, revenues went up 20 percent, from $139 billion in 1998 to $165 billion. Earnings also increased in 1999 by 21 percent, to nearly $5.4 billion. Industry analysts noted that this growth was in addition to an 18 percent compound annual growth rate over the past decade.

Wal-Mart Stores, Inc., revolutionized American retailing with its focus on low costs, efficient customer service, and everyday low pricing to drive sales. Although the company had suffered though some years of lagging performance, it had experienced big gains from its move into the grocery business with one-stop supercenters and in international markets with acquisitions and new ventures. To keep it all going and growing was a major challenge. As the largest retailer in the world, the company and its leadership were challenged to find new areas to continue to increase sales and profits into the future. H. Lee Scott knew that an ambitious expansion program was necessary to allow the company to meet these objectives.

Appendix A: Wal-Mart Stores, Inc., Consolidated Balance Sheets and Operating Statements, 1998–1999*

Consolidated Statements of Income

	Fiscal years ended January 31		
	2000	**1999**	**1998**
Revenues			
Net sales	**$ 165,013**	$ 137,634	$117,958
Other income—net	**1,796**	1,574	1,341
	166,809	139,208	119,299
Costs and expenses			
Cost of sales	**129,664**	108,725	93,438
Operating, selling, and general and administrative expenses	**27,040**	22,363	19,358
Interest costs			
Debt	**756**	529	555
Capital leases	**266**	268	229
	157,726	131,885	113,580
Income before income taxes, minority interest, equity in unconsolidated subsidiaries, and cumulative effect of accounting change	**9,083**	7,323	5,719
Provision for income taxes			
Current	**3,476**	3,380	2,095
Deferred	**(138)**	(640)	20
	3,338	2,740	2,115
Income before minority interest, equity in unconsolidated subsidiaries, and cumulative effect of accounting change	**5,745**	4,583	3,604
Minority interest and equity in unconsolidated subsidiaries	**(170)**	(153)	(78)
Income before cumulative effect of accounting change	**5,575**	4,430	3,526
Cumulative effect of accounting change, net of tax benefit of $119	**(198)**	—	—
Net income	**$ 5,377**	$ 4,430	$ 3,526
Net income per common share			
Basic net income per common share			
Income before cumulative effect of accounting change	**$ 1.25**	$ 0.99	$ 0.78
Cumulative effect of accounting change, net of tax	**(0.04)**	–	–
Net income per common share	**$ 1.21**	$ 0.99	$ 0.78
Average number of common shares	**4,451**	4,464	4,516
Diluted net income per common share			
Income before cumulative effect of accounting change	**$ 1.25**	$ 0.99	$ 0.78
Cumulative effect of accounting change, net of tax	**(0.04)**	0.00	0.00
Net income per common share	**$ 1.20**	$ 0.99	$ 0.78
Average number of common shares	**4,474**	4,485	4,533
Pro forma amounts assuming accounting change had been in effect in fiscal 2000, 1999, and 1998			
Net income	**$ 5,575**	$ 4,393	$ 3,517
Net income per common share, basic and diluted	**$ 1.25**	$ 0.98	$ 0.78

*Amounts in millions except per-share data.

Appendix B: Wal-Mart Stores, Inc., Consolidated Balance Sheets and Operating Statements, 1998–1999*

Consolidated Balance Sheets

	January 31	
	2000	**1999**
Assets		
Current assets		
Cash and cash equivalents	$ 1,856	$ 1,879
Receivables	1,341	1,118
Inventories		
At replacement cost	20,171	17,549
Less LIFO reserve	378	473
Inventories at LIFO cost	19,793	17,076
Prepaid expenses and other	1,366	1,059
Total current assets	24,356	21,132
Property, plant, and equipment, at cost		
Land	8,785	5,219
Building and improvements	21,169	16,061
Fixtures and equipment	10,362	9,296
Transportation equipment	747	553
	41,063	31,129
Less accumulated depreciation	8,224	7,455
Net property, plant, and equipment	32,839	23,674
Property under capital lease		
Property under capital lease	4,285	3,335
Less accumulated amortization	1,155	1,036
Net property under capital leases	3,130	2,299
Other assets and deferred charges		
Net goodwill and other acquired intangible assets	9,392	2,538
Other assets and deferred charges	632	353
Total assets	$70,349	$49,996
Liabilities and shareholders' equity		
Current liabilities		
Commercial paper	$ 3,323	$ —
Accounts payable	13,105	10,257
Accrued liabilities	6,161	4,998
Accrued income taxes	1,129	501
Long-term debt due within one year	1,964	900
Obligations under capital leases due within one year	121	106
Total current liabilities	25,803	16,762
Long-term debt	13,672	6,908
Long-term obligations under capital leases	3,002	2,699
Deferred income taxes and other	759	716
Minority interest	1,279	1,799
Shareholders' equity		
Preferred stock ($.10 par value; 100 shares authorized, none issued)		
Common stock ($.10 par value; 5,500 shares authorized, 4,457 and 4,448 issued and outstanding in 2000 and 1999, respectively)	446	445
Capital in excess of par value	714	435
Retained earnings	25,129	20,741
Other accumulated comprehensive income	(455)	(509)
Total shareholders' equity	25,834	21,112
Total liabilities and shareholders' equity	$70,349	$49,996

*Amounts in millions.

Appendix C: Wal-Mart Stores, Inc., Financial Summary, 1990–2000*

Eleven-Year Financial Summary

	2000	1999	1998
Net sales	$165,013	$137,634	$ 117,958
Net sales increase	20%	17%	12%
Comparative store sales increase	8%	9%	6%
Other income—net	1,796	1,574	1,341
Cost of sales	129,664	108,725	93,438
Operating, selling, and general and administrative expenses	27,040	22,363	19,358
Interest costs			
Debt	756	529	555
Capital leases	266	268	229
Provision for income taxes	3,338	2,740	2,115
Minority interest and equity in unconsolidated subsidiaries	(170)	(153)	(78)
Cumulative effect of accounting change, net of tax	(198)	—	—
Net income	5,377	4,430	3,526
Per share of common stock			
Basic net income	1.21	0.99	0.78
Diluted net income	1.20	0.99	0.78
Dividends	0.20	0.16	0.14
Financial position			
Current assets	$ 24,356	$ 21,132	$ 19,352
Inventories at replacement cost	20,171	17,549	16,845
Less LIFO reserve	378	473	348
Inventories at LIFO cost	19,793	17,076	16,497
Net property, plant and equipment, and capital leases	35,969	25,973	23,606
Total assets	70,349	49,996	45,384
Current liabilities	25,803	16,762	14,460
Long-term debt	13,672	6,908	7,191
Long-term obligations under capital leases	3,002	2,699	2,483
Shareholders' equity	25,834	21,112	18,503
Financial ratios			
Current ratio	.9	1.3	1.3
Inventories/working capital	(13.7)	3.9	3.4
Return on assets†	9.8%§	9.6%	8.5%
Return on shareholders' equity‡	22.9%	22.4%	19.8%
Other year-end data			
Number of domestic Wal-Mart stores	1,801	1,869	1,921
Number of domestic Supercenters	721	564	441
Number of domestic Sam's Club units	463	451	443
International units	1,004	715	601
Number of associates	1,140,000	910,000	825,000
Number of shareholders	341,000	261,000	246,000

*Dollar amounts in millions except per-share data.

†Net income before minority interest, equity in unconsolidated subsidiaries, and cumulative effect of accounting change/average assets.

‡Net income/average shareholders' equity.

§Calculated without giving effect to the amount by which a lawsuit settlement exceeded established reserves.

The effects of the change in accounting method for Sam's Club membership revenue recognition would not have a material impact on this summary prior to 1998. Therefore, pro forma information as if the accounting change had been in effect for all years presented has not been provided.

Acquisition of the ASDA Group PLC and the company's related debt issuance had a significant impact on the fiscal 2000 amounts in this summary.

1997	1996	1995	1994	1993	1992	1991	1990
$104,859	$ 93,627	$ 82,494	$ 67,344	$ 55,484	$ 43,887	$ 32,602	$ 25,811
12%	13%	22%	21%	26%	35%	26%	25%
5%	4%	7%	6%	11%	10%	10%	11%
1,319	1,146	914	645	497	404	262	175
83,510	74,505	65,586	53,444	44,175	34,786	25,500	20,070
16,946	15,021	12,858	10,333	8,321	6,684	5,152	4,070
629	692	520	331	143	113	43	20
216	196	186	186	180	153	126	118
1,794	1,606	1,581	1,358	1,171	945	752	632
(27)	(13)	4	(4)	4	(1)	—	—
—	—	—	—	—	—	—	—
3,056	2,740	2,681	2,333	1,995	1,609	1,291	1,076
0.67	0.60	0.59	0.51	0.44	0.35	0.28	0.24
0.67	0.60	0.59	0.51	0.44	0.35	0.28	0.24
0.11	0.10	0.09	0.07	0.05	0.04	0.04	0.03
$ 17,993	$ 17,331	$ 15,338	$ 12,114	$ 10,198	$ 8,575	$ 6,415	$ 4,713
16,193	16,300	14,415	11,483	9,780	7,857	6,207	4,751
296	311	351	469	512	473	399	323
15,897	15,989	14,064	11,014	9,268	7,384	5,808	4,428
20,324	18,894	15,874	13,176	9,793	6,434	4,712	3,430
39,604	37,541	32,819	26,441	20,565	15,443	11,389	8,198
10,957	11,454	9,973	7,406	6,754	5,004	3,990	2,845
7,709	8,508	7,871	6,156	3,073	1,722	740	185
2,307	2,092	1,838	1,804	1,772	1,556	1,159	1,087
17,143	14,756	12,726	10,753	8,759	6,990	5,366	3,966
1.6	1.5	1.5	1.6	1.5	1.7	1.6	1.7
2.3	2.7	2.6	2.3	2.7	2.1	2.4	2.4
7.9%	7.8%	9.0%	9.9%	11.1%	12.0%	13.2%	14.8%
19.2%	19.9%	22.8%	23.9%	25.3%	26.0%	27.7%	30.9%
1,960	1,995	1,985	1,950	1,848	1,714	1,568	1,399
344	239	147	72	34	10	9	6
436	433	426	417	256	208	148	123
314	276	226	24	10	—	—	—
728,000	675,000	622,000	528,000	434,000	371,000	328,000	271,000
257,000	244,000	259,000	258,000	181,000	150,000	122,000	80,000

Appendix D: Wal-Mart Stores, Inc., Board of Directors and Executive Officers, January 31, 2000

Directors

John A. Cooper, Jr.	H. Lee Scott
Stephen Friedman	Jack C. Shewmaker
Stanley C. Gault	Donald G. Soderquist
David D. Glass	Dr. Paula Stern
Roland Hernandez	Jose Villarreal
Dr. Frederick S. Humphries	John T. Walton
E. Stanley Kroenke	S. Robson Walton
Elizabeth A. Sanders	

Officers

S. Robson Walton
Chairman of the Board

H. Lee Scott
President and CEO

David D. Glass
Chairman, Executive Committee of the Board

Donald G. Soderquist
Senior Vice Chairman

Paul R. Carter
Executive Vice President and Vice President,
    Wal-Mart Realty

Bob Connolly
Executive Vice President, Merchandise

Thomas M. Coughlin
Executive Vice President and President and CEO,
    Wal-Mart Stores Division

David Dible
Executive Vice President, Speciality Division

Michael Duke
Executive Vice President, Logistics

Thomas Grimm
Executive Vice President and President and CEO,
    Sam's Club

Don Harris
Executive Vice President, Operations

John B. Menzer
Executive Vice President, President, and CEO,
    International Division

Coleman Peterson
Executive Vice President, People Division

Thomas M. Schoewe
Executive Vice President and Chief Financial Officer

Robert K. Rhoads
Senior Vice President, General Counsel, and Secretary

J. J. Fitzsimmons
Senior Vice President, Finance, and Treasurer

Source: Wal-Mart Stores, Inc., 2000 Annual Report.

REFERENCES

Albright, Mark, "Changes in Store," *New York Times,* May 17, 1999, pp. 10, 12.

Bergman, Joan, "Saga of Sam Walton," *Stores,* January 1988, pp. 129–130+.

Boudette, Neil E., "Wal-Mart Plans Major Expansion in Germany," *Wall Street Journal,* July 20, 2000, p. A21.

Cummins, Chip, "Wal-Mart's Net Income Increases 28%, but Accounting Change Worries Investors," *Wall Street Journal,* August 10, 2000, p. A6.

"David Glass's Biggest Job Is Filling Sam's Shoes," *Business Month,* December 1988, p. 42.

Feldman, Amy, "How Big Can It Get?" *Money,* December 1999, pp. 158+.

Friedland, Johnathan, and Louise Lee, "The Wal-Mart Way Sometimes Gets Lost in Translation Overseas," *Wall Street Journal,* October 8, 1997, pp. A1, A12.

Gustke, Constance, "Smooth Operator," *Worth,* March 2000, pp. 41+.

Helliker, Kevin, "Wal-Mart's Store of the Future Blends Discount Prices, Department-Store Feel," *Wall Street Journal,* May 17, 1991, pp. B1, B8.

Helliker, Kevin, and Bob Ortega, "Falling Profit Marks End of Era at Wal-Mart," *Wall Street Journal,* January 18, 1996, p. B1.

"How the Stores Did," *Wall Street Journal,* May 5, 2000, p. B4.

Huey, John, "America's Most Successful Merchant," *Fortune,* September 23, 1991, pp. 46–48+.

Johnson, Jay L., "The Supercenter Challenge," *Discount Merchandiser,* August 1989, pp. 70+.

Komarow, Steven, "Wal-Mart Takes Slow Road in Germany," *USA Today,* May 5, 2000, p. 3B.

Krauss, Clifford, "Wal-Mart Learns a Hard Lesson," *International Herald Tribune,* December 6, 1999, p. 15.

Larrabee, John, "Wal-Mart Ends Vermont's Holdout," *USA Today,* September 19, 1995, p. 4B.

Lee, Louise, "Discounter Wal-Mart Is Catering to Affluent to Maintain Growth," *Wall Street Journal,* February 7, 1996, p. A1.

Lee, Louise, and Joel Millman, "Wal-Mart to Buy Majority Stake in Cifra," *Wall Street Journal,* June 4, 1997, pp. A3+.

Loomis, Carol J., "Sam Would Be Proud," *Fortune,* April 17, 2000, pp. 131+.

"Management Style: Sam Moore Walton," *Business Month,* May 1989, p. 38.

Marsch, Barbara, "The Challenge: Merchants Mobilize to Battle Wal-Mart in a Small Community," *Wall Street Journal,* June 5, 1991, pp. A1, A4.

Mason, Todd, "Sam Walton of Wal-Mart: Just Your Basic Homespun Billionaire," *Business Week,* October 14, 1985, pp. 142–143+.

Mitchener, Brandon, and David Woodruff, "French Merger of Hypermarkets Gets a Go-Ahead," *Wall Street Journal,* January 26, 2000, p. A19.

Nelson, Emily, "Wal-Mart to Build a Test Supermarket in Bid to Boost Grocery-Industry Share," *Wall Street Journal,* June 19, 1998, p. A4.

Nelson, Emily, and Kara Swisher, "Wal-Mart Eyes Public Sale of Web Unit," *Wall Street Journal,* January 7, 2000, p. A3.

"Our People Make the Difference: The History of Wal-Mart," video cassette, Bentonville, Arkansas: Wal-Mart Video Productions, 1991.

Peters, Tom J., and Nancy Austin, *A Passion For Excellence,* New York: Random House, pp. 266–267.

Rawn, Cynthia Dunn, "Wal-Mart vs. Main Street," *American Demographics,* June 1990, pp. 58–59.

"Retailer Completes Purchase of Wertkauf of Germany," *Wall Street Journal,* December 31, 1997, p. B3.

Rudnitsky, Howard, "How Sam Walton Does It," *Forbes,* August 16, 1982, pp. 42–44.

"Sam Moore Walton," *Business Month,* May 1989, p. 38.

Schwadel, Francine, "Little Touches Spur Wal-Mart's Rise," *Wall Street Journal,* September 22, 1989, p. B1.

Sears, Roebuck & Co., *Annual Report,* Chicago, Illinois: Sears, 1999.

Sheets, Kenneth R., "How Wal-Mart Hits Main St.," *U.S. News & World Report,* March 13, 1989, pp. 53–55.

Target Corporation, *Annual Report,* Minneapolis, Minnesota: Target, 1999.

"The Early Days: Walton Kept Adding a Few More Stores," *Discount Store News,* December 9, 1985, p. 61.

Tomlinson, Richard, "Who's Afraid of Wal-Mart?" *Fortune,* June 26, 2000, p. 186.

Trimble, Vance H., *Sam Walton: The Inside Story of America's Richest Man,* New York: Dutton, 1990.

Voyle, Susanna, "Asda Criticised for Price Claims," *Financial Times,* December 8, 1999, p. 3.

"Wal-Mart's Asda Says CEO to Head Europe Expansion," *Wall Street Journal Europe,* December 3, 1999, p. 6.

"Wal-Mart Spoken Here," *Business Week,* June 23, 1997, pp. 138+.

Wal-Mart Stores, Inc., *Annual Report,* Bentonville, Arkansas: Wal-Mart, 2000.

"Wal-Mart Takes a Stand," *The Economist,* May 22, 1999, p. 31.

"Wal-Mart: The Model Discounter," *Dun's Business Month,* December 1982, pp. 60–61.

"Wal-Mart Wins Again," *The Economist,* October 2, 1999, p. 33.

Walton, Sam, with John Huey, *Sam Walton Made in America,* New York: Doubleday Publishing Company, 1992.

Wonacott, Peter, "Wal-Mart Finds Market Footing in China," *Wall Street Journal,* July 17, 2000, p. A31.

"Work, Ambition—Sam Walton," press release, Corporate and Public Affairs, Wal-Mart Stores, Inc.

Zellner, Wendy, "Someday, Lee, This May All Be Yours," *Business Week,* November 15, 1999, pp. 84+.

Zimmerman, Ann, "Wal-Mart Posts 19% Profit Rise, Exceeding Analysts' Expectations," *Wall-Street Journal,* May 10, 2000, p. B8.

Zimmerman, Ann, "Wal-Mart to Open Reworked Web Site for Sams-Club.com, June 6, 2000, p. B8.

26 Wal-Mart's Mexican Adventure

This case was prepared by Charles W. L. Hill, the University of Washington.

Introduction

Wal-Mart is America's and the world's largest retailer. It was founded by the legendary Sam Walton in the 1960s, and by 2001, Wal-Mart generated over $100 billion in annual sales from 4,000 stores, more than 1,000 of which were now located outside the United States. The company operates three basic store formats: the traditional Wal-Mart stores, which sell a wide range of basic consumer merchandise, from household products to clothes and electronics; Wal-Mart supercenters, which are larger stores that have groceries added to the basic merchandising mix; and Sam's Clubs, which are deep discount stores that carry a limited range of low-priced merchandise and food. Although the company was still opening new stores in the United States in 2001, it had recognized since the early 1990s that its U.S. growth prospects were ultimately limited by market saturation. Believing that its unique culture, format, and operating systems would give it a competitive edge in many foreign markets, Wal-Mart embarked on an international expansion strategy in 1991, when it opened the first Sam's Club store in Mexico City. A decade later, Mexico is the brightest star in the company's international division, with over 500 Mexican stores generating $9 billion in sales. Getting to this point, however, was not easy. Wal-Mart had suf-

fered several setbacks along the way that might have discouraged a less ambitious and near-sighted rival from continuing.

Wal-Mart's Competitive Advantage

Wal-Mart's spectacular four-decade growth from a small Arkansas retailer to a national powerhouse was based on a first-class management team that pursued several innovative operations strategies. These strategies backed up the company's commitment to deliver a large selection of high-value merchandise at low cost to consumers.

The firm's early success was based partly on a strategy of locating in small southern towns that had no other major retail presence. When Wal-Mart entered most of these towns, its primary competitors were small mom-and-pop stores that had a much higher cost structure than the discounter. Wal-Mart quickly gained significant share in these towns and did not have to face competition from other discounters, such as Kmart, which were focused on large urban areas.

As the number of stores grew, Wal-Mart pioneered the development of a hub-and-spoke distribution system, where central distribution warehouses were strategically located to serve clusters of stores. This system allowed Wal-Mart to replenish stock in its stores rapidly and to keep the amount of store space that needed to be dedicated to inventory to a minimum. The results included higher sales per square foot and more rapid inventory turnover. This combination helped to increase store sales and drive down inventory and logistics costs. The firm was also one of the first to utilize computer-based information systems to track in-store sales and transmit this information to suppliers. The information provided by these systems was used to determine pricing and stocking strategy and to manage inventories better. The combination of state-of-the art information systems and the hub-and-spoke distribution system allowed Wal-Mart to build the leanest supply chain in the industry. Wal-Mart is still a leader today in information systems. All Wal-Mart stores, distribution centers, and suppliers are linked together via sophisticated information systems and satellite-based communications systems that allow for daily adjustments to orders, inventories, and prices.

Wal-Mart is also famous for a dynamic and egalitarian culture that grants major decisionmaking authority to store managers, department managers, and individual employees (who Wal-Mart refers to as "associates"). Wal-Mart is renowned for treating its employees extremely well, but at the same time, for demanding commitment and excellent performance from them. This culture is backed up with generous profit sharing and stock ownership plans for all employees, including associates, which makes every employee "think and behave like an owner of the company." Wal-Mart has thus developed a culture and a control system that create incentives for associates and managers to give their best for the company. The result is higher employee productivity, which again translates into lower cost.

As Wal-Mart has grown, it has also garnered significant leverage with its suppliers, whether they are small manufacturers or global enterprises, such as Procter & Gamble, for whom Wal-Mart is the largest single account. Wal-Mart has used this leverage to demand lower prices from its suppliers, and it passes the savings on to its customers in the form of "everyday low prices."

Mexican Genesis

By 1990, Wal-Mart was concerned that its growth rate in the United States would inevitably slow down. This trend would slow stock price appreciation for Wal-Mart, which would be bad news for the thousands of Wal-Mart associates who were also stockholders. The company embarked on two strategies to recharge its growth rate. The first was expansion into the grocery business with the opening of Wal-Mart supercenters that would stock food products in addition to Wal-Mart's traditional merchandise. The second strategy was international expansion.

At the time that Wal-Mart was considering going international, the United States was entering negotiations with Mexico and Canada for creating a North American free-trade area (subsequently called NAFTA). This piqued Wal-Mart's interest in Mexico. Historically, significant barriers to cross-border trade and investment, substantial state involvement in business activity, and high inflation had characterized the Mexican economy. Under the government of Carlos Salinas, a Harvard trained economist, however, Mexico had embraced free-market reforms. State-owned enterprises were being privatized. Barriers to trade and investment with the United States had already been lowered significantly by Salinas and would fall much further under the NAFTA proposal. Tariffs on goods imported from the United States had come down from as much as 100 percent in the mid 1980s, to a maximum of 20 percent by the early 1990s. Under NAFTA, many of these tariffs would fall to zero. Many barriers to cross-border investment had been eliminated. Salinas had also imposed a tight monetary policy, which had lowered Mexico's inflation rate into the single digits. The country's economy was growing at a 4 to 5 percent annual rate by the early 1990s, faster than that of the United States, while disposable income had increased by some 70 percent since Salinas took office in 1988. Although Mexico was still a very poor country by U.S. standards, approximately 30 million of its 80 million people could now be classified as middle class. This segment was concentrated in three main urban areas: Mexico City, Guadalajara, and Monterrey.

Although the Mexican retail market was still fragmented and dispersed, four national supermarket chains had emerged and accounted for over 30 percent of the retail market. The largest of these, Cifra, operated about 120 discount and grocery stores in 1991 and generated sales of approximately $2.2 billion. Wal-Mart founder Sam Walton had first met one of Cifra's three founding brothers, Jeronimo Arango, in 1990. The two men immediately hit it off, and both agreed that the free-trade deal being negotiated among Canada, Mexico, and the United States opened opportunities for Wal-Mart to cooperate with Cifra in Mexico.

Having decided that Mexico would be a good proving ground for its foreign growth strategy, Wal-Mart employees debated several options for expansion, including licensing its brand name to franchisees, expanding via wholly owned subsidiaries, or entering into a joint venture with a Mexican company such as Cifra. The company quickly concluded that its competitive advantage was based on the combination of corporate culture and its supporting information and logistics systems, and that such a combination would be difficult to transfer to franchisees. The management know-how that underlay Wal-Mart's culture and systems was simply not amenable to franchising. At the same time, Wal-Mart realized that it knew little about the culture and business systems in Mexico, so the company decided to enter into a fifty-fifty joint venture agreement with Cifra.

Teething Problems

Wal-Mart's Mexican expansion began with the establishment of a single Sam's Club store in Mexico City in 1991. In 1992, Wal-Mart established six more stores, all Sam's Clubs, in Mexico. In 1993, the company began to open stores under the Wal-Mart name. When the first store in Mexico City opened its doors, an enormous crowd showed up, and all seventy-two cash registers were ringing constantly. It didn't last. Within months, the sales rate at Wal-Mart's Mexican stores had slowed down considerably, not surprising perhaps in a country where per-capita income was only about $2,000 per year. But according to critics, the problems had more to do with missteps by Wal-Mart than low income levels.

When Wal-Mart opened its first store in Monterrey in 1993, it had to bar the doors to control the crowds. Soon the local press was lambasting the company, however, for charging 15 to 20 percent more for merchandise than it did at its Wal-Mart store across the border in Laredo, Texas, a two-hour drive to the north. A Wal-Mart spokesperson pointed out that the higher prices reflected the transportation costs between the Wal-Mart distribution center in Laredo and its Monterrey store. In addition, the NAFTA agreement had not yet been implemented, and high tariffs contributed to the higher prices. But Wal-Mart also conceded that it was having problems replicating its U.S. distribution system in Mexico. Poor infrastructure, crowded roads, and a lack of leverage with local suppliers (many of whom would not or could not deliver directly to Wal-Mart's stores or distribution centers, as was common in the United States), all led to higher prices and lower margins for Wal-Mart.

Another problem was getting the right selection of merchandise. Many of the first Wal-Mart stores in Mexico carried items that were popular in the United States but were rarely used in Mexico, like ice skates, riding lawn mowers, leaf blowers, and fishing tackle. Managers would slash prices on these items to move the inventory, only to find that Wal-Mart's automated information systems ordered more to replenish the depleted inventory.

Then there were problems with government bureaucrats. After the implementation of NAFTA in January 1994, Wal-Mart believed that things would get easier, but it was not to be. In the summer of 1994, Mexican government inspectors made a surprise visit to Wal-Mart's new superstore in Mexico City. The inspectors found thousands of products that they claimed were improperly labeled or lacked instructions in Spanish. The store was ordered shut for seventy-two hours while the oversights were corrected. This brush with what they saw as overzealous inspectors sobered Wal-Mart's managers. The 200,000-square-foot supercenter that was inspected carried about 80,000 products. Each now had to be labeled in Spanish to indicate the country of origin, contents, instructions, and, in some cases, an import permit number. The inspectors charged that about 11,700 pieces of merchandise lacked such labels. Wal-Mart's managers responded by pointing out that many of the targeted goods—about 40 percent or more—were purchased from a local Mexican distributor. Nevertheless, the regulators insisted that the retailer had ultimate responsibility for the labeling. Some Wal-Mart managers wondered if this kind of bureaucratic red tape was a deliberate attempt by government officials to raise the costs of doing business in Mexico and thereby frustrate Wal-Mart's expansion plans.

The 1994 Peso Crisis

As if these problems were not enough, in late 1994 the Mexican economy took a sharp turn for the worse. The Mexican currency, the peso, had been pegged to the value of the U.S. dollar since the early 1980s and was allowed to depreciate by only about 4 percent per year against the dollar. Since the mid

1980s, prices in Mexico had risen by about 45 percent more than had prices in the United States, making the current exchange rate increasingly difficult to maintain. In 1993 and 1994, the Mexican economy responded to the drop in tariff barriers by importing products at a rapid rate. By late 1994, Mexico was running a $17 billion annual deficit on merchandised trade, which amounted to about 6 percent of the country's GDP. Currency traders began to place large bets that the Mexican government would be forced to devalue the peso against the dollar. Fearing this outcome, foreign investors who had rushed into the country in 1993 and early 1994, buying Mexican stocks and pushing the stock market up to record levels, reversed their course and moved a lot of money out of the country.

The Mexican government stepped into the foreign exchange market to defend its currency, using its foreign exchange reserves to buy pesos. But the outward flow of funds was so great that Mexico soon realized that its strategy would only deplete its foreign exchange reserves. Accepting the inevitable, in December 1994 the Mexican government announced that it would no longer peg the peso against the dollar and would let it float freely on the foreign exchange market. Immediately the peso plunged, losing about 40 percent of its value against the dollar in a matter of days. The Mexican economy plunged into an economic recession.

For Wal-Mart and other American firms that had moved into Mexico to take advantage of NAFTA, this was a severe blow. By this time, Wal-Mart had sixty-three stores in Mexico, but many of them were still stocked with goods imported from the United States. The fall in the value of the peso meant that it now cost even more to bring in goods from the United States, while the economic recession that now gripped Mexico meant that consumers had even less to spend. Over the next two years, retail sales in Mexico were to fall by 16 percent. Wal-Mart, which had planned to open another twenty-five stores in 1995, quickly put its Mexican expansion plans on hold.

Expansion Resumes

Although Mexico was to experience a two-year economic slowdown, the United States economy continued to grow. With Mexican goods now costing less in the United States and with trade barriers reduced or eliminated under NAFTA, Mexican exports boomed.

Foreign companies began to invest heavily in the country, seeing it as a low-cost location from which to export to its giant neighbor next door. The combination of an export boom and rapid foreign direct investment created jobs and helped to lift the Mexican economy out of its slump. Seeing that the corner was being turned, Wal-Mart's expansion plans were back on track by late 1995.

By mid 1997, Wal-Mart had about 145 stores in Mexico. Unlike several other foreign retailers, it had decided to take advantage of the economic slump to build its market share. The company was also making strong improvements in its operating efficiency. It had opened a distribution center in Mexico City, and it rapidly became the most efficient in the entire Wal-Mart system, in part due to very low labor costs. This allowed Wal-Mart to start reducing its inventory and logistics costs. Wal-Mart had also struck a three-way partnership with EASO, a Mexican trucking company, and MS Carriers Corp, a U.S. trucking company that does significant work for Wal-Mart in the United States. Under the agreement, MS Carriers shared its fleet of modern trucks, as well as its satellite systems designed to help plan delivery times, with EASO. This arrangement helped EASO cut its costs by 25 percent, and it passed the savings on to Wal-Mart, which now uses 200 of EASO's trucks to run its Mexican logistics system.

Wal-Mart also started to sell far more Mexican goods, in part because many of its suppliers had themselves located in Mexico to take advantage of lower production costs and the advantages under NAFTA. In an example of the savings this strategy produced, Wal-Mart officials cite the case of a Vega television from Sony. Imported from Japan, the combination of transportation costs and a 23 percent tariff meant that the television retailed for $1,600 in Wal-Mart's Mexican store, out of the reach of all but the most affluent Mexican consumers. But in 1999, Sony built a Vega television factory in Mexico to take advantage of NAFTA. The television now costs about $600 in Mexico, and sales are picking up.

Wal-Mart had also learned from its early mistakes and thus improved the mix of product offerings at its Mexican stores. Slow-moving items such as leaf blowers had been replaced by items that sold well in Mexico but would not in the United States, such as maids' uniforms. As its scale of operations in Mexico grew, Wal-Mart was also able to use its purchase volume to gain leverage with suppliers and bargain down prices in return for large purchase volumes. Wal-Mart then passed these prices on to consumers, enabling the company to gain market share and remain profitable even as total retail spending in Mexico shrank during 1995 and 1996. In contrast, Sears and Kmart, two U.S. competitors that had entered Mexico at the same time, left the country.

In mid 1997, Wal-Mart signaled its continuing commitment to Mexico by purchasing a controlling interest in its joint venture partner, Cifra. By combining Cifra's stores with the stores established by the joint venture, Wal-Mart now had 373 stores in Mexico, making it the largest retailer in the country by far. The new company was then listed on Mexico's stock exchange, the Bolsa, as Wal-Mart de Mexico (it soon become known as WalMex). The listing allowed Wal-Mart to begin introducing the same stock-based incentive plans for its associates in Mexico that had worked so well in the United States. Wal-Mart retained a 54 percent stake in WalMex, which it raised to 60 percent in April 2000.

By 1999, Wal-Mart felt that it had improved its cost structure in Mexico to such an extent that it could now start to be more aggressive about passing on cost savings to Mexican consumers. In August 1999, it closed down a supercenter in Mexico City for a single day and marked down all prices by 16 percent. It then reopened under the banner of "everyday low pricing." Sales surged, with the growth in volume more than making up for the lower prices. The experiment was such a success that Wal-Mart rolled out the program in all of its Mexican supercenters a month later. In May 2000, the program was extended to cover all Wal-Mart stores in Mexico. By July 2001, WalMex same-store sales growth exceeded that of competitors for eight out of the last twelve months, and for seven months in a row.

REFERENCES

DePalma, A., "Big Companies in Mexico Among the Peso's Worst Victims," *New York Times,* January 30, 1995, p. D4.

Ginns, J. J., "Wal-Mart Ventures into Mexico," Harvard Business School Case # 9-793-071, December 1992.

Luhnow D., "How NAFTA Helped Wal-Mart Reshape the Mexican Market," *Wall Street Journal,* August 31, 2001, pp. A1, A2.

Smith, G., "NAFTA: A Green Light for Red Tape," *Business Week,* July 25, 1994, p. 48.

"Wal-Mart: Mexico's Largest Retailer," *Chain Store Age,* June 2001, pp. 52–54.

Wal-Mart 10K reports, 1996–2000, news releases, and other information posted on the company's web site (www.wal-mart.com).

Walton, S., *Made in America,* New York: Bantam Books, 1992.

Kmart Corporation: Seeking Customer Acceptance and Preference

27

This case was prepared by James W. Camerius, Northern Michigan University.

On June 1, 2000, the search for the new chairman and chief executive officer of Kmart Corporation was over. Charles C. Conaway, a thirty-nine-year-old drugstore chain executive, was selected to fill the position. His appointment meant that the strategic direction of Kmart would come from a man who was previously unknown outside the drugstore industry. He would have to provide an answer to a crucial question: How can Kmart respond to the challenges of industry leader Wal-Mart Stores, Inc., in the extremely competitive arena of discount retailing?

As president and chief operating officer of CVS Corporation, Conaway was the number 2 executive at the nation's largest drugstore chain, whose annual sales were about half those of Kmart's annual revenues of $36 billion. By all accounts, Conaway had made a sizable contribution in sales, earnings, and market value at CVS, Inc., headquartered in Woonsocket, Rhode Island. CVS had 1999 sales of $18 billion, with 4,100 stores. Conaway, who became president and chief operating officer of CVS in 1998, was responsible for merchandising, advertising, store operations, and logistics. After joining the firm in 1992, he helped engi-

This case is intended to be used as a basis for class discussion rather than as an illustration of either effective or ineffective handling of the situation. Reprinted by permission of James W. Camerius.

neer the restructuring of the then parent Melville Corporation, a diversified retailer, into a successful drugstore chain. Conaway said in an interview upon assuming his new position with Kmart that his primary task would be to improve customer service, productivity of resources, and problems with out-of-stock merchandise. Setting the stage for a new direction, Conaway said, "Customer service is going to be at the top. We're going to measure it and we're going to tie incentives around it."

Floyd Hall, the previous chairman, president, and chief executive officer of Kmart since June 1995, appeared pleased with the appointment. He had announced two years earlier that he wanted to retire, and now he would be able to do so. In the last five years, Hall had restored Kmart profitability and made improvements in store appearance and merchandise selection. Analysts had noted, however, that the firm lacked a definable niche in discount retailing. Studies had shown that number 1 ranked Wal-Mart, originally a rural retailer, had continued to be known for lower prices. Target Corporation, number 3 in sales, had staked out a niche as a merchandiser of discounted upscale products. Kmart was left without a feature that would give it competitive distinction in the marketplace.

Kmart's financial results in the first quarter of fiscal 2000 reported that net income fell 61 percent, to $22 million. The decline ended a string of fifteen consecutive quarters of profit increases that Hall felt had signaled a turnaround at the discount chain. Hall was very optimistic, however, about the company's future. The financial information over the previous periods had convinced him that a new corporate strategy that he introduced would revitalize Kmart's core business, its 2,171 discount stores, and would put the company on the road to recovery. Industry analysts had noted that Kmart, once an industry leader, had posted eleven straight quarters of disappointing earnings prior to 1998 and had been dogged by persistent bankruptcy rumors. Analysts cautioned that much of Kmart's recent growth reflected the strength of the consumer economy and that uncertainty continued to exist about the company's future in a period of slower economic growth.

Kmart Corporation was one of the world's largest mass-merchandise retailers. After several years of restructuring, it was composed largely of general merchandise businesses in the form of traditional Kmart discount department stores and Big Kmart stores (general merchandise and convenience items) as well as Super Kmart Centers (food and general merchandise). It operated in all fifty states of the United States and in Puerto Rico, Guam, and the U.S. Virgin Islands. It also had equity interests in Meldisco subsidiaries of Footstar, Inc., which operated Kmart footwear departments. Measured in sales volume, it was the third largest retailer and the second largest discount department store chain in the United States.

The discount department store industry was perceived by many to have reached maturity. As part of that industry, Kmart had a retail management strategy that was developed in the late 1950s and revised in the early 1990s. The firm was in a dilemma in terms of corporate strategy. The problem was how to lay a foundation for providing a new direction that would reposition the firm in a fiercely competitive environment.

The Early Years

Kmart was the outgrowth of an organization founded in 1899 in Detroit by Sebastian S. Kresge. The first S. S. Kresge store represented a new type of retailing that featured low-priced merchandise for cash in low-budget, relatively small (4,000- to 6,000-

square-foot) buildings with sparse furnishings. The adoption of the "5¢ and 10¢" or "variety store" concept, pioneered by F. W. Woolworth Company in 1879, led to rapid and profitable development of what was then the S. S. Kresge Company.

Kresge believed it could substantially increase its retail business by centralizing buying and control, developing standardized store operating procedures, and expanding into heavy traffic areas with new stores. In 1912, the firm was incorporated in Delaware. It had eighty-five stores with sales of $10,325,000, and, next to Woolworth's, was the largest variety chain in the world. In 1916, it was reincorporated in Michigan. Over the next forty years, the firm experimented with mail-order catalogs, full-line department stores, self-service, several price lines, and the opening of stores in planned shopping centers. It continued its emphasis, however, on variety stores.

By 1957, corporate management became aware that the development of supermarkets and the expansion of drugstore chains into general merchandise lines had made inroads into market categories previously dominated by variety stores. It also became clear that a new form of store with a discount merchandising strategy was emerging.

The Cunningham Connection

In 1957, in an effort to regain competitiveness and possibly save the company, Frank Williams, then president of Kresge, nominated Harry B. Cunningham as general vice president. This maneuver was undertaken to free Cunningham, who had worked his way up the ranks in the organization, from operating responsibility. He was being groomed for the presidency and was given the assignment of studying existing retailing businesses and recommending marketing changes.

In his visits to Kresge stores and those of the competition, Cunningham became interested in discounting—particularly the discounting operations of a new store in Garden City, Long Island. Eugene Ferkauf had recently opened large discount department stores called E. J. Korvette. The stores had a discount mass-merchandising emphasis that featured low prices and margins, high turnover, large freestanding departmentalized units, ample parking, and a location typically in the suburbs.

Cunningham was impressed with the discount concept, but he knew he first had to convince the Kresge board of directors, whose support would be necessary for any new strategy to succeed. He studied E. J. Korvette for two years and presented Kmart with the following recommendation:

> We can't beat the discounters operating under the physical constraints and the self-imposed merchandise limitations of variety stores. We can join them—and not only join them, but with our people, procedures, and organization, we can become a leader in the discount industry.

In a speech delivered at the University of Michigan, Cunningham made his management approach clear by concluding with an admonition from the British author, Sir Hugh Walpole: "Don't play for safety, it's the most dangerous game in the world."

The board of directors at Kmart had a difficult job. Change is never easy, especially when the company has established procedures in place and a proud heritage. Before the first presentation to the board could be made, rumors were circulating that one shocked senior executive had said:

> We have been in the variety business for sixty years—we know everything there is to know about it, and we're not doing very well in that, and you want to get us into a business we don't know anything about.

The board of directors eventually accepted Cunningham's recommendations. When president Frank Williams retired, Cunningham became the new president and chief executive officer and was directed to proceed with his recommendations.

The Birth of Kmart

Management conceived the original Kmart as a conveniently located, one-stop shopping unit where customers could buy a wide variety of quality merchandise at discount prices. The typical Kmart store was 75,000 square feet, all on one floor. It generally stood by itself in a high-traffic, suburban area, with plenty of parking. All stores had a similar floor plan.

The firm made an $80 million commitment in leases and merchandise for thirty-three stores before the first Kmart opened in 1962 in Garden City, Michigan. As part of this strategy, management decided to rely on the strengths and abilities of its own people to make decisions rather than employing outside experts for advice.

The original Kresge 5¢ & 10¢ variety store operation was characterized by low gross margins, high turnover, and concentration on return on investment. The main difference in the Kmart strategy would be the offering of a much wider merchandise mix.

The company had the knowledge and ability to merchandise 50 percent of the departments in the planned Kmart merchandise mix, and contracted for operation of the remaining departments. In the following years, Kmart took over most of those departments originally contracted to licensees. Eventually, all departments, except shoes, were operated by Kmart.

By 1987, the twenty-fifth anniversary year of the opening of the first Kmart store in America, sales and earnings of Kmart Corporation were at all-time highs. The company was the world's largest discount retailer, with sales of $25,627 million, and operated 3,934 general merchandise and specialty stores. On April 6, 1987, Kmart Corporation announced that it agreed to sell most of its remaining Kresge variety stores in the United States to McCrory Corporation, a unit of the closely held Rapid American Corporation of New York.

The Nature of the Competitive Environment
A Changing Marketplace

The retail sector of the United States economy went through several dramatic and turbulent changes during the 1980s and early 1990s. Retail analysts concluded that many retail firms were negatively affected by increased competitive pressures, sluggish consumer spending, slower than anticipated economic growth in North America, and recessions abroad. As one retail consultant noted:

> The structure of distribution in advanced economies is currently undergoing a series of changes that are as profound in their impact and as pervasive in their influence as those that occurred in manufacturing during the nineteenth century.

This changing environment affected the discount department store industry. Nearly a dozen firms, like

E. J. Korvette, W. T. Grant, Arlans, Atlantic Mills, and Ames, filed for bankruptcy or planned a reorganization. Some firms, like Woolworth (Woolco Division), had withdrawn from the field entirely after years of disappointment. St. Louis–based May Department Stores sold its Caldor and Venture discount divisions, each with annual sales of more than $1 billion. Venture announced liquidation in early 1998.

Senior management at Kmart felt that most of the firms that had difficulty in the industry faced the same situation. First, they were very successful five or ten years ago but had not changed and therefore had become somewhat dated. Management that had a historically successful formula, particularly in retailing, was perceived as having difficulty adapting to change, especially at the peak of success. Management would wait too long when faced with a threat in the environment and then would have to scramble to regain competitiveness.

Wal-Mart Stores, Inc., based in Bentonville, Arkansas, was an exception. It was especially growth oriented and had emerged in 1991 as the nation's largest retailer as well as the largest discount department store chain in sales volume, and continued in that position through 2000. Operating under various names and formats, nationally and internationally, it included Wal-Mart stores, Wal-Mart supercenters, and Sam's Warehouse Clubs. The firm found early strength in cultivating rural markets, merchandise restocking programs, "everyday low pricing," and the control of operations through companywide computer programs that linked cash registers to corporate headquarters.

Sears, Roebuck & Co., in a state of stagnated growth for several years, completed a return to its retailing roots by spinning off to shareholders its $9 billion controlling stake in its Allstate Corporation insurance unit and the divestment of financial services. After unsuccessfully experimenting with an everyday low price strategy, management chose to refine its merchandising program to meet the needs of middle market customers, who were primarily women, by focusing on product lines in apparel, home, and automotive.

Many retailers, such as Target Corporation (formerly Dayton Hudson), which adopted the discount concept, attempted generally to go after an upscale customer. The upscale customer tended to have an annual household income of $25,000 to $44,000. Other segments of the population were served by firms like Ames Department Stores, Rocky Hill, Connecticut which appealed to outsized, older, and lower-income workers, and by Shopko Stores, Inc., Green Bay, Wisconsin, which attempted to serve the upscale rural consumer.

Kmart executives found that discount department stores were being challenged by several other retail formats. Some retailers were assortment oriented, with a much greater depth of assortment within a given product category. Toys "R" Us was an example of a firm that operated 20,000-square-foot toy supermarkets. Its prices were very competitive within an industry that was very competitive. When the consumers entered a Toys "R" Us facility, there was usually no doubt in their minds that if the product wasn't there, no one else had it. In the late 1990s, however, Toys "R" Us was challenged by Wal-Mart and other firms that offered higher service levels, more aggressive pricing practices, and more-focused merchandise selections.

Some retailers were experimenting with the off-price apparel concept, where name brands and designer goods were sold at 20 to 70 percent discounts. Others, such as Home Depot and Menards, operated home improvement centers that were warehouse-style stores with a wide range of hard-line merchandise for both do-it-yourselfers and professionals. Still others opened drug supermarkets that offered a wide variety of high-turnover merchandise in a convenient location. In these cases, competition was becoming more risk oriented by putting $3 or $4 million in merchandise at retail value in an 80,000-square-foot facility and offering genuinely low prices. Jewel-Osco stores in the Midwest, Rite Aid, CVS, and a series of independents were examples of organizations employing the entirely new concept of the drug supermarket.

The competition was offering something that was new and different in terms of depth of assortment, competitive price image, and format. Kmart management perceived this as a threat because these were viable businesses that hindered the firm in its ability to improve and maintain market share in specific merchandise categories. An industry competitive analysis is shown in Exhibit 1.

Expansion and Contraction

When Joseph E. Antonini was appointed chairman of Kmart Corporation in October 1987, he was charged with the responsibility of maintaining and eventually

EXHIBIT 1

An Industry Competitive Analysis, 1999

	Kmart	Wal-Mart	Sears	Target
Sales (millions)	$35,925	$165,013	$41,071	$33,702
Net income (millions)	403	5,575	1,453	1,144
Sales growth	6.6%	20%	2.7%	10%
Profit margin	1.1%	3.4%	2.8%	3.4%
Sales/square feet	233	374	318	242
Return/equity	6.4%	22.9%	23%	19.5%

Number of stores

Kmart Corporation
   Kmart Traditional Discount Stores—202
   Big Kmart—1,860
   Super Kmart Centers—105

Wal-Mart Stores, Inc. (includes international)
   Wal-Mart Discount Stores—2,373
   Supercenters—1,104
   Sam's Clubs—512

Sears, Roebuck & Company
   Full-line stores—858
   Hardware stores—267

Sears dealer stores—738
Sears automotive stores:
   Sears Auto Centers—798
   National Tire and Battery stores—310
Contract sales
The Great Indoors (prototype decorating)—2

Target Corporation
   Target—912
   Mervyn's—267
   Department store division—64

Source: Company annual reports.

accelerating the chain's record of growth, despite a mature retail marketplace. He moved to string experimental formats into profitable chains. As he noted:

> Our vision calls for the constant and never-ceasing exploration of new modes of retailing, so that our core business of U.S. Kmart stores can be constantly renewed and reinvigorated by what we learn from our other businesses.

In the mid 1970s and throughout the 1980s, Kmart became involved in the acquisition or development of several smaller new operations. Kmart Insurance Services, Inc., acquired as Planned Marketing Associates in 1974, offered a full line of life, health, and accident insurance centers located in twenty-seven Kmart stores, primarily in the South and Southwest.

In 1982, Kmart initiated its own off-price specialty apparel concept called Designer Depot. A total of twenty-eight Designer Depot stores were opened in 1982 to appeal to customers who wanted quality upscale clothing at budget prices. A variation of this concept, called Garment Rack,

was opened to sell apparel that normally would not be sold in Designer Depot. A distribution center was added in 1983 to supplement both. Neither venture was successful.

Kmart also attempted an unsuccessful joint venture with the Hechinger Company of Washington, D.C., a warehouse home-center retailer. After much deliberation, however, Kmart chose instead in 1984 to acquire Home Centers of America of San Antonio, Texas, which operated 80,000-square-foot warehouse home centers. The new division, renamed Builders Square, had grown to 167 units by 1996. It capitalized on Kmart's real estate, construction, and management expertise and on Home Centers of America's merchandising expertise. Builders Square was sold in 1997 to the Hechinger Company. On June 11, 1999, Hechinger filed for Chapter 11 bankruptcy protection. As a result, Kmart recorded a noncash charge of $354 million that reflected the impact of lease obligations for former Builders Square locations that were guaranteed by Kmart.

Waldenbooks, a chain of 877 bookstores, was acquired from Carter, Hawley, Hale, Inc., in 1984. It was part of a strategy to capture a greater share of the market with a product category that Kmart already had in its stores. Kmart management had been interested in the book business for some time and took advantage of an opportunity in the marketplace to build on its common knowledge base. Borders Books and Music, an operator of fifty large-format superstores, became part of Kmart in 1992 to form the "Borders Group," a division that would include Waldenbooks. The Borders Group, Inc., was sold during 1995.

The Bruno's, Inc., a joint venture formed a partnership with Kmart in 1987 to develop large combination grocery and general merchandise stores, or "hypermarkets," called American Fare. The giant, one-stop-shopping facilities of 225,000 square feet traded on the grocery expertise of Bruno's and the general merchandise of Kmart to offer a wide selection of products and services at discount prices. A similar venture, called Super Kmart Center, represented later thinking on combination stores with a smaller size and format. In 2000, Kmart operated 105 Super Kmart Centers, all in the United States.

In 1988, the company acquired a controlling interest in Makro Inc., a Cincinnati-based operator of warehouse club stores. With annual sales of about $300 million, Makro operated member-only stores that were stocked with low-priced fresh and frozen groceries, apparel, and durable goods in suburbs of Atlanta, Cincinnati, Washington, D.C., and Philadelphia. Pace Membership Warehouse, Inc., a similar operation, was acquired in 1989. The club stores were sold in 1994.

PayLess Drug Stores, a chain that operated superdrugstores in several western states, was sold in 1994 to Thrifty PayLess Holdings, Inc., an entity in which Kmart maintained a significant investment. Interests in the Sports Authority, an operator of large-format sporting goods stores that Kmart acquired in 1990, were disposed of during 1995.

On the international level, an interest in Coles Myer, Ltd., Australia's largest retailer, was sold in November 1994. Interests in thirteen Kmart general merchandise stores in the Czech and Slovak republics were sold to Tesco PLC, one of the United Kingdom's largest retailers, at the beginning of 1996. In February 1998, Kmart stores in Canada were sold to Hudson's Bay Co., a Canadian chain of historic full-service department stores. The interest in Kmart Mexico, S.A. de C.V., was disposed of in fiscal year 1997.

Founded in 1988, OfficeMax, with 328 stores, was one of the largest operators of high-volume, deep-discount office products superstores in the United States. It became a greater-than-90-percent-owned Kmart unit in 1991. Kmart's interest in OfficeMax was sold during 1995. In November 1995, Kmart also sold its auto service center business to a new corporation controlled by Penske Corporation. In connection with the sale, Kmart and Penske entered into a sublease arrangement concerning the operation of Penske Auto Service Centers.

During 1999, Kmart signed agreements with Supervalu, Inc., and Fleming Companies, Inc., under which both would assume responsibility for the distribution and replenishment of grocery-related products to all Kmart stores. Kmart also maintained an equity interest in Meldisco subsidiaries of Footstar, Inc., operators of footwear departments in Kmart stores.

The Maturation of Kmart

Early corporate research revealed that, on the basis of convenience, Kmart served 80 percent of the population. One study concluded that one out of every two adults in the United States shopped at a Kmart at least once a month. Despite this popular appeal, strategies that had allowed the firm to have something for everybody were no longer felt to be appropriate for the new millennium. Kmart found that it had a broad customer base because it operated on a national basis. Its early strategies had assumed the firm was serving everyone in the markets where it was established.

Kmart was often perceived as aiming at the low-income consumer. The financial community believed the original Kmart customer was blue collar, low-income, and upper lower class. The market served, however, was more professional and middle class because Kmart stores were initially built in suburban communities where that population lived.

Although Kmart had made a major commitment in more recent years to secondary or rural markets, these areas had previously not been cultivated. In its initial strategies, the firm perceived the rural consumer as different from the urban or suburban customer. In re-addressing the situation, it discovered that its product assortments in rural areas were too limited and there were too many preconceived notions about what the Nebraska farmer really wanted. The firm discovered that the rural consumer didn't always shop for bib overalls and shovels but for microwave ovens, in other words, the same things that everyone else shopped for.

One goal was not to attract more customers but to get the customer coming in the door to spend more. Once in the store, the customer was thought to demonstrate more divergent tastes. The upper-income consumer would buy more health and beauty aids, cameras, and sporting goods. The lower-income consumer would buy toys and clothing. In the process of trying to capture a larger share of the market and get people to spend more, the firm began to recognize a market that was more upscale. When consumer research was conducted and management examined the profile of the trade area and the profile of the person who shopped at Kmart in the past month, they were found to be identical. Kmart was predominately serving the suburban consumer in suburban locations. In 1997, Kmart's primary target customers were women between the ages of twenty-five and forty-five years, with children at home and with annual household incomes between $20,000 and $50,000. The core Kmart shopper averaged 4.3 visits to a Kmart store per month. The purchase amount per visit was $40. The purchase rate was 95 percent during a store visit. The firm estimated that 180 million people shopped at Kmart in an average year.

In lifestyle research in markets served by the firm, Kmart determined there were more two-income families, families were having fewer children, there were more working wives, and customers tended to be homeowners. Customers were very careful about how they spent their money and were perceived as wanting quality. This was in distinct contrast to the 1960s and early 1970s, which tended to have the orientation of a throwaway society. The customer now said, "What we want are products that will last longer. We'll have to pay more for them but we still want them and at the lowest price possible." Customers wanted better quality products but still demanded competitive prices. According to a Kmart annual report, "Consumers today are well educated and informed. They want good value and they know it when they see it. Price remains a key consideration, but the consumer's new definition of value includes quality as well as price."

Corporate management at Kmart considered the discount department store to be a mature idea.

Although maturity was sometimes looked on with disfavor, Kmart executives felt that naturity did not mean a lack of profitability or lack of opportunity to increase sales. The industry was perceived as being "reborn." In this context, in the 1990s a series of new retailing strategies designed to upgrade the Kmart image were developed.

The 1990 Renewal Program

The strategies that emerged to confront a changing environment were the result of an overall reexamination of existing corporate strategies. This program included accelerated store expansion and refurbishing, capitalization on dominant lifestyle departments, centralized merchandising, more capital investment in retail automation, an aggressive and focused advertising program, and continued growth through new specialty retail formats. The initial 1990, five-year, $2.3 billion program involved almost all Kmart discount stores. There would be approximately 250 new full-size Kmart stores, 620 enlargements, 280 relocations, and thirty closings. In addition, 1,260 stores would be refurbished to bring their layout and fixtures up to new-store standards. Another program introduced in 1996 resulted in an additional $1.1 billion being spent to upgrade Kmart stores. By year-end 1999, 1,860 new Big Kmart stores offered more pleasant shopping experiences thanks to the updated and easy-to-shop departmental adjacencies, better signing and lighting, wider aisles, and more attractive in-store presentations.

One area receiving initial attention was improvement in the way products were displayed. The traditional Kmart layout was by product category. Often the locations for departments were holdovers from the variety store. Many departments would not give up prime locations. As part of the new marketing strategy, the shop concept was introduced. Management recognized that it had a sizable "do-it-yourself" store. As planning management discussed the issue, "nobody was aware of the opportunity. The hardware department was right smack in the center of the store because it was always there. The paint department was over here and the electrical department was over there. All we had to do," management contended, "was put them all in one spot and everyone could see that we had a very respectable 'do-it-yourself' department." The concept resulted in several new departments such as "Soft Goods for the Home," "Kitchen

Korners," and "Home Electronic Centers." The goal behind each department was to sell an entire lifestyle-oriented concept to consumers, making goods complementary so shoppers would want to buy several interrelated products rather than just one item.

Name brands were added in soft and hard goods because management recognized that the customer transferred the product quality of branded goods to perceptions of private label merchandise. In the eyes of Kmart management, "If you sell Wrangler, there is good quality. Then the private label must be good quality." The company increased its emphasis on trusted national brands, such as Rubbermaid, Procter & Gamble, and Kodak, and on major strategic vendor relationships. In addition it began to enhance its private-label brands such as Kathy Ireland, Jaclyn Smith, Route 66, and Sesame Street in apparel. Additional private-label merchandise included K Gro in home gardening, American Fare in grocery and consumables, White-Westinghouse in appliances, and Penske Auto Centers in automotive services. Some private labels were discontinued following review.

Kmart hired Martha Stewart, an upscale Connecticut author of lavish best-selling books on cooking and home entertaining, as its lifestyle spokesperson and consultant. Martha Stewart was featured as a corporate symbol for housewares and associated products in advertising and in-store displays. Management visualized her as the next Betty Crocker, a fictional character created some years ago by General Mills, Inc., and a representative of its interest in lifestyle trends. The Martha Stewart Everyday home fashion product line was introduced in 1995 and was expanded in 1996 and 1997. A separate division was established to manage strategy for all Martha Stewart–label goods and programs. Merchandise was featured in the redesigned once-a-week Kmart newspaper circular, which carried the advertising theme: "The quality you need, the price you want."

Several thousand prices were reduced to maintain "price leadership across America." As management noted, "It is absolutely essential that we provide our customers with good value—quality products at low prices." Although lowering of prices hurt margins and contributed to an earnings decline, management felt that unit turnover of items with lowered prices enabled "Kmart to maintain its pricing leadership [and] will have a most positive impact on our business in the years ahead."

A centralized merchandising system was introduced to improve communication. A computerized, highly automated replenishment system tracked how quickly merchandise sold and, just as quickly, put fast-moving items back on the shelves. Satellite capability and a point-of-sale (POS) scanning system were introduced as part of the program. Regular, live satellite communication from Kmart headquarters to the stores allowed senior management to communicate with store managers and facilitated questions and answers. The POS scanning system allowed a record of every sale and transmission of the data to headquarters. This system enabled Kmart to respond quickly to what's new, what's in demand, and what would keep customers coming back.

The company opened its first Super Kmart Center in 1992. The format combined general merchandise and food with an emphasis on customer service and convenience. The stores ranged in size from 135,000 to 190,000 square feet, with more than 40,000 grocery items. The typical Super Kmart operated seven days a week, twenty-four hours a day, and generated high traffic and sales volume. The centers also featured wider shopping aisles, appealing displays, and pleasant lighting to enrich the shopping experience. Super Kmarts featured in-house bakeries, USDA fresh meats, fresh seafood, delicatessens, cookie kiosks, cappuccino bars, in-store eateries and food courts, and fresh-food carry-out salad bars. In many locations, the center provided customer services like video rental, dry cleaning, shoe repair, beauty salons, optical shops, express shipping services, and a full line of traditional Kmart merchandise. To enhance the appeal of the merchandise assortment, emphasis was placed on "cross-merchandising." For example, toasters were featured above the fresh baked breads, kitchen gadgets were positioned across the aisle from produce, and baby centers featured everything from baby food to toys. At the end of 1999, the company operated 105 Super Kmart stores.

The Planning Function

Corporate planning at Kmart was the result of executives, primarily the senior executive, recognizing change. The role played by the senior executive was to get others to recognize that nothing is good forever. "Good planning" was the result of getting involved. "Poor planning" was done by those who didn't recognize the need for it, and once they did, it was too late to survive. Good planning, if done regularly, was assumed to result in improved performance. Kmart's Michael Wellman, then director of planning and research, said, "Planning, as we like to stress, is making decisions now to improve performance tomorrow. Everyone looks at what may happen tomorrow, but the planners are the ones who make decisions today. That's where I think too many firms go wrong. They think they are planning because they are writing reports and are aware of changes. They don't say, 'because of this, we must decide today to spend this money to do this to accomplish this goal in the future.'"

Kmart management believed that the firm had been very successful in the area of strategic planning. "When it became necessary to make significant changes in the way we were doing business," Michael Wellman suggested, "that was accomplished on a fairly timely basis." When the organization made the change in the 1960s, it recognized there was a very powerful investment opportunity and capitalized on it—far beyond what anyone else would have done. We just opened stores at a great, great pace. Management, when confronted with a crisis, would state, 'It's the economy, or it's this, or that, but it's not the essential way we are doing business.'" He also noted, "Suddenly management would recognize that the economy may stay like this forever. We need to improve the situation and then do it." Strategic planning was thought to arise out of some difficult times for the organization.

Kmart had a reasonably formal planning organization that involved a constant evaluation of what was happening in the marketplace, what competition was doing, and what kinds of opportunities were available. Management felt a need to diversify because Kmart would not be a viable company unless it was growing. Management felt it was not going to grow with the Kmart format forever. It needed growth and opportunity, particularly for a company that was able to open 200 stores on a regular basis. Wellman felt that, "Given a 'corporate culture' that was accustomed to challenges, management would have to find ways to expend that energy. A corporation that is successful has to continue to be successful. It has to have a basic understanding of corporate needs and be augmented by a much more rigorous effort to be aware of what's going on in the external environment."

A planning group at Kmart represented several functional areas of the organization. Management described it as an "in-house consulting group" with some independence. It was made up of (1) financial planning, (2) economic and consumer analysis, and (3) operations research. The chief executive officer (CEO) was identified as the primary planner of the organization.

Reorganization and Restructuring

Kmart's financial performance for 1993 was disappointing. The company announced a loss of $974 million on sales of $34,156,000 for the fiscal year ended January 26, 1994. Antonini, noting the deficit, felt it occurred primarily because of lower margins in the U.S. Kmart stores division. "Margin erosion," he said, "stemmed in part from intense industrywide pricing pressure throughout 1993." He was confident, however, that Kmart was on track with its renewal program to make the more than 2,350 U.S. Kmart stores "competitive, on-trend, and cutting merchandisers." Tactical Retail Solutions, Inc., estimated that during Antonini's seven-year tenure with the company, Kmart's market share in the discount arena fell to 23 percent, from 35 percent. Other retail experts suggested that because the company had struggled for so long to have the right merchandise in the stores at the right time, it had lost customers to competitors. An aging customer base was also cited.

In early 1995, following the posting of its eighth consecutive quarter of disappointing earnings, Kmart's board of directors announced that Antonini would be replaced as chairman. It named Donald S. Perkins, former chairman of Jewel Companies, Inc., and a Kmart director, to the position. Antonini relinquished his position as president and chief executive officer in March. After a nationwide search, Floyd Hall, fifty-seven, former chairman and CEO of the Target discount store division of the Dayton-Hudson Corporation, was appointed chairman, president, and chief executive officer of Kmart in June 1995.

The company concluded the disposition of many noncore assets in 1996, including the sale of the Borders group, OfficeMax, the Sports Authority, and Coles Myer. During the 1990s, it also closed a large number of underperforming stores in the United States and cleared out $700 million in aged and discontinued inventory in the remaining stores.

In 1996, Kmart converted 152 of its traditional stores to feature a new design that was referred to as the high-frequency format. These stores were named Big Kmart. The stores emphasized the departments deemed the most important to core customers and offered an increased mix of high-frequency, everyday basics and consumables in the pantry area located at the front of each store. These items were typically priced at a one- to three-percentage differential from the leading competitors in each market and served to increase inventory turnover and gross margin dollars. In addition to the pantry area, Big Kmart stores featured improved lighting, new signage that was easier to see and read, and adjacencies that created a smoother traffic flow. In 1999, 588 stores were converted to the new Big Kmart format, bringing the total to 1,860. Other smaller stores would be updated to a "best of Big Kmart" prototype.

Kmart launched its first e-commerce site in 1998. The initial Kmart.com offered a few products and was not considered a successful venture. In 1999, Kmart partnered with Softbank Venture Capital, who provided technical expertise, experienced personnel, and initial capital, to create an Internet site 60 percent owned by Kmart. BlueLight.com increased the number of Kmart products it offered online to about 65,000, from 1,250. It planned to boost the number to 100,000 by year-end 2000 and possibly to millions of items in the future.

Major changes were made to the management team. In total, twenty-three of the company's thirty-seven corporate officers were new to the company's team since 1995. The most dramatic restructuring had taken place in the merchandising organization, where all four of the general merchandise managers responsible for buying organizations joined Kmart since 1995. In addition, fifteen new divisional vice presidents joined Kmart during 1997. Significant changes were also made to the board of directors, with nine of fifteen directors new to the company since 1995. A list of the board of directors and corporate officers from March 2000 is shown in appendix D.

At the end of his tenure, Floyd Hall announced that the company mandate in the year and century ahead was to create sustained growth that would profitably leverage all of the core strengths of the firm. The corporate mission in 2000 was "to become the discount store of choice for low- and middle-income households by satisfying their routine and seasonal shopping needs as well as or better than the competition." Management believed that the actions taken by Charles Conaway, the new president, would have a dramatic impact on how customers perceived Kmart, how frequently they shopped in the stores, and how much they would buy on each store visit. Increasing customers' frequency and the amount they purchased during each store visit were seen as having a dramatic impact on the company's efforts to increase its profitability.

Appendix A: Kmart Corporation, Consolidated Balance Sheets and Operating Statements, 1998–1999

	Years Ended January 26, 2000; January 27, 1999; and January 28, 1998		
	1999	**1998**	**1997**
Sales	$35,925	$33,674	$32,183
Cost of sales, buying, and occupancy	28,102	26,319	25,152
Gross margin	7,823	7,355	7,031
Selling, general, and administrative expenses	6,523	6,245	6,136
Voluntary early retirement programs	—	19	114
Continuing income before interest, income taxes, and dividends on convertible preferred securities of subsidiary trust	1,300	1,091	781
Interest expense, net	280	293	363
Income tax provision	337	230	120
Dividends on convertible preferred securities of subsidiary trust, net of income taxes of $27, $27, and $26	50	50	49
Net income from continuing operations	633	518	249
Discontinued operations, net of income taxes of $(124)	(230)	—	—
Net income	$ 403	$ 518	$ 249
Basic earnings per common share			
Net income from continuing operations	$ 1.29	$ 1.05	$ .51
Discontinued operations	(.47)	—	—
Net income	$ .82	$ 1.05	$ .51
Diluted earnings per common share			
Net income from continuing operations	$ 1.22	$ 1.01	$ .51
Discontinued operations	(.41)	—	—
Net income	$ .81	$ 1.01	$ .51
Basic weighted average shares (millions)	491.7	492.1	487.1
Diluted weighted average shares (millions)	561.7	564.9	491.7

	As of January 26, 2000, and January 27, 1999	
	1999	**1998**
Current assets		
Cash and cash equivalents	$ 344	$ 710
Merchandise inventories	7,101	6,536
Other current assets	715	584
Total current assets	8,160	7,830
Property and equipment, net	6,410	5,914
Other assets and deferred charges	534	422
Total assets	$15,104	$14,166
Current Liabilities		
Long-term debt due within one year	$ 66	$ 77
Trade accounts payable	2,204	2,047
Accrued payroll and other liabilities	1,574	1,359
Taxes other than income taxes	232	208
Total current liabilities	4,076	3,691
Long-term debt and notes payable	1,759	1,538

(continued)

Appendix A: Kmart Corporation, Consolidated Balance Sheets and Operating Statements, 1998–1999 *(continued)*

| | As of January 26, 2000, and January 27, 1999 | |
	1999	1998
Current assets *(continued)*		
Capital lease obligations	1,014	1,091
Other long-term liabilities	965	883
Company obligated mandatorily redeemable convertible preferred securities of a subsidiary trust holding solely 7¾% convertible junior subordinated debentures of Kmart (redemption value of $1,000)	986	984
Common stock, $1 par value, 1,500,000,000 shares authorized; 481,383,569 and 493,358,504 shares issued, respectively	481	493
Capital in excess of par value	1,555	1,667
Retained earnings	4,268	3,819
Total liabilities and shareholders' equity	$15,104	$14,166

Appendix B: Kmart Corporation, Financial Performance, 1990–1999*

Year	Sales (000)	Assets (000)	Net Income (000)	Net Worth (000)
1990	$32,070,000	$13,899,000	$756,000	$5,384,000
1991	34,580,000	15,999,000	859,000	6,891,000
1992	37,724,000	18,931,000	941,000	7,536,000
1993	34,156,000	17,504,000	(974,000)	6,093,000
1994	34,025,000	17,029,000	296,000	6,032,000
1995[†]	31,713,000	15,033,000	(571,000)	5,280,000
1996[†]	31,437,000	14,286,000	(220,000)	6,146,000
1997[†]	32,183,000	13,558,000	249,000	6,445,000
1998	33,674,000	14,166,000	518,000	6,963,000
1999	35,925,000	15,104,000	403,000	7,290,000

Source: Fortune financial analysis and Kmart annual reports.

*After taxes and extraordinary credit or charges.
[†]Data from 1995, 1996, and 1997 reflect disposition of subsidiaries.

Appendix C: Financial Performance, Wal-Mart Stores, Inc., 1990–1999

Year	Sales (000)	Assets (000)	Net Income (000)	Net Worth (000)
1990	$32,601,594	$11,388,915	$1,291,024	$ 5,365,524
1991	43,886,900	15,443,400	1,608,500	6,989,700
1992	55,484,000	20,565,000	1,995,000	8,759,000
1993	67,344,000	26,441,000	2,333,000	10,753,000
1994	82,494,000	32,819,000	2,681,000	12,726,000
1995	93,627,000	37,541,000	2,740,000	14,756,000
1996	104,859,000	39,604,000	3,056,000	17,143,000
1997	117,958,000	45,384,000	3,526,000	18,503,000
1998	137,634,000	49,996,000	4,393,000	21,112,000
1999	165,013,000	70,349,000	5,575,000	25,834,000

Source: Wal-Mart annual reports/*Fortune* financial analysis.

Appendix D: Board of Directors and Corporate Officers, Kmart Corporation, March 27, 2000

Board of Directors

James B. Adamson,[1]
Chairman, President, and
Chief Executive Officer,
Advantica Restaurant Group

Lilyan H. Affinito[1,3,5]
Former Vice Chairman of the Board,
Maxxam Group Inc.

Stephen F. Bollenbach[4]
President and Chief Executive Officer,
Hilton Hotels Corporation

Joseph A. Califano, Jr.[4]
Chairman and President,
The National Center on Addiction and
Substance Abuse at Columbia University

Richard G. Cline[2,3,5]
Chairman, Hawthorne Investors, Inc.,
Chairman, Hussmann International, Inc.

Willie D. Davis[2]
President,
All Pro Broadcasting, Inc.

Joseph P. Flannery[3,4,5]
Chairman of the Board, President,
and Chief Executive Officer,
Uniroyal Holding, Inc.

Floyd Hall[3]
Chairman of the Board, President,
and Chief Executive Officer,
Kmart Corporation

Robert D. Kennedy[2]
Former Chairman of the Board and
Chief Executive Officer,
Union Carbide Corporation

J. Richard Munro[3,4,5]
Former Co-Chairman of the Board and
Co-Chief Executive Officer,
Time Warner Inc.

Robin B. Smith[1,5]
Chairman and Chief Executive Officer,
Publishers Clearing House

Thomas Stallkamp[4]
Vice Chairman and Chief Executive
Officer, MSX International

James O. Welch, Jr.[2]
Former Vice Chairman, RJR
Nabisco Inc. and Chairman,
Nabisco Brands, Inc.

Committees:
1 = Audit
2 = Compensation and incentives
3 = Executive
4 = Finance
5 = Directors and corporate governance
* = Committee chair

Corporate Officers

Floyd Hall
Chairman of the Board, President,
Chief Executive Officer

Michael Bozic
Vice Chairman

Andrew A. Giancamilli
President and General Merchandise
Manager, U.S. Kmart

Donald W. Keeble
President, Store Operations, U.S. Kmart

Warren F. Cooper
Executive Vice President, Human
Resources and Administration

Ernest L. Heether
Senior Vice President, Merchandise
Planning and Replenishment

Paul J. Hueber
Senior Vice President, Store Operations

Cecil B. Kearse
Senior Vice President, General
Merchandise Manager—Home

Larry E. Carlson
Vice President, Real Estate Market Strategy

Ronald J. Chomiuk
Vice President, General Merchandise
Manager—Pharmacy/HBC/
Cosmetics/Photo Finishing

Timothy M. Crow
Vice President, Compensation, Benefits,
Workers Compensation and HRIS

Larry C. Davis
Vice President, Advertising

David R. Fielding
Vice President, Northwest Region

Larry J. Foster
Vice President, Training and
Organizational Development

G. William Gryson, Jr.
Vice President, Special Projects

Walter E. Holbrook
Vice President, Southeast Region

Shawn M. Kahle
Vice President, Corporate Affairs

Harry Meeth, III
Vice President, Design and Construction

Douglas M. Maissner
Vice President, Northeast Region

(continued)

Appendix D: Board of Directors and Corporate Officers, Kmart Corporation, March 27, 2000 (continued)

Corporate Officers (continued)

James L. Misplon
Vice President, Taxes

Ann A. Morgan
Vice President, Field Human Resources

Lorna E. Nagler
Vice President, General Merchandise
Manager—Kidsworld and Menswear

Gary J. Ruffing
Vice President, Merchandise
Presentation and Communication

Lucinda C. Sapienza
Vice President, General Merchandise
Manager—Ladieswear, Fashion
Accessories, and Lingerie

David L. Schuvie
Vice President, Electronic Sales
and Services

Brent C. Scott
Vice President, Grocery Operations

Jerome J. Kuske
Senior Vice President, General
Merchandise Manager—Hardlines

James P. Mixon
Senior Vice President, Logistics

Joseph A. Osbourn
Senior Vice President and Chief Information
Officer

E. Jackson Smailes
Senior Vice President, General
Merchandise Manager—Apparel

Martin E. Welch III
Senior Vice President and Chief Financial
Officer

Lorrence T. Kellar
Vice President, Real Estate

Nancie W. LaDuke
Vice President and Secretary

Ronald Laila
Vice President, Merchandise Controller

Thomas W. Lemke
Vice President, Data Base Marketing

Michael P. Lynch
Vice President, Southwest Region

Michael T. Macik
Vice President, Human Resources and
Labor and Associate Relations

Leo L. Maniago
Vice President, Mideast Region

David R. Marsico
Vice President, Store Operations

Stephen E. Sear
Vice President, Facilities Management
and Corporate Purchasing

Stephen W. St. John
Vice President, Great Lakes Region

E. Anthony Vaal
Vice President, Global Operations,
Corporate Brands, and Quality
Assurance

John S. Valenti
Vice President, Southern Region

Leland M. Viliborghi
Vice President, Central Region

Michael J. Viola
Vice President and Treasurer

Francis J. Yanak
Vice President, General Merchandise
Manager—Food and Consumables

REFERENCES

Berner, Robert, "Kmart's Earnings More Than Tripled in First Quarter," *Wall Street Journal*, May 14, 1998, p. A13.

Brauer, Molly, "Kmart in Black 'in 6 Months,'" *Detroit Free Press*, p. E1.

Business Week, "Where Kmart Goes Next Now That It's No. 2," June 2, 1980, pp. 109–110, 114.

Bussey, John, "Kmart Is Set to Sell Many of Its Roots to Rapid-American Corp's McCrory," *Wall Street Journal*, April 6, 1987, p. 24.

Carruth, Eleanore, "Kmart Has to Open Some New Doors on the Future," *Fortune*, July 1977, pp. 143–150, 153–154.

Coleman, Calmetta, "BlueLight.com Aims to Coax Kmart Shoppers Online," *Wall Street Journal*, June 19, 2000, p. B4.

Coleman, Calmetta, "Kmart Lease Pledge May Slow Rebound," *Wall Street Journal*, May 24, 1999, p. A3.

Coleman, Calmetta, "Kmart's New CEO Outlines Plans for Fast Changes," *Wall Street Journal*, July 27, 2000, p. B4.

Coleman, Calmetta, "Kmart Sees $740 Million Pretax Charge from Closing 72 Stores, Other Changes," *Wall Street Journal*, July 26, 2000, p. B10.

Coleman, Calmetta, "Kmart Selects CVS President to Be Its CEO," *Wall Street Journal*, June 1, 2000.

Coleman, Calmetta, "Kmart's Wave of Insider Sales Continues Amid Questions About Retailer's Plans," *Wall Street Journal*, June 23, 1999, p. A4.

Dewar, Robert E., "The Kresge Company and the Retail Revolution," *University of Michigan Business Review*, July 2, 1975, p. 2.

Duff, Christina, and Joann S. Lubin, "Kmart Board Ousts Antonini As Chairman," *Wall Street Journal*, January 18, 1995, p. A3.

Elmer, Vickie, and Joann Muller, "Retailer Needs Leader, Vision," *Detroit Free Press*, March 22, 1995, pp. 1A, 9A.

Frankel, Mark, "Attention, Kmart Grocery Shoppers," *Business Week*, August 2, 1999, p. 49.

Guiles, Melinda G., "Attention, Shoppers: Stop That Browsing and Get Aggressive," *Wall Street Journal*, June 16, 1987, pp. 1, 21.

Guiles, Melinda G., "Kmart, Bruno's Join to Develop 'Hypermarkets,'" *Wall Street Journal*, September 8, 1987, p. 17.

Ingrassia, Paul, "Attention Non Kmart Shoppers: A Blue-Light Special Just for You," *Wall Street Journal*, October 6, 1987, p. 42.

Kmart Corporation, *Annual Report*, Troy, Michigan, 1990.

Kmart Corporation, *Annual Report*, Troy, Michigan, 1995.

Kmart Corporation, *Annual Report*, Troy, Michigan, 1996.

Kmart Corporation, *Annual Report*, Troy, Michigan, 1997.

Kmart Corporation, *Annual Report*, Troy, Michigan, 1999.

Kmart Corporation, *Kmart Fact Book*, Troy, Michigan, 1997.

Kranhold, Kathryn, "Kmart Hopes to Steer Teens to Route 66," *Wall Street Journal,* July 27, 2000, p. B14.

Main, Jerry, "Kmart's Plan to Be Born Again," *Fortune,* September 21, 1981, pp. 74–77, 84–85.

Rice, "Why Kmart Has Stalled," *Fortune,* October 9, 1989, p. 79.

Saporito, Bill, "Is Wal-Mart Unstoppable?" *Fortune,* May 6, 1991, pp. 50–59.

Schwadel, Francine, "Kmart to Speed Store Openings, Renovations," *Wall Street Journal,* February 27, 1990, p. 3.

Sternad, Patrica, "Kmart's Antonini Moves Far Beyond Retail 'Junk' Image," *Advertising Age,* July 25, 1988, pp. 1, 67.

Talaski, Karen, "Kmart Profits Plunge Sharply," *Detroit News,* May 12, 2000, p. 1B.

Talaski, Karen, "Kmart to Invest $2 Billion," *Detroit News,* August 11, 2000, p. 1C.

Wellman, Michael, Interview with Director of Planning and Research, Kmart Corporation, August 6, 1984.

Woodruff, David, "Will Kmart Ever Be a Silk Purse?" *Business Week,* January 22, 1990, p. 46.

28 Tosco and the New Millennium

This case was prepared by M. Edgar Barrett with the assistance of Andrew Kimbrough, Research Assistant, Thunderbird, The American Graduate School of International Management.

. . . the refiner that Thomas D. O'Malley built into the nation's largest independent from a tiny base a decade ago still has trouble getting respect. Though the company has higher profits than any of its independent competitors as well as some of the lowest costs, the oil world has largely viewed Tosco as a garage-sale groupie on the prowl for major companies' castaways.[1]

Much to the consternation of Tosco's senior management, this quote seemed to capture the sentiments of many in both the worldwide oil community and the overall financial market. Tosco Corporation had annualized revenues approaching $25 billion (U.S.), was the third-largest refiner and the second-largest C-store chain in the United States, and easily ranked ahead of such firms as Phillips and Sunoco in retail gasoline sales (see Exhibits 1 and 2 for data on Tosco and its relative position prior to the major acquisitions of 2000).

Despite the existence of this data, Tosco's common shares traded at a price earnings (P/E) ratio of approximately nine during the latter half of 2000, whereas the domestic oil refining and marketing industry was selling at an average multiple of fourteen and the overall U.S. market was selling at a multiple of 30.[2]

Company Background

Hein Koolsbergen and a group of investors created The Oil Shale Corporation in Los Angeles, California, in 1955, a company formed specifically to develop oil shale reserves worldwide. Oil shale is a hard, porous substance that can contain oil deposits but requires specialized, and expensive, oil extraction techniques. Koolsbergen hoped to capitalize on the oil shale development processes available at the time to extract oil and gas from these difficult-to-develop deposits.

The Oil Shale Corporation's first project was in Brazil, where it hoped to profitably develop the country's oil shale reserves and assist the country in reducing its reliance on oil imports. The project fell through due to lack of financial support. In 1965, the company formed the Colony Shale Oil Project in partnership with Atlantic Richfield Corporation (Arco), a large oil company (which became part of BP in 2000)

1. Alexei Barrionuevo, "Tosco Ready to Join Big Leagues with Exxon Mobil Deal—Refiner's Purchase of Gasoline-Station Network Makes It a Major Player," *Wall Street Journal*, February 29, 2000.

2. Price earnings data taken from Charles Schwab Equity Report Card, August 24, 2000.

EXHIBIT 1

Relative Capacity: U.S.-Based Refineries

Rank	1 July 00[1] Firm	000 bpd	1 January 00[2] Firm	000 bpd	1 January 99[3] Firm	000 bpd	1 January 97[3] Firm	000 bpd	1 January 95[3] Firm	000 bpd
1	ExxonMobil[4]	1,785	ExxonMobil	1,913	BP Amoco	1,419	Chevron	1,047	Chevron	1,206
2	BP[4,5]	1,640	BP Amoco	1,430	Exxon	1,119	Exxon	1,017	Amoco	998
3	Tosco[4]	1,300	Chevron	1,049	Chevron	969	Amoco	1,010	Exxon	992
4	Chevron	1,050	Marathon	935	Marathon	935	Mobil	952	Mobil	929
5	Marathon	935	Tosco	920	Tosco	910	Shell	897	Shell	761
6	Motiva	850	Motiva	852	Motiva	849	Sunoco	704	BP America	701
7	Valero[4]	800	Equilon	748	Equilon	837	Star Enterprise[6]	605	Sunoco	700
8	Sunoco	725	Sunoco	724	Sunoco	724	Marathon	570	Star Enterprise	600
9	UDS[4]	568	Koch	557	Mobil	705	BP America	564	Marathon	570
10	Koch	557	Conoco	523	Koch	557	Koch	514	Citgo	503
11	Conoco	525	Clark	518	Clark	510	Citgo	506	Koch	485
12	Clark	520	Arco	512	Conoco	507	Conoco	491	Tosco	470
13	Citgo	470	Valero	494	Arco	486	Arco	484	Arco	453
14	Equilon	460	Citgo	473	Citgo	470	Tosco	466	Conoco	438
15	Phillips	384	UDS	412	UDS	465	Texaco	357	Texaco	351
Top 5		6,730 (40.8%)		6,267 (38.4%)		5,382 (33.5%)		4,923 (31.9%)		4,886 (31.7%)
Top 15		12,569 (76.2%)		12,060 (73.9%)		11,462 (71.5%)		10,184 (65.9%)		10,157 (65.8%)
Total U.S.		16,485 Est.[1]		16,312 Est.[1]		16,057		15,452		15,435

[1] *Source:* Casewriter estimates.
[2] *Source:* U.S. Energy Information data taken from website.
[3] *Source:* U.S. Energy Information Administration data as cited in *NPN Market Facts,* 1996 through 2000.
[4] Includes acquisitions or disposition completed or announced since 1/1/00.
[5] BP, Amoco, and Arco.
[6] Joint Venture of Texaco and Saudi Aramco.

EXHIBIT 2

Relative Market Share: U.S. Motor Gasoline Sales[1]

Rank	Firm	1999[2]			Firm	1998[3]			Firm	1997[3]		
		SOM[4]	Outlets[5]	States[6]		SOM	Outlets	States		SOM	Outlets	States
1	ExxonMobil[7]	18.61	15,913	36	BP Amoco[8]	10.40	15,500	37	Mobil	10.00	7,436	30
2	BP Amoco[8]	10.73	16,300	37	Mobil	9.97	7,413	34	Shell	9.83	9,300	39
3	Marathon[9]	8.24	3,482	16	Exxon	8.65	8,500	36	Citgo	9.53	14,885	48
4	Equilon LLC[10]	8.22	9,400	32	Marathon[9]	7.98	3,117	12	Exxon	8.53	8,500	40
5	Citgo	7.98	13,813	47	Shell	7.86	N.A.	N.A.	Amoco	8.26	9,184	33
6	Chevron	7.70	7,980	29	Chevron	7.77	8,126	28	Texaco	8.19	13,859	41
7	Sunoco	4.45	3,538	18	Texaco	6.96	N.A.	N.A.	Chevron	7.23	7,752	30
8	Motiva LLC[11]	4.35	14,200	26	Citgo	6.92	15,079	48	Marathon[9]	5.53	3,088	12
9	Arco[8]	3.63	1,760	5	A-H	4.90	637	N.A.	Sunoco	4.55	3,789	19
10	Phillips	3.58	5,913	32	Sunoco	4.43	3,721	18	Phillips	4.08	6,530	32
11	Tosco	3.35	4,143	36	Phillips	3.81	5,916	31	Arco	3.45	1,547	5
12	Conoco	3.34	4,958	20	Arco	3.68	1,760	5	Tosco	3.32	4,786	37
13	A-H[12]	3.28	701	N.A.	Tosco	3.48	4,527	36	Conoco	3.04	4,968	19
14	Shell	2.14	N.A.	N.A.	Conoco	3.12	4,897	20	BP America	N.A.	6,775	21
15	UDS[13]	1.96	3,779	17	Coastal	2.80	1,540	32	A-H	N.A.	N.A.	N.A.
Top 15 Share		**91.56**				**92.73**				**N.A.**		

[1] Source: NPN Market Facts, 1995 through 2000 and various annual reports.

[2] Preliminary data.

[3] Revised data, including firms in existence at that date.

[4] SOM = Share of Market

[5] Outlets = Branded Retail Outlets

[6] States = Number of States

[7] Exxon and Mobil merged in late 1999. They divested approximately 2,400 outlets in 2000.

[8] BP and Amoco merged in late 1998. BP acquired Arco in April 2000.

[9] Includes joint venture operations with Ashland since January, 1998.

[10] Shell/Texaco joint venture in 31 Western and Midwestern States, with Shell holding 56%.

[11] Shell/Texaco/Saudi Aramco joint venture, in 26 Eastern and Southern States; Shell: 35%, Texaco and Saudi Aramco. each 32.5%.

[12] AH = Amerada Hess.

[13] UDS = Ultramar Diamond Shamrock.

EXHIBIT 2 *(continued)*

Relative Market Share: U.S. Motor Gasoline Sales

Rank	1996				1995				1994			
	Firm	SOM	Outlets	States	Firm	SOM	Outlets	States	Firm	SOM	Outlets	States
1	Mobil	9.67	7,589	29	Mobil	9.90	7,689	32	Shell	8.85	8,609	41
2	Exxon	9.58	8,400	41	Shell	9.83	8,767	40	Mobil	8.75	7,705	27
3	Shell	9.36	8,609	41	Citgo	9.46	14,054	46	Citgo	8.22	13,116	46
4	Citgo	9.17	14,529	48	Exxon	8.44	8,250	37	Exxon	8.07	8,700	37
5	Texaco	8.10	13,785	25	Texaco	8.27	13,023	45	Chevron	7.95	7,903	27
6	Amoco	7.85	9,184	33	Amoco	8.04	9,600	30	Texaco	7.92	13,746	27
7	Chevron	6.92	8,614	25	Chevron	7.23	7,988	26	Amoco	7.91	9,608	30
8	Marathon	5.83	2,392	11	Marathon	5.83	2,380	11	Marathon	5.73	2,356	11
9	Phillips	4.08	6,888	32	Sunoco	4.70	3,861	19	BP America	5.32	6,750	27
10	BP America	3.51	6,752	21	BP America	4.60	6,800	25	Sunoco	4.01	4,115	19
11	Sunoco	3.33	3,806	19	Phillips	4.21	7,106	32	Phillips	3.98	7,247	33
12	Arco	3.31	1,547	5	Arco	3.40	1,700	5	Arco	3.27	1,547	5
13	Conoco	2.91	5,196	41	Conoco	3.11	5,017	37	Conoco	2.84	5,017	37
14	Unocal	1.88	1,421	7	Unocal	1.89	1,325	7	Unocal	2.26	1,421	7
15	Total	1.75	2,106	19	Total	1.87	1,991	18	Total	1.81	1,767	17
Top 15 Share		**87.25**				**90.78**				**86.85**		

Source: NPN Market Facts, 1995 through 2000 and various annual reports.

with substantial operations on the West Coast of the United States. The partnership acquired, and then attempted to develop, 7,000 acres of oil shale reserves in Colorado. This project had to be abandoned when U.S. environmental restrictions of the 1960s rendered it unprofitable.

Koolsbergen then decided to de-emphasize oil shale development and diversify The Oil Shale Corporation's operations. In 1970, the company purchased the Signal Oil and Gas refinery in Bakersfield, California, and in 1972 expanded its refining presence further by purchasing all of Monsanto's petroleum operations. In 1976, long-time Oil Shale executive Morton Winston became CEO of the company and renamed the firm Tosco, an acronym formed from The Oil Shale Corporation. Under Winston, Tosco purchased Phillips Petroleum's West Coast assets and became the largest petroleum product supplier to independent marketers in the United States.

When the increase in oil prices of the 1970s once again made oil shale development financially attractive, Tosco refocused on its oil shale business by making substantial investments in its Colony Shale partnership with Arco. Arco, however, was fearful of escalating costs in the partnership and sold its 60% partnership interest to Exxon in 1980.

When Colony Shale was unable to secure government funding to support the high cost of oil shale development, Exxon withdrew its support. The partnership was effectively terminated in 1982. Tosco's large investments in its oil shale subsidiary, however, left the company in serious financial distress. In 1983, Morton Winston resigned as CEO and was replaced by Matthew Talbot.

Talbot's tenure at the helm was reasonably short-lived. In 1988, by increasing its ownership interest in Tosco to 40%, Thomas O'Malley's Argus Energy investment company was in a position to install O'Malley as the company's Chief Executive Officer. Following his arrival in 1989, O'Malley initiated a series of moves to reorient the company toward refining and marketing.

Thomas O'Malley began his career as a trader after graduating from Manhattan College in 1968 and was initially employed by Phillip Brothers Inc. He later moved to Salomon Brothers Inc., where he rose to the position of Vice Chairman and CEO of Salomon Brothers Phibro Energy subsidiary. In the 1980s, O'Malley formed the Argus Energy investment partnership and in the mid-1980s took a 20% stake in

Tosco. In 1988, the partnership increased its stake to 40% and, near the end of 1989, took over management of the company, naming O'Malley CEO.

By early 1990, Tosco was a financially struggling, independent oil exploration and production firm with a modest refining presence on the U.S. West Coast. Its sole revenue-producing asset was its Avon refinery, which was located in the San Francisco Bay area and served the wholesale petroleum market in Northern California. The company also retained ownership of oil shale properties in Utah and Colorado.

Growth Through Acquisitions

During the early 1990s, both the domestic and worldwide oil and gas industries were well into a period of restructuring and consolidation. The decade of the 1980s had not been kind to the overall industry, with both falling and volatile crude oil prices and a general situation of over-capacity in virtually all aspects of the industry. While this scenario did not bode well for healthy, robust industry profits, it did provide a number of opportunities to buy assets at a discount to their replacement cost.

In addition, most refineries that were operating in the early 1990s were designed to process a particular crude oil feed of a relatively uniform chemical composition. Processing crude from a single field or region meant that the refining processes could be optimized for both maximum production output and, often, minimum operating costs. O'Malley, however, wanted to allow his refinery managers to vary their crude oil inputs so that they would have more flexibility in choosing a supply source. He believed that this would allow his managers to exercise more control over refining margins by being more selective with inputs. Additionally, he wanted to give his refinery managers more autonomy in choosing the products to be produced so that each refinery could produce the highest margin product mix for its particular market.

1993–1994   Tosco's first acquisition under O'Malley was the April 1993 purchase of Exxon's Bayway refinery in Linden, New Jersey. The addition of this refinery, which had a capacity of over 250,000 barrels per day (bpd), gave the firm a presence on both U.S. coasts and access to the retail and wholesale gasoline markets in both Northern California and the Greater New York City area. Within a year or so, O'Malley's team was able to increase daily production runs at the refinery by about 12%, contributing to a substantial per-unit cost saving.

Tosco also expanded into the retail gasoline marketing business in December 1993 with its acquisition of British Petroleum's (BP's) refining and marketing network in the Pacific Northwest region of the United States. Tosco made an initial payment of $125 million and committed to pay BP a portion of the profits earned from the acquired assets over the succeeding five years. This contingent payment was capped at $150 million.

The deal gave Tosco a refinery in Ferndale, Washington (on Puget Sound approximately 100 miles north of Seattle), and a retail marketing network of 105 company-owned stations, 27 leased stations, and a marketing structure serving 377 independently owned BP outlets located almost entirely in Oregon and Washington. One product tanker and product terminals in Renton and Tacoma, Washington, were also included. The acquisition gave Tosco an immediate 16% share of the retail gasoline market in the two states and an 85,000 bpd capacity refinery complex.

Tosco further expanded its U.S. West Coast petroleum products marketing presence in August 1994 when it acquired BP's Northern California operations under long-term lease arrangements. A total of 414 company-owned, company-leased, or independently owned outlets bearing the BP name were included in this transaction.[3] In December of the

same year, Tosco used a similar arrangement to acquire all 100 of the Exxon stations in Arizona. By early 1995, Tosco's refining and marketing operations included three refineries and approximately 1,050 owned, leased, or franchised service station sites in four states (see Exhibit 3).

1995–1996   Two significant acquisitions occurred during this two-year period, both of which were finalized in 1996. In early February, the firm acquired the U.S. Northeast refining and marketing assets of BP for $64.4 million, plus the value of the related inventories. Assets acquired included a 150,000 bpd (non-operating) refinery in Trainer, Pennsylvania, seven product terminals, and approximately 500 retail service station sites.

Later, in May 1996, the company completed its $772 million acquisition of the Circle K Corporation. This brought about 2,400 company-controlled convenience stores, approximately 2,000 of which sold gasoline, into the Tosco organization. The Circle K operations were located in a 28-state region, primarily across the southern half of the country.

Circle K Corporation was a Phoenix, Arizona-based firm that was originally founded in El Paso, Texas, in 1951. The company expanded dramatically

3. According to some industry observers at the time, BP shed its U.S. West Coast refining and marketing operations due, in part, to an inability to compete effectively against Arco. Ironically, BP Amoco acquired Arco in April, 2000.

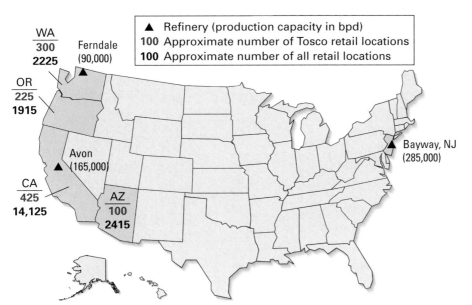

▲	Refinery (production capacity in bpd)
100	Approximate number of Tosco retail locations
100	Approximate number of all retail locations

WA
300
2225

Ferndale
(90,000)

OR
225
1915

Avon
(165,000)

CA
425
14,125

AZ
100
2415

Bayway, NJ
(285,000)

EXHIBIT 3

Early 1995 Refining and Marketing Operations

Source: Casewriter Estimates and Annual Reports.

during the late 1980s, a period during which many other C-store chains were growing and many of the major oil firms were adding merchandise offerings to their own gasoline retailing locations. The heightened competition, when combined with the heavy debt load incurred in financing a rapid expansion, led to a bankruptcy filing in 1990. The company shed approximately one-half of its assets while going through a court-supervised reorganization and emerged from the bankruptcy process in the mid 1990s. The company continued to struggle, however, as the competitive landscape remained difficult.[4]

Finally, in December 1996, Tosco entered into a definitive agreement to acquire the U.S. West Coast refining and marketing operations of Unocal Corporation at a price of approximately $1.4 billion. The assets in question included four California-based refineries, approximately 1,350 Union 76-branded retail outlets, and a variety of product distribution-related assets. By early 1997, Tosco was the largest independent refiner in the country. Its refining and marketing operations included seven refineries,

approximately 5,000 retail outlets (of which about half were company operated), 25 company-controlled wholesale terminals, and 1,300 miles of pipelines, and a lubricant blending, packaging and marketing business (see Exhibit 4).

1997–1998 The Unocal acquisition was finalized in late March 1997. With control of the additional set of assets, Tosco became the fifth-largest refiner in the United States and the second- or third-largest gasoline retailer in all of the major market areas within the state of California. The deal's primary benefits, however, appeared to lie in the increased operating efficiencies made possible with Tosco's now-enlarged asset base in California and the fact that it now had nearly total control over two nationally recognized brand names—Circle K in merchandise and 76 in petroleum products marketing.[5]

This two-year period also saw the continuation of Tosco's high-grading of individual operating assets. Various sources, including Hoover's Online and Paine Webber, reported the acquisition and disposition of assets such as product terminals, retail outlets,

4. In what later proved to be a precursor to future events, Circle K and Unocal seriously considered forming a co-branding joint venture which would have involved all Circle K stores in the Phoenix, Tucson, and Las Vegas metropolitan areas.

5. There were a few pre-existing license grants relating to 76 truck stops and the Uno-Ven joint venture with Petroleos de Venezuela S.A. in the U.S. Middle West.

EXHIBIT 4

Early 1997 Refining and Marketing Operations

Source: Casewriter Estimates, Annual Reports, and *NPN Market Facts,* Mid-July 2000.

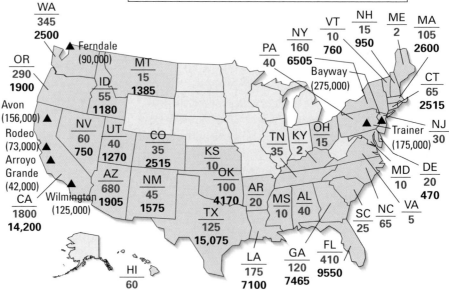

▲ Refinery (production capacity in bpd)
100 Approximate number of Tosco retail locations
100 Approximate number of all retail locations
(Not shown if Tosco is less than 1%)

and various pieces of vacant land. In general, the acquisitions were in geographic areas where Tosco already had a major presence, and the dispositions related to either overlapping assets from the recent large acquisitions or retail operations in areas where Tosco did not have a significant presence.

1999   The year 1999 contained no blockbuster deals. It did, however, see significant events occur in several diverse areas. In February, a fire at the Avon refinery near San Francisco resulted in four fatalities and a lengthy closure of the facility—which was not fully operating again until late July. The incident led to a flurry of negative press coverage, a thorough safety review, extensive employee training, and a public statement by the CEO that "We are not going to run a refinery that cannot be operated safely."[6] The firm also paid fines and other related payments totaling nearly $3 million and agreed to pay $21 million to settle wrongful death lawsuits filed by relatives of three of the workers killed. Two other lawsuits, one by the family of a fourth person killed and one by a worker disabled by the accident, were still pending in mid-2000.

In February, Tosco also signed a memorandum of understanding with Union Carbide Corp. to create a 50/50 joint venture to produce and market polypropylene (PP). Tosco would construct a $200 million, 775 million pounds-per-year (lb/yr) polypropylene plant at its Bayway refinery in Linden, New Jersey. Production from the new refinery would be combined with output from its existing propylene output at Bayway and production from Union Carbide's Seadrift, Texas, and Norco, Louisiana, refineries. The joint venture was scheduled to begin on the day that Tosco's new refinery began production, sometime in early 2001. Tosco was to use Union Carbide's Unipol PP process at its plant in exchange for payments to be made to Union Carbide over the life of the joint venture.

Polypropylene is a plastic used in products such as car bumpers, baby diapers, and plastic bottles and provides higher margins than most other refined petroleum products. Previous to the joint venture arrangement, Tosco produced 400 million lb./yr. of propylene and assumed substantial transportation costs to have it shipped to third-party refiners for conversion to polypropylene. The Tosco/Union Car-

bide venture would be one of the five-largest polypropylene suppliers in North America with a combined annual capacity (among the three plants) of approximately 1.6 billion lb./yr.

The year also saw an acceleration of Tosco's rebranding program with an increasing number of retail sites converted to the Circle K/76 format (Circle K merchandise and 76 petroleum products). In April, for example, it was announced that the BP name was being given up in the U.S. Pacific Northwest with all sites moving to the Circle K/76 format.

The retail site acquisitions and dispositions for the year continued the general theme of the prior several years, with the following transactions being the most prominent:

- March—Announced the sale of 320 retail sites in Colorado, Utah, Texas, and the U.S. Midwest.

- June—Sold 45 locations in Idaho to Jackson's Food Stores, making them the largest C-store operator in that state.

- July—Announced the acquisition of 137 sites in Pittsburgh and the U.S. Southeast from BP Amoco.

- October—Announced the acquisition of 87 sites in the U.S. Southeast from Boardman Petroleum.

Finally, Tosco was added to the Standard and Poor's 500 Index (S&P 500) in September 1999. Exhibit 5 provides data on Tosco's refining and marketing operations in mid-2000.

2000   Tosco returned to the large-deal mode in 2000. The largest of the year's deals was closed in February for $860 million and resulted in Tosco acquiring the Exxon system of retail gasoline and convenience store outlets from New York through Maine in the Northeastern U.S. and the Mobil system from New Jersey through Virginia in the Middle Atlantic region.[7]

Collectively, Tosco's acquisition consisted of 1,740 retail gasoline and C-store outlets as well as some undeveloped sites and distribution terminals. Tosco also acquired exclusive rights to the Exxon and Mobil brands in the applicable areas for a period of ten years. Many industry observers believed that Tosco

---

6. Tosco Corporation, 1999 Annual Report.

7. As a condition of approval for the merger of Exxon and Mobil in December 1999, the U.S. Federal Trade Commission required the combined firm to divest itself of approximately 2,450 service stations and the Benicia (California) refinery, among other items. The Tosco deal was closed less than 90 days after the finalization of the ExxonMobil merger.

EXHIBIT 5

Tosco: Mid-2000 Refining and Marketing Operations

Source: Casewriter Estimates, Annual Reports and *NPN Market Facts,* Mid-July 2000; and Tosco press releases and Investor Relations presentations.

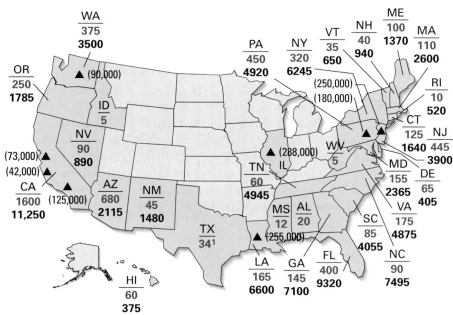

▲ Refinery (production capacity in bpd)
100 Approximate number of Tosco retail locations
100 Approximate number of all retail locations
(Not shown if Tosco is less than 1%)

[1] All located in Far West Texas

would gradually re-brand its new Mobil and Exxon locations with the Circle K and 76 brands.

Tosco moved again in the second quarter of the year with the $420 million acquisition of the Wood River Refinery and Chemical Complex from Equilon Enterprises LLC (a joint venture of Texaco, Inc. and Royal Dutch Shell). Equilon had been reported to be trying to focus primarily on its refining operations on the U.S. West Coast, and the disposition of the Wood River Refinery was consistent with this theme.[8] The 295,000 bpd facility raised Tosco's total refining capacity to 1.245 million bpd, making it the third-largest U.S. refiner after ExxonMobil (approximately 1.8 million bpd) and BP (approximately 1.7 million bpd). It also represented Tosco's initial refining foray into the Midwestern region of the country, where the Roxana, Illinois, facility was located. Initial estimates were that the refinery and chemical complex would add three billion dollars (U.S.) of revenue to Tosco on an annualized basis.

The Wood River acquisition was seen as an attractive one by most industry analysts. The price

agreed upon was reported to be significantly lower than the price Clark Refining and Marketing Company offered for the complex in 1999. The Clark deal fell apart due to the prospective buyer's inability to secure high-yield debt financing at the time. Tosco was also expected to be able to improve the returns at the refinery by broadening and varying the crude slate—with an emphasis upon more use of high sulfur crude.

Avon Refinery Sale In early July 2000, Tosco announced that it had entered into an agreement to sell its Avon (California) refinery to Ultramar Diamond Shamrock (UDS), another independent refiner and marketer, for $730 million. The $730 million net present value included a $650 million payment at closing and a participation payment of $150 million spread over the next eight years.[9] This deal closed in early September.

As noted by the Associated Press, the decision to sell the Avon Refinery Complex represented Tosco "throwing in the towel" on a long-troublesome asset.

---

8. "Tosco Fills Gap Between East, West Coasts with Acquisition of Wood River Refinery," *The Oil Daily,* April 2000, as reported by Northern Light Technology.

9. The Avon Refinery Complex was also expected to require capital investments of $300 million over the next three years to cover such things as complying with various environmental mandates.

"We retreated. That's the beginning, middle, and end of it. I think a new owner will do better with it," said Thomas O'Malley.[10]

UDS already owned a 125,000 bpd refinery in the Los Angeles area, which meant that they immediately became the fifth-largest refiner on the U.S. West Coast. Tosco, in turn, dropped to fourth-largest behind Chevron, BP, and Equilon Enterprise. It was expected that UDS would both invest heavily in the refinery to increase production and comply with environmental mandates and initiate a program to expand their retail presence in Northern California via the addition of more Beacon branded sites.

BP Amoco Alliance Refinery   Also in early July, Tosco announced a deal to acquire the BP Amoco Alliance Refinery on the U.S. Gulf Coast in Louisiana. The transaction, which was for approximately $760 million ($660 million, plus $100 million in working capital), closed in early September.

The Alliance refinery provided Tosco entry into the Gulf Coast market and (via product pipelines) allowed it to serve the Middle Atlantic and New York harbor region as well. The 250,000 bpd refinery, which was described as "world class" by one investment banking firm,[11] was more technologically sophisticated than most of its Gulf Coast peers with lower operating costs as well. In addition, near-term requirements for capital expenditures were believed to be quite modest.

Finally, in late July 2000, Tosco made a move into the international arena with the announcement that it intended to buy substantially all of the assets of the Irish National Petroleum Corporation Limited (INPCL) for $100 million, plus the cost of the crude oil and petroleum products at the time of closing. The main assets of INPCL were a modern 75,000 bpd refinery located in Cork and an 8.5 million barrel, deepwater crude oil and oil products complex located in Bantry Bay. The refinery had been upgraded, at a cost of $100 million over the past three years, so that it could meet the European Union requirements for low sulfur gasoline and diesel fuels.

Tosco was reported to be planning to lease half of the facilities at Bantry Bay on a long-term basis to the Irish government for their use as storage for the country's strategic petroleum reserves. It was also planning to use some of the refinery output, some 30,000 bpd of low sulfur fuel oil, as feedstock for the surplus upgrading facility at their Bayway and Trainer refinery complexes.

Other Sizeable Independents
The refining and marketing segments of the overall oil and gas industry in the United States had historically been dominated by large, integrated firms. For example, in early 2000, the five largest players in the domestic retail gasoline business were reported to hold about 57% of the overall market—and all five were portions (or affiliates) of major integrated firms.[12] Nonetheless, at least three independents[13] had been competing effectively with the integrated majors over the past few years. These three included Sun Oil Company (Sunoco), Tosco, and Ultramar-Diamond Shamrock (UDS) (see Exhibit 2).

On the refining side, however, the story was slightly different. Five of the ten largest refiners in the United States were independents, led by Tosco in the number three position.[14] The other four large independents included Valero, Sunoco, UDS, and Koch Industries (see Exhibit 1).

Over the next few pages, some brief background data is provided on two of these independents (UDS and Valero), as well as another major C-store chain (7-Eleven) and two alliance networks—one formed by Marathon and Ashland (MAP and Speedway SuperAmerica) and one formed by Shell and Texaco (Equilon and Motiva).

Ultramar-Diamond Shamrock
Ultramar-Diamond Shamrock (UDS) was the third-largest independent oil refiner and marketer in the United States, behind Tosco and Sunoco. The firm owned five refineries located in California, Oklahoma, and Texas with a combined capacity of

10. Associated Press Newswires, "Tosco, Ultramar execs see sale of Martinez refinery as 'classic win-win'," July 6, 2000.
11. Douglas T. Terreson, Paul J. Coppola and Jacques H. Rousseau, "Tosco Company Update: Tosco Strikes Again, Raising Estimates, PT $40/Sh.," Morgan Stanley Dean Witter, July 13, 2000, pg. 2.
12. BP Amoco and Arco presentation, 16 March 2000, as shown on BP: Alive: Alaska-Gas-Downstream (http//www.bpamoco.com).
13. Defined here to be primarily refining and marketing, as opposed to integrated oil and gas, firms.
14. Data is taken from NPN Market Facts, Mid-July 2000, pp. 110–111, and is based on refining capacity.

550,000 bpd and operated roughly 5,000 gas station/C-stores under the Diamond Shamrock, Ultramar, Beacon, and Total brand names in eighteen states. The company also owned a home heating oil business which served 236,000 households in New England and Eastern Canada and produced petrochemicals and natural gas liquids. Ultramar-Diamond Shamrock rounded out its marketing business with 4,000 wholesale branded outlets that sold diesel, jet fuel, lube oil, and asphalt to commercial customers and the military.

The National Convenience Stores chain, with 661 convenience stores in Texas, was purchased by Diamond Shamrock in 1995 for $260 million. By 1996, the firm had gained a 16% market share, making it the largest gasoline retailer in Texas, and operated 2,700 Corner Store, Stop-N-Go, and Diamond Shamrock C-stores. The company was also the second-largest gasoline retailer in New Mexico and Colorado. Its refineries in Three Rivers and Dumas, Texas, had a total capacity of 225,000 bpd. In 1996, Diamond Shamrock merged with Ultramar Corporation to form Ultramar Diamond Shamrock.

At the time of the merger with Diamond Shamrock, Ultramar operated refineries in Wilmington, California, and Quebec, Canada, with a combined capacity of 250,000 bpd. The company also sold gasoline at 360 California locations and 1,400 Eastern Canadian locations under the Ultramar and Beacon brands.

The Ultramar-Diamond Shamrock (UDS) merger was finalized in January 1997, creating what was then the fourth-largest refining and marketing firm in North America with $9 billion in revenue, 17,000 workers and 4,400 retail gasoline outlets.

In November 1997 UDS acquired Total Petroleum North American Ltd. for approximately $880 million in UDS stock and assumed debt. Total Petroleum operated three refineries (combined capacity 150,000 bpd) and owned eleven terminals, 1,136 miles of pipeline and 2,127 Total-branded gasoline stations. The deal gave Ultramar Diamond Shamrock a network of 6,381 retail outlets in 19 states and six Canadian provinces, a total refining capacity of 650,000 bpd, and boosted its total pipeline holdings to 5,679 miles.

In 1998, UDS signed a letter of intent to form the Diamond 66 joint venture with Phillips Petroleum. The highly publicized joint venture would have created a petroleum retailing organization with 12,000 gas station/C-stores and ten refineries in 36 states and six Canadian provinces. The original agreement had given UDS a 55% controlling interest in Diamond 66 in exchange for a $500 million cash payment to Phillips at the deal's close and an additional $300 million one year later. In the end, though, the two companies were unable to come to terms on the final agreement and the transaction was cancelled.

Valero Energy Corporation

Valero Energy Corporation, a San Antonio, Texas-based firm, was also one of the leading independent refiners of motor fuels in the United States. The company owned four refineries in Texas and Louisiana, one refinery in New Jersey, and a refinery in the San Francisco Bay area. Valero's products were marketed in 31 states and selected export markets. The company was transitioning into gasoline retail marketing with its acquisition of 340 Exxon-branded retail sites in Northern California.

Like Tosco, Valero had benefited from the asset divestitures of major oil companies in recent years. Valero bought Mobil's Paulsboro, New Jersey, refinery in 1998 and, most recently, purchased the Exxon-Mobil Benicia refinery in the San Francisco Bay area. Valero became one of the top five-to-seven refiners as measured by refining capacity in the United States and, with its acquisition of the Benicia refinery, obtained access to the large market for motor fuels in California. A summary of Valero's refining capacity as of mid-2000 is presented in Table 1.

Throughout Valero's growth period in the 1990s, the firm remained focused on upgrading its refineries to both increase overall output and to increase refining complexity and flexibility. This approach allowed Valero's refineries to process a wide slate of feedstocks that sold at a discount to the benchmark West Texas Intermediate crude oil.

On March 2, 2000, Valero agreed to purchase ExxonMobil's Benicia, California, refinery and all of the Exxon-branded California retail assets for a purchase price of $895 million, plus the value of inventories at the close of the transaction. This deal came as a result of the Federal Trade Commission and State of California Consent Decrees requiring divestiture of certain assets by Exxon and Mobil in order to satisfy antitrust issues associated with their merger. The Benicia Refinery, located on the Carquinez Straits of the San Francisco Bay, northeast of

TABLE 1

U.S. Refining Capacity (in bpd), Mid-2000, Valero

Refinery	Location	Capacity[1]	Capacity[2]
Corpus Christi Refinery	Corpus Christi, Texas	215,000	215,000[3]
Texas City Refinery	Texas City, Texas	200,000	152,000
Paulsboro Refinery	Paulsboro, New Jersey	170,000	152,000
Benicia Refinery	Benicia, California	160,000	129,500
Houston Refinery	Houston, Texas	120,000	72,500
Krotz Springs Refinery	Krotz Springs, Louisiana	85,000	78,000
Total		**950,000**	**799,000**

[1]As reported by Valero Energy Corporation on their website, www.valero.com (Benicia Slideshow Outline, 3/10/2000).
[2]As shown in *NPN Market Facts,* mid-July 2000. This report was based on US EIA data from 1998.
[3]Amended to reflect actual capacity as the cited source appeared to have inaccurate data.

the city of San Francisco, was a highly complex refinery with a rated crude oil capacity of 130,000 bpd.

The retail assets portion of the acquisition included 80 company-owned retail sites, 75 of which were in the San Francisco Bay Area. The Consent Decrees' requirements that ExxonMobil withdraw the Exxon brand name from these 75 stations allowed Valero to develop its own brand by rebranding these locations with the Valero name. Another 260 independently owned and operated retail facilities outside the Bay area included in the transaction were allowed to retain rights to the Exxon brand, continue to accept the Exxon credit cards and receive Exxon brand support. Valero received exclusive rights to the Exxon brand throughout California for a ten-year period, except in the San Francisco Bay area.

7-Eleven Incorporated

7-Eleven Incorporated was the Dallas, Texas-based operator of the 7-Eleven convenience store chain. In 1999, the company generated $8.3 billion in revenue through merchandise and gasoline sales at its outlets. The company also owned or had interests in stores in Canada and Mexico and licensed the 7-Eleven brand worldwide. Tosco became 7-Eleven's primary C-store competitor when it purchased the Circle-K convenience store chain in 1997.

7-Eleven purchased Citgo Gasoline Refining and Marketing Company in 1983. The deal included 300 Citgo service stations and use of the Citgo brand at its 7-Eleven outlets. In 1986, 7-Eleven sold a 50% interest in Citgo to the Venezuelan national oil company, Petroleos de Venezuela (PDVSA) in order to raise cash for other acquisitions. Following an attempted leveraged buyout, 7-Eleven filed for bankruptcy in 1990.

Ito-Yokado, 7-Eleven's Japanese partner and franchisee, entered the picture in 1991 when it purchased 70% of the company and named Clark Matthews as the new CEO. Matthews rationalized operations by closing under-performing stores, renovating the remaining stores and upgrading merchandise offerings. In 1992, the company's distribution system was sold to Wal-Mart, making Wal-Mart the nation's largest supplier to C-stores. In 1998, the company implemented an electronic Retail Information System (RIS) similar to that in use at its licensed outlets in Japan. The RIS connected all of the retail stores to a central network, allowing managers to optimize inventory management and product mix. 7-Eleven also introduced daily merchandise deliveries to 3,700 of its 5,800 retail outlets.

By late 1999, 7-Eleven, was positioning its U.S. retail outlets as an order fulfillment destination for online transactions initiated within its stores and at consumers' homes. The V.com, or virtual machine strategy, was established in 1998 as a pilot program for developing in-store product delivery and payment systems similar to those used successfully by Ito-Yokado's stores in Japan. Their long-term plan for V.com seemed to consist of a complete set of e-commerce services similar to those offered by 7-Eleven in Japan.

Marathon Ashland Petroleum LLC

Marathon Ashland Petroleum (MAP) was a 62/38 percent ownership joint venture between USX Corporation's USX-Marathon and Ashland Corporation. The venture was formed in 1998 to reduce costs and obtain economies of scale for the companies' refining and marketing assets. MAP operated seven refineries in the Midwestern states and Texas, representing a combined 935,000 bpd of crude oil capacity. MAP was the fifth-largest refiner in the U.S. with 6% of total U.S. refining capacity. The firm also sold motor gasoline through its 3,500 Marathon and Ashland-branded retail outlets. MAP had a retail presence in twelve primarily Midwestern states and had a 20% or greater market share in several of those states. MAP also had an interest in 8,000 miles of pipeline and operated over ninety asphalt and light product terminals in the Midwest and Southeast.

In addition to MAP, a related subsidiary of USX-Marathon, Speedway SuperAmerica LLC, owned and operated 2,300 locations in 19 states located in the Midwestern and Southeastern sections of the United States. Speedway SuperAmerica ranked first in the nation in company owned and operated truck stops (150 in a 12-state region) and third in the nation in company owned and operated convenience stores and gasoline outlets.

The Alliance Companies

The alliance companies were a collection of four related partnerships among Shell, Texaco, and the national oil company of the Kingdom of Saudi Arabia, Saudi Arabian Oil Company (Saudi Aramco). The three companies formed the alliance in 1998 by combining major portions of each participant's downstream operations (petroleum refining, distribution, and marketing) in the United States. The two major firms within the alliance were:

▪ Equilon Enterprises LLC

▪ Motiva Enterprises LLC

Both companies were based in Houston, Texas. The alliance companies posted combined gross revenues of $33.4 billion and controlled $17.1 billion in total assets in 1998. The overall enterprise was large, but each of the organizations operated semi-autonomously.

Equilon Enterprises LLC

Shell Oil Company and Texaco Incorporated combined major elements of their Western and Midwestern U.S. petroleum refining businesses to form Equilon. Shell and Texaco owned 56% and 44%, respectively. Equilon refined and marketed gasoline and petroleum products under both the Shell and Texaco brand names in 31 Western states and was responsible for the national transporation and lubricants businesses of the partner firms. The firm provided products to about 9,000 Shell and Texaco retail and wholesale outlets and had an 8.2% market share nationally. It was reported to have a 12% market share in the 31 states in which it operated and to be either number one or two in 14 of those states. Company assets included four refineries with a combined capacity of 563,000 bpd as of mid-2000. Three of them were located in California and one near Seattle.

Not long after Equilon was formed, Jim Morgan, president and CEO of the Equilon partnership, began looking for asset sale opportunities that would boost the firm's bottom line. In 1999 and early 2000, the company announced the sale of two of its then-owned refineries, representing almost half of Equilon's refining capacity. Equilon's intent was said to include a de-emphasis on refining and an expansion of its marketing, terminal, pipeline, lubricants, and trading businesses.[15]

Motiva Enterprises LLC

Motiva combined significant elements of Shell, Texaco, and Saudi Aramco's Eastern and Gulf Coast petroleum refining and marketing businesses. The previous Star Enterprise joint venture between Texaco and Saudi Aramco was dissolved and the assets from that partnership were rolled into Motiva Enterprises. The ownership split among the listed partners was 35%, 32.5%, and 32.5%, with Shell controlling the largest share of the company. Similar to Equilon, Motiva refined and marketed gasoline and petroleum products under the Shell and Texaco brand names. It operated in 26 states and Washington, D.C., providing product to 14,600 branded retail and wholesale

15. Former President of Shell Global Solutions International BV in the Netherlands, Rob J. Routs, succeeded Jim Morgan as Equilon's President and CEO in March 2000. Although it was officially stated that Mr. Morgan had chosen to retire, suspicion existed that the change was precipitated by dissatisfaction with Equilon's performance.

outlets. Motiva claimed to have a 15.4% market share in its operational region and to be either number one or two in 17 of its 26 states. The company's assets included four refineries with a combined capacity of 850 million bpd.

Turbulence in Refining and Marketing

By late 2000, the refining and marketing sector of the domestic oil and gas business had evolved such that it was quite different from what had prevailed as recently as a decade earlier. The independent refiners with Tosco leading the parade, had steadily increased their presence (see Exhibit 1). On the East Coast, for example, Tosco and Sun Oil Company (Sunoco) together controlled approximately 55% of the refining capacity. On the West Coast, the story was similar—but less dramatic—with Tesoro, Tosco, UDS, and Valero holding about 35% of industry capacity.[16]

Large, independent retail gasoline marketers such as Sunoco, Tosco, and UDS were providing meaningful competition for the majors in virtually every region of the country as well—with Tosco dominating in Arizona and UDS leading in Texas. British Petroleum (BP), meanwhile, had acquired both Amoco and Arco and reemerged as a major North American gasoline retailer. As of early 2000, they claimed to be the number one retailer in the United States, with 18,000 gas stations, a 15% share of the national market, and a 20% or greater market share in eight states including Washington, California, Nevada, Georgia, North and South Carolina, and Tennessee.[17]

Meanwhile, the C-store and retail gasoline industries had, for all practical purposes, converged to form an ill-defined, but sizeable, industry of his own. As of late 1999, the U.S. C-store industry had topped $160 billion in sales with nearly 100,000 locations nationwide. (See Exhibit 6 for more data on the U.S. C-store industry.)

The C-store industry, perhaps due to its relatively high gross margins and relatively stable return-on-

equity performance over the past few years, attracted a diverse set of companies. It counted majors, independents, and non-oil players among its largest firms. The top 20 firms, for example, included Tosco, Marathon-USX, UDS, and 7-Eleven as well as Exxon-Mobil, BP, Chevron, and Kampgrounds of America, Inc. (with 522 locations in 47 states).[18]

Despite the rosy picture that one might infer from the growth shown by some of the faster-changing players in the refining and marketing sector, the financial markets had not been looking favorably upon either the industry sector or its individual participants. In January 2000, for example, the average Price-to-Equity (P/E) and Price-to-Cash Flow (P/CF) ratios across Sunoco, Tosco, Valero, and UDS were 10.8 and 4.8, respectively.[19]

Among all the turbulence, however, some underlying truths appeared to have been present for some time in this sector of the overall oil and gas industry. The refining and marketing sector, for example, was still largely a game dominated by relatively large firms. Tosco's annualized revenues were running at approximately $25 billion (U.S.), when one considered its acquisitions and divestitures during 2000. Sunoco, UDS, and Valero, none of whom were among the top five refiners or gasoline marketers in the country, were all multibillion-dollar operations nonetheless. (See Exhibit 7 for data on the major geographic regions in terms of refinery capacity and utilization.) Finally, at least some of the independent players in this sector—and, in particular, Tosco—were reporting results that compared favorably with those of many of the so-called majors. (See Exhibit 8 for comparative financial and operating data across eight different firms for the 1995 to 1998 period.)

Tosco in the New Millennium

By late 2000, Toscos operations extended across 31 states encompassing all of the East, West and Gulf Coast states, as well as a few in the interior. The firm was also in a number of different segments of the overall oil and gas industry—ranging from petrochemicals at one extreme to pure C-store operations, with no gasoline retailing involved, at the other. As such, the firm competed with a wide range of firms

16. Michael Mayer, and Craig Ellis, *Tosco Corporation: Investment Conclusion and Valuation*, Schroder & Co., Inc., January 31, 2000, pp. 7 and 9, and *NPN Market Facts*, Mid-July 2000, pp. 110–111 and 114–115.

17. BP Amoco, "Alaska-Gas-US Downstream," BP Amoco and Arco Presentation, 16 March 2000, pp. 2 and 3, as reported on the BP website (http://www.bp.com).

18. "Top 50 U.S. Convenience Store Companies," *NPN Market Facts*, Mid-July 2000, p. 134.

19. The average for the S&P Industrials for the same time period was 29.2 and 17.7, respectively. Mayer, *Tosco Corporation*, p. 15.

EXHIBIT 6

Statistical Data on U.S. C-Stores: 1995–1999

	1999	1998	1997	1996	1995
Total Industry Sales	N.A.	$ 164B	$ 156.2B	$151.9B	$144.1B
In-Store	N.A.	$ 75.1B	$ 72.4B	$ 70.7B	$ 69.7B
Motor Fuel	N.A.	$ 88.9B	$ 83.8B	$ 81.2B	$ 74.4B
Total C-Stores	N.A.	96,700	95,700	94,200	93,200
Selling Motor Fuel	75.0%	77.0%	73.0%	73.0%	73.0%
Avg. Gallons/Month	110,500	95,100	84,500	82,000	81,000
Gross Margin/Gallon	13.4¢	12.6¢	13.4¢	13.1¢	13.4¢
Gross Margin	19.6%	20.8%	20.9%	20.3%	20.8%
In-Store	30.0%	31.2%	32.0%	31.2%	30.4%
Motor Fuel	11.7%	12.0%	11.3%	10.7%	11.8%
Average Store Sales/Year	N.A.	$ 1970m	$ 1876m	$1932m	$1842m
In-Store	$ 856m	$ 777m	$ 757m	$ 751m	$ 748m
Motor Fuel	N.A.	$ 1193m	$ 1199m	$1181m	$1094m
EBITDA[1]/Store	$ 83,500	$ 74,600	$ 65,300	N.A.	N.A.
Top Quartile	$140,200	$112,300	$101,400	N.A.	N.A.
Bottom Quartile	$ 31,400	$ 39,200	$ 26,000	N.A.	N.A.
Pre-Tax Profit/Store	2.0%	2.1%	1.6%	1.6%	2.2%
Top Quartile	2.9%	3.7%	3.0%	N.A.	N.A.
Bottom Quartile	(0.1%)	(0.1%)	(0.7%)	N.A.	N.A.
Performance Ratios					
Pre-Tax ROA	N.A.	10.5%	8.3%	6.1%	8.6%
Pre-Tax ROE	N.A.	24.9%	34.9%	21.5%	28.2%
Accts Pay. To Inventory	N.A.	1.5X	1.5X	1.3X	1.4X
Merchandise Shrinkage	N.A.	1.5%	1.8%	1.2%	1.4%

[1]EBITDA = Earnings Before Interest, Taxes, Depreciation and Amortization.

Source: Convenience Store Industry Fact Book, National Association of Convenience Stores; Alexandria, Virginia, 12th Edition, 1999, pp. 6–9, 24–27, 30, 46, 58, 59, and 104; and 2000 NACS/CS News Industry Databank as cited in *NPN Market Facts* 2000.

from ExxonMobil and BP at one extreme to Travel Centers of America and Stewart's Ice Cream Company, Inc. (both C-store chains with more than 150 units each) at the other. Finally, Tosco had become a rather sizeable firm as well (see Exhibit 9 for financial and operating data).

On the refining side, Tosco had become a significant player by almost any standard. They now controlled about 8% of the capacity available in the United States and were ranked behind only ExxonMobil and BP. On a worldwide basis, they had moved up to about the number 12 position—just above Texaco and the Kuwait National Petroleum Company.[20]

While they had built no new refineries on their own, Tosco's most recent acquisitions had all been purchased at a discount to replacement cost.[21] Each of them, in addition, was technologically sophisticated in terms that provided benefits at both the input process level and the outgoing products slate level. All of their refineries except one (Wood River) were located in or near a retail marketing region in which Tosco was a significant player.

The near-term outlook for refinery profits appeared to be quite positive as well. After a disastrous period during the late 1990s, the fundamentals seemed to have improved markedly. The incremental

20. Based on Year 2000 data used to update the rankings shown in "Worldwide Refining: How the World's Largest Refiners Rank," *Data Book 1999, Oil and Gas Journal,* 1999, p. 202.

21. The INPC acquisition, for example, involved paying $100 million for a facility that had been upgraded at that cost over the past three years. See Tosco press release dated July 31, 2000.

EXHIBIT 7

Refinery Capacity and Utilization: Selected Regions (barrels per calendar day, in thousands)

	1998	1997	1996	1995	1994	1993	1992	1991
TOTAL WORLD								
Refinery Capacity	80,440	79,845	77,800	76,885	75,575	74,240	73,390	74,830
Refinery Throughput	67,490	67,145	64,740	63,320	62,270	62,195	61,650	61,685
Capacity Utilization	83.9%	84.1%	83.2%	82.4%	82.4%	83.8%	84.0%	82.4%
UNITED STATES								
Refinery Capacity	16,155	15,705	15,450	15,335	15,435	15,030	15,120	15,700
Refinery Throughput	14,835	14,660	14,195	13,975	13,865	13,615	13,410	13,300
Capacity Utilization	91.8%	93.3%	91.9%	91.1%	89.8%	90.6%	88.7%	84.7%
Domestic Demand	18,917	18,620	18,309	17,725	17,718	17,237	17,033	16,714
WESTERN EUROPE								
Refinery Capacity	16,305	16,425	16,225	16,285	16,440	16,485	16,655	16,480
Refinery Throughput	15,265	14,835	14,670	14,430	14,370	14,245	13,975	13,800
Capacity Utilization	93.6%	90.3%	90.4%	88.6%	87.2%	86.4%	83.9%	83.7%
ASIA & AUSTRALASIA								
Refinery Capacity	19,390	18,755	17,860	17,110	15,945	15,385	14,575	13,740
Refinery Throughput	16,245	16,460	15,410	14,490	13,815	12,765	11,950	11,190
Capacity Utilization	83.8%	87.8%	86.3%	81.8%	86.6%	83.0%	82.0%	81.4%
MIDDLE EAST								
Refinery Capacity	5,935	5,835	5,660	5,555	5,335	5,020	4,680	4,450
Refinery Throughput	5,720	5,645	5,370	5,320	4,920	4,810	4,300	3,790
Capacity Utilization	96.4%	96.7%	94.9%	95.8%	92.2%	95.8%	91.9%	85.2%
CENTRAL & SOUTH AMERICA								
Refinery Capacity	6,465	6,555	6,145	6,210	6,090	6,110	6,140	6,075
Refinery Throughput	5,365	5,235	4,895	4,800	4,915	4,835	4,735	4,665
Capacity Utilization	83.0%	79.9%	79.7%	77.3%	80.7%	79.1%	77.1%	76.8%

Source: *National Petroleum New Market Facts*, Mid-July 2000, Adams Trade Press, Inc., Arlington Heights, Illinois, pp. 69 and 74.

EXHIBIT 8

Summary Performance Data for Selected Industry Firms

	Revenues		Net Income		Ident. Assets[2]		Return on Sales		Return on Assets[3]		Firm-Wide		Refinery Cap. Util.[6]
	Firm ($ Millions)	R&M[1] ($ Millions)	Firm ($ Millions)	R&M ($ Millions)	Firm ($ Millions)	R&M ($ Millions)	Firm (Percent)	R&M (Percent)	Firm (Percent)	R&M (Percent)	ROE[4] (Percent)	D/E[5] (Percent)	(Percent)
ARCO													
1995	15,819	5,555	1,376	200	23,999	3,165	8.70	3.60	5.73	6.32	20.36	99.26	104.0
1996	14,580	6,932	1,663	287	25,715	3,380	11.80	4.14	6.47	8.49	21.32	71.70	98.3
1997	14,757	6,853	1,771	325	22,425	3,564	12.35	4.74	7.90	9.12	20.40	41.69	97.9
1998	10,809	5,470	452	281	25,199	3,826	4.39	5.14	1.79	7.34	5.96	57.15	97.3
CHEVRON													
1995	36,310	N.A.	930	N.A.	34,330	N.A.	2.56	N.A.	2.72	N.A.	6.48	31.49	88.6
1996	43,893	29,580	2,607	419	34,854	N.A.	5.94	1.42	7.48	N.A.	16.69	25.53	91.1
1997	41,963	28,946	3,256	899	35,473	11,895	7.76	3.11	9.18	7.55	18.64	25.36	89.2
1998	30,557	21,070	1,339	600	36,540	11,643	4.38	2.84	3.66	5.15	7.86	25.79	83.1
EXXON													
1995	123,920	N.A.	6,470	1,272	91,296	N.A.	5.22	N.A.	7.09	N.A.	16.00	19.24	98.3
1996	134,249	106,755	7,510	885	95,527	32,538	5.59	0.83	7.86	2.72	17.25	16.67	95.2
1997	137,242	109,772	8,460	2,063	96,064	32,591	6.16	1.88	8.81	6.33	19.38	16.15	100.2
1998	117,772	95,216	6,370	2,458	92,630	33,752	5.41	2.58	6.88	7.28	14.56	10.35	95.4
MOBIL													
1995	75,370	62,362	2,376	894	42,138	22,463	3.15	1.43	5.64	3.98	13.24	25.79	92.0
1996	81,503	70,796	2,964	913	46,408	23,520	3.64	1.29	6.39	3.88	15.54	23.33	89.1
1997	65,906	55,871	3,272	1,025	43,559	20,212	4.96	1.83	7.51	5.07	16.81	18.86	105.5
1998	53,531	45,233	1,704	1,016	42,754	18,532	3.18	2.25	3.99	5.48	9.28	20.24	110.5

[1] R&M: Refining and Marketing
[2] Identifiable Assets
[3] Net income as a percentage of closing assets.
[4] Net income as a percentage of closing equity.
[5] Long-term debt as a percentage of stockholders' equity.
[6] Refinery capacity utilization for U.S.-based refineries only.

Source: *U.S. Oil and Gas Company Performance Report*, Third Edition, PennWell Publishing, July 1999, and Tosco and Valero annual reports.

EXHIBIT 8 (continued)
Summary Performance Data for Selected Industry Firms

| | Revenues | | Net Income | | Ident. Assets[2] | | Return on Sales (Percent) | | Return on Assets[3] (Percent) | | Firm-Wide | | Refinery |
	Firm ($ Millions)	R&M[1] ($ Millions)	Firm ($ Millions)	R&M ($ Millions)	Firm ($ Millions)	R&M ($ Millions)	Firm	R&M	Firm	R&M	ROE[4] (Percent)	D/E[5] (Percent)	Cap. Util.[6] (Percent)
SHELL (U.S.)													
1995	24,650	18,355	1,520	778	27,021	8,763	6.17	4.24	5.63	8.88	10.97	9.39	95.9
1996	29,151	22,944	2,021	336	28,709	9,326	6.93	1.46	7.04	3.60	14.06	5.52	99.3
1997	28,959	22,236	2,104	410	29,601	9,277	7.27	1.84	7.11	4.42	14.22	3.95	99.5
1998	15,451	4,193	(1,727)	169	26,543	5,970	(11.18)	4.03	(6.51)	2.83	(15.17)	4.30	96.2
TEXACO													
1995	36,787	19,411	607	486	24,937	N.A.	1.65	2.50	2.43	N.A.	6.38	57.81	101.7
1996	45,500	22,997	2,018	691	26,963	5,297	4.44	3.00	7.48	13.05	19.46	49.41	105.2
1997	46,667	24,322	2,664	789	29,600	5,861	5.71	3.24	9.00	13.46	20.87	43.14	108.4
1998	31,707	20,263	578	537	28,570	3,351	1.82	2.65	2.02	16.03	4.88	53.68	108.9
TOSCO													
1995	7,284	7,284	77	77	2,003	N.A.	1.06	1.06	3.84	N.A.	12.29	92.33	115.6[8]
1996	9,923	9,923	146	146	3,555	3,432	1.47	1.47	4.10	4.25	13.67	77.25	114.8[8]
1997	13,282	13,282	213	213	5,975	5,832[7]	1.60	1.60	3.56	3.65	10.94	72.80	102.2[8]
1998	12,022	12,022	106	106	5,843	5,755[7]	0.88	0.88	1.81	1.84	5.55	71.02	103.8[8]
[1999]	14,362	14,362	442	442	6,212	6,120[7]	3.07	3.07	7.11	7.22	20.95	64.17	92.4[8]
UDS													
1995	8,084	7,706	117	90	4,217	3,840	1.45	1.17	2.77	2.34	8.81	117.24	N.A.
1996	10,208	9,747	(36)	(44)	4,420	3,922	(0.35)	(0.45)	(0.81)	(1.12)	(2.89)	132.63	N.A.
1997	10,882	10,410	155	142	5,595	5,231	1.47	1.36	2.86	2.71	9.18	110.61	92.4[8]
1998	11,133	10,877	(78)	(72)	5,315	4,964	(0.70)	(0.66)	(1.47)	(1.45)	(5.64)	139.96	109.6[8]
[1999]	13,971	13,826	173	172	4,936	4,548	1.24	1.24	3.50	3.78	11.60	88.90	112.6[8]

[1] R&M: Refining and Marketing
[2] Identifiable Assets
[3] Net income as a percentage of closing assets.
[4] Net income as a percentage of closing equity.
[5] Long-term debt as a percentage of stockholders' equity.
[6] Refinery capacity utilization for U.S.-based refineries only.
[7] Does not include non-operating segment assets, which is consistent with other firms.
[8] Refinery input from annual report divided by US EIA data on capacity.

Source: U.S. Oil and Gas Company Performance Report, Third Edition, PennWell Publishing, July 1999, and Tosco and Valero annual reports.

EXHIBIT 9

Summary Financial and Operating Data for Tosco: 1991 to 1999

	1999	1998	1997	1996	1995	1994	1993	1992	1991
FINANCIAL DATA									
Total Sales ($ millions)	$ 14,362	$ 12,022	$ 13,282	$ 9,923	$ 7,284	$ 6,366	$ 3,559	$ 1,861	$ 1,609
Refining	8,550	6,796	7,654	6,960	N.A.	N.A.	N.A.	N.A.	N.A.
Marketing	5,812	5,226	5,628	2,963	N.A.	N.A.	N.A.	N.A.	N.A.
Merchandise	2,040	2,098	2,003	1,173	29	N.A.	N.A.	N.A.	N.A.
Motor Fuel	3,772	3,128	3,625	1,790	N.A.	N.A.	N.A.	N.A.	N.A.
Pre-Tax Income[1] ($ millions)									
Corporate	$ 766	$ 199	$ 381	$ 248	$ 127	$ 134	$ 132	N.A.	N.A.
Refining[2]	566	60	233	243	N.A.	N.A.	N.A.	N.A.	N.A.
Marketing[2]	216	154	163	19	N.A.	N.A.	N.A.	N.A.	N.A.
Pre-Tax ROA[3]									
Corporate	12.7%	3.4%	8.0%	8.9%	6.7%	N.A.	N.A.	N.A.	N.A.
Refining[2]	15.9%	1.7%	9.0%	N.A.	N.A.	N.A.	N.A.	N.A.	N.A.
Marketing[2]	9.1%	6.7%	8.0%	N.A.	N.A.	N.A	N.A.	N.A.	N.A.
Net Income ($ millions)	$ 441.7	$ 106.2	$ 212.7	$ 146.3	$ 77.1	$ 83.8	$ 80.6	$ (74.4)	$ 75.4
EPS (Diluted)	2.83	0.67	1.37	1.16	0.69	0.76	0.79	(0.96)	0.79
Closing Share Price (Year End)	27.06	25.47	36.88	25.53	12.15	9.11	8.92	6.13	7.46
OPERATING DATA									
Refining									
Capacity[4]	920,000	910,000	764,000	466,000	468,000	470,000	387,000	150,000	150,000
Throughput (bpd)	850,900	944,800	793,400	535,000	540,900	503,680	425,560	152,510	139,980
Gasoline Output—Tosco	53.7%	53.7%	52.4%	50.4%	50.4%	48.9%	53.8%	60.5%	57.3%
All U.S. Refineries[5]	43.2%	42.0%	41.6%	43.1%	44.0%	43.1%	43.0%	43.0%	43.1%
OTHER									
Retail Fuel Volume (million gallons)	4,452	4,490	4,159	2,061	1,047	769	N.A.	—	—
Gross Margin/Gallon	11.4¢	12.1¢	12.8¢	11.6¢	10.0¢	N.A.	N.A.	—	—
Gas Stations	4,143	4,476	4,652	3,270	1,015	995	520	—	—
C-Stores	2,070	2,313	2,395	2,400	115	75	N.A.	—	—
Employees[6]	24,600	26,300	26,200	24,300	4,000	3,600	3,000	1,000	900

[1]This number is also before distributions on Trust Preferred Securities

[2]Ignores those (relatively minor) expenses and assets shown in a non-operating segment.

[3]Based on average of opening and closing asset balance.

[4]Derived from EIA data, annual report data, and acquisition data for refineries purchased.

[5]Derived from *NPN Market Facts 2000*, Mid-July 2000, p. 145.

[6]Includes part-time employees at retail locations.

Source: Tosco Corporation Annual Reports (unless otherwise noted).

increase in refining capacity on a worldwide basis was expected to fall well below the increase in demand during both 2000 and 2001.[22] This, when combined with the regulatory move toward cleaner burning fuels in both the United States and the European Union,[23] was expected to mean that there could be shortages of both motor gasoline and distillate (primarily fuel oil) in the United States over the next 12 to 18 months. In fact, both motor gasoline stocks and distillate stocks were reported to be at the low end of the normal range by mid-2000.[24]

On the retail gasoline marketing side, Tosco had significantly enhanced their competitive position over the past few years. In addition to their strong West Coast operations, the recent acquisition of ExxonMobil properties on the East Coast had provided them with some areas of relatively high market share in the Middle Atlantic states. A recent presentation by Jay Allen, Tosco's president and CFO, had noted the following local market shares on a post-acquisition basis (see Table 2).

The same presentation had been used to assert that the U.S.-based refining and marketing earnings of Tosco had exceeded more of both Exxon and Chevron over the nine-month period ending 30 September 1999 and those of Exxon, Mobil, or Chevron for the three-month period ending on the same date.[25] This data, however, did not negate the overall volatility of refining and marketing earnings—where another observer noted that gasoline retailing margins had been nearly three times as high in California during the second quarter of 1999 (23.7¢ per gallon) as they were in the third quarter (8.9¢ per gallon).[26]

On the merchandise side, Tosco was now the first or second-largest C-store chain in the United States, depending on which source was cited, with over two billion dollars in annual revenue. While the margins in this business were quite positive (see Exhibit 6), there were a lot of players—some 22 of them had more than 500 locations each as of October 1999.[27]

TABLE 2

Projected Local Market Share in Selected Locations

Geographic Location	Share of Market
Greater Philadelphia	22.5%
Washington, D.C.	11.7%
Northern New Jersey	17.2%
New York City and Long Island	8.3%

Source: Jay Allen, Paine Webber presentation, February 15, 2000.

In terms of the newer ventures of Tosco, the firm was both moving up the value chain with its new polypropylene joint venture with Union Carbide and broadening its geographic reach with its acquisition of INPCL. The former was forecast to produce after-tax returns on capital of about 15% based on mid-cycle margins. The latter provided Tosco with an English-language entry point to the European Union as well as a source of 30,000 bpd of low sulfur fuel oil for use in the surplus upgrading capacity at the Bayway and Trainer refineries.[28]

Conclusion

Tosco, clearly, had changed markedly over the last few years. From a struggling firm with one significant asset, it evolved into a major player with operations in 31 states and plans to be in one European country as well. Yet, in some ways, the firm's approach toward its business had not changed much over the past decade. As its CEO, Thomas D. O'Malley, was quoted as saying:

> We are a patient buyer of assets, . . . the biggest opportunities for us will remain in the same areas that we've become expert in, and that's buying assets at reasonable prices, reorganizing them and then running them at a profit.[29]

The financial community, while not pricing Tosco's shares as high as its management would prefer, did nonetheless view that team in a fairly positive light. The firm had built a reputation with Wall Street

22. Douglas T. Terreson, Paul J. Coppola and Jacques H. Rousseau, "Tosco Company Update: Tosco Asset Sale Positive, Maintain Strong Buy, PT $40," Morgan Stanley Dean Witter, July 6, 2000, pp. 4 and 5.
23. Meaning that some smaller refineries would probably prove to be uneconomic in terms of cost required to upgrade (Editor).
24. Terreson, "Tosco Company Update," July 6, 2000.
25. Jay Allen, Paine Webber presentation, February 15, 2000.
26. Mayer, *Tosco Corporation*, p. 10.
27. "Top 50 U.S. Convenience Store Companies," p. 134.

28. "Tosco Corporation Announces Agreement to Buy the Operating Assets of the Irish National Petroleum Corporation Limited," Tosco Corporation Press Release, July 31, 2000.
29. "CEO Interview: Thomas D. O'Malley, Tosco Corporation," *The Wall Street Transcript*, DLJ Energy Supplement, March, 1999.

as having a very disciplined, even tight-fisted, approach to its operations. As one analyst described them: "O'Malley has simply done it leaner and meaner than the competition."[30]

The more positive among the analysts, particularly on the sell side of the industry,[31] were quite upbeat on the prospects for the firm over the next 12 to 18 months. Doug Terreson and his colleagues at Morgan Stanley Dean Witter (MSDW) for example, were predicting earnings-per-share figures of $3.10 and $4.05 for calendar 2000 and 2001, respectively, with a price target (PT) of $40 per share.[32] Attaining such a share price would represent a 35% improvement over that recorded on the date that MSDW released this particular company update.

O'Malley, quite clearly would be pleased with such a turn of events—particularly as he was reported to be holding some three million shares of the firm's stock. As he put it: "I own over three million shares of stock in this company. My interests are parallel with the shareholders."[33]

30. Fadel Gheit (Fahnestock & Co.) as quoted in Barrionuevo, "Tosco Ready to Join Big Leagues."
31. "Sell side" analysts work for firms that tend to underwrite or "sell" securities issues for corporate customers. "Buy side" analysts, on the contrary, work for large institutions such as insurance firms which tend to acquire ("buy") securities for their investment portfolios.
32. Terreson, "Tosco Company Update," July 21, 2000.
33. "CEO Interview," *The Wall Street Transcript.*

The Evolution of the Air Express Industry, 1973–2002

29

This case was prepared by Charles W. L. Hill, the University of Washington.

Introduction

The air express industry is that segment of the broader air cargo industry that specializes in rapid (normally overnight) delivery of small packages. It is generally agreed that the air express industry in the United States began with Fred Smith's vision for Federal Express Company, which started operations in 1973. Federal Express transformed the structure of the existing air cargo industry and paved the way for rapid growth in the overnight package segment of that industry. A further impetus to the industry's development was the 1977 deregulation of the U.S. air cargo industry. This deregulation allowed Federal Express (and its emerging competitors) to buy large jets for the first time. The story of the industry during the 1980s was one of rapid growth and new entry. Between 1982 and 1989, air express cargo shipments in the United States grew at an annual average rate of 31 percent. In contrast, shipments of air freight and air mail grew at an annual rate of only 2.7 percent.[1] This rapid growth attracted new entrants such as United Parcel Service (UPS) and Airborne Freight (which operates under the name Airborne Express). The entry of UPS triggered severe price cutting, which ultimately drove some of the weaker competitors out of the market and touched off a wave of consolidation in the industry.

By the mid 1990s, the industry structure had stabilized with three firms—Federal Express, UPS, and Airborne Express—accounting for approximately 70 percent of U.S. air express shipments. (See Table 1 for a comparison of the three companies.) During the first half of the 1990s, the air express industry continued to grow at a healthy rate, with express shipments expanding from 4,404 million ton miles in 1990 to 7,042 ton miles in 1994, an annual growth rate of slightly more than 16 percent.[2] Despite this growth, the industry was hit by repeated rounds of price cutting as the three biggest firms battled to capture major accounts. In addition to price cutting, the big three also competed vigorously on the basis of technology, service offerings, and the global reach of their operations. By the late 1990s and early 2000s, however, the intensity of price competition in the industry had moderated, with a degree of pricing discipline being maintained, despite the fact that the growth rate for the industry slowed down. Between 1995 and 2000, the industry grew at 9.8 percent per year. In 2001, however, the volume of express parcels shipped by air fell by 5.9 percent, partly due to an economic slowdown, and partly due to the aftereffects of the September 11 terrorist attack on the United States.[3]

This case is intended to be used as a basis for class discussion rather than as an illustration of either effective or ineffective handling of the situation. Reprinted by permission of Charles W. L. Hill.

TABLE 1

Main U.S. Air Express Operators, 2001

	Federal Express	**UPS**	**Airborne**
U.S. market share*	26%	53%	9%
Revenues	$18.3 billion	$29.7 billion	$2.85 billion
Average return on invested capital (ROIC), 1996–2001	17.9%	10.8%	8%
Aircraft fleet	662	560	118
Employees	215,000	359,000	22,500
Delivery vehicles	43,500	152,000	14,900

Sources: Standard & Poor's Airlines, *Industry Surveys,* March, 2002; Salomon Smith Barney Research; company 10K statements.

*Market share figures are for combined air and ground business.

The Industry in 1973

In 1973, roughly 1.5 billion tons of freight were shipped in the United States. Most of this freight was carried by surface transport, with air freight accounting for less than 2 percent of the total.[4] While shipment by air freight was often quicker than shipment by surface freight, the high cost of air freight had kept down demand. The typical users of air freight at this time were suppliers of time-sensitive, high-priced goods, such as computer parts and medical instruments, which were needed at dispersed locations but which were too expensive for their customers to hold as inventory.

The main cargo carriers in 1973 were major passenger airlines, which operated several all-cargo planes and carried additional cargo in their passenger planes, along with a handful of all-cargo airlines such as Flying Tiger. From 1973 onward, the passenger airlines moved steadily away from all-cargo planes and began to concentrate cargo freight in passenger planes. This change was a response to increases in fuel costs, which made the operation of many older cargo jets uneconomical.

With regard to distribution of cargo to and from airports, in 1973 about 20 percent of all air freight was delivered to airports by the shipper and/or picked up by the consignee. The bulk of the remaining 80 percent was accounted for by three major intermediaries: (1) Air Cargo Incorporated, (2) freight forwarders, and (3) the U.S. Postal Service. Air Cargo Incorporated was a trucking service, wholly owned by twenty-six airlines, which performed pickup and delivery service for the airlines' direct customers. Freight forwarders were trucking carriers who consolidated cargo going to the airlines. They purchased cargo space from the airlines and retailed this space in small amounts. They dealt primarily with small customers, providing pickup and delivery services in most cities, either in their own trucks or through contract agents. The U.S. Postal Service used air service for transportation of long-distance letter mail and air parcel post.[5]

The Federal Express Concept

Founded by Fred Smith, Jr., Federal Express was incorporated in 1971 and began operations in 1973. At that time, a significant proportion of small-package air freight flew on commercial passenger flights. Smith believed that there were major differences between packages and passengers, and he was convinced that the two had to be treated differently. Most passengers moved between major cities and wanted the convenience of daytime flights. Cargo shippers preferred nighttime service to coincide with late-afternoon pickups and next-day delivery. Because small-package air freight was subservient to the requirements of passengers' flight schedules, it was often difficult for the major airlines to achieve next-day delivery of air freight.

Smith's aim was to build a system that could achieve next-day delivery of small-package air freight (less than seventy pounds). He set up Federal Express with his $8 million family inheritance and $90 million in venture capital. Federal Express established a hub-and-spoke route system, the first airline to do so. The hub of the system was Memphis, chosen for its good weather conditions, central location, and the fact that it was Smith's hometown. The spokes were regular routes between Memphis and shipping facilities at public airports in the cities serviced by Federal Express. Every weeknight, aircraft would leave their home cities with a load of packages and fly down the spokes to Memphis (often with one or two stops on the way). At Memphis, all packages were unloaded, sorted by destination, and reloaded. The aircraft then returned back to their home cities in the early hours of the morning. Packages were ferried to and from airports by Federal Express couriers driving the company's vans and working to a tight schedule. Thus, from door to door, the package was in Federal Express's hands. This system guaranteed that a package picked up from a customer in New York at 5 P.M. would reach its final destination in Los Angeles (or any other major city) by noon the following day. It enabled Federal Express to realize economies in sorting and to utilize its air cargo capacity efficiently. Federal Express also pioneered the use of standard packaging with an upper weight limit of seventy pounds and a maximum length plus girth of 108 inches. This standard helped Federal Express to gain further efficiencies from mechanized sorting at its Memphis hub. Later entrants into the industry copied Federal Express's package standards and hub-and-spoke operating system.

To accomplish overnight delivery, Federal Express had to operate its own planes. Restrictive regulations enforced by the Civil Aeronautics Board (CAB), however, prohibited the company from buying large jet aircraft. To get around this restriction, Federal Express bought a fleet of twin-engine executive jets, which it converted to minifreighters. These planes had a cargo capacity of 6,200 pounds, which enabled Federal Express to get a license as an air taxi operator.

After 1973, Federal Express quickly built up volume. By 1976, it had an average daily volume of 19,000 packages, a fleet of thirty-two aircraft, 500 delivery vans, and 2,000 employees, and it had initiated service in seventy-five cities. After three years of posting losses, the company turned in a profit of $3.7 million on revenues of $75 million.[6] However, volume had grown so much that Federal Express desperately needed to use larger planes to maintain operating efficiencies. As a result, Smith's voice was added to those calling for Congress to deregulate the airline industry and allow greater competition.

Deregulation and Its Aftermath

In November 1977, Congress relaxed regulations controlling competition in the air cargo industry, one year before passenger services were deregulated. This involved a drastic loosening of standards for entry into the industry. The old CAB authority of naming the carriers that could operate on the various routes was changed to the relatively simple authority of deciding which among candidate carriers was fit, willing, and able to operate an all-cargo route. In addition, CAB controls over pricing were significantly reduced. The immediate effect was an increase in rates for shipments, particularly minimum- and high-weight categories, suggesting that prices had been held artificially low by regulation. As a result, the average yield (revenue per ton mile) on domestic airfreight increased 10.6 percent in 1978 and 11.3 percent in 1979.[7]

Freed from the constraints of regulation, Federal Express immediately began to purchase larger jets and quickly established itself as a major carrier of small-package air freight. Despite the increase in yields, however, new entry into the air cargo industry was limited, at least initially. This was mainly due to the high capital requirements involved in establishing an all-cargo carrier. Indeed, by the end of 1978, there were only four major all-cargo carriers serving the domestic market: Airlift International, Federal Express, Flying Tiger, and Seaboard World Airlines. While all of these all-cargo carriers had increased their route structure following deregulation, only Federal Express specialized in next-day delivery for small packages. Demand for a next-day delivery service continued to boom. Industry estimates suggest that the small-package priority market had grown to about 82 million pieces in 1979, up from 43 million in 1974.[8]

At the same time, in response to increasing competition from the all-cargo carriers, the passenger airlines continued their retreat from the all-cargo business (originally begun in 1973 as a response to high fuel prices). Between 1973 and 1978, there was a 45 percent decline in the mileage of all-cargo flights by the airlines. This decrease was followed by a 14 percent decline between 1978 and 1979. Instead of all-cargo flights, the airlines concentrated their attentions on carrying cargo in passenger flights. This practice hurt the freight forwarders badly. The freight forwarders had long relied on the all-cargo flights of major airlines to achieve next-day delivery. Now the freight forwarders were being squeezed out of this segment by a lack of available lift at the time needed to ensure next-day delivery.

This problem led to one of the major postderegulation developments in the industry: the acquisition and operation by freight forwarders of their own fleets of aircraft. Between 1979 and 1981, five of the six largest freight forwarders became involved in this activity. The two largest were Emery Air Freight and Airborne Express. Emery operated a fleet of sixty-six aircraft at the end of 1979, the majority of which were leased from other carriers. In mid 1980, this fleet was providing service to approximately 129 cities, carrying both large-volume shipments and small-package express.

Airborne Express acquired its own fleet of aircraft in April 1980 with the purchase of Midwest Charter Express, an Ohio-based all-cargo airline. Then, in 1981, Airborne opened a new hub in Ohio, which became the center of its small-package express operation. This enabled Airborne to provide next-day delivery for small packages to 125 cities in the United States.[9] Other freight forwarders that moved into the overnight mail market included Purolator Courier and Gelco, both of which offered overnight delivery by air on a limited geographic scale.

Industry Evolution, 1980–1986
New Products and Industry Growth

In 1981, Federal Express expanded its role in the overnight market with the introduction of an overnight letter service, with a limit of two ounces. This guaranteed overnight delivery service was set up in direct competition with the U.S. Postal Service's Priority Mail. The demand for such a service was illustrated by its expansion to about 17,000 letters per day within its first three months of operation.

More generally, the focus of the air express industry was changing from being predominantly a conduit for goods to being a distributor of information—particularly company documents, letters, contracts, drawings, and the like. As a result of the growth in demand for information distribution, new product offerings such as the overnight letter, and Federal Express's own marketing efforts, the air express indus-

try enjoyed high growth during the early 1980s, averaging more than 20 percent per year.[10] Indeed, many observers attribute most of the growth in the overnight delivery business at this time to Federal Express's marketing efforts. According to one industry participant, "Federal Express pulled off one of the greatest marketing scams in the industry by making people believe they absolutely, positively, had to have something right away."[11]

Increasing Price Competition

Despite rapid growth in demand, competitive intensity in the industry increased sharply in 1982 following the entry of UPS into the overnight-delivery market. UPS was already by far the largest private package transporter in the United States, with an enormous ground-oriented distribution network and revenues in excess of $4 billion per year. In addition, for a long time, UPS had offered a second-day air service for priority packages, primarily by using the planes of all-cargo and passenger airlines. In 1982, UPS acquired a fleet of twenty-four used Boeing 727-100s and added four DC-8 freighters from Flying Tiger. These purchases allowed UPS to introduce next-day air service in September 1982—at roughly half the price Federal Express was charging at the time.[12]

Federal Express countered almost immediately by announcing that it would institute 10:30 A.M. priority overnight delivery (at a cost to the company of $18 million). None of the other carriers followed suit, however, reasoning that most of their customers are usually busy or in meetings during the morning hours, so delivery before noon was not really that important. Instead, by March 1983, most of the major carriers in the market (including Federal Express) were offering their high-volume customers contract rates that matched the UPS price structure. Then three new services introduced by Purolator, Emery, and Gelco Courier pushed prices even lower. A competitive free-for-all followed, with constant price changes and volume discounts being offered by all industry participants. These developments hit the profit margins of the express carriers. Between 1983 and 1984, Federal Express saw its average revenue per package fall nearly 14 percent, while Emery saw a 15 percent decline in its yield on small shipments.[13]

Beginning around this time, customers began to group together and negotiate for lower prices. For example, Xerox set up accounts with Purolator and

Emery that covered not only Xerox's express packages but also those of fifty other companies, including Mayflower Corp., the moving company, and the Chicago Board of Trade. By negotiating as a group, these companies could achieve prices as much as 60 percent lower than those they could get on their own.[14]

The main beneficiary of the price war was UPS, which by 1985 had gained the number 2 spot in the industry, with 15 percent of the market. Federal Express, meanwhile, had seen its market share slip to 37 percent from about 45 percent two years earlier. The other four major players in the industry at this time were Emery Air Freight (14 percent of market share), Purolator (10 percent of market share), Airborne Express (8 percent of market share), and the U.S. Postal Service (8 percent of market share).[15] The survival of all four of these carriers in the air express business was in question by 1986. Emery, Purolator, and the U.S. Postal Service were all reporting losses on their air express business, while Airborne had seen its profits slump 66 percent in the first quarter of 1986 and now had razor-thin margins.

Industry Evolution, 1987–1996
Industry Consolidation

A slowdown in the growth rate of the air express business due to increasing geographic saturation and inroads made by electronic transmission (primarily fax machines) stimulated further price discounting in 1987 and early 1988. Predictably, this discounting created problems for the weakest companies in the industry. The first to go was Purolator Courier, which had lost $65 million during 1985 and 1986. Purolator's problems stemmed from a failure to install an adequate computer system. The company was unable to track shipments, a crucial asset in this industry, and some of Purolator's best corporate customers were billed 120 days late.[16] In 1987, Purolator agreed to be acquired by Emery. Emery was unable to effect a satisfactory integration of Purolator, and it sustained large losses in 1988 and early 1989.

Consolidated Freightways was a major trucking company and parent of CF Air Freight, the third largest heavy shipment specialist in the United States. In April 1989, Consolidated Freightways acquired Emery for $478 million. However, its shipment specialist, CF Air Freight, soon found itself struggling to cope with Emery's problems. In its first eleven

months with CF, Emery lost $100 million. One of the main problems was Emery's billing and tracking system, described as a "rat's nest" of conflicting tariff schedules, which caused overbilling of customers and made tracking packages en route a major chore. In addition, CF enraged corporate customers by trying to add a "fuel surcharge" of 4 to 7 percent to prices in early 1989. Competitors held the line on prices and picked up business from CF/Emery.[17]

As a result of the decline of the CF/Emery/Purolator combination, the other firms in the industry were able to pick up market share. By 1994, industry estimates suggested that Federal Express accounted for 35 percent of domestic air freight and air express industry revenues; UPS had 26 percent; Airborne Express was third with 9 percent; and Emery, DHL (a large Brussels-based international air express carrier), and the U.S. Postal Service each held onto 4 percent of the market. The remainder of the market was split among numerous small cargo carriers and several combination carriers, such as Evergreen International and Atlas Air. (Combination carriers specialize mostly in heavy freight but do carry some express mail.)[18]

The other major acquisition in the industry during this time was the purchase of Flying Tiger by Federal Express for $880 million in December 1988. Although Flying Tiger had some air express operations in the United States, its primary strength was as a heavy cargo carrier with a global route structure. The acquisition was part of Federal Express's goal of becoming a major player in the international air express market. However, the acquisition had its problems. Many of Flying Tiger's biggest customers, including UPS and Airborne Express, were Federal Express's competitors in the domestic market. These companies had long paid Tiger to carry packages to those countries where they had no landing rights. It seemed unlikely that these companies would continue to give international business to their biggest domestic competitor. Additional problems arose in the process of trying to integrate the two operations. These problems included the scheduling of aircraft and pilots, the servicing of Tiger's fleet, and the merging of Federal's nonunionized pilots with Tiger's unionized pilots.[19]

During the late 1980s and early 1990s, there were also hints of further consolidations. TNT Ltd., a large Australian-based air cargo operation with a global network, made an unsuccessful attempt to acquire

Airborne Express in 1986. TNT's bid was frustrated by opposition from Airborne and by the difficulties inherent in getting around U.S. law, which currently limits foreign firms from having more than a 25-percent stake in U.S. airlines. In addition, DHL Airways, the U.S. subsidiary of DHL International, was reportedly attempting to enlarge its presence in the United States and was on the lookout for an acquisition.[20]

Pricing Trends

In October 1988, UPS offered new discounts to high-volume customers in domestic markets. For the first time since 1983, competitors declined to match the cuts. Then in January 1989, UPS announced a price increase of 5 percent for next-day air service, its first price increase in nearly six years. Federal Express, Airborne, and Consolidated Freightways all followed suit with moderate increases. Additional rate increases of 5.9 percent on next-day air letters were announced by UPS in February 1990. Federal Express followed suit in April, and Airborne also implemented selective price hikes on noncontract business of 5 percent, or 50 cents, per package on packages up to twenty pounds.

Just as prices were stabilizing, however, the 1990–1991 recession came along. For the first time in the history of the U.S. air express industry, there was a decline in year-on-year shipments, with express freight falling from 4,455 million ton miles in 1989 to 4,403 million ton miles in 1990. This decline triggered off another round of competitive price cuts, and yields plummeted. Although demand rebounded strongly, repeated attempts to raise prices in 1992, 1993, and 1994 simply did not stick.[21]

Much of the price cutting was focused on large corporate accounts, which by this time accounted for 75 percent by volume of express mail shipments. For example, as a result of deep price discounting in 1994, UPS was able to lure home shopping programmer QVC and computer mail-order company Gateway 2000 away from Federal Express. At about the same time, however, Federal Express used discounting to capture retailer Williams-Sonoma away from UPS.[22] This prolonged period of price discounting depressed profit margins and contributed to losses at all three major carriers during the early 1990s. Bolstered by a strong economy, prices finally began to stabilize during late 1995, when price increases announced by UPS were followed by similar announcements at Federal Express and Airborne.[23]

Product Trends

Second-Day Delivery   Having seen a slowdown in the growth rate of the next-day document delivery business during the early 1990s, the major operators in the air express business began to look for new product opportunities to sustain their growth and margins. One trend was a move into the second-day delivery market, or deferred services, as it is called in the industry. The move toward second-day delivery was started by Airborne Express in 1991, and it was soon imitated by its major competitors. Second-day delivery commands a substantially lower price point than next-day delivery. In 1994, Federal Express made an average of $9.23 on second-day deliveries, compared to $16.37 on priority overnight service. The express mail operators see deferred services as a way to utilize excess capacity at the margin, thereby boosting revenues and profits. Since many second-day packages can be shipped on the ground, the cost of second-day delivery can more than compensate for the lower price.

In some ways, however, the service has been almost too successful. During the mid 1990s, the growth rate for deferred services was significantly higher than for priority overnight mail because many corporations came to the realization that they could live with a second-day service. At Airborne Express, for example, second-day delivery accounted for 42 percent of total volume in 1996, up from 37 percent in 1995.[24]

Premium Services   Another development was a move toward a premium service. In 1994, UPS introduced its Early AM service, which guaranteed delivery of packages and letters by 8:30 A.M. in select cities. UPS tailored Early AM toward a range of businesses that needed documents or materials before the start of the business day, including hospitals, who are expected to use the service to ship critical drugs and medical devices; architects, who need to have their blueprints sent to a construction site; and salespeople. Although demand for the service is predicted to be light, the premium price makes for high profit margins. In 1994, UPS's price for a letter delivered at 10:30 A.M. was $10.75, while it charged $40 for an equivalent Early AM delivery. UPS believes that it can provide the service at little extra cost because most of its planes arrive in their destination cities by 7:30 A.M. Federal Express and Airborne initially declined to follow UPS's lead.[25]

Logistics Services   Another development of some note was the move by all major operators into third-party logistics services. Since the latter half of the 1980s, more and more companies have been relying on air express operations as part of their just-in-time inventory control systems. As a result, the content of packages carried by air express operators has been moving away from letters and documents and toward high-value, low-weight products. By 1994, less than 20 percent of Federal Express's revenues came from documents.[26] To take advantage of this trend, all of the major operators have been moving into logistics services that are designed to assist business customers in their warehousing, distribution, and assembly operations. The emphasis of this business is on helping their customers reduce the time involved in their production cycles and gain distribution efficiencies.

In the late 1980s, Federal Express set up a Business Logistics Services (BLS) division. The new division evolved from Federal Express's Parts Bank. The Parts Bank stores critical inventory for clients, most of whom are based in the high-tech electronics and medical industries. On request, Federal Express will ship this inventory to its client's customers. The service saves clients from having to invest in their own distribution systems. It also allows their clients to achieve economies of scale by making large production runs and then storing the inventory at the Parts Bank.

The BLS division has expanded this service to include some assembly operations and customs brokerage and to assist in achieving just-in-time manufacturing. Thus, for example, one U.S. computer company relies on BLS to deliver electronic subassemblies from the Far East as a key part of its just-in-time system. Federal Express brings the products to the United States on its aircraft, clears them through customs with the help of a broker, and manages truck transportation to the customer's dock.

UPS moved into the logistics business in 1993 when it established UPS Worldwide Logistics, which it positioned as a third-party provider of global supply chain management solutions, including transportation management, warehouse operations, inventory management, documentation for import and export, network optimization, and reverse logistics. UPS's logistics business is based at its Louisville, Kentucky, hub. In 1995, the company announced that it would invest $75 million to expand the scope of

this facility, bringing total employment in the facility to 2,200 by the end of 1998.[27]

Airborne Express also made a significant push into this business. Several of Airborne's corporate accounts utilize a warehousing service called Stock Exchange. As with Federal Express's Parts Bank, clients warehouse critical inventory at Airborne's hub in Wilmington, Ohio, and then ship those items on request to their customers. In addition, Airborne has set up a commerce park on 1,000 acres around its Wilmington hub. The park is geared toward companies that want to outsource logistics to Airborne and can gain special advantages by locating at the company's hub. Not the least of these advantages is the ability to make shipping decisions as late as 2 A.M. Eastern time.

Information Systems

Since the late 1980s, the three major U.S. air express carriers have devoted more and more attention to competing on the basis of information technology. The ability to track a package as it moves through an operator's delivery network has always been an important aspect of competition in an industry where reliability is so highly valued. Thus, all the major players in the industry have invested heavily in bar-code technology, scanners, and computerized tracking systems. More recently, UPS, Federal Express, and Airborne have all invested in Internet-based technology that allows customers to schedule pickups, print shipping labels, and track deliveries online.

Globalization

Perhaps the most important development for the long-run future of the industry has been the increasing globalization of the air freight industry. The combination of a healthy U.S. economy, strong and expanding East Asian economies, and the move toward closer economic integration in Western Europe all offer opportunities for growth in the international air cargo business. The increasing globalization of companies in a whole range of industries from electronics to autos, and from fast food to clothing, is beginning to dictate that the air express operators follow suit.

Global manufacturers want to keep inventories at a minimum and deliver just in time as a way of keeping down costs and fine-tuning production, which requires speedy supply routes. Thus, some electronics companies will manufacture key components in one location, ship them by air to another for final assembly, and then deliver them by air to a third location for sale. This setup is particularly convenient for industries producing small high-value items (for example, electronics, medical equipment, and computer software) that can be economically transported by air and for whom just-in-time inventory systems are crucial for keeping down costs. It is also true in the fashion industry, where timing is crucial. For example, the clothing chain The Limited manufactures clothes in Hong Kong and then ships them by air to the United States to keep from missing out on fashion trends.[28] In addition, an increasing number of wholesalers are beginning to turn to international air express as a way of meeting delivery deadlines.

The emergence of integrated global corporations is also increasing the demand for the global shipment of contracts, confidential papers, computer printouts, and other documents that are too confidential for Internet transmission or that require real signatures. Major U.S. corporations are increasingly demanding the same kind of service that they receive from air express operators within the United States for their far-flung global operations.

As a consequence of these trends, rapid growth is predicted in the global arena. According to forecasts, the market for international air express is expected to grow at approximately 18 percent annually from 1996 to 2016.[29] Faced with an increasingly mature market at home, the race is on among the major air cargo operators to build global air and ground transportation networks that will enable them to deliver goods and documents between any two points on the globe within forty-eight hours.

The company with the most extensive international operations by the mid 1990s was DHL. In 1995, DHL enjoyed a 44 percent share of the worldwide market for international air express services (see Table 2).[30] Started in California in 1969 and now based in Brussels, DHL is smaller than many of its rivals, but it has managed to capture as much as an 80 percent share in some markets, such as documents leaving Japan, by concentrating solely on international air express. The strength of DHL was enhanced in mid 1992 when Lufthansa, Japan Airlines, and the Japanese trading company Nisho Iwai announced that they intended to invest as much as $500 million for a 57.5 percent stake in DHL.

TABLE 2

International Air Express Market Shares, 1995

Company	Market Share
DHL International	44%
Federal Express	21%
UPS	12%
TNT	12%
Others	11%

Source: Standard & Poor's, "Aerospace and Air Transport," *Industry Surveys,* February 1996.

Although Lufthansa and Japan Airlines are primarily known for their passenger flights, they are also among the top five air freight haulers in the world, both because they carry cargo in the holds of their passenger flights and because they each have a fleet of all-cargo aircraft.[31]

TNT Ltd., a $6 billion Australian conglomerate, is another big player in the international air express market, with courier services from 184 countries as well as package express and mail services. In 1995, its share of the international air express market was 12 percent, down from 18 percent in 1990.[32]

Among U.S. carriers, Federal Express was first in the race to build a global air express network. Between 1984 and 1989, Federal Express purchased seventeen other companies worldwide in an attempt to build its global distribution capabilities, culminating in the $880 million purchase of Flying Tiger. The main asset of Flying Tiger was not so much its aircraft, but its landing rights overseas. The Flying Tiger acquisition gave Federal Express service to 103 countries, a combined fleet of 328 aircraft, and revenues of $5.2 billion in fiscal year 1989.[33]

However, Federal Express has had to suffer through years of losses in its international operations. Start-up costs were heavy, due in part to the enormous capital investments required to build an integrated air and ground network worldwide. Between 1985 and 1992, Federal Express spent $2.5 billion to build an international presence. Faced also with heavy competition, Federal Express found it difficult to generate the international volume required to fly its planes above the break-even point on many international routes. Because the demand for outbound service from the United States is greater than the demand for inbound service, planes that left New York full often returned half empty.

Trade barriers have also proved very damaging to the bottom line. Customs regulations require a great deal of expensive and time-consuming labor, such as checking paperwork and rating package contents for duties. These regulations obviously inhibit the ability of international air cargo carriers to effect express delivery. Federal Express has been particularly irritated by Japanese requirements that each inbound envelope be opened and searched for pornography, a practice that seems designed to slow down the company's growth rate in the Japanese market.

Federal Express has also found it extremely difficult to get landing rights in many markets. For example, it took three years to get permission from Japan to make four flights per week from Memphis to Tokyo, a key link in the overseas system Then in 1988, just three days before the service was due to begin, the Japanese notified Federal Express that no packages weighing more than 70 pounds could pass through Tokyo. To make matters worse, until 1995 Japan limited Federal Express's ability to fly on from Tokyo and Osaka to other locations in Asia. The Japanese claimed, with some justification, that due to government regulations, the U.S. air traffic market is difficult for foreign carriers to enter, so they see no urgency to help Federal Express build a market presence in Japan and elsewhere in Asia.[34]

After heavy financial losses, Federal Express abruptly shifted its international strategy in 1992, selling off its expensive European ground network to local carriers to concentrate on intercontinental deliveries. Under the strategy, Federal Express relies on a network of local partners to deliver its packages. Also, Federal Express entered into an alliance with TNT to share space on Federal Express's daily trans-Atlantic flights. Under the agreement, TNT flies packages from its hub in Cologne, Germany, to Britain, where they are loaded onto Federal Express's daily New York flight.[35]

UPS has also built up an international presence. In 1988, UPS bought eight smaller European air freight companies and Hong Kong's Asian Courier Service, and it announced air service and ground delivery in 175 countries and territories. However, it has not been all smooth sailing for UPS either. UPS had been using Flying Tiger for its Pacific shipments. The acquisition of Flying Tiger by Federal Express left UPS in the difficult situation of shipping its parcels on a competitor's plane. UPS was concerned that its shipments would be pushed to the back of the aircraft. Since there were few alternative carriers, UPS pushed for authority to run an all-cargo route to Tokyo, but approval was slow in coming. "Beyond rights," to carry cargo from Tokyo to further destinations (such as Singapore and Hong Kong), were also difficult to gain.

In March 1996, UPS sidestepped years of frustrations associated with building an Asian hub in Tokyo by announcing that it would invest $400 million in a Taiwan hub, which would henceforth be the central node in its Asian network. The decision to invest in an Asian hub followed closely on the heels of a 1995 decision by UPS to invest $1.1 billion to build a ground network in Europe. In September 1996, UPS went one step further toward building an international air express service when it announced that it would start a pan-European next-day delivery service for small packages. UPS hopes that its recent moves will finally push the international operations of the carrier into the black after eight years of losses.[36]

The other U.S. carrier that is making a determined push overseas is Airborne Express. From the start, however, Airborne's strategy differed from that of Federal Express and UPS because it decided not to invest in its own international air fleet and ground operations. Airborne's strategy has two components. First, it will continue to fly its own planes in the United States but will book space on other air carriers for shipments going overseas. Second, it has been looking for strategic alliances with foreign companies that would give it market access and ground operations overseas. In 1989, the company announced an alliance with Mitsui & Co., a $125 billion-a-year Japanese trading and finance firm, and Tonami Transportation Co., operators of a ground-based express delivery service in Japan called Panther Express. The deal called for Mitsui to purchase $40 million worth of Airborne's stock and to provide $100 million in aircraft financing over five years and for the partners to collaborate in building volume in the Japan–U.S. air express market.

Industry Evolution, 1997–2002
Competitive Trends

The industry continued to grow at a solid rate through 2000, which helped to establish a stable pricing environment. In 2001, things took a turn for the worse, with recessionary conditions in the United States triggering a 7.6 percent decline in the number of domestic packages shipped by air. Even though the economy started to rebound in 2002, analysts were predicting only a 3 percent increase in the number of packages shipped by air.[37] Despite the weak environment, pricing discipline remained solid. Unlike the 1990–1991 recession, there was no price war. Indeed, in early 2002, UPS pushed through a 3.5 percent increase in prices, which was quickly followed by the other carriers. The carriers were also successful in tacking on a fuel surcharge to the cost of packages to make up for sharply higher fuel costs in 2001.[38]

During 1997–2002, several notable trends occurred in the industry. First, all three players continued to build their logistics services. UPS was reportedly the most successful in this area. By 2000, UPS's logistics business was the largest in the industry, with revenues of over $1 billion, an increase of 58 percent over the prior year. Growth forecasts were as high as 40 percent per year.[39] UPS was reportedly stealing share from FedEx in this area. (Federal Express changed its name to FedEx in 2000.) Most analysts expected logistics services to continue to be a growth area.

Second, all three carriers focused on supplementing their air networks with extensive ground networks and ground hubs to ship packages overnight. With more customers moving from overnight mail to deferred services, such as second-day delivery, this shift in emphasis has become a necessity. Demand for deferred services help up reasonably well during 2001, even as demand for overnight packages slumped. Prices for deferred and ground services are considerably lower than are prices for air services, but so are the costs (see Table 3). UPS has been the most aggressive in building ground delivery capabilities (of course, it already had extensive ground capabilities before its move into the air). In 1999, UPS decided to integrate overnight delivery into its huge ground transportation network. The company spent about $700 million to strengthen its ground delivery network by setting up regional ground hubs. By doing so, it found it could ship packages overnight on the ground within a 500-mile radius. Because ground shipments are cheaper than air shipments, the result was a significant cost savings for UPS. The company also deferred delivery of about 123 aircraft that were on order, reasoning that they would not be needed as quickly because more of UPS's overnight business was moved to the ground.[40]

FedEx has also accelerated the buildup of its ground network. In 1997, FedEx spent $500 million to acquire an established ground shipping company, supplementing its existing capability. It spent an additional $150 million in 2001 to strengthen the system and hopes to be able to provide ground service to all U.S. homes by the end of 2002, giving it a similar capability to UPS. In addition, FedEx struck a deal in 2001 with the U.S. Postal Service (USPS), under which FedEx will provide airport-to-airport transportation for 250,000 pounds of USPS Express Mail packages nightly and about 3 million pounds of USPS Priority Mail packages. The Priority Mail will be moved on FedEx planes that normally sit idle during the day. The deal could reportedly be worth $7 billion in additional revenues to FedEx over the seven-year term of the agreement. In addition, FedEx should reap cost savings from the better utilization of its lift capacity.[41]

The third trend has been a move toward selling various product offerings—including air delivery, ground package offerings, and logistics services—to business customers as a bundle. The basic idea behind bundling is to offer complementary products at a bundled price that is less than would have been the case if each item had been purchased separately. Yet again, UPS has been the most aggressive in offering bundled services to corporate clients. UPS is clearly aiming to set itself up as a one-stop shop offering a broad array of transportation solutions to customers. FedEx has also made moves in this area, and most recently, Airborne Express started to bundle its product offerings in mid 2001.[42]

The fourth trend of note has been ongoing speculation that further consolidation is likely in the

TABLE 3

Product Yield Comparisons, 2001

Company	Overnight Air	Deferred Air	Ground
Airborne	$9.16	$7.03	$5.60
FedEx	$14.96	$10.88	$5.98
UPS	$19.32	$12.52	$6.03

Source: Salomon Smith Barney Research, *Wrap It Up—Bundling and the Air Express Sector,* May 3, 2002.

industry. The source of most of the rumors has been Deutsche Post (DP). The recently privatized German postal service acquired in the late 1990s a 51 percent interest in DHL, whose U.S. airline, DHL Airways, has a small position in the U.S. air express market (remember, DHL is a major player in the international market). DP has made no secret about its desire to build a strong position in the global parcel express, forwarding, and third-party logistics businesses. DP spent approximately $5 billion to acquire several companies in the logistics business between 1997 and 1999. In November 2000, Deutsche Post went private with an initial public offering that raised $5.5 billion. In 2001 and 2002, it was rumored to be considering bids for two U.S. companies, Airborne Express and BAX Global, a freight forwarder. Other possible takeover candidates include Consolidated Freightways, another small player in the air express industry but one with a large ground network.

Currently, DP is theoretically constrained in its ability to operate an airline in the United States by the law that limits foreign ownership of a U.S. airline to 25 percent (air express operators are considered airlines for the purposes of this law). However, DP seems to have circumvented this law in the case of DHL by establishing a complex ownership structure. DP owns 51 percent of DHL, which in turn owns 23 percent of DHL Airways, the U.S. airline operations of DHL. The belief is that DP will use DHL Airways as the vehicle for any U.S. acquisitions, such as the rumored acquisition of Airborne Express. In early 2001, USPS and FedEx filed petitions against Deutsche Post with the U.S. Department of Transportation, contending that DP's ownership of DHL Airways was against the law (they argued that DP in effect controlled DHL Airways). However, the U.S. Department of Transportation rejected the petitions, potentially opening the way for DP to acquire Airborne Express under a similar ownership and control arrangement.[43]

ENDNOTES

1. Standard & Poor's, "Aerospace and Air Transport," *Industry Surveys,* February 1996.
2. Ibid.
3. Standard & Poor's, Airlines, *Industry Surveys,* March 2002.
4. Christopher H. Lovelock, "Federal Express (B)," Harvard Business School Case No. 579–040, 1978.
5. Standard & Poor's, "Aerospace and Air Transport," *Industry Surveys,* January 1981.
6. Lovelock, "Federal Express (B)."
7. Standard & Poor's, "Aerospace and Air Transport," *Industry Surveys,* January 1981.
8. Ibid.
9. Ibid.
10. Standard & Poor's, "Aerospace and Air Transport," *Industry Surveys,* January 1984.
11. Carol Hall, "High Fliers," *Marketing and Media Decisions,* August 1986, p. 138.
12. Standard & Poor's, "Aerospace and Air Transport," *Industry Surveys,* January 1984.
13. Standard & Poor's, "Aerospace and Air Transport," *Industry Surveys,* December 1984.
14. Brian Dumaine, "Turbulence Hits the Air Couriers," *Fortune,* July 21, 1986, pp. 101–106.
15. Ibid.
16. Chuck Hawkins, "Purolator: Still No Overnight Success," *BusinessWeek,* June 16, 1986, pp. 76–78.
17. Joan O'C. Hamilton, "Emery Is One Heavy Load for Consolidated Freightways," *BusinessWeek,* March 26, 1990, pp. 62–64.
18. Standard & Poor's "Aerospace and Air Transport," *Industry Surveys,* February 1996.
19. "Hold That Tiger: FedEx Is Now World Heavyweight," *Purchasing,* September 14, 1989, pp. 41–42.
20. Standard & Poor's, "Aerospace and Air Transport," *Industry Surveys,* April 1988.
21. Standard & Poor's, "Aerospace and Air Transport," *Industry Surveys,* February 1996.
22. David Greising, "Watch Out for Flying Packages," *BusinessWeek,* November 1994, p. 40.
23. Staff reporter, "UPS to Raise Its Rates for Packages," *Wall Street Journal,* January 9, 1995, p. C22.
24. Marilyn Royce, "Airborne Freight," *Value Line Investment Survey,* September 20, 1996.
25. Robert Frank, "UPS Planning Earlier Delivery," *Wall Street Journal,* September 29, 1994, p. A4.
26. Frank, "Federal Express Grapples with Changes in U.S. Market."
27. Company press releases (http://www.ups.com/news/).
28. Joan M. Feldman, "The Coming of Age of International Air Freight," *Air Transport World,* June 1989, pp. 31–33.
29. Standard & Poor's, "Aerospace and Air Transport," *Industry Surveys,* February 1996.
30. Ibid.
31. Peter Greiff, "Lufthansa, JAL, and a Trading Firm Acquire a Majority Stake in DHL," *Wall Street Journal,* August 24, 1992, p. A5.
32. Standard & Poor's, "Aerospace and Air Transport," *Industry Surveys,* February 1996.
33. "Hold That Tiger: FedEx Is Now a World Heavyweight."
34. Douglas Blackmon, "FedEx Swings from Confidence Abroad to a Tightrope," *Wall Street Journal,* March 15, 1996, p. B4.
35. Daniel Pearl, "Federal Express Plans to Trim Assets in Europe," *Wall Street Journal,* March 17, 1992, p. A3.
36. Company press releases (http://www.ups.com/news/).
37. C. Haddad and M. Arndt, "Saying No Thanks to Overnight Air," *Business Week,* April 1, 2002, p. 74.
38. Salomon Smith Barney Research, *Wrap It Up—Bundling and the Air Express Sector,* May 3, 2002.
39. C. Haddad and J. Ewing, "Ground Wars," *Business Week,* May 21, 2001, p. 64.
40. C. Haddad and M. Arndt, "Saying No Thanks to Overnight Air," *Business Week,* April 1, 2002, p. 74.
41. E. Walsh, "Package Deal," *Logistics,* February 2001, pp. 19–20.
42. Salomon Smith Barney Research, *Wrap It Up—Bundling and the Air Express Sector,* May 3, 2002.
43. P. Needham, "Coming to America," *Journal of Commerce,* April 22, 2002, p. 12.

30 Airborne Express in 2002

This case was prepared by Charles W. L. Hill, the University of Washington.

Introduction

Airborne Inc., which operates under the name Airborne Express, is an air-express transportation company that provides express and second-day delivery of small packages (less than seventy pounds) and documents throughout the United States and to and from many foreign countries. The company owns and operates an airline and a fleet of ground-transportation vehicles to provide complete door-to-door service. It is also an air freight forwarder, moving shipments of any size on a worldwide basis. As of 2002, Airborne Express held third place in the U.S. air express industry, with 9 percent of the market for small package deliveries. Its main domestic competitors are Federal Express, which has 26 percent of the market, and United Parcel Service (UPS), which has 53 percent of the market. There are several small players, including DHL Airways, Consolidated Freightways (CF), and the U.S. Postal Service, each of which holds less than 5 percent of the market share.[1]

This case was made possible by the generous assistance of Airborne Express. The information given in this case was provided by Airborne Express. Unless otherwise indicated, Airborne Express and the Securities and Exchange Commission's 10-K filings are the sources of all information contained within this case. The case is based on an earlier case, which was prepared with the assistance of Daniel Bodnar, Laurie Martinelli, Brian McMullen, Lisa Mutty, and Stephen Schmidt. The case is intended as a basis for classroom discussion rather than as an illustration of either effective or ineffective handling of an administrative situation. Reprinted by permission of Charles W. L. Hill.

The evolution of the air express industry and the current state of competition in the industry were discussed in a companion case: Case 29, "The Evolution of the Air Express Industry, 1973–2002." The current case (Case 30) focuses on the operating structure, competitive strategy, organizational structure, and cultures of Airborne Express.

History of Airborne Express

Airborne Express was originally known as Pacific Air Freight when it was founded in Seattle at the close of World War II by Holt W. Webster, a former Army Air Corps officer. (See Exhibit 1 for a list of major milestones in the history of Airborne Express.) The company was merged with Airborne Freight Corporation of California in 1968, taking the name of the California company but retaining management direction by the former officers of Pacific Air Freight. Airborne was initially an exclusive air freight forwarder. Freight forwarders such as Airborne arrange for the transportation of air cargo between any two destinations. They purchase cargo space from the airlines and retail this space in small amounts. They deal primarily with small customers, providing pickup and delivery services in most cities, either in their own trucks or through contract agents.

Following the 1977 deregulation of the airline industry, Airborne entered the air express industry by leasing the airplanes and pilots of Midwest Charter, a small airline operating out of its own airport in Wilmington, Ohio.

EXHIBIT 1

Major Milestones at Airborne Express[2]

1946: Airborne Flower Traffic Association of California is founded to fly fresh flowers from Hawaii to the mainland.

1968: Airborne of California and Pacific Air Freight of Seattle merge to form Airborne Freight Corporation. Headquarters are in Seattle, Washington.

1979–1981: Airborne Express is born. After purchasing Midwest Air Charter, Airborne buys Clinton County Air Force Base in Wilmington, Ohio, becoming the only carrier to own and operate an airport. The package sort center opens, creating the "hub" for the hub-and-spoke system.

1984–1986: Airborne is first carrier to establish a privately operated foreign trade zone in an air industrial park.

1987: Airborne opens the Airborne Stock Exchange, a third-party inventory management and distribution service. In the same year, service begins to and from more than 8,000 Canadian locations.

1988: Airborne becomes the first air express carrier to provide same-day delivery, through its purchase of Sky Courier.

1990: The International Cargo Forum and Exposition names Airborne the carrier with the most-outstanding integrated cargo system over the previous two years.

1991: Airborne is the first transportation company to receive Volvo-Flyg Motors' Excellent Performance Award. *Computerworld* ranks Airborne the "most effective user of information systems in the U.S. transportation industry." In addition, Airborne receives the "Spread the Word!" Electronic Data Interchange (EDI) award for having the largest number of EDI users worldwide in the air express and freight forwarding industry.

1992: Airborne introduces Flight-ReadySM—the first prepaid Express Letters and Packs.

1993: Airborne introduces Airborne Logistics Services (ALS), a new subsidiary providing outsourced warehousing and distribution services. IBM consolidates its international shipping operation with Airborne.

1994: Airborne opens its Ocean Service Division, becoming the first express carrier to introduce ocean shipping services. Airborne Logistics Services (ALS) establishes the first new film distribution program for the movie industry in fifty years. Airborne also becomes the first company to provide online communication to Vietnam.

1995: Airborne Alliance Group, a consortium of transportation, logistics, third-party customer service operations, and high-tech companies providing value-added services, is formed. Airborne opens a second runway at its hub, which is now the United States's largest privately owned airport. Airborne also expands its fleet, acquiring Boeing 767-200 aircraft.

1996: Airborne Express celebrates fifty years of providing value-added distribution solutions to business.

1997: Airborne Express has its best year ever, with net earnings increasing three-and-a-half-fold over the previous year. Airborne's stock triples, leading to a two-for-one stock split in February 1998.

1998: Airborne posts record profits and enters the Fortune 500. The first of thirty Boeing 767s is introduced to its fleet. *The Business Consumer Guide* rates Airborne as the Best Air Express Carrier for the fourth consecutive year.

1999: Airborne@home, a unique alliance with the United States Postal Service, is introduced. It enables etailers, catalog companies, and similar businesses to ship quickly and economically to the residential marketplace. Optical Village is created. Part of Airborne Logistics Services, this new division brings together some of the biggest competitors in the optical industry to share many costs and a single location for their assembly, storage, inventory, logistics, and delivery options.

2000: Airborne announces several changes in senior management, including a new president and chief operating officer, Carl Donaway. Several new business initiatives are announced, most notably a ground service scheduled to begin April 1, 2001. Airborne also wins the Brand Keys Customer Loyalty Award, edging out the competition for the second consecutive year.

2001: Airborne launches ground delivery service and 10:30 A.M. service, giving it a comprehensive, full-service industry competitive capability. Airborne.com launches its Small Business Center, as well as various enhancements to help all business customers speed and simplify the shipping process. Airborne also releases the Corporate Exchange shipping application, simplifying desktop shipping for customers while giving them greater control. Advanced tracking features are added to airborne.com and Airborne eCourier is released, enabling customers to send confidential, signed documents electronically.

Airborne quickly became dissatisfied, however, with the limited amount of control they were able to exercise over Midwest, which made it difficult to achieve the kind of tight coordination and control of logistics that was necessary to become a successful air express operator. Instead of continuing to lease Midwest's planes and facility, Airborne decided in 1980 to buy "the entire bucket of slop: company, planes, pilots, airport and all."

Among other things, the Midwest acquisition put Airborne in the position of being the only industry participant to own an airport. Airborne immediately began the job of developing a hub-and-spoke system capable of supporting a nationwide distribution system. An efficient sorting facility was established at the Wilmington hub. Airborne upgraded Midwest's fleet of prop and propjet aircraft by buying a modern fleet of DC-8s, DC-9s, and YS-11 aircraft. These planes left major cities every evening, flying down the spokes and carrying letters and packages to the central sort facility in Wilmington, Ohio. There, the letters and packages were unloaded, sorted according to their final destination, and then reloaded and flown to their final destination for delivery before noon the next day.

During the late 1970s and early 1980s, dramatic growth in the industry attracted many competitors. As a consequence, competition became intense, despite a high-growth rate price, forcing several companies to the sidelines by the late 1980s. Between 1984 and 1990, average revenues per domestic shipment at Airborne fell from around $30 to under $15 (today, they run at just under $9). Airborne was able to survive this period by pursuing several strategies that increased productivity and drove costs down to the lowest levels in the industry. Airborne's operating costs per shipment fell from $28 in 1984 to about $14 by 1990 (they fell to $9.79 by 2001). As a consequence, by the late 1980s, Airborne had pulled away from a pack of struggling competitors to become one of the top three companies in the industry, a position it still held in 2002.

Air Express Operations
The Domestic Delivery Network

As of 2002, Airborne Express had 305 ground stations within the United States. The stations are essentially the ends of the spokes in Airborne's hub-and-spoke system. The distribution of stations allows Airborne to reach all major population centers in the country. In each station are about fifty to fifty-five drivers plus staff. About 80 percent of Airborne's 115,300 full-time and 7,200 part-time employees work at this level. The stations are the basic units in Airborne's delivery organization. Their primary task is to ferry packages between clients and the local air terminal. Airborne utilizes approximately 14,900 radio-dispatch delivery vans and trucks to transport packages, of which 6,000 are owned by the company. Independent contractors under contract with the company provide the balance of the company's pickup and delivery services.

Airborne's drivers make their last round of major clients at 5 P.M. The drivers either collect packages directly from clients or from one of the company's more than 15,300 drop boxes. The drop boxes are placed at strategic locations, such as in the lobbies of major commercial buildings. To give clients a little more time, in most major cities there are also a few central drop boxes that are not emptied until 6 P.M. If a client needs still more time, the package can be delivered to the airport by 7 P.M. so it will make the evening flight.

When a driver picks up a package, he or she uses a hand-held scanner to read a bar code that is attached to the package. This information is then fed directly into Airborne's proprietary FOCUS (Freight, On-Line Control and Update System) computer system. FOCUS, which has global coverage, records shipment status at key points in the life cycle of a shipment. Thus, a customer can call Airborne on a twenty-four-hour basis to find out where their package is in Airborne's system. FOCUS also allows a customer direct access to shipment information through the Internet. All a customer needs to do is access Airborne's web site and key the code number assigned to a package, and FOCUS will tell the customer where the package is currently in Airborne's system.

When the driver has completed the pickup route, she or he takes the load to Airborne's loading docks at the local airport. (Airborne serves all ninety-nine major metropolitan airports in the United States.) There, the packages are loaded into C-containers (discussed later in this case study).

Several C-containers are then towed by hand or by tractor to a waiting aircraft, where they are loaded onto a conveyor belt and they pass through the passenger door of the aircraft. Before long, the aircraft is loaded and takes off. It will either fly directly to the company's hub at Wilmington or make one or two stops along the way to pick up more packages.

Sometime between midnight and 2 A.M., most of the aircraft will have landed at Wilmington. An old strategic air command base, Wilmington's location places it within a 600-mile radius (an overnight drive or one-hour flying time) of 60 percent of the U.S. population. Wilmington also has the advantage of good weather. In all the years that Airborne has operated at Wilmington, air operations have been fogged in on only a handful of days. In 1995, Airborne opened a second runway at Wilmington. Developed at a cost of $60 million, the second runway makes Wilmington the largest privately owned airport in the country. The runway expansion was part of a $120 million upgrade of the Wilmington sort facility.

After arrival at Wilmington, the plane taxis down the runway and parks alongside a group of aircraft that are already disgorging their load of C-containers. Within minutes the C-containers are unloaded from the plane down a conveyor belt and towed to the sort facility by a tractor. The sort facility has the capacity to handle 1.2 million packages per night. At the end of 2001, the facility handled an average of 1 million packages a night. The bar codes on the packages are read, and then the packages are directed through a labyrinth of conveyor belts and sorted according to final destination. The sorting is partly done by hand and partly automated. At the end of this process, packages are grouped together by final destination and loaded into a C-container. An aircraft bound for the final destination is then loaded with C-containers, and by 5 A.M. most aircraft have taken off.

Upon arrival at the final destination, the plane is unloaded and the packages are sorted according to their delivery points within the surrounding area. Airborne couriers then take the packages on the final leg of their journey. Packages have a 75 percent probability of being delivered to clients by 10:30 A.M., and a 98 percent probability of being delivered by noon.

Regional Trucking Hubs

Although about 71 percent of packages are transported by air and pass through Wilmington, Airborne has also established ten regional trucking hubs that deal with the remaining 29 percent of the company's domestic volume. These hubs sort shipments that originate and have a destination within approximately a 300-mile radius. The first one was opened in Allentown, Pennsylvania, which is centrally located on the East Coast. This hub handles packages that are being transported between points within the Washington, D.C.–Boston area. Instead of transporting packages by air, packages to be transported within this area are sorted by the drivers at pickup and delivered from the driver's home station by scheduled truck runs to the Allentown hub. There, they are sorted according to destination and taken to the appropriate station on another scheduled truck run for final delivery.

One advantage of ground-based transportation through trucking hubs is that operating costs are much lower than for air transportation. The average cost of a package transported by air is more than five times greater than the cost of a package transported on the ground. This cost differential is transparent to the customer, however, who assumes that all packages are flown. Thus, Airborne can charge the same price for ground-transported packages as for air-transported packages, but the former yields a much higher return. The trucking hubs also have the advantage of taking some of the load off the Wilmington sorting facility, which is currently operating at about 90 percent capacity.

International Operations

In addition to its domestic express operations, Airborne is also an international company providing service to more than 200 countries worldwide. International operations accounted for about 11 percent of total revenues in 2001. Airborne offers two international products: freight products and express products. Freight products are commercial-sized, larger-unit shipments. This service provides door-to-airport service. Goods are picked up domestically from the customer and then shipped to the destination airport. A consignee or an agent of the consignee gets the paperwork and must clear the shipment through customs. Express packages are small packages, documents, and letters. This service is door to door, and all shipments are cleared through customs by Airborne. Most of Airborne's international revenues come from freight products.

Airborne does not fly any of its own aircraft overseas. Instead, it contracts for space on all-cargo airlines or in the cargo holds of passenger airlines. Airborne owns facilities overseas in Japan, Taiwan, Hong Kong, Singapore, Australia, New Zealand, and London. These facilities function in a manner similar to Airborne's domestic stations (that is, they have their own trucks and drivers and are hooked into the FOCUS tracking system). The majority of foreign distribution, however, is carried out by foreign agents. Foreign agents are large, local, well-established surface delivery companies. Recently, Airborne has entered into several exclusive strategic alliances with large foreign agents. Currently it has alliances in Japan, Thailand, Malaysia, and South Africa. (The rationale for entering strategic alliances, along with Airborne's approach to global expansion, is discussed in greater detail later in this case.)

Another aspect of Airborne's international operations has been the creation at its Wilmington hub of the only privately certified foreign trade zone (FTZ) in the United States. While in an FTZ, merchandise is tax free and no customs duty is paid on it until it leaves. Thus, a foreign-based company may store critical inventory in the FTZ and have Airborne deliver it just in time to U.S. customers. This allows the foreign company to hold inventory in the United States without having to pay customs duty on it until the need arises.

Aircraft Purchase and Maintenance

As of 2001, Airborne Express owned a fleet of 118 aircraft, including twenty-four DC-8s, seventy-four DC-9s, and twenty Boeing 767s. In addition, approximately seventy smaller aircraft are chartered nightly to connect smaller cities with company aircraft that then operate to and from the Wilmington hub. To keep capital expenditures down, Airborne has traditionally purchased only used planes. Airborne converts the planes to suit its specifications at a maintenance facility based at its Wilmington hub. Once it gets a plane, Airborne typically guts the interior and installs state-of-the-art electronics and avionics equipment. The company's philosophy is to get all of the upgrades that it can into an aircraft.

Although this kind of overhaul can cost a lot up front, the payback is increased aircraft reliability and a reduction in service downtime. Airborne also standardizes cockpits as much as possible, which makes it easier for crews to switch from one aircraft to another if the need arises. According to the company, the total purchase and modification of a secondhand DC-9 costs about $10 million, compared with the cost of an equivalent new plane of $40 million. An additional factor reducing operating costs is that Airborne's DC-9 aircraft require only a two-person cockpit crew, as opposed to the three-person crews required in most Federal Express and UPS aircraft.

After conversion of the aircraft, Airborne strives to keep aircraft maintenance costs down by carrying out almost all of its own fleet repairs. (It is the only all-cargo carrier to do so.) The Wilmington maintenance facility can handle everything except major engine repairs and has the capability to machine critical aircraft parts if needed. The company sees this in-house facility as a major source of cost savings. It estimates that maintenance labor costs are 50 to 60 percent below the costs of having the same work performed outside.

In December 1995, Airborne announced a deal to purchase twelve used Boeing 767-200 aircraft between the years 1997 and 2000, and it announced plans to purchase an additional ten to fifteen used 767-200s between the years 2000 and 2004. These were the first wide-bodied aircraft in Airborne's fleet. The cost of introducing the first twelve aircraft was about $290 million, and the additional aircraft will cost another $360 million. The shift to wide-bodied aircraft was promoted by an internal study, which concluded that with growing volume, wide-bodied aircraft would lead to greater operating efficiencies.

During 2001, Airborne was using about 66.6 percent of its lift capacity on a typical business day. This compares with 76.7 percent capacity utilization in 1997, and 70 percent utilization in 2000. In late 2001, Airborne reduced its total lift capacity by approximately 100,000 pounds to about 4 million pounds a day, in an attempt to reduce excess capacity of certain routes and better match supply with demand conditions.

C-Containers

C-containers are uniquely shaped 60-cubic-foot containers developed by Airborne Express in 1985 at a cost of $3.5 million. They are designed to fit through the passenger doors of DC-8 and DC-9 aircraft. They replaced the much larger A-containers widely used in the air cargo business. At six times the size of a C-container, A-containers can be loaded only through specially built cargo doors and require specialized loading equipment. The loading equipment required for C-containers is a modified belt loader, similar to that used for loading baggage onto a plane, and about 80 percent less expensive than the equipment needed to load A-containers. The use of C-containers also means that Airborne does not have to bear the $1 million per plane cost required to install cargo doors that will take A-containers. The C-containers are shaped to allow maximum utilization of the planes' interior loading space. Fifty of the containers fit into a converted DC-9, and about eighty-three fit into a DC-8-62. A C-container filled with packages can be moved by a single person, making it easy to load and unload. Airborne Express has taken out a patent on the design of the C-containers.

Information Systems

Airborne utilizes three information systems to help boost productivity and improve customer service. The first of these systems is referred to as the LIBRA II system. LIBRA II equipment, which includes a metering device and PC computer software, is installed in the mailroom of clients. With minimum data entry, the metering device weighs the package, calculates the shipping charges, generates the shipping labels, and provides a daily shipping report. By December 2001, the system was in use at approximately 9,900 domestic customer locations. The use of LIBRA II not only benefits the customers but also lowers Airborne's operating costs because LIBRA II shipment data are transferred into Airborne's FOCUS shipment tracking system automatically, thereby avoiding duplicate data entry.

FOCUS is the second of Airborne's three main information systems. As discussed earlier, FOCUS is essentially a worldwide tracking system. The bar code on each package is read at various points (for example, at pickup, at sorting in Wilmington, at arrival, and so forth) with hand-held scanners, and this information is fed into Airborne's computer system. Using FOCUS, Airborne can track the progress of a shipment through its national and international logistics system. The major benefit is in terms of customer service. Through an Internet link, Airborne's customers can track their own shipments through Airborne's system on a twenty-four-hour basis.

For its highest-volume corporate customers, Airborne has developed Customer Linkage, an electronic data interchange (EDI) program and the third information system. The EDI system is designed to eliminate the flow of paperwork between Airborne and its major clients. The EDI system allows customers to create shipping documentation at the same time they enter orders for their goods. At the end of each day, shipping activities are transmitted electronically to Airborne's FOCUS, where they are captured for shipment tracking and billing. Customer Linkage benefits the customer by eliminating repetitive data entry and paperwork. It also lowers the company's operating costs by eliminating manual data entry. (In essence, both LIBRA II and Customer Linkage push a lot of the data-entry work into the hands of customers.) The EDI system also includes electronic invoicing and payment remittance processing. Airborne also offers its customers a program known as Quicklink, which significantly reduces the programming time required by customers to take advantage of linkage benefits.

Strategy
Market Positioning

In the early 1980s, Airborne Express tried hard to compete head-to-head with Federal Express with an attempt to establish broad market coverage, including both frequent and infrequent users. Frequent users are shippers that generate more than $20,000 of business per month, or more than 1,000 shipments per month. Infrequent users generate less than $20,000 per month, or less than 1,000 shipments per month.

To build broad market coverage, Airborne followed Federal Express's lead of funding a television advertising campaign designed to build consumer awareness. By the mid 1980s, however, Airborne decided that this method of building market share was expensive. The advertising campaign bought recognition but little penetration. One of the principal problems was that it was expensive to serve infrequent users. Infrequent users demanded the same level of service as frequent users, but Airborne would typically get only one shipment per pickup with an infrequent user compared with ten or more shipments per pickup with a frequent user. Far more pickups were required to generate the same volume of business. Given the extremely competitive nature of the industry at this time, such an inefficient utilization of capacity was of great concern to Airborne.

Consequently, in the mid 1980s, Airborne decided to become a niche player in the industry and focused on serving the needs of high-volume corporate accounts. The company slashed its advertising expenditure, pulling the plug on its television ad campaign, and invested more resources in building a direct sales force, which is now 460. By focusing on high-volume corporate accounts, Airborne could establish scheduled pickup routes and use its ground capacity more efficiently. This enabled the company to achieve significant reductions in its unit cost structure. Partly due to this factor, Airborne executives estimate that their cost structure is as much as $3 per shipment less than that of FedEx. Another estimate suggests that Airborne's strategy reduced labor costs by 20 percent per unit for pickup and 10 percent for delivery.

Of course, there is a downside to this strategy. High-volume corporate customers have a great deal more bargaining power than infrequent users, so they can and do demand substantial discounts. For example, in March 1987 Airborne achieved a major coup when it won an exclusive three-year contract to handle all of IBM's express packages weighing less than 150 pounds. To win the IBM account, however, Airborne had to offer rates up to 84 percent below Federal Express's list prices. Nevertheless, the strategy seems to have worked. As of 1995, approximately 80 percent of Airborne's revenues come from corporate accounts, most of them secured through competitive bidding. The concentrated volume that this business represents has helped Airborne to drive down costs.

Delivery Time, Reliability, and Flexibility

Another feature of Airborne's strategy was the decision not to try to compete with Federal Express on delivery time. Federal Express and UPS have long guaranteed delivery by 10:30 A.M. Airborne guarantees delivery by midday, although it offers a 10:30 guarantee to some very large corporate customers. Guaranteeing delivery by 10:30 A.M. would mean stretching Airborne's already tight scheduling system to the limit. To meet its 10:30 A.M. deadline, FedEx has to operate with a deadline for the previous day's pickups of 6:30 P.M. Airborne can afford to be a little more flexible and can arrange pickups as late as 7:00 P.M. if that suits a corporate client's particular needs. Later pickups clearly benefit the shipper, who is, after all, the paying party.

In addition, Airborne executives feel that a guaranteed 10:30 A.M. delivery is unnecessary. The extra hour and a half does not make a great deal of difference to most clients, and they are willing to accept the extra time in exchange for lower prices. In addition, Airborne stresses the reliability of its delivery schedules. As one executive put it, "A package delivered consistently at 11:15 A.M. is as good as delivery at 10:30 A.M." This reliability is enhanced by Airborne's ability to provide shipment tracking through its FOCUS.

Deferred Services

With a slowdown in the growth rate of the express mail market toward the end of the 1980s, Airborne decided in 1990 to enter the deferred-delivery business with its Select Delivery Service (SDS) product. SDS provides for next-afternoon or second-day delivery. Packages weighing 5 pounds or less are generally delivered on a next-afternoon basis, with packages of more than 5 pounds being delivered on a second-day basis. SDS shipments comprised approximately 42 percent of total domestic shipments in 1995. They are priced lower than overnight express products, reflecting the less time-sensitive nature of these deliveries. The company will utilize any spare capacity on its express flights to carry SDS shipments. In addition, Airborne will use other carriers, such as passenger carriers with spare cargo capacity in their planes, to carry less urgent SDS shipments.

Early in 1996, Airborne began to phase in two new services to replace SDS. Next Afternoon Service is available for shipments weighing 5 pounds or less, and Second Day Service is offered for shipments of all weights. By 2001, deferred shipments accounted for 46 percent of total domestic shipments.

Ground Delivery Service

In April 2001, Airborne launched a ground delivery service (GDS) in response to similar offerings from

FedEx and UPS. Airborne concluded that it was important to offer this service to retain parity with its principal competitors and to be able to offer bundled services to its principal customers (that is, to offer them air, ground, and logistics services for a single bundled price). Airborne also felt that they could add the service with a relatively minor initial investment, $30 million, because it leveraged existing assets, including trucks, tracking systems, and regional ground hubs and sorting facilities.

The new service has initially been introduced on a limited basis and is targeted at large corporate customers. GDS is priced less than deferred services, reflecting the less time-sensitive nature of the GDS offering. GDS accounted for 1.5 percent of domestic shipments in 2001, and 4 percent in the fourth quarter of 2001.

Logistics Services

Although small-package express mail remains Airborne's main business, the company is increasingly promoting a range of third-party logistics services through its Advanced Logistics Services Corp. (ALS) subsidiary. These services provide customers with the ability to maintain inventories in a 1-million-square-foot "stock exchange" facility located at Airborne's Wilmington hub or at sixty smaller stock exchange facilities located around the country. The inventory can be managed either by Airborne or by customer's personnel. Inventory stored at Wilmington can be delivered utilizing either Airborne's airline system or, if required, commercial airlines on a next-flight-out basis. ALS's central print computer program allows information on inventories to be sent electronically to customers' computers located at Wilmington, where Airborne's personnel monitor prints output and ships inventories according to customers' instructions.

For example, consider the case of Data Products Corp., a producer of computer printers. Data Products takes advantage of low labor costs to carry out significant assembly operations in Hong Kong. Many of the primary component parts for its printers, such as microprocessors, are manufactured in the United States and have to be shipped to Hong Kong. The finished product is then shipped back to the United States for sale. In setting up a global manufacturing system, Data Products had a decision to make: either consolidate the parts from its

hundreds of suppliers in-house and then arrange for shipment to Hong Kong, or contract someone to handle the whole logistics process. Data Products decided to contract, and they picked Airborne Express to consolidate the component parts and arrange for shipments.

Airborne controls the consolidation and movement of component parts from the component part suppliers to the Hong Kong assembly operation so that inventory-holding costs are minimized. The key feature of Airborne's service is that all of Data Products's materials are collected at Airborne's facility at Los Angeles International Airport. Data Products's Hong Kong assembly plants can then tell Airborne what parts to ship by air as they are needed. Thus, Airborne can provide inventory control for Data Products. In addition, by scheduling deliveries so that year-round traffic between Los Angeles and Hong Kong can be guaranteed, Airborne can negotiate a better air rate from Japan Air Lines (JAL) for the transportation of component parts.

International Strategy

One of the major strategic challenges currently facing Airborne (along with the other express mail carriers) is how best to establish an international service that is comparable to their domestic service. Many of Airborne's major corporate clients are becoming more global in their strategic orientation. They are increasingly demanding a compatible express mail service. In addition, the rise of companies with globally dispersed manufacturing operations that rely on just-in-time delivery systems to keep their inventory holding costs down has created a demand for a global air express service that can transport critical inventory between operations located in different areas of the globe (consider the example of Data Products discussed earlier in this case study).

The initial response of FedEx and UPS to this challenge was to undertake massive capital investments to establish international airlift capability and international ground operations based on the U.S. model. Their rationale was that a wholly owned global delivery network was necessary to establish the tight control, coordination, and scheduling required for a successful air express operation. More recently, however, FedEx pulled out of its European ground operations while continuing to fly its own aircraft overseas.

Airborne has decided on a quite different strategy. In part born of financial necessity (Airborne lacks the capital necessary to imitate FedEx and UPS), Airborne has decided to pursue what they refer to as a "variable cost strategy." This strategy involves two main elements: (1) the utilization of international airlift on existing air cargo operators and passenger aircraft to get their packages overseas, and (2) entry into strategic alliances with foreign companies that already have established ground delivery networks. With this strategy, Airborne hopes to be able to establish global coverage without having to undertake the kind of capital investments that Federal Express and UPS have.

Airborne executives defend their decision to continue to purchase space on international flights rather than fly their own aircraft overseas by making several points. First, Airborne's international business is currently 70 percent outbound and 30 percent inbound. If Airborne were to fly its own aircraft overseas, some would have to fly back half-empty. Second, on many routes, Airborne simply doesn't yet have the volume necessary to justify flying its own planes. Third, national air carriers are currently giving Airborne good prices. If Airborne began to fly directly overseas, the company would be seen as a competitor and might no longer be given price breaks. Fourth, getting international airlift space is currently not a problem. While space can be limited in the third and fourth quarters of the year, Airborne is such a big customer that it usually has few problems getting lift. On the other hand, the long-term viability of this strategy is questionable given the rapid evolution in the international air express business. Flying Tiger was once one of Airborne's major providers of international lift. Following the purchase of Flying Tiger by FedEx, however, Airborne has reduced its business with Flying Tiger. Apart from concerns about giving business to a competitor, Airborne fears that its packages will be pushed to the back of the plane whenever Flying Tiger has problems of capacity overload.

With regard to strategic alliances, Airborne currently has joint venture operations in Japan, Thailand, Malaysia, and South Africa. The alliance with Mitsui was announced in December 1989. Mitsui is one of the world's leading trading companies. Together with Tonami Transportation Co., Mitsui owns Panther Express, one of the top five express carriers in Japan and a company with a substantial ground network. The deal called for the establishment of a joint venture among Airborne, Mitsui, and Tonami. Known as Airborne Express Japan, the joint venture combined Airborne's existing Japanese operations with Panther Express. Airborne handles all the shipments to and from Japan. The joint venture is 40 percent owned by Airborne, 40 percent owned by Mitsui, and 20 percent owned by Tonami. The agreement specifies that board decisions must be made by consensus among the three partners. A majority of two cannot outvote the third. In addition, the deal called for Mitsui to invest $40 million in Airborne Express through the purchase of a new issue of nonvoting, 6.9 percent cumulative, convertible preferred stock and a commitment to Airborne from Mitsui of up to $100 million for aircraft financing. Airborne executives saw the Mitsui deal as a major coup, both financially and in terms of market penetration into the Japanese market. The primary advantage claimed by Airborne executives for expanding via strategic alliances is that the company gets an established ground-based delivery network overseas without having to make capital investments.

Organization

In 2001, Carl Donaway became CEO, replacing the longtime top management team of Robert Cline, the CEO, and Robert Brazier, the president and COO. Both had been with the company since the early 1960s. Prior to becoming CEO, Donaway was responsible for airline operations, including managing the Wilmington hub, the package sorting facility, and all aircraft and flight maintenance operations. The philosophy at Airborne is to keep the organizational structure as flat as possible, shorten the lines of communication, and allow for a free flow of ideas within the managerial hierarchy. The top managers generally feel that they are open to ideas suggested by lower-level managers. At the same time, the decision-making process is fairly centralized. The view is that interdependence between functions makes centralized decision making necessary. To quote one executive, "Coordination is the essence of this business. We need centralized decision making in order to achieve this."

Control at Airborne Express is geared toward boosting productivity, lowering costs, and maintaining a reliable high-quality service. These goals are achieved through a combination of budgetary controls, pay-for-performance incentive systems, and a corporate culture that continually stresses key values. For example, consider the procedure used to control stations (where about 80 percent of all employees work). Station operations are reviewed on a quarterly basis using a budgetary process. Control and evaluation of station effectiveness stress four categories. The first is service, measured by the time between pickup and delivery. The goal is to achieve 95 to 97 percent of all deliveries before noon. The second category is productivity, measured by total shipments per employee hour. The third category is controllable cost, and the fourth is station profitability. Goals for each of these categories are determined each quarter in a bottom-up procedure that involves station managers in the goal-setting process. These goals are then linked to an incentive pay system whereby station managers can earn up to 10 percent of their quarterly salary just by meeting their goals with no maximum on the upside if they go over the goals.

The direct sales force also has an incentive pay system. The target pay structure for the sales organization is 70 percent base pay and a 30 percent commission. There is no cap, however, on the commissions for salespeople. So in theory, there is no limit to what a salesperson can earn. There are also contests designed to boost performance. For example, there is a so-called top gun competition for the sales force in which the top salesperson for each quarter wins a $20,000 prize.

Incentive pay systems apart, however, Airborne is not known as a high payer. The company's approach is not to be the compensation leader. Rather, the company tries to set its salary structure to position it in the middle of the labor market. Thus, according to a senior human resources executive, "We target our pay philosophy [total package—compensation plus benefits] to be right at the 50th percentile plus or minus 5 percent."

A degree of self-control is also achieved by trying to establish a corporate culture that focuses employees' attention on the key values required to maintain a competitive edge in the air express industry. The values continually stressed by top managers at Airborne, and communicated throughout the organization by the company's newspaper and a quarterly video, emphasize serving customers' needs, maintaining quality, doing it right the first time around, and excellent service. There is also a companywide emphasis on productivity and cost control. One executive, when describing the company's attitude to expenditures, said, "We challenge everything. . . . We're the toughest sons of bitches on the block." Another noted, "Among managers I feel that there is a universal agreement on the need to control costs. This is a very tough business, and our people are aware of that. Airborne has an underdog mentality—a desire to be a survivor."

Airborne in 2002

The late 1990s and early 2000s were very difficult years for Airborne Express. A combination of weak volume growth (and an absolute decline in 2001); high fuel costs; a switch from premium overnight service to lower-margin deferred services; and strong competition from FedEx and UPS, both of whom had a superior capability to bundle products, pounded the company. After recording record earnings of $137 million in 1997, Airborne saw its profits slide over the next four years (see Exhibits 2–5 for details on Airborne's financial performance). In 2001, the company lost $19 million on revenues of $3.2 billion, even though this number represented an increase from the $2.9 billion revenues generated in 1997. For years, Airborne's niche strategy had served the company well and allowed it to make a return in a very competitive industry, but now analysts questioned whether Airborne could survive as an independent entity. The company, they said, simply lacked the global scale and scope of its larger rivals.

There was persistent speculation that Airborne would ultimately be acquired by DHL, which is 51 percent owned by Germany's Deutsche Post. DHL had a small position inside the United States but was the largest global shipper of express packages. Acquiring Airborne would give Deutsche Post the U.S. delivery network that it currently lacked to round out the global delivery and logistics business it is building. However, U.S. law currently prevents a foreign entity from owning more than 25 percent of a U.S. airline. Deutsche Post may be able to get around this restriction by using DHL Airways, a U.S.

EXHIBIT 2

Airborne Express Income Statement, 1997–2001 (in $ millions)

	Year Ended December 31				
	2001	**2000**	**1999**	**1998**	**1997**
Revenues:					
Domestic	$2,850,798	$2,895,818	$2,772,782	$2,712,344	$2,514,737
International	360,291	380,132	366,342	361,440	397,672
	3,211,089	3,275,950	3,139,124	3,073,784	2,912,409
Operating Expenses:					
Transportation purchased	1,046,954	1,042,541	965,722	944,357	922,885
Station and ground operations	1,067,764	1,055,142	975,669	914,919	858,238
Flight operations and maintenance	557,412	588,582	513,337	477,799	431,474
General and administrative	265,545	258,149	240,089	248,497	234,366
Sales and marketing	90,390	82,512	77,196	71,354	70,346
Depreciation and amortization	208,355	206,406	209,390	184,526	169,845
Federal legislation compensation	(13,000)	—	—	—	—
	3,223,420	3,233,332	2,981,403	2,841,452	2,687,154
Earnings (Loss) from Operations	(12,331)	42,618	157,721	232,332	225,255
Other Income (Expense):					
Interest, net	(19,868)	(23,425)	(17,262)	(12,882)	(27,790)
Discount on sales of receivables	(9,293)	(96)	—	—	—
Other	12,588	4,129	6,929	2,135	—
Earnings (Loss) Before Income Taxes	(28,904)	23,226	147,388	221,585	197,465
Income Taxes	(9,446)	8,940	56,187	84,300	77,393
Net Earnings (Loss) Before Change in Accounting	(19,458)	14,286	91,201	137,285	120,072
Cumulative Effect of Change in Accounting	—	14,206	—	—	—
Net Earnings (Loss)	($19,458)	$28,492	$91,201	$137,285	$120,072
Net Earnings (Loss) per Share:					
Basic					
Before change in accounting	($0.40)	$0.30	$1.88	$2.77	$2.68
Cumulative effect of change in accounting	—	0.29	—	—	—
Net earnings (loss)	($0.40)	$0.59	$1.88	$2.77	$2.68
Diluted					
Before change in accounting	($0.40)	$0.30	$1.85	$2.72	$2.44
Cumulative effect of change in accounting	—	0.29	—	—	—
Net earnings (loss)	($0.40)	$0.59	$1.85	$2.72	$2.44
Dividends per Share:	$0.16	$0.16	$0.16	$0.16	$0.15
Performance as a Percentage of Revenues:					
Operating margin	−0.4%	1.4%	5.0%	7.6%	7.8%
Pretax margin	−0.9%	0.7%	4.7%	7.2%	6.8%
Effective tax rate	32.7%	38.5%	38.1%	38.0%	39.2%
Net margin before change in accounting	−0.6%	0.4%	2.9%	4.5%	4.1%

EXHIBIT 3

Airborne Express, Shipment Revenue Statistics, 1997–2001

	Year Ended December 31				
	2001	**2000**	**1999**	**1998**	**1997**
Average Revenue per Pound:					
Domestic					
Overnight	$ 2.58	$ 2.45	$ 2.42	$ 2.36	$ 2.26
Next-afternoon service	3.65	3.61	3.34	3.05	3.03
Second-day service	1.26	1.23	1.24	1.19	1.18
Ground delivery service	0.57	—	—	—	—
100 lbs. and over	0.94	0.94	0.90	0.79	0.81
Total domestic	$ 2.02	$ 2.03	$ 2.03	$ 1.96	$ 1.89
International					
Express	$ 3.78	$ 3.83	$ 3.97	$ 4.02	$ 4.47
Freight	0.77	0.79	0.82	0.96	1.05
Total international	$ 1.03	$ 1.10	$ 1.17	$ 1.31	$ 1.35
Total shipments	$ 1.82	$ 1.89	$ 1.90	$ 1.85	$ 1.79
Average Revenue per Shipment:					
Domestic					
Overnight	$ 9.83	$ 9.74	$ 9.44	$ 9.26	$ 9.33
Next-afternoon service	6.99	6.63	6.43	6.27	5.86
Second-day service	7.03	7.45	7.49	7.22	7.15
Ground delivery service	5.60	—	—	—	—
100 lbs. and over	176.63	198.24	189.82	163.47	184.74
Total domestic	$ 8.76	$ 8.92	$ 8.76	$ 8.56	$ 8.45
International					
Express	$ 18.48	$ 19.00	$ 20.34	$ 20.72	$ 21.26
Freight	622.47	607.08	571.04	540.07	592.41
Total international	$ 57.33	$ 57.96	$ 52.05	$ 56.03	$ 69.78

EXHIBIT 4

Airborne Express Shipment Volume Statistics, 1997–2001

	Year Ended December 31				
	2001	**2000**	**1999**	**1998**	**1997**
Annual Growth Rates:					
Domestic					
Overnight	−8.1%	−0.5%	0.0%	7.8%	18.0%
Next-afternoon service	−4.1%	−3.5%	−3.4%	8.2%	92.5%
Second-day service	15.4%	12.3%	2.6%	2.3%	−11.8%
Ground delivery service	—	—	—	—	
100 lbs. and over	−15.5%	−3.4%	−19.8%	5.9%	13.8%
Total domestic	0.1%	1.9%	−0.1%	6.6%	16.8%
International					
Express	−4.3%	−7.3%	10.3%	15.2%	16.1%
Freight	−2.5%	0.5%	−8.1%	−8.8%	−11.2%
Total international	−4.2%	−6.8%	9.1%	13.2%	13.2%
Total shipments	0.1%	1.7%	0.1%	6.7%	16.8%
Shipments by Category as a Percentage of Total Shipments:					
Domestic					
Overnight	51.7%	56.3%	57.6%	57.7%	57.1%
Next-afternoon service	15.8%	16.5%	17.4%	18.0%	17.8%
Second-day service	29.0%	25.1%	22.7%	22.2%	23.2%
Ground delivery service	1.5%	—	—	—	
100 lbs. and over	0.1%	0.1%	0.1%	0.1%	0.1%
Total domestic	98.1%	98.0%	97.8%	98.0%	98.1%
International					
Express	1.8%	1.9%	2.1%	1.9%	1.7%
Freight	0.1%	0.1%	0.1%	0.1%	0.2%
Total international	1.9%	2.0%	2.2%	2.0%	1.9%
Total shipments	100.0%	100.0%	100.0%	100.0%	100.0%

EXHIBIT 5

Work Force and Productivity Statistics

	Year Ended December 31				
	2001	**2000**	**1999**	**1998**	**1997**
Labor:					
Number of employees					
Full-time	15,300	16,000	15,200	14,300	13,500
Part-time	7,200	8,100	8,300	8,700	9,000
Total employees	22,500	24,100	23,500	23,000	22,500
Labor Productivity:					
Total salaries, wages, and benefits (in thousands)	$1,212,122	$1,189,051	$1,098,557	$1,029,180	$945,562
Labor cost as a percentage of total revenues	37.7%	36.3%	35.0%	33.5%	32.5%
Labor cost as a percentage of operating expenses	37.6%	36.8%	36.8%	36.2%	35.2%
Labor cost per shipment	$3.68	$3.61	$3.40	$3.19	$3.12
Labor cost per FTE *	$ 60,354	$ 56,781	$ 53,963	$ 51,796	$ 50,100
Shipments per employee hour *	7.9	7.6	7.6	7.8	7.7
Shipments per FTE *	16,394	15,713	15,887	16,258	16,040
Full-time equivalents	20,084	20,941	20,358	19,870	18,874

*Computed on the basis of paid full-time equivalents and employee hours.

airline that is 23 percent owned by DHL, to acquire Airborne Express.

Meanwhile, Airborne went about its business, and in the first quarter of 2002 showed that it may be down but is not yet out. The company surprised analysts by earning a $5.3 million profit in the quarter (analysts had expected a $5 million loss). This profit was achieved despite a decline in the volume of overnight deliveries. The key to the performance was the new ground delivery service (GDS), which averaged 92,000 shipments a day, well above the company's own forecasts of 60,000 shipments a day.

Commenting on this performance, one analyst noted that the GDS is the key "to stopping the market share declines in the overnight express business, and it's the key to [Airborne] being more competitive in the bundling of freight services to fight back against FedEx and UPS."[3]

ENDNOTES

1. Standard and Poor's Industry Survey, Airlines, March, 2002.
2. Source: http://www.airborne.com/Company/History .asp?nav5AboutAirborne/CompanyInfo/History.
3. M. Schlangenstein, "Unexpected Delivery from Airborne," *Seattle Times*, April 30, 2002, p. C2.

31 Blockbuster in 2002

This case was prepared by Gareth R. Jones, Texas A&M University.

In June 2002, John Antioco, Blockbuster Inc.'s CEO, was reflecting on the challenges facing the company in the next five years. DVDs were increasingly becoming the rental medium of choice, and the video game market was booming. How long would the VHS market remain profitable, and how quickly would the threat of video-on-demand (VOD) bite into Blockbuster's revenues? With its nearly 8,000 global stores, 5,400 in the United States alone, Blockbuster had an enviable brand name and enormous marketing clout, but how could Antioco use it in a way to increase revenues and prevent the return of the problems that had plagued the company when he took over in 1997? What strategies needed to be developed to strengthen Blockbuster's business model in the coming years?

Blockbuster's History

David Cook, the founder of Blockbuster, formed David P. Cook & Associates, Inc., in 1978 to offer consulting and computer services to the petroleum and real estate industries. He created programs to analyze and evaluate oil and gas properties and to compute oil and gas reserves. When oil prices began to decline in 1983 due to the breakdown of the OPEC cartel, his business started to decline and Cook began evaluating alternative businesses in which he

could apply his skills. He decided to leave his current business by selling his company and to enter the video-rental business based on a concept for a video superstore. He opened his first superstore, called Blockbuster Video, in October 1985 in Dallas, Texas.

Cook developed his idea for a video superstore by analyzing the trends in the video industry occurring at that time. During the 1980s, the number of households that owned VCRs was increasing rapidly and so were the number of video-rental stores set up to serve their needs. In 1983, 7,000 video-rental stores were in operation; by 1985, there were 19,000; and by 1986, there were over 25,000, of which 13,000 were individually owned. These mom-and-pop video stores generally operated for a limited number of hours, offered customers only a limited selection of videos, and were often located in out-of-the-way strip shopping centers. These small stores often charged a membership fee in addition to the tape rental charge, and generally, customers brought an empty box to the video-store clerk, who would exchange it for a tape if it was available—a procedure that was often time-consuming, particularly at peak times such as evenings and weekends.

Cook realized that, as VCRs became more widespread and the number of available film titles steadily increased, customers would begin to demand a larger and more-varied selection of titles from video stores. They would also demand more convenient store locations and quicker in-store service than mom-and-pop stores could offer. He realized that the time was right for the development of the next generation of video stores, and he used this opportunity to implement his video superstore concept, which is still the center of Blockbuster's strategy.

The Video Superstore Concept

Cook's superstore concept was based on several components. First, Cook decided that, to give his video superstores a unique identity that would appeal to customers, the stores should be highly visible, stand-alone structures rather than part of a shopping center. In addition, his superstores would be large (between 3,800 and 10,000 square feet), well lit, and brightly colored (for example, each store has a bright blue sign with "Blockbuster Video" displayed in huge white letters). Each store would have ample parking and would be located in the vicinity of a large urban population to maximize potential exposure to customers.

Second, each superstore would offer a wide variety of tapes, such as adventure, children's, instructional, and video game titles. Believing that movie preferences differ in different locations, Cook decided to have each store offer a different selection of between 7,000 and 13,000 film titles organized alphabetically in over thirty categories. New releases were arranged alphabetically against the back wall of each store to make it easier for customers to make their selections.

Third, he created the concept of a three-day rental period for $3, based on the belief that many customers, particularly those with children, wanted to keep tapes for longer than a one-day period. (In 1991, a two-evening rental program was implemented, making new releases only $2.50 for two evenings during the first three weeks after release; after this period, the usual $3 for three evenings applied.) If the tape is available, it is behind the cover box. The customer takes the tape to the checkout line and hands the cassette and his or her membership card to the clerk, who scans the bar codes on both the tape and the card. The customer is then handed the tape and told that it is due back by midnight three days later. For example, if the tape were rented Thursday afternoon, it would be due back Saturday at midnight.

Fourth, Cook's superstores targeted the largest market segments, adults in the eighteen- to forty-nine-year-old group and children in the six- to twelve-year-old group. Cook believed that if his stores could attract children, then the rest of the family would probably follow. Blockbuster carries no X-rated movies and its goal is to be "America's Family Video Store." New releases are carefully chosen based on reviews and box-office success to maximize their appeal to families.

Finally, Cook decided that his superstores would offer customers the convenience of long operating hours and quick service, generally from 10:00 A.M. to midnight seven days a week, because he believed that customers want to choose a movie and get out of the store quickly. Members receive a plastic identification card that is read by the point-of-sale equipment developed by the company. This system uses a laser bar-code scanner to read important information from both the rental cassette and the ID card. The rental amount is computed by the system and due at the time of rental. Movie returns are scanned by laser, and any late or rewind fees are recorded on the account and automatically recalled the next time the member rents a tape. This system reduced customer checkout time and increased convenience. In addition, it provided Blockbuster with data on customer demographics, cassette rental patterns, and the number of times each cassette had been rented, all of which resulted in a database that increased in value over time as it grew bigger.

These five elements of Blockbuster's approach were successful, and customers responded well. Wherever Blockbuster opened, the local mom-and-pop stores usually closed down, unable to compete with the number of titles and the quality of service that a Blockbuster store could provide. By 1986, Blockbuster owned eight stores and had franchised eleven more to interested investors who could see the potential of this new approach to video rental. Initially, the company opened stores in markets with a minimum population of 100,000. Franchises were located in Atlanta, Chicago, Detroit, Houston, San Antonio, and Phoenix. New stores, which cost about $500,000 to $700,000 to equip, grossed an average of $70,000 to $80,000 a month.

Early Growth and Expansion

John Melk, an executive at Waste Management Corp. who had invested in a Blockbuster franchise in Chicago, would change the history of the company. He contacted H. "Wayne" Huizenga, a former Waste Management colleague, in February 1987 to tell him of the enormous revenue and profits his franchise was making. Huizenga had experience in growing small companies in fragmented industries. In 1955, he had quit college to manage a three-truck trash-hauling operation; in 1962, he bought his own operation, Southern Sanitation. In 1968, Southern Sanitation merged with Ace Partnership, Acme Disposal, and Atlas Refuse Service to form Waste Management. In succeeding years, Huizenga borrowed against Waste Management stock to buy over 100 small companies that provided services such as auto-parts cleaning, dry cleaning, lawn care, and portable-toilet rentals. He used their cash flows to purchase yet more firms. By the time Huizenga, vice chairman, resigned in 1984, Waste Management was a $6 billion Fortune 500 company and Huizenga was a wealthy man.

Although Huizenga had a low opinion of video retailers, he agreed to visit a Blockbuster store. Expecting a dingy store renting X-rated films, he was pleasantly surprised to find a brightly lit, family video supermarket. Detecting the opportunity to make Cook's superstore concept national, Huizenga, Melk, and Donald Flynn (another Waste Management executive) agreed to purchase 33 percent of Blockbuster from Cook for $18.6 million in 1986. (They also became directors at this time.) In 1987, CEO David Cook decided to take his money and leave Blockbuster to pursue another venture at Amtech Corporation. With the departure of the founder, Huizenga took over as CEO in April 1987, with the goal of making Blockbuster a national company and the industry leader in the video-rental market.

Recognizing his inexperience in retailing and franchising, Huizenga hired top managers who knew how to develop and grow a retail chain. First, he hired Luigi Salavaneschi, a former McDonald's executive who had gained considerable expertise in facility location during his involvement in the rapid expansion of McDonald's. He also hired Thomas Gruber, a former McDonald's marketing executive, as the chief marketing officer. Through their experience at McDonald's, these men had the background to orchestrate Blockbuster's rapid growth.

Blockbuster's Explosive Growth

Blockbuster's new top management team mapped out the company's growth strategy, the elements of which are discussed in this section.

Location

Store location is a critical issue to a video-rental store, and Huizenga moved quickly with Salavaneschi to obtain the best store locations in each geographic area into which Blockbuster expanded. They developed a "cluster strategy," whereby they targeted a particular geographic market, such as Dallas, Boston, or Los Angeles, and then opened new stores one at a time until they had saturated the market. Thus, within a few years, the local mom-and-pop stores found themselves surrounded and many, unable to compete with Blockbuster, closed down. Video superstores were always located near busy, well-traveled routes to establish a broad customer base. The cluster strategy eventually brought Blockbuster into 133 television markets (the geographic area that television reaches), where it reached 75 to 85 percent of the U.S. population.

Marketing

On the marketing side, Blockbuster's chief marketing officer, Tom Gruber, applied his knowledge of McDonald's family-oriented advertising strategy to strengthen Cook's original vision of the video-rental business. In 1988, he introduced Blockbuster Kids to strengthen the company's position as a family video store. This promotion, aimed at the six- to twelve-year-old age group, introduced four characters and a dog to appeal to Blockbuster's young customers. To demonstrate additional commitment to families, each store stocked forty titles recommended for children and provided a kids' clubhouse equipped with televisions and toys so that children could amuse themselves while their parents browsed for videos. In addition, Blockbuster allowed its members to specify what rating category of tapes (such as PG or R) may be rented through their account. A policy called Youth-Restricted Viewing forbade R-rated tape rentals to children under seventeen. Blockbuster also implemented the free Kidprint Program: a child's name, address, and height are recorded on a videotape given to parents and local police for identification purposes. In addition, Blockbuster has a program called America's Most Important Videos Are Free, which offers free rental of public-service tapes about topics such as fire safety and parenting. Finally, to attract customers and to build brand recognition, Gruber initiated joint promotions between Blockbuster and companies like Domino's Pizza, McDonald's, and Pepsi-Cola—something it continues to do today.

Operations

Blockbuster also made great progress on the operations side of the business. As discussed earlier, the operation of a Blockbuster superstore is designed to provide fast checkout and effective inventory management. The company designed its point-of-sale computer system, which is available only to company-owned and franchised stores, to make rental and return transactions easy.

Rapid expansion strains a company's operating systems. To support its stores, Blockbuster opened a 25,000-square-foot distribution center in Dallas in 1986. The distribution center has the capacity to store 200,000 cassette tapes that are removed from the original container. A label with a security device is affixed to the cassette. Each videotape is then bar-coded and placed into a hard plastic rental case. The facility has the capacity to process the initial inventory requirement of about 10,000 tapes for up to three superstores per day. In addition, Blockbuster supplies the equipment and fixtures, such as computer software and hardware, shelving, signs, and cash registers, needed to operate a new store. In 1987, the physical facilities of the distribution center were expanded to double capacity, to 400,000 videocassettes.

Blockbuster's growing buying power also gave it another operations advantage. As the largest single purchaser of prerecorded videotapes in the U.S. market, it could negotiate discounts off retail price. Cassettes are bought at an average of $40 per tape and rented for three nights at $3. Thus, the cash investment on hit videotapes is recovered in forty-five to sixty days, and the investment on nonhit titles is regained in two-and-a-half to three months. In its early days, Blockbuster could use its efficient distribution system to send extra copies of films declining in popularity to new stores, where demand is increasing. This ability to transfer tapes to locations where they are most demanded is very important for customers who want new tapes on the shelves when they are first released. It also allows the company to use its inventory to the best advantage and to receive the maximum benefit from each videotape.

Management and Structure

For Blockbuster, as for any company, rapid growth poses the risk of losing control over daily operations and allowing costs to escalate. Recognizing this predicament, Blockbuster established three operating divisions to manage the functional activities necessary to retain effective control over its operations as it grew. Blockbuster Distribution Corp. was created to handle the area licensing and franchising of new stores, and to service their start-up and operation—offering assistance with the selection, acquisition, assembly, packaging, inventory, and distribution of videocassettes, supplies, and computer equipment. Blockbuster Management Corp. was established to assist with the training of new store management, facility location and acquisition, and employee training. Finally, Blockbuster Computer Systems Inc. was formed to install, maintain, and support the software programs for the inventory and point-of-sale equipment. These three divisions provide all the support services necessary to manage store expansion.

Rapid growth also led Blockbuster to oversee store operations through a regional- and district-level organizational structure. In 1988, responsibility for store development and operations was decentralized to the regional level. However, corporate headquarters is kept fully informed of developments in each regional area, even in each store, through the computerized inventory and sales system. For example, Blockbuster's corporate inventory and point-of-sale computer systems track sales and inventory in each store and each region. The role of regional management is to oversee the stores in their regions, providing advice and monitoring stores' performance to make sure that they keep up Blockbuster's high standards of operation as its chain of superstores grow.

New-Store Expansion

With Blockbuster's functional-level competencies in place, the next step for Huizenga was to begin a rapid program of growth and expansion. Huizenga believed that expanding rapidly to increase revenue and market share was crucial for success in the video-rental industry. Under his leadership, Blockbuster opened new stores quickly, developed a franchising program, and began to acquire competitors to increase the number of its stores.

To facilitate rapid expansion, Blockbuster began to use its skills in store location, distribution, and sales. At first, Blockbuster focused on large markets, preferring to enter a market with a potential capacity for 500 stores—normally a large city. Later, Blockbuster decided to enter smaller market segments, like towns with a minimum of 20,000 people within driving distance. All stores were built and operated using the superstore concept described earlier. Using the services of its three divisions, it steadily increased its number of new-store openings until, by 1993, it owned over 2,500 video stores.

Blockbuster's rapid growth was also attributable to Huizenga's skills in acquisitions. Beginning in 1986, the company began to acquire many smaller regional video chains to gain a significant market presence in a city or region. In 1987, for example, the twenty-nine video stores of Movies to Go were acquired to expand Blockbuster's presence in the Midwest. Blockbuster then used this acquisition as a starting point for opening many more stores in the region. Similarly, in 1989, it acquired 175 video stores from Major Video Corp. and Video Library to develop a presence in southern California. In 1991, it took over 209 Erol's Inc. stores to obtain the stronghold that Erol's previously held in the mid-Atlantic states. All acquired stores were made to conform to Blockbuster's standards. Any store that could not was closed down. Most acquisitions were financed by existing cash flow or by issuing new shares of stock rather than by taking on new debt. These deals reflect Huizenga's reluctance to borrow money.

Licensing and Franchising

Recognizing the need to build market share rapidly and develop a national brand name, Huizenga also recruited top management to start an ambitious franchise program. Franchising, in which the franchisee is solely responsible for all financial commitments connected with opening a new store, allowed Blockbuster to expand rapidly without incurring debt. The downside of franchising is that Blockbuster had to share profits with the franchise owners. When franchising, it is important to maintain consistency in stores. Thus, the franchisees were required to operate their stores in the same way as company-owned stores and to follow the same store format for rental selection and the use of proprietary point-of-sale equipment.

Blockbuster's current method of franchising was established in January 1988. Under this plan, a franchisee is granted the right to open a store for twenty years, with renewal rights of an additional five years if the store is in compliance with agreements. All franchise owners pay an initial fee of up to $55,000 for the privilege of using the Blockbuster Video trademark. The capital investment required to open a store generally ranges from $425,000 to $650,000. All licensed and franchised stores must meet Blockbuster's design criteria and use its standardized operating systems so customers have no problems identifying and using the company's stores. A charge of up to $36,000 is assessed for software, and the monthly software-maintenance fee varies from $500 to $650. Franchise owners pay royalty fees from 3 to 8 percent of gross revenue, as determined by their agreement with Blockbuster; remit a certain percentage for marketing and promotions; and contribute 1 percent of gross receipts for national advertising. Contributions to national advertising began in 1989 when the five hundredth store was opened. All rental transactions must be recorded in the point-of-sale inventory control program, and any inventory must be approved by Blockbuster. Franchise owners are also required to buy from Blockbuster at least 5,000 videotapes of the required initial inventory of 7,000. In addition, the franchise owner must complete Blockbuster's training program or hire a manager who has completed Blockbuster's training program to run the store. Assistance with activities such as site selection and employee training are available for a fee.

Franchising facilitated the rapid expansion of Blockbuster Video. By 1992, the company had over 1,000 franchised stores, compared to 2,000 company-owned stores. Recognizing the long-term profit advantages of owning its own stores, however, Blockbuster began to repurchase attractive territories from franchisees. In 1993, the company spent $248 million to buy the 400 stores of its two largest franchisees and, with a new store opening every day, it owned over 2,500 stores by the end of 1993.

By the end of 1992, however, despite its rapid growth, Blockbuster still controlled only about 15 percent of the market—its 27,000 smaller rivals shared the rest. Consequently, in 1993, Blockbuster announced plans for a new round of store openings and acquisitions that would give it a 25 to 30 percent market share within two or three years.

The Home-Video Industry

By 1990, revenues from video rentals exceeded the revenues obtained in movie theaters. For example, video-rental revenues rose to $11 billion in 1991, compared to movie theater revenues of $4.8 billion and cable movie channel (like HBO) revenues of

$5.2 billion. The huge growth in industry revenues led to increased competition for customers, and as noted above, 28,000 video stores operated in the United States in 1990.

Blockbuster's rapid growth put it in a commanding position. In 1990, it had no national competitor and was the only company operating beyond a regional level. The next largest competitor, West Coast Video, had only $120 million in 1991 revenues, while Blockbuster had revenues of $868 million. However, Blockbuster faced many competitors at the local and regional levels. For example, various supermarket chains across the United States, such as Kroger and Winn Dixie, also expanded their video-rental operations and had video-rental revenues of $1.35 billion in 1991. In some markets, however, price wars started to break out. In the San Antonio market, for example, competition among video stores resulted in Blockbuster reducing its prices to $2.00, but then HEB (a supermarket chain) responded by dropping its price to $1.50 and offering $.99 specials, which started a new price war.

Mature Market

As the video-rental market matured, the level of competition in the industry changed. During the 1980s, video rentals grew rapidly due to the proliferation of VCRs. By 1990, however, 70 percent of households had VCRs, compared to 2 percent in 1980, and industry growth dropped from the previous double digits to 7 percent. The slow growth in VCR ownership and rentals made competition more severe. To a large degree, competition in the video-rental industry was fierce because new competitors could enter the market with relative ease; the only purchase necessary is videotapes. Unlike small video-rental companies, however, Blockbuster could negotiate discounts with tape suppliers because it buys new releases in such huge volumes.

New Technology

One growing problem facing Blockbuster by the early 1990s was the variety of new ways in which customers could view movies and enjoy other kinds of entertainment. Blockbuster has always felt competition both from other sources of movies—such as cable television and movie theaters—and from other forms of entertainment—such as bowling, baseball games, and outdoor activities. In the 1990s, technology began to give customers more ways to watch movies. New technological threats included pay-per-view or video-on-demand systems, digital compression, and direct broadcast satellites.

Pay-per-view movies could become a major competitive threat to video-rental stores. Currently, with pay-per-view systems, cable customers can call their local cable company and pay a fee to have a scheduled movie, concert, or sporting event aired on their television. Soon, a cable customer could call up their local "video company" and choose any movie to be aired on his or her television for a fee; the cable company would make the movie available when the customer wanted it. Telephone companies are becoming interested in the potential for pay-for-view because the networks of fiber-optic cable they are installing in ordinary households can transmit movies as well. Huizenga claims Blockbuster is not overly concerned about pay-per-view systems because only one-third of U.S. households have access to pay-per-view, and fiber-optic cables are expensive. It also claimed that home video rental is cheaper than pay-per-view and new releases are obtained thirty to forty-five days before pay-per-view.

Video-on-demand takes the pay-per-view concept further. Bellcore, the research branch of the regional Bell companies, invented video-on-demand. With this system (still in the trial stage), a customer will use an interactive box to select a movie from a list of thousands. The choice will be transmitted to an information warehouse that will store thousands of tapes in digital formats. The selected video will then be routed back to the customer's house through a series of switches, and a signal splitter will send the movie into the home through the phone lines. This technology bypasses the local video-rental store because the movies are stored on digital tape at the cable company's headquarters.

Movie companies or video stores like Blockbuster could function as the information warehouses from which the video selections are made. Blockbuster is interested in acting as the warehouse so that it can control the video-on-demand market, which could become a direct threat to video rental as the technology is refined. Blockbuster began discussions with Bell Atlantic Corporation, which developed a video-on-demand system for customers in northern Virginia. Bell hopes to offer between thirty and one hundred films, which would be instantly available to customers. Blockbuster, which would provide the movies for the video-on-demand system, views this move as an expansion of its business rather than a cannibalization of video rentals.

U.S. West, one of the baby bells, also announced plans to build a video-on-demand network to serve 13 million homes in fourteen states. With its partner, Time Warner, it planned eventually to reach 23 percent of the viewing market. The linking of phone companies with other entertainment companies could become a direct threat to Blockbuster, but Huizenga believes the local Blockbuster store could become the center or hub of the video-on-demand network. He feels that phone companies would prefer to deal with Blockbuster rather than with companies like Time Warner or Paramount, both of which lack Blockbuster's skills in video retailing and its established customer base—the 30 million customers who make 600 million trips per year to the local video store. Note that if Blockbuster did become the information warehouse of video-on-demand systems, videotape rentals would decrease, hurting Blockbuster's own rental revenues and likely finishing off the local mom-and-pop stores. If all worked out the way Huizenga envisions, in the long run, Blockbuster would seize control of both the video-rental and video-on-demand market.

Other new technologies include digital compression and direct broadcast satellites. Digital compression allows up to five television channels to be sent on the same bandwidth that can be used to carry only one channel. This provides more space for movies to be sent to customers. Direct broadcast satellites (DBS) were also an emerging threat because cable service could be obtained anywhere in the United States by installing a small, 2-foot-diameter satellite dish. The dishes, which first cost between $500 and $700, soon fell in price as companies like Hughes mass-produced them. Existing land-based cable companies responded by installing vast networks of fiber-optic cable also capable of carrying hundreds of channels. These new technologies allowed companies to transmit movies directly into people's homes, which would harm the video-rental industry because customers would no longer have to go to video-rental stores to get a movie.

Blockbuster's Emerging Strategies

Blockbuster also took advantage of its great size and secure financial position (provided by the large growth in its domestic revenues) to diversify into new industries and into global markets. It believed it could transfer the skills and capabilities it had developed in the domestic video-rental market to new markets and countries.

Global Expansion

Seventy percent of the world's VCRs are in countries outside the United States, and foreign countries account for half of total world video-rental revenues. In 1991, the United States was the largest video market, with revenues of $11 billion; Japan was second, with $2.6 billion, followed by the United Kingdom, with $1.4 billion, and Canada, with $1.2 billion. Blockbuster began to expand into international markets in 1989 when it saw the opportunity to exploit its marketing expertise, superstore concept, operating knowledge, financial strength, and ability to attract franchisees abroad.

Just as it did in the United States, Blockbuster started a program both to build new video superstores and to acquire foreign competitors abroad. Planning to be a leader in home entertainment around the world, Blockbuster's objective was to obtain a 25 percent share of international revenue by 1995 and to have 2,000 stores in international markets by 1996. In 1989, stores were opened in Canada and the United Kingdom. In 1990, Blockbuster opened its first store in Puerto Rico. It continued its expansion into the United Kingdom, Canada, the Virgin Islands, Venezuela, and Spain. Franchise agreements were also signed in Japan, Australia, and Mexico.

In Japan, Blockbuster formed a joint venture in March 1991 with Den Fujita & Co., Ltd., which runs McDonald's Co. Japan and has a stake in Toys "R" Us Japan Ltd. This venture opened fifteen stores in Japan in 1992, thirty stores in 1993, and 1,000 stores within ten years. Due to fierce price competition, the Japan stores are meeting only 90 percent of sales projections. Under the terms of this fifty-fifty joint venture agreement with Fujita & Co., Ltd., Blockbuster can franchise more stores in Japan. Blockbuster is importing its video concepts to a market that is very interested in video rentals. By forming a joint venture, Blockbuster can benefit from the expertise of Japanese locals in running a business in Japan.

To expand in the United Kingdom, in 1992 Blockbuster purchased Cityvision PLC, the United Kingdom's largest video retailer, for $81 million cash and 3.9 million shares of stock. At this time, Cityvision ran 875 stores in Britain and Austria under the name Ritz. Blockbuster transformed the Ritz outlets into Blockbuster stores and used the chain as a start for additional expansion into Europe, just as it had taken over large video chains in the United States on its way to becoming the national leader. Joint ventures were also negotiated in France, Germany, and Italy. Blockbuster increased the number of franchise stores in Mexico, Chile, Venezuela, and Spain. By the end of 1992, the company had 952 stores in nine foreign countries, with plans to establish at least 1,200 more by 1995.

Blockbuster created an international home-video division to oversee and manage its expansion into foreign markets. Besides having expertise in international operations, marketing, merchandising, product purchasing, distribution, franchising, real estate, and field support, this division is proficient at dealing with differences in entertainment, language, and business cultures in different countries and is successfully implementing Blockbuster's domestic strategy in its foreign operations.

Diversification

Blockbuster became a national video-rental chain because of the way it positioned itself in the market as a family-oriented store with a wide selection of videos, convenient hours and locations, and fast checkout. Blockbuster began to expand its entertainment concept into several new markets or industries, such as film entertainment programming and music retailing. To increase its revenue, Blockbuster also made deals to broaden its range of product offerings.

To enter the entertainment programming market, Blockbuster invested in Spelling Entertainment Group and Republic Pictures. Both companies have large film libraries—a source of inexpensive movies for Blockbuster's retail operations. For example, Blockbuster gained access to Spelling's library of 600 feature films and fifty-five television shows, including *Beverly Hills 90210*. The deal also provided Blockbuster with access to the broadcast and cable television markets. Spelling's proficiency in cable network programming could help Blockbuster, which was contemplating building its own cable channel. Republic's programming library includes classics such as *High Noon*, *The Quiet Man*, and *The Bells of St. Mary's*. This investment also strengthened Block-

buster's hold on the programming side of the entertainment industry because Republic has ongoing deals with the television, home-video, and theatrical markets.

Blockbuster also chose the music retail business as an area into which it could expand its entertainment concept. As in the video-rental industry, many music stores were mom-and-pop businesses or part of small, regional chains. Music stores had begun to market videos such as the Walt Disney collection, musicals, and family movies. Blockbuster saw a fit between selling records, cassettes, and compact discs (CDs) and renting or selling videos. So it decided to employ the same strategy it had used in the video-rental market: opening new stores and acquiring chains of music stores using the revenues from its video superstores. However, Blockbuster decided not to sell CDs and cassettes in its video stores. Instead, its music business was to be operated independently, with stores using the same superstore concept that was so successful in the video-rental business. The planned stores would be large and would offer a wide selection of music products such as recorded music, computer software, games, and even books. The proposed new name for the music-store chain was Chartbusters.

As part of its plan to diversify into the $8 billion record industry, Blockbuster agreed to buy Sound Warehouse and Music Plus, two record-store chains, for $185 million. At the time, Sound Warehouse was the seventh largest music retailer and Music Plus was the twelfth largest. These two retail chains had a total of 236 stores in thirty-five states, primarily in California and the South. This acquisition made Blockbuster the seventh largest music chain.

With 30 million video customers, Blockbuster felt it could transfer and share its resources and capabilities. For example, it could introduce joint promotions and advertising between its music and video stores, giving a customer a 15 percent discount on a CD for renting two videos. Customers who visit one of the video stores would be encouraged to visit Blockbuster's music stores, and vice versa. Because of its ability to attract families and young people, Blockbuster believed it had a considerable advantage. In 1991, 64 percent of record sales were made to people age fifteen to thirty-four, Blockbuster's main customer group.

The company also branched its entertainment concept. In 1990, it sponsored the first Blockbuster

Bowl—Florida State University versus Penn State. The company also saw an opportunity in themed, family-oriented entertainment centers, which would have batting cages, miniature golf, a high-tech video arcade, virtual-reality computer simulators, play areas for children, food service, and merchandising. It planned to open the first center in 1993. In June 1990, Blockbuster formed a joint venture to develop and operate three amphitheaters, circular outdoor arenas for rock concerts and other entertainment events. The first amphitheater was opened in Phoenix, Arizona, in November 1990. Other entertainment deals include gaining exclusive rights to distribute the 1990 World Series and other major-league baseball video productions and exclusive retail rights to the 1992 Summer Olympics from NBC. These events would be distributed on video.

In an effort to manage the companies it acquired and in its quest to become a full-service home entertainment retailer, Blockbuster reorganized in 1993, and split into several divisions: domestic home video, international home video, music retailing, international music retailing, new-technology ventures, and other entertainment ventures.

Huizenga Sells Blockbuster to Viacom

Blockbuster's stated goal in 1992 was to increase net income by at least 20 percent a year over the next five years. In October 1992, Blockbuster Video opened its three thousandth store and its one thousandth international store. Although Blockbuster, with its rapid growth and large positive cash flow, seemed poised to become an entertainment powerhouse, Huizenga knew that there were clouds ahead. The rapid advance in digital technology, including the Internet and broadband, meant that video-on-demand, a service in which customers could download new movies directly from their cable company or some other outlet, was a growing reality. Some analysts were even suggesting that Blockbuster was a dinosaur. And Huizenga soon found out that the music retailing industry was also highly competitive and that he faced fierce competition from large music retail chains. The music retail industry had many more experienced competitors than the video-rental industry. Some major competitors, like Sam Goody's and Tower Records, also had plans to accelerate the development of their own music megastores. Profit margins in music retailing were narrow, and large merchandisers like Wal-Mart were starting to lower the prices of CDs. Price wars were flaring up as a result. Even in the video-rental business, entrepreneurs who had watched Blockbuster's rapid growth still felt there was an opportunity for entry. Chains such as Hollywood Video began to expand rapidly, and increased competition seemed imminent in the video-rental business, too.

Huizenga decided that the time was ripe to sell the Blockbuster chain, just as he had sold other chains before, and an opportunity came when Sumner Redstone, chairman of Viacom, become involved in an aggressive bidding war to buy Paramount Studios, the movie company.

Redstone recognized the value of Blockbuster's huge cash flow in helping to fund the debt needed to take over Paramount. Ignoring the risks involved in taking over Blockbuster, Viacom acquired the company in 1994 for $8.4 billion in stock. (Further details about the logic behind the acquisition are found in the Viacom case later in the book.) Huizenga left the company and took his huge stockholdings with him.

Just the next year, in 1995, a tidal wave of problems hit the Blockbuster chain. First, a brutal price war broke out in the video-rental industry as new video chain start-ups fought for a niche in major markets and for some of the lucrative industry revenues. Second, movie studios started to lower the price of tapes, realizing that they could make more money by selling them directly to customers rather than letting companies like Blockbuster make the money through tape rentals. Third, as both Blockbuster's video and music operations expanded, it became obvious that the company did not have the materials management and distribution systems needed to manage the complex flow of products to its stores. Overhead costs started to soar. Combined with declines in revenues, the company turned from making a profit to incurring a loss. Blockbuster's cash flow was much less useful to Redstone now, burdened as he was by the huge debt for Paramount. Blockbuster's declining performance led to Viacom's stock price dropping sharply, and Redstone reacted by firing its top managers and searching for an experienced executive to turn the Blockbuster division around.

Blockbuster, 1996–1998

Given Blockbuster's soaring overhead costs, Redstone naturally looked for an executive who had experience in low-cost merchandising and information systems. In 1996, he pulled off a coup by hiring William Fields, the heir apparent to David Glass, Wal-Mart's CEO, and an information systems and logistics expert. Redstone saw Fields as the ideal person to turn Blockbuster's now 4,500 stores into broad-based entertainment retail outlets. Understanding Wal-Mart's sophisticated distribution system, Fields began planning a huge state-of-the-art distribution facility that would serve all Blockbuster's U.S. stores and replace its outdated facility. He also started the development of a new state-of-the-art point-of-sale merchandising information system that would give Blockbuster real-time feedback on which videos were generating the most money and when they should be transferred to stores in other regions to make the most of Blockbuster's stock of videos—its most important physical resource. Third, Fields added more retail merchandise, such as candy, comics, and audio books, to Blockbuster's product mix. The results of these efforts would take a couple of years to bear fruit, however. So to reduce debt, Viacom also scaled back expansion plans for the company, cutting by 25 percent the number of new video stores it planned to open in 1997 to 600, from the 800 it opened in 1996.

Some analysts believed that, by 1997, Redstone recognized the negative impact of Blockbuster's operations on its stock price and was trying to cut costs and thus boost short-term profits and harvest the company so that he could spin off Blockbuster. Redstone may also have sensed that the troubled division was not going to be fixed fast. Sales were expected to be flat in 1997.

Apparently, Fields and Redstone disagreed over Blockbuster's future in the Viacom empire. Its performance continued to decline in the first quarter of 1997, with a drop in profit of 20 percent. Only thirteen months after taking over at Blockbuster, Fields resigned in April 1997. Viacom's stock fell to a three-year low. Redstone argued that this was absurd because Blockbuster generated $3 billion in revenue and $800 million in cash flow for Viacom. In 1996, he argued it was due for a rebound in profitability. However, the specter of video-on-demand and increased price competition in the music and video business made analysts wonder if Blockbuster was going to recover. Furthermore, Fields was the expert in distribution and logistics. They wondered if Blockbuster would now be able to use its new distribution facility to cut costs when it opened. So many retail chains had filed for Chapter 11 bankruptcy in the 1990s, and many wondered if Blockbuster would be next on the list.

Once again, Redstone searched for an executive who could help turn Blockbuster around. John Antioco, the chief of PepsiCo's Taco Bell restaurants, was in the news at the time. In just eight months, Antioco introduced a new menu, new pricing, and a new store setup, thus engineering an about-face in Taco Bell's performance. A mounting loss was turned into rising profit. Antioco seemed to be the perfect choice as Blockbuster's CEO.

After Antioco took the helm, he assessed the situation. The video-rental market was still flat. Satellite services, with hundreds of movie channels, were becoming an increasingly popular way of watching new movies; sales of movie videos were soaring as their price came down in outlets such as Wal-Mart. Fields's strategy of enlarging the entertainment product lines carried in Blockbuster stores seemed like a logical move, but it had failed as costs continued to rise. Products had a short shelf life because changing fads and fashions made the value of Blockbuster's inventory unpredictable. What should Antioco do?

In fact, Antioco had once orchestrated a strategy similar to Fields's when he was in charge of taking the convenience store operator, CircleK, out of bankruptcy. At CircleK, Antioco had attempted to generate increased sales by encouraging customers who stopped for gas to enter the store and buy lottery tickets, prepared food, and so on. He had also redecorated the chain to attract customers and installed the then-new credit-card fuel machines to speed the fueling process. It seemed that Fields's basic approach was not wrong; the problem was defining Blockbuster's merchandising mix. And how should Antioco manage the purchase and distribution of Blockbuster's biggest ongoing expense, videotapes, to create a value chain that would lead to increased profitability?

Antioco realized that he needed to focus on reorganizing Blockbuster's value chain to reduce costs and generate more revenues simultaneously. Blockbuster's biggest expense and asset was its inventory of videos, so this was the logical place to start. Antioco and Redstone examined the way Blockbuster obtained its movies: from the big studios, MGM, Disney, and so on, at the high price of $65. Because it had to pay this high price, Blockbuster could not purchase enough copies of a particular hit movie to satisfy customer demand when the videotape was released. The result was that customers left unsatisfied and revenues were being lost. Perhaps there was a better way of managing the process for both the movie studios and Blockbuster to raise revenues from video rental.

Antioco and Redstone proposed that Blockbuster and the movie studios enter into a revenue-sharing agreement, whereby the movie studios would supply Blockbuster with tapes at cost, at around $8. This price would allow it to purchase 800 percent more copies of a single title. Blockbuster then would split rental revenues with the studios fifty-fifty. The hoped-for result would be growth in the market for rental tapes by 20 to 30 percent a year. Thus, both Blockbuster's and the movie studios' revenues would grow. This would also counter the threat from satellite programming, which was taking away all their revenues. Six million households were now subscribing to direct satellite services. While this deal was being negotiated in 1997, video rentals at Blockbuster dropped 4 percent more, and the studios that had been hesitating to enter into this radically different kind of sales agreement quickly signed. This agreement came at a crucial point for Blockbuster because its cash flow continued to drop as it faced higher write-off costs for outdated tapes. With the new revenue-sharing agreement signed, however, the profitability of its new business model would increase dramatically. (Blockbuster's market share increased from something less than 30 percent to over 40 percent in the next five years, and after a few years the division returned to profitability.) The movie studios also benefited because their stream of income increased.

Antioco's second major change in strategy was to abandon the attempt to transform Blockbuster's stores into general entertainment outlets and refocus on its core movie-rental business. In October 1998, it sold its 378 Blockbuster music chains to Wherehouse Entertainment for $115 million. Antioco still believed, however, as in case of CircleK, that it was a question of deciding what kinds of products would best fit the Blockbuster model, and how again to manage the value chain to keep operating expenses as low as possible while increasing revenues. In 1998,

one answer to this dilemma arrived when Citibank and Blockbuster announced a strategic alliance to install automated teller machines in up to 3,000 Blockbuster stores nationwide. Citibank would bear the costs of operating these machines and would pay Blockbuster a hosting fee, putting no drain on Blockbuster's resources, and helping cash-strapped customers. In 1998, Blockbuster also announced that it was testing home delivery of rental tapes to homes in the Boston area through a local distributor, Streamline. This strategy did not turn out to be successful, however.

Nevertheless, all these changes hurt Blockbuster's performance in the short term. In 1998, Viacom announced that it would record a $437 million charge in the second quarter to write down the value of its Blockbuster videotape inventory because it now had to revise the accounting method it adopted when it entered the new revenue-sharing agreement for tapes from Hollywood studios. (In 1997, it also had to take a charge of $323 million because of the problems noted above.) These charges wiped out Viacom's profits, and Redstone once again announced that a spinoff or initial public offering (IPO) of Blockbuster was likely because the unit was punishing Viacom's stock price and threatening Viacom's future profitability.

On the plus side, however, the revenue-sharing agreement resulted in a sharp increase in revenues; some video-store rentals increased by 13 percent in the second quarter of 1998, compared to a year earlier. Since rental tapes would now be amortized over only a three-month period—the time of greatest rental sales—not the old six to twenty-six months, the new business model seemed poised finally to increase cash flows. One good year for Blockbuster would allow Redstone, who had been increasingly criticized for his purchase of Blockbuster, to go forward with his desire to pursue an "IPO carve out," whereby Viacom would sell between 10 and 20 percent of the Blockbuster stock to the public in an IPO. This move would create a public market for the stock and make an eventual spinoff possible.

By the end of 1998, there were continuing signs of recovery. The revenue-sharing agreement had allowed Blockbuster's managers to develop strategies for increasing responsiveness to customers and allowed them to pursue their business model in a profitable way. With the huge increase in the supply of new videotapes made possible by the revenue-sharing agreement, Blockbuster was now able to offer the Blockbuster Promise to its customers: their chosen title would be in stock or next time it's free. Also, lower prices could now be charged for older video titles to generate additional revenues without threatening profitability. It turned out that the real threat to Blockbuster in the 1990s was not from new technology like video-on-demand, but from the lack of the right strategies to keep customers happy—having the products in stock that they wanted—and from a failure to understand the important dynamics behind the value chain, such as revenue sharing, that would grow the market.

Outside the United States, Blockbuster had been increasing the scope of its international operations. In 1994, it opened its first stores in Italy and New Zealand. In 1995, it entered Israel, Brazil, Peru, Columbia, and Thailand. In 1996, it entered Ecuador, Portugal, El Salvador, Panama, and Scandinavia, where it purchased Christianshavn Video in Denmark. In 1996, in entered Taiwan and Uruguay. In 1998, it acquired Video Flick's stores in Australia. In 1999, it entered Hong Kong as a gateway to China. In 1999, it opened its two hundredth store in Mexico, and in 2000, it expanded its operations in Central America to include Costa Rica and Guatemala. By 2002, it operated almost 2,600 stores outside the United States. The main advantage of its global operations is that it can constantly distribute copies of tapes that are less in demand domestically to other countries overseas, where they will appear as new releases and customers will be willing to pay the highest rental prices for them. In turn, the tapes will trickle down to other countries so that, even though revenues might be less, the cost of the tape has already been amortized and operations will still be profitable. On the other hand, it can also identify foreign-made movies that might attract a large U.S. viewing audience.

In 1998, Blockbuster finally opened its 820,000-square-foot distribution center in Kinney, Texas; now it was in a position to reduce costs and speed delivery of tapes to locations where they were most in demand, and to move them again when demand dropped. Also in 1998, Blockbuster began to offer Neighborhood Favorites, a program where each store would stock tapes customized to local tastes. In keeping with this differentiation approach, Blockbuster developed Blockbuster Rewards, its frequent renters program. The rewards program is designed to keep Blockbuster customers returning regularly to its stores with a coupon for a free video every month.

Blockbuster, 1999–2002

The year 1999 turned out to be a major turning point for Blockbuster. With its business model reestablished, Antioco orchestrated a successful IPO in August 1999. It was also the first of four consecutive years of increasing store sales as Antioco set about changing the entertainment mix in stores to increase revenues. It was clear to Antioco that by 1999, DVDs would become the next entertainment media of choice, and DVDs were a natural product-line extension for Blockbuster. In 1999, Blockbuster introduced DVDs into 3,000 of its stores to assess their promise; customer reaction was favorable because sales of DVD players and other digital media were soaring. In 2000, Blockbuster increased the number of DVD titles it carried because they had higher profit margins than tapes. Blockbuster also began to stock video game CDs and DVDs because the success of the Sony Playstation 2 made it clear that the video game rental business was becoming increasingly lucrative.

Recognizing the growing importance of satellite programming, Blockbuster also formed an alliance with DIRECTTV in 2000 to provide a cobranded pay-per-view service on DIRECTV. Blockbuster also became a new distribution channel for DIRECTV because it began to train its salespeople to sell dishes in its stores. Blockbuster receives a fee for each dish it sells and a share of future monthly payments, and every time a DIRECTV customer orders pay-per-view movies, Blockbuster will receive a payment that is higher than the net profit it makes from each current VHS rental. Antioco argued that this arrangement would give Blockbuster entry into the new technology, and would add between 5 and 15 percent to Blockbuster's revenues. Even a 5 percent increase each year over the next decade would have a substantial impact on its bottom line. DIRECTV gains because Blockbuster will use its database of 42 million households—an important asset—and its $200 million advertising budget to help guide DIRECTV's programming choices, increase market penetration, and increase its monthly pay-per-view order rate. Of course, this arrangement may reduce the number of customers coming into a Blockbuster store; however, Antioco wanted to become involved in in-house entertainment, regardless of the delivery channel.

In another attempt to get more control of the content, or entertainment software, end of the business, Blockbuster announced in 2000 an agreement with MGM to digitally stream and download recent theatrical releases, films, and television programming from the MGM library to Blockbuster's web site for pay-per-view consumption. Initial testing of the program started at the end of 2000. Blockbuster announced that it planned to have similar agreements in place with other movie studios shortly. In 2000, it also signed a deal with TiVo, a maker of set-top digital recorders, to offer a video-on-demand service through broadband using TiVo recorders. TiVo agreed to put demonstration kiosks in over 4,000 Blockbuster stores for its 65 million customers. The push toward video-on-demand was increasing.

The pace of change speeded up in 2001 when Blockbuster abandoned attempts to customize tape offerings to local markets and eliminated 25 percent of the company's less productive VHS tapes to focus on the booming market for DVDs. Once again, it took a loss to amortize these tapes, but then shipped them to its stores overseas to capitalize on growing global demand for these products. The result was that, by the end of 2001, the company achieved record revenues, strong cash flow, and increased profitability while it lowered its debt by more than $430 million. Since 1997, Antioco had increased Blockbuster's revenues from $3.3 billion to over $5 billion and had turned free cash flow from a negative position to over $250 million for 2001. Blockbuster's stock rose as investors realized that the company now had a business model that generated cash.

In August 2000, Antioco once again reaffirmed Blockbuster's goal to lessen its dependence on video rental by focusing more on delivering home entertainment. It started to roll out its "Blockbuster on demand" pay-per-view. He argued that video rental and pay-per-view could exist side by side. In 2001, as sales of DVDs soared, Antioco tried to repeat the success he had had in revenue-sharing with movie studios by arguing that falling DVD prices would not generate the highest long-term returns, and he lobbied for higher DVD wholesale prices to protect future DVD rental revenues. No revenue-sharing agreement was negotiated for DVDs, however, and Antioco did not see the rise in the wholesale price he had hoped for because of strong customer demand for DVDs.

In August 2001, however, five major movie studios—Sony, AOL Time Warner, Universal, MGM, and Paramount (also a Viacom division)—announced a plan to bypass powerful middlemen like Blockbuster and HBO and offer their own pay-per-view service directly to customers. In addition, it was reported that Disney and 20th Century Fox were planning their own pay-per-view service. All of a sudden, the threat of the new digital technology had become a reality because the studios sought to find the right platform on which to launch the service to customers. It had been Antioco's goal, just as it was Huizenga's before, that Blockbuster should provide this pivotal role. However, its own slow attempts to roll out pay-per-view revealed that it had no special competencies in the digital arena. It was still not clear how broadband downloads to customers would be handled in the future, nor was it clear which companies—movie studios, cable operators, satellite providers, and so on—would control the process.

All movies would be licensed to any video-on-demand service on a nonexclusive basis, so there would be no antitrust issues. Thus, in theory, Blockbuster could still operate its own pay-per-view through its stores. Each studio would control the pricing and availability of its films. To some degree, the studios were trying to limit digital piracy of their films and to prevent the emergence of a movie Napster. Service was planned to start sometime in 2002, after encryption and software problems were resolved. Consumers will pay a $3.99 fee similar to that charged by HBO and Blockbuster, and they will download an encrypted, digitally compressed film that can be stored on their hard drive for up to thirty days. The broadband download time would be twenty to forty minutes. Once the downloaded file is opened, however, it has to be watched in twenty-four hours. The file will play through a medium such as Real Networks or Microsoft Media Player.

In the short run, Antioco felt that the threat to Blockbuster posed by this development would be limited. Business travelers were expected to be the biggest customers for this kind of service. In the future, however, when PCs and televisions converge into one unit, the market could be huge and could annihilate Blockbuster's niche. The news hit Blockbuster's share price hard. Once again, the company seemed to be in trouble, although Antioco argued that Blockbuster would be able to license the rights to show pay-per-view movies on the same terms as any other distributor and that video-on-demand would not be a real threat for another five years. Anything could happen in that time, given the pace of technological change—perhaps Blockbuster might then have a viable format and be at the center of video-on-demand changes.

Nevertheless, realizing that the future is unclear, Antioco wondered again how to broaden the product line to keep revenues increasing and ward off any possible future declines in rental revenues. His answer came at the end of 2001, when Microsoft introduced its XBox video game console to compete with the Playstation 2 and Game Cube. The robust sales in the video game market became clear—it is a $15-billion-a-year revenue market. Blockbuster decided to carry a full line of Game Cube, XBox, and Playstation software and hardware for rental and to sell video games in its stores. It also began to work exclusive deals with game makers for old gaming systems and software because of the huge base of older generation video games. The attraction of these products to customers is that they can try any game they want before they must pay the high price for a game that they may not like. Also, rental makes variety possible. In the summer of 2002, Blockbuster began to offer $19.95 monthly rental service for unlimited video game rental. Also, this strategy fits Blockbuster's family profile because parents might come to the store to rent a DVD while their children can pick out a video game. Video games seemed to be a natural complementary product line. In May 2002, Blockbuster announced that it wanted to become "[g]amers' most comprehensive rental and retail resource."

In 2002, Blockbuster announced that it was switching even more quickly to high-margin DVDs and phasing out even more of its VHS. DVDs would thus account for 40 percent of the chain's rental inventory. Together, DVDs and video games now constitute more than half of Blockbuster's product offerings, and this percentage is expected to rise as DVDs sweep away VHS tapes much as CDs have swept away vinyl records. DVD rentals increased 115 percent in 2001 and the spring of 2002, and Blockbuster made $66 million in net income in the first quarter of 2002. During Memorial Day weekend in 2002, Blockbuster unveiled a new look for its video game section and added products in the push to double its video game rentals by 2003.

Finally, in June 2002, Blockbuster went to court to confront independent video retailers who claimed that its VHS revenue-sharing agreement, which had saved the company in 1999, violated antitrust laws by discriminating against them because they did not obtain preferential price treatment. Independents argued that before the revenue-sharing deals were negotiated, Blockbuster had only 24 percent of the market, while the independents had 55 percent. Today, Blockbuster has 40 percent and has real market power. Antioco argued that the outcome of the trial would have no real impact on his company because revenue-sharing deals do not exist for DVDs, and DVDs and video games were the key to the company's future.

The following question remains, however; how will video-on-demand and pay-per-view affect Blockbuster in the coming years if movie studios continue to increase their efforts to go directly to customers? Will the power of the Blockbuster brand name and huge store chain empire be enough to give it the bargaining power it needs to deal with that new competitive environment? Or will Blockbuster simply become a video game retail and rental chain?

REFERENCES

Apar, Bruce, "Ruminations on Burstyn, Bezos & Blockbuster," *Video Store*, January 14–January 20, 2001, p. 6.

Arnold, Thomas K., "Broadbuster," *Video Store*, August 6–August 12, 2000, pp. 1, 38.

Blockbuster 10Ks and annual reports, 1988–2001.

"Citibank Reaches Pact to Install Its ATMs in Blockbuster Stores," *Wall Street Journal*, May 28, 1998, p. A11.

Clarkin, Greg, "Fast Forward," *Marketing and Media Decisions*, March, 1990, pp. 57–59.

DeGeorge, G., *Business Week*, January 22, 1990, pp. 47–48.

DeGeorge, Gail, Jonathan Levine, and Robert Neff, "They Don't Call It Blockbuster for Nothing," *Business Week*, October 19, 1992, pp. 113–114.

Desjardins, Doug, "Blockbuster Scores with Games, DVDs," *DSN Retailing Today*, May 6, 2002, p. 5.

Fabrikant, Geraldine, "Blockbuster President Resigns: Video Chain Revamps to Adapt to New Units," *New York Times*, January 5, 1993, p. D6.

Frankel, Daniel, "Blockbuster Revamps Play Areas," *Video Business*, May 27, 2002, p. 38.

Gaudiosi, John, "Blockbuster Pushes PS2," *Video Store*, December 2–December 8, 2001, pp. 1, 38.

"Global Notes: Focus 1-Blockbuster Entertainment Corp. (BV)," *Research Highlights*, October 26, 1990, p. 9.

Grossman, Laurie, and Gabriella Stern, "Blockbuster to Buy Controlling Stake in Spelling in Swap," *Wall Street Journal*, March 9, 1993, p. B9.

Heller, Laura, "Radio Shack, Blockbuster Put Synergies to the Test," *DSN Retailing Today,* June 4, 2001, p. 5.

Hume, Scott, "Blockbuster Means More Than Video," *Advertising Age,* June 1, 1992, p. 4.

Kadlec, Daniel, "How Blockbuster Changed the Rules," *New York Times,* August 3, 1998, pp. 48–49.

Kirkwood, Kyra, "Blockbuster Moves into Used DVDs," *Video Store,* March 25, 2000, p. 1.

McCarthy, M., *Wall Street Journal,* March 22, 1991, pp. Al, A6.

Orwall, Bruce, "Five Studios Join Venture for Video on Demand," *Wall Street Journal,* August 17, 2001, p. A3.

QRP Merrill Lynch Extended Company Comment, November 16, 1990.

Roberts, Johnnie, "Blockbuster Officials Envision Superstores for Music Business," *Wall Street Journal,* October 28, 1992, p. B10.

Rosenblum, Trudi M., "Blockbuster to Add Audiobooks," *Publishers Weekly,* June 19, 2000, p. 14.

Sandomir, S., *New York Times,* June 19, 1991, pp. S22–S25.

Savitz, Eric, "An End to Fast Forward?" *Barron's,* December 11, 1989, pp. 13, 43–46.

Shapiro, Eben, "Heard on the Street: Chief Redstone Tries to Convince Wall Street There's Life Beyond Blockbuster at Viacom," *Wall Street Journal,* April 24, 1997, p. C2:3.

Shapiro, Eben, "Movies: Blockbuster Seeks a New Deal with Hollywood," *Wall Street Journal,* March 25, 1998, p. B1.

Shapiro, Eben, "Viacom Net Drops 70% as Cash Flow Slips on Weakness at Blockbuster Unit," *Wall Street Journal,* October 30, 1997, p. B8.

Shapiro, Eben, "Viacom Sets Major Charge Tied to Blockbuster," *Wall Street Journal,* July 23, 1998, p. A3.

Shapiro, Eben, "Viacom Trims Blockbuster's Expansion, Igniting Speculation of Eventual Spinoff," *Wall Street Journal,* March 28, 1997, p. B5:1.

Shapiro, Eben, and Nikhil Deogun, "Antioco Takes Top Job at Troubled Blockbuster," *Wall Street Journal,* June 4, 1997, p. A3:1.

Shapiro, Eben, and Susan Pulliam, "Heard on the Street: Viacom to Name Wal-Mart's Heir Apparent, William Fields, to Head Blockbuster Video," *Wall Street Journal,* March 29, 1996, p. C2.

Sweeting, Paul, "Big Blue Trimming Tapes," *Video Business,* September 17, 2001, p. 1.

Tarr, Greg, "DirecTV Teams with Blockbuster," *Twice,* May 15, 2000, p. 1.

Tedesco, Richard, "MGM, Blockbuster to Stream TV, Films," *Broadcasting & Cable,* January 24, 2000, p. 128.

"TiVo, Blockbuster Ink Cross-Promo Deal," *Twice,* January 17, 2000, p. 24.

"Video Stocks Stumbled," *Video Business,* September 3, 2001, p. 4.

Villa, Joan, "Blockbuster Game Exclusive," *Video Store,* January 20–January 26, 2002, pp. 1, 40.

Warren, Audrey, and Martin Peers, "Video Retailers Have Day in Court—Plaintiffs Say Supply Deals Between Blockbuster Inc. and Studios Violate Laws," *Wall Street Journal,* June 13, 2002, p. B10.

www. Blockbuster.com.

Video Concepts, Inc.

32

This case was prepared by John Dunkelberg and Tom Goho, Wake Forest University.

As Chad Rowan, the owner of Video Concepts, Inc., looked over his monthly income statement, he could only shake his head over how it could have been so much different. In many ways, he was a very successful entrepreneur, having started and grown a profitable business. In other ways, he felt trapped in a long-term, no-win situation. The question now was: what should he do given the current business environment? Basically, Rowan had a profitable business, but the profits were relatively small and had stopped growing since a strong competitor, Blockbuster Video, had moved into town. The profits, however, were not enough to pay off his long-term debts and provide him with any more than a subsistence living. In addition, the chances of selling his business for enough to pay off his debts and then start another business were not good. In reflecting on what might have been, Rowan commented:

> I had really hoped to expand Video Concepts into several similar-sized towns within a couple of hours' driving distance from here. The financial projections, which had been fairly accurate until Blockbuster arrived, indicated expansion was possible. I thought I was growing fast and had put about as much capital into the business as I could afford. I had even hoped to get a partner to go into this business with me, and one was very interested. Right now, however, I do not feel that I'm getting a very good return on my time and capital.

Talking about the current situation, Rowan said:

> I guess I'm getting a taste of my own medicine. As I grew, several local businesses went out of business, but the good news is that the total market has grown since Blockbuster opened its store. Their marketing clout has brought more people into the market.

To compete with Blockbuster, Rowan has tried everything he can think of to get market share. He has said, "The only way to increase revenues seems to be to raise the rental price, but my lower price is the best marketing strategy I have. If I raise the price, I'm afraid I will lose a lot of market share."

Background

Chad Rowan had been interested in having his own business since he had started and operated a lawn service business in high school. Rowan had started in the ninth grade mowing lawns for his neighbors using his family's lawn mower. By the time he had graduated from high school, his business had grown to a service that had purchased its own equipment: a riding mower, two smaller mowers, two blowers, a lawn aerator, an edger, and a trimmer. His business grew to the point that he employed three of his high school friends. The profits from this business were enough to pay his tuition to college, and he continued the business throughout his four college years.

Rowan majored in business and took the only two courses available in entrepreneurship and small-business management. During his senior year, he researched the video-rental business, which at that time was a relatively new industry. His research resulted in a paper on the video-rental business. The paper included a business plan for the start-up of a small video-rental store with an inventory of about 500 videotapes. By the middle of his senior year, Rowan knew he wanted to start in the video-rental business, and he had already chosen the site, a vacant retail store in the downtown business district of his hometown.

Starting a Business

After graduation in 1987, Rowan opened Video Concepts, a video-rental store with 200 square feet of retail space and a 500-tape rental library in Lexington, North Carolina, a town of about 28,000 people. Video Concepts started slowly but was profitable within six months. Rowan tried several innovative marketing techniques, including home delivery, a free rental after ten rentals, and selling soft drinks and popcorn both at the store and with the delivered videos. To help reduce the expense of the start-up business, Rowan lived at home with his parents and took only $500 a month for his own wages. Revenues that first year were $64,000, with all surplus cash flows used to buy additional videotapes. At the end of the first year's operation, Rowan decided to expand to a larger store.

A 1,000-square-foot retail store was available in a small shopping center that served a major neighborhood area. Using the value of some corporate stocks that he owned as collateral, Rowan borrowed $80,000 from his banker to open this store. The loan was a seven-year note with only interest due during the term of the loan and the entire principal due in seven years. The new store had 3,000 videotapes. Rowan purchased all his new releases through Major Video, one of the top three wholesale distributors in the United States. To increase the size of his video library, he purchased more than 2,000 used tapes from a firm that purchased tapes from bankrupt firms for resale.

Over the next two years, Video Concepts continued to grow rapidly and remained profitable. Rowan continued to put all profits into the purchase of additional tapes, however. Revenues during the second year increased to $173,000 and to $278,000 in the third year.

Growth Continues

The chance to open a third store became a reality when a furniture retail store, originally located in Lexington's busiest shopping district, decided to move to its own, larger building on the outskirts of town. The store contained 3,000 square feet of space, enough to hold more than 12,000 tapes on display. Rowan obtained a three-year lease on the store and opened his third video-rental store in the fall of 1990. Video Concepts now had stores in the three main shopping areas of Lexington.

The new Video Concepts store used open display racks for the videotapes, and customers could quickly and easily locate the type of movies they wanted by going to the appropriate section (for example, new releases, horror, science fiction, action, classic, and so forth) and walking down the aisle. Checking out was quick and easy thanks to a new computer software program that reduced checkout time to less than thirty seconds per customer. In addition, the software program allowed Rowan to keep track of the number of times each tape was rented, how many tapes each customer rented, and who had past-due tapes. The system also allowed Rowan to track sales easily on a daily, weekly, or monthly basis. The new store and the more efficient operation enabled Video Concepts to become a growing and fairly profitable business.

During the next year, growth at the three Video Concepts stores continued, with the majority of the growth coming from the new store. Rowan continued the policy of a free rental after ten rentals, reduced the price per rental to $1.99 per night, and introduced some advertising, which was centered primarily on local high school promotional events. The original two stores saw little growth in sales but remained profitable.

As his business had grown, the number of competitors had steadily decreased, and by the summer of 1991, only six of the original seventeen competitors were still operating. Rowan thought his aggressive pricing strategy, high-quality service, and good selection of new releases were factors in the demise of some of his smaller competitors. His six competitors averaged a tape inventory of less than 1,000 videos, and none had more than 1,600 videos. Rowan estimated that the annual revenues from video rentals in Lexington at the time was about $600,000.

The increase in video-rental chain stores nationally had not gone unnoticed by Rowan, and he had visited several competitors' stores in nearby cities. During his visits, Rowan primarily had tried to see what the competition was doing and learn what he must do to be more efficient and stay competitive. Although he had visited Blockbuster Video stores in several nearby cities, Rowan estimated that their stores would require annual revenues of at least $600,000 a store to be profitable. For this reason, Rowan believed that Lexington was too small to attract a major video-rental chain store. He also believed that he had a store operation that was as well stocked and efficiently operated as a chain-store operation.

With these thoughts in mind, he began paying himself a modest annual salary of $15,000. In addition, he was ready to start paying off the second loan of $200,000 that he had borrowed to open the new store. To obtain this last loan, Rowan had used all his assets as collateral because he believed that these stores were an excellent investment. In the summer of 1991, with sales increasing in every month, Rowan had reason to think that he had built a successful business.

Serious Competition Arrives

In August 1991, Blockbuster Entertainment announced that it would open a store in Lexington. Although a very young corporation, Blockbuster was the largest video-rental chain store in the United States. Blockbuster had grown from nineteen stores in 1986 to 2,028 (1,025 company-owned and 1,003 franchises) in 1991, with total revenues over $1.2 billion in 1992. The typical Blockbuster store carried 8,000 to 14,000 tapes, and the stores ranged in size from 4,000 to 10,000 square feet. In 1991 the 1,248 company-owned stores that had been in operation for more than a year were averaging monthly revenues of $74,984.

Although U.S. growth in consumer spending on video rentals seemed to have slowed, Blockbuster believed it had the opportunity to take market share away from the smaller competitors through its strategy of building large stores with a greater selection of tapes than most of its competitors. As the largest video-rental chain in the United States, Blockbuster also had advantages in marketing and in the purchase of inventory. Blockbuster's standard pricing was $3.50 per tape for two nights, but local stores had some pricing discretion.

In the fall of 1991, Blockbuster built a new store almost across the street from the main Video Concepts store. It purchased a vacant lot for $310,000 and then leased a 6,400-square-foot building that was built to its specifications under a long-term lease agreement for $8.50 per square foot for the first three years. The cost of completely furnishing the building, including stocking it with videotapes, was about $375,000, and Blockbuster spent more than $150,000 on the grand-opening promotions. Thus, Blockbuster spent about $835,000 to open its store, compared with the slightly more than $200,000 that Video Concepts had spent to open its similar-sized store. Blockbuster's operating costs were very similar to those of Video Concepts because the computer checkout equipment was similar and both firms had approximately the same personnel costs. Both firms depreciated their tapes over twelve months.

Blockbuster's Impact on Video Concepts

Rowan decided not to try to meet the grand-opening blitz by Blockbuster with an advertising promotion of his own, but he did start including brochures on Video Concepts with each rental. The brochure noted that the rental fee at Video Concepts was lower than Blockbuster's, that Video Concepts had a new game section with Nintendo games, that Video Concepts was a family entertainment store (that is, no X-rated videos), and that Video Concepts was a locally owned store that supported local school events. Rowan felt his past reputation for low prices ($1.99 versus $3.50 at Blockbuster), his hometown ownership, and courteous service were the appropriate responses to a well-financed competitor. He did not believe that he should even attempt to match Blockbuster's advertising budget and that he should not try to beat Blockbuster at its game. That is, he must continue to do what he did best and not try to match Blockbuster's marketing strategy. He did, however, increase the number of tapes purchased for each new release.

With the opening of the new Blockbuster store and its attendant grand-opening marketing campaign,

Video Concepts' revenues dropped about 25 percent for two months and then started slowly climbing back to its pre-opening levels. During this two-month period, Rowan had worked even harder to provide excellent customer service through brief training sessions for his employees. He had always had employee training sessions, but these new sessions emphasized the competitive threat from Blockbuster and the need to provide the best customer service possible. The primary points of these sessions were directed toward informing customers, as they checked out, of how many rentals they had before they could obtain a free rental, of the customer's ability to reserve videos, and of Video Concepts' willingness to deliver videos to a customer's home at no extra charge. (These were all services that Blockbuster did not offer.)

Unfortunately, Video Concepts' revenues hit a plateau of just under $40,000 per month and stayed there, with the normal minor seasonal variations, for the next twelve months. During this time, Rowan attempted several marketing promotions, including rent-one-get-one-free on the normally slow nights (Mondays, Tuesdays, and Wednesdays), mailing brochures to all Video Concepts customers that briefly highlighted the advantages of shopping at Video Concepts over Blockbuster (lower prices and additional services), and a free rental coupon.

The promotions seemed to help Video Concepts maintain the current revenue level, but they also decreased the profitability of the operation. To improve profitability, Rowan examined his operation for ways of making it more efficient. By studying the hour-by-hour sales patterns, he was able to schedule his employees more efficiently. He also used the information provided by the software program to determine when the rentals of hit and/or new releases had peaked. Rowan learned that there was a fairly good market for used tapes for a short period of time, but if the tapes were not sold during this time, he would end up with a tape that had very little rental demand and little resale value.

The problem with the hit videos was twofold. The first was the determination of how many tapes to purchase. There seemed to be little correlation between a hit at the box office and a hit from rentals. When the video was first released for rental, Rowan would buy forty to fifty videotapes at a cost of about $60 each. The demand for these videos would be very high for about six weeks to three months, after which the demand would drop significantly. The second

problem, therefore, was the determination of when and how many of the tapes to sell before the demand would drop to the level of nonhit videos. Rowan believed that he had solved the second problem by carefully watching the sales figures for the tapes. Analysis of this information helped to minimize his investment in the inventory of tapes, which marginally improved cash flow.

The Dilemma

Two years after Blockbuster had opened its store, Rowan carefully analyzed the financial statements for Video Concepts (see Tables 1 and 2). The company was profitable and had been able to maintain its market share. What was evident was the fact that the arrival of Blockbuster had increased the demand for video rentals in Lexington to an estimated $1,300,000 a year. Blockbuster's share was estimated to be about $700,000 a year, and the few remaining independents had approximately $100,000 a year in revenues.

To Rowan, the current situation was fairly straightforward. Video Concepts had a store that was comparable to Blockbuster's in tape selection, per-

TABLE 1

Video Concepts, Inc., Income Statement
One Year Ending June 30, 1993

Revenues		$465,958
Cost of goods*		192,204
Gross profit		$273,754
Expenses		
Salaries[†]	$108,532	
Payroll taxes	11,544	
Utilities	20,443	
Rent	23,028	
Office expenses	26,717	
Maintenance	6,205	
Advertising expenses	4,290	
Interest expenses	27,395	
Total expenses		228,154
Income before taxes		45,600
Taxes		10,944
Net income		$ 34,656

*Cost of goods = purchase price minus market value of tapes. This method is used because most of the tapes purchased are depreciated over a twelve-month period.
[†]Salaries include Chad's salary of $15,000.

TABLE 2

Video Concepts, Inc.
Balance Sheet, June 30, 1993

Cash	$ 15,274	Accounts payable	$ 15,429
Inventory	4,162	Sales taxes payable	2,415
Prepaid expenses	1,390	Withholding/FICA payable	3,270
Total current assets	$ 20,826	Total current liabilities	$ 21,114
Office equipment	$ 48,409	Bank term loan	$247,518
Furniture and fixtures	53,400	Common stock	20,800
Videocassette tapes	303,131	Retained earnings	24,153
Leasehold improvements	39,800		
Accumulated depreciation*	(151,981)		
Total assets	$ 313,585	Total liabilities and equity	$313,585

*Includes the depreciation of tapes.

sonnel costs, and efficiency of operation. Video Concepts had a cost advantage, with lower store leasing costs ($3.50 per square foot versus $8.50), but Blockbuster had a bigger advantage in the use of its purchasing power to purchase videotapes at a much lower cost. Video Concepts' major marketing strength was its lower rental price ($1.99 versus $3.00), but Blockbuster utilized a much larger advertising budget to attract customers. All of the Blockbuster stores in that region charged $3.50 for rental, except for the one in Lexington.

As had happened nationwide, the growth of video-rental revenue leveled off in the Lexington area starting in 1992. Nationwide in 1992, sales increased only 4.7 percent for Blockbuster stores that had been in operation more than one year. Future growth did not look bright. Advances in cable television technology could render video-store rentals obsolete because fiber optics allowed cable subscribers to order a wide variety of movies at home through pay-per-view services. This technology is still in development stages, however, and its spread to small towns is certainly many years away.

Looking to the future, Rowan felt that, for all his efforts, the net income from the Video Concepts operation would not provide him as high a return on his time and capital as he had expected. He was still paying only the interest on his long-term loans, and paying off the debt seemed several years away. From Rowan's viewpoint, he had several options. He considered raising the price of an overnight rental to $2.49 to make the business more profitable, but he was afraid of what the consequences of such a move might be. He also considered hiring someone to manage the business and find another job for himself. He had received offers of corporate jobs in the past and was considering exploring this option again. Another alternative was to try to sell the business. As Rowan pondered these alternatives, he tried to think of a solution that he might have overlooked. What he was sure of, however, was that he did not wish to keep working twelve-hour days at a business that did not seem to have a bright future.

REFERENCES

"Blockbuster Goes After a Bigger, Tougher Rep," *Variety,* January 25, 1993, p. 151.
"Blockbuster, IBM Plans Set Retailers Spinning," *Variety,* May 17, 1993, p. 117.
"Blockbuster Idea Might Work for Computer Industry," *Mac Week,* May 24, 1993, p. 62.
"Blockbuster Sizes Up PPV Potential: Talks Home Delivery with Bell Atlantic," *Billboard,* January 30, 1993, p. 11.
"Changes in Distribution Landscape Have Players Scouting Claims," *Billboard,* May 16, 1993, p. 52.
"Oscar Noms Mean Gold for Video Industry," *Variety,* February 24, 1992, p. 79.
"Play It Again and Again, Sam," *Newsweek,* December 16, 1991, p. 57.
"Recording Industry Hits Blockbuster," *Advertising Age,* May 17, 1993, p. 46.
"Record Store of Near Future: Computers Replace the Racks," *New York Times,* May 12, 1993, p. A1.
"Stretching the Tape," *New York Times,* April 22, 1993, p. B5.
"Video and Laser Hot Sheet," *Rolling Stone,* March 4, 1993, p. 72.
"VSDA Regaining Its Sense of Direction," *Variety,* June 8, 1992, p. 19.

33

AOL Time Warner: Creating a Colossus

This case was prepared by Charles W. L. Hill, the University of Washington.

Introduction

On January 10, 2000, America Online (AOL) and Time Warner stunned the business world by announcing plans to merge the two companies together into a powerhouse that would span both online and traditional media. The merger, which at the time was valued at $156 billion, was the largest ever. The plan called for AOL shareholders to get 55 percent of the stock in the combined company. Time Warner CEO Gerald Levin would become CEO of the new company. AOL's CEO, Steve Case, would become chairman, and Bob Pittman, AOL's president, would become copresident of the combined company and, in the view of many, heir apparent to Levin. The company would be called AOL Time Warner (AOL TW). The proposed merger would combine the largest online service provider of the Internet era with one of the blue chip companies of the old media world. Founded in 1923, Time Warner has a vast array of magazine, TV broadcasting, film, music, and cable service properties. These include *Time* and *Life* magazines, Warner's film and music properties, CNN, TNT, and HBO, and cable systems that serve 20 percent of the United States. AOL, founded only fifteen years ago, had just 20 percent of the revenue and 15 percent of the employees of Time Warner. However, most observers commented that, in this "marriage of equals," it was the upstart that was in effect acquiring the older company.[1]

In explaining why they were merging, executives from both companies cited a wide range of synergies. They claimed that Time Warner's cable system would help AOL to roll out a broadband version of its service, that AOL would be able to offer Time Warner content to its online subscribers, thereby enhancing the value of the service and guaranteeing continued growth, and that there were huge possibilities for cross-selling between AOL and Time Warner subscribers. They predicted that the combined company would be able to grow revenues at 12 to 15 percent per annum, earnings before interest, taxes, depreciation, and amortization (EBITDA) by 25 percent per annum, and free cash flow by 50 percent per annum.[2]

It took a year for the merger to close, primarily because the companies had to deal with a range of difficult antitrust issues. In the intervening period, the stock price of AOL fell from $68 to $47 a share, reflecting a slowdown in economic activity in the United States, and thus in advertising spending, a major component of revenue for both AOL and Time Warner. Still, the management of the new company stuck to their optimistic forecasts, predicting that they would grow EBITDA by 33 percent in 2001. It was not to be. Hit by weak advertising spending, AOL TW's EBITDA grew by only 18 percent and revenues by 5 percent.

In April 2002, AOL TW stock, which had hit a high of $56 in May 2001, was trading at $19 a share. The company announced that it would take a massive $54 billion charge against earnings, writing down the goodwill taken on as a result of the merger and essentially recognizing that the merger was based on an unrealistic valuation of the combined entity. CEO Gerald Levin had retired and was replaced not by AOL's Bob Pitman, as many initially expected, but by a Time Warner man, Richard Parsons. Parsons scaled back the bullish forecasts and stated that AOL TW would grow revenues by maybe 5 to 8 percent in 2002 and EBITDA by 8 to 12 percent. Even these scaled-back figures were viewed with suspicion by critics, who cited slow subscriber growth at the AOL division and a weak rollout of AOL's broadband offerings. Some were even speculating that AOL might be spun out of AOL TW.

The Rise of AOL

When AOL went public in 1992, it had fewer than 200,000 subscribers and revenues of just $27 million. By the time its merger was announced with Time Warner, the company was closing in on 22 million subscribers and was generating revenues of around $6 billion. The rise of the company had been dramatic and often controversial. It was initially seen as a distant third to two well-funded rivals, Prodigy and CompuServe, but by 2000 Prodigy had exited the industry, and AOL had acquired CompuServe in 1997. In addition, AOL acquired ICQ's instant messaging service in 1998, and shortly afterwards purchased Netscape, the company that had pioneered the Internet browser. Microsoft's MSN Network had emerged as a competitor mid decade, but in 2000 it was still a distant second to AOL, with just 3 million subscribers.

AOL offered subscribers access to a proprietary network that could be used to send and receive email, read bulletin boards, enter chat rooms, browse a wide range of media content, and purchase goods from e-commerce providers with a "storefront" on the network. In addition, from 1994 onward, AOL incorporated a web browser into its software, giving subscribers access to the rapidly growing World Wide Web (WWW). Much of AOL's success was attributed to the ease with which its software could be installed and used; the software organized content and features in a graphical user interface that was intuitively easy for computer neophytes to navigate. What also helped was the popularity of key features of the service such as email and chat rooms, the wide range of content that could be found on the service, and the company's own relentless and savvy marketing that had made AOL one of the best-known brands in America. For example, AOL "you've got mail" sound bite quickly became a signature of popular culture and the title of a highly successful film. Although sophisticated users of the Internet had derided AOL as the "Internet on training wheels," apparently that was what the mass market wanted— and AOL was, if nothing else, determined to give customers what they wanted.

AOL's Evolving Business Model

Over the course of the decade, AOL's business model had changed a number of times. Originally revenues were generated almost entirely from subscriptions, with usage being charged by the hour. In 1996, some 91 percent of AOL's revenues came from subscription fees, with the balance coming from advertising and commerce transactions. Through December 31, 1994, the standard monthly membership fee for AOL was $9.95 for five hours of access and $3.50 per hour thereafter. In January 1995, AOL reduced the per hour fee to $2.95, although it left the base fee unchanged. In May 1996, AOL announced an additional pricing plan for heavy users of the service. This included twenty hours of service for $19.95 per month and an hourly fee of $2.95 for use in excess of that.

However, by 1996 the Internet was becoming increasingly well organized due to the emergence of portals such as Yahoo.com, leading some critics to question the need for a proprietary online service like AOL. Internet service providers (ISPs) from small "mom-and-pop" operations to telecommunications giants like AT&T and MCI had sprung up and were starting to offer unlimited access to the Internet for $19.95 a month. Under AOL's pricing plan, the heaviest users could run up bills anywhere from $50 to $300 per month. Partly as a result, AOL's subscriber churn rate was unacceptably high. Estimates suggested that by mid 1996 the monthly churn rate was running at around 6 percent, implying that over 70 percent of AOL's customers would leave the service within one year of joining.[3] Since it cost AOL at least $45 in marketing expenses to get a new subscriber onto the service, the implication was that many subscribers were leaving before AOL had the chance to recoup the cost of acquiring them.[4] Moreover, among the customers who were leaving were longtime heavy users who were AOL's biggest spenders. Although representing only one-third of the subscriber base, these heavy users were accounting for two-thirds of AOL's revenues.

On October 10, 1996, Microsoft's MSN announced that it would adopt a flat rate pricing scheme of $19.95 per month for unlimited access to MSN's "proprietary content" and the Web. The move forced AOL's hand. On October 29, AOL announced that from December 1 it too would offer unlimited access for $19.95 per month.[5] Following the announcement of the move to flat rate pricing and unlimited access, AOL's membership surged. The service added over half a million new members in December alone. By early January, close to 8 million people were using the service, exceeding both the company's expectations and the capacity of its network. Hundreds of thousands of new members were joining the service—only to be greeted by busy signals! Complaints from irritated members overwhelmed the capacity of AOL's customer service operation. On January 16, AOL responded by announcing that it would invest an additional $100 million in its dial-up network over the next few months. The company also pledged to reduce its marketing expenditures and pull its TV ad campaign until the capacity of its network had been upgraded. The busy signals continued. A number of state attorneys general banded together and announced that they would sue AOL for deceptive selling practices, false advertising, and even fraud. By the end of January, AOL agreed to give a refund to any member who requested it as compensation for the inability to access the network. In return, the states agreed to drop their lawsuit.[6]

With revenue growth from subscribers now constrained by flat rate pricing, CEO Steve Case decided it was time to leverage the brand in order to maximize revenues from advertising and e-commerce—and AOL had to move quickly. Although it had already embarked on this road a year ago, the move to flat rate pricing gave the strategy new urgency. In October 1996, Case hired Bob Pittman as president of AOL Networks. It was to be Pittman's job to leverage the AOL brand and diversify the company's revenue sources. Then forty-two years old, Pittman had already left his mark on global pop culture. A one-time radio disk jockey, in 1981, together with John Lack, Pittman started an all-music cable TV channel called Music television, or MTV. Charismatic, photogenic, and charming, Pittman was in many ways the ultimate marketing *wunderkind*. In addition to MTV, Pittman also had a

hand in the creation of VH1 and the Nike at Nite cable TV channels.[7]

Pittman sharpened the focus of the strategy. Prior to Pittman's arrival, AOL had been considering entering all sorts of businesses itself, from selling books to long-distance telephone service. Pittman's view was that AOL had the most valuable real estate on the Internet and that AOL should leverage that, helping other organizations sell their goods and services to AOL members.

On February 25, 1997, Pittman announced the first of what was to become a steady stream of deals. Under this deal, Tel-Save Holdings, a long-distance telephone service reseller, paid AOL $100 million for the privilege of being able to sell long-distance services to AOL's members. Prior to the deal, Tel-Save had 500,000 customers. The $100 million was an advance on future commission payments that would be due to AOL for members Tel-Save signed up. For Tel-Save, the deal had two big attractions. It was a cost-effective way of reaching 8 million potential customers, and AOL would bill Tel-Save customers electronically and charge their credit cards for calls made using Tel-Save. Tel-Save estimated that electronic billing and credit card payments would reduce its unit costs by 30 percent, enabling it to offer customers long-distance rates 20 percent below those offered by rivals.[8] By March 1998, AOL and Tel-Save announced that the long-distance reseller had added 500,000 customers from AOL.[9]

On March 4, 1997, AOL opened to advertisers its 14,000 chat rooms, which logged 1 million hours daily. On June 10, CUC International agreed to pay AOL an advance of $50 million against future commissions in order to market its range of discount services directly to AOL subscribers. CUC expected to generate more than 1 million new interactive memberships per year from its AOL connection.[10] On July 7, Amazon.com, the Internet bookseller, agreed to pay AOL at least $19 million over three years in advances on commissions to be the featured bookseller on AOL's web site, aol.com. If Amazon.com sales through AOL exceeded targets, this figure would be increased. Barnes and Noble paid a similar amount (later increased to $40 million) to be the bookseller on AOL's proprietary service. Also in July 1997, 1–800-FLOWERS agreed to pay AOL at least $25 million in advances on commissions over four years to sell on the service. The flower company expected the deal to produce $250 million in sales over four years.[11]

Around the same time, AOL began to charge retailers "rents" of at least $250,000 per year for their spots on AOL, in addition to commissions. This represented a shift from the old practice by which AOL simply took a cut of the sales generated from sales over AOL. Revenues from this source had been disappointing, but Pittman felt that the change in incentive structure implied by the imposition of rents would yield significant dividends down the road.

In addition to taking a cut out of e-commerce transactions, AOL also began to change its relationship with content providers during this period. Under the old pricing scheme, AOL *paid* content providers a fee based on the time members spent at their sites. With the hourly fee now gone, AOL had no incentive to pay content providers. Instead, the company started requiring content providers to pay it a fee in exchange for the privilege of being able to offer content through AOL. In one of the first deals, announced in July 1997, AOL stated that it had signed CBS Sportsline to serve as an "anchor tenant" for the service's sports channel.[12] In addition to demanding fees, AOL started to weed out weak content providers, refusing to renew their contracts when they came due.

The fruits of this change in strategy started to become apparent by 1998. In fiscal 1995, AOL generated some $6 million in revenues from advertising and commercial fees. This increased to $100.2 million in 1996, $180 million in 1997, and $511 million in 1998. The figure for 1999 looked set to exceed $1 billion out of total AOL revenues of more than $4 billion. Moreover, there was no sign of a slowdown in the flow of deals bringing cash into AOL's coffers. In early 1999, AOL entered into a five-year agreement valued at $500 million with First USA under which First USA became the exclusive marketer of credit card products and service on AOL. Similarly, in July 1999 drkoop.com, an Internet-based health care site established by Dr. Everett Koop, the former surgeon general of the United States, agreed to pay AOL $89 million over four years. This was an advance on commissions for the chance to sell to AOL's members, which by then exceeded 19 million.[13] As of March 31, 1999, AOL's *backlog* of advertising and commerce revenues exceeded $1.3 billion (the *backlog* refers to future revenues guaranteed to AOL under the terms of agreements with content providers and online retailers).[14]

The Quest for Bandwidth

As 1999 progressed, it became increasingly clear that AOL needed to be able to offer its members greater bandwidth. *Bandwidth* refers to the rate at which digital data can be transferred between two points (the term *broadband* refers to a high-bandwidth connection). Currently most consumers only have relatively low-bandwidth connections to the Internet over standard telephone lines (a typical computer modem can transmit and receive data at 56 kilobytes per second). AOL CEO Steve Case had long argued that greater bandwidth connections would allow high-resolution video and audio data to be transmitted effectively to consumers over the Internet. In turn, this would dramatically expand the range of interactive service that consumers could access over the Internet, which could drive forward the growth in demand for AOL's various offerings.

There are various ways of delivering high-bandwidth connections to the home, all of which are in the early stages of being rolled out.[15] One way utilizes DSL (digital subscriber line) technology to increase the bandwidth of standard copper telephone lines. DSL technology typically moves data at between 128 K and 1.5 megabytes per second, with 640 K being the norm. This is the solution favored by telephone companies. By mid 1999 there were about 180,000 DSL subscribers in the United States. But DSL signals degrade with distance and typically won't work more than 3 miles from a phone switch.

Another solution involves adapting the coaxial cable used to transmit cable TV signals to carry two-way Internet traffic. Consumers with cable modems attached to their personal computers (PCs) would then be able to access the Internet at speeds up to five hundred times faster than with a standard 56-K telephone modem. TV cables run past 95 percent of homes in the United States. By mid 1999, 750,000 people in the United States were using services based on cable modems.

A third solution is to use digital satellite technology to beam down data at very high bandwidth rates. The problem with this solution right now is that the consumers can't beam data back at similar rates. Rather, they have to communicate requests for data through conventional telephone lines operating at 56 K. By mid 1999, some 25,000 consumers were using satellite services to connect to the Internet.

Steve Case is not the only one who believes that high-bandwidth connectivity is the key to expanding demand for interactive services over the Internet. Microsoft's Bill Gates also believes that high-bandwidth connectivity is crucial, and he sees high bandwidth driving forward demand for Microsoft software and services, including AOL rival MSN.[16] In 1998, Microsoft began to invest in cable TV companies as part of a strategy to create incentives for the cable companies to speed up their moves to upgrade their coaxial cable networks so that they could carry Internet traffic.

Microsoft started the ball rolling with a $5 billion investment in Comcast, a nationwide cable operator. Soon thereafter, AT&T jumped into the fray when it acquired the number one cable operator in the United States, TCI, for $75 billion. AT&T announced that it intended to provide phone service and Internet access over cable. Along with TCI came @Home, in which TCI had a controlling ownership stake. @Home was a leader in offering Internet access over coaxial cable. Then on May 10, 1999, AT&T acquired another major cable company, MediaOne, for $60 billion. MediaOne happened to be part owner of Roadrunner, which was a major competitor to @Home. As part of the AT&T-MediaOne deal, Microsoft agreed to invest $5 billion in AT&T and to purchase a 30 percent stake in MediaOne's European cable TV operating subsidiary, TeleWest (at one point, Microsoft was rumored to be preparing a rival bid for MediaOne).[17]

This flurry of deals led to speculation that AOL might be shut out of high-bandwidth access to the Internet via cable. Up to this point the cable networks had been closed to AOL because federal regulators had ruled that cable operators have the exclusive right to market data services to their own subscribers. AOL challenged this ruling, but met with little success. It lobbied regulators to allow it access to AT&T's now extensive cable network, which was reserved for AT&T's cable ISP, @Home, but again got nowhere. As an alternative, in early 1999 AOL entered into strategic alliances with two of America's telephone giants, Bell Atlantic and SBC Communications, to use DSL technology to make available a high-speed upgrade connection to AOL subscribers starting summer 1999.

This was followed by a May 12 announcement that AOL would make a record $1.5 billion investment in Hughes Electronics and jointly introduce new consumer offerings with Hughes's DirecTV satellite service.[18] The proposed offerings include AOL-Plus, which will provide high-speed Internet connection over satellite, and AOL TV for such television-based functions as interactive shopping, web surfing, email, and electronic chat, more commonly performed over the Internet. A set-top box, which the partners are developing jointly, will allow TV viewers to chat with friends, check their email, and engage in e-commerce. Although this deal put AOL back in the broadband race and positioned the company to enter the interactive TV market, the shortcomings of current satellite systems still left AOL at a potential disadvantage.

Time Warner

Time Warner, created in 1990 by the merger of Warner Communications and Time, was the world's largest media conglomerate.[19] In 2000 the company comprised six major segments: *cable networks*, principally interests in cable television programming; *publishing*, principally interests in magazine publishing, book publishing, and direct marketing; *music*, principally interests in recorded music and music publishing; *filmed entertainment*, principally interests in filmed entertainment, television production, and television broadcasting; *cable*, principally interests in cable television systems; and *digital media*, consisting principally of interests in Internet-related and digital media businesses.

In 1999, the year prior to the merger announcement, Time Warner had revenues of $27 billion and a net income of $1.95 billion. The revenue split between different businesses is given in Exhibit 1. The earnings split, measured by earnings before interest,

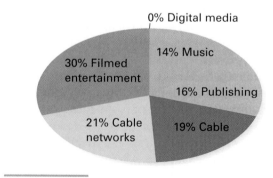

EXHIBIT 1

Time Warner Revenue Breakdown

Source: AOL Time Warner Form 10K, 2000.

tax, and amortization, is given in Exhibit 2. The digital media business was a start-up operation at this time; it generated no revenues and registered a loss.

Cable Networks

Time Warner owned a portfolio of cable television networks that included three of the top five networks in the United States, which accounted for 26 percent of all basic cable subscription revenue in the country and around 28 percent of basic cable advertising revenues. These networks included Turner Networks, which was acquired earlier in the decade when Time Warner bought Ted Turner's Turner Broadcasting (the acquisition left Ted Turner with a substantial shareholding in Time Warner and a seat on the board). Turner Networks included CNN, TBS, and TNT. CNN, the pioneering twenty-four-hour-a-day cable news service, had more than 77 million subscribers in the United States at the time of the merger announcement. Together with CNN International, CNN reached more than 200 million locations in 212 countries and territories by December 2001. When the merger was announced, TBS had approximately 77 million subscribers in the United States, and TNT approximately 75 million subscribers.

In addition, Time Warner owned HBO, which was the leading pay television service in the world and which together with its sister service, Cinemax, had approximately 36 million subscribers. A majority of HBO's programming and a large portion of that on Cinemax consist of recently released, uncut, and uncensored theatrical motion pictures. However, HBO was also gaining a reputation for developing its own compelling programming content. Two series,

The Sopranos and Sex in the City, had helped to boost HBO's rating and garnered the network a number of industry awards.

Time Warner also owned the Cartoon Network and a 50 percent interest in Comedy Central and Court TV. The Cartoon Network, which was number two to Nickelodeon, had around 61 million subscribers, and Court TV reached some 36 million.

Publishing

Time Warner's publishing interests were conducted primarily by Time Incorporated, which was a wholly owned subsidiary of the company. Time Inc. publishes some of the world's best-known magazines, including *Time, People, Sports Illustrated, Fortune, Money, Entertainment Weekly,* and *In Style,* and it accounted for 40 percent of magazine industry profits when the merger was announced. In 1999, Time magazines accounted for a leading 22.6 percent of the total advertising revenue in consumer magazines. *People, Time,* and *Sports Illustrated* were ranked 1, 2, and 3, respectively, in advertising revenue, and Time had eight of the thirty leading magazines in terms of advertising dollars. Advertising rates are a function of circulation, with high-circulation publications being able to demand higher rates from advertisers. Time has been experimenting, with considerable success, with brand extension strategies, publishing new offerings, such as *Teen People* and *Time for Kids,* that have swelled the overall circulation of Time publications.

Although single copies of magazines are sold through retail news dealers and other outlets that are supplied by wholesalers or directly by Time, most magazines are sold by subscription and delivered through the mail. Subscriptions are sold by direct mail and online solicitation, subscription sales agencies, television and telephone solicitation, and insert cards in magazines and other publications. Time was generally recognized as having one of the best subscription selling machines in the industry.

Time also has two major trade publishing houses, Warner Books and Little, Brown. In 1999, Time Warner Trade Publishing placed thirty-six books on the *New York Times* bestseller lists.

Music

Time Warner's music interests are run through Warner Music Group (WMG), whose record labels include Warner Bros., Atlantic, Elektra, and London-Sire. WMG is one of the five largest record labels in

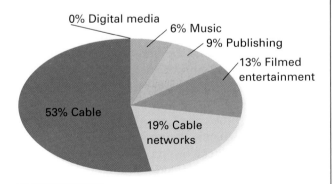

EXHIBIT 2

Earnings Breakdown (EBITA)

Source: AOL Time Warner Form 10K, 2000.

the world, with a 13 percent share of the U.S. music sales in 2000. WMG's artists include Madonna, Matchbox Twenty, Eric Clapton, Red Hot Chili Peppers, Brandy, Kid Rock, Goo Goo Dolls, Missy Elliot, Tim McGraw, Bare Naked Ladies, and Don Henley. However, WMG's market share had slipped from more than 20 percent just five years previously. Moreover, the entire recording industry was entering troubled waters, with the ease of distributing and swapping music files over the Internet potentially starting to disrupt the industry. The recording industry argued that the rise of file-sharing services such as Napster led to an increase in digital piracy rates in the United States and falling sales.

WMG is a vertically integrated music company. After an artist has entered into a contract with a WMG label, a master recording of the artist's music is produced and provided to WMG's manufacturing operation, which replicates the music primarily on CDs and audiocassettes. A WMG subsidiary, Ivy Hill, prints material that is included with CDs and audiocassettes and creates packaging for them. WMG's distribution arms sell product and deliver it, either directly or through subdistributors and wholesalers, to thousands of record stores, mass merchants, and other retailers throughout the country. CDs and audiocassettes are also increasingly being sold directly to consumers through Internet retailers such as CDnow and Amazon.com.

On January 24, 2002, just two weeks after the AOL–Time Warner merger had been announced, Time Warner announced that WMG and EMI's recording business would merge, forming a fifty-fifty joint venture, although Warner would control the board of the venture. The venture would create the largest music company in the world, with a huge catalog of around 2 million songs. In a news conference announcing the proposed venture, Time Warner executives argued that the combined company would be better positioned to deal with the opportunities and threats posed by the rise of the Internet as a primary medium for distributing music.

Filmed Entertainment

Time Warner's filmed entertainment businesses operate under the Warner Brothers, New Line Cinema, and Castle Rock film production names. The businesses produce and distribute theatrical motion pictures, television shows, animation, and other programming; distribute home videos; operate the WB Television Network; license rights to the company's characters; operate retail stores featuring consumer products based on the company's characters and brands; and operate motion picture theaters.

Warner Bros. Pictures's strategy includes building movie franchises, which will continue with the planned expansion of *The Matrix* into a series of films. In 2001 the first of a series of Harry Potter motion pictures and the first of the Lord of the Rings trilogy were introduced.

The WB Television Network (the WB) was established in 1995. During the l999–2000 broadcast season, the WB expanded its prime-time program line-up to six nights and started airing thirteen hours of series programming from Sunday to Friday nights. The network's line-up includes the family series *7th Heaven,* as well as programming aimed at a teen and young adult audience, such as *Dawson's Creek, Charmed, Buffy the Vampire Slayer, Felicity, Roswell, Popular,* and *Angel.* Total TV household coverage of the WB was 83 percent in 2000.

Cable

In 2000 Time Warner was the second-largest operator of cable TV systems in the United States, behind AT&T Broadband and ahead of Comcast. The company's cable business served some 12.6 million subscribers in 2000. These included approximately 6.7 million subscribers in a joint venture between TWE and Advance/Newhouse, a family-owned cable TV system. The joint venture is 66 percent owned by Time Warner.

During 1999, Time Warner Cable began an aggressive rollout of digital cable service in many of its cable systems. As of 2000, Time Warner Cable had approximately 430,000 digital service subscribers. The digitalization of signals allows them to be compressed so that they occupy less bandwidth, which substantially increases the number of channels that can be provided over a system. Digital set-tops delivered to subscribing customers offer a digital programming tier with up to one hundred networks, CD-quality music services, more pay-per-view options, more channels of multiplexed premium services, a digital interactive program guide, and other features such as parental lockout options.

In 1998 Time Warner, along with Microsoft, Compaq, and MediaOne, formed a joint venture, Road Runner, to operate and expand Time Warner Cable's and MediaOne's high-speed online service business (MediaOne was subsequently acquired by AT&T Broadband). Time Warner, through its various subsidiaries, has a 54.9 percent interest in Road Runner, which provides high-speed Internet access and also offers content optimized for broadband-capable networks. Road Runner affiliates with local cable television system operators, principally Time Warner Cable and MediaOne, in exchange for a percentage of the cable operator's retail revenue from subscribers for the Road Runner service. In early 2000, Road Runner had approximately 550,000 subscribers (of which approximately 330,000 were in Time Warner Cable systems).

Digital Media

In 1999 Time Warner created Time Warner Digital Media (TW Digital Media) to develop and implement a companywide digital media strategy, to fund and oversee digital media initiatives across Time Warner's divisions, and to identify and pursue digital media-related investment opportunities. The Digital Media business funds and participates in the oversight of the company's significant Internet sites, including CNN.com and CNNfn.com.

Merger Synergies

The management's of both AOL and Time Warner claimed that the merger was justified on the basis of the substantial synergies that the combined company could realize. In a show of editorial independence, an article in *Fortune* magazine, a Time Warner publication, quickly pointed out that the synergies would indeed have to be substantial, enormous actually, if the merger were to pay.[20] At the time, the combined market value of the two companies was around $290 billion, while the combined earnings were $2.7 billion, implying a price-to-earnings ratio of over 100. To make the merger pay, according to the article, the combined company would have to grow earnings at 22 percent per annum for the next fifteen years—not exactly an easy task even in the very best of times. Indeed, the article concluded that "getting there would be like pushing a boulder up an alp"! So how did the management of AOL and Time Warner plan to pull off this?

Distribution Synergies: Broadband Access

The merger would at a stroke help solve one of AOL's biggest problems, how to offer high-speed Internet service to its 22 million subscribers. As many Internet users have found out, downloading graphics-intensive web content over telephone lines using 56-K modems can be a very slow process, to say nothing of the wait required to download streaming video data. If the Internet is to fulfill its potential, the speed of Internet connections (the bandwidth) must be increased. Although AOL had made some headway with DSL and satellite systems, so far it had been shut out of the most-promising broadband distribution conduit, the coaxial cable used by cable TV. The merger would give AOL access to Time Warner's cable TV system with its 12.6 million subscribers. AOL could then offer these customers high-speed access to the Internet over Time Warner's cable TV systems. In effect, the merger allowed AOL to integrate forward into the distribution of its content.[21]

Content Synergies: Enhancing the Value of AOL

A second benefit claimed for the merger was that AOL would be able to offer Time Warner's rich array of content to its subscribers, thereby enhancing the value of its service. AOL has always seen itself as a media company offering compelling content to its customers. If content is indeed king on the Internet, the combination of AOL's web savvy and Time Warner's magazine and broadcasting properties opens up the potential for delivering a wide range of innovative content over the Internet to AOL's subscriber base. In addition to existing Time Warner services, such as CNN.com, these might include an ability to access TNT's vast film library on demand (assuming a cable modem), archived CNN news clips, web versions of *Time* magazine, and a range of web properties that have yet to be imagined. If the online version of this content were proprietary to AOL, it would help to justify a premium price for AOL's service, or growing subscriptions at a faster rate.

Operating Synergies: Cutting Costs

There were also some concrete operating synergies to be had from the merger. The two companies could combine sales and back-office functions such as customer support call centers. Managers claimed that these combinations alone could yield cost savings of $1 billion a year, according to the two companies, although a detailed breakdown of exactly where such savings would come from was hard to get. Then there was the potential for enhanced cross-selling between the subscribers of the two companies. Taken together, the two companies have access to more than 100 million subscribers. So in theory, for example, AOL installation CDs could be sold with Time publications, and AOL could use its service to market Time Warner's magazines, cable services, music, and so forth.[22]

Venture Synergies: The Creation of New Business

In addition to the above, there was also a belief that an AOL–Time Warner combination would be better positioned to create new businesses in the era of digital distribution of media, including films, magazines, and music. This would lead to much faster revenue growth than either AOL or Time Warner could achieve by themselves. It was music that was the focus on the most immediate speculation. The proposed merger between WMG and EMI's music interests would make AOL Time Warner the largest music company in the world, with access to a library of 2 million songs. The rapid rise of Napster, a company that was pioneering the digital distribution of music using peer-to-peer computer technology, was shaking the very foundations of the music industry. Although all of the big music companies were suing Napster for copyright infringement, and it seemed highly likely that the service would run into substantial legal problems, most observers still felt that the future of the music industry lay in the digital distribution of titles over the Internet. Not only would digital distribution cut significant costs out of the music industry, but it would also allow users to make their own music compellations, downloading choice content over the Internet. The massive popularity of Napster's service was a testament to this (although it must be admitted that getting music for free also had something to do with the popularity of the service).

Combine AOL's strong position in cyberspace, and its technology savvy, with WMG-EMI's music list, and the optimists argued that there should be a business model that would allow AOL Time Warner to profit from the disruptive technology represented by peer-to-peer computing and file-swapping technology. Exactly what such a business model might look like was not clear, but surely with all of the talent at its disposal, AOL Time Warner could solve the puzzle. Moreover, once AOL Time Warner had solved this puzzle for music, it could turn its attention to other areas where the technology promised both opportunities and threats—the digitalization and digital distribution of film and books. Again, AOL Time Warner's strong position in publishing and filmed entertainment positioned the company ideally for this brave new world.

Antitrust Issues

Before the proposed merger could be consummated, there were some thorny antitrust issues that had to be resolved. Regulators harbored fears that AOL Time Warner would deny competing providers—such as Earthlink, Juno, and Microsoft's MSN service—of Internet service access to its cable TV subscribers. To guard against this possibility, as a condition for approving the merger, officials at the Federal Trade Commission (FTC) required that AOL Time Warner commit to giving its cable customers the choice of three Internet service providers other than AOL. In addition, the FTC wanted AOL Time Warner to sign a deal with at least one competing provider as a precondition for the merger being approved. The reason that the FTC gave for taking this hard-line stance is that they did not want AOL Time Warner to offer its service first, before opening up the Time Warner cable system to competing providers. The irony in the FTC's stance was that a different government agency, the Federal Communication Commission (FCC), had not required that existing cable companies open up access to multiple Internet service providers!

On November 20, 2000, Time Warner announced that it had struck a deal with Earthlink that would allow this provider to offer Internet service to Time Warner's cable customers. The deal, which was contingent upon final approval of the merger, was aimed at satisfying the concerns of the FTC. Apparently satisfied, the FTC gave the merger the green light.

The FTC was not the only antitrust agency that AOL and Time Warner had to deal with, however. Since both companies were multinational concerns with substantial European interests, they also had to get approval from the European Union's (EU) Competition Commission. In recent years, the commission had not been shy about ruling on mergers between U.S.-based companies with substantial European activities. It had blocked a proposed merger between General Electric and Honeywell on antitrust grounds, and now it was making noises about the proposed combination between AOL and Time Warner. Its objection centered not on AOL and Time Warner per se, but on the potential market power that the WMG-EMI merger would give AOL Time Warner in the music industry, particularly given AOL's strong position in the online market.

A second concern of the EU was that AOL Europe was a joint venture with Germany's largest media company, Bertelsmann AG. The creation of AOL Time Warner would thus indirectly lead to greater concentration in the online distribution of media in Europe, with two of the world's largest media companies being effectively joined at the hip through AOL Europe.

After intense negotiation with the commission, the managements of AOL and Time Warner realized that they would have to make concessions on both of these issues if the merger was to win approval. They thus dropped the proposed linkup between WMG and EMI and agreed to buy out Bertelsmann's stake in AOL Europe. With this commitment in hand, on October 12, 2000, the commission gave its blessing to the merger.

Prework

Even before the merger was officially approved, AOL's Robert Pittman, who was slated to become copresident of the combined company with Time Warner's Richard Parsons, moved into Time Warner's head office and took the lead in integrating the two companies.[23] During 2000 the two companies signed between 150 and 200 commercial agreements. As an example, Warner music helped to sell AOL subscriptions by embedding AOL software on the latest CD from the rock group Match Box 20. AOL also generated 500,000 new subscribers for *Time* magazine. Perhaps most importantly, Pittman started holding regular meetings between AOL and Time Warner managers. For Time Warner, which has traditionally operated in a decentralized manner, this represented a big change. Reportedly, prior to Pittman's arrival many of the heads of Time Warner's divisions had not seen each other in years. Pittman told them to look at the potential for integration to produce cost savings and cross-selling both within Time Warner and between Time Warner and AOL. Pittman also told them that he would change the company's compensation system for senior executives. Historically, the compensation of divisional executives at Time Warner was based exclusively on the performance of their divisions. Pittman stated that he would link a good portion of it to the performance of the entire company after the merger.

Another Pittman initiative was the formation of a group loosely called the "Advertising Council." This group comprised every division's top people in sales, marketing, product licensing, and merchandising. Following final approval of the merger, the group planned to meet every two weeks to identify and monitor attempts for cross-selling. In 2000, one of the key collaborations between the two companies involved AOL TV, a device similar to Microsoft's Web TV that allows users to surf the Web and send email and instant messaging from their TV sets. Eventually, it will probably be integrated with Time Warner's set-top boxes to provide high-speed Internet access and allow users to interact with TV shows. AOL TV started promoting various Time Warner magazines and cable networks in 2000, and AOL did online promotions for various Warner music artists.

The First Year and Beyond

With approval from the FTC and EU Competition Commission in hand, the merger was formally consummated on January 11, 2001. The AOL unit was set up as a stand-alone division within AOL Time Warner's corporate structure (see Exhibit 3). The new company began 2001 by setting some high expectations. Revenues were expected to grow 10.5 percent in 2001 to $40 billion, while AOL Time Warner's preferred profit measure, EBITDA, was forecast by management to grow 33 percent to $11 billion. Although CEO Gerald Levin laid out the financial forecasts, Bob Pittman was widely regarded as the man behind them.

Initially, things seemed to be heading on the right track at the new company. In the first quarter of 2001, AOL Time Warner's EBITDA earnings measure grew by 20 percent, ahead of the company's 18 to 19 percent target for that quarter. The performance of the AOL unit was particularly strong. AOL overcame widespread softness in the online advertising market to post a 10 percent growth in online ad revenues, increasing its market share at the expense of competitors like Yahoo. In May 2001, with its subscriber base exceeding 23 million, AOL took advantage of its strong market position to raise the price of its online service 9 percent to $23.90 from $21.95 a month. The last time AOL increased prices was in 1998, when it had 11 million members. That time, it raised prices from $19.95. Its two largest competitors, Earthlink

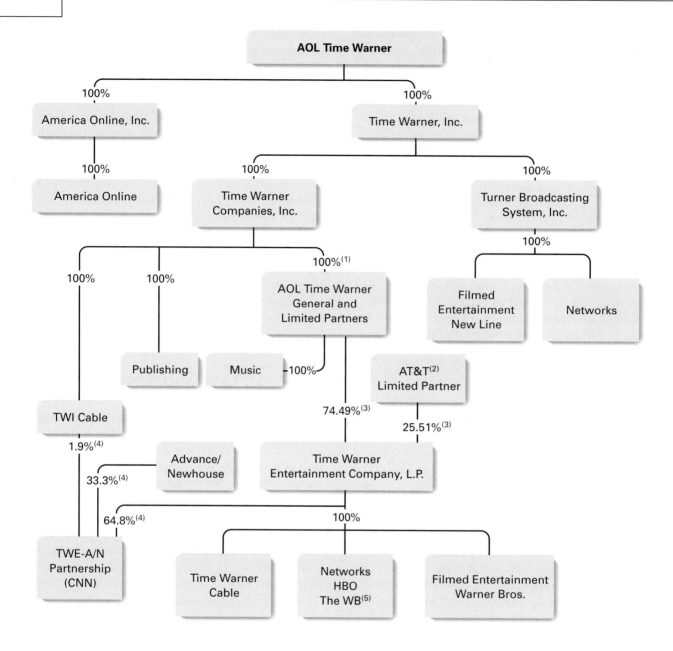

EXHIBIT 3

AOL Time Warner's Organization Structure

1. Time Warner Companies, Inc. directly or indirectly owns 100% of the capital stock of each of the AOL Time Warner General and Limited Partners.
2. Interest held by AT&T Corp.'s subsidiary, MediaOne TWE Holdings, Inc.
3. Pro rata priority capital and residual equity interests. In addition, the AOL Time Warner General Partners own 100% of the priority capital interests that are junior to the pro rata priority capital interests.
4. Direct or indirect common equity interests. In addition, TWI Cable indirectly owns preferred partnership interests.
5. Tribune Broadcasting owns a 22.25% interest in The WB.

Source: AOL Time Warner Form 10K, 2001.

and Microsoft's MSN network, did not announce plans to change their prices. Earthlink, with 4.8 million subscribers, charged $19.95 a month, and MSN, with 5 million subscribers, charged $21.95 a month.[24]

Several other divisions also registered strong performance as the year progressed. The filmed entertainment division had a banner year with several blockbuster films, including *Harry Potter and the Sorcerer's Stone,* the first of the *Lord of the Rings* trilogy, and *Oceans Eleven,* all registering impressive box-office numbers. The Harry Potter film was on track to become the highest grossing film of all time. Moreover, the strategy of building franchises in the movie business was looking as if it might pay long-term dividends. In 2002, there would be another *Harry Potter* and another *Lord of the Rings* film, plus a new *Austin Powers* movie and a new *Matrix* film. *Harry Potter and the Sorcerer's Stone* also provided investors with an early example of the enormous power of AOL Time Warner to leverage content across its divisions. The movie was made by Warner Brothers, and the soundtrack was recorded by WMG's Atlantic label. The film was on the cover of *Entertainment Weekly,* a Time Inc. publication, and AOL's web sites promoted the film through games, competitions, sneak previews, and advanced bookings. As Richard Parsons put it, the Harry Potter movie was an example of driving synergy both ways: "We use the different platforms to drive the movie, and the movie to drive business across the platforms."[25]

However, as the year lengthened it became increasingly clear that business conditions had deteriorated for AOL Time Warner, and in the end the ambitious goals set for the first year of the merger, and perhaps beyond, proved to be too much of a stretch (see Exhibit 4). For 2001, AOL Time Warner registered EBITDA of $7.43 billion on revenues of $38.2 billion. The stock price, which traded at $47.23 a share on the day of the merger, peaked at $56.60 on May 22, before falling to $32.10 by year end. As 2002 progressed, things got worse still for the company.

In April 2002, Time Warner announced that it would take a $54 billion charge against earnings to write down the goodwill on its books due to the merger. In effect, the company was admitting that when the merger was consummated, AOL's stock had been massively overvalued. Although this writedown impacted AOL's balance sheet, it did not impact the earnings potential of the company. However, the company also sharply reduced its long-term growth forecasts from 12 to 15 percent per annum for EBITDA to 8 to 12 percent per annum. What was going wrong?

Advertising Slowdown

The most obvious problem AOL Time Warner encountered in its first year was a sharp slowdown in

EXHIBIT 4

Revenue and EDITDA for AOL Time Warner, 2001 and 2000 Pro Forma ($ millions)

Segment	Revenue 2001	Revenue 2000	EBITDA 2001	EBITDA 2000
AOL	8,718	7,703	2,945	2,350
Cable	6,992	6,054	3,199	2,859
Filmed entertainment	8,759	8,119	1,017	796
Cable networks	7,050	6,802	1,797	1,502
Music	3,929	4,148	419	518
Publishing	4,810	4,645	909	747
Corporate	—	—	(294)	(304)
Merger related costs	—	—	(250)	(155)
Intersegment elimination	(2,024)	(1,258)	(86)	(46)
Total revenues and EBITDA	38,234	36,213	9,656	8,267
Depreciation and amortization	—	—	(9,203)	(8,650)
Total revenues and operating income (loss)	38,234	36,213	453	(383)

Source: AOL Time Warner Form 10K, 2001.

advertising expenditure in the United States, which entered a recession in 2001. Advertising spending tends to be very sensitive to the overall level of economic activity, and consequently very cyclical. It is often said that advertising spending is the first to feel the effects of an economic slowdown, and the last to recover. In 2000, with the United States enjoying its longest economic expansion in history, advertising spending in the United States surged 9.6 percent, partly thanks to advertising spending by dot.com companies. In 2001 the other shoe dropped, and U.S. advertising spending fell by 6.8 and 5.4 percent in the worlds' seven largest advertising markets. For 2002, forecasts suggested that advertising spending would slip by a further 3.3 percent in the United States and 1.9 percent globally.[26]

This slowdown presented an obvious problem for AOL Time Warner, which, as the world's largest media company, depends critically upon advertising spending for a good portion of its revenues and profits. As a whole, the company continued to grow revenues from advertising, but the rate of growth was slower than anticipated. Moreover, as 2001 turned to 2002, it began to look as if the rate of growth in advertising revenue at the AOL unit might fall. The problem for AOL was twofold. First, much of its advertising was from other dot.com's, and as they ran out of cash in 2001 this began to dry up. Second, Internet advertising in general fell out of favor with traditional companies in 2001, as many questioned the returns from banner ads.

Exhibit 5 shows the rise in advertising spending on the Internet from early 1996 through the first quarter of 2002. As can be seen, total online ad spending peaked at $2 billion in the first quarter of 2000 and started to fall of sharply after that, primarily because of the implosion of dot.com advertising. AOL was isolated from this effect for a while because it had signed many three-year ad deals in 1996–1999. As these deals expired, however, many were not renewed, and by late 2001 AOL was feeling the impact. In the first quarter of 2001, advertising and commerce revenue at AOL fell by 31 percent compared to the period a year earlier, to $501 million.[27]

AOL Subscription Growth Slows Down

Although subscriptions at AOL continued to grow, by late 2001 the rate of growth was slowing, and this trend continued in 2002. By March 2002, AOL had 34.6 million subscribers, a 20 percent year-to-year

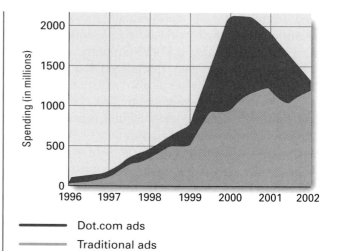

Dot.com ads
Traditional ads

EXHIBIT 5

Total Online Advertising Spending, 1996–2002

Source: Salomon Smith Barney estimates.

increase. While this might look impressive, the 5.8 million net gain year to year was 10 percent lower than the yearly gain to December 2001. Put another way, AOL added 1.3 million subscribers in the first quarter of 2002, 40 percent fewer than it added in the first quarter of 2001. The bulk of new subscribers came from outside the United States. The slowdown in the subscription growth rate was particularly bothersome given that the decline on online advertising spending meant that AOL now had to rely more on subscription revenue to hit its revenue and EBITDA targets (subscriptions accounted for 68 percent of AOL's revenue in the first quarter of 2002, the fourth consecutive quarter in which its share had grown).

AOL's Broadband Problem

A source of frustration for AOL throughout 2001 and early 2002 was its inability to make rapid headway in the broadband access market. Although the merger gave AOL access to Time Warner's cable system, and although AOL started to roll out broadband offerings on this system, it was unable to get access to other cable systems. Even though AOL Time Warner had to agree to open up its cable system to three competing Internet providers as a precondition for the merger, no such condition was placed on other cable systems. AOL had to convince other cable operators, such as Comcast and AT&T Broadband, to carry its service, and that proved difficult. The main sticking points were twofold: (1) whether the cable operators got any share of AOL's advertising revenue generated from high-speed business, and (2) who "controlled" the customer, meaning who would be responsible for selling the service to customers, billing them, and so on.[28] The cable companies wanted to retain control, primarily out of fear that if AOL customers could jump between cable and telephone companies' DSL offerings, they would have no loyalty to cable.

The impasse was serious, given that cable was fast emerging as the favored means to access the Internet at high speeds (see Exhibit 6).[29] By the end of 2001 there were 7 million cable customers in the United States using cable to access the Internet at high speeds, a 7 percent household penetration rate. This compared to 2.8 million DSL subscribers, a 3 percent penetration rate. While both cable and DSL Internet usage are growing at the same rate, cable is doing so from a much higher base. The most recent forecasts suggest that by 2006 broadband will account for 40 percent of all online households.[30]

AOL's problems were compounded in 2001 when it lost out to Comcast in an attempt to acquire AT&T Broadband, the cable unit of AT&T. AT&T had decided to exit the cable business and sold AT&T Broadband via an auction. Comcast was backed by Microsoft (which is an investor in both Comcast and AT&T). Assuming the merger is approved by regulators, Comcast will now be the largest cable provider in the United States, with 23 million subscribers. Given its relationship with Microsoft, there is an obvious fear that MSN will be given preferential access to Comcast's network and that AOL will have to pay a heavy price for access. Further clouding the situation, in March 2002 the FCC ruled that high-speed Internet access over cable pipes is an "information service," keeping it free from government oversight and effectively ensuring that cable companies did not have to open up access to competitors. It is still possible, however, that federal regulators might require Comcast to open up its cable network to other Internet service providers as a precondition for approving the proposed merger.

To further complicate issues, AT&T Broadband held a 25.5 percent stake in Time Warner Entertainment. That stake will now fall into Comcast's hands, which has indicated that it would like to unload the stake. Analysts have valued it at $10 billion, and some speculate that AOL Time Warner may have to buy the stake in order to get access to Comcast's network.[31] Compounding issues even further, the Newhouse family, which owns a cable network and is a partner in AOL Time Warner's cable system, has indicated that it is considering withdrawing from the partnership, effectively taking 2.3 million of AOL Time Warner's 12.8 million cable subscribers with it.[32]

Finally, there were signs that when AOL customers did switch to cable broadband offerings, they frequently dropped their AOL service. This was a particular problem in those regions where AOL Time Warner had no cable presence. Having to pay $40 a month for fast Internet access over a cable modem, consumers saw no reason to pay another $23.95 a month for AOL's slow dial-up network.

Strategic Issues in Mid 2002

With the performance of AOL Time Warner falling below expectations and the AOL unit, far from being the jewel in the crown, suddenly looking like a millstone around AOL Time Warner's neck, the company had to deal with some major strategic issues. First, there were management changes. In December 2001 Gerald Levin announced that he would step down in May, to be replaced not by Bob Pittman, as many had expected, but by Richard Parsons, a Time Warner man. Parsons immediately lowered expectations going forward, stating that "we will underpromise and overdeliver." Pittman would stay on as COO. This was followed by an announcement in April that Barry Schuler, the head of AOL, would step aside and

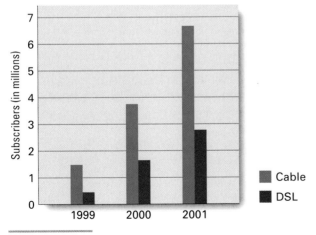

EXHIBIT 6

Broadband Internet Access in the United States

concentrate on developing digital services such as home networking and digital music delivery. Bob Pittman would once again head the AOL unit, while retaining his title as COO of the combined company. Pittman's job was clear—solve the emerging problems at AOL.

Meanwhile, speculation swirled about the company's strategy going forward. While Parsons stated that AOL would remain part of the company and that the Internet was central to the future of AOL Time Warner, outside voices called for the company to spin out the AOL unit.[33] The logic behind this suggestion was as follows: Time Warner's assets are worth between $16 and $20 a share, according to several Wall Street analysts. With AOL Time Warner stock trading at $18 a share in late April 2002, the stock market was effectively valuing the AOL unit at zero. In fact, analysts value the AOL unit at anywhere between $3 and $8 a share (which is down from a high of $83 a share immediately prior to the merger announcement). So by spinning off AOL, the combined value of the two companies would immediately trade higher (between $19 and $28 a share, according to these estimates).

Another issue concerned AOL Time Warner's financial position. The prospect of having to pay $10 billion to purchase Comcast's stake in Time Warner Entertainment (assuming that Comcast's bid for AT&T Broadband is approved by regulators) raised questions about AOL Time Warner's financial resources. Moreover, as part of the merger agreement with the FTC the company was still on the hook to pay $7 billion to acquire Bertelsmann's stake in AOL Europe. How was AOL Time Warner to finance this, particularly since the recent $54 billion writedown of its goodwill had reduced the strength of its balance sheet and would raise the costs of financing any debt offering? Potentially, AOL Time Warner also needed capital to purchase smaller cable TV providers to bolster its flagging broadband strategy. How could all of this be achieved?

There were also major concerns about the AOL unit going forward. Was the service now entering a slow-growth phase? How could the unit stop customers from defecting when they switched to high-speed Internet access over cable modems? What kind of concessions should AOL make to cable companies to get access to their pipes? Should it give up control over customers? When would advertising revenue come back, and how strong would the recovery be?

Finally, management had to grapple with how best to realize the potential gains from the merger. Were the synergies real? How might AOL Time Warner best realize them? What should AOL Time Warner do in the music businesses, where the online distribution of music seemed inevitable?

ENDNOTES

1. C. Yang et al., "Welcome to the 21st Century," *Business Week*, January 24, 2000, pp. 36–38.
2. C. J. Loomis, "AOL Time Warner's New Math," *Fortune*, February 4, 2002, pp. 98–102.
3. Kara Swisher, *AOL.COM: How Steve Case Beat Bill Gates, Nailed the Netheads, and Made Millions in the War for the Web* (New York: Random House, 1998).
4. Gene Koprowski, "AOL CEO Steve Case," *Forbes ASAP*, October 7, 1996, pp. 94–95.
5. David Hilzenrath, "Emergency Overhaul for AOL," *Washington Post*, October 30, 1996, p. A1.
6. Swisher, *AOL.COM*.
7. David Hilzenrath, "Turnaround Task at AOL," *Washington Post*, October 31, 1996, p. E1.
8. Jared Sandberg, "Firm Pays AOL $100 Million in Phone Pact," *Wall Street Journal*, February 26, 1997, pp. B4, B6.
9. "AOL and Tel-Save Approach Half a Million Long Distance Lines," AOL press release, March 25, 1998.
10. "AOL and CUC Announce Online Partnership," AOL press release, June 10, 1997.
11. Jared Sandberg, "Retailers Pay Big for Internet Space," *Houston Chronicle*, July 13, 1997, 2 STAR Edition, p. 8.
12. "AOL/SportsLine Deal," *New Media Age*, July 10, 1997, p. 6.
13. Paul Tolme, "AOL, Koop in $89 Million Alliance," *Associated Press*, July 8, 1999.
14. "America Online Reports FY99 Third Quarter Income," AOL press release, April 27, 1999.
15. Andy Reinhardt, "As the Web Spins," *Business Week*, May 24, 1999, p. 30.
16. Bill Gates interview with Charles W. L. Hill, June 1998.
17. Allan Sloan, "AT&T-MediaOne Soap Opera Has Just About Everything," *Business Week*, May 11, 1999, p. 3.
18. Sallie Hofmeister, "AOL, Hughes Link Up to Challenge Cable," *Los Angeles Times*, June 22, 1999, p. 1.
19. The following section draws on Time Warner's 1999 and 2000 10K reports filed with the SEC.
20. C. J. Loomis, "AOL+TWX=?" *Fortune*, February 7, 2000, pp. 81–84.
21. M. Peers, N. Wingfield, and L. Landro, "AOL, Time Warner, Leap Borders to Plan a Mammoth Merger," *Wall Street Journal*, January 11, 2000, p. A1.
22. C. Yang et al., "Welcome to the 21st Century," *Business Week*, January 24, 2000, pp. 36–38.
23. M. Peers and J. Angwin, "AOL, Time Warner Are Already Putting Operations Together," *Wall Street Journal*, November 10, 2000, p. A1.
24. J. Angwin, "America Online Boosts Price for Flagship Service," *Wall Street Journal*, May 23, 2001, p. A3.
25. "Harry Potter and the Synergy Test," *The Economist*, November 10, 2001, pp. 59–60.
26. A. Galloni, "Ad Report Suggests Delayed Recovery," *Wall Street Journal*, April 16, 2002, p. B5.

27. Salomon Smith Barney Research, *Internet–Online Media and eCommerce,* March 1st, 2002.

28. J. Angwin and M. Peers, "AOL Rethinks Its Game Plan on Internet Access," *Wall Street Journal,* April 19, 2002, p. A3.

29. Salomon Smith Barney Research, *Internet–Online Media and eCommerce.*

30. Ibid.

31. D. Henry. T. Lowery, and C. Yang, "AOL, You've Got Misery," *Business Week,* April 8, 2002, pp. 58–60.

32. D. Mermigas, "It's Getting Worse for AOL TW," *Electronic Media,* April 1, 2002, p. 16.

33. J. Angwin and M. Peers," AOL Breakup? Parlor Game for Wall Street," *Wall Street Journal,* April 22, 2002, p. C1.

34 The Viacom Empire

This case was prepared by Gareth R. Jones, Texas A&M University.

CBS Broadcasting established Viacom as in independent company in 1970 to comply with regulations set forth by the U.S. Federal Communications Commission (FCC) barring television networks from owning cable TV systems or from syndicating their own programs in the United States. The increasing spread of cable television and the continuing possibility of conflicts of interest between television networks and cable television companies made the spinoff necessary, and Viacom separated formally from CBS in 1971 when CBS distributed Viacom's stock to its shareholders at the rate of one share for every seven shares of CBS stock.

Viacom quickly became one of the largest cable operators in the United States, with over 90,000 cable subscribers. It also owned the syndication rights to a large number of popular, previously run CBS television series that it made available for syndication to cable TV stations. Revenue from these rights accounted for a sizable percentage of Viacom's income.

In 1976, to take advantage of Viacom's experience in syndicating programming to cable TV stations, its managers decided to establish the Showtime movie network to compete directly with HBO, the leading outlet for films on cable television. In 1977, Viacom earned $5.5 million on sales of $58.5 million. Most of its earnings represented revenues from the syndication of its television series, but they also reflected

growth of its own cable TV systems, which at this time had about 350,000 subscribers. Recognizing that both producing and syndicating television programming could earn greater profits, Viacom's managers decided to produce their own television programs in the late 1970s and early 1980s. Their efforts produced only mixed results, however, no hit series resulted from their work, and the Big Three television networks of ABC, NBC, and CBS continued to dominate the airwaves.

During the early 1980s, the push to expand the cable television side of its business became Viacom's managers' major priority. Cable television is a highly capital-intensive business, and Viacom made a large investment to build its cable infrastructure; for example, it spent $65 million on extending its customer base in 1981 alone. By 1982, Viacom had added 450,000 subscribers to the 90,000 it inherited from CBS, making it the ninth largest cable operator in the United States. Also, by 1982 Viacom sales had grown to $210 million, with about half its revenues coming from program syndication and about half from its cable operations.

Viacom's managers, however, continued to feel that its cable operations were not a strong enough engine for future growth. One reason was that cable TV prices were regulated at this time, and cable companies were limited in how much they could charge customers. Its managers continued to believe that real growth in earnings would come not from providing cable television service but providing the *content* of cable programming—television programs.

Given their previous failure in making their own programs, Viacom's managers sought to make acquisitions in the content side of the business—in companies that made entertainment programs. In 1981, Viacom started in a small way by buying a minority stake in Cable Health Network, a new advertiser-supported television network. Then, in September 1985, it made the acquisition that would totally change the company's future. Viacom purchased the MTV Networks from Warner Bros., a company that desperately needed cash because Warner's own cable TV system was suffering from a lack of investment.

The MTV Networks included MTV, a new popular music video channel geared toward the fourteen-to-twenty-four-age group; Nickelodeon, a channel geared toward children; and VH-1, a music video channel geared toward an older twenty-five-to-forty-four-age audience. MTV was the most popular property in the MTV Network. Its quick pace and flashy graphics were popular among young television viewers, and its young audience was a major target of large advertisers. The popularity of a station's programming determines how many advertisers it will attract and how much it can charge them. While MTV was performing well, Nickelodeon had been less successful and had not achieved any notable following among young viewers, which limited the revenues it could earn from advertisers. Viacom moved quickly to revamp Nickelodeon, giving it the slick, flashy look of MTV and developing unique programming that appealed to children, programming that was very different from that offered by competitors like the Disney Channel. In the next few years, Nickelodeon went from being the least popular channel on basic cable among children to being the most popular, and Viacom's managers were confident that they had in place the beginning of a new programming strategy to complement Viacom's cable TV interests and to guide the company to long-term profitability.

Enter Sumner Redstone

Viacom's hopes were shattered when its Showtime channel lost about 300,000 customers between March 1985 and March 1986 because of intense competition from HBO. HBO, under its then CEO Frank Biondi, was making itself the dominant pay movie channel by producing its own innovative programming and by forming exclusive agreements with major movie studios like Paramount to offer their movies to HBO first. As a result of the loss of customers, Viacom's cash flow dropped dramatically, and the company lost $9.9 million on sales of $919.2 million in 1986. Further weakened by the $2 billion debt load it had incurred to fund its cable expansion program and make its programming acquisitions, Viacom became a takeover target.

After a competitive six-month battle to acquire the company, Sumner M. Redstone bought Viacom for $3.4 billion in March 1986. Redstone was the owner of a closely held corporation, National Amusements Inc. (NAI), that owned and operated 675 movie screens in fourteen states in the United States and the United Kingdom. Redstone became chairman of Viacom's board and moved quickly to take control of the company. He had built NAI from fifty drive-in movie theaters to a modern theater chain. He is credited with pioneering the development of the multiplex movie theater concept, which offers moviegoers a choice of a dozen or more screens to choose from. However, running a chain of movie theaters was very different from running a debt-laden media conglomerate as complicated as Viacom.

Many analysts felt that Redstone had overpaid for Viacom, but he saw a great potential for growth. Besides its cable television systems and syndication rights, which now included the popular TV series *The Cosby Show*, Redstone recognized the potential of its MTV and Nickelodeon channels. Moreover, over the years Viacom had acquired five television and eight radio stations in major markets, which he saw as valuable investments. Redstone moved quickly to solve Viacom's problems, and with the "hands-on" directive management style for which he is well known, he fired Viacom's top managers and began the search for capable managers who would be loyal and obedient to him. To turn Showtime around, he immediately hired Frank Biondi, the chief executive who had made HBO the dominant movie channel, as CEO of Viacom.

Frank Biondi was just a few days away from moving to Hollywood to run Columbia Pictures when Redstone called and asked him to take over as CEO of Viacom. The forty-nine-year-old Biondi was known for his strong financial, deal-making, and strategic skills and a knack for managing a diverse group of young executives and building them into a cooperative unit. Unlike Redstone, who likes to be directly involved in the day-to-day operations of a business, however, Biondi felt that his job was to set challenging goals, find the resources—both capital and people—to achieve them, and then get out of the way to let his managers achieve them. His approach was to decentralize control to his managers and to let them get the job done. Analysts felt the combination of Redstone's hands-on approach and Biondi's future thinking style made them a very effective team to head the growing entertainment conglomerate.

Viacom Speeds Up

Redstone's takeover of Viacom was fueled by his belief that cable television programming would become the dominant means of providing consumers with their entertainment content in the future. With the acquisition of Viacom, Redstone now owned 76 percent of MTV and Nickelodeon, which together gave Viacom access to millions of viewers aged two to twenty-four. Redstone believed Viacom's cable networks were its "crown jewels" because they provided half the company's revenues and profits, which came both from subscribers (the cable companies that bought the programming) and from advertisers (who advertised on these channels). To strengthen the cable channel franchise and build its brand name, Redstone restructured MTV and installed a more aggressive advertising and sales staff. Against the expectations of many industry analysts, MTV and Nickelodeon experienced continued growth and profitability. In 1989, for example, the MTV Networks won 15 percent of all dollars spent on cable advertising. MTV was expanding throughout the world, broadcasting to Western Europe, Japan, Australia, and large portions of Latin America.

Despite the success of the MTV channels, Redstone still faced the problem of paying off the debt that he had incurred to acquire Viacom—debt that amounted to $450 million in interest in the first two years following the takeover. Several fortuitous events aided him. First, shortly after the buyout, Viacom began to earn millions of dollars from television stations wanting to show reruns of the blockbuster *Cosby Show*. Second, in 1987 Congress deregulated cable television and allowed cable television companies to charge what they liked for their programming. The result was that the prices charged for cable television service soared, and so did the price of cable television franchises. Redstone took full advantage of this situation to sell off some of Viacom's cable assets to help reduce debt. In February 1989, Viacom's Long

Island and suburban Cleveland cable systems were sold to Cablevision Systems Corp. for $545 million, or about twenty times their annual cash flow. Cablevision also bought a 5 percent stake in Showtime for $25 million, giving it an interest in promoting the channel to Cablevision's customers and helping Showtime get back in competition with HBO. These events enabled Redstone to significantly cut Viacom's debt and negotiate more favorable terms on its loans. However, it was rough going, and Viacom lost $154.4 million in 1987, even though its sales increased to almost $1 billion.

With Viacom's finances on a firmer footing and Showtime showing some renewed vigor, Redstone and Biondi began to plan how to make Viacom a leader in the production of creative entertainment. In a strategic alliance with the Hearst Corp. and Capital Cities/ABC Inc., Viacom introduced Lifetime, a channel geared toward women. Viacom Pictures was started in 1989 so that the company could make its own movies. Viacom Pictures produced ten feature films in its first year at a cost of about $4 million a film—a very low cost compared to the money the major studios like Paramount and Universal spent. Under Biondi, Viacom's television production operations, which had always achieved mixed results, started to achieve great success with programs like *Matlock* for NBC and *Jake and the Fatman* for CBS. To increase subscribers to the important Showtime channel, Redstone sold 50 percent of Showtime to TCI, a major cable systems operator, for $225 million in 1989. In November of 1989, Viacom bought five more radio stations for $121 million to add to the nine it already owned.

Together with the five television stations and the fourteen cable systems it owned, Viacom's many different properties and assets earned revenues of $1.4 billion in 1989 and generated profits of $131 million. In 1990 and 1991, however, while Viacom's sales continued to increase, Viacom experienced losses of $89 million and $49 million on sales of $1.6 billion and $1.7 billion, respectively, because of increased costs associated with developing new programming and the lackluster performance of its Showtime network.

Viacom in the Early 1990s

The problem facing Redstone and Biondi was how to position Viacom for profitable growth in the 1990s.

Both executives felt that developing and expanding Viacom's strengths in content programming—often referred to as entertainment software—were the key to its future success, despite how costly such programming was. They believed that the message or content that is sent is what really matters, not the medium or distribution channels that carry it. As Biondi put it, "In the end, a pipe is just a pipe. The customer doesn't care how the information is obtained; all that matters is the message."

To build its content programming strengths, Biondi worked hard to build and expand on the success of Viacom's MTV channels. His goal was to promote the MTV networks as global brands that were perceived as having something unique to offer. Since MTV's viewers dominate the record-buying audience, Biondi sought to negotiate exclusive contracts that give MTV the first crack at playing most major record companies' music videos—thus making it unique. At the same time, under Redstone and Biondi's control MTV went from being a purely music video channel to a channel that championed new kinds of programming to appeal to a young audience. The result was innovative programming such as *Beavis and Butthead, Road Stories,* and other kinds of youth-oriented programming interspersed with music videos. In addition, Redstone and Biondi did not neglect the lucrative licensing market that accompanies hit television series, such as the slew of activity toys made by Mattel for new Nickelodeon characters that hit the shelves in 1992. The *Beavis and Butthead* phenomenon also generated many lucrative spinoff products.

In developing its programming strategy, however, Viacom's interest was not in promoting certain specific programs or stars—all of which may have short-lived popularity of fame—but in building its networks as unique brands. For example, on the MTV channel, the goal was to attract viewers because of what the channel as a whole personifies—an appeal to youth. Its success is based not on any particular person but on what MTV stands for. Under its new management, MTV prospered and its franchise was extended into Europe, Asia, and Latin America. Soon, MTV reached 250 million households in seventy-four countries. Viacom began to perform much better: in 1992 it made profits of $48 million on sales of $1.86 billion, and in 1993 it made profits of $70 million on sales of $2 billion.

While the development of innovative new programming was one reason for Viacom's return to profitability, a second, very important reason was Redstone's emphasis on keeping costs under control. Redstone is well known for his frugal way of doing business. He runs Viacom in a cost-conscious manner, and this trend is evident throughout the organization, from the top executives to the lower levels of management. For example, Redstone has his office not in a prestigious Park Avenue, New York, location like the large networks, but in a small unimposing building a couple of blocks from New York's "red light" district. Despite his huge personal net worth, he was still walking to work every morning.

Redstone tries to instill his cost-conscious attitude down through the organization and across its many properties into specific business projects. For example, in the last decade costs have spiraled at many Hollywood studios and television networks because the producers are at the mercy of talent agencies that demand high prices for their stars, writers, and production companies. Not so with Viacom. Redstone demanded that all its own programming be produced by its own employees using low-cost, homegrown talent. An example of this is the production of its MTV shows. All of its hosts are virtually unknown and are paid little relative to network hosts like Dan Rather or Barbara Walters, who are paid millions of dollars a year. When one of the series produced by Viacom became a hit, the agent for the star of the show demanded that the actor receive a big increase in pay. Redstone decided not to pay the price and hired a new actor at a much lower cost. In 1990, Viacom opened a state-of-the-art production facility in Orlando, Florida—Nickelodeon Studios Florida—to produce its own programming for its kid's network and thus keep its costs down.

Changes in the Media and Entertainment Industry

In their efforts to build their companies' programming strengths, Redstone and Biondi realized that the environment around them was rapidly changing and that it was not at all clear how programming would be delivered to customers in the future. First, by the mid 1990s the U.S. cable television industry was in a state of flux. Emerging technologies such as wireless microwave transmission and satellite, and eventually broadband, threatened to bypass traditional cable systems, rendering Viacom's investment in wired cable much less valuable. Second, pressures were building to deregulate the telecommunications industry, and eventually companies in different industries, for example, cable companies, telephone companies, and Internet service providers (ISPs), were allowed to enter each other's markets. A number of regional phone companies interested in supplying television programming to their phone customers through new fiber-optic phone lines contacted Redstone. These companies wanted to take advantage of Viacom's programming capabilities and transit its channels through their phone lines.

This trend reinforced Redstone and Biondi's belief that during the coming decade the most successful companies would not be those that offered customers a channel into the home by cable, telephone wire, or wireless transmission. Instead, they believed that to prosper in this fast-changing environment an entertainment company should be the provider of the entertainment to all these channels. In other words, the most successful companies would be those that could offer the programming to go on the channels—the software providers. With its MTV, Nickelodeon, Showtime, and Cinemax channels, as well as its syndicated programming and ability to make its own programming, Viacom was in a good position to form alliances with the companies that provided the channels into the home. It would provide the software (the programming) to the companies that provided the hardware (the wired and wireless cable companies and telephone companies). Viacom's revenues would come both from the fees it charged to the hardware providers and most importantly from the advertising revenues it would obtain from selling spots on its many channels, revenues that are determined by the extent of the viewing audience. However, Redstone and Biondi had discovered how expensive it is to develop innovative programming and how devastating the effects of a flop of several movies or programs can be for profitability. The question was how to obtain high-quality programming at the right price, especially in an entertainment and media industry in which the value of companies was rocketing as stock prices increased.

The Paramount and Blockbuster Mergers

Viacom now had a new mission: it should become a software-driven company with a goal of driving its entertainment software through every distribution system, to every multimedia application, and to every region on earth. To achieve Viacom's mission, Redstone began to search for a company that possessed the software strengths that could produce the programming content for worldwide distribution. In particular, he went looking for an entertainment company that had an already established film studio that would round out Viacom's programming portfolio by supplying feature films and TV shows to its television channels. Paramount Pictures provided Redstone with his opportunity.

Paramount's many businesses include both entertainment and publishing. Its entertainment businesses include the production, financing, and distribution of motion pictures, television programming, and prerecorded videocassettes; and the operation of motion picture theaters, independent television stations, regional theme parks, and Madison Square Garden. Paramount also owned a large library of movies. Its publishing interests included Simon & Schuster, which publishes and distributes hardcover and paperback books for the general public and textbooks for elementary schools, high schools, and colleges; it also provides information services for businesses and professions.

Redstone and Biondi began to picture the extensive synergies that a merger with Paramount would provide Viacom in the future. As Redstone told reporters, "This merger is not about two plus two equaling four, but six, or eight, or ten." Redstone believed that together Viacom and Paramount would be a much more efficient and profitable organization. He had a vision, for example, of Paramount making films that featured MTV characters like Beavis and Butthead and new cable TV channels supported by Paramount's library of 1,800 films and 6,100 television programs. Both Redstone and Biondi believed that Paramount was a priceless asset for an entertainment company hoping to provide a broad range of programming content for future distribution to global customers. With its strengths not just in visual programming but also in publishing books and magazines, Viacom would become a multimedia entertainment powerhouse that could redraw the competitive map in the entertainment industry.

On September 12, 1993, after behind-the-scene talks between Redstone and Paramount executives, Paramount announced an $8.2 billion merger with Viacom. Soon, however, a bidding war for Paramount started. Barry Diller, the CEO of QVS Network Inc., another large entertainment company and the owner of the home shopping network, recognized the logic behind Viacom's strategy and announced a hostile bid for Paramount. On September 20, 1993, QVC announced an $80 per share or $9.5 billion bid for Paramount, and the battle between Viacom and QVC for ownership of Paramount Communications Inc. was on.

This unwelcome bid from QVS presented a significant problem for Redstone: Viacom still had substantial debt because of his original 1987 acquisition of Viacom and the rapid development of its own television programming. Redstone could not afford to counter QVS's bid unless he obtained other sources of financing, and he had to search around for partners to support his bid. After a career of financing deals with his own pocketbook, including the 1987 Viacom takeover, the seventy-year-old tycoon was forced to turn to other companies to rescue the Paramount deal. Redstone found two potential partners in Nynex and Blockbuster.

Nynex, one of the Baby Bell companies, anticipated that deregulation would allow it to enter the cable television market and wanted an alliance with a company that could supply it with programming content. Blockbuster, under its own energetic CEO Wayne Huizenga, had grown to become the largest chain of video stores in the nation. Blockbuster was cash rich as a result of its recent rapid growth. Huizenga, recognizing the threat that the growth in electronic movie mediums (such as video pay per view, wireless cable, and videos through fiber-optic phone lines) could pose to the sale and rental of videocassettes, was on the lookout for a way to reduce this risk. He agreed to support Redstone's bid for Paramount as a way to diversify Blockbuster's interests.

Redstone was not anxious to forge alliances with these companies, commenting that alliances are tricky: "No one who is not a hypocrite or a liar can guarantee how a relationship will look in the future." Moreover, Redstone also saw that Blockbuster's future was in doubt as a result of the growth in electronic means of providing home movie videos. However, his need for cash to outbid QVS for ownership of Paramount was stronger than his worries about forming the alliances. On October 21, 1993, after having aligned himself with these partners, Redstone obtained $600 million cash from Blockbuster and a $1.2 billion commitment from Nynex Corp. He then used this money to match QVS's offer of $80 per share for 51 percent of Paramount stock with the rest

in Viacom stock. Furthermore, anticipating a higher offer by QVC, Viacom raised its bid to $85 a share for 51 percent of the stock. Many analysts argued that this bidding war had become a personal battle between Redstone and QVC chairman Barry Diller and that whoever was the winner was doomed to pay much too much for Paramount—so much for low-cost programming.

On December 20, QVC raised its offer to $92 a share in cash for 50.1 percent, topping Viacom, which asked for more time to raise cash. On December 22, Paramount signed a merger agreement with QVC, but the bidding could continue, with a deadline for final bids on February 1, 1994. Redstone, desperate for more cash, went to Blockbuster CEO Wayne Huizenga for more money. Huizenga, increasingly convinced that it was in Blockbuster's shareholders' best interests to merge with Viacom, suggested that Viacom should take over Blockbuster for a hefty stock price. Redstone, recognizing the value of Blockbuster's cash reserves and huge cash flow from current operations, agreed.

On January 7, 1994, Viacom announced an $8.4 billion merger with Blockbuster; it also announced a new bid for Paramount for $105 a share in cash. After the bruising battle with QVC, Viacom gained full ownership of Paramount on July 7, 1994. Redstone hailed the new Viacom as an "entertainment colossus" and "a massive global media company."

Explosive Growth

In a few short years, Redstone had gone from controlling several hundred movie theaters to controlling the properties and franchises of three Fortune 500 companies; Viacom, Blockbuster, and Paramount. By engineering the three-way merger of Viacom, Paramount, and Blockbuster Entertainment, Redstone created one of the three largest media empires in the United States (the others being the Disney/Capital Cities ABC, and AOL Time Warner), with annual revenues in excess of $10 billion. This was a large jump from the $2 billion revenue that Viacom had just before these mergers. However, Redstone and Biondi faced several major challenges in managing Viacom's new entertainment empire.

Engineering Synergies

To justify the expensive purchase of Paramount and Blockbuster, it became essential that Redstone and

Biondi engineer synergies between Viacom's different entertainment properties, each of which was organized as a separate business division. Several efforts were immediately begun. Paramount executives were instructed to evaluate the potential of new shows developed by MTV for sale to television networks and TV stations. Viacom launched its new channel, the United Paramount Network (UPN), in January 1995 to take advantage of all the programming resources across its entertainment divisions. For example, MTV executives were instructed to quickly begin developing programming for the new network channel, which in 1996 was on the air only a few hours a day but today is on the air five days a week and through its TV broadcasting affiliates can reach almost all U.S. television households.

In another attempt to create synergies, Paramount executives were instructed to make their moviemaking skills available to the MTV Network and to help it make inexpensive movies that could be distributed through Paramount. One result of this was a Beavis and Butthead movie produced by Paramount and scheduled for late 1996. This was a first step in Redstone's strategy to boost the output of movies at the Paramount studio without having to finance a big increase in the studio's own movie budget and to find ways of making low-budget movies.

Redstone and Biondi also searched for synergies between Blockbuster and Viacom's other divisions. They hoped that Blockbuster could link its retail stores with Viacom's cable networks and Paramount's extensive film library. Perhaps Blockbuster could sell copies of Paramount's vast library of movies to encourage people to create their own video collections. Also, the release of a new Paramount movie on video could be timed to coincide with a major advertising campaign in Blockbuster stores to promote the launch. In addition, Viacom's publishing division, Simon & Schuster, would be able to release paperback books to coincide with the release, and perhaps even a multimedia CD-ROM product could be introduced to boost sales. Finally, the launch of new movies could be timed to coincide with a major advertising blitz on the MTV channel—something that happened when Paramount released *Mission Impossible*, a youth-oriented movie, in the summer of 1996.

Viacom's top executives also planned to use Blockbuster's massive database of 50 million video-rental customers to "reverse-engineer" Paramount movies. The idea was to look at the entertainment tastes of consumers in this database and tailor Paramount films to appeal to the customer—right down to the casting of actors. As Redstone said, "Viacom through its new combination of assets is poised to participate in, and in many ways define, the entertainment and information explosion about to engulf the globe." Clearly, there was potential for synergies to emerge between Viacom's various divisions.

Reducing Debt

While obtaining synergies was one major challenge facing Viacom's top managers, so too was the need to reduce debt. After the Paramount deal, Viacom had nearly $12 billion in debt against just $4.8 billion in equity, and Redstone realized the need to sell off some assets to reduce this debt. In keeping with Viacom's new strategy of being a provider of programming content, Redstone sought to protect his creative entertainment assets and decided to sell Viacom's distribution assets—some of Paramount's properties and its extensive cable system. The first asset to be put on the block was Madison Square Garden, which was sold to ITT and Cablevision for $1.08 billion in March 1995. Redstone also sold Viacom's 33 percent interest in the Lifetime cable network to its other partners, Capital Cities and Hearst, for about $318 million, the television station WTXF-TV in Philadelphia to Fox for $200 million, and various noncore television stations.

Redstone had no intention to sell Paramount's seven television stations, however, which distributed the new United Paramount Network (UPN) to many major markets. Simon & Schuster, Viacom's publishing division, was also instructed to sell nonessential assets, and six professional book divisions were sold off because they did not fit the publisher's strategy of focusing on consumer, education, business, reference, and international publishing. Also, Viacom did attempt to sell Spelling Entertainment for $1 billion in late 1994, but then withdrew from the sale after it could not find a buyer at this price. Then, in January 1995, Viacom announced that it would sell its cable television systems division to TCI Cable, one of the five biggest cable companies in the United States, for $1.6 billion. These asset sales reduced Viacom's debt by a few billion but still left it with a huge debt burden.

Structure and Management Challenges

As discussed previously, Sumner Redstone enjoys hands-on control of the day-to-day running of the company and is constantly involved in managing the problems facing the various divisions. To jump-start the process of leveraging competencies across divisions and reduce costs, he moved quickly to develop a hand-picked team of executives across Viacom's new divisions to install his cost-conscious frugal values in divisional managers. Before being acquired, Paramount was run by an all-powerful boss, Martin S. Davis, and a group of executives who indulged in luxuries like flying in corporate jets and spending company funds lavishly. Redstone sold Paramount's two corporate jets and installed his own cost-conscious managers to change Paramount's free-spending habits. In 1994, Viacom dismissed Richard E. Snyder, the headstrong chairman of Simon & Schuster, also an executive known for his free-spending ways, and replaced him with Jonathan Newcomb, who made his name as a competent administrator rather than as a visionary publisher. Newcomb still plans to continue Snyder's strategy of overseas expansion and technological innovation, however.

Media and Entertainment Industry Challenges

The fast-changing entertainment and media industry also created many new challenges for Redstone and Biondi. The major Hollywood players were changing rapidly. In the old Hollywood, seven major studios dominated film and TV production, while the Big Three networks—ABC, CBS, and NBC—delivered the programming to mass audiences. Now, the number of distribution channels was exploding and the well-established relationship between producers and distributors was eroding.

Government regulations that prevented broadcast networks from owning TV programs were phased out, and the competitive dynamics of the industry began to change dramatically. Viacom's strategy to develop a full line of entertainment programming fitted well with the changes occurring in the industry. Also, as discussed previously, the regulations that prohibit telephone and cable companies from invading each other's turf were eliminated. Many phone companies formed alliances with Viacom to obtain access to its innovative programming and network channels. Similarly, digital and wireless technology vastly expanded the carrying capacity of cable and television networks, and the operators of these distribution channels were also anxious to carry high-impact programming, such as that offered by Viacom's networks, to break through the clutter.

The media and entertainment industry was also experiencing rapid globalization as U.S. movies, news, and TV shows spread around the world. The U.S. market is still the largest indigenous market for entertainment, but as the standard of living rises in many other countries, opportunities for expansion abroad also grow quickly. A major challenge facing Viacom was to obtain access to the global marketplace—with a potential market of 900 million viewers in India and a billion-plus in China. As an example of Viacom's global push, in March 1995 Viacom won a cable television license to launch its Nickelodeon and VH-1 channels in Germany, Europe's biggest and potentially most lucrative media market, to complement the MTV pop music network, which has operated in Europe since 1987.

Technology challenges also confronted the media industry. Advances in digital and information technology, including streaming audio and video, began to offer viable new ways to distribute software content to customers. Just as the dominance of the Big Three networks—ABC, NBC, and CBS—has been eroded by the growth of companies like Viacom with its assorted networks, so now many new avenues for distributing content to consumers were emerging with the growth of the Internet and advances in broadband technology. Digital piracy was also becoming evident, as web sites were springing up to exchange digital files, and companies like Napster were just a few years away.

Finally, the growing strength of Viacom spurred the consolidation of the entertainment industry. In 1995, Time Warner announced that it would merge with Turner Broadcasting, and Disney announced that it would merge with Capital Cities/ABC. As a result, the industry was now composed of four major players: Disney, Viacom, Time Warner, and News Corp., which owns the Fox channel.

Problems for Viacom

Soon after Redstone's expensive decision to buy Paramount, the Paramount movie *Forrest Gump* became a surprise hit, generating over $250 million for Viacom and silencing those Redstone critics who had argued that he had spent too much to buy the movie company. Viacom's managers began to feel like Forrest Gump, with his philosophy that "life is like a box of chocolates: You never know what you're going to get." It seemed that Redstone and Viacom had been in the right place at the right time and had made a profitable acquisition. Just as Redstone had sensed the potential of MTV, so too had he sensed the potential of Paramount and Blockbuster.

By summer 1995, however, the selection of chocolates in Viacom's box did not seem as good as in 1994. Many of the hoped-for synergies had not been obtained or were taking longer to happen than Redstone and Biondi had thought. For example, before the merger Redstone claimed that Blockbuster would be valuable to Viacom as a distributor of its creative programming; however, few benefits of this kind had been achieved. Similarly, analysts argued that Paramount had to cooperate much more closely with Viacom's cable TV channels and with Blockbuster Video if synergies were to be forthcoming. Moreover, the performance of both the Paramount and Blockbuster divisions had been disappointing.

The Gump smash hit had been followed by a string of expensive failures. Redstone and Biondi had begun to realize that making movies is a very risky business and that past successes are no indication of future success. Paramount's share of the box office dropped from 14 percent in 1994 to 10 percent in 1995. Moreover, Redstone was annoyed about the high marketing and production costs of the movies that Paramount was making, and after a string of failures, including *Jade, Sabrina,* and *Home for the Holidays,* wanted to know why the studio had spent $20 million advertising another flop, *Nick of Time,* which was clearly a loser. Hit movies are vital to a movie studio because they provide the cash flow that pays for the flops and bankrolls the future. Paramount's poor performance was hurting Viacom's cash flow and ability to service its debt. Moreover, box-office hits are crucial because they drive the rest of a movie studio's profits from international markets to home video and television.

To compound the Paramount problem, the Blockbuster division was also not doing well. Viacom had bought Blockbuster at the peak of its success—when its revenues were doubling every year and its free cash flow was a valuable asset. After the acquisition Blockbuster began to run into intense competition from two sources. First, a number of new rival video chains such as Hollywood Video had recently sprung up that were giving it intense competition and creating a price war in some markets. Second, pay-per-view television was spreading rapidly, especially in large urban markets, and the emergence of electronically transmitted video—which could then be taped (illegally) for future use—was taking away its customers. Blockbuster's revenues were flat, and the hoped-for growth in cash flow to help service Viacom's debts had not occurred; indeed, Blockbuster's costs were increasing as it got into the music retailing business and began to expand its product line.

To make matters worse, Redstone had a falling-out with the top management teams of Paramount and Blockbuster, who he thought were doing a poor job. He forced the resignations of many key executives and went in search of new leadership talent. Then, in January 1996 he stunned the entertainment world when he announced that he was firing his second-in-command Frank Biondi, who was well respected throughout Hollywood, because he believed Biondi did not have the "hands-on skills" needed to manage the kinds of problems that Viacom was facing. Redstone felt that Biondi's decentralized management style was out of place in a company actively searching for synergies and cost reductions. In place of Biondi he promoted his two lieutenants, Phillipe Dauman and Tom Dooley, to orchestrate Viacom's strategy, even though they had little direct experience with the entertainment business.

Viacom's New Moves

In March 1996, Redstone hired William Fields, a senior Wal-Mart manager who had extensive experience in running efficient retail operations through advanced IT, to be the CEO of Blockbuster. Redstone hoped he could find a way to transform the Blockbuster Video stores into more broad based entertainment-software stores, given that it currently seemed likely that the video rental business would be swept away by the new wireless cable and direct broadcasting technologies.

Redstone himself became more involved in the day-to-day running of Paramount, spending more time with its marketing and production executives to understand the workings of the business. Many analysts wondered how good a job the seventy-year-old Redstone would do without the aid of a seasoned entertainment executive. Analysts also pointed to Viacom's lack of a strong global presence or any executives who had experience globally. They noted that Redstone did not have any personal international experience.

In the spring of 1996 Viacom's stock price plunged from a high of $54.50 to $35 as investors fled the stock because of problems at Blockbuster and Paramount. In the summer of 1996, after a string of flops (with the exception of one movie, *Mission Impossible*), Redstone announced plans to cut back the number of movies Paramount would make and to reduce their production costs as he searched for a new strategy. Chief among Viacom's problems was its huge debt, which had to be pruned by more asset sales. In addition, Redstone and his managers had to find ways to reduce rising operating costs and overheads as well as to find new ways of leveraging resources and competences across divisions to increase revenues and build cash flow.

On the cost side, flat revenues and soon-to-be losses at Blockbuster and Paramount were pulling down the performance of the whole corporation. Blockbuster was now a growing liability, and Field's efforts were not bearing quick results. In fact, Blockbuster's revenues were falling. In 1997, Fields left and Redstone brought in a new CEO, John Antioco. In 1998 they streamlined Blockbuster's operations and sold off its new music store business for $115 million in cash. (The Blockbuster case provides detailed information on Blockbuster's new strategy.) They also introduced the radical idea of video-rental revenue sharing with the movie studios, and within a few years Blockbuster's revenues were increasing again. Also, in 1998 Redstone sold off all the rest of Paramount Studios's publishing interests, except for its lucrative consumer publishing group, to Pearson for $4.6 billion and used this money to reduce debt.

On the revenue side, there were signs that some potential synergies were emerging. For example, an alliance between MTV and Simon & Schuster resulted in a successful line of "Beavis and Butthead" titles, and Paramount did produce a successful Beavis and Butthead movie. Also, Viacom's global presence was widening as Redstone formed alliances overseas and as its television studios were developing new channels, including a second MTV channel to be called MTV2, which would focus exclusively on music videos, since the regular MTV channel had become more involved in regular programming. In 1997 growing demand for its entertainment content led Viacom to offer to buy the rest of Spelling entertainment with its Star Trek franchise and Big Ticket Television Unit. Its content was perfect for Viacom's growing UPN network, although that network had

yet to make a profit. Redstone integrated Spelling into Paramount's television operations to obtain economies of scale and scope in the production of new television programming. He was clearly focused on reaping the long-term benefits from his entertainment empire, although the poor performance of Viacom's stock was a big personal embarrassment to him as his acquisitions were continually being criticized.

By 1999, Blockbuster's recovering revenues and cash flow allowed Redstone to announce an initial offering of Blockbuster stock so that the performance of that division could be separated from the rest of the company. Redstone believed it was impossible to assess Viacom's true value until a real market value was put on this unit. About 18 percent of Blockbuster's stock was sold at $16 to $18 a share, and the over $250 million raised was used to pay off its debt.

Also in 1999, Redstone hired the experienced media and entertainment manager and former head of CBS, Mel Karmazin, as Viacom's chief operating officer to help solve its ongoing problems. Karmazin was well known for his ability to select and manage hit programming and for his hands-on ability to find ways to leverage resources to improve operational effectiveness. He set to work restructuring Viacom's businesses to engineer cross-divisional synergies, create new programming content, and enhance its revenue and earnings stream.

Both Redstone and Karmazin also understood that one of the most important reasons to build an entertainment empire was to achieve economies of scale that arise from being able to offer potential advertisers the opportunity to advertise their products across multiple channels that attract different kinds of viewers. In other words, a potential advertiser could produce one or more themed commercials to run across all of Viacom's different TV networks as well as with its movies or in its books, theme parks, and so on. Redstone had also watched Disney merge with the ABC networks to provide it with a major new distribution channel for its Disney franchise, a move that also had made DisneyABC the biggest entertainment and media company in the world.

Since the majority of Viacom's future revenue stream would come from advertising, Redstone established a new unit, Viacom Plus, to provide a centralized advertising service that deals directly with large advertisers and handles advertising for *all* of Viacom's divisions. For example, in 2001 Procter &

Gamble and Viacom Plus negotiated a ground-breaking cross-platform deal whereby P&G would pay $300 million for advertising spread across nine of Viacom's major divisions; the success of this deal led it to pay $350 million in 2002 for advertising spread across fourteen of Viacom's divisions. P&G obtained a better deal than if it had negotiated with each Viacom property individually, and Viacom Plus reduced the costs associated with managing the vital advertising process. In 2002, Monster.com, the online job site, signed a $15 million deal with Viacom Plus to put all its "scatter money"—the money a company has to scatter across different channels and demographic groups—into the Viacom platform.

A new opportunity arose in 1999. CBS networks were in trouble because CBS ratings were dropping, and the company was interested in a merger in the consolidating entertainment industry. Redstone realized that with CBS's assets Viacom would reach the greatest number of viewers and listeners (CBS-owned Infinity Radio Broadcasting) of any media enterprise, spanning all ages and demographics from "cradle to cane." As such, it would become a premier outlet for advertisers around the world because it could now offer them the opportunity to achieve huge economies of scale and scope in their advertising efforts. Advertising content could be driven and promoted across virtually all media segments, including broadcast and cable television, radio, and outdoor advertising and new digital media. Also, channels such as MTV, MTV2, VH-1, and CMT could now be broadcast over Trinity's radio stations and over the Internet, and CBS's high-quality content, such as its news and sports programming, could be broadcast over all Viacom's properties. The huge scale would also give the combined company bargaining power with programming suppliers and allow it to maximize the effectiveness of its sales force across all its divisions—a major source of potential extra revenue and cost savings. Perhaps a part of Viacom's problems was that it was simply not big enough?

In September 1999 Viacom and CBS Corporation announced that they would merge the two companies in the largest media transaction to that date. All operations of the company would report to Mel Karmazin. The range of Viacom's properties was now staggering in its scope, especially because at the time of the merger CBS was in the process of taking control of radio station owner Infinity Broadcasting and King World productions, which syndicated such shows as *Jeopardy* and the *Oprah Winfrey Show.* Moreover, the merger was achieved through a stock swap so that no debt needed to be incurred to fund it, something Viacom could still little afford to do because its revenues and performance were still only slowly increasing.

Karmazin now gave his full attention to structuring and managing Viacom's assets to realize the gains from sharing and leveraging the competencies of its division across all its operations. It began to seem that with the CBS acquisition Viacom had achieved the critical mass that made such gains realizable. In May 2000, Karmazin announced the integration of the company's theme parks, Paramount Parks, into the Viacom entertainment group. This move would grow the parks faster by linking them to Viacom's other properties, such as its Nickelodeon and MTV cast of characters. In 2000, Karmazin integrated Paramount's and CBS's television groups, and the new division consisted of thirty-five television stations reaching eighteen of the top twenty television markets in the United States. This led to major operational and sales efficiencies, especially because all advertising and promotion could be linked to the company's Infinity radio stations and outdoor advertising operations, creating the "advertising bundle" mentioned above. CBS now could act as a local as well as a national broadcaster, and it could leverage its news, sports, and other programming across many more markets. In 2000, Viacom's television studios also formed a unit called MTV Films to produce movies for Paramount. Most of the low-budget movies, which generally cost around $30 million to make (less than half the normal Hollywood budget), have made a profit, including the rugrats movies and *Beavis and Butthead Do America.*

In 2001, in yet another move to make it the number one advertising platform in the world for advertisers with programming that appealed to every demographic category, Viacom acquired Black Entertainment Television (BET) for $3 billion. The BET network reaches 63.4 million U.S. households, and its other channels, like BET on Jazz and BET International, reach thirty countries in Europe and thirty-six in Africa. The BET acquisition was just one part of Viacom's push to become the dominant global media company. Continuing its strategy of leveraging value from its properties, BET is seeking more ways to integrate its activities with other Viacom properties, both by customizing various Viacom TV programming for BET's channels and vice versa, not only popular shows but also news and sports.

All of Viacom's networks were also instructed to follow MTV's lead and develop a global strategy to produce content locally in each country in which they were broadcast to increase the company's global viewing audience. MTV, for example, has a presence in most of the world's major markets; it reaches 125 million households and is a major revenue generator for Viacom. And, while it broadcasts its U.S. programming in countries abroad, it had also produced successful shows in countries abroad that are customized to local tastes; these have proved so popular that they have been transferred successfully to the United States and other countries. In 2001, Redstone met China's president Jaing in Beijing to affirm Viacom's commitment to China, and in May 2001 channels such as MTV and Nickelodeon started to be broadcast in China, also with extensive programming customized to the Chinese market.

Throughout the 2000s, Karmazin has continued his push to find the best way to integrate Viacom's many properties to realize economies of scale and scope. Appendix 1 describes Viacom's entertainment empire in 2002.

In 2001, the increasingly popular UPN and CBS broadcast networks were put under the CBS television unit. This linked the distribution and programming arms of the CBS television business, also making it easier to leverage resources and competencies across all business units and, once again, making it easier to sell services to advertisers. In 2002, Viacom integrated its Simon & Schuster consumer book operations into the Viacom Entertainment Group for similar reasons. By closely aligning its publishing and entertainment operations, managers could discover more revenue-enhancing opportunities to cross-develop and promote entertainment content. Viacom's organizational structure in 2002 is shown in Exhibit 1.

Talented leaders were continuing to emerge in the new Viacom divisions, and managers who had the ability to recognize these opportunities were being put in charge of bigger chunks of the Viacom empire. In 2001 Simon & Schuster had fourteen No.1 *New York Times* bestsellers, and it publishes more than two thousand books annually. Also, by 2002, the importance of the Infinity Radio division to Viacom was becoming increasingly apparent, since it contributed

more and more revenue and earnings to Viacom through its 183 radio stations as it became linked into Viacom's multichannel advertising strategy and enjoyed the benefits of carrying content from Viacom's MTV and country and western channels.

Viacom's stock climbed in the spring of 2002, despite the huge fall in advertising revenues caused by the recession in 2000 and the following September 11 tragedy—a fall that caused the earnings of its broadcast networks to drop by 20 percent. The over 10 percent fall in advertising revenues affected all entertainment and media companies and caused a plunge in the stock price of companies like Yahoo and AOL Time Warner. Indeed, the latter's stock price fell so far that Viacom became the number two global media company in 2002. Analysts now felt that Viacom was the best-positioned media company to benefit from the upswing in advertising that was expected in the latter half of 2002 because of its combination of large-scale operations, leading brands, and diverse revenue streams. While the broadcast groups' earnings fell by 20 percent, for example, the earnings of the cable network division rose by 12 percent, largely because of greater broadcasting in the United States and abroad. Redstone claimed in the summer of 2002 that the worst was over.

Still reeling from the downturn in advertising, Redstone and Karmazin continued to seek ways to counter future threats to the Viacom empire, particularly the threat from digital and broadband technology, which had hurt the Blockbuster unit and which might in the future threaten Viacom's distribution channels as TVs and computers would merge and more and more households would gain broadband connections to the Internet. Recognizing that Viacom and its Blockbuster unit had no particular competencies in digital technology, in May 2002 Viacom announced a major new initiative when it signed an agreement with IBM for IBM to build a companywide computing platform to support digital management of software content, wireless content delivery, and media applications delivered on demand, such as video-on-demand. The contract called on IBM to help properties such as Paramount pictures, MTV networks, CBS, and BET develop new computing initiatives that would help them leverage their resources and promote the cross-sharing of ideas. At the same time a standardized digital platform would help lower its cost structure and provide it with all the benefits of advanced IT in producing significant cost savings.

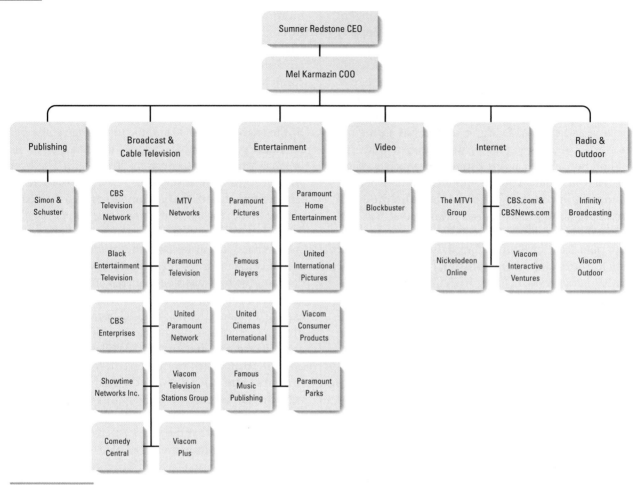

EXHIBIT 1

Viacom's Organizational Structure, 2002

There have been many reports since the hiring of Mel Karmazin that he and Redstone have locked heads on many occasions and that Karmazin was especially critical of Redstone's expensive acquisitions, which increased debt but had no clear future benefits. However, by June 2002, with the CBS merger and BET acquisition showing the value of Viacom's growth strategy, Karmazin was joking that their management styles were complementary and that he was in no rush to assume leadership of Viacom, especially since the seventy-nine-year-old Redstone was "good for another thirty to forty years—at least!" Redstone, however, joked that when Karmazin's contract expired in 2003, Karmazin "might want to retire." Karmazin's response, of course, was "never, never, never." After all, what COO would not want to control the Viacom empire?

REFERENCES

www.viacom.com.

Viacom Annual Reports and 10Ks, 1991–2001.

International Directory of Company Histories, vol. 7 (St. James Press, 1994,) pp. 560–562.

"The Paramount Takeover: The Drama Ended, Two Stars Get New Scripts; Viacom's Biondi Has to Stretch to Fill Big Role," *Wall Street Journal,* February 16, 1994, p. B1.

"The MTV Tycoon—Sumner Redstone is Turning Viacom into the Hottest Global TV Network," *Business Week,* September 21, 1992, pp. 56–62.

Matthew Schifrin, "I Can't Even Remember the Old Stars' Names," *Forbes,* March 16, 1992, pp. 44–45.

Nancy Hass, "The Message Is the Medium," *Financial World,* June 8, 1993, pp. 24–25.

"Redstone in Motion," *Financial World,* December 6, 1994, pp. 36–38.

"Paramount: Do I Hear $11 Billion?" *Business Week,* November 8, 1993, p. 36.

"The Ending of Paramount's Script May Not Be Written Yet," *Business Week,* September 27, 1993, pp. 38–39.

"Sumner Redstone Gets a Little Help from His Friends," *Business Week,* October 11, 1993, p. 36.

"The Paramount Takeover: Wall Street's Final Analysis: Might Made Right," *Wall Street Journal,* February 16, 1994, p. B1.

"Viacom Now Is a Full Owner of Paramount After Vote," *Wall Street Journal,* July 8, 1994, p. B9.

"Viacom Inc.: Paramount Gets 'First Look' at MTV Unit's TV Shows," *Wall Street Journal,* November 11, 1994.

"Viacom Firms Up Plans for Movies Produced by MTV," *Wall Street Journal,* Jun 14, 1994, p. B8.

"Sumner at the Summit," *Business Week,* February 28, 1994, p. 32.

"Deals Give Viacom Even More Muscle," *Wall Street Journal,* September 30, 1994, p. B1.

"Viacom Unit Continues Sell-off of Business That Don't Fit Strategy," *Wall Street Journal,* November 22, 1994, p. B4.

"Hollywood Scuffle," *Business Week,* December 12, 1994, pp. 38–38.

"Frank Biondi—A Media Tycoon's Take on the 21st Century," *Business Week,* 21st Century Capitalism, p. 190.

"Viacom Inc. Wins German License for Nickelodeon," *Wall Street Journal,* March 1, 1995, p. B10.

"Remaindered at Simon & Schuster," *Business Week,* June 27, 1994, p. 32.

"Gump Happens—and Viacom Is Thanking Its Lucky Stars," *Business Week,* August 8, 1994, p. 29.

Karissa S. Wang, "Mel Sez: CBS 'Pretty Darn Good,'" *Electronic Media,* June 3, 2002, p. 37.

Steve McClellan, "Viacom: Flat and Happy," *Broadcasting & Cable,* February 18, 2002, p. 8.

Martin Peers, "Viacom Posts $1.11 Billion Loss Largely Due to Goodwill Charge," *Wall Street Journal,* April 26, 2002, p. B4.

Marc Gunther, "MTV Films: It's a Sleeper," *Fortune,* April 29, 2002, pp. 24–28.

Dyan Machan, "Redstone Rising," *Forbes,* May 13, 2002, pp. 46–48.

Wayne Friedman, "Viacom Snares Monster TV Deal," *Advertising Age,* April 29, 2002, p. 1.

Jack Neff and Wayne Friedman, "P&G Broadens Deal with Viacom Plus," *Advertising Age,* June 17, 2002, p. 3.

Shirley Brady, "BET Seeks More Ways to Work with Viacom Family," *Cable World,* June 10, 2002, p. 24.

"IBM Thrusts into Entertainment via Viacom," *Communications Today,* May 8, 2002, p. 1.

Martin Peers, "Viacom Passes AOL in Market Value—CBS Acquisition Has Brought Shareholder Value to Media Company," *Wall Street Journal,* June 6, 2002, p. B3.

Appendix 1: The Viacom Empire in 2002

Broadcast and Cable Television

The CBS Television Network of more than two hundred affiliated stations provides viewers with some of the nation's best entertainment, news, and sports programming. Popular programs include *Everybody Loves Raymond,* the *Late Show* with David Letterman, and *60 Minutes.* Sports franchises include the NFL and the NCAA Basketball Championship. The daytime drama *The Young and the Restless* leads a daytime programming line-up that has been number one for more than twelve years.

MTV Networks owns and operates many of the most popular basic cable television programming services, including MTV: Music Television, the world's most widely distributed television network, reaching almost 400 million households in 164 countries and territories; Nickelodeon, which is seen in over 300 million households worldwide via localized channels, branded blocks, and individual programs; VH1, reaching over 96 million households around the world; and TNN, which serves 87 million homes in North America with the tops in pop culture programming. Other services include MTV2, Nick at Nite, TV Land, CMT, and the Digital Suite from MTV Networks. MTVN is also involved in a variety of entertainment businesses that extend its brands, including films, books, and online and consumer products.

BET comprises Black Entertainment Television, the largest national cable network serving African Americans, reaching 67 million U.S. households; BET on Jazz: The Jazz Channel, the country's only twenty-four-hour network devoted to jazz music; BET's publishing unit, BET Books; BET Pictures, which produces made-for-TV movies and documentaries; and BET.com, the leading online destination for African Americans.

Paramount Television is one of the largest suppliers of television programming for the broadcast, first-run syndication and cable markets, with over 55,000 hours of programming in its library. Its six production units are Paramount Network Television, Viacom Productions, Spelling Television, Big Ticket Television, Paramount Domestic Television, and Paramount International Television.

CBS Enterprises is a global leader in distribution. Its domestic syndication arm, King World Productions Inc., sells first-run programming such as *Wheel of Fortune, Jeopardy!,* and the *Oprah Winfrey Show.* Its off-network slate includes the hit CBS series *Everybody Loves Raymond.* Outside the United States, CBS Broadcast International is one of the premier distributors of U.S. network series programming, while its subsidiary, King World International Productions, is a leader in format sales and local production worldwide.

The United Paramount Network (UPN) reaches more than 86 percent of U.S. television homes through its affiliated stations, and it broadcasts ten hours of on-time, primetime programming each week. Popular programs include *Buffy the Vampire Slayer; Enterprise,* the latest installment in the Star Trek franchise; and *Roswell.*

Showtime Networks Inc. (SNI) owns the premium television networks Showtime, the Movie

Channel, and FLIX. SNI operates and manages the premium television network Sundance Channel, which is owned by SNI, Robert Redford, and Universal Studios. SNI also markets and distributes sports and entertainment events for exhibition to subscribers on a pay-per-view basis.

Viacom Television Stations Group consists of thirty-four television stations, reaching nine of the top ten television markets in the United States. The division includes sixteen owned and operated CBS stations and eighteen UPN-affiliated stations.

The CBS Television Stations Division includes duopolies in seven major markets, with CBS and UPN stations in Philadelphia, Boston, Dallas, Detroit, Miami, and Pittsburgh.

Comedy Central, the country's only all-comedy network, is jointly owned by Viacom and HBO and presents the biggest comedy stars from the past and present along with today's hottest newcomers.

Viacom Plus is the company's integrated sales and marketing arm. The group's mission is to create long-term marketing partnerships that build brands and drive revenue for both clients and the company.

Radio and Outdoor Advertising

Infinity Broadcasting is the radio and outdoor advertising unit of Viacom. Infinity Radio, the unit's radio division, operates over 180 radio stations, the majority of which are in the nation's largest markets. Infinity also manages and holds an equity position in Westwood One, Inc. Viacom Outdoor, Infinity's outdoor advertising division, has properties across North America and Europe, including the top one hundred markets in the United States.

Motion Pictures and Theatrical Exhibition

Paramount Pictures, one of the original major motion picture studios, has been a leading producer and distributor of feature films since 1912. Its more-than-2,500-title library includes Oscar winners such as *Forrest Gump, Braveheart,* and *Titanic* (the highest-grossing motion picture of all time) and recent releases *Jimmy Neutron: Boy Genius, Vanilla Sky,* and *Lara Croft: Tomb Raider.* Paramount Home Entertainment, a global leader in the distribution of filmed entertainment on videocassette and DVD, distributes theatrical releases from Paramount Pictures, Paramount Classics, Nickelodeon Movies, and MTV Films as well as nontheatrical releases both in the United States

and abroad. Recent successes include *Save the Last Dance* and *What Women Want.*

Famous Players, founded in 1920, is Canada's top-grossing, fastest-growing, and longest-operating theatrical exhibitor. The Toronto-based company offers audiences the best possible theatrical film experience through its 102 locations with 884 screens throughout Canada, including theaters in its joint venture with IMAX and its partnership with Alliance Atlantis. United International Pictures (UIP), in which Viacom has a 33 percent interest, handles general distribution of Paramount Pictures's films outside the United States and Canada. United Cinemas International (UCI), a joint venture between Viacom and Universal, operates approximately 970 screens in 113 theaters in the United Kingdom, Ireland, Germany, Austria, Spain, Japan, Italy, Taiwan, Poland, Argentina, Brazil, and Panama and is one of the largest operators of multiplex theaters outside the United States.

Viacom Consumer Products is a leader in the entertainment-licensing arena, merchandising properties on behalf of Paramount Pictures, Paramount Television, Viacom Productions, and Spelling Television, as well as third-party properties.

Famous Music Publishing is one of the top ten music publishers in the United States and one of the world's major suppliers of music to all mediums. Its diversified catalog of over 100,000 copyrights spans seven decades and includes music from Oscar-winning motion pictures such as *The Godfather, Forrest Gump,* and *Titanic* as well as every genre of contemporary music, including hits written or recorded by Blon-die, Bush, Montell Jordan, Garth Brooks, Ricky Martin, Eric Clapton, Whitney Houston, and Barbra Streisand.

Video

Blockbuster is the world's leading renter of videos, DVDs, and videogames, with nearly 7,800 stores throughout the Americas, Europe, Asia, and Australia. More than 3 million customers visit a Blockbuster store each day.

Internet

MTV.com is one of the leading music entertainment destinations on the Web, giving fans unlimited access and an intimate connection to their favorite artists, shows, and other fans. The site delivers unparalleled online programming with popular features like Radio

MTV.com, News, and unique community features, including MTV member profiles, instant messaging, and more. CBS.com and CBSNews.com, CBS's branded online offerings, promote and complement on-air programming, including *Survivor, CSI, Everybody Loves Raymond,* and *60 Minutes.* Nickelodeon Online is the leading portfolio of kids' and parents' destinations, featuring Nick.com, Nickjr.com, nick-at-nite.com, tvland.com, teachers.nick.com, and gas.nick.com. Viacom Interactive Ventures manages an Internet portfolio that includes equity relationships with over a dozen web sites, including CBS.MarketWatch.com, CBS.SportsLine.com, Hollywood.com, Switchboard.com, and the free-cash Internet portal iWon.com. VH1.com is a leading online destination for new music, entertainment, and artist information while serving as the online extension for the network's news and entertainment programming and its award-winning community-based initiative VH1 Save the Music.

Publishing

Simon & Schuster publishes more than 2,100 titles annually under thirty-eight well-known trade, mass market, children's, and new media imprints. The division published ninety-nine *New York Times* bestsellers in 2001, including fourteen at No. 1.

Parks

Paramount Parks is one of the largest theme park companies in the world and entertains approximately 13 million visitors annually at its five North American theme parks and its interactive attraction Star Trek: The Experience at the Las Vegas Hilton.

35

Monsanto (A): Building a Life Sciences Company

This case was prepared by Charles W. L. Hill, the University of Washington.

Introduction

As Monsanto entered the new millenium, Bob Shapiro, Monsanto's CEO, reflected on how much the company had changed during the last quarter of a century and on the vast opportunities and daunting challenges now confronting the enterprise. Monsanto was established in 1901 when John Queeny, a chemicals salesman, invested $5,000 in manufacturing facilities to produce saccharin, a synthetic sweetener. Over the next half a century, Monsanto moved into raw materials production, becoming an integrated chemical manufacturer. By the early 1970s, St. Louis–based Monsanto was one of the world's largest producers of high-volume, commodity chemical products. Then the first OPEC oil shock hit and Monsanto saw its margins drastically compressed by rising raw material prices and plunging demand.

It was at this point that Monsanto began on a journey that was to transform the company into a life sciences behemoth. From small beginnings, the company had grown to become one of the world's leading producers of agricultural and animal biotechnology products. Along the way it had acquired G. D. Searle, a second-tier pharmaceutical firm, thereby add-

ing human life sciences to its animal and agricultural life science businesses. By the late 1990s, twenty years of investment in life sciences seemed to be paying off. Monsanto had introduced genetically altered cotton, potatoes, canola, corn, and soybean seeds, engineered to produce natural herbicides and/or to resist damage from Roundup, Monsanto's best-selling chemical herbicide. Sales of these seeds were growing rapidly as farmers recognized their potential to boost crop yields. Furthermore, Monsanto had plans to roll out forty new genetically altered seed products during the 1999–2002 period.[1] Meanwhile, under Monsanto's tutelage, Searle had assembled one of the best new product pipelines in the pharmaceutical industry, and he expected to launch more than two dozen new products between 1999 and 2002, led by Celebrex, the first in a class of new painkillers.[2] To complete the transformation of Monsanto from a chemical to a life sciences company, in September 1997 Monsanto spun off its chemical operations as an independent company, Solutia. What remained was a company with sales of more than $9 billion that analysts thought could grow its earnings at an annual compound rate of 20 percent per annum for years to come.

Despite the growth potential of the new Monsanto, however, Shapiro had more than a few worries. Getting Monsanto to this position had been an expensive endeavor that had left the company straining under an $8.2 billion debt load, a debt-to-equity ratio of 1.25, and a $360 million annual interest bill. Given its debt, some analysts questioned whether Monsanto had the financial resources and the marketing and sales muscle to maximize the potential of its pharmaceutical and agricultural biotechnology pipelines. To address these concerns, in June 1998 Monsanto announced an agreement to merge with American Home Products (AHP). Many saw the potential merger as an ideal marriage of complementary assets, with AHP's financial resources and strengths in pharmaceutical distribution being a good match for Monsanto's bulging new product pipeline. However, in October 1998 the merger talks broke down, reportedly because of disagreements between senior executives at the two companies over operations and strategy. Now Shapiro had to devise an alternative strategy to maximize the value of Monsanto's pipeline.

If this were not enough, in September 2000 Monsanto's U.S. patent on glyphosate, the key ingredient in Roundup, would expire. Roundup was Monsanto's best-selling product, accounting for over $1.5 billion of its $4 billion in 1998 sales to agricultural markets. In countries outside of the United States where the patent had already expired, prices for Roundup had been cut in half. Many analysts believed that the same was about to occur in the United States. Of course, Shapiro's hope was that the slack would be taken up by the increased sales of Roundup-ready seeds, which should also boost demand for Roundup. Here too, however, there was a problem, for there was growing opposition to genetically engineered foodstuffs among the environmental community, which referred to transgenic crops as a form of "genetic pollution."[3] The resistance was strongest in Europe, where, in response to public disquiet, the European Union considered blocking imports of genetically altered agricultural products.[4]

Building Life Sciences at Monsanto

The life science business at Monsanto was constructed over a quarter of a century during the tenure of three CEOs: John Hanley, Richard Mahoney, and Robert Shapiro. At the outset of this twenty-five-year odyssey Monsanto was a major chemical company with substantial sales from low-margin, capital-intensive, commodity chemical operations that produced fibers, plastics, and agricultural chemicals. The main raw material input for these products was petrochemicals, leaving Monsanto highly vulnerable to fluctuations in the price of oil. Pushed by the OPEC oil price hikes of 1973 and 1979, both Hanley and Mahoney repeatedly emphasized the need for Monsanto to migrate its revenues away from low-margin commodity business toward proprietary, high-margin businesses. In the words of Richard Mahoney in a 1989 article:

> Our current strategy at Monsanto began to emerge in the mid 1970s, undertaken because we realized that, after thirty years of growth, many of our traditional chemical markets were maturing. In addition, oil companies and oil-producing nations were crowding into these markets. Not wanting to become a me-too player, we began to evaluate potential new directions. That decision liberated us to look at other technologies. Underlying that search was a determination to find technologies that would present whole new families of opportunities to exploit. We dedicated ourselves to becoming one of the truly great industrial enterprises by the early 1990s. In financial terms that means a 20 percent return on equity consistently, year after year.[5]

Hanley, who ran Monsanto from 1972 to 1983, made the first moves into biotechnology. Mahoney, his successor, built on this over the next ten years and in addition steered the company toward human pharmaceuticals with the 1985 acquisition of G. D. Searle. Shapiro, who succeeded Mahoney in 1993, completed the process.

Establishing Competencies in Biotechnology

The genesis of life sciences at Monsanto can be traced back to a 1973 decision to fund a small biotechnology skunkworks to carry out cellular research.[6] The skunkworks was the brain child of Ernie Jaworski, a senior research scientist at Monsanto. Jaworski had been following developments in plant genetics among the academic community. Like many other scientists, he had been stunned by the news in early 1973 that two California scientists, Stanley Cohn and Herbert Boyer, had managed to isolate fragments of a gene from one bacterium and insert them into another to create a bit of living cellular material that had never before existed.[7] Jaworski reasoned that it might be possible to use the Cohn-Boyer method—referred to as recombinant DNA technology—to genetically alter crop seeds to make them resistant to herbicides. The herbicides could then be used to kill the weeds around the crops as they were growing, without fear of harming the crops. This would help boost demand for one of Monsanto's newest products, the herbicide Roundup. Approved for market introduction in 1974, Roundup was a proprietary environmentally friendly herbicide developed by Monsanto. At the time, it could only be applied before crop growth, since it failed to discriminate between weeds and crops. Another possibility might have been to genetically alter crops so that they would express proteins that function as "natural" insecticides, repelling harmful pests. An example would be the cotton bollworm, which ate cotton plants and forced cotton farmers to spend significant sums on insecticides.

Jaworski proposed his idea to John Hanley, Monsanto's new CEO who joined Monsanto from Procter & Gamble in 1972. Hanley agreed to fund the establishment of the skunkworks, and Jaworski set up the operation with a staff of thirty-five scientists. The main focus of Jaworski's skunkworks, was on understanding cell biology with a view to creating crops with innate herbicide resistance. At the same time, Jaworski was cognizant of the opportunities that might exist if animal proteins could be produced using recombinant DNA technology. Back in the 1930s, Russian scientists had extracted growth hormone from the pituitary glands of slaughtered pigs and cows. They found that by injecting the hormone into a live animal, they could accelerate growth and, in the case of cows, increase milk production. However, the process was too expensive, and the technology required to mass-produce growth hormone proteins did not exist at that point in time, so for decades growth hormone remained little more than a scientific curiosity.[8] Now Jaworski realized that recombinant DNA technology might be used to mass-produce animal growth hormones, so he authorized research into growth hormones. However, progress was hindered by a lack of resources.

In 1976, Jaworski tried to persuade Monsanto to invest in Genentech, one of the first biotechnology start-ups. Herbert Boyer, one of the inventors of recombinant DNA technology, was one of the two founders of the company. At the time Genentech was seeking initial venture capital to finance basic research aimed at producing human proteins using recombinant DNA technology. Jaworski believed that Genentech might be an interesting way for Monsanto to get a foothold in this emerging field. However, Monsanto's top management was not enamoured by the growth possibilities that had them producing silicon for semiconductors, and expressed no interest in the possibility. In retrospect, this proved to be a mistake.

In 1978, Genentech produced the first human protein (somatostatin) in a microorganism (*E. coli* bacteria). Also in 1978, it succeeded in cloning human insulin using the same technology. The method involved using recombinant DNA technology to insert the piece of human DNA that carries instructions for producing the desired human protein (such as the gene to produce insulin) into the DNA of a microorganism (usually *E. coli* bacteria or some form of yeast). Because it now contained the gene for making the human protein, the microorganism expressed (produced) this protein. Cultures of the microorganism were then placed in fermentation tanks, where they multiplied and produced more of the desired protein. The microorganism was then harvested, and the desired protein was removed and converted into a drug, such as human insulin, that could be injected into people who lacked the protein (such as diabetics in the case of insulin).[9] In 1979, Genentech used this technology to engineer microorganisms to produce human growth hormone. The company went public in 1980 with an offering that leapt from $35 a share to a high of $88 after less than an hour on the market. At the time, this was one the largest stock run-ups ever.[10]

Against the background of rising interest in biotechnology, in 1979 Hanley hired Howard Schneiderman to head Monsanto's research and development (R&D) efforts. At the time he was hired, Schneiderman was the dean of biological sciences at the University of California, Irvine. As a member of the National Academy of Science and a recognized expert in the techniques of genetic engineering, Schneiderman struck Hanley as the ideal person to oversee Monsanto's biotechnology efforts. As Schneiderman later recalled it, Hanley posed a question to Schneiderman: "We spent $170 million on research in 1978. We probably should have spent $275 million. Do you have any good ideas?"[11] Schneiderman was instantly sold. "If you are a red-blooded American who has chosen research as a career, and a guy comes along and says, 'Do you have any good ideas for $100 million worth of research?' it's a fantastic temptation."[12] At Irvine, Schneiderman had administered an $8 million budget.[13] Hanley made Schneiderman senior vice president for research and development and gave him the charter to make Monsanto a "significant world force in molecular biology."[14]

Schneiderman moved quickly. Jaworski's group was transferred into central R&D under Schneiderman's direction. Jaworski was made the director of biological sciences within the corporate R&D staff and was given free rein to go on a hiring spree to attract brilliant young researchers. It wasn't easy; a surge of new biotechnology start-ups offering attractive stock option contracts to scientists were competing with Monsanto for scarce talent. Monsanto had an advantage, however. Its financial resources offered scientists the opportunity to engage in long-term research projects, free from financial worries. Schneiderman's reputation also helped, and the company hired 135 Ph.D.s in the first three years of his tenure. What also helped was the company's decision to invest $165 million to build a Life Sciences Research Center on a 210-acre campus 25 miles west of downtown St. Louis. Referred to within Monsanto as "the house that Howard built," the research center was a powerful symbol of Monsanto's commitment to basic biotechnology research. By 1990, the facility had 250 laboratories and 900 research scientists, making it one of the most powerful concentrations of life science research effort anywhere in the world.[15]

Research Alliances

Despite Monsanto's aggressive investment in R&D, Schneiderman was the first to admit that Monsanto could not do it all alone. Within three months of joining the company, Schneiderman entered into an alliance with Genentech. By this time, Genentech had already figured out how to use recombinant DNA technology to mass-produce human growth hormone. Monsanto was interested in using the same technology to mass-produce animal growth hormones. In return for the rights to the bovine somatotropin growth hormone (BST), Monsanto paid Genentech $990,000, agreed to make several subsequent milestone payments, and promised royalties on future sales of BST. Genentech delivered the first 600 milligrams of BST in December 1981, and initial tests showed that the product worked like natural BST.[16]

In 1982, Monsanto forged an alliance with nearby Washington University to get access to leading-edge academic research on molecular biology. This was Monsanto's second big involvement with a university. Back in 1974 the company had entered into a twelve-year, $23 million agreement with Harvard Medical School for research on the molecular basis of organ development. However, Monsanto was not satisfied with this arrangement. A major problem had been that the Harvard researchers refused to give Monsanto access to research findings until they had been published in academic journals. Moreover, the company had found it was unable to direct or influence the course of research at Harvard.[17]

This time, Monsanto structured the agreement to give the company greater access to research results and a greater ability to direct the research process. The agreement called for Monsanto to invest $23.5 million over five years for biomedical research into proteins and peptides, small proteins that modify the behavior of cells. About one-third of the effort was to be directed toward basic research, and the rest directed toward new pharmaceutical products aimed at treating a variety of ailments, including allergies. The contract specified that faculty members participating in projects funded by Monsanto would be free to publish all results of their findings and that Washington University would hold any resulting patents. Monsanto, on the other hand, would have exclusive marketing rights to such patents. Projects to receive funding would be selected by a committee that included four university and four Monsanto scientists. Monsanto scientists would be able to work side by side with university researchers in university laboratories, and vice versa.

This agreement raised concerns in some quarters that it might violate fundamental principles of academic research and freedom. Albert Gore, Jr., then a Democratic representative from Tennessee and chairman of the Investigation and Oversight Subcommittee of the House Committee on Science and Technology, commented, "You don't have to know algebra to figure out how that committee works. No research can be done unless the company gives permission."[18] In reply, Schneiderman insisted that "everything is carefully designed to enable the university to be true to its fundamental purpose."[19]

The Washington University deal was followed by a series of other research deals structured along similar lines. These included a $5 million five-year agreement with Oxford University in the United Kingdom to sequence the structure of certain plant proteins and a $4 million five-year agreement with Rockefeller

University to investigate the structure and regulation of plant genes involved in photosynthesis. Smaller agreements were also signed with the California Institute of Technology, the University of California (San Francisco), and Harvard University. In 1985, the Washington University agreement was extended to cover eight and a half years, and the total funds committed increased to $62 million, making it the largest collaborative agreement of its kind.[20] According to Schneiderman, such contracts provide "a powerful insight into the future," fund research that is "more likely to make a leap," keep Monsanto researchers "in the front line of academic research," and "can be a magnet for attracting good people to Monsanto."[21]

Acquiring Searle

As Monsanto embarked on its journey into the life sciences business, it was not altogether clear what the focus of the company would ultimately be. Jaworski's skunkworks, and many of the scientists hired after Schneiderman arrived, focused primarily on applying the principles of molecular biology to plants. This made good sense given Monsanto's strong position in agricultural herbicides, a position that was getting stronger all the time due to the success of Roundup, which by the early 1980s was generating over $500 million a year in sales and was Monsanto's most profitable product.[22] On the other hand, the alliance with Genentech signaled an interest in animal proteins, and the agreement with Washington University was in large part directed at producing human pharmaceuticals.

Within Monsanto, the debate was not so much about whether the company should leverage its growing life science expertise to enter the human pharmaceutical business, as it was about how best to achieve this. By 1983, Monsanto, in collaboration with its university partners, was beginning to identify some interesting candidates for clinical investigation. An example was atrial peptide, a human protein that had been isolated from the atrium of the heart by researchers at Washington University. The protein dilates the vascular system, and Monsanto believed that it might have value as a drug for controlling blood pressure.[23] However, Monsanto lacked both the regulatory experience with the FDA and the distribution network required to maximize the potential of such pharmaceuticals.

The slow pace of Monsanto's move away from its low-margin commodity chemicals business added

urgency. By 1984, the company was still generating 60 percent of its sales from its traditional chemical operations, even though 65 percent of its operating profits came from agricultural chemicals, and most of those could be attributed to just two products, Roundup and another herbicide, Lasso (the patent on Lasso was set to expire in 1988). Monsanto's new CEO, Richard Mahoney, wanted to accelerate the shift away from commodity chemicals and simultaneously gain a pharmaceutical distribution network. To further attainment of these objectives, in 1983 Monsanto hired the investment banker Goldman, Sachs & Co. to identify acquisition candidates in the pharmaceutical business. In 1984, Monsanto acquired a small Belgian drug company, Continental Pharma, but a large acquisition candidate eluded it. G. D. Searle was on the list compiled by Goldman, Sachs & Co., but the company was 34 percent owned by the Searle family, and they seemed unlikely to sell. This changed in 1984 when the Searle family indicated that they wanted to sell their stake, effectively putting Searle on the block. Searle's pharmaceutical business had been a lackluster performer in recent years. The company had not introduced a significant new drug for eight years. It did, however, have a powerful antiulcer drug, Cytotec, in late-stage clinical trials. There were also a number of interesting drug candidates further down the product development pipeline. Searle also had aspartame (NutraSweet), the artificial sweetener that generated $600 million in annual sales—roughly half of Searle's total revenues. However, the patent on aspartame was due to expire in 1992. Initially, Monsanto wanted to purchase Searle's pharmaceutical business, leaving Searle with NutraSweet, but Searle refused to deal and negotiations broke down.

In 1985, Monsanto approached Searle again, this time with an offer to buy the entire company. The change in Monsanto's position was in part due to a reassessment of the value of NutraSweet. Searle had just won regulatory approval to use 100 percent NutraSweet in diet soda. Mahoney believed that this would expand sales for NutraSweet to close to $1 billion before the patent expired, throwing off significant free cash flow in the process. In Mahoney's words, "NutraSweet brings a very interesting earnings stream in the time between now and when our biotechnology begins to pay off."[24]

In July 1985, Monsanto announced that it had agreed to purchase Searle for $2.7 billion, or about seventeen times Searle's estimated 1985 earnings. While many analysts commented that the acquisition was too expensive and that Monsanto was paying a hefty premium for a mediocre drug company that had not introduced any significant new products for some time, Monsanto seemed pleased with its purchase. One business development executive in the company noted that "Searle's marketing and distribution operations will be the vehicle by which we can go forward and commercialize new products worldwide. Now Monsanto has the infrastructure to realize the benefits of biotechnology."[25] Mahoney also noted that "Searle has done a very good job of finding product leads of its own. We are engaged in a long-term strategic move to have Searle's and Monsanto's strengths melded together."[26] In fact, by mid 1986, Searle had twenty-one new chemical or biological entities in various stages of clinical development, one of the best pipelines in the pharmaceutical industry. These included cardiovascular drugs for hypertension and irregular heartbeat; central nervous system drugs for depression, epilepsy, and pain; immunoinflammatory drugs for arthritis; and an ulcer medication.[27] However, most of these products were still in the early stages of clinical testing, there was no guarantee that they would show the desired combination of efficacy and manageable side effects in clinical trials, and even if they did, they were years from market introduction.

Developing Products

With the 1985 acquisition of Searle, Monsanto had assembled the main building blocks required to embark on the transformation from a major chemical company into a life sciences concern. At the time, Ernest Jaworski commented that "by 1990 Monsanto will be the greatest biotechnology company in the world."[28] Executives in other biotechnology firms characterized such comments as "absolutely ridiculous" and an "extraordinary boast."[29] They noted that it was small entrepreneurial biotechnology enterprises such as Amgen, Genentech, and Biogen that had succeeded in moving biotechnology products to market, not large corporations like Monsanto. Large companies, the critics noted, lacked the required sense of urgency, drive, and creativity of smaller biotechnology enterprises. In 1986, only two biotechnology products were on the market, insulin and human growth hormone. Genentech, not a large

pharmaceutical firm, produced both of these. Moreover, all five biotechnology products then in phase III (final-stage) clinical trials belonged to entrepreneurial biotechnology companies, not large pharmaceutical enterprises. More than anything else, the critics felt that Monsanto was underestimating the problems involved in developing biotechnology products and bringing them to market.

Ps-3732

By 1986 Monsanto was already beginning to get a taste for the problems involved in developing biotechnology products. On May 20 of that year the Environmental Protection Agency (EPA) turned down an application from the company to field-test its first genetically altered microbe, dealing a body blow to one of the company's most-advanced agricultural biotechnology research projects.[30] The microbe in question was a genetically engineered bacteria that produced a protein that functioned as a natural insecticide and was capable of killing insects that fed on corn. In denying the company's request to proceed with field testing, the EPA was bowing to pressure from environmental activists, who had criticized Monsanto's testing procedures and questioned the safety of releasing genetically altered organisms into the environment.

The research project that produced the bacteria was begun in 1980 when a twenty person team of scientists, led by thirty-two-year-old Robert Kaufman, received approval to develop microbes that produced "natural" insecticides. The thinking was straightforward; farmers around the world were spending about $7 billion on chemical pesticides, but these pesticides also killed animals, polluted ground water and rivers, and showed up in traces in foods. Surely, Monsanto executives believed, farmers would buy a genetically engineered product that was cheaper, easier to use, and did not harm the environment or human health.

By late 1982, after collecting and analyzing hundreds of bacteria that colonized the roots of corn, Dr. Kaufman and his team isolated a single microbe, dubbed Ps-3732, that was capable of mass reproduction and able to compete with other microorganisms for space around the roots of corn plants. The team had also identified a natural toxin capable of killing caterpillar-type pests and generated by one of the three to five thousand genes in the chromosomes in another common bacterium, *Bacillus thuringiensis*. By the end of 1983, the team had isolated the gene and had succeeded in inserting it into the chromosomes of Ps-3732 using recombinant DNA technology.

The team now believed that they had a means to deliver a natural insecticide. The plan was to sell corn seeds coated with the genetically modified bacteria. After the farmer planted the seeds, the bacteria would multiple in the soil and form a barrier around the roots of the corn, preventing damage from cutworms, a common pest. Before field testing the bacteria, Kaufman's team undertook seventeen safety studies designed to establish the environmental impact of the genetically modified Ps-3732. The bacteria were fed to mice, quail, fish, and bees, and a wide variety of other plants were exposed to it. No adverse effects were observed. Armed with these data, Monsanto submitted a request to the EPA to move forward with a field test.

At this point, Jeremy Rifkin entered the picture. A well-known radical activist, Rifkin was president of the Foundation for Economic Trends, a policy study group largely funded from sales of Rifkin's own books. Rifkin had already established a reputation as a vocal and effective critic of the imperialism of modern science in general, and biotechnology in particular. In Monsanto's request, he saw an opportunity to nip the emerging agricultural biotechnology movement in the bud.

Rifkin's attack on Monsanto had two thrusts. First, he argued that once released into the environment, genetically altered bacteria could spread uncontrollably. Such "genetic pollution" might cause problems that had not yet been identified. Second, he requested from the EPA access to all of Monsanto's data on safety studies. He then had these data reviewed and critiqued by several ecologists and microbiologists that he had worked with for several years. These experts criticized Monsanto's safety studies as poorly conducted and scientifically inconclusive. Armed with this finding, Rifkin formally petitioned the EPA to deny Monsanto a permit to field-test Ps-3732.

The EPA subsequently issued a report on Monsanto's safety study tests. Written by microbiologists on the EPA's staff, the report stated that thirteen of the seventeen studies were either inconclusive or scientifically flawed. Kaufman acknowledged that some of the safety studies were scanty, but he argued that Monsanto was breaking new ground, that many of the tests were the first of their kind, and that the EPA ignored a lot of good data and instead simply focused on those tests where there was some question about the sample design. Kaufman subsequently met with the EPA's advisory panel—which was composed of independent academic advisors—after which the panel indicated that it would "reverse" the staff evaluation and recommend that the EPA allow Monsanto to proceed with the experiment. In reaching its decision, the panel acknowledged that some of Monsanto's safety studies were poorly designed, but it added that it had enough data from other sources to know that if Monsanto's microbe were released into the environment, it would not be a hazard.

Unfortunately for Monsanto, the panel's advice is not binding, although reversal of the panel's recommendation is a rare event. Alerted by EPA insiders as to what the panel recommendation would be, Rifkin continued to put pressure on the EPA, indicating that he would sue the agency if it approved the field test. This put Dr. John Moore, the head of the EPA, in a difficult position. Although privately he acknowledged that Monsanto's microbe was in all probability not harmful, he recognized that a lawsuit would give Rifkin the opportunity to probe Monsanto and the EPA in public. Cognizant of Rifkin's eloquence and his influence among certain U.S. Congress members, and aware of the holes in some of Monsanto's studies, Moore decided to deny the request, although he urged the company to undertake several safety studies and resubmit the request. In a short letter to the company, Moore noted, "I believe that it is in the best interests of Monsanto and the EPA that the general public develop a feeling of trust and confidence that all decisions to permit experiments of this sort be based on expert evaluation of reliable data." Later Moore commented that "we do not have the knowledge to completely understand the interactions of organisms in the environment. I think caution is absolutely justified."[31] Commenting on the decision, Rifkin stated that "we owe it to ourselves and the next generation to raise these issues and ask these questions. We are talking about the ability to change the genetic code of life, and that's ominous power. We ought to have a thorough, reasonable, and well thought out public debate. It ought not to be left in the hands of Monsanto."[32]

In the aftermath of the EPA's decision, Kaufman resigned from Monsanto to join a start-up biotechnology company, his team was reassigned, and Monsanto decided to shelve the project and pursue other avenues in the agricultural biotechnology research arena.

Genetically Altering Plants

One of the other avenues that the company was pursuing was the genetic manipulation of plant DNA. Unknowingly, human beings have been manipulating plant DNA since the dawn of the agricultural revolution thousands of years ago, but they have done it through the slow and highly imprecise methods of selective breeding and hybridization. By harnessing biotechnology, Monsanto hoped to dramatically reduce the time required to produce new varieties of crops and to design crops that had specific desirable traits. To this end, in 1981 a twenty-eight-year-old scientist within Monsanto, Robert Fraley, was put in charge of the plant molecular biology group and given the task of developing better crops through genetic engineering.[33]

Fraley's group first had to confront the problem of how to alter a plant's DNA. They settled on the novel approach of harnessing bacteria that have the natural ability to invade plant cells without destroying the cells. The bacterium they chose, *Agrobacterium tumefaciens*, invades a plant's cell and produces tumorous crown galls on infected species. The utility of this bacterium as a gene transfer system was first recognized when it was demonstrated that the crown galls were actually produced as a result of the transfer and integration of genes from the bacterium into the genome of the plant cells. The scientists theorized that if they could disable the disease-causing genes in *Agrobacterium,* it would prove to be a useful vector for transporting foreign genes into the DNA of a plant.[34]

It took two years to disassemble *Agrobacterium's* genetic code and remove the regions of DNA that produced crown gall. They then took another bacteria, *E. coli,* and isolated the gene that made *E. coli* resistant to an antibiotic called kanamycin. They cut the kanamycin-resistant gene out of the *E. coli* and spliced it into the DNA of the *Agrobacterium.* They then infected cells from a petunia plant with the modified *Agrobacterium.* The significance of this is that kanamycin is normally lethal to petunias. When they exposed *Agrobacterium*-infected petunia cells to kanamycin, however, the petunia cells continued to divide. In 1983, Fraley announced that Monsanto produced a kanamycin-resistant petunia that was the world's first genetically engineered plant.[35] Subse-

quent experiments found that traits introduced into the DNA of host plants were stable over multiple generations during crossbreeding.[36]

Fraley then used the same methodology for more elaborate, and commercially important, plant transformations. The first successful gene-altering experiment with a staple crop came in 1987, when Fraley's group succeeded in modifying soybeans to resist damage from glyphosate, the active ingredient in the company's best-selling herbicide, Roundup. The glyphosate gene had been isolated from bacteria and then inserted into the soybean cells' genetic structure using recombinant DNA technology.

While Monsanto claimed Roundup-resistant plants would boost yields, critics in the environmental community opposed Monsanto's attempt to create crops resistant to Roundup. Because Roundup does not discriminate between weeds and crops, farmers must use it with extreme care and avoid it altogether in soybean, corn, and cotton fields. The development of Roundup-resistant crops, however, allowed farmers to spray the herbicide freely, a fact that troubled environmentalists. As one put it: "Monsanto's rhetoric is low or no pesticide agriculture, but in fact what they are delivering is a whole new generation of herbicide-tolerant plants that will shackle us to chemicals for the foreseeable future."[37] For its part, Monsanto pointed out that Roundup is an environmentally friendly herbicide. Glyphosate becomes inert on contact with the soil, breaking down into nitrogen and other nontoxic elements that are naturally found in the soil.

A series of other crop modifications followed the creation of Roundup-resistant soybeans. These included the engineering of an array of crops—tomatoes, potatoes, alfalfa, tobacco, and cucumber—that were resistant to viral infections. By 1990, the company had also succeeded in engineering transgenic cotton, tomato, and potato plants that contain genes from bacteria that produce proteins fatal to budworms, bollworms, and other common farm pests.[38] The insect-resistant crops were based on genes from a family of bacteria called *Bacillus thuringiensis,* commonly referred to as Bt. The Bt genes are a code for assembling proteins that can kill certain pests while having no effect on beneficial insects and animals. Bts have been used in sprays for decades, mostly by organic farmers, who forgo the use of manmade chemicals. But the sprays were not effective enough to make much of a dent in the chemical-pesticides market. Monsanto wanted to change that, in the process saving farmers millions of dollars per year in spending on insecticides. Once more, however, the environmental community protested loudly. A big concern was that over time common pests would develop resistance to the Bt protein. In particular, they worried that insects and weeds would quickly build up resistance to the transgenic plants and the herbicides used in conjunction with them, possibly leaving farmers worse off than before after a short burst of extra productivity.[39]

BST

Monsanto licensed the rights to bovine somatotropin growth hormone (BST) from Genentech in 1981 and received the first batch of BST in December of that year. Monsanto planned to perfect BST so that it could be used to boost milk production in dairy cattle (subsequently, studies at universities and at dairy farms have found that the drug increases milk production 10 to 20 percent in well-managed herds). It took twelve years and an estimated $300 million in R&D before the company finally won approval to sell BST in the marketplace.[40]

Monsanto's product is produced by inserting the BST gene from cows into *E. coli* bacteria, which are then multiplied in fermentation tanks. The bacteria are then harvested and the BST protein is removed, purified, and converted into the drug that can be injected into cows. This process might sound straightforward, but it is not. It took several years for Monsanto's scientists to find the ideal environment in fermentation vats for the care and feeding of the BST-producing *E. coli*. *E coli* turned out to be difficult to mass-produce, requiring just the right amount of oxygen and nutrients and the correct temperature. If any one of these variables was not right, other bacteria could swamp *E. coli*, dramatically lowering BST yields from the fermentation process. Then researchers ran into problems when they tried to kill the bacteria and "crack open" the organisms. Cracking open bacteria involves submitting the organisms to very high pressure and then releasing that pressure. The sudden drop in pressure causes the bacteria to pop open and release their contents. Monsanto found that the BST-laden bacteria quickly wore down the stainless steel valves on pressure equipment. The reason: BST protein particles have the consistency of superhard grains of sand. As a result, the pressure equipment was breaking down constantly. Solving the problem

required the invention of ceramic valves that could withstand the wear and tear from BST. After cracking, Monsanto found that it needed to conduct seven more purification steps to separate the BST molecules from thousands of other proteins, fats, and carbohydrates in the *E. coli* mix. To perfect the purification process, Monsanto had to develop special filters that prevented BST from becoming contaminated.

Another problem was finding the correct formulation of the drug. Early BST tests required scientists to inject cows every day, but Monsanto concluded that such a regime would be too expensive and cumbersome for farmers, and it developed a formulation that only needed to be injected weekly. Then there was also the issue of where to produce BST. United States regulations prohibit the export of drugs that have not been approved for marketing by the FDA in the United States. Monsanto reasoned that it might get approval to market BST from foreign regulators before it received FDA approval (correctly, as it turned out), so the company decided to locate the manufacturing facilities in Austria.

Difficult as they were, however, solving all of these production problems was minor compared to the political and regulatory problems that Monsanto had to solve before BST could be marketed. The problems started in 1985, when researchers at Cornell University reported that the results of early field trials found that the drug increased milk production by as much as 40 percent. The widely publicized results dismayed dairy farmers in New York, Wisconsin, Minnesota, and other milk-producing states. They came at a time when large dairy surpluses were pushing prices down, forcing family farms out of business. Thousands of farmers in the Upper Middle West joined with Jeremy Rifkin in a grassroots campaign that in 1990 succeeded in persuading the state legislatures of Wisconsin and Minnesota to enact temporary moratoriums on the use of the drug in the event it was approved. The moratoriums expired in 1991. In the same year, an unprecedented review by a panel of experts convened by the National Institutes of Health declared the drug safe.

In November 1993, the FDA got its turn. After extensive testing and review, the FDA approved Monsanto's BST. This represented the first time the government would allow food to be produced using a genetically engineered drug. The decision was made by Dr. David A. Kessler, the commissioner of food and drugs, who noted, "There is virtually no difference in milk from treated and untreated cows. In fact, it's not possible using current scientific techniques to tell them apart. We have looked carefully at every single question raised, and we are confident this product is safe for consumers, for cows and for the environment." Jeremy Rifkin was defiant in response. To quote: "We have said since 1986 that if the F.D.A. ever approved this drug that the final battleground would be the grocery stores, restaurants and convenience stores. This is the beginning of food politics in this country. If Monsanto succeeds with this product, they open the floodgates on the biotechnology age. If we succeed, it will send a chilling message through the agricultural business that people don't want genetically engineered foods."[41]

COX-2 Inhibitor

In 1999, Monsanto's Searle unit introduced Celebrex, the first in a new class of pain treatments for arthritis that offers the same benefit as existing pain relief medications for arthritis (such as aspirin), but with a sharp reduction in the harmful—and often dangerous—side effects of stomach irritation, ulcers, and internal bleeding. The product was the result of a fifteen-year quest by Philip Needleman to understand the role of cyclo-oxygenase (COX) enzymes in the regulation of prostaglandins, hormonelike fatty acids that are crucial to the body's maintenance.[42] As a researcher in the medical school at Washington University, Needleman studied complex chemicals that act as on-off switches in the body. Needleman and a colleague discovered a chemical inhibitor that affects prostaglandins. He learned more from an English researcher, who discovered that aspirin and aspirinlike drugs block the production of prostaglandins and thus reduce pain. But too much blocking is dangerous. Prostaglandins help regulate blood flow through the kidneys and aid in blood clotting. Without prostaglandins producing a protective coating, the stomach would eat itself because of the acid it secretes during digestion. As a result of this effect, patients taking drugs that block COX enzymes, such as aspirin, can suffer from serious stomach lesions. The resulting internal bleeding contributed to the death of some sixteen thousand people a year in the United States alone.

Needleman found that there are two COX enzymes: COX-1 handles the body's housekeeping; injury or disease triggers COX-2. Aspirin and other similar painkillers, referred to as nonsteroidal anti-inflammatory drugs (NSAIDs), block both enzymes—hence the side effects. Needleman wanted to block just COX-2. If that could be achieved, it would be possible to develop a pain medicine that lacked the side effect profile of NSAIDs. By the late 1980s, Needleman was convinced that this was possible, but he did not have the resources to do much about it. At this point he was also chair of the Department of Pharmacology at Washington University. In this role he had helped negotiate the original Monsanto–Washington University research agreement and now helped the company to allocate funds to Washington University researchers. The company was looking for a successor to Schneiderman and was favorably disposed towards hiring another academic. Needleman had the combination of scientific credentials and leadership skills that Monsanto was looking for, and he was also a known quantity to the company. Like Schneiderman before him, Needleman found the possibilities enticing: "I became enthralled with the idea of what it's like to have all of the people and resources to attack a problem."[43] In 1989, he joined the company as chief scientist.

At Monsanto's Searle division, Needleman found a company that had a long history of household-name products, but the new product pipeline seemed relatively bare to him, and he found the research effort to be diffused. Moreover, Needleman was aware of the costs and risks involved in bringing a new drug to market. Producing human pharmaceuticals is if anything a more expensive and risky business than producing transgenic crops. On average, it can take twelve years and cost $300 million to take a drug from the laboratory to the marketplace. To make matters worse, some 80 percent of products that enter clinical trials fail to make it to the market. A drug candidate must go through three sets of increasingly expensive clinical trials to test for safety, dosage, and efficacy (referred to as phase I, II, and III trials). It then faces a rigorous review at the hands of the FDA. On average, 70 percent of drug candidates that enter into phase I trials make it through to phase II, 47 percent entering phase II make it to phase III, and 82 percent entering phase III make it to the FDA, where 74 percent are approved.[44]

Realizing that Searle lacked the resources of its larger pharmaceutical industry rivals, Needleman developed a two-pronged strategy for Searle's R&D.[45] First, he directed research effort toward three main therapeutic areas: arthritis, oncology, and cardiovascular problems. By concentrating resources,

Searle could match or exceed the dollars spent per therapeutic area by larger rivals. In 1998, for example, Searle spent $280 million per therapeutic area, compared to $250 million at Pfizer and $200 million at Merck.[46] Second, he developed the discipline of killing off drug development projects early if they didn't survive what he characterized as "killer experiments."

As part of this strategy, Needleman "exploded the budget for COX-2." The search for a COX-2 inhibitor became the biggest project Searle had ever undertaken. For three years a team of thirty chemists and thirty biologists examined two thousand chemical compounds in the quest to find a COX-2 inhibitor. Urgency was added to the quest by the fact that Merck was also racing to develop a COX-2 inhibitor. When the Searle team found the compound that eventually became Celebrex, they submitted it to a "killer experiment" while it was being tested in a phase I trial as an arthritis treatment. The killer experiment was to discover whether the drug relieved severe tooth pain. Needleman reasoned that if the drug alleviated dental pain, it would also get arthritis. Celebrex survived the experiment, and the phase I and II trials suggested that the drug not only relieved pain, but also had none of the dangerous side effects associated with other treatments. After a 8,000-patient phase III trial produced favorable results, Searle filed with the FDA for approval to market the drug in August of 1998. Because the drug was the first COX-2 inhibitor to come up for review, the FDA granted Celebrex a propriety review, which meant that it would announce a decision within six months (normally, FDA approval can take as long as twelve months). Approval was granted in December 1998, and Celebrex was launched in mid January, 1999, the first in a new class of "superaspirin" painkillers.

Product Launches

Monsanto launched BST in February 1994. It was to be the first in a series of new product launches over the next five years that was to finally generate significant revenues for the company, almost a quarter of a century after Jaworski's skunkworks started Monsanto down the biotechnology road.

BST

By early 1999, BST, which Monsanto sold under the brand name Posilac, was being regularly injected in some 30 percent of dairy herds in the United States. Follow-up data showed that BST boosted milk production by about 10 percent on average. Robust demand for milk and milk products in the United States meant that the supply glut feared by dairy farmers did not materialize. Monsanto and the FDA continued to monitor BST for possible adverse effects. As of 1999, the FDA continued to state that milk from BST-treated cows posed no health risks. The American Medical Association, the World Health Organization, and the National Institutes of Health have issued similar findings. According to Monsanto, BST has enjoyed robust sales gains and in 1998 passed 100 million doses—at $5.80 per dose.[47]

Despite its success in the United States, however, Monsanto has still not been able to get the product approved for sale in either Canada or the European Union (EU). In early 1999, Health Canada, the Canadian version of the FDA, rejected Monsanto's application to market BST. While a review of existing data by Canadian scientists found no significant risk to human beings who ingest products from animals treated with BST, they noted that short-term tests on lab rats suggest that further study is needed. Health Canada concluded that there was sufficient concern to warrant not approving the drug.[48]

In 1989, the European Union imposed a moratorium on the use of animal growth hormones, or the sale of products produced by those hormones, on the grounds that European farmers were already producing too much milk and beef, and there was no need for greater production. The moratorium was extended in 1996 and 1997 and was due to expire at the end of 1999. In early 1999, the animal health and welfare committee of the EU concluded that BST should not be injected into cattle. Its report cited increased likelihood of mastitis, foot problems, and injection site reactions, which would also lead to welfare problems besides human health risks. In contrast, another EU committee, the committee for veterinary medicinal products, had ruled in 1998 that BST was perfectly safe.[49] More generally, public opinion in the EU seemed to be strongly against not just BST, but genetically modified foods in general. In the United States, the Clinton administration considered appealing to the World Trade Organization (WTO) on the grounds that the EU ban on BST represented an unfair restraint of trade that was at variance with WTO rules, of which the EU was a signatory.

Genetically Modified Crops

Following regulatory approval, in 1996 Monsanto introduced the first wave of its genetically modified crops: Roundup Ready Soybeans, Bollgard Insect Protected Cotton, and New Leaf Insect Protected Potatoes. Getting to this point had required sixteen years of research and, according to various estimates, cost between $300 million and $500 million in R&D spending. A series of other products were scheduled to follow over the next few years, including Roundup-ready canola, cotton, and oil seed rape, Yield Guard insect-protected corn, insect-protected tomatoes, corn rootworm–protected cotton, and Roundup Ready insect-protected soybeans (which adds Bt to Roundup Ready soybeans to provide both insect resistance and herbicide tolerance).

Although it was acknowledged as a technology leader and the first to bring a substantial number of products to market, Monsanto did not have the field entirely to itself. It faced the prospect of competition from several large companies, including DuPont and Swiss-based Novartis. DuPont had developed soybeans that tolerated the company's powerful Synchrony herbicide. Novartis had genetically altered corn seed so that it produced a protein that killed a common pest, the European corn borer. Both companies also had active research programs that promised to produce a range of genetically modified crops over the next decade.

Several smaller agricultural biotechnology companies had also been developing genetically altered crops, including DeKalb Genetics and Calgene. Calgene had introduced the first genetically engineered crop the previous year, a tomato that ripened more slowly and would stay fresh longer on supermarket shelves. Calgene was also developing a variety of soybean that was resistant to glyphosate, the active ingredient in Roundup. Similarly, DeKalb was developing corn seed that was resistant to glyphosate. Monsanto purchased Calgene in April 1997 for $240 million.

Distribution Agreements   The delivery vehicle for all of Monsanto's genetic improvements was seed. However, the company had not traditionally been a strong player in the seed business. Thus, to produce and deliver genetically modified seed to farmers, Monsanto needed to find a way to participate in the seed industry. Companies in this industry grow seeds and then distribute them to farmers. The issue was further complicated by the fact that the genes that Monsanto created provided only one specific trait to the farmer. It was crucial that Monsanto's genes be incorporated in the best germplasm available, necessitating that Monsanto find some way to cooperate with leading seed companies. In its 1998 annual report, the company explained the issue as follows:

> Seed is the delivery vehicle for biotechnology traits. Integrating seed into our life sciences system will accelerate the development of new traits and their introduction into new varieties. The combination of breeding and genomics will accelerate the development of new varieties with better quality. Germplasm, the basic genetic structure of a plant, determines the characteristics of that variety, such as yield potential or drought resistance. Germplasm is crucial to grower acceptance; our traits must be available in the varieties that growers prefer. While we license our technology for use in other companies' germplasm—and that's an integral part of our overall strategy—we need to be involved from the start in developing new varieties that include the best traits.

The seed industry itself was highly concentrated, with a small number of players dominating the market. Different seed companies also focused on different product and vertical segments of the seed market. For example, Delta & Pine Land had a 55 percent share of the U.S. market for cotton seeds, but a zero percent share of the market for corn seeds, and only 1 percent of the market for soybean seeds. In contrast, Pioneer Hi-Bred had a 44 percent share of the market for corn seeds, a 19 percent share of the soybean market, and no position in the market for cotton seeds. Other large seed companies included DeKalb Genetics, Northrup King (owned by Sandoz), Cargill, Ciba Seeds (owned by Ciba Geigy), Asgrow (owned by ELM of Mexico), and Holden's Foundation Seeds. DeKalb Genetics and Holden's were among the companies that focused on producing seeds, which they then sold to distributors.

Monsanto's initial approach was to explore a variety of relationships with seed companies. It decided to license its Roundup Ready Soybean technology to a broad range of seed companies. It also entered into an exclusive licensing agreement with Delta Pine & Land to produce and market Bollgard Cotton. In early 1996, the company acquired a minority position in DeKalb, which would produce Monsanto's Yield Guard corn. Independent of Monsanto, DeKalb Genetics had developed a strain of corn that was resistant to glyphosate. In September 1996 Monsanto acquired one of its Roundup Ready Soybean technology licensees, Asgrow, for $240 million. At the time of the acquisition, Asgrow ranked second among U.S. soybean seed companies, with an 18 percent market share for licensed and proprietary products. Monsanto stated that it would continue to license its technology to other soybean seed companies.

In January 1997, Monsanto acquired Holden's Foundation Seeds and Corn States Hybrid Service and Corn States International, which marketed Holden's products worldwide, for around $1 billion. Like DeKalb, Holden's specializes in developing corn germ plasma, the genetic foundation for seed corn varieties. It licenses the germ plasma to independent companies, which in turn create corn hybrids for commercial use. Although Holden's doesn't sell seeds directly to farmers, it supplies one-third of the corn seed parent stock planted in the United States every year. Along with DeKalb and leading corn seed seller Pioneer Hi-Bred International, Holden's owns one of the three largest pools of corn genetics in the world. It's stored in the form of millions of kernels in cooled storage rooms. According to Monsanto's CEO, Holden's would give Monsanto "an excellent delivery mechanism for our biotechnology innovations in corn. These acquisitions mean the latest technological advances will be made available to the greatest possible number of seed companies of all sizes with unparalleled speed."[50] Holden's had been the subject of acquisition rumors for months before the Monsanto takeover. The company reportedly got bids or inquiries from several multinational companies that were moving into agricultural biotechnology, including DuPont, Dow-Elanco, AgrEvo, and Novartis.[51]

The acquisition spree continued in 1998 when Monsanto purchased DeKalb Genetics outright for $2.3 billion, Delta Pine & Land for $1.3 billion, wheat seed company AgriPro, and the international seed business of Cargill. As a result of these acquisitions, Monsanto controlled an estimated 86 percent of the U.S. cotton seed market and nearly 50 percent of the corn and soybean seed markets.[52] To finance these acquisitions, Monsanto offered about $1.5 billion in common and preferred stock and took on $2.5

billion in long-term debt, adding significant leverage to its balance sheet.[53] Monsanto's view of the industry value chain in early 1999 and its position in it are summarized in Figure 1. The companies listed under the "seed" box in Figure 1 are biotechnology companies with which Monsanto had research alliances in 1999.

Monsanto was not alone is buying its way into the seed business. In May 1997, DuPont invested $1.7 billion to acquire a 20 percent stake in Pioneer High Breeds, the largest seed producer in the United States. Like Monsanto, DuPont made the purchase to speed up the process of commercializing its discoveries in agricultural biotechnology and bring genetically altered seeds to the market more rapidly. Many independent observers worried that in their race to become the Coke and Pepsi of agricultural biotechnology, Monsanto and DuPont were fast creating an oligopolistic situation in the seed business.[54] Their fears intensified in March 1999 when DuPont offered $7.7 billion to purchase all of Pioneer. If regulators approve the DuPont-Pioneer deal, three companies—DuPont, Monsanto, and Novartis—will control two-thirds of the North American seed corn market, 45 percent of the soybean seed market, and 85 percent of the U.S. cotton seed market.[55]

Pricing Strategy   A big issue for Monsanto was how to price genetically altered seeds to capture the value implied by its proprietary position and its years of heavy investment in R&D. With regard to Bollgard cotton, which was distributed by Delta Pine & Land, Monsanto decided to price the seed at market rates but to tack on a separate technology fee of $32 per acre that the farmers had to pay directly to Monsanto. The pricing strategy presented farmers with something of a gamble; would it cost more to fight pests using traditional methods, or should they pay the fee to Monsanto? And would the cotton survive if they didn't use Bollgard? Depending on the year, most farmers estimate that they spend anywhere from $20 to $100 per acre spraying against pests. While some of this cost is saved if they plant Bollgard cotton, they might still have to use some sprays to fight other pests.[56]

According to Monsanto, in its first full year, 1996, more than 5,700 U.S. farmers purchased Bollgard cotton and planted 1.8 million acres, or 13 percent of the total cotton acres in the United States. Approximately 60 percent of Bollgard users were able to

FIGURE 1

The Value Chain for
Transgenic Crops

*Pending closure
Source: Monsanto Investment
Conference, May 3, 1999.

Global Platform Spans Value Chain

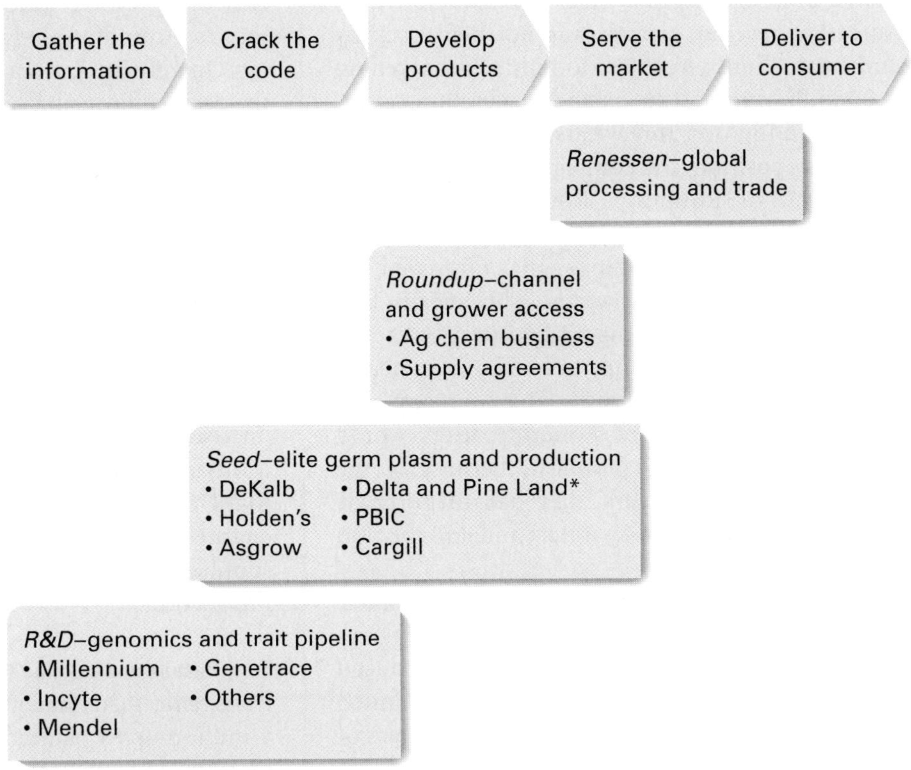

Gather the information → Crack the code → Develop products → Serve the market → Deliver to consumer

Renessen–global processing and trade

Roundup–channel and grower access
• Ag chem business
• Supply agreements

Seed–elite germ plasm and production
• DeKalb • Delta and Pine Land*
• Holden's • PBIC
• Asgrow • Cargill

R&D–genomics and trait pipeline
• Millennium • Genetrace
• Incyte • Others
• Mendel

totally eliminate insecticides, saving the average grower $33 per acre on land planted with Bollgard. Crop yields from fields planted with Bt cotton increased by 8 to 10 percent. Four out of five users said they were either satisfied or very satisfied with the cotton's overall performance. Only 2 percent said that they would not use it again.[57]

With regard to Roundup-ready soybeans, Monsanto decided to charge a technology fee of $5 per 50-pound bag of seed. A 50-pound bag of soybean seeds was selling for between $13 and $15 in 1996. Roundup-ready soybeans cost between $18 and $20 per bag, depending on the seed company (Monsanto did not control the retail price; distributors did). Monsanto also required farmers to sign an agreement promising not to reuse the patented seed—which annoyed many farmers who were in the habit of doing so. The farmers also had to agree to use Roundup, and not any competing glyphosate-based herbicide. The contract also allowed Monsanto to visit their farms for three years to make sure they kept their promise. In response to numerous complaints, Monsanto later dropped the requirement that farmers allow the com-

pany to inspect their operations, but it raised the technology fee to $6.50 per bag in 1998.[58]

Monsanto's marketing pitch for Roundup-ready soybeans emphasized two things. First, the company extolled the virtues of being able to use the environmentally friendly broad-spectrum Roundup herbicide to control weeds *after* crops began to sprout, rather than more expensive crop-specific herbicides. The company estimated that this would save farmers $12 to $16 per acre in reduced weed control costs, which of course had to be offset against the $5 technology fee. Second, Monsanto emphasized that if farmers made greater use of Roundup, they could reduce their use of traditional deep tillage weed control methods. This would have a long-term benefit in terms of reduced soil erosion. Put differently, it would facilitate the adoption of conservation tillage methods.

Roundup Strategy If Monsanto's push into Roundup ready crops generated the sales that the company hoped for, the result would be a substantial surge in demand for Roundup that should expand sales past the expiration of its U.S. patent on glyphosate in

September 2000. By 1996, Roundup was generating over $1 billion in annual sales for Monsanto. To ensure that revenue growth was not held back by volume constraints, in 1996 Monsanto embarked on a $200 million project to expand production capacity for Roundup over three years. To help protect its proprietary position, the company developed a new formulation of Roundup, Roundup Ultra, and applied for a patent on Ultra. Roundup Ultra contained surfactants and additives that improved the herbicide's absorption by weeds. This means that Ultra has less chance of being washed away by rain—it is absorbed by weeds in one to two hours, whereas basic Roundup takes six hours. The company estimated that 90 percent of Roundup users would switch to Ultra by 1997, primarily because of the convenience (prior to Ultra, they had to purchase surfactants and additives separately and add them to Roundup).[59]

At the same time, Monsanto continued a move begun ten years previously to price Roundup aggressively. Between 1992 and 1998, Monsanto reduced the price of Roundup by 9 percent in the United States market. This, coupled with the tie-in to sales of Monsanto's genetically altered crops, produced a 201 percent increase in the volume of Roundup sales. Even larger volume increases were observed in other nations, where Monsanto's patent had already expired. In Brazil, for example, Monsanto cut the price of Roundup by 45 percent between 1992 and 1998 and was rewarded by a 685 percent surge in volume. In Canada, a 34 percent reduction in price over the same time period led to a 310 percent increase in Roundup volume.[60]

In 1998 and 1999, Monsanto took additional steps to deal with the increased threat of competition after the U.S. patent on glyphosate expired. The catalyst was an attempt by Zeneca to test its own brand of glyphosate-based herbicide, Touchdown, on Monsanto's Roundup-ready soybeans. Zeneca already sold Touchdown outside of the United States and was preparing to sell in the United States after September 2000. In mid 1998, Monsanto sued Zeneca, saying it had illegally acquired Roundup-ready soybean seed for testing Touchdown. The British company responded by suing Monsanto, charging that the company's requirement that farmers use its brand of glyphosate on Roundup-ready crops was anticompetitive. In March 1999 the companies dropped their lawsuits against each other. Monsanto agreed to allow Zeneca to use its Touchdown on seeds using Monsanto's Roundup-ready herbicide-tolerant technology. In return, Zeneca agreed to pay Monsanto an unspecified licensing fee.[61]

While the lawsuits were still pending, Monsanto entered into a number of separate agreements to sell glyphosate to five other agricultural chemical companies, including Dow Chemicals and Novartis. Under the terms of these agreements, which extended for five years and could be renewed thereafter, Monsanto also agreed to allow U.S. farmers to use glyphosate herbicides from these companies on Roundup-ready cotton and soybeans in 2000, and on corn in 2001. Commenting on the Dow deal, a Monsanto spokesman noted, "We were concerned that Dow would go and build glyphosate plants and engage in a price war. By having Monsanto provide supplies of glyphosate, Dow will have better costs of production."[62]

Early Results and Looking Ahead   Since 1996, the use of transgenic seeds has increased exponentially, from 4 million acres planted in 1996 to 70 million acres in 1998. In 1997, sales of transgenic crops totaled $4 billion. The worldwide market was projected to double by 2002. In 1996, only 1 million acres of Monsanto's Roundup-ready soybeans were planted. In 1998, around half of the United States's 75-million-acre soybean crop would be Roundup-ready. If growth continued, in 1999 Monsanto would earn almost $300 million in royalties from sales of soybean seeds alone. Bt cotton was also expected to be used on more than half of the U.S. cotton acreage planted in 1999. Moreover, adoption was also occurring quickly overseas. China used Monsanto's Bt cotton for about a quarter of its planting in 1999. Of the nearly 70 million acres planted with genetically modified crops worldwide in 1998, Monsanto varieties accounted for over 70 percent. Monsanto claims that they could have sold a lot more if they had had the seed (see Figure 2 for details).[63]

Human Pharmaceuticals

During the 1990s Monsanto's Searle unit launched a number of products, culminating in the launch of Celebrex, the COX-2 inhibitor, in early 1999. The first of these, Ambien, a treatment for insomnia, was introduced in 1993 and by 1998 was generating over $450 million in annual revenues. This was followed by Daypro, a once-a-day NSAID treatment for osteoarthritis and rheumatoid arthritis that generated annual sales of $308 million in 1998, and Arthrotec, another NSAID drug that also has ulcer prevention properties, which generated revenues of $346 million in 1998. Revenues from all three of these drugs, however, could well be dwarfed by sales of Celebrex.[64]

Aware that Merck's competing COX-2 inhibitor, Vioxx, would probably be on the market by mid 1999, Searle entered into a comarketing agreement with Pfizer. The goal was to leverage the reach of Pfizer's large sales force, reckoned by many to be among the best in the industry. To jump-start market adoption, Searle and Pfizer sent 45,000 "patient starter kits" to physicians and pharmacies. In each free kit there were ten bottles, each containing a twenty-five-day supply of Celebrex. Using a sophisticated database, Searle gave its samples to doctors who most often prescribe arthritis-related painkillers (NSAIDs)—rheumatologists, orthopedic surgeons, and podiatrists. Searle also aimed the kits at physicians in big medical practices who prescribe large amounts of NSAIDs.[65]

As might be expected, the marketing pitch emphasized that Celebrex offers the same pain relief as traditional NSAIDs but causes fewer side effects, such as intestinal bleeding and ulcers. Pricing was perhaps the most difficult issue. Searle and Pfizer tested some seven hundred different pricing models before settling on a cost to consumers of about $2.42 per day. This was significantly more than generic NSAIDs, which can cost as little as 10 cents per day, but less than most analysts had initially expected. In part, the lower price was a concession to managed care organizations that were trying to get control of soaring prescription costs. Following a formal launch meeting of February 22, hundreds of sales representatives from both companies fanned out to doctors' offices in what was one of the most intense marketing efforts ever. The aim was to acquaint the nation's 150,000 doctors with the virtues of Celebrex within six months. This was to be followed by a consumer advertising blitz. The cost of this effort was forecasted to exceed $100 million.[66]

The initial results from this launch effort were nothing short of spectacular. By April, Searle was reporting that it had already directly contacted 70 percent of the nation's doctors. According to independent research data, two months after the launch some 100 percent of rheumatologists surveyed were aware of the drug and 98 percent had prescribed it. This compared with averages of 85 percent and 54 percent for new arthritis treatments.[67] It was soon apparent that Celebrex was experiencing the second fastest sales ramp-up of any drug product launch in U.S. history, outpaced only by sales of

FIGURE 2

Major Players in the Agricultural Seed and Chemical Industry: Projected 1999 Revenues

Source: Monsanto Investment Conference, May 3 1999.

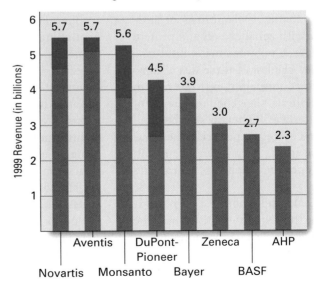

Agriculture Industry Leaders

Pfizer's male impotence drug, Viagra. Two months after the launch, analysts predicted first-year sales in excess of $550 million and sales of $3 billion annually by 2002. To put this in context, in 1998 Monsanto's total sales were $8.65 billion, and those of its Searle unit $2.42 billion.

Looking Ahead

In September 1997, Monsanto confirmed its commitment to life sciences when it spun off its commodity chemical businesses to stockholders as an independent unit with sales of close to $3 billion. What remained of Monsanto was focused on agricultural and human life sciences. In both areas, the company had ambitious long-term plans.

Agriculture

The success of the first wave of Monsanto's transgenic crops was based on the benefits farmers gained in the form of improved yield and economies in the use of inputs. Although these products offered no direct benefits to consumers, there was an indirect benefit from the increase in productivity; consumers needed to spend less of their disposable incomes on food. The second wave of transgenic crops, which Monsanto and others were set to introduce in the 1999–2004 time period, offered quality and nutrition traits; in other words, valued-added outputs. Examples include oilseed rape with high lauric, stearate, oleic, and GLA contents (all nutritionally beneficial); soybeans containing proteins that reduce cholesterol or have a medical value in combating osteoporosis or hormonal cancer; maize with enhanced oil and protein contents; and high-starch potatoes that would take up less fat when fried. The last of these was a Monsanto product scheduled for market introduction in 2000. Monsanto had altered the genetic sequence of the potatoes to make them higher in starches and lower in water. When cut into french fries, the potatoes absorbed less fat in the deep fryer. The result: the fries tasted the same, but they had fewer calories and a better texture.[68]

A third wave of genetically modified crop products further down the pipeline could best be described as "plants as factories." Examples under development at Monsanto, DuPont, and Novartus included using tobacco plants to produce albumin and growth hormones, maize to produce humanized

monoclonal antibodies for treating diseases, and transgenic oilseed rape for producing modified fatty acids. Rape could also be modified to produce high levels of beta carotene, much greater than the amounts produced in crops such as carrots. This could be significant for meeting dietary deficiencies in some developing countries. There is also research under way to engineer plants that produce fibers, polymers, or intermediaries that otherwise could come from petrochemicals.

To accelerate the process of developing new transgenic crop varieties, in 1997 Monsanto entered into an alliance with Millenium, a biotechnology firm with expertise in screening genes to identify the causes of diseases—an area known as genomics. The terms of the deal called for Monsanto to pay Millenium $118 million over five years for *exclusive* access to Millennium's gene research in agriculture. In addition, Monsanto stated that it would start a gene research unit in Cambridge, Millenium's base, which would employ up to 150 scientists by the end of 1998. Millennium would hire most of the staff. According to a Monsanto spokesman, "By greatly increasing the speed and precision with which we can analyze new product leads, this agreement will help us rapidly bring future Monsanto life sciences products to market."[69] The Millennium announcement came one day after Monsanto said it was extending an existing collaboration with another genomics firm, Incyte Pharmaceutical, also in agricultural genetics.

Pharmaceuticals

In pharmaceuticals, Monsanto set itself the goal of continuing to grow its product portfolio and development pipeline in arthritis, oncology, and cardiovascular diseases by adding one new chemical or biological entity to the pipeline every year (on average) and one new "technology platform" every three years. A technology *platform* refers to the notion of adding multiple indications for the same drug or using an understanding of a basic biological process to develop a family of drugs.

The concept of a technology platform can best be understood by considering how Monsanto hoped to exploit its technology platform in COX-2 inhibitors (see Figure 3). COX-2 enzyme expression is suspected of playing a role in Alzheimer's and some cancers, such as colon cancer (FAP). This raises the possibility that a COX-2 inhibitor, such as Celebrex, might be a useful treatment for these diseases. Searle conducted phase III trials to explore the use of Celebrex in treating FAP, had data from a phase II trial using Celebrex to treat Alzheimer patients, and on the basis of this intended to move forward with a phase III Alzheimer trial. Searle was also looking at producing different COX-2 inhibitors, such as deracoxib for the veterinary market or valdecoxib, a second-generation COX-2 inhibitor.

The Concerns of Analysts

While impressed by Monsanto's plans, analysts worried that the company lacked the resources required to grow its business given its debt load. Of particular concern was the pharmaceutical area, where Monsanto was still a small player relative to industry lead-

ers. With a smaller research budget and sales force presence, there were fears that the Searle company would not be able to fully exploit and extend its strong product pipeline.

In mid 1998, the company seemed to have found a solution to these issues when it announced a merger with American Home Products (AHP). AHP had a world-class pharmaceutical sales force and a strong financial position, but lacked Monsanto's deep product pipeline. However, the merger talks collapsed in October 1998, reportedly because of clashes between the top management of both companies over layoffs and attitudes toward R&D spending and risk taking. In the aftermath of the collapse, Monsanto's management vowed to go it alone.[70]

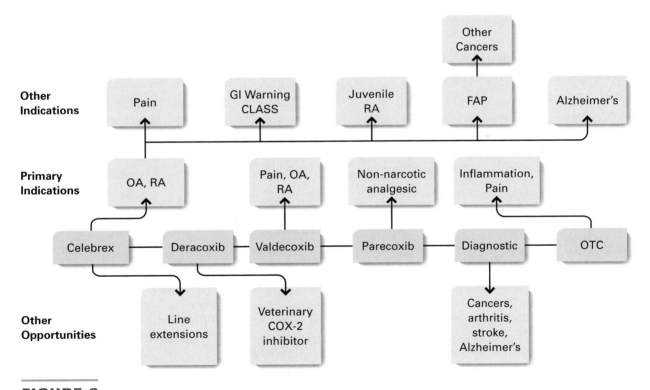

FIGURE 3

COX-2 Inhibitor Technology Platform

Source: Monsanto.

Appendix 1: Monsanto's Financial Position, 1996–1998

Monsanto Company and Subsidiaries Statement of Consolidated Income
(dollars in millions, except per share), Unaudited

	Three Months Ended December 31,		Twelve Months Ended December 31,	
	1998	1997	1998	1997
Net sales	$ 2,148	$ 1,820	$ 8,648	$ 7,514
Costs, expenses and other				
Cost of goods sold	971	749	3,593	3,091
Selling, general and administrative expenses	675	557	2,421	2,023
Technological expenses	391	326	1,358	1,044
Acquired in-process research and development	213	75	402	684
Amortization of intangible assets	281	59	487	173
Restructuring and other special charges—net	307		272	
Interest expense	98	59	312	170
Interest income	(11)	(9)	(50)	(45)
Other expense—net	69	7	96	8
Income (loss) from continuing operations before taxes	(846)	(3)	(243)	366
Income taxes	(243)	(8)	7	72
Income (loss) from continuing operations	(603)	5	(250)	294
Income from discontinued operations				176
Net income (loss)	$ (603)	$ 5	$ (250)	$ 470
Basic earnings / (loss) per share				
Continuing operations	$ (1.00)	$ 0.01	$ (0.41)	$ 0.50
Discontinued operations				0.30
Total	$ (1.00)	$ 0.01	$ (0.41)	$ 0.80
Diluted earnings / (loss) per share				
Continuing operations	$ (1.00)	$ 0.01	$ (0.41)	$ 0.48
Discontinued operations				0.29
Total	$ (1.00)	$ 0.01	$ (0.41)	$ 0.77
Weighted average common shares—basic (in millions)			603.5	590.2
Weighted average common shares—diluted (in millions)			603.5	610.5
Earnings before interest and tax expense (EBIT)	$ (748)	$ 56	$ 69	$ 536

Monsanto Companies and Subsidiaries Segment Data (dollars in millions), Unaudited

	EBITDA *			
	Three Months		Twelve Months	
	1998	1997	1998	1997
Segment				
Agricultural products	$ 35	$ (11)	$ 1,092	$ 939
Nutrition and Consumer products	88	109	405	440
Pharmaceuticals	222	197	451	422
Corporate and other	(25)	(26)	(183)	(94)
Total	$ 320	$ 269	$ 1,765	$1,707

* EBITDA (earnings before interest expense, taxes, depreciation and amortization excluding unusuals) is EBIT excluding depreciation, amortization, and the effects of unusual items.

Appendix 1: Monsanto's Financial Position, 1996–1998 *(continued)*

Monsanto Company and Subsidiaries Statement of Consolidated Financial Position
(dollars in millions), Unaudited

	Dec. 31, 1998	Dec. 31, 1997
Assets		
Current assets		
Cash and cash equivalents	$ 89	$ 134
Trade receivables	2,404	1,823
Prepaid assets and other Receivables	1,141	692
Deferred income tax benefit	567	243
Inventories	2,004	1,374
Total current assets	6,205	4,266
Net property, plant and equipment	3,254	2,400
Intangible assets	6,047	2,837
Investment and other assets	1,233	1,271
Total assets	$16,739	$10,774
Liabilities and Shareowners' Equity		
Current liabilities		
Payables and accruals	$ 2,998	$ 1,813
Short-term debt	1,069	1,726
Total current liabilities	4,067	3,539
Long-term debt	6,259	1,979
Postretirement liabilities	871	735
Other liabilities	536	417
Shareowners' equity	5,006	4,104
Total liabilities and shareowners' equity	$16,739	$10,774
Working capital	$ 2,138	$ 727
Debt to capital ratio	59%	47%

ENDNOTES

1. J. Vorman, "China Seen Swiftly Adopting Transgenic Cotton," *Reuters*, April 26, 1999.
2. Monsanto, "In the Pipeline," www.monsanto.com.
3. J. Rifkin, "Perils of Unnatural Science," *Financial Times*, June 20, 1998, p. 9.
4. C. Blackledge, "Benefits That Go Against the Grain," *Financial Times*, March 15, 1999, p. 4.
5. R. J. Mahoney, "The Player's Point of View," *Institutional Investor*, June 1989, p. 23.
6. D. Leonard Barton and G. Pisano, "Monsanto's March Into Biotechnology," Harvard Business School Case 9-690-009.
7. K. Schneider, "Betting the Farm on Biotechnology," *New York Times*, June 10, 1990, section 3, part 2, p. 26.
8. R. Steyer, "BST Is Monsanto's Splice of Life," *St. Louis Post-Dispatch*, April 25, 1994, p. 12.
9. K. Drlica, *Understanding DNA and Gene Cloning* (New York: Wiley, 1997).
10. Company history summarized at www.gene.com.
11. Schneider, "Betting the Farm."
12. Ibid.
13. "Offer of Top R&D Post Lured Him Off Campus," *Chemical Week*, January 23, 1980, p. 48.
14. "The Reworking of Monsanto," *Chemical Week*, January 12, 1983, p. 42.
15. K. Schneider, "Betting the Farm."
16. Steyer, "BST."
17. E. B. Fiske, "Monsanto Research Pact Aims to Cut Academic Controversy," *New York Times*, June 4, 1982, p. 21A; D. Sanger, "Corporate Links Worry Scholars," *New York Times*, October 17, 1982, Late City Final Edition, section 3, p. 4.
18. Sanger, "Corporate Links."
19. Fiske, "Monsanto Research Pact."
20. B. J. Spalding, "Monsanto's Bid for the Lead in Biotechnology," *Chemical Week*, June 11, 1986, p. 41.
21. Ibid.
22. "Reworking of Monsanto."
23. "Monsanto-Searle: A Biotech Coupling," *Chemical Engineering*, August 19, 1985, p. 26.
24. J. E. Ellis, and E. K. Spragius, "Why Monsanto Is Bucking the Odds," *Business Week*, August 5, 1985, p. 76.
25. "Monsanto-Searle."
26. Ibid.
27. Spalding, "Monsanto's Bid."
28. Ibid.
29. Ibid.
30. K. Schneider, "Biotech's Stalled Revolution," *New York Times*, November 16, 1986, section 6, p. 43.
31. Ibid.
32. Ibid.
33. Schneider, "Betting the Farm."
34. C. S. Gasser and R. T. Fraley, "Genetically Engineering Plants for Crop Improvement," *Science*, June 16, 1989, vol. 244, no. 4910, p. 1293.
35. "Plant-Genetics Advance: Antibiotic-Resistant Petunias," *Popular Science*, April 1983, vol. 222, p. 19.
36. Gasser and Fraley, "Genetically Engineering Plants."
37. Schneider, "Betting the Farm."
38. Ibid.
39. B. J. Feder, "Out of the Lab, a Revolution on the Farm," *New York Times*, March 3, 1996, p. 3.
40. Steyer, "BST."
41. K. Schneider, "U.S. Approves Use of Drug to Raise Milk Production," *New York Times*, November 6, 1993, p. 1.
42. R. Steyer, "Discovery of Arthritis Drug Began in WU Lab." *St. Louis Post-Dispatch*, April 6, 1998, p. A1.
43. Ibid.
44. These figures come from the FDA's own database and were compiled by Analysis Group Economics, a drug industry consulting firm.
45. T. M. Burton, "A Pharmaceutical Plumb in Monsanto's Basket," *Wall Street Journal*, June 2, 1998, p. B1.
46. Figures come from Monsanto's May 3, 1999, presentation to securities analysts, posted at www.monsanto.com.
47. M. Groves, "Canada Rejects Hormone That Boosts Cow's Milk Output," *Los Angeles Times*, January 15, 1999, p. C1.
48. Ibid.
49. K. O'Sullivan, "EU Scientific Committee Casts Doubt on Safety of Injected Hormone Used to Boost Milk Yield," *Irish Times*, March 17, 1999, p. 2.
50. J. Swiatek, "Business of Seeds Changing in Big Ways," *Indianapolis Star*, January 12, 1997, p. E1.
51. R. Steyer, "Monsanto Buys Seed Corn Firm," *St. Louis Post-Dispatch*, January 7, 1977, p. C6.
52. P. Downs, "Badseed; Company Has Near Monopoly on the Seed Industry," *The Progressive*, February, 1999, vol. 63, no. 2, p. 36.
53. T. M. Burton, "Monsanto's Cost Cutting Steps to Raise Cash for Seed Company Acquisitions," *Wall Street Journal*, November 12, 1998, p. A4.
54. S. Kilman and S. Warren, "Old Rivals Fight for New Turf Biotechnology Crops," *Wall Street Journal*, May 27, 1998, p. A4.
55. R. Steyer, "DuPont's Purchase of Pioneer Validates Big Bet Monsanto Made on Seed Companies," *St. Louis Post-Dispatch*, March 21, 1999, p. E1.
56. S. J. Willis, "Farmers Torn over Use of Pest Fighter," *Arizona Business Gazette*, May 29, 1997, p. 16.
57. Monsanto, Bollgard Cotton Update, March 1997.
58. R. Steyer, "Super Soybean," *St. Louis Post-Dispatch*, February 25, 1996, p. E1.
59. R. Steyer, "Monsanto Reports Success for New Roundup," *St. Louis Post-Dispatch*, December 22, 1996, p. 1E.
60. Figures come from Monsanto's May 3, 1999, presentation to securities analysts, posted at www.monsanto.com.
61. R. Steyer, "Monsanto, British Firm End War over Herbicides," St. Louis Post-Dispatch, March 19, 1999, p. C9.
62. R. Steyer, "Monsanto Will License Roundup Rights to Dow," *St. Louis Post-Dispatch*, January 20, 1999, p. C1.
63. R. F. Service, "Chemical Industry Rushes Toward Greener Pastures," *Science*, October 23, 1998, vol. 282, p. 608; J. Vorman, "China Seen Swiftly Adopting Transgenic Cotton," *Reuters*, April 26, 1999.
64. Data from Monsanto's May 3, 1999, presentation to securities analysts, posted at www.monsanto.com.
65. "Safe Painkiller Set to Launch Pharmaceuticals World War," *Financial Times*, February 5, 1999, p. 26.
66. A. Barrett and R. A. Melcher, "Why Searle Is Feeling No Pain," *Business Week*, February 15, 1999, p. 36.
67. Data from Monsanto's May 3, 1999, presentation to securities analysts, posted at www.monsanto.com.
68. R. Lenzner and B. Upbin, "Monsanto v Malthus," *Forbes*, March 10, 1997, pp. 58–60.
69. R. Rosenberg, "Millennium Inks Pact Worth as Much as $218 m," *Boston Globe*, October 29, 1997, p. C2.
70. T. M. Burton and E. Tanouye, "Another Drug Industry Megamerger Goes Bust," *Wall Street Journal*, October 14, 1998, p. B1.

Monsanto (B): Merger and Rebirth

36

This case was prepared by Charles W. L. Hill, the University of Washington.

Introduction

On December 20, 1999, the boards of Pharmacia and Monsanto formally approved a merger between the two enterprises, valued at $27 billion. For Pharmacia's CEO, Fred Hassan, the merger represented the latest and most dramatic move in his quest to transform Pharmacia from a perennial "also ran" into one of the leading growth companies in the pharmaceutical industry. Hassan had joined Pharmacia in 1997 after holding a high-ranking position at rival American Home Products. In the two and a half years since he had become CEO, Hassan had received accolades from Wall Street for reducing costs at Pharmacia and rationalizing the company's product pipeline. But Hassan knew that if the company was to grow, it needed some blockbuster drugs. There were not enough of those in Pharmacia's product development pipeline, but Monsanto's Searle unit had several, including its recently approved COX-2 inhibitor, Celebrex.[1]

As for Monsanto and its CEO, Robert Shapiro, the merger came at the end of a tough year during which the value of the company's stock was cut in half. What ailed Monsanto was a combination of high debt and environmental protests against its genetically modified seeds. In 1997 and 1998, Monsanto built up some $6 billion in debt as it acquired six seed companies. The debt would not have mattered had

demand for Monsanto's genetically modified seeds continued to grow as forecasted, but a rising wave of environmental protests scuttled growth projections. Responding to continent-wide protests against genetically modified foodstuffs, in 1998 the European Union placed a moratorium on the approval of any more genetically engineered crops. At the same time, many large European food companies bowed to public opinion and announced that they would not use any genetically modified ingredients in their foods.[2]

For Monsanto, which had pioneered the use of biotechnology to produce genetically modified seeds, this was a major setback. Monsanto had naively believed that environmentalists would embrace its "feed the world" vision in which it promised to use the wonders of biotechnology to produce "environmentally friendly" crops that did not need to be treated so often with harmful chemical pesticides and would produce better yields. Instead, environmentalists fretted about the unknown risks of growing and consuming genetically modified food. They argued that Monsanto's genetically modified seed corn, which was engineered to produce natural herbicides, would lead to the evolution of "superbugs" that would soon be immune to the natural herbicides. They expressed fears that genetically modified foodstuffs could have yet unknown adverse consequences on human health, including a rise in cancers. They argued that the introduction of genetically modified crops might lead to "genetic pollution," with engineered traits that seem to be desirable in crops producing

This case is intended to be used as a basis for class discussion rather than as an illustration of either effective or ineffective handling of the situation. Reprinted by permission of Charles W. L. Hill.

unanticipated harmful side effects. When a species of rare and harmless butterfly was apparently killed by the herbicide that Monsanto had engineered into some of its seed corn, the environmentalists thought they had found the smoking gun.

Monsanto asserted that these fears were unfounded. The company produced reams of scientific data to back up its position, but in the court of public opinion this received short shift. While the American consumer apparently cared little about all of this, things got worse for Monsanto when some American food companies that exported products to Europe, such as Gerber and Archer Daniels Mills (ADM), also began to reduce their demand for genetically modified crops. While agreeing with Monsanto that there was no evidence that genetically modified crops produced any harmful effects, they were apparently mindful of the need to cater to public opinion. This raised the specter that American farmers, who had been among the most enthusiastic adopters of Monsanto's genetically altered food stuffs, would reduce their demand for the seeds too; this would effectively blow a hole right through the heart of Monsanto's growth assumptions.[3]

Gains from the Merger

Hassan's justification for the merger was straightforward. Pharmacia was too small a player to compete effectively in the global pharmaceutical industry. It needed the scale of a larger firm to support the R&D, marketing, and sales expenses required to discover, produce, and market new pharmaceuticals. It also needed a pipeline of promising drugs under development, and Monsanto's Searle unit had one of the best in the industry. As for Monsanto, it too needed a better sales and marketing presence to leverage its drug pipeline. Shapiro had realized this for some time. In 1998 he had unsuccessfully pursued a merger proposal with American Home Products that would have achieved this goal. According to unofficial company sources, that merger was scuttled by personality clashes between Shapiro and the CEO of American Home Products. This did not seem to be a problem this time around. Hassan would be the CEO of the new company and Shapiro would be the chairman.

Hassan told investors that the new Pharmacia would have pharmaceutical sales of $9 billion, a strong development pipeline, a $2 billion R&D budget, and the potential to achieve a 20 percent annual

growth rate in pharmaceuticals. He also believed that some $600 million in annual cost savings could be realized by eliminating duplication between the two businesses. As for Monsanto's agricultural biotechnology business, Hassan agreed that this had problems, although he also stated that in the long run he thought that the world would come round to Monsanto's view. Monsanto, he said, was simply five to ten years ahead of its time.

Still, recognizing the drag on Pharmacia that Monsanto's agriculture business might produce, he announced that this part of Monsanto would be spun out of the merged company within a year. The plan was to initially offer about 20 percent of the agricultural company for sale to the public and to spin out the remainder two years later. This would leave two companies, a pure-play pharmaceutical enterprise that combined the old Pharmacia and Monsanto's Searle unit, and a pure-play agricultural biotechnology unit that would trade under the Monsanto name.

The New Monsanto

In preparation for the partial spinoff of Monsanto from the new Pharmacia, in mid 2000 the Monsanto unit sold off its NutraSweet and Equal artificial sweetener businesses for $1.7 billion, using the proceeds to pay down some of Monsanto's debt load. In October 2000, Pharmacia sold 14 percent of Monsanto via an initial public offering, raising some $700 million in the process. This would be used to further pay down Monsanto's debt. Pharmacia planned to spin off the remainder of Monsanto's agricultural unit in late 2002, while holding onto the Searle unit.[4]

The new Monsanto is the second largest seed company in the world and the third largest agrochemical company, and it remains the leader in genetically engineered seed corn. Despite the debate over genetically modified foods, sales of food made from genetically modified crops material surged from some $4 billion in 1997 to $19 billion in 1999.[5] Monsanto is a major beneficiary of this shift. Going forward, Monsanto plans to reduce operating costs by $225 million per annum by integrating the operations of six seed companies bought during the 1997–1998 period. Monsanto has also scaled back its R&D spending on agricultural biotechnology from $700 million to $600 million and refocused attention on a limited number of major areas such as corn, wheat, cotton, and soybeans, where returns promise to be largest, while dropping potatoes, vegetables, and other crops.

Clearly, the new Monsanto faces significant challenges going forward. One of the biggest is to convince a skeptical public and Wall Street that agricultural biotechnology is not a dead end. Although genetically modified seeds have been widely accepted in the United States, Canada, and Argentina, serious problems are evident elsewhere. The situation in Europe is a difficult one for Monsanto, but at least it was contained to that region in 1998 and 1999. The task became harder in late 2000 when a court in Brazil, a key developing market for Monsanto and one of the world's largest agricultural producers, blocked the sale of Monsanto's genetically altered soybeans. The court was ruling on a suit filed by environmental activists in Brazil. Although Monsanto may still ultimately win the case on appeal, the development is a serious one. Licensing genetically modified soybean seeds to Brazil was projected to add at least $1 billion to Monsanto's annual revenues. That would have been just the beginning, since Monsanto has plans to introduce at least another ten genetically engineered crops into Brazil, which is already the company's largest export market. It is also worth noting that a range of countries, including Australia and Japan, have recently announced plans to regulate the sale of genetically modified foodstuffs. Moreover, some U.S. farmers are reportedly having second thoughts about genetically modified crops, primarily because the export market for such crops is now limited by actions taken in Europe and elsewhere.

Monsanto's other major problem is the expiration in late 2000 of its patent on Roundup, its single biggest product, with global sales of over $3.2 billion. Sales of Roundup have been robust in recent years, growing at 20 percent per annum, thanks in large part to the tie-in with Roundup-ready seeds. However, the combination of a backlash against genetically modified seeds, a slowing farm economy, and the emergence of close substitutes for Roundup seemed likely to reduce the growth rate for Roundup sales going forward to closer to 5 percent.[6]

The First Year

Monsanto's first year as an independent unit was better than many expected. The stock rose some 75 percent since Pharamacia listed the company. Net profits increased 8 percent in 2001, and were projected to increase another 5 percent in 2002. While hardly spectacular, this increase was achieved against the background of a weak economy.

More importantly for the long run, there were signs that things were beginning to turn in Monsanto's favor. A turning point seemed to come in mid 2001, when StarLink, a Monsanto genetically modified corn approved only for animal feed, found its way into taco shells and other U.S. foods. Critics expected the incident to become a rallying cry in the United States against genetically modified foodstuffs, but the American consumer just shrugged and went on eating tacos. This was followed by a report from the United Nations that came out in support of biotechnology crops, stressing the benefits for the 800 million people worldwide who suffer from malnutrition. In October, the Environmental Protection Agency in the United States approved the sale of Monsanto's genetically modified corn seed for another seven years after finding that it posed no risk to humans or animals. Perhaps even more importantly, in the 2001 growing season U.S. farmers planted 11 percent more genetically modified seeds from Monsanto than in 2000. Biotech soybean planting rose 16 percent, and some 63 percent of the total U.S. soybean crop came from biotech seeds. Despite progress, problems still remain. Monsanto still cannot market its biotech soybean seeds in Brazil, the second largest soybean producer in the world behind the United States. Moreover, in Europe resistance to genetically modified foodstuffs remains strong, with no new biotech seeds or food stuffs having received regulatory approval since 1998.[7]

As for Roundup, as expected, sales started to fall in 2001 and 2002 as the expiration of patent protection resulted in greater competition and lower prices. Despite this, in the first quarter of 2002 Monsanto's sales grew 7 percent as a 17 percent increase in sales of Monsanto's seeds offset a fall in Roundup revenues. Going forward, the company's CEO, Hendrik Verfaillie, has stated that Monsanto is poised to deliver significant shareowner value by growing earnings and increasing cash flow. According to Verfaillie, "Monsanto is uniquely positioned to deliver integrated solutions to farmers today. Our strong core businesses are complemented by a leadership position in biotechnology solutions, seeds and genomics. These strengths, together with a disciplined approach that focuses on the growth segment of the agricultural industry, will add even more value in the medium to long term as we realize global expansion of current and future products."[8]

According to Verfaillie, Monsanto is continuing its transformation from a traditional chemical company to a company offering high-tech, value-added solutions. In 2001, nearly 70 percent of the company's revenues were from traditional agricultural products such as Roundup, but by 2007 Verfaillie expects that more than half of Monsanto's revenues will come from its seeds and genomics segment. Likewise, the company continues to focus the vast majority of its R&D investment in the seeds and technology solutions, while most competitors spend their R&D dollars on agricultural chemicals.

ENDNOTES

1. R. Langreth, "Monsanto Merger Is Just Latest of Bold Moves by Pharmacia CEO," *Wall Street Journal,* December 20, 1999, p. A3.
2. A. Barrett, "Rocky Ground for Monsanto?" *Business Week,* June 12, 2000, pp. 72–76.
3. S. Kilman and T. M. Burton, "Farm and Pharm: Monsanto Boss's Vision of 'Life Sciences' Firm Now Confronts Reality," *Wall Street Journal,* December 21, 1999, p. A1.
4. "Monsanto Raises $700 Million in IPO," *Los Angeles Times,* October 18, 2000, p. C4.
5. J. Epstein, "Brazilians Boil over Ban on Altered Beans," *Christian Science Monitor,* August 25, 2000, p. 1.
6. A. Barrett, "Rocky Ground?"
7. J. Forster and G. Smith, "A Genetically Modified Comeback," *Business Week,* December 24, 2001, pp. 60–61.
8. Taken from CEO statement on Monsanto's web site. See: **http://www.monsanto.com/monsanto/media/02/02May1_Shareowners.html.**

Eli Lilly & Company: The Global Pharmaceutical Industry

37

This case was prepared by Elizabeth Petrovski and Marc E. Gartenfeld under the direction of Dr. Robert J. Mockler, St. John's University.

The company under study was Eli Lilly & Company, a major pharmaceutical company within the health care industry. Eli Lilly, which had previously suffered from a sloppy, unfocused strategy and had recovered strongly in the mid 1990s due its highly successful antidepressant Prozac, was facing another bout of corporate depression in 1998–1999. Eli Lilly was fighting to keep patent protection on Prozac, which was to expire in 2003, and was involved in legal battles to stop the encroachment of generic drug companies into the antidepressant market. Prozac sales were almost $3 billion, or 30 percent of Lilly's total revenues, and a loss of the patent would seriously hurt company earnings. In February 1999, management at Eli Lilly had to design a strategy to protect future earnings in the case of losing the Prozac patent.

Eli Lilly was a research-based, global pharmaceutical firm that concentrated on research, development, and marketing in the following areas: neuroscience, endocrinology, oncology, cardiovascular disease, infectious diseases, and women's health. In addition to the Prozac patent woes, the company entered into

This case is intended to be used as a basis for class discussion rather than as an illustration of either effective or ineffective handling of the situation. This case was prepared by Elizabeth Petrovski, Marc E. Gartenfeld, and Robert J. Mockler, under whose supervision the case was written. Reprinted by permission of the authors.

an agreement with Sepracor Inc. to allow it to acquire exclusive rights to market a new form of Prozac. This would allow Lilly to keep the drug patented and thus keep a monopoly on the antidepressant market for another fifteen years. For this they were under investigation by the Federal Trade Commission (FTC) for alleged antitrust activity. Future Prozac sales were also being challenged by new antidepressant compounds entering the market. Lastly, sales for Evista, a postmenopausal osteoporosis drug rolled out in early 1998, had been disappointing. These more or less represented Lilly's major issues at home.

Prozac was not alone in its pending expirations; in the U.S. industry, there were a number of blockbuster drugs nearing expiration around the year 2000 that would create an assault on earnings not easily overcome. On the upside, the U.S. market itself was still offering great growth potential, and the late 1990s trends of globalization, an aging worldwide population, longer life expectancy, opening of new markets, and increased demand from Third World nations experiencing rising standards of living offered pharmaceutical firms worldwide continued sales growth.

Research and development (R&D) had been said to be the lifeblood of the pharmaceutical industry (Gerstein, 1997; Sharpe and Keelin, 1998). Those firms able to innovate and bring new drugs to the market were those that prospered. In an arena of rapidly increasing R&D costs, pharmaceutical firms that wished to remain competitive had been finding merger partners throughout the 1990s to spread these costs over a broader base of sales. U.S. pharmaceutical firms concerned about future growth in the United States increased their sales of drugs in foreign markets fourfold between 1980 and 1998. European-based companies attracted by the high growth of U.S. pharmaceuticals wanted a piece of the pie and thus were seeking U.S. merger partners.

In the midst of globalization across all industries where firms looked to capture new geographical markets to remain competitive—and specifically in the pharmaceutical industry, where there was talk of a global launch being a byproduct of industry consolidation—Eli Lilly's percent of revenues derived from sales abroad decreased dramatically, from 44 percent in 1995 to 36 percent in 1998. The company's U.S. sales remained strong after a revamped strategy in the early 1990s; however, the U.S. market's future was uncertain in light of the dominance of managed care companies and an ever-expanding generics market.

With 30 percent of their revenues at stake, Eli Lilly's short-term future partially lay in the hands of the U.S. court system and simultaneously in the company's ability to bring new products to the market. Did Lilly have enough R&D and marketing muscle to go it alone in an industry in the midst of a consolidation trend? Should Lilly have considered the option of purchasing or teaming up with a generic subsidiary to fend off the encroachment of an expanding generic market? Would the addition of over-the-counter medicines be an appropriate hedge against patent losses? What kind of product mix in terms of therapeutic class, the area of disease for which a drug was created, was optimal? In light of pressures at home from generic drug companies and specifically Lilly's being threatened with the loss of Prozac's patent or at least its approaching expiration, could the company afford to allow foreign sales as a percent of total revenues to continue to decrease? The main question to be resolved was how to differentiate Eli Lilly & Company from its competition and so achieve a winning edge over competitors in intensely competitive, rapidly changing immediate, intermediate, and long-term time frames.

Industry and Competitive Market

The health care industry, as shown Figure 1, consisted primarily of the following entities: not-for-profit and for-profit health benefit providers, governments, research institutions, biotechnology companies, and foreign markets. For-profit health care benefit providers were broken down into service organizations, which provide hospital management, health care plans, or long-term care; and product organizations such as drug companies (drugmakers) and medical products and supplies companies. Drugmakers collaborated with research institutes, including universities, national agencies, and biotechnology companies, to develop therapeutic medicines. They were also one of the most-regulated industries on the globe and had to answer to government regulatory bodies with regard to drug approval as well as industry practices. The amount of government interference depended on the country's political system and tended to vary around the globe.

The dynamics surrounding the industry in the United States had changed in the 1990s. Previously, pharmaceutical companies sunk massive funds into R&D of new drugs and heavily emphasized the sales to physicians. The companies and their one-sided pricing strategy were protected by patents and the public's general indifference to pricing due to reimbursement from health insurance programs. Managed care's emergence changed all this, since it provided service to entire companies for fixed fees and thus was highly sensitive to pricing. Also entering the picture were pharmacy benefits management companies (PBMs), which processed prescription drug claims for managed-care companies and large employers. In this way, buyers of drugs were able to decide which drug purchases to reimburse based on volume discounts provided by drug companies, putting pressure on the prices that pharmaceutical companies charge (Anonymous, 1999B).

The Pharmaceutical Industry

The pharmaceutical industry, as shown in Figure 2, consisted then of the product organizations, such as drug companies (drugmakers), and product and supplies organizations. Also included in this group were diversified companies, those that combined different aspects of the production end of health care benefit providers.

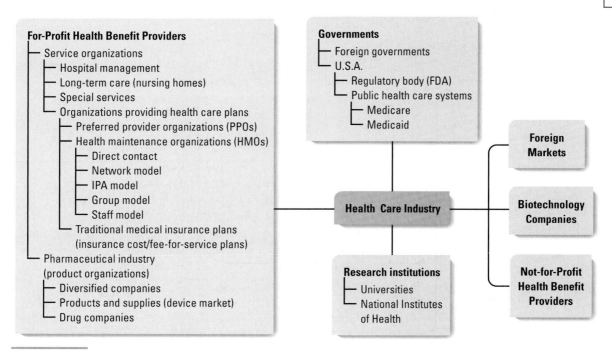

FIGURE 1

Health Care Industry

Industry growth rates had been gargantuan since the end of World War II due to an ever-increasing demand for pharmaceuticals worldwide, with the world per capita consumption of drugs increasing 70 percent between 1975 and 1990. The industry had actually grown dramatically during the time of the war in response to demand for penicillin and anti-infectives. Impressive growth rates at the end of the 1990s were tied to several factors both external and internal. External factors included increased demand due to the aging population and a large untreated population; a highly distinct internal factor was the tendency for firms to use cooperation (joint ventures and alliances) as a business strategy, which often resulted in increased margins. The most pervasive industry trend at the end of the 1990s, however, was the tendency for companies to combine forces. Mostly the merging craze was said to be the result of quickly escalating R&D costs, and in an industry whose major preoccupation was bringing new drugs to market, this was seen as a means to beef up research capabilities and seize economies of scale, thereby protecting future profits. Thus at this point in time, size was often considered to be a key to success.

The size of the global industry was $250 billion in 1999, and 6 to 7 percent annual worldwide sales growth was predicted for the years 1999–2003, shown in Figure 3. In addition, discoveries in rational drug design and molecular biology were cited as contributing to industry growth (Standard & Poor's, 1998). Rational drug design involves the use of computer technology to study cellular targets in order to modify them in the treatment of disease. In the United States toward the end of the 1990s, the Food and Drug Administration (FDA) adopted practices that allowed for the swifter passage of new drugs to market while the European Union established its own FDA counterpart.

The pharmaceutical industry in general was not subject to the fluctuations of the business cycle from which other companies' sales suffered. Related was the fact that the price of pharmaceuticals was relatively inelastic; that is, individuals would not decrease consumption of a particular drug because of an increase in price.

Participants

The participants consisted of producers and marketers of ethical, proprietary, and generic types of

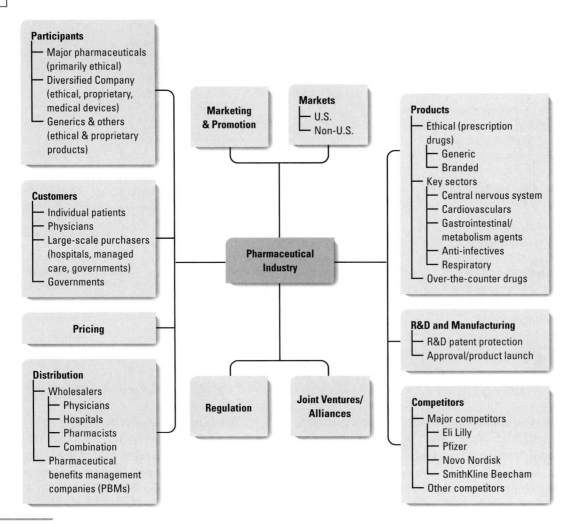

FIGURE 2

Pharmaceutical Industry

drugs. Ethical drugs were those sold to patients only through a prescription, while proprietary were those sold over the counter without the consultation of a physician. Ethical drugs fell into either the branded or generic categories. The major pharmaceutical companies primarily produced ethical products, and this end of the producing groups was fairly concentrated at the end of the 1990s; that is, the top ten companies accounted for almost 40 percent of world retail sales, as shown in Figure 4. Another trend during this period was that drug companies that were making headway into the lifestyle drug segment were actually creating new markets with new drug discoveries, such as Merck's Proscar treatment for enlarged prostrate glands and Pharmacia & Upjohn's Rogaine hair growth stimulant (Standard & Poor's, 1998). A

key to success then was the ability to direct research toward not only therapeutic treatment for disease but also lifestyle improvement drugs.

Major Pharmaceuticals Major pharmaceuticals or research-based firms included those companies whose most distinguishing characteristic was their ability to devote a significant portion of their earnings to research and development. Most of the largest firms were spending between 14 and 18 percent of their earnings on R&D in the late 1990s, as opposed to the average U.S. manufacturing firm, which spent less than 4 percent of its revenues on R&D (Standard & Poor's, 1998). These firms concentrated primarily on the research, development, manufacture, and marketing of ethical/prescription products. Thus a

FIGURE 3

Projected World Pharmaceutical Market
by Region by 2002

Market/Region	Projected Market Size (U.S.$ billions)
North America	169.9
Europe	100.8
Japan	45.8
Latin America & Caribbean	30.5
South-East Asia & China	20.1
Middle East	10.6
Eastern Europe	7.4
Indian subcontinent	7.3
Australasia	5.4
Africa	5.3
CIS	3.2

Source: IMS Health (1999), "Global Pharma Forecast 1998–2002" [Online]. ***http://ims-global.com/insight/report/generics/report.htm.*** Accessed March 20.

key to success in this sector was the ability to devote a significant portion of earnings to R&D.

Diversified Companies   Other pharmaceutical companies produced combinations of ethical and propri-

etary drugs, and still some others also manufactured medical devices. In this latter case, company revenues were normally equally divided between ethical and proprietary pharmaceuticals and medical devices. Proprietary or over-the-counter drugs were consumer oriented in that they tended to be mass marketed and thus carried much lower margins than the ethical category. Most over-the-counter medications had their start as prescription drugs and came into being as the result of the expiration of the patent. Thus R&D was no longer the most crucial aspect in this sector; instead it was the ability of the firm to support large schemes of advertising and promotion.

Generic Companies   Lastly, other companies produced primarily generic products and thus, in the interest of competition, provided the customer with added choices of medications. Generic drugs were compounds that contained the same active ingredient as the branded counterpart. Moreover, they acted as the motivating force for innovation by the ethical producers, since once a product patent expired, its profit potential was all but finished. The modern generic industry evolved in the United States by 1984 legislation that gave any generic company challenging a branded drug the right to sell their version for six months before other generics were allowed to compete (Sherrid, 1999). Thus a key to success for

FIGURE 4

Leading Companies in 1998 Global Pharmaceutical Sales*

Companies	Sales (U.S.$ billions)	World Market Share(%)	Growth from Previous Year (%)
Novartis	$10.6	4.2%	5.0%
Merck & Co.	10.6	4.2	8.0
Glaxo Wellcome	10.5	4.2	1.0
Pfizer	9.9	3.9	21.0
Bristol-Myers Squibb	9.8	3.9	11.0
Johnson & Johnson	9.0	3.6	8.0
American Home Products	7.8	3.1	1.0
Roche	7.6	3.0	6.0
Lilly	7.4	2.9	17.0
SmithKline Beecham	7.3	2.9	6.0
Leading 10 Corporations	*90.7*	*36.1*	*8.0*

*Proposed mergers not included.

Source: IMS Health (1999), "Global Pharma Forecast 1998–2002" [Online]. *http://ims-global.com/insight/report/generics/report.htm.* Accessed March 20.

ethical producers was the ability of a company to defend patents against the encroachment of generic substitutes.

Glaxo Wellcome's Zantac was a shining example of how a company's profits could be eroded upon the entrance of a generic substitute. When the patent on this drug expired in July of 1997, generic rivals entered the market at prices 80 percent less than the original. This brought the company's sales from $3 billion in 1996 to 2.1 billion in 1997 (Standard & Poor's, 1998). Thus in order to stay profitable, the ethical producers had to continue to bring innovation to the market. Some ethical producers owned a generic-producing subsidiary as a means of protecting their earnings from patent losses.

The top ten world generic markets were valued at $14.3 billion in 1997, with growth rates almost double that of the total retail sector. Between 1997 and 2002, 120 patented molecules representing $15 billion were scheduled to expire, including top sellers Prozac, Losec, and Renitec. Some loss of market share was imminent in all cases of patent expiration; however, the exact loss would depend on specific conditions in the market. The United States, United Kingdom, and Germany were all considered to have relatively sophisticated generic markets at the end of the 1990s, attested to by high volume and low prices (IMS Health, 1999).

Customers

With an industry such as this, customers ranged from individuals who purchased pharmaceutical products over the counter to those hospital patients who were administered medications where choice might not have played a role in the decision. The importance of these varied by geographical market in the late 1990s, since countries were in the midst of altering public health care systems, and thus the dynamics in certain markets were going through a process of change. For example, in countries where direct-to-consumer (DTC) advertising was gaining in acceptance and practice, such as in the United States, individual customers were being increasingly targeted. In other markets where governments heavily subsidized pharmaceutical care, governments were the customer and in 1999 were still strongly influencing the practices of drug manufacturers.

Individual Patients Individual patients purchased ethical pharmaceuticals on the recommendation of a physician whose counsel they sought or received through treatment of a debilitating illness. Through the growing use of DTC advertising, buyers of ethical products were becoming more informed, and therefore were playing a larger role in the drug purchase decision process. The decision being only on the part of a physician was occurring less often. Individuals selected over-the-counter drugs, sometimes termed self-medications, and thus personal decision and marketing constituted a much larger role in this sector.

Growth in the pharmaceutical industry beyond 1999 took into account a lengthening of life expectancy in Western cultures and an aging of the world population (the over-sixty-five population was expected to rise from 380 million in 1997 to 800 million by the year 2025) (World Health Organization, 1998), translating to greater demand for pharmaceuticals. Long life expectancy would not necessarily translate, however, to healthier geriatric-age individuals. Pharmaceutical companies that would be able to target conditions such as heart disease, stroke, arthritis, cancer, depression, impotence, osteoporosis, and Alzheimer's disease would experience the strongest growth. In addition, the World Health Organization (WHO) was predicting a doubling of cancer cases in many countries during the period 2000–2025, with a 33 percent increase in lung cancer in women and a 40 percent increase in prostate cancer for men in Europe by the year 2005 (Standard & Poor's, 1998). A key to success therefore was the ability of companies to identify and develop treatments for future widespread maladies.

Physicians In the United States, physicians were typically the target of pharmaceutical marketing practices prior to the 1990s and thus carried much influence in treatment decisions affecting the final customer, the patient. The emergence and dominance of managed care in the health care industry was reducing the influence of the physician in the purchase decision.

Large-Scale Purchasers Large-scale buyers such as hospitals and managed care health providers received discounted pricing due to the size of their purchases. In the United States during the 1990s, the dominance of managed care in the health care provider industry was changing the way pharmaceutical firms reaped profits. Sixty-five percent of all prescriptions by mid

1998 were for persons covered by managed care organizations, an increase from 30 percent at the beginning of the 1990s. This percentage was expected to reach 75 in the year 2000 (Standard & Poor's, 1998). Because of increased large-scale purchases by managed care companies, pharmaceutical companies had to provide discounting while increasing their volumes to stay profitable. This would support size as being another key to success.

Governments   Governments also acted as customers when they purchased for different government agencies and public health care systems. In the United States, Medicare and Medicaid, the two major government health care programs, were expected to account for almost one-fifth of drug sales. In countries with public health care systems, governments were the customers and therefore had much more control over industry practices, contracts, and, most importantly, pricing. In Europe, government interference in the industry in the form of price controls was the norm in order to keep national drug budgets under control. Attempts at deregulation by the European Union were unsuccessful in 1998.

Pricing

Pricing of pharmaceutical products varies by geographical market, but mainly followed two paths: pricing set by the market (in the United States and the United Kingdom) and prices set by governments (most others) (Vilas-Boas and Tharp, 1997). Other governments were taking part in efforts to reduce regulation including that of pricing; however, prices set by the market were still mainly prevalent in the United States and the United Kingdom. In the U.S. market specifically, prices were being put under pressure in the 1990s by large purchasers who could command volume discounts; however, volume sales were still providing strong revenue growth. This obviously was expected to have a profound effect on geographical choices of marketing by drug manufacturers. In countries with a national health plan that covered pharmaceutical care, pharmaceutical companies had practically no influence over product decisions by governments. In terms of pricing, then, access to the U.S. market was a key to success. However, having acute awareness of deregulation in other markets around the globe in order to make wise market-entry decisions was also considered a key to success.

Distribution

Distribution of pharmaceutical products was accomplished through wholesalers, physicians, hospitals, and retailers (pharmacists). In the United States, approximately 70 percent of prescription pharmaceuticals were distributed through wholesalers to hospitals, health maintenance organizations (HMOs), and retail pharmacies. The remaining were sold by manufacturers to physicians, hospitals, retailers, and others (Standard & Poor's, 1998).

In the United States, wholesalers could potentially wield much power, as they were able to influence the breadth of a product's distribution through exclusive agreements with drug manufacturers to distribute specific drugs in specific regions.

Pharmaceutical firms worldwide counted on salespeople to market their products through relationship building with doctors and pharmacists and dissemination of literature. This practice was taking on a more multidimensional twist in the United States, and as the industry went through transformation, marketing was also directed toward managed care organizations, including HMOs, and directly to patients. At the end of 1998, several companies were greatly increasing their sales forces, otherwise known as "detail people" within the industry, in order to handle the introduction of new products. Thus a key to success involved a company's possession of a sizable sales force.

Pharmaceutical Benefits Management Companies (PBMs)
PBMs acted as intermediaries between pharmaceutical manufacturers and large drug purchasers by means of aiding large drug purchasers in managing pharmaceutical costs. They sold pharmaceuticals to large employers, HMOs, hospitals, and other large health benefit providers. Thus they carried immense purchasing clout and were able to pass on savings to large customers. Specifically, their principal aim was to process prescription drug claims for managed care companies and large employers. In this way, drug buyers could choose which prescriptions they wanted to reimburse based on volume discounts (Anonymous, 1999B). They emerged in the United States as an offshoot of managed care and thus were partly responsible for the altering of pharmaceutical distribution in the 1990s. As a result of their intermediary role, they were able to wrestle away some of the drugmakers' profits. To counteract this profit-squeezing phenomenon, some pharmaceutical manufacturers

acquired PBMs as part of their business portfolios. This approach had mixed success.

Because of major differences in health care systems around the globe, the role of PBMs outside the United States was limited. However, as early as 1997, U.S. PBM companies were seeking ways to enter pharmaceutical markets abroad (Edlin, 1997). At this point in time, it appeared that their role would be slightly different in a place such as Europe. PBMs had more of the role of medical care information coordinator in order to provide European patients with more informed decision making capability in terms of choosing medicines (Edlin, 1997). It was also apparent in the late 1990s that the European system of health care was on the verge of being changed, since countries could not afford to continue the systems they had enjoyed. Some European firms were involved in ventures with U.S. companies in the interest of introducing a type of managed care to Europe.

Products

Products in the industry could be classified by their therapeutic benefit—the class of disease they treated. They could also be classified by how they were prescribed: through a doctor's prescription only or through over-the-counter sales. Further, prescription drugs could be either branded products, which were the direct result of lengthy and costly R&D trials, or of the generic type, those that mimiced their branded counterpart in terms of therapeutic benefit and thus emerged when patents expired.

Ethical (Prescription) Drugs: Branded and Generic At the end of the 1990s, prescription drugs fell into these five main therapeutic sectors: central nervous system, cardiovascular, gastrointestinal/metabolism agents, anti-infective, and respiratory drugs. Most major pharmaceutical producers concentrated their efforts in selected areas because of the high cost of research and development. For example, Merck & Co. traditionally had specialized in antihypertensive and cholesterol-lowering products, while Glaxo-Wellcome had dominated the respiratory drug category. With managed care service providers dominating the U.S. market, there was speculation that offering wider spectrums of products would increasingly become a key to success.

These therapeutic sectors could be further classified into therapeutic classes, that is, by the specific maladies that they treated. For example, the central nervous system sector included the classes of sedatives, antidepressants, drugs for Alzheimer's disease, Parkinson's disease, and ALS (Lou Gehrig's disease). The top ten therapeutic classes accounted for 30 percent of total revenues worldwide in 1998, and three of these leading ten were experiencing 20 percent sales growth per year and more (IMS Health, 1999), as shown in Figure 5.

FIGURE 5

Leading Therapy Classes in 1998 Global Pharmaceutical Sales

Class	Sales (U.S.$ billions)	% of Market	1998 Growth (%)
1. Antiulcerants	$12.9	5.1%	3.0%
2. Cholesterol and triglyceride reducers	9.6	3.8	20.0
3. Antidepressants	9.4	3.7	21.0
4. Calcium antagonists plain	8.7	3.4	1.0
5. Cephalosporins and combinations	6.8	2.7	−1.0
6. ACE inhibitors plain (antihypertensive)	6.5	2.6	4.0
7. Non-narcotic analgesics	6.2	2.5	−4.0
8. Antirheumatics	6.0	2.4	4.0
9. Antipsychotics	3.9	1.6	30.0
10. Broad-spectrum penicillins	3.8	1.5	4.0

Source: IMS Health (1999), "Global Pharma Forecast 1998–2002" [Online]. *http://ims-global.com/insight/report/generics/report.htm.* Accessed March 20.

An industry trend gaining momentum in the late 1990s in response to the higher R&D cost was the tendency for drug companies to seek second and third therapeutic benefits from a previously marketed drug. This practice helped to bring down a company's R&D expenditure. There were several success stories, including Glaxo-Wellcome's discovery that their antidepressant drug marketed under the name Zyban had been found to be an effective smoking cessation treatment (Morrow, 1999), while Viagra, Pfizer's blockbuster impotence drug, had been originally tested to treat angina (heart drug).

In general, when assessing the strength of a pharmaceutical company, the product portfolio was one of the main focuses, in addition to R&D capabilities. One had to appraise not only the sales potential of current products, but the future potential of those products, including pending patent registrations, and finally, products in the company's pipeline. What new drugs would it be bringing to market in the future? These were all keys to success in the 1990s.

Related to this was the actual business portfolio, which companies had to design from a strategic point of view quite carefully. The merger and acquisition situation reflected a need to increase company size; however, attention had to be paid to the types of business in which a company participated. At the end of the 1990s, among the firms that had experienced success, there existed varying types of business portfolio strategies, which included areas of ethical drugs, over-the-counter drugs, animal products, pharmacy benefit management, and medical devices, all related businesses. Within pharmaceutical units, companies had to choose among therapeutic areas. A company's business unit portfolio depended on its known strengths and its management's preferences. One common denominator was having a clear and defined focus. That is, the choice of areas in which to concentrate was not necessarily vital, but recognizing where the company could succeed and then moving in that direction was. Firms whose focus was unclear, such as SmithKline Beecham, ended up having to defend weak earnings reports and to make excuses to shareholders. Thus a key to success was the ability to select and effectively manage the combination of business units in operation under any one firm's control.

Generic Drugs   Also relevant in this sector of producers was the participation of generic drug companies.

In the United States, growth in generics had been spurred by a growth in the service sector of managed care and the number of branded drugs that were to lose patents around the year 2000. The former situation was a response to a larger trend of cost control within the health care industry in general. The philosophy behind managed care was preventative maintenance to keep costs down, that is, treating patients before any serious type of malady occurred. Generic drugs, which were chemical equivalents to branded drugs, entered the market at a time when a patent on a branded drug expired. Generic drugmakers avoided the costs of R&D, FDA approval, and advertising, necessary investments by their counterpart brand producers. They were able to pass these cost savings (50–90 percent) on to customers, and thus generics were highly appropriate for the cost-conscious managed care service sector. This obviously did not bode well for the brand producer who had lost the patent.

Over-the-Counter Drugs   Over-the-counter drugs came into existence when the patent on an ethnic/prescription drug expired. In fact, in the United States most of the ethical products on the market started out as ethical products (Standard & Poor's, 1998). After the expiration of an ethical drug's patent, a company might apply to the FDA for over-the-counter status, which could be a very lucrative road to take. Over-the-counter drugs faced a very different market than the ethical sector, since they more or less responded to the forces of supply and demand. They could actually be considered part of the consumer products industry, where heavy spending on marketing was essential to build brand recognition and customer loyalty to retain market share. Companies had often used line extensions to increase sales in other segments, such as children's versions of adult medicines. Further, like consumer products, over-the-counter drugs had low margins. All these characteristics were dissimilar to the ethical sector. Over-the-counter drugs did not have the heavy FDA reporting requirements characteristic of the ethical sector. A key to success in this sector was therefore the company's portfolio of recognizable brands.

Research and Development/Manufacturing

There were three main stages in the life cycle of a prescription drug: research and development, patent protection, and FDA approval/product launch.

Research and Development   The development of new drugs, which required years of laborious research, started in either an academic or an industrial laboratory and might have been an accidental discovery but most often was the result of work completed with a specific objective in sight. Raw materials used in the production of drugs included plant substances, animal substances, and inorganic compounds (Standard & Poor's, 1998). The work involved the screening of multitudinous combinations of compounds, most of which in the end were discarded. Compounds that looked successful began the long process of animal tests for useful properties, potency, and toxicity (Gerstein, 1997). If the compound was proven to be effective with animals, it began the process of human trials, which could take from one to five years. The FDA identified three phases through which a new drug had to pass before it was brought to market.

- Phase I: Drug was given to a small number of healthy people to test its safety.

- Phase II: Drug was administered to people with the disease that it was intended to treat.

- Phase III: Rigorous tests were performed involving larger groups of ill patients.

Out of twenty drugs passing through these three stages, one or two actually gained approval for marketing. More staggering perhaps was the fact that only one in five thousand compounds discovered ever reached the pharmacy shelf, and fewer than one-third of companies recouped their R&D investment (Hoover's Online: Pharm. & Medical Equip.,1999).

A new drug was given three designations: (1) a chemical name based on the structure of the compound, (2) a generic name, simpler than the chemical name, and (3) a brand name used to identify it to the public as well as for registering for trademarks (Gerstein, 1997).

Above all, R&D—specifically, a company's product portfolio and pipeline—was said to indicate the health of a company, not to mention direct its strategic objectives (Saldanha, Pesanello, and Harrington, 1997), as shown in Figure 6.

R&D in the industry in the late 1990s was attracting major attention because companies were under continuous pressure to innovate. R&D expenditures more than doubled between 1991 and 1998, while the industry was expected to grow approximately 7 percent beyond 1998. This translated to a requirement of twenty-four to thirty-six new products launched by 2005, earning over $1 billion each, in order to support this growth. Thus, the pressures on companies with regard to R&D investment were tremendous approaching the year 2000 (Anonymous, 1999D).

Patent Protection   Patent protection usually began after the compound had been discovered and had a duration of twenty years. This was stipulated under the rules of the World Trade Organization (WTO) for protection of intellectual property. Since the process

FIGURE 6

Pipeline Importance*

	Company A (Multinational)	Company B (Global)	Company C (Regional/Transnational)
Organization	Decentralized	Centralized	Integrated teams
Strategy	Locally driven and implemented	Established globally Implemented locally	Established globally Refined regionally Implemented locally
Communication	Bottom up	Top down	Team based
Product portfolio	Aging; me-too	Narrow & innovative	Broad & innovative
Pipeline (five-year horizon)	Limited potential for innovation	High potential for innovation	High to moderate potential for innovation

*The quality of a company's product portfolio and its R&D pipeline affect its global marketing strategy and organizational structure.

Source: G. Saldanha, P. Pesanello, and E. Harrington (1997), "Building Value Through Global Markets," *Pharmaceutical Executive,* December 17(12): 72–78 [Online]. *http://proquest.umi.com.* Accessed April 14, 1999.

of clinical development and human trials was taking up to ten years in the 1990s, the shelf life of a drug would normally be ten or twelve years (Moran, 1999). Some industry analysts put it another way—companies would have to create five new drugs per year to keep up with industry growth rates (Moran, 1999).

By the end of the 1990s, companies were facing a changing environment in the area of intellectual property protection due to intended global streamlining of patent protection from country to country, especially under the efforts of the WTO. In many cases, patent protection outside the United States, however, was still much weaker than that inside the United States and companies had to guard their intellectual property well.

In the late 1990s, an industry trend involved not only protecting patented drugs from generics entering the market, but also trying to extend a patent in some form or another to protect the earnings captured by a particular drug, especially for those that had so-called blockbuster status. One way for companies to do this was to change the drug product ever so slightly, just enough to require a new patent: for example, changing a drug from injectable to tableted form. In the United States, this was a major complaint by generic companies. Upon the entrance of a generic drug, it was more important then for ethical producers to turn to marketing for product differentiation. When a drug arrived on the market, its therapeutic benefit was its selling point; however, with the arrival of generic challengers, it now became more important to distinguish the branded drug from competitors, and therefore marketing and product differentiation were the new goals. Thus a key to success was the ability of companies to protect patents, find creative ways to extend patent protection, and lastly, in the event of competitors entering the market, creatively differentiate a drug from those of competitors.

Approval/Product Launch   In the United States, a drug had to be approved by the FDA before it could be brought to market, which involved the company filing complete information about the new compound, including its material composition, formulation materials, manufacturing methods, controls, packaging, and proposed text for the label (Gerstein, 1997). It also had to be proven to be effective for the treatment for which it was intended. Outside the United

States, a regulatory body within the country where the drug would be marketed must give approval. At the end of the 1990s, the FDA was still considered the world's drug approval organization, since many drugs were being developed in the United States, where pharmaceutical firms were strongest and R&D was successful. Many drugs started their existences here and would be marketed overseas after a successful U.S. launch.

In general, when assessing the value of a drug company, the number of drugs in the research and development pipeline was critical. Furthermore, much attention was given to the phase (I, II, or III) in the development cycle that drugs had achieved, this being an indication of a company's success in terms of future profit growth potential.

Marketing and Promotion

Marketing and promotion (DTC) played a significant role in the over-the-counter sector of the pharmaceutical industry, whereas within the ethical sector, research and development had traditionally been the lifeblood for survival. This distinguishing factor between the two sectors started to become somewhat blurred in the 1990s in the United States. Within the ethical sector, total advertising expenditures between 1993 and 1997 went from $183 million to $875 million. Underlying factors included a loosening of advertising regulations in the ethical sector by the FDA, customers' desire to be informed about health care and medications, and the widespread use of the Internet.

With the growth in DTC marketing, the dynamics of industry distribution were somewhat altered. In the past, doctors were alone in being able to prescribe drugs, with pharmacists being the only ones to distribute them. With the increase in DTC advertising, patients began to request name brands from their physicians. Ethical producers found DTC advertising to be extremely effective because it served not only as a selling device but also as a means of keeping the medical profession abreast about specific drugs. The use of DTC advertising could also create a stronger association between ethical product brand names and company names in the eyes of consumers—now more than ever, patients themselves. This would make a company's image even more critical as a part of marketing and promotion.

The trend toward DTC advertising in the ethical sector, however, had not yet arrived in Europe, where health care was still mostly not privatized. It was clear, however, that DTC practices were beginning to spread outside the United States. In the United Kingdom, DTC advertising was still illegal; however, to overcome this DTC advertising had taken the form of centering ads around a disease with only a mention of a drug company for the cure (Yates, 1999). The International Federation of Pharmaceutical Manufacturers Association (IFPMA), an agency that promoted cooperation between countries in terms of health care and pharmaceutical practices and whose members were regional and national associations representing research-based pharmaceutical companies, required all members and those they represented to accept the association's provisions in the *IFPMA Code of Pharmaceutical Marketing Practices.*

Publicity, as with other industries, especially adverse publicity, could influence markets more powerfully than any form of paid advertising or promotion, and this industry was very sensitive to any negative publicity because of the nature of the products. Negative publicity in the past had usually been the result of ineffective drugs or, worse-case scenario, drugs that had a strong debilitating effect on patients. Thus a key to success was efficacy and safety of products.

Regulation

The FDA had always been considered the world's "gold standard" in terms of safely approving drugs for marketing. With a newly unified Europe, the European Medicines Evaluations Agency (EMEA) was created by the European Council in 1995 to streamline practices among countries within the EU, which then seriously challenged the stand-alone authority of the FDA. In the early 1990s the FDA moved to bring drugs to market more swiftly, shortening approval times from thirty-five months in 1992 to twenty-two months in 1997.

Further steps were being taken to deregulate the European licensing system in the mid 1990s. Greatly affecting the European market were regulations on pricing within the industry. Price controls enforced by European governments, which were usually footing the health care bills, ensured that prices did not get out of control and put increased pressure on European companies' profits. As late as December 1998, the European Council was still not willing to pass deregulation laws and was more concerned with

cost containment (Moore, 1998). With center-left governments dominating the environment in Europe, there was not much hope for deregulation in the late 1990s.

Regulation streamlining at the end of the 1990s was one of the dynamics changing the global industry as well. Worldwide, regulation existed to accomplish two main objectives: allow the entrance of pharmaceutical products into markets and protecting the health of the public. Regulation and compliance in different markets had always led to difficulty for drug marketers seeking to expand outside their home markets. Specifically, regulation systems in the United States, Europe, and Japan varied greatly and profoundly affected the means of achieving profitability by outsiders in those markets.

Japan's Ministry of Health and Welfare (the Koseisho), responsible for operation of Japan's health care system, including the surveillance and regulation of drugs, traditionally did not allow companies to submit foreign clinical studies on drug treatments, but only those studies carried out on Japanese patients.

The International Conference on Harmonization (ICH) was founded in 1991. Since its inception, it concentrated its efforts on streamlining and bringing uniformity to drug approval processes across the three geographical markets, which happened to be the three largest pharmaceutical markets at the end of the 1990s: the United States, Japan, and Europe. This effort had a profound effect on marketing practices within the global pharmaceutical industry because approval times between these three countries varied considerably, with the EMEA having the shortest guaranteed completion of an application. In addition, the application and market maintenance fee structures for drugs varied across these markets, with those of the European Union being the least costly. It thus appeared that testing, manufacturing, and marketing a new drug in Europe had its advantages over doing the same in other markets. Therefore, a key to success was having a presence in Europe in order to benefit from these advantages, as well as to participate in a region comprising 30 percent of the global pharmaceutical market. In addition, firms had to be in an optimal position to participate in these three geographical markets in time for harmonization of drug approval laws, which were expected to have a profound effect on the industry.

Joint Ventures/Strategic Alliances to Mergers and Acquisitions

Since the 1980s, combining forces, in agreements ranging from joint ventures, or strategic alliances, to the most extreme form of union, mergers and acquisitions, had been a common strategy in the industry that was used to put more muscle behind costly research, development, and scientific breakthrough. The marketing arm of the business also became a factor, since firms would join forces in order to have a more extensive sales force.

Joint Ventures and Strategic Alliances Joint ventures and alliances had long been a common strategy because pharmaceutical firms did well to create alliances with smaller biotechnology or biopharmaceutical companies that were possibly developing new drugs. Conversely, smaller pharmaceutical firms sought alliances with larger firms that had more marketing muscle in order to bring a new discovery to the market. In addition, companies often had relationships with university scientists and, in the United States, with the National Institutes of Health, which had the power to forward products still in the research chain of development to drug companies. As with joint venture strategy in many industries, the advantages of having a foreign partner when entering foreign markets lie in the foreign partner's familiarity with business practices in a particular country. Lastly, alliances between foreign companies allowed drugmakers to license drugs discovered in foreign countries in the home market. In the late 1990s, U.S. drugmakers were increasingly collaborating with biotechnology firms to develop therapeutic compounds through genomics (genetics) research. Thus a key to success was a company's ability to create joint ventures and strategic alliances.

Mergers and Acquisitions Mergers and acquisitions, the most extreme form of joint ventures, had been increasingly evident in the business environment of the pharmaceutical industry since the beginning of the 1990s. One study states that in the first six months of 1990 alone, 151 mergers in this industry were announced. Some of the more famous mergers had been Beecham with Smithkline, Merrell Dow with Marion, Bristol-Myers with Squibb, and Upjohn with Pharmacia (Agrawal, 1997).

During the late 1990s, a new wave toward consolidation appeared with mergers and acquisitions. This trend had the same catalyst seen in joint ventures, but it incorporated other factors into the equation. In general, the new European single market and the recent entrance of the euro ushered in a flood of mergers and acquisitions in Europe. Specifically, the pharmaceutical industry was ripe for these unions because of the steep costs of R&D, said to be the lifeblood of any pharmaceutical company. In 1999 the cost of bringing a new drug to market was estimated to be $350 to $500 million, and the process generally took fifteen years. Therefore, there were many who supported the argument that "size mattered" when it came to pharmaceuticals. The industry's global revenues of $250 billion in 1999 were expected to reach $400 billion by the year 2003, yet no one company had been able to boast more than 5 percent of total market share.

Prior to 1980, pharmaceutical companies had as their strengths innovation, patent protection of drugs, and pricing flexibility. While U.S. pharmaceutical firms had been able to boast strong growth over the years, as reflected in high equity drug stock prices, this growth (once in double-digit figures) was expected to slow in 1999 to a level of 9 percent (IMS Health, 1999). European firms' growth rates were at a level of approximately 6 percent and were expected to remain flat, along with those of Japan. U.S. growth was boosted by the increase in managed care facilities, while in Europe national governments were mainly responsible for health care systems and thus used price controls. No movement toward privatization was necessarily in sight. In the United States, managed care represented 50 percent of the medical products market and was expected to reach 90 percent by the end of the year 2000. Thus European players were seeking U.S. partners to gain exposure in the strong U.S. market and to realize economies of scale.

Initially, the move toward consolidation was driven by weakness in comparison to U.S. companies. Specifically, this indicated that companies might not have enough projects in the R&D arena to protect future earnings. With the surge in mergers and acquisitions, average company size was on the increase, and thus the optimum company size for this industry would likely have to be redefined. This was exemplified by the fact that the largest pharmaceutical firm in 1997, Glaxo Wellcome, boasted $11.6 billion in sales;

the proposed mergers, if realized, would put the top company, AHP-SmithKline Beecham, at $27.0 billion in sales, as Figure 7 indicates.

All mergers were not necessarily successful. Three large mergers in 1998 did not happen as intended, and although the real issues were not disclosed, there appeared to be unwillingness on the part of management in all three cases to give up the reins. Moreover, despite the presence of the single European market, many practices still varied from country to country, including tax, accounting, and auditing standards; pension provisions; corporate and shareholding structures; culture and language; industry structure; and regulatory requirements (Curwen, 1999). At one point it appeared that these failures would put a damper on future unions, but in late 1998, Hoechst and Rhone-Poulenc, Sanofi SA and Synthelabo, and Zeneca and Astra all announced their intention to join forces. European companies were said to be looking for American partners to seize a part of the massive U.S. market; however, lofty equity prices in early 1999 kept them at bay.

In general, global consolidation in this industry protected future earnings through cost cutting, which in turn gave companies more time for development of new drugs. It also insured against earnings risk when patents expired. Lastly, it enhanced a company's research and development prospects and expanded its global market reach. However, the benefits of mergers and acquisitions even during the consolidation trend of the late 1990s were in contin-

uous debate. It was noted that size did not always contribute to strength, while it could certainly contribute to logistical headaches. Past success stories exemplified the fact that smaller entities could be just as valid. An example was the European division of Pfizer, which was responsible for three-quarters of the company's output with a mere one-third of the R&D resources (LLY NEWS, 1999). In the late 1990s, it appeared that on mergers the jury was still out.

Markets

Typically, one of the main difficulties in marketing pharmaceuticals abroad was considered to be the differing regulatory environments, which appeared to be moving toward convergence at the end of the 1990s.

North America (U.S.)   The North American market boasted 40 percent of world market share as of early 1999, as well as the highest growth rates among all the regions worldwide. This rate was supported by product innovation and volume sales to managed care facilities. It was the market that European companies had their eyes on for expansion and was partially responsible for the great industry consolidation in progress in 1998. European and smaller firms looked for merger partners to compete with stronger U.S. players or actually sought U.S. merger partners in order to capture part of the U.S. market. In various research studies on the U.S. pharmaceutical industry in the 1980s, predictions varied on the future competitiveness of American companies. One study cited the fact that FDA regulations and longer regulatory review periods would hamper future competitiveness, but by 1999 this issue had already been addressed and perhaps rectified by new FDA regulation passed in 1998, which shortened the average review period for new drugs. Essentially, the U.S. market was extremely attractive, and healthy pharmaceutical firms derived significant portions of their earnings from it. Thus strong operations and sales in this market were keys to success.

Foreign Markets (Non-U.S.)   Between 1999 and 2004, in addition to North America, the fastest-growing markets in the industry were predicted to be the Middle East, Australasia, and Southeast Asia, including China (IMS Health, 1999) (see Figure 8). Europe was expected to continue to be plagued by price controls. Southeast Asia, which was experiencing rapid growth

FIGURE 7

Proposed Mergers
(combined pro forma sales)

Drug Deals	
AHP-SmithKline Beecham (canceled)	$27.0 billion
AHB-Monsanto (canceled)	23.0 billion
Glaxo Wellcome-SmithKline Beecham (canceled)	19.0 billion
Zeneca-Astra	15.9 billion
Hoechst-RP	13.0 billion
Sanofi-Synthélabo	6.1 billion

Source: A. Scott, (1999), "Drug Makers Consolidate," *Chemical Week*, January 6, 161(1): 29 [Online]. *http://proquest.umi.com.* Accessed March 23.

FIGURE 8

Five-Year Forecast of the Global Pharmaceutical Markets (1998–2002)

Regions	CAGR %	Regions	CAGR %
North America	9.8%	Eastern Europe	8.6%
Europe	5.8	Middle East	10.6
Japan	4.9	Africa	3.3
Latin America and Caribbean	8.4	Indian Subcontinent	8.6
Southeast Asia/China	11.0	Australasia	9.8
Eastern Europe	8.6	CIS	6.7
Total World Market	**8.0%**		

Source: IMS Health (1999), "Global Pharma Forecast 1998–2002" [Online]. *http://ims-global.com/insight/report/generics/report.htm.* Accessed March 20.

before the Asian crisis, was expected to return to that phase by 2001–2002.

U.S. and foreign markets varied by the ways in which drugs were brought to market, by regulatory procedures, and by ways in which market forces worked. Outside the United States, even though it was less difficult and costly to move a drug through the phases of development, actual sales practices between the drug company and the customer, usually the government, involved more relationship building, covert pacts, and price controls. Thus market forces took a backseat position.

Europe   At the same time that the American market was experiencing strong growth at the end of the 1990s, Europe's growth was expected to be approximately 7 percent. The European market was considered to be lagging at the end of the 1990s and not necessarily the place to be for pharmaceutical players. The fault lay partially with the European socialized health care system, which, in maintaining price controls and other government intervention tools, squeezed drug company budgets. The hope in Europe was for deregulation to take hold, which would unleash price controls and increase volume. European companies in the midst of this situation speculated that they would not be sought out for merger partners, but rather as takeover candidates.

China and Asia   As with other industries in China, the pharmaceutical industry faced large prospects for growth due to current small per-capita consumption, an already rapidly growing industry, and the tendency for Chinese consumers to switch to Western-style medicines in lieu of traditional Chinese medicines (homeopathic). A major drawback of marketing in China lay in the fact that although China had laws protecting intellectual property, the laws did not cover pharmaceuticals; the law specifically permitted copying of patented medicines (Mauer Fron and Smith, 1998). In the past, companies for whom this had been an issue had registered complaints with Chinese authorities without necessarily achieving success (Mauer Fron and Smith, 1998). Even with this major impediment, China's market was considered to be too great to overlook. In 1999 this market was expected to grow by 14 percent; however, because of the continuing Asian financial crisis, products planned for export were to be offered in the domestic market, adding to severe competition pressures. Profits earned in the industry in China were expected to decrease by 250 million yuan in the same year. A key to success therefore in this market was to establish a presence, with the expectation that rewards would not necessarily be near term (Anonymous, 1999A).

Japan   Japan boasted the highest per-capita prescription drug market outside the United States in 1998, and thus was the second largest market in the world. However, at that time Japan's government still exercised stiff control over drug prices, including required across-the-board price cuts on drugs every few years (Standard & Poor's, 1998). In the mid 1990s, Japan was seen as an ideal geographical location to facilitate expansion into Asia, specifically into South Korea and China (Yoshida, 1995).

Competitors

Because of the business structure of the pharmaceutical industry, the structure of competition was also unique. One could witness a strategy dichotomy. On the one hand, the high cost of R&D bore witness that size was important and specialization of R&D in certain therapeutic areas would help to keep costs down. On the other hand, being able to offer various types of products allowed companies to offer one-stop shopping to customers, that is, drug wholesalers and hospitals. The competition appeared to be more focused on the former situation and thus concentrated in certain therapeutic areas. Geographies were also an important consideration, since not only did therapeutic area dictate competitive strength, but breadth of sales and marketing—strength in specific geographical areas—would also indicate more or less the type of competition, direct or nondirect.

Another important consideration was the fact that drug companies, as in other industries, could decide how to design their business portfolios. Some companies concentrated solely on ethical products, often including some participation in the animal health care market, which was seen as providing synergies with human health care. Some firms included over-the-counter product manufacturing in their portfolios; thus they were also participating in the consumer products industry, where emphasis was on brand recognition and consumer loyalty. Even though the emphasis in this sector was different, it was a way to protect earnings when patents for strong-selling products expired.

Because of the nature and structure of the pharmaceutical industry at the end of the 1990s, competition in a particular therapeutic area could emerge from any corner of the industry. Companies could seek out alliances for product development and marketing, and thus competition could emerge from companies that previously might not have had a strength in a particular area. Once a product entered the market, even nongeneric companies could try to mimic the product by studying its patent application.

Major Competitors   By classifying competition according to therapeutic strengths, one can identify the following competitors: Novo Nordisk A/S, Pfizer, Inc., and SmithKline Beecham plc.

Novo Nordisk A/S   This Danish company was still the world's leading producer of insulin and industrial enzymes. Health care products comprised 75 percent of the company's sales in 1997. The company also produced insulin injection and monitoring systems, treatments for osteoporosis and menopause, growth hormones, antidepressants, and epilepsy treatments. More than half of the company's sales were within Europe at the end of the 1990s.

The company's most prevalent strengths were its health products for diabetes, which, until 1998, were mainly marketed in Europe. In 1998, the company signed an agreement with Schering-Plough to make inroads into the U.S. market with their diabetes drugs. This move proved to be successful, since the company experienced a 20 percent increase in insulin sales in the United States in 1998 (Moore, 1999). Prevalent products included Seroxat, introduced in 1992 for depression, and Gabitril for epilepsy and NovoSeven for hemophilia, both introduced in 1995.

The company portfolio's inclusion of industrial enzymes represented another way that pharmaceutical firms diversified to take advantage of manufacturing synergies. In early 1999, however, the company embarked on a major strategy shift when it revealed that the two businesses would be split into separate legal entities. This decision was a result, in part, of the industry's merger mania, which created powerful rivals with which Nordisk felt it could not compete with its business portfolio. The company was also following an industry trend of sharpening its focus around core strengths. It also caused massive speculation that the pharmaceutical entity would be seeking a merging partner.

The merger speculation about Novo Nordisk was also born out of the fact that the company had a relatively small size in terms of annual sales ($2.5 billion in 1997), and smaller firms like Nordisk, seeking out R&D and marketing muscle, were ripe to merge with other firms. Novo Nordisk had been strong in terms of R&D expenditure as a percentage of sales—in 1997, the company spent 16.3 percent of earnings on R&D.

Pfizer, Inc.   Pfizer was one of the leaders in the production of ethical drugs (number one in the U.S.) and was a producer of animal health treatments and consumer health products sold over the counter. Pfizer was the creator of the anti-impotence drug Viagra, launched in 1998. Prescription drugs produced included treatment for cardiovascular disease, antidepressants, antibiotics, and cholesterol-lowering drugs. Health care products accounted for 85 percent of the company's revenues. Pfizer's strength lay in its R&D capabilities, and the company had 170 drugs in its research pipeline in 1999. It also had a strong presence in the consumer products market with such known brands as BenGay muscle rub, Visine eyedrops, and Bain de Soleil sunscreens.

Pfizer was an example of a company that had both ethical and over-the-counter products in its business portfolio. It was considered one of the powerhouses in the industry, with a formidable R&D team that consistently used 15 percent of the company's revenues. Its drug pipeline was the envy of the industry, with sixty new drugs in the early stages of development and an approximate total of 170 drugs in the pipeline in 1998 (Moran, 1999). Pfizer had overcome hard times during the 1980s when it experienced gaps in the product pipeline. After suffering through years of weak earnings due to strong investment in R&D and a vast sales force, the company came back with a vengeance and during the early 1990s had moved from number thirteen in terms of worldwide prescription drug sales to number four. Pfizer's sales force reached 14,500 in 1998 (Stipp, 1998). The company had a few top-selling drugs in its portfolio at the end of the 1990s, including Viagra, Norvasc, a hypertension drug that had sales of $2.2 billion in 1997, and Zoloft, an antidepressant that was a strong competitor to Prozac.

SmithKline Beecham plc.   SmithKline Beecham, based in the United Kingdom, produced both prescription and over-the-counter treatments. Prescription drugs included antidepressants and vaccines for illnesses such as diphtheria, tetanus, and hepatitis. It was also a leader in workplace drug testing. Planned mergers with Glaxo Wellcome and American Home Products failed; however, the company was still actively seeking a merger partner in 1998–1999.

The company's total revenues in 1998 were over $13 billion, 60 percent of which were derived from pharmaceutical sales and 30 percent from consumer products. The antidepressant Paxil/Seroxat was the company's second best-selling drug in that year, behind the antibiotic Augmentin. In 1998, SmithKline found itself continuing on a path of strategic missteps. Previously, CEO Mr. Jan Leschly had tried to lead the company toward more broadened strategic goals, which included the purchase of a pharmacy benefit management business. A mere increase of 4 percent in sales in 1998 was proof that this approach had failed. Other players in the industry had been doing just the opposite at the end of the 1990s—streamlining businesses and focusing their strategies. Other signs of difficulty included the closing of excess manufacturing plants and layoffs of approximately three thousand people. Smith-Kline's R&D expenditure, reduced to 10 percent in 1998 from 17 percent in the previous year, also demonstrated a sign of trouble.

Other competitors   Other competitors produced both ethical drugs for humans and animals, over-the-counter drugs, and generic drugs. They included Schering-Plough Corporation, Merck & Co., Inc. (tied for the number one selling company by worldwide sales with Novartis AG), Scheim Pharmaceutical, Inc., a producer of generic drugs, Bristol-Myers Squibb Co., Glaxo Wellcome plc, and Novartis AG.

In general, competition dynamics were unique within this industry in the sense that in any given period, companies could be direct competitors because of the products they were developing or marketing at a particular time. Other companies would be considered indirect competitors, since their business portfolios could contain drug treatments for different therapeutic areas. Competition pressures could change instantly, since even drugs in the late stages of development did not necessarily "make it" into the market and thus could completely change a company's therapeutic strengths. Given the consolidation trend in the 1990s, the composition of the industry was changing, and consequently the dynamics of competition were changing.

The Company

Colonel Eli Lilly, pharmacist and Union officer in the Civil War, founded Eli Lilly & Company in 1876, and the company remained family owned until 1953. Eli Lilly expanded into the world market in the 1950s and 1960s, and over the years experimented with different business portfolio strategies, including diversifying with the purchase of Elizabeth Arden in 1971 (it was sold in 1987) and of IVAC (a medical instruments manufacturer) in 1977. Lilly's launch of Humulin (synthetic insulin) in 1982 made it the first pharmaceutical firm to market a genetically engineered drug.

Prior to the 1990s, drugmakers used a common strategy in the eternal struggle for profit growth.

Heavy emphasis was placed on R&D in the interest of developing new drugs, while the nurturing of strong sales forces enabled companies to move products by selling to physicians. Drugs protected by patents were not vulnerable to price competition. Further, patients covered by traditional health insurance plans were unaffected by price in general.

In the 1990s, in a move sanctioned by the Clinton administration, managed care became the approach to low-cost health care and changed the dynamics of the American industry. Pharmacy benefits management firms (PBMs) emerged to help large companies control the costs of pharmacy benefits programs. They emphasized use of alternatives to branded pharmaceuticals carrying lofty prices and thus put earnings pressure on pharmaceutical firms. In the early 1990s, weakened equity prices of pharmaceutical firms reflected this pressure. Lilly lost $11 billion in market capitalization in eighteen months (Eli Lilly, 1998).

Some U.S. firms responded by beating the PBMs at their own game—they purchased them. In 1994, Lilly purchased PCS Health Systems for $4 billion. However, the distinct strategic advantage that Lilly anticipated, funneling its own products through PCS, did not happen. Partially responsible were perceived conflicts of interest by drug customers as well as by the U.S. Federal Trade Commission (FTC). Lilly sold off PCS Health Systems in 1997, which resulted in a substantial write-off. Since PBMs had proven to be profitable entities, other pharmaceutical companies such as Merck were willing to retain them as part of their business portfolios.

Selling PCS was to be part of a general transformational strategy that Randall Tobias, then CEO of Lilly, implemented in the mid 1990s. After an evaluation of the business portfolio of the company, Mr. Tobias realized that Lilly's strength was in its core business: pharmaceuticals. As a result he divested some of the noncore entities, including medical device businesses, cosmetics, agricultural products, and a hard gelatin capsule business. In addition, acquisitions were made and relationships fostered to strengthen the core business, including a strategic alliance to develop and market a blood substitute product; ownership of Sphinx Pharmaceuticals, primarily a research and development division; and a stake in a biotechnology firm to have access to the testing of cutting-edge chemical substances.

It appeared that some of these efforts had paid off by the end of the 1990s. In 1997 Lilly's earnings per share boasted growth of 21 percent versus 20 percent for Merck and 13 percent for Pfizer (Stipp, 1998).

Products

In the mid to late 1990s, Lilly's structure was revamped around the five core therapeutic areas in which it had already carried a strong presence by that time: infectious diseases, cancer, cardiovascular products, endocrinology, and neuroscience. Between 1995 and 1998, new Lilly products accounted for 78 percent of the company's sales growth. Some of the major drugs are shown in Figure 9.

Prozac   This product accounted for almost 30 percent of company sales. It was used for treatment of depression and bulimia. Prozac (fluoxetine) was part of the company's group of neuroscience products, their largest-selling product group. The pending expiration on the patent for this product in the year 2003 was making company executives nervous and sent them scrambling for ways to hang onto its success, including an agreement with Sepracor to develop a new version of Prozac minus the side effects. Prozac's success was challenged in some geo-

FIGURE 9

Eli Lilly & Company Net Sales in 1998 (U.S.$ millions)

Class	Sales	% Change from 1997	% of Total
Prozac	$2,811.5	10%	30%
Zyprexa	1,442.7	98	16
Anti-infectives	1,160.9	(9)	13
Insulins	1,154.9	8	13
Animal health	614.4	4	7
Axid	418.0	(20)	4
ReoPro	365.4	44	4
Gemzar	306.8	76	3
Humatrope	268.0	3	3
Evista	144.1	N/M	1

Source: Eli Lilly and Company (1999), 10K report for the fiscal year ended December 31, 1998 [Online]. http://www.sec.gov/Archives/edgar/data/59478/0000950131-99-001772.txt. Accessed April 17.

graphic markets, such as in Australia and Canada, where generic competition had made some inroads, and in France, where competition had put pressure on sales.

Lilly's impressive results at the end of 1998 were due mostly to Prozac, whose sales grew 8 percent worldwide, mostly supported by U.S. sales, which grew by 10 percent. International sales of Prozac remained essentially flat due to competition in foreign markets. Prozac had been the company's savior, responsible for Lilly's turnaround in the mid 1990s. But in April of 1999, Lilly reported first-quarter Prozac sales down 4 percent from the previous year, with U.S. sales down 6 percent and a 2 percent rise in world sales (Anonymous, 1999C).

One way Lilly tried to protect its patent on Prozac was to market the drug in other forms, such as a once-a-week pill. This new form of Prozac was submitted to the FDA for approval in early 1999.

Even if Lilly were able to retain patent protection on Prozac until 1993, there were competitors producing other antidepressants that were showing promise, such as Celexa, marketed by Warner-Lambert and Forest Laboratories, Inc., and Pfizer's Zoloft and SmithKline Beecham's Paxil, which were second and third, respectively, in terms of sales in the antidepressant market. In addition, even though Prozac had shown strong sales growth overseas and sales had increased 10 percent in the United States in 1998, some experts were not necessarily optimistic about its future with Lilly. Lilly stock suffered a blow in March 1999, dropping over 5 percent after one securities analyst lowered estimates for Prozac sales in 1999 (Anonymous, 1999E).

During February 1999, Lilly and Barr Laboratories Inc. reached a partial settlement with regard to Barr's patent-rights lawsuit, which was a victory for Lilly in that it barred Barr from manufacturing generic versions of Prozac. However, the case was not completely resolved because of appeals filed by Barr.

Anti-infectives (Antibiotics) Comprising 15 percent of company sales in 1997, Lilly's sales of anti-infectives decreased 13 percent. This was one therapeutic area where strong competition from generics in the United States and overseas led to a sales decline. Sales outside the United States accounted for approximately 75 percent of anti-infectives sales.

Insulins Insulins included Humulin and Humalog. The production of insulins constituted 13 percent of the company's sales in 1998.

Other The following newer products (launched in 1996) accounted for 13 percent of company sales in 1997:

- *Zyprexa.* This product was an antischizophrenic— a treatment for schizophrenia and related psychoses. Zyprexa boasted sales of $1.4 billion, 16 percent of the company's sales, in its first year of existence on the world market. Whether it would become another Prozac remained to be seen.

- *Gemzar.* This was a product treating cancer.

- *ReoPro.* This was a cardiovascular agent.

- *Evista.* An estrogenlike compound that prevented osteoporosis and perhaps breast cancer, representing Lilly's late 1990s efforts toward moving into women's health care, this had disappointing sales in the first year of only $144 million, or 1 percent of the company's sales in 1998. The British drug company Zeneca Inc. sued Lilly in February 1999 for making claims about Evista as a treatment for breast cancer, since research in this area had not been completed. Lilly executives responded by saying that this had been identified as part of the company's long-term strategy for Evista, but as of yet they said Lilly had not made such claims.

All other products in addition to the ones discussed above comprised 13 percent of company sales.

Lilly also had devoted a portion of its efforts to the animal health sector, which comprised 7 percent of the company's sales in 1998 (Eli Lilly, 1998).

Patent protection of a company's products was a good indicator of the strength of future profits, especially in the light of high R&D costs. Lilly's product patent expiration scenario at the end of the 1990s was centered around Prozac, whose patent was due to expire in 2001; the patent for how it functioned was to expire in 2003, as shown in Figure 10.

Distribution

Within the United States, Lilly used two hundred independent wholesale outlets to distribute its pharmaceutical products. The company's primary objective in distribution was ensuring that customers— physicians, pharmacies, hospitals, and health care

FIGURE 10

Eli Lilly & Company Patent Expirations
for Major Therapeutic Products

Product	Year	Product	Year
Prozac	2001, 2003	ReoPro	2015
Axid	2002	Gemzar	2006*
Zyprexa	2011	Evista	2012*
Humalog	2013		

Source: Eli Lilly and Company (1999), 10K report for the fiscal year
ended December 31, 1998 [Online]. *http://www.sec.gov/Archives/
edgar/data/59478/0000950131-99-001772.txt.* Accessed April 17.

professionals—had immediate access to its products.
In 1998, four primary wholesale distributors were
responsible for 55 percent of the company's consolidated net sales; the remainder was distributed by
smaller wholesalers, none of which accounted for
more than 7 percent of consolidated net sales (Eli
Lilly, 1998).

Distribution outside the United States was
accomplished through salaried sales representatives.
Neuroscience products made up the largest therapeutic class of drugs marketed outside the United States.
In the late 1990s, Lilly stepped up marketing efforts
in certain emerging markets, such as Central and
Eastern Europe, Latin America, Asia, and Africa.
However, sales outside the United States remained at
37 percent of company sales, down from 44 percent
in 1995.

Alliances

Consistent with the strategic industry-wide business
model, Lilly was heavily involved in alliances to perform research. At the end of 1997, the company was
involved in fifty significant research alliances, thirty
of which were signed in 1997 (Eli Lilly, 1999).

Other alliances and agreements involved crucial
aspects of drug marketing and served to lengthen
Lilly's so-called monopoly on patented drugs. In late
1998, Lilly signed an agreement with Sepracor, a
company that specialized in removing side effects
from drugs currently on the market and licensing the
rights to market the new product back to the original
company. In this case, Sepracor was researching a
new form of Prozac, which, if successful, would allow
Lilly to continue with their exclusive rights to Prozac,
the blockbuster drug that in 1998 was responsible for

30 percent of Lilly's revenues. It was not without
opposition from other industry participants that
Lilly was proceeding with this agreement. The U.S.
FTC was investigating the agreement in early 1999
because of a lawsuit against Lilly by Barr Laboratories, a generic drugmaker, which stood to lose the
marketing of a generic form of Prozac and thus the
entry of competition if the Lilly-Sepracor deal was
allowed to proceed. Other research alliances included
collaboration with Takeda Chemical Industries, Ltd.,
a Japanese pharmaceutical company, to comarket the
company's oral diabetes treatment, which was still
under regulatory approval in 1999. In 1998, Lilly
made an agreement with ICOS Corporation to enter
into an eventual joint venture for the study of treatments for sexual dysfunction.

Overseas Markets

In the late 1990s, Lilly was selling in 159 countries.
The company had R&D facilities in nine countries,
including North America, Europe, and Japan. It had
manufacturing facilities in twenty countries, including locations in Australia, South America, China, the
Middle East, Europe, and the United States.

In 1997, while the company's overall sales
increased 16 percent, sales in the United States
increased 28 percent and outside the United States by
merely 1 percent. The weakness in overseas sales was
in part due to unfavorable exchange rates and price
decreases. In 1998, overseas sales experienced a turnaround because of the successes of some of the new
drugs, but foreign sales as a percentage of total sales
still remained at approximately 36 percent of total
revenues in 1998, as shown in Figures 11 and 12.

FIGURE 11

Eli Lilly & Company Overseas Sales
(U.S.$ millions)

Year	Amount	Year	Amount
1989	1,335.7	1994	2,430.2
1990	1,636.9	1995	2,950.9
1991	1,807.0	1996	3,081.0
1992	1,996.2	1997	3,105.9
1993	2,097.5	1998	3,400.6

Source: Eli Lilly and Company (1999), 10K report for the fiscal year
ended December 31, 1998 [Online]. *http://www.sec.gov/Archives/
edgar/data/59478/0000950131-99-001772.txt.* Accessed April 17.

FIGURE 12

Eli Lilly & Company Sales, 1998,
by Geographic Area

Region	U.S.$ millions	% of Total
U.S.	5,837	63
Western Europe	1,692	18
Other regions	1,708	18
Total	9,237	100

Source: Hoover's Online (1999), Company Capsules [Online].
http://www.hoovers.com. Accessed March 29.

Research and Development

Lilly Research Laboratories (LRL) was the division of the company responsible for R&D for pharmaceutical products and animal health products. In 1997, Lilly's expenditures for R&D were $1.3 billion, or 16 percent of sales. This was in line with major competitors, for whom the percentage spent on R&D ranged from 14 to 18 percent. In 1998, research and development costs increased by 27 percent. The company stated that the increase was due to greater R&D efforts as well as the development of external R&D collaborations. One of the industry benchmarks was comparing the rate of sales growth to the rate of R&D expenditure growth. When R&D growth was higher, pressure was put on earnings. In Lilly's case, although sales growth had been strong, R&D expenditures were increasing at a faster rate. This might have been the result of Prozac earnings being directed toward new research and development.

Toward the Future

The most prevalent industry factor at work at the end of the 1990s was the quickly escalating R&D costs, which necessitated choosing core businesses wisely in order to enjoy higher margins. The tendency for companies to join forces to confront this phenomenon was beginning to change the average size of pharmaceutical manufacturing organizations. Lilly had already experienced some success with reorganizing its business around its core competencies, five specific therapeutic categories in the mid 1990s, after the entrance of a new CEO, Randall Tobias, in 1993. It was through this reorganization that the blockbuster product Prozac emerged, boosting the company's sales and making Lilly a top ten contender within the industry. Lilly realized that Prozac had boosted it into this prestigious group of players; however, it had to design a new strategy to continue strong growth post Prozac in light of market and internal conditions.

The U.S. market, which had usually boasted strong growth rates throughout the second half of the century, had once again been booming because of product innovation and strong volume sales. Smaller pharmaceutical firms, especially those outside the United States wanting to get a piece of the action, looked for merger partners with whom they could join either to increase their R&D muscle or to have immediate access to the American market. However, even the U.S. market's strong growth rates could not be counted on because of the dominance of managed care, which was changing the dynamics of the industry and putting downward pressure on prices. The industry also had to focus on global launching, even though markets outside the United States appeared to be less attractive with socialist governments and price controls.

An additional prevailing external factor was the aging of the world population and the lengthening of life expectancy. Experts had cited several conditions from which the oldest age groups would suffer in this environment, and a key to success in the future would be the ability to address these particular areas with treatment.

Lilly realized that it was in a middle-of-the-road position. In the current environment of rising R&D costs, its pipeline of drugs contained some decent candidates to create strong future sales growth. However, it remained to be seen whether the company could manage the loss of Prozac and still provide excellent growth and shareholder value. Wall Street analysts were on the fence about Lilly, and some recommendations were: yes, buy pharmaceuticals, but hold off on Lilly. Internally, Lilly was going through some of its own transitions. Randall Tobias, who had led the company through the mid 1990s reorganization and had guided the Prozac success story, decided to retire in 1998. The new CEO, Sidney Taurel, had to decide on a strategic direction toward which to carry the company into the new millennium in light of industry and company conditions.

At a meeting of the Board of Directors in the spring of 1999, Mr. Laurel was evaluating possible alternatives provided by various directors. Mr. Charles E. Golden, executive vice president and chief financial officer, realized that Lilly had already tightened its therapeutic focus onto five basic areas that would help it capture and take advantage of an aging world population—it already had a presence here. Mr. Golden recognized that Lilly, like many other pharmaceutical firms, was at the mercy of its drug pipeline, since at the time it was approaching a possible loss of Prozac. There were some promising drugs in its pipeline, specifically, Zyprexa, which had blossomed in its second year of sales to a USD 1.4 billion selling drug. The other promising candidates were ReoPro and Gemzar, but neither of these looked like it would have the strength of Prozac. Thus the company had to devise a way to maintain its main contender status within the industry by continuing the growth rates it had achieved with Prozac. It did not want this success story to be a onetime deal.

Mr. Golden felt that he had to expand the company by locating a merger partner by which he could enter a compatible sector that would provide earnings with a type of insurance when the drug pipeline had possible gaps. In this way, Lilly could continue to pursue pharmaceuticals and use its strength in R&D, as it had done previously, but would have the added protection of consumer products that focused more on marketing and sales, an area in which Lilly had been strong. While both consumer product and pharmaceutical demand were considered to be relatively insensitive to swings in the business cycle, a consumer goods unit would equal revenues minus the pipeline problem. Golden cited Pfizer, the powerhouse company whose drug pipeline had been formidable against the competition but which at the same time had been able to focus on building strong brand recognition with consumer products. The fact was that strength in one sector had not deterred Pfizer from performing well in the other. In other words, the businesses were compatible, and this addition could be strategically beneficial. In addition, since most over-the-counter medicines had their beginnings as ethical products, Lilly would be able to make this transition on its own upon expiration of patents. It seemed a logical move on the part of Mr. Golden.

Mr. Taurel listened carefully to these arguments. The idea of making strides toward becoming a powerhouse like Pfizer had always attracted him, and the theory behind Mr. Golden's presentation was certainly logical. Pfizer was living proof that this strategy of having varying business units could work; however, he felt rather uneasy about such a radical strategy change. After all, his predecessor had refocused Lilly's strategy around the company's core competencies and had sold off other business units, making strong focus one of the company's strengths. He felt that although the loss of Prozac might have serious consequences for earnings, Lilly's pipeline was still promising and had been effective against competition in similar therapeutic areas. He added that the company should perhaps be keeping its eggs in this strategic basket and not be so quick to reverse the internal trend of the mid 1990s. He was willing to listen to other proposals.

Another officer at Lilly, Mr. Gerhard N. Mayr, president of intercontinental operations, although not opposed to finding a merger partner, had a different idea. He noted that Lilly had excellent success in the United States, a market that had provided strong growth potential and the most attractive market in the industry. However, he recognized that other competitors were experiencing higher sales percentages overseas and that Lilly, if it wanted to retain its status in the industry, could not necessarily rely only on the U.S. market for future growth. Secondly, the company size in terms of sales was changing because of the trend toward mergers and acquisitions, and at least in the near term, it was losing its position as a top contender in terms of sales.

Lilly's success story with Prozac had become, in 1998, mostly a U.S. phenomenon. That is, Prozac sales overseas had been basically flat because of competition from European firms. Even though Lilly was already operating in some 150 countries, sales outside the United States did not well represent the company's investment in those markets. If it had better representation in those markets, perhaps in the form of a European partner with compatible therapeutic competencies, it would be able to accomplish a threefold objective: further strengthen its R&D capabilities, since R&D in Europe was highly respected; pick up synergies with a foreign partner while increasing its capital base in an environment of mergers and acquisitions that were quickly expanding the average size of firms in the industry; and increase its presence in Europe so it could participate in more opening markets in the future. In this way, the company could also remain focused on its core competencies, an industry key to success in the late 1990s. Mayr noticed that companies like SmithKline Beecham were experiencing problems because of too broadly designed strategies. Thus Lilly had to stick with its therapeutic competencies—however, with a partner.

Mr. Laurel had listened to both of these arguments intently, but he was not necessarily intent on making an immediate decision. Both his board members had put forth ideas that had strategic sense; however, he felt that the situation merited deeper thought and analysis.

REFERENCES

Agrawal, M. (1997). "Global Competitiveness in the Pharmaceutical Industry: An Examination of the Factors." Center for Global Education, St. John's University, September.

Anonymous (1999A). "Boost for China's Pharmaceutical Industry for 1999," Intelli-Health, Inc. [Online]. *http://www.intelihealth.com/ IH/ihtIH*. Accessed April 20.

Anonymous (1999B). "Business: Pill Pushing." *Economist*, February 13, 350(8106): 66 [Online]. *http://proquest.umi.com*. Accessed March 23.

Anonymous (1999C). "Eli Lilly Sales Higher but Prozac Down." *Financial Times*, April 1999 [Online]. *http://www.ft.com/ hippocampus/qb266e.htm*. Accessed April 19.

Anonymous (1999D). "Experts Predict Growing Revenue, Greater Expense in Global Market." *Medical Marketing and Media*, February, 34(2): 18 [Online]. *http://proquest.umi.com*. Accessed April 14.

Anonymous (1999E). "Lilly Shares Drop on Concern About Prozac." *New York Times*, March 18: C4 [Online]. *http://proquest .umi.com*. Accessed April 14; Curwen, A. (1999). "Acquisitions in Europe," *European Venture Capital Journal*, March 1 [Online]. *http://proquest.umi.com*. Accessed March 18.

Edlin, M. (1997). "Pharmacy Benefits Go Global." *Managed Healthcare*, December, 7(12): 30 [Online]. *http://proquest.umi.com*. Accessed March 18, 1999.

Eli Lilly & Company (1998). Annual Report [Online]. *http://www.elililly.com*. Accessed March 15, 1999.

Eli Lilly & Company (1999). 10K report for the fiscal year ended December 31, 1998 [Online]. *http://www.sec.gov/Archives/edgar/ data/59478/0000950131-99-001772.txt*. Accessed April 17.

Gerstein, A. (1997). "Pharmaceutical Industry." *Collier's Encyclopedia* [Online]. *http://web7.infotrac-custom.com/*. Accessed March 10, 1999.

Hoover's Online (1999). Company Capsules [Online]. *http://www .hoovers.com*. Accessed March 29.

IMS Health (1999). "Global Pharma Forecast 1998–2002" [Online]. *http://ims-global.com/insight/report/generics/report.htm*. Accessed March 20.

LLY NEWS (1999). *Corporate Communications Internal Publication*, March 12.

Mauer Fron, J., and Craig S. Smith (1998). "Drugs: Prozac's Maker Confronts China over Knockoffs." *Wall Street Journal*, March 25: B1 [Online]. *http://proquest.umi.com*. Accessed April 19, 1999.

Moran, C. (1999). "Industry Snapshot: Pharmaceuticals and Medical Equipment." *Hoover's Online Industry Zone* [Online]. *http://www.hoovers.com/features/industry/pharm.html*. Accessed April 19.

Moore, S. D. (1998). "Hopes Dwindle That EU Would Dismantle Draconian Price Controls on Medicines." *Wall Street Journal*, December 7: 1 [Online]. *http://proquest.umi.com*. Accessed March 10, 1999.

Moore, S. D. (1999). "Novo Nordisk, Following Rivals' Path, Opts to Split into Two Separate Entities." *Wall Street Journal*, February 24: 1 [Online]. *http://proquest.umi.com*. Accessed April 12.

Morrow, D. J. (1999). "Companies Find Bonus in Drugs That Cure Several Ills." *New York Times*, March 19: C1 [Online]. *http:// proquest.umi.com*. Accessed April 12.

Saldanha, G., P. Pesanello, and E. Harrington (1997). "Building Value Through Global Markets." *Pharmaceutical Executive*, December, 17(12): 72–78 [Online]. *http://proquest.umi.com*. Accessed April 14, 1999.

Scott, A. (1999). "Drug Makers Consolidate." *Chemical Week*, January 6, 161(1): 29 [Online]. *http://proquest.umi.com*. Accessed March 23.

Sharpe, P., and Tom Keelin (1998). "How SmithKline Beecham Makes Better Resource-Allocation Decisions." *Harvard Business Review*, March–April, 76(2): 45–52 [Online]. *http://proquest.umi.com*. Accessed April 12, 1999.

Sherrid, P. (1999). "A Big Downer for Prozac." *U.S. News and World Report*, February 1, 126(4): 42–43 [Online]. *http://proquest .umi.com*. Accessed March 15.

Standard & Poor's Industry Surveys (1998). "Healthcare: Facilities, Managed Care, Pharmaceuticals, Products and Supplies," December 17.

Stipp, D. (1998). "Why Pfizer was So Hot." *Fortune*, May 11 [Online]. *http://www.pfizer.com/pfizerinc/about/fortune2.html*. Accessed April 10, 1999.

Vilas-Boas, I. M., and C. Patrick Tharp (1997). "Practitioner Update: The Drug Approval Process in the U.S., Europe, and Japan: Some Marketing and Cost Implications." *Journal of Managed Care Pharmacy*, July–August, 3(4) [Online]. *http://www.amcp.org/public/ pubs/journal/vol3/num4/drug.html*. Accessed April 13, 1999.

Yates, K. (1999). "Fit for the World." *Campaign*, January 8: 3–5 [Online]. *http://proquest.umi.com*. Accessed April 14.

Yoshida, M, (1995). "Pharmaceuticals: West Meets East in the Asian Markets." *Tokyo Business Today*, August, 63(8): 36–37 [Online]. *http://proquest.umi.com*. Accessed April 12, 1999.

38

Kikkoman Corporation in the Mid 1990s: Market Maturity, Diversification, and Globalization

This case was prepared by Norihito Tanaka, Kanagawa University, Marilyn L. Taylor, University of Missouri at Kansas City, Joyce A. Claterbos, University of Kansas, and NACRA.

In early 1996, Mr. Yuzaburo Mogi, president of Kikkoman Corporation, faced a number of challenges. Analysts indicated concern with Kikkoman's slow sales growth and noted that the company's stock had underperformed on the Nikkei Exchange in relation to the market

The authors express deep appreciation to Kikkoman Corporation, which provided encouragement to this study, including access to the U.S. manufacturing and marketing facilities in addition to time in the corporate offices in Japan. The authors also gratefully acknowledge the support for this study provided by the Japanese Department of Education and the Institute for Training and Development in Tokyo. Quotes and data in this case study were drawn from a variety of personal interviews in the United States and Japan, company documents, and public sources. Documents and public sources appear in the list of references at the conclusion of the case.

This case is intended to be used as a basis for class discussion rather than as an illustration of either effective or ineffective handling of the situation.

and to its peers for several years. Throughout the world, ongoing changes in taste preferences and dietary needs presented threats to the company's traditional food lines. The company marketed its branded products in ninety-four countries and had to consider which products and markets to emphasize as well as which new markets to enter. As Mr. Mogi described the company's focus, "We are now concentrating on further enhancing our ability to serve consumers in Japan and overseas. The basic keynotes of this effort are expansion of soy sauce markets, diversification, and globalization."

In Japan, Kikkoman had long dominated the soy sauce market, and its mid 1990s market share position of 27 percent was well beyond the 10 percent of its next closest competitor. However, its share of the soy sauce market had continued to decline from its high of 33 percent in 1983, falling from 28 percent in 1993 to 27.2 percent in 1994. Further, although the company's worldwide sales had increased slightly overall from 1994 to 1995, sales of soy sauce in Japan had decreased over 1 percent during that period.

The U.S. market had provided significant opportunity in the post–World War II period. However, the company's U.S. market share for soy and other company products was essentially flat. In addition, three competitors had built plants in the United States beginning in the late 1980s. Mr. Mogi was aware that Kikkoman's choices in the U.S. market would provide an important model for addressing higher income mature markets.

With a market capitalization of nearly ¥160 billion,[1] Kikkoman Corporation was the world's largest soy sauce producer, Japan's nineteenth largest food company, and also Japan's leading soy sauce manufacturer. The company was the oldest continuous enterprise among the two hundred largest industrials in Japan. It began brewing shoyu, or naturally fermented soy sauce, in the seventeenth century and had dominated the Japanese soy industry for at least a century. The company held 50 percent of the U.S. soy sauce market and 30 percent of the world market. Kikkoman had thirteen manufacturing facilities in Japan and one each in the United States, Singapore, and Taiwan. The company was one of the few traditional manufacturers

to successfully establish a presence worldwide. (Exhibits 1 and 2 have the locations of and information on the company's principal subsidiaries. Exhibits 3 and 4 list the consolidated financial statements.)

Kikkoman in Japan

The Beginnings in Noda

In 1615, the widow of a slain samurai warrior fled three hundred miles from Osaka to the village of Noda near Edo (now called Tokyo). With her five children, the widow Mogi embarked upon rice farming and subsequently began brewing shoyu, or soy sauce. The quality of the Mogi family's shoyu was exceptional almost from its beginnings. At the time, households produced shoyu for their own use, or local farmers made and sold excess shoyu as a side enterprise to farming. As more people moved to the urban areas in the seventeenth and eighteenth centuries, there was increased demand for nonhome production. Households developed preferences for the product of a particular brewer. (See Appendix A: The Making of Soy Sauce.)

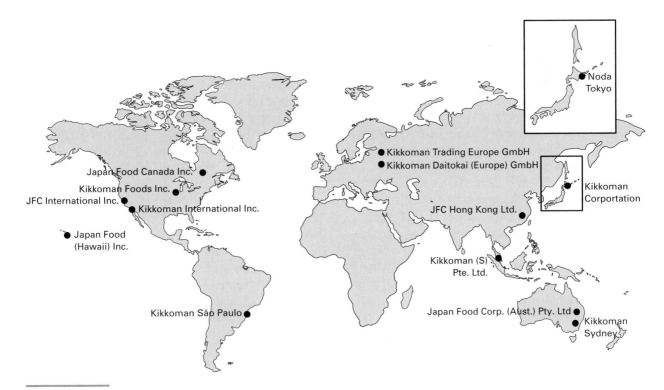

EXHIBIT 1

Locations of Principal Subsidiaries

Source: "Flavors That Bring People Together," Kikkoman Corporation Brochure, 1994.

EXHIBIT 2

Consolidated Subsidiaries as of FY 1995

Subsidiary	Country	Paid-In Capital (¥)m/$m)	Kikkoman Equity (%)
Japan Del Monte	Japan	900	99.7%
Mann's Wine	Japan	900	100.0
Pacific Trading	Japan	72	66.7
Morishin	Japan	30	66.7
Kikkoman Foods, Inc.	U.S.	U.S.$ 6	100.0
Kikkoman International	U.S.	U.S.$ 3.5	92.6
JFC International	U.S.	U.S.$ 1.2	98.0
Kikkoman Trading Europe	Germany	DM 1.5	75.0
Kikkoman Pte	Singapore	S$ 7.5	100.0
Kikkoman Trading Pte	Singapore	S$ 0.4	100.0
Tokyo Food Processing	U.S.	U.S.$ 0.02	100.0
Hapi Products	U.S.	U.S.$ 0.05	100.0
Rex Pacific	U.S.	U.S.$ 1.5	100.0

Source: Table 4: Consolidated Subsidiaries, UBS Securities Limited, May 28, 1996, as reported by *Investext*.

Shoyu had come to Japan with the arrival of Buddhism in the sixth century. The teachings of Buddhism prohibited eating meat and fish. Residents of the Japanese islands turned from meat-based to vegetable-based flavorings. One of the favorites became a flavorful seasoning made from fermented soybeans. A Japanese Zen Buddist priest who had studied in China brought the recipe to Japan. The Japanese discovered that adding wheat gave the sauce a richer, more mellow flavor.

Over the eighteenth century, Noda became a major center for shoyu manufacturing in Japan. Shoyu's major ingredients, soybeans and wheat, grew readily in the rich agricultural Kanto plain that surrounded Noda. The trip to the major market of Edo took only one day on the Edo River. The various shoyu-producing families in the Noda area actively shared their knowledge of fermentation. The Mogi family and another Noda area family, the Takanashi family, were especially active in the industry. By the late eighteenth century, the two families had become interrelated through marriage. Their various enterprises made considerable investment in breweries, and family members began ancillary enterprises such as grain brokering, keg manufacture, and transportation.

Japan's Shoyu Distribution System and Industry Structure

Japan's neophyte and fragmented shoyu industry had two distribution systems during this time. In the rural areas, the shoyu breweries sold their products directly to households. In the cities, urban wholesalers distributed shoyu, vinegar, and sake. The wholesalers purchased bulk shoyu and established their own brands. The wholesalers controlled pricing, inventory, distribution, and marketing knowledge. They would distribute branded shoyu only on consignment. During the 1800s, the wholesalers formed alliances that gave them near monopolistic power over the Tokyo market. As the shoyu manufacturers became more efficient, they found it impossible to lower prices or make other adjustments to increase their market share.

The Mogi and Takanashi families took several steps to counteract the wholesalers' dominance. The Takanashi family had diversified into wholesaling some years prior and were part of the wholesalers' alliance. One Mogi family intermarried with a wholesaler's family—a traditional strategy in Japan for cementing strategic alliances. In addition, the Mogi and Takanashi families worked to increase brand recognition and dominance. In 1838, Mogi Saheiji

EXHIBIT 3

Consolidated Profit and Loss Statement ((¥) m)

	1989	1990	1991	1992	1993	1994	1995
Sales	195,851	196,925	206,861	211,671	203,491	200,976	203,286
COGS	117,062	118,808	122,872	124,882	118,504	117,809	119,656
Gross profit	78,789	78,117	83,989	86,789	84,987	83,167	83,629
Gross profit margin (%)	40.2	39.7	40.6	41	41.8	41.4	41.1
SG&A expenses	71,227	71,876	74,181	76,019	74,320	72,689	72,836
SG&A exp. (%)	36.4	36.5	35.9	35.9	36.5	36.2	35.8
Operating profit	7,562	6,240	9,807	10,769	10,666	10,477	10,792
Operating margin (%)	3.9	3.2	4.7	5.1	5.2	5.2	5.3
Net non-op. income	−572	−1,042	−1,564	−1,895	−2,282	−2,197	−2,305
Recurring profit	6,990	5,197	8,243	8,873	8,384	8,280	8,487
Recurring margin (%)	3.6	2.6	4	4.2	4.1	4.1	4.2
Net extraordinary income	181	1,165	1,317	59	108	1,434	−1,177
Pretax profit	7,170	6,363	9,559	8,932	8,493	9,714	7,310
Tax	3,327	3,299	4,726	5,178	4,597	4,157	3,569
Tax rate (%)	46.4	50.7	49.4	58	54.1	42.8	48.8
Minority interest	56	78	37	34	1	−52	46
Amortization of consol. dif.	0	0	−35	1	5	0	−314
Equity in earnings	1,097	1,464	1,188	1,245	887	1,002	996
Net profit	4,697	4,694	6,166	4,928	4,688	6,614	4,447
Shares outstanding (m)	169.08	169.71	169.97	178.61	187.62	187.77	197.2
EPS	27.8	27.7	31.3	25	23.8	33.5	22.6
EPS change (%)	80	−0.4	13.3	−20.2	−4.9	41	−32.8
Cash flow per share	20.8	46.5	48	41.9	44.4	58.5	46.8
Average exchange rate (¥/USD)	137.96	144.79	134.71	126.65	111.20	102.21	94.06

Sources: Table 9: UBS Securities Limited, May 28, 1996; *The World Almanac,* 1998 (original source: IMF).

applied for and received the shogunate's recognition of his family's premier brand, named Kikkoman. He aggressively promoted the brand by sponsoring professional storytellers and sumo wrestlers, embossing paper lanterns and umbrellas with the Kikkoman trademark, and putting ornate gold labels from Paris on his Kikkoman shoyu kegs. In the latter part of the nineteenth century, Kikkoman shoyu won recognition in several world's fairs.

In reaction to depressed market prices and fluctuating costs of inputs, a number of the Noda shoyu brewers formed the Noda Shoyu Brewers' Association in 1887. The association purchased raw materials, standardized wages, and regulated output quality. The members' combined efforts resulted in the

largest market share at the time, 5 to 10 percent of the Tokyo market, and widespread recognition of the high quality of Noda shoyu.

Noda brewers, and especially the Mogi and Takanashi families, began research and development activities early. The Japanese government encouraged the Noda shoyu brewers to conduct research in the recovery and processing of the two byproducts of shoyu manufacture, shoyu oil and shoyu cake. In the early 1900s, the association began to fund a joint research and development laboratory.

The Shoyu Industry in the Twentieth Century

In 1910, there were still fourteen thousand known makers of shoyu in Japan. However, a number of

EXHIBIT 4

Consolidated Balance Sheet ((¥) m)

	1990	1991	1992	1993	1994	1995
Current Assets	81,611	88,092	89,705	103,152	105,220	107,339
Cash and deposits	13,254	17,570	18,261	28,826	36,381	37,366
Accounts receivable	43,579	44,661	44,503	46,009	44,246	44,439
Securities	315	1,012	1,316	3,310	3,306	3,307
Inventories	21,769	21,300	22,484	21,469	18,579	19,258
Fixed assets	94,631	97,999	105,231	113,940	112,183	119,411
Tangible assets	52,087	53,254	59,276	67,649	65,795	72,684
Land	11,768	12,011	11,910	15,156	15,613	11,540
Investments	26,371	29,597	31,771	33,051	34,083	35,006
Total Assets	177,583	187,316	195,955	218,561	218,805	228,308
Liabilities and Owner's Equity						
Current liabilities	48,040	52,626	54,014	50,272	46,663	63,400
Short-term borrowings	18,846	18,908	19,046	17,462	14,838	15,741
Fixed liabilities	58,374	58,850	62,351	85,532	85,143	71,710
Long-term borrowings	4,457	4,549	4,723	3,274	3,091	2,312
Bonds and CBs[a]	26,565	26,346	26,231	46,170	44,776	29,921
Minority interest	1,223	1,166	1,157	1,103	1,024	427
Total liabilities	107,638	112,643	117,522	136,909	132,832	135,538
Shareholders' equity	69,945	74,673	78,434	81,651	85,973	92,770
Total Liabilities and Equity	177,583	187,316	195,955	218,561	218,805	228,308

[a]There were two CBs issued January 90 exercisable at (¥) 1,522. The other two were issued July 93 and were exercisable at (¥) 969. With the share price at approximately (¥) 100, the total dilution factor was about 18 percent, with 80 percent of that dependent on the two CBs exercisable at (¥) 969. Of 228 ((¥) m) in 1995, about 170 belonged to the parent (i.e., Japan corporation) company.

Source: Nikkei Needs as reported in Table 12: Consolidated Balance Sheet, UBS Securities Limited, May 28, 1996.

changes led to consolidation. Manufacturing shifted from a small-batch, brewmaster-controlled production process to a large-batch, technology-controlled process. Mogi families in Noda invested in modernized plants, and a fifth-grade Japanese geography reader featured a state-of-the-art Kikkoman facility. A national market also developed, thanks to the development of a railway system throughout most of the country. In addition, consumer tastes shifted to the Tokyo-style shoyu produced by eastern manufacturers such as the Noda Shoyu Brewers' Association.

Consumers also began to purchase shoyu in smaller glass bottles rather than in the traditional large wooden barrels that sometimes leaked and were expensive to build and difficult to store. Raw materials also became more expensive as the brew-

ers increasingly sought higher-quality imported soybeans (from Manchuria, China, and Korea) and salt (from England, Germany, and China). The association members controlled costs by purchasing in bulk and demanding high-quality materials from suppliers.

The Noda Shoyu Company: 1918–1945—A Family *Zaibatsu*[2]

In 1918, seven Mogi families and a related Takanashi family combined their various enterprises into a joint stockholding company called the Noda Shoyu Company. The merger was in reaction to the market upheaval caused by World War I. The new company was a small *zaibatsu* with nearly a dozen companies in manufacturing fermented grain-based products, transportation, and finance. Unlike early shoyu manufacturing, where ownership, management, and operations were clearly separated, the Mogi and Takanashi families owned, managed, and operated their firm. Initially, the family produced thirty-four different brands of shoyu at various price points. The Kikkoman brand had a history of heavy promotion for over forty years, greater Tokyo market share, and a higher margin than the company's other brands. The Kikkoman brand became the company's flagship brand. The new corporation continued its long-standing emphasis on research and development and aggressively pursued new manufacturing processes, increased integration, and acquisition of other shoyu companies.

After the Mogi Takanashi coalition, the company aggressively pursued a strong nationwide sole agent system and direct distribution. The combined company also continued Kikkoman's well-known advertising activities. Kikkoman had carried out the first newspaper advertising in 1878. In 1922, the company carried out the firm's first advertising on the movie screen.

During the 1920s, the company aggressively modernized with machines such as hydraulic presses, boilers, conveyors, and elevators. The company's modernization efforts were emulated by competitors, and the results were increased supply and heightened industry competition. The changes brought about by increased automation led to severe labor unrest. One particularly long strike against the Kikkoman company in the late 1920s almost destroyed the participating labor union. After the strike ended, Kikkoman rehired about a third of the striking employees. The company centralized and reorganized the work processes to accommodate improved technology, restructured work practices, and established methods to monitor and reward workers for their performance. However, the company also established efforts to improve the identity of the workers with the company. Internal communications carried the message that all employees were members of one family, or ikka, united in a common purpose—the production of shoyu. The Noda Shoyu Company was also heavily involved in the city of Noda and supported many of its cultural and charitable activities as well as the local railroad, bank, town hall, cultural center, library, fire station, elementary school, hospital, recreation facilities and association, and much of the city's water system.

Kikkoman's International Activities

Kikkoman's initial export activities began in the late seventeenth century with Dutch and Chinese traders. The Dutch began to export shoyu to Holland and the rest of Europe, while the Chinese served the southeast Asian markets. The shoyu brewers relied on agents for these early export transactions. During the nineteenth century, one Mogi patriarch opened a factory in Inchon, Korea. Demand for the increasing export, marketing, and direct investment continued to come primarily from Japanese and other peoples living abroad whose traditional cuisines called for shoyu. In 1910, the Noda city brewers' international activities were recognized when the Japanese government selected Noda shoyu to appear in a public relations publication introducing Japan's industries overseas.

Noda Shoyu Company continued to expand internationally between World War I and World War II. Acquisition of raw materials from abroad continued. The company added a manufacturing facility for shoyu and miso in Manchuria and two shoyu factories in North America. Other facilities in Japan were expanded or updated to support increasing international sales.

The company established sales offices in China and Korea to market shoyu, miso, and sake. By the late 1930s, the company exported 10 percent of its output, about half to the Asian region—especially Korea, China, and Indonesia—and half to Hawaii and California. Almost all of the exports were the Kikkoman brand and were sold through food import/export firms to the company's traditional customers.

Post–World War II Kikkoman in Japan

At the end of World War II, Kikkoman operated only in Japan. Activities elsewhere had been closed. To meet the need for capital, Kikkoman issued publicly traded stock in 1946, reducing family ownership markedly. (Exhibit 5 shows the changes in ownership from 1917 to 1993.) The post–World War II period brought a number of social changes to Japanese society. Japanese families began the change to nuclear- rather than extended-family formation. Food tastes changed, leading among other trends, to a decline in per-capita consumption of shoyu. Compared with other industries, demand for soy sauce grew very slowly. In 1942, demand for soy sauce in Japan was 1.7 times greater than in 1918. Demand in the 1960s was expected to be 2.2 times greater than that in 1918. However, modernization led to increased output.

EXHIBIT 5

Noda Shoyu Company and Kikkoman Corporation Ownership

Shareholder Name	Holdings (% of total shares or assets)			
	1917	1925	1955	1993
Mogi-Takanashi-Horikiri brewing families	100.0%[a]	34.6%	15.0%[b]	2.3%
Senshusha holding company		62.0	3.1	3.4
Insurance and banking companies			9.9[c]	20.5[c]
All others		3.6	71.1	73.6

[a]Eight holdings ranging from 1.4 percent to 29.3 percent.
[b]Five holdings ranging from 1.5 percent to 4.4 percent.
[c]In 1955 and 1993, including Meiji Mutual Insurance Co., Mitsubishi Trust Bank; in 1955, including Kofukan Foundation and Noda Institute of Industrial Science; in 1993, including Nitsuit Trust Bank, Nippon Life Insurance, Sumitomo Trust, and Yasuda Trust.

Sources: W. Mark Fruin, *Kikkoman—Company, Clan, and Community* (Cambridge, MA: Harvard University Press, 1983), pp. 98, 121, 249; *Japan Company Handbook,* Toyo Keizai, Inc., 1993, p. 207.

Kikkoman had received considerable recognition for its advertising efforts prior to World War II. After the war, the company began to market even more aggressively in Japan. These efforts included establishing the company's strong nationwide distribution system throughout Japan; mounting aggressive activities in marketing research, advertising, and consumer education; and changing to a new and more Western image. As a result of Kikkoman's marketing efforts, the company's market share rose sharply. (Exhibit 6 shows the national output of shoyu and the company's market share from 1893 to 1994.) In 1964 the company officially changed its name to Kikkoman Shoyu, and in 1980 it became Kikkoman Corporation. The word *Kikkoman* is a combination of "kikko" (the shell of a tortoise) and "man" (ten thousand). It was taken from an old Japanese saying, "A crane lives a thousand years and a tortoise ten thousand years" (implying, in other words, "May you live as long!"). In essence, the Kikkoman brand connotes a long-lasting living thing. Kikkoman had become well known for its advertising skill in Japan and had found that the word *Kikkoman* was easy for Americans to pronounce.

The company also diversified its product line using its expertise in shoyu manufacture, fermentation, brewing, and foods marketing. This diversification included a 1963 venture to market Del Monte products in Japan. In 1990, the company bought the Del Monte assets and marketing rights for the Del Monte brand name in the Asia–Pacific region.

EXHIBIT 6

National Output and Company Market Share of Shoyu (in kiloliters)[a]

Year	National Output (Japan)	Noda Shoyu Share (%)
1893	230,360	3.5%
1903	317,500	4.5
1913	430,435	6.1
1923	624,764	5.1
1933	576,026	10.1
1943	680,955	12.0
1953	822,179	14.1
1963	1,051,730	21.4
1973	1,277,887	31.4
1983	n.a.	33.0
1993	n.a.	28.0
1994	1,323,529[b]	27.2

[a]1 kiloliter = 264 gallons.
[b]Derived from Kikkoman's production of 360,000 kl and its 27.2 percent market share. Residents of Japan consumed about 2.6 gallons of soy sauce per capita yearly. In contrast, U.S. citizens consumed about 10 tablespoons.
[c]As reported by UBS Securities Limited, May 28, 1996, in *Investext.* This source also reported that demand for soy sauce was flat in Japan and production between 1984 and 1994 had declined about 5.1 percent.

Source: W. Mark Fruin, *Kikkoman—Company, Clan, and Community* (Cambridge, MA: Harvard University Press, 1983), pp. 40–41.

(Exhibit 7 shows Kikkoman Corporation's product lists as of 1949, 1981, and 1994.) Kikkoman's R&D expertise led to activities in biotechnology and products such as enzymes, diagnostic reagents, and other biologically active substances used to test for microorganisms in water samples in hospitals, food-processing factories, and semiconductor plants. The company also developed a number of patents at home and overseas. The company became involved in both the import and export of wines. It also undertook activities in food-processing machinery. In spite of the diversification, Kikko-

man's domestic sales were still about 55 percent soy sauce related.

In the 1990s, soy sauce continued as a perennial favorite in Japan's cuisine, although demand was essentially flat. Among the remaining three thousand shoyu companies in Japan, Kikkoman produced 360,000 kl in Japan, or about 27 percent of the country's output. (Exhibit 6.) The company faced price pressures, especially on its base product of soy sauce, mainly because of the competitive pressures at the retail level in Japan and the aggressive introduction of private brands. Sales in the Del Monte line also

EXHIBIT 7

Kikkoman Corporation Products and Product Lines

1949	1981	1994
Kikkoman Brand soy sauce, sauce, memmi and tsuyu (soup bases)	**Kikkoman Brand** soy sauce, mild soy sauce (lower salt, 8%), light color soy sauce (usu-kuchi), teriyaki barbecue marinade and sauce, Worcestershire sauce, tonkatsu sauce, memmi and tsuyu (soup bases), sukiyaki sauce, instant soy soup mix, instant osumono (clear broth soup mix)	**Kikkoman Brand** soy sauce, mild soy sauce (lower salt, 8%), light color soy sauce (usu-kuchi), teriyaki sauce, Worcestershire sauce, tonkatsu sauce, memmi (soup base), sukiyaki sauce, sashimi soy sauce, lemon-flavored soy sauce, mirin (sweet rice wine), Aji-Mirin, plum wine, instant miso (soybean paste) soups, egg flower soup mixes, rice crackers, tofu, neo-genmai (puffed brown rice), genmai soups, oolong tea, tsuyu-dakono (soup base), ponzu soy sauce, soy sauce dressing, oyster sauce, bonito stock
Manjo Brand mirin (sweet rice wine), sake, shochu, whiskey	**Manjo Brand** mirin (sweet rice wine), shochu, plum wine	**Manjo Brand** triangle, komaki
	Yomonoharu Brand sake	**Yomonoharu Brand**
	Del Monte Brand tomato ketchup, juice, puree, paste, chili sauce, Mandarin orange juice	**Del Monte Brand** tomato ketchup, juice, fruit drinks, Mandarin orange juice
	Disney Brand fruit juice (orange, pineapple, grape), nectar (peach, orange)	
	Mann's Brand[a] wine and sparkling wine, brandy	**Mann's Brand** koshu, koshu (vintage), zenkoji, blush, brandy
	Higeta Brand shoyu, tsuyu, Worcestershire sauce	
	Ragu Brand spaghetti sauces	
	Kikko's Brand tomato ketchup	**Beyoung** protein powder, wheat germ
	Monet Brand cognac	**Imported Wines** aujoux, chateau tatour, boriemanoux, franz reh and sohn, pol roger

*Marketed, not manufactured, by Kikkoman.

[a]The company established its Mann Wine subsidiary in 1964.

Sources: W. Mark Fruin, *Kikkoman—Company, Clan, and Community* (Cambridge, MA: Harvard University Press, 1983), pp. 275–276; "Flavors That Bring People Together," Kikkoman Corporation Brochure, 1994.

decreased in the early 1990s. To improve performance, Kikkoman began to reduce its product line from a high of 5,000 items to an expected eventual 2,500. One bright spot was the growth in wines and spirits. In addition, Kikkoman also introduced successful new soy-sauce-related products in 1993, 1994, and 1995 in the form of two soup stocks and Steak Soy Sauce. Profit increases in the early 1990s came primarily from higher-priced luxury products. (Exhibits 8 and 9 display the parent company financial statements.) The company recognized that continuing success in its mature domestic market would depend on continuous development of new applications and variations of its older products as well as development of new products.

Kikkoman in the United States in the Post–World II Era

U.S. Market Potential

The various Mogi family branches and Noda Shoyu Company had been expanding company efforts beyond Japan since the early 1800s. Japanese expatriates living in various countries and other peoples whose traditional cuisine used shoyu constituted the company's primary pre–World War II markets. By the end of World War II, however, the various family enterprises and the Noda Shoyu Company had ended all activities outside Japan. Then in 1949 Kikkoman started to export soy sauce, mainly to the United States. In the 1950s, consumption of soy sauce began to decline in Japan. Noda Shoyu Company decided to invest heavily in expanding the international sales of Kikkoman brand shoyu to overseas markets. Whereas prior to World War II, Noda Shoyu's major overseas

markets were Asia and Hawaii, after the war, the company decided to focus on the mainland United States because (1) political and economic conditions in Asia were very unstable, (2) the Japanese community in Hawaii had relearned shoyu brewing during World War II, and there were many small Hawaiian shoyu breweries that would have made competition intense in that market, and (3) the United States had a healthy and rapidly growing economy.

Several changes in the U.S. market made that market attractive to Noda Shoyu Company. First, Americans who had been in Asia during or just after World War II developed a taste for Japanese goods, including food. Second, the company expected that as Asians in the United States became more Americanized, their consumption of traditional foods including soy sauce would decline. Third, American eating habits were shifting to more natural foods and to food that could be prepared quickly. Noda Shoyu Company moved to target both Asians and non-Asians in its marketing efforts.

During the 1956 U.S. presidential election, Noda Shoyu bought air time to advertise Kikkoman brand products. Yuzaburo Mogi, son of the head of the company's planning department, urged this move to U.S. television advertising.

U.S. Distribution Activities

During the years immediately after World War II, Japanese companies in general relied on a small group of internationalized and entrepreneurial Japanese and Japanese-American individuals. Sale of food products in the United States involved a complex distribution system with heavy reliance on food brokers as promoters to local wholesalers and retail-

EXHIBIT 8

Parent Company Revenues by Product Line ((¥) m)

	1994	1995	% Change	1996E	% Change
Soy sauce	74,666	73,843	−1.1%	75,000	1.6%
Food	15,091	16,310	8.1	18,500	13.4
Del Monte	24,692	19,857	−19.6	19,000	−4.3
Alcohol	24,993	25,925	3.7	27,000	4.1
Others	4,159	4,285	3	4,500	5
Total	143,601	140,220	−2.4	144,000	2.7

Source: Table 5: UBS Securities Limited, May 28, 1996, as reported by *Investext.*

EXHIBIT 9

Parent Company Balance Sheet ((¥) m)

	1993	1994	1995
Current assets	78,463	81,805	80,749
Fixed assets	88,007	86,029	89,599
Total	166,802	168,000	170,348
Short-term liabilities	33,469	32,033	46,762
Long-term liabilities	79,898	79,527	66,567
Equity	53,434	56,440	57,019
Total liabilities and equity	166,802	168,000	170,348

Source: Table 11: UBS Securities Limited, May 28, 1996, as reported by *Investext.*

ers. Food brokers required careful training by a knowledgeable sales team in how to use the product, especially where the product was unusual or unfamiliar to consumers. Food brokers marketed the product to wholesalers and large retailers, took orders for the product, and relayed the orders to the manufacturer or, in the case of foreign manufacturers, the manufacturer's agent. The manufacturer or agent then made delivery of the product to the wholesaler or retailer and handled all billing and accounts, paying the broker a commission for his or her marketing representation. The food broker was an important link between the manufacturer and the wholesaler or retailer. Food brokers were evaluated based on their ability to persuade retailers and wholesalers to carry products and to feature them prominently.

In 1957, the company formed Kikkoman International, Inc. (KII), a joint venture between Noda Shoyu Company in Japan and Pacific Trading of California. KII was incorporated in San Francisco to serve as the marketing and distribution center for Kikkoman products in the United States. Most of the products were produced by Noda Shoyu Company, but some were purchased from other manufacturers and sold under the Kikkoman label.

Over the next ten years, sales grew 20 to 30 percent a year. In 1960, the Safeway grocery store chain agreed to have some of its stores carry Kikkoman Soy Sauce. Noda Shoyu opened regional sales offices for KII in Los Angeles (1958), New York City (1960), Chicago (1965), and Atlanta (1977). Retail marketing activities included in-store demonstrations, advertis-

ing campaigns in women's magazines that emphasized soy sauce use in American cuisine, and limited television commercials. The company used brokers as their distribution channels to supermarkets and wholesalers for the small oriental retail stores. It encouraged food brokers through contests and training. For the food service and industrial market segments, the company carried out industrial magazine ad campaigns and special educational programs. It also formed partnerships with the American Veal Manufacturers' Association and the Avocado Association to feature Kikkoman Soy Sauce in their product advertisements.

Other major international companies had to modify their products for the United States. However, Kikkoman marketed the same soy sauce in the United States as in Japan. The company's experience in its campaign to "Westernize" soy sauce for the Japanese market applied to the campaign in the United States. In the United States, Kikkoman provided traditional, low-sodium preservative-free, and dehydrated soy sauce. The company also marketed tailor-made sauces, other food extracts, and agents.

Exploration of Potential U.S. Manufacturing Capacity

As early as 1965, Kikkoman Corporation began to explore the possibility of manufacturing in the United States. However, the company determined that sales in North America were insufficient to support the economies of scale required for a minimum efficient scale production facility. Instead, in 1968 Kikkoman Corporation contracted with a subsidiary of Leslie Salt Company of Oakland, California, to bottle the Kikkoman soy sauce shipped in bulk from Japan and to blend and bottle teriyaki sauce, a major ingredient of which was soy sauce. These bottling efforts constituted Kikkoman's first post–World War II manufacturing efforts in the United States. Bottling in the United States reduced customs and tariff costs. However, moving goods back and forth from the United States and Japan added considerably to the company's costs. In the mid 1980s, Japan imported 95 percent and 88 percent of its soybeans and wheat, respectively. The United States was Japan's major source of supply. Transportation of raw materials (such as soybeans and wheat) to Japan was between 5 and 20 percent of preproduction costs; transportation costs of brewed soy sauce from Japan to the United States was 25 percent of production costs. Various import/export restrictions and tariffs increased the risk and expense of importing raw materials to Japan and exporting finished goods to the United States.

The North American market was potentially much larger than the Japanese market, and Kikkoman had a greater share of the North American market than the company had in Japan. Yuzaburo Mogi hired a Columbia University classmate as a consultant, and the company formed a team to work with him to consider a U.S. plant. By 1970, the analyses, in spite of higher U.S. labor costs, favored construction of a U.S. manufacturing facility. As Yuzaburo Mogi put the company's motivation, "We made a decision to go after the American consumer."

Selection of Walworth, Wisconsin

The team considered over sixty potential sites in the East, West, and Midwest. The team chose the Midwest because of its central location and crop production. Ultimately, the team selected a 200-acre dairy farm site in Walworth, Wisconsin. Walworth provided the best fit with the five criteria established by the company: (1) access to markets (it was close to Milwaukee and Chicago, and the geographic convenience of a midway point between the East and West Coasts made shipping relatively efficient); (2) ample supplies of wheat and soybeans (soybeans came from Wisconsin, wheat from North Dakota, and salt from Canada); (3) a dedicated work force; (4) a strong community spirit; and (5) an impeccable supply of water. Kikkoman also appreciated Wisconsin's emphasis on a clean environment.

Walworth, Wisconsin, was situated about two hours northwest of Chicago and about one hour west of Milwaukee. A community of about 1,100, Walworth was surrounded by some of the most productive farmland in the United States. The area included a number of other smaller communities whose economies depended primarily on farming and summer vacation home residences. The company hired a local consultant, lawyer Milton Neshek, who ultimately became general counsel of Kikkoman Foods, Inc. Mr. Neshek described the original reaction to Kikkoman's purchase of prime farmland as mixed, "with a small faction on the town board opposed to the company coming in." Yuzaburo Mogi described the opposition as strong. Residents of the small, rural, close-knit farming community expressed concerns about the impact of a large, especially foreign,

corporation in a small community, the potential inflation of land values, and the possibility of industrial pollution.

One of Neshek's partners, Thomas Godfrey, visited Kikkoman facilities in Noda City, Japan. "When Kikkoman called me in 1971," said Godfrey, "and asked me to create a Wisconsin corporation for them so they could make soy sauce, I didn't even know what the hell soy sauce was. Nobody else around here did either." Walworth's plant manager, Bill Wenger, recalled his introduction to the company. In 1972, he was stationed with the U.S. Marines in Hawaii. His mother sent a newspaper clipping about the soy sauce plant, suggesting that it might be a good place to begin his return to civilian life. Wenger and his wife didn't know what soy sauce was either, but his wife went to the local grocery store and bought a bottle. As Wenger described it, the purchase was "some horrible local Hawaiian brand. She brought it home and opened it. We looked at one another and said, '*@& . . . , this stuff is terrible.'" Another of the three American production managers employed at the plant had a similar tale. The production manager said, "The first year I worked here, we never had any soy sauce in my home. My wife wouldn't buy it, wouldn't even allow it in the house. I finally brought home a bottle and put it on some meatloaf. Now we use it on just about everything. I put it on peaches. And we even have a local minister who puts it on his ice cream. . . . I do too. It's good."

No other Japanese-owned manufacturing facility had been constructed in the United States at the time. Neshek's partner, Godfrey, visited Noda because, as he put it, "I had to see for myself what it was they were talking about. I had to make sure the factory wasn't going to pollute the air and water and stink up the place." Local Kikkoman representatives met with organizations such as the local Grange, Farm Bureau groups, church groups, Rotary, and ladies' clubs. Wisconsin's governor, Patrick Lucey, came to one of the seven town meetings held to discuss the plant and explain the state's role and position. Yuzaburo Mogi described the process as "removing the fears of the local people and local council about the building of the new factory." The company was able to convince area residents that Kikkoman would not pollute the environment and would use local labor and other resources. The final vote of the county zoning board was 53 for, 13 against. The town board declined to oppose the zoning board's action. Among other issues, Kikkoman put a great deal of effort into reducing potential pollution. In talking about this process of "nemawashi," or root tending, Mr. Mogi emphasized the importance of a prosperous coexistence between the company and the local community. He said, "We've been doing business in Noda for 360 years. We learned a long time ago that to survive you need to coexist with the surrounding community."

Opening the New Plant

In January 1971, Kikkoman executives along with Japanese, Walworth, and Wisconsin officials held a ceremonial ground breaking on the 200-acre site. A Cleveland, Ohio, design and construction firm built the plant. Other American companies, many located in the region, built many of the critical components. The initial investment in the 10,000-kiloliter facility was $8 million, and the plant was finished just in time to avoid the 1973 American embargo on the sale of soybeans to Japan. Kikkoman's Walworth plant was the first Japanese investment in production capacity in the United States in the post–World War II period and the first plant Kikkoman built outside Japan after World War II. Opening ceremonies included dignitaries and officials from Wisconsin, Kikkoman, Japan, and the United States. The seven hundred invited guests heard the texts of telegrams from the Japanese prime minister and President Richard Nixon. President Nixon referred to the plant as a "visionary step (that) will mean meaningful trade relations and balance of trade and will enhance further friendships between our two countries."

From its opening in 1972 through the mid 1990s, the company expanded the Walworth facility eight times to 500,000 square feet. Kikkoman invested in facilities or equipment every year, with production increasing 8 to 10 percent per year. Originally, the plant produced two products, soy sauce and teriyaki sauce. In the mid 1990s, the plant produced eighteen products, including regular and light soy sauce, teriyaki steak sauce, sweet and sour sauce, and tempura dip. All but one used a soy base. The company had been very careful about pollution, treating its wastewater carefully so that there was no threat to nearby popular Geneva Lake. The Walworth town clerk said, "There's no noise, no pollution. I live about three-quarters of a mile from them, and once a day, I get a whiff of something that's like a sweet chocolate odor. It's no problem." The company marketed the plant's output in all fifty states plus Canada

and Mexico. Soy sauce was shipped in many varieties, including bottles ranging from 5 to 40 ounces, 1- to 5-gallon pails, and sometimes in stainless steel tank trucks for large customers. McDonald's, for example, used soy sauce in one of the Chicken McNuggets condiments.

Management of the Walworth Plant

The company maintained a state-of-the-art laboratory at the Walworth facilities. However, plant management pointed out that the most accurate test during production was the human nose. "Our people have worked with the product for so long, a whiff can tell them something is not quite right," said one Kikkoman director. The venture was described as "a prime example of the best combination of Japanese and American business and industrial savvy." As the plant's general manager, Michitaro Nagasawa, a Ph.D. in biochemistry from the University of Wisconsin, put it, "The productivity of this plant is the highest of all our plants. . . . It's an exceptional case in Kikkoman history. We took the sons and daughters of farmers, trained them and taught them about total quality management. They were raw recruits with no experience in making soy sauce. People with farm backgrounds are very diligent workers. They will work 7 days a week, 24 hours a day if necessary. They understand what hard work is."

The plant opened with fifty employees. Originally, fourteen Japanese Kikkoman employees and their families came to Walworth to train employees and get the plant functioning. The Japanese families scattered in groups of two or three to settle in Walworth and various nearby communities. Local women's community organizations "adopted" the Japanese wives, formed one-to-one friendships, and helped the Japanese wives become acclimated to the communities, including learning to drive, using the local supermarkets, and hiring baby sitters for their children. The Japanese husbands joined local service clubs. "That helped achieve an understanding between the Americans and Japanese and helped them to assimilate faster. It exposed Japanese people to a farming town that had had no Asian people before," noted Bill Nelson, Kikkoman Foods vice president. Kikkoman established the practice of rotating its Japanese employees back to Japan after an average of five years in the United States. In the mid 1990s, only seven Japanese families remained in the Walworth area, still spread throughout the local communities.

Community Contributions

Kikkoman Foods, Inc., was an active and contributing member of the community. The company donated time and funds on three levels. At the local level, the company established Kikkoman Foods Foundation in 1993. The foundation, which was to be ultimately funded at the $3 million level, was formed to support area charitable activities. The company supported as many as thirty local projects a year, including college scholarships for area students, local hospital activities, a vocational program that assisted people in developing employment-related skills, and a nearby facility that preserved circus-related items. As Walworth's town clerk put it, "They sponsor just about everything—Community Chest (an organization similar to the United Way), Boy Scouts, Girl Scouts, all the way down the line. They're very good neighbors." The clerk treasurer from a nearby town said, "You see their name in the paper almost every week, helping out some organization."

At the state level, Kikkoman Foods, Inc., supported the University of Wisconsin educational system, established up to four Beloit College scholarships to honor Governor Lucey at his alma mater, and funded a Mogi Keizaburo scholarship at the Milwaukee School of Engineering. Members of the board of directors served on several public service boards and commissions. At the national level, Kikkoman Corporation, through its U.S. subsidiary Kikkoman Foods, Inc., supported Youth for Understanding exchange programs. At the fifth anniversary celebration, Kikkoman's chairman reported that the plant had developed better than had been anticipated. At the tenth anniversary celebration of the Kikkoman plant, the local Walworth paper reported, "In the 10 years that Kikkoman Foods, Inc., has been located here, it has become an integrated part of the community. The company has truly become a part of the Walworth community, and not only in a business sense." In 1987, reflecting Kikkoman's contributions, Wisconsin's governor appointed Yuzaburo Mogi as Wisconsin's honorary ambassador to Japan.

Kikkoman's Japanese–American Management in the United States

In the mid 1990s, Kikkoman operated its U.S. activities through two subsidiaries, Kikkoman Foods, Inc. (KFI), and Kikkoman International, Inc. (KII). KFI owned and operated the Walworth manufacturing plant. KII in San Francisco, California, undertook marketing responsibilities, including wholesaler and distributor activities throughout the United States. The boards of directors for both subsidiaries had several members from the parent corporation but were primarily Americans from among local operations officers or local Walworth citizens (for KFI) or the broader U.S. community (for KII). The KFI board met as a whole once a year and rotated the site of its annual stockholders' meeting between Japan and Wisconsin. An executive committee met monthly to consider operational decisions. The executive committee included Yuzaburo Mogi, who attended two to three meetings in the United States every year, and the head of Kikkoman Corporation's International Division. The remaining members of the executive committee included American and Japanese officers from the U.S. corporation. The KII board operated in a similar manner but met only in the United States.

Yuzaburo Mogi believed that a long-term commitment was essential for international success. A 1961 alumnus of Columbia University's Graduate School of Business, Mr. Mogi was the first Japanese to graduate from a U.S. university with an M.B.A. degree. In the years following graduation, he worked in various departments in Kikkoman, including accounting, finance, computers, long-range planning, and new product development. In time, he took on other roles, including member of Kikkoman's board of directors (1979), managing director of the company (1982), executive management director (1989), and executive vice president (1994). The seventeenth generation of his family to brew soy sauce, Mr. Mogi had become Kikkoman's president in early 1995. He explained his view regarding the necessity of a long-term perspective: "We should do business from a longer range viewpoint. It will be very difficult to expect fruitful results in the short run under different and difficult circumstances. Failure will be inevitable in foreign countries if one proceeds with a short-range view. In fact, it took Kikkoman 16 years to become established in the United States."

Of the five senior managers at the Walworth facility, three were Japanese and two were American. The plant manager, the finance manager, and the laboratory manager were Japanese. It was expected that these three positions would continue to be Japanese appointments. One American manager described the situation: "We know we will only attain a certain level, but that's OK, though. I can accept that. Soy sauce has been made in Japan for centuries. It's their product, their technology. They have the history, the research."

The general manager, that is, the plant manager, was the most senior person in authority at the plant and was responsible directly to headquarters in Japan. The appointment would be a person who had been with the company for many years. The finance manager's position required someone who was familiar with Japanese accounting systems and who was steeped in the Japanese emphasis on long-range profits. Japanese corporate headquarters controlled their foreign branches through their accounting and finance sections.

Mr. Mogi explained the Japanese appointment to the position of laboratory manager: "The production of soy sauce is very sophisticated. Normally, we recruit graduates with a master's degree in Japan who have gone to universities that have specialized programs in soy sauce production. In America, there is no university that teaches soy sauce production techniques, so it is difficult to promote Americans into general manager positions." As Dr. Magasawa, general manager at the Walworth plant, put it in explaining the discriminating tastes the Japanese have developed since childhood, "The sensory system, passion, feeling, or sensitivity can't transfer. That is based on just experience. Our vice president is a kind of god in this plant because he recognizes (even) a slight difference. . . . I don't have that. That's why I can't be manufacturing vice president. I am a general manager—nothing special. I am a biochemist (with) 39 years in Kikkoman, mostly in research."

Decisions at the Walworth plant, when possible, were made by consensus. KFI vice president Bill Nelson described the plant management as American in content and Japanese in style, with decisions arrived at from the bottom up and most matters of importance needing a consensus of employees. "It's hard, really, to get at because of the fact that nothing . . . here should run in an American style or a Japanese style or what have you. It was just simply—let's see what happens when you have both parties participate," he said. Nelson gave the example of an idea for changing summer working hours to start at 7 A.M. instead of 8 A.M. so that workers could leave earlier and enjoy more daylight. It was, Nelson, pointed out, unusual for a company to even entertain the idea. Nelson explained the process: "Instead of simply exploring it on a management level, here we started the process by asking individual employees what per-

sonal inconvenience would be experienced if the hours were changed."

Milton Neshek observed that Japanese management and the middle management at the Walworth plant worked well together with long-range budgeting and strategic planning carried out by the Japanese executive team. He described the situation: "Our 30 employees feel like part of our family. That makes management more responsive to employees. Decisions, whenever possible, are made by consensus." The fact that the plant has no labor union was no surprise to Nelson. As he put it, a union "has never been an issue here."

Yuzaburo Mogi summarized Kikkoman's approach to its U.S. operations and, in particular, its Walworth plant as a five-point approach:

> Kikkoman has been successful doing business in the United States by adapting to American laws, customers, and most importantly, its culture. . . . (An) important matter to consider, especially when establishing a manufacturing plant in a foreign country, is the maintenance of what has come to be called "harmony" with society and the local community. A foreign concern should try to prosper together with society and the local community. . . . It is important to try to localize the operation. . . . (Our) . . . first commitment is the employment of as many local people as possible. Second we try to participate in local activities . . . trying to be a good corporate citizen (in Wisconsin) and contributing to society through our business activities. Third, we have been trying to avoid the so-called "Japanese-village" . . . by advising our people from Japan not to live together in one single community, but to spread out and live in several separate communities in order to become more familiar with the local people. Fourth, we try to do business with American companies. The fifth commitment is our practice of delegating most authority to local management in order to better reflect local circumstances. Through this process we are better able to make the most responsible decision. If we have an opinion, for example, we discuss it with other members at a local meeting in our American plant before reaching a decision. Kikkoman attempts to avoid a remote-control situation with letters or telephone calls from Japan. . . . If we have an opinion, we discuss it with other members at a local meeting in our American plant before reaching a decision.

The plant did encounter intercultural issues, however. For example, plant manager Bill Wenger pointed out, "Communication can be a problem sometimes. The language barrier is one reason. Then there's the problem of saving face. If a mistake is made, the Japanese tend to cover up for one another so the person who made the mistakes doesn't lose face."

The company was a popular local employer in Walworth. Local unemployment was phenomenally low at 2 percent, but the Walworth plant had over one thousand active applications on file for the plant's 136 positions. However, turnover among plant employees was negligible. "No one quits unless it is a move by a spouse. Our absenteeism is minimal and as for tardiness—we just don't have it. We offer competitive wages and good benefits. . . . [E]mployees feel like part of our family," said general counsel Neshek. Company officials stated that they paid about 10 percent more than the state average of $9.71 per hour, and employees did not have to contribute to the cost of their health insurance. As the company's vice president Shin Ichi Sugiyama put it, "In management, our primary concern is always the employee." The employees reported, "We feel like they listen to us. Our opinion counts, and we have the ability to make change, to better the company."

Mr. Sugiyama pointed out that the Walworth plant's productivity and quality had been about equal to that of Japanese plants. Productivity improved following the plant opening and by 1993 was actually the best of all the company's plants.

The U.S. Market in the 1990s[3]

U.S. Demand in the 1990s

After the opening of the Walworth plant, Kikkoman's U.S. sales growth slowed somewhat. However, Ken Saito, Kikkoman's brand manager for the Midwest, summarized the company's hopes: "Americans are more adventurous than Japanese when it comes to trying new foods. That's why we have developed some products only for the American market. But most Americans still are not familiar with how to use soy sauce." Thus, the company developed a number of nonoriental recipes that call for soy sauce and other Kikkoman products, for example, teriyaki chicken wings and Pacific Rim pizza with sweet and sour sauce, beef and chicken fajitas, and grilled salmon with confetti salsa flavored with "lite" soy sauce. Kikkoman clearly expected Americans to increasingly use soy sauce for applications beyond oriental foods and expected significant growth in the company's base product in the United States. According to Saito, "We figure the market in the United States will increase 100 times in the next decade." Kikkoman marketing coordinator, Trisha MacLeod, articulated the goal as "to get consumers to realize soy sauce is the oldest man-made condiment, and that it can also be used in meatloaf, barbecue—across the spectrum."

MacLeod pointed out, "Americans eat a lot more soy sauce than they realize." However, America's per-capita consumption was barely ten tablespoons, translating into $300 million in North American sales. In contrast, Japanese per-capita consumption was about 10.5 quarts per person, which translated into about $1.4 billion in annual sales in Japan.

The population of Asian immigrants and families of Asian descent was projected to grow significantly in the United States. The California population increased 127 percent to 2.8 million during the 1980s. The total population of Asian Americans in the United States was estimated at 7.3 million in 1990, up 108 percent over the 1980s. Asian peoples represented the traditional mainstay market for oriental foods. Asians had higher income and educational levels than any other ethnic groups in the United States. However, each country represented a different cuisine, and the different Asian ethnic groups required different marketing approaches. Asian populations had spread throughout many parts of the United States, and retail outlets were learning how to highlight and display oriental foods to spur sales. Restaurants greatly influenced American food-buying habits. One industry executive observed that almost all U.S. restaurant kitchens in the 1990s had soy sauce. A 1996 National Restaurant Association study indicated that ethnic foods were increasing in popularity. Thus, oriental food manufacturers and distributors expected that oriental food sales would increase sharply.

Some information in the mid 1990s suggested strong and increasing popularity for oriental foods. U.S. sales of oriental foods had slowed considerably. The most recent aggregate information regarding the demand for oriental food in the United States in the mid 1990s is shown in Exhibit 10.

EXHIBIT 10

U.S. Oriental Food Sales ($000,000)

	1992	1993	1994
Sales	$275	$305	$301

Source: Information Resources, Inc., Chicago, Illinois.

By the late 1980s, consumers began to indicate dissatisfaction with canned entrees, at $81 million in sales the second largest subcategory of oriental foods. Sales of this subcategory had declined as much as 10 percent (1991 to 1992) and showed no signs of abating. Competition was intense, with a third of all products sold on the basis of feature, price, and/or display promotion.

U.S. Major Competitors

Kikkoman's two major competitors in the United States were Chun King and LaChoy. Both companies made soy sauce by hydrolyzing vegetable protein. This European-derived method was faster and less expensive than the six-month fermentation process Kikkoman used. By 1971, Kikkoman had surpassed Chun King in supermarket sales of soy sauce, becoming number two in the American marketplace. In 1976, Kikkoman outsold LaChoy brand soy sauce and became the number one retailer of soy sauce in the United States, a position it continued to hold in the mid 1990s. However, the company faced strong competitors in the oriental foods category and in the sauces and condiments subcategory.

The new consumer focus was on oriental food ingredients that individuals could add to home-cooked dishes. "People are cooking more oriental foods at home," said Chun King's vice president of marketing. "Over 40 percent of U.S. households stir-fry at least once a month. Sauces are an opportunity to get away from the canned image." Indeed, sauces were the only growth area on the oriental food category, with 1992 sales rising 11 percent over the previous year. Rivals Chun King and LaChoy were flooding the oriental foods aisle in American supermarkets with new products. LaChoy had about 40 percent of the shelf products in oriental foods, and Chun King had about 20 percent.

However, there were more changes than just new products. In the early 1990s, LaChoy and Chun King had revved up their marketing efforts under new ownership. LaChoy was owned by ConAgra's Hunt-Wesson division. Among other initiatives, ConAgra, a major U.S. food company, hired a new advertising firm for LaChoy.

A Singapore-based firm purchased Chun King in 1989 and brought in a new management team. As one observer put it, "The brand had really been neglected as part of Nabisco (its previous owner). It was just a small piece of a big pie." The new management team introduced a line of seasoned chow mein noodles and another of hot soy sauces. The firm's marketing plan included consumer promotions and a print ad campaign in women's magazines. Chun King's 1992 oriental food sales were estimated at $30 million. In mid 1995, ConAgra purchased Chun King from the Singapore company and added the brand to its Hunt-Wesson division. ConAgra was no stranger to the Chun King brand. The large U.S. competitor had purchased Chun King's frozen food line in 1986 from Del Monte. It was expected that Hunt-Wesson would eventually consolidate manufacturing but continue to aggressively advertise the two brands separately. As a Hunt-Wesson executive put it, "They're both established leaders in their field, and they both have brand strength."

LaChoy advertised itself as "the world's largest producer of oriental foods created for American tastes." The company led the oriental foods category with sales (excluding frozen) of $87 million in 1992 and $104.4 million in 1994. Its products included chow mein noodles, bamboo shoots, sauces, and miscellaneous foods. About $28 million of the 1992 sales came from sauce and marinade sales. La Choy's manager of corporate communications indicated that the Chicago-based firm planned no increase in marketing spending in reaction to the new Chun King initiatives. However, the company did plan to advertise two new lines—Noodle Entrees and Stir-Fry Vegetables 'N Sauce. The company expected to expend most of its marketing support for the latter product line, a set of vegetables in four sauces formulated for consumers to stir-fry with their choice of meat.

Kikkoman and Other Competitors

Kikkoman remained the one bright spot in the oriental food category of sauces and marinades. It controlled $63 million of the $160 million sauces/marinades segment and supported its position with a moderate amount of advertising—$3.2 million in 1992, about the same as in 1991. In its major product lines, Kikkoman controlled about two-thirds of the California market and had about one-third market share in other major U.S. sales regions. The company was test-marketing a new line of sauces for addition to the consumer's own vegetables and meat.

Kikkoman also had to consider recent moves by several other competitors. Yamasa Shoyu Co., Ltd., Japan's second largest soy sauce maker, had announced plans to build a factory in Oregon in mid 1994. This multigenerational company was founded in 1645 in Choshi City, Japan. Estimates on the cost of the Oregon factory ranged from $15 million to $20 million, and the plant was expected to eventually employ fifty workers. Yamasa intended to produce soy sauce for the U.S. market by using soybeans shipped from the midwest. It took Yamasa four years to select the final site for its new plant. The company produced a number of products in addition to soy sauce, including other food and drugs made from biological raw materials such as soybean protein and wheat starch.

Hong Kong–based Lee Kum Kee was a producer and importer of Chinese-oriented sauces and condiments. Lee Kum Kee had opened a sauce-manufacturing plant in Los Angeles in 1991 to keep up with rising U.S. demand and to reduce dependence on imports, thus avoiding payment of import duties, which could be as high as 20 percent. The company was a Hong Kong subsidiary of one of Japan's leading soy sauce brewers. Lee Kum Kee retailed its sauces in big supermarket chains in all fifty states. Historically, the company imported its soy sauce through an independent U.S.-based importer of the same name. The U.S. importer also imported about forty other food products, mostly marinades, curries, and sauces from the East. Lee Kum Kee found its sales propelled by the population doubling of Americans of Asian or Pacific Island descent.

Competitor San-J International of the San-Jirushi Corporation of Kuwana, Japan, built a soy sauce plant in Richmond, Virginia, in 1988. Hawaiian competitor Noh Foods of Hawaii innovated a line of oriental dried seasonings and powdered mixes. In reaction, other manufacturers, including Kikkoman, produced copycat products. Noh Foods distributed its products in the United States, Europe, and Australia through distributors and trade show activities.

Kikkoman's International Position

The Kikkoman Vision

In the mid 1990s, Kikkoman manufactured in four countries and marketed its brand products in over ninety countries. (Exhibit 11 compares domestic and non-Japan sales and operating profits.) Of the company's 3,200 employees, over 1,000 were in international subsidiaries, and only 5 percent of those were Japanese. The company saw at least part of its mission as contributing to international cultural exchange. Yuzaburo Mogi explained,

> Kikkoman believes that soy sauce marketing is the promotion of the international exchange of food culture. In order to create a friendlier world, I believe we need many types of cultural exchanges. Among these, there is one that is most closely related to our daily lives—the eating of food. Soy sauce is one of the most important food cultures in Japan. Hence, the overseas marketing of soy sauce means the propagation of Japanese food culture throughout the world.

As one U.S. scholar who had studied the company extensively in the 1980s put it, "There is an evident willingness on the part of Kikkoman to experiment with new products, production techniques, management styles, and operational forms in the international arena." Yuzaburo Mogi put it similarly when he said, "It should be understood that adjustment to different laws, customs, and regulations is imperative, instead of complaining about those differences."

Kikkoman in Europe

Kikkoman began its marketing activities in Europe in 1972. It found Europeans more conservative and slower to try new tastes than Americans. The firm

EXHIBIT 11

Consolidated Results FY 1995 ((¥) m)

	Domestic	Non-Japan
Sales	162,426	40,860
Operating profit	6,640	4,152
Operating margin	4.0	10.1

Source: Table 7: UBS Securities Limited, May 28, 1996, as reported by *Investext*.

found Germany the least conservative and opened restaurants there in 1973. By the early 1990s, the company had opened six Japanese steak houses in Germany. The restaurants gave their customers, over 90 percent of who were non-Asian, the opportunity to try new cuisine. The Kikkoman trading subsidiary in Germany was the company's European marketing arm. Said the managing director for Kikkoman's European marketing subsidiary located in Germany, "Germany and Holland are big business for us, as both countries are very much into interesting sauces and marinades." Kikkoman's managing director of Europe made it clear that he had aggressive plans to grow sales both by increasing the sales of soy sauce as well as by extending the markets in which the company operated. The massive ready-made meal business in both the United States and Europe had huge potential for Kikkoman. The firm would need to market to end consumers at the retail level as well as to food manufacturers.

The company established its second overseas manufacturing facility in 1983. This facility supplied soy sauce to Australian and European markets. By the early 1990s, Kikkoman had about 50 percent of the Australian soy sauce market. The United Kingdom brand debut occurred in 1986, and the 1992 U.K. market was estimated at 1 billion pounds. In 1993, the firm opened a 25,000-square-foot warehouse in London. With $1.66 billion (U.S.) in sales, Kikkoman had come a long way with "just" soy sauce. Overall, analysts noted that the United States had experienced about 10 percent annual growth in soy sauce demand and expected Europe to expand similarly.

Kikkoman in Asia

In Asia, the company opened a production facility in Singapore in 1983 and incorporated a trading company in 1990. Industry observers expected the company to enter the soy sauce market in China in the near future. In addition, other Asian countries offered various opportunities in sauces, condiments, and foods.

Kikkoman—The Challenges

The company the Mogi family had headed for nearly four hundred years confronted a number of challenges on the global stage in the latter part of the 1990s. Kikkoman executives realized that the company's future could depend primarily on its mature

domestic market. The multigeneration family firm would have to change its image as a maker of a mature product. As Mr. Mogi stated, "We . . . take pride in our ability to contribute to the exchange of cultures by using some of the world's most familiar flavors. We are now concentrating on further enhancing our ability to serve consumers in Japan and overseas. Kikkoman continues as a company that is proud of its heritage, but nevertheless willing and able to adapt to the constantly evolving requirements of our customers and markets."

ENDNOTES

1. In early 1996, the exchange rate was about 95 yen per U.S. dollar. Thus, in U.S. dollars, Kikkoman's market value was about $1.7 billion. Sales at year end 1995 for the consolidated company were ¥203 billion, or slightly less than $2 billion (see Exhibits 2 and 3 for consolidated financial data and Exhibits 8, 9, and 11 for parent company and domestic versus non-Japan revenues plus other selected financial information).

2. *Zaibatsu:* Industrial and financial combines dissolved by occupation fiat after World War II, but which have reemerged as somewhat weaker entities. Some of these *zaibatsu* have developed into large conglomerates such as Mitsubishi. However, they should be distinguished from *keiretsu* (of which Mitsubishi is also one of largest). *Keiretsu* are informal enterprise group-based associations of banks, industrials, and so forth.

3. Information on the market and competitors was drawn primarily from InfoScan.

REFERENCES

Allen, Sara Clark. "Kikkoman, a Good Neighbor in Wisconsin," *Business,* Tuesday, June 11, 1996.

Bergsman, Steve. "Patience and Perseverance in Japan," *Global Trade,* Vol. 109, Issue 8 (August 1989), pp. 10, 12.

Campbell, Dee Ann. "Del Monte Foods to See European Foods Business," *Business Wire,* April 17, 1990.

Demestrakakes, Pan. "Quality for the Ages," *Food Processing,* Vol. 70, No. 6 (September 1996).

"Fireflies Help Kill Germs," *Times Net Asia,* January 1, 1996.

Forbish, Lynn. "Grand Oriental Celebration Held for Opening of Kikkoman Foods," *Janesville Gazette,* June 18, 1973.

Forrest, Tracy. "Kikkoman: a Way of Life," *Super Marketing,* January 28, 1994.

Fruin, W. Mark. *Kikkoman: Company, Clan, and Community* (Cambridge, MA: Harvard University Press, 1983).

Hewitt, Lynda. "Liquid Spice," *Food Manufacture,* February, 1993, p. 23.

Hostveldt, John. "Japan's Kikkoman Corp. Brews Success Story in Walworth," *Business Dateline: The Business Journal—Milwaukee,* Vol. 3, No. 31, Sec. 3 (May 19, 1986), p. 17.

"In-Store: Happy New Year's Feast," (Article on Kikkoman's In-Store Promotion), *Brandsweek,* Vol. 37 (January 1, 1996), pp. 14–15.

Jansen, Leah. "Kikkoman Spices Up Walworth's Quality of Life," *Janesville Gazette,* January 21, 1984.

Jensen, Debra. "Kikkoman Executive Lauds Wisconsin, Lucey," *Gazette,* January 13, 1989, p. 1B.

Jensen, Don. "A Stainless Success Story," *Kenosha News,* Business Section, August 1, 1993.

"The Joy of Soy: How a Japanese Sauce Company Found a Happy Home in Walworth, Wisc.," *Chicago Tribune Magazine*, January 31, 1993, p. 13.

Kikkoman Corporation: Flavors That Bring People Together (Company Brochure).

Kinugasa, Dean. "Kikkoman Corporation," 1979 (Private Translation by Norihito Tanaka and Marilyn Taylor, 1994).

La Choy's home page (**www.hunt-wesson.com/lachoy/main/mission/**).

LaGrange, Maria L. "RJR Sells Del Monte Operations for $1.4 Billion," *Los Angeles Times*, September 26, 1989, p. 2.

Mogi, Yuzaburo. "The Conduct of International Business: One Company's Credo—Kikkoman, Soy Sauce and the U.S. Market" (available from Company).

Mogi, Yuzaburo. *"Masatsunaki Kokusai Senryaku"* (Tokyo, Japan: Selnate Publishing Co., Ltd., 1988—in English translation).

Ostrander, Kathleen. "Kikkoman's Success Tied to Proper Blend," *Business Datelines (Wisconsin State Journal)*, March 1, 1992 p. 29.

Plett, Edith. "Kikkoman Foods Marks Fifth Year," *Janesville Gazette*, January 26, 1979.

Redman, Russell. "Hunt-Wesson Acquires Chun King," *Supermarket News*, Vol. 45, No. 19 (May 8, 1995), p. 101.

SBA home page, Wisconsin Gallery.

Schoenburg, Lorraine. "Governor Supports Kikkoman," *Janesville Gazette*, September 14, 1989.

Shima, Takeshi. "Kikkoman's Thousand-Year History," *Business JAPAN*, January, 1989, p. 65.

Wilkins, Mira. "Japanese Multinational in the United States: Continuity and Change, 1879–1990," *Business History Review*, Vol. 64, Issue 4 (Winter 1990), pp. 585–629.

Yates, Ronald E. "Wisconsin's Other Brew," *Chicago Tribune Magazine*, January 31, 1993, p. 14.

In addition to personal interviews in Tokyo, Walworth, Wisconsin, and San Francisco, information and quotations were also drawn from these references. This list is part of a much broader set of sources that the authors consulted.

Appendix A: The Making of Soy Sauce

The Chinese began making jiang, a precursor of soy sauce, about 2,500 years ago. The most likely story of soy sauce's origins relates how Kakushin, a Japanese Zen priest who studied in China, returned to Japan in the middle of the thirteenth century and began preparing a type of miso, or soybean paste produced through fermentation, that became a specialty of the area. By the end of the thirteenth century, the liquid was called *tamari* and sold commercially along with the miso. Experimentation with the raw ingredients and methods of fermentation began. Vegetarianism also became popular in Japan during this time, and people were eager for condiments to flavor their rather bland diet. Soldiers also found the transportability of the seasonings useful.

Soy sauce evolved from tamari and miso by adding wheat to the soybean fermentation mash. The Japanese modified the shoyu to include wheat to gentle the taste so that it did not overwhelm the delicate flavors of Japanese cuisine. Most households made their shoyu during the slack time in agricultural cycles. Families harvested grains in the fall and processed them into mash. The mash fermented from October–December to January–March, when the shoyu was pressed from the mash.

Regional differences among the soy sauces developed depending upon the mix of soybean, wheat, and fermentation techniques. Even in the last decade of the twentieth century, there were hundreds of local varieties of soy sauce available commercially in Japan.

Produced in the traditional way, soy sauce was a natural flavor enhancer. In the later part of the twentieth century, ingredient-conscious consumers shied away from artificial flavor enhancers. Soy sauce responded to the challenge of finding ingredients to flavor foods. For vegetarian manufacturers, the "beefy" taste provided by the soy sauce without any meat extract was highly desirable.

There were two methods of manufacturing soy sauce—the traditional fermentation process used by Kikkoman and the chemical method.

Soy Sauce Through Fermentation— Kikkoman's Traditional Method

Kikkoman's process was the traditional one and involved processing soy and wheat to a mash. Kikkoman had developed an innoculum of seed mold that the company added. The seed mold produced a growth, the development of which was controlled by temperature and humidity. The resulting mash (*koji*) was discharged into fermentation tanks where selected microorganism cultures and brine were added. The product (*moromi* mash) was aerated and mixed, then aged. During this process, enzymes formed in the cells of the *koji* and provided the characteristics of the brewed sauce. The soybean protein changed to amino acid, and the enzymatic reaction that occurred between the sugar and amino acids produced the taste and color. Enzymes changed the wheat starch to sugars for sweetness, and a special yeast developed, changing some of the sugars to alcohol. Fermentation changed other parts of the sugars to alcohol that produced tartness. The brewing process determined flavor, color, taste, and aroma. The brine added to the *koji* mixture stimulated the enzymes and produced the reddish brown liquid mash. This process resulted in *umami*—or flavor-enhancing—abilities, as well as the brewed flavor components. The final mash was pressed between layers of cloth under constant pressure. After a pasteurization process to intensify color and aromas, the shoyu was filtered again and bottled. There were no flavorings, coloring, additives, or artificial ingredients in the product. According to produce developers, these complex flavors were not present in brewed soy sauce.

Chemically Produced Soy Sauce

Nonbrewed soy sauce could be made in hours. Soybeans were boiled with hydrochloric acid for fifteen to twenty hours. When the maximum amount of amino acid was removed from the soybeans, the mixture was cooled to end the hydrolysis action. The amino acid liquid was then neutralized, mixed with charcoal, and finally purified through filtration. Color and flavor were introduced via varying amounts of corn syrup, salt, and caramel coloring. The resulting soy sauce was then refined and bottled.

39

CenturyTel in a Bear Hug

This case was prepared by Lawrence R. Jauch and Melissa V. Melancon, University of Louisiana at Monroe.

Glen Post, CEO of CenturyTel (CTL), was in his office at company headquarters in Monroe, Louisiana, on a hot day in late August, 2001, when word arrived that AllTel had given him a "bear hug." "Bear hug" acquisitions are unsolicited, publicly announced offers to buy a company. They have been turning up recently in communications-related industries. Companies sometimes resort to bear hugs after being rejected through traditional channels out of the public eye. Even if the private offer includes a significant premium to a company's current stock price, top executives and directors may turn it down if they believe the stock market is putting an unduly cheap price on the shares. That could be why CTL spurned AllTel, despite the potential of a 40 percent premium above CTL's current market price. Alternatively, it could be just a matter of wanting to stay independent. AllTel and CenturyTel are regional rivals. Offered one analyst, "I think it's pride, rather than price. . . . It's understandable."

A CEO can easily turn down an offer made in private, but a bear hug forces a corporate board to consider any reasonable bid because directors have a responsibility to provide shareholders with the best financial returns. It steps up the pressure. Sometimes, the only way to get

past unwilling board members is to use public pressure. Alltel and its advisers have to convince large shareholders of CenturyTel to pressure the board. Bear hug acquisitions require massive public relations offensives directed at institutional shareholders and other board members besides the chair and CEO. "It's PR directed toward people whose decision making matters." Despite the pressure, companies can and do adopt takeover defenses. One of the key defenses is voting rights. In the case of CenturyTel, owners of stock prior to 1988 have 10 votes per share. The founder of CTL, Clarke Williams, controls the board so tightly that it may be impossible to win a proxy fight.

Some bear hug announcements are mainly designed to be disruptive to rivals. The communications industry has been ravaged over the past year, and its companies have been left vulnerable to mergers and acquisitions. Competitive local exchange carriers face potential problems, since many observers believe there are too many companies chasing the same customers. Many overbuilt, leaving themselves stuck with unused networks. Therefore, the industry is ripe for consolidation, and wireless services companies will be among the first to merge or buy each other.

CenturyTel had been shopping around for its wireless unit and had approached AllTel as a potential buyer of its wireless operations. However, apparently AllTel wanted the whole company, because the rural fixed-wire business was highly profitable and having a ready customer base made CTL's wireless business more valuable. (See Table 1 for financial data on CenturyTel and AllTell.)

Now Glen and CTL were faced with some key decisions. Should CTL counteroffer AllTel? How could he get rid of the bear hug? Should he continue to try to sell the wireless operations? Should CTL continue its past strategy?

A Brief History of CenturyTel

William and Marie Williams gave the Oak Ridge Telephone Company as a gift to their son Clarke on his return from World War II (see Table 2). The sleepy little local exchange telephone company began its first of many acquisitions in 1972. After forays in and out of larger metropolitan areas, Century decided to stay focused mainly in rural and suburban areas. It was first listed on the New York Stock Exchange in 1978; the firm became one of the S&P 500 companies in 1999. Mainly through acquisitions, the company has added long-distance, Internet, data transmission, and cellular services to its local exchange offerings.

As of June 30, 2001, CenturyTel was the eighth largest local exchange telephone company in the United States based on access lines (1,807,950). Its network was 100 percent digital [Centrex; Integrated Services Digital Network (ISDN); Advanced Intelligent

---

TABLE 1

Selected Financial Results (9/01/2001)

	CenturyTel	AllTel	Industry Average	Industry High	Industry Low	S&P 500
Growth rates						
Revenue—5-year growth rate	23.4%	17.8%	15.6%	1,857.6%	(100.0)%	15.2%
EPS—5-year growth rate	13.4%	27.3%	11.5%	171.8%	(71.0)%	17.4%
Dividend—5-year growth rate	5.3%	5.7%	(0.8)%	463.7%	(100.0)%	8.7%
Capital spending—5-year growth rate	18.0%	31.9%	29.4%	2,662.8%	(100.0)%	7.2%
Financial strength						
Quick ratio (MRQ)	0.5	0.9	0.8	21.2	0.0	1.1
Current ratio (MRQ)	0.6	1.0	1.0	32.2	0.0	1.7
LT debt/equity (MRQ)	1.3	0.8	1.2	25.2	0.0	0.7
Total debt/equity (MRQ)	1.3	0.8	1.2	25.2	0.0	0.7
Interest coverage (TTM)	2.4	5.0	4.4	481.6	(7,039.5)	9.1
Management effectiveness						
Return on assets—5-year average	5.6%	9.4%	5.5%	26.9%	(4,884.2)%	8.3%
Return on investment—5-year average	6.1%	10.7%	7.8%	190.1%	(800.3)%	13.2%
Return on equity—5-year average	15.6%	25.2%	21.2%	743.0%	(518.5)%	22.2%
Profitability ratios						
Gross margin—5-year average	49.3%	37.2%	44.4%	100.0%	(95.2)%	47.9%
EBITD margin—5-year average	49.3%	35.1%	29.9%	82.5%	(98.2)%	21.9%
Operating margin—5-year average	29.7%	21.4%	14.4%	58.0%	(99.0)%	18.4%
Profit margin—5-year average	17.4%	14.4%	7.4%	58.6%	(99.9)%	11.5%
Effective tax rate—5-year average	39.8%	41.4%	40.9%	94.9%	0.0%	35.5%
Operating efficiency						
Revenue/employee	$298,070	$269,399	$299,080	$3,335,333	$118	$718,012
Net income/employee	$ 47,421	$ 49,184	$ 30,998	$ 985,194	$ 0	$ 96,034
Asset turnover	0.3×	0.6×	0.4×	7.6×	0.0×	1.0×
Stock prices						
High, 52 weeks	39.87	68.68				
Low, 52 weeks	25.45	49.43				
Capital structure—debt	57%	43%				
Capital structure—equity	43%	57%				
Beta	.81	.80				

TABLE 2

CenturyTel Highlights

1930	William Clarke and Marie Williams purchase Oak Ridge Telephone Company in Oak Ridge, Louisiana.
1946	The Williams's son, Clarke McRae, today chairman of the board, assumes management of CTL.
1972	Century acquires La Crosse Telephone Corporation in Wisconsin.
1978	Century's common stock first traded on the New York Stock Exchange as CTL. (Later also listed on the Berlin Stock Exchange.) Century begins replacing mechanical switches with digital computer technology.
1983	Century files for FCC approval to operate cellular systems in three areas in Michigan.
1989–92	Acquires Universal Telephone and Central Telephone Company of Ohio.
1993	Acquires San Marcos Telephone Company; provides long-distance and operator services. Acquires Interactive Communications, Inc; provides interactive information services nationwide. Forms competitive access provider (CAP)—Metro Access Networks (MANs) to compete with local exchange carriers in metropolitan areas.
1994	Acquires Celutel (five cellular systems in metropolitan areas in Mississippi and Texas); renamed Century Cellunet. Acquires Kingsley Telephone Company; 2,400 in northern Michigan near other Century properties. Acquires Pine Bluff, Arkansas, Metropolitan Statistical Area (MSA), and buys additional ownership in a cellular system operated by Century in Michigan.
1995	Acquires Tele-Max, Inc., in Denton County, Texas, that owns part of a limited cellular partnership operating a cellular system in Dallas MSA. Acquires cellular operations in Michigan RSA, adjacent to cellular properties Century operates. Acquires cellular systems serving Mississippi RSAs adjacent to Century's Jackson, Mississippi, cellular market.
1996	Acquires Ringgold (Louisiana) Telephone Co.; ownership in North LA Cellular Partnership increases to 87 percent. Surpasses the half-million customer mark in its local exchange operations. Surpasses the 100,000-customer milestone in its long-distance operations. Acquires Mississippi RSA in central Mississippi, adjacent to Century's Jackson MSA and cellular systems.
1997	Acquires Pecoco, Inc., in Randolph, Wisconsin; minority interest in two cellular partnerships serving Madison and Milwaukee representing approximately 35,000 pops. Divested Metro Access Networks, Inc. (MAN). Created a strategic alliance with Brooks Fiber Properties, Inc.; became Brooks Fiber's largest shareholder; alliance consisted of developing CLEC networks in seven Texas cities; opportunity for Century and Brooks to develop additional CLEC networks in Century's wireless markets in Michigan on a 50-50 joint venture basis. Largest acquisition to date with purchase of Pacific Telecom, Inc. (PTI); gained about 660,000 telephone access lines in twelve states, bringing access lines to nearly 1.2 million. Acquired nearly 1.9 million cellular pops in six states.
1998	Introduced the name CenturyTel to communicate CTL's ability to offer multiple services in a bundled or packaged manner. Purchase of Ameritech's telephone operations and directory publishing business in twenty-one communities in Wisconsin.
1999	Declared a 3-for-2 stock split. CenturyTel was added to the Standard & Poor's (S&P) 500 Index. Closed the sale of its Alaska-based operations to Fox Paine Capital. Acquired the cellular system serving the Vicksburg and Greenville, Mississippi, markets. Sold the assets of its wireless operations in the Brownsville and McAllen, Texas, markets. Purchased the Internet service provider DigiSys, Inc., in Kalispell, Montana.

(continued)

TABLE 2 *(continued)*

CenturyTel Highlights

2000	Acquired GTE properties in Arkansas and Missouri; added 230,500 access lines to its existing 46,000 in Arkansas; partnered with Spectra Communications to service 127,000 access lines.
	Completed two transactions to purchase seventy-seven Wisconsin local exchange properties from Verizon; paid Verizon about $195 million in cash to purchase 70,000 access lines; in a joint venture with Telephone USA of Wisconsin, LLC, bought an additional 62,650 access lines in thirty-five Wisconsin exchanges for $170 million.
2001	Acquisition pending of ninety-eight exchanges in Missouri and ninety in Alabama for $2.159 billion from Verizon.
	Announced an increase in common dividends for a twenty-eighth consecutive year.

Network (AIN)]. Services offered included local number Internet access, custom local area signaling services (CLASS), videoconferencing, and long distance (414,000 subscribers).

The latest Verizon acquisition, if approved, would increase CenturyTel's wireline ownership 37 percent, from 1.8 million to 2.5 million access lines, and add 369,000 access lines in Missouri as well as 306,000 in Alabama, taking CTL into its twenty-second state. Glen Post commented, "This advances our strategy to expand our wireline business in rural and suburban areas that cluster with our existing operations. We're still in the process of considering separation of our wireless business in some form."

Through acquisitions and internal development, CenturyTel also became the eighth largest cellular operator in the United States based on population equivalents owned. Operating in six states, CTL had 779,958 cellular units in service (majority-owned markets), with 9,512,571 pops (the portion of the population of the service areas based on ownership interest). Using digital-ready platforms and a nationwide Signaling System 7 (SS7) network, CTL operated 855 cell sites (including personal communications services, or PCS). CTL cellular distribution was based on company-owned retail locations, agents, and Wal-Mart Kiosks.

The Telecommunications (Telecom) Services Industry

The telecommunications industry encompasses the movement of voice, video, and data over distances long or short. The broad industry comprises local exchange, wireless service of all types (including cellular phones, pagers, and palm-type devices), satellite broadcast, fiber optics, copper wire, undersea and coaxial cable, the Internet, microwave, private networks, long-distance service, and videoconferencing. In telecom services, some of the most important influences come from government action, technological change, and competitor behavior.

Government Influence on Competition

Twenty years ago, there was AT&T the Great. This firm reigned supreme over the entire telecom system of the United States. AT&T owned the long-distance business, most of the local phone companies, the labs that created the latest telephone technology, and the companies that manufactured much of the industry's equipment. It was the largest employer in the United States, with about 1 million workers. Telephone service was excellent but relatively expensive.

In a bout of deregulation during the 1980s, the U.S. government's antitrust people stepped in and made AT&T spin off its seven "Baby Bells," the local phone companies, into independent regional corporations (such as Verizon, Bellsouth). Deregulation allowed intense competition in long-distance services from MCI (WorldCom), Sprint, and an increasingly long list of upstarts. As a result, the cost of making a long-distance call plummeted. However, deregulation was far from complete; AT&T was restrained from offering local phone services while the Baby Bells were restrained from offering long-distance services, keeping their monopolies on local phone lines.

Congress enacted sweeping deregulation with the Telecommunications Act of 1996. It was anticipated that this act would lead to vigorous competition in local telephone services. The theory was that allowing cable television companies and long-distance carriers to serve local markets while allowing the former Bell companies to enter the domestic long-distance and international markets would spur innovation and competition that would benefit consumers.

The 1996 act created a new breed of company called competitive local exchange carriers (CLECs). The nascent CLEC industry competes with the Baby Bells in the $100+ billion local telecommunications market, providing voice and data services to business and residential consumers alike. CLECs have competed vigorously with the Baby Bells and now claim 6 to 8 percent of the local telecom market. The Baby Bell phone companies were allowed to sell long-distance phone services to compete against AT&T, WorldCom/MCI, and Sprint. However, the Baby Bells had to give up their monopolies on local phone services. The former Baby Bells and other existing local phone companies became known as incumbent local exchange carriers (ILECs).

ILECs have operated as monopolies regulated by the Federal Communications Commission (FCC) and various state agencies (public service commissions or public utility commissions). Most of such commissions have regulated pricing and intrastate access charges through "rate of return" regulation that allows authorized levels of earnings. Most of these commissions also (1) regulate the purchase and sale of ILECs, (2) prescribe depreciation rates and certain accounting procedures, and (3) regulate various other matters, including certain service standards and operating procedures. Legislatures and regulatory commissions in most states have reduced the regulation of ILECs or intend to do so. Such reduced oversight may allow ILECs to offer new and competitive services faster.

The 1996 act also focused especially on advanced services in rural and high-cost areas. Section 254 of the act specifies that "consumers in all regions of the nation, including low-income consumers and those in rural, insular, and high cost areas, should have access to telecommunications and information services, including interexchange services and advanced telecommunications." The act authorized the establishment of new federal and state "universal service funds" to provide support to eligible carriers. Some allege that the act established contradictory objectives of promoting universal service by maintaining billions of dollars of industry subsidies for local telephone service while encouraging competition in the same market, where the costs of service have been skewed in favor of rural and residential users. In areas where prices have been subsidized historically, competition can result in an increase, not a decrease, in prices as they rise toward the true costs. If the FCC implements new universal support mechanisms for rural carriers based on forward-looking cost models (as it did for nonrural carriers in October 1999), revenues of ILECs could be negatively impacted. (The federal Universal Service Fund represented 7.9 percent of CenturyTel's year 2000 revenue.)

FCC and FAA Regulation   The FCC regulates interstate services by regulating the access charges that are billed to long-distance companies for use of a local network in connection with the origination and termination of interstate telephone calls. Additionally, the FCC prescribes certain rules and regulations for telephone companies, including regulations regarding the use of radio frequencies; a uniform system of accounts; and the separation of costs between jurisdictions and, ultimately, between interstate services.

During the 1980s and early 1990s, the FCC awarded two ten-year licenses to provide cellular service in each MSA and RSA market (metropolitan or rural statistical areas). Initially, one license was reserved for companies offering local telephone service in the market (the wireline carrier), and one license was available for firms unaffiliated with the local telephone company (the nonwireline carrier). The FCC has permitted telephone companies to acquire control of nonwireline licenses in markets in which they do not hold interests in the wireline license. The completion of an acquisition involving a cellular system requires prior FCC approval and, in certain cases, receipt of other federal and state regulatory approvals.

The FCC has also taken steps to (1) require certain cellular towers and antennas to comply with radio frequency radiation guidelines, (2) require cellular carriers to work with public safety or law enforcement officials to process 911 calls and conduct electronic surveillance, and (3) enable cellular subscribers to retain their existing telephone numbers when they change service providers. These increase the cost of providing cellular service.

In 1997, the FCC established new programs to provide discounted telecom services to schools, libraries, and rural health care providers. Local, cellular, and long-distance operators are required to contribute to these programs. Firms recover their contributions in their rates for interstate services (passing charges on to their customers). Other FCC initiatives have resulted in the allocation of additional radio spectrum or the issuance of licenses for emerging mobile communications technologies that are competitive with cellular and telephone operations. In late 2001 the FCC decided to phase out limits as to how much of the airwaves mobile phone companies can hold in a single market. Such action could lead to greater industry consolidation. Carriers say this allows service improvements, but critics fear this will dampen competition and lead to higher prices.

Cellular systems are subject to certain Federal Aviation Administration (FAA) tower height regulations as well as state or local zoning and land use regulations concerning transmitters and antennas. Moreover, there is an increasing possibility of local community opposition to new towers.

Technology

Improvement in telecom infrastructure has made distance irrelevant to the cost of an in-country phone call. Speed advantages are possible in new phone technology. For example, ATM (asynchronous transfer mode) allows voice, video, and data signals to be transmitted digitally over advanced phone switches at speeds from 25 million to 1 billion bits per second, much faster than traditional analog phone lines, which only move at 2 million bits per second.

However, new technologies—wireless phones, email, instant messaging, and cable modems—are siphoning business off the old telephone networks. New technologies account for 10 to 15 percent of communications that would have traveled over the traditional phone network two to three years ago. A reduction in access lines may begin to characterize the industry. Before, when consumers started using the Internet, they often bought second and third phone lines. Now, as households sign up for high-speed access, about half of these disconnect their second phone lines.

An important development to watch is "instant messaging" on America Online and other Internet services. Currently a method of chatting in real time, online, with friends and associates via sophisticated email, this technology will evolve into a voice-based system as broadband access increases and more PCs become equipped for Internet telephony. At that point, instant voice-based chatting will be a no-cost,

viable alternative to some telephone calls. Because of its base of registered subscribers, AOL provides instant text messaging to 100 million people worldwide.

Telephone service and email are beginning to converge. Companies such as jfax.com offer local telephone numbers all over the world for customers who spend a lot of time traveling. The customer gets a personalized phone number in the area code of choice. Fax and voice messages are translated into email. The user then checks email to get faxes, voice mail, and email all in one place. Net2Phone, using voice over Internet protocol (IP) technology, allows people to place inexpensive telephone calls over a computer, telephone, or fax machine to any telephone or fax machine worldwide, allowing a savings of up to 95 percent when calling internationally. IP telephony is efficient because the line is used for other purposes when people are not talking. Moreover, it does not need costly phone switches to route calls to a particular line. That would make IP telephony cheaper and more profitable than today's phone technology.

Several large wireless carriers have taken initial steps to provide wireless data, short messaging, and other enhanced "next generation" digital wireless services. Several large domestic carriers that currently use the TDMA (time division multiple access) standard either have announced their intention to abandon TDMA or have begun to overlay their TDMA systems with additional network elements permitting packet data transmissions. Functions that might require a $5 million circuit switch can be done by a Cisco router that costs $20,000. Some cable companies have considered this as a substitute technology.

However, the leading supporter of phone via cable—AT&T Broadband—is in limbo. Comcast and AOL Time Warner have their home phone plans on hold. They are waiting for perfection of cheaper Internet call-handling technology to replace today's costly circuit switch system. Too many digital packets still take too long to arrive, creating delays and interruptions, and garble like a bad cell phone call. The cable industry also must hammer out standards for IP telephony so it can provide the security and features required for a company to offer primary phone service. To be sold as a home's only phone, for example, the line must be able to connect directly to 911 emergency centers. Cox, the only other cable provider committed to phone, still believes cable is the next best technology for telecom services. "We have always thought that being able to offer voice, video, and data was the Holy Grail." Some research indicates that the most attractive piece of the bundle is high-speed data. If a goal is to make the customer relationship deeper, then high-speed data may perform better than phone lines. However, consumers may trust their phone companies more than they trust cable operators to carry their conversations.

The cellular telephone industry has been in existence for over sixteen years in the United States. The industry has grown significantly during this period, and cellular service is now available in substantially all areas of the United States. In June 2000 there were estimated to be over 97 million wireless customers across the United States.

Technological developments involving the application of digital radio technology offer certain advantages over analog technologies, including expanding the capacity of mobile communications systems, improving voice clarity, permitting the introduction of new services, and making such systems more secure.

Competition

Competition is rising as the lines between telecom, computing, and data networking blur. The Telecommunications Act of 1996 opened the door for competition in the marketplace, but few consumers are aware of all the options now at their disposal. Competition is generally restricted to large urban business markets. Competition in the rural and suburban areas has not developed or at least does not yet benefit residential customers. ILECs increasingly face competition from CLECs, particularly in high-population areas. CLECs provide competing services through reselling the ILECs' local services, through use of the ILECs' unbundled network elements, or through their own facilities.

ILECs increasingly face competition from alternative communication systems constructed by long-distance carriers, large customers (private networks), or alternative access vendors. These systems are capable of originating or terminating calls without use of the ILECs' networks. Customers may also use wireless or Internet voice service to bypass ILECs' switching services.

There are two thousand companies and subsidiaries providing local telephone services in the United States. One hundred fifty (150) firms offer long-distance services over network facilities of which they own at least a part. Another 350 companies provide toll services by reselling the long-distance services of the large carriers that have built their own nationwide networks. About 300 CLECs have built fiber networks in urban business districts that connect with the networks of long-distance carriers. The precise number of firms providing telecommunications services in the United States is unknown, since many are unregulated, small, privately held enterprises. The total probably is around 4,100. Although well over 90 percent of wireline service revenues are controlled by a few large companies, new services based on new or improved technologies provide ample scope for niche market players in telecom services. Competition between providers of wireless communications services is conducted principally on the basis of price, services, and enhancements offered, the technical quality and coverage of the system, and the quality and responsiveness of customer service.

Mergers continue to occur at all levels of the telecommunications industry, and that trend is expected to continue in the absence of sharp antitrust or regulatory opposition. The antitrust environment under President Bush is expected to be easier. With a weak economy and overcapacity evident, consolidation is more likely. For those with financial muscle, assets can be acquired more cheaply since stocks of weaker companies are often available at bargain prices. Changes in the accounting rules ending the practice of amortizing goodwill will spur hostile offers since earnings of the takeover firms will no longer be diluted. Some predict that ultimately only three of the original seven Bell regional companies may remain, each allied or merged with one of the two or three big U.S. long-distance carriers or with a foreign carrier. In a few years, there may only be a handful of truly global telecommunications carriers.

Market capitalization in the telecommunications services industry ranges from a high of $62.3 billion (AT&T) to less than $1 billion. By way of comparison, AllTel's market capitalization was about $17.7 billion, and CenturyTel had about $4.8 billion in market capital as of September 2001.

Table 3 shows selected economic data and company data from CenturyTel and AllTel.

The number of companies that have requested authorization to provide local exchange service in CenturyTel's service areas has increased substantially,

TABLE 3
Selected Economic and Company Data

P E	1996	1997	1998	1999	2000	2001*
AllTel	16.0	16.1	21.6	29.6	23.1	20.20
CenturyTel	15.3	14.8	22.1	25.6	21.3	20.1

EPS	1996	1997	1998	1999	2000	
AllTel	1.92	2.12	2.09	2.39	2.70	
CenturyTel	0.98	1.89	1.67	1.72	1.65	1.50

Bond rating	Coupon	Maturity	YTM*			
AllTel (selected issues)**						A
Debenture	7.25	2004	5.12*			
Debenture	6.75	2005	5.46*			
Debenture	6.50	2013	6.80*			
Debenture	7.00	2016	6.72*			
Debenture	6.80	2029	7.77*			
CenturyTel (selected issues)						BBB+
Sr. note A	7.75	2004	5.58*			
Sr. note B	8.25	2024	8.14*			
Sr. note C	6.55	2005	5.79*			
Sr. note D	7.20	2025	8.03*			
Sr. note E	6.15	2005	5.33*			
Sr. note F	6.30	2008	6.13*			
Sr. note G	6.875	2028	8.02*			

	1996	1997	1998	1999	2000	2001
AAA corporate	7.37%	7.26%	6.53%	7.04%		
BAA	8.05%	7.86%	7.22%	7.87%		
GDP growth		3.20%	4.77%	4.41%	2.81%	
Unemployment rate		4.95%	4.51%	4.23%	4.01%	
Rf (10-year treasury)	6.44%	6.35%	5.26%	5.64%	6.03%	5.17%
S&P 500 Index returns	17.2%	23.4%	26.7%	19.5%	−10.1%	−11.3%
S&P 500 P/E	19.1	24.2	32.6	30.5		26.2
S&P 500 yield	1.97	1.60	1.32	1.14		1.8%
S&P 500 index	740.43	970.43	1229.2	1469.3		
Prime rate	8.27%	8.44%	8.36%	7.97%	9.23%	7.81%

*Figures through July 2001.
**Figures as of September 2001.

especially in CTL's newly acquired Verizon markets. Others may take similar action in the future.

Economic Outlook

When the economic bubble burst during the latter half of 2000, one of the hardest hit industry sectors was the dot-com industry. The telecommunications industry followed the decline foreshadowed by the dot-coms. This downturn in the economy spread to all sectors of the economy. Stock values declined 20 to 40 percent during this time, and the Federal Reserve cut interest rates eleven times, suggesting that there was grave concern about the economic future. Pessimists in the economy suggest that the current trend presages the advent of another recessionary period in the United States.

Industry Trends and Outlook

With the demand for communications more insatiable than ever, the U.S. market reached a value of $285 billion in 2000. High-volume business customers account for 43 percent of the market, with residential users accounting for 30 percent of the market. The number of telephone access lines in the United States was estimated to exceed 180 million in the year 2000. A healthy overall 4 percent annual growth rate can be anticipated because of continued increases in the number of households with demand for second or third lines, unless wireless and broadband offset this. The number of business access lines has been growing 7 percent annually.

Wireline telecommunications services generated 85 percent of telecom services revenue in 1998. Wireless could increase from the current 15 percent to 20 percent of total revenues in 2004. Analysts agree that wireless will continue to draw significant amounts of voice telephony traffic from wireline, especially in highly penetrated markets. An increasing percentage of consumers are using wireless handsets as a primary, as opposed to secondary, means of communication.

Growth in total long-distance use should continue to increase at a 10 percent annual rate, but prices may decline somewhat, particularly when the Baby Bells enter the market. Toll services represent fewer than 4 percent and should be close to 3 percent of total industry revenues; toll revenues could reach $118 billion in 2004.

Several plausible scenarios facing the industry have been suggested by different industry analysts. According to optimists, the industry future is very positive. They see:

1. Continued rapid growth in wireless communications;

2. Convergence of wireless phones and the Internet;

3. Deregulation and the breaking down of barriers among telecommunications industries;

4. Bundling of cable TV, telephone, Internet, and wireless services for consumers;

5. "Instant messaging" online as an alternative to telephone calls;

6. Companies offering flat-rate pricing, eliminating the need for separate sales staffs and offices.

With broadband service now available to over half of the nation's consumers, analysts predict that almost 40 percent of U.S. households may subscribe to broadband services in 2003. As consumers use more-advanced Internet applications that require greater bandwidth, carriers will rush to meet the insatiable demand for high-speed connectivity. It took the United States almost fifty years to achieve 30 percent penetration for electric service, almost forty years for telephone service, and almost twenty years for television. On the other hand, it has taken only seven years to achieve such penetration for the Internet, and it is estimated that broadband service will achieve a 30 percent penetration rate in only five years.

Such a scenario could result in greater consolidation in the industry. Merger inquiries are not unusual in a competitive industry facing an uncertain economy, and some expect more mergers between long-distance and local phone carriers. Traditional telecom companies (providing basic voice and data services) would become information and communications companies (offering integrated voice, enhanced data, video, and multimedia services) and would look for partners that could increase the ability of the combined firms to compete in the global marketplace. Telecom companies would likely seek partners that offered different types of services in adjacent markets or that had developed expertise in new technologies to offer "bundling." Bundling is the practice of offering a bundle of services for one price. Customers may get multiple services such as an Internet connection, local and long-distance wireline service, and wireless phone or cable TV, all from the same company. A typical middle-income family in the United States may be willing to spend $100 to $150 monthly for cable TV, telephone service, and Internet access. Bundled services provide simplified billing as the customer only has to pay one monthly bill for a range of services. A company that wants to provide its customers with one-stop shopping for all their communications needs is unlikely to have the necessary resources and expertise in-house and will need to buy or form a joint venture with other companies.

However, some pessimists view the future another way. Some consolidation that has already created "one-stop shops" in telecom has slowed. The meltdown in Internet stocks created a profound change in market psychology. Cash-strapped carriers have found it difficult to raise money, especially as revenue growth slowed. Hence, carriers may begin to cut back on capital spending. The optical revolution that began transforming the long-distance network in the 1980s is about to go local to speed data transfer; but this requires large capital investments, even as telecom revenue growth is likely to slow. Smaller companies are being forced into alliances with larger corporations for access to capital and customers. Still, a volatile market makes it difficult to value a takeover target. Hence, "focus" instead of "bundling" may be the new mantra, and the leaders could be companies such as Vodafone (which concentrates on wireless). Players in the high-growth wireless market and carriers in the dying long-distance phone business may both be at risk, especially as falling prices and the routing of more traffic over private line networks and the Internet take place.

Like everything else, the terrorist attacks and their aftermath will impact the telecom industry. Immediately following September 11, many travelers used videoconferencing instead of airplanes to make business connections. The attacks changed the perceptions of many that a cell phone was no longer a luxury, but a necessity. Some expect that growth rates of wireless may be up 30 percent annually for several years because of this. Security and privacy concerns will affect the ways in which people communicate thereby affecting the development and use of the telecom system. Therefore, the forecasts and scenarios will be altered in as yet unforeseen ways.

Corporate Governance

Top Management

Most of CenturyTel top management has been with the firm for over fifteen years. The key personnel include the following:

- **Clarke M. Williams,** founder and chairman of the board; mother and father gave him Oak Ridge Telephone Company.

- **Glen F. Post III,** president, chief executive officer, and vice chairman of the board, joined CenturyTel in 1976. Senior vice president and treasurer 1984; executive vice president and chief operating officer 1988; president, chief executive officer, and vice chairman of the board 1992; M.B.A.

- **Karen A. Puckett,** executive vice president and chief operating officer, joined CenturyTel in 2000; M.B.A., directs all of CTL's telecommunications operations, including sales, marketing, engineering, and other support functions: twenty years of communications experience; served as area president of GTE's Texas wireless region.

- **R. Stewart Ewing, Jr.,** executive vice president and chief financial officer, joined CenturyTel in 1983; vice president and controller 1984; executive vice president and chief financial officer 1999; B.S. in business; certified public accountant (CPA); key role in CenturyTel's acquisition strategy by negotiating all stages of purchase agreements from legal and regulatory to folding new companies into CenturyTel's corporate structure and philosophy.

- **Harvey P. Perry,** executive vice president and chief administrative officer, joined CenturyTel in 1984; general counsel 1984; executive vice president and chief administrative officer 1999; J.D.; Bar Association; responsible for the human resources and administrative services functions within CenturyTel as well as the operation of CenturyTel Air.

- **David D. Cole,** senior vice president, operations support, joined CenturyTel in 1982; director of regulatory affairs 1982; president, Wireless Group 1996; senior vice president, Operations Support 1999; M.B.A.; operational finance, billing and revenue assurance, government relations, revenues, and customer service areas.

- **Mike Maslowski,** senior vice president and chief information officer, joined CenturyTel in 1999; responsible for all of CTL's information systems activities; thirty years of experience working in the telecommunications business with Illinois Bell, AT&T, and Lucent Technologies; focus is on developing information systems that identify customer needs, help package products and services, and enhance ease of acquisition.

Board of Directors

Six of the fourteen board members are present or former executives of CenturyTel. Ten of the fourteen have served on the board for fifteen years or more. The composition of the board is as follows:

- **William R. Boles, Jr.,** age 44; a director since 1992; an executive officer, director, and practicing attorney.

- **Virginia Boulet,** age 47; a director since January 1995; partner, Phelps Dunbar, L.L.P., a law firm.

- **Ernest Butler, Jr.,** age 72; a director since 1971; chairman, president, and a director of I. E. Butler Securities Inc., an investment banking firm, since February 1998; for over thirty years prior to such time, Mr. Butler served as an executive officer of Stephens Inc., an investment banking firm.

- **Calvin Czeschin,** age 65; a director since 1975; president and chief executive officer of Yelcot Telephone Company and Czeschin Motors.

- **James B. Gardner,** age 66; a director since 1981; managing director of the capital markets division of Service Asset Management Company, a financial services firm; a director of Ennis Business Forms, Inc.; prior to April 1994, Mr. Gardner served as an executive officer of various financial institutions or other financial service companies.

- **W. Bruce Hanks,** age 46; a director since 1992; interim athletic director of the University of Louisiana at Monroe; vice president–strategic issues; executive vice president–chief operating officer; senior vice president–corporate development and strategy; president–telecommunications services.

- **R. L. Hargrove, Jr.,** age 69; a director since 1985; retired as executive vice president of CTL in 1987 after twelve years of service as an officer.

- **Johnny Hebert,** age 72; a director since 1968; president of family-owned electrical contracting business.

- **F. Earl Hogan,** age 79; a director since 1968; managing partner of EDJ Farms Partnership, a farming enterprise, for several years prior to his retirement in December 1997.

- **C. G. Melville, Jr.,** age 60; a director since 1968; private investor since 1992; retired executive officer of an equipment distributor.

- **Harvey P. Perry,** age 56; a director since 1990; executive vice president and chief administrative officer of CTL since May 1999; senior vice president of CTL; general counsel and secretary of CTL since 1984 and 1986, respectively.

- **Glen F. Post III,** age 48; a director since 1985; vice chairman of the board, president and chief executive officer of CTL.

- **Jim D. Reppond,** age 59; a director since 1986; retired; vice president of Telephone Group of CTL from January 1995 to July 1996; president of Telephone Group of CTL from May 1987 to December 1994.

- **Clarke M. Williams,** age 79; a director since 1968; chairman of the board of CTL. Mr. Williams, who is the father-in-law of Harvey P. Perry, founded CTL's telephone business in 1946.

Stock Ownership and Control

CenturyTel's Articles of Incorporation specify that each share of common stock beneficially owned continuously by the same person since May 30, 1987, generally entitles the holder thereof to ten votes per share. The holders of 10.6 million shares of common stock were entitled to ten votes per share. Seven hundred twenty-eight (728) institutions own 71.1 percent of the 141 million CTL common shares outstanding. The average institutional ownership of the Communications Services Industry is 35.0 percent, and the average institutional ownership of the S&P 500 as a whole is 58.6 percent. Table 4 identifies the distribution and voting power of selected common shareholders.

CenturyTel Business Operations (as of the end of fiscal year 2000)

CenturyTel's local exchange telephone subsidiaries operated over 1.8 million telephone access lines, primarily in rural, suburban, and small urban areas in twenty-one states, with the largest customer bases located in Wisconsin, Arkansas, Washington, Missouri, Michigan, Louisiana, and Colorado. CTL is the eighth largest local exchange telephone company in the United States based on the number of access lines served (see Table 5).

CenturyTel's cellular systems (1) served approximately 751,000 customers in nineteen metropolitan

TABLE 4

Nature and Amount of Ownership of Common Shares

	Number of Shares	Percent of Shares	Percent of Voting Power
Capital Research and Management Company	10,597,250	7.5%	4.5%
Regions Bank, as trustee of the Stock Bonus Plan and ESOP (the "Benefit Plans")	8,460,064	6.0%	28.1%
	310,582	—	—
	202,922	—	—
All directors and executive officers as a group (18 persons)	3,581,604	2.5%	2.9%

statistical areas (MSAs) and twenty-two rural service areas (RSAs) in Michigan, Louisiana, Arkansas, Mississippi, Wisconsin, and Texas and (2) had access to approximately 7.6 million cellular pops (the estimated population of licensed cellular telephone markets multiplied by CTL's proportionate equity interest in the licensed operators). CTL also owned minority equity interests in ten MSAs and sixteen RSAs representing approximately 1.9 million cellular pops. CTL's 9.5 million aggregate pops make it the eighth largest cellular telephone company in the United States (see Table 6).

CTL also provides long-distance, Internet access, competitive local exchange carrier, broadband data, security monitoring, and other communications and business information services in certain local and regional markets.

CEO Glen Post says CenturyTel's vision is to be the leading provider of integrated communications services to rural areas and smaller cities in America.

CenturyTel continually evaluates the possibility of acquiring additional telecom assets and at any given time may be engaged in discussions or negotiations regarding additional acquisitions. CTL generally does not announce its acquisitions until it has entered into a preliminary or definitive agreement. Over the past few years the number and size of communications properties on the market have increased substantially. Although CTL's primary focus will continue to be on acquiring telephone and wireless interests that are proximate to its properties or that serve a customer base large enough for CTL to operate efficiently, other communications interests may also be acquired.

CTL had approximately 6,860 employees, approximately 1,270 of whom were members of seventeen different bargaining units, including the International Brotherhood of Electrical Workers and the Communications Workers of America. Relations with employees are generally good.

TABLE 5

CenturyTel Access Lines (6/30/2001)

Arizona	1,920	Arkansas	274,783	Colorado	96,696	Idaho	6,331
Indiana	5,471	Iowa	2,060	Louisiana	103,948	Michigan	117,406
Minnesota	31,114	Mississippi	23,520	Missouri	130,493	Montana	66,345
Nevada	486	New Mexico	6,369	Ohio	85,328	Oregon	79,696
Tennessee	27,967	Texas	50,947	Washington	190,869	Wisconsin	500,818
Wyoming	5,383						
				Total	**1,807,950**		

TABLE 6

CenturyTel Wireless Operations

	Year Ended December 31		
	2000	**1999**	**1998**
Majority-owned and operated MSA and RSA systems			
Cellular systems operated	41	42	44
Cell sites	743	711	644
Population of systems operated	8,219,411	8,267,140	9,026,150
Customers			
At beginning of period	707,486	624,290	569,983
Gross units added internally	339,247	240,084	214,767
Disconnects	284,880	146,325	160,460
Net units added internally	54,367	93,759	54,307
Effect of property dispositions	(10,653)	(10,563)	
At end of period	751,200	707,486	642,290
Market penetration at end of period	9.1%	8.6%	6.9%
Churn rate	1.95%	2.02%	2.23%
Average monthly service revenue per customer	$ 49	$ 53	$ 57
Construction expenditures (in thousands)	$58,468	$58,760	$57,326

Telephone Operations

CTL's local exchange telephone subsidiaries derive revenue from providing (1) local telephone services (33 percent), (2) network access services (58 percent), and (3) other related services (9 percent) (see Table 7). Network access revenues primarily relate to services provided by CTL to long-distance carriers, wireless carriers, and other customers in connection with the use of CTL's facilities to originate and terminate inter-state and intrastate long-distance telephone calls. Other revenues include revenues related to (1) leasing, selling, installing, maintaining, and repairing customer premise telecommunication equipment and wiring, (2) providing billing and collection services for long-distance companies, and (3) participating in the publication of local directories.

CTL has experienced growth in its telephone operations over the past several years, a substantial portion of which was attributable to the acquisitions of telephone properties from Verizon and PTI and the expansion of services (see Table 8). A portion of CTL's access line growth was offset by the sale of CTL's Alaska telephone operations. CTL expects future growth in telephone operations from (1) acquiring additional telephone properties, (2) providing service to new customers, (3) increasing network usage, and (4) providing additional services made possible by advances in technology, improvements in CTL's infrastructure, and changes in regulation.

All of CTL's access lines are digitally switched. The installation of digital switches, high-speed data circuits, and related software has been an important component of CTL's growth strategy. This allows CTL to offer enhanced voice services (such as call forwarding, conference calling, caller identification, selective call ringing, and call waiting) and data services. This increases utilization of access lines. CTL has expanded its list of premium services (such as voice mail) offered in certain service areas and has aggressively marketed these services. CTL is installing fiber-optic cable in certain of its high-traffic routes and provides alternative routing of phone service over fiber-optic cable networks in several strategic operating areas. Subsidiaries had over ten thousand miles of fiber-optic cable in use.

Certain large communications companies for which CTL currently provides billing and collection services continue to indicate their desire to reduce their expenses, which has resulted and may continue to result in future reductions of CTL's billing and collection revenues.

TABLE 7

CenturyTel Income Sources (dollars in thousands)

	Year Ended December 31		
	2000	**1999**	**1998**
Operating Revenues			
Local service	$ 408,538	$ 353,534	$ 331,736
Network access*	727,797	654,003	629,583
Other	117,634	118,575	116,024
Total	**$1,253,969**	**$1,126,112**	**$1,077,343**
Operating Expenses			
Plant operations	$ 290,062	$ 251,704	$ 233,896
Customer operations	105,950	88,552	90,331
Corporate and other	163,761	160,631	157,142
Depreciation and amortization	317,906	273,666	261,370
Total	**$ 877,679**	**$ 774,553**	**$ 742,739**
Operating Income	**$ 376,290**	**$ 351,559**	**$ 334,604**

	2000	**1999**
*Network access revenues increased due to the following factors:		
Acquisitions	$75,938	17,645
Increased recovery from the federal Universal Service Fund (USF)	15,753	8,193
Disposition of Alaska properties	(23,348)	(39,985)

Wireless Operations

The development strategy for wireless operations is to secure operating control of service areas that are geographically clustered. This aids CTL's marketing efforts and provides various operating and service advantages. Because most cellular markets are located in rural, suburban, or small urban areas, CTL believes that most of its customers typically require only local or regional services. CenturyTel lacks the facilities and national brand name necessary to compete effectively for business customers requiring nationwide services, and CTL does not actively target these customers in its marketing campaigns. CTL has targeted roaming service revenues, but there is no formal roaming venture with any national carrier.

CTL has access to approximately 9.5 million cellular pops, of which 65 percent were applicable to MSAs and 35 percent were RSA pops. Approximately

TABLE 8

CenturyTel Growth in Telephone Operations (dollars in thousands)

	Year Ended December 31			
	2000	**1999**	**1998**	**1997**
Access lines	1,800,565	1,272,867	1,346,567	1,203,000
% residential	76	75	74	74
% business	24	25	26	26
Operating revenues	$1,253,969	$1,126,112	$1,077,343	$526,000
Capital expenditures	$ 275,523	$ 233,512	$ 233,190	$115,000

19 percent of cellular customers currently subscribe to digital services. Revenue results from charges to subscribers for access to its systems, for minutes of use, and for enhanced services, such as voice mail (see Table 9). A subscriber may purchase rate plans that bundle these services in different ways and are designed to fit different customer requirements. Average monthly cellular revenue per customer declined to $49 in 2000 from $53 in 1999 and $57 in 1998. Average revenue per customer is expected to further decline as additional lower-usage customers are activated, as CTL continues to receive pressure from other cellular operators to reduce roaming rates, and as competitive pressures intensify.

CTL markets its wireless services through several distribution channels, including its direct sales force, retail outlets owned by CTL, and independent agents. Advertising includes direct mail, billboard, magazine, radio, television, and newspaper advertisements. The sales and marketing costs of obtaining new subscribers include advertising and a direct expense applicable to most new subscribers, in the form of either a commission payment to an agent or an incentive payment to a direct sales employee. CTL typically purchases cellular phones in bulk and typi-cally resells them at a loss to meet competition or to stimulate sales by reducing the cost of becoming a cellular customer. The average cost of acquiring each new customer ($289 in 2000) remains one of the larger expenses in conducting wireless operations. CenturyTel seeks to lower this average cost by focusing on its direct distribution channels. CTL opened its first retail outlet in 1994 and currently operates 143 such outlets.

Churn rate (the average percentage of cellular customers that terminate service each month) is an industrywide concern. A significant portion of the churn in CTL's markets is due to disconnecting service to cellular customers for nonpayment of their bills. In addition, CTL faces substantial competition from other wireless providers, including PCS providers. CTL's average monthly churn rate, excluding prepaid customers, in its majority-owned and -operated markets was 1.95 percent in 2000 and 2.02 percent in 1999. CTL is attempting to lower its churn rate by increasing its proactive customer service efforts and implementing additional customer retention programs.

The construction and maintenance of cellular systems are capital intensive. CTL has continued to

TABLE 9

CenturyTel Wireless Income (dollars in thousands)

	Year Ended December 31		
	2000	**1999**	**1998**
Operating revenues*			
Service	$328,956	$305,006	$302,468
Roaming	99,791	106,486	96,271
Equipment sales	14,822	10,777	9,088
	$443,569	$422,269	$407,827
Operating expenses			
Cost of equipment sold	$ 30,064	$ 21,408	$ 16,992
System operations	69,641	56,866	60,049
General, administrative	78,087	79,569	81,350
Sales and marketing	82,673	61,903	57,967
Depreciation and amortization	65,239	68,593	62,345
	$325,704	$288,339	$278,703
Operating income	$117,865	$133,930	$129,124
Minority interest—wireless operations	(11,598)	(12,911)	(12,635)
Income from unconsolidated cellular entities	26,986	27,675	32,869
	$133,253	$148,694	$149,358

*All of CTL's wireless customers are located in Michigan, Louisiana, Wisconsin, Mississippi, Texas, and Arkansas.

add cell sites to increase coverage, provide additional capacity, and improve the quality of these systems. CTL operated 743 cell sites in its majority-owned markets.

CTL owned licenses to provide PCSs representing approximately 3.0 million pops and thirty-six local multipoint distribution system (LMDS) licenses representing approximately 12.2 million pops. CenturyTel plans to use a portion of its LMDS licenses in connection with its new competitive local exchange business. CTL is currently evaluating its options with respect to the remainder of these licenses, some of which will lapse if not used by specified dates.

A substantial number of the cellular systems in MSAs and RSAs operated by CTL are owned by limited partnerships in which CTL is a general partner. Partnership agreements include customary provisions concerning capital contributions, sharing of profits and losses, and dissolution and termination of the partnership. Most of these agreements vest complete operational control with the general partner.

Other Operations

CenturyTel expects that the growth of operating income for its other operations will slow in future periods as it incurs increasingly larger expenses in connection with expanding its fiber network and competitive local exchange carrier businesses (see Table 10). CTL expects to incur a combined operating loss ranging from $15 to $20 million in 2001 in its fiber network and competitive local exchange carrier businesses.

CenturyTel Financial Activities

CenturyTel's financial statements appear in Tables 11–13. A few explanations may help in the interpretation of the data.

The interest expense increase in FY 2000 was primarily related to the Verizon acquisition and higher interest rates. CTL acquired over 490,000 telephone access lines and related assets from Verizon in four separate transactions for approximately $1.5 billion in cash. To finance these acquisitions on a short-term basis, CTL borrowed $1.157 billion on a floating-rate basis under its new $1.5 billion credit facility with Bank of America, N.A., and Citibank, and borrowed $300 million on a floating-rate basis under its existing credit facility with Bank of America. CenturyTel then issued $500 million of 8.375 percent Notes and $400 million of 7.75 percent Notes. Net proceeds were used to repay a portion of debt in connection with the Verizon acquisitions. Because the Wisconsin Public Service Commission rejected CenturyTel's request to increase the access rates previously charged by Verizon, these acquisitions would dilute CTL's 2001 earnings more than expected.

Excluding acquisitions, CenturyTel relies on cash provided by operations to provide for its cash needs.

TABLE 10

CenturyTel Other Operations (dollars in thousands)

	Year Ended December 31		
	2000	**1999**	**1998**
Operating revenues			
Long distance	$ 104,435	$ 83,087	$53,027
Internet	23,491	16,818	14,267
Call center	3,765	11,749	9,701
Other	116,697	16,634	14,920
Total	$ 148,388	$128,288	$91,915
Operating expenses			
Cost of sales and operating expenses	$ 112,219	$ 99,151	$70,993
Depreciation and amortization	4,911	6,557	4,839
Total	$ 117,130	$105,708	$75,832
Operating income	$ 31,258	$ 22,580	$16,083

TABLE 11

CenturyTel, Inc., Annual Income Statement (in thousand U.S. dollars, except per share amounts)

	Year Ended December 31				
	1996	1997	1998	1999	2000
Telephone	$451,538	$530,597	$1,077,343	$1,126,112	$1,253,969
Mobile communication	250,243	307,742	407,827	422,269	443,569
Paging/other	47,896	63,182	91,915	128,288	148,388
Total revenues	**$749,677**	**$901,521**	**$1,577,085**	**$1,676,669**	**$1,845,926**
Cost-sales/operating	$394,360	$474,256	$768,720	$819,784	$932,457
Depreciation/amortization	132,021	159,495	328,554	348,816	388,056
Total expenses	**$526,381**	**$633,751**	**$1,097,274**	**$1,168,600**	**$1,320,513**
Interest expense	(44,662)	(56,474)	(167,552)	(150,557)	(183,302)
Other, net	25,008	197,045	75,199	71,760	44,074
Income before taxes	**$203,642**	**$408,341**	**$ 387,458**	**$ 429,272**	**$ 386,185**
Income taxes	74,565	152,363	158,701	189,503	154,711
Income after taxes	**$129,077**	**$255,978**	**$ 228,757**	**$ 239,769**	**$ 231,474**
Preferred dividend	(420)	(460)	(408)	(403)	(399)
Common dividend/share	$ 0.16	$ 0.1647	$ 0.1733	$ 0.18	$ 0.19

Phone operations are a stable source of cash flow and help the long-term program of capital improvements. Budgeted capital expenditures for 2001 are projected to be $400 million for telephone operations, $70 million for wireless operations, and $80 million for other operations. This includes the installation of fiber-optic cable and the upgrading of plant and equipment, including digital switches, to provide enhanced services, particularly in newly acquired markets. Expenditures in wireless focus on constructing additional cell sites. Capital expenditures for other operations include $20 million for construction of competitive local exchange networks.

CenturyTel continually evaluates the possibility of acquiring additional telecommunications properties. The firm has 4.6 million shares of common, and 200,000 shares of CenturyTel preferred are available for future acquisitions.

AllTel (AT)

AllTel is aiming to become a dominant rural communications carrier. Its ILEC operations (second largest in the United States) accounted for 38.6 percent of FY 2000 profit. AT's wireless telephone services (50.8 percent) are the sixth largest in the United States. All-

Tel is leveraging strong cash flows from its ILEC operations to fund Emerging Businesses (generating operating losses of $23.9 million in 2000), including competitive local exchange (CLEC) operations outside its incumbent service territory and long-distance services. AT expanded its CLEC service into seventeen additional markets in four new states, bringing its total CLEC presence to forty-three markets covering ten states. At the end of 2000, AllTel had approximately 1.1 million long-distance customers, up about 20 percent from 1999.

AT's goal for its Emerging Businesses unit is to expand margins through cross-selling of additional services to existing customers. In AT's ILEC service territory (including 2.6 million customer lines), about 44 percent of all local phone customers also subscribed to CTL's long-distance phone service at the end of 2000. Approximately 50 percent of AT's ILEC service territory is covered by its wireless phone services, with 13 percent of covered local customers also subscribing to wireless services. In its CLEC markets, AllTel provides bundled services (including local, long-distance, and wireless) to higher-volume medium and small business customers. These bundled services are provided at a discount and are billed on a single, consolidated billing statement.

TABLE 12

CenturyTel, Inc., Annual Balance Sheet (in thousand U.S. dollars)

	Year Ended December 31				
	1996	**1997**	**1998**	**1999**	**2000**
Assets					
Cash/ST investments	$ 8,402	$ 26,017	$ 5,742	$ 56,640	$ 19,039
Receivable—customers	86,444	143,613	130,289	128,338	182,454
Other accounts receivable	0	83,659	55,109	64,719	124,711
Materials/supplies	8,222	21,994	23,709	28,769	38,532
Other	6,166	8,197	11,389	7,607	11,768
Total current assets	$ 109,234	$ 283,480	$ 226,238	$ 286,073	$ 376,504
Property/plant/equipment	$1,685,693	$3,845,498	$4,289,658	$0	$0
Telephone	0	0	0	3,439,469	4,999,808
Wireless	0	0	0	472,725	522,684
Other properties	0	0	0	281,713	392,024
Depreciation	(536,681)	(1,586,935)	(1,938,205)	(1,937,449)	(2,955,223)
Goodwill	532,410	1,767,352	1,956,701	1,644,884	2,509,033
Other assets	237,849	400,006	401,063	517,992	548,460
Total assets	$2,028,505	$4,709,401	$4,935,455	$4,705,407	$6,393,290
Liabilities					
Note payable	$0	$0	$0	$0	$276,000
Current portion long-term debt	19,919	55,244	53,010	62,098	149,962
Accounts payable	60,548	83,378	87,627	78,450	127,287
Accrued salaries	0	38,225	36,900	34,570	33,859
Other current liabilities	63,677	124,340	90,381	96,827	104,251
Accrued interest	0	20,821	36,926	37,232	52,011
Total current liabilities	$ 144,144	$ 322,008	$ 304,844	$ 309,177	$ 743,370
Total Long-Term Debt	$ 625,930	$2,609,541	$2,558,000	$2,078,311	$3,050,292
Deferred liabilities	230,278	477,580	541,129	469,927	567,549
Total liabilities	$1,000,352	$3,409,129	$3,403,973	$2,857,415	$4,361,211
Shareholder Equity					
Preferred stock	$10,041	$8,106	$8,106	$7,975	$7,975
Common stock	59,859	91,104	138,083	139,946	140,667
Paid in capital	474,607	469,586	451,535	493,432	509,840
Retained earnings	494,726	728,033	932,611	1,146,967	1,351,626
Treas. Stk/Other	0	11,893	0	0	0
Other equity	(11,080)	(8,450)	1,147	59,672	21,971
Total equity	$1,028,153	$1,300,272	$1,531,482	$1,847,992	$2,032,079
Total Liabilities and Shareholder Equity	$2,028,505	$4,709,401	$4,935,455	$4,705,407	$6,393,290
Shares outstanding	134,682	136,656	138,083	139,946	140,667

TABLE 13

CenturyTel, Inc., Annual Cash Flow Statement (in thousand U.S. dollars)

	Year Ended December 31				
	1996	1997	1998	1999	2000
Cash from (Used by) Operations					
Net income	$129,077	$ 225,978	$228,757	$239,769	$ 231,474
Depreciation	132,021	159,495	328,554	348,816	388,056
Cellular entities	(26,952)	(27,794)	(32,869)	(27,675)	(26,986)
Minority interest	6,675	5,498	12,797	27,913	10,201
Deferred taxes	7,935	16,230	17,713	(17,139)	41,820
Property sales	(815)	(169,640)	(49,859)	(62,808)	(20,593)
Accounts receivable	(4,353)	7,649	(15,277)	(15,181)	(82,252)
Accounts payable	5,103	(25,440)	4,249	(11,469)	48,653
Accrued expenses	1,285	58,205	(34,908)	(59,571)	(967)
Current assets	6,220	7,263	15,033	(1,354)	3,605
Noncurrent assets	0	0	0	0	(46,026)
Other noncurrent liabilities	4,305	2,173	(1,706)	(5,311)	4,087
Other, net	4,151	7,702	(4,760)	(7,288)	11,394
Cash from operations	**$264,652**	**$ 297,319**	**$467,774**	**$408,702**	**$ 562,466**
Plus: Cash from (Used by) Investment Activities					
Acquisitions	($ 46,327)	($1,543,814)	($222,569)	($ 20,972)	($1,540,856)
Capital expenditures	(222,885)	(181,225)	(310,919)	(389,908)	(449,537)
Property sales	0	202,705	132,307	484,467	29,495
Minority/cellular	14,904	16,015	26,515	22,219	35,842
Insurance, investment	(5,944)	(12,962)	(2,786)	(2,545)	(5,753)
Note receivable	1,667	22,500	0	0	0
Other	(2,106)	(6,346)	4,807	(23,416)	(3,267)
Other investing	18,900	0	0	0	20,000
Cash from investing	**($241,791)**	**($1,503,127)**	**($375,645)**	**$ 69,773**	**($1,914,076)**
Plus: Cash from (Used by) Financing Activities					
Debt issuance	$ 59,649	$1,312,546	$957,668	$ 15,533	$2,715,852
Debt, net	(71,220)	(79,203)	(1,015,015)	(438,399)	(1,375,895)
Common stock issue	10,089	14,156	15,033	19,182	7,996
Dividends (paid)	(21,775)	(22,671)	(24,179)	(25,413)	(26,815)
Other	258	(1,405)	951	1,520	1,490
Hedge contracts	0	0	(40,237)	0	(4,345)
Debt issuance costs	0	0	(6,625)	0	(4,274)
Cash from financing	**($ 22,999)**	**$1,223,423**	**($112,404)**	**($427,577)**	**$1,314,009**
Equals: Increase (Decrease) in Cash					
Net Change in Cash	**($ 138)**	**$ 17,615**	**($ 20,275)**	**$ 50,898**	**($ 37,601)**
Free cash flow	$ 19,992	$ 93,423	$132,676	($ 6,691)	$ 86,114

In addition to communications, AT has an Information Services division (10.7 percent of 2000 operating profit) that provides data processing and account management services to financial institutions and telecommunications industries. The unit's clients include forty-eight of the fifty leading U.S. banks. During FY 2000, Information Services processed 50 percent of all U.S. residential mortgages and 34 percent of all U.S. consumer loans. To improve the operating efficiency of its information services business, AllTel recorded a restructuring charge of $10.1 million to account for severance and employee benefit costs related to a planned work force reduction and for lease termination costs related to the consolidation of operating locations.

Recent AllTel Transactions and Agreements

During FY 1999, AllTel completed mergers with Liberty Cellular Inc., Aliant Communications Inc., Standard Group, Inc., Advanced Information Resources, Ltd., and Southern Data Systems. In connection with these mergers, about 6.5 million shares of AllTel common stock were issued.

During FY 2000, AT and the Georgia Public Service Commission reached a settlement to resolve all pending litigation, requiring AllTel to issue a one-time credit of about $25 to approximately 450,000 wireline customers in Georgia. Also in FY 2000, AllTel, Bell Atlantic Corporation, GTE Corporation, and Vodafone Airtouch agreed to exchange wireless properties in thirteen states. The companies also signed a new national roaming agreement that allows their customers to roam on one another's networks at reduced rates across a footprint covering almost 95 percent of the U.S. population. These agreements required AllTel to sell its Personal Communications Services operations in Mobile, Alabama, and Pensacola, Florida. The sale of these PCS assets was necessary in order for AT to meet the U.S. Department of Justice guidelines regarding the overlap of wireless properties. In connection with the exchange of wireless assets with Bell Atlantic and GTE, AllTel also recorded integration expenses and other charges consisting of severance and employee benefit costs related to work force reduction and branding and signage costs.

AllTel's Results

AllTel has acquired interests in twenty-seven wireless markets representing about 14.6 million pops and approximately 1,467,000 wireless customers, while divesting interests in 42 wireless markets representing 6.9 million pops and approximately 778,000 customers. Thus, at the end of FY 2000, the wireless division had more than 6.3 million customers in twenty-one states. The unit is undergoing two important transitions. The first is an effort to move analog customers to digital service. AllTel projects that more than 70 percent of its subscriber base will be digital by the end of 2001, up from nearly 40 percent in 2000 and 10 percent in 1999. The second transition is to eliminate roaming fees and move toward simple, one-rate pricing plans.

For telephone operations as a whole, average revenue per customer per month was $49.32 in FY 2000. Reductions in average revenue per customer per month reflect expansion of local, regional, and national calling plans, decreased roaming rates, and continued penetration into competitive market segments. New roaming agreements with Bell Atlantic, GTE, and Vodafone offer new rate plans that provide customers with national wireless coverage with no toll or roaming charges. AllTel expects that these national rate plans will increase customer usage and increase its ability to compete effectively for the high-volume, roaming customer.

A financial snapshot for AllTel is found in Tables 14 and 15.

The Future

When the latest acquisition from Verizon is completed, CenturyTel expects that its new properties will generate revenues of up to $550 million and produce a cash flow of up to $300 million during the first full year of operations. The properties experienced more than 19 percent population growth between 1990 and 2000. CenturyTel will absorb about 950 Verizon employees after the sale closes in 2002.

The acquisition may signal that CenturyTel executives believe that the wireline business offers better long-term growth prospects in rural markets. It can serve as the distribution pipe for business and residential customers. Says one analyst, "I believe there is greater value to be seen for CenturyTel by separating its wireless." CenturyTel's wireless business has come under some pressure since it lacks a roaming arrangement with a larger carrier. AllTel has such an agreement with Verizon Wireless.

TABLE 14

AllTel Corporation Annual Income Statement (in thousand U.S. dollars, except per share amounts)

	Year Ended December 31				
	1996	**1997**	**1998**	**1999**	**2000**
Total revenue	$4,239,467	$4,906,958	$5,780,700	$6,461,400	$7,067,000
Total expenses	$3,427,997	$3,777,767	$4,754,800	$4,936,300	$5,399,500
Interest expense	(237,196)	(274,917)	(278,400)	(280,200)	(310,800)
Other, net	4,514	232,157	357,400	85,900	1,994,000
Income before taxes	$ 578,788	$1,086,431	$1,104,900	$1,330,800	$3,350,700
Income taxes	227,532	433,950	501,800	547,200	1,385,300
Income after taxes	$ 351,256	$ 652,481	$ 603,100	$ 783,600	$1,965,400
Preferred dividend	(1,071)	(1,233)	(1,200)	(900)	(100)
Common dividends/share	$1.055	$1.115	$1.175	$1.235	$1.29

Glen Post still faces the $8.75 billion acquisition bear hug from AllTel. The open letter from AllTel's CEO, Scott Ford, said he was "mystified by CenturyTel's refusal to negotiate." Ford's letter called CenturyTel's wireless business "subscale," saying that it had underperformed regional cellular peers, including AllTel, over the past eighteen months. Alltel also said a successful sale of the wireless business could leave CenturyTel with large tax liabilities. CenturyTel officials in the past have asserted that separation of the business could be done in a tax-friendly way.

Ford has commented that CenturyTel's board was out of touch with its shareholder base and was denying the group a fair return on their investments. Glen Post released a letter to Ford stating, "There is no reason to reconsider [our] decision. While we believe your letter is clearly misleading, we have no intention of engaging in your public letter-writing campaign." CenturyTel later revealed that it had considered and rejected takeover offers from AllTel twice before.

Shareholders said they might be more supportive of CenturyTel's planned separation of its wireless and traditional telephone businesses if the firm

TABLE 15

AllTel Corporation Annual Balance Sheet (in thousand U.S. dollars)

	Year Ended December 31				
	1996	**1997**	**1998**	**1999**	**2000**
Total current assets	$ 709,468	$ 880,791	$ 1,102,561	$ 1,167,200	$ 1,780,700
Depreciation	(2,072,789)	(2,904,507)	(3,814,390)	(4,556,400)	(5,564,400)
Total assets	$5,359,183	$8,570,405	$10,155,454	$10,774,200	$12,182,000
Total current liabilities	$ 590,696	$1,004,492	$ 1,301,841	$ 1,194,000	$ 1,515,900
Total long-term debt	$1,756,142	$3,699,519	$ 3,678,626	$ 3,750,400	$ 4,611,700
Deferred taxes	$ 674,887	$ 710,723	$ 1,001,143	$ 917,500	$217,000
Other long-term liabilities	233,896	437,864	541,812	706,600	742,000
Total liabilities	$3,255,621	$5,852,598	$ 6,523,422	$ 6,568,500	$ 7,086,600
Total equity	$2,103,562	$2,717,807	$ 3,632,032	$ 4,205,700	$ 5,095,400
Total liabilities and shareholder equity	$5,359,183	$8,570,405	$10,155,454	$10,774,200	$12,182,000
Shares outstanding	187,200	273,411	306,015	314,258	312,984

explained adequately why that plan was more attractive financially. A survey of roughly a dozen large CenturyTel shareholders supports AllTel's claim that it is gaining support among CTL's large investors. Victory Capital Management earlier in 2001 owned as many as 2 million CenturyTel shares, but reduced that to more than 300,000 shares over concern that CTL's main growth vehicles were slowing down. "To have a company just place their stake in the sand and say CTL is not for sale and we're just going to pursue this wireless spinoff without coming to the table one more time. I'm still at a loss as to why."

However, many shareholders find AllTel's current offer far too low. Scott Mayo, comanager of John Hancock's Large Cap Value Fund, who manages around a million CenturyTel shares, says, "Putting these two companies together really makes a lot of sense. But I think they could sweeten the offer a little bit." CTL is worth closer to $55 per share. AllTel's current bid values CTL at about $41.38 per share. (This was before the CTL acquisition announcement.) If the acquisition were to be consummated, excellent synergies between the companies could contribute to long-term EPS growth and enhance the value of AllTel's wireless unit. Ford would not comment on whether his company would sweeten its offer, and said he has never been told it was inadequate in the first place. "They've said we don't want to talk. They've said we've talked to our bankers and our lawyers and CTL is not for sale. Do they think it's inadequate? If that's what they're saying, then they need to say that."

Growing animosity between the two firms makes friendly talks unlikely—even if AllTel sweetens its bid. CenturyTel filed a lawsuit seeking to keep its rival from unfairly promoting its unsolicited bid, asking the U.S. district court to keep AllTel from interfering with the auction of its wireless business. Investors and analysts concede that it would take an enormous amount of shareholder pressure to bring the two parties to the table; and given the preventative takeover measures, they believe the merger is unlikely to take place.

Therefore, Glen Post was pondering several options. Should CenturyTel keep its wireless operation or seek another buyer? How much would the wireless operation be worth to a buyer? If AllTel sweetens the bid, how high would the offer have to be for the board to approve it? Would a suitor other than AllTel be friendlier?

Appendix: A Glossary of Telecommunications Terminology

access charge   A fee charged subscribers or other telephone companies by a local exchange carrier for the use of its local exchange networks.

analog signal   A signaling method that uses continuous changes in the amplitude or frequency of a radio transmission to convey information.

bandwidth   The capacity of a telecom line to carry signals. The necessary bandwidth is the amount of spectrum required to transmit the signal without distortion or loss of information. FCC rules require suppression of the signal outside the band to prevent interference.

broadband   A descriptive term for evolving digital technologies that provide consumers with a signal switched facility offering integrated access to voice service, high-speed data service, video-demand services, and interactive delivery services.

cellular technology   Term often used for all wireless phones regardless of the technology they use, derives from cellular base stations that receive and transmit calls. Both cellular and PCS phones use cellular technology.

common carrier   In the telecommunications arena, the term used to describe a telephone company.

cramming   Practice by which customers are billed for enhanced features such as voice mail, caller-ID, and call-waiting that they have not ordered.

dial around   Long-distance services that require consumers to dial a long-distance provider's access code (or "10-10" number) before dialing a long-distance number to bypass or "dial around" the consumer's chosen long-distance carrier in order to get a better rate.

landline   Traditional wired phone service.

land mobile service   A public or private radio service providing two-way communication, paging, and radio signaling on land.

network   Any connection of two or more computers that enables them to communicate. Networks may include transmission devices, servers, cables, routers, and satellites. The phone network is the total infrastructure for transmitting phone messages.

personal communications services (PCS)   Any of several types of wireless, voice, and/or data communications systems, typically incorporating digital technology. PCS licenses are most often used to provide services similar to advanced cellular mobile or paging services. However, PCS can also be used to provide other wireless communications services, including services that allow people to place and receive communications while away from their home or office, as well as wireless communications to homes, office buildings, and other fixed locations.

pops   Portion of the population of the service area.

service provider   A telecommunications provider that owns circuit-switching equipment.

spectrum   The range of electromagnetic radio frequencies used in the transmission of sound, data, and television.

subscriber line charge (SLC)   A monthly fee paid by telephone subscribers that is used to compensate the local telephone company for part of the cost of installation and maintenance of the telephone wire, poles, and other facilities that link your home to the telephone network. These wires, poles, and other facilities are referred to as the "local loop." The SLC is one component of access charges.

telephony   Word used to describe the science of transmitting voice over a telecommunications network.

unbundling   The access provided by a local exchange carrier so that other service providers can buy or lease portions of its network elements, such as interconnection loops, to serve subscribers.

REFERENCES

AllTel Corporation. *Standard & Poor's Stock Report.* September 8, 2001.

CenturyTel Corporation. *Standard & Poor's Stock Report.* October, 2001.

CenturyTel, 10-K, U.S. Securities and Exchange Commission. 2001.

CenturyTel Notice of Annual Meeting and Proxy Statement. May 10, 2001.

"CenturyTel History." Retrieved 9/24/01 from **www.centurytel.com/index.cfm?action=About%20Us&subaction=History.**

Centurytel, Inc., ProVestor Plus Company Report. September 17, 2001.

"CenturyTel Increases Quarterly Cash Dividend." February 28, 2001. Retrieved 9/24/01 from **www.centurytel.com/index.cfm?action=News&subaction=Financial%20News&pr_id=126.**

"CenturyTel Leadership." Retrieved 9/24/01 from **www.centurytel.com/index.cfm?action=About%20Us&subaction=CenturyTel%20Leadership.**

"CenturyTel Media Contacts." Retrieved September 21, 2001, from **http://centurytel.com/index.cfm?action=About%20Us&subaction=Media%20Contacts.**

"CenturyTel to Acquire 675,000 Access Lines from Verizon for $2.159 Billion." Retrieved October 22, 2001, from **www.centurytel.com/index.cfm?action=News&details=Acquisitions&pr_id=305.**

"FCC Votes to Cut Airwaves Phone Limits." *USA Today,* November 9, 2001, p. B1.

Haddad, Charles. "The Bells Aren't Ringing." *Business Week,* November 12, 2001, pp. 118–120.

Hilburn, Greg. "CenturyTel to Buy Verizon Lines." *News-Star,* October 23, 2001, p. A1.

Johnson, Tom. "Alltel Renews Public Pressure on CenturyTel." Retrieved September 17, 2001, from **http://tools.fidelity.com/news/RM/index.cfm?story=RM-20010828-N28299487.**

Johnson, Tom. "CenturyTel Investors Ready to Talk, but Want Higher Price." Retrieved September 17, 2001, from **http://tools.fidelity.com/news/rc/index.cfm?story=rc-20010831-n31328542.**

Kagan, Jeffrey. "Analysts Predict AT&T Merger Talk May Set Off New Trend." *News-Star.* October 7, 2001, p. D1.

Lieberman, David. "Cost Break from Phone, Cable Link Creeps Along." *USA Today,* October 8, 2001, p. B1.

"Management Discussion: Alltel Corp (AT)." Retrieved 9/18/01 from **http://excite.elogic.com/sec_mgmt.asp?defview=FULL&ticker=at&Submit2=Go.**

Non, Sergio G. "Embracing an Acquisition Trend: The Bear Hug." *CNET News.com,* August 22, 2001. Retrieved from **http://quickenexcite.cnet.com/news/0-1007-200-6943204.html.**

"Overview of the Telecommunications Industry." Retrieved September 24, 2001, from **http://www.plunkettresearch.com/telecommunications/telecom_trends.htm.**

Rosenbush, Steve. "Telecommunications." *Business Week Online,* January 8, 2001. Retrieved September 24, 2001, from **http://www.businessweek.com:2001/01_02/b3714089.htm.**

"Telecommunications Services." *U.S. Industry & Trade Outlook 2000.* New York: McGraw-Hill Companies, Inc., 1999, pp. 30–1 to 30–26.

Thomton, Emily. "It Sure Is Getting Hostile." *Business Week,* January 14, 2002, pp. 28–30.

U.S. Department of Commerce, Bureau of Economic Analysis.

Wolcott, David A. "An ALTS Analysis: Local Competition Policy & The New Economy." February 2, 2001. Retrieved from **http://www.alts.org/Filings/020201Analysis.pdf.**

Whirlpool Corporation's Global Strategy

40

This case was prepared by Meredith Martin, Simon Algar, and Vipon Kumar under the supervision of Professor Andrew C. Inkpen, Thunderbird, the Graduate School of International Management.

We want to be able to take the best capabilities we have and leverage them in all our companies worldwide.

—David Whitman, Whirlpool CEO, 1994
Quoted in the Harvard Business Review

In 1989, Whirlpool Corporation (Whirlpool) embarked on an ambitious global expansion with the objective of becoming the world market leader in home appliances. Beginning with the purchase of a majority stake in an appliance company owned by Philips, the Dutch electronics firm, Whirlpool purchased a majority stake in an Indian firm, established four joint ventures in China, and made significant new investments in its Latin America operations.

However, by the mid-1990s, serious problems had emerged in the company's international operations. In 1995, Whirlpool's European profit fell by 50% and in 1996, the company reported a $13 million loss in Europe. In Asia, the situation was even worse. Although the region accounted for only 6% of corporate sales, Whirlpool lost $70 million in Asia in 1996 and $62 million in 1997. In Brazil, Whirlpool found

itself a victim in 1997, and again in 1998, of spiraling interest rates. Despite the company's investments of hundreds of millions of dollars throughout the 1990s to modernize operations there, appliance sales in Brazil plummeted by 25% in 1998. Whirlpool expected that 1999 would be the third straight year of declining sales for the Brazilian subsidiary.

In response to these problems, Whirlpool began a global restructuring effort. In September 1997, the company announced that it would cut 10% of its global workforce over the next two years and pull out of two joint ventures in China. In announcing the cuts, Whirlpool's CEO David Whitwam said, "We are taking steps to align the organization with the marketplace realities of our industry."[1] In Latin America, 3,500 jobs were abolished, and significant investments were made to upgrade plants and product lines.

After the optimism of the early 1990s, what went wrong with Whirlpool's global strategy? Was the company overly ambitious? Was there

1. C. Quintanilla and J. Carlton, "Whirlpool Announces Global Restructuring Effort," *Wall Street Journal*, 19 Sept. 1997: A3, A6.

a lack of understanding about how to create an integrated global strategy? Or, were the problems the result of changes in the competitive and economic environments in Europe, Asia, and Latin America? Should Whirlpool have foreseen the problems and reacted earlier?

The Appliance Industry in the late 20th Century

Approximately 120 million home appliances are sold in developed countries each year.[2] The appliance industry is generally classified into four categories: laundry, refrigeration, cooking, and other appliances. Appliances are constructed in capital intensive plants, and design usually varies among countries and regions.

The North American Industry

Although it was estimated that 46 million appliances were sold in North America annually, the market was expected to grow little in the late 1990s. Saturation levels were high, with virtually 100% of households owning refrigerators and cookers and over 70% owning washers. Because of the limited growth opportunities, competition was fierce. In the United States, the industry had consolidated in the 1980s, leaving four major competitors: Whirlpool, General Electric, Electrolux, and Maytag (see Exhibit 1 for more detail). These four firms controlled about 80% of the market.[3] Each firm offered a variety of products and brands segmented along price lines. Distribution of these appliances was generally through sales to builders for new houses or to retailers, such as department stores and specialty resellers.

In a *Harvard Business Review* article in 1994 called "The Right Way to Go Global," David Whitwam, Whirlpool's CEO, described the competitive situation that existed in the early 1990s:

> Even though we had dramatically lowered costs and improved product quality, our profit margins in North America had been declining because everyone in the industry was pursuing the same course and the local market was mature. The four main players—Whirlpool,

General Electric, Maytag, and White Consolidated, which had been acquired by Electrolux—were beating one another up everyday.[4]

With limited growth opportunities and a handful of major players in the United States, it was critical that firms focus on cost reduction, productive efficiency, and product quality. Product innovation was also critical, although few major innovations had occurred in recent years. The appliance firms segmented their products according to different consumers' needs, and each strived to achieve greater economies of scale. Still, by the end of the 1990s, the competitive landscape remained unattractive. Profit margins continued to decline for most firms. Many analysts believed that the market for appliances was saturated and that there would be little increase in growth rates. This saturation had left the distributors focusing primarily on replacement purchases and purchases for new housing developments.

The European Industry

In the early 1980s, there were approximately 350 producers of household appliances in Europe. With consolidation in the industry, by the late 1980s the number had shrunk to about one hundred.[5] By early 1995, it was estimated that five of the companies, including Electrolux (with a 25% market share), Philips Bauknecht, and Bosche-Siemens, controlled over 70% of the market.[6] The industry was highly regionalized, with many of the companies producing a limited number of products for a specific geographic area.

The European market consisted of more than 320 million consumers whose preferences varied by country and by region. For example, Swedes preferred galvanized washing machines to withstand the damp salty air.[7] The British washed their clothes more often than the Italians did, and wanted quieter machines. The French liked to cook on gas at high temperatures, splattering grease on cooking surfaces, and so preferred self-cleaning ovens, while the Ger-

2. Weiss, David D. and Andrew C. Gross, "Industry Corner: Major Household Appliances in Western Europe," *Business Economics,* Vol. 30, Issue 3, July 1995: 67.
3. Echikson, William. "The Trick to Selling in Europe," *Fortune,* 20 Sept. 1993: 82.
4. Maruca, Regina Fazio. "The Right Way to Go Global: An Interview with Whirlpool CEO David Whitwam," *Harvard Business Review,* March–April 1994: 137.
5. Weiss and Gross.
6. Jancsurak, Joe, "Holistic Strategy Pays Off," *Appliance Manufacturer,* Feb. 1995: W-3, W-4.
7. Steinmetz, Greg and Carl Quintanilla. "Tough Target: Whirlpool Expected Easy Going in Europe, and It Got a Big Shock," *Wall Street Journal,* 10 April 1998: Sec. A:1.

EXHIBIT 1

Major Competitors in the United States

GE Appliance	General Electric Appliance was the second-largest manufacturer of household appliances in the U.S. (behind Whirlpool). Other brand names produced by the company included Monogram, Profile, Profile Performance, Hotpoint, and some private brands for retailers. GE Appliance comprised approximately 6% of the parent company's sales and had the top market share position in India and Mexico. In addition, the company had a 50-50 joint venture with General Electric Co., the leading appliance firm in the United Kingdom.
Maytag	Maytag's products were generally aimed at the mid-to-high end of the market and commanded a premium price based on product quality and reliability. Other brand names produced by Maytag included Jenn-Air, Magic Chef, Performa, and Hoover. Maytag entered the European market in 1989, but after a decline in profits, pulled out of Europe in 1995. Maytag had a limited presence in China.
AB Electrolux	AB Electrolux was the world's largest producer of household appliances. Other Electrolux brand names included Frigidaire, Tappan, and Kelvinator. The Swedish company had the number one market share in Europe and number four market share in North America. Electrolux entered the United States when it bought White Consolidated Industries in 1986. The firm was actively expanding overseas into Eastern Europe, China, India, South East Asia, and Latin America.

Sources: Hoovers Online. Accessed 2/9/00. Remich/Norman C. "A Kentucky Thoroughbred that is Running Strong," *Appliance Manufacturer,* July 1995: GEA-3. Steinmetz, Greg and Carl Quintanilla. Tough Target: Whirlpool Expected Easy Going in Europe, and It Got a Big Shock," *Wall Street Journal,* 10 April 1998; Sec. A:1.

mans liked to cook on electric stoves at lower temperatures and did not need such features.[8]

Distribution of the appliances in Europe was different than in the United States. Most appliances were sold through independent retailers, who had become organized in buying groups or as multiple store chains.[9] A smaller channel was through independent kitchen specialists who sold complete kitchen packages, including appliances.[10]

The Asian Industry

Asia, the world's second largest home appliance market, was also the fastest growing market of the 1980s. By the mid-1990s, it was growing at a rate of between 8% and 12% annually, a rate that was expected to continue well past the year 2000.[11] The industry was highly fragmented, consisting of manufacturers primarily from Japan, Korea, and Taiwan. Matsushita,

the market leader, held less than 10% market share outside Japan.

Asian consumer preferences were different from those in Europe or North America. Kitchen appliances needed to be smaller to fit in Asian kitchens. Lack of space sometimes required the consumer to store the appliance in an outside hallway and transport it into the kitchen for use.[12] Therefore, high value was placed on appliances that were portable, usually lightweight and on wheels, and easily hooked up to electrical and water supplies. Refrigerators also tended to be smaller and more colorful. Indeed, when Asian countries first began to experience significant economic growth, some East Asians viewed their refrigerators as status symbols and liked to display them prominently, perhaps even in the sitting room. Clothes dryers and dishwashers were uncommon in most Asian countries, but most homes had microwaves.

Appliances in Asia were traditionally sold through small retail shops. However, the industry was beginning to witness a shift away from these small

8. Schiller, Zachary, et al., "Whirlpool Plots the Invasion of Europe," *Business Week,* 5 Sept. 1988: 70.
9. Jancsurak, Joe, "Group Sales: Channel Focused," *Appliance Manufacturer,* Feb. 1995: W-14.
10. "Group Sales," W-14.
11. Babyak, Richard J, "Strategic Imperative," *Appliance Manufacturer,* Feb. 1995: W-21.

12. Babyak, Richard J, "Demystifying the Asian Consumer," *Appliance Manufacturer,* Feb. 1995: W26.

shops and towards distribution through national, power retailer organizations, especially in China and parts of Southeast Asia.

The Latin American Industry

The economic stability in Latin America in the 1990s made the region an attractive growth proposition. The appliance makers hoped that the days of hyper-inflation and economic mismanagement were over, and they were pleased to see that governments were reducing tariffs. Distributors in Latin America were generally responsible for marketing a company's appliances to small independent retailers in the region.[13] In 1994, there were over 65 competitors in the Latin American market, many of them sub-sidiaries of U.S. parents.

Whirlpool Corporation

Whirlpool was founded in 1911 as The Upton Machine Co. in St Joseph, Michigan, to produce an electric motor-driven wringer washer. The company merged with The Nineteen Hundred Washer Company in 1929 and began to sell their first automatic washing machine through Sears, Roebuck & Co. in 1947. The Whirlpool brand was introduced in 1948 and steadily built a strong retail relationship with Sears. Through a series of acquisitions and mergers, the company emerged as a leading force in the U.S. appliance industry with annual revenue reaching $2 billion in 1978 (see Exhibit 2 for more detail on Whirlpool's history). Whirlpool's headquarters was in Benton Harbor, Michigan.

As of 1998, Whirlpool Corporation claimed to be the world's leading manufacturer of major home appliances. The company manufactured in thirteen countries and marketed its products under eleven major brand names (including Kenmore, Sears, KitchenAid, Roper, Inglis, and Speed Queen) to over 140 countries. Whirlpool's sales were $8.2 billion in fiscal year 1997.

The Globalization of Whirlpool

Whirlpool's first international investment was in 1957 when the firm acquired an equity interest in Multibras S.A., a Brazilian manufacturer of white goods. In 1969, the company entered the Canadian market by purchasing an equity interest in Inglis Ltd. and acquired sole ownership in 1990.

By the mid-1980s, Whirlpool saw that, despite increasing efficiencies and product quality, its profit margins were rapidly decreasing in North America. Top management believed that if the company continued to follow its current path, the future would be "neither pleasant nor profitable."[14] They considered restructuring the company financially or diversifying into related businesses but eventually settled on further global expansion for two main reasons: the company wished to take advantage of less mature markets around the world and it did not want to be left behind by its competitors, which had already begun to globalize.

Whitwam's Vision and Platform Technology

David Whitman joined Whirlpool in 1968 as a marketing management trainee and rose through the sales and marketing ranks to succeed Jack Sparks as CEO in 1987. Although Whitwam admitted that he had never actually run a multinational company until Whirlpool bought Philips in 1989, he believed that:

> The only way to gain lasting competitive advantage is to leverage your capabilities around the world, so that the company as a whole is greater than the sum of its parts. Being an international company—selling globally, having global brands or operations in different countries—isn't enough.[15]

Whitwam was convinced that most companies with international divisions were not truly global at all, as their various regional and national divisions still operated as autonomous entities rather than working together as a single company. He believed that the only way to achieve his vision of an integrated international company, or one company worldwide, was through intensive efforts to understand and respond to genuine customer needs and through products and services that earn long-term customer loyalty.

Whitwam talked about his vision of integrating Whirlpool's geographical businesses so that the company's expertise would not be confined to one location or product. He forecast appliances such as a World Washer, a single machine that could be sold anywhere,

---

13. Janesurak, Joe, "South American Sales Co.: Linking the Americas, Europe," *Appliance Manufacturer*, Feb. 1995: W-39.

14. Maruca, p. 136.
15. Maruca, p. 137.

EXHIBIT 2

Whirlpool History

1911	Upton Machine Co. is founded in St. Joseph, Michigan, to produce electric motor-driven wringer washers.
1916	First order for washers is sold to Sears, Roebuck and Co.
1929	Upton Machine merges with Nineteen Hundred Washer Company of Binghamton, New York. The new firm, Nineteen Hundred Corp., operates plants in Michigan and New York until Binghamton is closed in 1939.
1942	All facilities are converted to wartime production until end of World War II in 1945.
1947	The company's first automatic washer is introduced to the market by Sears.
1948	A Whirlpool brand automatic washer is introduced, thus establishing dual distribution—one line of products for Sears, another for Nineteen Hundred.
1950	Nineteen Hundred Corporation is renamed Whirlpool Corporation. Automatic dryers are added to the product line.
1951	LaPorte, Indiana, plant is acquired. It will become the company's parts distribution center. Whirlpool merges with Clyde (Ohio) Porcelain Steel and converts the plant to washer production. All washers eventually will be produced here.
1955	Manufacturing facilities are purchased in Marion, Ohio, from Motor Products Corp., and dryer production is transferred there. Whirlpool merges with Seeger Refrigerator Co. of St. Paul, Minnesota, and the Estate range and air conditioning divisions of R.C.A. RCA Whirlpool is established as the brand name; Whirlpool-Seeger Corporation, as the company name. A refrigeration plant is acquired in Evansville, Indiana, from International Harvester.
1956	First full line of RCA Whirlpool home appliances is introduced. RCA will be used with the Whirlpool brand name until 1967. New administrative center is completed on 100-acre site in Benton Harbor.
1957	Company name is changed back to Whirlpool Corporation. Appliance Buyers Credit Corporation is established as a wholly owned finance subsidiary. It will be renamed Whirlpool Financial Corporation in 1989.
1957	Whirlpool invests in Brazilian appliance market through purchase of equity interest in Multibrás S.A. It is renamed Brastemp S.A. in 1972.
1966	The Norge plant in Fort Smith, Arkansas, is acquired, adding more than one million sq. ft. of refrigeration manufacturing space.
1967	Toll-free Cool-Line® Telephone Service begins. Renamed the Consumer Assistance Center in 1990, it gives customers direct, 24-hour access to Whirlpool. The company's first totally new manufacturing facility is completed in Findlay, Ohio. Dishwashers and, later, ranges will be manufactured there.
1968	The Elisha Gray II Research & Engineering Center is completed in Benton Harbor. For the first time, annual revenues reach $1 billion.
1969	The company enters the Canadian appliance market through purchase of an equity interest in Inglis Ltd. Sole ownership is established in 1990.
1970	Construction is completed on a new plant in Danville, Kentucky. Production of trash compactors and, later, vacuum cleaners is transferred there.
1976	Whirlpool increases its investment in the Brazilian market through purchase of equity interests in Consul S.A., an appliance manufacturer, and Embraco S.A., a maker of compressors.
1978	Annual revenues reach $2 billion.
1983	The company announces a phaseout of washer assembly at St. Joseph. All washers will be made at Clyde.
1984	The St. Paul Division is closed. Production of freezers and ice makers moves to Evansville.
1986	Whirlpool purchases the KitchenAid division of Hobart Corporation. A majority interest is purchased in Aspera s.r.l., an Italian compressor manufacturer. Whirlpool will become sole owner before the business is sold to Embraco of Brazil in 1994. Whirlpool closes most of its St. Joseph Division. The remaining machining operation is renamed the Benton Harbor Division.

(continued)

EXHIBIT 2 *(continued)*

Whirlpool History

1987	Whirlpool and Sundaram-Clayton Limited of India form TVS Whirlpool Limited to make compact washers for the Indian market. Whirlpool will acquire majority ownership in 1994.
1988	A joint venture company, Vitromatic S.A. de C.V., is formed with Vitro, S.A. of Monterrey, to manufacture and market major home appliances for Mexican and export markets. Whirlpool acquires the Roper brand name, which it will use to market a full line of value-oriented home appliances.
1989	Whirlpool and N.V. Philips of the Netherlands form a joint venture company, Whirlpool Europe B.V., from Philips major domestic appliance division, to manufacture and market appliances in Europe. Whirlpool will become sole owner in 1991. Appliance operations in the United States, Canada, and Mexico are brought together to form the North American Appliance Group (NAAG). Annual revenues catapult over the $6 billion mark.
1990	A program is launched to market appliances in Europe under the dual brands Philips and Whirlpool. Whirlpool Overseas Corporation is formed as a subsidiary to conduct marketing and industrial activities outside North America and Western Europe. An Estate brand of appliances targeted to national accounts is introduced.
1991	The company commits globally to its Worldwide Excellence System, a total quality management program dedicated to exceeding customer expectations. NAAG repositions its refrigeration business. The Port Credit, Ontario, plant is closed. Top- and bottom-mount refrigerators are consolidated at Evansville, side-by-side refrigerators at Fort Smith.
1992	Whirlpool assumes control of SAGAD S.A., of Argentina. Whirlpool Hungarian Trading Ltd. is formed to sell and service appliances in Hungary. Whirlpool Tatramat is formed to make and sell washing machines and market other major home appliances in Slovakia. Whirlpool will take controlling interest in 1994. A Small Appliance Business Unit is formed to operate on a global basis. Revenues top $7 billion. The South American Sales Co. (SASCo), a joint venture with Whirlpool's Brazilian affiliates, begins directing export sales to 35 Latin American countries.
1993	Whirlpool Overseas Corporation is replaced by two separate regional organizations: Whirlpool Asia and Whirlpool Latin America. Whirlpool Asia sets up headquarters in Tokyo with regional offices in Singapore, Hong Kong, and Tokyo. Sales subsidiaries are opened in Poland and the Czech Republic, adding to Whirlpool Europe's growing presence in Eastern Europe. Whirlpool wins the $30 million Super Efficient Refrigerator Program sponsored by 24 U.S. utilities. Inglis Ltd. becomes Canada's leading home appliance manufacturer.
1994	Whirlpool Asia and Teco Electric & Machinery Co. Ltd. form Great Teco Whirlpool Co. Ltd. to market and distribute home appliances in Taiwan. Whirlpool becomes a stand-alone brand in Europe. Brazilian affiliates Consul and Brastemp merge to form Multibrás S.A. Electrodomésticos. Whirlpool breaks ground in Tulsa, Oklahoma, for a new plant to make freestanding gas and electric ranges. Whirlpool's Asian headquarters is moved to Singapore, and the number of operating regions is increased from three to four. Whirlpool exits vacuum cleaner business. To strengthen competitiveness, a major restructuring is announced in North America and Europe. One U.S. and one Canadian plant close. Total revenues top $8 billion.
1995	An executive office is formed in Whirlpool Asia to lead the company's rapid growth and manage strategic deployment in the region. Whirlpool acquires controlling interest in Kelvinator of India Ltd., one of India's largest manufacturers and marketers of refrigerators. TVS Whirlpool Ltd. changes name to Whirlpool Washing Machines Ltd. (WWML). Construction is completed on a new plant in Greenville, Ohio. KitchenAid small appliances will be manufactured there. Whirlpool begins to sell appliances to Montgomery Ward. Whirlpool Europe opens representative office in Russia. Whirlpool Financial Corporation (WFC) is established in India. Whirlpool assumes control of Beijing Whirlpool Snowflake Electric Appliance Group Co. Ltd., a refrigerator and freezer manufacturing joint venture. Beijing Embraco Snowflake Compressor Co. Ltd., a compressor manufacturing joint venture, is formed between Embraco and Beijing Snowflake. Whirlpool has a minority position in the joint venture. Whirlpool acquires controlling interest in

(continued)

EXHIBIT 2 *(continued)*

Whirlpool History

1995 *(continued)*	Whirlpool Narcissus (Shanghai) Co. Ltd., a washing machine manufacturing joint venture. Whirlpool acquires majority ownership of SMC Microwave Products Co. Ltd., a microwave oven manufacturing joint venture. Shenzhen Whirlpool Raybo Air-Conditioner Industrial Co. Ltd., an air conditioner manufacturing joint venture, is formed with Whirlpool having a majority stake. Whirlpool investments in Asia increase to over US$350 million, and employees total more than 9,300.
1996	Whirlpool Europe opens sales subsidiaries in Romania and Bulgaria. Production of electric and gas ranges officially begins in Whirlpool's new plant in Tulsa, Oklahoma. The company's new Greenville, Ohio, plant, which manufactures KitchenAid small appliances, begins production. The Ft. Smith Division in Arkansas begins production of trash compactors. Whirlpool Asia employees total more than 12,000. Whirlpool Europe acquires the white goods business of Gentrade of South Africa. The acquisition provides Whirlpool a sales and manufacturing base in this country.

Source: <http://www.whirlpool.com>

and he wanted to standardize the company's manufacturing processes. According to Whitwam,

> Today products are being designed to ensure that a wide variety of models can be built on the same basic platform. . . . Varying consumer preferences require us to have regional manufacturing centers. But even though the features . . . vary from market to market, much of the technology and manufacturing processes involved are similar.[16]

Given this view that standardization should be the focus, Whirlpool planned to base all its products, wherever they were built or assembled, on common platforms. These platforms would produce the technological heart of the product, the portion of the product which varied little across markets. The products could then be diversified to suit individual and regional preferences. In this way, the parts that the customer sees—the dimensions of the appliance, the metal case, and the controls—could be varied by segment or market to fulfill consumers' needs. The products would also have to meet rigorous quality and environmental standards to ensure that they could be used in different countries around the world.

Whitwam believed that the platform technology would bring a $200 million annual savings in design and component costs by the time it was fully implemented in the year 2000.[17] In addition, management was convinced that the platform strategy would put the company two to three years ahead of its competitors.

Platform technology, however, represented only the beginning of Whirlpool's globalization strategy.

According to Whitwam in the 1994 interview, Whirlpool could not truly achieve its goal of globalization until:

> . . . we have cross-border business teams . . . running all of our operations throughout the world . . . There will also come a day when we'll identify a location where the best skills in a certain product area should be concentrated, and that place will become the development center for that type of product . . . [but] while we may have only one major design center for a given product, not everyone associated with that product will have to be located there.[18]

Developing and Implementing the Global Strategy

By 1987 Whirlpool had adopted a five-year plan to develop a new international strategy. The company's 1987 Annual Report included the following statement:

> The U.S. appliance industry has limited growth opportunities, a high concentration of domestic competitors, and increasing foreign competition. Further, the United States represents only about 25% of the worldwide potential for major appliance sales. Most importantly, our vision can no longer be limited to our national borders because national borders no longer define market boundaries. The marketplace for products and services is more global than ever before and growing more so every day.

16. Maruca, p. 136.
17. Whirlpool Corporation, Annual Report, 1997.
18. Maruca, p. 145.

Recent industry forecasts indicated that approximately three-quarters of the growth in domestic appliance sales between 1995 and 2000 would be in East Asia (including Australia), Eastern Europe, and South and Central America. According to the forecasts, by 2000 these three regions (excluding Japan) would account for about 34% of sales.

European Expansion

In 1989, Whirlpool bought a major stake in N.V. Philips, a struggling Dutch appliance operation, and then purchased the remaining equity in 1991 for a total of $1.1 billion.[19] Whitwam believed that the U.S. and European markets were very similar and hoped that Whirlpool would be able to replicate their successes in the United States in the new market through implementation of a pan-European strategy. Whirlpool management also believed that the European market was becoming more "American." Research performed by the company indicated that European integration was making it more difficult for smaller companies to survive and that the industry was ripe for consolidation. Whirlpool's plan was to be one of the big players following this consolidation, and Whitwam was expecting a 20% share of the $20 billion market by the year 2000.[20] Whirlpool's strategy was to focus on brand segmentation and operational efficiency. It was believed that the company that produced the most innovative products while reducing costs would capture the market.

The European subsidiary, Whirlpool Europe BV (WEBV), created a brand portfolio segmented by price. Bauknecht (Philip German brand) served as the company's high-end product while Ignis served as the lower-end, value brand. The Philips/Whirlpool brand filled the middle range.[21] However, the company decided to heavily market the Whirlpool brand name at the expense of managing its other European brands. Managers at Bauknecht in Germany saw their marketing budgets slashed, and Bauknecht's market share fell from 7% to 6%.[22] By 1995, however, consumer research showed Whirlpool to be the most recognized appliance brand name in Europe, despite the fact that many Germans, Italians, and French had a problem pronouncing the name.

To better manage sales and service throughout the region, Whirlpool set up two centralized distribution centers: one in Cassinetta, Italy, and one in Schorndorf, Germany. Operations were streamlined in order to achieve reduced costs through economies of scale and considerable efforts were put toward product innovation and increasing operational efficiency. This strategic focus was overlaid with a global outlook, and managers were regularly rotated between Europe and the United States. The rotation generated a crossover of ideas but annoyed retail clients who felt that they had no continuity when dealing with senior managers.

The early years of European expansion were successful. Sales and profits increased steadily, and Whirlpool made a profit of $129 million in Europe in 1993. The company was able to cut costs by reducing the number of suppliers it dealt with and by using common parts in its appliances.

However, Whirlpool was not the only company aggressively attacking the market, and competition subsequent to Whirlpool's entry grew fierce. Electrolux and Bosch-Siemens both greatly improved their efficiency, along with many of the smaller European companies. The European companies laid off large numbers of workers, built up their core businesses, and concentrated on generating profits. Bosch-Siemens expanded its overseas operations while keeping production local and the company managed to raise its non-German revenue by more than 30% in five years. Electrolux shed all of its non-appliance businesses and cut its workforce by 15,000, closing 25 factories. Electrolux invested in new factories and achieved higher efficiency. Both Electrolux and Bosch-Siemens increased their profitability.

Across the industry, European plants doubled their output from 1990 to 1998 and cut the time needed to build a washing machine from five days to eight hours. Companies embraced computer-aided design techniques to speed the development of products. In 1997, it was reported that a new washing machine could move from the ideas stage to the shops in just 2-1/2 years, twice as fast as only a few years before. The "value gap" which existed between appliances in the United States and Europe also closed by an estimated 15% to 20% for all appliances.[23]

19. Steinmetz and Quintanilla, A:6.
20. Steinmetz and Quintanilla, A:1, A:6.
21. "Holistic Strategy," W-3.
22. Steinmetz and Quintanilla, A:6.

23. Jancsurak, Joe, "Marketing: Phase 2," *Appliance Manufacturer,* Feb. 1995: W-10.

The state of the retail sector also changed. Traditionally, the producers had determined price in the European appliance industry. These producers had been able to reduce their costs through greater operational efficiencies and had allowed the retailers to keep their margins constant. However, by the 1990s, the number of retail outlets across Europe had fallen significantly, giving the larger surviving retailers more power when dealing with manufacturers. Recession in Europe also caused consumers to become more cost-conscious, and brands such as the low-price firm Indesit won considerable market share.

With all companies becoming more efficient as producers, there was a shift towards product innovation as the basis for competition. For example, Whirlpool increased the size of the entrance of its front-loading washing machines, thus allowing clothes to be pushed into the machine more easily and contributing to increased sales. Companies also attempted to improve customer service and to create appliances that were more friendly to the environment. Such changes were not going unnoticed, but the industry appeared to be extremely mature. Not only were new entrants, such as Whirlpool, GE, Daewoo of South Korea, and Malaysia's Sime Datby, trying to build up sales from a small base, but the traditional European producers had become more aggressive. More than that, few were making tactical or strategic errors. Seeing the increased costs of competition and the growing intensity of rivalry, Maytag left the European market in 1995, selling its Hoover unit at a $130 million loss. Leonard Hadley, Maytag's chairman, commented, "Europe isn't an attractive place to try to go in and dislodge the established players."[24]

Eastern Europe was seen as the next great battleground and Whirlpool expanded its operations in 1996 to newly developing countries in Eastern and Central Europe. In 1997, Whirlpool opened new offices in Romania, Bulgaria, Turkey, Morocco, and South Africa from its European headquarters. Sales in the initial years were disappointing.

Problems for Whirlpool

Whirlpool's sales leveled off in the mid-1990s and profits began to fall. Sales only increased 13% from 1990 to 1996, which was far from the levels management had expected. The company initiated a major restructuring in 1995 and laid off 2,000 employees. The restructuring did not solve the problems and in 1996, the company's European operations recorded a loss of $13 million. Between 1995 and 1997 the company also witnessed a rise in materials and labor costs. Exhibit 3 shows Whirlpool's stock prices versus the S&P 500. Exhibits 4 and 5 show Whirlpool corporate and business unit financial information.

24. Steinmetz and Quintanilla, A:6.

EXHIBIT 3

Whirlpool Share Price*

*The Whirlpool share price is on the bottom.

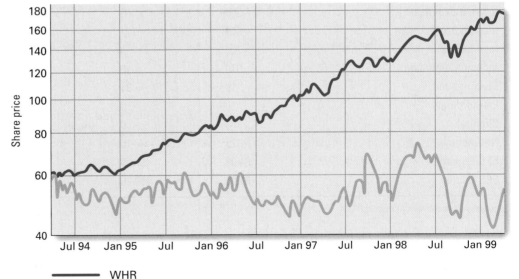

EXHIBIT 4

Whirlpool Financial Statements

Balance Sheet	Dec-98 US$MM	Dec-97 US$MM	Dec-96 US$MM	Dec-95 US$MM
Cash	636	578	129	149
Securities	0	0	0	0
Receivables	1,711	1,565	2,366	2,117
Allowances	116	156	58	81
Inventory	1,100	1,170	1,034	1,029
Current Assets	3,882	4,281	3,812	3,541
Property and Equipment, Net	5,511	5,262	3,839	3,662
Depreciation	3,093	2,887	2,041	1,883
Total Assets	7,935	8,270	8,015	7,800
Current Liabilities	3,267	3,676	4,022	3,829
Bonds	1,087	1,074	955	983
Preferred Mandatory	0	0	0	0
Preferred Stock	0	0	0	0
Common Stock	83	82	81	81
Other Stockholders' Equity	1,918	1,689	1,845	1,796
Total Liabilities and Equity	7,935	8,270	8,015	7,800

Income Statement	Dec-98 US$MM	Dec-97 US$MM	Dec-96 US$MM	Dec-95 US$MM
Total Revenues	10,323	8,617	8,696	8,347
Cost of Sales	9,596	8,229	8,331	6,311
Other Expenses	39	377	65	31
Loss Provision	45	160	63	50
Interest Expense	260	168	165	141
Income Pre Tax	564	−171	130	242
Income Tax	209	−9	81	100
Income Continuing	310	−46	156	209
Discontinued	15	31	0	0
Extraordinary	0	0	0	0
Changes	0	0	0	0
Net Income	325	−15	156	209
EPS Primary	$4.09	($0.20)	$2.08	$2.80
EPS Diluted	$4.06	($0.20)	$2.07	$2.76

Sources: Whirlpool Annual Reports

EXHIBIT 5

Whirlpool Business Unit Sales and Operating Profit

	Sales (in millions of US dollars)			
	Dec-97	**Dec-96**	**Dec-95**	**Dec-94**
North America	5263	5310	5093	5048
Europe	2343	2494	2428	2373
Asia	400	461	376	205
Latin America	624	268	271	329
Other	−13	−10	−5	−6
Total	8617	8523	8163	7949

	Operating Profit (in millions of US dollars)			
	Dec-97	**Dec-96**	**Dec-95**	**Dec-94**
North America	546	537	445	522
Europe	54	−13	92	163
Asia	−62	−70	−50	−22
Latin America	28	12	26	49
Restructuring charge	343	−30		−248
Business dispositions	−53			60
Other	159	−158	−147	−154
Total	11	278	366	370

Sources: Whirlpool Annual Reports

Whirlpool announced a second restructuring in 1997. The company planned to cut a further 4,700 jobs worldwide, or about 15% of its workforce, mostly in Europe. In 1998, WEBV had a 12% market share and held the number three market position. However, in 1998, the profit margin had reduced further to 2.3%, compared to 10% in the U.S.

Whirlpool's managers blamed a number of causes—reduced consumer demand, poor economic growth, the rising Italian lira, intense competition, and even the European Monetary Union—for its poor performance in Europe but shareholders were unimpressed. Indeed, Scott Graham, analyst at CIBC Oppenheimer, commented in 1998, "The strategy has been a failure. Whirlpool went in big [into overseas markets] and investors have paid for it."

In 1998, Whirlpool's goals remained the same, but the timeframes for delivery grew. Whitwam attributed the performance to temporary problems in the newer regions of activity and believed that Whirlpool was now coming through the challenges." He and the rest of his management team remained resolute.

> We were convinced when we first bought [the Philips operation] and we're convinced now. The benefits from Europe have begun to flow. But they have yet to be recognized.[25]

Asian Expansion

Whirlpool's strategy in Asia consisted of five main points: partnering to build win-win relationships; attracting, retaining, and developing the best people; ensuring quality in all aspects of the business; exceeding customer needs and expectations; and offering four key products (refrigerators, washers, microwaves, and air conditioners). Although Whirlpool announced in 1987 a full-scale cooperation with Daiichi, a department store retailer in Japan, the company

25. Steinmetz and Quintanilla, A:6.

decided to focus its efforts in Asia primarily on India and China. There were two main reasons for this decision. First, recent changes in government regulations in both countries made it possible for foreign corporations to own a controlling interest in a manufacturing company. Second, the large populations of India and China reduced the risk of establishing large-scale operations there.

Whirlpool decided that the best way to enter the Asian market was through joint ventures, as they would allow the company to quickly establish a manufacturing presence in Asia. Once it had accomplished this goal, Whirlpool planned to build its own manufacturing facilities in the region. In 1987, Whirlpool announced an agreement with Sundram Clyton of India to manufacturer compact washers for the Indian market, a joint venture which later became known as Whirlpool Washing Machines Limited. In 1993, the Asian group established regional headquarters in Tokyo and a pan-Asian marketing, product development, and technology center in Singapore.

Whirlpool intensified its Asian acquisition strategy in 1995 with various acquisitions and joint ventures in both India and China. The company bought controlling interest in Kelvinator in India, combined it with Whirlpool Washing Machines Limited, and renamed the new entity Whirlpool of India (WOI). In addition to giving Whirlpool a 56% interest in WOI, the Kelvinator purchase gave the company direct access to more than 3,000 trade dealers in India. Between 1994 and 1995, the company also set up four joint ventures in China, as it believed that China's market for appliances was likely to equal or surpass that of North America within ten years. By 1996, Whirlpool's investment in Asia had reached $350 million and they employed over 12,000 people. In 1997, the Asian businesses generated over $400 million in sales.

Despite its investments, however, the company suffered operating losses in Asia of $70 million in 1996 and $62 million in 1997. In 1997, Whirlpool decided to restructure its Chinese operations when overcapacity in the refrigerator and air-conditioning markets drove prices down significantly. In 1997, Whirlpool decided to find strategic alternatives for the two money-losing joint ventures which catered to these two markets.

Smaller Chinese companies were also seizing considerable market share away from the multinational foreign competition. Haier, a Chinese producer of air conditioners, microwave ovens, refrigerators, and

dishwashers publicly announced plans to become a global brand by 2002 and had already expanded into Indonesia and the Philippines. In addition, the Chinese government was strongly encouraging consumers to "buy Chinese."[26] Too many producers were making similar goods, and production soon outpaced demand. For example, although Whirlpool believed it would take approximately five to six years for the market to become saturated, the refrigerator and air conditioning markets were deemed saturated just two years after Whirlpool established its joint ventures in China. In addition, the company's Asian operations produced products of poorer quality than its Japanese rivals.[27]

Competition and overcapacity were not the only problems for Whirlpool. The company had overestimated the size of the market. The Chinese middle class that could afford new home appliances numbered only about 120 million, and there was no tradition in China of changing appliances that worked properly.

Once in China, Whirlpool also realized that it had not properly understood the distribution system. The company discovered that there were huge geographical distances between Chinese cities and that the country lacked strong distribution channels. The company had not expected to face major problems with telecommunications and, despite the country's huge labor supply, Whirlpool had difficulties finding qualified people for its factories.

The situation in India was similar. Despite having invested heavily in advertising and promotions, Whirlpool blamed overcapacity and difficult trading conditions in the refrigerator sector for its losses. Nevertheless, Whitwam remained confident:

> Our lower cost structure and focus on the remaining majority-owned joint ventures in China, combined with our strong market position in India and Asia-Pacific sales subsidiaries, leave Whirlpool well positioned for future growth and profitability in this region . . . Our growing knowledge of Asia and ability to draw on the other global resources of Whirlpool will lead to continued improvement in our operating performance in 1998 and beyond, especially as we manage through a difficult market and economic environment.[28]

26. Shuchman, Lisa, "Reality Check," *Wall Street Journal,* 1998 April 30: Global Investing Section: 1.
27. Vlasic, Bill and Zachary Schiller. "Did Whirlpool Spin Too Far Too Fast?" *Business Week,* 24 June 1996: 136.
28. Whirlpool Corporation. Annual Report, 1997.

Whirlpool continued to invest money in India and committed over $100 million to build a new plant near Pune to produce chlorofluorocarbon-free and frost-free refrigerators for the Indian market. The company began construction of the new facility in 1997 and the factory began commercial production in the first quarter of 1998.

Latin American Expansion

Throughout most of the 1990s, Brazil was Whirlpool's most profitable foreign operation.[29] The company first bought into the Brazilian market in 1957 and held equity positions in three companies: Brasmotor S.A., Multibras, and Embraco. These companies held a 60% market share and after 40 years of operating in Brazil, had extremely high brand recognition and brand loyalty. Whirlpool took over Philips Argentine subsidiary, SAGAD, in 1992. In the mid-90s, sales and profit figures were good, with sales up 28% in 1994–1995, and 15% in 1996. In 1997, Brazilian operations recorded approximately $78 million in earnings.

Because Latin America had lower appliance penetration rates than Europe and the United States (e.g., only 15% of Brazilian homes owned microwaves, compared with 91% in the United States), the region appeared to be a good target for expansion. By the mid-1990s, Latin America was beginning to achieve economic stability, and growth was sure to follow. Consumers felt the same way. Many consumers were now able to replace old and worn-out appliances using budget plans and credit arrangements.

In 1997 in Brazil, Whirlpool spent $217 million to increase its equity share in Brasmotor from 33% to 66%. Whirlpool then invested another $280 million in 1997 and 1998 to renew plants and product lines. The company introduced data transfer systems, flexible production lines, and launched new products. Shortly after Whirlpool made these large investments in Brazil, however, interest rates in the country began to climb. The Brazilian government doubled interest rates in October 1997 and again in 1998. As a result, the currency depreciated and the economy suffered. In real terms, the *real* fell more than 50% in the six months prior to January 1999. Total foreign investment in Brazil slumped, and the country was eventually forced to request a $41.5 billion credit line from the International Monetary Fund in order to help rescue the economy.

Worse yet, Whirlpool's market research told them that consumers had reacted quickly to the economic problems. Many were afraid of job cuts in the worsening economy and were wondering whether Brazil would resort to the traditional solution of printing money to solve the economic problems. Consumers foresaw inflation and realized that they would not be able to afford to purchase Whirlpool's appliances, especially on credit. As Antonio da Silva, a thirty-seven-year-old maintenance worker said, "I'm afraid to pay over many months because you don't know if interest rates or inflation will rise again."[30]

In 1998, Whirlpool's Brazilian sales fell by 25%, or $1 billion.[31] Equally important, Whirlpool's *real* reserves had shrunk in value against the dollar, and the company was expecting inflationary pressures. As a result, in late 1998 the company announced more restructuring to its Latin American operations. Whirlpool immediately cut 3,200 jobs (about 25% of the workforce) to improve efficiency, and the company planned to cut out levels in the production chain in its seven factories in Brazil, Argentina, and Chile. At the same time, the company increased its marketing efforts in the region.

As of 1998, Whirlpool was still confident of a return to profitability in Latin America. The company believed that industry shipments to Brazil in 1999 would equal those in 1997. *Business Week* characterized the company as bullish:

> The experience of surviving Brazil's many debt crises, bouts of hyperinflation, and military governments has given Whirlpool a been-there, done-that aura of confidence.[32]

But, given Whirlpool's poor showing in the earlier phases of its globalization plan, it still had far to go in convincing the many sceptics and disappointed shareholders that globalization was the best strategy. Many analysts were unsure whether Whirlpool's self-confidence was actually deserved or if it was little more than self-delusion.

29. Katz, Ian, "Whirlpool: In the Wringer," *Business Week,* 14 Dec. 1998: 83.

30. Katz, 83.
31. Katz, 83.
32. Katz, 87.

41

"You Push the Button, We Do the Rest": From Silver Halide to Infoimaging at Eastman Kodak

This case was prepared by Gareth R. Jones, Texas A&M University.

In April 2002, Daniel Carp, the chief executive officer (CEO) of the Eastman Kodak Company, was reflecting on Kodak's situation. Kodak had just reported a 74 percent drop in first-quarter earnings on a 9 percent decline in sales, with no growth in sales for 2002 in sight, and Kodak's stock had dropped by 10 percent. Was Kodak's new "infoimaging" business model—based on strategies to counter the threats posed to Kodak's traditional silver halide–based technology by the convergence of imaging and digital information technology—working? Did the company have the digital products in place to rebuild its profitability and fulfill its "You press the button, we do the rest" promise? Or, after ten years of declining sales and profits, was the company just on the verge of another downward slope in the face of intense global competition on all its product fronts? Carp, a thirty-year Kodak veteran, thought it was a pity that Colby Chandler, Kodak's CEO in the late 1980s, had chosen to lessen Kodak's dependence on the photo-

graphic products industry and counter competition from other imaging techniques by engaging in an ambitious program of diversification. If only that money had been invested early in digital photographic technology . . .

Kodak's History

Eastman Kodak Company was incorporated in New Jersey on October 24, 1901, as successor to the Eastman Dry Plate Company, the business originally established by George Eastman in September 1880. The Dry Plate Company had been formed to develop a dry photographic plate that was more portable and easier to use than other plates in the rapidly developing photography field. To mass-produce the dry plates uniformly, Eastman patented a plate-coating machine and began to manufacture the plates commercially. Eastman's continuing interest in the infant photographic industry led to his development in 1884 of silver halide paper–based photographic roll film. Eastman capped this invention with his introduction of the first portable camera in 1888. This camera used his own patented film, which was developed using his own proprietary method. Thus Eastman

This case is intended to be used as a basis for class discussion rather than as an illustration of either effective or ineffective handling of the situation. Reprinted by permission of the author.

had gained control of all the stages of the photographic process. His breakthroughs made possible the development of photography as a mass leisure activity. The popularity of the "recorded images" business was immediate, and sales boomed. Eastman's inventions revolutionized the photographic industry, and his company was uniquely placed to lead the world in the development of photographic technology.

From the beginning, Kodak focused on four primary objectives to guide the growth of its business: (1) mass production to lower production costs, (2) maintaining the lead in technological developments, (3) extensive product advertising, and (4) the development of a multinational business to exploit the world market. Although common now, those goals were revolutionary at the time. In due course, Kodak's yellow boxes could be found in every country in the world. Preeminent in world markets, Kodak operated research, manufacturing, and distribution networks throughout Europe and the rest of the world. Kodak's leadership in the development of advanced color film for simple, easy-to-use cameras and in quality film processing was maintained by constant research and development in its many research laboratories. Its huge volume of production allowed it to obtain economies of scale. Kodak was also its own supplier of the plastics and chemicals needed to produce film, and it made most of the component parts for its cameras.

Kodak became one of the most profitable American corporations, and its return on shareholders' equity averaged 18 percent for many years. To maintain its competitive advantage, it continued to invest heavily in research and development in silver halide photography, remaining principally in the photographic business. In this business, as the company used its resources to expand sales and become a global business, the name *Kodak* became a household word signifying unmatched quality. By 1990, approximately 40 percent of Kodak's revenues came from sales outside the United States.

Starting in the early 1970s, however, and especially in the 1980s, Kodak ran into major problems, reflected in the drop in return on equity. Its preeminence was being increasingly threatened as the photographic industry and industry competition changed. Major innovations had taken place within the photography business, and new methods of

recording images and memories beyond silver halide technology, most noticeably digital imaging, were emerging.

The New Industry Environment

In the 1970s, Kodak began to face an uncertain environment in all its product markets. First, the color film and paper market from which Kodak made 75 percent of its profits experienced growing competition from Japanese companies, led by Fuji Photo Film Co. Fuji invested in huge, low-cost manufacturing plants, using the latest technology to mass-produce film in large volume. Fuji's low production costs and aggressive, competitive price cutting squeezed Kodak's profit margin. Finding no apparent differences in quality and obtaining more vivid colors with the Japanese product, consumers began to switch to the cheaper Japanese film, and this shift drastically reduced Kodak's market share.

Besides greater industry competition, another liability for Kodak was that it had done little internally to improve productivity to counteract rising costs. Supremacy in the marketplace had made Kodak complacent, and it had been slow to introduce productivity and quality improvements. Furthermore, Kodak (unlike Fuji in Japan) produced film in many different countries in the world rather than in a single country, and this also gave Kodak a cost disadvantage. Thus the combination of Fuji's efficient production and Kodak's own management style allowed the Japanese to become the cost leaders—to charge lower prices and still maintain profit margins.

Kodak was also facing competition on other product fronts. Its cameras had an advantage because of their ease of use as compared with complex 35-mm single-lens reflex models. They were also inexpensive. However, the quality of their prints could not compare with those of 35-mm cameras. In 1970 Kodak had toyed with the idea of producing a simple-to-use 35-mm camera but had abandoned it. In the late 1970s, however, the Japanese did develop an easy-to-use 35-mm pocket camera featuring such innovations as auto flash, focus, and rewind. The quality of the prints produced by these cameras was far superior to the grainy prints produced by the smaller Instamatic and disk cameras, and consumers began to switch to these products in large numbers.

This shift led to the need for new kinds of film, which Kodak was slow to introduce, thus adding to its product problems.

Shrinking market share due to increased competition from the Japanese was not Kodak's only problem. In the early 1980s, it introduced several less-than-successful products. In 1982 it introduced a new disk camera as a replacement for the pocket Instamatic. The disk camera used a negative even smaller than the negative of the Instamatic and was smaller and easier to use. Four and a half million units were shipped to the domestic market by Christmas, but almost a million of the units still remained on retailers' shelves in the new year. The disk cameras had been outsold by pocket 35-mm cameras, which produced higher-quality pictures. The disk camera also sold poorly in the European and Japanese markets. Yet Kodak's research showed that 90 percent of disk camera users were satisfied with the camera and especially liked its high "yield rate" of 93 percent printable pictures, compared with 75 percent for the pocket Instamatic.

A final blow on the camera front came when Kodak lost its patent suit with Polaroid Corp. Kodak had forgone the instant photography business in the 1940s when it turned down Edwin Land's offer to develop his instant photography process. Polaroid developed it, and instant photography was wildly successful, capturing a significant share of the photographic market. In response, Kodak set out in the 1960s to develop its own instant camera to compete with Polaroid's. According to testimony in the patent trial, Kodak spent $94 million perfecting its system, only to scrub it when Polaroid introduced the new SX-70 camera in 1972. Kodak then rushed to produce a competing instant camera, hoping to capitalize on the $6.5 billon in sales of instant cameras. However, on January 9, 1986, a federal judge ordered Kodak out of the instant photography business for violating seven of Polaroid's patents in its rush to produce an instant camera. The cost to Kodak for closing its instant photography operation and exchanging the 16.5 million cameras sold to consumers was over $800 million. In 1985 Kodak reported that it had exited the industry at a cost of $494 million. However, the total costs of this misadventure were finally realized on July 15, 1991, when Kodak agreed to pay Polaroid a sum of $925 million to settle out of court a suit that Polaroid had brought against Kodak for patent infringement.

On its third product front, photographic processing, Kodak also experienced problems. It faced stiff competition from foreign manufacturers of photographic paper and from new competitors in the film-processing market. Increasingly, film processors were turning to cheaper sources of paper to reduce the costs of film processing. Once again the Japanese had developed cheaper sources of paper and were eroding Kodak's market share. At the same time, many new independent film-processing companies had emerged and were printing film at far lower rates than Kodak's own official developers. These independent laboratories had opened to serve the needs of drugstores and supermarkets, and many of them offered twenty-four-hour service. They used the less expensive paper to maintain their cost advantage and were willing to accept lower profit margins in return for a higher volume of sales. As a result, Kodak lost markets for its chemical and paper products—products that had contributed significantly to its revenues and profits.

The photographic industry surrounding Kodak had changed dramatically. Competition had increased in all product areas, and Kodak, while still the largest producer, faced increasing threats to its profitability as it was forced to reduce prices to match the competition. To cap the problem, by 1980 the market was all but saturated: 95 percent of all U. S. households owned at least one camera. Facing increased competition in a mature market was not an enviable position for a company used to high profitability and growth.

The second major problem that Kodak had to confront was due not to increased competition in existing product markets but to the emergence of new industries that provided alternative means of producing and recording images. The introduction of videotape recorders, and later video cameras, gave consumers an alternative way to use their dollars to produce images, particularly moving images. Video basically destroyed the old, film-based home movie business on which Kodak had a virtual monopoly. After Sony's introduction of the Betamax machine in 1975, a video industry grew into a multibillion-dollar business. VCRs and 16-mm video cameras became increasingly hot-selling items as their prices fell with the growth in demand and the standardization of technology. The development of compact 8-mm video cameras that were much smaller than the 16-mm version, and then the later introduction of laser disks, compact disks, and, in the 1990s, DVDs were also significant developments. The vast amount of data that can be recorded on these disks gave them a great advantage in reproducing images through electronic means. It was increasingly apparent that the whole nature of the imaging and recording process was changing from chemical methods of reproduction to electronic, digital methods. Kodak's managers should have perceived this transformation to digital-based methods as a disruptive technology because its technical preeminence was based on sliver halide photography. However, as is always the case with such technologies, the real threat lies in the future.

These changes in the competitive environment caused enormous difficulties for Kodak. Between 1972 and 1982 profit margins from sales declined from 15.7 to 10.7 percent. Kodak's glossy image lost its luster. It was in this declining situation that Colby Chandler took over as chairman in July 1983.

Kodak's New Strategy

Chandler saw the need for dramatic changes in Kodak's businesses and quickly pioneered four changes in strategy: (1) he strove to increase Kodak s control of its existing chemical-based imaging businesses; (2) he aimed to make Kodak the leader in electronic imaging; (3) he spearheaded attempts by Kodak to diversify into new businesses to increase profitability; and (4) he began on major efforts to reduce costs and improve productivity. To achieve the first three objectives, he began a huge program of acquisitions, realizing that Kodak did not have the time to venture new activities internally. Because Kodak was cash rich and had low debt, financing these acquisitions was easy.

For the next six years. Chandler acquired businesses in four main areas, and by 1989 Kodak had been restructured into four main operating groups: imaging, information systems, health, and chemicals. In a statement to shareholders at the annual meeting in 1988, Chandler announced that with the recent acquisition of Sterling Drug for $5 billion the company had achieved its objective: "With a sharp focus on these four sectors, we are serving diversified markets from a unified base of science and manufacturing technology. The logical synergy of the Kodak growth strategy means that we are neither diversified as a conglomerate nor a company with a one-product family."

The way these operating groups developed under Chandler's leadership is described in the following text.

The Imaging Group

Imaging comprised Kodak's original businesses, including consumer products, motion picture and audiovisual products, photo finishing, and consumer electronics. The unit was charged with strengthening Kodak's position in its existing businesses. Kodak's strategy in its photographic imaging business has been to fill gaps in its product line by introducing new products either made by Kodak or bought from Japanese manufacturers and sold under the Kodak name. For example, in attempting to maintain market share in the camera business, Kodak introduced a new line of disk cameras to replace the Instamatic lines. However, in addition, Kodak bought a minority stake and entered into a joint venture with Chinon of Japan to produce a range of 35-mm automatic cameras that would be sold under the Kodak name. This arrangement would capitalize on Kodak's strong brand image and give Kodak a presence in this market to maintain its camera and film sales. That venture succeeded; Kodak sold 500,000 cameras and gained 15 percent of the market. In addition, Kodak invested heavily in developing new and advanced film. It introduced a whole new range of "DX" coded film to match the new 35-mm camera market film that possesses the vivid color qualities of Fuji film. Kodak had not developed vivid film color earlier because of its belief that consumers wanted "realistic" color.

Kodak also made major moves to solidify its hold on the film-processing market. It attempted to stem the inflow of foreign low-cost photographic paper by gaining control over the processing market. In 1986 it acquired Texas-based Fox Photo Inc. for $96 million and became the largest national wholesale photograph finisher. In 1987, it acquired the laboratories of American Photographic Group. In 1989, it solidified its hold on the photo-finishing market by forming a joint venture between its operations and the photo-finishing operations of Fuqua industries. The new company, Qualex Inc., had ninety-four laboratories nationwide. These acquisitions provided Kodak with a large, captive customer for its chemical and paper products as well as control over the photo-finishing market. Also, in 1986 Kodak introduced new improved one-hour film-processing labs to compete with other photographic developers. To accompany the new labs, Kodak popularized the Kodak "Color Watch" system that requires these labs to use only Kodak paper and chemicals. Kodak hoped that this would stem the flow of business to one-hour mini-labs and also establish the industry standard for quality processing.

New and improved film products, including Kodak Gold Label film and Ektachrome film, were announced during 1988, as were new types of 35-mm cameras. Kodak also formed a battery venture with Matsushita to produce a range of alkaline batteries for Kodak. A gold-topped battery was introduced to compete with Duracell's copper-top battery. Moreover, Kodak internally ventured a new lithium battery that lasted six times as long as conventional batteries. As a result of these moves, Kodak regained control over the processing end of the market and made inroads into the camera, film, and battery ends as well. In 1988, Kodak earnings were helped by the decline in value of the dollar, which forced Fuji Photo, its main competitor, to raise its prices. Consequently, Kodak was able to increase its prices. All these measures increased Kodak's visibility in the market; Kodak was protecting its mission of "You push the button, we do the rest."

Kodak also engaged in a massive internal cost-cutting effort to improve the efficiency of the photographic products group. Beginning in 1984 it introduced more and more stringent efficiency targets aimed at reducing waste while increasing productivity. In 1986, it established a baseline for measuring the total cost of waste incurred in the manufacture of film and paper throughout its worldwide operations. By 1987 it had cut that waste by 15 percent, and by 1989 it announced total cost savings worth $500 million annually.

Despite these strategic moves, the net earnings of Kodak's photographic business dropped dramatically in 1989. Although Kodak's volume and sales of its products were up, profit margins were down. Polaroid with its new One Film product was advertising aggressively to capture market share. Fuji, realizing the strong threat posed by Kodak's reassertion of industry control, responded with an intense competitive push. Both Fuji and Kodak were spending massive amounts to advertise their products in order to increase market share. In 1989, Kodak had 80 percent of the $7 billion film market while Fuji had 11 percent, but Fuji increased its advertising budget by 65 percent in 1989 to increase its market share and

simultaneously offered discount coupons on its film products. Moreover, Fuji announced plans for a major new filmmaking plant in Europe—a plant the size of its Japanese plant, which by itself can produce enough film for one-quarter of the world market. The result was a huge amount of excess capacity in global film production as Fuji, the cost leader, went all out to build global market share through aggressive pricing.

Kodak's losses mounted as it was forced to reduce prices to counter Fuji's attempts to build market share and to give multipack discounts on its products. Also to fight back, Kodak announced a fifteen-year agreement with the Walt Disney Company to use Disney characters in its advertising. However, these moves were very expensive for Kodak and slashed profits. They also offset most of the benefits from Kodak's cost-cutting effort, and the slow growth in Kodak's core photographic imaging business meant that there was little prospect of increasing profitability.

It was because of this slow industry growth that Chandler saw the need for diversification. Because sales increased only 5 percent a year and Kodak already had 80 percent of the market, it was tied to the fortunes of one industry. While this made Kodak cash-rich when competition was weak, it made Kodak poor when competition increased. This fact, plus the increasing use and growing applications of digital imaging techniques, led to Chandler's second strategic thrust: an immediate policy of acquisition and diversification into the electronic imaging business with the stated goal of being "first in both industries"—imaging and digital.

The Information Systems Group

In 1988, when Sony introduced an electronic camera that could take still pictures and then transmit them back to a television screen, it became increasingly obvious that the threat to Kodak from new electronic imaging techniques would continue to increase. Although pictures taken with video film could not match the quality achieved with chemical reproduction, the advent of compact disks offered the prospect of an imaging medium that could meet such standards in the future. To survive and prosper in the imaging business, Kodak's managers began to realize that it required expertise in a broad range of technologies to satisfy customers' recording and imaging needs—they began to see the threat posed by the disruptive technology. Kodak's managers saw that a large number of different types of electronic markets were emerging. Electronic imaging had become important in the medical sciences and in all business, technical, and research activities, driven by the advent of powerful personal computers. However, Kodak's managers did not choose to focus on imaging products and markets close to "photographs." They began to target any kind of imaging applications in communications, computer science, and various hard-copy-output technologies that they felt might be important in the imaging markets of the future. Since Kodak had no expertise in digital imaging, it began to buy companies its managers perceived did have these skills, and then pursued its strategy of marketing the products of these companies under its own famous brand name—for instance, an electronic publishing system for corporate documents and an automated microfilm-imaging system.

Kodak thus began a strategy of acquisitions and joint ventures to invest its excess cash in new imagining technologies that it hoped, somehow, would lead to increased future profitability. In the new Information Systems group several acquisitions were made, including Atex Inc., Eikonix Corp., and Disconix Inc. Atex, acquired in 1981, made newspaper and magazine electronic publishing and text-editing systems to newspapers and magazines worldwide as well as to government agencies and law firms. Eikonix Corp. was a leader in the design, development, and production of precision digital imaging systems. Further growth within the Information Systems group came with the development of the Ektaprint line of copier-duplicators. The copiers achieved good sales growth and reached new standards for quality, reliability, and productivity in the very competitive high-volume segment of the copier marketplace. In 1988, Kodak announced another major move into the copier service business. It purchased IBM's copier service business and copier sales agreements in the United States. Kodak also announced that it would market copiers manufactured by IBM while continuing to market its own Ektaprint copiers. This service agreement was eventually extended to sixteen countries outside the United States.

Kodak also announced two new image management packages: the Kodak Ektaprint Electronic Publishing System (KEEPS) and the Kodak Imaging Management System (KIMS). KIMS electronically scans, digitizes, and stores film images and transmits image information electronically. The system enables users with large, active databases to view and manipulate information stored on microfilm and magnetic or optical disks. KEEPS was a high-quality electronic publishing package that had the ability to edit, print, and update text and graphics for publications. However, the KEEPS package included a computer made by Sun Microsystems, software produced by Interleaf Inc. and just enhanced by Kodak, and a printer manufactured by Canon. In 1988, Kodak announced that it would begin marketing a "VY-P1" printer developed in a joint venture with Hitachi to make high-quality still images from VCRs and camcorders. Although Kodak had begun to spend more and more of its R&D budget on digital imaging, it still had not internally ventured any important new products.

Moreover, these new markets did not overlap much with its core photography business. With these moves, Kodak extended its activities into the electronic areas of artificial intelligence, computer systems, consumer electronics, peripherals, telecommunications, and test and measuring equipment. Kodak was hoping to gain a strong foothold in these new businesses to make up for losses in its traditional business—not to strengthen its core business.

Soon, Kodak's managers began to purchase imaging companies that made products as diverse as computer workstations and floppy disks. It aggressively acquired companies to fill in its product lines and obtain technical expertise in information systems. After taking more than a decade to make its first four acquisitions, Kodak completed seven acquisitions in 1985 and more than ten in 1986. Among the 1985 acquisitions—for $175 million—was Verbatim Corporation, a major producer of floppy disks. This acquisition made Kodak one of the three big producers in the floppy disk industry.

Entry into the information systems market, like the expansion in its core photographic products business, produced new competitive problems for Kodak. In entering office information systems, Kodak entered areas where it faced strong competition from established companies such as IBM, Apple, and Sun. The Verbatim acquisition brought Kodak into direct competition with 3M. Entering the copier market brought Kodak into direct competition with Japanese firms such as Canon that competitively marketed their own lines of advanced, low-cost products. Kodak was entering new businesses where it had little expertise, where it was unfamiliar with the competitive problems, and where there was already strong competition.

Thus Kodak was forced to retreat from some of these markets. In 1990, it announced that it would sell Verbatim to Mitsubishi. (Mitsubishi was immediately criticized by Japanese investors for buying a company with an old, outdated product line.) Kodak was soon forced to withdraw from many other areas of business by selling assets or closing operations and taking a write-off. For example, to reduce costs it sold Sayett Technology, Kodak Video programs and videocassettes, and Aquidneck Data Corporation. The decline in the performance of the Information Systems group, attributed to increased competition, a flat office systems market, and delays in bringing out new products, reduced earnings from operations from a profit of $311 million in 1988 to a loss of $360 million in 1989.

The Health Group

Kodak's interest in health products emerged from its involvement in the design and production of film for medical and dental x-rays. The growth of imaging in medical sciences offered Kodak an opportunity to apply its skills in new areas, and it began to develop such products as Kodak Ektachem—clinical blood analyzers. It developed other products—Ektascan laser imaging films, printers, and accessories—for improving the display, storage, processing, and retrieval of diagnostic images.

However, Kodak did not confine its interests in medical and health matters to imaging-based products. In 1984, it established within the health group a life sciences division to develop and commercialize new products deriving from Kodak's distinctive competencies in chemistry and biotechnology. One of the division's objectives was to focus on product opportunities in markets with relatively few competitors and high profit potential—products such as nutritional supplements that can be delivered orally or intravenously, as well as nutrition products for sale over the counter to consumers. Another objective was to develop innovative ways to control the absorption of pharmaceutical drugs into the body so that a drug would remain therapeutically effective for the optimum amount of time. A third objective involved developing new applications for existing products and processes. Kodak had in its files about 500,000 chemical formulations on which it could base new products.

Within life sciences was the bioproducts division, which engaged in joint research with biotechnology companies such as Cetus Corporation, Amgen, and Immunex. Bioproducts pursued an aggressive strategy to scale up and commercialize products based on biotechnology derived from in-house as well as outside contract research. Ventures entered into by the bioproducts division included an agreement with Advanced Genetic Sciences for the commercial production of SNOW-MAX, a product useful in making artificial snow for ski areas.

Kodak began to enter into joint ventures in the biotechnical industry, both to build its business and to enter new businesses. In April 1985 Kodak and ICN Pharmaceuticals jointly announced the formation of a research institute that would explore new biomedical compounds aimed at stopping the spread of viral infections and slowing the aging process. Kodak and ICN were to invest $45 million over six years to form and operate the Nucleic Acid Research Institute, a joint venture located at ICN's Costa Mesa, California, facility. The institute would dedicate much of its research exclusively to preclinical studies of new antiviral and anti-aging substances.

However, these advances into biotechnology proved expensive, and the uncertainty of the industry caused Kodak to question the wisdom of entering this highly volatile area. In 1988, to reduce the costs of operating the bioproducts division, a joint venture incorporating bioproducts was formed between Kodak and Cultor Ltd. of Finland, and Kodak essentially left the market. The remaining parts of the life sciences division were then folded into the health group in 1988, when Chandler completed Kodak's biggest acquisition, the purchase of Sterling Drug for more than $5 billion.

The Sterling acquisition once again totally altered Kodak's strategy for the health group. Sterling Drug is a worldwide manufacturer and marketer of prescription drugs, over-the-counter medicine, and consumer products. It has such familiar brand names as Bayer aspirin, Phillips' milk of magnesia, and Panadol. Chandler thought this merger would provide Kodak with the marketing infrastructure and international drug registration that it needed to become a major player in the pharmaceuticals industry. With this acquisition Kodak's health group became pharmaceutically oriented, its mission being to develop a full pipeline of major prescription drugs and a world-class portfolio of over-the-counter medicine.

Analysts, however, questioned the acquisition. Once again Chandler was taking Kodak into an industry where competition was intense and the industry itself was consolidating because of the massive cost of drug development. Kodak had no expertise in this area, despite its forays into biotechnology, and the acquisition was unrelated to the other activities of the health group. Some analysts claimed that the acquisition was aimed at deterring a possible takeover of Kodak and that it was too expensive.

The acquisition of Sterling dramatically increased the sales of the health group but dampened Kodak's earnings and helped lead to a reversal in profits in 1989. Moreover, by purchasing Sterling, Kodak had obtained Sterling's Lehn & Fink products division, which produced products as diverse as Lysol and Minwax wood-care products. Far from wishing to sell this division, Kodak believed that this acquisition would lead to long-term profits. Analysts asked whether this was growth without profitability.

The Chemicals Group

Established more than sixty-five years ago as a supplier of raw materials for Kodak's film and processing businesses, the Eastman Chemical Company has been responsible for developing many of the chemicals and plastics that have made Kodak the leader in the photographic industry. The company has also been a major supplier of chemicals, fibers, and plastics to thousands of customers worldwide. Kodak has been enjoying increased growth in its plastic material and resins unit because of outstanding performance and enthusiastic customer acceptance of Kodak PET (polyethylene terephthalate), a polymer used in soft-drink bottles and other food and beverage containers. The growth in popularity of 16-ounce PET bottles spurred a record year for both revenue and volume in 1985. Kodak announced the opening of a major new PET facility in England in 1988. In 1986, three new businesses were established within the chemicals group: specialty printing inks, performance plastics, and animal nutrition supplements. They all had the common objective of enabling the chemicals group to move quickly into profitable new market segments where there is the potential for growth.

In its chemical business, too, Kodak ran into the same kinds of problems experienced by its other operating groups. There is intense competition in the plastics industry, not only from U.S. firms like Du-Pont but also from large Japanese and European firms like Imperial Chemical Industries PLC and Hoech, which compete directly with Kodak for sales. In specialty plastics and PET, for example, volume increased but Kodak was forced to reduce prices by 5 percent to compete with other firms in the industry. This squeeze in profit margins also contributed to the reversal in earnings in 1989.

Logical Synergies?

With the huge profit reversal in 1989 after all the years of acquisition and internal development, analysts were questioning the existence of the "logical synergy" that Chandler claimed for Kodak's businesses. Certainly, the relative contributions of the various operating groups to Kodak's total sales differed from the past, and Kodak was somewhat less dependent on the photographic industry. But was Kodak positioned to compete successfully in the 1990s? What was the rationale for Kodak's entry into different businesses? What were the synergies that Chandler was talking about? Wasn't the improvement on profits in 1990 due to corporate restructuring to reduce costs?

Corporate Restructuring and Cost Reduction

As Chandler tackled changes in strategy, he also directed his efforts at reshaping Kodak's management style and organizational structure to (1) reduce costs and (2) make the organization more flexible and attuned to the competitive environment. Because of its dominance in the industry, in the past Kodak had not worried about outside competition. As a result, the organizational culture at Kodak emphasized traditional, conservative values rather than entrepreneurial values. Kodak was often described as a conservative, plodding monolith because all decision making had been centralized at the top of the organization among a clique of senior managers. Furthermore, the company had been operating along functional lines. Research, production, and sales and marketing had operated separately in different units at corporate headquarters and dispersed to many different global locations. Kodak's different product groups also operated separately. The result of these factors was a lack of communication and slow, inflexible decision making that led to delays in making new product decisions. When the company attempted to transfer resources between product groups, conflict often resulted, and the separate functional operations also led to poor product group relations, for managers protected their own turf at the expense of corporate goals. Moreover, there was a lack of attention to the bottom line, and management failed to institute measures to control waste.

Another factor encouraging Kodak's conservative orientation was its promotion policy. Seniority and loyalty to "mother Kodak" counted nearly as much as ability when it came to promotions. Only twelve presidents had led the company since its beginnings in the 1880s. Long after George Eastman's suicide in 1932, the company followed his cautious ways: "If George didn't do it, his successors didn't either."

Kodak's technical orientation also contributed to its problems. Traditionally, its engineers and scientists had dominated decision making, and marketing had been neglected. The engineers and scientists were perfectionists who spent enormous amounts of time developing, analyzing, testing, assessing, and retesting new products. Little time, however, was spent determining whether the products satisfied consumer needs. As a result of this technical orientation, management passed up the invention of xerography, leaving the new technology to be developed by a small Rochester firm named Haloid Company (later Xerox). Similarly, Kodak had passed up the instant camera business. Kodak's lack of a marketing orientation allowed competitors to overtake it in several areas that were natural extensions of the photography business, such as 35-mm cameras and video recorders.

Kodak's early management style, while profitable throughout the 1960s because of the company's privileged competitive position, was thus creating difficulties. With its monopoly in the photographic film and paper industry gone, Kodak was in trouble. Chandler had to alter Kodak's management orientation. He began with some radical changes in the company's culture and structure.

Firmly committed to cost cutting, Chandler orchestrated a massive downsizing of the work force to eliminate the fat that had accumulated during Kodak's prosperous past. Traditionally, Kodak had prided itself on being one of the most "Japanese" of all U.S. companies, hiring college graduates and giving them a permanent career. Now it had to go against one of its founding principles and reduce its work force. Kodak's policy of lifetime employment

was swept out the door when declining profitability led to a large employee layoff. Chandler instituted a special early retirement program, froze pay raises, and ordered the company's first layoffs in more than a decade. By 1985, the "yellow box factory" had dropped 12,600 of its 136,000 employees. To further reduce costs in 1986, divisions were required to cut employment by an additional 10 percent and to cut budgetary expenditures by 5 percent. These measures helped, but because of Kodak's deteriorating performance, new rounds of cost cutting came in 1988 and 1989. Additional 5 percent reductions in employment aimed at saving $1 billion. The effect of these huge cuts was seen in 1990 when profits rebounded; however, it was not clear whether their effect on earnings would be short run or long run.

Although these measures had an effect on Kodak's culture, Chandler still needed to reshape Kodak's structure. In 1985 he began by shedding the old, stratified corporate structure for what he called an "entrepreneurial" approach. The first step was to reorganize the imaging group into seventeen operating units. Each of the seventeen lines of business contained all the functions necessary for success, including marketing, financial, planning, product development, and manufacturing. Each unit was treated as an independent profit center and was managed by a young executive with authority over everything from design to production. All units had the common goal of improving quality and efficiency and eliminating problems in the transfer of resources and technology among operating groups. The purpose behind this change was to eliminate the old divisional orientation, which had led to competition and reduced integration within the company. Chandler hoped the changes in organizational control and structure would promote innovation, speed reaction time, and establish clear profit goals. With this restructuring, Chandler also reduced Kodak's top-heavy management to decentralize decision making to lower levels in the hierarchy. This reorganization was a sign that the company was at last shedding its paternalistic approach to management.

With its new risk-taking attitude, Kodak also attempted to create a structure and culture to encourage internal venturing. It formed a "venture board" to help underwrite small projects and make conventional venture capital investments. In addition, the company created an "office of submitted ideas" to screen outside projects. Kodak received more than three thousand proposals, but only thirty survived the screening process. This aggressive research program led to a breakthrough in tubular silver halide grains, which improve the light-gathering capability of film. The discovery resulted in the new line of 35-mm products. However, Kodak's attempts at new venturing were generally unsuccessful. Of the fourteen ventures that Kodak created, six were shut down, three were sold, and four were merged into other divisions. One reason was Kodak's management style, which also affected its new businesses. Kodak's top managers never gave operating executives real authority or abandoned the centralized, conservative approach of the past. One example is Kodak's managing of Atex Inc., the manufacturer of desktop publishing systems that Kodak bought in 1981. Because of Kodak's overbearing management style, the top executives and employees of Atex resigned, creating serious management problems for Kodak. The Atex executives claimed that Kodak executives were hardworking but bureaucratic and did not understand the competitive nature of computer technology. Kodak managers should have been reacting to the computer marketplace weekly. They did not, and Atex executives could not handle Kodak's slow pace.

Another reason for the failure at managing new ventures and acquisitions was that Kodak did not give managers an equity stake in the new ventures, so they felt that they had no stake in the ventures' success. Having learned its lesson, Kodak announced that throughout the company pay would be more closely related to performance. For example, in 1990 up to 40 percent of a manager's annual compensation was to be based on corporate performance. Even at the middle-manager level, 15 percent of compensation was to be linked to company results. Kodak hoped by these measures to make the company more entrepreneurial and to move it along the cost reduction path.

Kodak also reorganized its worldwide facilities to reduce costs. International divisions were turning out identical products at higher cost than their counterparts in the United States. In a plan to coordinate worldwide production to increase productivity and lower costs, Kodak streamlined European production by closing duplicate manufacturing facilities and centralizing production and marketing operations, and it also brought some foreign manufacturing home. As a result, Kodak gained $55 million in productivity savings. However, Fuji's new European facility posed a severe challenge. Starting from scratch and employing production techniques learned from low-cost Japanese operations, Fuji remained the clear cost leader with the ability to start a price war to increase market share.

George Fisher Changes Kodak

Chandler retired as CEO in 1989 and was replaced by his chief operating officer, Kay Whitmore, another Kodak veteran. Whitmore immediately was forced to confront the problem of dealing with the poor performance of Chandler's misguided acquisitions. As Kodak's performance continued to plunge under his leadership, however, he came under intense scrutiny from analysts, who began to question the whole logic behind Kodak's aggressive diversification efforts. Whitmore responded by hiring managers from outside Kodak to help him restructure the company, but when they proposed selling off most of Kodak's new acquisitions and laying off many more thousands of employees to reduce costs, Whitmore resisted. He, too, was entrenched in the old Kodak culture and was unwilling to take such drastic steps. Finally, after continued criticism from analysts, Kodak's board of directors ousted Whitmore as CEO and in 1993 George Fisher, the first outsider to lead Kodak in 117 years, became the new CEO. George Fisher left his job as CEO of Motorola to join Kodak. At Motorola, he had been credited with leading that company into the digital age, and it was his expertise in the digital sector that led to his appointment. Fisher was given 2 million Kodak stock options at around $90 a share, Kodak's then stock price, to reward him for what many felt would be a fast turnaround in Kodak's fortunes.

Fisher's strategy was to reverse Chandler's diversification into any industry in the digital sector. Kodak's principal thrust, Fisher decided, should be to strengthen its competencies in the digital photography industry. However, given that Kodak had spent so much money on making its acquisitions, the question was what to do about its other businesses, especially as the company was now burdened with increasing debt from its acquisitions and falling profits. Fisher's solution was dramatic.

Looking at Kodak's four business groups, he decided that the over-the-counter drugs component of the Health Products Group was doing nothing to add value to Kodak's profitability, and he decided to divest Sterling Drugs to pay off debt. Soon, all that was left of this group was the health imaging business. Fisher also decided that the Chemicals Group, despite its expertise in the invention and manufacture of chemicals, no longer fitted with his new digital strategy. Henceforth Kodak would buy its chemicals in the open market, and in 1995 he spun this group off and gave each Kodak shareholder a share in the new company, Eastman Chemicals, whose stock price soon increased rapidly. The Information Systems Group with its diverse businesses was a more difficult challenge; the issue was which components would help promote Kodak's new digital strategy and which were superfluous and could be sold off. In the end, Fisher decided that Kodak would focus on building its presence in the document imaging industry with a focus on photocopiers, commercial inkjet printers, and commercial digital imaging and either sold or closed down the various other parts of the business that did not fit this theme. However, he also decided to outsource the sales and service end of the business, and in 1995 Kodak announced an agreement with Danka Business Systems for them to sell and service Kodak's high-volume copiers throughout the United States and Canada.

With these actions, within two years Fisher had pared down Kodak's debt by $7 billion, dumped chemicals and health, and boosted Kodak's stock price—all this signaled good times ahead. However, Fisher still had to confront the problems inside Kodak's core photographic imaging group, and here the solution was neither easy nor quick. Kodak was still plagued by high operating costs that were still 27 percent of annual revenue, and Fisher knew he needed to get these costs down to about 15 to 20 percent to compete effectively in the digital world. Kodak's work force had shrunk to 95,000 by 1993, and he wanted to avoid further layoffs, which would demoralize an already shaken work force. But with Kodak's current revenue in 1995 of $16 billion, this would mean finding ways to squeeze another couple of billion out of operating costs.

At the same time, Fisher also knew that Kodak had to invest more and more of its R&D budget into digital imaging. Kodak had no particular competency in making either digital cameras or the software necessary to allow them to operate efficiently. Soon Kodak was spending over $400 million a year on digital projects. However, new digital products were slow

to come on line. Also, consumers were slow to embrace digital photography, the cameras were expensive and bulky, the software was complicated to use, and printing digital photographs was both expensive and difficult at this time. Neither Kodak nor its customers had ramped up the digital photography learning curve, and by 1997 its digital business was still losing over $100 million a year.

To compound matters, in 1995 Fuji Film decided to open up a state-of-the-art filmmaking operation in the United States to further attack the $6 billion film market with "home-grown" products. Fuji also snatched the biggest photo-finishing contract in the United States, the Wal-Mart account, away from Kodak in 1995, and soon after sales of Fuji film in Wal-Mart started to rocket. Through 1995–1997 Fuji also lowered its prices and started a price war, and by 1997 Kodak's share of the U.S. film market had fallen to 78 percent, down a further 4 percent from 1996, while Fuji's had risen to 14 percent. This loss of four points cost Kodak about $125 million in lost sales, and sales of private-label film were beginning to increase, putting more pressures on revenues and costs.

To speed product development, Fisher reorganized Kodak's product groups into fourteen autonomous business units based on serving the needs of distinct groups of customers, such as those for its health products or commercial products. The idea was to decentralize decision making, thus putting managers closer to their major customers and escaping from Kodak's suffocating centralized style of decision making. Fisher also changed the top managers in charge of the film and camera units; however, he did not bring in many outsiders to spearhead the new digital efforts. This new emphasis on customer groups also meant that overhead costs rose because each unit had its own complement of functions; thus sales forces and so on were duplicated.

Fisher had been performing the roles of Kodak's chairman, CEO, president, *and* COO—something that analysts now started to complain about bitterly. How could Kodak get rid of its centralized decision-making style when its new leader apparently wanted to centralize all important decision making in his own hands? The reorganization into fourteen autonomous business units had not decentralized control to business unit leaders, and Fisher and his top management team were still overseeing all important strategy decisions. This explained the slow pace of change at Kodak. Thus while Fisher had brought Kodak's focus back to its core photography business, he had not put in place the infrastructure that would allow its managers to achieve its new digital mission.

In 1996, Fisher finally realized his dilemma, and with pressure from the board Daniel A. Carp was named Kodak's president and COO, the appointment to COO meaning that he was Fisher's heir apparent as Kodak's CEO. Carp was a Kodak veteran who had spearheaded the global consolidation of its operations and its entry into major new international markets such as China. He was widely credited with having had a major impact on Kodak's attempts to fight Fuji on a global level and help it to maintain its market share. Henceforth, Kodak's Digital and Applied Imaging, Business Imaging, and Equipment manufacturing—almost all its major operating groups—would now report to Carp. Carp also retained control of the Greater China region, where potential future film sales were seen as crucial to Kodak's future in its battle with arch-rival Fuji.

However, Kodak's revenues and profits continued to decline during the mid to late 1990s. It was slowly but steadily losing market share in its core film business to Fuji, but now generic film brands were also attracting customers and putting squeezes on profit margins. By 2000 analysts estimated it only had 66 percent percent of the U.S. market. Although the major price war with Fuji was over, sales of private-label film were still rising, and Kodak was periodically forced to use tactics such as multipack price discounts and rebates to prevent even further erosions to its market share, even at the cost of profits. Fisher knew that Kodak must preserve its market share to protect its future profitability and to give time both for it to develop its own digital competencies and for customers to develop an understanding and appetite for digital cameras. Meanwhile, the quality of the pictures taken by digital cameras was advancing rapidly as more and more pixels were being crammed into them. Also, at the low end, the price of a basic digital camera was falling rapidly because of economies of scale in production. Perhaps, finally, the digital photography market was taking off, but would Kodak be able to meet the challenge?

Despite early enthusiasm from analysts, Kodak's slow progress on all fronts and Fisher's leadership had become a major disappointment. When in July 1997 Fisher announced poor second-quarter results, many analysts and shareholders who had bought into his new strategy for Kodak began to bail out. Its share price soon tumbled to below $70 from $90, and Fisher's stock options that had been granted at $90 were now valueless at this price. Many analysts wondered if Kodak's board had been right in February 1997 to extend Fisher's contract for three more years to December 31, 2000.

Carp's Growing Influence

With Carp now in control of both Kodak's digital and global operations, the pace of change started to quicken. In 1997, Kodak announced it would open an office of the COO in Hong Kong to capitalize on trends in emerging markets, especially because of China's low-cost manufacturing advantages. In addition, in April 1997 Kodak increased its stake in the Japanese camera manufacturer Chinon to 50.1 percent effectively taking control of the company that now was making its advanced digital cameras and scanners. In 1997, Kodak announced it would operate the largest photo lab in the world in Fuji's home territory at the 1998 Olympic Winter Games in Nagano, Japan. It would loan all journalists its new digital cameras and provide them with the ability to scan ordinary negatives, convert their pictures into digital form, and send them anywhere around the world. This was a major advertising coup for Kodak and promoted its rapidly developing digital capabilities.

In 1998, Kodak announced its lowest-priced-yet digital camera with "megapixel" (million pixels per inch) image quality. This camera also, looked and operated like a conventional point-and-shoot camera. In the same month Kodak bought Picturevision Inc., whose digital Photonet online network products, combined with Kodak's brand name, would attract more customers who could now scan their pictures into its digital network, transmit the images and share them with others, and also receive outputs ranging from reprints to enlargements. Photo retailers also named Kodak's digital picture–maker kiosks the "top product of the year." Customers could take their ordinary photographs and use the kiosks to remove red eye, do quick and easy color corrections, and zoom or crop to select and print the best part of a photo. Essentially, Kodak was using these kiosks and to help customers learn about the advantages of digital photography and to help develop the market.

Kodak and Intel also formed an agreement to use Intel digital scanning equipment in Kodak's Qualex photo-finishing labs to make it easy for customers to put photos onto CD-ROM for use in home computers. In 1998, America Online and Kodak announced a strategic alliance to offer AOL members an exclusive online service, "You've Got Pictures," whereby AOL members could have their regular processed pictures delivered in digital format to their AOL mailbox. Customers were becoming increasingly familiar with how the new digital products worked, and Kodak was in the forefront of online efforts to capture customers and promote the Internet for transmission of digital images.

Thus Kodak was beginning to make steady progress in its "infoimaging mission." Under Carp's leadership its digital cameras were growing in popularity, in large part because of its developing competencies in making easy-to-use camera-printer software. Also, its digital kiosks and photo-finishing operations were being increasingly visited by customers, and their number was increasing rapidly both in the United States and globally. In recognition of his progress, in June 1999 Kodak's board named Carp as new CEO of Kodak, and he was to keep his other roles of president and COO. Fisher was to remain chairman until January 2001.

In the next few years Kodak's developing digital skills led to new products in all its major businesses. In 1999, its Health Imaging group announced the then fastest digital image management system for echocardiography labs. It also entered the digital radiography market with three state-of-the-art digital systems for capturing x-ray images. Its Document Imaging group announced several new electronic document management systems. It also teamed up with inkjet maker Lexmark to introduce the stand-alone Kodak Personal Picture Maker by Lexmark, which could print color photos from both compact flash cards and Smart Media. Its Commercial and Government Systems group announced advanced new high-powered digital cameras for uses such as in space and in the military. This group also became increasingly involved with Japanese Sanyo in developing full-color, active-matrix, organic electroluminescent (OEL) displays, which are much easier to view than conventional liquid crystal displays (LCDs). OEL displays are also as thin as a dime and require much less power. Since they are perfectly matched to mobile digital devices such as Smart Phones and personal digital assistants (PDAs), they had a huge market potential.

With these developments, Kodak's net earnings shot up between 1998 and 2000, and its stock price recovered somewhat. However, one reason for the increase in net revenues was that the devastating price war with Fuji that had raged from 1979 to 1999 had ended as both companies saw that continuing to offer price discounts simply reduced both companies' profits. Kodak also was still not getting quickly to the market the range of new digital imaging products it needed to drive its future profitability, since there was intense competition in the core film businesses, which had traditionally given it 30 to 40 percent of its profits. Here, as in film products, Kodak's high operating costs overwhelmed the benefits it obtained from its new product introductions and hurt its bottom line—its profits were not increasing.

Kodak in the 2000s

New digital product developments and changing industry conditions in most of its markets began to punish Kodak as it entered the 2000s. In the Consumer Imaging group, for example, Kodak launched a new camera, the EasyShare, in 2001. Over 4 million digital cameras were sold in 2000 and over 6 million in 2001, and over a half-million of the easy-to-use new Kodak camera were sold. However, given the huge development costs and intense competition from Japanese companies like Sony and Canon, who also make advanced cameras and "digicams," Kodak has not yet made any money from its digital cameras. Moreover, every time it sells one it reduces demand for its high-margin film; thus Kodak is cannibalizing a profitable product for an unprofitable one!

Kodak argued that it would make more money in the future from sales of the paper necessary to print these images and from its photo-finishing operations. However, it is becoming increasingly obvious that consumers are not printing out many of the photographs they take, preferring to save many in disk form and only selecting and printing out the few best ones to send to their friends. With chemical films, one could not pick and choose; the whole roll had to be developed. So revenues are not increasing on this front. Moreover, it is the ink sellers such as Hewlett-Packard (HP) and Lexmark, who have been charging monopoly prices for ink cartridges, that have been making the money in printing images, and Kodak has failed to use its strengths in chemicals to get into the printer ink business.

On the photo-finishing end, Kodak's future revenues and profits depend on it maximizing the number of its in-store kiosks or the number of photo-finishing contracts with large chain stores. After Kodak lost the Wal-Mart contract to Fuji, it signed new agreements with Walgreen's (the second largest U.S. film processor, with over three thousand stores) and with Kmart. It also operated its own Fox and Qualex photo-finishing labs. However, in 2001, Kmart declared Chapter 11 bankruptcy, and the Fox photo store chain, which was primarily finishing traditional roll film, went bankrupt, causing a large loss to Kodak. To compound matters, in June 2002 it was reported that Walgreen's was testing Fuji's new photo-finishing laboratory system in thirty of its stores and that it might award this important contract to Fuji when it came up for renewal sometime in 2002.

While Kodak is fighting back with its own advanced digital finishing labs, by 2002 advances in digital photo-finishing technology had brought down the price of digital kiosks so far that in the future an easy-to-use kiosk is expected to be found in every corner store. However, there are other major players in the market. Hewlett-Packard, long a leader in printing, has also developed state-of-the-art consumer photo-finishing products. Indeed, Kodak has teamed up with HP to unveil Phogenix, a joint partnership program for on-site photo finishing using HP's print technology, which will provide a product indistinguishable from the silver halide product. Fuji and Olympus have also developed their own systems that they are aggressively marketing.

In fact, in June 2002, recognizing that Fuji was gaining a competitive edge in the vital photo-finishing systems market, Kodak announced that it was buying key components of its new digital system from Agfa, a European imaging firm, since it did not have the time to develop them itself. This suggests that Kodak's technology is no better than that of competitors, and it might be even behind that of competitors like Fuji. Thus it is not clear that Kodak has a lead in all the activities—cameras, software, paper, and photo finishing—necessary to dominate the photography market as it had in the past. It does have its powerful brand name going for it, however,

which is why it has been so concerned to protect its market share at any cost to its profits.

At the industry level, the emergence of powerful buyers in many markets has seriously hurt Kodak's performance. In photo finishing, large store chains like Wal-Mart and Walgreen's are in a strong bargaining position and can threaten Kodak's profitability (it has been estimated that 10 percent of Kodak's photo-finishing operations are with Walgreen's). This same situation occurred in the health imaging industry. Here, Kodak's state-of-the-art imaging products were widely expected to generate large revenues and boost its profitability. However, after a good start, in 2000 Kodak faced the problem of bargaining over prices with Novation Group Purchasing organization, a major buyer of health equipment, and therefore a powerful buyer as well. Kodak was forced to slash its prices to win the contract against agile competitors, and this experience was repeated with many other large health care providers. So intense was competition in this segment that in 2001 sales of laser printers and health-related imagining products, which make up Kodak's second biggest business, fell 7 percent while profit in the segment fell 30 percent, causing a large drop in Kodak's share price.

While in 2001 Kodak had over $19 billion in revenues, in 2002 it was expected to earn around $13 billion, and its profits have stagnated. By early 2002, analysts were once again beginning to wonder if Kodak under Carp was really faring any better than Kodak under Fisher. In an embarrassing turn of events, Kodak's new COO, Patricia Russo, a well-respected executive who had left Lucent to take over the important job of restructuring Kodak, abruptly left the company and returned to Lucent. Analysts once again attributed this to Kodak's entrenched, inbred, and unresponsive management that persists in doing all it can to frustrate real efforts to reduce costs and streamline its operations. For despite all the advances in its digital skills, Kodak is still burdened with high operating costs, well out of proportion with its declining revenues. In 2000, after its profits fell drastically, it announced another two thousand job cuts, and in 2001 it announced another five thousand, for a total of seven thousand, bringing Kodak's work-force down to about seventy-eight thousand.

In 2001 Carp also announced another major reorganization of Kodak's businesses in line with a plan suggested by Russo before her departure. To give it a sharper focus on its products and customers, Kodak announced that it was moving from a structure based on customer groups to one based on strategic product lines. It disbanded its three global area groups and moved Entertainment Imaging into the Photography group, which now contains all its silver halide and digital photography operations. Health Imaging was to be operated as a totally self-contained stand-alone business. Commercial Imaging continues to manage its document systems and inkjet business. The Components group handles Kodak's display products and its new OLE optics business, which Kodak hopes will allow it to diversify into a high-growth product market. Thus, with this reorganization Kodak is once again involved in four distinct lines of business that appear to have little in common, as in the Chandler era.

Analysts are still wondering if the layoffs or reorganization will be enough to turn the company's performance around. The bottom line is that Kodak's film business is a huge generator of cash, but the company has so far failed either to reduce costs or to use that cash to fund entry into businesses that will generate a future stream of profits. Perhaps Kodak should sell off or spin off its health, commercial, and optics operations, eliminate its debt, and focus on reducing costs and building its digital presence in its core photography group. Amazingly enough, it still pays shareholders one of the top ten dividends of all companies in the Fortune 500. Analysts argue that it should be run for profit now, not in the future. Kodak's managers reply that the economic recession and events of 2000–2002 are to blame for a large part of its problems and that it has all the pieces in place for a sustained recovery and for dominance in the digital arena using its powerful brand name once the market has recovered. Its other businesses will only boost its future profitability. Only time will tell, but Kodak's stock price plunged in 2002 and was selling in the $30s in June—a far cry from the $90s when Fisher took over and a continuing sign of the fall of this once economic powerhouse.

REFERENCES

www.Kodak.com, 2002.

Kodak Annual Reports, 1980–2001.

Thomas Moore, "Embattled Kodak Enters the Electronic Age," *Fortune*, August 22, 1983, pp. 120–128.

"Kodak's New Lean and Hungry Look," *Business Week*, May 30, 1983, p. 33.

Charles K. Ryan, Eastman Kodak, Company Outline, Merrill Lynch, Pierce, Framer & Smith Incorporated, May 7, 1986.

John Greenwald, "Aiming for a Brighter Picture," *Time*, January 9, 1984, p. 49.

Barbara Buell, "Kodak Is Trying to Break Out of Its Shell," *Business Week*, June 10, 1985, pp. 92–95.

Barbara Buell, "Kodak Scrambles to Fill the Gap," *Business Week*, February 8, 1986, p. 30.

"Kodak's New Image: Electronic Imaging," *Electron Business*, January 1986, pp. 38–43.

Barbara Buell, "A Gust of Fresh Air for the Stodgy Giant of Rochester," *Business Week*, June 10, 1985, p. 93.

"Yellow at the Edges," *Economist*, December 7, 1984, p. 90.

James S. Hirsch, "Kodak Effort at 'Intrapreneurship' Fails," *Wall Street Journal*, August 17, 1990, p. 32.

"Agfa to Supply Kodak with Lab Equipment," Yahoo.com, Friday, June 7, 2002.

Franklin Paul, "Sony to Muscle into Kodak's Digital Printing Arena," Yahoo.com, Wednesday, June 5, 2002.

"Citigroup Moves to Stress Global Products," Yahoo.com, Tuesday, June 11, 2002.

Daniel P. Palumbo, "Kodak Embraces Disruptive Technology," *Journal of Business Strategy*, July–August 2001, p. 11.

Franklin Paul, "Kodak Digital Camera, Software Sims to Ease Printing," Yahoo.com, Tuesday, May 21, 2002.

"Kodak, Walt Disney Sign Multiyear Alliance Agreement," Yahoo.com, Tuesday, May 28, 2002.

Daniel Eisenburg, "Kodak's Photo Op," *Time*, April 30, 2001, p. 46.

Emily Nelson and Joseph B. White, "Blurred Image: Kodak Moment Came Early for CEO Fisher, Who Takes a Stumble—Bet on Digital Photography Has Been a Money Loser; Fuji Is Gaining Ground—Dennis Rodman's Film Flop," *Wall Street Journal*, July 25, 1997, p. A1.

James Bandler, "Kodak Will Acquire Ofoto in a Move to Expand Services," *Wall Street Journal*, May 1, 2001, p. B9.

"Business Brief—Kmart Corp.: Retailer Teams with Kodak in an Online Photo," *Wall Street Journal*, May 9, 2001.

James Bandler, "Kodak's Net Fell 93% in Second Quarter on Weakness in Film," Medical Divisions," *Wall Street Journal*, July 18, 2001, p. B4.

Fauziah Muhtar, "Kodak Zooms In with New Digital Cameras," *Computimes Malaysia*, May 2, 2002, p. 1.

"Moody's Downgrades Kodak's Debt Rating on Digital Concerns," *Wall Street Journal*, March 20, 2002, p. B5.

Laura Heller, "PMA Highlights Print Kiosks, but Digital Imaging Steals Show," *DSN Retailing Today*, March 11, 2002, p. 6.

"Business Brief—Eastman Kodak Co.: Suit Is Filed Charging Sun with Infringement of Patents," *Wall Street Journal*, February 15, 2002, p. B8.

Andy Serwer, "Kodak: In the Noose," *Fortune*, February 4, 2002, pp. 147–148.

Adrienne Carter, "Kodak's Promising Developments," *Money*, February 2002, p. 39.

Geoffrey Smith and Faith Keenan, "Kodak Is the Picture of Digital Success," *Business Week*, January 14, 2002, p. 39.

James Bandler and Joann Lublin, "Russo's Departure Is a Blow to Kodak as It Seeks to Move into the Digital Age," *Wall Street Journal*, January 8, 2002, p. B4.

James Bandler, "Kodak Advances in Market Share of Digital Cameras," *Wall Street Journal*, December 21, 2001, p. B2.

Doug Olenick, "Kodak, Sanyo Plan to Produce OEL Flat-Panel Displays," *Twice*, December 17, 2001, p. 90.

James Bandler, "Kodak, Sanyo Agree to Make New Type of Screen Display," *Wall Street Journal*, December 4, 2001, p. B7.

James Bandler, "Kodak Will Offer Its Staff a Chance to Upgrade Options," *Wall Street Journal,* November 30, 2001, p. B7.

"Business Brief—Eastman Kodak Co.: Photo Concern Is Shutting Its Picture Vision Operation," *Wall Street Journal,* November 20, 2001.

"Eastman Kodak to Acquire Encad," *Daily Deal,* November 16, 2001.

John Hechinger, "Kodak to Reorganize Its Business Again," *Wall Street Journal,* November 15, 2001, p. B12.

James Bandler, "Kodak Stock Falls on Credit Downgrade, Signs Film Market Share Is Decreasing," *Wall Street Journal,* November 1, 2001, p. B8.

James Bandler, "Kodak Net Plummments 77% on Weak Sales," *Wall Street Journal,* October 25, 2001, p. B9.

James Bandler, "Kodak Slashes Earnings Forecast, Citing Weak Sales," *Wall Street Journal,* September 20, 2001, p. B4.

"Eastman Kodak Rating May Fall a Rung Lower," *Wall Street Journal,* July 24, 2001.

42 Restructuring Exide

This case was prepared by Charles W. L. Hill, the University of Washington.

Introduction

In March 1999, Exide Corporation announced that Robert Lutz, the flamboyant sixty-seven-year-old former Chrysler executive who helped turn that company around in the early 1990s, would become chairman, president, and chief executive officer of Exide. Lutz, an outspoken former marine known for his love of good cigars, fine wine, and flying jet fighters, would have his work cut out for him. Exide was a company in trouble. The world's largest manufacturer of lead acid batteries, the company had reportedly sacrificed profitability in its quest for market share leadership. For the financial year ending March 1999, Exide lost $9 million on global sales of $2.37 billion. A series of bank-financed acquisitions during the 1990s had left the company with a weak balance sheet, including $1.3 billion in debt that cost $100 million in annual interest payments to serve. Moreover, a price war in the lead battery industry was squeezing profit margins.

Exide's Business

Market Segments and Customers

Exide manufactures batteries for customers in two broad areas: industrial and automotive. The industrial area, which accounts for around 37 percent of Exide's revenues, is broken down into two segments. One, the motive power business, is engaged in the manufacture of batteries for electric vehicles, including fork lift trucks, golf carts, wheel chairs, and electric floor cleaning equipment. The other industrial segment, network power, makes standby batteries used for backup power applications, to ensure continuous power supply in case of main (primary) power failure or outage. The largest customers here are manufacturers of telecommunications equipment, who incorporate the batteries in their equipment to ensure that it continues to function in the case of a power outage (which is why you can still make phone calls, even if you do not have power at home). A second customer group is businesses that use standby batteries in computer installations so that the computer system stays up even if the power goes down.

In the industrial motive power business, most of Exide's batteries are sold through independent lift truck dealers or sold directly to large users of lift trucks, such as Wal-Mart and Kroger. Exide's customers in the industrial network power business include manufacturers of telecommunications equipment, as well as telecommunications service providers. Customers include Lucent, Motorola, and Nokia, all major global producers of telecommunications equipment, and AT&T, British Telecom, China Telecom, Deutsche Telekom, GTE, and Nippon Telephone and Telegraph, all service providers.

The automotive area of Exide's business, which accounts for 67 percent of global revenues, is composed primarily of the manufacture and sale of lead acid batteries to automobile manufacturers and to "aftermarket" distributors. Principal OEM customers include Daimler-Chrysler, for whom Exide is the primary global battery supplier, Ford, Toyota, Mack Trucks, John Deere, Volvo, the Renault Group, Volkswagen, and BMW. Aftermarket batteries are sold principally though retail automotive parts chains and mass merchandisers. Customers in the United States include NAPA Distribution Centers, Wal-Mart, Kmart, and Les Schwab Tire. Customers in Europe include large national distributors such as Kwik Fit in the United Kingdom. In the United States, Exide batteries are sold in the aftermarket under the Exide and Champion brand names. In Europe the brand names in the aftermarket vary from country to country and include Exide, Fulmen, DETA, Tudor, SONNAK, and Centra.

Competition

Exide is the global market share leader in both the motive power and network power segments of the industrial area. Major competitors include U.K.-based Invensys's Hawker battery group, C&D Technologies (another U.S. firm), and Yuasa of Japan. In the automotive area, Exide again leads with a 36 percent share of the global market for automobile batteries (both OEM and aftermarket). Exide's largest competitors in the United States automotive segment include Delphi Automotive and Johnson Controls. In Europe, Exide faces a number of strong local competitors, including Varta, Fiamm, and Hoppeke. Price competition has long been intense in all markets, with major customers using their buying power to bargain down battery prices. Exide's financial troubles in the late 1990s, however, were due in part to an outbreak of extremely aggressive price competition in Europe.

Manufacturing, Employees, and Facilities

Lead is the principal material used in the manufacturing of batteries, accounting for about one-fifth of the cost of goods sold. Exide operates a number of lead recycling plants in both the United States and Europe. It reclaims lead from used batteries that end users returned to distributors. Exide fulfills most of its lead requirements from its recycling plants. Other key raw materials include lead oxide and bulk chemicals.

Exide employs some 20,000 people, 8,500 in the United States and approximately 10,900 in Europe.

The company operates some fifty facilities, the bulk of which are in Europe and North America, where most of the company's sales are concentrated. Exide has some fourteen manufacturing facilities in North America, sixteen in Western Europe, two in Australia, one in New Zealand, and one in Turkey. In Western Europe, there are manufacturing and lead recycling facilities in each major national market.

Lutz's Changes

Lutz moved rapidly to make a number of changes in Exide's business. One of his first decisions was to pull out of a supply agreement with Sears. Exide sold over 4.5 million batteries per year to Sears, but to get the agreement the company had to slash prices. The result was that Exide was making less from the Sears deal than it was from deals one-fifth the size. Lutz also pushed the company to shift demand from low-priced battery models to higher-priced branded products, particularly in the automotive segment. Consistent with this theme, in June 1999 Exide introduced a new lead acid battery, the Select Orbital battery. While the battery cost $125, Exide claimed that it was based on a radically new design and would retain its charge for over a year, substantially longer than a conventional battery. Moreover, while a conventional battery has a life of around thirty to forty months, Exide claimed that the Orbital would last five years and stand up to far more abuse.

Lutz also pushed the company to quickly solve its legal problems. The company was being sued in the United States for recycling old batteries and selling them as new through distributors such as Sears. Under Lutz's direction, instead of fighting the lawsuits, Exide quickly settled them for a few million dollars and took a one-time charge against earnings.

Within some fifteen months of his arrival, Lutz had replaced the entire board of directors and the majority of senior executives in both Europe and North America. Worldwide battery product capacity had been cut by some 20 percent through plant closures, the company's debt load had been substantially pared back by issuing additional stock and using the proceeds to pay down debt, and Exide had made a major acquisition, paying $368 million in stock and cash for GNB Technologies, a major supplier in the fast-growing market for standby batteries in telecommunications and computer equipment. Perhaps the most difficult change Lutz initiated, however, was one in the organization structure of Exide's business.

Changing the Organization Structure: Product or Geography?

When he arrived at Exide, Lutz found a structure that was based on geography with ten different country organizations. The genesis of this structure was rooted in history. Many of the country organizations had previously been independent businesses that Exide had acquired in its rush to gain global market share. After being acquired, the majority continued to function as self-contained operations with their own brands, manufacturing facilities, and distribution systems. Exide managed the different subsidiaries on an arms-length basis, setting profit goals for each and awarding local executives big bonuses if they exceeded those goals.

It soon became apparent to Lutz that this structure was causing problems for Exide, particularly in Europe. When Lutz arrived, Exide's European business was losing money. The various country managers in Europe blamed the losses on significant price discounting. After talking to competitors and customers, Lutz found that there indeed was significant price discounting in Europe, but in many cases this was because different Exide subsidiaries were competing against each other for major customers. They were exporting into each other's territories or competing aggressively for a share in third countries. Thus, for example, the British subsidiary was gaining share in Australia from the German subsidiary by underselling the latter by 10 to 15 percent. Part of the blame for this competition could be laid at the feet of an incentive system that rewarded country managers for increasing the performance of their unit, irrespective of whether that was at the expense of another Exide unit.

Convinced that the structure had to change, Lutz held five management retreats between June 1999 and January 2000. "Where does our future lie?" Lutz asked the thirty senior executives assembled for the first meeting. "Does it lie in country management or in global business units?" Many of the country managers reacted with apprehension to the question. Several argued that their regions were in good shape and that any problems that existed were due to weaknesses elsewhere or to general industry conditions.

Between retreats managers working in teams were assigned to grapple with the various dilemmas confronting the company, using existing and alternative models of the organization as solutions. In a typical assessment, one team looked at Exide's Asian expansion strategy. It concluded that the geographic focus encouraged construction of manufacturing plants in each country Exide entered, even though it was not profitable to keep putting up plants like that. On the third retreat, the teams started to report their findings, and it quickly became apparent that many were concluding that only a product line structure could cure Exide's ills. After a vigorous debate, Lutz stood up and announced, "We don't have consensus yet. . . . But I'm going to make a decision, and we are going to a global business unit structure."

Under the proposed structure that Lutz revealed at the next meeting, six global business units replaced the geographic organization. Each business unit was built around a distinct product line, such as network power, industrial motive power, and so on. It was the global business units that were now given responsibility for major strategic and operational decisions, such as what to produce where, how much to charge customers, and selling to major regional or global customers. Country managers were given a coordinating role and the responsibility for local sales efforts and distribution.

Although by now expected, the announcement was a severe blow for many country managers. Effectively, it meant a demotion. When one country manager frowned at the announcement, Lutz looked at him and asked, "Why don't you give this a try?" "No," the manager replied, "I'm out of here!" Another country manager told a consultant: "Being a country manager is my life. It's something I've worked for my entire life. I don't see how I'll have a role going forward." Subsequently, the manager was given the option of moving from Naples to Frankfurt, for less money, or leaving the company. He chose the former option, but his family refused to move and stayed in Naples. Other country managers came out of the process quite well. Albrecht Leuschner, the head of the German unit, found himself promoted to lead the global network power business unit, which was to be headquartered in Germany.

The Acquisition of GNB Technologies

Leuschner found himself in this position for just six weeks. In May 2000, Exide acquired GNB Technologies for its fast-growing network power business and industrial motive power businesses. The acquisition gave Lutz a problem; he feared that Mitchell Bregman, the well-regarded president of GNB's operation, might leave once Exide folded his industrial battery business into its global network power and industrial motive power business units. Instead, Lutz approached Bregman and told him that after the acquisition he would retain control over the North American industrial battery business. In effect, after only six weeks, the global business unit structure was being amended. There was now a European business unit for network power headed by Leuschner, a European business unit for industrial motive power that was run out of the United Kingdom, and a North American industrial battery business headed by Bregman.

Initially, the decision gave rise to a turf battle between Leuschner and Bregman. The point of contention was over who should run China for Exide. Bregman wanted to form and direct a Chinese subsidiary, because China represented his unit's fastest-growing market. Leuschner lobbied to form a joint venture in China that would be under his command. Bregman was finally persuaded to give in to Leuschner, but only after he had been given control over South American operations and had been guaranteed control over operations in Korea, Japan, and Taiwan.

Now all parties claim that the structure is working well. The company still maintains separate industrial battery sales forces in North America and Europe, in what has become a de facto regional structure. However, teams from the European and North American units have begun making joint pitches to global customers such as Ford and Lucent.

REFERENCES

L. Chappell, "Lutz Put Exide in Recovery," *Automotive News*, August 6, 2001, p. 49.

Exide 2000 and 2001 10K filed with Securities and Exchange Commission.

J. S. Lublin, "Place vs Product: It's Tough to Choose a Management Model," *Wall Street Journal*, June 27, 2001, pp. A1, A4.

M. Maynard, "Lutz Gets a Charge Out of a New Career: Exide CEO Achieves a Dream," *USA Today*, June 1, 1999, p. 12B.

D. W. Nauss, "Ex-Chrysler Exec Robert Lutz to Head Troubled Exide Corporation," *Los Angeles Times*, November 17, 1998, p. 3.

A. Puchalsky, "Exide Makes Tough Choices in Comeback," *Wall Street Journal*, March 26, 1999.

R. Sherefkin, "New One Two Punch at Exide," *Automotive News*, June 12, 2000, p. 22.

A. Taylor, "Getting Back in the Fast Lane," *Fortune*, March 6, 2000.

43

First Greyhound, Then Greyhound Dial, Then Dial: What Will Happen in 2002?

This case was prepared by Gareth R. Jones, Texas A&M University.

It was June 2002 and Herbert Baum, Dial's CEO, was reflecting on the performance of the company since he had been brought in to engineer a turnaround in 2000. He had sold off underperforming product lines and invested heavily in building Dial's core products like Dial soap. By April 2002 he had been happy to report a rebound in Dial's earnings, which sent its share soaring from the lows it had reached in April 2001, when its earnings plunged by 69 percent due to the poor strategic decisions of his predecessor. Now the question was what to do? Should he continue to build Dial's portfolio of brand name products and strive to keep the company independent? Or, should he sell off the company, either as a whole or in parts, to other companies that would now be prepared to pay a high price for its strong brand name products? While pondering this question, Baum thought that the history of the company, which had started out as Greyhound, might provide him with some important clues.

Greyhound's Early History and Growth

Greyhound was founded in Hibbing, Minnesota, in 1914. Its first business was providing bus transportation to carry miners to work at

This case is intended to be used as a basis for class discussion rather than as an illustration of either effective or ineffective handling of the situation. Reprinted by permission of the author.

the Mesabi Iron Range. Because Greyhound was the sole provider of bus service for these workers, it was immediately successful. In its very first year, the new corporation started expanding its routes and acquiring interests in bus companies operating near Chicago. For the next sixteen years, the young company continued purchasing interests in bus companies, extending its route structure from New York to Kansas City. In 1930, the name *Greyhound Corporation* was adopted, and the now-familiar running-dog logo was painted on the buses.

For the next twenty-seven years, Greyhound continued to acquire bus interests in order to consolidate its routes and link its various bus operations. Growth proceeded sometimes by purchase, sometimes by stock swaps, and sometimes by merger. However, the result was always the same to the traveling public: it saw more and more of the familiar running dog. By 1960, Greyhound had substantially achieved its objective of operating a bus system that could carry passengers to most destinations in the continental United States and Canada.

By 1962, however, Greyhound was facing the prospect of increasingly limited opportunities to expand its route system; in the company's favor was the fact that bus operations were generating large sums of excess cash, which could fund expansion into new businesses. So Greyhound's board of directors decided to diversify into operations outside the bus transportation industry.

In that same year, Greyhound began the program of acquisition that turned it into a conglomerate. It solidified its bus-manufacturing operations into Motor Coach Industries, which became the foundation of Greyhound Dial's transportation manufacturing operating division. Also in 1962, the corporation acquired Boothe Leasing Company, an enterprise that specialized in equipment leasing. Boothe Leasing was renamed Greyhound Leasing and became the core business around which Greyhound's financial services division was to be built. Thus, by the end of 1963, Greyhound Corporation was operating in three major businesses: bus transportation, bus manufacturing, and financial services. Bus manufacturing supplied buses to bus transportation as well as to other bus companies.

Acquisitions Between 1966 and 1970

Gerry Trautman was appointed CEO in 1966, and he wasted no time in accelerating Greyhound's new strategy for expansion and growth. From Trautman's installation as CEO until 1970, Greyhound acquired more than thirty widely different companies and formed a new operating division—services—that specialized in managing transportation-related businesses, such as Border Brokerage Company, which operated two duty-free shops at the Canadian border, and Florida Export Group, which also handled duty-free commerce. In addition, the services division included Manncraft Exhibitors, a company that specialized in building displays for major exhibitions; Nassau Air Dispatch, a Caribbean shipping company; and Freeport Flight Services, a Bahamian aircraft-servicing business. Trautman also brought in a line of cruise ships in the Caribbean, the Bahama Cruise Line Company. Then he added companies as diverse as Ford Van Lines of Lincoln, Nebraska, a company specializing in furniture moving; Red Top Sedan Service, a Florida limousine service; two regional intercity bus lines; Washington Airport Transport, a commuter carrier from the Washington, D.C., suburbs to Dulles Airport; and Gray Line New York Tours Corporation, a sightseeing bus line. Furthermore, he added Hausman Bus Parts to the bus-manufacturing unit.

Not all the companies that Trautman acquired proved to be as profitable or as manageable as he had hoped. What he was looking for was value as well as some synergy with Greyhound's existing transporta-

tion activities. However, as the acquisition process continued, synergy became a secondary objective. When Trautman became dissatisfied with an acquisition, he would divest it as quickly as he had acquired it, and many companies were spun off. Near the end of his tenure as CEO, Trautman would boast that Greyhound had achieved "diversification within diversification." What he meant was that in his view the operating groups had become diversified, so that each individually was recession-proof and all were enhancing the financial strength of the holding company.

Trautman's boldest maneuver and biggest acquisition came in 1970. He acquired Armour & Co., another large conglomerate that had many diverse business interests in food and consumer products. Trautman paid $400 million in cash, notes, and stock to take over Armour, which was primarily a large meat-packing company with more than $2 billion of sales in marginally profitable businesses. However, Armour also had interests in pharmaceuticals, cosmetics, and consumer products such as soap, through its very profitable Dial division. Trautman knew that it appeared as though he had overpaid for Armour-Dial. However, he soon reduced the price of the acquisition by selling off, for some $225 million, a number of Armour's divisions that he considered to be peripheral to Armour's core food and consumer businesses. In 1977, he sold off Armour's pharmaceutical division for $87 million, reducing Greyhound's net investment to $88 million. What remained after the divestitures were Armour's food operations and Armour's Dial division, from which would emerge Greyhound Dial's consumer products operating division.

Trautman hoped that his new acquisition would be more recession-proof than the bus business, if not countercyclical to it. However, the Armour acquisition brought to Greyhound new businesses that had management problems of their own in areas in which Greyhound had no experience, such as the price of pork bellies, cycles for meat packers' contracts, and foreign competition.

Trautman's Acquisitions and Divestitures Between 1970 and 1978

For the next eight years, Greyhound under Trautman continued buying businesses and increasing the size of the operating divisions in its corporate portfolio. By 1978, Greyhound's holding company consisted of five operating divisions: transportation, bus manufacturing, food and consumer products, financial, and services/food service. Each of these operating divisions acquired many new businesses, so that Greyhound was still undergoing "diversification within diversification." Many of the new acquisitions, however, were failures. Businesses as diverse as a chicken hatchery, a European acquisition to expand the financial services group, and various transportation businesses (Caribbean Gray Cruise Line, Ltd., VAVO Greyhound N.V. of Schoonhoven, Netherlands, Shannon-Greyhound Coaches, and Hausman Bus Parts) proved unprofitable.

Greyhound's portfolio of businesses kept changing during this period, and Trautman continued to feel that he was shaping a diversified company that would have a powerful base in many lines of business. He was willing to take the risk of acquiring some companies that would be failures as long as the overall health of the company was strengthened. However, Greyhound became more and more distant from its core business—bus transportation.

In April 1978, Trautman engineered another major acquisition by acquiring 97 percent of the stock of Verex Corporation, the largest private insurer of residential mortgages in the United States. The Verex acquisition was intended to strengthen the operations of Greyhound's financial operating division. Verex insured first mortgages on residential real estate generally having loan-to-value ratios in excess of 80 percent.

By 1978, Greyhound had grown nearly as large as it would grow under Trautman's leadership. The collection of businesses that he had assembled—some by acquisition, some by internal growth, and some by selling off pieces of larger businesses—was designed to make Greyhound more resistant to economic downturns. The activities of Greyhound's five major operating divisions are summarized below.

- *Transportation.* This operating division comprised the intercity services division and the travel services division. Transportation operated regularly scheduled passenger bus service between most metropolitan areas in North America and engaged in related operations, such as package shipping, sightseeing services, airport ground transportation, and deluxe tour and charter bus services.

- *Bus manufacturing.* The largest maker of intercity buses in North America, the bus-manufacturing division had operations that were vertically integrated to fabricate bus shells of intercity design, assemble buses, and manufacture bus parts for final assembly. In addition, this operating division warehoused and distributed replacement parts to meet its own requirements and the larger requirements of the bus industry. Greyhound bus manufacturing was the principal U.S. supplier of buses to charter operators and sightseeing companies.

- *Food and consumer products.* The companies in this operating group manufactured and marketed products to independent retailers under private-label arrangements and distributed several products under their own trademarks. These trademarks included Dial, Tone, and Pure & Natural soaps, Armour Star and Armour Tree canned meat and meat food products, Dial antiperspirants and shampoos, Appian Way pizza mixes, Parsons' ammonia, Bruce floor care products, Magic sizing and prewash, and Malina handknitting yarns and needle products.

- *Services/food service.* Companies in this operating division provided a broad range of services directed primarily to business markets, although duty-free shops located at airports and on cruise ships were targeted toward the consumer market. Greyhound convention services (GCS) specialized in designing, fabricating, warehousing, shipping, and setting up exhibits for trade shows, conventions, and exhibitions. GCS also served as a decorating contractor at conventions and trade show sites. The food service division, generally known as Greyhound food management (GFM), served approximately 2,400 locations in industrial plants, bus terminals, airports, office buildings, schools, colleges, and other facilities.

- *Financial.* This operating division consisted of Greyhound Computer Corporation, a company specializing in computer leasing and sales in the United States, Canada, Mexico, and Europe; Greyhound Leasing and Financial Corporation, a company specializing in worldwide industrial equipment leasing; Pine Top Insurance, an entity that reinsured commercial property and provided excess casualty insurance for large policyholders; and Verex Corporation, the leading private insurer of highly leveraged residential mortgages for primary lenders. Travelers Express Company, Inc., another company in the financial division, specialized in providing travelers' checks and check-cashing services in 32,000 retail establishments and financial institutions in the mainland United States and Puerto Rico.

Together, those five operating divisions were generating combined revenues of nearly $4.5 billion. Trautman had accomplished his objective of using profits from the bus operations to move Greyhound into other businesses.

Trautman Selects Teets to Take over Greyhound

Serious problems became apparent at Armour when the food and consumer products operating division went from a profit of $22 million in 1979 to a loss of $1.7 million in 1980. Armour's problems came at a very inconvenient time for Trautman because he had planned to retire in 1980. Trautman wanted to solve Armour's difficulties while he kept business rolling at Greyhound's other groups and prepared a successor to take over the collection of companies that he had assembled. That successor was to be John Teets.

Teets was very different from Trautman. His background did not include Harvard Business School or law practice. Instead, Teets had learned to be an effective hands-on manager by staying as close to the action as possible. He had worked for his father's construction company but decided that he wanted to operate a restaurant. He borrowed money, started his own restaurant, and quickly made it successful. However, soon after he had paid back his loan money and his restaurant was earning a profit, it burned to the ground. In search of a new business opportunity, Teets answered a newspaper advertisement about a position managing a Greyhound food service concession stand at the New York World's Fair in 1964.

After joining the services/food service operating group, Teets quickly distinguished himself as a tight-fisted cost cutter who could make money on a miserly budget. He seemed to have a talent for squeezing every last penny out of everything he managed. Teets moved up quickly, gaining a reputation as an extremely effective manager. By 1975, he was put in charge of the food service group, which primarily operated a conglomeration of marginally profitable, obscure, franchised restaurants. His aggressive management style produced quick results, and in 1980 he

was named the outstanding executive in the food industry. Also in 1980, in addition to Teets's responsibilities as CEO of the food service group, Trautman named Teets to head Armour and turn around the division's performance.

In 1981, Armour's major problem, as Teets saw it, was that it was paying 30 to 50 percent more in wages and fringe benefits than its competitors. Teets asked Armour's unions for immediate wage concessions. He told the unions that if he failed to get the concessions, he would have to start closing plants. After a bitter strike, wage concessions in excess of 15 percent were obtained. Given these concessions, the cost cutting from plant closings, and more efficient operating procedures, it looked as though Armour had bought itself some time.

With Armour running more efficiently, the bus business cruising along on excess profits because of the recession and energy crunch in 1979–1980, and high profits in its financial operating division generated by high interest rates in the early 1980s, it seemed that the stage was set for Trautman's retirement. In fact, all that remained was to formally select a successor. It was not difficult for Trautman to make up his mind about who that should be. He was impressed with Teet's successes in managing the services/food service group and also with the way in which Teets had dominated Armour's labor unions.

Teets Seeks Solutions

In 1981, John Teets succeeded Gerry Trautman as the chief executive officer of the Greyhound Corporation. The challenge facing Teets was to manage Greyhound's diverse businesses so that he would be able to achieve at least a 15 percent return on equity. However, many problems on the horizon might hinder the achievement of this goal. Some were the direct consequence of Trautman's ambitious expansion and diversification efforts. Others resulted from changes in environmental factors and consumer preferences. Still others stemmed from internal inefficiencies that Teets hoped he would be able to remedy.

Two challenges in particular caused Teets to feel uneasy about the corporation's overall profit picture. The first problem was Armour's high production costs, which made it a weak competitor. The second was the challenge faced by Greyhound Bus Lines: the need to compete in a newly deregulated bus transportation market. He knew that if he did not find solutions for these two problems, they would seriously diminish the Greyhound Corporation's earnings. The contribution of each operating division to Greyhound's total sales revenues in 1981 is presented in Figure 1.

Dealing with Armour's High Production Costs

Having been president of Armour, Teets was very familiar with the division's problems: its high production costs, the reluctance of union leadership and rank-and-file workers to agree with Greyhound's assessment of Armour's problems, and its utter inability to successfully change its marketing orientation to compete effectively. In addition, Teets was concerned about Armour's inefficient plants and the volatility of hog and pork-belly prices, which cyclically depressed Armour's 1981 profit of $9 million and represented a profit margin of less than 0.39 percent on sales of more than $2.3 billion. Teets sensed that it was not going to be easy to make Armour a low-cost leader. Thus, he decided to divest Armour.

In preparation for the sale, he separated the Armour Food Company from Armour-Dial. On December 18, 1983, the food company was sold to ConAgra, Inc., for $166 million. With the Armour sale, Teets was chopping off nearly half of Greyhound's business. Nevertheless, even with Greyhound's revenues dropping from $5 billion in 1982 to less than $3 billion in 1984 without Armour, the sale gave Teets the opportunity to put Greyhound in better shape than it had been in years.

The Bus Line Divestiture

Teets was also concerned about the 1981 passage of House bill H.R. 3663, which deregulated the intercity

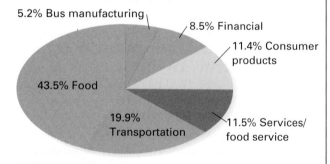

FIGURE 1

Greyhound in 1981

Source: Data from Greyhound Dial Corporation, Annual Report, 1990.

bus business. Greyhound Bus Lines had based its route system on the competitive conditions that had existed in the earlier business environment. Teets, however, sensed that future success in the bus business would be based not on the extensiveness of Greyhound's route system or its fifty years of experience in operating in a regulated industry but on its ability to make money by charging competitive fares.

With the beginning of deregulated competition in the intercity bus business and declining passenger revenues resulting from the end of the energy crunch, Greyhound found itself paying wages and benefits that were 30 to 50 percent higher than those paid by its competitors. Furthermore, its chief competitor, Trailways, having negotiated significant wage concessions from the Amalgamated Transit Union, had immediately passed the savings on to customers in the form of lower fares. Trailways's action was a frontal assault on Greyhound's most lucrative routes in an attempt to gain market share. Greyhound's response was to match every one of Trailways's price cuts. Although Greyhound preserved its market share, it lost millions of dollars.

For Greyhound Bus Lines, the legacy of deregulation was a total inability to be a low-cost provider of bus transportation. Deregulation had brought about the emergence of lower-cost competitors in regional markets, competitors that were able to be responsive and flexible in pricing and in reacting to Greyhound's actions. As a result, Greyhound lost its competitive edge. In 1986, in an effort to save the bus lines, Teets converted 120 company-owned terminals to commission agencies, trimming a huge overhead burden. He also created four stand-alone regional bus companies and a new travel and charter company. Finally, he franchised several of Greyhound's least profitable routes to independent operators, licensing them to use the Greyhound logo and trademark.

However, the one factor that Teets could not control was winning a new labor contract. In February 1986, an offer to freeze wages was rejected by the union. In October, in a deteriorating market, a second offer involving concessions was presented with the understanding that its rejection would prompt the sale of the company. The offer was subsequently rejected, and fifteen days later Teets announced the sale of Greyhound Bus Lines for approximately $350 million to an investor group headquartered in Dallas. Teets claimed that the actions taken by management in an effort to salvage the bus business were exactly the ones that made it an attractive acquisition for the Currey Group in Dallas.

The sale of Greyhound Bus Lines brought in $290 million in cash and equivalents, including a 22.5 percent interest in a new holding company established by the Dallas investor group.

Divestitures in the Financial Operating Division

Besides selling Greyhound Bus Lines in 1987, Teets also sold Greyhound Capital Corporation (GCC). The decision to sell GCC reportedly reflected Teets's conviction that "some businesses just fit better into Greyhound's plans than others." What this statement really meant was that GCC had become an underperformer in the face of lowered interest rates and changes in the tax laws that disallowed investment tax credits. GCC was sold for $140 million, realizing a one-time gain of $79.7 million for Greyhound.

In early 1987, Greyhound announced its intention to sell Verex. The timing of the acquisition had been a disaster, given the recession in the real estate market caused by the oil bust in the early 1980s. Verex suffered huge losses generated by insurance claims from business generated before 1985. These claims were originating in states where severe downturns in farming, auto production, and oil drilling had led to a widespread inability to keep up with mortgage payments.

Not surprisingly, Teets could not find a buyer for Verex. In January 1988, Greyhound announced that it had stopped taking applications for new mortgage insurance and that it was discontinuing its mortgage insurance business. It also announced that 1987 results would reflect a one-time after-tax charge of $45 million as a result of reclassifying Verex as a discontinued operation; then Greyhound would manage Verex's existing portfolio to minimize continuing losses from the company's operations. Management hoped the remnants of Verex would not be a drain on corporate resources.

With the sale of Greyhound Bus Lines, Greyhound Capital Corporation, and Armour, and with the discontinuation of Verex, Teets announced that he was near the end of his mammoth task of restructuring Greyhound and shedding businesses that seemed to lack sufficient growth potential. By late 1987, Greyhound Corporation was primarily a consumer products and services company. Figure 2 sum-

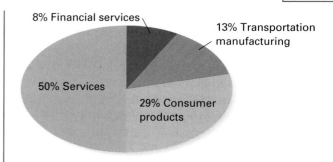

FIGURE 2

Total Revenues: 3.3 Billion

Source: Data from Greyhound Dial Corporation, Annual Report, 1990.

marizes the contribution of the different operating groups to total revenues in 1988. Compare the Greyhound Corporation that Teets structured (Figure 2) with the corporation he inherited in 1982 (Figure 1).

With the restructuring in place, Wall Street looked for an improvement in Greyhound's performance. However, it soon became obvious that the stack of businesses created by Teets was not proving much more profitable than the ones he had divested. There was only an 8.8 percent return on equity in 1987, and net income after nonrecurring losses was $25.1 million, the lowest for many years. Revenue was $2.5 billion. Teets maintained that the problems with Greyhound's various divisions could not have been foreseen as the restructuring was taking place but that Greyhound was set for "substantial profits in the future." Teets began a program of acquisitions and new product developments to strengthen Greyhound's presence in the four business areas identified in Figure 2 and to begin the turnaround process.

Consumer Products

In the midst of the divestiture of Armour and Greyhound Bus Lines, Teets had made one major acquisition. On February 21, 1985, he announced the purchase of Purex Industries and its thirty household cleaning products for $264 million. Teets's aim with this acquisition was to boost profits in Greyhound's Consumer Products operating division (principally composed of the old Dial division) by using the Dial sales force and marketing expertise to sell Purex products—Purex bleach, Brillo soap pads, Old Dutch cleanser, and Sweetheart and Fels-Naptha soap, among others.

The Purex acquisition drew mixed reviews from Wall Street. It did not meet Teets's goal of a

15 percent return, but Teets believed that it would by 1988. Analysts were also unimpressed with the purchase because Greyhound had not been successful in managing Armour. Teets responded that Dial was capable of marketing consumer products, although it had not been successful at developing its own lines. He cited as evidence the fact that Dial was marketing the number one deodorant soap in its Dial brand. Analysts did concede that Teets should be able to realize increased profitability by using the same sales force to sell Purex and Dial products. Along with Purex's household cleaners, Greyhound also got Elio's Pizza as part of the Purex acquisition. Teets was enthusiastic about expanding this frozen pizza business nationwide from its East Coast base. This was to be done by means of the Dial sales force.

The Dial operating division, as it was now known, became the center of Teets's attention and the flagship of the Greyhound Corporation. In the past Dial had not had much success in launching new products, but Teets was determined to change the situation, recognizing that growth in revenue had to come from the manufacture and marketing of new products. The first product introduced by the Dial division was Lunch Buckets, a range of microwavable meals with a stable shelf life of two years. This was a new market segment. Previously all microwavable meals had been frozen. Lunch Buckets meals were very successful and surpassed early expectations by a wide margin. By 1988, they had national distribution. By 1990, they had seized a 30 percent market share, becoming the market leader. In 1990, Dial announced new low-calorie Lunch Buckets.

Another new product introduced in 1987 was Liquid Dial antibacterial soap. This product, too, was very successful, and by 1990 it had achieved a 20 percent market share and was the second-best-selling liquid soap in the market, after Procter & Gamble's Ivory liquid. Another successful new product was Mountain Fresh Dial, a highly scented version of Dial's deodorant soap. Additional developments were liquid Purex detergent and other cleaning products.

In 1988, Teets acquired the household products and industrial specialties businesses of the 20 Mule Team division of United States Borax and Chemical Corporation. Teets announced a new advertising campaign to reestablish the market presence of Borax bleaches and cleaning powders. Teets's formula for increasing the Dial division's market share called for further extensions of the Dial brand, fur-

ther extensions of the Purex brand name, and Parsons' ammonia.

Greyhound Dial, Then Dial

On June 4, 1990, Teets learned that Greyhound Bus lines, the bus transportation company that he had sold in 1987, had declared bankruptcy and Greyhound's stake was now valueless. To distance his "new" company from Greyhound, he changed the company's name to Greyhound Dial in February 1990, and the next year it became simply Dial. The name change also marked the company's new focus on its consumer products division. However, the price of Dial's stock, which had been more or less unchanged for the last six years, started to plunge in 1990 after Dial reported a loss. Analysts wondered whether Teets would ever be able to improve the company's profitability.

In September 1990, another consumer products acquisition was announced: Breck hair care products. Breck had 1989 revenues of $60 million. Teets announced that integrating Breck into Dial would result in annual sales of more than $1 billion for the Dial division. Teets said that "Breck has been a household name for 60 years. It's a perfect fit with our other Dial products and under Dial management the power of the Breck name will flourish." Under its previous owners, Breck had languished. Teets hoped to turn the product around by applying Dial's marketing skills.

From the changes he had orchestrated, Teets was hoping for sizable revenue growth and profit from the Dial division, and in March 1991, as an indication of the company's future strategy, the company's name was again changed, to the Dial Corporation.

Services

By 1987, the restaurant food services division was contributing the most to total revenues. It was natural, therefore, that Teets should seek to strengthen food operations. In 1987, Dial purchased the nation's second biggest airline catering and airline retailing business. The new operation had three units: Dobbs International Services, the nation's second largest provider of in-flight meals for airlines; Dobbs Houses, the operator of restaurants at many airports; and Carson International, which operated the food and beverage concession at Chicago's O'Hare Airport. In 1990, Teets announced that Dobbs had had a record year—the company had served sixty scheduled airlines in forty cities. Moreover, it had added five new accounts, including Houston International Airport.

Teets strengthened Dial's Travelers Express money order business with the purchase of Republic Money Orders, Inc., of Dallas. This acquisition made Dial the leader in the money order business, ahead of the U.S. Postal Service. Teets had returned to the cruise ship industry in 1984 with the takeover of Premier Cruise Lines. In 1986, he negotiated an agreement with the Walt Disney Company that made

Dial's Premier Cruise Line Disney's exclusive cruise ship line, with three- and four-day sailing to the Bahamas from Cape Canaveral in Florida. The cruise line business enjoyed record sales, and in 1989 another line was added.

The New Look of the Dial Corporation

The new look of Dial's businesses after the acquisitions and divestitures is shown in Table 1. Teets acknowledged the wide diversity of businesses in the

TABLE 1

Greyhound's Businesses

Consumer Products	Services	Transportation Manufacturing	Financial Services
The Dial Corporation	Brewster Transport Company, Ltd.	Motor Coach Industries (MCI)	Greyhound Financial Corporation
Food	Consultants and Designers, Inc.	Transportation Manufacturing Corporation (TMC)	Greyhound Financial and Leasing
Personal care	Carson International, Inc.	• Custom Coach	Greyhound Financial Services, Ltd.
Laundry and household	Dobbs Houses, Inc.		Greyhound Bank PLC
	Dobbs International Services, Inc.		

Greyhound Airport Services Companies

Greyhound Exhibitgroup Inc.

Greyhound Exposition Services, Inc.

Greyhound Food Management, Inc.
- Faber Enterprises, Inc.
- Glacier Park, Inc.
- GFM Engineering and Design Group
- GFM Fast Food Division
- GFM Public Service Division
- GFM Truckstop Systems
- Restaura
- Restaura, S.A.

Greyhound International Travel, Inc. (GITI)

Greyhound Leisure Services, Inc. (GLSI)
- Florida Export Warehouse
- International Cruise Shops
- Greyhound Leisure Services Duty-Free Shops
- Premier Cruise Lines, Ltd.

Greyhound Lines of Canada, Ltd.

Travelers Express Company, Inc.
- Republic Money Orders, Inc.

Universal Coach Parts, Inc.

Source: Greyhound Dial Corporation, Annual Report, 1990.

company's portfolio. However, he contended that the businesses did fit together. In his words, "We are a multiservice business. We operate in niches and were number one or two in most of these niches. From a recession standpoint, I think we're going to feel it less than most major companies." Teets argued that Dial was making acquisitions to strengthen its presence in existing niches. By concentrating on a niche, the corporation avoided going head-to-head with major competitors. Moreover, the niches were recession-proof, small-ticket items such as Lunch Buckets and soap, not refrigerators and cars. Teets argued that Dial was positioned for growth and that management expected revenues to increase steadily over the next few years. See Table 2.

Some analysts, however, felt that the organization was still a hodgepodge of different businesses in need of rationalization. They pointed to the lack of fit between a cruise ship line and hotel operations in Glacier National Park and contract catering, saying that Dial was still a collection of companies with no real connection. They also argued that Greyhound Dial's breakup value was more than $60 a share, while its stock price had been in the range of $25 to $35 for years. Teets agreed that some minor divestitures were necessary, but he believed that the best way to proceed was to stay in the same niches and manage the existing businesses more efficiently.

Dial, 1990–1996

In 1991, it appeared that, at last, things were going Dial's way. Dial's share price, which had plummeted to less than $10 a share at the end of 1990, rose to almost $25 a share by the end of 1992. This turnaround occurred for several reasons. First, Dial had finally spun off its loss-making financial services group to stockholders so that the liabilities no longer affected its balance sheet. Second, its consumer products group, and in particular the Dial soap division, was performing strongly. Dial had become the number one selling deodorant soap in the United States, with more than 20 percent of the market. Third, Teets had orchestrated a major downsizing, or what he had called "rightsizing," reducing the number of corporate managers from four hundred to three hundred. Also, all of Dial's different businesses were subjected to close scrutiny to try to reduce costs, and employment was reduced across the board, even in the successful Dial division. Teets also reduced corporate debt from a high of $850 million to $550 million

through the sales of certain assets such as Dobbs House, its airport catering company. Analysts hoped that all these events were the first signs of a turnaround in the company's performance.

These hopes were doomed, however, by a series of problems that emerged in Dial's various businesses. In the 1990s, businesses in Dial's transportation manufacturing unit began to perform poorly, draining the company's profits. In 1993, Teets decided to dispose of it. Also, its Purex bleach business was doing poorly and losing money. It began to seem that just when Dial was making strides in one of its businesses, problems in another were wiping out the effects of the improvement. Investors began to wonder again about Teets's claims for his recession-proof niche strategy.

By 1995, major problems were affecting many areas of the company, including the pivotal Dial division. Teets, desperate to increase the company's return on equity and stock price, which had been flat since its high in 1992, began again to slash costs. One way he did this was by reducing the advertising budget for Dial soap products from $8.7 million to $4.9 million. However, this was something that no niche player could afford to do when battling such industry giants as Procter & Gamble and Unilever, whose new soap Lever 2000 made major inroads into sales of Dial soap. Dial soap's market share dropped to 17.6 percent from 19.7 percent of the market in 1995, which was a severe blow to the Dial Corporation's most important product line and a disaster for the company.

The Purex division also was not performing well. The Purex bleach line was phased out in 1995 because of mounting losses. Late in 1995, Purex detergent, the low-priced detergent that had been selling well, came under intense pressure from Procter & Gamble, which introduced a competing low-priced brand, Ultra Bonus, that was aimed directly at Purex. Dial was forced to slash the price of Purex by 10 percent to compete, further cutting into the company's profits. Furthermore, Dial's successful Lunch Buckets, the line of microwave products, had generated a host of imitators from major food companies that quickly introduced their own competing products. Having lost this niche and no longer able to compete, Dial phased out Lunch Buckets in 1995. It began to seem to Dial's managers that even when they found a winning strategy their larger competitors just stole the idea away from them.

TABLE 2

The Dial Corporation: Consolidated Balance Sheet
(000 omitted, except per-share data)

	Year-ended December 31		
	1995	**1994**	**1993**
Revenues	$ 3,575,070	$ 3,546,847	$ 3,000,342
Costs and expenses			
Costs of sales and services	$ 3,271,151	$ 3,216,627	$ 2,725,049
Restructuring charges and asset write downs	191,100		
Unallocated corporate expense and other items, net	43,194	43,938	42,734
Interest expense	75,994	61,195	57,292
Minority interests	4,346	3,392	3,618
	$ 3,585,785	$ 3,325,152	$ 2,828,693
Income (loss) before income taxes	$ (10,715)	$ 221,695	$ 171,649
Income taxes (benefit)	(11,852)	81,384	61,376
Income from Continuing Operations	$ 1,137	$ 140,311	$ 110,273
Income from discontinued operations			32,120
Income before extraordinary charge and cumulative effect of change in accounting principle	$ 1,137	$ 140,311	$ 142,393
Extraordinary charge for early retirement of debt net of tax benefit of $11,833			(21,908)
Cumulative effect net of tax benefit of $7,544 to January 1, 1995 of initial application of SFAS No. 121, "Accounting for the Impairment of Long-Lived Assets and for Long-Lived Assets to Be Disposed Of"	(17,696)		
Net income (loss)	$ (16,559)	$ 140,311	$ 120,485
Income (Loss) per Common Share			
Continuing operations	$ 0.00	$ 1.61	$ 1.28
Discontinued operations			0.38
Income before extraordinary charge and cumulative effect of change in accounting principle	$ 0.00	$ 1.61	$ 1.66
Extraordinary charge			(0.26)
Cumulative effect, to January 1, 1995, of initial application of SFAS No. 121	(0.20)		
Net income (loss) per common share	$ (0.20)	$ 1.61	$ 1.40

Dial's other businesses were also suffering problems. Its cruise ship line, Premier Cruise Lines, which had formed an agreement with the Walt Disney Company to operate Disney's theme cruises on the Big Red Boat, lost its license in 1995 when Disney decided that it would launch its own cruise line. With four aging ships, and lacking any differentiated appeal in the increasingly competitive cruise ship industry in the 1990s, the company put its ships up for sale and withdrew from the cruise ship business— one more recession-proof niche gone.

Then, Dial's airline food business began to suffer in the 1990s when, to cut down on costs in an increasingly competitive airline industry, the major airlines cut back on the quality of the food they offered their customers. Airlines that had offered full meals began to offer snacks, and airlines such as Southwest offered passengers nothing. In airports, too, there had been a move to allow fast-food chains to set up their franchises on site to increase the variety of foods offered to customers. All this hurt Dial's catering businesses.

It was becoming increasingly obvious to industry analysts that Dial was nothing more than a hodgepodge of different businesses that had nothing in common, were not recession-proof, and did not even have a secure niche.

Dial, 1996–2002

With its profits flat or eroding and no turnaround in sight, the question became how to create new value from Dial's different businesses. The movement of many diversified companies to break up their operations and let individual businesses go it alone in the early 1990s gave Teets his answer. He would split apart Dial's consumer products and services operations—thus dismantling the empire he had built since 1984—into two different companies. One, which would still be known as the Dial Corp., would consist of all its consumer product interests and would have revenues of about $1.3 billion. The other, to be called Viad Corp., would manage its remaining financial, catering, and exhibition businesses and have revenues of about $2.2 billion.

Initially, analysts thought that the breakup would allow the two new companies to realize more value. For example, since they operated separately, a downturn in the business of one division would no longer hurt the performance of the other. Moreover, after the breakup managers would be able to make decisions that could promote their own businesses, not corporate interests. However, analysts later came to realize that in the future there would be two sets of managers who would have to be paid to manage the two companies and two sets of overhead costs. Moreover, the question arose as to whether there was any value to be created by the breakups, because all of Dial's businesses were under threats from more efficient and aggressive competitors such as Procter & Gamble, Colgate-Palmolive, and Unilever. Analysts came to believe increasingly that more value could be made for shareholders if the company dismantled itself and sold off its assets separately to the highest bidder. A bidder could then merge a particular Dial business into its own operations and thus reduce manufacturing, distribution, or marketing costs or even use its skills to increase the division's differentiation advantage.

In July 1996, John Teets's plan came under increasing attack from Michael Price, president of Heine Securities Corp. Price was the advisor to Mutual Series Funds, a large mutual fund company that owned 9.9 percent of Dial's stock. Price, along with other analysts, however, argued that Teet's plan would reduce, not increase, value for shareholders and that what Teets should do was to divest Dial's many different businesses and return the proceeds to shareholders. Of course, the selloff would mean that many of Dial's managers might find themselves out of well-paying jobs, including Teets, who had earned many millions of dollars over the years. On the other hand, these managers had not created much value for their shareholders.

In 1996, Teets answered his critics with half-page ads in the *Wall Street Journal* arguing that his strategy was a "strategy for empowered growth" that would allow each of the two new companies to "aggressively pursue acquisition opportunities without worry about upsetting the balance in Dial's existing mix of business." However, he did not explain how new value would be created by the two companies or how the proposed acquisitions might create value. Since Teets's acquisition strategy had met with little success for the last twelve years, what reason would shareholders have to suppose it would improve in the future?

This question remained unanswered, but in 1996 Viad was spun off to stockholders, Teets stepped down as CEO, and a new CEO, Malcolm Jozoff, was appointed to head what was now a consumer products company, albeit one that sold canned beef and shampoo. Jozoff was recruited from Procter & Gamble because Dial's board believed that a P&G veteran would understand how to fashion a business model to promote the profitability of a soap and detergent maker. What they forgot was that P&G is a differentiator whose claim to fame is developing new and improved products and marketing them successfully to consumers. While it is true that Dial, the best-selling antibacterial soap, was their flagship differentiated product, Dial's other main products, such as Purex detergent, Breck Shampoo, and even Armour corned beef, were not bought for their differentiated qualities but because of their low price. Even Dial soap did not command much of a premium price compared to P&G's and Unilever's brands; it sold because of the advertising expenditures used to promote its brand name.

Jozoff, however, given his immersion in P&G's "differentiation" culture, saw Dial's problems as the lack of a differentiated appeal of its products, not the fact that its high-cost structure was eroding the profitability of a low-price cost leadership strategy. Jozoff's efforts were thus directed toward increasing customer demand by differentiating Dial's brands. To promote Purex washing powder, he entered into a joint venture with Germany's Henkel group to use that company's expertise in stain removal to boost Purex's cleaning power (not its strong point); he proposed to call the new powder "Purex Advanced," and to recoup the extra costs it would cost a few dollars more a pack. He felt these moves would position it against Tide, the leading brand. Knowing that P&G was entering the home dry-cleaning market, he introduced a new Purex home dry-cleaning kit, and also knowing that P&G and Unilever were introducing washing powder in tablet form, he put in motion Purex Tablets. To push Dial into higher-end personal care products, he bought two companies, Sarah Michaels and Freeman Cosmetics, that specialized in producing upscale soaps, bath powders, and oils for gift boxes, although he did not propose to sell these under the Dial name. Also, knowing that rivals were developing new kinds of antibacterial soap with more fragrant scents and better foaming qualities, he reformulated Dial soap to position it against tough future competition. Jozoff also agreed to acquire the Plusbelle brand hair care business from Revlon for $46.5 million. Plusbelle was the leader in the Argentinean market. These acquisitions cost over $300 million and pushed up Dial's debt to over $550 million. Teets had left Dial saddled with a $300 million debt during the Viad spinoff, whereas Viad emerged virtually debt free.

In changing Dial's business-level strategy, Jozoff plunged the company into a whole new set of problems. First, the movement to a differentiation strategy raised Dial's cost structure, especially because of the extra debt it had to assume, so he was betting the company's future on consumers' acceptance of Dial's new products and higher-pricing structure. At the same time, Jozoff brought the company into more direct competition with the rivals such as P&G and Unilever that had much more money to spend on the expensive business of promoting new brand products. For example, it was estimated that in 1994 it would cost $5 million in fees to retailers to promote a new consumer product in the greater New York area; that figure had risen to $25 million by 1999 because

of increasing competition for shelf space caused by the consolidation both of consumer product companies and of retailers and supermarkets such as Kroger's.

When Dial's new products started to be manufactured and introduced in 1998 and 1999, at first things looked good; sales increased by 12 percent in 1998 and by 13 percent in 1999 to $1.7 billion, and operating profits grew 13 percent in 1998 and 17 percent in 1999. However, it turned out that things were not as good as they seemed. While sales did increase in 1998, largely as the result of a big increase in marketing expenditures to sell the new, wider product range, by 1999 consumers were turning away from Dial's brands. By the middle of 1999 Dial's top managers knew there were problems, but to disguise the issue from the board, the company's sales team was instructed to boost the end-of-year sales figures by "stuffing the channel" with Dial products, that is, sending huge inventories of products, particularly Dial soap, to retailers that counted as sales in the company's books, and by offering retailers big promotions to sell its products at discounted prices to move them off the shelves.

Major errors were also made. First, expecting customers to stock up on canned goods because of Y2K glitches, the company loaded up stores with extra Armor Star Vienna Sausage and then raised prices hoping its competitors would follow. When there was no Y2K panic and competitors didn't raise prices, most of this product was left unsold and was either returned or sold at cost. Second, although it seemed to Jozoff that the Sarah Michaels and Freeman Cosmetics acquisitions were natural, albeit "upmarket," extensions to Dial's product line, Dial was not prepared for the huge manufacturing challenges involved in custom-packing gift boxes and matching them to the needs of the customers. As Baum (see next section) later said, upmarket products such as scented lotions, bath oils, and aromatherapy products are "fashion products," whereas Dial's business was "bread-and-butter" products where low-cost production and distribution were vital. Third, it turned out that the market for home dry cleaning was far smaller than anticipated, and Dial's dry-cleaning product was simply left on the shelf because of its rivals' higher advertising budgets.

Even in the vital soap business, problems arose. Because Dial had stuffed the channels with its old soap product, when its new improved scented mois-turizing soap came out in late 1999, retailers would not sell it until they had sold the old soap product. This gave a leg up to P&G and Unilever, which had also introduced a new range of soap to compete with Dial. Finally, Dial discovered that customers didn't understand the properties of the new improved Purex washing powder or why they should spend a lot more for it. As Baum later commented, he pleaded with Jozoff to introduce it under another upmarket name to differentiate it, but this was not done, and the powder was left stuck in the middle—not differ-entiated and not low cost.

Dial Gets a New CEO

As a result of all these problems, estimates for Dial's 2000 operating profits dropped from $73 million to $60 million in the summer of 2000, wiping out all its previous gains. The board became increasingly aware of the problems that had been taking place, and in August 2000 they ousted Jozoff as CEO and replaced him with a vocal board member, Herbert M. Baum. Baum, a former Campbell Soup executive and CEO of Quaker State (which he had sold to Pennzoil) and then the COO of Hasbro, the toy maker, was sur-prised to be asked to take over yet one more turn-around effort at Dial, but he accepted the challenge. Since his experience was with bread-and-butter products—canned soups and oil—he was familiar with the problems of managing a company's cost structure to get the most value out of its products. He also recognized the importance of finding the right strategy to compete against rivals like P&G and pow-erful retail chains like Kroger and Wal-Mart, both of which were launching private-label low-price wash-ing powders and soaps at the low end of the market. The problem was that he had to move fast because Dial's performance and stock price were collapsing.

Baum took a close look at how Dial's brands were managed internally. He reorganized them into a product structure with five product groups—per-sonal cleansing, washing powders, air fresheners, food products, and Dial International. For the first time, Baum made the product line managers accountable for their own inventory management and profit-and-loss figures. Previously, these had been spread across brands so that each line's relative performance had been hidden. Now it was possible to identify specific underperforming brands and decide

what to do about them—turn them around, sell them off, or close them down.

Baum then turned his attention to the various problems that emerged in launching Dial's new prod-ucts. Recognizing the importance of protecting Dial soap's market share, he pumped money into advertis-ing its improved products to regain their momentum and build their profitability. With Purex, he decided to go ahead with the introduction of Purex tablets, but ended the joint venture with Henkel and went back to the old low-cost strategy. He also decided to sell off the Sarah Michaels and Freeman upscale lines, which had only resulted in losses, and he used the money to reduce Dial's debt. He also withdrew from the home dry-cleaning market and took Purex's product off the shelf. The savings in operating costs from abandoning these product lines both provided money to fund Dial's core soap, Purex, and Renuzit air freshener products and lowered its cost structure.

In September 2001, Baum announced that, given the increasing competitive pressures in all its brand categories from companies like P&G and Unilever, he and the board felt that it would be better if Dial were part of a larger enterprise. Various possible acquirers came forward to look at the company's books in the next months, but it appeared that none of them wanted to buy the whole company. In the meantime, Baum's business model and strategies began to pay off for Dial. Its inventory stocking and manufactur-ing problems were gone; brand managers were squeezing out costs now that they were directly responsible for their brand's performance; and top managers were not distracted by searching for elusive new product opportunities but were focusing, per-haps for the first time, on managing all aspects of the value chain to reduce costs. With its well-known products, sold at the right price, there was no reason why Dial should not be able to increase revenues and profits and build cash flow.

In fact, the company astounded analysts when in April 2002, only six months after it put itself up for sale, it raised its first-quarter earnings estimates, cit-ing stronger-than-expected domestic sales. Dial's share reached $20, up from just $12 only a year before. Since no buyer for Dial had emerged, Baum also announced in April that Dial itself, to strengthen and protect its core businesses, would be looking to make acquisitions in the coming year. However, rec-ognizing that nobody wanted to buy the whole of

Dial because of its many different product lines, Baum emphasized that Dial would be buying brands, not companies—those with high volumes and those that used the same sales channels as Dial to make better use of the company's resources.

It seems that the future of the company depends on how quickly Baum can build up Dial's competencies in product development and brand management on the one hand, and on manufacturing and inventory control on the other. If these improve as time goes on, then Dial with its pruned and cleaner product lines will become an even more attractive takeover target; indeed, if Baum can find a buyer for Armor foods, its divestiture is almost certain. However, the meat-packing business is notoriously risky, and its low profit margins are not attractive. The question is which course of action—remaining independent or a effecting a breakup—will Baum, Dial's board, and outside analysts think will create most value for shareholders?

REFERENCES

Moody's Transportation Manual, 1987.

A. Stuart, "Greyhound Gets Ready for a New Driver," *Fortune,* March 3, 1966, pp. 34–38.

Greyhound Corporation, Annual Reports, 1966–1990.

Dial Corporation, Annual Reports and 10K Reports, 1971–2002.

"Greyhound: A Big Sell-off Leaves It Built for Better Speed," *Business Week,* July 25, 1983, pp. 88–90.

"Greyhound's New Strategy: Slimmed Down and Decentralized, It's After More Market Share, 15% on Equity," *Dun's Business Month,* February 1984, pp. 66–68.

S. Toy and J. H. Dobrzynski, "Will More Soap Help Greyhound Shine?" *Business Week,* March 11, 1985, pp. 73–78.

"The Greyhound Corporation," *Wall Street Journal Transcript,* February 5, 1990, pp. 96, 204.

"Dial Corp.: Firm's Loss of $26.2 Million Is Due to Special Charges," *Wall Street Journal,* October 25, 2000, p. B8.

Jack Neff and Kate MacArthur, "Beleaguered Dial Cuts Product Lines," *Advertising Age,* September 25, 2000, p. 128.

"Dial Corp.: Loss of $7.5 Million Posted, Partly from a Restructuring," *Wall Street Journal,* January 25, 2001, p. B5.

Rebecca Flass, "Dial Shifts Direction," *Adweek,* May 21, 2001, p. 8.

"Dial Agrees to Buy Plusbelle," *Wall Street Journal,* March 30, 2000, p. C14.

Steven Lipin and Anna W. Mathews, "Dial Board, Hit by New Profit Shortfall, Ousts Top Executives and Turns to Baum," *Wall Street Journal,* August 8, 2000, p. A3.

Arlene Weintraub and Christopher Palameri, "Wish Everyone Used Dial? Dial Does," *Business Week,* September 25, 2000, pp. 132–134.

Kerri Walsh, "Dial Raises First-Quarter Earnings Estimates; Eyes Brand Acquisitions," *Chemical Week,* April 17, 2002, p. 36.

"Dial Jettisons Underperforming Unit," *SPC Soap, Perfumery, and Cosmetics,* London, September, 2001, p. 4.

Brent Shearer, "Under Competitive Pressures, Dial Puts Itself Up for Sale," *Mergers and Acquisitions,* October 2001, p. 23.

"Dial Corp.: Earnings Forecast Climbs Again to as Much as 25 Cents a Share," *Wall Street Journal,* April 10, 2002, p. A8.

Jack Neff, "Clorox, Dial Exit Dry Cleaning Biz," *Advertising Age,* September 10, 2001, p. 4.

Kerri Walsh, "Dial May Be Broken Up," *Chemical Week,* August 15, 2001, p. 25.

"Dial Puts Itself Up for Sale Despite Portfolio, Analysts Say Company Could Fetch $2 Billion," *Chemical Market Reporter,* August 13, 2001, p. 3.

"Dial Corp.: Quarterly Earnings Surge, Outlook for Year Is Raised," *Wall Street Journal,* July 26, 2001.

Gene G. Marcial, "With Dial, Clorox Could Clean Up," *Business Week,* October 4, 1999, p. 247.

"Dial Corp.: Laundry-Products Venture to Tap Henkel Technology," *Wall Street Journal,* April 21, 1999.